EUROPEAN COMPETITION LAW

European Competition Law

A Practitioner's Guide

Third edition

Lennart Ritter W. David Braun

KLUWER LAW
INTERNATIONAL

Published by:
Kluwer Law International
P.O. Box 85889
2508 CN The Hague, The Netherlands

Sold and distributed in North, Central and South America by:
Aspen Publishers, Inc.
7201 McKinney Circle
Frederick, MD 21704, USA

Sold and distributed in all other countries by:
Extenza-Turpin Distribution Services
Stratton Business Park
Pegasus Drive
Biggleswade
Bedfordshire SG18 8TQ, United Kingdom

Library of Congress Cataloging-in-Publication Data

Ritter, Lennart.
European competition law : a practitioner's guide / Lennart Ritter, David Braun.-- 3rd ed.
p. cm.
Rev. ed. of: EC competition law. 2nd ed. c2000.
Includes bibliographical references and index.
ISBN 90-411-2200-1 (alk. paper)
1. Antitrust law--European Union countries. 2. Restraint of trade--European Union countries. 3. Competition--European Union countries. I. Braun, W. David, 1950- II. Ritter, Lennart. EC competition law. III. Title.

KJE6456.R58 2004
343.4'0721--dc22

2004053781

ISBN 90 411 2200 1

Printed on acid-free paper

For Titia and Jeanne

Foreword

When the second edition of this work appeared in 1999, EC competition law had undergone dramatic changes. But no one would have expected that the nex developments of the last four years would be even more dramatic. The administrative and judicial experience gathered under the 'old' rules induced the Commission to modernize its competition rules. This modernization process aims at improving both procedure and methodogy, including a more economic approach in interpreting, developing and applying EC competition law. The most important change is the removal of the Commission's exclusive competence to grant exemptions under Article 81 (3). The modernization process includes a briskly flowing stream of regulations, guidelines and notices, sometimes dealing with the same issues from different standpoints. However, these new rules are based on the previous case law of the Court of Justice and decisions by the Commission, which therefore remain relevant for the interpretation and application of the new rules and consequently are extensively referred to in this Third Edition.

This modernization process includes a more active role of the national competition authorities and national courts in the application of EC competition law, including the ten new member states as from May 1, 2004. This constitutes a challenge for both the 'old' and the 'new' member states to apply the new rules with the view of realizing the objective of the EC Treaty: an open market economy with free competition within the enlarged Community.

Commenting these new rules at this early stage of their application (as from May 1, 2004) without any administrative or judicial experience having yet developed in applying them implies risks and errors: the wide range of topics and the impressive quantity of Commission documents dealing with the different issues (sometimes in parallel and not always in harmony in the Commission regulations, guidelines, notices and Commission decisions) makes it sometimes difficult for our small team to digest, analyse and find the common thread and the transparency which is the Commission's objective. However, we trust it may be helpful for the reader to be informed as quickly as possible – even if in an imperfect way – on the new developments of the EC competition law.

This edition misses the collaboration of Francis Rawlinson who has shifted to another directorate and was unable to develop and update his original thoughts and comments. Therefore, only Lennart Ritter and David Braun are responsible for the undoubtably numerous committed errors, trusting that the reader will be indulgent and hopefully also stimulated to carefully check our analysis, in particular with the view of taking account of the ongoing process of further 'modernization' of the EC competition rules.

We want to express our thanks to those whose ideas and criticism have been most helpful: Kurt Riechenberg, Massimo Merola, Aurelio Pappalardo, Gloria Crichlow, Valeria Passalacqua, Maria Christina Santacroce and Bettina Volpi. No less do we thank our families, who have suffered again under the obstinate efforts and pains of the authors, who have become recidivists once more in the repeat offense 'stealing' their time and talents in order to make the old and new members of the enlarged European family more familiar with the quite complex application of the new competition rules on the Community and the national level.

Brussels and Chicago
June, 2004

Table of Contents

List of Abbreviations

BGE	Entscheidungen des Schweizerischen Bundesgerichts
BGH	Bundesgerichtshof (German Federal Supreme Court)
BkartA	Bundeskartellamt (German Federal Cartel Office)
CFI	Court of First Instance
CMLR	Common Markt Law Reports
CMLRev	Common Market Law Review
D.Comm.	Decisions of the EC Commission
DG COMP	Directorate-General for Competition
EC	European Community
ECJ	European Court of Justice
ECR	European Court Reports
ECSC	European Coal and Steel Community
ECU	European Currency Unit
EEA	European Economic Area
EFTA	European Free Trade Association
EFTACR	EFTA Court Reports
EIPR	Euroepan Intellectual Property Review
ELR	European Law Reporter (St. Gallen)
ELRev	European Law Review
EP	European Parliament
EuR	Europarecht
EUR	Euro €
EuZW	Europäische Zeitschrift für Wirtschaftsrecht
Foro.It	Il Foro Italiano
Fordham Corp.L.Inst.	Annual Proceedings of the Fordham Corporate Law Institute (Hawk ed)
Fordham Int.L.J.	Fordham International Law Journal
GATT	General Agreement of Tariffs and Trade
ICLQ	International and Comparative Law Quarterly
IIC	International Review of International Property and Copyright Law
IP	Information à la presse (Commission press release)
NJW	Neue Juristische Wochenschrift
OECD	Organisation for Economic Cooperation and Development
OJ	Official Journal (L = legislatio, C = communicatio)
PCT	Patent Cooperation Treaty
Rev.int.dr.ec	Revue internationale du droit économique
RevMC	Revue du Marché Commun
Rev.trim.dr.eur	Revue trimestrielle de droit européen
RIW	Recht der Internationalen Wirtschaft
SEW	Sociaal-Economische Wetgeving

TRIPs	Trade-Related Aspects of Intellectual Property Rights
UNCTAD	United Nations Conference on Trade and Development
World Competition	World Competition Law and Economics Review (Kluwer)
WTO	World Trade Organisation
WuW	Wirtschaft und Wettbewerb (WuWE = Entscheidungssammlung Kartellrecht)
ZWR	Zeitschrift für Wettbewerbsrecht

Table of EC Competition Rules

A. The Treaties

1. **The EC Treaty**
   applying, from July 22, 2002, also in the coal and steel sectors, thereby replacing Articles 65 and 66 of the ECSC Treaty
2. **The EEA Agreement**
   1994 OJ L 1/1
3. **The Documents Concerning the Accession of the Ten New Member States**
   2003 OJ L 236

B. General Notices of the Commission

1. ***De Minimis* Notices**
   (a) **Notice on Agreements of Minor Importance**
   2001 OJ C 368/13, with respect to Article 53 of the EEA Agreement: 2003 OJ C 67/20
   (b) **Commission Recommendation on the Definition of Small and Medium-Sized Undertakings**
   2003 OJ L 124/36
2. **Notice on the Definition of the Relevant Market**
   1997 OJ C 372/3
3. **Guidelines on the Effect on Trade Concept Contained in Articles 81 and 82**
   2004 OJ C 101/81
4. **Guidelines on the Application of Article 81 (3) of the EC Treaty**
   2004 OJ C 101/97

C. Regulations and Notices on Horizontal Cooperation

1. **Council Regulation 2821/71 (Block exemption enabling regulation)**
   1971 OJ L 285/46
2. **Regulation 2658/2000 on Specialization Agreements**
   2000 OJ L 304/3
   Replacing Regulation 417/85, 1985 OJ L 53/14
3. **Regulation 2659/2000 on R&D Agreements**
   2000 OJ L 304/7
   Replacing Regulation 418/85, 1985 OJ L 53/5
4. **Notice on the Applicability of Article 81 to Horizontal Cooperation**
   2001 OJ C 3/2
   Commission Brochure 'The Competition Rules for Supply and Distribution Agreements' (containing a Flow Chart on how to proceed to the assessment of vertical agreements)
   ISBN 92-894-3905-X

D. Regulations on Vertical and Licence Agreements

1. **Regulation 19/65 (Block exemption enabling regulation)**
   1965 OJ 533
2. **Regulation 2790/1999 on Vertical Restraints**
   1999 OJ L 336/21
   Replacing Regulation 1983/83 on Exclusive Dealing Agreements, 1983 OJ L 173/1, Regulation 1984/83 on Exclusive Purchasing Agreements, 1983 OJ L 173/5 and Regulation 4087/88 on Franchising Agreements, 1988 OJ L 359/46
3. **Guidelines on Vertical Restraints**
   2000 OJ C 291/1
4. **Regulation 1400/2002 on Vertical Agreements in the Motor Vehicle Sector**
   2002 OJ L 203/30
   Replacing Regulation 1475/95 on Motor Vehicle Distribution and Servicing Agreements, 1995 OJ L 145/25
   Explanatory Brochure, IP/02/1392,
   http://europa.eu.int/comm/competition/car_sector/explanatory_brochure_en.pdf
5. **Regulation 772/2004 on Technology Transfer Agreements**
   2004 OJ L 123/11
   Replacing Regulation 240/96 on Technology Transfer Agreements, 1996 OJ L 31/2
6. **Guidelines on the Application of Article 81 to Technology Transfer Agreements**
   2004 OJ C 101/2
   Replacing the Notice on Subcontracting Agreements, 1979 OJ C 1/2

E. Provisions Governing the Procedure of the Commission Relating to Procedings Pursuant to Articles 81 and 82

1. **Regulation 1/2003 on the Implementation of the Rules of Competition Laid Down in Articles 81 and 82 of the EC Treaty**
   2003 OJ L 1/1
   Replacing, from May 1, 2004, Regulation 17, 1962 OJ 204, as amended by Regulation 1216/99, 1999 OJ L 148/5, and Regulation 2988/74 on Prescription, 1974 OJ L 319/1;
   Amending Regulation 1017/68 on Rail, Road and Waterway Transport, Regulation 4056/86 on Sea Transport and Regulation 3795/87 on Air Transport
2. **Regulation 773/2004 Relating to the Conduct of Proceedings by the Commission Pursuant to Articles 81 and 82 of the EC Treaty**
   2004 OJ L 123/18
   Replacing, from May 1, 2004, Regulation 3385/94, 1994 OJ L 377/28

3. **Notice on the Handling of Complaints by the Commission under Articles 81 and 82 of the EC Treaty**
   2004 OJ C 101/65
4. **Notice on Informal Guidance Relating to Novel Questions concerning Articles 81 and 82 that Arise in Individual Cases *(Guidance Letters)***
   2004 OJ 101/78
5. **Guidelines on the Method of Setting Fines**
   2003 OJ C 10/16
   Replacing Guidelines on the Method of Setting Fines, 1998 OJ C 9/3
6. **Notice on the Non-Imposition or Reduction of Fines in Cartel Cases**
   2002 OJ C 45/3
   Replacing Notice on the Non-Imposition or Reduction of Fines, 1996 OJ C 207/4
7. **Notice on Cooperation within the Network of Competition Authorities (European Competition Network – ECN)**
   2004 OJ C 101/43
   Replacing Notice on Cooperation between National Competition Authorities and the Commission, 1997 OJ C 313/3
8. **Notice on the Cooperation between the Commission and the Courts of the EU Member States**
   2004 OJ C 101/54
   Replacing Notice on Cooperation between National Courts and the Commission, 1993 OJ C 39/5
9. **Agreement between the European Communities and the United States Regarding the Application of their Competition Laws**
   1995 OJ L 96/45

F. Provisions on Mergers

1. **Regulation 139/2004**
   2004 OJ L 24/1
   Replacing Regulation 1310/97
2. **Notice on the Concept of Concentration**
   1998 OJ C 66/5
3. **Notice on the Concept of Undertakings Concerned**
   1998 OJ C 66/14
4. **Notice on the Calculation of Turnover**
   1998 OJ C 66/25
5. **Notice on the Concept of Full-Function Joint Ventures**
   1998 OJ C 66/1
6. **Guidelines on the Assessment of Horizontal Mergers**
   2004 OJ C 31/5
7. **Notice on Restrictions Directly Related and Necessary to Concentrations** (Ancillary Restrictions)
   2001 OJ C 188/5

Draft 2004 Commission Notice on Ancillary Restrictions
http://europa.eu.int/comm/competition/mergers/legislation/consultation/restrictions

8. **Notice on Remedies Acceptable under the Merger Control Regulation**
2001 OJ C 68/3
9. **Best Practice Guidelines for Divestiture Commitments**
http://europa.eu.int/comm/competition/mergers/legislation/divestiture_commitments
10. **Procedural Provisions**
(a) **Commission Regulation 802/2004 Implementing Council Regulation 139/2004 on the Control of Concentrations between Undertakings**
2004 OJ L 133/1
Replacing Regulation 447/98, 1998 OJ L 61/1
(b) **Commission Notice on a Simplified Procedure for Treatment of Certain Concentrations**
2000 OJ C 217/32
Draft 2004 Commission Notice on a Simplified Procedure
http://eu.int/comm/competition/mergers/legislation/consultation/simplified.pdf
(c) **Draft 2004 Commission Notice on Case Allocation (Notice on case Referral in Respect of Concentrations)**
http://europa.eu.int/comm/competition/mergers/legislation/consultation/case_allocation
(d) **Best Practices on the Conduct of EC Merger Control Proceedings**
http://europa.eu.int/comm/competition/mergers/legislation/best_practices.pdf

G. Provisions Governing Special Sectors

1. **General Interest**
Communication on Services of General Interest in Europe
2001 OJ C 17/4
2. **Agriculture**
Regulation 26/62 Applying the Competition Rules to Production of and Trade in Agricultural Products
1962 OJ 993
3. **Inland Transport**
Regulation 1017/68 on Rail, Road and Inland Waterway Transport
1968 OJ L 175/1
Amended by Article 36 of Regulation 1/2003, 2003 OJ L 1/1
4. **Maritime Transport**
Regulation 4056/86 Applying the Competition Rules to MaritimeTransport
1986 OJ L 378/4

Amended by Article 38 of Regulation 1/2003, 2003 OJ L 1/1
Regulation 823/2000 on the Application of Article 81 (3) to Liner Shipping Companies (Consortia)
2000 OJ L 100/24
Amended by Regulation 463/2004
2004 OJ L 77/23

5. **Air Transport**
Regulation 3975/87 Applying the Competition Rules to Air Transport
1987 OJ L 374/1
Amended by Article 39 of Regulation 1/2003, 2003 OJ L 1/1
Regulation 847/2004 on the Negotiation and Implementation of Air Service Agreements between Member States and Third Countries
2004 OJ L 157/7
6. **Insurance**
Council Regulation 1534/91 (block exemption enabling regulation)
1991 OJ L 143/1
Regulation 358/2003 on Agreements in the Insurance Sector
2003 OJ L 53/8
7. **Energy**
Directive 2003/54/EC Concerning Common Rules for the Internal Market in Electricity
2003 OJ L 176/37
Repealing Directive 96/92/EC
Directive 2003/55/EC Concerning Common Rules for the Internal Market in Natural Ggas
2003 OJ L 176/57, corr. 2004 OJ L 16/74
Repealing Directive 98/30/EC
8. **Telecommunications**
Guidelines on the Application of EC Competition Rules in the Telecommunications Sector
1991 OJ C 233/2
Directive 2002/21/EC on a Common Regulatory Framework for Electronic Communications Networks and Services (Framework Directive)
2002 OJ L 108/33
Access Interconnection Directive 2002/19/EC
2002 OJ L 108/7
Authorization Directive 2002/20/EC
2002 OJ L 108/21
Universal Service Directive 2002/22/EC
2002 OJ L 108/51
Directive 2002/77/EC on Competition in the Markets for Electronic Communications Networks and Services
2002 OJ L 249/21

Commission Guidelines on Market Analysis and the Assessment of Significant Market Power under the Community Regulatory Framework for Electronic Communications Networks and Services
2002 OJ C 165/6

9. Postal Services

Notice on the Application of the Competition Rules to Postal Services and the Assessment of State Measures Relating to Postal Services
1998 OJ C 39/2

Directive 97/67/EC on Common Rules for the Development of Community Postal Services and Improved Quality Services as amended by Directive 2002/39/EC
2002 OJ L 176/21

Chapter I

Fundamentals of EC Competition Law

CONTENTS

A. EC Competition Policy

The process of European integration has led to numerous changes in its framework of supranational law. This book is devoted to the competition rules in the EC Treaty and the corresponding secondary legislation, including the rules on procedure and the rules on merger control. The principal competition rules were originally adopted as Articles 85 and 86 of the Treaty of Rome and entered into effect in 1958. These provisions have remained unchanged after the ratification of the Amsterdam Treaty, but they are renumbered as Articles 81 and 82 according to Article 12 of the Amsterdam Treaty.[1]

1. Sources of Law

The European Community Treaties.
The European Community is based on three Treaties: the 1951 European Coal and Steel Community Treaty (the 'ECSC Treaty'), the 1957 European Economic Community Treaty (the 'EC Treaty'[2]) and the 1957 European Atomic Energy Treaty (the 'Euratom Treaty'). These three treaties are referred to jointly as the 'Community Treaties' (or 'EC Treaties'). The ECSC Treaty, concluded for 50 years, entered into effect on July 22, 1952, and the EEC and the Euratom Treaties on January 1, 1958, between the same six nations, Belgium, France, Germany, Italy, Luxembourg and the Netherlands. By 1993 the number of member states of the Community had expanded to a total of fifteen. Denmark, Ireland and the United Kingdom became members in 1973, followed by Greece in 1981, by Spain and Portugal in 1986 and by Austria, Finland and Sweden in 1993.[3] The Community has legal personality (Article 281 of the EC Treaty). On 23 July 2002 the ECSC Treaty expired and is now integrated in the EC Treaty. In May 2004 ten additional countries joined the EU, making the total number of member states twenty-five European countries.[4]

The Maastricht Treaty – The European Union.
The European Union was established by the Maastricht Treaty, which was signed in Maastricht on February 7, 1992 by the then twelve members of the European Community (the 'EU Treaty' or the 'Maastricht Treaty').[5] This 'European Union' is based on three pillars: (i) the existing EC Treaties, (ii) a Common Foreign

1. 1997 OJ C 340/85.
2. The EEC Treaty was later renamed the European Community Treaty.
3. Norway had decided to join in 1973, but withdrew its application after a national referendum voted against membership.
4. 2003 OJ L 236. The ten new member states are: Cyprus, Czech Republic, Estonia, Hungary, Latvia, Lithuania, Malta, Poland, Slovakia, and Slovenia.
5. 1992 OJ C 224/1.

and Security Policy (Article 11) and (iii) the Fields of Justice and Home Affairs (Article 29). The latter two pillars (created by the EU Treaty) are quite distinct from the first one in that the jurisdiction of the Court of Justice does not apply to these fields (Article 46). However, the other European institutions, the European Parliament, the Council of Ministers and the Commission, exercise responsibilities with respect to all aspects of the European Union. The main objectives of the Maastricht Treaty are the strengthening of economic and social cohesion and the establishment of economic and monetary union, including a single currency (Articles 2 and 4). With the entry into force of the third stage of the European Monetary Union in January 1999, the currency exchange rates among the participating member states were locked and a new currency, the Euro, was born.[6]

The Amsterdam Treaty.
The Amsterdam Treaty, signed in 1997 and entered into force on May 1, 1999,[7] consolidates the European Union, it strengthens the position of the Parliament and adds in particular to the EU Treaty provisions on fundamental rights of citizens. The EC competition rules remain unchanged. However, Article 12 of the Amsterdam Treaty provides for a renumbering of the articles of the EC Treaty as amended by the Maastricht and the Amsterdam Treaty as mentioned above.

The Nice Treaty.
The Nice Treaty, signed in 2001 and entered into force on February 1, 2003, aims at preparing the accession of ten European countries to the EU as of May 2004.[8] It provides for changes within the institutions during the enlargement process, a new distribution of seats in the European Parliament, a change to the qualified majority system within the Council, a new composition of the Commission, major reforms to the Union's legal system in order to tackle the Court's case overload and to introduce greater flexibility, and a preventive instrument in the case of a serious and persistent breach of fundamental rights. The EC competition rules remain unchanged.

The Agreement on the European Economic Area.
The European Economic Area entered into force at the beginning of 1994 and is based on the European Economic Area Agreement (the 'EEA Agreement').[9] The Agreement provides for free movement of goods, persons, services and capital

---

6. Participating members are Belgium, Germany, Spain, France, Ireland, Italy, Luxembourg, the Netherlands, Austria, Portugal and Finland. The exchange rates between the national currencies and the EUR are laid down in Council Regulation 2866/98 of Dec. 31, 1998, 1998 OJ L 359/1.
7. 1997 OJ C 340/1. The ratification procedure terminated with the ratification of the Amsterdam Treaty by the last member state.
8. 2003 OJ C 24/11. A consolidated version of the Treaty has been published in 2003 OJ C 325/1.
9. 1994 OJ L 1/1.

similar to those in the EC Treaties and almost identical rules on competition policy. The EEA Agreement was originally concluded between the European Community, its member states and the members of the European Free Trade Association ('EFTA'), namely Austria, Finland, Sweden, Iceland, Norway, Liechtenstein and Switzerland. Since Austria, Finland and Sweden have become members of the European Community, at present the EEA members are now only Iceland, Norway and Liechtenstein. Switzerland failed to ratify the EEA Agreement.

Secondary Sources of EU Law.
The secondary sources of EU law comprise:

- Council regulations and Commission regulations based on a Council enabling regulation, which are binding in their entirety and directly applicable in all member states,[10]
- Directives of the Council, the Parliament or the Commission, which are binding, as to the result to be achieved, upon each member state to which they are addressed,[11] and
- Commission guidelines and notices, which have no binding force,[12] but do have a certain self-binding effect on the Commission.

2. The Legal Instruments of the European Community

The Assigned Tasks of the European Community.
The assigned tasks of the Community are, by establishing a common market and progressively approximating the economic policies of member states, to promote 'a harmonious development of economic activities, a continuous and balanced expansion, an increase in stability, an accelerated raising of the standard of living and closer relations between the states belonging to it'[13] with the aim of establishing a barrier-free EC internal market.[14] To this end, the activities of the Community include, *inter alia,* the elimination of customs duties, quantitative restrictions on imports and exports between member states and all other measures having equivalent effect, the establishment of a common external customs tariff and of a common commercial policy toward third countries, the abolition of obstacles to freedom of movement for persons, services and capital, the adoption of a common policy in the spheres of agriculture and transport, the application of procedures to

---

10. Article 249 (2) of the EC Treaty.
11. Article 249 (3) of the EC Treaty.
12. Article 249 (5) of the EC Treaty.
13. Article 2 of the EC Treaty.
14. Article 14 of the EC Treaty. In 1986 the EC member states decided upon a crash program of measures to complete the process of establishing the 'internal market' by adopting the 'Single European Act', 1987 OJ L 169/1.

coordinate the economic policies of the member states, and the harmonization of laws to the extent required for the proper functioning of a common market.[15] Not the least among these activities of the Community is 'the institution of a system ensuring that competition in the common market is not distorted'.[16]

Free Movement of Goods and Services Principle.
Articles 28 to 30 and 49 to 55 of the EC Treaty are designed to assure the free movement of goods and services within a single European market. The free movement of goods and services is ensured by a prohibition against any quantitative restrictions and all measures having equivalent effects except those justified on grounds of public morality, public policy or public security, the protection of health and life or the protection of industrial or commercial property. The prohibition is addressed to member states, but it may also be enforced before national courts by individuals and firms. The EEA Agreement contains similar provisions on free movement of goods and services.[17]

Competition Rules Fundamental to Free Movement of Goods and Services.
The principle of free competition is the basic principle for all economic activity within the Community. Economic policy is to be 'conducted in accordance with the principle of an open market economy with free competition' (Article 4 (1)). Free competition may be distorted by the behavior of firms or by practices of member states. The EC Treaties and the EEA Agreement provide for a unique set of legal instruments to act against both forms of distortion: Competition rules that apply to undertakings and other competition rules that apply to member states.

Competition Rules Applying to Undertakings.
The principal competition rules of the EC Treaty and the EEA Agreement that apply to undertakings are:

- Article 81 of the EC Treaty and Article 53 of the EEA Agreement prohibit *agreements* between firms, *decisions* by associations of firms and *concerted practices* which may affect trade between member states of the EU and/or the EEA and which have as their object or effect the prevention, restriction or distortion of competition, subject to clearance criteria set forth in these provisions,
- Article 82 of the EC Treaty and Article 54 of the EEA Agreement prohibit any *abuse* by one or more firms of a dominant position in so far as it may affect trade between member states of the EU and/or of the EEA, and

15. Article 3 of the EC Treaty.
16. Article 3 (g) of the EC Treaty.
17. Articles 8–13 (free movement of goods) and 28 (free movement of services) of the EEA Agreement.

- Article 2 (3) of the merger regulation[18] and Article 57 of the EEA Agreement prohibit *concentrations* (mergers, acquisitions and certain joint ventures) which significantly impede effective competition within the EU or EEA or a substantial part thereof, in particular as a result of the creation or strengthening of a dominant position. These articles apply in principle to trade in goods and services by firms in all industries, including the field of nuclear energy,[19] and to the coal and steel sectors.[20]

Regulations and Notices: Supplements to the Competition Rules.
The main supplements to the competition rules set forth in Articles 81–89 of the EC Treaty are:

- *Council and Commission Regulations:* Regulations on substantive law, in particular block exemption regulations, and procedural regulations, in particular Regulation 1/2003 on the enforcement of the competition rules, and its implementing regulation. They are legally binding upon those to whom they are addressed,[21]
- *Commission Notices:* Notices (also called 'communications' or 'guidelines') that explain the competition rules and how the Commission intends to apply them. They do not have the force of law but bind the Commission in its administrative proceedings. [22]

Competition Rules Applying to Member States.
Article 86 of the EC Treaty and Article 59 of the EEA Agreement are designed to ensure that firms that are in state ownership, or are granted special or exclusive rights, do not evade the rules on competition. Articles 87 and 88 of the EC Treaty and Articles 61 and 62 of the EEA Agreement prohibit government subsidies ('state aids') that threaten to distort competition insofar as they may affect trade

18. Regulation 139/2004.
19. The Euratom Treaty does not contain specific competition rules. Article 305 (2) of the EC Treaty makes the EC rules applicable.
20. The ECSC Treaty contained a prohibition of cartels (Article 65), powers to act against the abuse of a dominant position (Article 66 (7)), and merger control (Article 66 (1)–(6)). These provisions expired when the EC competition rules became applicable to the coal and steel sectors on July 23, 2002. Article 305 of the EC Treaty establishes the principle of subsidiarity of the ECSC Treaty, which implies the applicability of the EC rules after the expiry of the ECSC Treaty. However, the substantive rules of the ECSC Treaty remain applicable with respect to conduct committed under ECSC law (although there are no transitionary provisions): Commission's Communication of June 26, 2002, 2002 OJ C 152/5, point 31; *Concrete reinforcing bar cartel*, D.Comm. Dec. 17, 2002, IP/02/1908 (appeal still pending).
21. Article 249 of the EC Treaty.
22. *Peugeot*, CFI April 22, 1993, 1993 ECR II-493, paras 71–74; *Auffass*, CFI Dec. 12, 1996, 1996 ECR II-2169, para. 57; *LR af 1998 (Carton)*, CFI March 20, 2002, 2002 ECR II-1705, para. 360.

between member states of the EU and/or the EEA, subject to certain exceptions and exemptions to be granted by the Commission.

Market Integration Function.
The Commission, which is charged with the responsibility to enforce the competition rules, has described competition policy under the EC Treaty as having dual and largely complementary objectives, namely:

> 'first it must enable competition to perform its traditional role in helping to improve the allocation of resources, increase businessmen's capacities for adjustment and better satisfy the requirements of consumers; secondly, it must reinforce the unity of the Community market by eliminating obstacles to trade between Member States.'[23]

Thus, the Community's competition policy is not only an instrument to assure that competition is not unduly restrained; it also serves as a crucial instrument within the overall purpose of the EC Treaty to promote integration of national markets into a unified, 'internal market' (Article 14). Unlike the United States economy which blossomed in an environment with minimal governmental or private restrictions on trade between its states, the Community's integration objective reflects a strong desire to dismantle longstanding government-imposed or privately implemented barriers to trade that have insulated European firms from sources of competition in neighbouring countries. The simultaneous pursuit of vigorous competition policy and elimination of trade barriers between the member states is designed to foster an economic and legal environment in which competitively viable firms will expand output and increase efficiency as a result of a larger home market extending over the whole of the EU and EEA.

3. The Institutions of the European Community

The four governing institutions of the Community are the European Parliament, the Council, the Commission and the Court of Justice.

Council.
The Council is the Community's primary decision-making body and its principal legislator. The Council is composed of ministers from the governments of the member states, and it acts on proposals by the Commission. In the field of competition law, the Council is empowered under Article 83 of the EC Treaty to adopt appropriate regulations or directives to implement the competition rules set out in Articles 81 and 82.

23. Twelfth Report on Competition Policy, p. 12.

Commission.

The Commission is the executive arm of the Community. Article 211 of the EC Treaty empowers the Commission to apply its provisions and the regulations, directives and decisions made under the Treaty by the institutions of the Community, to formulate recommendations and deliver opinions on matters dealt with in the Treaty, itself to exercise powers of decision and to propose measures to be taken by the Council and the European Parliament, and to exercise other powers which the Council confers for the implementation of its rules. The Commission is composed, as of May 2004, of 30 members ('Commissioners')[24] nominated by the governments of the member states and approved by the European Parliament. The Commission's administration is organized into Directorate Generals which cover the major subject matters. The Directorate-General for Competition ('DG-COMP') is charged with enforcing the competition rules under the instructions of the member of the Commission responsible for competition matters.[25]

Parliament.

The European Parliament is directly elected by voters in each member state. The reforms introduced by the 1986 'Single European Act' and by the Treaty of the European Union (the 'Maastricht Treaty') have increased the influence Parliament can exert on legislation. Article 192 of the EC Treaty empowers the Parliament to participate in the process leading up to the adoption of Community acts, by delivering advisory opinions or submitting appropriate proposals and by exercising co-decision or co-operation powers (Articles 247 and 248). The European Parliament is furthermore empowered to approve or disapprove the Commission's budget (Article 276), to dismiss the entire Commission by motion of censure (Article 201) and to obtain answers from the Commission to its questions (Article 197 (3)). The European Parliament may also hear petitions of any natural or legal person residing in a member state (Article 193), and it has appointed an Ombudsman empowered to receive complaints from any citizen of the European Union (Article 194). The Amsterdam Treaty will further increase the powers of Parliament.

Court of Justice.

The European Court of Justice is the final arbiter of legal disputes arising under Community law. The Court of Justice is, as from May 2004, composed of 25 judges and assisted by eight advocates general. It has three principal functions. First, the Court provides judicial review over acts of the Council, the Commission and the European Parliament.[26] Second, it gives rulings on preliminary questions

24. As from Nov. 1, 2004 reduced to 25 members (one per country), *see* Treaty of Nice and MEMO/04/61 of March 16, 2004.
25. *See* in greater detail Chapter X.A.2 (a).
26. Article 230 of the EC Treaty.

as to the interpretation of the Treaties or Community legislation referred to it by courts of the member states.[27] Third, it determines whether a member state has infringed its obligations under the Treaties.[28] Since November 1989, the Court of Justice has been assisted by a lower court called the Court of First Instance.[29] The Court of First Instance, with 25 judges, has jurisdiction in all actions brought against the Commission by natural or legal persons.[30] This includes all competition cases. All other actions, in particular actions brought by a member state or an institution of the Communities against another institution or a member state, and the appeal against judgments of the Court of First Instance, are heard by the Court of Justice.

The Institutions of the European Economic Area (EEA).
The institutions of the EEA Agreement are the EEA Council,[31] the EEA Joint Committee,[32] the EFTA Surveillance Authority (ESA)[33] and the EFTA Court.[34] Both the Commission and the ESA can apply the competition rules of the EEA Agreement in close cooperation and consultation of each other.[35] According to Article 56 of the EEA Agreement, the ESA deals with cases which only affect trade between EFTA countries and cases involving companies realizing at least one third of their turnover in EFTA countries, i.e. Norway, Iceland and Liechtenstein. Given the limited importance and the geographic dispersion of the EFTA countries, most competition cases are in fact dealt with by the Commission, which applies in parallel Article 81 of the EC Treaty and Article 53 of the EEA Agreement, Article 82 of the EC Treaty and Article 54 of the EEA Agreement as well as the merger control regulation and Article 57 of the EEA Agreement. Actions against decisions of the ESA may be brought before the EFTA Court,[36] whereas decisions adopted by the Commission under both the EU Treaty and the EEA Agreement may be brought before the Court of First Instance and the Court of Justice.[37] The final interpreter of the EEA Agreement is the Court of Justice.[38]

---

27. Article 234 of the EC Treaty.
28. Articles 226 and 227 of the EC Treaty.
29. Council Decision 88/591, 1988 OJ L 319/1. *See infra* Chapter X.G.
30. Articles 230 (4) and 232 (3) of the EC Treaty.
31. Article 89 of the EEA Agreement.
32. Article 92 of the EEA Agreement.
33. Article 108 (1) of the EEA Agreement. The Authority is located in Brussels.
34. Article 108 (2) of the EEA Agreement. The Court is located in Geneva.
35. Article 109 (1) and (2) of the EEA Agreement. *See* Article 58 of the EEA Agreement and Protocols 23 and 24.
36. Article 108 of the EEA Agreement.
37. Article 110 of the EEA Agreement.
38. Article 111 of the EEA Agreement. *See* the Court of Justice's opinions expressed in *EEA I*, Dec. 14, 1991, 1991 ECR I-6079, and *EEA II*, April 10, 1992, 1992 ECR I-2825.

B. Application of the Community's Competition Rules

1. Scope of Applicability

Direct Applicability.
The EC Treaty and the EEA Agreement are more than treaties that establish mutual obligations between signatory nations.[39] In contrast to most international treaties,[40] the EC and ECSC Treaties establish bodies of law that have become a part of the law of each member state and are directly enforceable by their national courts. The directly applicable provisions of the Treaties create rights and obligations between individuals *inter se* and between individuals and governments of the member states.[41] This is because under the Treaties the member states have created a supranational legal regime that is binding both on their subjects and on themselves. They have established the Community for an unlimited period, equipped it with governing organs, with legal and executive capacities, with diplomatic powers, and have transferred to it sovereignty in certain fields.[42]

A condition for the direct application of Community law is that the relevant provisions are 'self-executing'; they must be suited according to their legal nature, system and wording to have direct application in the legal relationships of the Community and its subjects.[43] Despite the necessarily general wording of the rules of competition, the Court of Justice has held that they are sufficiently specific and conceived and written as directly applicable rules.[44] Under Article 1

39. *See EEA I*, ECJ Dec. 14, 1991, 1991 ECR I-6079, para. 21.
40. Including the GATT Agreement: ECJ May 2, 2001, 2001 ECR I-3159.
41. *See* in particular: *Van Gend & Loos*, ECJ Feb. 5, 1963, 1963 ECR I, 12; *BRT/SABAM I*, ECJ Jan. 30, 1974, 1974 ECR 51, 62–63, paras 16–17; *Delimitis/Henninger Bräu*, ECJ Feb. 28, 1991, 1991 ECR I-935, para. 45; *Automec II*, CFI Sept. 18, 1992, 1992 ECR II-2223, para. 90. The view advanced in the early years of the Community that the Treaty competition provisions constituted only guidelines or a grant of authority was superseded not later than 1962 with the enactment of Regulation 17 and the *Bosch* decision of the Court of Justice: *Bosch*, ECJ April 6, 1962, 1962 ECR 45.
42. *Costa/ENEL*, ECJ July 15, 1964, 1964 ECR 585, 593. With respect to the EEA Agreement the EFTA Court of Justice ruled in *Erla Maria Sveinbjörndottir* (Dec. 10, 1998, E-9/97): 'The Court concludes from the foregoing considerations that the EEA Agreement is an international treaty *sui generis* which contains a distinct legal order of its own. The EEA Agreement does not establish a customs union but an enhanced free trade area ... The depth of integration of the EEA Agreement is less far-reaching than under the EC Treaty, but the scope and the objective of the EEA Agreement goes far beyond what is usual for an agreement under public international law'. (para. 59).
43. The conditions for direct effect were summed up by the Advocate General in *Reyners v. Belgium*, ECJ June 21, 1974, 1974 ECR 631, 659–663. *See also* Chapter III. 1.
44. *BRT/SABAM I*, ECJ Jan. 30, 1974, 1974 ECR 51, paras 16–17. *See also Hoffmann-La Roche*, ECJ Feb. 13, 1979, 1979 ECR 461, paras 128–134. Article 81 has only been directly applicable since the enactment of implementing rules under Article 87 of the EC Treaty. For most industries this has been so since 1962 when Regulation 17 came into force: *Bosch*, *supra* note

(1) and (3) of Regulation 1/2003, any infringement of Article 81 or Article 82 is prohibited without any prior decision to that effect being required. By their very nature these provisions have direct effect on the relationships among natural and legal persons, the member states and Community bodies; they also create direct rights to be exercised by and against natural and legal persons which the courts of the member states must protect.[45]

Application by National Courts and National Competition Authorities. As a consequence of direct applicability, Articles 81 and 82 cannot only be applied by the Commission but also by national courts and national competition authorities.[46] They can be the basis for remedies in civil proceedings, such as the nullity of prohibited agreements or actions for damages. They are also part of the public policy (or *ordre public*) under the national law of each member state and may not be derogated from by contract.[47] In *van Schijndel* the Court decided that national courts have to apply Articles 81 and 82 even if the parties to a procedure have not expressly relied on them.[48] Finally, the right to grant an exemption under Article 81 (3) that was formerly reserved to the Commission can now also be exercised by national competition authorities and national courts.[49]

Sector-Wide Applicability of the Community Competition Rules. The Community's competition rules, i.e., principally Articles 81 and 82 of the EC Treaty, apply generally to all economic sectors (including, since July 23, 2002,

---

41. This applies to any industry not specifically excluded, such as insurance: *Fire Insurance*, ECJ Jan. 27, 1987, 1987 ECR 405, 451, paras 11–14. For the transport sector, which was excluded from the scope of Regulation 17 and covered by special procedural rules issued later, Article 81 has been directly applicable since the entry into force of those rules: *Nouvelles Frontieres*, ECJ April 30, 1986, 1986 ECR 1425, paras 60–64; *Ahmed Saeed*, ECJ April 11, 1989, 1989 ECR 803, para. 20.

45. *BRT/SABAM I*, ECJ Jan. 30, 1974, 1974 ECR 51, para. 16 ('As the prohibitions of Articles 85 [81] (1) and 86 [82] tend by their very nature to produce direct effects in relations between individuals, these Articles create direct rights in respect of the individuals concerned which the national courts must safeguard.'). *See also Sacchi/Tele Biella*, ECJ April 30, 1974, 1974 ECR 409, 430, para. 18; *Marty/Estée Lauder*, ECJ July 10, 1980, 1980 ECR 248/1, 2500, para. 13; *Sugar I (intervention)*, Dec. 11, 1973, 1973 ECR 1465, para. 7 ('Since it is the particular objective of the Union to represent and protect consumers, it can show an interest in the correct application of Community provisions in the field of competition, which not only ensure that the common market operates normally but which also tend to favor consumers.'); *Delimitis/Henninger Bräu*, ECJ Feb. 28, 1991, 1991 ECR I-935, para. 45.

46. From May 1, 2004 national authorities and national courts will also be empowered to apply Article 81 (3): Articles 5 and 6 of Regulation 1/2003.

47. *See*, e.g., *BMW-Importe*, German Federal Supreme Court (BGH) Oct. 23, 1979, WuWE BGH 1643, 1645; *Sacem*, French Cour de Cassation, Dec. 13, 1983, 1984–3 CMLR 233.

48. *Van Schijndel and van Veen v. Stichting Pensioenfonds*, ECJ Dec. 14, 1995, 1995 ECR I-4705, para. 15. However, this is limited to jurisdictions where the relevant national law of procedure allows a court to rely on provisions not invoked by a party to the proceedings.

49. Articles 5 and 6 of Regulation 1/2003.

to the coal and steel sectors) with a narrow exception for agriculture and certain fields of transport.[50]

Territory of the EC Treaty.
As from May 2004 the competition rules apply in the territories of all 25 member states (the earlier 15[51] and the additional 10 new member states[52]), including the French Overseas Departments,[53] the Channel Islands[54] and the Portuguese islands of Madeira and the Azores, whereas the Danish territories of Greenland and the Faeroe Islands are excluded.[55] They also apply in the European territories for whose external relations a member state is responsible.[56] In practice, the latter category only covers Gibraltar since the Channel Islands, the Isle of Man and the United Kingdom Sovereign Base Areas in Cyprus are also subject to special arrangements which generally excludes them from the Community.[57] The competition rules do *not* apply to the independent 'states within states' of San Marino, Monaco and the Vatican, nor to the co-principality of Andorra.[58]

Territory of the EEA Agreement.
The EEA Agreement applies to EC member states and the other 'Contracting Parties', namely Norway, Iceland and Liechtenstein.[59]

Competition Rules Applying to Other European Countries.
Provisions similar to those of Community's competition rules are contained in the Agreement on the European Free Trade Association ('EFTA') concluded on January 1, 1977. However, these provisions are principles rather than directly applicable law.[60] The EFTA Agreement is practically limited to restrictions on

---

50. *See* in greater detail Chapter VIII.B. and C.
51. Austria, Belgium, Denmark, Finland, Germany, Greece, France, Ireland, Italy, Luxembourg, the Netherlands, Portugal, Spain, Sweden and the United Kingdom.
52. Cyprus, Czech Republic, Estonia, Hungary, Latvia, Lithuania, Malta, Poland, Slovakia and Slovenia, Norway, Iceland and Liechtenstein are members of the EEA; Switzerland is not a member of the Community.
53. Guadeloupe, Guyana, Martinique, Réunion and St. Pierre-et-Miquelon. *See Somaco*, ECJ July 7, 1998, 1998 ECR I-2587.
54. *See Konica*, D.Comm. Dec. 18, 1987, 1988 OJ L 78/34, point 23.
55. The Faeroe Islands were excluded at the time Denmark acceded to the Community. *See* Article 299 (5) (a) of the EC Treaty. Greenland was excluded from the Community at its own request in 1985 and, despite its status as part of the Danish Kingdom, is now treated as one of the overseas countries and territories under Part Four of the EC Treaty (Articles 182–186). *See* 1985 OJ L 29/1.
56. Article 299 (4).
57. Article 299 (5) (c).
58. These are effectively independent states which do not fall into any of the categories referred to in Article 299.
59. Article 126 of the EEA Agreement.
60. Anticompetitive agreements and practices are 'incompatible', but not 'prohibited' as under the EC Treaty.

imports to and exports from Switzerland.[61]

2. Economic Policy Objectives

(a) Market Economy as Foundation of the Community

Market Economy/Federal Structure.
The original member states of the Community, and those which joined later, have mainly market economies, as opposed to the centrally planned economies of socialist countries. The treaties therefore reflect market economy principles,[62] the basis of which is the belief that optimal economic efficiency is achieved when economic decision-making is left to businesses operating in competition with one another in the marketplace. The market economy can take various forms. The Community is not designed to replace or harmonize the economic order of the member states; this would contradict the federal structure of the Community in which the member states retain a considerable degree of sovereignty. Member states are free to pursue their own economic policies to the extent that they do not jeopardize the attainment of the objectives of the Community.[63]

National Competition Rules.
All member states have national competition laws, which apply – after the expiration of the ECSC Treaty in July 2002 – also to the coal and steel sectors. Member states may pursue their own competition policy in relation to domestic restrictive practices. Accordingly, the competition laws of individual member states need not be identical to achieve an effective competition policy; the harmonization of these laws is not a central purpose but may be a consequence of the Community's competition rules. However, member states are prohibited from discriminating on grounds of nationality when applying their competition law,[64] and the application of national law must not prejudice the full and uniform application of Community law or the effects of measures taken or to be taken to implement Community law,[65] i.e., the application of national law must not render virtually impossible or excessively difficult the exercise of rights conferred by Community law.[66] The

---

61. EFTA Agreement with Switzerland, 1972 OJ L 300/188.
62. *See* new Article 4 of the EC Treaty: Principle of open market economy with free competition.
63. Article 10 of the EC Treaty. This freedom includes according to Article 86 (2) the freedom of member states to reserve the operation of services of general economic interest (as defined by them and possibly in a different way from member state to member state) to undertakings entrusted by them, provided however that the application of the competition rules is not excluded (they are inapplicable only insofar as they would 'obstruct' the performance of the tasks assigned to the undertakings). *See* in greater detail Chapter IX.C.
64. Article 12 of the EC Treaty; *Walt Wilhelm*, ECJ Feb. 13, 1969, 1969 ECR 1, 15–16.
65. Article 10 of the EC Treaty; *Walt Wilhelm*, ECJ Feb. 13, 1969, 1969 ECR 1, 14.
66. *Commission/Italy (Law 428/1990)*, ECJ Dec. 9, 2003, C-129/00, para. 25. *See* in greater detail section F.2. *infra*.

EC competition rules have dramatically influenced the harmonization of national competition laws in order to avoid or reduce contradictions or conflicts when applying either EC or national competition rules or both in cases of parallel application to the same facts.[67] Member states that until recently had no national competition laws 'modeled' their national competition rules on the EC competition rules, whereas member states which had longstanding national competition laws have moved toward a greater integration of EC standards.[68] The applicable national competition laws are the following:[69]

- *Austria*: Federal Act on the establishment of a Federal Competition Authority (BGBl. I Nr 62/2002 Article I) and Federal Act of October 19, 1988 on cartels and other restrictive practices (1988 Cartel Act: initial version: Federal Law Gazette No. 600/1988 and Amendment of 1988 Cartel Act published in BGBl. I Nr. 33/2003).
- *Belgium*: Act on the Protection of Economic Competition, co-ordinated on July 1, 1999 (Belgian Official Gazette, 01.09.1999).
- *Denmark*: Consolidated Competition Act No. 539 of June 28, 2002 (Act No. 384 of June 10, 1997 as amended by Act No. 416 of May 31, 2000) and Act No. 426 of June 6, 2002).
- *Finland*: Act on Competition Restrictions (480/1992), amended by (447/94), (448/94), (600/1995), (908/1995) and (303/1998); Act on the Finnish Competition Authority of July 28, 1998 (711/1988) amended by (482/1992).
- *France*: New Economic Regulations Act of May 15, 2001 (amendment to Book IV of the Code of Commercial Law); Book IV of the Code of Commercial Law on the freedom to set prices and compete.
- *Germany*: Act against Restraints of Competition of January 1, 1958 (as amended in January 2002, BGBl. 1998 I-2546).
- *Greece*: Competition Act (703/77) on the control of Monopolies and Oligopolies and the Protection of Free Competition.
- *Ireland*: Competition Act 2002.
- *Italy*: Law No. 287 of October 10, 1990, Competition and Fair Trading Act.
- *Luxembourg*: Law of May 17, 2004; Memorial No. 76 of May 26, 2004.
- *Netherlands*: New Regulations on Economic Competition (Competition Act) 1997.
- *Portugal*: Law No. 18/2003 of June 11 Approving the Legal Framework for Competition.
- *Spain*: Competition Act 16/1989 of July 17, 1989 (as amended by Act 62/2003, of December 30, 2003).

---

67. *See Bronner/Mediaprint*, ECJ Nov. 26, 1998, 1998 ECR I-7791 (preliminary ruling on the interpretation of Article 82 in order to permit the application of national (Austrian) law in the light of Community law).
68. However, the new Swiss competition law of April 1, 2004 is based on a system of prior notification (with immunity from fines); *see* WuW 2004–5, 495, 506.
69. Further information is available on http://www.europa.eu.int/comm/competition/other_sites/

- *Sweden*: Competition Act (entered into force on July 1, 1993).
- *United Kingdom*: Competition Act of 1998 and Enterprise Act 2002.

The applicable national competition laws in the new member states are as follows:[70]

- *Cyprus*: Protection of Competition Law, 1989, and Control of Concentrations between Enterprises Law, 1999.
- *Czech Republic*: Antitrust Act, 144/2001.
- *Estonia*: Competition Act 2001, anticipating the EC competition rules, in particular with respect to the assessment of horizontal and vertical agreements (including *de minimis* thresholds) and mergers.
- *Hungary*: Act on Prohibition of Unfair and Restrictive Market Practices, LXX/2001.
- *Latvia*: Competition Act 2002.
- *Lithuania*: Law of Competition, Resolution 45/2002.
- *Malta*: Competition Act 1994.
- *Poland*: Law on Competition and Consumer Protection, 2000, which is modeled on the EC competition rules.
- *Slovakia*: Act on Protection of Competition Act 136/2001 as amended by Act 465/2002.
- *Slovenia*: Prevention of Restrictions of Competition Act, 2000.

(b) 'Effective Competition' as a Starting Point

'Effective Competition'.
The Court has stated that the competition rules are designed to maintain 'effective competition', meaning that in each market there must be sufficient competition to ensure the observance of the basic requirements and the attainment of the objectives of the Treaty, in particular the creation of a single market achieving conditions similar to those of a domestic market.[71] A central focus of the Court's decisions is the principle of independent decision-making by firms active in the marketplace. Competition may function effectively only if firms make autonomous business decisions. This freedom of economic decision making includes the right to adapt to the conduct of competitors, but it strictly precludes contacts whose object or effect is to influence the conduct of an actual or potential competitor or to disclose the firm's own future conduct.[72] There is no regulation or law that orders firms to

70. *See* Global Counsel Handbooks, 2003/2004.
71. *Continental Can*, ECJ Feb. 21, 1973, 1973 ECR 215, paras 25–26; *Hoffmann-La Roche*, ECJ Feb. 13, 1979, 1979 ECR 461, para. 38; *SABA I*, ECJ Oct. 25, 1977, 1977 ECR 1875, paras 20–22.
72. *Sugar*, ECJ Dec. 16, 1973, 1973 ECR 1663, paras 172–174; *John Deere*, ECJ May 28, 1998, 1998 ECR I-3111, para. 86.

compete. The competition rules are infringed only if actual or potential competition is restrained through an agreement or a concerted practice that causes at least one of the parties to surrender some of its freedom to compete (Article 81) or if its ability to compete is restricted by an abuse of a dominant position (Article 82).

Interpretation in the Light of the Basic Principles in Articles 2 and 3. The competition rules are to be interpreted in their legal and economic context.[73] They protect both competition as an economically beneficial institution and preserve individual economic freedom as part of the foundation of political freedom guaranteed by a democracy.[74] In relation to the first of these goals, the principles stated in Articles 2 and 3 of the EC Treaty provide guidance as to the interpretation of the competition rules in Articles 81 and 82. Under Article 2, the Community has as its task, by establishing a common market, including a monetary union, and progressively approximating – not standardizing – the economic policies of member states, to promote throughout the Community a harmonious development of economic activities, a continuous and balanced expansion, an increase in stability, an accelerated raising of the standard of living and closer relations between the member states. One of the several means of attaining these goals, set forth in Article 3 (g) of the Treaty, is 'the institution of a system ensuring that competition in the common market is not distorted'. The Court of Justice has ruled that these basic principles in Articles 2 and 3 are merely given concrete expression in Articles 81 and 82. Thus, the Court has repeatedly made reference in its decisions on competition issues to Articles 2 and 3 as the basic principles underlying the EC Treaty's rules of competition,[75] In the *SABA* case the Court of Justice stated that 'the requirement of Article 3 (g) that competition shall not be distorted implies the existence on the market of workable competition, that is to say the degree of competition necessary to ensure observance of the basic requirements and the attainment of the objectives of the Treaty, in particular the creation of a single market achieving conditions similar to those of a domestic market'.[76]

Evaluation of Pro- and Anticompetitive Effects under Article 81. The prohibition of anticompetitive agreements and concerted practices in Article 81 (1) is tempered by a possibility of exemption under Article 81 (3) where the agreements or practices also have significant procompetitive effects, such as to

73. Constant practice of the Court of Justice, *see Langnese-Iglo*, CFI June 8, 1995, 1995 ECR II-1533, para. 99.
74. *See Sugar I (Intervention)*, ECJ Dec. 11, 1973, 1973 ECR 1465, para. 7.
75. E.g., *Continental Can*, ECJ Feb. 21, 1973, 1973 ECR 215, paras 22–26; *Hoffmann-La Roche*, ECJ Feb. 13, 1979, 1979 ECR 461, para. 38; *SFEI*, CFI Jan. 15, 1997, 1997 ECR II-4, para. 56. Similarly, the Court of First Instance ruled that the competition rules of the ECSC Treaty must be interpreted in the light of the fundamental objectives of Articles 2–5: *Steel Beams -British Steel*, CFI March 11, 1999, 1999 ECR II-629, para. 276.
76. *SABA I*, ECJ Oct. 25, 1977, 1977 ECR 1875, paras 20–21.

contribute to improving the production or distribution of goods or to promoting technical or economic progress. This evaluation was formerly left exclusively with the Commission. Under Regulation 1/2003 the exclusive competence of the Commission to grant an exemption under Article 81 (3) is abolished from May 1, 2004. This extends the competence to apply the provisions of Article 81 (3) beyond the Commission: national authorities and national courts may decide whether the conditions for exemption set forth in Article 81 (3) have been satisfied. The evaluation of pro- and anticompetitive effects under Article 81 (3) must be based on both existing and future competitive conditions. Accordingly, the evaluation must take into account, *inter alia,* the nature and quantity of the products or services covered by the agreement, the position and importance of the parties in the market for the products concerned, and the isolated nature of the disputed agreement or, alternatively, its context in a series of agreements.[77] The competition rules are not designed to establish uniform competitive conditions in all member states. The Court of Justice has recognized that market conditions may vary from one member state to the next,[78] even after the Community's single 'internal market' is established (Article 14) without, however, leading to completely uniform conditions for many reasons: varying consumer preferences, currencies, languages, tax and regulatory measures and competitive advantages based on the physical location of competing firms.

Interpretation in Context with Overall Objectives of the Community – Competition Policy v. Industrial Policy.
Although the competition rules have not been amended by the Maastricht and the Amsterdam Treaties, competition policy must be seen in the context of the overall objectives of the EC Treaty as it has been amended by both Treaties. As expressed in the Commission's Twenty-sixth Report on Competition Policy, the aim of competition policy is 'to ensure that markets acquire or maintain the flexibility they need to allow scope for initiative and innovation and to allow an effective and dynamic allocation of society's resources'.[79] This means that competition policy interacts with most other broadly based policies, such as the development of the internal market, the policy on growth and competitiveness,[80] the policy of cohesion,[81] research and development policy,[82] environmental policy[83] and consumer

77. Long-standing practice: *Maschinenbau Ulm*, ECJ June 30, 1966, 1966 ECR 235, 250; *Haecht I*, ECJ Dec. 12, 1967, 1967 ECR 407, 415; *Bilger/Jehle*, ECJ March 18, 1970, 1970 ECR 127, 135, para. 5; *Beguelin*, ECJ Nov. 25, 1971, 1971 ECR 949, 960, para. 18; *Delimitis/Henninger*, ECJ Feb. 28, 1991, 1991 ECR I-935, paras 15–22.
78. *See Parke Davis*, ECJ Feb. 29, 1968, 1968 ECR 55, 71–73.
79. Twenty-sixth Report on Competition Policy, point 1.
80. Articles 3 (1) and 157.
81. Article 158.
82. Article 163.
83. Article 174. *See Eco-Emballage*, D.Comm. June 15, 2001, 2001 OJ L 233/37; *DSD (Green dot)*, D.Comm. Sept. 17, 2001, 2001 OJ L 319/1.

protection.[84] These additional aspects are therefore relevant for the application of the competition rules,[85] as stated in the Council's Conclusions on the Contribution of Industrial Policy to European Competitiveness:[86]

> '... all policies related to enhancing competitiveness should be based on a careful analysis of the relevant aspects, as well as on an equilibrium between the economic, social and environmental pillars of sustainable development'.

3. Modernization of the EC Competition Rules

The Scope of Competition Rules in the Light of the Enlargement and the Progressive Integration of the Community.

As a result of the accession of new member states, the progressive integration of national markets and the globalization of the economy, an ever increasing number of agreements and concerted practices became subject to the competition rules requiring clearance by the Commission under Article 81 (3). The consequence is that a disproportionally large amount of the Commission's resources have been devoted to clearance of agreements and concerted practices, and too few resources were devoted to investigation of serious offenses that remain unnotified, such as market allocation and price fixing. Therefore, Regulation 1/2003, which replaces Regulation 17 from May 1, 2004, provides for an 'adjustment' of the actual enforcement system through the decentralized application of both Article 81 and Article 82 by national authorities and national courts. Regulation 1/2003 is based on the Commission's Green Paper on Vertical Restraints and its White Paper on Modernization of the EC competition rules.

The Commission Green Paper on Vertical Restraints.

In its *Green Paper on Vertical Restraints*[87] the Commission recommended a shift from the former policy on clause-related rules with sector-specific regulation to a system based on economic effects covering virtually all sectors of distribution. The proposal aimed at simplifying administrative supervision and the legislative framework, thereby ensuring effective protection of competition and providing adequate legal certainty for firms. Following this proposal the Council adopted on June 10, 1999 two regulations:

84. Article 153.
85. *See* e.g. the consideration of social aspects in *SABA*, ECJ Oct. 25, 1977, 1977 ECR 1875, para. 43; *Nestlé-Perrier*, CFI April 27, 1995, 1995 ECR II-1213, paras 30–31.
86. 2003 OJ C 317/2. *See also* Twenty-first Report on Competition Policy, point 45.
87. Jan. 22, 1997, COM(96)721 final, Twenty-sixth Report on Competition Policy, points 263–271.

- *Regulation 1215/99 amending Regulation 19/65 on the Application of Article 81 (3) of the EC Treaty to Certain Categories of Agreements and Concerted Practices.*[88] The regulation empowers the Commission to issue block exemption regulations covering all types of vertical restraints, including exclusive purchasing agreements concerning the supply of goods or services intended for processing or incorporation and selective distribution agreements. On the basis of this regulation the Commission has issued a single *block exemption Regulation 2790/1999* replacing the existing block exemptions on exclusive distribution, exclusive purchasing and franchising agreements.[89] The Commission also adopted Regulation 772/2004 on transfer of technology agreements replacing Regulation 240/96. The new regulations no longer enumerate the exempted clauses ('white clauses') but rather (i) define those restrictions which fall outside the regulation ('black clauses' or 'hardcore restrictions'), such as resale price maintenance and absolute territorial protection, and (ii) define a market share limitation below which all other (non-black) clauses are deemed compatible with Article 81. In addition the Commission adopted guidelines with respect to the assessment of agreements and concerted practices between parties having market shares above the new market share thresholds beyond which the block exemptions will not apply.[90] The result is a greater decentralization in the application of the EC competition rules, including a new power given to national competition authorities to withdraw the benefit of the block exemption in cases where the anticompetitive effects of an agreement or of a network of agreements are felt in their territory.
- *Regulation 1216/99 Amending Regulation 17.*[91] This regulation dispenses vertical restrictive agreements from the requirement of prior notification. Such agreements may be notified at any time and exempted with retroactive effect going back to the date of their conclusion irrespective of the date of their notification, provided they fulfill the conditions of Article 81 (3) and do not contain hardcore restrictions. This regulation permits the implementation of agreements without prior notification at the parties' own risk, including damage claims and fines, and the possibility of exemption with retroactive effect. This would apply in particular to exclusive purchasing agreements between companies with market shares of 30–40% or more, which will not be covered by the block exemption regulation and will thereby be left to an individual assessment under Article 81 (3).

88. 1999 OJ L 148/1.
89. 1999 OJ L 336/21.
90. 2000 OJ C 291/3.
91. 1999 OJ L 148/5.

The Commission White Paper on Modernization of the EC Competition Rules.

The White Paper[92] aimed at modernizing the EC competition rules through their more efficient implementation, thereby ensuring the role of competition as the driving force of the economy throughout a more and more integrated economic and monetary union (creating a 'culture of competition'). This approach must be seen in the context of the results of the hitherto existing application of the EC competition rules: the abundant case-law, clearly established basic principles and details, which remain the *substance* of the EC competition rules. The reform aims at 'streamlining' the EC competition rules, namely simplifying the *modalities* in order to focus more systematically on economic analysis, easing the administrative burden on companies, reinforcing the role of national authorities and courts and concentrating the Commission's activities on infringements that are the most damaging to competition and to an open 'common' market.

In its White Paper the Commission reviewed its policy *on horizontal restraints,* in particular the former centralized exemption system, i.e., the system of prior notification to, and exemption by, the Commission, thereby preventing national authorities and national courts from effectively applying the EC competition rules.[93] The Commission admitted that the centralized exemption system was formerly necessary to establish uniform application of Article 81 throughout the Community and to promote market integration, but a more decentralized system to implement competition policy was unavoidably necessary as the Community adds many new member states and the proactive role of national competition authorities to enforce both national and (where they are empowered to do so) EC competition law has steadily expanded.[94] Therefore, the Commission adopted Regulation 1/2003, which implemented a directly applicable exception system and *ex post* control to reduce the number of burdensome and time-consuming notification procedures. National authorities and courts also play a more active role in the enforcement of the EC competition rules, thereby enabling the Commission to concentrate its activities on the most serious infringements and on cases having a Community interest and ensure the effective application of the competition rules by means of regulations and guidelines. In addition, the Commission increased the market share thresholds which apply under the new *De Minimis* Notice.[95] The Commission 'modernized' the *block exemptions* on specialization and R&D agreements by simplifying their applicability, provided the market share thresholds are not exceeded,[96] and issued Guidelines in the applicability of Article 81 to

92. 1999 OJ C 132/1.
93. *See* Articles 5 and 6 of Regulation 1/2003.
94. White Paper, point 3.
95. 2001 OJ C 149/18.
96. Regulation 2658/2000 on specialization agreements and Regulation 2659/2000 on R&D agreements, 2000 OJ L 304/3 and 7.

horizontal cooperation, in particular in those cases which are not covered by the block exemption regulations.[97] The modernization of the EC competition rules is reflected by an impressive package of regulations, guidelines, communications, notices and best practices.[98]

4. Influence of Governmental Measures

Non-Discriminatory Treatment of Entrepreneurial and Governmental Restrictions of Competition.

Despite a general commitment on the part of governments to preserve freedom of market access and independence to enter into commercial agreements, firms' decisions are inevitably influenced by a variety of governmental measures. However, such influences cannot serve to justify an anticompetitive agreement between competitors, even if arguably needed as a counterbalancing or a self-help measure. The Court of Justice has repeatedly so held under both the EC Treaty[99] and the ECSC Treaty.[100] Only if a firm's conduct is so fundamentally restricted by governmental measures that it cannot engage in meaningful competitive conduct do the competition rules not apply.[101] In this case the Community must give priority to action against the governmental measures if they are incompatible with the Treaty. Examples of government measures affecting competition are regulations of a member state that reinforce private anticompetitive agreements,[102] that

97. 2001 OJ C 3/2.

98. The most recent commentaries on modernization include D.G. Goyder, *EC Competition Law*, 4th edition, Oxford University Press, 2003; Jones/Van der Woude, *EC Competition Law Handbook*, 2003/2004; Valentine Korah, *Recent Developments in EC Competition Law*, 2003/2004; J. Parisi, *Developments in EU Competition Law & Policy*, 2003, ABA, Washington, March 4, 2004; H. Schröter/Jakob/Mederer, *Kommentar zum Europäischen Wettbewerbsrecht*, Baden-Baden, 2003; R. Wish, *Competition Law*, 5th edition, LexisNexis Butterworth.

99. *Centrafarm/Sterling Drug*, ECJ Oct. 31, 1974, 1974 ECR 1147, paras 22–25; *Musik Membran/GEMA*, ECJ Jan. 20, 1981, 1981 ECR 147, paras 23–26; *Van den Hazel*, ECJ May 18, 1977, 1977 ECR 901, paras 21–23; *INNO/ATAB*, ECJ Nov. 16, 1977, 1977 ECR 2115, paras 39–41; *FEDETAB*, ECJ Oct. 29, 1980, 1980 ECR 3125, paras 82–84; *Pioneer*, ECJ June 7, 1983, 1983 ECR 1825, paras 99–100; SSI, ECJ Dec. 10, 1985, 1985 ECR 3831, paras 38–40; *Dutch Construction Works*, CFI Feb. 21, 1995, 1995 ECR II-289, para. 310; *Dutch Cranes*, CFI Oct. 22, 1997, 1997 ECR II-1739, paras 194–200; *Polypropylene – Montecatini*, ECJ July 8, 1999, 1999 ECR II-4539, paras 127–128. *See under* Article 82 *AAMS*, D.Comm. June 17, 1998, 1998 OJ L 252/47.

100. *Valsabbia*, ECJ March 18, 1980, 1980 ECR 907, 1021–1022, paras 138–141; *Welded Steel Mesh – Baustahlgewerbe*, CFI April 6, 1995, 1995 ECR II-987, para. 108; *Steel Beams – Eurofer*, CFI March 11, 1999, 1999 ECR II-263, paras 209–217.

101. 'Conduct unilaterally imposed by national authorities through the exercise of irresistible pressure': *Strintzis Lines Shipping* (Greek Ferries), CFI Dec. 11, 2003, T-65/99, para. 122. *See also Sugar*, ECJ Dec. 16, 1975, 1975 ECR 1663, 1916–1924, paras 29–72 (accepted); *FEDETAB*, ECJ Oct. 29, 1980, 1980 ECR 3125, paras 123–134 (denied).

102. *Flemish Travel Agents*, ECJ Oct. 1, 1987, 1987 ECR 3801, 3829, para. 24.

impede free trade in goods or services, including through the operations of state monopolies,[103] that restrict competition to the benefit of public enterprises or firms to which a member state has granted special or exclusive rights,[104] or that distort competition by the grant of state aid.[105] Thus, unlike other antitrust laws, the EC Treaty provides for legal instruments for acting against both private and governmental anti-competitive conduct, and the Commission has authority to intervene in both instances using whatever Treaty provisions are appropriate. Accordingly, EC competition policy has two roles to play, as stated in the Commission's Twenty-fourth Report on Competition Policy:

> 'First, with the removal of regulatory trade barriers, the main obstacles to trade between Member States stem from the behaviour of firms or from practices by Member States wishing to grant privileges or aid to some of their enterprises. Economic operators may wish to avoid the consequences of the opening-up of the markets, which bring them face to face with more intense competition from firms from elsewhere. Competition policy is a key instrument of ensuring that the benefits resulting from the opening-up of markets are not thwarted by some. Secondly, competition policy can also be used to open up sectors that still remain closed despite the establishment of the internal market (for example, a large part of the energy sector and most of the telecommunications sector and postal services), with Member States having entrusted their operation to undertakings on which they have conferred exclusive or special rights.'[106]

Modernization of the EC State Aid Rules.

In parallel to its proposals for modernizing the EC competition rules the Commission has also put forward since 2002, measures for the reorientation and modernization of state aid monitoring. The aim is to improve transparency and legal certainty by simplifying procedures in clear-cut cases and concentrating the Commission resources on the most serious distortions of competition.[107]

Chapter IX deals in greater detail with government-induced distortions of competition, including state aid.

---

103. *See* Article 31 of the EC Treaty.
104. *See* Article 86 of the EC Treaty; *Greek Insurance*, D.Comm. April 24, 1985, 1985 OJ L 152/25; upheld ECJ June 30, 1988, 1988 ECR 3611; *see* Chapter IX.B.3.
105. Articles 87–89 of the EC Treaty; *Philip Morris*, ECJ Sept. 17, 1987, 1987 ECR 2671. *See* Chapter IX.G.
106. Twenty-fourth Report on Competition Policy, point 6. *See also* Thirty-second Report on Competition Policy, point 332.
107. Thirty-first Report on Competition Policy, points 336–342; Thirty-second Report on Competition Policy, points 329–337.

C. The Arena of Competition: The Relevant Market

1. The New More Systematic Approach

Analysis of Market Power v. Analysis of Restrictive Agreements.
The definition of the relevant market or markets is the first step in the evaluation of any anticompetitive agreement, conduct or structural change of the competitive conditions.[108] The market definition is a tool to identify and define the boundaries, the 'arena', of competition between the parties directly concerned and between the parties and with third parties, such as actual or potential competitors, customers or suppliers. The Commission used to apply Article 81 by analyzing the restrictive agreements or behavior without a detailed description of the markets and products concerned,[109] whereas any application of Article 82 clearly required such analysis.[110] In its early judgments the Court of Justice examined whether an agreement was likely to appreciably restrict competition and to affect trade between member states without making its analysis dependent on the parties' market shares and the market structure.[111] In more recent judgments the Court of Justice has required the definition of the relevant market as a necessary precondition of any assessment under Article 81 (1).[112] In the *European Night Services* case[113] the Court of First Instance stated that, in the absence of any analysis of the relevant market by the Commission, it was unable to make any findings as to whether the alleged restrictions had an appreciable effect on competition and annulled the Commission decision for that reason.[114]

Need for Uniform Criteria when Defining the Relevant Market.
The Commission realized that a more consistent, realistic and systematic analysis was necessary. This led to issuing its Notice on the Definition of the Relevant Market in 1997.[115] The main purpose was to identify in a systematic way the

108. *See Italian Flat Glass*, CFI March 10, 1992, 1992 ECR II-1403, para. 159; *SPO (Dutch Construction Works)*, CFI Feb. 21, 1995, 1995 ECR II-295 para. 74.
109. *See Roquette*, ECJ Oct. 22, 2002, C-94/00, para. 82; *CSA CGM FETTCSA*, CFI March 19, 2003, T-213/00, para. 206.
110. Commission Notice on the Definition of the Relevant Market, 1997 OJ C 372/3, point 2. *See United Brands*, ECJ Feb. 14, 1978, 1978 ECR 207, paras 12–35 (relevant product market) and 36–57 (relevant geographic market).
111. *Maschinenbau Ulm*, ECJ June 30, 1966, 1966 ECR 235, 249–250; *Völk/Verwaecke*, ECJ July 9, 1969, 1969 ECR 295, paras 5–7; *Cadillon/Höss*, ECJ May 6, 1971, 1971 ECR 351, paras 5–9; *Tepea*, ECJ June 20, 1978, 1978 ECR 1391, paras 52–56; *Pioneer*, ECJ June 7, 1983, 1983 ECR 1825, paras 81–87; *Hasselblad*, ECJ Feb. 21, 1984, 1984 ECR 883, paras 19–23.
112. *See Far Eastern Freight Conference*, CFI Feb. 28, 2002, 2002 EC R II-1101, para. 116.
113. *European Night Services*, CFI Sept. 15, 1998, 1998 ECR II-3141.
114. *Ibid.*, para. 93.
115. 1997 OJ C 372/4. Hereafter 'Notice on the Relevant Market'.

competitive constraints that the companies involved face. The assessment of any allegedly anticompetitive agreement or behavior requires the proper definition of the relevant product market and the relevant geographic market in order to determine, *inter alia:*

- whether an agreement is one of minor importance, that is probably not caught by Article 81 (1), because the market share does not exceed 10% in the case of a horizontal agreement or 15% in the case of a vertical agreement,
- whether the agreement is caught by Article 81 (1) but does not exceed the maximum market shares set by a block exemption regulation and is therefore exempted,
- whether an agreement exceeds the market share limits of a block exemption regulation or notice but may nevertheless satisfy the conditions for exemption under Article 81 (3) because it does not afford the participating undertakings 'the possibility of eliminating competition in respect of a substantial part of the products in question',
- whether an agreement is not capable of appreciably affecting trade between member states and therefore not caught by Article 81 (1), which is normally the case when the parties' market shares do not exceed 5% and their aggregate annual turnover does not exceed EUR 40 million,[116]
- whether a dominant position exists under Article 82, or
- whether a merger or a full function joint venture is likely to significantly impede effective competition, in particular as a result of the creation or strengthening of a dominant position under the merger control regulation.

Prospective Analysis v. Analysis of Past Behaviour.
Although the criteria for defining the relevant market are uniform, they must be applied in view of the anticompetitive behaviour or transaction to be assessed. An anticompetitive arrangement or abusive conduct must be based on the past and current market conditions,[117] whereas a merger leading to a structural change also requires a prospective analysis.[118] This different methodology might lead to different results depending on the competitive issue to be examined. For instance, the scope of the relevant product or geographic market may be broader when analyzing a merger because of the need to take into account future competitive conditions, including potential competition, which must be included in the assessment together with an analysis of past and current market conditions. Accordingly, structural cooperation between such a firm and a competitor, such as Michelin and Continental, is likely to affect a wide range of products and the competitive

116. Commission Guidelines on the effect on trade concept, 2004 OJ C 101/81.
117. *See* Guidelines on market analysis and assessment of significant market power in telecommunications, 2002 OJ C 165/6.
118. *See Tetra Laval*, CFI Oct. 25, 2002, 2002 ECR II-4381, para. 251.

conditions throughout several member states or the entire Common Market.[119] In contrast, an analysis of abusive behavior of a dominant firm under Article 82 may be limited to a narrow product line or to customers in a single member state.[120]

The Three Main Sources of Competitive Constraints.
The Commission identifies three main sources of competitive constraints: demand substitutability, supply substitutability and potential competition. Demand substitution constitutes the most immediate and effective disciplinary force on the suppliers of a given product, in particular to their pricing decisions. The competitive constraints arriving from *supply substitutability* are in general less immediate and in many cases require an analysis of additional factors. The conditions under which *potential competition* will actually represent an effective competitive constraint depend on the analysis of specific factors and circumstances related to the conditions of market entry.

2. The Relevant Product Market

(a) Criteria of Defining the Relevant Product Market

Definition of the Court of Justice.
In *Hoffmann La Roche* the Court of Justice referred to the concept of the relevant market as follows:

> 'The concept of the relevant market … implies that there can be effective competition between the products which form part of it and this presupposes that there is a sufficient degree of interchangeability between all the products forming part of the same market in so far as a specific use of such products is concerned'.[121]

In *Deutsche Bahn* the Court of First Instance stated that:

> '… it must be possible to distinguish the service or the good in question by virtue of particular characteristics that so differentiate it from other services or other goods that is only to a small degree interchangeable with those alternatives and affected by competition from them …. In that context, the degree of interchangeability between products must be assessed in terms of

---

119. *Continental/Michelin*, D.Comm. Oct. 11, 1988, 1988 OJ L 305/33 (exemption for Community-wide cooperation).

120. *Michelin I*, ECJ Nov. 9, 1983, 1983 ECR 3461, para. 26 (application of fidelity rebates in the Netherlands); *Michelin II*, CFI Sept. 30, 2003, T-203/01, paras 235–245 (application of fidelity rebates in France).

121. *Hoffmann/La Roche*, ECJ Feb. 13, 1979, 1979 ECR 461, para. 28.

their objective characteristics, as well as the structure of supply and demand on the market, and competitive conditions ....'[122]

Accordingly, the definition of the relevant market requires the analysis of demand substitutability, supply substitutability and, to a certain extent, potential competition.

(b) Demand Substitution

Criteria for Demand Substitutability.
The main criteria for demand substitutability are listed in the standard definition of substitute products that the Commission has used, in accordance with the Court of Justice's definition, in block exemption regulations[123] and in the notification Forms A/B and CO,[124] namely '... all those products and/or services which are regarded as interchangeable or substitutable by the consumer, by reason of the products' characteristics, their price and intended use'.[125]

Characteristics.
A product or service is distinct from other products or services if its characteristics are particularly apt to satisfy an inelastic need of customers.[126] Homogeneous products normally are easily interchangeable, such as basic chemicals.[127] Products which satisfy different needs belong to distinct markets, such as pharmaceuticals having different therapeutic effects,[128] spices[129] or plant species (seeds).[130] However, a product's functional characteristics are more important in this connection than its appearance or physical or chemical make-up. Thus, bottles and cans can belong to the same beverage container market[131] and different pharmaceuticals may have the same therapeutical effect.[132]

---

122. *Deutsche Bahn*, CFI Oct. 21, 1997, 1997 ECR II-1689, para. 54.
123. E.g. Article 9 of Regulation 2790/1999 on vertical agreements.
124. 1994 OJ L 377/28.
125. Example: *Deutsche Telekom*, D.Comm. May 21, 2003, 2003 OJ L 263/9, points 78–91.
126. *Langnese-Iglo*, CFI June 8, 1995, 1995 ECR II-1533, para. 61; *aff'd* ECJ Oct. 1, 1998, 1998 ECR I-5609.
127. *See*, with respect to polyethylene: *Exxon/Shell*, D.Comm. May 18, 1994, 1994 OJ L 144/20 (under Article 81); *BASF/Shell*, D.Comm. Dec. 23, 1997, M.1041 (under the merger control regulation). *See*, however, *VEBA/Degussa*, D.Comm. Dec. 3, 1997, 1998 OJ L 201/102, points 32–33 (diamines as a separate market from alleged diamines/polyamines market).
128. *Beecham/Parke Davis*, D.Comm. Jan. 17, 1979, 1979 OJ L 70/11, point 45; *Ciba-Geigy/Sandoz*, D.Comm. July 17, 1996, 1996 OJ L 201/1; *Hoffmann/La Roche*, D.Comm. Feb. 4, 1998, 1998 OJ L 234/1; *Aventis/Merck*, D.Comm. Nov. 27, 2002, IP/02/1746.
129. *McCormick/CPC/Rabobank/Ostmann*, D.Comm. Oct. 29, 1993, M.330, point 40.
130. *Sicasov*, D.Comm. Dec. 14, 1998, 1999 OJ L 4/27, point 45.
131. *Continental Can*, ECJ Feb. 21, 1973, 1973 ECR 215, paras 28–36.
132. *Ciba-Geigy/Sandoz*, D.Comm. July 17, 1996, 1996 OJ L 201/1, point 42.

Relevant Products v. Relevant Services.
The characteristics of a product must be distinguished from those of services provided for the product.[133] In the *Magill – RTE* case[134] the Court of First Instance stated that the relevant product market, the weekly program listings and the television guides in which those listings are published, must be distinguished from the market for more general information about television programs.

Price.
Price is an important factor in evaluating whether products are substitutes.[135] If similar products sell at widely differing prices in the same geographic market, they are unlikely to be close substitutes. In its *Tetra Pak I* case which concerned aseptic milk cartons and carton filling machines the Commission stated:

> 'the lack of demand and supply substitution reflected in the fact that a small but significant rise in the price of aseptic packages (or machines) will neither bring about a large and immediate reduction in demand for that package (or machine) with a corresponding increase in demand for the other packages (or machines), nor will it encourage immediate entry by new producers. This lack of price sensitivity on either demand side or supply side for aseptic cartons and machines allows producers of these products to act independently of either consumers or producers of other packaging materials and machines.'[136]

Different product markets have consequently been recognized for similar products sold at different price levels, such as soft drinks and spring water,[137] nylon fibers and polyester fibers,[138] lower, higher and middle class categories of records and cameras,[139] cosmetics sold in supermarkets and in pharmacies,[140] different generations of mobile telecommunication systems[141] or copying systems.[142] A measure of

133. E.g., *Deutsche Telekom*, D.Comm. May 21, 2003, 2003 OJ L 263/9, points 59–63.
134. *Magill – RTE*, CFI July 10, 1991, 1991 ECR II-485 paras 61–62; *aff'd* ECJ April 6, 1995, 1995 ECR I-743.
135. *Crown Cork & Seal/Carnaud Metalbox*, D.Comm. Nov. 14, 1995, 1996 OJ L 75198, point 15. *See* Briones Alonso, 'Market Definition in the Community's Merger Control Policy', 1994–4 ECLR 195, 200–204.
136. *Tetra Pak I*, D.Comm. July 26, 1980, 1980 OJ L 272/27, 34, *aff'd* CFI Oct. 6, 1994, 1994 ECR II-755, paras 63–71.
137. *Nestlé/Perrier*, D.Comm. July 22, 1992, 1992 OJ L 356/1.
138. *DuPont/ICI*, D.Comm. Sept. 30, 1992, 1993 OJ L 7/13.
139. *Miller International*, ECJ Feb. 1, 1978, 1978 ECR 131, paras 8–10; *Hasselblad*, ECJ Feb. 21, 1984, 1984 ECR 883, paras 19–21.
140. *Vichy*, CFI Feb. 27, 1992, 1992 ECR II-415, para. 63.
141. *O2 UK Limited/T-Mobile*, D.Comm. April 30, 2003, 2003 OJ L 200/59, points 5–10.
142. *Carbonless Paper*, D.Comm. Dec. 20, 2001, IP/01/1892 (carbonless paper distinct from computer printer).

the degree of substitutability between products is price cross-elasticity of demand, i.e., the ratio of the change in quantity demanded of another product to a change in the price of the product in question.[143] If a small increase in prices would cause consumers to switch to alternatives, these substitutes must be included in the relevant product market.[144] However, substitutes must be excluded in cases of barriers and costs associated with switching consumption, such as a need for different refrigeration equipment to purchase aseptic or non-aseptic packages[145] or a government production quota limiting the quantities available for substitution.[146] The Commission quantified this price sensitivity in its Notice on the Definition of the Relevant Market: the question is whether the parties' customers would switch to readily available substitutes 'in response to a hypothetical small (in the range of 5% to 10%) but permanent relative price increase.'[147] The Commission often asks selected customers about substitutability in the case of (hypothetical) price changes.[148]

Intended Use.

Whether the intended use of products is sufficiently similar to make them part of the same market is evaluated by both the Commission and the Court of Justice by reference to the structure of demand. This may lead to markets being defined more narrowly or more widely than the inherent characteristics of the products would suggest. Accordingly, different markets may be distinguished for the same product used in different applications, for example:

- impulse ice cream or take-away ice cream,[149]
- individual vitamins for bio-nutritive (pharmaceuticals, food and animal feed)[150] or for technological uses (for antioxydants, fermentation agents and additives),[151]

---

143. *AngloAmerican Corp/Lonrho*, D.Comm. April 23, 1997, 1998 OJ L 149/21, points 80–82. However, price cross-elasticity as a way of measuring substitutability may be misleading when trying to assess the competitive constraints faced by the parties after the merger and should be, and in fact is, used with care and only if the results are coroborated by other criteria; *see* Briones Alonso, 'Market Definition in the Community's Merger Control Policy', 1994–4 ECLR 195, 202.
144. *See United Brands*, ECJ Feb. 14, 1978, 1978 ECR 207, paras 32–33.
145. *Tetrapak/Alfa-Laval*, D.Comm. July 22, 1991, 1991 OJ L 290/35; *Tetra Laval*, CFI Oct. 25, 2002, 2002 ECR II-4381, paras 226–251.
146. *Eridania/ISI*, D.Comm. July 30, 1991, M.62.
147. 1997 OJ C 372/3, point 17.
148. Notice on the Relevant Market (1997 OJ C 372/3), point 34. *See Saint Gobain/Wacker*, D.Comm. Dec. 4, 1996, 1997 OJ L 247/1, point 59; *Coca Cola/Amalgated Beverages*, D.Comm. Jan. 22, 1997, 1997 OJ L 218/15, point 26; *Coca Cola/Carlsberg*, D.Comm. Sept. 11, 1997, 1999, M.833.
149. *Langnese-Iglo*, CFI June 8, 1995, 1995 ECR II-1533, para. 61.
150. E.g., *Methionine*, D.Comm. July 2, 2002, 2003 OJ L 355/1
151. *Hoffmann/La Roche*, ECJ Feb. 13, 1979, 1979 ECR 461, paras 25–30; *Industrial and Medical Gases*, D.Comm. July 24, 2002, 2003 OJ L 84/1. *See Commercial Solvents*, ECJ March 6,

- sugar for retail sale or for industrial customers,[152]
- pharmaceuticals for human and veterinary use,[153]
- pharmaceuticals for hospitals, pharmacies and non-specialized outlets,[154]
- products sold to original equipment manufacturers (OEMs) for reprocessing and products sold through dealers to final consumers,[155]
- citric acid for food and beverages, household detergents and cleaners,[156]
- spare parts supplied to car manufacturers for original equipment and spare parts supplied to dealers for repairing cars,[157]
- raw materials as opposed to finished products incorporating them,[158] or to products for other industrial purposes,[159]
- different types of industrial and medical gases,[160]
- products leased as opposed to products purchased outright,[161]
- internet sales as distinct from mail orders, sales in stores or supermarkets, [162]
- credit cards for use as payment card schemes as distinct from credit cards for card-related services between financial institutions,[163]
- new cars[164] and aircraft[165] as opposed to used cars and aircraft.

1974, 1974 ECR 223 (distinction between the pharmaceutical and other industrial markets for the intermediary chemical product aminobutanol).

152. *British Sugar*, D.Comm. July 18, 1988, 1988 OJ L 284/41, 50; *British Sugar, Tate & Lyle*, D.Comm. Oct. 14, 1998, 1999 OJ L 24/1; *Eridania/IS*, D.Comm. July 30, 1991, M.62. *See also Sugar*, ECJ Dec. 16, 1975, 1975 ECR 1663 (distinction between sugar for human consummation and for denaturation purposes).
153. *See* the field-of-use restrictions white-listed under Article 2 (1) (8) of Regulation 240/96 on Technology Transfer Agreements.
154. *Hoffmann-La Roche/Boehringer Mannheim*, D.Comm. Feb. 4, 1998, 1998 OJ L 234/1, para. 11; *Vichy*, CFI Feb. 27, 1992, 1992 ECR II-265, para. 63 (cosmetics of a certain image).
155. *Pilkington/SIV*, D.Comm. Dec. 21, 1993, 1994 OJ L 158/24, point 19.
156. *Citric Acid*, D.Comm. Dec. 5, 2001, 2002 OJ L 239/18, points 6–14.
157. *Michelin*, ECJ Nov. 9, 1983, 1983 ECR 3461, para. 38; *BMW/Rover*, D.Comm. March 14, 1994, M.416.
158. For instance, the market for aminobutanol, the basic ingredient of the anti-tuberculosis drug, ethambutol, as against the market for the drug itself *Commercial Solvents*, ECJ March 6, 1974, 1974 ECR 223, paras 19–22.
159. *Saint Gobain/Wacker*, D.Comm. Dec. 4, 1996, 1997 OJ L 247/1, point 40; *Stark/Wienerberger*, D.Comm. April 4, 1996, M.702, point 13.
160. *Industrial and Medical Gases*, D.Comm. July 24, 2002, 2003, OJ L 84/1, points 4–14.
161. *Dutch Cranes*, CFI Oct. 22, 1997, 1997 ECR II-1739, paras 141–147. *See Industrial Gases*, Nineteenth Report on Competition Policy, point 62.
162. *Bertelsmann/Mondadori*, D.Comm. April 22, 1999, M. 1407; *Babcock Borsig, mg technologies and SAP*, D.Comm. Nov. 8, 2000, M.2172; *Otto Versand/Sabre*, D.Comm. Dec. 20, 2001, IP/01/1881.
163. *Visa International*, D.Comm. Aug. 9, 2001, 2001 OJ L 293/24, point 34.
164. *See* new Motor Vehicle Regulation 1400/2002, 2002 OJ L 203/30.
165. *Boeing/McDonnell Douglas*, D.Comm. July 30, 1997, 1997 OJ L 336/16, para. 19.

Different relevant product markets may exist even in the case where identical products are marketed with or without a trademark or with the producer's or a private label.[166] On the other hand, if different products are substitutes for the same use, as for example metal or glass containers are for processed foods, they may be regarded as belonging to the same market.[167]

Demand for Individual Products v. Demand for a Range of Similar Products.
Different product types (e.g., spices[168] or fruits[169]) or dimensions (e.g., truck or bus tires[170]) may not be substitutable as far as the final user (e.g., the fruit consumer or the trucking company) is concerned. However, the full range of such products may be found to form a single market if they are supplied to the same customers or dealers who purchase a full range of products from one supplier.[171] Similarly, insurance coverage for different risks is not substitutable for the consumer and may constitute distinct (sub)markets,[172] whereas a merger between insurance companies is assessed on the basis of the parties' position in the three main markets: life, non-life and reinsurance.[173]

Primary v. Secondary Products and Services.
Product characteristics and intended use may be insufficient to show whether two products or services are demand substitutes. In particular, the original equipment market for a car component and the spare parts market may be subject to different competitive constraints because of different price, distribution or service characteristics although there is no difference in the product characteristics.[174] Thus, for repair shops that are dependent on supplies of spare parts for a specific

166. *Mannesmann/Vallourec/Ilva*, D.Comm. Jan. 31, 1994, 1994 OJ L 102/1, para. 20; *Kimberley-Clark/Scott Paper*, D.Comm. Jan. 16, 1996, 1996 OJ L 183/1, point 48.
167. *Continental Can*, ECJ Feb. 21, 1973, 1973 ECR 215, paras 28–36.
168. *McCormick/CPC/Ostmann*, D.Comm. Oct. 29, 1993, M. 330.
169. Bananas: *United Brands*, ECJ Feb. 14, 1978, 1978 ECR 207, paras 32–33.
170. *Michelin I*, ECJ Nov. 9, 1983, 1983 ECR 3461, para. 44; *Kish Glas*, CFI March 30, 2000, 2000 ECR II-1885, para. 62.
171. *Michelin I*, ECJ Nov. 9, 1983, 1983 ECR 3461, paras 42–44; *McCormick/CPC/Rabobank/Ostmann*, D.Comm. Oct. 29, 1993, M.330, point 40; *Kesko/Tuco*, D.Comm. Nov. 20, 1996, 1997 OJ L 110/53, point 18 ('basket of daily consumer goods'); *Blokker/Toys 'R' Us*, D.Comm June 26, 1997, 1998 OJ L 316/1, point 27 (retailer of toys). Similarly with respect to wholesale services for information technology: *Tech Data/Computer 2000*, D.Comm. June 3, 1998, M.1179, points 8–14, and for the distribution of chemicals: *Metallgesellschaft/Klöckner Chemiehandel*, D.Comm. Jan. 29, 1998, M.1073.
172. *Allianz/Vereinte*, D.Comm. Nov. 11, 1996, M.812; *Axa/UAP*, D.Comm. Dec. 20, 1996, M.862; *BAT/Zürich*, D.Comm. Feb. 16, 1998, M. 1043, point 9.
173. *Schweizer Rück/NCM*, D.Comm. June 26, 1998, M.1150.
174. *See ABB/Daimler Benz*, D.Comm. Oct. 18, 1995, 1997 OJ L 11/29, point 19.

make of fastening systems,[175] cash register[176] or car,[177] the relevant market may be spare parts for that make. Services provided for overhauling and repairing products (e.g., industrial gas turbines) constitute a separate market ('after market').[178] For assessing whether there is sufficient interrelation between the primary and secondary market (e.g., original cartridges and empty, refillable cartridges for photocopiers), the Commission applies four criteria, namely (i) whether the customer can make an informed choice, (ii) whether the customer is likely to make an informed choice, (iii) whether a sufficient number of customers would purchase on the primary market if the sales conditions on the after-market appear to be abusive, and (iv) whether the customer would react within a reasonably short period of time.[179]

Consumer Preferences.

Consumer preferences and the motivation of the consumer are taken into account. In order to evaluate how consumers value different product or service characteristics the Commission often contacts purchasers to inquire into their views about substitutability and to obtain the necessary factual evidence.[180] Consumer preferences may be influenced according to the brands used for the same product (producer's own brand – premium brands).[181] However, it may be difficult to gather reliable views of consumers. Marketing studies which have been commissioned by the parties in the past may be useful, whereas consumer surveys carried out after the Commission's investigation has begun are usually scrutinized with utmost care.[182]

Distinct Categories of Customers.

A distinct category of customers may constitute a narrower, distinct market when such a group could be subject to price discrimination.[183] This will, according to

175. *HILTI*, CFI Dec. 12, 1991, 1991 ECR II-1439, paras 70–78; *aff'd* ECJ March 2, 1994, 1994 ECR I-667.
176. Notice on the Relevant Market, points 36 and 56. *See Hugin/Liptons*, ECJ May 31, 1979, 1979 ECR 1869, paras 3–10.
177. *Michelin I*, ECJ Nov. 9, 1983, 1983 ECR 3461, para. 38; *Renault*, ECJ Oct. 5, 1988, 1988 ECR 6039, para. 16; *Volvo/Veng*, ECJ Oct. 5, 1988, 1988 ECR 6211, paras 8–9.
178. *TPM/Wood Group*, D.Comm. July 20, 1998, M.1224, points 7–8.
179. *Info-Lab/Ricoh*, D.Comm. Jan. 7, 1999 (rejection of complaint); *Pelikan/Kyocera*, Twenty-fifth Report on Competition Policy, p. 140.
180. Notice on the Relevant Market, point 33.
181. *Coca Cola/Amalgated Beverages*, D.Comm. Jan. 22, 1997, 1997 OJ L 218/15, para. 26; *Cargill/Vandenmoortele*, D.Comm. July 20, 1998, M. 1227, point 16.
182. Notice on the Relevant Market, point 41.
183. *See Price Waterhouse/Coopers & Lybrand*, D.Comm. May 20, 1998, 1999 OJ L 50/27, points 21–54 (accounting services provided to large and small and medium sized customers); *BT/AT&T*, D.Comm. March 30, 1999 (global telecommunication services for multinational corporate customers as separate market).

the Commission's notice,[184] be the case when two conditions are met: (i) it is possible to identify clearly which group an individual customer belongs to at the moment of selling the relevant products to him, and (ii) trade among customers or arbitrage by third parties is not feasible. In the *United Brands* case the very young and the old and sick were identified as a distinct group of banana consumers[185] although they could hardly be subject to price discrimination and would therefore not constitute a distinct market according to the Commission's present criteria.[186]

Sufficient Degree of Substitutability.
Perfect substitutability is not required for goods to be regarded as belonging to the same market, but they must be substitutable more than to a very limited degree.[187] Thus, flat glass, though in competition with plastic in certain uses, such as for greenhouses and verandas, has certain mechanical, thermal, optical and decorative properties and a certain price level which means that in most of its uses it is not substitutable by other products.[188] Similarly, in the *British Plaster Board* case the Commission refused to consider plasterboard and wet plastering as a single market because wet plastering was substitutable only to a limited extent for users of plasterboard.[189] Transport markets are determined according to the customers' point of view, thereby distinguishing between different routes.[190]

Economic Dependence.
If the supply of products or services is subject to a statutory monopoly, the customers seeking those services are in a position of economic dependence on the supplier without having any realistic alternative to the extent that those products or services constitute a distinct market.[191] This applies even if the services provided are linked to a product which is itself in competition with other products, such as the issuance of certificates for vehicle conformity.[192]

---

184. Notice on the Relevant Market, point 43.
185. *United Brands*, ECJ Feb. 14, 1978, 1978 ECR 207, 23–33, paras 19–21.
186. *See VEBA/Degussa*, D.Comm. Dec. 3, 1997, 1998 OJ L 201/102, point 33.
187. *Continental Can*, ECJ Feb. 21, 1973, 1973 ECR 215, 32; *Hoffmann/La Roche*, ECJ Feb. 13, 1979, 1979 ECR 461, para. 28; *Michelin*, ECJ Nov. 9, 1983, 1983 ECR 3461, paras 48–52.
188. *Italian Flat Glass II*, D.Comm. Dec. 7, 1988, 1989 OJ L 33/44, 65.
189. *British Plasterboard*, D.Comm. Dec. 5, 1988, 1989 OJ L 10/50, 51–52, 64–65; *aff'd* CFI April 1, 1993, 1993 ECR II-389; *aff'd* ECJ April 6, 1995, 1995 ECR I-865.
190. *Austrian Airlines/Lufthansa*, D.Comm. July 5, 2002, 2002 OJ L 242/25, points 46–61 (routes between Austria and Germany); *Marlines – Greek Ferries*, CFI Dec. 11, 2003, T-56/99 (ferry services between Greece and Italy).
191. *Deutsche Bahn*, CFI Oct. 21, 1997, 1997 ECR II-1689, 57. paras 53–56.
192. *General Motors*, ECJ Nov. 13, 1975, 1975 ECR 1367, paras 5–10; *British Leyland*, ECJ Nov. 11, 1986, 1986 ECR 3263, paras 3–10.

(c) Supply Substitution

Reasonable Alternatives.
Supply-side substitutability may be taken into account when defining the relevant markets when its effects are equivalent, or constitute at least a 'reasonable alternative,[193] to those of demand substitution in terms of effectiveness and immediacy, i.e., when producers of other products are able to switch production capacity or resources to producing the relevant product or existing producers of the relevant product are able to expand their production in the short term without incurring significant additional costs or risks.[194] The main criteria of supply substitutability are:

- the characteristics of the production technology, i.e., whether plants producing other products could be rapidly switched to production of the relevant product, or the production technology for the relevant products is so specific that considerable investment would be required to bring new production capacity on stream (technical entry barriers);[195]
- the presence of idle capacity for the relevant products which could easily be activated;[196]
- the possibility of firms already producing the product for their own consumption expanding their output for sale on the market;[197]
- the possibility of a customer entering the market by producing the product on its own;[198]
- the presence of barriers to access to the necessary production technology[199] or regulatory barriers such as monopoly rights.[200]

---

193. *Hilti*, CFI Dec. 12, 1991, 1991 ECR II-1439, para. 69.
194. Notice on the Relevant Market, point 20.
195. *Continental Can*, ECJ Feb. 21, 1973, 1973 ECR 215, para. 33.
196. *Hoffmann/La Roche*, ECJ Feb. 13, 1979, 1979 ECR 461, para. 42.
197. *Continental Can*, ECJ Feb. 21, 1973, 1973 ECR 215, para. 36.
198. *Hoffmann/La Roche*, ECJ Feb. 13, 1979, 1979 ECR 461, paras 112–115.
199. Owing to patents or know-how: *Tetra Pak I*, D.Comm. July 26, 1988, 1988 OJ L 272/27, 38–39; *aff'd* ECJ Nov. 14, 1996, 1996 ECR I-5951; *Hilti*, D.Comm Dec. 22, 1987, 1988 OJ L 65/19, 34, *aff'd* ECJ March 2, 1994, 1994 ECR I-67. Owing to copyrights: *Deutsche Grammophon*, ECJ June 8, 1971, 1971 ECR 487, paras 16–18. Owing to trademarks: *United Brands*, ECJ Feb. 14, 1978, 1978 ECR 207, paras 88–93. Note that the possession of industrial or intellectual property right does not automatically define the relevant market *(Renault*, ECJ Oct. 5, 1988, 1988 ECR 6039, para. 15), but may strengthen a dominant position: *Tetra Pak I*, ECJ Nov. 14, 1996, 1996 ECR I-5951; *Coca Cola/Orangina (Pernod)*, French Ministry of Financial and Economic Affairs, WuW 1999–3, 260 (decision prohibiting the proposed acquisition of the Orangina brand beverages by Coca Cola).
200. *General Motors*, ECJ Nov. 13, 1975, 1975 ECR 1367, paras 4–10 (exclusive right to issue certificates for vehicle conformity); *British Leyland*, ECJ Nov. 11, 1986, 1986 ECR 3263, paras 3–10; *Deutsche Bahn*, CFI Oct. 21, 1997, 1997 ECR II-1689, para. 57.

A finding of supply-side substitutability often leads to a broader market definition.[201]

Relevant Market in Cases of Buying Power.
In the case of buying power by a dominant purchaser, the relevant product market is judged by similar criteria but based primarily upon the standpoint of the seller. Therefore, supply substitution constitutes the most immediate and effective disciplinary force on the supplier of a given product to a powerful purchaser, in particular in relation to the supplier's pricing decisions. A customer cannot have a significant impact on the prevailing conditions of sale, such as prices, if its suppliers are in a position to switch easily to other customers, in particular customers located elsewhere, or to adjust or to switch their production to other uses without incurring significant additional costs. When a customer issues instructions as to the technical[202] or quality specifications[203] of the product in accordance with its specific needs, the supplier may be effectively prevented from switching to another customer because he has undertaken significant investments in order to meet that customer's special needs and would incur significant costs to switch his production to satisfy other customers. Similarly, national suppliers may be dependent on national customers which enjoy exclusive rights[204] or a statutory monopoly, e.g. with respect to rail transport services,[205] to the supply of telecommunications products or services[206] or to the supply of construction works conforming to specifications issued in accordance with the rules on public bids.[207]

---

201. Hence the generally broader product market definitions in the United States, where the practice of scrutinizing both the demand and supply sides of the hypothetical product market is well established.
202. The customer may grant a license which is limited to the customer's specific use: *EUROFIMA*, points 68–69 (railroad rolling stock manufacturers); *General Electric/Pratt & Whitney*, 1998 OJ C 339/3 (engines for new aircrafts of Boeing and Airbus).
203. Car manufacturers with respect to the supply of spare parts, *see* Article 4 (1) (j) of Regulation 1400/2002 on motor vehicle agreements.
204. E.g., copyright collecting societies: *GEMA I*, D.Comm. June 2, 1971, 1971 OJ L 134/15; television stations dealing with film distributors: March 28, 1985, 1985 ECR 1105, paras 21–22 (however, in this case, the question of dominant position was not discussed by the Court since it agreed with the Commission that the alleged abuse of imposing unfair prices was not proven).
205. *Deutsche Bahn*, D.Comm. CFI Oct. 21, 1997, 1997 ECR II-1689, para. 57.
206. Commission's Guidelines on the Application of the EC Competition Rules in the Telecommunications sector, 1991 OJ C 233/2, point 82.
207. *SPO (Dutch Construction Works)*, Feb. 15, 1995, 1995 ECR II-267, paras 73–83.

(d) Potential Competition

Potential Competition as Competitive Constraint.
The Commission Notice on the Definition of the Relevant Market[208] states that the third source of competitive constraint, potential competition, is normally *not* taken into account when defining the relevant market, since the conditions under which potential competition will actually represent an effective competitive constraint depend on the analysis of specific factors and circumstances related to the conditions of market entry. 'If required, this analysis is only carried out at a subsequent stage, in general once the position of the companies involved in the relevant market has already been ascertained, and when such position gives rise to concerns from a competition point of view.' However, the assessment of supply substitutability includes the analysis of whether suppliers are able to switch production to the relevant products and market them in the *short term* without incurring significant additional costs or risks. When these conditions are met, the additional production that is put on the market will have a disciplinary effect on the competitive behavior of the companies involved. Such a (potential) impact in terms of effectiveness and immediacy is equivalent to the demand substitution effect.[209] Thus, in certain cases potential competition may be taken into account when defining the relevant market but, more generally, only at the subsequent stage when assessing whether the parties' position on the so defined relevant market constitutes a dominant position (Article 82), is likely to significantly impede effective competition, in particular as a result of the creation or strengthening of a dominant position (Article 2 of the merger control regulation), or affords the parties the possibility of eliminating competition in respect of a substantial part of the product in question (Article 81 (3)). The decisive criterion, although difficult to apply, may be that of immediacy, i.e., of whether suppliers are able to switch production or the provision of services to the relevant product or services in the *short* or *longer term*. However, the methodology for assessing potential competition should be consistent: the ability of potential suppliers to switch production in the short term should result in a broader relevant market, including products or services of potential competitors, thereby reducing the parties' market shares. If suppliers require a long lead time to switch production, this will lead to a narrower market with higher market shares that excludes these potential competitors from the relevant market. However, the impact of potential competition which prevents the parties from impeding significantly effective competition over the medium term may nevertheless be of key importance to structural cases under the merger control regulation. This may be demonstrated by the following cases.

---

208. 1997 OJ C 372/3.
209. Notice on the Relevant Market, point 20.

Cases where Potential Competition is Taken into Account when Defining the Relevant Market.
In *DHL/Deutsche Post,*[210] which concerned a merger in the expedited transport industry, the Commission held that parcel deliveries (by Deutsche Post) and express deliveries (by DHL) compete at least at the margins and that these two services *may* become closer in terms of supply side substitutability although the further delineation of the relevant markets was left open. In *Price Waterhouse/Coopers & Lybrand*[211] the Commission defined the relevant market by taking into account the possibility of the big auditing firms to expand their auditing activities 'relatively easily'[212] in the banking and insurance sector. In *Ciba-Geigy/Sandoz*[213] the Commission looked, when defining the relevant market for pharmaceutical products, at R&D potentials in terms of its importance for existing, but also for future markets even if these future markets must, by their very nature, be defined in a less clear-cut manner than in the case of existing markets. In *Continental Can*[214] the Court of Justice did not consider light metal containers for meat and fish as distinct markets 'as long as it has not been proven that competitors from other sectors of the market for light metal containers are not in a position to enter the market, by a simple adaptation, with sufficient strength to create a serious counterweight.' The Commission tends to consider potential competition only at the subsequent stage when assessing the parties' market position, although the customers' ability to start producing their own requirements[215] or to switch to potential sources of supply, such as from electricity to gas,[216] or the suppliers' ability to switch production to other qualities or grades or other fields of use, to increase capacity or production output, or to sell part of their captive production on the market,[217] may have 'a disciplinary effect on the competitive behavior of the companies involved'[218] and determine the relevant market rather than the assessment of the market position.

---

210. Clearance of the acquisition of joint control of DHL by Deutsche Post and Lufthansa, *DHL/Deutsche Post*, D.Comm. June 26, 1998, M.1168, points 15–18 (Deutsche Post's subsequent proposal to merge with *Schnell-Lieferdienst (Trans-o-flex)* was opposed by the Commission and withdrawn by the parties on Feb. 4, 1999). The acquisition of sole control of DHL by Deutsche Post was cleared on Oct. 21, 2002, M.2908.
211. *Price Waterhouse/Coopers & Lybrand*, D.Comm. May 20, 1998, 1999 OJ L 50/27, point 47.
212. *See* discussion in *VEBA/Degussa*, D.Comm. Dec. 3, 1997, 1998 OJ L 201/102, point 33.
213. *Ciba-Geigy/Sandoz*, D.Comm. July 17, 1996, 1996 OJ L 201/1, points 42–44.
214. *Continental Can*, ECJ Feb. 21, 1973, 1973 ECR 215, para. 33.
215. *Hoffmann/La Roche*, ECJ Feb. 13, 1979, 1979 ECR 461, paras 112–115. *See Continental Can*, ECJ Feb. 21, 1973, 1973 ECR 215, para. 36.
216. *EDFI/ESTAG*, D.Comm. March 17, 1998, M.1107, point 10; *Gaz de France/BEWAG/GASAG*, D.Comm. Jan. 20, 1999, M.1402.
217. *Continental Can*, ECJ Feb. 21, 1973, 1973 ECR 215, para. 36. However, the Commission tends to consider captive production only when assessing the parties' market position, *see Mannesmann/ Boge*, D.Comm. Sept. 23, 1991, M.134, point 12; *Lucas/Eaton*, D.Comm. Dec. 9, 1991, M.149, point 22; *DuPont/ICI*, D.Comm. Sept. 30, 1992, 1993 OJ L 7/13.
218. Notice on the Relevant Market, point 20.

Cases where Potential Competition is Taken into Account when Assessing the Parties' Position on the Relevant Market.
In cases where the suppliers' ability to switch production to other products or markets entails a significant and *longer-term* adjustment of existing tangible or intangible assets[219] the Commission considers the impact of such potential competition at the subsequent stage of assessing the parties' position on the (smaller) relevant market. In *Mannesmann/Vallourec/Ilva,*[220] which concerned the clearance of a merger in the sector of seamless stainless steel tubes, the Commission held that eastern European competitors held the necessary means to enter the market rapidly and to have 'a more significant impact on the western European market in the near future'. On the other hand, in *WorldCom/MCI*[221] the Commission denied the potential competitors' ability to enter the market of internet-related services and to counterbalance the merging parties' dominant position; the Commission therefore declared the merger compatible with the Common Market only subject to the condition of compliance with their commitments, *inter alia,* to divest MCI's intemet business.[222] Obviously, a dominant position will be strengthened if the parties to a merger or restrictive behavior are capable of eliminating potential competition.[223]

3. THE RELEVANT GEOGRAPHIC MARKET

Definition.
'The relevant geographic market comprises the area in which the undertakings concerned are involved in the supply and demand of products or services, in which the conditions of competition are sufficiently homogeneous and which can be distinguished from neighboring areas because the conditions of competition are appreciably different in those areas.'[224]

219. Notice on the Relevant Market, point 20, note 4.

220. *Mannesmann/Vallourec/Ilva*, D.Comm. Jan. 31, 1994, 1994 OJ L 102/15, points 116–124.

221. *WorldCom/MCI*, D.Comm. July 8, 1998, 1999 OJ L 116/1, point 129–131.

222. Other examples of cases where the Commission concluded potential competition was an insufficient competitive constraint include: *DuPont/ICI*, D.Comm. Sept. 30, 1992, 1993 OJ L 7/13, points 22–23; *Nestlé/Perrier*, D.Comm. July 22, 1992, 1992 OJ L 356/1, points 90–107; *Pilkington/SIV*, D.Comm. Dec. 21, 1993, 1994 OJ L 158/24, point 44; *Procter & Gamble/Schickedanz*, D.Comm. June 21, 1994, 1994 OJ L 354/32, point 73; *Crown Cork & Seal/CarnaudMetalbox*, D.Comm. Nov. 14, 1995, 1996 OJ L 75/38, points 80–83; *Agfa-Gevaert/DuPont*, D.Comm. Feb. 11, 1998, 1998 OJ L 211/22, points 84–105.

223. Under the merger control regulation: *MSG Media Service*, D.Comm. Nov. 9, 1994, 1994 OJ L 364/1, points 56–59. Under Article 82: *AAMS (Italian tobacco monopoly)*, D.Comm. June 17, 1998, 1998 OJ L 252/47; *TACA*, D.Comm. Sept. 16, 1998, 1999 OJ L 95/1. Under Article 81: *TransAtlanticAgreement*, D.Comm. Oct. 19, 1994, 1994 OJ L 376/1, points 165–188.

224. Commission Notice, point 8. This definition accords with that of the Court of Justice in *United Brands*, ECJ Feb. 14, 1978, 1978 ECR 207, paras 44 and 53; *SCPA/Kali + Salz-MdK*, ECJ March 31, 1998, 1998 ECR I-1375, para. 143.

Evidence of Defining the Relevant Geographic Market.
For the purposes of defining a 'distinct' market, the geographic market consists, according to Article 9 (7) of the merger control regulation, of the area

> 'in which the undertakings concerned are involved in the supply and demand of products or services, in which the conditions of competition are sufficiently homogeneous and which can be distinguished from neighbouring areas because, in particular, conditions of competition are appreciably different in those areas. This assessment should take into account in particular of the nature and characteristics of the products or services concerned, of the existence of entry barriers or of consumer preferences, of appreciable differences of the undertakings' market shares between the area concerned and neighboring areas or of substantial price differences'.

Thus, 'the objective conditions of competition applying to the product in question must be the same for all traders'.[225] However, the definition of the relevant geographic market does not require the objective conditions to be perfectly homogeneous; it is sufficient if they are 'similar' or 'sufficiently homogeneous' as opposed to 'heterogeneous' conditions.[226] The outer limits of the relevant geographic market are set in some cases by government measures, [227] statutory[228] or natural monopolies.[229] In other cases the decisive factors are:

– significant price differences between different geographic areas;[230]

---

225. *United Brands*, ECJ Feb. 14, 1978, 1978 ECR 207, paras 44 and 53.
226. *Deutsche Bahn*, CFI Oct. 21, 1997, 1997 ECR II-1689, para. 92.
227. *United Brands*, ECJ Feb. 14, 1978, 1978 ECR 207, paras 11 and 53; *Tetra Pak*, CFI Oct. 6, 1994, 1994 ECR II-755, paras 91–92; *Deutsche Bahn*, CFI Oct. 21, 1997, 1997 ECR II-1689, para. 92. *United Brands*, ECJ Feb. 14, 1978, 1978 ECR 207, paras 36–57; *Price Waterhouse/ Coopers & Lybrand*, D.Comm. May 20, 1998, 1999 OJ L 50/27, point 55; *Bertelsmann/Kirch/ Première*, D.Comm. May 27, 1998, 1999 OJ L 53/1, point 23; *Sicasov*, D.Comm. Dec. 14, 1998, 1999 OJ L 4/27, points 31–36.
228. *Deutsche Bahn*, CFI Oct. 21, 1997, 1997 ECR II-1689, para. 57; *Electricity Monopolies – Italy*, ECJ Oct. 23, 1997, 1997 ECR I-5789, paras 23–25. *See Télémarketing*, ECJ Oct. 3, 1985, 1985 ECR 3261, 3274–3275, paras 11–19. The Luxembourg television station had a legal monopoly and in Belgium TV advertising was banned.
229. Switching to another port or airport is no realistic alternative; ports: *Silvano Raso (Porto di Genova II)*, ECJ Feb. 12, 1998, 1998 ECR I-593, para. 26; airports: *Airport of Frankfurt*, D.Comm. Jan. 14, 1998, 1998 OJ L 72/30; *Portuguese Airports*, D.Comm. Feb. 10, 1999, 1999 OJ L 69/31, point 17; *Air Alliances*, D.Comm. Oct. 29, 2002, IP/02/1569; *Ilmailulaitos/ Luftartsverket*, D.Comm. Feb. 10, 1999, 1999 OJ L 69/24, points 24–32 (under Article 86 in conjunction with Article 82.
230. *Kimberley-Clark/Scott Paper*, D.Comm. Jan. 16, 1996, 1996 OJ L 183/1, point 109. This applies even if the price differences are the result of governmental measures with respect to national social security systems, *see Ciba-Geigy/Sandoz*, D.Comm. July 17, 1996, 1997 OJ L 201/1, points 47, 195; *Hoffmann-La Roche/Boehringer Mannheim*, D.Comm. Feb. 4, 1998, 1998 OJ L 234/1, point 16.

- significant transport costs,[231] in particular in the case of low value products;[232]
- broadcasting transmission capacity;[233]
- significant differences of the firms' market shares between the area concerned and neighboring areas;[234]
- different market strategies in different geographic areas;[235]
- past evidence of diversion of orders to other areas (habit or ability of switching demand to other actual or potential suppliers);[236]
- basic demand characteristics and views of customers and competitors, in particular consumer preferences[237] and habits;[238]
- trade flow/pattern of shipments based on sufficiently detailed information.[239]

Importance of the Firms' Conduct.
In the case of restrictive or abusive behavior, the relevant geographic market is defined by the area in which the firm concerned 'may be able to engage in abuses which hinder effective competition',[240] and in the case of mergers by the area in which the firms are 'involved in the supply and demand of the products or services concerned'.[241] The definition of the relevant geographic market must

231. E.g., *Industrial and Medical Gases*, D.Comm. July 24, 2002, 2003 OJ L 84/1, points 14 and 422–424 (gases in cylinders and bulk).
232. *Continental Can*, ECJ Feb. 21, 1973, 1973 ECR 215, para. 35 (geographic limits between 150 and 300 kilometers for transporting large cans and between 500 and 1000 kilometers for transporting smaller cans); *Kali + Salz/MdK II*, D.Comm. July 9, 1998, M.308, point 16. Examples of larger (EC-wide) markets without transport costs limits: *ECS/Akzo*, D.Comm. Dec. 14, 1985, 1985 OJ L 374/1, 17; *aff'd* ECJ July 3, 1991, 1991 ECR I-3359; *Hilti*, D.Comm. Dec. 22, 1987, 1988 OJ L 65/19, 31; *aff'd* CFI Dec. 12, 1991, 1991 ECR II-1439, paras 80–81; *SCPA/Kali + Salz-MdK*, ECJ March 31, 1998, 1998 ECR I-1375, paras 127–151; *WorldCom/MCI*, D.Comm. July 8, 1998, 1999 OJ L 116/1, point 79 (transatlantic carrier services).
233. *Nordic Satellite Distributor*, D.Comm. July 19, 1995, 1996 OJ L 53/20, points 65–72; *Bertelsmann/ Kirch/Première*, D.Comm. May 27, 1998, 1999 OJ L 53/1, point 25.
234. *See* Article 9 (7) of Regulation 139/2004 on merger control.
235. Community-wide: *Hoffmann-La Roche*, ECJ Feb. 13, 1979, 1979 ECR 461, para. 22; *Nordic Satellite*, D.Comm. July 19, 1995, 1996 OJ L 53/20, point 73. A single member state: *Michelin*, ECJ Nov. 9, 1983, 1983 ECR 3461, para. 26.
236. Community-wide: *Agfa-Gevaert/DuPont*, D.Comm. Feb. 11, 1998, 1998 OJ L 211/22, points 37–41. National markets: *WorldCom/MCI*, D.Comm. July 8, 1998, 1999 OJ L 116/1, point 80 (provision of local loop services). *See also Sugar*, ECJ Dec. 16, 1975, 1975 ECR 1663, para. 371.
237. E.g., for national brands, language, culture and life style, *see Thorn/EMI/Virgin Music*, D.Comm. April 27, 1992, M.202, point 58; *MSG/Media Service*, D.Comm. Nov. 9, 1994, 1994 OJ L 364/1, point 47.
238. *Bertelsmann/Kirch/Première*, D.Comm. May 27, 1998, 1999 OJ L 53/1, point 22.
239. Notice on the Relevant Market, point 49. *See Agfa-Gevaert/DuPont*, D.Comm. Feb. 11, 1998, 1998 OJ L 211/22, points 37–41; *Shell/Montecatini*, D.Comm. June 8, 1994, 1994 OJ L 332/48.
240. *United Brands*, ECJ Feb. 14, 1978, 1978 ECR 207, para. 44. *See also BPB*, CFI April 1, 1993, 1993 ECR II-389, para. 66.
241. Article 9 (7) of Regulation 139/2004 on merger control.

therefore take into account the geographic scope of the conduct in question.[242] The conduct may constitute a general, Community-wide strategy, as in cases involving sale of a product throughout the Community.[243] It may also be directed only at distributors or customers in a single member state. It may even be directed at distributors in part of a member state.[244] However, parts of a member state may be added to a larger market if they are interlinked, in particular by a centralized pricing policy,[245] comparable to the cumulative effect of parallel anticompetitive agreements.[246]

Substantial Part of the Common Market.

If the relevant market is not the whole Common Market, it must be at least 'a substantial part of the Common Market'. A part of a single member state may constitute a substantial part of the Common Market as in the *Sugar* case in which one of the abuses contrary to Article 82 was limited to the southern part of Germany.[247] In *Crespelle* the Court of Justice stated:

> '[B]y thus establishing, in favour of those undertakings, a contiguous series of monopolies territorially limited but together covering the entire territory of a Member State, those national provisions create a dominant position, within the meaning of the Common Market'. [248]

A fortiori a contiguous series of monopolies controlled by the same undertaking may represent a substantial part of the Common Market, which may be corroborated where the traffic volume for the port or airport in question constitute a considerable part of the total traffic volume of the member state concerned.[249] On the other hand, part of a member state will not always be a substantial part of the Common Market. For example, if competitive conditions throughout a national

---

242. However, this does not exclude the application of Article 82 to a dominant firm which abuses its dominant position on one market in order to extend its monopoly or eliminate potential competitors to another market, *see Télémarketing*, ECJ Oct. 3, 1985, 1985 ECR 3261, paras 25–27.
243. Under Article 82: *Hoffmann-La Roche*, ECJ Feb. 13, 1979, 1979 ECR 461, para. 22; under the merger control regulation: *Nordic Satellite*, D.Comm. July 19, 1995, 1996 OJ L 53/20, point 73.
244. Under Article 82: *Michelin*, ECJ Nov. 9, 1983, 1983 ECR 3461, para. 26 (tires retailing in the Netherlands); under the merger control regulation: *Blokker/Toys 'R' Us*, D.Comm. June 26, 1997, 1998 OJ L 316/1, point 42 (toys retailing in the Netherlands).
245. *Delhaize/PG*, D.Comm. Aug. 22, 1994, M.471, points 10–11; *Blokker/Toys 'R' Us*, D.Comm. June 26, 1997, 1998 OJ L 316/1, point 40.
246. *Ilmailulaitos/Luftartsverket*, D.Comm. Feb. 10, 1999, 1999 OJ L 69/24, point 36.
247. *Sugar*, ECJ Dec. 16. 1975, 1975 ECR 1663, paras 441–448.
248. *Crespelle*, ECJ Nov. 5, 1994, 1994 ECR I-5077, para. 17. *See also Almelo*, ECJ April 27, 1994, 1994 ECR I-1477.
249. *Portuguese Airports*, D.Comm. Feb. 10, 1999, 1999 OJ L 69/31, point 21.

market are constant so that the national market must be regarded as the relevant market, a strong position on a regional market will not suffice to bring the holder's conduct under Article 82.[250]

Trend to a 'Europeanization'or 'Globalization' of National Markets.
The Commission takes into account the continuing process of market integration, especially in the field of mergers and structural joint ventures. A process of market integration, including the ongoing process of liberalization, may lead to wider geographic markets,[251] i.e., to a 'Europeanization'[252] or even 'globalization' of national markets.[253] This accords with the prospective analysis of the anticompetitive effects of structural changes caused by a merger. By contrast, the analysis of abusive conduct of a dominant firm is based on its past and current behavior and is limited to past and current market conditions. Similarly, potential competition can only be considered if its effects are short-term and prevent a firm from behaving to an appreciable extent independently of such potential competitive constraint, thereby affording it the possibility to abuse its market position. Longer-term competitive constraints, however, may be taken into account when assessing changes of the competitive structure of the market, thereby leading to a wider definition of the relevant geographic market.

4. Determination of Parties' Position on the Relevant Market

Calculation of Market Shares.
The parties' position on the relevant market is calculated on the basis of their turnover (sales) of the relevant products compared to the total turnover of all suppliers. The total turnover may be determined from industry statistics, consultants, trade associations or estimates. The Commission may ask each supplier to provide its own turnover figure. In some cases it may seem more appropriate to base the calculation on other indications, such as volume, capacity,[254] reserves (stocks),[255] orders firmly booked,[256] advertising revenue,[257] or a family of products or services, which may be used as 'leverage'.[258]

---

250. *Alsatel/Novasam*, ECJ Oct. 5, 1988, 1988 ECR 5987, 15 and 18–19.
251. Notice on the Relevant Market, point 32.
252. *Procter & Gamble/Schickedanz*, D.Comm. June 21, 1994, 1994 OJ L 354/32, point 104.
253. Twenty-eighth Report on Competition Policy, point 134 (insert 5).
254. E.g. fleet capacity: *Air France/Sabena*, D.Comm. Oct. 5, 1992, M.157.
255. *See Gencor*, CFI March 25, 1999, 1999 ECR II-753, para. 255.
256. *Aérospatiale-Alenia/DeHavilland*, D.Comm. Oct. 2, 1991, 1991 OJ L 334/42, points 21–25.
257. Notice on the Relevant Market, points 53–55.
258. *Schneider*, CFI Oct. 22, 2002, 2002 ECR II-4091, para. 240.

Potential Competition.
Any competitive assessment must include 'the structure of all markets concerned and the … potential competition from undertakings'.[259] The Commission treats a firm as a potential competitor 'if there is evidence that, absent the agreement, this firm could and would be likely to undertake the necessary additional investments or other necessary switching costs so that it could enter the relevant market in response to a small and permanent increase in relative prices'.[260] The impact of potential competition is not measurable in mathematical terms. The impact of potential competition from a neighbouring geographic market may be estimated on the basis of that part of capacity which may be diverted, activated or enlarged to satisfy the needs of customers on the relevant market.[261] In the context of a merger or a joint venture it must be established 'to the requisite legal standard' that potential competition is expected to be eliminated or significantly reduced by finding that the implementation of the operation 'would place [the acquiror] … in a position where it could be more independent than in the past in relation to its competitors …'.[262]

D. Addressees of Competition Rules

1. Undertakings and/or Member States as Addressees

Introduction.
Unlike other antitrust laws, the EC Treaty provides for a complete set of legal instruments to prevent distortions of competition regardless of whether they are caused by private undertakings, by public undertakings or by member states themselves. Undertakings are addressees of the competition rules of Articles 81 and 82 and Regulation 139/2004 on merger control. The member states are addressees of:

(i) the prohibitions against quantitative restrictions or restrictions having equivalent effects on trade between member states on goods (Articles 28–30) or on the freedom to provide services (Articles 49–55),
(ii) the obligation to adjust existing state trading monopolies (Article 31),

259. Article 2 (1) (a) of Regulation 139/2004 on merger control.
260. Guidelines on Horizontal Cooperation, FN 9.
261. *See Mannesmann/Hoesch*, D.Comm. Nov. 12, 1992, 1993 OJ L 114/34, points 103–111.
262. *Tetra Laval*, CFI Oct. 25, 2002, 2002 ECR II-4381, para. 324. The foreseeable impact may be estimated, in particular in the case of a new product, on the basis of the firm's own sales targets on the market of those products which will be improved or replaced by the new product (*see* Article 4 (2) of Regulation 2658/2000 on R&D agreements). In the case of the development and future marketing of new products a key question is whether the parties will obtain patents that may have a blocking effect and lead to a structural danger of foreclosing the future market (e.g., *Ciba-Geigy/Sandoz*, D.Comm. July 17, 1996, 1996 OJ L 201/1, points 95–107).

(iii) the prohibition against distorting competition by granting state aids (Articles 87–89) or by imposing discriminatory taxes (Articles 90–93), and
(iv) the prohibition against inducing distortions of competition by undertakings (Article 10 in conjunction with Articles 81 and 82 and Article 86).

Consequently, the Commission may act against any author of a distortion of competition, although under different procedures: Regulation 1/2003 in cases of infringement of Articles 81 and 82 or Regulation 139/2004 in the case of mergers; and under the specific procedures of Articles 31, 86 and 88 or the general provision of Article 226 in cases of infringement by a member state.

2. Concept of 'Undertaking'

Businesses as 'Undertakings'.
The term 'undertaking' as used in Articles 81 and 82 of the EC Treaty is not defined. However, the terms used in the languages of the original EC member countries, from which the English version of the Treaties was translated, show that it is simply another word for firm, business or enterprise. An 'undertaking' therefore need not have legal personality under national law.[263] Article 31 (1) (2) of the EC Treaty uses, in the context of a state monopoly, the term 'any body' through which a member state supervises or influences imports and exports. For the specific purposes of the ECSC Treaty, the Court of Justice has defined an undertaking as 'a single organization of personal, tangible and intangible elements, attached to an autonomous legal entity pursuing a given long term economic aim.'[264] For the purposes of the EC Treaty, the Court of Justice adopts a similarly broad definition by stating that Article 81 (1) is aimed at 'economic units which consist of a unitary organization of personal, tangible and intangible elements which pursues a specific economic aim on a long-term basis'.[265] The term 'undertaking' may therefore refer to any entity engaged in business activities (supplying goods or services)[266] irrespective of its financing and of its legal status.[267] 'Undertakings'

263. *See Albany*, ECJ Sept. 21, 1999, 1999 ECR I-5751, paras 77–87.
264. *Klöckner/Hoesch*, ECJ July 13, 1962, 1962 ECR 325, 341.
265. *Shell*, CFI March 10, 1992, 1992 ECR II-757, para. 311; *HFB Holding*, CFI March 20, 2002, 2002 ECR II-1487, para. 54.
266. *Airport of Milano*, ECJ Jan. 18, 2001, 2001 ECR I-385, paras 107–108; *Aéroports de Paris*, ECJ Oct. 24, 2002, 2002 ECR I-9297, paras 75–79 (purely administrative activities to be distinguished from management and operation of airports); *FENIN*, CFI March 4, 2003, T-319/99, paras 35–36 (public hospitals).
267. *CNSD*, ECJ June 18, 1998, 1998 ECR I-3851, para. 36. *See also Transparency Directive II*, ECJ June 16, 1987, 1987 ECR 2599, 2620–2622, par-as. 3–11; *Höffner/Macrotron*, ECJ April 23, 1991, 1991 ECR I-1979, para. 21; *Dutch Cranes*, CFI Oct. 22, 1997, 1997 ECR II-1739, para. 120.

therefore include partnerships,[268] sole proprietorships[269] and natural persons who engage in commercial activities. The business activity undertaken must involve the performance of economic services in return for payment, and normally – but not necessarily – with the objective of making a profit.[270] The business activity must be of some duration.[271] However, the term 'commercial activities' excludes purely 'social' activities[272] and the exercise of sovereign powers.[273] Likewise, executing government instructions cannot be regarded as 'commercial activity.[274]

Natural Persons as 'Undertakings'.
Natural persons may be 'undertakings' if they engage in business activities. The competition rules have been applied, for example, to commercial agents, except where they only execute orders of their principal,[275] to customs agents, even if they may be associated with a 'liberal' profession,[276] to patent agents,[277] to inventors who may enter into anticompetitive agreements with respect to the exploitation of their inventions,[278] or auditors helping to run a cartel[279] (but not to independent experts[280]), to artists to the extent that their artistic works may be commercial

268. *Roses*, D.Comm. Dec. 13, 1985, 1985 OJ L 369/9, point 22.
269. *Tepea*, ECJ June 20, 1978, 1978 ECR 1391.
270. *GEMA I*, D.Comm. June 2, 1971, 1971 OJ L 134/15. Pension funds may be 'undertakings' even if they are not profit-making: *Albany*, ECJ Sept. 21, 1999, 1999 ECR I-5751, paras 77–87. 'Associations of undertakings' in particular need not be profit-making.
271. *Klöckner/Hoesch*, ECJ July 13, 1962, 1962 ECR 325, 341.
272. *FENIN*, CFI March 4, 2003, T-319/99, para. 37.
273. *Cf.* Article 45 (1) of the EC Treaty ('exercise of official authority'). *See* in greater detail Chapter IX.A.
274. *SAT/Eurocontrol*, ECJ Jan. 19, 1994, 1994 ECR I-43. However, the mere approval of commercial behavior or a decision or the assistance of public representatives does not exempt the undertaking from its responsibility under the competition rules: *BNIC*, ECJ Jan. 30, 1985, 1985 ECR 391; *Gebrüder Reiff*, ECJ Nov. 17, 1993, 1993 ECR I-5801, para. 16.
275. *Peugeot*, ECJ June 16, 1994, 1994 ECR I-2727, paras 33–36; *Union internationale des chemins de fer (UIC)*, CFI June 6, 1995, 1995 ECR II-1503, paras 38–40.
276. *COAPI*, D.Comm. Jan. 30, 1995, 1995 OJ L 122/37, paras 36–47; *CSND II*, CFI March 30, 2000, 2000 ECR II-1807, paras 54–55; Belgian Architects, D.Comm. June 24, 2004, IP/04/800. *See* Commission Report on Competition in Professional Services, COM(2004)83 final, http://europa.eu.int/comm/competition/liberal_professions/final_communication_en.pdf.
277. *COAPI*, D.Comm. Jan. 30, 1995, 1995 OJ L 122/37, paras 32–33; *EPI*, D.Comm. April 7, 1999, 1999 OJ L 106/14, points 23–24 (narrower interpretation by CFI March 28, 2001, 2001 ECR II-1087, para. 50, which partially annulled the Commission decision).
278. *Vaessen/Moris*, D.Comm. Jan. 10, 1979, 1979 OJ L 19/32, 34; *AOIP/Beyrard*, D.Comm. Dec. 2, 1975, 1976 OJ L 6/8, 12.
279. 'Fides' in *Italian Cast Glass*, D.Comm. Dec. 17, 1980, 1980 OJ L 383/19, 23–24, 26; *Fides*, D.Comm. Jan. 31, 1979, 1979 OJ L 57/33 (order to submit to investigations); *Organic Peroxides Cartel*, D.Comm. Dec. 10, 2003, IP/03/1700 (fining a Swiss-based company for playing a key role in the cartel by organizing meetings and hiding incriminating evidence).
280. *CSND I*, ECJ June 18, 1998, 1998 ECR I-3851, para. 44; *CSND II*, CFI March 30, 2000, 2000 ECR II-1807, para. 55.

objects,[281] to sports figures to the extent that they undertake commercial activities within the meaning of Article 2 of the Treaty,[282] and to the owner of a business who sells it but who may remain a potential 'undertaking' in spite of the sale.[283]

3. Parent and Subsidiary: The 'Intra-Enterprise Doctrine'

Parent and Subsidiary Operated as One Enterprise.
Article 81 does not normally apply to intracorporate agreements or practices between a parent and its subsidiaries if they form an economic unit in which the subsidiary has no real freedom to determine its course of action on the market, and if the agreements or practices are concerned merely with the internal allocation of tasks within the group,[284] which may include the allocation of territories protected against active or passive sales of other companies under common control within the same group.[285] Similarly, Article 81 does not apply to a license agreement between a parent company and its controlled subsidiary[286] or to arrangements on selective distribution between companies belonging to the same group.[287] On the other hand, companies belonging to a group that operates as a single enterprise are subject to Article 82 if a dominant position is abused,[288] and remain subject to Articles 28–30 and Articles 49–55 if the free movement of goods or services within the group is impeded.[289] Several natural or legal persons (companies) are regarded

281. *Deutsche GrammophonMetro*, ECJ June 8, 1971, 1971 ECR 487, 501, para. 18; *RAI/Unitel*, D.Comm. May 26, 1978, 1978 OJ L 157/39, 40 (opera singers).
282. *Deliège*, ECJ April 11, 2000, 2000 ECR I-2549, para. 53; *Lehtonen*, ECJ April 13, 2000, 2000 ECR I-2681, paras 39–46; *Union Cycliste*, ECJ Dec. 12, 1974, 1974 ECR 1405, 1417, para. 4. *See* Thirtieth Report on Competition Policy, points 226–229.
283. *Reuter/BASF*, D.Comm. July 26, 1976, 1976 OJ L 254/40, 45.
284. *Carton – Stora*, CFI May 14, 1998, 1998 ECR II-2111, para. 79; *Micro Leader/Microsoft*, CFI Dec. 16, 1999, 1999 ECR II-3989, para. 38. *See also Dyestuffs – ICI*, ECJ July 14, 1972, 1972 ECR 619, paras 132–141; *Johnson & Johnson*, D.Comm. Nov. 25, 1980, 1980 OJ L 377/16, 26; *Ford I*, ECJ Feb. 28, 1984, 1984 ECR 1129, paras 12–13; *Hydrotherm/Compact*, ECJ July 12, 1984, 1984 ECR 2999, 3016, paras 10–12; *Funeral Services*, ECJ May 4, 1988, 1988 ECR 2479, 2513, para. 19; *Ahmed Saeed*, ECJ April 11, 1989, 1989 ECR 803, paras 35–36; *Viho/Parker Pen*, ECJ Oct. 24, 1996, 1996 ECR I-5457, para. 16.
285. *Viho/Parker Pen*, ECJ Oct. 24, 1996, 1996 ECR I-5457, para. 16; *Interbrew*, Twenty-sixth Report on Competition Policy, p. 139.
286. *Christiani & Nielsen*, D.Comm. June 18, 1969, 1969 OJ L 165/12, 13–14; *Centrafarm/Sterling Drug*, ECJ Oct. 31, 1974, 1974 ECR 1147, para. 41; *Dyestuffs – ICI*, ECJ July 14, 1972, 1972 ECR 619, para. 134.
287. *Viho/Parker Pen*, CFI Jan. 12, 1995, 1995 ECR II-17, para. 47; *aff'd* ECJ Oct. 24, 1996, 1996 ECR I-5457.
288. *Viho/Parker Pen*, ECJ Oct. 24, 1996, 1996 ECR I-5457, para. 17. *See Funeral Services*, ECJ May 4, 1988, 1988 ECR 2479, 2513, para. 21; *AlsatelNovasam*, ECJ Oct. 5, 1988, 1988 ECR 5987, 6010, para. 20; *British Plaster Board*, CFI April 1, 1993, 1993 ECR II-389, paras 149–154.
289. *Deutsche Grammophon/Metro*, ECJ June 8, 1971, 1971 ECR 487, paras 2 and 9–13.

as a single 'undertaking' if they carry on business as one economic unit.[290] For the purposes of legal enforcement, however, the activities must be attributed to a legal entity or individual to which a decision can be addressed.[291] Auxiliary activities performed by commercial agents or subcontractors are attributed to their principal; they are only an extended arm of their principal.[292]

Control Required for an Economic Entity.
Under the 'intra-enterprise doctrine', several businesses can only form an 'economic entity' if a control relationship exists between them.[293] Article 81 (1) does not apply to agreements between undertakings belonging to the same group as parent company and subsidiary if those undertakings form an economic unit within which the subsidiary has no real freedom to determine its course of action on the market, and if the agreements or practices are concerned merely with the internal allocation of tasks within the group.[294] However, the 'intra-enterprise doctrine' presupposes the possibility of exercising 'control'. A minority shareholding which results in a blocking minority stake but that does not result in actual control (e.g. 25.001%) is too weak a relationship to establish 'control' or an economic entity.[295] Further, no economic entity will be deemed to exist between companies by virtue of joint control over another enterprise, as is ordinarily the case with joint ventures which are autonomous and independent undertakings. It follows that agreements concluded between one parent and the joint venture

290. *Hydrotherm/Compact*, ECJ July 12, 1984, 1984 ECR 2999, paras 10–12; *ICI-Dyestuffs*, ECJ July 14, 1972, 1972 ECR 619, paras 132–141.

291. *Polypropylene – Enichem-Anic*, CFI Dec. 17, 1991, 1991 ECR II-1623, para. 55; *Carton – SCA Holding*, CFI May 14, 1998, 1998 ECR II-1373, para. 63; *Carton – Stora*, CFI May 14, 1998, 1998 ECR II-2111, para. 79. For purposes of imposing fines the Commission must (i) identify the natural or legal person responsible, and (ii) determine whether the natural or legal person is still in business or, in the case of a legal person, whether it has been wound up or absorbed by another company: *PVC II*, D.Comm. July 27, 1994, 1994 OJ L 239/14, paras 40–46; *Aalborg – Cement*, ECJ Jan. 7, 2004, C-204/00, paras 354–360.

292. *See* Chapter IV.A.3.b.

293. *ICI-Dyestuffs*, ECJ July 14, 1972, 1972 ECR 619, paras 125–141; *Commercial Solvents*, ECJ March 6, 1974, 1974 ECR 223, paras 36–41; *SABA II*, ECJ Oct. 22, 1986, 1986 ECR 3021, paras 82–84; *Centrafarm/Sterling Drug*, ECJ Oct. 31, 1974, 1974 ECR 1147, para. 41; *Funeral Services*, ECJ May 4, 1988, 1988 ECR 2479, para. 19; *Viho*, ECJ Oct. 24, 1996, 1996 ECR I-5457, para. 16; *Krupp Thyssen*, CFI Dec. 13, 2001, 2001 ECR II-3757, paras 315–319.

294. *Centrafarm/Sterling Drug*, ECJ Oct. 31, 1974, 1974 ECR 1147, para. 41; *Ford I*, ECJ Feb. 28, 1984, 1984 ECR 1129, paras 12–13; *Hydrotherm/Compact*, ECJ July 12, 1984, 1984 ECR 2999, paras 10–12; *SABA II*, ECJ Oct. 22, 1986, 1986 ECR 3021, paras 82–84; *Funeral Services*, ECJ May 4, 1988, 1988 ECR 2479, para. 19.

295. *Welded Steel Mesh – Tréfilunion*, CFI April 6, 1995, 1995 ECR II-791, para. 129. *See also Philip Morris/Rothmans*, ECJ Nov. 17, 1987, 1987 ECR 4487, para. 65. An arrangement between the minority shareholder and the company may therefore not be regarded as mere internal allocation of tasks.

may be caught by Article 81 (1).[296] However, an economic entity may be formed gradually between previously independent companies on the basis of links established over a period of time. The companies can be regarded as an economic unit once a contract confers actual control or leads to actual consolidation of the activities of the enterprises; until that time their cooperation is subject to Article 81.[297] No economic entity will be assumed to exist among several government-owned enterprises if they are subject to the control of different governmental agencies that do not coordinate their operations on the basis of an internal allocation of functions.[298]

Responsibility within a Group.

The parent company that controls a subsidiary and determines its commercial behavior is *prima facie* responsible for anticompetitive acts committed by the subsidiary.[299] A mere holding function does not suffice to establish the parent's responsibility,[300] unless it assumes responsibility for the affiliate's conduct.[301] A subsidiary that has a certain autonomy in determining its commercial policy may be held responsible for its own anticompetitive behavior.[302] If both parent and

---

296. *Welded Steel Mesh – Baustahlgewerbe*, CFI April 6, 1995, 1995 ECR II-987, paras 107–108.
297. *IMI/Heilmann I*, Seventh Report on Competition Policy, points 29–32. *See also Montedison/Hercules (Himont)*, Seventeenth Report on Competition Policy, point 69; *Funeral Services*, ECJ May 4, 1988, 1988 ECR 2479, para. 19.
298. In the case of a merger between two French state-owned steel companies, the Commission saw the need to issue an authorization under Article 66 of the ECSC Treaty: *Usinor/Sacilor-Normandie*, D.Comm. April 2, 1982, 1982 OJ L 139/1, 3.
299. Under Article 81: *ICI Dyestuffs*, ECJ July 14, 1972, 1972 ECR 619, paras 125–141; *AEG/Telefunken*, ECJ Oct. 25, 1983, 1983 ECR 3151, para. 50; *Polypropylene Shell*, CFI March 10, 1992, 1992 ECR II-757, para. 315; *Polypropylene*, D.Comm. April 23, 1986, 1986 OJ L 230/1, 30–33; *aff'd Linz*, CFI March 10, 1992, 1992 ECR II-1275: Chemie Linz and not its majority-owned subsidiaries located in the Common Market since their marketing policy was decided by the head office. Under Article 82: *British Plaster Board*, CFI April 1, 1993, 1993 ECR II-389, paras 149–151; *Carton – Stora*, CFI, May 14, 1998, 1998 ECR II-2111, para. 79.
300. E.g., *Polypropylene – Shell*, CFI March 10, 1992, 1992 ECR II-757, para. 315 (Shell International Chemical Company was responsible and therefore was the appropriate addressee of the decision, and not the parent holding company Shell, because Shell International Chemical Company had overall responsibility for the planning and coordination of the activities of the Shell group companies in polypropylene).
301. *Carton – SCA Holding*, CFI May 15, 1998, 1998 ECR II-1373, para. 63; *PVC II*, CFI April 20, 1999, 1999 ECR II-931, paras 983–989 (*aff'd* ECJ Oct. 15, 2002, 2002 ECR I-8375). *See Polypropylene – Enichem-Anic*, CFI Dec. 17, 1991, 1991 ECR I-1623, para. 55.
302. Under Article 81: *Deutsche Philips*, D.Comm. Oct. 5, 1973, 1973 OJ L 293/40; *BMW Belgium*, D.Comm. Dec. 23, 1977, 1978 OJ L 46/33, 42; *Italian Flat Glass II*, D.Comm. Dec. 7, 1988, 1989 OJ L 33/44, 45 (Italian subsidiaries of French and U.S. companies, in this respect *aff'd* CFI March 10, 1992, 1992 ECR II-1403, para. 358); *Sandoz*, D.Comm. July 13, 1987, 1987 OJ L 222/28, 33 (Italian subsidiary of Swiss company); *Konica*, D.Comm. Dec. 18, 1987, 1988 OJ L 78/34, 42. Under Article 82: *Michelin*, D.Comm. Oct. 7, 1981, 1981 OJ L 353/33 (Dutch subsidiary of French parent).

subsidiary play a role and have their own interest in anticompetitive behavior, they may be held jointly responsible.[303]

4. Associations and Government Bodies

Associations.

Any association of undertakings, whether or not it has legal personality, is subject to Articles 81 and 82, provided they exercise a commercial activity[304] and may take action on their own initiative.[305] The form the association takes, in particular its legal personality, is not determinative;[306] Article 81 applies to associations,[307] cooperatives[308] and consortia in the form, for instance, of a 'groupement d'intérêt économique' in French law, a 'vennootschap onder firma' or 'stichting' in Dutch law,[309] a 'European Economic Interest Grouping' under EC law,[310] or trade unions

303. Under Article 81: *Johnson & Johnson*, D.Comm. Nov. 25, 1980, 1980 OJ L 377/16, 26. Under Article 82: *Commercial Solvents*, D.Comm. Dec. 14, 1972, 1972 OJ L 299/51, 54.

304. A professional organization is *not as such* restrictive: *Eurovision II*, D.Comm. May 10, 2000, 2000 OJ L 151/68, point 68 (*rev'd* CFI Oct. 8, 2002, 2002 ECR II-3805, because of unjustified application of Article 81 (3)). Trade Unions are not subject to Article 8: *Albany*, ECJ Sept. 21, 1999, 1999 ECR I-5751, paras 59–60.

305. *Woodpulp I*, ECJ Sept. 27, 1988, 1988 ECR 5193, paras 24–27; *Steel Beams – Eurofer*, CFI March 11, 1999, 1999 ECR II-263, paras 98–99; *Wirtschaftsvereinigung Stahl*, CFI April 5, 2001, 2001 ECR II-1217. Social activities *see FENIN*, CFI March 4, 2003, T-319/99, para. 37. Cultural activities *see Sacchi/Tele Biella*, ECJ April 30, 1974, 1974 ECR 409, paras 13–14; *IFPI Simulcasting*, D.Comm. Oct. 8, 2002, 2003 OJ L 107/58.

306. *CEWAL*, ECJ March 16, 2000, 2000 ECR I-1365, para. 144.

307. *FEG*, D.Comm. Oct. 10, 1999, 2000 OJ L 39/1; *French Federations in the beef sector*, D.Comm. April 2, 2003, IP/03/479. *See also FEDETAB*, ECJ Oct. 29, 1980, 1980 ECR 3125, 3250, paras 87–88; *Fire Insurance*, ECJ Jan. 27, 1987, 1987 ECR 405, paras 26–32; *Wood Pulp I*, ECJ Sept. 27, 1988, 1988 ECR 5193, paras 24–28. Association without legal personality: *CEWAL*, D.Comm. Dec. 23, 1992, 1993 OJ L 34/20; *aff'd* CFI Oct. 8, 1996, 1996 ECR II-1201, para. 232, but partially *rev'd* on procedural grounds ECJ March 16, 2000, 2000 ECR I-1365, paras 142–147 (line conferences). Including federations of associations: *VBBB/VBVB*, D.Comm. Nov. 25, 1981, 1982 OJ L 54/36, 37, 50; *Eurocheque – Helsinki*, CFI Feb. 23, 1994, 1994 ECR II-49, para. 76; *Jahrhundertvertrag*, D.Comm. Dec. 22, 1992, 1993 OJ L 50/14; *FENEX*, D.Comm. June 5, 1996, 1996 OJ L 181/28, para. 32–42.

308. *Rennet*, ECJ March 25, 1981, 1981 ECR 851, paras 9–13; *Meldoc*, D.Comm. Nov. 26, 1986, 1986 OJ L 348/50; *Hudson's Bay I*, D.Comm. Oct. 28, 1988, 1988 OJ L 316/43, 48; *aff'd* CFI July 2, 1992, 1992 ECR II-1931, para. 50; *Gottrup-Klim*, ECJ Dec. 15, 1994, 1994 ECR I-5641.

309. *Dutch Construction Works*, D.Comm. Feb. 5, 1992, 1992 OJ L 92/1, para. 141; *aff'd* SPO, ECJ March 25, 1996 ECR I-1611; SSI, D.Comm. July 15, 1982, 1982 OJ L 232/1; *Dutch Cranes*, CFI Oct. 22, 1997, 1997 ECR II-1739, para. 120.

310. *See*, respectively, *Air-Forge*, Twelfth Report on Competition Policy, point 85; *De Laval/Stork*, D.Comm. July 25, 1977, 1977 OJ L 215/11; *Orphé*, D.Comm. Dec. 6, 1990, IP (90) 991. The EEIG is a new legal form for transnational consortia introduced into EC law by Council Regulation 2137/85, 1985 OJ L 199/1.

insofar as they assist in the conclusion and implementation of restrictive agreements or conduct.[311] Agreements between associations are also covered by Article 81 (1).[312] An association may act on its own initiative or coordinate its members' activities.[313] The association may be held responsible for any activity infringing Article 81,[314] except where its members use the association as tool of coordinating their own anticompetitive behavior.[315] However, fines may only be imposed on entities having legal personality (for reasons of enforcement);[316] in the absence of a legal status of the association its members are subject to fines insofar as they can be held responsible for the infringement.[317]

State Agencies, Public Bodies and Governments.
The state itself and its agencies, public bodies, and bodies to which the state has granted special or exclusive rights may also be 'undertakings' to the extent that they engage in business activities as opposed to exercising sovereign powers[318] irrespective of whether they are vested with legal personality or not.[319] Article

311. *French Federation in the Beef Sector*, D.Comm. April 2, 2003, IP/03/479; *National Farmers' Union*, ECJ Oct 22, 2002, 2002 ECR I-9079.
312. *See VBBB/VBVB*, D.Comm. Nov. 25, 1981, 1982 OJ L 54/36, *aff'd* ECJ Jan. 17, 1984, 1984 ECR 19.
313. *Fire Insurance*, ECJ Jan. 27, 1987, 1987 ECR 405; *Dutch Cranes*, CFI Oct. 22, 1997, 1997 ECR II-1739, paras 170 and 254; *Steel Beams – Eurofer*, CFI March 11, 1999, 1999 ECR II-263, para. 131. Coordination function denied: *Woodpulp I*, ECJ Sept. 27, 1988, 1988 ECR 5249, paras 24, 27.
314. *Nederlandse Federatieve Vereniging voor de Groothandel op Elektrotechnisch Gebied (FEG)*, CFI Dec. 16, 2003, T-5/00, paras 390–393. *See Steel Beams – Eurofer*, CFI March 11, 1999, 1999 ECR II-263, paras 98–99, 131 and 180. *Hudson's Bay*, D.Comm. Oct. 28, 1988, 1988 OJ L 316/43; *Soda Ash – ANSAC*, D.Comm. Dec. 19, 1990, 1991 OJ L 152/54. Fines may be imposed on associations (provided they have legal personality: *CEWAL*, CFI Oct. 8, 1996, 1996 ECR II-1201, para. 232, but partially *rev'd* on procedural grounds ECJ March 16, 2000, 2000 ECR I-1365, paras 142–147) on the basis of their members' aggregate turnover: *Dutch Cranes*, CFI Oct. 22, 1997, 1997 ECR II-1739, para. 253; *Carton*, D.Comm. July 13, 1994, 1994 OJ L 243/1, points 173–175; *aff'd Carton – Finnboard*, CFI May 14, 1998, 1998 ECR II-1617; *EPI*, D.Comm. April 7, 1999, 1999 OJ L 106/14, point 25 (narrower interpretation by CFI March 28, 2001, 2001 ECR II-1087, para. 50, which partially annulled the Commission decision); *see* Commission White Paper on Modernization, 1999 OJ C 132/1, point 127.
315. *Woodpulp I*, ECJ Sept. 27, 1988, 1988 ECR 5193, paras 24–27.
316. However, the amount of fines must be limited to 10% of the association's turnover: *FNCBV – French Federations in the Beef Sector*, CFI Jan. 21, 2004, T-217/03R, para. 52.
317. *Eurofer*, CFI March 11, 1999, 1999 ECR II-263, paras 98–99 and 131; *CEWAL*, ECJ March 16, 2000, 2000 ECR I-1365, paras 144–146.
318. *Höfner/Macrotron*, ECJ April 23, 1991, 1991 ECR I-1979, para. 21. *See Ameyde/UCI*, ECJ June 9, 1977, 1977 ECR 1091, para. 18; *INNO/ATAB*, ECJ Nov. 16, 1977, 1977 ECR 2115, paras 28–34; *British Telecommunications*, ECJ March 20, 1985, 1985 ECR 873, paras 16–20; *Cafeteros de Colombia*, D.Comm. Dec. 10, 1982, 1982 OJ L 360/31, 32, 34; *Euglucon*, Thirteenth Report on Competition Policy, points 107–109.
319. *Decoster*, ECJ Oct. 27, 1993, 1993 ECR I-5335, para. 11.

81 applies to agreements between household waste collection undertakings and local authorities insofar as they carry on an economic activity by granting financial support in return for establishing a selective collection service and proof that the waste is recovered.[320] However, Article 81 does not apply to sovereign acts, regardless of whether the sovereign act is carried out by the state itself or delegated to a public body or to a private body.[321] However, non-sovereign activities, whether performed by the state itself, by a public body, a state-owned or controlled enterprise, or by a private firm entrusted with the activity by the state, are subject to the rules on competition.[322] For instance, the Commission has applied the competition rules to a government-appointed board of wine growers and dealers that fixed the price of cognac,[323] a car manufacturer that had a *de facto* monopoly from the government for the issuance of automotive type approvals for imported vehicles and charged excessive prices for this service,[324] to national telecommunications authorities holding a monopoly for certain services that used their position to curb the activities of private operators on markets not covered by the monopoly,[325] to state-owned banks,[326] to rail transport authorities[327] and to postal authorities.[328]

320. *Eco-Emballages*, D.Comm. June 15, 2001, 2001 OJ L 233/37, points 70–71.
321. *SAT/Eurocontrol*, ECJ Jan. 19, 1994, 1994 ECR I-43; *BRD/Delta*, ECJ June 9, 1994, 1994 ECR I-2517; *Diego Cali & Figli*, ECJ March 18, 1997, 1997 ECR I-1547, paras 23–24 (whether an activity is subject to a fee or not is irrelevant: the exercise of sovereignty is not necessarily free of charge).
322. *Transparency Directive II*, ECJ June 16, 1987, 1987 ECR 2599, paras 3–11; *Funeral Services*, ECJ May 4, 1988, 1988 ECR 2479, para. 21.
323. *BNIC I*, ECJ Jan. 30, 1985, 1985 ECR 391, paras 16–26.
324. *British Leyland*, ECJ Nov. 11, 1986, 1986 ECR 3263, para. 9.
325. *British Telecommunications*, ECJ March 20, 1985, 1985 ECR 873, paras 16–20; *Bundespost I-III*, Fifteenth Report on Competition Policy, points 259–26 1; Sixteenth Report on Competition Policy, point 294.
326. *Austrian Banks – Lombard Club*, D.Comm. June 11, 2002, IP/02/844 (fines of EUR 124.26 million), suspension rejected, CFI Dec. 20, 2002, T-213/01R.
327. *Union internationale des chemins de fer (UIC)*, CFI June 6, 1995, 1995 ECR II-1503; *GT-Link/De Dansk Statsbaner*, ECJ July 17, 1997, 1997 ECR I-4449; *Deutsche Bahn*, CFI Oct. 21, 1997, 1997 ECR II-1689, para. 57; *Eurotunnel*, D.Comm. Dec. 13, 1994, 1994 OJ L 354/66 (condition attached to exemption annulled: CFI Oct. 22, 1996, 1996 ECR II-1491); *Night Services*, D.Comm. Oct. 21, 1994, 1994 OJ L 259/20.
328. *Deutsche Post/GZS*, ECJ Feb. 10, 2000, 2000 ECR I-825; *Express International*, DHL, ECJ June 16, 1994, 1994 ECR I-2681; Commission notice on the application of the competition rules in the postal sector, 1998 OJ C 39/2, points 2.6.–2.9.; *Belgian Poste*, D.Comm. Dec. 5, 2001, 2002 OJ L 61/32.

E. Scope of Application

1. Effect on Trade between Member States

Effect on Trade.

The jurisdictional reach of the EC competition rules and of the rules governing governmental distortions of competition is limited to conduct that 'may affect trade between Member States'.[329] The nations that founded the EC reasoned that, given the federal structure of the Community, the policing of anticompetitive conduct that had only localized effects should be left to the member states.[330] The Court of Justice has stated that the test of effect on trade between member states is met whenever it is possible to foresee with a sufficient degree of probability, on the basis of a set of objective factors of law or fact, that the agreement or concerted practice in question may have an influence, *direct or indirect, actual or potential*, on the pattern of trade in goods or services between member states.[331] As the Court of First Instance stated in the *Irish Sugar* case, 'it is therefore not necessary to demonstrate that the conduct complained of actually affected trade between member states in a discernable way; it is sufficient to establish that the conduct is capable of having that effect.'[332] The effect on the flow of trade must be such as to give rise to a danger that the realization of a single market between member states might be impeded[333] or affect the competitive structure of the market[334] without the

329. Commission Guidelines on the effect on trade concept, 2004 OJ C 101/810. In contrast, the ECSC competition rules applied regardless of whether trade between member states is affected but are, after the expiration of that Treaty on July 22, 2002, replaced by the EC competition rules. This implies that agreements and conduct likely to affect trade between member states are now subject to the EC competition rules whereas agreements and conduct the effects of which are limited to one member state must be assessed under national competition law. *See Concrete reinforcing bar cartel*, D.Comm. Dec 17, 2002, IP/02/1908 (appeal still pending).

330. Report to the foreign ministers by the heads of delegations to the intergovernmental committee set up by the Conference of Messina (Spaak Report), April 1956, pp. 55 and 59 respectively.

331. *See Grundig/Consten*, ECJ July 13, 1966, 1966 ECR 299, 341; *Maschinenbau Ulm*, ECJ June 30, 1966, 1966 ECR 235, 249, and more recently in *Polypropylene – Montecatini*, ECJ July 8, 1999; 1999 ECR I-4539, para. 170; *Tate & Lyle*, CFI July 12, 2001, 2001 ECR II-2035, para. 78 (and the case law cited therein). Similarly EFTA Court of Justice in *Jaeger/Norge*, April 1, 1998, E-3/97, para. 79.

332. *Irish Sugar*, CFI Oct. 7, 1999, 1999 ECR II-2969, para. 170 (*aff'd* ECJ July 10, 2001, 2001 ECR I-5333).

333. *See* Article 14 of the EC Treaty. The effects may concern upstream or downstream markets, derivative products or services (*see BNIC*, ECJ Dec. 18, 1987, 1987 ECR 4789, para. 18; *Woodpulp*, ECJ March 31, 1993, 1993 ECR I-1307, para. 142; *Asahi/Saint Gobain*, D.Comm. Dec. 16, 1994, 1994 OJ L 354/87, para. 23) or secondary products or services (*see* Twenty-fifth Report on Competition Policy, point 86).

334. *Magill*, CFI July 10, 1991, 1991 ECR II-485, para. 77 and ECJ April 6, 1995, 1995 ECR I-743, para. 70; *Ladbroke I*, CFI Oct. 27, 1994, 1994 ECR II-1015, para. 41; *Compagnie Belge Transports*, CFI Oct. 8, 1996, 1996 ECR II-1201, para. 203.

need to prove any actual anticompetitive effect[335] nor harm to the consumer;[336] the effect may be indirect and potential.[337] This broad definition agrees with the one adopted by the Court of Justice for the prohibition against quantitative restrictions on imports in Article 28 of the Treaty.[338] The Court has used a similar approach for state aid under Article 87.[339] The same jurisdictional reach is attributed to Articles 53 and 54 of the EEA Agreement which mirror Articles 81 and 82 of the EC Treaty.[340]

Indirect Effect on Trade.

The effect on trade may also be indirect. The Court has stated that conduct which affects the structure of the market within the Community, e.g., a refusal to supply, may also be deemed to affect trade between the member states even when the behaviour in question does not itself significantly affect interstate trade.[341] Nor is it necessary to establish that each clause of an agreement has such an effect.[342] In the *BNIC II* case[343] it ruled that a cartel that fixes prices of a raw material (*eaux de vie*) that is itself normally not exported to other member states but that is ultimately exported throughout the Community after processing into another end product (cognac) affects trade between the member states.[344]

335. *British Plaster Board*, ECJ April 1, 1993, 1993 ECR I-389, para. 134; *Welded Steel Mesh – Ferriere Nerd*, ECJ July 17, 1997, 1997 ECR I-4411, paras 19–20; *Bagnasco*, ECJ Jan. 21, 1999, 2001 ECR I-135, para. 48; *PVC II*, CFI April 20, 1999, 1999 ECR II-931, para. 753; *aff'd* ECJ Oct. 15, 2002, 2002 ECR I-8375. Interstate trade is likely to be 'affected' by anticompetitive practices even if the volume of trade increases (under Article 37: *Swedish Alcohol Monopoly*, ECJ Oct. 23, 1997, 1997 ECR I-5909, para. 32) or if the trade is affected by fiscal, technical or administrative difficulties (*FEDETAB*, ECJ Oct. 29, 1980, 1980 ECR 3125, para. 172; *Fire Insurance*, ECJ Jan. 27, 1987, 1987 ECR 405, paras 21–22).
336. *Dunlop-Slazenger*, CFI July 7, 1994, 1994 ECR II-441, para. 171.
337. Commission Guidelines on the effect on trade concept, points 38 and 41.
338. *See Dassonville*, ECJ July 11, 1974, 1974 ECR 837, para. 5.
339. *Philip Morris*, ECJ Sept. 17, 1980, 1980 ECR 2671, para. 11.
340. *See Jaeger/Opel Norge*, EFTA Court of Justice April 1, 1998, E-3/97, para. 71; *Graphite Electrodes*, D.Comm. July 18, 2001, 2002 OJ L 100/1, points 111–112.
341. *Commercial Solvents*, ECJ March 6, 1974, 1974 ECR 223, 252–253, paras 30–35; *United Brands*, ECJ Feb. 14, 1978, 1978 ECR 207, 294, paras 197–203; Guidelines on the effect on trade concept, points 15 and 49.
342. *Windsurfing*, ECJ Feb. 25, 1986, 1986 ECR 611, para. 96. Therefore, in a cartel case the degree of individual contribution of the members is not decisive but rather the collective likely affect on trade between member states: *FEDETAB*, ECJ Oct. 29, 1980, 1980 ECR 3125, para. 172; *Polypropylene – Herkules*, CFI Dec. 17, 1991, 1991 ECR II-1715, para. 279.
343. *BNIC II*, ECJ Dec. 3, 1987, 1987 ECR 4789, paras 16–18. Similarly, the Court ruled under Article 87 in *Dutch Natural Gas Prices I*, ECJ Feb. 2, 1988, 1988 ECR 219, 276, para. 59, that subsidization of the price of natural gas to Dutch glasshouse crop producers by 5.5% affected trade between member states because of the importance of energy costs (25–30% of the selling price) and of the market share (65%) and the exports (9.1%) of the firms receiving the state aid.
344. *See also* Commission Guidelines on the effect on trade concept, point 38. Similarly: *Woodpulp*, ECJ March 31, 1993, 1993 ECR I-1307, para. 142; *Asahi/St. Gobain*, D.Comm. Dec. 16, 1994, 1994 OJ L 354/87, para. 23.

Potential Effect on Trade.

The jurisdictional reach of Articles 81 and 82 extends to mere *potential*, not only actual effects on trade between member states. Potential effects are those that may occur in the foreseeable future with a sufficient degree of probability, excluding however abstract, hypothetical and speculative effects.[345] In the *Miller International* case,[346] the Court of Justice stated that:

> 'the Treaty does not require proof that such agreements have in fact appreciably affected such trade, which would moreover be difficult in the majority of cases to establish for legal purposes, but merely requires that it be established that such agreements are *capable* of having that effect.'[347]

On the other hand, in *Hugin Liptons* the Court of Justice ruled that since the sale of spare parts for cash registers in the United Kingdom was an entirely local matter the alleged abusive refusal of supply did not implicate interstate trade.[348]

2. Substantial Part of the Common Market

Part of a Member State can Suffice.

The relevant geographic market affected by the restraint must be at least 'a substantial part of the Common Market' and must have such dimension as to possibly affect trade between member states under Article 81 or 82 or Article 2 of Regulation 139/2004 on merger control. A 'substantial part of the Common Market' has been a single member state[349] or even a 'not negligible' part of a member state,[350] such as ports or airports, since the amount of trade passing there and via other ports or airports within the Common Market clearly affects trade between

345. Commission Guidelines on the effect on trade concept, points 41–43.
346. (Emphasis added.) *Miller International*, ECJ Feb. 1, 1978, 1978 ECR 131, 151, para. 15. *See also Michelin*, ECJ Nov. 9, 1983, 1983 ECR 3461, paras 103–104; *British Leyland*, ECJ Nov. 11, 1986, 1986 ECR 3263, para. 20. Under the EEA Agreement: *Jaeger/Opel Norge*, EFTA Court of Justice April 1, 1998, 1998 EFTACR 38, para. 71.
347. *See also John Deere*, ECJ May 28, 1998, 1998 ECR I-3175, para. 91.
348. *Hugin/Liptons*, ECJ May 31, 1979, 1979 ECR 1869, paras 17–26.
349. Under Article 81: *Welded Steel Mesh*, CFI April 6, 1995, 1995 ECR II-987, paras 80–92. Under Article 82: *Sugar*, ECJ Dec. 16, 1975, 1975 ECR 1663, 1976–1977, paras 370–375 (Belgium/Luxembourg); *British Leyland*, ECJ Nov. 11, 1986, 1986 ECR 3263, 3299–3300, paras 4–9 (UK); *British Telecommunications*, ECJ March 20, 1985, 1985 ECR 873, 886, paras 21–22(UK); *BRT/SABAM II* ECJ March 27, 1974, 1974 ECR 313, 316, para. 5 (Belgium); *Deutsche Bahn*, D.Comm. Oct. 21, 1997, 1997 ECR II-1689, para. 58. Under the merger regulation: *MSG Media Service*, D.Comm. Nov. 9, 1994, 1994 OJ L 364/1; *Blokker/Toys 'R' Us*, D.Comm. June 27, 1997, 1998 OJ L 316/1, points 39–42. However, in cases of a dominant position on a market which presents all the characteristics of a 'distinct' market the Commission may refer the case to the national authority according to Article 9.
350. *BASF Coatings*, CFI May 19, 1999, 1999 ECR II-1581, para. 133.

member states.[351] However, part of a member state will not always be a substantial part of the Common Market. For example, if competitive conditions throughout a national market are constant so that the national market must be regarded as the relevant market for the purposes of establishing a dominant position, a strong position on only a regional market will not suffice to bring the holder's conduct within Article 82.[352] On the other hand, regional markets may be added to a larger market if they are sufficiently linked, in particular if the firms operate according to national concepts.[353]

3. 'Appreciable' Effect on Trade

The Court of Justice's Concept of Appreciability.

The Court of Justice has clarified that Article 81 (1) is not applicable where the impact of the agreement on intra-Community trade or on competition is not 'appreciable.'[354] Agreements which are not capable of significantly affecting trade between member states are not caught by Article 81 (1) but may be subject to national competition law. The Court of Justice has not given a definition of an 'appreciable' restriction of trade, and has avoided attempting to quantify 'appreciable. In the cases in which the Court has addressed the issue, important factors have been the stringency of the restriction, the type and quantity of the goods or services affected, the market position of the parties and generally the economic and legal setting, particularly the cumulative effects of similar agreements.[355] Appreciable effects on interstate trade were found to result even from agreements that increased trade[356] as well as agreements between important producers in a single member state in which imports had only a minor share of the market.[357]

---

351. *Aeroports de Paris*, CFI Dec. 12, 2000, 2000 ECR II-3929, paras 137–138 (*aff'd* ECJ Oct. 24, 2002, C-82/01P). *See also Silvano Raso (Porto di Genova II)*, ECJ Feb. 12, 1998, 1998 ECR I-593, para. 26; *Airport of Frankfurt*, D.Comm. Jan. 14, 1998, 1998 OJ L 72/30; *Portuguese Airports*, D.Comm. Feb. 10, 1999, 1999 OJ L 69/31, point 21.
352. *Alsatel/Novasam*, ECJ Oct. 5, 1988, 1988 ECR 5987, 6009–6010, paras 15 and 18–19. In this case, the telephone equipment company Alsatel held a dominant position in Alsace, but the relevant market was judged to be the whole of France.
353. *Tesko/Tuco*, D.Comm. Nov. 20, 1996, 1997 OJ L 110/53, point 23.
354. *Maschinenbau Ulm*, ECJ June 30, 1966, 1966 ECR 235, 249–250; *Völk/Verwaecke*, ECJ July 9, 1969, 1969 ECR 295, 302; *Béguelin*, ECJ Nov. 25, 1971, 1971 ECR 949, paras 10–18); *Net Book Agreement*, CFI July 9, 1992, 1992 ECR II-1995, para. 55; *Parker Pen*, CFI July 14, 1994, 1994 ECR II-549, para. 39; *CMA CGM FETTSCA*, CFI March 19, 2003, T-213/00, para. 207.
355. *See Haecht I*, ECJ Dec. 12, 1967, 1967 ECR 407, 415, 416; *Béguelin*, ECJ Nov. 25, 1971, 1971 ECR 949, paras 10–18; *Delimitis/Henniger Bräu*, CFI Feb. 28, 1991, 1991 ECR I-935, para. 91; *Whitbread*, D.Comm. Feb. 24, 1999, 1999 OJ L 88/26, points 107–138 (*aff'd* CFI March 21, 2002, 2002 ECR II-2033).
356. *See* under Article 31 *Swedish Alcohol Monopoly*, ECJ Oct. 23, 1997, 1997 ECR I-5909, para. 32.
357. *CSV*, D.Comm. July 20, 1978, 1978 OJ L 242/15, 30.

Qualitative v. Quantitative Criteria of Appreciability of Agreements and Concerted Practices.

(i) Notices on Agreements of Minor Importance.
The Court of Justice bases its assessment of 'appreciability' on *qualitative* criteria by reference to the parties' market position and the overall economic and legal setting. The Commission has taken a more *quantitative* approach in the interest of providing legal certainty about the circumstances when it considers the consequences of challenged conduct to be too minor so that the competition rules should not apply and the matter left to national enforcement rules. In its 1970 Notice on agreements of minor importance ('*De Minimis* Notice')[358] the Commission set quantitive criteria (minimum market share of 5% and minimum turnover of ECU 15 million) for both the restriction of competition and the effect on trade between member states. The subsequent Notices increased the quantitative requirements.[359] The most recent 2001 Notice[360] sets a minimum market share threshold of 10% in the case of horizontal and 15% in the case of vertical agreements without any reference to the parties' turnover,[361] thereby stating that the Notice does not apply with regard to the effect on trade between member states, but rather solely on the issue of whether the restriction is 'appreciable' and thereby justifies the application of the EU competition rules at all.[362]

(ii) Guidelines on the Effect on Trade Concept.
With respect to the effect on trade the Commission issued specific Guidelines on the Effect on Trade Concept[363] in which it sets quantitative criteria for assessing the effect of agreements on trade, thereby referring to rulings of the Court of Justice which suggest that the appreciability can be appraised in particular by reference to the position and importance of the relevant undertakings on the market for the products concerned.[364] In these Guidelines the Commission holds the view that, in principle, agreements are not capable of appreciably affecting trade between member states when the following cumulative conditions are met:

---

358. 1970 OJ C 64/1.
359. 1977 Notice, 1977 OJ C 313/3 (5% market share and ECU 50 million in sales), 1986 Notice, 1986 OJ C 231/2 (5% market share and ECU 200 million in sales) and 1994 Notice, 1994 OJ C 368/20 (5% market share and ECU 300 million in sales). Specific *de minimis*-thresholds have been established for the brewery sector: Commission's Notice 1992 OJ C 121/2
360. 2001 OJ C 368/13; similarly with respect to Article 53 of the EEA Agreement: Notice of the EFTA Surveillance Authority of March 20, 2003, 2003 OJ C 67/20.
361. A turnover limit still applies to agreements between small and medium-sized undertakings: 2003 OJ L 124.
362. 2001 OJ C 368/13, point 3.
363. Commission Guidelines on the Effect on Trade Concept.
364. *Javico*, ECJ April 28, 1998, 1998 ECR I-1983, para. 17; *BPB Industries*, ECJ April 1, 1993, 1993 ECR II-389, para. 138.

– The aggregate market share of the parties on the relevant market within the Community affected by the agreement does not exceed 5%,[365] and
– In the case of horizontal agreements, the aggregate annual Community turnover of the undertakings concerned[366] in the products covered by the agreement does not exceed EUR 40 million;[367] in the case of vertical agreements the relevant turnover is that of the supplier in the products, in the case of buying power that of the buyer and in licence agreements that of the licensor and the licensee(s).[368]

With respect to agreements between small and medium-sized undertakings the Commission repeats its previous statement that such agreements are 'rarely capable of appreciably affecting trade between member states'.[369] Small and medium-sized undertakings are currently defined in the Commission Recommendation on small and medium-sized undertakings[370] as undertakings which have fewer than 250 employees and have either an annual turnover not exceeding EUR 40 million or an annual balance-sheet total not exceeding EUR 27 million.[371]

Commission Guidelines as a Rule of Thumb.
The Guidelines establish a rebuttable positive presumption that an agreement is capable of affecting trade between member states when the parties' turnover exceeds EUR 40 million or, even when the turnover is below EUR 40 million, the parties' market share exceeds 5%.[372] The Guidelines establish a rebuttable negative presumption that effects on trade are not appreciable when both the market share and turnover limits are not exceeded irrespective of the nature of the restrictions contained in the agreement, including hard-core restrictions.[373] This seems to conflict with the Commission's *De Minimis* Notice, which states that a hard-core restriction of competition is appreciable irrespective of the parties' market shares.

365. The 5% limit may be exceeded by not more than 10% during two successive calendar years: Guidelines on the effect on trade concept, point 52.
366. 'Undertakings concerned' include connected undertakings as defined in point 12.2. of the Commission 2001 Notice on agreements of minor importance.
367. The turnover limit may be exceeded up to 10% during two successive calender years.
368. Guidelines on the Effect on Trade Concept, point 52. With respect to the cumulative effect of parallel networks of similar agreements, *see* Guidelines, points 49 and 56.
369. 2001 *De Minimis* Notice, point 3.
370. 2003 OJ L 124/36.
371. Example: *Luxembourg Breweries*, D.Comm. Dec. 5, 2001, 2002 OJ L 253/21, point 82.
372. Guidelines on the Effect on Trade Concept, point 53. This must be seen in the context of the parallel application of national and Community competition law in order to foster coherent parallel application of both laws by the competent national authority (and not by the Commission) according Article 3 (2) of Regulation 1/2003.
373. Guidelines, point 50. This corresponds to the Court of Justice's ruling in *Völk/Verwaecke*, ECJ July 1969, 1969 ECR 295, where the Court held that an agreement between companies with small market shares was not caught by Article 85 *[now 81]* (1) although it provided for an absolute territorial protection by way of export bans.

Moreover, the Guidelines on the Effect on Trade Concept are contradictory by stating that some types of agreements are 'by their very nature capable of affecting trade between member states' in particular because they concern imports or exports or cover several member states.[374] The Guidelines on the Effect on Trade Concept must be understood as allowing the Commission and the national competition authorities to concentrate on cases presenting a major interest, thereby leaving minor infringements for civil actions before the national courts.[375]

Appreciability of Abuses of a Dominant Position.
The appreciability of abuses of a dominant position depends on the nature of the abusive conduct[376] and the position of the undertakings on the market for the products in question.[377] Abusive conduct – whether exploitative or exclusionary – is prohibited by Article 82 if it is 'liable to exercise a sufficiently significant real or potential influence on intra-Community trade'.[378]

Appreciability of Agreements and Abusive Practices Involving Imports from, and Exports to, Third Countries.
Such agreements and abusive practices affecting imports into the Community from third countries must have appreciable, i.e., immediate, foreseeable and substantial, effects within the Community.[379] These effects are assessed according to the general rules, which require, in particular, the existence of an 'appreciable' difference between the prices of the products charged in the Community and those charged outside the Community.[380]

The Court of Justice's Position on the Commission's *De Minimis* Notice.
The Court of Justice accepts the Commission's *de minimis* thresholds for quantifying the appreciability of a restriction of competition, in particular the foreclosure effect of a vertical restraint.[381] However, the Court continues its qualitative approach towards the actual or potential effect on trade between member states calling for a detailed market analysis without reference to the Commission Notice

374. Guidelines, points 48, 59 and 62–65.
375. *See De Minimis* Notice, 2001 OJ C 368/13, point 4.
376. Guidelines, points 58–59.
377. Guidelines, point 44.
378. *BPB Industries*, CFI April 1, 1993, 1993 ECR II-389, para. 139.
379. *Gencor/Lonrho*, CFI March 25, 1999, 1999 ECR II-753, para. 90.
380. Guidelines, points 100–105. *See* Section E.3 *below*.
381. *See Langnese-Iglo*, CFI June 8, 1995, 1995 ECR II-1533, para. 98 (where the Court states that agreements are not automatically caught by Article 81 (1) if the parties' market shares exceed the *de minimis* thresholds. In its judgment of March 21, 2002, T-1431/99, the Court of First Instance upheld the Commission exemption decision *Whitbread* (Feb. 24, 1999, 1999 OJ L 88/26) without expressly dealing with the appreciability of the exclusive purchasing obligations in the beer leases in question, which was discussed by the Commission on the basis of the *De Minimis* Notice.

or to specific sales or market share thresholds, provided it is established that sales of at least one of the parties to an anticompetitive agreement represent a 'not inconsiderable proportion of the market'.[382] In any event, as an administrative document a notice does not have the force of law and can bind neither the Court of Justice nor national courts;[383] but it does bind the Commission in its administrative practice, thereby creating legitimate expectations.[384] Thus, the Commission is estopped by it from imposing fines in such cases, but it may not limit the field of application of Article 81.[385]

4. Case Law on Effect on Trade between Member States or EEA Countries

(a) Practices by One or More Firms in Several Member States or EEA Countries

Under Article 81 or Article 53 of the EEA Agreement.
The actual or potential effects of an anticompetitive agreement between firms in several member states or EEA countries will ordinarily not be limited to the market of a single state, but will extend to trade between different national markets. Showing an effect on trade between the member states has not posed a problem in any of the cases brought by the Commission against cartels among firms located in different member states. There is no doubt that arrangements to share markets or to set prices or allocate quotas between competitors from different member states affect trade between member states and/or EEA countries.[386]

Under Article 82 or Article 54 of the EEA Agreement.
An abuse of a dominant position under Article 82 need not be targeted against trade between member states so long as the abuse affects the territory of more than

382. *Miller International*, ECJ Feb. 1, 1978, 1978 ECR 131, paras 8–10; *Bagnasco*, ECJ Jan. 21, 1999, 1999 ECR I-135, paras 34 and 53. However, when the Commission has failed to make adequate findings on the issue of interstate trade, the Court of Justice has overruled its decisions: *Belgian Wallpaper*, ECJ Nov. 26, 1975, 1975 ECR 1491, paras 22–34; *Hugin/Liptons*, ECJ May 31, 1979, 1979 ECR 1869, paras 15–26; *Parker Pen*, CFI April 14, 1994, 1994 ECR II-549, paras 45–46.
383. *De Minimis* Notice, point 6; Guidelines on the effect on trade doctrine, point 3.
384. *Hercules*, CFI, Dec. 12, 1991, 1991 ECR II-1715, para. 53.
385. Guidelines, point 50. *See* Advocate General De Lamotte in *Cadillion/Höss*, ECJ May 6, 1971, 1971 ECR 351, 361; Advocate General De Lamotte in *Béguelin*, ECJ Nov. 25, 1971, 1971 ECR 949, 968; Advocate General Warner in *Miller International*, ECJ Feb. 1, 1978, 1978 ECR 131, 157–158.
386. Guidelines, points 64–69. *See Welded Steel Mesh*, CFI April 6, 1995, 1995 ECR II-987, paras 103–104. Recent examples: *Graphite Electrodes*, D.Comm. July 18, 2001, 2002 OJ L 100/1, points 111–112; *Vitamins*, D.Comm. Dec. 5, 2001, 2003 OJ L 6/1, points 596–605; *Citric Acid*, D.Comm. Dec. 5, 2001, 2002 OJ L 239/18, points 168–172.

one member state, e.g. by foreclosing competitors from other member states.[387] It suffices if an abuse committed in several member states causes the flow of trade to develop along potentially different lines than in the absence of the abuse.[388]

Under the Merger Control Regulation.
The merger control regulation applies to mergers having a Community dimension, i.e. a minimum turnover within the Community, without express reference to whether the merger is likely to affect trade between member states. However, 'national' mergers, i.e. mergers between firms each of which earns more than two-thirds of its aggregate Community-wide turnover within one and the same member state, are excluded and subject to national merger regulations.[389] Moreover, the Commission may refer mergers to the national competition authorities insofar as they affect competition on a market within a member state that presents all the characteristics of a distinct market.[390] The merger control regulation applies to firms established in third countries, provided they have immediate and substantial effects within the Community.[391] Mergers which create or strengthen a dominant position within the territory covered by the EEA Agreement are subject to Article 57 and must be assessed by the EFTA Surveillance Authority or the Commission in close cooperation[392] according to the amount of the combined turnover achieved in the EFTA countries and within the Community.[393]

(b) Practices by Firms in a Single Member State

Direct Nexus to Trade – Horizontal Agreements.
Restraints of competition caused by firms located in a single member state may nevertheless affect trade between member states. A direct effect on trade between member states will result from an agreement, decision or concerted practice that

387. *United Brands*, ECJ Feb. 14, 1978, 1978 ECR 207, 294, paras 197–202; *Hilti*, CFI Dec. 12, 1991, 1991 ECR II-1439, paras 123–125; *aff'd* ECJ March 2, 1994, 1994 ECR I-667; *Tetra Pak I*, D.Comm. July 26, 1988, 1988 OJ L 272/27, 40; *aff'd* CFI July 10, 1990, 1990 ECR II-309.
388. *Hilti*, CFI Dec. 12, 1991, 1991 ECR II-1439, paras 123–125.
389. Article 1 (2) of Regulation 139/2004.
390. Article 9 (2) of Regulation 139/2004.
391. *Gencor/Lonrho*, CFI March 25, 1999, 1999 ECR II-753, paras 79, 85 and 90. *See General Electric/Honeywell*, D.Comm. July 3, 2001, M.2220 (appeal still pending).
392. Protocol 24 to the EEA Agreement. Examples: *Orkla/Volvo*, D.Comm. Sept. 20, 1995, 1996 OJ L 66/17, points 7–9; *Multimedia/Telenor-Nextel/Telia*, D.Comm. May 27, 1999, JV.1.
393. There are no cases decided by the EFTA Surveillance Authority, and it is unlikely that a merger will fulfill the thresholds in the EFTA countries (Norway, Iceland and Liechtenstein). In *Gencor/Lonrho* the Commission applied both the EC merger regulation and Article 57 of the EFTA Agreements: D.Comm. April 24, 1996, 1994 OJ L 11/42, points 14–18 (*aff'd* CFI March 25, 1999, 1999 ECR II-753).

restricts exports to another member state[394] or prevents or makes more difficult imports from other member states.[395] This will be the case, for instance, with a joint selling (and exporting) agency representing the majority of national suppliers[396] or with a price-fixing agreement between several manufacturers in a single member state, because the operation of such cartels invariably requires measures to protect the national market against free imports.[397] A *direct* nexus to interstate trade is also evident where in relation to a product[398] that is traded between member states several manufacturers in a single state agree on production or sales quotas,[399] production specialization,[400] or increases in production capacity.[401]

Direct Nexus – Vertical Agreements.

The Court has held consistently that agreements concluded between a supplier and a reseller within one and the same member state and intended to deprive the reseller of its commercial freedom to choose its customers by requiring the reseller to sell only to customers established in the contractual territory[402] or not to resell the products outside the contractual territory[403] constitute by their very nature a restriction of competition[404] and are capable of affecting trade between member states if 'it is possible to foresee with a sufficient degree of probability, on the basis of objective factors of law of fact, that they have an influence, direct

394. Export bans are, by their very nature, capable of affecting trade between member states: *BASF Coatings*, CFI May 19, 1999, 1999 ECR II-1581, para. 133; Guidelines on the effect on trade concept, points 59, 62, 78–82.
395. *VCH*, ECJ Oct. 17, 1972, 1972 ECR 977, paras 26–31; *Langnese-Iglo*, CFI June 8, 1995, 1995 ECR II-1533, para. 120.
396. *Gottrup-Klim*, ECJ Dec. 15, 1994, 1994 ECR I-5641, point 4 of the operative part.
397. *Belasco*, ECJ July 11, 1989, 1989 ECR 2117, paras 32–38; *CSV*, D.Comm. July 20, 1978, 1978 OJ L 242/15, 29–30; *Meldoc*, D.Comm. Nov. 26, 1986, 1986 OJ L 348/50, 63.
398. *VISA International*, D.Comm. July 24, 2002, 2002 OJ L 318/17, point 72 (services being cross-border related); *German Banks*, D.Comm. Dec. 11, 2001, 2003 OJ L 15/1; *Austrian Banks*, D.Comm. June 11, 2002, IP/02/844. *See also Greenwich/SACEM*, ECJ Oct. 25, 1979, 1979 ECR 3275, 3288–3289; *GVL*, ECJ March 2, 1983, 1983 ECR 483, paras 34–39; *Anseau*, ECJ Nov. 8, 1983, 1983 ECR 3369, para. 35; *Flemish Travel Agents*, ECJ Oct. 1, 1987, 1987 ECR 3801, para. 18; *Funeral Services*, ECJ May 4, 1988, 1988 ECR 2479, paras 24–25; *Herlitz*, CFI July 14, 1994, 1994 ECR II-531, paras 29–34.
399. *Welded Steel Mesh*, CFI April 6, 1995, 1995 ECR II-987, paras 80–92.
400. *BP Chemicals/ICI*, D.Comm. July 19, 1984, 1984 OJ L 212/1, 7–8; *ENI/Montedison*, D.Comm. Dec. 4, 1986, 1987 OJ L 5/13, 18.
401. *Cimbel*, D.Comm. Dec. 22, 1972, 1972 OJ L 303/24, 34–35; Guidelines on the effect on trade concept, point 77.
402. *Hasselblad*, ECJ Feb. 21, 1984, 1984 ECR I-883, para. 46; *BMW/ALD*, ECJ Oct. 24, 1995, 1995 ECR I-3459, paras 19 and 21; *Javico/Yves St. Laurent*, ECJ April 28, 1998, 1998 ECR I-1983, para. 13.
403. *Tipp-ex*, ECJ Feb. 8, 1990, 1990 ECR I-261, para. 22; *Javico/Yves St. Laurent*, ECJ April 28, 1998, 1998 ECR I-1983, para. 14.
404. *Miller International*, ECJ Feb. 1, 1978, 1978 ECR 131, para. 7; *JCB Service*, CFI Jan. 13, 2004, T-67/01, paras 148–155; Guidelines, points 70–72.

or indirect, actual or potential, on the pattern of trade between Member States in such a way as to cause concern that they might hinder the attainment of a single market between Member States'.[405] The effect must not be insignificant, which must be appraised in particular by reference to the position and the importance of the parties on the relevant market.[406] Agreements between market players having a weak market position may may have insignificant effects even if they impose absolute territorial protection.[407] Agreements between larger market players may have a significant effect on trade even if the export ban is not systematically enforced and has rather 'a visual and psychological effect'.[408]

Indirect Nexus to Trade.
Even when no direct nexus is shown, trade between the member states may still be affected, except in cases which cover only part of a member state.[409] However, in these cases a distinction should be drawn between horizontal and vertical agreements.

Indirect Nexus – Horizontal Agreements.
A horizontal agreement 'extending over the whole of the territory of a member state by its very nature has the effect of reinforcing the compartmentalization of markets on a national basis, thereby holding up the economic interpenetration which the Treaty is designed to bring about and protecting domestic production.'[410] This is the case when a restrictive national agreement covers an appreciable proportion of the imports from other member states. In the *FEDETAB* case, a national tobacco cartel whose members accounted for half the imports of cigarettes (these

405. *Javico/Yves St. Laurent*, ECJ April 28, 1998, 1998 ECR I-1983, para. 16; Guidelines, points 86–88.
406. *Völk/Verwaecke*, ECJ July 9, 1969, 1969 ECR 295, para. 5; *Lancôme*, ECJ July 10, 1980, 1980 ECR I-2511, para. 24; *Parker Pen*, CFI July 14, 1994, 1994 ECR II-549, para. 39; *Javico/Yves St. Laurent*, ECJ April 28, 1998, 1998 ECR I-1983, para. 16.
407. *Musique Diffusion*, ECJ June 7, 1983, 1983 ECR 1825, para. 85; *Javico/Yves St. Laurent*, ECJ April 28, 1998, 1998 ECR I-1983, para. 17.
408. *See Volkswagen*, CFI July 6, 2000, 2000 ECR II-2707, para. 231; *Glaxo*, D.Comm. May 8, 2001, 2001 OJ L 302/1, points 145–146; *Daimler Chrysler*, D.Comm. Oct. 10, 2001, 2002 OJ L 257/1, points 191–198; *Nintendo*, D.Comm. Oct. 30, 2002, IP/02/1584. *See also Parker Pen*, CFI July 14, 1994, 1994 ECR II-549, para. 55; *BASF Coatings*, CFI May 19, 1999, 1999 ECR II-1581, para. 156.
409. Guidelines, points 89–95 and 97–99.
410. *VCH*, ECJ Oct. 17, 1972, 1972 ECR 977, para. 29; *Remia/Nutricia*, ECJ July 11, 1985, 1985 ECR 2545, para. 22; *Dutch Construction Work*, CFI Feb. 21, 1995, 1995 ECR II-289, paras 227–236; *CNSD*, ECJ June 18, 1998, 1998 ECR I-3851, para. 48. *See also Anseau*, ECJ Nov. 8, 1983, 1983 ECR 3389, paras 26–27; *Dutch Bricks*, D.Comm. May 3, 1994, 1994 OJ L 131/15 (national capacity coordination); *COAPI*, D.Comm. Jan. 30, 1995, 1995 OJ L 122/37, para. 41. In relation to services: *Fire Insurance*, ECJ Jan. 27, 1987, 1987 ECR 405, paras 44–50; *Funeral Services*, ECJ May 4, 1988, 1988 ECR 2479, paras 24–25; *Belgian Banks*, D.Comm. Dec. 11, 1986, 1987 OJ L 7/27, 32.

imports representing 5% of the domestic market) and 12–14% of imports of cigars (10% of the domestic market) was considered to have an appreciable effect on trade.[411] The Court of Justice, however, requires a concrete demonstration of the effect the anticompetitive conduct has on trade between member states. In the *Belgian Wallpaper* case the Court of Justice reversed the Commission's decision because it failed to explain how an agreement with respect to the 10% of Belgian imports of wallpaper sold by the defendants, which represented 5% of the Belgian market, was likely to affect trade between the member states.[412] If a national agreement prevents imports or makes them more difficult, trade between member states is affected. This has been found to apply, for instance, in cases where imported goods were subjected to a system of checks involving the use of conformity labels which could be obtained only by manufacturers and sole importers, with the effect of making parallel imports more difficult,[413] and where suppliers operated a collective aggregated rebate system only for national producers, thereby placing producers from other member states at a competitive disadvantage and restraining imports.[414] In *CSV*, which concerned an agreement between the Dutch nitrogenous fertilizer producers on joint marketing within the Netherlands and third countries (but not other member states), complemented by an agreement on production and exchange of information, the Commission decided the arrangement would inevitably have repercussions on sales to other member states since it affected the whole production and sales policy and would discourage foreign manufacturers from competing in the Dutch market.[415] Restrictive agreements between banks located in a single member state fixing the rate of interest paid on customer accounts are likely to affect trade between member states,[416] whereas agreements between such banks standardizing conditions which apply to bank accounts rarely used by foreign customers may not affect trade between member states, and therefore not infringe Article 81 (1).[417]

---

411. *FEDETAB*, ECJ Oct. 29, 1980, 1980 ECR 3125, paras 169–173. *See also SSI*, ECJ Dec. 10, 1985, 1985 ECR 3831, paras 46–51; *Dutch Cranes*, CFI Oct. 22, 1997, 1997 ECR II-1739, para. 181; *FENEX*, D.Comm. June 5, 1996, 1996 OJ L 181/28, para. 76; *FEG*, D.Comm. Oct. 26, 1999, 2000 OJ L 39/1, *aff'd* CFI Dec. 16, 2003, T-5/00, paras 63–64 and 319–328.

412. *Belgian Wallpaper*, ECJ Nov. 26, 1975, 1975 ECR 1491, paras 22–34.

413. *Anseau*, ECJ Nov. 8, 1983, 1983 ECR 3369, paras 22–25.

414. *NSO*, ECJ Dec. 10, 1985, 1985 ECR 3801, paras 50–56; *German Ceramic Tiles Discount Agreement*, D.Comm. Dec. 29, 1970, 1971 OJ L 10/15, 20.

415. *CSV*, D.Comm. July 20, 1978, 1978 OJ L 242/15, 29–30. With this decision the Commission abandoned its earlier *'Cobelaz doctrine'* which denied in such case an effect on trade between member states: *Cobelaz/Febelaz*, D.Comm. Nov. 6, 1968, 1968 OJ L 276/13, 17–18.

416. *German Banks*, D.Comm. Dec. 11, 2001, IP/01/1796; *Austrian Banks*, D.Comm. June 11, 2002, 2004 OJ L 56/1, points 438–442.

417. *Bagnasco*, ECJ Jan. 21, 1999, 1999 ECR I-135, paras 51–53 (standard bank conditions relating to the provision of general guarantees to secure current-account credit facilities).

Indirect Nexus – Vertical Agreements.
Vertical agreements concluded among firms located in the same member state that contain no express import or export prohibition may affect trade between the member states. This is true, for example, of exclusive or selective distribution agreements which have repercussions on the sale of imported products[418] or which prevent dealers from trading or expanding their business activities to other member states.[419] License agreements between firms in a single member state solely with respect to the use of technology in that member state but which restrict production or distribution are also likely to affect trade between the member states.[420] In all cases the economic and legal context in which the agreement operates must be considered,[421] including the existence of similar agreements by the same or other suppliers and the cumulative effect of such a network of agreements within one member state which may collectively have an appreciable effect on interstate trade.[422] The applicability of Article 81 (1) therefore depends largely on the degree of the 'foreclosure effect', i.e., on the scope remaining for manufacturers in other member states to find distributors for their products on the market.[423] Indirect effects on trade between member states also occur when a manufacturer limits the validity of its warranty to purchasers in a particular member state where the product was supplied through the supplier's authorized dealers, thereby creating disincentives for customers in other member states to source products from other channels because they would not be able to invoke the warranty.[424]

Indirect Nexus – Abuse of a Dominant Position.
If an abuse of a dominant position appears to be limited to a single member state, the competitive structure of the market and consequently the pattern of trade between member states may nevertheless be affected, for example by applying predatory practices,[425] discriminating between national and foreign customers,[426] by discriminating among customers according to whether they purchased ex-

---

418. *Salonia*, ECJ June 16, 1981, 1981 ECR 1563, paras 11–20.
419. *AEG-Telefunken*, ECJ Oct. 25, 1983, 1983 ECR 3151, paras 54–66; *Pronuptia*, ECJ Jan. 28, 1986, 1986 ECR 353, para. 26.
420. *Windsurfing*, ECJ Feb. 25, 1986, 1986 ECR 611, paras 95–97.
421. *See* Vertical Guidelines, 2000 OJ C 291/1, point 7.
422. *Haecht I*, ECJ Dec. 12, 1967, 1967 ECR 407, *Concordia*, ECJ Feb. 1, 1977, 1977 ECR 65, paras 25–33; *Hesbignonne*, ECJ April 19, 1988, 1988 ECR 1919, paras 17–19; *Delimitis/Henninger*, ECJ Feb. 28, 1991, 1991 ECR I-935, para. 19; *Vichy II*, CFI Feb. 27, 1992, 1992 ECR II-415, paras 80–81; *Parker Pen*, CFI July 14, 1994, 1994 ECR II-549, paras 39–40; *Langnese-Iglo*, CFI June 8, 1995, 1995 ECR II-1533, paras 119–120.
423. *John Deere*, CFI Oct. 27, 1994, 1994 ECR II-957, para. 101; Guidelines, point 71.
424. *Swatch/ETA*, ECJ Dec. 10, 1985, 1985 ECR 393, paras 12–13.
425. Guidelines, points 93–96. *See CNSD*, CFI March 30, 2001, 2001 ECR II-1807, para. 82.
426. *GVL*, ECJ March 2, 1983, 1983 ECR 483, paras 46–56; *Höfner/Macrotron*, ECJ April 23, 1991, 1991 ECR I-1979, para. 33.

clusively from the dominant firm or also from foreign suppliers,[427] by applying discriminatory transport tariffs[428] or discriminatory landing charges according to whether the airlines are domestic or from other member states,[429] by making it necessary or desirable for competitors or customers to obtain supplies from other member states,[430] by including imports from other member states in the dominant firm's distribution outlets,[431] by making market access more difficult for suppliers in other member states[432] or by forcing a competitor from a market.[433] The Court of Justice has stated that 'when the holder of a dominant position obstructs access to the market by competitors it makes no difference whether such conduct is confined to a single Member State as long as it is capable of affecting patterns of trade and competition on the common market'.[434] The market concerned may be only part of a member state if this part is relatively self-contained.[435] However, an abuse whose effects are not felt beyond the frontiers of a single member state does not have the requisite effect on interstate trade.[436] For instance, trade between member states is not likely to be affected by the application of discriminatory landing fees if the traffic is either entirely domestic or from third countries.[437]

(c) Practices Governing Exports to Non-EU Countries

Introduction.
A restraint of competition relating to exports to countries outside the Community ('non-EC countries') is 'not in itself likely to restrict or distort competition

427. *Michelin*, ECJ Nov. 9, 1983, 1983 ECR 3461, paras 100–105; *British Plaster Board*, CFI April 1, 1993, 1993 ECR II-389, paras 134–137; *German Post*, D.Comm. March 20, 2001, 2001 OJ L 125/27, point 42.
428. *Deutsche Bahn*, CFI Oct. 21, 1997, 1997 ECR II-1689, paras 78–86.
429. *Portuguese Airports*, D.Comm. Feb. 10, 1999, 1999 OJ L 69/31, point 20.
430. *Michelin*, ECJ Nov. 9, 1983, 1983 ECR 3461, 3522–3523, paras 100–105; *British Leyland*, ECJ Nov. 11, 1986, 1986 ECR 3263, para. 20; *Aeroports de Paris*, CFI Oct. 24, 2002, 2002 ECR I-9297, para. 91.
431. Conflict of interests affecting competition between imported and national products: *Telecommunication Directive Terminal Equipment*, ECJ March 19, 1991, 1991 ECR I-935, paras 48–52; *Greek Television*, ECJ June 23, 1991, 1991 ECR I-2925, paras 22–23; *RTT/GB-Inno-BM*, ECJ Dec. 13, 1991, 1991 ECR I-5941; *Decoster*, ECJ Oct. 27, 1993, 1993 ECR I-5335, paras 18, 22.
432. *GEMA I*, D.Comm. June 2, 1971, 1971 OJ L 134/15, 26; *Sabena*, D.Comm. Nov. 8, 1988, 1988 OJ L 317/47, 52; *British Plaster Board*, CFI April 1, 1993, 1993 ECR II-389, paras 134–137.
433. *Boosey & Hawks*, D.Comm. July 29, 1987, 1987 OJ L 286/36, 41.
434. *Michelin*, ECJ Nov. 9, 1983, 1983 ECR 3461, para. 103.
435. *Sugar*, ECJ Dec. 16, 1975, 1975 ECR 1663, paras 441–448 (affirmed); *Alsatel/Novasam*, ECJ Oct. 5, 1988, 1988 ECR 5987, para. 11 (denied).
436. *Hugin/Liptons*, ECJ May 31, 1979, 1979 ECR 1869, paras 15–26; *Alsatel/Novasam*, ECJ Oct. 5, 1988, 1988 ECR 5987, paras 15–19.
437. *Portuguese Airports*, D.Comm. Feb. 10, 1999, 1999 OJ L 69/31, point 20, fourth subparagraph.

within the common market.'[438] Such restraints of competition are subject to the Community competition rules only if they have appreciable repercussions within the Community.[439] The repercussions must be appreciable enough to affect not only one particular part of the territory of the Community, but specifically trade between member states. However, restrictions of competition relating to exports to EEA countries are likely to affect trade between the EC and EEA countries and are prohibited under Article 53 (1) of the EEA Agreement.

Exports to Non-Member Countries – Horizontal Agreements.
The mere coordination of exports to third countries between suppliers within the Community or with non-Community firms are unlikely to have an appreciable repercussion on trade between member states, and therefore are beyond the scope of Article 81 (1), unless they have repercussions on trade between member states. For instance, an exchange of information aiming at defending interests of European industry on export markets outside the EU is covered by Article 81 (1) if the restriction of competition is likely to affect trade within the Community.[440] When several manufacturers from member countries with excess production agreed to divert the excess to non-EC countries, the inference was drawn that by reducing supplies in the Community they restrained the intensity of competition and altered the pattern of trade within the Community. Such agreements channeling production surplus to third countries may serve as an essential part of a scheme that also extends to the sales activities of the parties within the Community, thereby restricting competition between themselves with regard to a substantial part of their businesses and affecting trade between member states such that Article 81 (1) is infringed,[441] provided there is sufficient evidence.[442] Agreements between competitors inside and outside the Community that expressly coordinate exports

---

438. *Bulk Oil v. Sun*, ECJ Feb. 18, 1986, 1986 ECR 559, 589, para. 44.

439. Guidelines, points 100–109. Horizontal: *TACA II*, D.Comm. Nov. 14, 2002, 2003 OJ L 26/53, point 74 (price fixing for the provision of scheduled maritime transport services between ports in Northern Europe and ports in the US and Canada); *Citric Acid*, D.Comm. Dec. 5, 2001, 2002 OJ L 239/18, points 173–176. Vertical: *Junghans*, D.Comm. Dec. 21, 1976, 1977 OJ L 30/10, 14; *Javico*, ECJ April 28, 1998, 1998 ECR I-1983, para. 17.

440. *Rheinzink*, ECJ March 28, 1984, 1984 ECR 1679, paras 24–31; *Welded Steel Mesh*, CFI April 6, 1995, 1995 ECR II-987, paras 115–116; *Cement*, CFI March 15, 2000, 2000 ECR II-491, para. 3785.

441. Guidelines, point 105. *See Sugar*, ECJ Dec. 16, 1975, 1975 ECR 1663, paras 564, 580, 596–601 (effect on trade between member states affirmed); *CSV*, D.Comm. July 20, 1978, 1978 OJ L 242/15, 29–30. *See also Cewal*, CFI Oct. 8, 1996, 1996 ECR II-1201, paras 196–199; *Trans Atlantic Agreement*, D.Comm. Oct. 19, 1994, 1994 OJ L 376/1, para. 300; *French-West-African Shipowners Committee*, D.Comm. April 1, 1992, 1992 OJ L 134/1; *Far East Freight Conference*, D Comm. Dec. 21, 1994, 1994 OJ L 378/17, para. 137; *aff'd* CFI Feb. 28, 2002, 2002 ECR II-1101, para. 147.

442. This was denied in *DECA*, D.Comm. Oct. 22, 1964, 1964 OJ 2761, and in *Cement*, CFI March 15, 2000, 2000 ECR II-491, paras 3790 and 3849–3850.

to and imports from the Community are obvious market-sharing arrangements likely to affect trade between member states.[443] However, when a firm in the Community enters into cooperation with an actual or potential competitor in a non-EC or EEA country in order to develop that foreign market, such as through an exclusive dealership or joint venture, this alone will not establish an appreciable effect on trade between the member states or may at least justify an exemption under Article 81 (3).[444]

Exports to Non-Member Countries – Vertical Agreements.
In the case of vertical agreements governing exports to non-member countries, a more rigorous inquiry needs to be made. Even agreements prohibiting exports outside the Community do not have, by their very nature, an anticompetitive object within the Community[445] but may, according to their economic and legal context, have such an effect.[446] Prohibitions against exporting to or re-importing from non-EC countries contained in vertical or license agreements are therefore caught by Article 81 (1) only if they have appreciable anticompetitive effects within the Common Market. This may be the case if the structure of the Community market is oligopolistic, allowing only limited competition within the Community network and if substantial price differences exist between the non-EC country and the Community which cannot be explained by customs duties[447] and transport costs.[448] Insofar as they may have such appreciable effect on trade between member states, the block exemption regulations on exclusive distribution, exclusive purchasing and technology transfer agreements apply to the same extent as they would to agreements that apply to territories within the Common Market.[449] On the other hand, Article 81 of the Treaty and the corresponding Article 57 of the EEA Agreement apply directly to agreements that have an effect on trade with Norway, Iceland and Liechtenstein. The elimination of customs duties between the Community and EFTA countries in 1977 removed the argument

443. *EMI/CBS*, ECJ June 15, 1976, 1976 ECR 811, 871 and 913; *Siemens/Fanuc*, D.Comm. Dec. 18, 1985, 1985 OJ L 376/29; *Quantel International-Continuum/Quantel*, D.Comm. July 27, 1992, 1992 OJ L 235/9; *Graphite Electrodes*, D.Comm. July 18, 2001, 2002 OJ L 100/1, points 111–112.

444. *BT/MCI*, D.Comm. July 27, 1994, 1994 OJ L 223/36, para. 47; *Banque Nationale de Paris/ Dresdner Bank*, D.Comm. June 26, 1996, 1996 OJ L 188/37 (exemption decisions).

445. However, they are caught by the prohibition of Article 53 of the EEA Agreement if they concern (or include) export bans towards EEA countries.

446. *Almelo*, ECJ April 27, 1994, 1994 ECR I-1477, para. 37; *Javico/Yves St. Laurent*, ECJ April 28, 1998, 1998 ECR I-1983, paras 21–22.

447. The existence of a double taxation was the main reason for granting negative clearance in *Grosfillex/Fillistorf* D.Comm. March 11, 1964, 1964 OJ 9/15; *Rieckermann/AEG-Elektrotherm*, D.Comm. Nov. 6, 1968, 1968 OJ L 276/25, 27–28; *Kodak*, D.Comm. June 30, 1970, 1970 OJ L 147/24, 26; *Distillers I*, D.Comm. Dec. 20, 1977, 1978 OJ L 50/16, 24.

448. Guidelines on the Effect on Trade Concept, point 109.

449. *Javico/Yves St. Laurent*, ECJ April 28, 1998, 1998 ECR I-1983, paras 23–26.

that tariffs would prevent re-importation to the Community from EFTA countries, thereby increasing the likelihood of finding that export bans to EFTA countries have appreciable effects in the Community. The Commission included an explicit reservation to this effect in the *Junghans* decision[450] and required the deletion of a prohibition on exports to these third countries in the *SABA I* decision.[451]

Exports – Abuse of a Dominant Position.
If a dominant firm abuses its position in relation to a firm in the territory of a non-EC or EEA country, the abuse may still affect trade between member states if the competitive market structure within the Community is affected.[452] Equally, the refusal by a dominant firm to supply a customer in the Community who intends to export the goods to third countries may affect trade between member states if the competitiveness of this customer in the Community depends heavily on this non-EC export activity.[453]

(d) Practices Governing Imports into the Community

Restrictive Agreements Relating to both Trade within the Community and between the Community and Non-EU Countries.
Agreements relating to the trade between the Community and non-EU countries may have as their *object* the restriction of competition inside the Community likely to affect trade between member states, in particular where they bring about an isolation of the internal market.[454] Agreements between competitors inside and

450. *Junghans*, D.Comm. Dec. 21, 1976, 1977 OJ L 30/10, 14. This case is still relevant, *see* Guidelines, point 108.
451. *SABA I*, D.Comm. Dec. 5, 1975, 1976 OJ L 28/19, 22 and 26 (*aff'd* ECJ Oct. 25, 1977, 1977 ECR 1875, but the decision was not appealed on this ground).
452. *Greenwich/SACEM*, ECJ Oct. 25, 1979, 1979 ECR 3275, para. 12 ('Where an association exploiting composers' copyrights is to be regarded as an undertaking abusing a dominant position within the Common Market or in a substantial part of it, the fact that such abuse, in certain cases, relates only to the performance in non-member countries of contracts entered into in the territory of a Member State by parties within the jurisdiction of that State does not preclude the application of Article 82 of the Treaty').
453. *Commercial Solvents*, ECJ March 6, 1974, 1974 ECR 223, para. 33 ('When an undertaking in a dominant position within the Common Market abuses its position in such a way that a competitor in the Common Market is likely to be eliminated, it does not matter whether the conduct relates to the latter's exports or its trade within the Common Market, once it has been established that this elimination will have repercussions on the competitive structure within the Common Market'); *United Brands*, ECJ Feb. 14, 1978, 1978 ECR 207, 294, para. 201 ('Furthermore, if the occupier of a dominant position, established in the Common Market, aims at eliminating a competitor who is also established in the Common Market, it is immaterial whether this behavior relates to trade between Member States once it has been shown that such elimination will have repercussions on the patterns of competition in the Common Market').
454. E.g., *Siemens/Fanuc*, D.Comm. Dec. 18, 1985, 1985 OJ L 376/29. *See* Notice on the Effects on Trade, points 102–103.

outside the Community that expressly coordinate exports to and imports from the Community are obvious price[455] and market-sharing arrangements likely to affect trade between member states.[456] Worldwide price cartels involving the transfer of goods within and outside the Community fall, as a whole, within Article 81 (1).[457] Agreements relating to trade with non-EU countries may also have restrictive *effects* on imports, e.g., in the case of agreements between shipping companies operating between the Community ports and West-African ports because they affected the activities of undertakings that relied on the parties for transportation services either as a means of transporting goods purchased in third countries or as an important imput into services that the ports offered themselves.[458]

Third Country Imports – Horizontal Agreements.

In the case of *horizontal* agreements, any agreement between firms within or outside the EC and EEA to channel, control or otherwise restrict imports from third countries is also likely to restrict trade between the member states. In such cases the intensity of competition between the parties in the Community is lessened and thereby a nexus to interstate trade is established even though the imports do not themselves involve interstate trade. This applies to agreements halting imports altogether,[459] channeling imports through the hands of competing producers in the Community,[460] subjecting imports to quantitative restrictions[461] or operating joint selling or price-fixing arrangements for imports[462] or including them in general market coordination schemes between producers located both within and outside the Common Market.[463] The Commission has pointed out that generally measures

455. *See Far Eastern Freight Conference*, CFI Feb. 28, 2002, 2002 ECR II-1101, para. 146–148; *TACA I – Transatlantic Conference Agreement*, D.Comm. Sept. 16, 1998, 1999 OJ L 95/1, points 386–396 (the findings of the Commission on the effect on trade between member states was not appealed: CFI Sept. 30, 2003, T-191/98); *TACA II*, D.Comm. Nov. 14, 2002, 2003 OJ L 26/53, point 78.
456. E.g., *EMI/CBS*, ECJ June 15, 1976, 1976 ECR 811, 871, and 913; *Graphite Electrodes*, D.Comm. July 18, 2001, 2002 OJ L 100/1, points 111–112.
457. E.g., *Vitamins*, D.Comm. Nov. 21, 2001, 2003 OJ L 6/1, point 600; *Citric Acid*, D.Comm. Dec. 5, 2001, 2002 OJ L 239/18, points 170–172.
458. *CEWAL – Compagnie Maritime Belge de transport*, CFI Oct. 8, 1996, 1996 ECR II-1101, paras 194–203, *aff'd* in this respect: ECJ March 16, 2000, 2000 ECR I-1365.
459. *EMI/CBS*, ECJ June 15, 1976, 1976 ECR 811, paras 25–39; *Siemens/Fanuc*, D.Comm. Dec. 18, 1985, 1985 OJ L 376/29; *ICI/Fujitsu*, Sixteenth Report on Competition Policy, point 72.
460. *Aluminium Imports from Eastern Europe*, D.Comm. Dec. 19, 1984, 1985 OJ L 72/1, 46–47.
461. *French-Taiwanese Mushroom Packers*, D.Comm. Jan. 8, 1975, 1975 OJ L 29/26, 28; *Asia Motors France I*, CFI Sept. 18, 1992, 1992 ECR II-2285.
462. Joint selling: *ANSAC*, D.Comm. Dec. 19, 1990, 1991 OJ L 152/54; price fixing: *Wood Pulp I*, ECJ Sept. 27, 1988, 1988 ECR 5193; *Polypropylene*, CFI March 10, 1992, 1992 ECR II-1275; aligning prices: *Franco-Japanese Ballbearings Agreement*, D.Comm. Nov. 29, 1974, 1974 OJ L 343/19.
463. *IFTRA-Aluminium*, D.Comm. July 15, 1975, 1975 OJ L 228/3; *Carbonless Paper*, D.Comm. Dec. 20, 2001, IP/01/1892.

which directly restrain imports to the Community or which regulate quantities, prices, quality or other terms of trade and thereby indirectly prevent or restrict imports from third countries are subject to the rules of competition.[464] Restrictions of competition relating to imports from EEA countries into EC countries directly affect trade between EEA and EC countries and are prohibited under Article 53 (1) of the EEA Agreement. Restrictions of competition relating to imports from third countries to EEA or EC countries may affect trade between the EEA or EC countries and may be prohibited under Article 53 (1) of the EEA Agreement or Article 81 (1) of the EC Treaty irrespective of whether the agreements are concluded between firms located in third countries, between such firms and firms located in an EEA or EC country or between firms located inside the EEA or EC countries.[465]

Third Country Imports – Vertical Agreements.
An agreement by which a producer established outside the EC and EEA grants to a distributor within a member state the exclusive right to distribute its products solely in that country nevertheless affects trade between member states if the arrangement may prevent the distributor from exporting the products to other member states or may prevent parallel imports from other member states.[466] Particular consideration has to be given to the structure of competition within the Community[467] and the existence of similar agreements entered into by the same producer with exclusive distributors established in other member states.[468] An agreement by which a producer grants to a dealer outside the Community (who is not his actual or potential competitor) the exclusive distribution rights for the whole Community may affect trade between member states by precluding the grant of similar rights to another dealer in the Community who might have competed with the first dealer; in this case, however, the agreement qualifies for exemption[469] and in fact benefits from the block exemption for vertical agreements, Regulation 2790/1999.[470] Agreements between a licensor inside and a licensee outside the Community which prevent direct and indirect imports from the third country are normally justified, unless the licensor has substantial market

464. Commission Notice on Japanese Imports, 1972 OJ C 111/13.
465. Notice of the EFTA Surveillance Authority (Annex VII to Decision 3/94/COL of Jan. 12, 1994 according to Annex XIV of the EEA Agreement.
466. *Béguelin*, ECJ Nov. 25, 1971, 1971 ECR 949, 959, paras 10–12; *Tepea*, ECJ June 20, 1978, 1978 ECR 1391, paras 47–48; *but see Cane Sugar Supply Agreements*, D.Comm. Dec. 7, 1979, 1980 OJ L 39/64, 69–70 (no appreciable effects found).
467. This was the reason why the Commission opposed the obligation imposed on a dealer outside the Community not to resell the product (soda) within the Common Market: *Solvay/Sisecam*, D.Comm. Sept 25, 1999, 1999–5 CMLR 1444, point 21 (clearance of a joint venture after removal of the obligation).
468. *Béguelin*, ECJ Nov. 25, 1971, 1971 ECR 949, paras 13–18.
469. *Duro-Dyne/Europair*, D.Comm. Dec. 19, 1974, 1975 OJ L 29/11.
470. Article 1 (c) of Regulation 2790/1999.

power such that competing products are not readily available and the only available source for such products is imports from the non-EU licensee.[471]

Refusal to Deal or Other Abuses by a Dominant Firm in a Non-Member Country.

If a manufacturer or a dealer in the Community is cut off by his supplier located in a non-EC or EEA country but who nevertheless holds a *dominant position* in the Community, then competition within the Community has been harmed[472] unless the affected party has no regular business activities in other member states and operates only in a single member state.[473] The quantity of the affected party's exports to other member states is irrelevant if his entire supplies are affected by the abuse of a dominant position.[474] Similarly, there is an infringement of Article 82 where a dominant foreign supplier ties the sale of other products to that of the product for which it has a dominant position.[475]

5. Extraterritorial Application

'Effects Doctrine'.

The 'effects doctrine' was developed principally under the antitrust laws of the United States[476] and the Federal Republic of Germany[477] and has gradually been adopted in Community decisions.[478] The 'effects doctrine' holds that a state has

471. *See Raymond/Nagoya*, D.Comm. June 9, 1972, 1972 OJ L 143/39. With respect to the exhaustion of industrial propery rights, *see Silhouette*, ECJ June 16, 1998, 1998 ECR I-4799, para. 26.
472. *United Brands*, ECJ Feb. 14, 1978, 1978 ECR 207, paras 197–203; *Commercial Solvents*, ECJ March 6, 1974, 1974 ECR 223, paras 30–35; *Tetra Pak II*, D.Comm. July 24, 1991, 1992 OJ L 72/1; *aff'd* CFI Oct. 6, 1994, 1994 ECR II-755 and ECJ Nov. 14, 1996, 1996 ECR I-5951 (the Commission's competence with respect to the Swiss firm Tetra Pak was, in this case, not even contested).
473. *Hugin/Liptons*, ECJ May 31, 1979, 1979 ECR 1869, paras 15–26.
474. *Commercial Solvents*, ECJ March 6, 1974, 1974 ECR 223, para. 33.
475. *Hilti*, D.Comm. Dec. 22, 1987, 1988 OJ L 65/19, 38; *aff'd* CFI Dec. 12, 1991, 1991 ECR II-1439 and ECJ March 2, 1994, 1994 ECR I-667). *See also Belgian Post*, D.Comm. Dec. 5, 2001, 2002 OJ L 61/32.
476. *See* 15 U.S.C. § 7a *et seq.*, which requires a direct, substantial and reasonably foreseeable effect on import commerce or trade within the U.S. E.g., *United States v. Aluminium Company of America*, 148 F.2d 416, 444 (2d Cir. 1945).
477. *See* § 130 (2) of the German Law Against Restraints of Competition (GWB), which declares the law applicable to restrictions which have effects within Germany even if they are brought about outside Germany. E.g., *Ölfeldrohre*, German Federal Supreme Court (BGH) July 12, 1973, WuW/E BGH 1276; *Morris-Rothmans*, Berlin Appeals Court (Kammergericht) July 1, 1983, WuW/E OLG 3051.
478. Article 81: *Wood Pulp I*, ECJ Sept. 27, 1988, 1988 ECR 5193, paras 11–18; Article 82: *Commercial Solvents*, ECJ March 6, 1974, 1974 ECR 223, paras 44 and 48–49; merger control regulation: *Continental Can*, ECJ Feb. 21, 1973, 1973 ECR 215, 241–242, paras 14–16; *Gencor/Lonrho*, CFI March 25, 1999, 1999 ECR II-753, para. 90; Article 7 (non-discrimination): *Union Cycliste*, ECJ Dec. 12, 1974, 1974 ECR 1405, paras 26–29.

jurisdiction to prohibit restraints of competition committed by parties located outside its territory if the restraint causes anticompetitive effects within its territory. Although it is not stated in Community legislation, the Commission has derived the effects doctrine from the territoriality principle of customary international law that permits every nation to subject to its jurisdiction conduct which bears a sufficient relationship to its territory, i.e. when it is foreseeable that it has an immediate and substantial effect in the Community.[479] The infringement of a fundamental legal principle – here, the principle of free and undistorted competition in the territory of the Community – by implementing an anticompetitive agreement or engaging in abusive conduct in the Community is regarded as a sufficient basis for the assertion of jurisdiction.

Some Conduct within the Community.
Articles 81 and 82 have been applied to anticompetitive conduct that takes place within the Community even though the firms' headquarters are located outside the Community. A direct nexus to competition within the Community is evident if competitors inside and outside the Community agree on prices,[480] or agree to isolate the Community from imports from a non-member country, as in the *EMI/CBS* case.[481] Frequently the objectionable conduct has been by a subsidiary or agent located in the Community.[482] However, the competition rules apply only insofar as the anticompetitive conduct may affect trade between the member states; anticompetitive effects on trade between the Community and third countries do not count. Consequently, fines on non-EC firms are generally related to their sales within the Community.[483] The same principle applies to Articles 53 and 54 of the EEA Agreement. Mergers are subject to the EC merger control regulation and Article 57 of the EEA Agreement irrespective of whether the merger is carried out within the Community or in EEA countries; it suffices that the merger has an immediate and substantial effect within the Community or the EEA territory.[484]

---

479. *Gencor/Lonrho*, CFI March 25, 1999, 1999 ECR II-753, para. 90.

480. *ICI – Dyestuffs*, ECJ July 14, 1972, 1972 ECR 619, paras 125–141; *Franco-Japonese Ballbearings Agreement*, D.Comm. Nov. 29, 1974, 1974 OJ L 343/19, 25; *Polypropylene – Linz*, CFI March 10, 1992, 1992 ECR II-1275, para. 350; *Lysine cartel*, D.Comm. June 7, 2000, 2001 OJ L 152/14; *Graphite Electrodes*, D.Comm. July 18, 2001, 2002 OJ L 100/1; *Vitamins*, D.Comm. Dec. 5, 2001, 2003 OJ L 6/1.

481. *EMI/CBS*, ECJ June 15, 1976, 1976 ECR 811, paras 25–29. *See also Siemens/Fanuc*, D.Comm. Dec. 15, 1985, 1985 OJ L 376/29, 35 (in such a case of market sharing between firms inside and outside the Common Market, the potential of the non-EC firm to make sales in the Common Market must be evaluated).

482. *See Tetra Pak II*, D.Comm. July 24, 1991, 1992 OJ L 72/1, *aff'd* ECJ July 10, 1991, 1991 ECR II-309.

483. *Polypropylene – Linz*, CFI March 10, 1992, 1992 ECR II-1275, para. 350; *Nintendo*, D.Comm. Oct. 30, 2002, 2003 OJ L 255/33, points 381–383.

484. Article 82: *Hilti*, CFI March 2, 1994, 1994 ECR II-667 (*aff'd* ECJ Nov. 14, 1996, 1996 ECR I-5951 Merger control regulation: *Gencor/Lonrho*, CFI March 25, 1999, 1999 ECR II-753, paras 79 and 90.

Conduct outside the Community/Implementation inside the Community. In the *Wood Pulp* case[485] the Commission charged solely non-EC firms located in Finland, Sweden, Norway, Canada, Spain, Portugal and the United States with infringement of Article 81 for coordinating prices of wood pulp sold to purchasers in the Community. While the defendants either exported directly to purchasers within the Community or were doing business in the Community through branches, subsidiaries, agencies or other establishments, the anticompetitive coordination of prices was accomplished solely outside of the Community. On appeal to the Court of Justice, the defendants argued that international law precludes any claim by the Community to regulate conduct restricting competition adopted outside the territory of the Community merely by reason of the economic repercussions which that conduct produces within the Community. In other words, the defendants asked the Court to reject the 'effects doctrine'. The Court answered:

> 'Where wood pulp producers established in those [non-EC] countries sell directly to purchasers established in the Community and engage in price competition in order to win orders from those customers, that constitutes competition within the Common Market.
>
> It follows that where those producers concert on the prices to be charged to their customers in the Community and put that concertation into effect by selling at prices which are actually coordinated, they are taking part in concertation which has the object and effect of restricting competition within the Common Market within the meaning of Article 85 ….
>
> It should be observed that an inftingement of Article 85, such as the conclusion of an agreement which has the effect of restricting competition within the Common Market, consists of conduct made up of two elements, the formation of the agreement, decision or concerted practice and the implementation thereof. If the applicability of prohibitions laid down under competition law were made to depend on the place where the agreement, decision or concerted practice was formed, the result would obviously be to give undertakings an easy means of evading those prohibitions. The decisive factor is therefore the place where it is implemented.
>
> The producers in this case implemented their pricing agreement within the Common Market. It is immaterial in that respect whether or not they had recourse to subsidiaries, agents, sub-agents, or branches within the Community in order to make their contacts with purchasers within the Community.
>
> Accordingly the Community's jurisdiction to apply its competition rules to such conduct is covered by the territoriality principle as universally recognized in public international law'.[486]

485. *Wood Pulp I*, ECJ Sept. 27, 1988, 1988 ECR 5193.
486. *Ibid.*, paras 6, 12–18.

Application of Article 81 to Government-Authorized Export Cartels.
In the *Wood Pulp* case Court of Justice also ruled that the Commission had jurisdiction to impose fines under Article 81 on members of a United States export cartel whose concerted pricing practices were expressly exempted from United States antitrust rules under the Webb-Pomerene Act and therefore were legal in the United States. The Court noted that the United States antitrust exemption did not subject the members of the United States export cartel to conflicting requirements by the United States and EC authorities; the statutory exemption for export cartels from the application of United States antitrust laws 'does not require such cartels to be concluded'.[487] Accordingly, in the absence of compulsion to engage in the conduct prohibited under the Community's competition rules, these rules apply and can be enforced.[488]

Investigations of Non-EC Firms.
The Commission's power to carry out on-the-spot investigations on firms are for jurisdictional reasons limited to the territory of the Community. This includes the EC subsidiaries of firms based outside the Community. The same applies under the EEA provisions.[489] However, the Commission may, and occasionally does, request information from firms located outside the Community to the extent this is needed to investigate a possible infringement that is carried out in the Community. In this case the request does not refer to possible sanctions. If an enterprise located outside the Community has a subsidiary or affiliate in the Community, then the Commission's request for information will normally be directed at both enterprises through the subsidiary or affiliate located in the Community. The Commission may give prior notice of its request to the antitrust authorities of the foreign country whose interest is affected under a notification procedure that applies between OECD member countries[490] and under antitrust cooperation

487. *Ibid.*, para. 20. In the *Franco-Japanese Ballbearings Agreement* decision the Commission similarly held that measures resulting from agreements or concerted practices between Japanese firms that were merely authorized by the Japanese authorities under Japanese law (as opposed to measures that were imposed on Japanese firms by the Japanese authorities or measures taken in pursuance of trade agreements between the Community and Japan) could be subject to Article 81 because the firms would be free not to enter into the agreements or engage in the concerted practices. Article 81 is applicable, *a fortiori*, to measures resulting solely from agreements, concerted practices, or decisions by associations of firms, entered into or engaged in either unilaterally by Japanese firms or in concert with European firms: *Franco-Japanese Ballbearings Agreement*, D.Comm. Nov. 29, 1974, 1974 OJ L 343/19, 23.

488. *See also ANSAC*, D.Comm. Dec. 19, 1990, 1991 OJ L 152/54 (export organization of the U.S. soda ash producers).

489. Protocol 21 to the EEA Agreement, 1994 OJ L 1/1, 182. *See* Chapter X at p. 1062.

490. 1995 OECD Revised Council Recommendation concerning Cooperation Between Member Countries on Anticompetitive Practices Affecting International Trade, COM/TD/DAFFE/CLP(98)25, 97 and 98; Twenty-eighth Report on Competition Policy, point 347.

agreements with major trading partners including the United States,[491] Canada,[492] and Japan,[493] and with competition authorities of other OECD countries, in particular Australia, New Zealand, Korea and Switzerland.[494] The Commission reports regularly on the application of these agreements.[495]

F. Parallel Application of Competition Law on Community and on National Level

1. Application of Community Competition Rules on Community and National Level

The Principle of Parallel Application.
The EC competition rules have direct effects on the relationships among natural and legal persons creating rights and obligations which the Commission, the national authorties and the national courts must protect and enforce. Regulation 1/2003 is based on a system of parallel competences.[496] The Community competition rules may be applied:

- by the *Commission* using its powers conferred by Regulation 1/2003, which include investigation powers, interim measures, cease and desist orders and the imposition of fines; the Commission has equivalent powers and similar functions under Article 55 of the EEA Agreement and Article 1 of its Protocol 21;
- by a *single national competition authority* or by *several national competition authorities* designated by the member states[497] using their procedural powers conferred by their respective national laws to apply Community competition rules, which also include investigation powers, interim measures, cease and desist orders and the imposition of fines; and

491. Agreement between the European Communities and the United States regarding the application of competition laws, 1995 OJ L 95/45.
492. Agreement of June 10, 1999, similar to that concluded with the United States: 1999 OJ L 175/49.
493. COM(200)230 final.
494. Thirty-second Report on Competition Policy, point 64.
495. *See* Report of Sept. 17, 2002, COM(2002)505 final and Thirty-second Report on Competition Policy, points 655–665.
496. Notice on cooperation within the the network of competition authorities (European Competition Network – 'ECN'), point 5. The notice replaces the previous Commission Notice on cooperation between national authorities and the Commission, 1997 OJ C 313/3.
497. Article 5 of Regulation 1/2003 and the competition laws of the member states conferring the respective powers to their antitrust authorities.

– by the *national courts* applying the civil consequences of infringements of Articles 81 and 82 including nullity (governed by Article 81 (2)), restitution[498] and damages.[499]

The Principle of Parallel Application within the European Competition Network.
The European Competition Network ('ECN') comprises the Commission and the national competition authorities which must ensure both an efficient division of work and an effective and consistent application of the EC competition rules. The division of work takes place according to the principle of subsidiarity, as enshrined in Article 5 (2) of the EC Treaty:

> 'In areas which do not fall within its exclusive competence, the Community shall take action, in accordance with the principle of subsidiarity, only if and only in so far as the objective of the proposed action cannot be sufficiently achieved by the Member States and can therefore, by reason of the scale of effects of the proposed action, be better achieved by the Community'.

This means that although a case might be handled in parallel on the Community and national levels, it should be handled by that authority within the ECN which is best placed to take the most appropriate action for effective protection of competition,[500] except where the Commission assumes exclusive competence.

Cases of Exclusive Competence of the Commission.
Parallel application is excluded in those areas which fall within the exclusive competence of the Commission:

– The Commission's former exclusive competence to grant an individual exemption under Article 81 (3) is repealed by Regulation 1/2003, and is now shared with national competition authorities[501] and national courts.[502] The Commission's exclusive competence to apply Articles 65 and 66 of the ECSC Treaty lapsed as of July 22, 2002 so that the coal and steel sectors are now fully subject to Articles 81 and 82 and to the principle of parallel application by the Commission, the national authorities and courts. However, exemptions granted under the former Regulation 17 continue to have effect for the purposes of ap-

498. *Courage*, ECJ Sept. 20, 2001, 2001 ECR I-6297, para. 30.
499. *Ibid.*, paras 27–29. The modalities governing Community actions must be not less favorable than those governing similar domestic actions: *Palmisani*, ECJ July 10, 1997, 1997 ECR I-4025, para. 27. Overview on the application of Articles 81 and 82 by national courts: http://europa.eu.int/comm/competition/publications/art8586_en.pdf (1997).
500. Recital 18 to Regulation 1/2003; Notice on ECN, points 8–15.
501. Article 5 of Regulation 1/2003.
502. Article 6 of Regulation 1/2003.

plying Regulation 1/2003,[503] subject to the possibility to withdraw the benefit of such an exemption.[504]

- The Commission has exclusive competence to issue block exemptions under Article 81 (3).[505]
- The Commission may initiate proceedings for the adoption of decisions under Article 11 (6) of Regulation 1/2003, which relieves the national competition authorities[506] of their competence to apply Articles 81 and 82.[507] National authorities may apply national competition law only in a manner consistent with the outcome of a parallel application of Articles 81 and 82 because national law can be applied only together with Articles 81 and 82.[508] However, national courts are not automatically relieved of their competence to apply Articles 81 and 82 but must 'avoid giving decisions which would conflict with a decision contemplated by the Commission in proceedings it has initiated'.[509] The provision is therefore a powerful right to establish exclusive competence,[510] subject, however, to certain guarantees: the Commission must first consult the national competition authority which is already acting on a case[511] and the case must, at the request of the national authority, be included on the agenda of the Advisory Committee.[512] The regulation does not address whether the Commission can pursue its proceedings without taking action or defining its position within a certain time limit (thereby re-opening parallel actions by a national authority or court).[513]
- The Commission has sole jurisdiction to assess mergers (including ancillary clauses) that have a Community dimension, thereby precluding national authorities from applying national law.[514] This is without prejudice to the possibility

503. Article 34 (2) of Regulation 1/2003.
504. Article 29 of Regulation 1/2003.
505. Regulation 19/65 and Regulation 2821/71 delegate powers to exempt certain categories of vertical and horizontal agreements.
506. Including national courts that exercise the function of an administrative authority (Article 35 (2)–(4) of Regulation 1/2003).
507. Article 11 (6) of Regulation 1/2003. The Commission may in particular initiate proceedings when the outcome of a civil dispute before a national court depends on them: Notice on cooperation between Commission and national courts, point 12.
508. Article 3 of Regulation 1/2003; Notice on ECN, point 28(b). An exception is made allowing enforcement of stricter national competition law rules against unilateral conduct: Article 3 (2) of Regulation 1/2003.
509. Article 16 (1) of Regulation 1/2003.
510. In cases where a national authority is already acting on a case, the Commission must consult the national authority (Article 11 (6)) and, at the authority's request, the Advisory Committee (Article 14 (7) of Regulation 1/2003).
511. Notice on ECN, points 50–57.
512. Article 14 (7) of Regulation 1/2003.
513. *See*, however, Article 232 (2) of the EC Treaty, which fixes a two-month period.
514. Article 21 (1) and (2) of the merger control regulation.

of referring a transaction, at the request of a member state, to the competent authorities of this member state.[515]

Modalities of Cooperation for the Purposes of Case Allocation.
The Commission and the competition authorities retain full discretion in deciding whether or not to investigate a case. The authority that receives a complaint or starts an *ex-officio* proceeding remains in charge of the case, except where reallocation issues arise.[516] However, whenever the Commission initiates proceedings according to Article 11 (6) of Regulation 1/2003, in particular in cases involving more than three member states or concerning new competition issues,[517] this automatically relieves the national competition authorities of their competence to apply Articles 81 and 82,[518] and whenever the Commission adopts a decision under Article 81 or 82, national authorities and national courts are prevented from taking decisions which would run counter to the Commission decision in order to respect uniform application of Community competition law.[519] In order to detect multiple proceedings the members of the ECN have to be informed at an early stage. Article 11 of Regulation 1/2003 creates the mechanism of mutual notification before or without delay after commencing the first formal investigative measure. This cooperation also applies between the Commission and the EFTA surveillance authority with respect to the concurrent application of the EC competition rules and those of the EEA Agreement.[520] The information, including confidential information, may also be made available to other competition authorites.[521] Where it results from the information exchanged that a particular authority is better placed than another the case may be reallocated by mutual agreement, thereby avoiding parallel proceedings and conflicts, except in cases where the Commission and the national authorities decide to proceed to a joint investigation with the view to taking separate decisions.[522] The objective of such a reallocation is to achieve a quick and efficient process that should be resolved within two months and without delaying ongoing investigations.[523]

Stay or Closure of Proceedings.
Where the same infringement on the same relevant product and geographic market is subject to multiple proceedings, some authorities may suspend or close the

515. Article 9 of the merger control regulation.
516. Notice on ECN, points 6, 16–19. The allocation of cases is not subject to appeal: point 31.
517. Notice on ECN, points 14–15.
518. Article 11 (6) of Regulation 1/2003.
519. Article 16 (1) and (2) of Regulation 1/2003 without prejudice to the rights and obligations of the national courts under Article 234 of the EC Treaty.
520. Protocol 23 to the EEA Agreement.
521. Notice on ECN, points 26–36.
522. Article 22 of Regulation 1/2003; Notice on ECN, points 8–15.
523. Notice on ECN, points 7 and 18.

proceedings before them, including the possibility of rejecting a complaint. This also applies to the Commission, which may reject a complaint on the ground that a national competition authority is dealing with the case.[524] However, in cases of complaints of Community interest the Commission may initiate proceedings, which automatically relieves the national competition authorities of their competence to apply Article 81 or 82.[525] Complaints that lack Community interest may be rejected by the Commission.[526]

Avoiding Conflicting Decisions by Applying the Principle of *Non Bis in Idem.* The Commission has the ultimate responsibility for ensuring consistent application of the EC competition rules.[527] To this end, national competition authorities must inform the Commission by sending, no later than 30 days before adopting a final decision, a summary of the case, the envisaged decision or any other document indicating the proposed course of action.[528] The ultimate purpose is to avoid inconsistent or conflicting decisions. In the *PVC* case[529] the Court of Justice stated:

> '... the principle of *non bis in idem,* which is a fundamental principle of Community law enshrined in Article 4 (1) of Protocol No 7 of the ECHR,[530] precludes, in competition matters, an undertaking from being found guilty or proceedings from being brought against it a second time on the grounds of anti-competitive conduct in respect of which it has been penalized or declared not liable by a previous unappealable decision.
>
> The application of that principle therefore presupposes that a ruling has been given on the question whether an offence has in fact been committed or that the legality of the assessment has been reviewed. Thus, the principle of *non bis in idem* merely prohibits a fresh assessment in depth of the alleged commission of an offence which could result in the imposition of either a second penalty, in addition to the first, in the event that liability is established a second time, or a first penalty in the event that liability is not established by the first decision is established by the second. On the other hand, it does not in itself preclude the resumption of proceedings in respect to the same anti-competitive conduct where the first decision was annulled for procedural reasons without any ruling having been given on the substance of the facts alleged, since the annulment decision cannot in such circumstances

524. Article 13 of Regulation 1/2003.
525. Article 11 (6) of Regulation 1/2003.
526. Notice on ECN, point 25.
527. *See Foto Prost*, ECJ Oct. 22, 1987, 1987 ECR 4199, para. 15.
528. Article 11 (4) of Regulation 1/2003; Notice on ECN, points 43–49.
529. *LVM – PVC*, ECJ Oct. 15, 2002, 2002 ECR I-8375.
530. European Charter of Human Rights, Protocol No. 11 (ETS No. 140) of the Council of Europe (1998).

> be regarded as an 'acquittal' within the meaning given to that expression in penal matters. In such a case, the penalties imposed by the new decision are not added to those imposed by the annulled decision but replace them'.[531]

Consequences.
It follows that a Commission decision finding an infringement of Article 81 or 82,[532] imposing a fine,[533] concluding that the conditions of Article 81 (3) are fulfilled or declaring an undertaking 'not liable' for an alleged infringement (concluding that there is no infringement)[534] precludes a second decision by a national authority which would conflict with the first decision (principle of *res iudicata).*[535] However, this applies only where actions are taken or considered against the *same* infringement on the same product and geographic market.[536] For instance, there is no identity of infringement where the infringement is 'predominantly different'[537] with respect to the basic facts, duration and territorial scope, in particular:

- where the infringement has effects on trade within the Community, without counting the effects outside the Community,[538] or
- where the effects are limited to a national territory presents all the characteristics of a *distinct* market and within other markets of the Community.[539]

531. Paras 59–62. The first *PVC* decision of Dec. 21, 1988 (1989 OJ L 74/1) was declared non-existent by CFI Feb. 27, 1992, 1992 ECR II-315, annulled by ECJ June 15, 1994, 1994 ECR I-2555, and renewed by the Commission on July 29, 1994, 1994 OJ L 239/14, which was unsuccessfully appealed: CFI April 20, 1999, 1999 ECR II-931, and ECJ Oct. 15, 2002, 2002 ECR I-8375.
532. Article 7 of Regulation 1/2003.
533. Articles 23 and 24 of Regulation 1/2003.
534. Article 10 of Regulation 1/2003.
535. *PVC*, ECJ Oct. 15, 2002, 2002 ECR I-8375, paras 59–62. *See also* Article 16 of Regulation 1/2003.
536. It follows that a fine imposed on an undertaking by the Commission or a national competition authority (or court) precludes the imposition of a fine on individuals by another authority under its national law that provides for such a sanction, provided both fines would sanction the same anti-competitive conduct (double jeopardy), without prejudice to the possibility of exchanging information: Notice on ECN, point 28 (b).
537. *See* Article 3 (3) of Regulation 1/2003.
538. *Quinine – Boehringer*, ECJ Dec. 14, 1972, 1972 ECR 1281; *Pre-insulated Pipes – Ke Kelit*, CFI March 20, 2002, 2002 ECR II-1647, para. 189; *Lysine Cartel*, CFI July 9, 2003, T-220/00. However, it may be argued that in the case of a worldwide cartel that affects trade within *and* outside the Community and therefore falls '*as a whole*' under Article 81 the rule of taking account of the prior sanction (wherever imposed) should apply: *see Vitamins*, D.Comm. Nov. 21, 2001, 2003 OJ L 6/1, point 600; *Citric Acid*, D.Comm. Dec. 5, 2001, 2002 OJ L 239/18, points 170–172.
539. *See* the distinct market concept of Article 9 of the merger control regulation.

For instance, a merger which is notified to the Commission may be referred, according to Article 9 of the merger control regulation, to national competition authorities with respect to the part of the merger that affects competition within a market, which presents all the characteristics of a distinct market, so that the effects of a merger on the distinct market are assessed by the national competition authority and on the other markets by the Commission. The Court of First Instance affirmed the legality of such a partial referral even by recognizing that the referral may lead to inconsistent and conflicting ('irreconcilable') decisions, which must be accepted.[540] However, where both the Commission and the national authority arrive at the same conclusion that the operation is incompatible and subject to fines, then equity requires, in order to avoid 'double jeopardy', that the earlier sanctions should be taken into account in determining the level of the later sanctions to be imposed,[541] irrespective of which authority is the first to impose sanctions.[542]

The principle of *res iudicata* does not apply when the Commission does not adopt a decision which states the inapplicability of Article 81 or 82 but *settles* the case without decaring a conduct 'not liable'. Such an act does not bind the national courts, which are not precluded from applying national or Community competition law with respect to the same suspected infringement on the basis of fresh evidence.[543]

The Obligation of National Courts to Apply the Community Competition Rules.

National courts are free to assess a case involving the application of Community law under their own responsibility, which follows from the full and direct applicability of both Article 81 (1) and Article 81 (3). However, it is clear from the case-law of the Court that the member states' duty under Article 10 of the EC Treaty and Article 16 of Regulation 1/2003 to take all appropriate measures, whether general or particular, to ensure fulfillment of the obligations arising from Community law and to abstain from any measure which could jeopardize the

540. *Royal Philips Electronics – SEB/Moulinex*, CFI April 3, 2003, T-119/02, paras 367 and 380. The merger was cleared by the French authority with respect to the French 'distinct' market without commitments (despite the particularly high market share on this market), and cleared by the Commission with respect to other markets only under the condition of important commitments.
541. *Walt Wilhelm*, ECJ Feb. 13, 1969, 1969 ECR 1,15; *Pre-insulated Pipes – Ke Kelit*, CFI March 20, 2002, 2002 ECR II-1547, para. 189. Article 90 of the ECSC Treaty expressly provided for the EC authorities to take account of prior national enforcement actions when determining EC penalties.
542. *Cast Iron and Steel Rolls*, D.Comm. Oct. 17, 1983, 1983 OJ L 317/1, 15; *Welded Steel Mesh*, D.Comm. Aug. 2, 1989, 1989 OJ L 260/1, 41–42; *aff'd Sotralentz*, CFI April 6, 1995, 1995 ECR II-1127, paras 26–29.
543. *Sateba II*, ECJ July 17, 1998, 1998 EC R I-4913, paras 38–39.

attainment of the objectives of the Treaty, is binding on all the authorities of member states including the national courts for matters within their jurisdiction.[544] No conflict arises where a national court applies the civil remedies of an infringement of Article 81 or 82 with respect to *past* illegal conduct, in particular damage claims, even if the Commission has imposed,[545] or granted immunity from, fines with respect to the same conduct.[546] Civil damages claims must be distinguished from administratice sanctions because they pursue different objectives. However, a national court is prevented from applying the civil consequences with respect to *future* conduct, in particular declaring an agreement valid and enforceable, which the Commission has prohibited or considers prohibiting, or from adopting mandatory orders with respect to an agreement which is block exempted or which the Commission has declared compatible with the EC competition rules. Such a decision would constitute an irreconcilable actual conflict with a Commission decision, i.e., compel the defendant to disobey a Commission decision with respect to the same conduct.[547] In such a case the national court is obliged under Article 10 of the EC Treaty to adopt the appropriate measures in order to resolve such a conflict, including by suspending enforcement or ordering restitution.[548] When national courts apply Article 81 or 82 to agreements or conduct which are already the subject of a Commission decision, they are obliged, under Article 16 (1) of Regulation 1/2003, not to take decisions running counter to the Commission decision. Accordingly, national courts have to respect legally binding acts of the Commission, such as findings of the inapplicability of Article 81 (1) or Article 82,[549] decisions making commitments binding on the parties,[550] and

544. *Masterfoods*, ECJ Dec. 14, 2000, 200 ECR I-11369, para. 49, referring to *IP v. Borsana*, Dec. 17, 1998, 1998 ECR I-8597, para. 26; *Consorzio Industrie Fiammiferi*, ECJ Sept. 9, 2003, C-198/01, paras 45–47. *See* recital 17 to Regulation 2790/1999 on vertical restraints.

545. *Bank Austria Creditanstalt*, CFI Nov. 7, 2003, T-198/03 R, para. 52 (affirming the decision of the Hearing Officer to publish the non-confidential version of the Commission decision of June 11, 2002, 2004 OJ L 56/1, imposing a fine on the Austrian Banks, despite the risk that the published decision might lead to damage claims). *See*, however, the civil actions for treple damage under § 4 of the Clayton Act, which may be brought by natural persons injured or by any attorney general of a State, acting as *parens patriae* on behalf of natural persons (§ 4C of the Clayton Act), thereby underlining the closer link between civil and administrative proceedings.

546. *See* Commission Notice on Immunity from Fines and Reduction of Fines in Cartel Cases, 2002 OJ C 45/3, point 31: 'The fact that immunity or reduction in respect of fines is granted cannot protect an undertaking from the civil law consequences of its participation in an infringement of Article 81'. *See also* the liability of member states for damage caused to individuals by breaches of Community law under both national law (*Gerhard Köbler*, ECJ Sept. 30, 2003, C-224/01, para. 100) and Community law (Article 228 (2)).

547. *Consorzio Industrie Fiammiferi*, ECJ Sept. 9, 2003, C-198/01, para. 48.

548. *Masterfood/HB Ice Cream*, Dec. 14, 2000, 2000 ECR I-11369, para. 60.

549. *PVC II – LVM*, ECJ Oct. 15, 2002, 2002 ECR I-8375, para. 59.

550. Article 9 of Regulation 1/2003. Since commitments are made legally binding on the parties the national courts may be asked to enforce such commitments under the procedural conditions

decisions finding the inapplicability of Article 81 (1) or of the applicability of Article 81 (3),[551] and to take duly into account any other act by the Commission, such as its rejection of a complaint,[552] issuance of an informal guidance letter[553] or entering into a settlement following a statement of objections and amendment of the challenged agreements.[554]

Cooperation between National Courts and the Commission.
In order to avoid conflicts, Article 10 of the EC Treaty is interpreted by the Court of Justice as imposing on the national courts and the Commission the obligation of constant and loyal cooperation and of reciprocal assistance.[555] Following the Court of Justice's reasoning in its *Delimitis/Henninger Bräu* judgment,[556] the Commission issued a Notice on the Cooperation Between the National Courts and the Commission in 1993,[557] which is replaced by Articles 15 and 16 of Regulation 1/2003 and the Commission Notice on the cooperation between the Commission and the national courts. The cooperation includes the following rights and obligations:

- The national competition authorities may request a national court to transmit any documents necessary for the assessment of a case under Article 81 or 82.[558] This presupposes that the national authorities are informed by the national court about any case which it is hearing that involves the application of Article 81 or 82.[559] The Commission may not directly address a national court but must request the national authority to do so.
- The national courts may ask the Commission to transmit to them information in its possession[560] or its opinion on questions relating to the application of Article

---

set out by national law: Commission Notice on the cooperation between the Commission and the national courts, points 7 and 36.

551. Article 10 of Regulation 1/2003.
552. *Koelman*, CFI Jan. 9, 1996, 1996 ECR II-1, para. 41.
553. *Guerlain*, ECJ July 10, 1980, 1980 ECR 2327, para. 13.
554. *See Philip Morris*, D.Comm. Fourteenth Report on Competition Policy, points 98–100; *aff'd* ECJ Nov. 17, 1987, 1987 ECR 4487; *IRI/Nielsen*, Twenty-sixth Report on Competition Policy, point 64.
555. *Zwartveld*, ECJ July 13, 1990, 1990 ECR I-3365, para. 8; *Delimitis/Henninger Bräu*, ECJ Feb. 28, 1991, 1991 ECR I-935, para. 53; *Postbank*, CFI Sept. 18, 1996, 1996 ECR II-921, paras 66–67. *See* Notice on the cooperation between the Commission and the national courts, point 15.
556. *Delimitis/Henninger Bräu***,** ECJ Feb. 28, 1991, 1991 ECR I-935, paras 49–53.
557. 1993 OJ C 39/5.
558. Article 15 (3), second subparagraph of Regulation 1/2003. *See* the broader powers under national law (Article 15 (4) of Regulation 1/2003, which indirectly refers to provisions, such as §90 of the German Law Against Restraints of Trade).
559. The national court may be obliged to do so under national law, e.g., under German law (§ 90 of the German Law Against Restraints of Trade).
560. Including confidential information, *see* Notice on ECN, points 26–28. *See also* Notice on the cooperation between the Commission and the national courts, points 21–26.

81 or 82,[561] without prejudice to the possibility to apply for a preliminary ruling of the Court of Justice according to Article 234 of the EC Treaty.[562]
- To that effect, the national court may ask the Commission whether it has initiated proceedings and on the likelihood of a decision.[563]
- The national competition authorites and the Commission may submit written and oral observations to the national courts on issues relating to the application of Article 81 or 82 ('*amicus curiae*').[564]
- The national court may stay its proceedings in order to avoid giving a decision which would conflict with a decision which is contemplated by the Commission.[565] The national courts may come to a contrary conclusion after having duly consulted the Commission.[566] However, the national court cannot avoid the binding effects of a Commission decision[567] but may refer a question on the validity of the Commission's interpretation of Community law to the Court of Justice and while awaiting such a preliminary ruling suspend its proceedings.[568]
- The national competition authorities are obliged to forward a copy of the full written judgment of a national court deciding on the application of Article 81 or 82.[569]

These rules put a heavy responsibility on the national courts, in particular in cases which *prima facie* do not affect trade between member states and where the need for initiating the complicated information and coordination process is not evident. Where a national court has already adopted a decision that conflicts with Community law the court may even be obliged under Article 10 of the EC Treaty

561. Article 15 (1) of Regulation 1/2003.
562. *See* Article 16 (1) of Regulation 1/2003; Notice on the cooperation between the Commission and the national courts, points 27–30. By analogy to the consequences of a non-respect of the obligation of national courts under Article 234 (3) of the EC Treaty: Where a national court considers that a decision of the Court of Justice on the interpretation of the EC Treaty is necessary to enable it to give judgment and where there is no judicial remedy against this judgment under national law, the national court must bring the matter before the Court of Justice. The non-respect of this obligation may be imputed on the member state and constitute a proceeding under Article 226 of the EC Treaty. There is no specific case law yet, however, *see* with respect to the repayment of tax charges levied in breach of Community rules: *Commission/Italian Republic*, ECJ Dec. 9, 2003, C-129/00, paras 25–41.
563. Notice on the cooperation between the Commission and the national courts, point 12.
564. Article 15 (3) of Regulation 1/2003; Notice on the cooperation between the Commission and the national courts, points 17–20 and 31–35.
565. Article 16 (1) of Regulation 1/2003.
566. Notice on the cooperation between the Commission and the national courts, point 12.
567. *See Foto-Frost*, ECJ Oct. 22, 1987, 1987 ECR 4199, para. 16.
568. Notice on the cooperation between the Commission and the national courts, point 13; *Masterfoods/HB Ice Cream*, ECJ Dec. 14, 2000, 2000 ECR I-11369, paras 52–60.
569. Article 15 (2) of Regulation 1/2003; Notice on the cooperation between the Commission and the national courts, point 37.

to suspend enforcement,[570] to adopt interim measures in order to safeguard the interests of the parties[571] or to order restitution for its improper decision.[572] The Commission is not prevented from applying Article 81 and 82 even though it shares competence with national courts and even where an agreement or practice has already been the subject of a decision by a national court and the decision contemplated by the Commission conflicts with the national court's decision.[573]

2. Parallel Application of Community and National Competition Law

Principle of Parallel Application but in Case of Conflict Community Law Governs.

Both EC competition rules and national competition law contribute to achieving the functioning of the internal market by ensuring a system of a free and undistorted competition. As a rule, both Community and national law may apply concurrently. Articles 81 and 82 judge anticompetitive conduct by its effects on interstate trade. National law may judge the same anticompetitive conduct from the standpoint of its domestic effects according to different criteria.[574] Consequently, a restrictive practice may become the object of parallel legal proceedings, one pursuant to Community law before the Commission and the other pursuant to national law before national competition authorities and courts subject to the coordination rules of Articles 15 and 16 of Regulation 1/2003. Where national authorities and courts apply national law they must apply it under their domestic procedural rules, which likewise apply when acting under the Community competition rules.[575] In order to be compatible with Community law the national rules must provide for:[576]

- effective, proportionate and dissuasive sanctions,
- the possibility of claiming damages, and

570. Notice on the cooperation between the Commission and the national courts, point 13.
571. *Masterfoods/HB Ice Cream*, ECJ Dec. 14, 2000, 2000 ECR I-11369, para. 5.
572. *See Woodpulp – Assi Domän*, ECJ Sept. 14, 1999, 1999 ECR I-5363, paras 57–63.
573. *Van den Bergh Foods*, CFI Oct. 23, 2003, T-65/98, para. 199 (in this case the Commission 'overruled' the decision adopted by the Irish High Court in *Masterfoods Ltd v. HB Ice Cream*, May 28, 1992, paras 221–229: the High Court granted HB a permanent injunction restraining Mars – the complainant in the Commission proceedings – from inducing retailers to stock Mars ice cream in freezer cabinets belonging to HB, thereby relying on the exclusivity clause which constituted, according to the Commission, an infringement of Article 81 (1). The Irish Supreme Court decided to stay proceedings and to refer to the Court of Justice. This reference was the subject of the judgment *Masterfoods/HB Ice Cream*, ECJ Dec. 14, 2000, 2000 ECR I-11369, paras. 47–48.
574. Applying different criteria is inherent to a system of parallel application of law: *Cabeleurope*, CFI Sept. 30, 2003, T-346/02, para. 197.
575. *Van Schijndel*, ECJ Dec. 14, 1995, 1995 ECR I-4705, paras 13–22; Notice on the cooperation between the Commission and the national courts, point 3.
576. Notice on the cooperation between the Commission and the national courts, point 10.

– procedural rules which do not make enforcement of Community law excessively difficult or pratically impossible (principle of effectiveness) and are not less favorable than the rules applicable for the enforcement of equivalent national law (principle of equivalence).[577]

Primacy of Community Law.
In the *Walt Wilhelm* case[578] the Court of Justice has acknowledged the principle of concurrent jurisdiction in recognition of the fact that the competition laws of the Community and of member states protect different interests:

> '... conflicts between the rules of the Community and national rules in the matter of the law on cartels must be resolved by applying the principle that Community law takes precedence.
>
> It follows from the foregoing that should it prove that a decision of a national authority regarding an agreement would be incompatible with a decision adopted by the Commission at the culmination of the procedure initiated by it, the national authority is required to take proper account of the effects of the latter decision.
>
> Where, during national proceedings, it appears possible that the decision to be taken by the Commission at the culmination of a procedure still in progress concerning the same agreement may conflict with the effects of the decision of the national authorities, it is for the latter to take the appropriate measures'.[579]

This statement accords with the principle of Article 10 of the EC Treaty, which obliges the member states to abstain from any measure which could jeopardize the attainment of the objectives of the Treaty.[580] Accordingly, the Commission stated in its block exemption regulations:

> 'In accordance with the principle of the primacy of Community law, no measure taken pursuant to national laws on competition should prejudice

577. *Courage and Crehan*, ECJ Sept. 20, 2001, 2001 ECR I-6297, paras 26–29. *See also International Power/NALOO*, ECJ Oct. 2, 2003, C-172/01 P, para. 88.
578. *Walt Wilhelm*, ECJ Feb. 13, 1969, 1969 ECR 1, 13.
579. *Walt Wilhelm*, ECJ Feb. 13, 1969, 1969 ECR I, 14–15; *see also Pre-insulated Pipes – Ke Kelit*, CFI March 20, 2002, 2002 ECR II-1647, para. 189.
580. *AEB (Spanish Banks)*, ECJ July 16, 1992, 1992 ECR I-4785, para. 44: 'Parallel application of national competition law may be permitted only to the extent to which it does not undermine the uniform application, throughout the Common Market, of the Community competition rules and the full effect of the measures based on those rules'. *See also Consorzio Industrie Fiammiferi*, ECJ Sept. 9, 2003, C-198/01, para. 45 (referring in particular to *Van Eycke*, ECJ Sept. 21, 1988, 1988 ECR 4769, para. 16, and *Reiff*, ECJ Nov. 17, 1993, 1993 ECR I-5801, para. 14).

the uniform application throughout the common market of the Community competition rules or the full effect of any measures adopted in implementation of those rules'.[581]

Regulation 1/2003 aims at avoiding conflicts:

- by obliging the national authorities and national courts to apply, in close cooperation with the Commission, both national and Community competition rules in cases which may affect trade between member states in order to stimulate a coherent application and to avoid any conflict from the very beginning of a procedure. However, the application of national competition law may not lead to a different outcome, in particular to the prohibition of agreements or conduct which do not infringe Article 81 (1) or fulfill the conditions of Article 81 (3);[582]
- by empowering the Commission to initiate proceedings.[583] However, unlike national authorities, national courts are not relieved of their competence to apply both national and Community competition law with respect to the consequences of an infringement under national civil law, such as damage issues. However, a national court is obliged under Article 10 of the EC Treaty to adopt the appropriate measures in order to avoid or to resolve a conflict.[584]

Duty to Disapply National Law in Case of Conflict with Community Law. In the *Consorzio Industrie Fiammiferi* case the Court of Justice ruled that the primacy of Community law requires any provision of national law which contravenes a Community rule to be disapplied by both national authorities and national courts, regardless of whether it was adopted before or after that rule.[585] It follows that national law that conflicts with Community law cannot legitimize conduct contrary to Article 81 or 82. For instance, it is immaterial whether a loyalty-inducing rebate system applied by a firm holding a dominant position that is contrary to Article 82 is compatible with national law or approved by a national competition authority.[586] When a national authority disapplies an anti-competitive national

581. Recital 19 to Regulation 2658/2000 on Specialization Agreements, recital 23 to Regulation 2659/2000 on R&D Agreements and recital 17 to Regulation 2790/1999 on Vertical Restraints.
582. Article 3 (2) and Article 15 of Regulation 1/2003; Notice on cooperation between Commission and national courts, point 6.
583. Article 11 (6) of Regulation 1/2003.
584. *See* end of this section *below*.
585. *Consorzio Industrie Fiammiferi*, ECJ Sept. 9, 2003, C-198/01, paras 48–49.
586. *Michelin II*, CFI Sept. 30, 2003, T-203/01, para. 112. *A fortiori*, it is immaterial whether conduct that is contrary to Community law reflects a *traditional* practice common to all member states or third countries: *Atlantic Container Line AB – TACA II*, CFI Sept. 30, 2003, T-191/98, paras 569–570, 1124 and 1406.

law, no criminal or administrative penalties may be imposed on the parties for past conduct that was required by national legislation.[587] Since the relevant national legislation set the framework for the undertaking's *past* conduct, it constitutes a justification which shields the undertakings from all the consequences of an infringement of Articles 81 and 82.[588] With respect to conduct *subsequent* to a decision finding an infringement of Article 81 or 82 and disapplying such an anticompetitive national law the undertakings can no longer rely on that national law and are subject to sanctions, once the decision has become definitive in their regard.[589]

No Conflict in Cases of Different Conduct.

National competition law applies without conflicting with Community law where the conduct pursued under national law is different from the conduct pursued under Community law. For instance, there is no identity of conduct where undertakings are engaged in:

- practices which are clearly severable, e.g. predatory practices in the overall context of a price cartel;[590]
- the same conduct but subsequent or prior to the conduct which was the subject of a Commission decision (constituting a distinct infringement);[591]
- similar conduct on different geographic markets within the Community,[592] in particular within a different national market which presents all the characteristics of a *distinct* market and within other markets of the Community;[593] or
- the same or a similar conduct within the Community and within a third country.[594]

587. *Consorzio Industrie Fiammiferi*, ECJ Sept. 9, 2003, C-198/01, para. 53.
588. *Ibid.*, para. 54. However, a national law which merely encourages, or makes it easier for undertakings to engage in anticompetitive conduct does not preclude penalties with respect to such an autonomous conduct (para. 80).
589. *Ibid.*, para. 55. However, the national legal framework may be a mitigating factor: para. 57.
590. E.g., *Aalborg Portland A/S*, ECJ Jan. 7, 2004, T-204/00 P, para. 339: the anticompetitive supply contracts between cement producers which sought to prevent imports and to protect home markets (sanctioned by the Commission) had a different object from the cooperation agreements between one of the parties and three Italian cement producers (pursued by the Italian competition authority).
591. Except where a prior conduct was the subject of the Commission's proceedings but was not held to constitute an infringement (*ne bis in idem).*
592. E.g. *Michelin I*, ECJ Nov. 9, 1983, 1983 ECR 3461 (fidelity rebates on the Dutch market); *Michelin II*, CFI Sept. 30, 2003, T-203/01 (fidelity rebates on the French market).
593. *See* the distinct market concept of Article 9 of the merger control regulation. A partial referral leads to a parallel application of Community and national law with the inherent risk of a different evaluation: *Cabeleurope*, CFI Sept. 30, 2003, T-346/02, para. 197.
594. *Quinine – Boehringer*, ECJ Dec. 14, 1972, 1972 ECR 1281; *Pre-insulated Pipes – Ke Kelit*, CFI March 20, 2002, 2002 ECR II-1647, para. 189; *Lysine Cartel*, CFI July 9, 2003, T-220/00. However, it may be argued that in the case of a worldwide cartel that affects trade within *and*

However, the same conduct may not be pursued under a different legal aspect (e.g. under Article 82 instead of Article 81), which would conflict with the *ne bis in idem* principle as described above.

No Conflict where the Scope of National Competition Law and the Scope of the Community Competition Law do not Overlap.
National competition law applies without conflicting with Community law where its scope is different from the scope of the Community competition law, in particular in the following cases:

- agreements or conduct that are unlikely to affect trade between member states;[595]
- unilateral anticompetitive conduct of non-dominant undertakings[596] and unilateral price recommendations,[597]
- provisions of national law which predominantly pursue an objective different from that pursued by Articles 81 and 82,[598] such as provisions on unfair competition (e.g, protecting the consumer as opposed to provisions on exclusionary practices protecting competitors);[599]
- national competition laws protecting competition against offences committed by undertakings of third countries, which are clearly distinct from offences committed by the same undertakings inside the Community market,[600] and, more generally,

outside the Community and therefore falls '*as a whole*' under Article 81 the rule of taking account of the prior sanction (wherever imposed) should apply: *see Vitamins*, D.Comm. Nov. 21, 2001, 2003 OJ L 6/1, point 600; *Citric Acid*, D.Comm. Dec. 5, 2001, 2002 OJ L 239/18, points 170–172

595. In particular purely national anticompetitive agreements or conduct without effect on trade between member states.
596. Article 3 (2). This exception concerns national provisions which prohibit or sanction abusive behaviour toward economically dependent undertakings without involving undertakings having a dominant position, such as under French and German law, *see* Recital 8 to Regulation 1/2003.
597. Example: §23 of the German Act against Restraints of Trade.
598. Article 3 (3) of Regulation 1/2003.
599. Recital 9 to Regulation 1/2003.
600. *Quinine – Boehringer*, ECJ Dec. 14, 1972, 1972 ECR 1281, paras 1–7; *Welded Steel Mesh – Sotralentz*, CFI April 6, 1995, 1995 ECR II-1127, paras 26–29. However, in cases such as *Vitamins*, D.Comm. Nov. 21, 2001, 2003 OJ L 6/1, point 600, and *Citric Acid*, D.Comm. Dec. 5, 2001, 2002 OJ L 239/18, points 170–172, the Commission stated that a worldwide price cartel which involves the transfer of goods within and outside the Community may fall 'as a whole' within Article 81 (1), thereby constituting one single infringement under the different applicable competition laws. In such cases the principle of taking account of each other's sanction may apply.

- the imposition of fines on natural persons (which is not provided for under Community competition law), except to the extent that such sanctions are the means whereby competition rules applying to undertakings are enforced;[601]
- mergers and full-function joint ventures without coordination effects, which do not have a Community dimension[602] and provisions of national law authorizing mergers that are not subject to the merger control regulation for reasons of public interest.[603]

No Conflict in Cases of Stricter Community Law.
No conflict arises whenever Community law is stricter than national law. In this case, the stricter Community rules set the legal standard. Community rules also apply to conduct that is permitted, capable of being exempted or expressly exempted from national competition rules[604] or is 'common practice' without being opposed by national authorities or courts.[605] A restrictive agreement or conduct that is permitted or authorized under national law may still be prohibited under Community competition rules.[606]

No Conflict in Cases of Non-Intervention by the Commission.
No conflict arises if the Community does not intervene against an agreement or conduct under the competition rules on grounds of policy or opportunity . Such a 'non-action' presents no conflict with stricter national law which allows national competition authorities or national courts to intervene against the same conduct.

Deference to a Commission Clearance.
The most apparent conflict arises where a national authority or national court were to apply a prohibition provision of national competition law contrary to a Commission clearance.

- A Commission decision finding that the conditions of Article 81 (3) are fulfilled[607] (which substitutes for the former exemption decision) precludes the

---

601. Recital 8 to Regulation 1/2003. *See* §81 of the German Law against Restraints of Trade. The *Walt Wilhelm* case concerned fines imposed *i.a.* on a natural person which was one of the managers of the dyestuff cartel (ECJ July 14, 1972, 1972 ECR 713).
602. Article 22 (1) of the merger control regulation. With respect to joint ventures *see* Statements for Council minutes *re* Article 22 of Regulation 1310/97.
603. Article 3 (3) of Regulation 1/2003.
604. *Guerlain*, ECJ July 10, 1980, 1980 ECR 2327, paras 15–17.
605. *TACA I*, CFI Sept. 30, 2003, T-191/98, paras 568–569.
606. *See Atlantic Container Line – TACA II*, CFI Sept. 30, 2003, T-191/98, para. 1406. With respect to third countries *see ANSAC*, D.Comm. Dec. 19, 1990, 1991 OJ L 152/54 (prohibition by the Commission of a joint sales arrangement which was permitted under the U.S. Webb Pomerene Act).
607. Article 10 of Regulation 1/2003.

application of national law because it constitutes a 'positive, although indirect action' within the meaning of the *Walt Wilhelm* doctrine.[608]

- This also applies with respect to exemption decisions which have been granted within the Commission's sole competence under Article 9 (1) of Regulation 17 and which continue in effect under Regulation 1/2003.[609]
- An agreement which fulfils the conditions of a block exemption regulation is exempted with the same effects as an individual exemption decision.[610] The national authorities and national courts are legally bound and prevented from applying stricter national law.[611]
- A Commission decision stating that the conditions of Article of 81 (1) are not fulfilled[612] represents a 'positive, although indirect, action' of the Commission which precludes the applicability of stricter national law,[613] as stated by the Court of Justice in the *AEB (Spanish Banks)* case:[614]

  'Parallel application of national competition law may be permitted only to the extent to which it does not undermine the uniform application, throughout the Common Market, of the Community competition rules and the full effect of the measures based on those rules'.
- Comfort letters or 'informal guidance' letters[615] by which the Commission grants clearance to an agreement in the form of a simple administrative letter are not legally binding on national authorities or courts[616] but constitute an element of persuasive authority which must be taken into account,[617] in particular where such a comfort letter is preceeded by a detailed publication of the content of the agreement in question and its provisional evaluation.[618]

---

608. *Walt Wilhelm*, ECJ Feb. 13, 1969, 1969 ECR 1, 13.
609. Article 34 (2) of Regulation 1/2003.
610. *Delimitis/Henninger Bräu*, ECJ Feb. 28, 1991, 1991 ECR I-935, para. 46; *Automec II*, CFI Sept. 18, 1992, 1992 ECR II-223, paras 92–95.
611. *Delimitis/Henninger Bräu*, ECJ Feb. 28, 1991, 1991 ECR I-935, para. 46.
612. Article 10 of Regulation 1/2003.
613. Such a decision is different from the negative clearances under the former Regulation 17, by which the Commission stated 'that, on the basis of the facts in its possession, there are no grounds under Article 81 (1) or Article 82 for action'; such a negative clearance did not preclude the application of stricter national law, *see Guerlain*, ECJ July 10, 1980, 1980 ECR 2327, paras 17–19.
614. *AEB (Spanish Banks)*, ECJ July 16, 1992, 1992 ECR I-4785, para. 12.
615. Recital 38 to Regulation 1/2003.
616. Notice on Guidance Letters, point 26.
617. *Guerlain*, ECJ July 10, 1980, 1980 ECR 2327, para. 13.
618. Example of a publication under Article 19 (3) of Regulation 17 in the Official Journal: *REIMS II – Terminal Dues*, 2003 OJ C 94/3. Example of publication in the Commission's Report on Competition Policy: *Long-term Gas Supply Agreements*, Thirty-second Report on Competition Policy, points 80–81. The Commission is not prevented from proceeding to a similar form of publication under Article 30 of Regulation 1/2003.

Remedies in Cases of Conflicts.
Despite close cooperation conflicts may arise, which was recognized by the Commission in the *Van der Bergh Foods* case:[619]

> 'It is not inconsistent with the principles governing the concurrent powers of the national courts and the Commission in the application of Article 85 (1) [*now 81 (1)*] and Article 86 [*now 82*] of the Treaty, for the Commission to take a decision which differs from a judgment delivered by a national court, provided that there exists a sufficient Community interest in doing so'.

Answering a preliminary question relating to the same case the Court of Justice ruled:

> '...in order to fulfill the role assigned to it by the Treaty, the Commission cannot be bound by a decision given by a national court in application of Articles 85 (1) and 86 [*now 81 and 82*] of the Treaty. The Commission is therefore entitled to adopt at any time individual decisions under Articles 85 and 86 of the Treaty, even where an agreement or practice has already been subject of a decision by a national court and the decision contemplated by the Commission conflicts with that national court's decision'.[620]

The national court is obliged under Article 10 of the EC Treaty to adopt the appropriate measures in order to resolve such a conflict, including by suspending enforcement or ordering restitution. Likewise the Commission may examine whether a merger that has been notified to and cleared by the national competition authority had a Community dimension and therefore fell within the exclusive competence of the Commission (and not that of the national authority) even if the possibile legal remedies against the decision of the national authority are exhausted.[621]

---

619. *Van der Bergh Foods*, D.Comm. March 11, 1998, 1998 OJ L 264/1, point 279.
620. *Masterfoods*, ECJ Dec. 14, 2000, 2000 ECR I-11369, para. 48. In this case the exclusive purchasing obligation imposed on Masterfoods was held legal under Article 81 by the national court but illegal (constituting an infringement of Article 81) by the Commission.
621. *Schlüsselverlag Moser*, ECJ Sept. 25, 2003, C-170/02, paras 36–37.

Chapter II

Article 81 – General Principles

CONTENTS

A. Introduction

Anticompetitive Agreements, Decisions and Concerted Practices.
Article 81 (1) constitutes a general prohibition against agreements between undertakings, decisions by associations of undertakings and concerted practices which may affect trade between member states of the Community 'and which have as their object or effect the prevention, restriction or distortion of competition within the common market'.[1] The rule is addressed broadly in scope to both formal and informal agreements, decisions and concerted practices among all forms of business enterprise. The principal objective of this rule is to assure that each enterprise determines independently its business policies and market conduct in the Community. The requirement of independent decision-making is not meant to prevent businesses from adapting intelligently to the existing and anticipated conduct of their competitors, but it does preclude any direct or indirect contact the object or effect of which is to influence the market conduct of a competitor or to disclose future competitive conduct.[2] Although Article 81 refers expressly only to products it applies also to services.[3]

Unilateral Measures not Governed by Article 81.
Article 81 applies only to agreements, collective decisions and concerted practices. Unilateral measures, such as mere refusal to supply parallel importers or the decision to reduce output of a product, are not within the scope of Article 81. Under some circumstances, however, unilateral measures may be an abuse of a dominant position under Article 82, and measures that appear unilateral may in fact be the result of an agreement or concerted action that infringes Article 81.[4]

Object or Effect.
The restraint of competition may be *either* the 'object' *or* 'effect' of the enterprise's conduct. Accordingly, no actual effect on the market is necessary for the rule to apply.[5] This corresponds to the preventive nature of the rule. Therefore, even an

---

1. Article 81 is complemented by Article 53 of the EEA Agreement to the extent that anticompetitive agreements, decisions and concerted practices are prohibited insofar as they 'may affect trade between the Contracting Parties' which include the member states and the EFTA states with the exception of Switzerland.
2. *Sugar*, ECJ Dec. 16, 1975, 1975 ECR 1663, paras 173–174; *Polypropylene – Rhône Poulenc*, CFI Oct. 24, 1991, 1991 ECR II-867, para. 121; *UK Agricultural Tractor Registration Exchange*, CFI Oct. 27, 1994, 1994 ECR II-957, paras 50–52; *aff'd John Deere*, ECJ May 28, 1998, 1998 ECR I-3175, paras 86–87.
3. *Parker Pen (Herlitz)*, CFI July 14, 1994, 1994 ECR II-531, paras 29–34.
4. *See Bayer – Adalat*, CFI June 5, 1996, 1996 ECR II-381, para. 54; *Volkswagen II*, CFI Dec. 3, 2003, T-208/01, para. 351.
5. *Miller International*, ECJ Feb. 1, 1978, 1978 ECR 131, para. 15; *Tréfileurope*, CFI April 6, 1995, 1995 ECR II-797, para. 122; *BASF Coatings*, CFI May 19, 1999, 1999 ECR II-1581, paras 133–136.

anticompetitive agreement just made, but not yet implemented[6] or not intended to be implemented,[7] is prohibited and unenforceable. Whether and to what extent fines are to be imposed under such circumstances is a separate issue.[8]

Types of Restrictive Agreements Covered.
Article 81 applies at and between all levels in the production and distribution chain, from research and development to retailing. The prohibition of anticompetitive practices applies to both horizontal agreements among competitors and to vertical agreements among a supplier and its dealers, including agreements on franchising, licensing, specialization and joint research and development.[9] The different categories of restrictions are dealt with in the following chapters: horizontal agreements (Chapter III), vertical agreements and franchise agreements (Chapter IV), mergers and joint ventures (Chapter VI), and technology transfer agreements (Chapter VII).

Appreciability Criterion.
The broad prohibition of Article 81 (1) against agreements that prevent, restrict or distort competition has been limited in the enforcement practice of the Commission and in the decisions of the European Court of Justice by the principle that the restriction must be 'appreciable', i.e., significant, before Article 81 will apply. Appreciability has both quantitative and qualitative aspects. The quantitative aspect is that the Commission considers agreements between firms with small market shares (together less than respectively 10% of the relevant market in cases of horizontal agreements and 15% in cases of vertical agreements) as normally not capable of having an 'appreciable effect' on competition that would justify application of Article 81. Such agreements are treated as negligible or *de minimis*.[10]

---

6. *Grundig/Consten*, ECJ July 13, 1966, 1966 ECR 299, 342 ('… there is no need to take account of the concrete effects of an agreement once it appears that it has as its object the prevention, restriction or distortion of competition'.); *PVC II*, ECJ Oct. 15, 2002, 2002 ECR I-8375, para. 509; *Eurochèques – Cartes Bancaires 'CB'*, CFI Feb. 23, 1994, 1994 ECR II-49, para. 87; *UK Agricultural Tractor Registration Exchange – John Deere*, CFI Oct. 27, 1994, 1994 ECR II-957, para. 92; *aff'd New Holland*, ECJ May 28, 1998, 1998 ECR I-3175, para. 91 ('potential effects').
7. *Zinc Producer Group*, D.Comm. Aug. 6, 1984, 1984 OJ L 220/27, 38; *Dutch Industrial and Medical Gases*, D.Comm. July 24, 2002, 2003 OJ L 84/1, point 351.
8. *Polypropylene – Hercules*, CFI Dec. 17, 1991, 1991 ECR II-1715 para. 344.
9. *Grundig/Consten*, ECJ July 13, 1966, 1966 ECR 299, 339; *Italy v. Council and Commission*, ECJ July 13, 1966, 1966 ECR 389, 407 (vertical agreements); *FEDETAB*, ECJ Oct. 29, 1980, 1980 ECR 3125, para. 132 (horizontal and vertical agreements); *Maize Seed*, ECJ June 8, 1982, 1982 ECR 2015, paras 44–66 (licence agreements); *Pronuptia*, ECJ Jan. 29, 1986, 1986 ECR 353, paras 14–27 (franchise agreements); *Jaz/Peter I*, D.Comm. July 22, 1969, 1969 OJ L 195/5, 7–8 (specialization); *Henkel/Colgate I*, D.Comm. Dec. 23, 1971, 1972 OJ L 14/14 (joint research and development).
10. Commission Notice of Dec. 22, 2001, 2001 OJ C 368/13, replacing the preceding notices which were based on a market share thresholds of respectively 5% and 10% (1997 OJ C 372/4)

However, the quantitative definition of 'appreciable' is not an absolute yardstick. First, cases falling below these thresholds may be caught by Article 81 (1) if the agreement is part of a 'bundle' of agreements having a cumulative restrictive effect,[11] and the Commission may still intervene in cases of a 'hardcore' restriction of competition such as fixing prices or sharing customers or markets. In addition, the thresholds do not prevent private challenges to conduct or to the validity of agreements which do not meet the Commission's 'appreciability' standard.[12] Finally, even in cases exceeding the thresholds it may be argued that the restrictive effects are not appreciable yet.[13]

Clearance.
Where restrictive agreements meet the 'appreciability' test and affect trade between member states, they may nevertheless be cleared by way of a Commission block exemption, individual exemption or individual assessment:

- *'Block exemption' regulations.* The Commission may exempt a class of similar restrictive agreements whose pro-competitive benefits are considered to outweigh their anticompetitive detriments under a so-called 'block exemption' regulation. Such regulations automatically exempt agreements of the relevant type from the application of Article 81 (1) if they do not exceed the limits set forth in the regulation. Block exemption regulations have been adopted for various categories of agreements to date.[14] The benefit of a block exemption may be withdrawn in particular cases by the Commission or (from 1 May 2004) also by national authorities.
- *Individual clearance.* Up to 1 May 2004 the Commission had exclusive competence to grant exemption under Article 81 (3) for an individual agreement, a so-called 'individual exemption', where its benefits significantly outweigh the anticompetitive detriments. Individual exemptions required formal notification of the agreement to the Commission and a public notice under Article 19 (3) of Regulation 17 inviting comments from third parties. Then the Commission

---

and, in addition, of a minimum turnover threshold (that increased periodically and was eliminated in 1997) of EUR 50 million (Notice of 1977, 1977 OJ C 313/3), EUR 200 million (Notice of 1986, 1986 OC C 231/2) and EUR 300 million (Notice of 1994, 1994 OJ C 368/20).

11. *See below* section 5(b).
12. *Pronuptia*, ECJ Jan. 29, 1986, 1986 ECR 353, in which the restraints challenged in a German court related to only a single franchisee of wedding garments. *See also De Minimis* Notice 2001 OJ C 368/13, point 11.
13. *Langnese-Iglo*, CFI June 8, 1995, 1995 ECR II-1533, para. 98.
14. These are Regulation 2790/1999 on Vertical Restraints; Regulation 1400/2002 on Vertical Agreements in the Motor Vehicle Sector, Regulation 772/2004 on technology transfer agreements; Regulation 2658/2000 on Specialization Agreements; Regulation 2659/2000 on Research and Development Agreements and various regulations in the field of insurance and transport (*see* Chapter VIII). These regulations also apply under the EEA Agreement: Appendix XIV to the EEA Agreement, 1994 OJ L 1/446.

issued a formal exemption or negative clearance decision or an informal comfort letter. From 1 May 2004 the Commission's exclusive competence is abolished by Regulation 1/2003, thereby enabling not only the Commission but also the national authorities and courts to apply Article 81 (3) without any formal notification being required. The Commission will no longer issue exemption decisions but may, in appropriate cases, find that the conditions of Article 81 (1) are not fulfilled or that the conditions of Article 81 (3) are satisfied.[15]

- *Informal guidance letter*. In lieu of the forms of clearance discussed above, the Commission may now issue an 'informal guidance letter' in cases which give rise to genuine uncertainty.[16]

Direct Effect of Articles 81 and 82.
The prohibition of Article 81 (1) is a directly applicable part of the law of each member state, and therefore may be enforced in the national courts of each state with all the legal consequences, including the unenforceability of the agreement under Article 81 (2), the possible award of damages and issuance of an injunction.[17] From 1 May 2004 national authorities and national courts may also directly apply Article 81 (3). The application of Article 81 is without prejudice to the application of Article 82; both provisions may be applied in parallel.[18]

B. System of Article 81 (1)

1. Prohibited Forms of Cooperation: Agreements, Decisions and Concerted Practices

Substance instead of Form Decisive.
Article 81 prohibits all anticompetitive agreements between firms, decisions by associations of firms and concerted practices. It is the substance and not the form of the collaboration that matters. Although generally speaking it can be said that an agreement involves a higher degree of consensus between the parties than a concerted practice, the distinctions between agreements, decisions and concerted practices are not clear-cut; the various types of action form a continuum with similar anticompetitive consequences which are treated alike.[19] This corresponds

---

15. Article 10 of Regulation 1/2003.
16. Recital 38 to Regulation 1/2003 and Notice on Informal Guidance. Informal guidance letters may be compared to comfort letters, containing, however, a more detailed reasoning.
17. Under Article 81: *BRT/SABAM*, ECJ Jan. 30, 1974, 1974 ECR 51, paras 16–17; *Masterfood/HB Icecream*, ECJ Dec. 14, 2000, 2000 ECR I-11369, paras. 51–60. Under Article 53 of the EEA Agreement: *Erla Maria Sveinbjörnsdottir*, EFTA Court of Justice Dec. 10, 1998, 1998 EFTACR 95, para. 58.
18. *CEWAL*, ECJ March 16, 2000, 2000 ECR I-1365, para. 33.
19. Block exemption regulations therefore apply equally to agreements and concerted practices.

to economic reality since many types of collusion involve elements of agreements, decisions and concerted practices.[20] In order to find Article 81 (1) applicable, the Court of Justice requires evidence of coordination or cooperation between firms that is likely to influence their conduct so as to restrict or distort competition;[21] it does not have the issue turn on whether the cooperation is the result of a formal agreement or a concerted practice. Likewise, the Commission tends in complex cases to be content with finding a combination of agreements and concerted practices that have led to 'institutionalized and systematic collusion' and does not attempt to distinguish between them.[22] The Court upheld this practice arguing as follows:[23]

> 'The Commission was also entitled to characterize that single infringement as an "agreement and concerted practice", since the infringement involved at one and the same time elements to be characterized as "agreements" and factual elements to be characterized as "concerted practices". Given such a complex infringement, the dual characterization by the Commission in Article 1 of its Decision must be understood not as requiring, simultaneously and cumulatively, proof of each of those factual elements presents the constituent elements both of an agreement and a concerted practice, but rather as referring to a complex whole comprising a number of factual elements some of which were characterized as agreements and others as concerted practices for the purposes of Article 85 (1) of the EEC Treaty [now Article 81 (1)], which lays down no specific category for a complex infringement of this type.'

The key distinction is therefore not between the various forms of collusion, be it agreement, decision or concerted practice,[24] but rather between collusion (an

20. *Polypropylene*, D.Comm. April 23, 1986, 1986 OJ L 230/1, 27–28; *aff'd* CFI 24 Oct. 1991, 1991 ECR II-867, paras 121–122; *Polypropylene – Petrofina*, CFI Oct. 24, 1991, 1991 ECR II-1087, paras 35–36. Similar principles apply when proving an illegal 'conspiracy' under United States antitrust law, section 1 of the Sherman Act, 15 U.S.C. §1, which the Supreme Court has referred to as 'a unity of purpose or a common design and understanding, or a meeting of the minds in an unlawful arrangement'. *American Tobacco* v. *United States*, 328 U.S. 781, 810 (1946).
21. *See*, e.g., *Philip Morris/Rothmans*, ECJ Nov. 17, 1987, 1987 ECR 4487, paras 32–64.
22. *Cf. Polypropylene*, D.Comm. April 23, 1986, 1986 OJ L 230/1, 36 (Article 1): 'an agreement *and* concerted practice'; *Pre-insulated Pipes*, D.Comm. Oct. 21, 1998, 1999 OJ L 24/1, paras 129–134, *aff'd HFB Holding*, CFI March 20, 2002, 2002 ECR II-1487, para. 186.
23. *Polypropylene – Rhône-Poulenc*, CFI Oct. 24, 1991, 1991 ECR II-867, para. 127; *Polypropylene – Montecatini*, ECJ July 8, 1999, 1999 ECR I-4539, para. 195.
24. *Carton – LR af 1998*, CFI March 20, 2002, 2002 ECR II-1705, para. 158; *HFB Holding*, CFI March 20, 2002, 2002 ECR II-1847, para. 186.

'overall plan'[25]) and independent, 'mere parallel behaviour with no element of concertation'.[26]

(a) Agreements

Broad Interpretation.
The term 'agreement' is not interpreted so narrowly as under contract law, under which legal or quasi-legal duties are preconditions for the enforcement of a contract before a court of law. It is not necessary for the 'agreement' to be intended as legally binding upon the parties for Article 81 to apply.[27] According to the decisions of the Court of Justice,

> 'the minimum requirement for there to be an "agreement" is an expression of a joint intention of the parties involved to conduct themselves on the market in a specific way, the object or effect of the conduct being the prevention, restriction or distortion of competition.'[28]

A general agreement to reach a more detailed and finalized agreement ('heads of agreements') may be qualified as an 'agreement', in particular where the agreement is accompanied by an exchange of confidential information which, as such, may already lead to a certain coordination in the sector concerned, whereas mere negotiations which 'have not yet culminated in an expression of a joint intention' or a unilateral offer made for the conclusion of a contract do not qualify as an 'agreement' because they lack the necessary 'minimum of consensus'. An agreement exists if the parties reach a consensus between themselves or via a third party, e.g., a common supplier or licensor, which limits or is likely to limit their commercial freedom by determining the pattern of their action or abstention from action in the market.[29] No contractual sanctions or enforcement procedures are

25. *Cement – Aalborg Portland*, ECJ Jan. 7, 2004, C-204/00P, para. 258.
26. *Woodpulp II*, ECJ March 31, 1993, 1993 ECR I-1307, paras 70–72. Examples of the close relationship between agreement and concerted practice in a horizontal context: *Polypropylene – Atochem*, CFI Oct. 24, 1991, 1991 ECR II-1177, paras 125–126; *PVC II*, CFI April 20, 1999, 1999 ECR II-931, paras 694–698; *aff'd* ECJ Oct. 15, 2002, 2002 ECR I-8375; in the vertical context: *Dunlop-Slazenger*, CFI July 7, 1994, 1994 ECR II-441, para. 54. Under Article 65 ECSC Treaty: *Steel Beams*, D.Comm. Feb. 16, 1994, 1994 OJ L 116/1, para. 291; *aff'd* CFI March 11, 1999, 1999 ECR II-347, paras 266–273.
27. *FEDETAB*, ECJ Oct. 29, 1980, 1980 ECR 3125, paras 85–86; *Sandoz II*, ECJ Jan. 11, 1990, 1990 ECR I-45, para. 13; *Polypropylene*, D.Comm. April 23, 1986, 1986 OJ L 230/1, 26–21*; aff'd CFI Polypropylene-Atochem*, CFI Oct. 24, 1991, 1991 ECR II-1177. Under Article 65 ECSC Treaty: *Welded Steel Mesh*, D.Comm. Aug. 2, 1989, 1989 OJ L 260/1, 35; *aff'd* CFI April 6, 1995, 1995 ECR II-987.
28. *Jaeger/Opel Norge*, EFTA Court of Justice April 1, 1998, E-3/97, paras 35–36. *Cf. Polypropylene – Hercules*, CFI Dec. 17, 1991, 1991 ECR I-1711, para. 256; *aff'd* ECJ July 8, 1999, 1999 ECR I-4539, para. 162.
29. *Polypropylene – Rhône-Poulenc*, CFI Oct. 24, 1991, 1991 ECR II-867, paras 120 and 211.

required.[30] Nor is it necessary for such an agreement to be made in writing: an oral agreement or tacit understanding suffices.[31] Agreements settling national court proceedings may also be caught by Article 81 (1) if they determine the parties' future conduct. Even a judicial settlement that is approved by the court to make it enforceable between the parties is subject to the ordinary requirements of the law and public policy (*ordre public*), which include the EC rules of competition.[32]

Need for Consensus.

Any consensus between the parties to regulate their future competitive conduct will suffice to establish a prohibited restraint on their autonomy and independence.[33] All that is required is the intent to take account of others' interests and to submit oneself to economic, social or moral pressure[34] (mutual understanding, 'joint intention' or 'concurrence of wills'[35]). According to consistent case law, in order for there to be an 'agreement' within the meaning of Article 81 (1), it is sufficient for the undertakings in question to have expressed their joint intention to conduct themselves in the market in a particular way; the tacit acceptance by an undertaking or the participation in a meeting suffices to prove the participation to the agreement, unless it manifestly opposes or indicates to the other parties that it was participating in a spirit different from those of the other parties.[36] The joint monitoring system of an agreement on target prices or target quantities may indicate participation in that agreement so that the participants needed to explain and justify conduct that was inconsistent with those targets.[37]

---

30. *Polypropylene – Petrofina*, CFI Oct. 24, 1991, 1991 ECR II-1087, paras 152–156.
31. *Tepea*, ECJ June 20, 1978, 1978 ECR 1391, paras 40–41. Identical restrictions (e.g., to observe minimum prices) imposed on the licensees of industrial property rights have also been held to be equivalent to a horizontal agreement between the fellow licensees even though there may have been no contact between them: *Hesbignonne*, ECJ April 19, 1988, 1988 ECR 1919, para. 15.
32. *Maize Seed*, ECJ June 8, 1982, 1982 ECR 2015, paras 80–89; *Bayer/Süllhöfer*, ECJ Sept. 27, 1988, 1988 ECR 5249, paras. 14–15; *ECO Swiss/Benetton*, ECJ June 1, 1999, 1999 ECR I-3055. *See* Article 5 (5) of Regulation 4056/86 on maritime transport ('awards at arbitration').
33. *Polypropylene*, D.Comm. April 23, 1986, 1986 OJ L 230/1, 26–27; *aff'd* CFI 24 Oct. 1991, 1991 ECR II-1177, paras 162–169. *See* Guidelines on Article 81 (3), points 14–15.
34. 'Creating a visible and psychological climate': *Hasselblad*, ECJ Feb. 21, 1984, 1984 ECR 883, para. 46; *Parker Pen*, CFI July 14, 1994, 1994 ECR II-549, para. 55; *BASF Coatings*, CFI May 19, 1999, 1999 ECR I-1581, para. 156; *Polypropylene – Montecatini*, ECJ July 8, 1999, 1999 ECR I-4539, para. 162.
35. In a horizontal context: *Cement*, CFI March 15, 2000, 2000 ECR II-491, para. 2061; *aff'd* ECJ Jan. 7, 2004, C-204/00P; *Pre-insulated Pipes – HFB Holding*, CFI March 20, 2002, 2002 ECR II-1847, para. 199; in a vertical context: *Volkswagen II*, CFI Dec. 3, 2003, T-208/01, para. 32. Under the EEA agreement: *Jaeger/Opel Norge*, EFTA Court of Justice, April 1, 1998, 1998 EFTACR 38, para. 35.
36. *Greek Ferries – Marlines*, CFI Dec. 11, 2003, T-56/99, paras. 20–21 (with further references); *Aalborg – Cement*, Jan. 7, 2004, T-204/00 P, para. 81.
37. *Polypropylene – Rhône-Poulenc*, CFI Oct. 24, 1991, 1991 ECR II-867, para. 120.

The concerted activity need not necessarily be made known to purchasers and recognized or recognizable as having been coordinated.[38] A confidential agreement on price targets can be no less anticompetitive than a published common price list.[39] In a case of exchange of information between competitors the Court of First Instance ruled:

> '… the undertakings in question … did not confine themselves to merely exchanging information on their price "forecasts" or "estimates" but expressed their common desire to conduct themselves on the market in a particular manner in regard to prices, that is to say, to act in such a way as to ensure that the prices agreed at the meetings in question would be achieved or, in some cases, maintained. The Court finds that such a common intention constitutes an "agreement" within the meaning of Article 65 (1) of the [ECSC] Treaty. Moreover, the Court sees no reason here to interpret the concept of "agreement" in Article 65 (1) of the Treaty differently from the concept of "agreement" in Article 85 [*now 81*] (1) of the EC Treaty.'[40]

Gentlemen's Agreements.
An agreement need not be legally binding[41] or have the outer appearance or the specificity of a contract. Gentlemen's agreements that cannot be enforced in a court of law are also the 'faithful expression of the joint intention of the parties with regard to their conduct in the Common Market' and therefore an agreement within the meaning of Article 81.[42] The temporary formal suspension of an agreement followed by conduct indicating that the consensus continued may indicate only that the agreement was not strictly followed for a time.[43] A party who for a time applies the agreement passively or reluctantly, or who attempts to turn it to his own interest or advantage, cannot necessarily be assumed to be an unwilling participant in the agreement, as long as he shows a readiness to continue to

---

38. *Polypropylene*, D.Comm. April 23, 1986, 1986 OJ L 230/1, 28; *aff'd Polypropylene – Atochem*, CFI Dec. 17, 1991, 1991 ECR II-1715, paras 340–341.
39. *Belasco*, D.Comm. July 10, 1986, 1986 OJ L 232/15, 19, 23; *see also Zinc Producer Group*, D.Comm. Aug. 6, 1984, 1984 OJ L 220/27, 30–32, 37–38.
40. *Steel Beams – Thyssen Stahl*, CFI Oct. 2, 2003, T-194/99 P, para. 262.
41. Restrictive clauses of an agreement cannot be legally enforced anyway because of their nullity according to Article 81 (2). *See Pre-insulated Pipes*, D.Comm. Oct. 21, 1998, 1999 OJ L 24/1, points 133–134.
42. *ACF Chemiefarma-Quinine*, ECJ July 15, 1970, 1970 ECR 661, paras 106–113; *Boehringer-Quinine I*, ECJ July 15, 1970, 1970 ECR 769, paras 27–28; *FEDETAB*, ECJ Oct. 30, 1978, 1978 ECR 2111, para. 86; *Welded Steel Mesh – Tréfilunion*, CFI April 6, 1995, 1995 ECR II-791, paras 95–96.
43. *ACF Chemiefarma-Quinine*, ECJ July 15, 1970, 1970 ECR 661, para. 169; *Boehringer-Quinine I*, ECJ July 15, 1970, 1970 ECR 769, para. 49.

participate.[44] An agreement will be deemed to exist even if it is loosely applied[45] or if a restrictive rule is applied flexibly, i.e., violations overlooked or exceptions granted.[46] The formal termination of an agreement does not preclude the application of Article 81 to anticompetitive effects that continue to be felt; such effects will be assumed if the conduct of the parties continues to display features of collusion and coordination producing the same result as an agreement.[47]

Agreements Imposed on One of the Parties.
The economic dependence of one party on another for supplies – even in a parent-subsidiary relationship – does not preclude a divergence in conduct or interests between the firms so that their relationship will be based on an agreement imposed by the more powerful firm which may infringe Article 81.[48] Even an 'unwilling' acceptance may constitute an agreement; a mental reservation is irrelevant.[49] Thus a firm may be considered as participating actively or passively in an association's anticompetitive decision[50] even if it subscribes to the decision with the intention of ignoring it.[51] However, the Commission has exercised leniency with regard to firms that acted only negligently or took part in an anticompetitive agreement under duress.[52] For instance, it has refrained from fining dealers upon whom an

---

44. *Belasco*, D.Comm. July 10, 1986, 1986 OJ L 232/15, 19–21, 25; *aff'd* ECJ July 11, 1989, 1989 ECR 2117, paras 21–23; *Polypropylene – Petrofina*, CFI Oct. 24, 1991, 1991 ECR II-1087, paras 92–93, 128–130, 254; *HFB Holding*, CFI March 20, 2002, 2002 ECR II-1847, para. 227.
45. *Miller International*, ECJ Feb. 1, 1978, 1978 ECR 131, paras 6–7; *Belasco*, ECJ July 11, 1989, 1989 ECR 2117, para. 14.
46. *Hasselblad*, ECJ Feb. 21, 1984, 1984 ECR 883, para. 46; *Belasco*, ECJ July 11, 1989, 1989 ECR 2117, para. 15; *Sandoz II*, ECJ Jan. 11, 1990, 1990 ECR I-45, paras 14 and 18.
47. Affirmed: *EMI/CBS*, ECJ June 15, 1976, 1976 ECR 811, paras 30–31; *Binon/AMP*, ECJ July 3, 1985, 1985 ECR 2015, paras 16–17; *Rendo/IJsselcentrale*, CFI Nov. 18, 1992, 1992 ECR II-2417, para. 110; *Pre-insulated Pipes*, D.Comm. Oct. 21, 1998, 1999 OJ L 24/1, point 142 (*aff'd Preinsulated Pipes – LR af 1998*, CFI March 20, 2002, 2002 ECR II-1847); *BASF Coatings*, CFI May 19, 1999, 1999 ECR II-1581, para. 139. Denied because of too long time interval: *Soda Ash – Solvay*, CFI June 29, 1995, 1995 ECR II-1775, paras 72–73.
48. *BMW Belgium*, ECJ July 12, 1979, 1979 ECR 2435, para. 36; *Tipp-Ex*, D.Comm. July 10, 1987, 1987 OJ L 222/1, 7; *aff'd Tipp-Ex*, ECJ Feb. 8, 1990, 1990 ECR I-261, para. 23.
49. *Polypropylene – Hercules*, CFI Nov. 17, 1991, 1991 ECR II-1711, para. 232; *HFB Holding*, CFI March 20, 2002, 2002 ECR II-1847, para. 137.
50. *Pre-insulated Pipes – LR af 1998*, CFI March 20, 2002, 2002 ECR II-1705, para. 39.
51. *FEDETAB*, ECJ Oct. 29, 1980, 1980 ECR 2913, paras 90–91; *Polypropylene*, D.Comm. April 23, 1986, 1986 OJ L 230/1, 27; *Belasco*, D.Comm. July 10, 1986, 1986 OJ L 232/15, 27.
52. In cases of a horizontal cartel: *Cement*, D.Comm. Nov. 30, 1994, 1994 OJ L 343/1, para. 64.9.b. (*aff'd* in this respect CFI March 15, 2000, 2000 ECR II-491); *Preinsulated Pipes – LR af 1998*, CFI March 20, 2002, 2002 ECR II-1705, paras. 142 and 165. In cases of vertical restrictions: *Sandoz*, ECJ Jan. 11, 1990, 1990 ECR I-45, paras 10–13; *Pioneer*, ECJ June 7, 1983, 1983 ECR 1825, paras 10–13.

export prohibition had been imposed,[53] unless the dealer had actively contributed to conclude or implement the restrictive agreement.[54]

Evidence of Agreement.
The creation of an institutional framework – such as regular meetings at which confidential sales and price information are exchanged to coordinate sales and price policies – may serve as evidence of an agreement.[55] Even if undertakings which are present at at such meetings do not expressly agree to the results, they may give the impression to the other participants that they intend to follow the scheme discussed between the parties at the meetings, unless they publicly distance themselves from the results.[56] Hence, it is not necessary to show that the parties give their formal consent to the agreement if they act generally in accordance with it.[57] Indeed, outsiders may be drawn into an agreement without ever having openly expressed support for it.[58] Also, as noted above, an agreement can be found even when one of the parties is so dependent on the other that it has little choice but to accept the other's wishes. In *BMW Belgium*, for example, the Court of Justice ruled that a circular to dealers which was signed by its recipients constituted an agreement.[59] BMW's Belgian subsidiary had sent a circular to its Belgian dealers to halt exports to Germany which were made attractive by Belgian price controls on cars. By gaining the consent of the dealers to halt their exports (albeit against their will), BMW Belgium and its dealers had entered into an agreement

---

53. E.g., *VW/Audi*, D.Comm. Jan. 28, 1998, 1998 OJ L 124/60 (*aff'd* CFI July 6, 2000, 2000 ECR II-2707).
54. *BMW Belgium*, D.Comm. Dec. 23, 1977, 1978 OJ L 46/33,42; *Tipp-Ex*, D.Comm. July 10, 1987, 1987 OJ L 222/1 (*aff'd* ECJ Feb. 8, 1990, 1990 ECR I-261); *Dunlop – Slazenger*, D.Comm. March 18, 1992, 1992 OJ L 131/32 (*aff'd* CFI April 28, 1994, 1994 ECR II-211); *Viho/Parker Pen*, D.Comm. July 15, 1992, 1992 OJ L 233/27 (*aff'd* CFI July 14, 1994, 1994 ECR II-549); *Tretorn*, D.Comm. Dec. 22, 1994, 1994 OJ L 378/45 (*aff'd* CFI Dec. 11, 1996, 1996 ECR II-1799); *BASF Lacke + Farben*, D.Comm. July 12, 1995, 1995 OJ L 272/16, para. 105 (*aff'd* CFI May 19, 1999, 1999 ECR II-1581).
55. *Polypropylene*, D.Comm. April 23, 1986, 1986 OJ L 230/1, 26–27; *aff'd CFI* Oct. 24, 1991, 1991 ECR II-1177, paras 43–44.
56. Polypropylene – *Hercules*, CFI Dec. 17, 1991, 1991 ECR II-1711, para. 232; *Nederlandse Federatieve Vereniging voor de Groothandel op Elektrotechnisch Gebied*, CFI Dec. 16, 2003, T-5/00, para. 359; *Greek Ferries – Marlines*, CFI Dec. 11, 2003, T-56/99, paras. 20–21 (with further references); *Aalborg – Cement*, Jan. 7, 2004, T-204/00 P, para. 81.
57. *Polypropylene*, D.Comm. April 23, 1986, 1986 OJ L 230/1, 28 ('… in a complex cartel, some producers at one time or another might not express their definite assent to a particular course of action agreed by the others but nevertheless indicate their general support for the scheme in question and conduct themselves accordingly'); *aff'd* CFI Oct. 24, 1991, 1991 ECR II-867 and 1177.
58. *Belasco*, D.Comm. July 10, 1986, 1986 OJ L 232/15, 30; *aff'd Belasco*, ECJ July 11, 1989, 1989 ECR 2117, para. 13.
59. *BMW Belgium*, ECJ July 12, 1979, 1979 ECR 2435, paras 28–36.

which supplemented their regular contractual relationship.[60] On the other hand, it may be argued that if a circular is neither signed by the recipients, nor followed by them nor enforced, then it may remain only a unilateral declaration of intent.[61]

Unwritten Agreements.
An unwritten agreement will be found to exist if one party sufficiently communicates to the other parties its expectations as to a particular form of conduct and the other parties recognize the consequences of failure to observe the agreement from their own experience, from the experience of others or from an explicit threat. Thus, a selective distribution system will infringe Article 81 if the manufacturer makes the admission of dealers dependent not just on meeting the established written criteria, but also on other criteria such as price loyalty or not exporting to other member states.[62] The same conclusion will be reached if the manufacturer threatens his customers with termination or short supplies if the customer exports any of the goods.[63] Coordinated conduct that extends beyond the terms of a written agreement reflecting a policy of market compartmentalization may still be regarded as a concerted practice.[64] However, where practices are systematically applied, for example action to prevent parallel imports under a distribution agreement, and where the consequences are known to the parties, they may become a supplemental unwritten but integral part of the ongoing contractual relations between the manufacturer and its dealers or customers.[65]

(b) Decisions

Coordination between Members of an Association.
Decisions of associations are more easily distinguishable from agreements. They are typically articles of incorporation, by-laws, or rules of a trade association. Such decisions may be binding not only on the members who participated in and

---

60. *See also Peugeot*, CFI April 22, 1993, 1993 ECR II-495 para. 63; *Volkswagen/Audi*, D.Comm. 28 Jan. 1998, 1998 OJ L 124/60, paras 128–129 and 151–152, *aff'd* CFI July 6, 2000, 2000 ECR II-2707 and ECJ Sept. 18, 2003, C-338/00 P, para. 60.
61. *Jaeger/Opel Norge*, EFTA Court of Justice, April 1, 1998, 1998 EFTACR 38, para. 36. Practical difficulties of distinguishing between agreement and unilateral behaviour: *Bayer-Adalat*, ECJ Jan. 6, 2004, C-2/01 P, paras. 21–29 (annulling the Commission's decision because of lack of evidence that the wholesalers 'acquiesced' in Bayer's policy of restricting supplies in order to prevent parallel trade); *General Motors – Opel*, CFI Oct. 21, 2003, T-368/00, paras. 78–88.
62. *AEG/Telefunken*, ECJ Oct. 25, 1983, 1983 ECR 3151, paras 31–39.
63. *Sandoz*, D.Comm. July 13, 1987, 1987 OJ L 222/28, 32; *aff'd* CFI Jan. 11, 1990, 1990 ECR II-45.
64. *Hasselblad*, D.Comm. Dec. 2, 1981, 1982 OJ L 161/18, 26.
65. *General Motors – Opel*, CFI Oct. 21, 2003, T-368/00, paras. 97–105. *See also Ford II*, ECJ Sept. 17, 1985, 1985 ECR 2725, paras 16–26; *Sandoz II*, ECJ Jan. 11, 1990, 1990 ECR I-45, paras 10–12; *Mercedes-Benz*, D.Comm. Oct. 10, 2001, 2002 OJ L 257/1, points 124–130.

approved of the decision in question,[66] but also on those who did not agree to them and may not have taken part in the decision-making process;[67] decisions reflect the association's intention at coordinating the market behaviour of its members.[68] For instance, a member of a trade association may be bound by a decision of that body if the decision was made as authorized in its rules, even though the member had no part and did not concur in the decision.[69] Similarly, non-members of an association can become parties to its decisions if they abide by them.[70]

(c) Concerted Practices

Form or Substitute of Coordination.

The Court of Justice has described concerted practices under Article 81 as 'a form of coordination between undertakings which, without having reached the stage where an agreement properly so called has been concluded, knowingly substitutes practical cooperation between them for the risks of competition'[71] contrary to the requirement of economic independence.[72] The concerted practice must relate to

---

66. Tantamount to an agreement between the members who agree: *Cement*, CFI March 15, 2000, 2000 ECR II-491, para. 1328. However, members which did not participate cannot be held responsible: *Eurofer*, CFI March 11, 1999, 1999 ECR II-263, paras. 98–99 and 131.
67. This is the main difference between a decision of an association and an agreement between the members of that assocication. *Polypropylene – Petrofina*, CFI Oct. 24, 1991, 1991 ECR II-1087, para. 210; *Eurochèque Helsinki – Cartes Bancaires 'CB'*, CFI Feb. 23, 1994, 1994 ECR II-49, para. 76; *Cement*, D.Comm. Nov. 30, 1994, 1994 OJ L 343/1, point 53.5; *COAPI*, D.Comm. Jan. 30, 1995, 1995 OJ L 122/37, paras 34–35.
68. *FENEX*, D.Comm. June 5, 1996, 1996 OJ L 181/28, para. 41; *Steel Beams-Eurofer*, CFI March 11, 1999, 1999 ECR II-263, paras 109–118. *See under* Article 65 of the ECSC Treaty: *SOREMA I*, ECJ March 19, 1964, 1964 ECR 151, 164.
69. *Fire Insurance*, ECJ Jan. 27, 1987, 1987 ECR 405, paras 26–32. In this case the statutes of the association provided that it was empowered to coordinate the activities of its members, especially in relation to competition. A specialist committee on industrial risks was to coordinate the policy of the members with regard to premium rates and the decisions or recommendations of the committee were deemed to be definitive. Therefore, 'the recommendation, regardless of what its precise legal status may be, constituted the faithful reflection of the applicant's resolve to coordinate the conduct of its members on the German insurance market in accordance with the terms of the recommendation.'
70. *Belasco*, D.Comm. July 10, 1986, 1986 OJ L 232/15, 30; *aff'd* ECJ July 11, 1989, 1989 ECR 2117, para. 13.
71. *ICI-Dyestuffs*, ECJ July 14, 1972, 1972 ECR 619, para. 64; *Polypropylene*, D.Comm. April 23, 1986, 1986 OJ L 230/1, 27; *aff'd Polypropylene – Herkules*, CFI Dec. 17, 1991, 1991 ECR II-1715, paras 258–260; *P&O/Stena/Brittany Ferries*, D.Comm. Oct. 30, 1996, 1997 OJ L 26/33, para. 56; *HFB Holding*, ECJ March 20, 2002, 2002 ECR II-1847, para. 211.
72. *Steel Beams – Thyssen Stahl*, CFI Oct. 2, 2003, T-194/99 P, para. 266. *See also Sugar*, ECJ Dec. 16, 1975, 1975 ECR 1663, paras 173–174; *Züchner*, ECJ July 14, 1981, 1981 ECR 2021, paras 13–14; *Polypropylene – Rhône-Poulenc*, CFI Oct. 24, 1991, 1991 ECR II-867, para. 121; *UK Agriculture Registration Exchange – John Deere*, CFI Oct. 27, 1994, 1994 ECR II-957, paras 87, 97 and 101; *aff'd* ECJ 28 May 1998, 1998 ECR I-3175, paras 86–88.

future conduct, but it is not necessary for a coherent plan of action to have been devised.[73] As the Court of Justice held in the *Sugar* case,[74] competition presupposes:

> 'that each economic operator must determine independently the policy which he intends to adopt on the Common Market including the choice of the persons and undertakings to which he makes offers or sells. Although it is correct to say that this requirement of independence does not deprive economic operators of the right to adapt themselves intelligently to the existing or anticipated conduct of their competitors, it does however strictly preclude any direct or indirect contact between such operators, the object or effect whereof is either to influence the conduct on the market of an actual or potential competitor or to disclose to such a competitor the course of conduct which they themselves have decided to adopt or contemplate adopting on the market.'[75]

Concerted practices that infringe Article 81 need not necessarily lead to visible anticompetitive effects in the marketplace; the less apparent effects of a concerted practice which prevent prices from falling to a lower level or maintain prices within a certain range are equally prohibited.[76]

Evidence of Concerted Practices.
Two main sources of evidence of a concerted practice are:

- direct evidence of coordination, i.e., plans, meetings, minutes of meetings, exchange of confidential market information or other close contacts,[77] and
- indirect evidence of coordination inferred from the participation in an information exchange system and joint discussions of the exchanged data,[78] or from the

73. *Polypropylene-Rhône Poulenc*, CFI Oct. 24, 1991, 1991 ECR II-867, para. 121; *UK Agricultural Registration Exchange*, ECJ May 28, 1998, 1998 ECR I-3175, para. 86; *Carton – Stora*, CFI May 15, 1998, 1998 ECR II-2111, paras 111–112.
74. *Sugar*, ECJ Dec. 16, 1975, 1975 ECR 1663, paras 173–174.
75. *See also British Sugar, Tate & Lyle*, CFI July 12, 2001, 2001 ECR II-2035, paras. 55–56.
76. *Polypropylene*, D.Comm. April 23, 1986, 1986 OJ L 230/1, 29; *aff'd* CFI Oct. 24, 1991, 1991 ECR II-867, para. 121; *aff'd* ECJ July 8, 1999, 1999 ECR I-4539, paras 122–123; *PVC II*, D.Comm. July 29, 1994, 1994 OJ L 239/14; *aff'd* CFI April 20, 1999, 1999 ECR II-931, para. 743.
77. *Polypropylene – Atochem*, CFI Oct. 24, 1991, 1991 ECR II-867, paras 120–127; *PVC II*, CFI April 20, 1999, 1999 ECR II-931, paras 715–730; *Polypropylene – Montecatini*, ECJ July 8, 1999, 1999 ECR I-4539, paras 133–148.
78. *See* in an horizontal context: *Polypropylene – Atochem*, CFI Oct. 24, 1991, 1991 ECR II-1177, paras 43–44 and 52–57; in a vertical context: *Dunlop-Slazenger*, CFI July 7, 1994, 1994 ECR II-441, para. 106.

market behaviour of the parties which cannot be explained otherwise than by collusion,[79] e.g., similarity of timing and amount of price increases, systematic refusal to deal with certain customers or to deliver to certain destinations.[80]

Usually the Commission's findings are supported by direct documentary evidence showing that market behaviour was coordinated.[81] If the case rests on indirect, circumstantial evidence, this must be clear and not be rebutted by other objective circumstances.[82] The evaluation of whether a concerted practice exists must be made in the overall context of the particular market and its structure.[83] An examination must always be made of whether the parallel conduct can be explained by normal market conditions or *must* have been coordinated.[84] Such coordination has been found if several competitors create an institutional framework which unavoidably leads to agreement, e.g.:

79. *SACEM III*, ECJ July 13, 1989, 1989 ECR 2521, paras 20–26; *P&O/Stena/Brittany Ferries*, D.Comm. Oct. 30, 1996, 1997 OJ L 26/23, para. 58.
80. *See* in an horizontal context: *Cement – Aalborg*, ECJ Jan 7, 2004, C-204/00 P, paras. 279–297; in a vertical context: *Volkswagen*, CFI July 6, 2000, 2000 ECR II-2707, para. 234, *aff'd* ECJ Sept. 18, 2003, C-338/00P; *JCB*, CFI Jan. 13, 2004, T-67/01, paras. 85–108; *Nintendo*, D.Comm. Oct. 30, 2002, 2003 OJ L 255/3, points 102–238 (evidence of collusion to empede parallel imports). In the *Italian Flat Glass* case the Court partly upheld the Commission's decision with respect to the conclusion that parallel announcements of similar price lists constitute an infringement, but partly annulled the decision for lack of proof: *Italian Flat Glass*, CFI March 10, 1992, 1992 ECR II-1403, paras 314–333. *See also Sugar*, ECJ Dec. 16, 1975, 1975 ECR 1663, paras 285–294; *Asturienne – Rheinzinc*, ECJ March 28, 1984, 1984 ECR 1679, paras 10–20. The Court accepted, however, other economic explanations as contradicting a concertation in: *Woodpulp*, ECJ March 31, 1993, 1993 ECR I-1307, paras 72, 118.
81. *See*, e.g., *Graphite Electrodes*, D.Comm. July 18, 2001, 2002 OJ L 100/1, points 51–59; *Dutch Industrial and Medical Gases*, D.Comm. July 24, 2002, 2003 OJ L 84/1, points 332–353 (system of regular meetings proving a cartel).
82. E.g., *Nederlandse Federatieve Vereniging voor de Groothandel op Elektrotechnisch Gebied*, CFI Dec. 16, 2003, T-5/00, paras. 192–209 (Commission decision upheld); *Italian Flat Glass II*, D.Comm. Dec. 7, 1988, 1989 OJ L 33/44, 61; *rev'd* CFI March 10, 1992, 1992 ECR I-1407, paras 172–173 (Commission decision annulled). It must be established, as Advocate General Mayras suggested in the *Dyestuffs* case: 'first, that the conscious parallel behaviour is not exclusively or even mainly due to economic conditions or to the structure of the market; secondly, that, where there is no express meeting of minds, sufficiently clear, unequivocal presumptions lead to the conviction that the parallel conduct was the result of concertation, of a coordinated policy'. *See ICI-Dyestuffs*, ECJ July 14, 1972, 1972 ECR 619, 673.
83. *See* the analysis made in *ICI-Dyestuffs*, ECJ July 14, 1972, 1972 ECR 619, paras 64–119; *Philip Morris/Rothmans*, ECJ Nov. 17, 1987, 1987 ECR 4487, paras 40–51.
84. *Sugar*, ECJ Dec. 16, 1975, 1975 ECR 1663, paras 295–304, 311–364; *Asturienne-Rheinzinc*, ECJ March 28, 1984, 1984 ECR 1679, paras 10–20; *Polypropylene – Petrofina*, CFI Oct. 24, 1991, 1991 ECR II-1087, paras 92–93, 128–130, 156 and 254.

- if the participants announce price increases in advance,[85]
- if a manufacturer enters into an arrangement to supply markets outside of its home market only through a competing manufacturer located there and refuses to supply dealers or consumers there except at prices coordinated with the local manufacturer,[86]
- if an ongoing information exchange system is established covering competitively sensitive data, such as prices and sales,[87]
- if a reciprocal distribution system is implemented whereby competitors agree to supply one another's customers in their own home market in the competitor's name,[88] or
- if market conduct is coordinated through a joint venture network[89] or through common board members.[90]

It is not necessary to prove that the participants invariably followed the concerted strategy; evidence of collusion is not rebutted by instances of independent behavior.[91] Article 81 (1) forbids any collusion that allows competitors to rely upon the market conduct of the others at least at critical moments, such as when responding to price increases.[92] Evidence of a concerted practice may be confirmed by the fact that the participants stand to gain from coordination of their conduct, for example

85. *ICI-Dyestuffs*, ECJ July 14, 1972, 1972 ECR 619, paras 83–119; *Polypropylene*, D.Comm. April 23, 1986, 1986 OJ L 230/1, 28; *aff'd* CFI Oct. 24, 1991, 1991 ECR II-1177, paras 125–126.
86. *Sugar*, ECJ Dec. 16, 1975, 1975 ECR 1663, paras 126–192; *Vegetable Parchment*, D.Comm. Dec. 23, 1977, 1978 OJ L 70/54, 61 ('These facts confirm that ... there was a concerted practice between Wiggins Teape and the member manufacturers of the GVPA, who delivered vegetable parchment regularly to the British undertaking. The concerted practice consisted in the continental manufacturers ... refraining from supplying other United Kingdom users while at the same time agreeing to supply Wiggins Teape with the quantities of the product it needed to fill its production gap and thus meet the entire British demand for vegetable parchment').
87. *Züchner*, ECJ July 14, 1981, 1981 ECR 2021, paras 12–21; *Woodpulp II*, ECJ March 31, 1993, 1993 ECR I-1307, paras 131–132, 160–161; *SPO-Dutch Construction Works*, CFI 21 Feb. 1995, 1995 ECR II-289, para. 117; *Cement*, CFI March 15, 2000, 2000 ECR II-491, para. 1465 and 1514. *See Methionin*, D.Comm. July 2, 2002, IP/02/976; *Plasterboard*, D.Comm. Nov. 27, 2002, IP/02/1744; *Food Flavor Enhancer Cartel*, Dec. 17, 2002, IP/02/1907. Any decision prohibiting price collusion may extend to the restrictive patterns of price information: *Carton – Stora*, CFI May 14, 1998, 1998 ECR II-2111, paras. 111–112 (*aff'd* ECJ Nov. 16, 2000, 2000 ECR I-9925).
88. *Fison-UCB/Hoechst*, Sixth Report on Competition Policy, points 126–128.
89. *Optical Fibers*, D.Comm. July 14, 1986, 1986 OJ L 236/30, 36–37.
90. *IMI/Heilmann I*, Seventh Report on Competition Policy, points 29–32; *Pilkington/BSN*, Tenth Report on Competition Policy, points 152–155; *Philip Morris/Rothmans*, ECJ Nov. 17, 1987, 1987 ECR 4487, paras 46–47.
91. *Polypropylene – Petrofina*, CFI Oct. 24, 1991, 1991 ECR II-1087, paras 152–183 (affirming D.Comm. April 23, 1986, 1986 OJ L 230/1, 29–30).
92. *Ibid.*, *Sugar*, ECJ Dec. 16, 1975, 1975 ECR 1663, paras 172–176, 293.

because it is the only way of raising prices on a depressed market,[93] or by the opposite, namely that parallel conduct runs counter to the economic interests of individual participants to increase their own market share,[94] especially if there are substantial cost differences between producers or major variations in market conditions across the various markets affected.[95] However, the Commission is obliged to evaluate whether the circumstances do not permit another explanation of the suspicious conduct. In the *Asturienne* case, an alleged concerted practice to protect the German market was contradicted by evidence that the Belgian producer had filled orders from the customer suspected of exporting to Germany and that the termination of deliveries to the customer could be explained by ordinary commercial reasons, namely non-payment of invoices.[96] In the *Woodpulp* case, an alleged price coordination deduced from parallel price increase announcements was contradicted by the existing price transparency on the oligopolistic market, insignificant cost differences and the prompt reports on price initiatives by agents and the press.[97]

Vertical Concerted Practices.

The prohibition of concerted practices that have an anticompetitive object or effect[98] also encompasses vertical arrangements involving firms at different stages of production and distribution.[99] Typically the parties have entered into a long-term supply, distribution or sales agreement which is supplemented by informal anticompetitive arrangements extending beyond the text of the agreement to certain other market conduct of the purchaser (e.g., not to export, or to maintain resale prices), and it is obvious to the purchaser that observance of those arrangements is an unwritten condition for obtaining supplies.[100] Here, too, it is not necessary

---

93. *Polypropylene*, D.Comm. April 23, 1986, 1986 OJ L 230/1, 28–29; *aff'd* CFI Oct. 24, 1991, 1991 ECR II-1177, para. 228.
94. *Italian Flat Glass II*, D.Comm. Dec. 7, 1988, 1989 OJ L 33/44, 63–64; *aff'd* – in this respect – CFI March 10, 1992, 1992 ECR II-1403, paras 193–196.
95. *ICI-Dyestuffs*, ECJ July 14, 1972, 1972 ECR 619, paras 107–110.
96. *Asturienne-Rheinzinc*, ECJ March 28, 1984, 1984 ECR 1679, paras 10–20.
97. *Woodpulp II*, ECJ 31 March 1993, 1993 ECR I-1307, paras 85–88, 123–124, overruling D.Comm. 19 Dec. 1984, 1985 OJ L 85/1, 16–19.
98. *JCB*, CFI Jan. 13, 2004, T-67/01, para. 117; *General Motors – Opel*, CFI Oct. 21, 2003, T-368/00, para. 104.
99. *Pioneer*, ECJ June 7, 1983, 1983 ECR 1825, paras 72–80; *Hasselblad*, ECJ Feb. 21, 1984, 1984 ECR 883, paras 24–29.
100. *AEG/Telefunken*, ECJ Oct. 25, 1983, 1983 ECR 3151, paras 35–39; *Tipp-Ex*, ECJ Feb. 8, 1990, 1990 ECR I-261, para. 21; *Johnson & Johnson*, D.Comm. Nov. 25, 1980, 1980 OJ L 377/16, 23; *Peugeot*, D.Comm. Dec. 4, 1991, 1992 OJ L 66/1; *aff'd* CFI April 22, 1993, 1993 ECR II-495; *Dunlop – Slazenger*, CFI July 7, 1994, 1994 ECR II-441, paras 54–56; *Van Megen/Tretorn*, CFI Dec.11, 1996, 1996 ECR II-1791; *VW/Audi*, CFI July 7, 2000, 2000 ECR II-2707, paras 162–169); *Accinauto*, CFI 19 May 1999, 1999 ECR II-1635, para. 83; *Nintendo*, D.Comm. Oct. 30, 2002, IP/02/1584. *See also Volkswagen II*, D.Comm. June 29,

to distinguish clearly between 'agreement' and 'concerted practice', provided the parties engage in coordinated conduct on the market in some form.[101] However, agreements and concerted practices must be clearly distinguished from unilateral conduct.[102]

Acting on Complaints by Customers or Competitors.
If a firm receives complaints from a competitor about competition from its products and adapts its conduct accordingly, the conduct is likely to amount to a concerted practice. It does not matter who took the initiative, who acted first and who reacted. Such actions are common not only in horizontal relations between competitors,[103] but also in vertical relations where a manufacturer receives complaints from a dealer in one country about parallel imports from another country and takes measures in order to halt the parallel imports, thereby restricting competition between the dealers.[104]

(d) Recommendations

Recommendations are not expressly mentioned as means of anticompetitive coordination. However, they may be the object of an agreement or decision, and they may also constitute or lead to a concerted practice.

Horizontal Recommendations.
Recommendations that are the object or effect of a horizontal agreement between competitors or stem from a decision taken by an association of such competitors are judged critically because of the element of horizontal cooperation. In this case, the recommendation need not lead to uniform behaviour. For instance, a price recommendation that has no binding effect on members of the association and is only partly followed is prohibited because it permits the membership to identify their competitors' price policy and thereby is likely to have an appreciable effect on price competition.[105] Price recommendations may be tantamount to fixing prices

---

2001, 2001 OJ L 262/14; *Daimler Chrysler*, D.Comm. Oct. 10, 2001, 2002 OJ L 257/1, point 125 (concertation by means of circular letters).

101. *AEG-Telefunken*, ECJ Oct. 25, 1983 ECR 3151, paras 35–39; *Ford II*, ECJ Sept. 17, 1985, 1985 ECR 2725, paras 25–26.
102. *Dunlop-Slazenger*, CFI July 7, 1994, 1994 ECR II-441, para. 54 , and *Volkswagen I*, ECJ Sept. 18, 2003, C-338/00 P, para. 60; *Volkswagen II*, CFI Dec. 3, 2003, T-208/01, paras 33–36 (collusive behavior); *Bayer*, Oct. 26, 2000, 2000 ECR II-3383, paras. 66–71, and *General Motors – Opel*, CFI Oct. 21, 2003, T-368/00, paras. 78–88 (unilateral behavior).
103. *Sugar*, ECJ Dec. 16, 1975, 1975 ECR 1663, paras 279–283.
104. *Tipp-Ex*, D.Comm. July 10, 1987, 1987 OJ L 222/1, 7–8 (*aff'd* ECJ Feb. 8, 1990, 1990 ECR I-261); *Volkswagen*, CFI July 6, 2000, 2000 ECR II-2707, para 117.
105. *Dutch Cranes*, CFI Oct. 22, 1997, 1997 ECR II-1739, para. 157; *FENEX*, D.Comm. June 5, 1996, 1996 OJ L 181/28, para. 72–73. *See VCH*, ECJ Oct. 17, 1972, 1972 ECR 977, paras 15–25; *FEDETAB*, ECJ Oct. 29, 1980, 1980 ECR 3125, paras 85–89; *Anseau*, ECJ Nov. 8,

when they are published, in particular when they aim at improving margins.[106] The Commission has frequently challenged horizontal recommendations by associations which clearly seek to coordinate the conduct of the addressees.[107]

Vertical Recommendations.
A simple *unilateral recommendation* – such as where a manufacturer suggests retail prices to its distributors – may bring about a certain uniformity of market conduct without infringing Article 81.[108] However, a recommendation addressed by a seller to a buyer may lead to a concerted practice if it is followed by the buyer and monitored or policed by the seller. This is especially the case with selective distribution systems that are ostensibly based on objective qualitative criteria for admission to the network, but in fact succeed in maintaining recommended prices and/or to limit or halt parallel imports.[109]

2. Object or Effect

The Economic Context.
Article 81 (1) prohibits agreements, decisions and concerted practices whose 'object or effect' is the prevention, restriction or distortion of competition within the Common Market. The 'object or effect' of an agreement, decision or concerted practice must be assessed as a whole in its economic context and in particular in the light of the situation on the relevant market.[110] A written agreement must be evaluated not only by reference to what is written but also to the context in which it is made.[111] In the *Philip Morris* case, for instance, the Court of Justice analysed whether the acquisition by one company of a minority interest in a competitor had an anticompetitive object or effect. The Court reviewed not only whether the agreements included clauses with an anticompetitive object, but also whether the actual

1983, 1983 ECR 3369, paras 18–21; *Fire Insurance*, ECJ Jan. 27, 1987, 1987 ECR 405, paras 26–32 (*see also* Advocate General Darmon at 1987 ECR 436–439).

106. *Dutch Cranes*, CFI Oct. 22, 1997, 1997 ECR II-1739, para. 159; *FENEX*, D.Comm. June 5, 1996, 1996 OJ L 181/28, para. 61.

107. *Italian Banks*, D.Comm. Dec. 12, 1986, 1987 OJ L 43/51, 52–53; *Steel Stockholders*, D.Comm. Feb. 8, 1980, 1980 OJ L 62/28, 34; *Vimpoltu*, D.Comm. July 13, 1983, 1983 OJ L 200/44, 48; *Dutch Cranes*, D.Comm. Nov. 29, 1995, 1995 OJ 312/79 (fine of ECU 11.5 million, *aff'd* CFI Oct. 22, 1997, 1997 ECR II-1739); *FENEX*, D.Comm. June 5, 1996, 1996 OJ L 181/28 (symbolic fine because of parties' cooperation in the Commission's investigation). Under Article 65 ECSC Treaty: *Steel Stockholders*, D.Comm. Feb. 8, 1980, 1980 OJ L 62/28; *Preinsulated Pipes – LR af 1998*, CFI March 10, 2002, 2002 ECR II-1705, para. 39.

108. *Pronuptia*, ECJ Jan. 28, 1986, 1986 ECR 353, para. 25. *See* Guidelines on Article 81 (3), point 12.

109. *Hasselblad*, ECJ Feb. 21, 1984, 1984 ECR 883, paras 47–52; *AEG/Telefunken*, ECJ Oct. 25, 1983, 1983 ECR 3151, paras 40–43.

110. *General Motors – Opel*, CFI Oct. 21, 2003, T-368/00, para. 102.

111. *Philip Morris/Rothmans*, ECJ Nov. 17, 1987, 1987 ECR 4487, paras 32–64.

effect of the acquisition agreement would be to restrict competition and whether it was potentially an instrument for influencing the commercial conduct of a competitor.[112] Therefore, a clear distinction between object and effect is not necessary for applying Article 81 (1), particularly if potential effects are taken into account as they were by the Court of Justice in the *Philip Morris* case.[113] However, the question whether an arrangement had restrictive effects is relevant when it comes to assessing the gravity of the violation for the purpose of imposing fines.[114]

Anticompetitive 'Object'.

The object to restrict competition must result from the agreement itself without need to prove intention on the part of the parties to restrict competition.[115] If an object to restrain competition is evident, then the agreement itself, or at least any anticompetitive clause in the agreement, constitutes a restraint of competition 'by its very nature', and its effects on the market[116] and damage to customers need not be examined.[117] Agreements create an institutional framework through which the parties sacrifice their autonomous competitive conduct and instead observe group

112. *Philip Morris/Rothmans*, ECJ Nov. 17, 1987, 1987 ECR 4487, paras 37–59. The Court said (at paras 37–40) that the acquisition of an equity stake could 'serve as an instrument for influencing the commercial conduct of the companies in question so as to restrict or distort competition on the market on which they carry on business. That will be true in particular where, by the acquisition of a shareholding or through subsidiary clauses in the agreement, the investing company obtains legal or *de facto* control of the commercial conduct of the other company or where the agreement provides for commercial cooperation between companies or creates a structure likely to be used for such cooperation. That may also be the case where the agreement gives the investing company the possibility of reinforcing its position at a later stage and taking effective control of the other company. Account must be taken not only of the immediate effects of the agreement but also of its potential effects and of the possibility that the agreement may be part of a long-term plan. Finally, every agreement must be assessed in its economic context and in particular in the light of the situation on the relevant market. Moreover, where the companies concerned are multinational corporations which carry on business on a world-wide scale, their relationships outside the Community cannot be ignored. It is necessary in particular to consider the possibility that the agreement in question may be part of a policy of global cooperation between the companies which are party to it'.
113. *Philip Morris/Rothmans*, ECJ Nov. 17, 1987, 1987 ECR 4487, paras 54–59.
114. *BMW Belgium*, ECJ July 12, 1979, 1979 ECR 2435, paras 39–48; *Belasco*, D.Comm July 10, 1986, 1986 OJ L 232/15, 26, 30–31.
115. *CMA CGM – FETTCSA*, CFI March 19, 2003, T-213/00, para. 183. *See* Guidelines on Article 81 (3), points 21–22.
116. *Welded Steel Mesh – Ferrière Nord*, ECJ July 17, 1997, 1997 ECR I-4411, paras 14–15; *Volkswagen*, CFI July 6, 2000, 2000 ECR II-2707, para. 178 (with further references); *Pre-insulated Pipes – LR af 1998*, CFI March 20, 2002, 2002 ECR II-1847, para. 47. *See also UK Agricultural Tractor Exchange System – John Deere*, CFI Oct. 27, 1994, 1994 ECR II-1957, paras 61, 92; *Alloy Surcharge*, D.Comm. Jan. 21, 1998, 1998 OJ L 100/55, point 49; *Polypropylene – Montecatini*, ECJ July 8, 1999, 1999 ECR II-4539, paras 122–123 (*horizontal*); *BASF Coatings*, CFI May 19, 1999, 1999 ECR II-1581, para. 139 (vertical).
117. *Krupp Thyssen*, CFI Dec. 13, 2001, 2001 ECR II-3757, paras. 151–154.

discipline. For this reason merely entering into an anticompetitive agreement is prohibited, even if, temporarily, it may not be followed or its objects achieved.[118] Thus, anticompetitive agreements that have not yet been implemented[119] or have not been strictly implemented[120] infringe Article 81 (1) and may be held valid only if the conditions of Article 81 (3) are fulfilled. This accords with the purpose of Article 81, which is to combat actions which threaten competition; the provision is designed to discourage even the possibility of anticompetitive effects occurring.

Object must be Clear but not Necessarily Achieved.
The object of the agreement, decision or concerted practice must be sufficiently clear. Agreements and decisions are often explicit enough for an anticompetitive purpose to be evident without confirmation from other sources. Nevertheless, the circumstances and context of the agreement or decision are usually relevant and in many cases crucial for removing any possible doubt as to the purpose behind it.[121] In the case of concerted practices, i.e., collusion falling short of a formal agreement, the anticompetitive intent of the participants can be inferred from their actions and the background against which the conduct took place.[122] As already noted, the presence of an anticompetitive object does not depend on the apparent effectiveness of the restrictive practice.[123] For example, the fact that a distributor fails to observe an export prohibition strictly or does not apply sanctions to violators does not prove that the threatened sanctions were ineffective. Even an export prohibition which is not strictly observed or vigorously enforced may nevertheless act as a strong psychological barrier to exporting and thus succeed in its object of dividing markets.[124] Similarly, the fact that prices that were fixed or coordinated

118. *Belasco*, ECJ July 11, 1989, 1989 ECR 2117, para. 15; *Sandoz ll*, ECJ Jan. 11, 1990, 1990 ECR I-45, para. 13; *Polypropylene – Atochem*, CFI Oct. 24, 1991, 1991 ECR II-1177, paras 100, 187.
119. Under Regulation 17, *see Henkel/Colgate I*, D.Comm. Dec. 23, 1971, 1972 OJ L 14/14; *Franco-Japanese Ballbearings Agreement*, D.Comm. Nov. 29, 1974, 1974 OJ L 343/19. Under Regulation 1/2003 the scope of Article 81 (1) is automatically limited by the exception of Article 81 (3).
120. *JCB*, CFI Jan. 13, 2004, T-67/01, para. 117.
121. *Maschinenbau Ulm*, ECJ June 30, 1966, 1966 ECR 235, 249–250; *AEG-Telefunken*, ECJ Oct. 25, 1983, 1983 ECR 3151, paras 39 and 44–46; *Anseau*, ECJ Nov. 8, 1983, 1983 ECR 3369, paras 22–25.
122. *PVC II*, D.Comm. July 27, 1994, 1994 OJ L 239/14, paras 35–38 (*aff'd* CFI April 20, 1999, 1999 ECR II-931, and ECJ Oct. 15, 2002, 2002 ECR I-8375).
123. *See* in case of a bid-rigging cartel: *SPO Dutch Construction Works*, CFI Jan. 12, 1993, 1993 ECR II-1, paras 199–203; in case of anticompetitive exchange of commercially sensitive information: *Woodpulp II*, ECJ March 31, 1993, 1993 ECR I-1307, para. 132.
124. *Miller International*, ECJ Feb. 1, 1978, 1978 ECR 131, paras 6–7; *Sandoz II*, ECJ Jan. 11, 1990, 1990 ECR I-45, para. 18; *Parker Pen*, CFI July 14, 1994, 1994 ECR II-549, para. 55.

were not strictly followed by all or certain participants[125] or that higher discounts were granted than were allowed in an agreement does not indicate that the agreement was totally ineffective.[126] The anticompetitive effect of coordinated attempts to implement price increases may result from the exchange of information about prices when deviations from the targets are discussed and from the monitoring system that is set up.[127] Almost inevitably, some convergence of prices will result. Likewise, the fact that price recommendations based on an agreement or a decision by a trade association do not entirely succeed in securing the recommended behaviour does not disprove their anticompetitive object.[128]

Anticompetitive 'Effects'.

Even if no anticompetitive object is established, an agreement, decision or concerted practice will still infringe Article 81 (1) if it has anticompetitive *effects*. The effects must arise from the agreement, decision or concerted practice. Only those consequences of the agreement that are inherent or obvious are relevant; this requires a determination of the 'natural and probable consequences'.[129] The Court of Justice has stated that where an analysis of the clauses of an agreement 'does not reveal the effect on competition to be sufficiently deleterious, the consequences of the agreement should then be considered and for it to be caught by the prohibition it is then necessary to find that those factors are present which show that competition has in fact been prevented or restricted or distorted to an appreciable extent'.[130] The effects of the agreement include not only the immediate effects but also the potential future effects and the possibility that the agreement may be part of a long-term plan or wider cooperation.[131] It is also possible that parts of the agreement that individually do not infringe Article 81 (1) produce anticompetitive effects in combination with one another.[132] The anticompetitive effects need not have an impact immediately in the marketplace or be perceptible to other market operators.[133] Some of the restrictive practices to which Article 81 (1) applies concern immediately only relations between the participants, such as

125. The individual abstention does not preclude an infringement as long as the cartel has an overall impact on the market (= passive participation): *Polypropylene-Atochem*, CFI Oct. 24, 1991, 1991 ECR II-1117, paras 262–277; *Polypropylene-Herkules*, CFI Dec. 17, 1991, 1991 ECR II-1715, paras 271–272.
126. *See Belasco*, ECJ July 11, 1989, 1989 ECR 2117, para. 15.
127. *Steel Beams – Thyssen Stahl*, CFI March 11, 1999, 1999 ECR II-347, paras 373–378, 398.
128. *Fire Insurance*, ECJ Jan. 27, 1987, 1987 ECR 405, paras 39–42.
129. *IFTRA Aluminium*, D.Comm. July 15, 1975, 1975 OJ L 228/3, 8. *See* Guidelines on Article 81 (3), points 24–26.
130. *Maschinenbau Ulm*, ECJ June 30, 1966, 1966 ECR 235, 249.
131. *Philip Morris/Rothmans*, ECJ Nov. 17, 1987, 1987 ECR 4487, paras 37–59; *Cement – Aalborg Portland*, ECJ Jan. 7, 2004, C-204/00P, para. 258.
132. *Philip Morris/Rothmans*, ECJ Nov. 17, 1987, 1987 ECR 4487, paras 60–63.
133. *PVC II*, D.Comm. July 27, 1994, 1994 OJ L 239/14, para. 38, *aff'd* ECJ Oct. 15, 2002, 2002 ECR I-8375.

agreements to limit production or coordinate technical development or investment. Likewise, the exchange of commercially sensitive information, which may not have an immediately perceptible impact in the marketplace, has been found to violate Article 81 (1) insofar as it enables competitors to take their business decisions with knowledge of each other's market strategy and intentions.[134] Even agreements which have been formally terminated may still have anticompetitive effects.[135]

Effect of Parallel Agreements.

The effects of an anticompetitive agreement may be reinforced if there are parallel agreements between the same firms or between third parties.[136] An example is where several suppliers impose parallel exclusive purchasing obligations or have selective distribution networks, which may prevent suppliers in other member states from gaining access to the national market where such parallel restrictions are employed. The existence of such parallel agreements 'is a circumstance which, together with others, is capable of being a factor in the economic and legal context within which the contract must be judged';[137] agreements which are, as such, of minor importance, may infringe Article 81 (1) by the cumulative effects of parallel networks of similar agreements.

3. RESTRAINT OF COMPETITION

Restrictions – Non-Exhaustive List of Examples.

Article 81 (1) prohibits the 'prevention, restriction or distortion of competition', i.e. the restriction of the freedom of the parties individually and autonomously to decide their own market policy, contrary to the requirement of economic independence.[138] Article 81 (1) gives as examples:

---

134. *Wood Pulp*, D.Comm. Dec. 19, 1984, 1985 OJ L 85/1, 20; *Fatty Acids*, D.Comm. Dec. 2, 1986, 1987 OJ L 3/17, 22–23; *Polypropylene – Atochem*, CFI Oct. 24, 1991, 1991 ECR II-1177, paras 54, 166, 112; *John Deere*, CFI Oct. 21, 1994, 1994 ECR II-957, para. 101; *SPO – Dutch Construction Works*, CFI 21 Feb. 1995, 1995 ECR II-289, para. 117.
135. *EMI/CBS*, ECJ June 15, 1976, 1976 ECR 811, paras 30–32; *Binon/AMP*, ECJ July 3, 1985, 1985 ECR 2015, para. 11; *Polypropylene-Herkules*, CFI Dec. 17, 1991, 1991 ECR II-1715, para. 257.
136. *SABA II*, ECJ Oct. 22, 1986, 1986 ECR 3021, paras 40–47; *Hesbignonne*, ECJ April 19, 1988, 1988 ECR 1919, para. 18.
137. *Haecht I*, ECJ Dec. 12, 1967, 1967 ECR 407, 416; *Concordia*, ECJ Feb. 1, 1977, 1977 ECR 65, paras 25–33; *Henninger Bräu*, ECJ Feb. 28, 1991, 1991 ECR I-935, paras 14–27; *Langnese-Iglo*, CFI June 8, 1995, 1995 ECR II-1533, para. 99; *VGB*, CFI May 14, 1997, 1997 ECR II-759.
138. *See VISA International*, D.Comm. July 24, 2002, 2002 OJ L 318/17, points 64–66; *Sugar*, ECJ Dec. 15, 1975, 1975 ECR 163, paras 173–174.

- fixing purchase or selling prices or other terms of trade;
- limiting or controlling production, markets, technical development or investment;
- sharing markets or sources of supply;
- discriminatory practices; and
- tying arrangements.

This list of examples is not exhaustive. Competition may be restricted by other means. For example, Article 81 (1) prohibits not only agreements discriminating against purchasers or suppliers (Article 81 (1) (d)) but also those directed at third parties.[139] Furthermore, agreements may restrict third parties by foreclosing the market as in the case of collective aggregated rebate schemes[140] or collective boycott.[141] These examples represent only special cases of the application of a general clause. Article 81 (1) may therefore also apply to anticompetitive restrictions not expressly included in any of these examples. The various forms of restraint of competition are addressed in later chapters as follows:

- horizontal agreements in Chapter III,
- vertical agreements in Chapter IV,
- restrictions in the framework of mergers, joint ventures and minority shareholdings in Chapter VI, and
- technology transfer agreements in Chapter VII.

No Substantial Difference between Prevention, Restriction and Distortion of Competition.

An agreement or concerted practice infringes Article 81 (1) if it has as its object or effect the 'prevention, restriction or distortion of competition'. The term 'prevention' is the most severe form of anticompetitive conduct and the most easily identified. It includes the elimination of existing or potential competitive activities by, for instance, dividing markets among competitors or prohibiting exports by dealers. The term 'restriction' implies that the extent of competitive activity is reduced or virtually eliminated. Consequently, 'prevention' and 'restriction' can sometimes apply to identical conduct. Competition is considered to be restricted whenever firms cease to determine their market behaviour independently, but co-ordinate it with others. The term 'distortion' is the broadest concept, which has been applied only in rare cases.[142] It denotes an artificial alteration of competitive conditions in favour of the parties, such as when a private levy is charged on the

139. *Sugar*, ECJ Dec. 15, 1975, 1975 ECR 1663, paras 522–527.
140. *NSO*, ECJ Dec. 10, 1985, 1985 ECR 3801, paras 32–49.
141. *See Dutch Cranes*, CFI Oct. 22, 1997, 1997 ECR II-1739, paras 141–146.
142. *Cf.* Article 87 (1) of the EC Treaty in which distortion of competition is the basis for the prohibition of government subsidies to the industry.

parties' domestic production in order to subsidize their exports[143] or when a levy on both domestic and foreign operators is refunded only to domestic firms or the proceeds are mainly used for their benefit.[144]

Horizontal v. Vertical Restrictions of Competition.
Article 81 (1) applies to agreements concluded by two or more enterprises operating at the same level of the supply chain (horizontal agreements) or between two or more enterprises operating at different levels of supply (vertical agreements) irrespective of whether they concern *intra-brand* and *inter-brand* competition.[145] Although vertical agreements are generally less harmful than horizontal agreements, they may retard the process of market integration which is one of the Community's prime objectives.[146]

Restriction of Competition between the Parties or *vis-à-vis* Third Parties.
Competition may be restricted between the parties (inter-party competition) or with respect to third parties (third-party competition).[147]

- *Restrictions of competition between the parties*: Such a restriction is defined by the Court of Justice, in a *horizontal* context, strictly in the sense of a limitation of the parties' freedom of independence and autonomous action by knowingly substituting practical cooperation between them for the risks of competition. As the Court of Justice held in the *Sugar* case,[148] competition presupposes

  > 'that each economic operator must determine independently the policy which he intends to adopt on the Common Market including the choice of the persons and undertakings to which he makes offers or sells. Although it is correct to say that this requirement of independence does not deprive economic operators of the right to adapt themselves intelligently to the existing or anticipated conduct of their competitors, it does however strictly preclude

---

143. *Cimbel*, D.Comm. Dec. 22, 1972, 1972 OJ L 303/24, 33; *Milk Promotion Fund*, D.Comm. Dec. 7, 1984, 1985 OJ L 35/35, 40; *Dutch Construction Works*, D.Comm. Feb. 5, 1992, 1992 OJ L 92/1, point 96; *aff'd* CFI Feb. 21, 1995, 1995 ECR II-289 and ECJ March 25, 1996, 1996 ECR I-1611.
144. *EATE*, D.Comm. July 10, 1985, 1985 OJ L 219/35, 41–42; *aff'd ANTIB*, ECJ May 20, 1987, 1987 ECR 2201, paras 19–23.
145. *Langnese-Iglo*, CFI June 8, 1995, 1995 ECR II-1533, para. 94. *See* in greater detail Chapter IV.A.2. *See also* Guidelines on Article 81 (3), points 17, 18 and 26.
146. *See* Commission's Follow-up to the Green Paper on Vertical Restraints, 1998 OJ C 365/3, 9. Leading cases: *Grundig/Consten*, ECJ July 13, 1966, 1966 ECR 299, 339 (distribution); *Pronuptia*, ECJ Jan. 29, 1986, 1986 ECR 353, paras 24–26 (franchise); *Maize Seed*, ECJ June 8, 1982, 1982 ECR 2015, paras 64–67 (licence).
147. *Langnese-Iglo*, CFI June 8, 1995, 1995 ECR II-1533, para. 94; *aff'd* ECJ Oct. 1, 1998, 1998 ECR I-5609. *See* Commission guidelines on the application of the EC competition rules in the telecommunications sector, 1991 OJ C 233/2, point 65.
148. *Sugar*, ECJ Dec. 16, 1975, 1975 ECR 1663, paras 173–174.

any direct or indirect contact between such operators, the object or effect whereof is either to influence the conduct on the market of an actual or potential competitor or to disclose to such a competitor the course of conduct which they themselves have decided to adopt or contemplate adopting on the market.'[149]

– *Restrictions of competition* vis-à-vis *third parties*: Vertical restraints may also restrict competition by one of the parties or third parties. The Court of Justice ruled in the *Delimitis/Henninger Bräu* case with respect to exclusive purchase obligations in beer agreements:[150]

  'In order to assess whether the existence of ... agreements impedes access to the market as so defined, it is further necessary to examine the nature and the extent of those agreements in their totality, comprising all similar contracts tying a large number of points of sale to several national producers. The effect of those networks of contracts on access to the market depends specifically on the number of outlets thus tied to national producers in relation to the number ..., the duration of the commitments entered into, the quantities of beer to which the commitments relate, and on the proportion between those quantities and the quantities sold by free distributors .... In that connection it is necessary to examine whether there are real concrete possibilities for a new competitor to penetrate ... or to circumvent the bundle of contracts ....'

  Thus, exclusive purchasing agreements may not prevent, restrict or distort competition appreciably between two parties, but a *network* of exclusive purchasing agreements may *collectively* reinforce barriers to entry that make access to the market by third parties an appreciable restraint of competition.[151] This applies with even greater force to non-compete clauses in horizontal agreements between competitors which aim at preventing competing activities likely to frustrate the success of their joint efforts to enter a new market.[152]

Actual v. Potential Competition.

A restraint of competition exists not only if actual, but also if potential, competition is restrained. The reason for treating actual and potential competitors similarly is that the firms already operating on the market are influenced in their

149. *See also Züchner*, ECJ July 14, 1981, 1981 ECR 2021, paras 13–14; *Polypropylene – Rhône-Poulenc*, CFI Oct. 24, 1991, 1991 ECR II-867, para. 121; *Wood Pulp II*, ECJ March 31, 1993, 1993 ECR I-1307, paras 131–132; *UK Agriculture Registration Exchange – John Deere*, CFI Oct. 27, 1994, 1994 ECR II-957, paras 87, 97 and 101; *aff'd* ECJ May 28, 1998, 1998 ECR I-3175, paras 86–88.

150. *Delimitis/Henninger Bräu*, ECJ Feb. 28, 1991, 1991 ECR I-935, paras 19 and 21.

151. *Schöller*, CFI June 8, 1995, 1995 ECR II-1611, para. 75.

152. *VGB*, May 14, 1997, 1997 ECR II-759, para 140. With regard to a network of joint ventures, *see Optical Fibers*, D.Comm. July 14, 1986, 1986 OJ L 236/30, 34–35. *See* Commission Telecommunications Guidelines, 1991 OJ C 233/2, points 56–59.

market conduct by the possibility of entry by a potential competitor. Whether potential competition is likely to be restrained depends on an analysis of the facts and circumstances of the relevant market (e.g. taking into account increasing globalization and innovation in the markets[153]) and the parties' individual competitive capacities and the conditions of market entry. In the *European Night Service* case,[154] which concerned an agreement between different railways to run night passenger trains between the United Kingdom and the Continent, the Court of First Instance ruled:

> 'It must be stressed that the examination of the conditions of competition is based not only on existing competition, in order to ascertain whether, in the light of the structure of the market and the economic and legal context within which it functions, there are real concrete possibilities for the undertakings concerned to compete among themselves or for a new competitor to penetrate the relevant market and compete with the undertakings already established.'[155]

The Commission treats a firm as *an actual competitor*

> 'if it is either active on the same relevant market or if, in the absence of the agreement, it is able to switch production to the relevant products and market them in the short term without incurring significant additional costs or risks in response to a small and permanent increase in relative prices (immediate supply-side substitutability). The same may lead to the grouping of different geographic areas.'[156]

The Commission treats a firm as *a potential competitor*

---

153. Twenty-sixth Report on Competition Policy, points 53–65; Twenty-seventh Report on Competition Policy, points 70–80; Twenty-eigth Report on Competition Policy, point 134 (insert 5).
154. *European Night Service*, CFI Sept. 15, 1998, 1998 ECR II-3141, para. 137.
155. *See also Delimitis/Henniger Bräu*, ECJ Feb. 28, 1991, 1991 ECR I-935, para. 21; Commission Notice on the assessment of cooperative joint ventures (Appendix 6), point 18. Potential competition affirmed but exemption under Article 81 (3) granted: *ACI* (*Allied Continental Intermodal Services*), D.Comm. July 27, 1994, 1994 OJ L 224/28 (implicitly confirmed by the Court of First Instance in *European Night Services*, CFI Sept. 15, 1998, 1998 ECR II-3141, para. 156); *Ford/Volkswagen*, D.Comm. Dec. 23, 1992, 1993 OJ L 20/14; *aff'd Matra/Ford-Volkswagen*, CFI July 15, 1994, 1994 ECR II-595 (setting-up of a joint venture for producing a new van); *ACI* (*Eurotunnel*), D.Comm. July 27, 1994, 1994 OJ L 224/28 (setting-up of a joint venture for providing combined rail transport for vehicles and containers through the Channel tunnel). Potential competition affirmed by the Commission but denied by the Court of First Instance: *European Night Service*, D.Comm. Sept. 21, 1994, 1994 OJ L 259/20; *rev'd* CFI Sept. 15, 1998, 1998 ECR II-3141.
156. Commission Notice on horizontal cooperation, 2001 OJ C 3/2, fn. 8.

> 'if there is evidence that, absent the agreement, this firm could and would be likely to undertake the necessary additional investments or other necessary switching costs so that it could enter the relevant market in response to a small and permanent increase in relative prices. This assessment has to be made on realistic grounds, the mere theoretical possibility to enter a market is not sufficient.'[157]

Accordingly, a firm has been regarded as *a potential competitor*, thereby necessitating individual exemption when establishing a joint venture

- in cases of a *new product market*, e.g. an engine alliance for producing and marketing a new engine,[158] and a joint venture for entering the pay TV market,[159] in both cases subject to commitments because of the possible spill-over effect on neighbouring markets;
- in cases of a *new geographic market*, e.g. the creation by two competitors within the Community of a joint venture for starting production outside the Community.[160]

Potential competition has been *denied*, thereby justifying negative clearance in the case of a joint venture for providing combined rail transport for vehicles and containers through the Channel tunnel,[161] and an agreement assuring waste disposal[162] where the joint venture partners did not have the resources necessary for entering the market individually.

Express v. Implied Restrictions of Competition.

A restriction of competition may be the result of an express contractual obligation or may be implied by agreements which do not contain express restrictive clauses but provide for a long-term technical or commercial relationship. Long-term supply agreements on an important part of the purchaser's requirements may, even if they do not include an express exclusivity obligation, prevent the purchaser from switching to other suppliers and thereby restrict competition between suppliers.[163]

157. Commission Notice on horizontal cooperation, fn. 9.
158. *GEAE/P&W*, D.Comm. Sept. 14, 1999, 2000 OJ L 58/16 (*see* point 86).
159. *British Interactive Broadcasting*, D.Comm. Sept. 15, 1999, 1999 OJ L 312/1 (*see* points 139–141).
160. *Solvay/Sisecam*, D.Comm. Sept. 25, 1999, 1999 OJ C 272/14 (comfort letter after removal of active sales bans).
161. *European Night Services*, CFI Sept. 15, 1998, 1998 ECR II-3141, thereby overruling the Commission which affirmed potential competition and granted an exemption: D.Comm. Sept. 21, 1994, 1994 OJ L 259/20.
162. *Green Dot*, D.Comm. Sept. 17, 2001, 2001 OJ L 319/1; *ARA*, D.Comm. Oct. 16, 2003, 2004 OJ L 75/59.
163. *See* in greater detail Chapter IV.B.10.(d).

Competitors may enter into joint ventures and renounce competing activities in the joint ventures' field of activity, thereby restricting competition between them or between them and third parties ('group effect' and 'spill-over effect').[164] Competitors may conclude partnership agreements with respect to a well-defined part of their businesses: development and production of a new product, rationalization or coordination of strategic decisions (therefore frequently called 'strategic alliances'). The common features of such agreements are the lack of precise clauses, the statement of vague objectives, and a system of reciprocal ongoing exchanges on technical and/or commercial data necessary for defining the objectives and means of the work in the field in which the partnership or strategic alliance is to operate. Such agreements may be caught by Article 81 (1) in so far as they institutionalize between competitors a framework which affects the 'requirement of independence' by substituting practical cooperation for the risks of competition.[165] However, such a restriction may be held 'ancillary' and compatible with Article 81 (1) if it is strictly necessary, in scope and duration, for a proper functioning of the agreement and if that agreement itself is compatible with the competition rules.[166]

Voluntary v. Compelled Anticompetitive Conduct.
Government involvement does not change the character of an agreement between firms nor take the agreement out of reach of Article 81 so long as the government does not assert its sovereign authority to compel the anticompetitive conduct,[167] or to require observance of an anticompetitive agreement,[168] and as long and in so far as the firms, although possibly influenced by the government,[169] retain their own initiative and a discretion of action.[170] For example, the existence of an agricultural market organization and the fixing of production quotas do not preclude

164. *See* in greater detail Chapter VI.F.2.
165. The 'requirement of independence' may therefore be used twice for both sides of the same coin: for detecting a 'concerted practice' as well as for identifying a 'restriction of competition'.
166. *See* section C.2. *infra*. *See also* Guidelines on Article 81 (3), points 28–31.
167. *BNIC I*, ECJ Jan. 30, 1985, 1985 ECR 391, paras 16–25; *British Telecommunications*, ECJ March 20, 1985, 1985 ECR 873, paras 18–20; *Woodpulp I*, ECJ Sept. 27, 1988, 1988 ECR 5193, para. 20; *Ladbroke III*, ECJ Nov. 11, 1997, 1997 ECR I-6265, para. 33; *Polypropylene-Montecatini*, ECJ July 8, 1999, 1999 ECR II-4539, para. 127. *See* in greater detail *infra* Chapter VI.
168. *Flemish Travel Agents*, ECJ Oct. 1, 1987, 1987 ECR 3801, paras 22–24; *Höfner/Macrotron*, ECJ April 23, 1991, 1991 ECR I-1979, paras 26–27; *Greek Television Monopoly*, ECJ June 23, 1991, 1991 ECR I-2925, para. 38; *Almelo*, CFI Nov. 18, 1992, 1992 ECR II-2417, para. 106; *Ladbroke II*, CFI Sept. 18, 1995, 1995 ECR II-2568, paras 46–48; *Asia Motors*, CFI Sept. 18, 1995, 1995 ECR II-961, paras 60–69.
169. *COAPI*, D.Comm. Jan. 30, 1995, 1995 OJ L 122/37, paras 44–48.
170. *Ladbroke III*, ECJ Nov. 11, 1997, 1997 ECR I-6265, paras 33–34; *Flower Auctions Aalsmeer*, D.Comm. July 26, 1988, 1988 OJ L 262/27.

the responsibility of the firms for their own anticompetitive initiative within such governmental framework.[171] The mere participation of government representatives in the drafting of the agreement[172] or retroactive governmental approval[173] is not sufficient. Similarly, the setting of a regulatory framework for fixing tariffs does not preclude a 'restriction of competition' if the firms agree among themselves on a fixed amount and modalitites of that tariff.[174] 'Voluntary agreements' between industry and public administrations are agreements that can restrict competition and therefore need clearance under Article 81 (3).[175] However, pressures by government bodies to enter into anticompetitive agreements may be taken into consideration as mitigating factor.[176]

4. Relevant Market

Need to Define the Relevant Market.
The relevant market and the parties' shares of that market are key parameters for the evaluation under Article 81, under Article 82 and under the merger control regulation.[177] In Article 81 cases involving hardcore restrictive practices, such as price fixing, allocation of customers and territories, etc., that are not eligible for exemption under Article 81 (3) and so do not require an assessment of whether the parties can eliminate competition, the Commission and the Court did not always evaluate the precise position of the parties in the relevant market. The Commission's decisions contained only a general description of the products concerned, the structure of the market and competitive conditions on the market, without determining the exact market shares of the parties and their competitors.[178] Recently, the Commission[179] and the Court of Justice[180] have considered the definition of the relevant market in a more systematic way as a 'necessary precondition of

171. *Sugar*, ECJ Dec. 16, 1975, 1975 ECR 1663, paras; 36–73; *Welded Steel Mesh – Ferrière Nord*, ECJ July 17, 1997, 1997 ECR I-4411, para. 25.
172. *BNIA*, D.Comm. July 26, 1976, 1976 OJ L 231/24, 27; *BNIC I*, ECJ Jan. 30, 1985, 1985 ECR 391, paras 18–25.
173. *Franco-Japanese Ballbearings Agreement*, D.Comm. Nov. 29, 1974, 1974 OJ L 343/19, 23.
174. *CNSD I*, ECJ June 18, 1998, 1998 ECR I-3851, paras 58–60; *CNSD II*, CFI March 20, 2000, 2000 ECR II-1807, paras. 56–74. But *see Albany*, ECJ Sept. 21, 1999, 1999 ECR I-5751, paras 59–60 (collective agreements between employers and workers).
175. Twenty-fourth Report on Competition Policy, paras 83–85; *Franch-Taiwanese Mushroom Packers*, D.Comm. Jan. 8, 1975, 1975 OJ L 29/26. *See Asia Motor France*, CFI Sept. 18, 1996, 1996 ECR II-961, para. 60.
176. *French Federations in the beef sector*, D.Comm. April 2, 2003, IP/03/479.
177. *See* in greater detail Chapter I.C.
178. Guidelines on Article 81 (3), point 27. *See*, e.g., *Dutch Construction Works*, D.Comm. Feb. 5, 1992, 1992 OJ L 92/1; *aff'd* CFI Feb. 21, 1995, 1995 ECR II-289 and ECJ March 25, 1996, 1996 ECR I-1611.
179. Commission notice on the definition of the relevant market, 2001 OJ C 368/13.
180. *See Italian Flat Glass* (*SIV*), CFI March 10, 1992, 1992 ECR II-1407, para. 159.

any judgment concerning allegedly anticompetitive behaviour'. In the *European Night Services* case[181] the Court of First Instance ruled:

> 'it must be borne in mind that in assessing an agreement under Article 85 (1) of the Treaty, account must be taken of the actual conditions in which it functions, in particular the economic context in which the undertakings operate, the products or services covered by the agreement and the actual structure of the market concerned'.[182]

The Commission and the Court of Justice therefore undertake a precise market analysis particularly in order to evaluate:

- Whether the effects of an agreement are appreciable or '*de minimis*'.[183]
- Whether an agreement qualifies for the application of a block exemption regulation within the limits of any applicable market shares thresholds.
- Whether the agreement appreciably limits market access of third parties.[184]
- Whether the agreement is concluded between actual or potential competitors.[185]
- Whether the agreement affords the possibility of eliminating competition with respect to a substantial part of the relevant market (Article 81 (3) (b)).
- Whether the gravity of the infringement merits substantial fines.[186]

However, the exact definition of the relevant market is not necessary for the purposes of Article 81 where an infringement concerns different markets and the parties have a strong position on each of those markets.[187]

Definition of the Relevant Market.
The definition of the relevant market is addressed in Chapter I.C. The relevant market is defined mainly by an analysis of the relevant products and geography and sometimes the relevant time period.

---

181. *European Night Services*, CFI Sept. 15, 1998, 1998 ECR II-3141, para. 136.
182. *See also* in case of horizontal agreements: *Gottrup Klim*, Dec. 15, 1994, 1994 ECR I-5641, para. 31; *Oude Luttikhuis Coberco*, ECJ Dec. 12, 1995, 1995 ECR I-4515, para. 10; *VGB*, CFI May 14, 1997, 1997 ECR II-759, para. 140. In case of vertical agreements: *Delimitis/Henninger Bräu*, ECJ Feb.28, 1991, 1991 ECR I-935, paras 19–20; *Langnese-Iglo*, CFI June 8, 1995, 1995 ECR II-1533, para. 60 *aff'd* ECJ Oct. 1, 1998, 1998 ECR I-5609.
183. Commission notice on agreements of minor importance (*De Minimis* Notice) 2001 OJ C 368/13.
184. *See*, e.g., *Delimitis/Henninger Bräu*, ECJ Feb. 28, 1991, 1991 ECR I-935, paras 19–22.
185. *European Night Services*, CFI Sept. 15, 1998, 1998 ECR II-3141, para. 136.
186. *See*, e.g., *Cement*, CFI March 15, 2000, 2000 ECR II-491, para. 4846.
187. *Nederlandse Federatieve Vereniging voor de Groothandel op Elektrotechnisch Gebied*, CFI Dec. 16, 2003, T-5/00, paras. 117–124.

The *relevant product market* generally includes all those products and/or services which are regarded as interchangeable or substitutable by the customer, by reason of the product's characteristics, price and intended use.[188]

The *relevant geographic market* generally comprises the area in which the undertakings concerned are involved in the supply and demand of products or services, in which the conditions of competition are sufficiently homogeneous and which can be distinguished from neighbouring areas because the conditions of competition are appreciably different in those areas.[189]

The *relevant time period* has played a role mainly in cases involving the assessment of trade fairs under Article 81.[190] In such cases the relevant time period is the period between trade fairs organized by the same organizer; the portion of that period in which non-compete obligations (i.e., not to take part in a competing trade fair) are imposed on exhibitors determines whether the agreement between organizer and exhibitors is unduly restrictive.

No Need of Systematic Market Analysis in Case of Hardcore Restrictions. The Commission[191] and the Court of Justice[192] consider that agreements containing hardcore ('*per se*') restrictions, such as price fixing, market-sharing, resale price maintenance or territorial protection, may infringe Article 81 (1) even if the aggregate market shares of the parties remain below the *de minimis* thresholds. This may explain why the Commission did not proceed to a detailed market analysis in cases of horizontal and vertical agreements containing hardcore restrictions although the assessment of the gravity needs careful consideration of the effects on the relevant market. Often a restrictive agreement defines itself the relevant market because otherwise the restriction would not be effective.[193] However, the evaluation of whether the agreement is likely to eliminate competition in relation to a substantial part of the products in question (Article 81 (3) (b)) necessarily presupposes the determination of the relevant market.[194]

188. Commission 1997 Notice on the Definition of the Relevant market , point 7.
189. *Ibid.*, point 8.
190. E.g., *ANCIDES*, ECJ July 9, 1987, 1987 ECR 3131, paras. 19–20 (restrictive trade fair agreement).
191. Commission notice on the definition of the relevant market, point 11.
192. *Volkswagen I*, CFI July 6, 2000, 2000 ECR II-2707, paras. 179 and 230–231.
193. *Recent examples: Pre-insulated Pipes*, D.Comm. Oct. 21, 1998, 1999 OJ L 24/1, *aff'd* CFI March 20, 2002, 2002 ECR II-1845 (horizontal prices and quota fixing arrangement); *VW/Audi*, D.Comm. Jan. 28, 1998, 1998 OJ L 124/60, *aff'd* CFI July 6, 2000, 2000 ECR II-2707 (vertical market sharing).
194. E.g., *M6 – Eurovision II*, CFI Oct. 8, 2002, 2002 ECR II-3805, para. 51.

5. Appreciability of Restrictions of Competition

(a) Appreciability v. Rule of Reason

Economic Assessment.
The system of Article 81 – a general prohibition of restraints attenuated by the grant of exemption – implies a rather broad interpretation of 'restraints' to be covered by Article 81 (1) leaving the evaluation of any economic advantages to the Commission's scrutiny under Article 81 (3). Unlike the U.S. antitrust law, no automatic '*rule of reason*' test applied.[195] However, the Court of Justice stated in its early decisions that a restraint of competition and its effect on trade between the member states must be 'appreciable' for the restraint to infringe Article 81 (1).[196] The Court judges appreciability in the light of the economic and legal setting of the agreement and its object and effects, including the cumulative effects of possible parallel agreements without anticipating or supplanting the assessment under Article 81 (3).[197] The Court does not apply a quantitative test for appreciability, but in several cases has concluded that appreciable effects would be lacking, in spite of absolute territorial protection of an exclusive distributor, if the agreement 'has only an insignificant effect on the markets, taking into account the weak position which the persons concerned have on the market of the product in question'[198] without commenting on the Commission's notices on Agreements of minor importance although the Advocate General has referred to it in several cases.[199] However, in its more recent decisions the Court seems not to exclude any qualitative test similar to the 'rule of reason'. In the *Polypropylene* case the Court stated:

> 'Furthermore, the fact that the infringement of Article 81 (1) of the EEC Treaty, in particular subparagraphs (a), (b) and (c), is a clear one precludes the application of a rule of reason assuming such rule to be applicable in Community competition law, since in that case it must be regarded as an infringement *per se* of the competition rules'.[200]

---

195. *M6 Métropole télévision*, CFI Sept. 18, 2001, 2001 ECR II-2459, paras 72–78.
196. *See also supra* Chapter I.B.2 and the Commission's recent proposals in its White Paper, 1999 OJ C 132/1.
197. *Maschinenbau Ulm*, ECJ June 30, 1966, 1966 ECR 235, 249–250; *Haecht I*, ECJ Dec. 12, 1967, 1967 ECR 407, 415–416; *Bilger/Jehle*, ECJ March 18, 1970, 1970 ECR 127, para. 5; *Delimitis/Henninger Bräu*, ECJ Feb. 28, 1991, 1991 ECR I-935, para. 19; *Langnese-Iglo*, CFI June 8, 1995, 1995 ECR II-1533, paras 98–99.
198. *Volk/Verwaecke*, ECJ July 9, 1969, 1969 ECR 295, 302; *Cadillon/Hoss*, ECJ May 6, 1971, 1971 ECR 351, paras 9–10. *See* Guidelines on Article 81 (3), point 18 (2).
199. *See* Advocate General De Lamotte in *Cadillon/Hoss*, ECJ May 6, 1971, 1971 ECR 351, 360–362; Advocate General De Lamotte in *Beguelin*, ECJ Nov. 25, 1971, 1971 ECR 949, 968; Advocate General Warner in *Miller International*, ECJ Feb. 1, 1978, 1978 ECR 131, 157–160.
200. *Polypropylene – Montedipe*, CFI March 10, 1992, 1992 ECR II-1155, para. 265.

An appreciability test in the sense of a detailed market analysis is therefore not necessary in cases of hardcore or '*per se*' restrictions.[201] Such restrictions may infringe Article 81 (1) even if the parties' market shares do not exceed the thresholds of the *De Minimis* Notice.[202] This approach has been generalized in its notice on the definition of the relevant market.[203] However, the appreciability test is still not to be confused with the substantially broader 'rule of reason' in the United States, which calls for a general evaluation of relevant facts and includes the type of analysis made when determining whether or not to grant an exemption under Article 81 (3).[204]

*(b) Quantitative Appreciability: The Commission's Notice on Agreements of Minor Importance (*De Minimis *Notice)*

Market Share Thresholds Only.

The Commission's 2001 *De Minimis* Notice sets minimum quantitative thresholds before the Commission considers there to be an appreciable restriction of competition.[205] The Commission holds the view that agreements do not give grounds for action by the Commission[206] and even do not fall under Article 81 (1) at all[207] if the aggregate market shares held by all participants do not exceed:

- 10% where the agreement is made by undertakings operating on the same market level ('horizontal' agreements),
- 15% where the agreement is made between undertakings operating on different economic levels ('vertical' agreements);[208]

---

201. *Volkswagen*, CFI July 6, 2000, 2000 ECR II-2707, point 179 (with further references).
202. In a horizontal context: *European Night Services*, CFI Sept. 15, 1998, 1998 ECR II-3141, para. 136; in a vertical context: *Delimitis/Henninger Bräu*, ECJ Feb. 28, 1991, 1991 ECR I-935, para. 26; *BASF Coatings*, CFI May 19, 1999, 1999 ECR II-1581, para. 133.
203. 1997 OJ C 372/5, point 11.
204. *M6 Metropole télévision*, CFI Sept. 18, 2001, 2001 ECR II-2459, paras 72–78.
205. Notice on Agreements of Minor Importance which do not Appreciably Restrict Competition, 2001 OJ C 368/13; similarly with respect to Article 53 of the EEA Agreement: Notice of the EFTA Surveillance Authority of March 20, 2003, 2003 OJ C 67/20. The effect on trade between member states is 'quantified' according to different criteria: Notice on the effect on trade concept, point 52, namely a market share exceeding 5% and a minimum turnover of EUR 40 million: Commission's Guidelines on the Effect on Trade Concept.
206. *De Minimis* Notice, point 5. *See* the *Relais & Chateaux* case which has been settled for this reason, DG IV Newsletter 1998–1, p. 49.
207. This statement extends to the consequences under civil law, however without binding the national courts (*De Minimis* Notice, point 7).
208. 2001 OJ C 368/13, point 7. This 2001 Notice supersedes that of 1997 which fixed market share thresholds of respectively 5% (horizontal) and 10% (vertical) (1997 OJ C 372/6) and the previous notices which fixed a single market share threshold of 5% for both horizontal and vertical agreements but whose turnover limit steadily increased over time: 1970 Notice: ECU 15 million (1970 OJ C 64/1); 1977 Notice: ECU 50 million (1977 OJ C 313/3); 1986

- 10% in the case of mixed horizontal/vertical agreements,[209] and
- 5% in the case of agreements having a cumulative effect[210] (which may exist where the cumulative foreclosure effect is more than 30%[211]).
  All these thresholds may be exceeded by two percentage points during two successive calender years and can still be considered as *de minimis*.[212]

In addition, the Commission considers that agreements between small and medium-sized undertakings [213] having fewer than 250 employees and either an annual turnover not exceeding EUR 40 million or an annual balance-sheet total not exceeding EUR 27 million do not fall under Article 81 (1).[214]

Effects of the *De Minimis* Notice.
The *De Minimis* Notice does not set absolute yardsticks:

- Agreements between undertakings having a aggregate market share of less than the minimum thresholds may nevertheless infringe Article 81 (1) if their object is to fix prices or to limit production or sales or to share markets or sources of supply.[215] These restrictions constitute hardcore or '*per se*' restrictions[216] although they may, under exceptional circumstances, qualify for an exemption under Article 81 (3). However, the Commission does not intend to take action against such agreements except in cases of Community interest, unless the agreements impair the proper functioning of the internal market.
- Agreements between companies with market shares *exceeding* the thresholds of the *De Minimis* Notice may still have only a negligible effect on competition and may therefore not be prohibited by Article 81 (1).[217] Such agreements may nevertheless escape the prohibition of Article 81 (1) on account of (i) their 'exclusively favourable impact on competition'[218] (which may be understood as anticipating a more general '*rule of reason*') or (ii) the qualification of the participants as small and medium-sized undertakings as defined in the *De Minimis*

Notice: ECU 200 million (1986 OJ C 231/2); and 1994 Notice: ECU 300 million (1994 OJ C 368/20).

209. *De Minimis* Notice, point 7.
210. *Ibid.*, points 7 and 8.
211. *Ibid.*, point 8.
212. *Ibid.*, point 9.
213. As defined in Commission Recommendation 2003/361/EC (2003 OJ L 124) replacing Recommendation 96/280/EC.
214. *De Minimis* Notice, point 3.
215. This is in accordance with the Commission's previous case law, *see Miller International*, ECJ Feb. 1, 1978, 1978 ECR 131, paras 8–10; *BASF Coatings*, CFI May 19, 1999, 1999 ECR II-1581, para. 133 (absolute territorial protection in an exclusive distribution agreement).
216. *Volkswagen*, CFI July 6, 2000, 2000 ECR II-2707, point 179.
217. *De Minimis* Notice, point 2; *Bagnasco*, ECJ Jan. 21, 1999, 1999 ECR I-135, paras 34–35.
218. *De Minimis* Notice, point 3.

Notice, as noted above.[219]

- The Notice expresses the Commission's view and does not bind the Court of Justice or national competition authorities and courts which may take enforcement action under the EC competition rules or under national legislation irrespective of the parties' market shares, in particular in cases of '*per se*' restrictions. The jurisdiction of national courts to apply Article 81 (1) as well as to enforce Article 81 (2) derives from the direct effect of the competition rules irrespective of the Commission's views on its priorities. The Notice is nevertheless a factor which such courts may take into account when deciding a pending case.[220]
- The Notice gives legal certainty and immunity from fines. The Commission will not consider imposing fines in cases where the parties assumed in good faith that the agreement was covered by the Notice.[221] However, in cases of doubt the parties will, from 1 May 2004, no longer be free to notify the agreement to the Commission in order to obtain individual clearance[222] but only to request informal guidance in cases of 'genuine uncertainty'.[223]
- The Notice states that *individual* suppliers or distributors with a market share not exceeding 5% normally do not contribute significantly to a *cumulative* foreclosure effect[224] and that a cumulative foreclosure effect is unlikely to exist if less than 30% of the relevant market is covered by a parallel network of similar restrictive agreements. Regulation 2790/1999 on vertical restraints exempts agreements by *individual* suppliers or distributors whose market share does not exceed 30%.[225] However, the Commission is permitted to withdraw the benefit of the exemption where the *cumulative* effect of parallel networks covers more than 50% of the relevant market.[226] It may therefore be concluded

219. *Ibid.*, point 3. Small and medium-sized undertakings are defined according to their turnover and number of employees but without reference to their market shares.
220. *De Minimis* Notice, point 7; *European Night Services*, CFI Sept. 15, 1998, 1998 ECR II-3141, para. 136. *See supra* Chapter I.B.1, and *infra* Chapter X.I.
221. *De Minimis* Notice, point 5. *See Relais & Chateaux*, Twenty-seventh Report on Competition Policy, pp. 141–142.
222. *De Minimis* Notice, point 4.
223. Recital 38 to Regulation 1/2003.
224. *De Minimis* Notice, point 8. In its administrative practice the Commission applied a lower market share threshold: no significant contribution where the undertakings had a market share of less than 1% or 1.3% (Notice of 13 May 1992, 1992 OJ C 121/2; *Roberts/Greene King*, D.Comm. Nov. 30, 1998, points 99–106) but significant contribution and need of exemption under Article 81 (3) where the threshold of 1% was exceeded (*Whitbread*, D.Comm. Feb. 24, 1999, 1999 OJ L 88/26, point 130, *aff'd* CFI March 21, 2002, 2002 ECR II-2033).
225. This accords with the findings of the Court of First Instance in the case *Langnese-Iglo*, CFI June 8, 1995, 1995 ECR II-1533, paras. 94, 99–108. In the case *Van den Bergh Foods*, CFI Oct. 23, 2003, T-65/98, paras. 113–118 and 140, the level of market foreclosure was 40%.
226. Article 8 of Regulation 2790/1999. *See also* Article 6 of Regulation 1400/2002 on motor vehicle agreements.

that parallel networks of similar restrictive agreements are exempted under Regulation 2790/1999, unless (i) one of the suppliers or distributors contributing to the network has an *individual* market share exceeding 30% or (ii) the network covers *cumulatively* more than 50% *and* the Commission adopts a withdrawal decision, which has only a prospective effect.[227] This is likely to reduce the burden on national courts when assessing the legality of an agreement with a view of its contribution to a cumulative restrictive effect.[228]

(c) Qualitative Appreciability

Introduction.
It is also possible that the effect of an agreement is *qualitatively* not appreciable enough for Article 81 (1) to apply. Qualitative appreciability is a test which has been applied by the Court of Justice and the Commission under which a restriction that is objectively necessary to protect certain rights recognized as legitimate by the legal system escapes the application of Article 81 (1). One of the foremost examples of qualitative appreciability is the distinction between the *existence* and the *exercise* of intellectual property rights, which the Court of Justice has referred to since the *Deutsche Grammophon* decision[229] and which has been further developed and extended by both the Commission and the Court of Justice.[230] The basic principle is as follows: Whereas the Treaty does not affect the *existence* of rights recognized by the intellectual property law of a member state, the *exercise* of such rights may infringe the Treaty if it involves restrictions that are not justified for the purpose of safeguarding rights which constitute the essential function ('specific subject-matter') of such property. In the following other specific cases the Commission and the Court have acknowledged that the need to protect legitimate rights absolved the restraint of any qualitatively appreciable effect:

- A simple exclusive licence (without absolute territorial protection) for the production and marketing of newly developed products that is associated with

227. In the case *Langnese-Iglo*, CFI June 8, 1995, 1995 ECR II-1533, the Court of First Instance considered the degree of the cumulative effect as confidential (most probably it was about 2/3). *See* Chapter IV at p. 376.
228. The difficulties of assessing the cumulative foreclosure effect are highlighted in cases such as *Dymond v. Button*, English High Court July 24, 1975, 1976–1 CMLR 133; *Chemidus Wavin*, English High Court July 9, 1976, 1976–2 CMLR 387; *Eismann*, German State Appeals Court Koblenz, Oct. 26, 1984, WuWE OLG 3451; Karlsruhe, June 13, 1990, WuWE OLG 4577, and Stuttgart, Oct. 2, 1992, WuWE OLG 5073, 5080 *et seq.*; German Supreme Court (BGH), NJW 1992, 1456.
229. *Deutsche Grammophon*, ECJ July 8, 1971, 1971 ECR 487, paras 4–7.
230. *Coditel I*, ECJ March 18, 1980, 1980 ECR 881, paras 11–17; *Maize Seed*, ECJ June 8, 1982, 1982 ECR 2015, paras. 48–58; *Pronuptia*, ECJ Jan. 28, 1986, 1986 ECR 353, paras 15–22.

some risk;[231] licences granting absolute territorial protection[232] or reciprocal licence agreements between competitors, on the other hand, are considered as restraints of competition under Article 81 (1).[233]

- An exclusive licence agreement to show films, as long as the agreement is not excessively long and associated with unduly high royalties.[234]
- The licensing of intellectual property rights for specific fields of use.[235]
- An obligation not to grant sub-licences.[236]
- An obligation to maintain the confidentiality of licensed know-how.[237]
- The obligation to maintain the image and quality standards of a franchising system.[238]
- A non-competition clause upon the sale of a business if its substantive scope, geographic coverage and duration are necessary to guarantee the value of the assets transferred.[239]
- 'Ancillary' restrictions in connection with a merger or joint venture, i.e., restrictions which in duration, geographic scope and subject matter are directly related and necessary to implementation of the merger or are strictly necessary for the formation and operation of the joint venture.[240]
- Restrictions in subcontracting[241] and agency agreements[242] where the sucontrator is dependent on the principal's technology to carry out the work and the agent does not trade independently in the marketplace.

---

231. *Maize Seed*, ECJ June 8, 1982, 1982 ECR 2015, paras 48–58; *Sicasov*, D.Comm. Dec. 14, 1998, 1999 OJ L 4/27, point 53.
232. *Maize Seed*, ECJ June 8, 1982, 1982 ECR 2015, paras 60–65; *Sicasov*, D.Comm. Dec. 14, 1998, 1999 OJ L 4/27, point 62.
233. *Siemens/Fanuc*, D.Comm. Dec. 18, 1985, 1985 OJ L 376/29, 35–36. *See also* Article 4 (1) of Regulation 772/2004 on technology transfer agreements.
234. *Coditel II*, ECJ Oct. 6, 1982, 1982 ECR 3381, paras 8–20. Similarly, the exercise of design copyrights to prevent imports does not infringe Article 82, provided there is no discrimination and unduly high prices are not charged: *Renault*, ECJ Oct. 5, 1988, 1988 ECR 6039, paras 14–17; *Volvo/Veng*, ECJ Oct. 5, 1988, 1988 ECR 6211, paras 7–10.
235. Article 4 (1) (c) (i) of Regulation 772/2004. *See* Article 2 (1) (8) of Regulation 240/96.
236. *Sicasov*, D.Comm. Dec. 14, 1998, 1999 OJ L 4/27, point 53. *See* Article 2 (1) (2) of Regulation 240/96.
237. *See* Article 2 (1) (1) of Regulation 240/96.
238. *Pronuptia*, ECJ Jan. 28, 1986, 1986 ECR 353, paras 17–19. Under Regulation 2790/1999 included in the block exemption: Guidelines on vertical restraints, 2000 OJ C 291/2, points 184 and 199–201.
239. *Remia/Nutricia*, ECJ July 11, 1985, 1985 ECR 2545, paras 17–36.
240. On ancillary restraints in mergers *see* Commission's Notice on ancillary restraints, 2001 OJ C 188/5. Regarding ancillary restrictions in joint ventures *see infra* Chapter VI.F.1. and *Mitchell Cotts/Sofiltra*, D.Comm. Dec. 17, 1986, 1987 OJ L 41/31, 35–36. *See* Guidelines on Article 81 (3), points 28–31.
241. Notice on Subcontracting Agreements, 1979 OJ C 1/2; under Regulation 2790/1999 included in the block exemption up to the market share limit of 30%: Guidelines on horizontal cooperation, 2001 OJ C 3/2, point 80, and Article 4 (e) of Regulation 2790/1999.
242. Guidelines on vertical restraints, 2000 OJ C 281/2, points 12–20.

- The non-discriminatory application of objective, qualitative criteria for selecting dealers for a selective distribution system justified by the distribution requirements for the particular product and prohibiting authorized dealers from reselling to non-authorized dealers.[243]
- Prohibiting wholesalers in a selective distribution system from selling to private customers, in order to maintain the separation of functions of wholesaler and retailer.[244]
- Prohibiting any multi-disciplinary partnership between members of the bar and accountants, in so far as it is necessary for the proper practice of the legal profession.[245]

This principle of qualitative appreciability must be seen as a precursor of the more systematic economic evaluation of restrictions promoted by the Commission's White Paper,[246] its Green Paper[247] and Regulation 1/2003,[248] except when the agreement contains 'obvious' restrictions, such as price fixing, market sharing, resale price maintenance or absolute territorial protection.

6. Restrictions to Prevent Unfair Competition

Fair v. Unfair Competition.
The EC Treaty aims at removing existing obstacles 'in order to guarantee … fair competition' and at ensuring that competition in the Common Market is not 'distorted'.[249] Fair competition is primarily protected by the respective national unfair competition laws.[250] However, Article 81 also prohibits collective arrangements

243. *SABA I*, ECJ Oct. 25, 1977, 1977 ECR 1875, paras 20 and 26–27. Selective distribution systems are included in the block exemption granted by Regulation 2790/1999 even if they are based on objective, qualitative criteria, Article 4 (b).
244. *SABA I*, ECJ Oct. 25, 1977, 1977 ECR 1875, paras 28–30. Such restraints are included in the block exemption granted by Regulation 2790/1999: Article 4 (d).
245. *Orde van Vlaamse Balies*, D.Comm. Sept. 3, 2003, 2003 OJ C 207/22 (comfort letter), which accords with *Wouters*, ECJ Feb. 19, 2002, 2002 ECR I-1577, para. 123.
246. 1999 OJ C132/1.
247. Jan. 22, 1997, COM(96)72 final.
248. 2003 OJ L 1/1.
249. Preamble, Recital 4 and Article 3 (g) of the EC Treaty.
250. The differences between national unfair competition laws are significant, in particular in Germany and Austria with a very (probably overly) extensive protection of 'fair' competition on the one side while the United Kingdom prohibits only the most flagrant forms of unfair competition. Harmonization by Community directives is, up to now, rare and limited to comparative and deceptive publicity that is likely to mislead consumers: First Directive 84/450/EEC relating to the Approximation of the Laws, Regulations and Administrative Provisions of the Member States Concerning Misleading Advertising, 1984 OJ L 250/20, and Proposal for a Directive Concerning Comparative Advertising and Amending Directive 84/450/EC, 1994 OJ C 136/4.

on using means of unfair competition, in particular exclusionary practices, collusive tendering (bid-rigging),[251] the joint institution of a private levy on domestic production in order to subsidize exports[252] and boycotts.[253] Similarly, some forms of abuse of a dominant position prohibited under Article 82 constitute acts of unfair competition, such as exploitative abuses (unfair purchase or selling prices or other unfair trading conditions)[254] and predatory abuses (practices aiming at eliminating or impeding competitors).[255] Commitments to respect national unfair competition laws are as such compatible with EC competition law. However, if such commitments to prevent unfair competition are undertaken collectively by the majority of competitors in different member states they risk, in view of the considerable differences between national unfair competition laws, regulating behaviour on a Community-wide scale that may not be qualified as unfair competition in some member states and might therefore constitute an infringement of Article 81; i.e., comparative price advertising is very restricted in Germany but liberally permitted in the United Kingdom. Furthermore, it is often the implementation of such an agreement that is of key importance. If the definition of what is fair or unfair is left to the parties, a trade association, a trustee or a private arbitral tribunal that supplants the jurisdiction of the courts, then the arrangement may subject the parties to a joint discipline which, under the guise of a measure to halt unfair competition, is in fact designed to coordinate their conduct and to replace national courts by cartel-like behavior.[256]

National Unfair Competition Law and EC Free Movement of Goods and Competition Rules.

There are numerous differences in the scope of application and the practices covered by unfair competition laws of the member states. This may give rise to conflicts with Community law. The Court of Justice has held under Articles 28 and 30 that national unfair competition laws are enforceable, by states or by private parties, against the importation and marketing of goods insofar as necessary[257] to satisfy essential requirements of consumer protection or fair

251. *SPO – Dutch Construction Works*, CFI Feb. 21, 1995, 1995 ECR II-289, paras 157–158; *Preinsulated Pipes*, D.Comm. Oct. 21, 1998, 1998 OJ L 24/1 (*aff'd* CFI March 20, 2002, 2002 ECR II-1705).
252. *Milk Promotion Fund*, D.Comm. Dec. 7, 1984, 1985 OJ L 35/35.
253. *Belgian Wallpaper*, D.Comm. July 23, 1974, 1974 OJ L 237/3, 9 (annulled by ECJ because of insufficient proof of effects on trade between member states: ECJ Nov. 26, 1975, 1975 ECR 1491); *Preinsulated Pipes*, D.Comm. Oct. 21, 1998, 1999 OJ L 24/1, point 147 (*aff'd LR af 1998*, CFI March 20, 2002, 2002 ECR II-1705, para. 137).
254. *Ahmed Saaed*, ECJ April 11, 1989, 1989 ECR 803, para. 43.
255. *AKZO*, ECJ July 3, 1991, 1991 ECR I-3359, paras 72, 140, 146.
256. *SPO – Dutch Construction Works*, CFI Feb. 21, 1995, 1995 ECR II-289, para. 310. *See* Guidelines on Article 81 (3), point 47.
257. Proportionality test: *Yves Rocher*, ECJ May 18, 1993, 1993 ECR I-2361.

trading.[258] However, importation cannot be prevented if the goods have been marketed in accordance with the law of the member state of origin and this law satisfies the same essential requirements merely in a different manner from that of the state of importation.[259] In all cases the actual risk of the consumer being misled by the imported goods is the decisive factor.[260] This danger may sometimes be a real one, as when imported goods of substandard quality are passed off as the genuine article.[261] The Court has followed a similar approach in applying Article 81. It has held that agreements that abusively provide for or permit the enforcement of rights under national unfair competition law or of intellectual property rights in order to prevent parallel imports and to reinforce absolute territorial protection are caught by Article 81 (1).[262] On the other hand, the enforcement of such rights to the extent necessary to allow a commercial arrangement such as an exclusive distributorship to operate normally without conferring absolute territorial protection does not infringe the Article.[263] Nor

---

258. *Robertson*, ECJ June 22, 1982, 1982 ECR 2349, para. 9 (concerning the importation of silver-plated cutlery for which there are no EC-wide regulations governing hallmarking to protect the consumer).
259. *Ibid.*, paras 7–12.
260. *Ringelhan*, ECJ Nov. 6, 1984, 1984 ECR 3651 (impermissible under Articles 28 and 30 to apply German unfair competition law to prevent the importation of goods bearing a lawfully applied French trademark on the ground that the trademark, which was previously well-known as that of a now defunct German firm, would mislead consumers and thereby harm competitors); *GB-INNO-BM/CCL*, ECJ March 7, 1990, 1990 ECR I-667 (freedom of cross-frontier advertising not overridden by law on unfair competition which prohibits traders from advertising the duration of cut-price offers and the previous price of the goods); *Pall/Dahlhausen*, ECJ Dec. 13, 1990, 1990 ECR I-4844 (impermissible under Articles 28 and 30 to apply German unfair competition law to prevent the importation of goods lawfully marked in Italy with a trademark accompanied with the 'registered' sign ® on the ground that the trademark is not registered in Germany and the 'registered' sign is not permitted there and would mislead the consumer).
261. *Dansk Supermarked*, ECJ Jan. 22, 1981, 1981 ECR 181, paras 13–18. Here the issue was whether Danish unfair competition law could be relied upon to prevent the importation and sale in Denmark of substandard specimens of a china dinner service which a Danish trader had commissioned from a British manufacturer on terms which included a clause that rejects could be sold in the UK but not exported to Denmark. Dansk Supermarked had obtained stocks of the substandard items from UK dealers and was selling them in Denmark. The Court held that while the actual importation of goods that had been legally marketed in another member state could not be considered as an improper or unfair act, their marketing in such circumstances might legitimately be restrained under national unfair competition law.
262. *Béguelin*, ECJ Nov. 25, 1971, 1971 ECR 949, para. 14 (exclusive dealing agreement may infringe Article 81 if, owing to the combined effects of the agreement and of national legislation on unfair competition, the dealer is able to prevent parallel imports from other member states); *VAG Händlerrat/SYD*, ECJ June 5, 1997, 1997 ECR I-3223 (validity of selective distribution systems under Article 81 irrespective of the right or possibility to invoke unfair competition law under the respective national law in order to prevent parallel trade).
263. *Hydrotherm/Compact*, ECJ July 12, 1984, 1984 ECR 2999, paras 17–22.

does the exemption of distribution agreements between a manufacturer and its selected distributors under Article 81 (3) imply the qualification of the activity of parallel importers of motor vehicles as unfair competition.[264]

Private Agreements to Prevent Unfair Competition.
Agreements by which the parties enter into obligations to halt certain unfair competitive activities may be basically permissible and appropriate. This may apply to agreements in which the owners of trademarks define the limits of use of their marks in order to avoid confusion, conflicts or misleading consumers, as the Court of Justice held in the *Toltecs/Dorcet* case.[265] However, these worthy objectives will not excuse the use of such agreements for anticompetitive purposes or effects. Referring to its *Grundig/Consten* decision,[266] the Court went on to say that while trademark delimitation agreements are lawful and useful to define the areas within which trademarks may be used, such agreements are not beyond the scope of Article 81 if they also have the aim of dividing the market or restricting competition in other ways.[267] In the *Windsurfing* case the Court of Justice stated with respect to a requirement imposed on licensees, allegedly to prevent slavish imitation, a specific form of unfair competition, that they should submit their designs of sailboards for approval although the licensed patent covered only the windsurfing rig, not the board:

> 'In so far as the clause at issue enabled Windsurfing International to detect and prevent the slavish imitation of boards by licensees, there can be no doubt that the clause constituted a restriction on the freedom of competition. It substituted Windsurfing International's discretion for the decisions of national courts, which were the proper forum for actions by licensees who wished to obtain a finding that slavish imitation had taken place'.[268]

Cartels Disguised as Unfair Trading Rules.
Privately agreed 'fair trading' rules between the majority of sellers in a market under which the competitors as a group determine what is unfair, instead of leaving this to a court, may mask a comprehensive cartel covering a substantial part or the whole of an industry. Examples of agreements designed to prevent unfair competition but which have in fact anticompetitive effects that infringe Article 81 are the IFTRA cases concerning an agreement between glass manufacturers

264. *Nissan France*, ECJ Feb. 15, 1996, 1996 ECR I-677, para. 20.
265. *Toltecs/Dorcet*, ECJ Jan. 30, 1985, 1985 ECR 363, para. 33. *See also Terrapin/Termnova*, ECJ June 22, 1976, 1976 ECR 1039, para. 7 (trademark owner entitled to protection against importation of goods bearing confusingly similar mark).
266. *Grundig/Consten*, ECJ July 13, 1966, 1966 ECR 299, 344–346.
267. *Toltecs/Dorcet*, ECJ Jan. 30, 1985, 1985 ECR 363, paras 33–37.
268. *Windsurfing*, ECJ Feb. 25, 1986, 1986 ECR 611, para. 52.

prohibiting discriminatory prices, discounts or conditions or any secret departure from price lists[269] and an agreement between aluminium manufacturers prohibiting 'destructive sales below cost' or 'dumping'.[270] Price cartels tend to qualify the existing price competition as 'unfair' or even 'ruinous' even though it does not conflict with national unfair competition law at all but merely represents an inconvenient and undesired form of competition.[271] The protection of fair conditions of competition is a task for the courts and law enforcement agencies in compliance with Community law and not for the undertakings to regulate themselves.[272] Collusive tendering (bid-rigging) is clearly prohibited under Article 81 (1) even if the agreement aims at preventing 'unfair' competition.[273] The object of eliminating or preventing unfair competition (i.e. ruinous competition) may eventually be taken into account when considering the conditions of Article 81 (3) but normally fails the indispensability test and thus does not qualify for exemption.[274]

---

269. *IFTRA-Glass*, D.Comm. May 15, 1974, 1974 OJ L 160/1, 12.
270. *IFTRA-Aluminium*, D.Comm. July 15, 1975, 1975 OJ L 228/3, 8–9. Other examples include: *VCH*, D.Comm. Dec. 16, 1971, 1972 OJ L 13/34, 40 (agreement prohibiting price cutting); *Rolled Zinc*, D.Comm. Dec. 14, 1982, 1982 OJ L 362/40, 48 (obligation to comply with 'rules of fair competition' when selling goods obtained from third parties). The Commission's decision in the latter case was not overruled in this respect in *Asturienne-Rheinzinc*, ECJ March 28, 1984, 1984 ECR 1679. *See also Vimpoltu*, D.Comm. July 13, 1983, 1983 OJ L 200/44, 46 ('fair trading rules' covering discounts, payment and delivery terms, and sales promotions); *VBVB/VBBB*, ECJ Jan. 17, 1984, 1984 ECR 19, paras 35–37 (prohibition of 'loss leading'); *Aluminium Imports from Eastern Europe*, D.Comm. Dec. 19, 1984, 1985 OJ L 92/1, 43–44 (agreement between competitors within and outside the Community to control imports in order to avoid alleged dumping); *Meldoc*, D.Comm. Nov. 26, 1986, 1986 OJ L 348/50, 62 (Dutch cartel's 'dumping' of cheap milk on the Belgian market allegedly in retaliation for anticompetitive practices on the Belgian market by Belgian producers); *Zinc Producer Group*, D.Comm. Aug. 6, 1984, 1984 OJ L 220/27, 39 (alleged anticompetitive practices by competitors is no justification for coordinated retaliation); *Flemish Travel Agents*, ECJ Oct. 1, 1987, 1987 ECR 3801, paras 13–21 (agreement prohibiting travel agents from passing on part of their commission to customers); *Belasco*, ECJ July 11, 1989, 1989 ECR 2117, paras 17–18 (prohibition of free gifts and selling below cost); *Dutch Cranes*, CFI Oct. 22, 1997, 1997 ECR II-1739, paras 159–160 (recommending 'reasonable' rates to remedy instability in the market).
271. *Valsabbia*, ECJ March 18, 1980, 1980 ECR 907, para. 155; *Polypropylene – Montedipe*, CFI March 10, 1992, 1992 ECR II-1155, paras 289–297.
272. Guidelines on the application of Article 81 (3), point 42.
273. *SPO – Dutch Construction Works*, CFI Feb. 21, 1995, 1995 ECR II-289, paras 178, 280–290; *Pre-insulated Pipes*, D.Comm. Oct. 21, 1998, 1998 OJ L 24/1, point 147 (*aff'd* CFI March 20, 2002, 2002 ECR II-1705, para. 137) (collective boycott).
274. *VBVB*, ECJ Jan. 17, 1984, 1984 ECR 19, para. 37; *COAPI*, D.Comm. Jan. 30, 1995, 1995 OJ L 122/37, para. 42; *SPO-Dutch Construction Works*, CFI Feb. 21, 1995, 1995 ECR II-289, para. 310.

Vertical Agreements on Unfair Competition.
Distribution agreements may place an obligation on the dealer to observe national unfair competition laws, infringement of which may lead to the termination of the dealership status. Again it is the manufacturer who determines what is fair or unfair, for example whether low resale prices by the dealer are to be regarded as below cost and therefore unfair. The discretion the manufacturer typically has under such a clause may allow him to stop practices which are in fact quite legal and may serve as a disguised form of anticompetitive resale price maintenance.[275] In *SABA II* the Commission solved this problem by requiring that an alleged infringement of rules on unfair trading might lead to a termination of the contractual relationship only if the infringement was established in a national court or admitted by the dealer concerned.[276]

C. System of Article 81 (3)

1. The General Principle of Exemption

Competence to Grant Exemption.
Article 81 (3) provides for an exemption for anticompetitive agreements that infringe Article 81 (1). Exemption may be granted by regulation for certain categories of agreements (block exemption) or for clearance in individual cases (individual exemption) if the four conditions of Article 81 (3) are cumulatively fulfilled.[277]

(i) *Block exemption*: A block exemption requires a Council regulation delegating powers to the Commission to adopt a block exemption regulation for a specific category of agreements or practices. Such regulations have been adopted for certain horizontal agreements by Regulation 2821/71, for certain vertical agreements by Regulation 19/65 and Regulation 1534/91 for certain agreements in the insurance sector.[278] These regulations remain applicable under Regulation 1/2003.[279] However, the benefit of a block exemption may

275. *Hasselblad*, ECJ Feb. 21, 1984, 1984 ECR 883, paras 38–53.
276. *SABA II*, D.Comm. Dec. 21, 1983, 1983 OJ L 376/41, 43; *see also Grundig I*, D.Comm. July 10, 1985, 1985 OJ L 233/1, 5; *Grundig II*, D.Comm. Dec. 21, 1993, 1994 OJ L 20/15, point 33.
277. *See Eurovision I*, CFI July 11, 1996, 1996 ECR II-649, para. 93.
278. Regulation 2658/2000 on specialization agreements (2000 OJ L 304/3), Regulation 2659/2000 on R&D agreements (2000 OJ L 304/7), Regulation 2790/1999 on vertical restraints (1999 OJ L 36/21), Regulation 1400/2002 on vertical agreements in the motor vehicle sector (2002 OJ L 203/30), Regulation 772/2004 on technology transfer agreements (2004 OJ L 123/11) and Regulation 358/2003 on agreements in the insurance sector (2003 OJ L 53/8).
279. Guidelines on Article 81 (3), points 2 and 35–37.

be withdrawn not only by the Commission but also by a national competition authority when an agreement has effects that are incompatible with Article 81 (3).[280]

(ii) *Individual exemption*: According to Regulation 1/2003, Article 81 (3) may be applied directly by the Commission, the national authorities and the national courts; the exclusive competence of the Commission under Article 9 (1) of Regulation 17 is abolished from 1 May 2004:
   - Agreements and practices caught by Article 81 (1) which *satisfy* the conditions of Article 81 (3) are not prohibited, no prior decision to that effect being required.[281]
   - Agreements which *do not satisfy* the conditions of Article 81 (3) are prohibited, no prior decision to that effect being required.[282] Where the conditions of Article 81 (3) are not fulfilled the competent authority may propose changes or amendments in order to render the agreement compatible with Article 81 (3) but is under no obligation to do so.

Formal Decisions v. Informal Guidance.
Under the old Regulation 17 the Commission granted exemptions in numerous cases only after having objected to, and obtained, amendments to the notified agreements in order to eliminate or modify clauses which were not considered indispensable under Article 81 (3) (a). In such cases the Commission proceeded to the settlement of the case or the issuance of a comfort letter rather than to the adoption of a formal decision. Formal decisions rejecting an exemption or granting an exemption under Article 81 (3) subject to commitments are therefore limited in number, but have had a greater impact than expressed by their numbers. Due to its limited resources, the Commission tended to concentrate on certain leading cases in order to clarify key legal issues and to give guidance for its administrative practice. There was, however, insufficient transparency in this practice. Only a small portion of all notifications were followed by a publication in the Official Journal; the majority are 'short form' publications without giving any detail on the content of the notified agreements, and comfort letters are normally not reasoned except for a very limited number reported in the Annual Reports on Competition Policy. It may be expected that this practice will not change under the new Regulation 1/2003 since the issuance of 'informal guidance' will be limited to cases of 'genuine uncertainty' at the discretion of the Commission,[283] and there may be also little transparency of the clearances granted by national authorities and courts, even if

280. Article 29 of Regulation 1/2003; the withdrawal by a national authority is limited to cases where the effects are incompatible in their territory with represents all the characteristics of a distinct market.
281. Article 1 (2) of Regulation 1/2003.
282. Article 1 (1) of Regulation 1/2003.
283. Recital 38 to Regulation 1/2003.

they consider carefully the four conditions of Article 81 (3). A possible remedy could be more systematic and detailed reports on such cases in the Annual Report on Competition Policy on the cooperation between the Commission and national authorities and courts according to the Notices and the more specific provisions in Regulation 1/2003.[284]

Broad Discretion Subject to Limited Judicial Review.
The application of Article 81 (3) requires balancing the pro- and anticompetitive effects of an agreement or a concerted practice, which implies a certain latitude (discretion) in making the assessment. Under the new broadened system of review provided under Regulation 1/2003, this discretion is no longer lodged exclusively in the Commission, but is also lodged in the national courts and national competition authorties, subject to limited intervention by the Commission and appeal ultimately to the Court of Justice. The judicial review of the assessment undertaken in the exercise of this discretion is therefore limited to ascertaining whether the procedural rules have been complied with, whether proper reasons have been provided, whether the facts have been accurately stated and whether there has been a manifest error of appraisal or misuse of powers;[285] it is not for the Court of First Instance to substitute its own assessment.[286] Decisions which state that the conditions of Article 81 (3) are fulfilled may be appealed:

- by the parties to the agreement where the clearance is made subject to conditions (commitments) and time limits, which may be likely to affect in particular the long-term investment strategy of the parties;[287]
- by third parties which are 'directly and individually concerned' because they are prevented from relying on the prohibition of the agreements under Article 81 (1). In the *Eurovision* case, which concerned the broadcast of television programs (especially sports) and the joint purchasing of the relevant broadcasting rights, the Court of First Instance annulled the Commission's exemption

284. *See* Article 11 of Regulation 1/2003 (cooperation with national competition authorities) and Article 15 (cooperation with national courts). *See also* the bilateral agreements on cooperation with third country authorities (Chapter X).
285. Even within these limits, the Court of First Instance may come to a different evaluation of the prospective developments, in particular the foreseeable reactions of current and future competitors and consumers, as under the merger control regulation in *Airtours*, CFI June 6, 2002, 2002 ECR II-2585, paras. 207–210.
286. *Van den Bergh Foods*, CFI Oct. 23, 2003, T-65/98, paras. 80 and 135. *See La Cinq*, CFI Jan. 24, 1992, 1992 ECR II-1, para. 86; *Net Book Agreements*, ECJ Jan. 17, 1995, 1995 ECR I-23, paras. 39–41; *Eurovision I*, CFI July 11, 1996, 1996 ECR II-649, para. 93; *Matra/Ford-Volkswagen*, CFI July 15, 1995, 1995 ECR II-595, para. 104; *SPO – Dutch Construction Works*, CFI Feb. 21, 1995, 1995 ECR II-289, para. 262 (*aff'd* ECJ March 25, 1996, 1996 ECR I-1611); *Langnese-Iglo*, CFI June 8, 1995, 1995 ECR II-1533, para. 179.
287. *See*, under the merger control regulation, *Air France*, CFI May 19, 1994, 1994 ECR II-323, paras 42–46.

decision, which was appealed by the competitor Gestevision, for erroneous application of Article 81 (3)[288] and the renewed exemption decision was again successfully appealed.[289]

The Four Conditions of Article 81 (3).
The conditions for the grant of exemption are stated in Article 81 (3). To qualify for exemption an arrangement must cumulatively[290] meet the following four conditions:

(1) the agreement must contribute to improving production or distribution or to promoting technical or economic progress;
(2) consumers must be allowed a fair share of the resulting benefit, namely the economic advantages;
(3) any restrictions imposed must be indispensable to attaining the preceding objectives; and
(4) the agreement must not be capable of eliminating competition in relation to a substantial part of the products in question.[291]

Burden of Proof.
With regard to the burden of proof, the general legal standards apply:[292]

- The burden of proving an infringement of Article 81 (1) is on the party or the authority that alleges the infringement;
- The burden of proving that all the conditions of Article 81 (3) are fulfilled is on the undertaking or association of undertakings that claim the benefit of an exemption.[293] Parties which request informal guidance must therefore provide sufficient data (similar, although not as detailed as in a notification under Regulation 17) to allow a comprehensive assessment.[294]

288. *Eurovision (EBU) I*, D.Comm. June 11, 1993, 1993 OJ L 179/23; *rev'd* CFI, 11 July 1996, 1996 ECR II-1201, para. 123.
289. *Eurovision II – M6, Antena 3, Gestévision*, CFI Oct. 8, 2002, 2002 ECR II-3805.
290. *Eurovision I*, CFI July 11, 1996, 1996 ECR II-649, para. 93; *Van der Bergh Foods*, ECJ Oct. 23, 2003, C-65/98, para. 137 (with further references). *See* Guidelines on Article 81 (3), point 42.
291. Under Article 65 (2) of the ECSC Treaty a restrictive agreement can only be exempted ('authorized') in cases of specialization, joint selling, joint buying and in 'strictly analogous' cases: *Wirtschaftsvereinigung Stahl*, D.Comm. Nov. 26, 1997, 1998 OJ L 1/10, para. 62.
292. Article 2 of Regulation 1/2003. *See* Guidelines on Article 81 (3), points 35, 41 and 78.
293. *See JCB*, CFI Jan. 13, 2004, T-67/01, para. 162; *Van der Bergh Foods*, ECJ Oct. 23, 2003, C-65/98, para. 136.
294. *See* the information to be supplied in the case of a request for informal guidance: Notice on guidance letters, point 15.

Benefits must Outweigh Detriments to Competition.
The essential concern and the ultimate criterion for the evaluation of whether an agreement satisfies the conditions of Article 81 (3) is set forth in Article 3 (g) of the EC Treaty, namely ensuring the maintenance of effective competition in the Common Market with a view of promoting consumer welfare and to ensuring an efficient allocation of resources.[295] Thus, the public interest in ensuring the maintenance of effective competition rather than the private interests of the parties is determinative in an evaluation under Article 81 (3). When an agreement involving a restriction of competition brings about an improvement in production or distribution, the restriction of competition must be 'indispensable' to the improvement in question, and '[t]his improvement must in particular show appreciable objective advantages of such a character as to compensate for the disadvantages which they cause in the field of competition'.[296] In fact, the four conditions set forth in Article 81 (3) overlap and constitute only different viewpoints to consider in an evaluation of the benefits and detriments of an agreement or a contractual clause. It is hardly conceivable to affirm a valuable contribution to improving technological progress, production or distribution if it is to the obvious disadvantage of customers or clearly not indispensable.[297] Any exemption decision may not be based on criteria which are extraneous to Article 81 (3). In particular, it may not anticipate a decision of the Commission under Articles 87 and 88 of the Treaty on state aid granted by a member state in order to promote implementation of the notified agreement.[298]

---

295. Guidelines on the Application of Article 81 (3), point 28.
296. *Grundig/Consten*, ECJ July 13, 1966, 1966 ECR 299, 348; Guidelines on horizontal cooperation, point 32. There must be a sufficient link between the restrictions and the claimed efficiencies: Guidelines on Article 81 (3), points 53–54.
297. *See SPO Dutch Construction Works*, CFI Feb. 21, 1995, 1995 ECR II-289, paras 327–328 (denying the indispensability of cooperation with respect to offers to public procurement agencies because of the manifested opposition of the communes ('consumers')).
298. *CEWAL*, CFI July 11, 1996, 1996 ECR II-1201, para. 121; *TNT Post Group/Jet Services*, D.Comm. Feb. 15, 1999, M.1405, point 47. Examples include long-term supply arrangements concerning subsidized German coal: *Steelwork Agreement*, D.Comm. March 30, 1989, 1989 OJ L 101/35, para. 25 (Article 65 of the ECSC Treaty); *Jahrhundertvertrag*, D.Comm. 22 Dec. 1992, 1993 OJ L 50/14 (Article 81 of the EC Treaty and Article 65 of the ECSC Treaty), rev'd *RJB Mining*, CFI Jan. 31, 2001, 2001 ECR II-337 because of state aid implications); *RAG/Saarbergwerke/Preussag Anthrazit*, D.Comm. July 29, 1998, ECSC 1252, point 54, and the creation of a subsidized joint venture for manufacturing a new type of car: *Ford/Volkswagen*, D.Comm. Dec. 23, 1992, 1993 OJ L 20/14, *aff'd* CFI July 14, 1994, 1994 ECR II-595 (under Article 81) and *Matra/Ford-Volkswagen*, ECJ June 15, 1993, 1993 ECR I-3250, para. 44 (affirming the Commission's favourable decision on the grant of state aid).

Complex and Prospective Evaluation.
Balancing the pro- and anticompetitive effects requires a very complex evaluation, and it is difficult to accurately estimate efficiencies, the consumer pass-on rate and the development of the market structure, in particular the possibility for new market entry.[299] This may cause major problems for the effective enforcement of Article 81, in particular by national courts which do not dispose of the broad investigation powers of competition authorities and the economic experience required for taking into account, *i.a.*, the characteristics and the structure of the market, the nature and the estimated magnitude of the cost efficiency gains and the likely effect on prices as suggested by the Commission in its Guidelines on the application of Article 81 (3).[300] The assessment is particularly difficult where the agreement is not yet in effect or is in effect for only a short period, and where the actual effects on the market are as yet entirely or largely unknown. The assessment of such cases under Article 81 (3) therefore requires a *prognosis* of the present and future pro- and anticompetitive effects of the agreement in the expected market conditions, based upon a hypothetical comparison with the situation that would have existed had the agreement not been made.[301] The decision adopted by the Commission, the national competition authority or the national court is based on the facts and information in their possession at the time and does not prejudge the subsequent assessment of the same agreement or conduct.[302] Thus, the implementation of a long-term agreement involving important investments may give rise to multiple disputes which necessitate a fresh analysis on the basis of changing facts and forecasts, likely to lead to different conclusions, thereby affecting legal security.

Possibility of Imposing Fines v. Legitimate Expectations.
Under the former Regulation 17 the parties to a restrictive agreement were entitled to cure legal uncertainty about the application of Article 81 (3) by notifying the agreement with the effect that the Commission was precluded from imposing fines in respect of acts taking place between the date of the notification and its decision in application of Article 81 (3), except where the parties were informed that after preliminary examination an application of Article 81 (3) was not justified.[303] This safeguard against the danger of fines no longer exists under Regulation

299. Guidelines on the application of Article 81 (3), points 56–57.
300. *Ibid. See* in particular points 45–47, 59, 87 and 103.
301. *See Van der Bergh Foods*, ECJ Oct. 23, 2003, C-65/98, para. 107. The balance of the pro- and anticompetitive effects presupposes that the agreement or concerted practice in question comes within Article 81 (1) and is therefore not to be confused with the – broader – rule of reason. (*Métropole television (M6)*, CFI Sept. 18, 2001, 2001 ECR II-2459, paras 72–78).
302. By contrast, the exemption granted under Article 81 (3) and Article 8 of Regulation 17 was legally binding for the duration of the exemption unless the Commission withdraws the benefit of the exemption.
303. Article 15 (5) and (6) of Regulation 17.

1/2003.[304] However, it may be argued that the principle of legitimate expectations[305] may protect against the competition authority imposing fines in cases of 'genuine uncertainty because they present novel and unsolved questions'.[306]

2. The Substantive Conditions of Exemption

Introduction.
An agreement is exempted from the prohibition of Article 81 (1) if all the four conditions of Article 81 (3) are fulfilled. The exemption may not be made subject to other Treaty provisions,[307] unless they can be subsumed to one of the four conditions.[308] The assessment must be made in the actual context in which the agreement in question occurs on the basis of the facts pertaining at the time of its implementation.[309] Article 81 (3) is not precluded *a priori* from application to any type of agreements. However, agreements containing hardcore restrictions are unlikely to fulfill the conditions of Article 81 (3).[310]

First Condition: Improving Production or Distribution or Promoting Technical or Economic Progress.
To make a contribution to improving the production or distribution of goods or services (efficiency gains)[311] an agreement must at least be capable of materially contributing to achievement of these objectives.[312] The Commission has stated:

> 'The fundamental principle in this respect, established at the time the Common Market was formed, lays down that fair and undistorted competition is the best guarantee of regular supply on the best terms. Thus, the question of a contribution to economic progress within the meaning of Article 81 (3) can

304. *See* Article 7 of Regulation 1/2003. Under Regulation 17 agreements were not safe from fines even if they were dispensed from notification for the purpose of exemption, unless they were nevertheless notified: *See SSI*, ECJ Dec. 10, 1985, 1985 ECR 3831, paras 73–78.
305. *See Sugar*, ECJ Dec. 16, 1975, 1975 ECR 1663, para. 556; *Fleuron Compost*, CFI Jan. 14, 2003, T-109/01, para. 142; *Atlantic Container Line*, CFI Sept. 30, 2003, T-191/98, para. 1631.
306. Recital 38 to Regulation 1/2003.
307. E.g., industrial policy, environment, social and economic cohesion.
308. *Matra*, CFI July 15, 1994, 1994 ECR II-595, para. 139.
309. Guidelines on the application of Article 81 (3), points 44–47.
310. Guidelines on the application of Article 81 (3), point 40. *See VISA International*, D.Comm. July 24, 2002, 2002 OJ L 318/17, point 79.
311. Guidelines on Article 81 (3), points 48–72. *See Parker Pen* (*Herlitz*), CFI July 14, 1995, 1995 ECR II-531, paras 29–34. *See also* the exemptions granted for trade fairs (e.g., *ANCIDES*, ECJ July 9, 1987, 1987 ECR 3131) and in the banking and insurance sector (*see infra* Chapter VIII. D).
312. Guidelines on the application of Article 81 (3), points 53–56. *See Fire Insurance*, D.Comm. Dec. 5, 1984, 1985 OJ L 35/20, 28; *aff'd* ECJ Jan. 27, 1987, 1987 ECR 405.

> only arise in those exceptional cases where the free play of competition is unable to produce the best result economically speaking'.[313]

The parties which bear the burden of proof must demonstrate that the efficiencies are substantial and cannot be achieved by less restrictive means and that cost savings are realistic and not speculative; the Commission does not take into account cost savings that arise from output reduction, market sharing, or from the mere exercise of market power.[314]

Benefits must be Expressly Provided for.

Cooperation may be justified and can lead to substantial economic benefits, in particular where companies need to respond to increasing competitive pressure and to a changing market driven by globalization, the speed of technological progress and the more dynamic nature of markets.[315] Efficiency claims must identify the nature of the efficiencies, the link with the agreement, the likelihood and magnitude, the means and any cost of achieving the efficiencies.[316] The efficiencies may include cost efficiencies through synergies, economies of scale or the dissemination of a new technology or qualitative efficiencies.[317] This requirement of Article 81 (3) will not be met if the agreement does not provide expressly for such a contribution to improving production or distribution or to promoting technical or economic progress. For instance, such a contribution is placed in doubt if a research and development agreement does not define the framework of the joint research program,[318] if no detailed plan for reducing overcapacity[319] or specializing production is provided,[320] if the improvement in distribution is only incidental to a wider anticompetitive arrangement[321] or if the financial implications are not clearly established.[322] Improvements to production or distribution cannot be claimed for arrangements which set uniform prices[323] or discounts[324]

---

313. *Bayer/Gist I*, D.Comm. Dec. 15, 1975, 1976 OJ L 30/13; *Cimbel*, D.Comm. Dec. 22, 1972, 1972 OJ L 303/24.
314. Guidelines on horizontal cooperation, points 32–33.
315. *Ibid.*, point 3; *IFPI Multicasting*, D.Comm. Oct. 8, 2002, 2003 OJ L 107/58, point 84.
316. Guidelines on the application of Article 81 (3), point 56.
317. *Ibid.*, points 64–71.
318. This is no longer a regulatory requirement under Regulation 2659/2000 as it was under Article 2 (a) of Regulation 418/85.
319. *Synthetic Fibers II*, D.Comm. July 4, 1984, 1984 OJ L 207/17, 19–21.
320. The specialization must be the primary object of the agreement: Article 1 (2) of Regulation 2658/2000 on specialization agreements.
321. *Ideal Standard*, D.Comm. Dec. 10, 1984, 1985 OJ L 20/38, 43; *Grohe*, D.Comm. Dec. 10, 1984, 1985 OJ L 19/17, 22; *CRN*, D.Comm. Dec. 18, 1972, 1972 OJ L 303/7, 15–16.
322. *CEWAL*, CFI July 11, 1996, 1996 ECR II-1201, paras 119–121.
323. *VISA International*, D.Comm. July 24, 2002, 2002 OJ L 318/17, point 79. *See SSI*, ECJ Dec. 10, 1985, 1985 ECR 3831, para. 85; *Dutch Cranes*, CFI Oct. 22, 1997 ECR II-1739, para. 159–164. Exceptionally, minimum commissions have been exempted in the *Eurochèques I* case in order

or for simple market sharing[325] or output limitation arrangements,[326] joint sales organizations,[327] or for coordination of competitors' behaviour through an information exchange system[328] or through a joint venture.[329] Production or distribution must be effectively and substantially improved by the cooperation. The Commission has found improvements to production particularly in cases of specialization that exploit economies of scale,[330] reduce production costs, increase output, close down uneconomic production units, or bring about a wider range of output or improved quality.[331] Adoption of common standards or types may also improve production.[332] Long-term improvements to production have been accepted in cases of structural overcapacity where firms that were unable to reduce capacity independently agreed on a coordinated, definitive reduction of capacity which the Commission found to be on a sufficient scale to make a permanent improvement in conditions in the industry.[333] Exclusive dealing agreements may improve security and regularity of supply and thereby improve production planning. Exclusive distribution arrangements commonly improve distribution by having the exclusive distributor concentrate his marketing efforts on certain sales areas, and selective distribution systems contribute to better quality service to the consumer.[334] Agreements on national roaming between third generation mobile network operators improve distribution by providing better coverage, quality and transmission rates, including service in less populated and less commercially attractive areas.[335]

---

to promote the acceptance by local banks of Eurocheques drawn abroad in foreign currency: D.Comm. Dec. 10, 1984, 1985 OJ L 35/43, 49. *See also Reims II*, D.Comm. Sept. 15, 1999, 1999 OJ L 275/17; *IFPI Multicasting*, D.Comm. Oct. 8, 2002, 2003 OJ L 107/58, point 120.

324. *NSO*, ECJ Dec. 10, 1985, 1985 ECR 3801, 3828, paras 61–62; *Vimpoltu*, D.Comm. July 13, 1983, 1983 OJ L 200/44, 50.
325. *SNPE/Leafields Engineering Ltd.*, D.Comm. June 12, 1978, 1978 OJ L 191/41, 44; *Quantel/Continuum*, D.Comm. July 27, 1992, 1992 OJ L 235/9.
326. *French-West African Shipowners' Committee*, D.Comm. April 1, 1992, 1992 OJ L 134/1, para. 46. *See* Guidelines on horizontal cooperation, points 11 and 18.
327. CSV, July 20, 1978, 1978 OJ L 242/15, 32–34; *ANSAC*, D.Comm. Dec. 19, 1990, 1991 OJ L 152/54.
328. *Wirtschaftsvereinigung Stahl*, D.Comm. Nov. 26, 1997, 1998 OJ L 1/10.
329. *Blackpowder*, D.Comm. Oct. 20, 1978, 1978 OJ L 322/26, 34.
330. *Ford/Volkswagen*, D.Comm. Dec. 23, 1992, 1993 OJ L 20/14, para. 33, *aff'd* CFI July 15, 1994, 1994 ECR II-595.
331. *See* Chapter III.C.3.
332. *X/Open Group*, D.Comm. Dec. 15, 1986, 1987 OJ L 35/36, 41–42; *CECED I*, D.Comm. Jan. 24, 1999, 2000 OJ L 187/47.
333. *Synthetic Fibers II*, D.Comm. 4 July, 1984, 1984 OJ L 207/17, 22–24.
334. Recital 8 to Regulation 2790/1999.
335. *O2 UK Limited/T-mobile (UK Network Sharing Agreement)*, D.Comm. April 30, 2003, 2003 OJ L 200/59, points 137–141.

Promoting Technical or Economic Progress.
The benefits which make an agreement eligible for exemption include promoting technical or economic progress. In relation to joint research and development and licensing of technology the Commission has expressed a generally positive attitude to such collaboration through the adoption of the block exemption Regulation 2659/2000 on joint research and development agreements and Regulation 772/2004 on technology licensing agreements. Promotion of technical progress may consist of more rapid and more efficient development and introduction of a new technology,[336] including the bundling of complementary technologies in order to optimize the production process.[337]

Improving Supply by Product Market Extension Agreements.
Agreements between firms that are not capable of entering a new product market alone because of a lack of the necessary technical knowledge, the availability of inputs, a minimum scale of production facilities, access to the necessary distribution channels, the ability to bear the technical and financial risks or activities in related businesses,[338] and aiming at facilitating penetration of a new product market are normally likely to improve production and/or distribution.[339] The Commission and the Court of Justice also include in this favourable assessment restrictions which are necessary to penetrate that new product market for a limited period, in particular non-compete clauses accompanying the creation of joint ventures as long as they are necessary for the implementation and functioning of the joint venture.[340] Because it is usually quite difficult to determine the appropriate duration of such a temporary market penetration period, it is advisable or even necessary to submit such agreements for guidance to the Commission.

336. *Continental/Michelin*, D.Comm. Oct. 11, 1988, 1988 OJ L 305/33, 39–40 (common development of a new run-flat tire); *Matra/Ford-Volkswagen*, CFI July 15, 1994, 1994 ECR II-595, paras 109–110 (common development of a new van).

337. *Matra/Ford-Volkswagen*, CFI July 15, 1994, 1994 ECR II-595, paras 109–110.

338. *See European Night Services*, CFI Sept. 15, 1998, 1998 ECR II-3141; *Elopak/Metalbox*, D.Comm. July 13, 1990, 1990 OJ L 209/15; *Konsortium ECR*, D.Comm. July 27, 1990, 1990 OJ L 228/31. *International Private Satellite Partners*, D.Comm. Dec. 15, 1994, 1994 OJ L 354/75, para. 55.

339. *GEAE/P&W*, D.Comm. Sept. 14, 1999, 2000 OJ L 58/16. *See Matra/Volkswagen-Ford*, CFI July 15, 1994, 1994 ECR II-595; *Continental/Michelin*, D.Comm. Oct. 11, 1988, 1988 OJ L 305/33; *Philips/Osram*, D.Comm. Dec. 21, 1994, 1994 OJ L 378/37; *ATLAS* and *Phoenix/Global One*, D.Comm. July 17, 1996, 1996 OJ L 239/23 and 57; *Uniworld* and *Unisource I*, D.Comm. March 19, 1997, 1997 OJ L 318/24 (*see*, however, *Unisource II*, D.Comm. Dec. 21, 2000, 2002 OJ L 52/30).

340. Indispensability affirmed: *Unisource* and *Uniworld*, D.Comm. Oct. 29, 1997, 1997 OJ L 318/1 and 24; indispensability accepted under time limitation: *Ford/Volkswagen*, D.Comm. Dec. 23, 1992, 1993 OJ L 20/14, point 41; *aff'd* CFI July 15, 1994, 1994 ECR II-595; indispensability denied: *ASTRA*, D.Comm. Dec. 23, 1992, 1993 OJ L 20/23, paras 19–31.

Improving Supply by Geographic Market Extension Agreements.
In any market that is relatively open to new entry, it is likely that a seller who reaches a certain minimum size is capable not only of supplying its home market but also neighbouring markets either as a direct exporter or indirectly through local intermediaries, provided that transport costs are not prohibitively high. For this reason the Commission has not hesitated to consider agreements to share markets between firms operating in the same product market that have not yet made sales into each others' respective geographic markets as infringements of Article 81 (1) and not meriting exemption under Article 81 (3),[341] in particular in cases in which suppliers in one member state agreed to make sales in another member state only jointly, as in the *Floral* case,[342] or in a coordinated manner, as in *CSV*[343] and *ANSAC*.[344] Reciprocal exclusive distribution agreements between competitors may, although excluded from the scope of block exemption Regulation 1983/83 on exclusive distribution agreements, qualify for clearance under Article 81 (3) if the markets are difficult to penetrate and the agreement genuinely facilitates each other's market access.[345] Distribution opportunities may be improved and transaction costs significantly reduced in cases where suppliers have a limited reach on other markets due to technical reasons (terrestrial means instead of the use of internet).[346]

Improving Supply by New Product/Geographic Market Extension Agreements.
The Commission has granted exemptions under Article 81 (3) for limited forms of cooperation in which one of the parties was found to be a potential competitor of the other as a result of its production capacity, size, structure and activities in other markets. The *Rockwell/Iveco* case,[347] for example, concerned a joint venture

341. *Siemens/Fanuc*, D.Comm. Dec. 18, 1985, 1985 OJ L 376/29, 31; *Zinc Producer Group*, D.Comm. Aug. 6, 1984, 1984 OJ L 220/27, 34–36. The Commission denied a potential competitive relationship in cases where the partners were unable to export individually to third countries: *Machine Tools*, D.Comm. July 17, 1968, 1968 OJ L 201/1; *SAFCO*, D.Comm. Dec. 16, 1971, 1972 OJ L 13/44.
342. *Floral*, D.Comm. Nov. 28, 1979, 1980 OJ L 39/51. Similarly, joint selling in the EC by non-EC suppliers: *ANSAC*, D.Comm. Dec. 19, 1990, 1991 OJ L 152/54.
343. *CSV*, D.Comm. July 20, 1978, 1978 OJ L 242/15.
344. *ANSAC*, D.Comm. Dec. 19, 1990, 1991 OJ L 152/54 (joint venture created by non-EC producers of soda ash for joint distribution in the Community).
345. Exemption granted: *Banque Nationale de Paris/Dresdner Bank*, D.Comm. June 24, 1996, 1996 OJ L 188/37; *Fluke/Philips*, Nineteenth Report on Competition Policy, point 47. Exemption rejected: *Siemens/Fanuc*, D.Comm. Dec. 18, 1985, 1985 OJ L 376/29.
346. *IFPI – Simulcasting*, D.Comm. Oct. 8, 2002, 2003 OJ L 107/58, points 89–92. This is the reason why the Commission tends to consider the internet market as a separate market, *see* Chapter IV.B.5 (e).
347. *Rockwell/Iveco*, D.Comm. July 13, 1983, 1983 OJ L 224/19.

to produce truck axles in the EC between an American axle manufacturer (which had already exported axles to the EC and owned an axle-making subsidiary in the EC) and the European truck manufacturer Iveco (which had heretofore produced axles only for internal consumption). The Commission decided to grant an exemption because the joint venture spared Iveco costly development on its own, promoted production on a more economic scale and the joint venture partners accounted for a minor share of the EC truck axle market. In the *Carlsberg* case[348] the Commission granted an individual exemption for an agreement between the Danish brewery, Carlsberg, and a British brewer to help Carlsberg enter the British market by having the British brewer sell Carlsberg's lager beer through its network of tied public houses (bars). The successful penetration of this new geographic market required cooperation with a domestic brewery having the requisite distribution network until Carlsberg was able to build up a network of its own, which it was thought would take eight years, the period of the exemption. Substantial economic benefits have been recognized for the simulcasting licenses for the use of the licensed rights in more than one territory, thereby allowing for a wide spread legitimate use of the rights, in accordance with the global reach of internet and giving rise to a new product, a multi-territorial, multi-repertoire simulcasting license covering the repertoires of different collecting societies, and enabling a simulcaster to obtain a single license from a single collecting society ('one-stop-shop').[349]

Maintenance of Employment and Rationalization as a Contribution to Improving Production or Distribution.

Maintenance of employment may, as the Court of Justice held in the *SABA I*[350] and *Remia/Nutricia*[351] cases, be taken into account as a contribution to improving production under Article 81 (3) in times of economic recession. The same applies to agreements on coordinated rationalization in an industry suffering from overcapacity. The agreement must contain concrete plans for reducing capacity and for economic or technical improvements to the remaining production facilities.[352]

348. *Carlsberg*, D.Comm. July 12, 1984, 1984 OJ L 207/26. *See also Moosehead/Whitbread*, D.Comm. March 23, 1990, 1990 OJ L 100/32.

349. *IFPI – Simulcasting*, D.Comm. Oct. 8, 2002, 2003 OJ L 107/58, points 86–87. However, this reasoning may not be generalized with regard to exclusive patent pools. Non-exclusive patent pools may, by contrast, justify negative clearance: *DVD Standard*, D.Comm. Oct. 9, 2000, IP/00/1135 (comfort letter); *Mobilfunkdienste*, D.Comm. Nov. 12, 2002, IP/02/1651.

350. *SABA I*, ECJ Oct. 25, 1977, 1977 ECR 1875, para. 43.

351. *Remia/Nutricia*, ECJ July 11, 1985, 1985 ECR 2545, para. 42.

352. *Synthetic Fibers II*, D.Comm. July 4, 1984, 1984 OJ L 207/17, 22–24. However, agreements tending merely to adapt output without reducing production capacity have been considered as unexemptible quota arrangements: *Cimbel*, D.Comm. Dec. 22, 1972, 1972 OJ L 303/24, 37–38; *Polyester Fibers*, Second Report on Competition Policy, point 31. *See also*, under Article 65 of the ECSC Treaty, the Opinion of the Court of Justice of Dec. 13, 1961, 1961 ECR

If the agreement or concerted practice is only designed to reduce the effects of a recession among competitors without reducing capacity, it will not improve production or distribution but merely restrict competition, which through the operation of market forces would probably lead to a solution. Arrangements which provide for a fair allocation of the available quantities of a commodity which is in short supply due to a serious crisis, such as the 1973–74 oil crisis, are likely to improve distribution but the terms must be limited to that which is strictly necessary.[353]

Safety Considerations.

The Commission has considered improvements to safety as among the benefits justifying the application of Article 81 (3) in the case of agreements which improved the nuclear reprocessing service offered to nuclear power plants by raising safety standards and by stabilizing the service.[354] The need to ensure high safety standards in car servicing has been recognized as justifying an exemption for selective distribution systems in the automobile sector,[355] whereas in relation to plumbing fittings consumer protection did not justify a selective distribution system that excluded all dealers who were not themselves plumbing contractors.[356]

Environmental Considerations.

Environmental considerations may be included in the general economic assessment of an agreement.[357] The Commission welcomes voluntary initiatives to improve environmental conditions in a given sector and is not opposed to the possible passing on to the customers of 'polluter pays' investment costs but has to ensure that undertakings competing in that sector do not resort to agreements

---

243, 258–263 (rejecting a proposed new provision for authorizing agreements for 'adaptation to new marketing conditions' because it would give the Commission too wide a discretion).

353. *Ford/Volkswagen*, D.Comm. Dec. 23, 1992, 1993 OJ L 20/14, para. 36, (*aff'd* CFI July 15, 1994, 1994 ECR II-595); *International Energy Agency*, D.Comm. Dec. 12, 1983, 1983 OJ L 376/30, 35. *Cf. ABC/Oil Companies*, D.Comm. April 19, 1977, 1977 OJ L 117/1. In this case the Commission held that BP had abused its temporary dominant position during the oil crisis in refusing to supply a certain dealer instead of dividing the available quantities equally between its customers. However, the Court of Justice reversed the decision, holding that the dealer in question was not a regular customer: *BP*, ECJ June 29, 1978, 1978 ECR 1513.

354. *United Reprocessors*, D.Comm. Dec. 23, 1975, 1976 OJ L 51/7, 11; *Amersham/Buchler*, D.Comm. Oct. 29, 1982, 1982 OJ L 314/34, 36. *See* Guidelines on Article 81 (3), point 70.

355. *BMW*, D.Comm. Dec. 13, 1974, 1975 OJ L 29/1, 6–7.

356. *Grohe*, D.Comm. Dec. 10, 1984, 1985 OJ L 19/17, 22–24; *Ideal-Standard*, D.Comm. Dec. 10, 1984, 1985 OJ L 20/38, 43–45.

357. *See Concordia Bus Finland*, ECJ Sept. 17, 2002, 2002 ECR I-7213, para. 85 (with regard to public procurement).

which go beyond what is necessary to achieve that goal, to the detriment of competition.[358]

- In the *VOTOB* case[359] the Commission intervened against an agreement between undertakings offering tank storage facilities for third parties on the uniform application of a fixed 'environmental charge' which was to cover (although in part only) the costs of investments required to reduce vapour emissions from members' storage tanks (although the members employed different techniques to reduce emissions). The Commission argued that by fixing a uniform charge members would have less incentive to make investments as cheaply and efficiently as possible. The case was settled following the agreement of the VOTOB members to renounce its uniform charging system.
- In the *Mineral Water* case[360] the Commission acted against the Genossenschaft Deutscher Brunnen (GDB), a cooperative of mineral water producers, in order to obtain from GDB its consent to grant access to its pool of refillable glass bottles to mineral water producers from other member states, in particular the Belgian producer Spa Monopole. The pool of standardized refillable glass bottles was set up to conform with the German legislation providing that packaging may only be used when it can be recycled. GDB established a collection system with German supermarket chains which did not want a second collecting system for other bottles and therefore made it impossible for other producers to penetrate the German market. The case was settled following the admission by GDB of other mineral water producers.
- The *DSD* case[361] concerned an agreement between a recycling undertaking and suppliers of liquids in plastic bottles on the collection and recycling of plastic packaging and on the use of the trademark 'Grüner Punkt' identifying recyclable plastic packaging. The Commission issued a comfort letter after obtaining commitments to avoid discrimination against producers and suppliers of plastic packaging within the Community, including licensing the 'Grüner Punkt' trademark.[362] Although the Commission did not give detailed reasoning, it may be assumed that the agreements in question were covered by Article 81 (1) because of their market foreclosure effects and, although improving distribu-

358. Twenty-fourth Report on Competition Policy, points 177 and 185; Twenty-eighth Report on Competition Policy, points 129–134. *See* F.O.W. Vogelaer, 'Towards an Improved Integration of EC Environmental Policy and EC Policy', in Barry Hawk, ed., *Annual Proceedings of the Fordham Corporate Law Institute: International Antitrust Law & Policy 1994*, p. 529 (Kluwer 1995).

359. *VOTOB*, Twenty-fourth Report on Competition Policy, points 178–184. *See also ACEA* and *EUCAR*, Twenty-eighth Report on Competition Policy, points 131–132.

360. *Mineral Water* (*Spa Monopole/GDB*), Twenty-third Report on Competition Policy, point 240.

361. *DSD* (*'Grüner Punkt'*), D.Comm. Sept. 17, 2001, 2001 OJ L 319/1. *See also IFCO II*, DG IV News Letter 1998–2, p. 48, and *Valpak*, Twenty-eighth Report on Competition Policy, points 133–134.

362. Abusive and predatory conditions of using this system lead to the prohibition decision under Article 82: *Duales System*, D.Comm. April 20, 2001, 2001 OJ L 166/1.

tion of goods and promoting economic progress which includes environmental protection, they contained restrictions which were not indispensable to the attainment of those objectives.[363]
- Similar systems for the collection and recycling of used packaging were cleared by the Commission in the French *Eco*[364] and the Austrian *ARA* case.[365] In both cases the Commission was mainly concerned with ensuring unrestricted access for competing systems to the collection infrastructure.

The basic principles that a packaging waste system must comply with have been summarized by the Commission as follows:[366]

- Companies required to recover and recycle waste must have the choice between several systems in order to avoid dominant positions.
- Any exclusivity must be limited in scope and duration.[367]
- Collectors should have unrestricted access to the collections infrastructure.
- The collectors must be as free as possible to find the appropriate reprocessing channel.

Industrial Policy and Social and Economic Cohesion.
The criteria of Article 81 (3) are exhaustive and cannot be complemented by other considerations to which Articles 4 and 5 of the Treaty refer without affecting, and even presupposing, effective competition. Article 4 expressly states that economic policy must be 'conducted in accordance with the principle of an open market economy with free competition'.[368] In the *Glaxo* case the Commission dealt with the problem whether the significant delays between the application for a product license in Spain and the actual marketing of those products there justified resale

363. *See* the requirement of 'proportionality' which the Court of Justice applies under Article 28: *Plastic Bottles*, ECJ Sept. 20, 1988, 1988 ECR 4607, paras 10–22; *Waste Oil II*, ECJ Feb. 7, 1985, 1985 ECR 531, 549, para. 15. However, agreements to improve environmental conditions, such as agreements for joint collecting and recovery of household packaging, have been amended in such a way as to eliminate restrictions and to justify negative clearance, e.g., *DVD Standard*, D.Comm. Oct. 9, 2000, IP/00/1135; *COMBAT*, D.Comm. Nov. 23, 2000, IP/00/1351; *Eco-Emballage*, D.Comm. June 15, 2001, 2001 OJ L 233/37. Furthermore, an agreement between competitors or their association to limit production of energy-non-efficient washing machines has been held restrictive because of the reduction of output but exempted because of their collective environmental benefits: *CECED I*, D.Comm. Jan. 24, 1999, 2000 OJ L 187/47. In *CECED II* the Commission issued a comfort letter for additional measures to improve energy efficiency: D.Comm. Nov. 26, 2001, IP/01/1659.
364. *Eco Emballage*, D.Comm. June 15, 2001, 2001 OJ L 233/37.
365. *ARA*, D.Comm. Oct. 16, 2003, 2004 OJ L 75/59.
366. Thirty-first Report on Competition Policy, point 79, Box 3.
367. A recommended duration was not indicated by the Commission, but probably not more than 3 to 5 years.
368. *See* Chapter I.B.2. *supra*.

price maintenance (dual pricing) in order to ensure adequate supplies of innovative medicines on that market. However, the Commission concluded that Glaxo failed to demonstrate that parallel trade has caused undue harm to distributors and consumers.[369]

Second Condition: Consumers Receive a Fair Share of the Resulting Benefit.

Consumers must be allowed a fair share of the resulting benefit in order to justify the grant of an exemption under Article 81 (3), e.g., for gaining access to a larger range of products or services.[370] Cost savings will be passed on the consumer by way of lower prices[371] or new products, provided there are sufficient competitive constraints.[372] Consumers' benefit may be questionable if distribution outlets are reduced by agreements preventing parallel trade by direct export bans or by an indirect dual pricing policy,[373] or a selective distribution system where the characteristics of the product do not require the retailer to hold special qualifications.[374] However, consumers may receive a fair share of the resulting benefit of joint development and production of a new product necessitating high and risky investments,[375] of an agreement between banks to improve payment facilities within the Common Market,[376] or of an agreement improving the quality and a wider coverage of a mobile network.[377] 'Consumers' is not to be interpreted narrowly and includes industrial purchasers and processors in the case of agreements concerning, for instance, joint rationalization of raw material production.[378] Savings

369. *Glaxo*, D.Comm. May 8, 2001, 2001 OJ 302/1, points 89, 147 and 151.
370. *IFPI – Simulcasting*, D.Comm. Oct. 8, 2002, 2003 OJ L 107/58, point 94.
371. *VISA International II*, D.Comm. July 24, 2002, 2002 OJ L 318/17, points 82–95 (a negative clearance had been granted after amendments in *VISA International I*, D.Comm. August 9, 2001, 2001 OJ L 293/24). *See* with regard to environmental agreements Thirty-first Report on Competition Policy, point 79, Box 3.
372. Guidelines on horizontal cooperation, point 34.
373. *Glaxo*, D.Comm. May 8, 2001, 2001 OJ 302/1, points 177–186.
374. For example, cosmetics do not justify distribution via qualified dispensing chemists; the exclusion of other distributors is of no benefit to consumers: *Vichy II*, CFI Feb. 27, 1992, 1992 ECR II-415, para. 98.
375. *Matra/Ford-Volkswagen*, CFI July 15, 1994, 1994 ECR II-595, para. 122; *Philips/Osram*, D.Comm. Dec. 21, 1994, 1994 OJ L 378/37, para. 27.
376. Even the terms and conditions for accepting and clearing cheques were initially determined in common (which might be regarded as joint price fixing): *Eurocheques*, D.Comm. Dec. 10, 1984, 1985 OJ L 35/43; but in its *Eurocheques Helsinki* cease and desist order decision the Commission took a stricter position: D.Comm. March 25, 1992, 1992 OJ L 95/50. *See also SPO – Dutch Construction Works*, CFI Feb. 21, 1995, 1995 ECR II-289, paras 146–152; *UIC*, CFI June 6, 1995, 1995 ECR II-1503, para. 50.
377. *O2 UK Limited/T-mobile (UKL Network Sharing Agreement)*, D.Comm. April 30, 2003, 2003 OJ L 200/59, point 142.
378. *Bayer/Gist*, D.Comm. Dec. 15, 1975, 1976 OJ L 30/13, 19. Guidelines on the application of Article 81 (3), point 84.

in costs and improvements in distribution or standards of service may directly benefit consumers, while improvements in quality may indirectly benefit them if the higher quality is achieved without price increases, or indeed with price reductions.[379] In some cases benefits in certain respects may be outweighed by losses in others. For example, the benefit of achieving greater market transparency in an oligopolistic market may have the effect of restricting price competition among the parties to the agreement, which is to the detriment of consumers.[380] As a general rule, the extent to which benefits are likely to reach consumers will depend upon the competitive pressures to which the contracting parties are subject. If this competitive pressure is minimal, the parties to the agreement will attempt to keep the benefits for themselves.[381] If it is great, they will be compelled to pass the benefits on to consumers at least in the longer term.[382] As a rule, cost efficiencies will occur with a certain time lag, which does not exclude the application of Article 81 (3).[383] Hence, the intensity of actual and likely future competition must be carefully evaluated.[384]

Third Condition: The Indispensability Criterion.
The indispensability criterion is central to the evaluation under Article 81 (3).[385] It has to be compared to the general proportionality principle as established by Article 30 and, in particular, Article 86 (2) of the EC Treaty: 'The development of trade must not be affected to such an extent as would be contrary to the interests of the Community'.[386] According to the Court of Justice the proportionality principle requires the evaluation of whether legitimate objectives can be achieved with less restrictive means,[387] or, as formulated by the Commission, whether or

379. *See Optical Fibers*, D.Comm. July 4, 1986, 1986 OJ L 236/30, 38.
380. *IFTRA Glass*, D.Comm. May 15, 1974, 1974 OJL 160/1, 15; *IFTRA Aluminium*, D.Comm. July 15, 1975, 1975 OJ L 228/3, 12; *COBELPA*, D.Comm. Sept. 8, 1977, 1977 OJ L 242/10, 18. With respect to the (rather hypothetical) pass-on and balancing of cost efficiencies: Guidelines on Article 81 (3), points 95–104.
381. *Gerofabriek*, D.Comm. Dec. 22, 1976, 1977 OJ L 16/8; *Vimpoltu*, D.Comm. July 13, 1983, 1983 OJ L 200/44.
382. *United Reprocessors*, D.Comm. Dec. 23, 1975, 1976 OJ L 51/7, 11.
383. Guidelines on the application of Article 81 (3), point 87; however, future gains for consumers are worth less than present gains, which may therefore to be 'discounted'.
384. *Synthetic Fibers II*, D.Comm. July 4, 1984, 1984 OJ L 207/17, 24.
385. E.g., *IFPI – Simulcasting*, D.Comm. Oct. 8, 2002, 2003 OJ L 107/58, points 96–115. *See FRUBO*, ECJ May 15, 1975, 1975 ECR 563, paras 40–43.
386. *See Commission/Italy*, ECJ Oct. 23, 1997, 1997 ECR I-5789, paras 62–63.
387. *VISA International II*, D.Comm. July 24, 2002, 2002 OJ L 318/17, points 99–103; *IFPI – Simulcasting*, D.Comm. Oct. 8, 2002, 2003 OJ L 107/58, point 97. *See Cassis de Dijon*, ECJ Feb. 20, 1979, 1979 ECR 649, para. 8; *Pall/Dahlhausen*, ECJ Dec. 13, 1990, 1990 ECR I-4844, para. 12; *Yves Rocher*, ECJ May 18, 1993, 1993 ECR I-2361, para. 12; *Mars*, ECJ July 6, 1995, 1995 ECR I-1923, para. 15; *Graffioni/Fransa*, ECJ Nov. 26, 1996, 1996 ECR I-6039, para. 17.

not the restrictive agreement and individual contractual restrictions make it possible to perform the activity in question more efficiently than would have been in the absence of the agreement or the restriction concerned without the intention to second guess the business judgement of the parties.[388] Under Article 81 (3) a restriction of competition must not extend beyond what is necessary, in scope, territory and duration, for achieving the legitimate objectives of the agreement in the sense of the first and the second conditions of this article noted above (which leaves substantial discretion to the assessing authority or court).[389] The restrictions of competition must not only produce concrete benefits,[390] but also be indispensable to obtain the advantages and benefits of the agreement (for example the access to a new geographic or product market)[391] or for recapturing the costs of the necessary investments.[392] In practice it is often because of the failure of specific clauses to meet this indispensability test that the Commission has refused to grant an exemption or requires amendment of the agreement prior to the grant of an exemption or issuance of a comfort letter.[393] Thus, agreements to reduce capacity may not be supplemented by price[394] and quota agreements;[395] agreements on specialization or research and development will not be regarded as justifying joint selling; and discrimination by nationality will never be accepted as indispensable because of the clear prohibition of discrimination in Article 17 of the EC Treaty.[396] Most block exemption regulations include a 'blacklist' of restraints of competition that will disqualify an agreement from receiving the benefit of the block exemption because normally these practices are not indispensable to achieve the otherwise legitimate objects of the agreement. However, agreements containing 'blacklisted' clauses may receive an individual exemption after careful consideration of the justification for the clauses.[397] In the case of a long-term supply agreement the indispensability test implies a balancing of duration and quantity.[398]

---

388. Guidelines on the application of Article 81 (3), points 73–76.
389. Guidelines on horizontal cooperation, point 35. *See SABA I*, ECJ Oct. 25, 1977, 1977 ECR 1875, para. 21; *Eurocheque Helsinki Agreement*, CFI Feb. 23, 1994, 1994 ECR II-49, para. 114; *John Deere UK Agricultural Tractor Registration Exchange*, CFI Oct. 27, 1994, 1994 ECR II-957, para. 105.
390. Under exceptional circumstances, even price arrangements may be held indispensable: *VISA International*, D.Comm. July 24, 2002, 2002 OJ L 318/17, points 98–103.
391. *Matra/Ford-Volkswagen*, CFI July 15, 1994, 1994 ECR II-595, para. 138. Parties need to prove that restrictions are indispensable for guaranteeing a reasonable redeem of the investments: *Eurovision*, CFI July 11, 1996, 1996 ECR II-649, para. 118.
392. *Eurovision I*, CFI July 11, 1996, 1996 ECR II-649, para. 118.
393. *See Dual System DSN*, 1997 OJ C 100/14, paras 55–67.
394. *Finnish Timber*, Twenty-sixth Report on Competition Policy, point 126.
395. *Synthetic Fibers I*, Eighth Report on Competition Policy, point 42.
396. Under Article 82*: GVL*, ECJ March 2, 1983, 1983 ECR 483, 509.
397. *See M6 – Eurovision*, CFI Oct. 8, 2002, 2002 ECR II-3805, para. 51.
398. *Philip Morris/Tabacalera*, D.Comm. Feb. 23, 2001, IP/01/249. *See* in greater detail Chapter IV.B.6. (c).

An agreement between record producers' rights administration societies satisfies the indispensability criterion only if the country-of-origin determination of tariffs clearly distinguishes the administrative fee from the royalty fee (without amalgamating them) in order to avoid any country-related discrimination.[399]

Indispensability v. Ancillarity.
In cases of structural joint ventures the Commission used to evaluate restrictions agreed in relation to the creation and functioning of the joint venture under the 'indispensability' standard.[400] Its more recent practice tends to limit the applicability of Article 81 (1) to the creation of the joint venture, whereas collateral restrictions are examined under the 'ancillary' standard, i.e. whether they are necessary for the creation and implementation of the joint venture.[401]

Fourth Condition: No Substantial Elimination of Competition.
The criterion of elimination of competition for a substantial part of the products in question is related to the question of dominance[402] and calls therefore for the determination of the relevant market.[403] Whether the anticompetitive agreement affords the parties the possibility of eliminating competition in respect of a substantial part of the products in question (the relevant product market) calls for an extensive qualitative and quantitative analysis of the magnitude of remaining sources of actual competition,[404] including the assessment of entry barriers and the real possibility for new entry.[405] The main issues are:

- How much competition remains *between the parties* (inter-party competition), and
- How much competition remains with *other firms* in the market (third-party competition).

(a) Inter-Party Competition

The question of how much competition remains between the parties depends on whether the cooperation between them extends to all competition parameters

399. *IFTRI*, D.Comm. Oct. 8, 2002, 2003 OJ L 107/58, points 99–107. *See* the possibility of withdrawing the benefit of the block exemption in the case of price discrimination under Article 6 (1) (d) of Regulation 1400/2000.
400. *See Optical Fibers*, D.Comm. July 14, 1986, 1986 OJ L 236/30.
401. Guidelines on the application of Article 81 (3), points 29–31. *See Philips/Osram*, D.Comm. Dec. 21, 1994, 1994 OJ L 378/37, Article 2 of the operative part of the decision.
402. Guidelines on horizontal cooperation, point 36.
403. Guidelines on the application of Article 81 (3), points 107–108.
404. Guidelines on the application of Article 81 (3), point 109.
405. The relevant criteria are listed in point 115 of the Guidelines on the application of Article 81 (3).

(R&D, production and marketing) or whether it leaves to the parties the possibility of individual marketing[406] and, in particular, independent pricing,[407] provided there is sufficient third party competition which effectively constrains the parties to behave independently. If competition between the parties is eliminated or severely curtailed, as in the case of a production joint venture which also distributes the products[408] or a selective distribution system in which intra-brand competition is reduced,[409] exemption will depend on the intensity of outside (third-party) competition, as shown principally by the market shares of the parties and their competitors. On the other hand, if an agreement restrains competition only in specific fields, as in the case of joint research and development,[410] of combination of wireless mobile technology,[411] joint production of part of a model range,[412] coordinated reductions in production capacity,[413] reciprocal specialization of production,[414] development of standards,[415] joint purchasing of part of the parties' requirements,[416] joint sales promotion and advertising,[417] uniform procedures or technical rules in services,[418] or agreed allocation of quantities in emergencies such as an oil shortage,[419] then substantial areas of competition between the parties, in particular marketing, should remain unaffected.[420] In these cases high market share alone will not prevent the grant of an exemption. Even agreements

406. *See Exxon/Shell*, D.Comm. May 18, 1994, 1994 OJ L 144/20; *GEAE/P&W*, D.Comm. Sept. 14, 1999, 2000 OJ L 58/16, point 96 (both exemptions providing for a 'Chinese wall' as guaranteeing the independence of the parties).
407. *IFPI – Simulcasting*, D.Comm. Oct. 8, 2002, 2003 OJ L 107/58, point 120.
408. E.g., *Rockwell/Iveco*, D.Comm. July 13, 1983, 1983 OJ L 224/19.
409. *SABA II*, ECJ Oct. 22, 1986, 1986 ECR 3021, paras 34–46; *Grundig II*, D.Comm. Dec. 21, 1993, 1994 OJ L 55/52, paras 39–41.
410. *Henkel/Colgate I*, D.Comm. Dec. 23, 1971, 1972 OJ L 14/14, 17; *Beecham/Parke Davis*, D.Comm. Jan. 17, 1979, 1979 OJ L 70/11, 20; *Continental/Michelin*, D.Comm. Oct. 11, 1988, 1988 OJ L 305/33, 42; *Alcatel/ANT*, D.Comm. Jan. 12, 1990, 1990 OJ L 32/19.
411. *O2 UK Limited/T-mobile (UK Network Sharing Agreement)*, D.Comm. April 30, 2003, 2003 OJ L 200/59, points 145–147.
412. *VW/MAN*, D.Comm. Dec. 5, 1983, 1983 OJ L 376/11, 15; *Ford-Volkswagen*, D.Comm. Dec. 23, 1992, 1993 OJ L 20/14, paras 37–38, *aff'd* CFI July 15, 1994, 1994 ECR II-595.
413. *Synthetic Fibers I*, Eighth Report on Competition Policy, point 42; *Synthetic Fibers II*, D.Comm. July 14, 1984, 1984 OJ L 207/17, 24.
414. *Bayer/Gist*, D.Comm. Dec. 15, 1975, 1976 OJ L 30/13, 20–21.
415. *X/Open Group*, D.Comm. Dec. 15, 1986, 1987 OJ L 35/36, 42.
416. *National Sulphuric Acid Association I*, D.Comm. July 9, 1980, 1980 OJ L 260/24, 27, 31; *National Sulphuric Acid Association II*, D.Comm. June 9, 1989, 1989 OJ L 190/22, 24.
417. *VIFKA*, D.Comm. Sept. 30, 1986, 1986 OJ L 291/46, 49; *ANCIDES*, ECJ July 9, 1987, 1987 ECR 3131, paras 12–16.
418. *Belgian Banks*, D.Comm. Dec. 11, 1986, 1987 OJ L 7/27, 34–35; *Italian Banks*, D.Comm. Dec. 12, 1986, 1987 OJ L 43/51, 60–61.
419. *International Energy Agency*, D.Comm. Dec. 12, 1983, 1983 OJ L 376/30, 36.
420. *Matra/Ford-Volkswagen*, CFI July 15, 1995, 1995 ECR II-595, para. 155.

that include all or nearly all of the competitors in a particular market have been exempted if they do not affect price competition and the free movement of goods between member states.[421] However, exemption has been refused if the coordination of behaviour has spilled over into other fields.[422] In the case of collaborative research programs, the Commission also looks at the presence of competing research activity by third parties.[423]

(b) Third-Party Competition

Even in cases where agreements do not affect substantial areas of competition between the parties, the effectiveness of competition by third parties has to be assessed. The more inter-party competition is restricted or eliminated, the greater attention has to be dedicated to the intensity of third-party competition.[424] This assessment is based on the same factors as are taken into consideration under Article 82 to determine whether or not there is a dominant position,[425] namely:

- Market structure: Number, strength and size of actual and potential competitors and the parties' market share and the possibilities of market access.
- Firm-level elements: Technical and commercial knowledge, control over raw materials, capital, means of transport, and processors and distributors.[426]

However, the finding of a threat to competition under Article 81 (3) does not require that the parties hold a dominant position, but only that the agreement will put them in a position to substantially eliminate effective competition. Market shares below the thresholds of the respective block exemption regulations are, as such, not sufficient but may give rise to a collective dominant position, provided there is a connection enabling the operators to act together.[427] The individual market share thresholds fixed by block exemptions may be exceeded under exceptional circumstances justifying exemption in cases where companies having high market shares

421. *Synthetic Fibers II*, D.Comm. July 4, 1984, 1984 OJ L 207/17.
422. *Flower Auctions Aalsmeer I*, D.Comm. 26 July 1988, 1988 OJ L 262/27, 43.
423. *Beecham/Parke Davis*, D.Comm. Jan. 17, 1979, 1979 OJ L 70/11; *Vacuum Interrupters II*, D.Comm. Dec. 11, 1980, 1980 OJ L 383/1, 8.
424. Exemption rejected: *Trans Atlantic Agreement*, D.Comm. Oct. 19, 1994, 1994 OJ L 376/1, paras 428–461.
425. *See infra* Chapter V.C.3.
426. *See* in greater detail Guidelines on the application of Article 81 (3), point 115.
427. E.g., *CEWAL*, D.Comm. Dec. 23, 1992, 1993 OJ L 34/20, *aff'd* CFI Oct. 8, 1996, 1996 ECR II-1201, but *rev'd* ECJ March 16, 2000, 2000 ECR I-1365. The Commission decision was based on the assumption of a collective dominant position infringing both Article 81 and 82 but only the infringement of Article 82 lead to the imposition of fines which the Court of Justice annulled whereas the findings on Article 81 were not appealed. Similarly, *TACA II*, CFI Sept. 30, 2003, T-191/98.

cooperate in order to develop and manufacture a new product in competition with existing products without any restrictive spill-over effect.[428] No exemption would be possible for a cartel that included all major firms in the relevant market and eliminated competition in most respects.[429]

Relevance of Potential Competition and Barriers of Market Access.
The evaluation of third party competition must include potential competition.[430] The benefit of Article 81 (3) may be denied where potential competition is insufficient to counterbalance the parties' strong position on the market and may necessitate appropriate remedies.[431]

The Criterion of Elimination of Competition in the Light of the *Eurovision* Case.
Eurovision is a television program exchange system based on the understanding that member radio and television organizations will offer other members their coverage of national sporting and cultural events likely to be of interest for them. The members, grouped in the European Broadcasting Union (EBU), participate in the joint acquisition and sharing of television rights to international sporting events ('Eurovision rights'). Four free-to-air television channels with national coverage contested the rules governing the joint acquisition of television rights and the contractual access for third parties to that system, in particular the sub-licensing system governing access for third parties' broadcasting free-to-air.

A first exemption decision of the Commission[432] was annulled by the Court of First Instance mainly because the system was likely to lead to a discriminatory treatment by the Eurovision system when accepting certain commercial broadcasters as members and excluding others. The Court of First Instance made a distinction between live and deferred transmissions: even if it were acceptable for EBU members to reserve the first category for themselves, nothing justifies their extending that right to all the competitions in a given event (including restrictions

428. *GEAE/P&W*, D.Comm. Sept. 14, 1999, 2000 OJ L 58/16, point 86. *See Asahi/St.Gobain*, D.Comm. Dec. 16, 1994, 1994 OJ L 354/87; *Exxon/Shell*, D.Comm. May 18, 1994, 1994 OJ L 144/20, paras 79–82 (joint additional capacity); *GEAE/P&W*, D.Comm. Sept. 14, 1999, 2000 OJ L 58/16, point 86.

429. *Vimpoltu*, D.Comm. July 13, 1983, 1983 OJ L 200/44, 50 (90% of the Dutch market); *Rennet*, D.Comm. Dec. 5, 1979, 1980 OJ L 51/19, 25 (90% of the Dutch market); *SSI*, D.Comm. July 15, 1982, 1982 OJ L 232/1, 5, 32–34 (96% of the Dutch market); *Flemish Travel Agents*, ECJ Oct. 10, 1987, 1987 ECR 3801, paras 12–18 (industry-wide agreement imposed by law on 100% of the Belgian market); *Stichting Kraanhuurbedrijf*, D.Comm. April 13, 1994, 1994 OJ L 117/30 (Article 15 (6) decision).

430. The Commission may apply the HHI test as additional parameter for balancing the importance of market shares. *See* Chapter VI.D.2.(c).

431. *See Austrian Airlines/Lufthansa*, D.Comm. July 15, 2002, 2002 OJ L 242/25, points 103 and 115.

432. *Eurovision I*, D.Comm. June 11, 1993, 1993 OJ L 179/23.

as regards embargo times and the editing of programs) when they do not intend to broadcast those competitions live.[433]

Subsequently, the EBU adopted new provisions which were considered as offering wider opportunities for live and deferred transmission for non-members.[434] However, this exemption decision was, again, annulled by the Court of First Instance.[435] Although the joint acquisition of transmission rights was not in itself held a restriction of competition, the exercise of these rights none the less lead to barring access to programs[436] which deprives non-EBU channels of potential revenue and to an unjustified exclusivity: if the same rights were bought by a media group, operators could negotiate to obtain them for their respective markets. The Court of First Instance concluded that the sublicence scheme did not allow genuine access of third parties to the programme acquired by EBU and that therefore the condition of Article 81 (3) (b) was not fulfilled.[437]

3. Modalities of Applying Article 81 (3)

New Modalities of Applying Article 81 (3).
Under the old Regulation 17 the Commission had sole competence to grant an exemption under Article 81 (3). The exemption had a prospective effect: it was granted (and created legal certainty) for a specific period and could be made subject to conditions or obligations. The exemption was legally binding for its entire duration unless the Commission withdrew the benefit of the exemption according to Article 8 (3) of Regulation 17.

Regulation 1/2003 (which supersedes Regulation 17 as of 1 May 2004) makes Article 81 (3) directly applicable in parallel by the Commission, national competition authorities and national courts, thereby requiring an assessment of Article 81 in its entirety, including infringement of Article 81 (1) and the conditions for exemption under Article 81 (3). Any decision adopted is based on the facts and information available at the time of the decision and *does not have a prospective effect*. Thus, the decision does not prejudge a re-assessment of the same agreement or conduct in the light of new facts at a later time, although account may be taken of the previous decision in the framework of the cooperation within the European Competition Network (ECN).[438]

433. *Metropole Télévision/Eurovision I*, CFI July 11, 1996, 1996 ECR II-649, paras. 117–121.
434. *Eurovision II*, D.Comm. May 10, 2000, 2000 OJ L 151/18.
435. *M6, Antena 3, Gestevision/Eurovision II*, CFI Oct. 8, 2002, 2002 ECR II-3805.
436. *Ibid.*, para. 64.
437. *Ibid.*, paras. 84–85.
438. Articles 11 and 15 of Regulation 1/2003 and the notices on cooperation between then Commission and the national authorities and the national courts.

Types of Acts Finding that the Conditions of Article 81 (3) are Fulfilled.

- The *Commission* may adopt a formal decision stating that the conditions for exemption under Article 81 (3) are satisfied where the Community public interest so requires,[439] in particular with a view of clarifying a legal situation and to preventing similar infringements.[440] Such a formal exemption is not granted for a specified period and may not be made subject to conditions or obligations. However, the parties may submit commitments which the Commission may accept with a view to rendering the agreement compatible with Article 81 and declare these commitments binding for a specific period according to Article 9 of Regulation 1/2003. Where the parties fail to comply with such commitments the Commission may impose fines[441] or penalty payments,[442] and third parties may rely on the commitments before national courts. This is without prejudice to the Commission's right to reopening proceedings.[443]

  However, the Commission may prefer not to proceed to a formal decision but to settle the case and to issue an informal guidance letter,[444] thereby finding that the conditions of a block exemption are fulfilled or that an agreement that is *not* covered by any block exemption satisfies the conditions of Article 81 (3), possibly following amendments to the agreement. Such a guidance letter is not binding on any subsequent assessment by the Commission or a national competition authority, but the Commission will take a previous guidance letter into account unless there are new facts or developments in the case law of the European Courts.[445] Such informal guidance letters are comparable to comfort letters issued under Regulation 17: they are not legally binding on national authorities or national courts but are of persuasive authority and constitute a factor to be taken into account when examining the same agreement under Article 81.[446]
- The *national competition authorities* may find that the conditions of Article 81 (3) are satisfied (possibly following commitments) and decide on the basis of the information in their possession that there are no grounds for action on their part.[447] Such a decision is similar to a negative clearance under Article 2 of Regulation 17 and does not prejudge a subsequent assessment of the same

---

439. Article 10 of Regulation 1/2003.
440. *See*, under Regulation 17, *GVL*, ECJ March 2, 1983, 1983 ECR 483, paras. 16–28.
441. Article 23 (2) (c) of Regulation 1/2003 (up to 10% of total turnover in the preceding business year).
442. Article 24 (1) (c) of Regulation 1/2003 (up to 5% of average daily turnover in the preceding business year per day).
443. Article 9 (2) (b) of Regulation 1/2003. The principle of *non bis in idem* does not apply because it is limited to the same facts: *LVM – PVC II*, ECJ Oct 15, 2002, 2002 ECR I-8375, para. 59.
444. Recital 38 to Regulation 1/2003 and Commission Notice on informal guidance.
445. Commission Notice on informal guidance, point 25.
446. *Guerlain*, ECJ July 10, 1980, 1980 ECR 2327, para. 13.
447. Article 5 second subparagraph of Regulation 1/2003.

conduct by the Commission or another authority. However, a national authority is obliged to inform the Commission without delay after commencing investigative measures[448] and provide the Commission a summary of the case, the envisaged decision or other document indicating the proposed course of action at least 30 days before adoption in order to facilitate uniform application of the Community competition rules.[449]

- The *national courts* must apply both Article 81 (1) and Article 81 (3). National courts are not required to notify the Commission about their cases[450] but they may ask the Commission for advice, and both the Commission and the national competition authorities may submit written observations.[451] The Commission may do so acting on its own initiative and, with permission of the court, may also make oral observations.[452]
- The *parties* to a restrictive agreement may themselves assess whether the conditions of Article 81 (3) are fulfilled. They may prefer to implement pro-competitive obligations into the original agreement, thereby alleviating the need for a review and the probable delay associated with a clearance (possibly subject to conditions) by the Commission or the national competition authority.

Effects of Acts Finding that the Conditions of Article 81 (3) are Fulfilled. The application of Article 81 (3) under Regulation 1/2003 renders the prohibition of Article 81 (1) automatically inapplicable with effect as of the date when the conditions of Article 81 (3) are fulfilled. This may be the date of the conclusion of the agreement irrespective of the date when the agreement is brought to the attention of the competent competition authority,[453] or the date when the parties amend the agreement in order to satisfy the conditions of Article 81 (3). During any period of the agreement while the conditions of Article 81 (3) are not fulfilled, the parties are subject to administrative and civil sanctions.[454] Since Regulation 1/2003 does not provide for any formal notification and consequently for no immunity from fines, but only a request for informal guidance, the parties bear entirely the risk of the past infringement subject to the discretion of the authority to impose, or to abstain from imposing, fines.[455]

Types of Acts Finding that the Conditions of Article 81 (3) are *not* Fulfilled. Where the conditions of Article 81 (3) are *not* satisfied:

---

448. Article 11 (3) of Regulation 1/2003.
449. Article 11 (4) of Regulation 1/2003.
450. However, they may be required under national law to inform the national competition authority (*cf.* §90 of the German Law Against Restraints of Competition).
451. Article 15 of Regulation 1/2003.
452. Article 15 (3) of Regulation 1/2003.
453. Under Article 6 of Regulation 17 this was the date of notification to the Commission.
454. Article 1 (1) of Regulation 1/2003.
455. Under Article 15 (5) of Regulation 17 notification guaranteed immunity from fines. *See*, however, the principle of legitimate expectation discussed at fn. 305 *supra*.

- the *Commission* may adopt interim measures,[456] order the termination of the infringement, including behavioral and structural remedies[457] and/or impose fines and penalty payments if the infringement is not be brought to an end;[458]
- the *national competition authorities* may order interim measures, require the infringement be brought to an end and impose fines or penalty payments or any other penalty provided for under their national law;[459]
- the *national courts* may apply the civil consequences of an infringement of Article 81 (1) provided for under their national law: nullity, damages or restitution.[460]

Transitional Provisions.
According to Article 34 of Regulation 1/2003 the notifications made under Regulation 17 'lapse' as of 1 May 2004, the date of application of Regulation 1/2003, whereas exemptions granted pursuant to notifications submitted under Regulation 17 will continue to apply until their stated date of expiration. However, the immunity from fines will lapse as well. Thus, an agreement or conduct is, despite having duly been notified or communicated to the Commission, subject to fines, unless the Commission exercises its discretion by refraining from using this power.

The adhesion Treaty with the ten new member states[461] contains transitional provisions which allow the parties to an agreement that is subject to a block exemption regulation and exists at the date of accession and which, by reason of accession, falls within the scope of Article 81 (1), to amend the agreements within a grace period of six months so that it is brought into compliance with the existing block exemption regulations.[462] In such a case, the agreement does not constitute an infringement of Article 81 (1) even during the grace period and even with respect to hardcore restrictions, provided they are duly eliminated or amended within the grace period.[463]

Implications of the New Scheme of Applying Article 81 (3).
The new system established by Regulation 1/2003 constitutes a fundamental change of the system of Regulation 17:

456. Article 8 of Regulation 1/2003.
457. Article 7 of Regulation 1/2003.
458. Articles 23 and 24 of Regulation 1/2003. An infringement ceases to exist where the parties terminate the restrictive agreement or implement the agreement in a way that no longer violates Article 81 (1), e.g., by making an exclusive arrangement non-exclusive.
459. Article 5 of Regulation 1/2003.
460. Discussed in greater detail in Chapter X.H. *See* Guidelines on Article 81 (3), point 41.
461. 2003 OJ L 236. The ten new member states are: Cyprus, Czech Republic, Estonia, Latvia, Lithuania, Hungary, Malta, Poland, Slovenia and Slovakia.
462. 2003 OJ L 236/344–346.
463. However, agreements which are not covered by a block exemption (horizontal agreements other than R&D or specialization agreements) and do not qualify for exemption under Article 81 (3) fall within the scope of the prohibition of Article 81 (1) without having a grace period for amendment.

- *Lack of legal certainty*: The parties to an agreement are prevented from obtaining legal certainty as to the compatibility of their agreement with Article 81, except in cases of 'genuine uncertainty' with respect to novel or unresolved questions. They have to assess their agreements themselves in the light of the Commission's practice and guidelines. Their agreements may become the subject of Community or national proceedings any time, which may lead to an assessment 'within the actual context in which they occur and on the basis of the facts existing at any given point of time'.[464] There is an inherent risk of inconsistent and even irreconcilable decisions.[465] However, the parties may have a legitimate interest in requesting a formal decision or at least informal guidance from the Commission on the compatibility of agreements when they involve costly or long-term investment decisions.
- *Lack of transparency*: In the absence of any publication or notice in advance of decisions by the Commission, national competition authorities or national courts, third parties are not informed of the proceedings and therefore not able to comment on whether the agreements restrict competition but are likely to satisfy the conditions of Article 81 (3). This thwarts their right to be heard: they are unable to comment and to complain or to appeal any administrative act which may erroneously find the conditions of Article 81 (3) to be satisfied.

A possible way-out would be to publish a summary of the agreement for which informal guidance is requested,[466] thereby inviting third parties an opportunity to comment, and to make a summary of the advice public in an appropriate form, such as a press release or annual report. In this case the informal guidance letter could have a persuasive authority and be more easily taken into account in subsequent proceedings on the Community or national level.

D. Legal Consequences of Infringement of Article 81

Clearance.
When the Commission finds that an agreement, a decision or a concerted practice does not infringe Article 81 (1) or fulfills the conditions of Article 81 (3), it may issue a clearance decision under Article 10 of Regulation 1/2003, provided that the Community public interest so requires. According to Recital 38 the Commission may issue informal guidance in cases that give rise to genuine uncertainty because they present novel or unresolved questions.[467]

---

464. Notice on the application of Article 81 (3), point 39.
465. As in the case of a partial referral under the merger control regulation: *Royal Philips Electronics/ SEB-Moulinex*, CFI April 3, 2003, T-119/02, para. 380.
466. E.g., under Regulation 17: *REIMS II*, 2003 OJ C 94/3.
467. *See* Commission Notice on Informal Guidance (Guidance letters), 2004 OJ C 101/78.

Fines.
The size of fines for clear breaches of Article 81 are often quite large and have shown a rising trend in recent years.[468] Article 23 (2) of Regulation 1/2003 allows undertakings to be fined up to 10% of their total turnover in the preceding business year for infringement of Article 81.

Termination of Infringement.
When the Commission finds that a violation of Article 81 has occurred it may issue a decision under Article 7 of Regulation 1/2003 finding an infringment and ordering it to be terminated, if it has not already been so.[469] The Commission may impose periodic penalty payments up to 5% of the average daily turnover per day in order to compel the undertakings to comply with its decision under Article 24 (1) of Regulation 1/2003.

Civil Remedies.
Article 81 has direct effect in the member states so that the prohibition can be enforced by individuals before the national courts. The Community provides only one consequence of civil law in Article 81 (2): the offending agreements are automatically void, no prior decision to that effect being required. The question whether the agreement is entirely or partly void and whether the infringement justifies injunctions, restitution and damage claims is a matter of national law.[470]

468. *See* the list of fines at the end of Chapter X.
469. *See* Chapter X.F.2.
470. *See* in greater detail Chapter X.I.

Chapter III

Permitted, Prohibited and Exemptible Forms of Horizontal Cooperation between Actual or Potential Competitors

CONTENTS

A. Applicability of Article 81 (1) to Horizontal Cooperation

1. More Economic Approach

Objective of Article 81 (1).

The objective of Article 81 (1) is to protect competition on the market as a means of enhancing consumer welfare and of ensuring an efficient allocation of resources.[1] The prohibition rule of Article 81 (1) applies to restrictive agreements, decisions and concerted practices in so far as they are likely to affect trade between member states. Article 81 (1) is complemented by Article 53 of the EEA Treaty which contains the same prohibition with respect to trade between the countries of the EEA, thereby including Norway, Iceland and Liechtenstein.[2] Both prohibition rules imply that each economic operator must determine independently the policy he intends to adopt on the market[3] without depriving companies of the right to adapt themselves intelligently to the existing or anticipated conduct of their competitors.[4] Such unilateral market conduct is subject only to Article 82, whereas Article 81 (1) applies to anticompetitive coordination whereby at least one undertaking undertakes *vis-à-vis* another undertaking to adopt a certain concerted conduct on the market or to reduce the degree of uncertainty in regard to their competitive conduct.[5] Anticompetitive coordination that infringes Article 81 (1) therefore includes any form of obligation that regulates or influences competitive market conduct.[6] Coordination of market conduct may have as its object or effect[7] a negative impact on the parameters of competition between the parties or between them and third parties (competitors) with respect to prices, output, markets, or innovation. The question whether such negative effects are outweighted by pro-competitive effects (economic efficiencies) is reserved for Article 81 (3).[8] The most important forms of restrictions of competition are enumerated in Article 81 (1) and will be discussed hereafter before dealing with those forms of coordination which are likely to satisfy the conditions of Article 81 (3).

The Commission's White Paper.

The Commission's White Paper on modernization of the EC competition rules[9] aims at making the application of these rules simpler, more expedient, more ef-

---

1. Guidelines on Article 81 (3), point 12. The coal and steel sectors are, after the expiration of the ECSC Treaty on July 23, 2002, subject to the competition rules of the EC Treaty.
2. Agreement on the European Economic Area, 1994 OJ L 1/1.
3. *Polypropylene – Anic*, ECJ July 8, 1999, 1999 ECR I-4125, para. 116.
4. *Thyssen Steel*, ECJ Oct. 2, 2003, C-194/99 P, paras 82 and 83.
5. *Thyssen Steel*, ECJ Oct. 2, 2003, C-194/99 P, para. 89; Guidelines on Article 81 (3), point 14.
6. Guidelines on Article 81 (3), point 13.
7. *See* Chapter II.B.2.
8. *Métropole télévision (M6)*, CFI Sept. 18, 2001, 2001 ECR II-2459, para. 107.
9. White Paper, Commission Program No. 99/027, 1999 OJ C 132/1.

ficient and more transparent. The Commission intends to adopt a more economic approach to the application of Article 81. The general rule is that agreements – horizontal or vertical – must be evaluated in their economic context. This economic analysis may lead to more horizontal cooperation agreements falling outside the scope of Article 81 (1) than before and to a broader application of block exemptions and clearances by the Commission and by national authorities and national courts. This implies a change of the role of the Commission. At the beginning the focus of its activity was on establishing and clarifying rules on restrictive practices interfering directly with the goal of market integration. Sharing the burden of enforcement with national authorities and courts has the advantage of concentrating more on ensuring effective competition by detecting and stopping cross-border cartels, maintaining or restoring competitive market structures, enforcing merger control and liberalizing hitherto monopolized markets.[10] The decentralization of powers implies a closer cooperation between national authorities, national courts and the Commission in order to ensure coherent application of the rules throughout the Community, which is complemented by international cooperation with antitrust authorities of third countries.[11]

Facilitating Assessment of Agreements and Practices under Article 81. The assessment of agreements and concerted practices is facilitated by:

- a broader application of the *de minimis* rule between competitors, which considers agreements and practices as falling outside Article 81 (1) if the parties have combined market shares of no more than 10%[12] (previously 5%[13]), assuming that the negative effects on competition are only likely to occur where at least one of the parties has or obtains some degree of market power;[14]
- block exemptions which are no longer based on a legalistic approach and ensure legal certainty ('safe harbor') up to certain market share thresholds;[15]
- hardcore restrictions which, as a rule, infringe Article 81 (1) irrespective of the parties' market shares;[16]
- Guidelines on Horizontal Cooperation between Competitors[17] and the more general Guidelines on the Application of Article 81 (3);[18]

10. White Paper, points 8–10.
11. E.g. with antitrust authorities in US, Canada, Japan.
12. 2001 OJ C 368/13, point 7.
13. 1997 OJ C 372/4, point 9.
14. Guidelines on Article 81 (3), point 25.
15. Regulation 2658/2000 on Specialization Agreements and Regulation 2659/2000 on R&D Agreements.
16. Article 5 of both regulations.
17. 2001 OJ C 3/2. The same Guidelines are adopted by the EFTA Surveillance Authority: 2002 OJ C 266/1.
18. 2004 OJ C 101/97.

- Direct applicability of Article 81 (3), which, as from May 1, 2004, no longer requires notification to the Commission so that agreements which satisfy the conditions of Article 81 (3) are not prohibited, no prior decision to that effect being necessary.

Plan of this Chapter.
The general conditions of Article 81 (1) are discussed hereafter, in particular the hardcore restrictions, such as fixing of prices, limiting output or sales, or allocating markets or customers, which are almost *per se* infringements and may only under exceptional circumstances satisfy the conditions of Article 81 (3). The block exemption regulations and guidelines are commented upon in Sections B and C below.

2. Fixing Prices or Other Terms of Sale

(a) Prices

Importance of Price Competition.
Article 81 (1) (a) prohibits agreements or concerted practices that 'directly or indirectly fix purchase or selling prices'. Price competition is the most visible and important, but by no means the only, form of competition.[19] Price competition holds prices to the lowest possible level and encourages trade in goods between the member states, thereby making possible an optimal allocation of resources based on the relative productivity and adaptability of firms, and giving consumers the benefits of a wide selection of goods and services.[20] Price is closely related to supply, so production quotas may directly affect price competition.[21]

Reducing Price Disparities between Member States.
For many products there are still substantial price differences from one member state to the next. The Commission has concluded that these differences may be explained to varying extents by:

- differences in national tax policies,
- exchange rate fluctuations,
- differences in the level of economic activity and in rates of inflation,
- differences in consumer preferences and tastes, and
- national purchasing power disparities.

---

19. *SABA I*, ECJ Oct. 25, 1977, 1977 ECR 1875, paras 20–21.
20. *ICI-Dyestuffs*, ECJ July 14, 1972, 1972 ECR 619, 660, para. 115.
21. *Polypropylene – Petrofina*, CFI Oct. 24, 1991, 1991 ECR II-1087, paras 92–93, 128–130; *PVC I*, D.Comm. July 27, 1994, 1994 OJ L 239/14, point 35 (*aff'd* – after eight years – ECJ Oct. 15, 2002, 2002 ECR I-8375); *Trans Atlantic Agreement*, D.Comm. Oct. 19, 1994, 1994 OJ L 376/1, point 8.

Opening – or keeping open – national markets to competition from firms in other member states enables market forces to erode unjustifiably wide price disparities. Accordingly, any form of price-fixing, quota or market-sharing agreement that preserves existing price disparities or reinforces the isolation of national markets will be considered particularly suspect. Article 81 is designed not only to maintain effective competition, but also to act as an important instrument in establishing an integrated, unified Community market.

Examples of Prohibited Price-Fixing Agreements.
The following are examples of the kind of price-fixing agreements which Article 81 (1) prohibits:

- Jointly setting prices for goods or services[22] (irrespective of whether the jointly fixed prices lead to price increases[23] or price erosion[24]) at specific levels; setting minimum,[25] maximum[26] or mutually 'acceptable'[27] prices, frequently accompanied by allocating sales volumes or quotas;[28]
- Jointly observing list prices,[29] even if the prices being set are designed to counter a market crisis or increased processing costs[30] or are subject to government controls or receive government approval;[31]

22. *See* the collective fixing of bank commissions in *Austrian Banks*, D.Comm. June 11, 2002, IP/02/844.
23. *Dutch Cranes*, CFI Oct. 22, 1997, 1997 ECR II-1739, para. 240; *Speciality graphites*, D.Comm. Dec. 17, 2002, IP/02/1907.
24. *Polypropylene – Atochem*, ECJ Oct. 24, 1991, 1991 ECR II-1177, para. 100 (joint fixing of the eroding prices in order to 'share the pain').
25. E.g. *French Beef*, D.Comm. April 2, 2003, IP/03/479. Prohibition of minimum prices intended to end a 'price war': *Plasterboard*, D.Comm. Nov. 27, 2002, IP/02/1744.
26. *Cement*, D.Comm. Nov. 30, 1994, 1994 OJ L 343/1, point 47, *aff'd* CFI March 15, 2000, 2000 ECR II-491, para. 4517. However, maximum commissions may in certain cases be to the advantage of customers and therefore exemptible: *Belgian Banks*, D.Comm. Dec. 11, 1986, 1987 OJ L 7/27, 30–31; *VISA*, D.Comm. July 24, 2002, 2002 OJ L 318/17, points 91.
27. *Nederlandse Federatieve FEG*, D.Comm. Oct. 26, 1999, 2000 OJ L 39/1, point 120, *aff'd* CFI Dec. 16, 2003, T-5/00, para. 168.
28. E.g. *Sorbates*, D.Comm. Oct. 1, 2003, IP/03/1330.
29. *Far East Trade Tariff Charges*, D.Comm. May 16, 2000, 2000 OJ L 268/1, points 127–130 and 134 (precluding any price reductions or discounts on the price lists), *aff'd* CFI Feb. 28, 2002, 2002 ECR II-1101, paras 398–400 (although annulling the fine).
30. *Dutch Cranes*, Oct. 22, 1997, 1997 ECR II-1739, para. 159; VCH, ECJ Oct. 17, 1972, 1972 ECR 977, paras 19 and 21; *Fire Insurance*, ECJ Jan. 27, 1987, 1987 ECR 405, para. 41. Price increase because of increased costs representing a substantial part of the end price: *Alloy Surcharge*, D.Comm. Jan. 21, 1998, 1998 OJ L 100/55, points 43–49 (under Article 65 ECSC Treaty).
31. *SSI*, ECJ Dec. 10, 1985, 1985 ECR 3831, para. 40; *Welded Steel Mesh – Société de Treillis*, CFI April 6, 1995, 1995 ECR II-1191, para. 99; *CSND*, D.Comm. *Benelux Flat Glass*, D.Comm. July 23, 1984, 1984 OJ L 212/13, 18–19; *Zinc Producer Group*, D.Comm. Aug. 6, 1984, 1984 OJ L 220/27, 39; *Belasco*, D.Comm. July 10, 1986, 1986 OJ L 232/15, 24–25. Frequently,

- Jointly setting prices through an agreement on joint marketing or a joint sales organization[32] or an association with the primary purpose of promoting a quality standard but in reality used as platform for price-fixing and market-sharing talks;[33]
- Jointly agreeing on the price to be offered by one party in cases of bid-rigging;[34]
- Jointly agreeing on the rate, time and place of price increases;[35]
- Jointly agreeing on the use of a common price list or on price increases to be announced publicly by one participant which the other competitors are prepared to follow;[36]
- Jointly agreeing on an essential part of the price, e.g., on an environmental charge to cover the costs of investments;[37]
- Jointly setting prices for different customers [38] or for different countries of sale;[39]
- The direct or indirect setting of prices under arrangements for sharing revenue, profits or losses (including compensation schemes);[40]

---

government price controls only relate to maximum prices: *Cimbel*, D.Comm. Dec. 22, 1972, 1972 OJ L 303/24, 32*;* or to price increases in general without fixing a specific amount: *CSND*, D.Comm. June 30, 1993, 1993 OJ L 203/27 (*see CNSD*, ECJ June 18, 1998, 1998 ECR I-3851, paras 58–60).

32. E.g. *Scottish Salmon Board*, D.Comm. July 30, 1992, 1992 OJ L 246/37; *Far East Trade Tariff Charges*, D.Comm. May 16, 2000, 2000 OJ L 268/1 (line conference),
33. *Industrial Copper Tubes Cartel*, D.Comm. Dec. 16, 2003, IP/03/1746.
34. *SPO – Dutch Construction Works*, CFI Feb. 21, 1995, 1995 ECR II-289, paras 154–158; *Pre-insulated Pipes*, D.Comm. Oct. 21, 1998, 1999 OJ L 24/1, point 147 (*aff'd* CFI March 20, 2002, 2002 ECR II-1487).
35. *ICI-Dyestuffs*, ECJ July 14, 1972, 1972 ECR 619, 660–661, paras 118–119; *Cast Iron and Steel Rolls*, D.Comm. Oct. 17, 1983, 1983 OJ L 317/1, 12–13; *PVC II*, D.Comm. July 29, 1994, 1994 OJ L 239/14; CFI April 20, 1999, 1999 ECR II-931, paras 637–661 (*aff'd* ECJ Oct. 15, 2002, 2002 ECR I-8375); *British Sugar – Tate & Lyle*, D.Comm. Oct. 14, 1998, 1999 OJ L 76/1; *aff'd* CFI July 12, 2001, 2001 ECR II-2035 (although reducing the fine); *Organic Peroxides Cartel*, D.Comm. Dec 10, 2003, IP/03/1700.
36. *Pre-insulated Pipes*, D.Comm. Oct. 21, 1998, 1999 OJ L 2411, point 147 (*aff'd* CFI March 20, 2002, 2002 ECR II-1487); *Polypropylene-Herkules*, CFI Dec. 17, 1991, 1991 ECR II-1715, para. 152.
37. *VOTOB*, Twenty-second Report on Competition Policy, points 177 and 185; *Dutch Industrial and Medical Gases*, D.Comm. July 24, 2002, 2003 OJ L 84/1, points 289–305; *Far East Freight Conference*, CFI Feb. 28, 2002, 2002 ECR II-110, para. 148.
38. *Pre-insulated Pipes*, D.Comm. Oct. 21, 1998, 1999 OJ L 24/1, point 147 (*aff'd* CFI March 20, 2002, 2002 ECR II-1647)
39. *IFTRA Glass*, D.Comm. May 15, 1974, 1974 OJ L 160/1, 8–9, 12–13; *IFTRA Aluminium*, D.Comm. July 15, 1975, 1975 OJ L 228/3, 11–12; *Cast lron and Steel Rolls*, D.Comm. Oct. 17, 1983, 1983 OJ L 3 1711, 11–13.
40. *Supexie*, D.Comm. Dec. 23, 1970, 1971 OJ L 10/12, 13–14; *Lightweight Papers*, D.Comm. July 26, 1972, 1972 OJ L 182/24, 25; *Cimbel*, D.Comm. Dec. 22, 1972, 1972 OJ L 303/24, 33; *Meldoc*, D.Comm. Nov. 26, 1986, 1986 OJ L 348/50; *CEWAL Line Conferences*, D.Comm.

- Jointly setting purchase prices;[41]
- Jointly setting price surcharges insofar as they represent a significant part of the total costs of transport;[42]
- Jointly setting target prices for basic grades of a product which are communicated to customers and serve as the basis for negotiating varying prices with individual customers;[43]
- Jointly prohibiting trade discounts in excess of a certain percentage,[44]even in cases where retail prices are fixed by the government[45] or prohibiting the rebate of part of a commission to the customer;[46]
- Jointly prohibiting discriminatory prices;[47]
- Jointly setting recommended sales prices which may or may not actually be followed but which make it possible to predict with a reasonable degree of certainty what the pricing policy pursued by competitors will be;[48]
- Jointly publishing recommended sales prices by which to engage in price coordination;[49]

Dec. 23, 1992, 1993 OJ L *34/20; aff'd* CFI Oct. 8, 1996, 1996 ECR II-1201; *Dutch Cranes*, CFI Oct. 22, 1997, 1997 ECR II-1739, paras 165–170; *Pre-insulated Pipes*, D.Comm. Oct. 21, 1998, 1999 OJ L 24/1, point 147 (*aff'd* CFI March 20, 2002, 2002 ECR II-1647).

41. Prohibited as part of an overall cartel arrangement: *Aluminium Imports from Eastern Europe*, D.Comm. Dec. 19, 1984, 1985 OJ L 92/1, 40; *Zinc Producer Group*, D.Comm. Aug. 6, 1984, 1984 OJ L 220/27, 37–38; *Industrial Timber*, Fifth Report on Competition Policy, points 36–37; *Finnish Timber*, Twenty-sixth Report on Competition Policy, p. 126.
42. *Alloy Surcharge*, D.Comm. Jan. 21, 1998, 1998 OJ L 100/55, point 71, *aff'd* CFI Dec. 13, 2001, 2001 ECR II-3501, para. 96; *CGM CMA FETTCSA*, CFI March 19, 2003, T-213/00, para. 178.
43. *PVC II*, CFI April 20, 1999, 1999 ECR II-931, paras 637–644 (*aff'd* ECJ Oct. 15, 2002, 2002 ECR I-8375); *Industrial Copper Tubes*, D.Comm. Dec. 16, 2003, IP/03/1746, points 214–215.
44. *FEDETAB*, ECJ Oct. 29, 1980, 1980 ECR 3125, paras 130–134; *Vimpoltu*, D.Comm. July 13, 1983, 1983 OJ L 200/44, 48–49; *IFTRA Glass*, D.Comm. May 15, 1974, 1974 OJ L 150/1, 12–13; *Italian Flat Glass II*, D.Comm. Dec. 7, 1988, 1989 OJ L 33/44, 62; *Net Book Agreement*, D.Comm. Dec. 12, 1988, 1989 OJ L 22/12, 19–20 *(rev'd* ECJ Jan. 17, 1995, 1995 ECR I-23 because of insufficient economic evaluation under Article 81 (3)).
45. *NSO*, ECJ Dec. 10, 1985, 1985 ECR 3801, 3819–3820, paras 23–27.
46. *Flemish Travel Agencies*, ECJ Oct. 1, 1987, 1987 ECR 3801, para. 17; *UIP*, CFI June 6, 1995, 1995 ECR II-1503, para. 50
47. *IFTRA Glass*, D.Comm. May 15, 1974, 1974 OJ L 160/1, 12–13; *IFTRA Aluminium*, D.Comm. July 15, 1975, 1975 OJ L 228/3, 9–20; *Meldoc*, D.Comm. Nov. 26, 1986, 1986 OJ L 348/50, 61–62 (collective dumping).
48. *VCH*, ECJ Oct. 17, 1972, 1972 ECR 977, paras 15–25; *Fire Insurance*, ECJ Jan. 27, 1987, 1987 ECR 405, 455–458, paras 34–43; *FENEX*, D.Comm. June 5, 1996, 1996 OJ L 181/28, para. 61; *Dutch Cranes*, CFI Oct. 22, 1997, 1997 ECR II-1739, para. 157; *Pre-insulated Pipes*, Oct. 21, 1998, 1999 OJ L 24/1, point 147 (*aff'd* CFI March 20, 2002, 2002 ECR II-1847). However, recommended prices which are clearly considered (*and* practised) as non-binding may qualify for exemption: *Uniworld*, D.Comm. March 19, 1997, 1997 OJ L 318/24.
49. *Dutch Cranes*, CFI Oct. 22, 1997, 1997 ECR II-1739, para. 159. An agreement between competitors setting 'recommended' prices can restrict competition just as effectively as fixed prices: *VCH*, ECJ Oct. 17, 1972, 1972 ECR 977, paras 15–25.

- Regular exchange of price information, which is a typical means of arriving at and monitoring concerted prices;[50]
- Jointly calculating price components,[51] particularly costs[52] or fees,[53] and joint preparation of the underlying calculation formula may be a restraint of competition when more extensive agreements among competitors are involved;[54]
- Jointly influencing or stabilizing commodity prices to prevent violent price fluctuations.[55]
- Jointly observing 'fair' or 'reasonable' prices and avoiding 'unfair' or 'unreasonable' pricing practices, with the consequence that the limits between fair and unfair or reasonable and unreasonable pricing are decided collectively and result in fixing minimum prices.[56]
- Jointly employing a system of uniform delivered prices regardless of the location of the purchaser, which disadvantages nearby purchasers and those wishing to pick up their orders themselves.[57]

---

50. *Thyssen Stahl*, ECJ Oct. 2, 2003, C-194/99, para. 89; *PVC II*, CFI April 20, 1999, 1999 ECR II-931, paras 674–687 (meetings between producers as means of monitoring concerted prices) (*aff'd* ECJ Oct. 15, 2002, 2002 ECR I-8375); *British Sugar, Tate & Lyle*, CFI July 12, 2001, 2001 ECR II-2035, paras 58–66; *Methionine*, D.Comm. July 2, 2002, 2003 OJ L 255/1, points 423, 435 and 530.
51. E.g. jointly setting price components for environmental charges: *VOTOB*, Twenty-second Report on Competition Policy, points 177–186, or jointly calculating tank rental for liquid gas customers: *Dutch Industrial and Medical Gases*, D.Comm. July 24, 2002, 2003 OJ L 84/1, point 306.
52. *NSO*, CFI Feb. 21, 1995, 1995 ECR II-289, para. 152; jointly setting part of transport costs: *Transatlantic Agreement*, D.Comm. Oct. 19, 1994, 1994 OJ L 376/1, para. 295; *Far Eastern Freight Conference*, D.Comm. Dec. 21, 1994, 1994 OJ L 378/17, para. 54; indirectly by joint comparison of costs: *Dutch Construction Works*, D.Comm. Feb. 5, 1992, 1992 OJ L 92/1; *aff'd* CFI Feb. 21, 1995, 1995 ECR II-289; *Nederlandse Federatieve FEG*, D.Comm. Oct. 26, 1999, 2000 OJ L 39/1, points 114–122, *aff'd* CFI Dec. 16, 2002, T-5/00. *See* Horizontal Guidelines, point 25.
53. *Christie's and Sotheby's*, D.Comm. Oct. 30, 2002, IP/02/1585. *See also Far Eastern Freight Conference*, D.Comm. Dec. 21, 1994, 1994 OJ L 378117 (18.6% of the total costs); *Tariff Structures in the Combined Transport of Goods*, D.Comm. Feb. 24, 1993, 1993 OJ L 73/38, para. 33, unless the fee is only a marginal component of price (1%) (para. 53).
54. *IFTRA Glass*, D.Comm. May 15, 1974, 1974 OJ L 160/1, 13–14; *IFTRA Aluminium*, D.Comm. July 15, 1975, 1975 OJ L 228/3, 11; *SPO (Dutch Construction Works)*, CFI Feb. 21, 1995, 1995 ECR II-289, para. 146; *Alloy Surcharge*, D.Comm. Jan. 21, 1998, 1998 OJ L 100/55, points 55 and 62.
55. *Zinc Producer Group*, D.Comm. Aug. 6, 1984, 1984 OJ L 220/27, 38–39; *Aluminium Imports from Eastern Europe*, D.Comm. Dec. 19, 1984, 1985 OJ L 95/1, 42–43; *British Sugar, Tate & Lyle*, D.Comm. Oct. 14, 1998, 1998 OJ L 76/1.
56. Agreements preventing 'unfair' pricing: *IFTRA Glass*, D.Comm. May 15, 1974, 1974 OJ L 160/1, 11; *IFTRA Aluminium*, D.Comm. July 15, 1975, 1975 OJ L 228/3, 8–9; *Aluminium Imports from Eastern Europe*, D.Comm. Dec. 19, 1984, 1985 OJ L 95/1, 43–45; *Meldoc*, D.Comm. Nov. 26, 1986, 1986 OJ L 348/50, 61–62; *Belasco*, D.Comm. July 10, 1986, 1986 OJ L 232/15, 22.
57. *NCH*, D.Comm. Dec. 23, 1971, 1972 OJ L 22/16, 24–25; *IFTRA Glass*, D.Comm. May 15,

– Jointly imposing fixed resale prices through collective resale price maintenance, which has frequently been associated with schemes to divide national markets and restrict imports.[58]

Normally no Applicability of Article 81 (3).
Normally the anticompetitive practices listed above do not satisfy the conditions of Article 81 (3) because of their severe detriment to consumer interests[59] even if they concern price components or fees constituting only a part of the end-consumer price.[60] Only in the most rare and exceptional cases may the Commission see fit to grant an exemption. One such exception was the *Eurocheques* case where the Commission exempted an agreement between national banking associations of the member states on the charging of uniform rates of commission for clearing 'Eurocheques' (a standardized European payments medium) when these were drawn abroad in local currency. The standard rates of commission were found to be essential for the system, which facilitated the acceptance of the cheques abroad and avoided unnecessary and lengthy bilateral negotiations between the associated banks.[61] However, this example should not be generalized since the Commission changed its position when adopting a decision in the *Eurochèques Helsinki Agreement* cases. The Commission ruled that an agreement under which French banks charged French retailers the same commission for cashing foreign eurocheques as they charged for paying by bank card infringed Article 81 and imposed a fine.[62] Similarly, the Commission ruled that German and the Austrian

---

1974, 1974 OJ L 160/1, 14; *Cement*, D.Comm. Nov. 30, 1994, 1994 OJ L 343/1, points 10.3–10.5. (*aff'd* CFI March 15, 2000, 2000 ECR II-491).

58. *Belgian Wallpaper*, ECJ Nov. 26, 1975, 1975 ECR 1491, paras 6–21; *FEDETAB*, ECJ Oct. 29, 1980, 1980 ECR 3125, paras 158–162; *VBVB/VBBB*, ECJ Jan. 17, 1984, 1984 ECR 19, 66, para. 45; *Binon/AMP*, ECJ July 3, 1985, 1985 ECR 2015, paras 44–47; SSI, ECJ Dec. 10, 1985, 1985 ECR 3831, paras 23–32; *ASPA*, D.Comm. June 30, 1970, 1970 OJ L 148/9, 11; *GISA*, D.Comm. Dec. 22, 1972, 1972 OJ L 303/45, 48; *Stoves and Heaters*, D.Comm. June 3, 1975, 1975 OJ L 159/22, 26; *GERO-fabriek*, D.Comm. Dec. 22, 1976, 1977 OJ L 16/8, 11.
59. *SSI*, ECJ Dec. 10, 1985, 1985 ECR 3831, paras 83–85; *Peroxygen*, D.Comm. Nov. 23, 1984, 1985 OJ L 35/1, 16; *Methionine*, D.Comm. July 2, 2002, 2003 OJ L 255/1 and IP/02/976.
60. *Dutch Construction Works*, CFI Feb. 21, 1995, 1995 ECR II-289, paras 146–152; *VOTOB*, Twenty-second Report on Competition Policy, points 177–186.
61. *Eurocheques I*, D.Comm. Dec. 10, 1984, 1985 OJ L 35/43, 50. The exemption was not renewed because some banks were deducting commission from the face value of the checks, thus reducing their acceptability as a commercial payments medium, which was one of the main justifications for the system: Commission Press Release No. IP/88/496. Similarly *Reims II*, D.Comm. Sept. 15, 1999, 1999 OJ L 275/17, point 87; *VISA*, D.Comm. July 24, 2002, 2002 OJ L 318/17, points 79–95 (clearance of an agreement on multilateral interchange fee); *IFTI Simulcasting*, D.Comm. Oct. 8, 2002, 2003 OJ L 107/58, points 70–78 (obligation to respect the tariffs of the country of destination).
62. *Eurocheques – Helsinki*, D.Comm. March 25, 1992, 1992 OJ L 95/50; *aff'd* CFI Feb. 23, 1994, 1994 ECR II-49, paras 85–91 (this agreement was not covered by the package deal which had been exempted in the 1984 decision).

banks infinged Article 81 (1) by fixing deposit, lending and other rates to the detriment of businesses and consumers.[63] However, the exceptional circumstances of specific sectors, such as the maritime sector, may justify joint fixing of freight rates because of the stabilizing role of such agreements,[64] which can, however, not be generalized.[65]

Influence of National Price Regulation.
The competition rules of the EC Treaty apply despite widely differing competitive conditions in the member states. Article 81 (1) applies even if an anticompetitive pricing agreement:

- is made known to national regulatory authorities beforehand;[66]
- is a subject of consultation with national regulatory authorities;[67]
- is submitted to national regulatory authorities who approve the principle of an increase,[68] an average[69] or maximum price increase;[70]
- is authorized by the national regulatory authorities before or after it was reached;[71] or
- accords with national practice, even if common to all member states, which cannot prevail over the application of the competition rules.[72]

National government price controls must be examined to determine whether or not they leave the parties substantial freedom to compete on price[73] and whether

63. *German Banks*, D.Comm. Dec. 11, 2001, 2003 OJ L 15/1; *Austrian Banks*, D.Comm. June 11, 2002, IP/02/844.
64. *CGM CMA FETTCSA*, CFI March 19, 2003, T-213/00, para. 98; *Compagnie Générale Maritime*, CFI Feb. 28, 2002, 2002 ECR II-1011, para. 254.
65. For instance, the fixing of common rates for maritime services is prohibited even if they are ancillary and necessary for maritime transport: *TACA – Atlantic Container Line*, CFI Sept. 30, 2003, T-191/98, paras 568.
66. *Zinc Producer Group*, D.Comm. Aug. 6, 1984, 1984 OJ L 220/27, 39 ('... the fact that member state authorities had knowledge of, participated in or approved price-fixing agreements does not protect them from the application of the EEC competition rules'.)
67. *SSI*, ECJ Dec. 10, 1985, 1985 ECR 3831, paras 38–40; *Belasco*, D.Comm. July 10, 1986, 1986 OJ L 232/15, 24–25.
68. *CNSD*, D.Comm. June 30, 1993, 1993 OJ L 203/27, *aff'd* ECJ June 18, 1998, 1998 ECR I-3851, paras 58–60.
69. *Benelux Flat Glass*, D.Comm. July 23, 1984, 1984 OJ L 212/13.
70. *Benelux Flat Glass*, D.Comm. July 23, 1984, 1984 OJ L 212/13, 18–19; *CNSD*, D.Comm. June 30, 1993, 1993 OJ L 203/27 (*aff'd* ECJ June 18, 1998, 1998 ECR I-3851).
71. *BNIC I*, ECJ Jan. 30, 1985, 1985 ECR 391, paras 18–26.
72. *TACA – Atlantic Container Line*, CFI Sept. 30, 2003, T-191/98, para. 569.
73. *FEDETAB*, ECJ Oct. 29, 1980, 1980 ECR 3125, paras 123–134. *See also Autotrasporti Librandi*, ECJ Oct. 1, 1998, 1998 ECR I-5955, para. 52; *Polypropylene-Montecatini*, ECJ July 8, 1999, 1999 ECR I-4539, paras 127–128.

the regulations themselves violate Community law.[74] *A fortiori*, commercial practices of non-member states cannot dictate the application of Community law.[75] In any event, if there is a substantial residual field for operation of some price competition, then Article 81 is infringed by an agreement or concerted practice that prevents, restricts or distorts the price competition that could still operate.

Strict Observance of Fixed Prices v. Loose Co-ordination of Prices and Concerted Practices.

Strict observance of a price-fixing agreement leading to a higher price than the market price merits particularly high fines[76] but is not necessary for the agreement to be prohibited by Article 81[77] and subject to heavy fines.[78] Fixing price targets is prohibited even if the targets are not achieved, as demonstrated in the *Polypropylene* cartel where the fixed price levels actually achieved generally fell short of the targets, and initiatives to increase prices tended to run out of momentum, sometimes resulting in a temporary drop in prices; whenever a sudden price 'collapse' occurred, it was arrested by fixing a new, lower target and an upward price trend was re-established.[79] Price recommendations may be caught by Article

---

74. *Sugar*, ECJ Dec. 16, 1975, 1975 ECR 1663, paras 65–72; *CNSD*, ECJ June 18, 1998, 1998 ECR I-3851, para. 53.
75. *TACA – Atlantic Container Line*, CFI Sept. 30, 2003, T-191/98, para. 569.
76. *See* in particular *Austrian Banks*, D.Comm. June 11, 2002, IP/02/844 (fine of EUR 124.26 million).
77. No need to prove the concrete effects: *Pre-insulated Pipes – LR af 1998*, CFI March 20, 2002, 2002 ECR II-1705, para. 47.
78. Most recently: *Lysine*, D.Comm. June 7, 2000, 2001 OJ L 152/14 (fines of EUR 109.9 million); *Graphite electrodes*, D.Comm. July 18, 2001, 2002 OJ L 100/1 (fines of EUR 218.8 million); *Sodium gluconate*, D.Comm. Oct. 2, 2001, IP/01/1355 (fines of EUR 57.53 million); *Vitamins*, D.Comm. Dec. 5, 2001, 2002 OJ L 239/18 (fines of EUR 855.22 million); *Belgian Brewers*, D.Comm. Dec. 5, 2001, IP/01/1739 (fines of EUR 91 million); *Zinc phosphate*, D.Comm. Dec. 11, 2001, IP/01/1797 (fines of EUR 11.95 million); *German Banks*, Dec. 11, 2001, IP/01/1796 (fines of EUR 100.8 million); *Carbonless paper*, D.Comm. Dec. 20, 2001, IP/01/1892 (fines of EUR 313.7 million); *Austrian Banks*, D.Comm. June 11, 2002, IP/02/844 (fines of EUR 124.26 million); *Methionine*, D.Comm. July 2, 2002, IP/02/976 (fines of EUR 127 million); *Dutch industrial gases*, D.Comm. July 24, 2002, IP/02/1139 (fines of EUR 25.72 million); *Christie's and Sotheby's*, D.Comm. Oct. 30, 2002, IP/02/1585 (fine of EUR 20.4 million); *Methylglucamine*, D.Comm. Nov. 27, 2002, IP/02/1746 (fines of EUR 2.85 million); *Plasterboard*, D.Comm. Nov. 27, 2002, IP/02/1744 (fines of EUR 478 million); *Food flavour enhancer*, D.Comm. Dec. 17, 2002, IP/02/1907 (fines of EUR 20.56 million); *Concrete reinforcing bar*, D.Comm. Dec. 17, 2002, IP/02/1908 (fines of EUR 85 million); *Specialities graphites*, D.Comm. Dec. 17, 2002, IP/02/1906 (fines of EUR 60.6 million); *Sorbates*, D.Comm. Oct. 2, 2003, IP/03/1330 (fines of EUR 138.4 million); *Organic Peroxides*, D.Comm. Dec. 10, 2003, IP/03/1700 (fines of EUR 70 million); *Industrial Copper Tubes Cartel*, D.Comm. Dec. 16, 2003, IP/03/1746 (fines of EUR 78.6 million).
79. *Polypropylene – Atochem*, CFI Oct. 24, 1991, 1991 ECR II-1177, para. 100 (not appealed). *See also Methionine*, D.Comm. July 2, 2002, 2003 OJ L 255/1, point 437; *Tokai Carbon*, CFI April 29, 2004, T-236/01, para. 369.

81 even if they do not lead to the setting of identical prices,[80] although this may justify lower fines.[81] Whether or not a party intends to abide by the agreement that it has made or the decision to which it is subject without publicly distancing itself from what was agreed is irrelevant ('mental reservation').[82] Fines may be imposed even after the infringement ceased.[83] The continuation of an exchange of information or of an institutionalized discussion mechanism is evidence of the continuation of the agreement or the concerted practice.[84] The Commission's practice of imposing heavy fines on price fixing cartels is in general upheld by the Court,[85] in some cases with minor corrections, principally due to an erroneous assessment of the duration[86] and the gravity of the infringement,[87] the extent of involvement of the individual companies[88] and the degree of their cooperation with the Commission.[89]

---

80. *Dutch Cranes*, CFI Oct. 22, 1997, 1997 ECR II-1739, para. 159 (published recommended price may be tantamount to price fixing). *See Fire Insurance*, ECJ Jan. 27, 1987, 1987 ECR 405, 457, paras 39–42; *FENEX*, D.Comm. June 5, 1996, 1996 OJ L 181/28, points 61–73; *Pre-insulated Pipes*, Oct. 21, 1998, 1999 OJ L 24/1, point 147 (*aff'd* CFI March 20, 2002, 2002 ECR II-1847).
81. *Eurochèques Helsinki*, CFI Feb. 23, 1994, 1994 ECR II-49, paras 142–144.
82. *Polypropylene – Herkules*, CFI Dec. 17, 1991, 1991 ECR II-1711, para. 232; *Welded Steel Mesh – Tréfilunion*, CFI April 6, 1995, 1995 ECR II-791, paras 85–86; *HFB Holding*, CFI March 20, 2002, 2002 ECR II-1487, paras 137 and 227; *Aalborg – Cement*, ECJ Jan. 7, 2004, C-204/00P, para. 81.
83. *Polypropylene – Hercules*, CFI Dec. 17, 1991, 1991 ECR II-1715, para. 310, *Polypropylene – Montecatini*, ECJ July 8, 1999, 1999 ECR I-4539, para. 195; *Krupp Thyssen*, CFI Dec. 13, 2001, 2001 ECR II-3757, para. 313 (*aff'd* ECJ Oct. 2, 2003, C-194/99).
84. *EMI/CBS*, ECJ June 15, 1976, 1976 ECR 811, paras 30–31; *PVC II*, D.Comm. July 29, 1994, 1994 OJ L 239/14, point 31; *aff'd* CFI April 20, 1999, 1999 ECR II-931, paras 674–686, and ECJ Oct. 15, 2002, 2002 ECR I-8375; *Steel Beams – Thyssen Stahl*, CFI March 11, 1999, 1999 ECR II-347, paras 373–378 (*aff'd* ECJ Oct. 2, 2003, C-194/99).
85. The Commission was not prevented from raising the previous general level of fines in order to increase their deterrent effect: *Ke Kelit*, CFI March 20, 2002, 2002 ECR II-1647, para. 128.
86. *Carton – KNP*, ECJ Nov. 16, 2000, 2000 ECR I-9641, para. 66; *British Sugar, Tate & Lyle*, CFI July 12, 2001, 2001 ECR II-2035, para. 162.
87. In the *Italian Flat Glass* case the fines imposed by Commission decision (D.Comm. Dec. 7, 1988, 1989 OJ L 33/44; April 23, 1986, 1986 OJ L 230/1) were considerably reduced by the Court for lack of sufficient proof for the main infringement: CFI March 10, 1992, 1992 ECR II-1403. *See also Steel Beams – British Steel*, CFI March 11, 1999, 1999 ECR II-629; *Far Eastern Freight Conference*, Feb. 28, 2002, 2002 ECR II-1101, para. 485 (existence of reasonable doubt).
88. *Cement*, CFI March 15, 2000, 2000 ECR II-491, para. 4815, *aff'd* ECJ Jan. 7, 2004, C-204/00 P, paras 78–92 and 328.
89. *Krupp Thyssen*, CFI Dec. 13, 2001, 2001 ECR II-3757, paras 315–319 (*aff'd* ECJ Oct. 2, 2003, C-194/99); *ABB Brown Boveri*, CFI March 20, 2002, 2002 ECR II-1881, para. 244.

(b) Discounts

Discounts as an Element of Price Competition.
Agreements or concerted practices between competitors with respect to discounts of wholesale or retail list prices are merely an indirect means of fixing or regulating prices that is expressly prohibited under Article 81 (1) (a). Examples of such prohibited restrictions of competition are agreements:

- prohibiting discounts,[90] which is, in fact, a form of indirect price fixing;[91]
- fixing uniform rates of discount or dealers' margins.[92]
- setting maximum discounts;[93]
- prohibiting any public announcement of discounts while allowing discounts to be given;[94]
- prohibiting discounts deviating from those announced to the public;[95]
- prohibiting secret discounts, which are sometimes the last vestige of competition in oligopoly markets with homogeneous products that are ordinarily sold at virtually identical prices;[96]
- prohibiting indirect discounts in the form of gifts[97] or other benefits or trade-in prices for second-hand vehicles higher than agreed maximum levels;[98]
- operating a collective discount scheme toward large retail customers in order to prevent them from switching to another supplier.[99]

Collective Aggregated Rebate Schemes among Competitors.
Collective aggregated rebate schemes among competitors under which annual rebates are based on customers' total purchases from all the parties combined

---

90. *CMA CGM – FETTCSA*, CFI March 19, 2003, T-213/00, paras 175–176; *CB and Europay – Eurocheques*, CFI Feb. 23, 1994, 1994 ECR II-49, paras 84–86; *Flemish Travel Agents*, ECJ Oct. 1, 1987, 1987 ECR 3801, para. 17; *Belasco*, ECJ July 11, 1989, 1989 ECR 2117, para. 12; *IFTRA Glass*, D.Comm. May 15, 1974, 1974 OJ L 160/1, 12; *IFTRA Aluminium*, D.Comm. July 15, 1975, 1975 OJ L 228/3, 10; *UIP II*, CFI June 6, 1995, 1995 ECR II-1503, para. 50.
91. *CMA CGM – FETTCSA*, CFI March 19, 2003, T-213/00, para. 175.
92. *FEDETAB*, ECJ Oct. 29, 1980, 1980 ECR 3125,3264–3267, paras 131–146; *SSI*, ECJ Dec. 10, 1985, 1985 ECR 3831, paras 33–40; *Italian Flat Glass I*, D.Comm. Sept. 28, 1981, 1981 OJ L 326/32, 39–40.
93. *Vimpoltu*, D.Comm. July 13, 1983, 1983 OJ L 200/44, 48.
94. *Belgian Wallpaper*, ECJ Nov. 26, 1975, 1975 ECR 1491, 1511, paras 6–11.
95. *IFTRA Glass*, D.Comm. May 15, 1974, 1974 OJ L 160/1, 2, 12; *IFTRA Aluminium*, D.Comm. July 15, 1975, 1975 OJ L 228/3, 4–6, 10–11.
96. *Ibid.*; *see also Industrial and Medical Gases*, D.Comm. July 24, 2002, 2003 OJ L 84/1, points 334–353.
97. *SSI*, D.Comm. July 15, 1982, 1982 OJ L 232/1, 17–18, 28–29; *Belasco*, D.Comm. July 10, 1986, 1986 OJ L 232/15, 23, *aff'd* ECJ July 11, 1989, 1989 ECR 2117, paras 17–18.
98. *Vimpoltu*, D.Comm. July 13, 1983, 1983 OJ L 200/44, 48–49.
99. *British Sugar – Tate & Lyle*, D.Comm. Oct. 14, 1998, 1999 OJ L 76/1, *aff'd* CFI July 12, 2001, 2001 ECR II-2035, paras 58–66.

(usually only domestic suppliers) are likely to infringe Article 81 . This is because such schemes have the effect of denying sales opportunities to third parties and concentrating purchases on the rebate scheme participants and limiting imports from other Member States.[100] In the *Dutch Cigarettes* case, [101] the associations of Dutch retail tobacconists (NSO) and of Dutch cigarette manufacturers and importers (SSI) unsuccessfully challenged a Commission decision refusing to grant an exemption under Article 81 (3) for an annual bonus (rebate) scheme for qualifying retail tobacconists run by the SSI. Under the bonus scheme, the retailers received a standard end-of-year rebate based on their total purchases of cigarettes from all the manufacturers and importers participating in the scheme. The Dutch tobacco duty legislation prohibited the sale of tobacco products to the final consumer at a price other than that indicated on the revenue stamps or the setting of different retail prices for identical products within the same market without special authorization, but the law still left room for competition between manufacturers/importers and between wholesalers on trade discounts and end-of-year rebates. Thus, the introduction of a uniform rebate scheme eliminated an important competitive tool and infringed Article 81. The Court of Justice also rejected the argument that the uniform bonus scheme was necessary to preserve an effective network of specialist retailers.

Justifiable Discounts.
Discounts may be granted it they are economically justified on the basis of cost savings, such as quantities supplied, promotion or transport costs, provided they are applied in a non-discriminatory way.[102]

(c) Terms and Conditions of Sale

Joint Setting of Terms or Conditions of Sale Normally Prohibited.
Article 81 (1) (a) not only prohibits price-fixing; it also prohibits directly or indirectly fixing 'any other trading conditions'. Thus, agreements or concerted practices among competitors to co-ordinate terms and conditions of services,

---

100. *NSO*, ECJ Dec. 10, 1985, 1985 ECR 3801, paras 32–49; *FEDETAB*, ECJ Oct. 29, 1980, 1980 ECR 3125, paras 142–146, affirming consistent Commission practice with regard to such schemes: *German Ceramic Tiles Discount Agreement*, D.Comm. Dec. 29, 1970, 1971 OJ L 10/15, 18; *Gas Water Heaters*, D.Comm. July 3, 1973, 1973 OJ L 217/34, 36–37.

101. *NSO*, ECJ Dec. 10, 1985, 1985 ECR 3801, paras 28–49 and 58/62; *SSI*, ECJ Dec. 10, 1985, 1985 ECR 3831, paras 33–45 and 83–85.

102. *See* the discount schemes accepted in *British Plaster Board II* (Twenty-second Report on Competition Policy, p. 443), *notified* in the context of the proceedings under Article 82 (D.Comm. Dec. 5, 1988, 1989 OJ L 10/50; *aff'd* ECJ April 6, 1995, 1995 ECR I-865): *Super Stock Scheme* (1992 OJ C 321/9), *Buying Societies Plasterboard Rebate Scheme* (1992 OJ C 321/10), *Efficiency Rebate Scheme* (1992 OJ C 321/11), *Accessories and Do-it-yourself Promotion Schemes* (1992 OJ C 321/12).

103. *FEDETAB*, ECJ Oct. 29, 1980, 1980 ECR 3125, paras 154–156.

such as transport, or of sale that include competitively sensitive price components such as payment terms including credit periods and interest charges,[103] customer services and guarantees are likely to infringe Article 81.[104] The same applies to agreements between competitors on uniform pricing methods[105] and collusive tendering (bid-rigging).[106] The Commission has also condemned agreements on uniform delivered prices and on 'basing point' ('phantom freight') systems for the calculation of freight charges regardless of the actual location of the supplier, both of which lead to alignment of prices by ignoring differences in freight costs between customers and suppliers at nearby or distant locations.[107]

The *IFTRA* Fair Trading Rules Case.
An example of a cartel masked as fair trading rules was the standard contract on fair trading rules adopted by European manufacturers of glass containers. Among other things the so-called 'IFTRA rules' prohibited discriminatory prices, discounts or other conditions of sale, and any secret departure from published offers or price lists. Under arrangements made to implement the IFTRA rules the parties also agreed to exchange information on prices, discounts and sales terms so as to prevent one manufacturer from gaining any secret competitive advantage over its rivals, and fostered price co-ordination by providing a uniform system for calculating costs and a delivered pricing system whereby customers located closest to a supplier were not permitted to gain a price advantage from this act. The Commission condemned the offending rules and agreements and refused the request for an exemption.[108]

3. Limiting or Controlling Production, Markets, Technical Development, or Investment

Introduction.
Article 81 (1) (b) prohibits agreements or concerted practices that 'limit or control production, markets, technical development or investment'. Technical development, investment and production restrictions of various kinds may be a means of achieving important rationalization benefits in the form of new products, uniform product standards or specialization of production which may yield economies of

104. *TACA II*, D.Comm. Sept. 16, 1998, 1999 OJ L 95/1, points 442–448; *aff'd Atlantic Container Line*, CFI Sept. 30, 2003, T-191/98, paras 495–507.
105. *IFTRA Glass*, D.Comm. May 15, 1974, 1974 OJ L 160/1, 9, 13–14; *Steel Stockholders*, D.Comm. Feb. 8, 1980, 1980 OJ L 62/28, 33–35 (under Article 65 of the ECSC Treaty).
106. *Dutch Construction Works*, D.Comm. Feb. 5, 1992, 1992 OJ L 92/1; *aff'd* CFI Feb. 21, 1995, 1995 ECR I-289; *Pre-insulated Pipes*, D.Comm. Oct. 21, 1998, 1999 OJ L 24/1 (*aff'd LR af 1998*, CFI March 20, 2002, 2002 ECR II-1705, para. 141).
107. *See* 'Spatial Pricing and Competition', EC Commission, Competition – Approximation of Legislation Series, No. 29 (1976).
108. *IFTRA Glass*, D.Comm. May 15, 1974, 1974 OJ L 160/1.

scale and lower production costs.[109] Such cooperation arrangements will normally qualify for clearance – either by block or individual exemption – and are therefore discussed in the context of the block exemption regulations and the Commission's Horizontal Guidelines. [110] However, investment, capacity and production restrictions may also be part of an overall market-sharing or price-fixing cartel or aim at controlling the output of an industry, in particular by fixing quotas, and artificially influencing the supply/demand balance,[111] or at restructuring of industries with structural overcapacity during which the older and less efficient plants are closed down and the industry as a whole becomes more efficient.[112] Such agreements normally contain hardcore restrictions, such as 'the limitation of output or sales'[113] and do not satisfy the conditions of Article 81 (3) and are discussed in the context of the other examples of hardcore restrictions enumerated in Article 81 (1). However, agreements to stop production with a view of improving the environmental performance of the products may satisfy the conditions of Article 81 (3).[114]

Restrictions of Investment or Capacity.

Decisions on investment or capacity belong to the most confidential and sensitive business decisions of actual or potential competitors. Any agreement between competitors limiting or controlling each other's strategic plans in these respects is likely to be prohibited and normally ineligible for exemption. This applies to the non-expansion of capacity, [115] non-use[116] or reciprocal information on the use of capacity[117] or provisions on mutual deliveries or payments in order to compensate

109. *See* Guidelines on Article 81 (3), points 48–72.

110. Sections B.and C. *infra.*

111. *Italian Cast Glass*, D.Comm. Dec. 17, 1980, 1980 OJ L 383/19; *Benelux Flat Glass*, D.Comm. July 23, 1984, 1984 OJ L 212/13; *Zinc Producer Group*, D.Comm. Aug. 6, 1984, 1984 OJ L 220/27; *Pre-insulated Pipes*, D.Comm. Oct. 21, 1998, 1999 OJ L 24/1, point 147 (*aff'd* CFI March 20, 2002, 2002 ECR II-1487). *See also Boehringer-Quinine*, ECJ July 15, 1970, 1970 ECR 769, paras 45–46; *Cimbel*, D.Comm. Dec. 22, 1972, 1972 OJ L 303/24, 33–34; *Zinc Producer Group*, D.Comm. Aug. 6, 1984, 1984 OJ L 220/27, 38; *Polypropylene – Atochem*, CFI Oct. 24, 1991, 1991 ECR I-1177, paras 125–126, 162–164; *aff'd* ECJ July 8, 1999, 1999 ECR I-4539; *Lysine*, D.Comm. June 7, 2000, 2001 OJ L 152/14 (fixing prices and quotas), *aff'd* (in substance) CFI July 9, 2003, T-220/00.

112. *See Polyester Fibers Agreement*, Second Report on Competition Policy, point 31; *Synthetic Fibers I*, Eighth Report on Competition Policy, point 42.

113. *De Minimis* Notice, 2001 OJ C 149/18, point 12 (1) (b).

114. *CEC ED*, D.Comm. Feb. 11, 2000, 2000 OJ L 187/47.

115. New Capacity: *Cimbel*, Dec. 22, 1972, 1972 OJ L 303/24, 33–34; *CRN*, D.Comm. Dec. 22, 1972, 1972 OJ L 303/7, 8; *Rolled Zinc Products*, D.Comm. Dec. 14, 1982, 1982 OJ L 362/40; new investment: *Zinc Producer Group*, D.Comm. Aug. 6, 1984, 1984 OJ L 220/27; preventing the use of a new technology: *Pre-insulated Pipes*, D.Comm. Oct. 21, 1998, 1999 OJ L 24/1, point 147 (*aff'd* CFI March 20, 2002, 2002 ECR II-1845).

116. *Transatlantic Agreement (TAA)*, D.Comm. Oct. 19, 1994, 1994 OJ L 376/1, point 319.

117. *Carton*, D.Comm. July 13, 1994, 1994 OJ L 243/1, point 136 (*aff'd* CFI March 11, 1999, 1999 ECR II-2111, para. 134, referred back ECJ Nov. 16, 2000, 2000 ECR I-9925 (because of erroneous calculation of the fine).

under- or over-utilization of capacity.[118] The same applies to agreements limiting the parties' output of certain products[119] or coordinating production levels.[120] In many cases such output and investment restrictions are a means of controlling supply to particular markets in order to maintain prices and are thus associated with sales quotas and are unlikely to satisfy the conditions of Article 81 (3).[121]

Industrial Restructuring Agreements (Crisis Cartels).
Neither the EC Treaty nor the ECSC Treaty specifically provides an express exception from the rules on competition for cartels formed to deal with problems of structural adjustment in an industry. The Treaties assume that the problems of declining industries, which are inherent in any market economy, can normally be resolved through the market. The policy followed by the Commission is that if exceptions are to be permitted, it is only when the principal objective of the agreement is to provide a direct solution to the structural adjustment problem by means of orderly reductions of capacity.

Structural v. Cyclical Crisis.
A difficulty in evaluating agreements claimed to be necessary for restructuring purposes is in distinguishing structural from mere cyclical problems. In a cyclical downturn (recession), capacity should be maintained for the expected upturn. A structural crisis in an industry, on the other hand, involves industry-wide overcapacity which results in some or all producers operating at inefficient output levels and often at a loss. In these circumstances, a significant reduction in industry production capacity is necessary. The Commission has stated that adjustments to an industry's capacity are best achieved by market forces[122] and the Court

---

118. *Rolled Zinc Products*, D.Comm. Dec. 14, 1982, 1982 OJ L 362/40; *Trans Atlantic Agreement*, D.Comm. Oct. 19, 1994, 1994 OJ L 376/1, para. 20; *French-West-African Shipowners Committee*, D.Comm. April 1, 1992, 1992 OJ L 134/1.

119. Agreement not to produce synthetic quinine: *Boehringer-Quinine*, ECJ July 15, 1970, 1970 ECR 769, paras 45–46.

120. *Zinc Producer Group*, D.Comm. Aug. 6, 1984, 1984 OJ L 220/27, 38; *Transatlantic Agreement*, D.Comm. Oct. 19, 1994, 1994 OJ L 376/1, para. 300.

121. *Carton – Sarrio*, CFI May 14, 1998, 1998 ECR II-1439, para. 328, *aff'd* ECJ Nov. 16, 2000, 2000 ECR I-9641; *Sorbates*, D.Comm. Oct. 2, 2003, IP/03/1330. Setting sales quotas: *Quinine – Boehringer*, ECJ July 15, 1970, 1970 ECR 769, para. 41–44; *Welded Steel Mesh – Société des Treillis*, CFI April 6, 1995, 1995 ECR I-1191, para. 60; *NCH (Cement)*, D.Comm. Dec. 23, 1971, 1972 OJ L 22/16; *Auditel*, D.Comm. Nov. 24, 1993, 1993 OJ L 306/50 (agreeing on audience ratings); *Transatlantic Agreement*, D.Comm. Oct. 19, 1994, 1994 OJ L 376/1, point 8; *Pre-insulated Pipes*, D.Comm. Oct. 21, 1998, 1999 OJ L 24/1, point 147 (*aff'd* CFI March 20, 2002, 2002 ECR II-1845). Fixing sales targets: *Polypropylene – Atochem*, CFI Oct. 24, 1991, 1991 ECR I-1177, paras 162–166, 169. Under Article 65 (2) ECSC Treaty: *Stainless Steel*, D.Comm. July 18, 1990, Twentieth Report on Competition Policy, point 123.

122. *Cimbel*, D.Comm. Dec. 22, 1972, 1972 OJ L 303/24, 36; *Steel Beams*, D.Comm. Feb. 16, 1994, 1994 OJ L 116/1, *aff'd* CFI March 11, 1999, 1999 ECR II-629, paras 251–274.

confirmed this statement in accepting the crisis argument only as a justification for mitigating fines.[123] More generally, the Court of Justice rejected a proposed amendment of the ECSC Treaty to allow restructuring agreements, holding that virtual antitrust waivers for agreements promoting adjustment to 'new market conditions' were not justified.[124] However, the members of an industry with severe and chronic structural overcapacity may be able to justify to the Commission the adoption of anticompetitive measures to deal with the problem. The measures must be reasonable and limited to those necessary to achieve a significant reduction in capacity.[125] Coordinating pricing policy[126] or fixing production quotas, for example, is strictly prohibited.[127] The key to gaining an exemption under Article 81 (3) is to set forth a detailed plan that will achieve non-discriminatory and effective capacity reductions, specifying which firms are to reduce capacity at

---

123. *Welded Steel Mesh – Baustahlgewerbe*, CFI April 6, 1995, 1995 ECR I-987 paras 55–56, 121.
124. The Court stressed the importance of the final condition for the authorization of specialization and joint buying or selling agreements, set out in subparagraph (c) of the first paragraph of Article 65 (2) of the ECSC Treaty, namely the maintenance of competition. The condition was 'intended to ensure that no agreement, no matter how acceptable it is and no matter even its intrinsic merits, can be permitted to enable the persons concerned, by virtue of their power in a specific sector, to control the market for those products and indeed, with regard to such products, to frustrate the very objectives of the Common Market'. (Opinion of the Court of Justice, Dec. 13, 1961, 1961 ECR 243, 260).
125. *Polyester Fibers Agreement*, Second Report on Competition Policy, point 31; *Synthetic Fibers I*, Eighth Report on Competition Policy, point 42 (restrictive agreements merely coordinating output or sales policies in order to overcome the overcapacity problems did not qualify for exemption); *Stichting Baksteen (Dutch Bricks)*, D.Comm. May 3, 1994, 1994 OJ L 131/1 5.
126. *French Beef*, D.Comm. April 2, 2003, IP/03/479 (reduction in the fine because of the successive crises leading to pressure and threat of violence from farmers).
127. Overcapacity has frequently been claimed to justify cartels, but at most has been regarded as a mitigating factor: *CRN*, D.Comm. Dec. 18, 1972, 1972 OJ L 303/7, 15 (no fine); *Cimbel*, D.Comm. Dec. 22, 1972, 1972 OJ L 303/24 (no fine); *Italian Cast Glass*, D.Comm. Dec. 17, 1980, 1980 OJ L 383/19, 26 (no fine); *White Lead*, D.Comm. Dec. 12, 1978, 1979 OJ L 21/16, 23 (no fine); *Rolled Zinc Products*, D.Comm. Dec. 14, 1982, 1982 OJ L 362/40 (no fine); *Welded Steel Mesh*, D.Comm. Aug. 2, 1989, 1989 OJ L 260/1, 35, 41 (fines of between ECU 13,000 and 4.5 million because part of an overall cartel), *aff'd* CFI April 6, 1995, 1995 ECR I-987, para. 121 and II-1191, para. 108 (no 'force majeure'). *See also* the Commission's decisions under Article 65 (1) of the ECSC Treaty: *Cockerill/Klöckner*, D.Comm. Jan. 12, 1979, 1979 OJ L 19/37 (exemption); *Special Steel Producers*, Tenth Report on Competition Policy, points 109–110 (fines totalling ECU 900,000); *Steel Stockholders*, D.Comm. Feb. 8, 1980, 1980 OJ L 62/28, 37 (no fine); *Stainless Steel*, D.Comm. July 18, 1990, Twentieth Report on Competition Policy, point 123 (fines totalling ECU 425,000). In *EATA*, D.Comm. April 30, 1999, 1999 OJ L 193/23, the Commission found that an arrangement between shipping lines on rates (conferences) and capacity (consortia) was likely to reduce significantly the advantages which would accrue the more efficient of them (point 166) and could not be justified under Article 81 (3) by the need of ensuring stability and preventing destructive price competition (point 197). *See also TACA II*, D.Comm, Sept. 16, 1999, 1999 OJ L 95/1, points 415–441.

what time.[128] Such a plan may also provide for enforcement, including penalties for non-compliance, and include an obligation not to build new capacity during the period of the agreement.[129] Capacity reduction often calls for plant closures and workforce reductions among the parties according to a fixed schedule, which therefore justifies only a short-term exemption. In *Synthetic Fibers*[130] the exemption was granted for three years. In *Dutch Brick Producers*[131] a five-year exemption was granted after eliminating price and quota restrictions. The plan also must not serve to shift the losses arising from unutilized capacity onto consumers.

Restructuring Arrangements Evaluated under Article 81.
Firms may try to overcome chronic overcapacity problems in an industry by various types of arrangement, multilateral and bilateral:

- *Multilateral agreements* involving most or all producers in an industry have generally had all the classic ingredients of cartels, namely price-fixing, quotas and market-sharing. The Commission has refused to grant exemption for alleged attempts to deal with overcapacity problems by this means, as in *Cimbel*[132] and *Polyester.*[133] On the other hand, multilateral schemes may bring about genuine rationalization if they are limited to and are effective at achieving a reduction of capacity. Such rationalization schemes may satisfy the conditions of Article 81 (3), as in the *Synthetic Fibers* and the *Dutch Brick* cases.[134]
- *Bilateral agreements* involving only two competing producers are the most likely form of rationalization agreement to satisfy the conditions of Article 81 (3), provided that they are effective at achieving a reduction of capacity, genuinely rationalize production and are not capable of eliminating competition with respect to a substantial part of the products in question. The advantage of bilateral agreements is that successful rationalization and specialization measures are more certain and effective between two firms than among numerous firms across an entire industry. The principal disadvantage is that the number of independent competitors is reduced. The *Bayer/BP Chemicals* case exempted

---

128. *Rolled Zinc Products*, D.Comm. Dec. 14, 1982, 1982 OJ L 362/40; *Synthetic Fibers II*, D.Comm. July 4, 1984, 1984 OJ L 207/17, 20–21, 23–24; *Krupp/Thyssen*, ECJ Oct. 15, 1985, 1985 ECR 3409; *Stichting Baksteen (Dutch Bricks)*, D.Comm. May 3, 1994, 1994 OJ L 131/15.
129. Restrictive agreements merely coordinationg output or sales policy in order to overcome the overcapacity problems did not qualify for exemption: *Dutch Bricks*, D.Comm. May 3, 1994, 1994 OJ L 131/15.
130. *Synthetic Fibers II*, D.Comm. July 4, 1984, 1984 OJ L 207/17, 23.
131. *Dutch Bricks*, D.Comm. May 3, 1994, 1994 OJ L 131/15.
132. *Cimbel*, D.Comm. Dec. 22, 1972, 1972 OJ L 303/24.
133. *Polyester Fibers Agreement (Synthetic Fibers I)*, Second Report on Competition Policy, point 31.
134. *Synthetic Fibers II*, D.Comm. July 4, 1984, 1984 OJ L 207/17, 20–21; *Dutch Bricks*, D.Comm. May 3, 1994, 1994 OJ L 131/15.

a joint restructuring and modernization of plants in order to avoid overcapacity.[135] The *EnichemICI* case may be close to the limits of what is acceptable since the agreement led to the creation of a non-dominant EC market leader with a 22–23% market share in PVC, followed closely by several other firms with slightly smaller shares.[136] The criteria used for exempting under Article 81 (3) a bilateral arrangement motivated by the need to restructure and avoid overcapacity are quite similar to those used under the merger control regulation when assessing merger-type operations.[137]

- *Private 'voluntary restraint agreements'* with suppliers from non-Community countries, whereby the latter agree to reduce the volume of their imports of a particular product into the Community or one of its member states, or to raise their prices, are sometimes made with the avowed intention of reducing overcapacity. However, as they merely reduce imports or monitor minimum price levels without allowing or promoting industrial restructuring, they have the character of a cartel that yields no substantial benefits and tends to maintain the existing overcapacity. As a result, up to now the Commission has refused to grant exemption for such agreements.[138]
- *Intergovernmental* voluntary restraint agreements setting maximum import quantities or quotas do not fall within Article 81 but may come into conflict with Community trade policies established under Article 133 of the EC Treaty.[139] They may also be complemented by private agreements between importers partitioning the global quota between them, which clearly infringe Article 81 (1).[140]
- In the *transport* sector, the prohibition of restrictive agreements may be set aside under Article 6 of Regulation 1017/68 for agreements designed to reduce 'disturbances' on the transport market in question. This provision is, however, repealed by Article 36 of Regulation 1/2003. According to Regulation 823/2000 on liner shipping companies (consortia),[141] it has been clarified that the non-

135. *Bayer/BP Chemicals*, D.Comm. May 5, 1988, 1988 OJ L 150/35.
136. *Enichem/ICI*, D.Comm. Dec. 22, 1987, 1988 OJ L 50/18.
137. *Kali + Salz/MDK (Treuhand)*, D.Comm. Dec. 14, 1993, 1994 OJ L 186/38; *rev'd* ECJ March 31, 1998, 1998 ECR I-1375, but clearance renewed: D.Comm. July 9, 1998, M.308; *SIV/Pilkington*, D.Comm. Dec. 21, 1993, 1994 OJ L 158/24. *See* Chapter VI.D.2.(d) and, with respect to similar problems under the state aid provisions, Commission's Notice Dec. 23, 1994, 1994 OJ C 368/12.
138. Commission's Notice on Japanese Imports (1972 OJ C 111/13). *France-Japanese Ballbearings Agreement*, D.Comm. Nov. 29, 1974, 1974 OJ L 343/19; *French-Taiwanese Mushroom Packers*, D.Comm. Jan. 8, 1975, 1975 OJ L 29/26.
139. *Asia Motor France II*, CFI Sept. 18, 1996, 1996 ECR I-961, para. 61. *See* in greater detail Chapter IX.
140. *Asia Motor France I*, CFI June 29, 1993, 1993 ECR I-669, paras 39–55, 69–71.
141. 2000 OJ L 100/24, as amended by Regulation 463/2004, 2004 OJ L 77/23.

utilisation of vessel capacity within a consortia is *not* an essential feature of consortia[142] whereas temporary capacity adjustments are block exempted.[143]

Quota Arrangements as Prohibited Means of Market Sharing.
A quota agreement sets or controls the quantities of goods or services which competitors are to produce or market. The quota may limit total output or restrict the volume of sales within a certain territory. Quota arrangements are a classic form of market sharing.[144] They have consistently been found by the Commission to infringe Article 81 (1) and to be ineligible for exemption under Article 81 (3).[145] Quotas typically aim at fixing the market shares of the parties at certain levels, often based on the participants' sales in prior years and adapted to shifts in production capacity and the market situation. In order to be effective, quota arrangements commonly control the quantities sold and compensate for under- and over-deliveries.[146] However, they also infringe Article 81 (1) even if they only fix quota targets which are not in fact observed because this still leads to anticompetitive joint discipline of the market strategy among competitors. Their purpose and

142. Recital 7 and Article 4.
143. Article 3 (2) (b).
144. *Soda Ash II – Solvay/CSK*, D.Comm. Dec. 13, 2000, 2003 OJ L 10/1. *See Carton – Sarrio*, CFI May 14, 1998, 1998 ECR II-1439, para. 328, *aff'd* ECJ Nov. 16, 2000, 2000 ECR I-9641). *See French- West African Shipowners Committees*, D.Comm. April 1, 1992, 1992 OJ L 134/1; *Pre-insulated Pipes*, D.Comm. Oct. 21, 1998, 1999 OJ L 24/1, points 135 and 147 *(aff'd* CFI March 20, 2002, 2002 ECR II-1847); *PVC II*, CFI April 20, 1999, 1999 ECR II-931, paras 588–590 ('sharing the pain' expressing quota arrangement), *aff'd* ECJ Oct. 15, 2002, 2002 ECR I-8375. Under Article 65 of the ECSC Treaty: *Welded Steel Mesh – Baustahlgewerke*, CFI April 6, 1995, 1995 ECR II-987, para. 60; *Steel Beams – Thyssen Stahl*, CFI March 11, 1999, 1999 ECR II-347, paras 331–349.
145. *Lysine*, D.Comm. June 7, 2000, 2001 OJ L 152/14. *See NCH*, D.Comm. Dec. 21, 1971, 1972 OJ L 22/16; *CRN*, D.Comm. Dec. 18, 1972, 1972 OJ L 303/7; *Cimbel*, D.Comm. Dec. 22, 1972, 1972 OJ L 303/24; *French-Taiwanese Mushroom Packers*, D.Comm. Jan. 8, 1975, 1975 OJ L 29/26; *White Lead*, D.Comm. Dec. 12, 1978, 1979 OJ L 21/16; *Italian Cast Glass*, D.Comm. Dec. 17, 1980, 1980 OJ L 383/19; *Italian Flat Glass I*, D.Comm. Sept. 28, 1981, 1981 OJ L 326/32; *Benelux Flat Glass*, D.Comm. July 23, 1984, 1984 OJ L 212/13; *Zinc Producer Group*, D.Comm. Aug. 6, 1984, 1984 OJ L 220/27; *Aluminium Imports from Eastern Europe*, D.Comm. Dec. 19, 1984, 1985 OJ L 92/1; *Polypropylene*, D.Comm. April 23, 1986, 1986 OJ L 230/1; *aff'd* CFI Oct. 24, 1991, 1991 ECR I-1177 paras 162–169; *Belasco*, D.Comm. July 10, 1986, 1986 OJ L 232/15; *aff'd* ECJ July 11, 1989, 1989 ECR 2117; *Meldoc*, D.Comm. Nov. 26, 1986, 1986 OJ L 348/50; *PVC I*, D.Comm. July 29, 1994, 1994 OJ L 239/14; *Welded Steel Mesh*, D.Comm. Aug. 2, 1989, 1989 OJ L 260/1; *aff'd* CFI April 6, 1995, 1995 ECR II-987, para. 60. *See also* under Article 65 of the ECSC Treaty: *Special Steel Producers*, Tenth Report on Competition Policy, points 109–110; *Stainless Steel*, D.Comm. July 18, 1990, Commission Press Release No. IP/90/584; *Steel Beams*, D.Comm. Feb. 16, 1994, 1994 OJ L 116/1.
146. *Pre-insulated Pipes*, D.Comm. Oct. 21, 1998, 1999 OJ L 24/1, point 147 (including compensation for deliveries on other markets), (*aff'd* CFI March 20; 2002, 2002 ECR II-1847); *PVC I*, CFI April 20, 1999, 1999 ECR II-931, paras 554–575 *(aff'd* ECJ Oct. 15, 2002, 2002 ECR I-8375).

effect is often to maintain or raise prices.[147] Frequently production quota agreements also back up a tacit or express price coordination agreement.[148]

Practical Application of Quota Arrangements.
Quota systems often involve the gathering of detailed information about each of the participants' production and/or sales to ensure that they do not exceed their allotted quotas.[149] It is also common for administrative machinery to be set up to monitor sales and to set future quota allocations.[150] In some cases the arrangements go so far as to provide for balancing deliveries or payments among the parties to adjust for output or sales in excess of quota.[151] However, in any system deviations from quota generally must be explained by the offender, so that group discipline is maintained.[152] An agreement merely on target delivery levels[153] may therefore be just as effective in restricting supply and creating artificial market conditions conducive to price rises[154] as a more formally managed system. Nor is

147. *See Polypropylene*, D.Comm. April 23, 1986, 1986 OJ L 230/1,28, *aff'd* CFI Oct. 24, 1991, 1991 ECR I-867, paras 85–93; *Meldoc*, D.Comm. Nov. 26, 1986, 1986 OJ L 348/50, 60; *PVC I*, D.Comm. July 27, 1994, 1994 OJ L 239/14, para. 35; *Carton*, D.Comm. July 13, 1994, 1994 OJ L 243/1, paras 133–137, *aff'd* CFI May 14, 1998, 1998 ECR II-1373, para. 143; *Far Eastern Freight Conference*, D.Comm. Dec. 21, 1994, 1994 OJ L 378/17, paras 119–133 (*aff'd* CFI Feb. 28, 2002, 2002 ECR II-1101).

148. In the form of supply quotas: *Sorbates*, D.Comm. Oct. 2, 2003, IP/03/479; *Quinine – Boehringer*, July 15, 1970, 1970 ECR 769, paras 41–44; *NCH (cement)*, D.Comm. Dec. 23, 1971, 1972 OJ L 22/16; *Welded Steel Mesh – Société des Treillis*, CFI April 6, 1995, 1995 ECR I-1191, para. 60; or of supply targets: *Polypropylene – Atochem*, CFI Oct. 24, 1991, 1991 ECR I-1177, paras 162–164, 169; *aff'd* ECJ July 8, 1999, 1999 ECR I-4539; or exchange of detailed information on orders received and goods supplied: *Carton*, D.Comm. July 13, 1994, 1994 OJ L 243/1, para. 136, *aff'd* CFI May 14, 1998, 1998 ECR II-1439, paras 111–112; *Cement*, D.Comm. Nov. 30, 1994, 1994 OJ L 343/1, paras 47 and 62; *Pre-insulated Pipes*, D.Comm. Oct. 21, 1998, 1999 OJ L 24/1, point 147 (*aff'd* CFI March 20, 2002, 2002 ECR II-1647).

149. E.g., *Welded Steel Mesh*, D.Comm. Aug. 2, 1989, 1989 OJ L 260/1, 35, *aff'd* CFI April 6, 1995, 1995 ECR I-1191, paras 72–73; *Polypropylene – Petrofina*, CFI Oct. 24, 1991, 1991 ECR I-1087 paras 171–177.

150. *Carton*, D.Comm. July 13, 1994, 1994 OJ L 243/1, para. 134; *aff'd Stora*, CFI May 14, 1998, 1998 ECR I-2111, para. 111.

151. *PVC I*, CFI April 20, 1999, 1999 ECR II-931, paras 592–598 (*aff'd* ECJ Oct. 15, 2002, 2002 ECR I-8375); *Transatlantic Agreement*, D.Comm. Oct. 19, 1994, 1994 OJ L 376/1, para. 20; *Pre-insulated Pipes*, D.Comm. Oct. 21, 1998, 1999 OJ L 24/1, point 147 (*aff'd* CFI March 20, 2002, 2002 ECR II-1845).

152. *Polypropylene – Atochem*, CFI Oct. 24, 1991, 1991 ECR I-1177, paras 162–164, 169, 187; *CRN*, D.Comm. Dec. 18, 1972, 1972 OJ L 303/7, 14; *Aluminium Imports from Eastern Europe*, D.Comm. Dec. 19, 1984, 1985 OJ L 92/1, 40; *Belasco*, ECJ July 11, 1989, 1989 ECR 2117, paras 19–20.

153. *Polypropylene*, D.Comm. April 23, 1986, 1986 OJ L 230/1, 16–17, 29–30; *aff'd* ECJ Oct. 24, 1991, 1991 ECR I-1177, paras 162–164, 169, 187; *Preinsulated Pipes*, D.Comm. Oct. 21, 1998, 1999 OJ L 24/1, point 147 (*aff'd* CFI March 20, 2002, 2002 ECR II-1845).

154. Quota arrangements may make price arrangements superfluous because producers have no incentive to cut prices: *PVC*, D.Comm. July 27, 1994, 1994 OJ L 239/14, para. 35; *aff'd* CFI

it necessary that the quotas are always meticulously observed. The Commission stated in the *White Lead* decision that 'a quota agreement conflicts with this provision [Article 81 (1)] even if it has the limitation or control of markets merely as its object … An agreement does not cease to be anticompetitive simply because it is temporarily or even repeatedly circumvented by one of the parties to it'.[155] Even a system that is limited to an exchange of detailed individualized information on deliveries, as in the *Fatty Acids* case,[156] has been found to infringe Article 81 (1) as equivalent to a quota scheme. In *White Lead*, the Commission also ruled that even without a formal quota scheme the exchange of sales information between competitors restricted competition:

> 'In this way they reduce or even remove the risks which would arise if they were not aware of each other's market policy and the amounts they delivered through the absence of reliable statistics and the lack of knowledge of demand in the two different sectors of paints and plastic material. The information provided on deliveries during the previous month is very precise. It makes it possible to recognize another party's intentions in good time, where he plans for instance to begin supplying a market which he has hitherto supplied only occasionally if at all, or to raise the quantities sold, which on a shrinking market would sooner or later lead to price cuts and thus increase the danger of a general collapse in prices, which was exactly what cooperation was intended to prevent.'[157]

4. Sharing Markets or Sources of Supply

Geographic Market Sharing.
A division of markets may be achieved not only by express export restrictions, but also by agreements to limit exports to shipments between the parties to the agreement,[158] reciprocal exclusive distribution agreements between competing

---

April 20, 1999, 1999 ECR II-931, paras 656–660 (*aff'd* ECJ Oct. 15, 2002, 2002 ECR I-8375); *Welded Steel Mesh*, D.Comm. Aug. 2, 1989, 1989 OJ L 260/1, 34, *aff'd* CFI April 6, 1995, 1995 ECR I-1191.

155. *White Lead*, D.Comm. Dec. 12, 1978, 1979 OJ L 21/16, 21. *Polypropylene-Atochem*, CFI Oct. 24, 1991, 1991 ECR I-1177, para. 187.

156. *Fatty Acids*, D.Comm. Dec. 2, 1986, 1987 OJ L 3/17, 22–23.

157. *White Lead*, D.Comm. Dec. 12, 1978, 1979 OJ L 21/16, 21; the Commission affirmed this approach in: *Carton*, D.Comm. July 13, 1994, 1994 OJ L 243/1, para. 136 (*aff'd* ECJ Nov. 16, 2000, 2000 ECR I-9925); *Cement*, D.Comm. Nov. 30, 1994, 1994 OJ L 343/1, para. 62.

158. *See Sugar*, ECJ Dec. 16, 1975, 1975 ECR 1663, 1943, paras 181–182; *Cement*, D.Comm. Nov. 30, 1994, 1994 OJ L 343/1, paras 54.1 and 55.3. Similarly under Article 31: *Telecommunication Directive – Terminal Equipment*, ECJ March 19, 1991, 1991 ECR I-1223, paras 34–36.

manufacturers[159] or by the numerous cases prosecuted by the Commission of collective exclusive dealing agreements and aggregated rebate schemes, both of which raise barriers to entry by third parties and thereby protect markets. The sharing out of geographic markets within the EC – often on national lines – is, by definition, likely to affect trade between member states. The same also applies to agreements between competitors within and outside the Community isolating the EC from competitive third country producers, whereas import and export restrictions solely concerning non-member countries require careful evaluation to see whether they have an appreciable effect on interstate trade.

Market Sharing within the EC/EEA.
Arrangements between competitors having the object or effect of dividing member states' markets from one another clearly affect trade between member states, infringe Article 81 (1) and do not meet the criteria for exemption under Article 81 (3)[160] and are subject to heavy fines.[161] For instance, the Commission fined a market sharing agreement between SAS and Maersk Air, according to which Maersk Air would cease flying between Copenhagen and Stockholm and, as com-

159. *Greek Television*, ECJ June 18, 1991, 1991 ECR I-2925, paras 23–25 (conflict of interest when distributing its own and a foreign competitor's products). *See Fisons-UCB/Hoechst*, Sixth Report on Competition Policy, points 126–128 (this was a swap agreement under which Fisons-UCB supplied Hoechst customers in Belgium in Hoechst's name, and Hoechst supplied Fison-UCB customers in Germany under Fisons-UCB's name in order to save on freight costs. Although the parties were theoretically free to determine the price for sales to their customers in the other country, in practice the price was always the same as, or only very slightly below, that charged by the domestic producer. The Commission concluded that the system led to coordination between the companies on distribution policy); *Siemens/Fanuc*, D.Comm. Dec. 19, 1985, 1985 OJ L 376/29 (this was a reciprocal exclusive distribution agreement under which Siemens granted Fanuc exclusive selling rights for its computerized numerical controls for machine tools in Asia, and Fanuc granted the same rights to Siemens for Europe. Siemens was the leading seller of numerical controls in Europe, and Fanuc was the leader in Asia. The Commission fined the firms ECU 1 million each). *See also SNEAP/Cansulex*, Twelfth Report on Competition Policy, point 81; *CSK/Gist Brocades*, Twenty-sixth Report on Competition Policy, p. 143. Exceptionally, such arrangements may be exempted insofar and so long as they are necessary to penetrate new markets: *see Carlsberg/Watney*, D.Comm. July 12, 1984, 1984 OJ L 207/26.

160. *Boehringer-Quinine*, ECJ July 15, 1970, 1970 ECR 759, paras 30–34; *Julien/Van Katwijk*, D.Comm. Oct. 28, 1970, 1970 OJ L 242/18, 20; *Potassium Salts*, D.Comm. May 11, 1973, 1973 OJ L 217/3,4–5; *SNPE/Leafields Engineering*, D.Comm. June 12, 1978, 1978 OJ L 191/41, 43; *Cast Iron and Steel Rolls*, D.Comm. Oct. 17, 1983, 1983 OJ L 317/1, 12–13; *Benelux Flat Glass*, D.Comm. July 23, 1984, 1984 OJ L 212/13, 19; *Peroxygen*, D.Comm. Nov. 23, 1984, 1985 OJ L 35/1, 13; *Woodpulp II*, ECJ March 31, 1993, 1993 ECR I-1317, paras 168–177.

161. *See Seamless Steel Tubes*, Dec. 8, 1999, Twenty-ninth Report on Competition Policy, p. 137; *Graphite Electrodes*, D.Comm. July 18, 2001, 2002 OJ L 100/1; *Citric Acid*, D.Comm. Dec. 5, 2001, 2002 OJ L 239/18; *Belgian Brewers*, D.Comm. Dec. 5, 2001, IP/01/1739; *Carbonless Paper*, D.Comm. Dec. 20, 2001, IP/01/1892.

pensation, SAS would stop operating the route between Copenhagen and Venice, on which Maersk Air would start operations.[162] Market sharing arrangements may include a general non-aggression pact, the allocation of customers, price-fixing in the retail sector the limitation of investments and advertising, and a detailed exchange of information, as in the *Belgian Beer* case, a market sharing agreement between the two biggest beer suppliers on the Belgian market.[163] The prohibition of Article 81 (1) applies even if the market sharing is limited to a smaller, although substantial, part of Common Market.[164] Written agreements exist only under specific circumstances, e.g. in the framework of liner conferences (freight pooling)[165] or in cases of reciprocal exclusive distribution arrangements.[166] In other cases, a market sharing arrangement must be proved by circumstantial evidence. A strong indication of national market sharing may be when a producer supplies competing producers in other member states with substantial quantities of his output on a regular basis and refrains from selling to others in those territories.[167] However, in *Asturienne-Rheinzinc*,[168] the Commission failed in its case against Belgian and German zinc producers for allegedly conspiring to isolate the German market against parallel imports from Belgium because its evidence was susceptible to different interpretations. Agreements on the use of trademarks[169] or

162. *SAS/Maersk Air*, D.Comm. July 18, 2001, 2003 OJ L 265/15, point 69 (fines of respectively EUR 40 and 13 million). The agreement between British Midland, Lufthansa and SAS to coordinate their services to and from London Heathrow and Manchester was exempted subject to the commitments to make slots available so as to allow a new entrant to increase its frequencies: *British Midland, Lufthansa and SAS*, D.Comm. June 12, 2001, 2001, IP/01/831.
163. *Belgian Breweries*, D.Comm. Dec. 5, 2001, 2003 OJ L 200/1, point 265 (fines of EUR 91 million).
164. *Luxembourg Breweries*, D.Comm. Dec. 5, 2001, 2002 OJ L 253/21, points 77–81.
165. Trans Atlantic Agreement – *TACA I*, D.Comm. Oct. 19, 1994, 1994 OJ L 376/1 (including express compensation provision in the case of overdelivery) (suspended CFI March 10, 1995, 1995 ECR II-595, *aff'd* ECJ July 19, 1995, 1995 ECR I-2165); stricter approach in *Trans Atlantic Conference I*, D.Comm. Nov. 26, 1996, Twenty-fifth Report on Competition Policy, point 73 (Article 15 (6) decision) (*aff'd* CFI Nov. 22, 1995, 1995 ECR II-2895); *TACA II*, D.Comm. Dec. 3, 2001, IP/01/1713 (clearance only after abolition of information exchange and capacity coordination); *Far Eastern Freight Conference*, D.Comm. Dec. 21, 1994, 1994 OJ L 378/17 *aff'd*, although annulling the symbolic fine, CFI Feb. 28, 2002, 2002 ECR II-1101, paras 484–485).
166. E.g., *Siemens/Fanuc*, D.Comm. Dec. 19, 1985, 1985 OJ L 376/29.
167. *Sugar*, ECJ Dec. 16, 1975, 1975 ECR 1663, 1933–1945, paras 131–192; *Welded Steel Mesh*, D.Comm. Aug. 2, 1989, 1989 OJ L 260/1, 37, *aff'd* CFI April 6, 1995, 1995 ECR I-987 paras 103–104; *aff'd* ECJ July 17, 1997, 1997 ECR I-4411; *Cement*, D.Comm. Nov. 30, 1994, 1994 OJ L 343/1, paras 54.1 and 55.3. (*rev'd* in this respect because of lack of proof CFI March 15, 2000, 2000 ECR II-491, paras 3790, 3798, 3811, 3821, 3848).
168. *Asturienne-Rheinzinc*, ECJ March 28, 1984, 1984 ECR 1679, paras 10–23 (suspect conduct explained by failure of one party to pay invoices). *See also Sugar*, ECJ Dec. 16, 1975, 1975 ECR 1663, paras 295–304, 342–354.
169. *Toltecs/Dorcet*, ECJ Jan. 30, 1985, 1985 ECR 373.

product certificates[170] in order to prevent or control imports may also be a form of market sharing.

Agreements that Limit or Control Imports into the EC.
Competing purchasers of a good or service imported from outside the EC sometimes agree to pool their buying power in order to negotiate more favorable prices and other terms from foreign suppliers. An import cartel which restricts the quantities or coordinates the prices of imports into the Community[171] or allocates territories between non-Community countries and the Community[172] infringes Article 81 (1) of the EC Treaty if it has an effect on trade between the member states. This can be so even in the case of an import agreement between producers in a single member state where its effects are not limited to the territory of that country, but extend directly or indirectly to other member states.[173] The Court of Justice has also found that it could be a restriction of competition affecting intra-EC trade for the owners of the same trademark within and outside the Community to agree that the non-Community trademark owner will not attempt to import the trademarked goods into the Community although it has subsidiaries there that could distribute the goods.[174]

Jurisdiction over Import Cartels between Non-EC Firms.
In the *Wood Pulp* case[175] the Court of Justice confirmed the Community's jurisdiction to apply Article 81 to import cartels involving solely non-Community firms. The decisive factor was where the anticompetitive agreement was *implemented* rather than where it was formed. It had been implemented within the Community through the parties' sales of wood pulp to customers in the EC. It was irrelevant how their conduct within the Community was organized, whether via direct sales

170. System of certificates issued by an association for cranes of its members which did not permit acceptance of equivalent product guarantees from other systems: *Dutch Cranes (Stichting Certificatie Kraanhuurbedrijf)*, D.Comm. Nov. 29, 1995, 1995 OJ L 312/79, *aff'd* CFI Oct. 22, 1997, 1997 ECR I-1739, para. 149. *See Anseau*, D.Comm. Dec. 17, 1981, 1982 OJ L 167/39, *aff'd* ECJ Nov. 8, 1983, 1983 ECR 3369.

171. *Zinc Producer Group*, D.Comm. Aug. 6, 1984, 1984 OJ L 220/27, 40–41; *Aluminium Imports from Eastern Europe*, D.Comm. Dec. 19, 1984, 1985 OJ L 92/1, 3940.

172. *EMI/CBS*, ECJ June 15, 1976, 1976 ECR 811, 848, paras 28–29; *Siemens/Fanuc*, D.Comm. Dec. 18, 1985, 1985 OJ L 376/29, 35.

173. *France-Japanese Ballbearings Agreement*, D.Comm. Nov. 29, 1974, 1974 OJ L 343/19, 25; *French-Taiwanese Mushroom Packers*, D.Comm. Jan. 8, 1975, 1975 OJ L 29/26, 28. *See Asia Motor France I*, CFI June 29, 1993, 1993 ECR I-669, where the (rejected) appeal concerned the non-intervention of the Commission against a quota sharing arrangement between the five biggest importers of Japanese cars.

174. *EMI/CBS*, ECJ June 15, 1976, 1976 ECR 811, 848–850, paras 28–29 and 38–39; *Gillette/Wilkinson*, D.Comm. Nov. 10, 1992, 1993 OJ L 116/21.

175. *Wood Pulp*, ECJ Sept. 27, 1988, 1988 ECR 5193, paras 16–23. *See Carton*, D.Comm. July 13, 1994, 1994 OJ L 243/1, para. 139, *aff'd* CFI May 14, 1998, 1998 ECR II-2111.

to customers or through subsidiaries, agents, sub-agents or branches within the Community making sales contacts with purchasers in the Community. The Court also ruled that the United States export cartel that participated in the anticompetitive pricing scheme with wood pulp producers from other nations was subject to Article 81. The Court noted that the United States antitrust exemption did not *compel* its members to engage in anticompetitive conduct but merely *permitted* such conduct. Since the statutory exemption did not compel conduct contrary to Community law, Article 81 applied and could be enforced. This policy was applied against a similar U.S. export cartel in the *Soda Ash* case.[176] Similarly, in *Cansulex*[177] the Commission opposed a proposal for the world's leading sulphur exporter, Cansulex of Canada, to transfer sole distribution rights for Western Europe and North Africa to Elf Aquitaine Production, the biggest sulphur producer in the Community. Elf would then have controlled the sale of competing Canadian sulphur in Europe. Following the Commission's intervention, the firms abandoned the project.

Cooperation in Exporting outside the Community.
Export agreements may be established among competing sellers of a good or service to coordinate advertising, shipment, warehousing, pricing and terms of sale in foreign markets. Agreements between large competitors governing their exports from the Community to non-member countries run a risk of having anticompetitive market sharing effects within the EC.[178] Two categories of export agreements can be distinguished. Export agreements between firms within the Community whose cooperation extends solely to exports to non-member countries may have no impact within the Community and thus qualify for exemption, or may not infringe Article 81 at all.[179] On the other hand, export agreements that 'channel' production surplus to third countries, thereby avoiding[180] or prohibiting[181] sales

176. *Soda Ash – ANSAC*, D.Comm. Dec. 19, 1990, 1991 OJ L 152/54.
177. *SNEAP/Cansulex*, Twelfth Report on Competition Policy, point 81.
178. In the CSV case (D.Comm. July 20, 1978, 1978 OJ L 242/15) the Commission refused an exemption for a joint sales organization established by the two largest Dutch producers of fertilizers for sales in Holland and in non-EC countries, because the Commission found that the agreement led in fact to a more far-reaching coordination affecting trade between member states.
179. *DECA*, D.Comm. Oct. 22, 1964, 1964 OJ 2761; *VVVF*, D.Comm. June 25, 1969, 1969 OJ L 168/22, 24.
180. *Cement*, CFI March 15, 2000, 200 ECR II-491, paras 3849–3850; *CEWAL*, CFI Oct. 8, 1996, 1996 ECR I-1201, paras 194–204. *See also Linoleum Manufacturers' Export Convention*, Fifth Report on Competition Policy, point 35; *CSV*, D.Comm. July 20, 1978, 1978 OJ L 242/15, 29.
181. An obligation imposed on a customer inside the Common Market to resell the products only in non-EC countries may be a disguised prohibition to export into other member states: *Asturienne – Rheinzinc*, ECJ March 28, 1984, 1984 ECR 1679, paras 24–30; *Welded Steel Mesh – Baustahlgewerbe*, CFI April 6, 1995, 1995 ECR I-987, paras 24 and 28.

within the common market or obliging buyers within the common market to resell the product to a given third country which prevents them from reselling into other member states are likely to infringe Article 85 (1). In the *Sugar* case[182] it was shown that the parties' collusive bidding for subsidies ('refunds') to export sugar to the world market had the effect of restricting competition between them within the Community: First, it resulted in exchanges of information that led to concerted practices with respect to prices. Secondly, it involved the diversion of excess supply to non-member countries, thereby reducing supplies of sugar within the Community and diminishing competition to an appreciable extent. By contrast, in the *Dutch Paint Producers* case[183] no significant repercussions were found within the Common Market since the minimum prices fixed for exports to non-EC countries were considerably lower than actual prices and were unlikely to influence the firms' prices within the Common Market, where they faced fierce competition.

Sharing Sources of Supply.
Agreements made by competitors to limit sources of supply may also infringe Article 81,[184] except where the agreements set minimum quality specifications or technical or safety standards which are necessary for the proper exploitation of a technology or product.[185]

Sharing Customers.
Agreements made by competitors to share out customers between them or to supply only certain customers according to a system agreed between them – whether or not at the request of the customer – clearly infringe Article 81.[186] The same applies to agreements between manufacturers to supply only certain distribution channels, usually in return for the distributors undertaking to buy only those manufacturers' products. The Commission normally considers such systems of collective selection of customers under which groups of manufacturers control distribution channels and thereby make market entry and parallel imports more difficult as infringements of Article 81, and therefore not capable of an exemption.[187] Even if the selection criteria are objective, the scheme is still likely to fall

182. *Sugar*, ECJ Dec. 16, 1975, 1975 ECR 1663, paras 558–602.
183. *VVVF*, D.Comm. June 25, 1969, 1969 OJ L 168/22, 24.
184. *VGB*, CFI May 14, 1997, 1997 ECR II-759, para. 120.
185. *See* Article 2 (1) (5) of Regulation 240/96 on technology transfer agreements.
186. *Dutch Industrial and Medical Gases*, D.Comm. July 24, 2002, 2003 OJ L 84/1, point 340; *Methylglucamine*, D.Comm. D.Comm. Nov. 27, 2002, IP/02/1746; *Food flavour enhancer*, D.Comm. Dec. 17, 2002, IP/02/1907.
187. *Convention Faïence*, Recommendation of Comm. July 24, 1963, First Report on Competition Policy, point 20; *ASPA*, D.Comm. June 30, 1970, 1970 OJ L 148/9, 10; *Belgian Central Heating Agreement*, D.Comm. Oct. 20, 1972, 1972 OJ L 264/22, 28; *GISA*, D.Comm. Dec. 22, 1972, 1972 OJ L 303/45, 49; *Gas Water Heaters*, D.Comm. July 3, 1973, 1973 OJ L 217/34, 38; *Belgian Wallpaper*, D.Comm. July 23, 1974, 1974 OJ L 237/3, 7; *Stoves and*

foul of Article 81 (1) and not to justify an exemption because of its character as a horizontal agreement between competitors.[188] Agreements between competing manufacturers selecting one of them to win the right to supply public administrations or bodies subject to public procurement (collusive tendering or bid-rigging) is a market sharing arrangement which is prohibited under Article 81 (1) and does not justify exemption under Article 81 (3).[189] However, joint bidding with the knowledge and consent of the purchaser – especially when one of the bidders acting alone would not qualify for lack of capacity, skills or product range – may be pro-competitive and does not infringe Article 81 (1).[190]

5. Applying Dissimilar Conditions to Equivalent Transactions

Rules in Articles 81 and 82.
The EC Treaty has no general provision that prohibits discrimination. However, discrimination based on nationality (Article 17) or sex (Article 141) is specifically prohibited.[191] In the realm of business the EC Treaty is based upon the assumption that every seller is basically free to select the persons or firms with whom it wishes to deal. The competition rules prohibit discrimination only where it is the object, means or effect of an anticompetitive agreement (Article 81 (1) (d)) or represents an abuse of a dominant position (Article 82 (c)).[192]

Collective Discrimination is Prohibited.
While the unilateral act of a firm to discriminate in price or other terms of sale may be contrary to Article 82, agreements between firms jointly to apply discriminatory prices or other terms infringe Article 81 (1). Agreements and concerted practices to discriminate against purchasers or suppliers are specifically prohibited in Article 81 (1) (d) insofar as the discrimination[193] has the effect of 'placing

Heaters, D.Comm. June 3, 1975, 1975 OJ L 159/22, 26; *Bomée Stichting*, D.Comm. Nov. 21, 1975, 1975 OJ L 329/30, 32–33.

188. *See FEDETAB*, ECJ Oct. 29, 1980, 1980 ECR 3125, paras 134–141; *Salonia*, ECJ June 16, 1981, 1981 ECR 1563, paras 11–20; *VBVB/VBBB*, ECJ Jan. 17, 1984, 1984 ECR 19, 55, paras 9,54–60; *Binon/AMP*, ECJ July 3, 1985, 1985 ECR 2015, paras 18, 27–35.
189. *SPO Dutch Construction Works*, D.Comm. Feb. 5, 1992, 1992 OJ L 92/1 (fines totalling 22.5 million ECU), *aff'd* CFI Feb. 21, 1995, 1995, II-289, para. 185; *Pre-insulated Pipes*, D.Comm. Oct. 21, 1998, 1999 OJ L 24/1, point 147 (*aff'd* CFI March 20, 2002, 2002 ECR II-1647).
190. Commission Notice on cooperation between enterprises, 1968 OJ C 75/3, para. 11.5. *See Independent Power Generators*, 1992 OJ C 92/4; *Twinning Program Engineering Group*, 1992 OJ C 148/8 and *ENAC*, 1993 C 175/12 (comfort letters granted for consortia beween EDF, Framatome and Siemens designed to improve safety of the East European atomic reactors).
191. *See* Chapter V.D.7.
192. *Parker Pen (Viho)*, CFI Jan. 12, 1995, 1995 ECR II-17, paras 61–69; *aff'd* ECJ Oct. 24, 1996, 1996 ECR I-5457.
193. Discrimination is defined as different treatment of comparable situations without objective justification: *SFEI*, CFI Jan. 15, 1997, 1997 ECR II-1, para. 101.

them at a competitive disadvantage'.[194] The discrimination may also be directed at third parties (other than purchasers or suppliers) and still be prohibited, since the list of examples given in Article 81 (1) is not exhaustive.[195] Cases of collective discrimination that have been found to infringe Article 81 (1) have involved nation-wide collective reciprocal exclusive dealing arrangements,[196] collective predatory pricing,[197] the collective exercise or pooling of patent rights[198] or trade marks,[199] or trade discriminatory practices in organizing trade fairs[200] and collective aggregated rebate systems which tend to tie customers to the group of participating firms as a whole and exclude competitors.[201] Examples of prohibited discrimination concerted or organized between competitors include:

- jointly prohibiting discriminatory prices;[202]
- jointly applying discriminatory ('dumping') prices in order to harm competitors;[203] and
- collective boycott.[204]

---

194. Collective system of certificates for cranes preventing thirds from competing: *Dutch Cranes*, CFI Oct. 22, 1997, 1997 ECR I-1739, para. 149. Collective system of aggregated (recognized) suppliers and distributors: *Convention Faïence*, D.Comm. July 24, 1963, First Report on Competition Policy, point 28.
195. *See under* Article 82 *Sugar*, ECJ Dec. 16, 1975, 1975 ECR 1663, paras 522–527.
196. *VCH*, D.Comm. Dec. 16, 1971, 1972 OJ L 13134; *aff'd* ECJ Oct. 17, 1972, 1972 ECR 977, 991, para. 30; *Sugar Beet*, D.Comm. Dec. 19, 1989, 1990 OJ L 31/32; *Irish Timber Importers' Association*, Commission Press Release No. IP/90/110.
197. *Belasco*, D.Comm. July 10, 1986, 1986 OJ L 232/15, *aff'd* ECJ July 11, 1989, 1989 ECR 2117 (concerted action aiming at discouraging other manufacturers from taking away customers); *Meldoc*, D.Comm. Nov. 26, 1986, 1986 OJ L 348/50 (jointly applying discriminatory 'dumping' prices in order to harm competitors); *CEWAL*, D.Comm. Dec. 23, 1992, 1993 OJ L 34/20; *aff'd* CFI Oct. 8, 1996, 1996 ECR I-1201 (collective low-pricing in order to drive out competitors); *British Sugar – Tate & Lyle*, D.Comm. Oct. 14, 1998, 1999 OJ L 76/1 (collective discount policies toward large retail customers) (*aff'd* in this respect CFI July 17, 2001, 2001 ECR II-2035).
198. *IGR Stereo Television I*, Eleventh Report on Competition Policy, point 94; *IGR Stereo Television II*, Fourteenth Report on Competition Policy, point 92 (restrictions on access to two patents for stereo television reception held by a body set up by German television manufacturers).
199. *Anseau*, ECJ Nov. 8, 1983, 1983 ECR 3369, 3413, para. 35 (refusal to make conformity labels available to importers into Belgium that were not sole importers); *Poroton*, Tenth Report on Competition Policy, points 130–132 (restrictions on access by French insulating brick manufacturers to the 'Poroton' quality label used by German producers).
200. *UNIDI*, D.Comm. July 17, 1975, 1975 OJ L 228/14; *British Dental Trade Association*, D.Comm. July 11, 1988, 1988 OJ L 233/15, 16–17 and 22–23.
201. *NSO*, ECJ Dec. 10, 1985, 1985 ECR 3801, 3823–3824, paras 39–42.
202. *IFTRA Glass*, D.Comm. May 15, 1974, 1974 OJ 160/1, 8–9, 12–13; *Dutch Electrotechnical Federation*, D.Comm. Oct. 26, 1999, 2000 OJ L 39/1, point 120.
203. *Meldoc*, D.Comm. Nov. 26, 1986, 1986 OJ L 348/50, 61–62.
204. *Pre-insulated Pipes*, D.Comm. Oct. 21, 1998, 1999 OJ L 24/1, point 147 (*aff'd LR af 1998* CFI March 20, 2002, 2002 ECR II-1705, para. 137).

Different Treatment of Like Situations.
Discrimination may not only consist in the different treatment of like situations, but also in equal treatment of different ones.[205] Agreements among competing firms not to discriminate in prices or other terms of sale have therefore been found to infringe Article 81 (1) as likely to restrain discounting. Examples of such cases include:

- A prohibition agreed among competitors against offering discriminatory prices, which may amount to collective resale price fixing[206] or an illegal price cartel;[207]
- A prohibition against granting different rates of discount to individual customers, which amounted to an illegal price cartel.[208]
- Joint implementation of an identical pricing scheme irrespective of the location of the customer.[209]

Boycott as a Special Form of Discrimination.
A boycott consists of unilateral or collective action to cut off supplies or purchases to or from a particular customer or supplier or the application of conditions to that customer or supplier which make continued dealings impractical. Boycotts are often used to force a trader to adopt conduct that is anticompetitive (a predatory boycott) or to punish violations of agreements that restrain competition (a defensive boycott). A common type of boycott starts when a dealer demands that his supplier 'blacklist' other dealers who are selling outside their assigned sales area, engaging in price cutting or failing to meet selective distribution criteria. The Commission's experience in boycott cases is limited. Up to now the Commission has applied Article 81 (1) in cases where the boycott was organized by a trade association under an agreement between competing suppliers and was designed to strengthen the anticompetitive effect of contractual obligations (e.g., to charge certain prices or use specified distribution channels) even though the boycott remained only a threat or was only occasionally enforced.[210] Access to advertising

205. *Italy v. Commission*, ECJ July 17, 1963, 1963 ECR 165, 177–178.
206. *IFTRA Glass*, D.Comm. May 15, 1974, 1974 OJ L 160/1, 12; *IFTRA Aluminium*, D.Comm. July 15, 1975, 1975 OJ L 228/3, 10.
207. *Net Book Agreement*, D.Comm. Dec. 12, 1988, 1989 OJ L 22/12 (this part of the decision has been upheld by both CFI July 9, 1992, 1992 ECR II-1995 and ECJ Jan. 17, 1995, 1995 ECR I-23).
208. *FEDETAB*, ECJ Oct. 29, 1980, 1980 ECR 3125, paras 130–132.
209. *NCH*, D.Comm. Dec. 23, 1971, 1972 OJ L 22/16, 24–25; *IFTRA Glass*, D.Comm. May 15, 1974, 1974 OJ L 160/1, 14.
210. *Belgian Wallpaper*, D.Comm. July 23, 1974, 1974 OJ L 237/3, 9; Fourth Report on Competition Policy, point 66 (the boycott 'amounted to a particularly severe violation of the rules of competition, since its aim was to eliminate a troublesome competitor'). The decision was not overruled on appeal in this respect: ECJ Nov. 26, 1975, 1975 ECR 1491). *See also ASPA*, D.Comm. June 30, 1970, 1970 OJ L 148/9; *Dutch Cranes*, D.Comm. Nov. 29, 1995, 1995 OJ

in trade journals must not be restricted by agreements between competitors (who influence the journal) to discontinue such advertisements. For instance, in the Commission's *Boat Equipment* investigation,[211] the only two Belgian specialist journals in the boat equipment trade refused to continue to carry advertisements for a British supplier of boat equipment similar to those that they had published in the past. The journals had been approached by Belgian manufacturers who alleged that they were competing under serious cost and tax disadvantages. The British supplier complained to the Commission that his sales in Belgium had suffered seriously. In response to the Commission's intervention the journals agreed to accept advertisements from suppliers in other member states on the same basis as from their Belgian competitors.

Associations Defending Legitimate Interests or Discriminating against Non-Members.
Associations defending the professional interests of their members are unlikely to infringe Article 81 (1), provided they do not discriminate against non-members, in particular by refusing access without objective justification or applying discriminatory fees.[212] Associations pursuing an anticompetitive object, such as exchange of commercially sensitive information, fixing prices or tariffs or allocating quotas, strengthen the anticompetitive effect by exerting pressure on non-members to join their organization, thereby preventing potential competition contrary to Article 81 and possibly Article 82.[213]

6. Tying Arrangements

Definition.
Article 81 (1) (e) prohibits making 'the conclusion of contracts subject to acceptance by the other parties of supplementary obligations which, by their nature

---

L 312/79, point 28 (blacklisting members of an association which do not respect the association's certification requirement); *aff'd* CFI Oct. 22, 1997, 1997 ECR I-1739, paras 141–146); *Pre-insulated Pipes*, D.Comm. Oct. 21, 1998, 1999 OJ L 24/1, point 147 (*aff'd* CFI March 20, 2002, 2002 ECR II-1847).

211. *Boat Equipment*, Tenth Report on Competition Policy, points 119–120.

212. *VGB*, CFI May 14, 1997, 1997 ECR II-759, paras 115–128; *British Cattle and Sheep Breeders Association*, Twenty-second Report on Competition Policy, points 56–566. *See* section 20 (6) of the German Act against Restraints of Competition: professional associations may not deny admission of an enterprise if the denial constitutes unequal treatment and unfairly places the enterprise at a disadvantage in competition.

213. *SPO – Dutch Construction Works*, CFI Feb. 21, 1995, 1995 ECR II-285, paras 199–200 (restrictive exchange of information system); *Dutch Cranes*, CFI Oct. 22, 1997, 1997 ECR II-1739, paras 141–146 (restrictive bid-rigging); *French – West-African Shipowners' Committee*, D.Comm. April 1, 1992, 1992 OJ L 134/1, point 68 (restrictive liner shipping conference); *CEWAL*, CFI Oct. 22, 1996, 1996 ECR II-1201, para. 149; *TACA II*, D.Comm. Sept. 16, 1998, 1999 OJ L 95/1, point 560 (maritime transport organization preventing potential competition from non-members).

or according to commercial usage, have no connection with the subject of such contracts'. This is commonly known as a 'tying' arrangement involving a 'tying product' for which the customer has a special need or demand and which is therefore used by the supplier as a 'leverage', and the 'tied product' upon whose purchase the seller conditions sale of the tying product. Tying affects the competitive freedom of the purchaser to find a better substitute or obtain better terms of sale for the tied product. Conversely, it also harms the right of third parties to sell their products to a purchaser who would be free to purchase from them if he were not forced to purchase the tied product. Tying between a seller and a purchaser of goods or services is rarely contrary to Article 81 if the seller imposing the tie does not have a meaningful market position in the tying product, but is likely to infringe Article 81 and 82 if the supplier holds a dominant position in the tying product, which is discussed in Chapter V.[214] Tying practices in a vertical context are discussed in Chapter IV.[215]

Scarce Case Law.
The leading case is the *Windsurfing* case[216] where the Commission ruled (and the Court of Justice confirmed) that it was a violation of Article 81 for a licensor to require its licensees to sell the patented sailboard rig only in conjunction with the (unpatented) sailboards, thereby impeding competitors from supplying boards to the licensees. This case concerned a licence agreement between non-competitors. Collective tying agreements between competitors are rarely qualified as 'tying' arrangements even if they contain clauses which make the supply of a product or service dependent on the supply of another related product or service. Such practices are assessed rather as a restriction of competition between the parties and *vis-à-vis* third parties contrary to Article 81 (1), similar to other forms of collective exclusionary restrictive practices, such as exclusionary pricing or collective aggregated rebate schemes. Such agreements normally involve companies having a significant (not necessarily dominant) position on the market of the tying products or services. Examples include:

- collective application of a system of uniform delivered prices regardless of the location of the purchasers, which disadvantages those wish to pick up their orders themselves or via other transporters (thereby tying the sale of the product and transport services);[217]
- collectively supplying inland transport services as part of the multimodal transport of cargo (by container), thereby preventing independent contractors from

214. Chapter V.D.5.
215. Chapter IV.B.10.(g).
216. *Windsurfing,* ECJ Feb. 25, 1986, 1986 ECR 611, paras 54-59.
217. E.g., *IFTRA Glass Containers,* D.Comm. May 15, 1974, 1974 OJ L 160/1, point 48.

carrying out inland transport services (on-carrying and off-carrying of containers);[218]
- collectively selling a complete range of products, also known as 'full line forcing';[219]
- collectively conditioning the supply of industrial gases to the supply also of cryogenic tanks;[220]
- collectively (via a partial-function joint venture) covering both uplink and transponder capacity by satellite communications operators;[221] and
- collective pooling intellectual property rights (package licensing).[222]

Tying may be justified where the tied product is necessary for a technically or qualitatively proper use of the tying product[223] or for safety reasons[224] or where the products are normally not sold separately.[225]

Tying v. Commercial Usage.
A major problem is determining whether the 'tied product' is or is not 'connected' by its nature or commercial usage to the 'tying product'. However, the mere fact that the tying corresponds to commercial usage does not preclude the applicability of Article 81 (1). With regard to Article 82 (d), which defines 'tying' in the same way as Article 81 (1) (e), the Court of Justice stated in the *Tetra Pak II* case:[226]

---

218. *Far Eastern Freight Conference,* D.Comm. Dec. 21, 1994, 1994 OJ L 378/17, points 43–55 and 119–123; *aff'd* CFI Feb. 28, 2002, 2002 ECR II-1101, paras. 118–131.
219. In *FEDETAB* the Commission held an agreement between competitors on the sale of a complete range of tobacco products restrictive of competition (D.Comm. July 20, 1978, 1978 OJ L 224/29, 39) whereas the Court of Justice left this question undecided (ECJ Oct. 29, 1980, 1980 ECR 3125, para. 164).
220. *Industrial Gases,* Nineteenth Report on Competition Policy, point 62 and, more explicitly, IP/89/426.
221. *ASTRA,* D.Comm. Dec. 21, 1992, 1993 OJ L 20/23, point 24
222. E.g., *IGR Stereo Television,* Eleventh Report on Competition Policy, point 94 and Fourteenth Report on Competition Policy, point 92 (restrictions on access to two patents for stereo television held by a body set up by the German television manufacturers); *DVD,* D.Comm. Oct. 9, 2000, IP/00/1135; *Antena 3/Eurovision*, CFI Oct. 8, 2002, 2002 ECR II-3805, paras 56–79; *UEFA Champions League,* D.Comm. July 23, 2003, 2003 OJ L 291/25, points 32–39 and 117–124; *Sogecable/Via Digital,* D.Comm. May 8, 2003, IP/03/655; *Bundesliga Broadcasting Rights*, D.Comm. July 24, 2003, IP/03/1106. For exceptions *see Philips/Sony,* D.Comm. Aug. 7, 2003, IP/03/1152.
223. Not black listed under the new Regulation 772/2004 on technology transfer agreements, even in agreements between competitors (white listed under Article 2 (1) (5) of Regulation 240/96). *See* Guidelines on technology transfer agreements, point 191.
224. *Industrial Gases,* Nineteenth Report on Competition Policy, point 62 and, more explicitely, IP/89/426.
225. E.g., complete range of products (portfolio), *see* Article 2 (3) (a) of Regulation 1983/83.
226. *Tetra Pak II*, ECJ Nov. 14, 1996, 1996 ECR I-5951, paras 34–37.

> 'It must, however, be stressed that the list of abusive practices set out in the second paragraph of of Article 86 of the Treaty [now 82] is not exhaustive. Consequently, even where tied sales of two products are in accordance with commercial usage or there is a natural link between the two products in question, such sales may still constitute an abuse within the meaning of Article 86 unless they are objectively justified. The reasoning of the Court of First Instance is not therefore in any way defective'.[227]

It may be concluded that this reasoning also applies to Article 81 (1) (e) with the result that tying of two products or services in accordance with commercial usage may still constitute a restriction of competition under Article 81 (1), unless the tying is objectively justified.

B. Block Exemptions on Horizontal Cooperation

1. Introduction

New Regulations Replacing Previous Regulations 417/85 and 418/85.
On November 29, 2000 the Commission adopted new competition rules concerning horizontal cooperation agreements, namely Regulation 2658/2000 on Specialization Agreements[228] and Regulation 2659/2000 on R&D Agreements.[229] These new regulations entered into force on January 1, 2001. They replace their predecessors, Regulations 417/85 and 418/85.

New Guidelines.
The Commission issued Guidelines for the application of Article 81 (3) in general[230] and for the assessment of horizontal agreements under Article 81 in particular,[231] in order to provide guidance on agreements which are not covered by the new regulations and on other horizontal agreements between competitors: production, standardization, joint purchasing and joint commercialization agreements. The Guidelines replace those on cooperation between enterprises (1968),[232] on the assessment of cooperative joint venture agreements (1993)[233] and on subcontracting agreements (1979).[234] They apply to cooperation concerning both products and

227. *See also TACA II – Atlantic Container Line*, CFI Sept. 30, 2003, T-191/98, paras 1124–1126.
228. 2000 OJ L 304/3.
229. 2000 OJ L 304/7.
230. Guidelines on the Application of Article 81 (3), 2004 OJ C 101/97.
231. Guidelines on the Applicability of Article 81 to Horizontal Cooperation, 2001 OJ C 3/2.
232. 1968 OJ C 75/3.
233. 1993 OJ C 43/2.
234. 1979 OJ C 1/2. This notice is formally replaced by the Guidelines on technology transfer agreements, point 36.

services but do not apply to cooperation in agriculture, transport or insurance which are subject to sector-specific rules.[235]

Main Objectives of the New Rules.
The new rules[236] complement those adopted with respect to vertical restraints. The Commission's objectives are the same:

- to modernize the EC competition rules;
- to shift from the previous formalistic approach to a more economic assessment;
- to reduce the regulatory burden on companies;
- to ensure effective control of cartels and agreements that have appreciable anticompetitive effects because the parties hold, gain or increase market power through the cooperation;[237]
- to benefit consumers.

Main Characteristics of the New Rules.
The new rules are less complex, in particular by replacing the previously exempted 'white listed' clauses (which were seen as a 'straight-jacket') by a broader approach exempting all restrictions except certain hardcore restrictions (price-fixing, output limitation, allocation of markets or customers and certain harmful restrictions in R&D agreements, similar to the previous 'black clauses'). The market share threshold of 20% has been maintained for specialization agreements, whereas the threshold for R&D agreements has been increased from 20% to 25%. The new rules on horizontal cooperation are less revolutionary than the new rules on vertical restraints. Although the Commission aims at simplification and clarification, the new rules do not remove legal uncertainty for agreements which are not covered by the block exemptions, in particular joint venture agreements which are on the borderline between a merger and a form of cooperation, hardly addressed in the Guidelines.[238]

Need for Individual Assessment.
Agreements that do not fulfill the conditions of the block exemption because of higher market shares and/or hardcore restrictions must be assessed individually in the light of the new Guidelines as to whether they fall within Article 81 (1) and, if so, whether they meet the conditions of Article 81 (3). The possibility of notification to and individual exemption by the Commission disappeared on May

235. Guidelines on Horizontal Cooperation, point 13; *see* Chapter VIII *infra*.
236. As summarized in IP/00/1376.
237. Guidelines on Horizontal Cooperation, point 27.
238. *See* Guidelines on Horizontal Cooperation, point 12.

1, 2004;[239] from that date Articles 81 and 82 may be applied in full by the Commission, the national competition authorities and the national courts. However, the Commission may, if requested, issue informal guidance in cases which give rise to genuine legal uncertainty.[240]

2. Regulation 2658/2000 on Specialization Agreements

(a) General

Common Forms of Specialization.
A 'specialization agreement' refers to a form of cooperation between actual or potential competitors whereby each of the parties limits its production activities to different fields in order to concentrate resources and thereby improve quality or technology or lengthen production runs. Each party ordinarily agrees to supply its partner with the products that it produces, and to purchase from its partner the products that it has agreed not to produce. Any business is naturally free to limit its activities to specific fields of its choice. Article 81 (1) applies if this limitation is co-ordinated with other firms and has any of the following anticompetitive effects:

- *Production Restrictions.* A party is obliged for the duration of the specialization agreement to cease production of competing products or is not permitted to expand its product range in response to changed market conditions or innovations nor to co-operate with any third party.
- *Purchase Restrictions.* A party that has given up the manufacture of certain products and purchases them from its partner is not allowed to obtain them from third parties that offer more favorable terms or higher quality standards.
- *Distribution Restrictions.* Consumer choice is restricted by an agreement that only one of the partners is to sell certain categories of products or that provides for joint distribution.

Favorable Approach toward Specialization.
Many forms of specialization agreements may be caught by Article 81 (1) because they restrict competition between actual or potential competitors and are likely to affect the competitive structure of the market and therefore trade between member states. However, the Commission takes a generally favorable attitude to specialization agreements which it considers normally satifying the conditions of Article 81 (3) because they allow the parties to concentrate on the manufacture of certain

---

239. Regulation 1/2003 abandons the Commission's exclusive competence to apply Article 81 (3) and, consequently, notification to the Commission, including the possibility to get immunity from fines as provided by Article 15 (5) of Regulation 17.

240. Recital 38 of Regulation 1/2003. *See* in greater detail Chapter X.C.4.(b).

goods or services and therefore normally contribute to improving the production of goods or services.[241] Over the years it has issued block exemption Regulation 2779/72,[242] amended by Regulation 417/85,[243] extended by Regulation 151/93[244] and now replaced and extended by Regulation 2658/2000 on specialization agreements.

Structure of the Regulation.
The structure of Regulation 2658/2000 is as follows:

- Unlike the previous regulation, there is no exhaustive 'white list' of exempted clauses but a 'black list' of clauses[245] that precludes the applicability of the block exemption and normally do not satisfy the conditions of Article 81 (3) in the case on an individual assessment.
- The block exemption covers, as the previous regulation, certain purchasing and marketing arrangements, provided they do not constitute black listed clauses.[246]
- The limits for the automatic application of the block exemption are, as under the previous regulation, a combined market share of 20%.[247] No lower market share threshold is established for specialization agreements extending to joint distribution, which were exempted under the previous regulation only insofar as the specialized products did not represent more than 10% of the relevant market.[248] Finally, the previous additional aggregate turnover limit[249] is abandoned.
- There is a withdrawal procedure which corresponds to that of the previous regulation.[250]

(b) Scope of Regulation 2658/2000

Definition of Specialization. According to Article 1 (1) of Regulation 2658/2000, the new regulation applies to the following specialization agreements between competitors:

241. Recital 8.
242. 1972 OJ L 292/23.
243. 1985 OJ L 53/1.
244. 1993 OJ L 21/8.
245. Article 5. Regulation 417/85 did not provide for a black list.
246. Article 3 (a).
247. Articles 4 and 6.
248. *See* Article 3 (2) (a) of Regulation 417/85.
249. *See* Article 3 (1) (b) of Regulation 417/85.
250. Article 7 of Regulation 417/85.

- **Unilateral specialization**, by virtue of which one party agrees to cease production of certain products[251] or to refrain from producing those products and to purchase them from a competing firm, while the competing undertaking agrees to produce and supply those products. This is new. Unilateral specialization agreements were excluded from the previous regulation[252] but qualified for individual exemption, as in *Prym/Beka*.[253] Regulation 2658/2000 applies to unilateral specialization agreements, including outsourcing, subcontracting and OEM agreements, between actual or potential competitors, provided they do not contain hardcore restrictions, such as market or customer sharing as in the *Siemens/Fanuc* case.[254]
- **Reciprocal specialization**, by virtue of which two or more parties on a reciprocal basis agree to cease production or refrain from producing certain goods or services and to purchase them from the other parties (normally competitors), who agree to supply them. Reciprocal specialization agreements were the classic forms of exemptible agreements, provided the parties' market shares are not particularly high. A typical case, such as *Jaz/Peter*,[255] concerns an agreement between two or more partners who enter into reciprocal obligations neither to manufacture nor to subcontract the manufacture of certain finished products. Both companies continued to manufacture their other product lines, and to sell a full range of products. The parties agreed to several anticompetitive restrictions as part of the specialization arrangement: (1) to supply certain types of contract products in its partner's home country exclusively to its partner and under the partner's trademark, (2) not to purchase from third parties any articles of the same nature as those in which its partner was specializing and had agreed to supply to it, (3) to grant to its partner the exclusive distribution rights in the partner's home country for any new products which it developed, and (4) to exchange know-how and to consult on all common problems. The Commission granted an exemption under Article 81 (3) because there was strong competition from many other suppliers both within and outside the Community.
- **Joint production agreements,** by virtue of which two or more paries agree to produce certain products jointly, mostly by way of creating a joint venture,

251. 'Products' including services, *see* Recital 11.
252. The reason was lack of administrative experience.
253. *Prym/Beka*, D.Comm. Oct. 8, 1973, 1973 OJ L 296/24 (agreement between competitors in the sewing machines sector by which one party agreed to terminate its needles production and to purchase its requirements from the other). *See also Billiton/M&T*, Seventh Report on Competition Policy, point 131 (exclusive purchase obligation in the tin tetrachloride sector combined with the obligation not to start manufacturing this product).
254. *Siemens/Fanuc*, Dec. 18, 1985, 1985 OJ L 376/29 (decision imposing a fine). *See ICL/Fujitsu*, D.Comm. 1986 OJ C 210/3 (comfort letter following amendments).
255. *Jaz/Peter I*, D.Comm. July 22, 1969, 1969 OJ L 195/5; *Jaz/Peter II* (extension of exemption), D.Comm. Dec. 23, 1977, 1978 OJ L 61/17.

which may also be entrusted with the distribution of the specialized products.[256] Such agreements may concern:

- *Joint production of new products*: The parties may specialize their production by pooling their expertise and efforts in order to develop, manufacture and distribute a new product by means of a joint venture while leaving undisturbed all their other business activities. An example is the *Vacuum Interruptors* case,[257] in which two English manufacturers of switchgear apparatus agreed to develop and manufacture jointly a new vacuum-type interruptor for switchgear. Although the parties could have carried out this development independently, they decided, because of the scale of the technical and financial resources required, to set up a jointly owned company for this purpose, while remaining competitors in conventional switchgear apparatus and other heavy electrical equipment. The principal danger of such an arrangement is the total elimination of competition between the parent firms in the field assigned to the joint venture, but the Commission granted an exemption because the parties would face strong competition from abroad and the joint venture allowed their product to be brought to the market in competition with foreign suppliers sooner than if the parents had borne the technical and financial burden of the development individually. Although such cooperation may be objectively necessary for the purposes of penetrating the new market and therefore may not fall under Article 81 (1),[258] Regulation 2658/2000 provides a 'safe harbour' for reasons of legal certainty, provided the market share thresholds are not exceeded.
- *Joint production of basic or intermediate products*: A specialization agreement may apply solely to the production of basic or intermediate products, leaving further processing and distribution of derived products to the parties independently. In the *Bayer/Gist* case[259] each of the parties agreed to specialize in the manufacture of one of the basic or intermediate products and to exchange the results of their research in these product fields. One party increased its production capacity for the intermediate product and halted its production of the further processed product, whereas the other party stopped its production in intermediates and increased its production in the processed product. The Commission granted an exemption because the two partners remained independent suppliers that continued to take their own output and investment decisions and to compete at the distribution and sales level.

---

256. Article 3 (b). Example: *Fiat/Hitachi*, D.Comm. Dec. 21, 1992, 1993 OJ L 20/10 (individual exemption because the then applicable block exemption did not extend to joint distribution).
257. Leading case: *Vacuum Interruptors I*, D.Comm. Jan. 20, 1977, 1977 OJ L 48/32; *Vacuum Interruptors II* (exemption extended), D.Comm. Dec. 11, 1980, 1980 OJ L 383/1.
258. Guidelines on Article 81 (3), point 18 (2); Guidelines on technology transfer agreements, point 17.
259. *Bayer/Gist*, D.Comm. Dec. 15, 1975, 1976 OJ L 30/13.

- *Joint creation of additional capacities.* The block exemption extends to agreements by which two or more competitors refrain from enlarging their existing capacities and instead jointly create additional capacity in the framework of a joint venture for satisfying the needs of the parent companies which continue to sell their own products and those purchased from the joint venture independently. Such agreements have satisfied the conditions of individual exemption by the Commission, subject to assurances as to the parties maintaining independence on the distribution level.[260]
- *Joint production in order to restructure the parties' existing businesses*: Two firms may agree to swap certain assets, such as production facilities and related industrial property rights, as part of a restructuring of their overall businesses to *reduce* capacity by closing down obsolete plants and improving the efficiency of the assets that remain and to refocus their businesses on core activities. The parties may transfer their assets in a specific market to a joint venture, but retain separate operations in one or more other markets. In the leading case *Enichem/ICI*[261] the Commission granted an exemption for five years under Article 81 (3) for the creation of a non-dominant EC market leader with a 22–23% market share in PVC. Subsequently the Commission determined that, as a result of substantial changes in its structure, the joint venture had gained a market identity which was distinct from their shareholders and that therefore Article 81 (1) no longer applied.[262]

Types of Specialization Agreements that are Excluded from the Block Exemption.

The following types of specialization agreements are excluded from the block exemption:

– *Unilateral specialization agreements between non-competitors.* Such agreements are excluded from Regulation 2658/2000, which is designed to cover only agreements between competitors.[263] However, outsourcing and subcontracting agreements between non-competitors normally do not infringe Article 81 (1) at all, including exclusive supply obligations (which may be held ancillary).[264] Such agreements may have to be assessed under Regulation 2790/1999

260. Under Article 65 of the ECSC Treaty: *Sidmar*, Commission (High Authority), April 25, 1962, Eleventh ECSC General Report, points 346–349. Under Article 81: *Exxon/Shell*, D.Comm. May 18, 1994, 1994 OJ L 144/20. Under the merger control regulation: *Asahi Glass/Mitsubishi/F2 Chemicals*, D.Comm. March 21, 2000, JV.42.
261. *Enichem/ICI I*, D.Comm. Dec. 22, 1987, 1988 OJ L 50/18.
262. *Enichem/ICI II*, Twenty-first Report on Competition Policy, p. 336.
263. Recital 10 to Regulation 2658/2000.
264. *See* Guidelines on Horizontal Cooperation, points 80–81, and Guidelines on technology transfer agreements, point 44.

on vertical restraints or, if they involve the transfer of secret and substantial know-how,[265] under Regulation 772/2004 on technology transfer agreements.[266] Unlike its previous approach under the 1979 Notice on subcontracting agreements, the Commission takes a somewhat stricter view considering that such agreements may be caught by Article 81 (1) in the light of possible foreclosure problems and spill-over effects where the input is an important component of costs and the parties have a strong position in the downstream market for the final product.[267]

- *Agreements where specialization is only a secondary or long-term goal.* In the *CSV*,[268] *Italian Cast Glass*[269] and *Siemens/Fanuc*[270] cases, specialization played too small a part in the arrangements to justify the wide-ranging cooperation between the parties which had anticompetitive effects at the distribution level. For the block exemption to apply, specialization must be the core of the agreement: specialization between competitors in the distribution of their products is inherently suspect as a device for market or customer sharing.
- *Agreements where the manufacture and distribution of the specialized products is entrusted to a joint venture.* Such a joint venture may have all the functions of an autonomous economic entity, which is subject to the merger control regulation (and not to Regulation 1/2003), provided the matter has a Community dimension; only a joint venture that does not have a Community dimension must be assessed under Article 81 and the block exemption, provided it has a cooperative object or effect.[271]

Market Share Threshold of 20%.

The block exemption is limited to specialization agreements between firms whose combined market share does not exceed 20% of the relevant market.[272] Unlike its predecessor regulation, there is no turnover limitation and no reduced market share threshold in cases where the cooperation extends beyond production to joint marketing.[273] Market shares are calculated according to Article 6 and Article 2 (3) on the basis of the sales volumes realized by the participating and connected undertakings in the preceding calender year or estimates based on other reliable market information. The block exemption applies if the parties' market share is initially not more than 20% but subsequently exceeds this threshold:

265. This is the main difference between simple outsourcing and subcontracting agreements: Guidelines on technology transfer agreements, point 44.
266. *See* Guidelines on technology transfer agreements, points 41–45.
267. Guidelines on Horizontal Cooperation, point 100.
268. *CSV*, D.Comm. July 20, 1978, 1978 OJ L 242/15, 32.
269. *Italian Cast Glass*, D.Comm. Dec. 17, 1980, 1980 OJ L 383/19, 25.
270. *Siemens/Fanuc*, D.Comm. Dec. 18, 1985, 1985 OJ L 376/29.
271. Article 21 (1) of Regulation 139/2004.
272. Article 4 and Article 2 (6).
273. The exemption of joint marketing was limited to 10% and a turnover of EUR 1 billion under Article 3 (2) of the previous regulation.

- if the market share rises up to 25% the exemption applies for two consecutive calender years, and
- if the market share rises above 25% the exemption applies for one calender year, following the year in which the threshold was first exceeded.

The definition of the relevant market is based on the Commission's 1997 Notice on the definition of the relevant market,[274] which remains applicable.[275] The relevant market may be that for important components or other inputs to the parties' final products.[276] With respect to the evaluation of market shares the Guidelines refer to the Herfindahl-Hirschman Index,[277] without, however, indicating why it is an appropriate additional test.[278] Specialization agreements between parties with market shares below these limits normally fulfill the conditions of Article 81 (3).[279] However, hardcore restrictions are unlikely to satisfy the conditions of this provision.

(c) Restrictions Covered by the Block Exemption v. Hardcore Restrictions

Restrictions Covered by the Block Exemption.
According to Article 3 the block exemption applies:

- to exclusive purchase and/or supply obligations in the context of a unilateral or reciprocal specialization agreement or a joint production agreement;[280]
- to arrangements not to sell the products which are the subject of the specialization independently but provide for joint distribution or agree to appoint a third party distributor on an exclusive or non-exclusive basis, provided the third party is not a competiting undertaking;[281]
- to provisions which are not the primary object of a specialization agreement but that are directly related and necessary ('ancillary') to its implementation, in particular where the specialization is implemented by the assignment or use of intellectual property rights.[282]

---

274. 1997 OJ C 372/3.
275. Guidelines on Horizontal Cooperation, point 27.
276. Guidelines on Horizontal Cooperation, point 99.
277. This index, which is used in merger cases, is defined as the sum of the squares of the market shares of all the firms in the market and captures the notion of market power.
278. Guidelines, point 29 and note 19. The Commission tends, however, to use the Herfindahl-Hirschmann index more generally as market power indicator.
279. Guidelines, point 37.
280. This corresponds to Article 2 (3) of Regulation 417/85.
281. Article 3 (b) of Regulation 2658/2000. 'Competitors' include actual and potential competitors: Article 1 (7).
282. Article 1 (2).

Hardcore Restrictions.

The hardcore restrictions are listed in Article 5 which also applies to restrictions having the same object as the listed restrictions.[283]

(i) *Restrictions on prices*: The parties may not fix prices when selling to third parties.[284] However, the parties may agree upon the price that their *production joint venture* charges to its immediate customers.[285] By contrast, Article 5 (2) (b) of Regulation 2659/2000 on R&D agreements is more generous: it exempts the fixing of prices charged to immediate customers in the case of joint distribution of the contract products *without* joint production. In any event, the joint venture may not impose on its immediate customers fixed *resale* prices to end-consumers.[286]

(ii) *Limitation of output or sales*: The parties may not collude on output or sales, subject to two exceptions:

- The parties may agree on the 'amount of products' in the context of a unilateral or reciprocal specialization agreement,[287] which, at first glance, seems to reverse the rule. However, the term 'provisions on the agreed amount of products' may be understood as 'setting of production targets' in the sense of Regulation 2659/2000 on R&D agreements.[288]
- The parties may set the capacity and production volume of a production joint venture. However, the parties to a joint venture are anyway capable, by exercising their rights of joint control, to influence the joint venture's activity, including the capacity and production volume.

The rule prohibiting the limitation of output or sales applies where two competitors continue to manufacture a certain product independently and also agree on joint *additional* production because fixing capacity and volume of the joint additional production can lead to coordination of their own individual production. In its previous case law the Commission tried to reduce such a restrictive effect by imposing a 'Chinese wall' between them in order to prevent the exchange of commercially sensitive information on their independent production and output.[289]

(iii) *Allocation of markets or customers*: Territorial and customer limitations are hardcore restrictions. The parties must be free to sell the specialized products (manufactured by themselves or purchased from other parties or the joint venture) without any limitation. Thus, neither active nor passive sales bans

283. Article 1 (2) second subparagraph.
284. Article 5 (1) (a). Example: *Welded Steel Mesh*, D.Comm. Aug. 2, 1989, 1989 OJ L 260/1; *aff'd* CFI April 6, 1995, 1995 II-987 and ECJ Dec. 17, 1998, 1998 I-8417 (decision imposing fines).
285. Article 5 (2) (b).
286. This agreement is subject to Regulation 2790/1999 on vertical restraints, which black lists resale price fixing according to Article 4 (a).
287. Article 5 (1) (b) and (2) (a) of Regulation 2658/2000.
288. Article 5 (2) (a) of Regulation 2659/2000.
289. *Exxon/Shell*, D.Comm. May 18, 1994, 1994 OJ L 144/20. Similarly under Article 2 (4) of the merger control regulation: *BT/AT&T*, D.Comm. March 30, 1999, JV.15.

are permitted between the parties (unlike Regulation 2659/2000 on R&D agreements which permitted active sales bans). The distribution agreements concluded by each of them are not covered by the Regulation 2658/2000 but must be assessed under Regulation 2790/1999.

(d) Withdrawal of the Block Exemption

The Commission may, on its own initiative or upon request of a member state, a natural or legal person, withdraw the benefit of the block exemption if it finds that an agreement, although covered by the block exemption, nevertheless has effects that are incompatible with Article 81 (3).[290] The main examples are cases where the specialization does not yield significant benefits to consumers or is likely to endanger effective competition, in particular by the cumulative effect of parallel specialization agreements which individually do not exceed the thresholds of the regulation.

3. Regulation 2659/2000 on R&D Agreements

(a) General

Favorable Attitude toward Joint Research.
The Commission takes a generally positive attitude toward joint research and development ('R&D') agreements. They are normally pro-competitive because they aim, by their very nature, at developing and marketing *new* products or new applications of existing products. Cooperation in R&D and in the exploitation of the results generally promotes technical and economic progress by increasing dissemination of technical knowledge between the parties and avoiding duplication of R&D work, by stimulating new advances through the exchange of complementary technical knowledge, and by rationalizing the manufacture of products or application of the processes arising out of the R&D.[291] However, R&D agreements between powerful and potentially very innovative competitors may slow the pace of technical progress by reducing competition in innovation and may facilitate coordination of prices and production or division of markets or customers and can therefore not be excluded from the scope of Article 81.[292]

A Leading Case: *Henkel/Colgate*.
The *Henkel/Colgate* case[293] concerned an R&D agreement between two large enterprises in the washpowder sector with world-wide markets which were

290. Article 7, which corresponds to Article 8 of Regulation 417/85 (which was never applied).
291. Recitals 10–11 to Regulation 2659/2000.
292. *Ibid.*, Recitals 16–18.
293. *Henkel/Colgate*, D.Comm. Dec. 23, 1971, 1972 OJ L 14/14.

characterized by their oligopolistic structure and great technical homogenity of products offered, as well as by particularly intensive and costly advertising, which made penetration of the market very difficult for other manufacturers who wished to compete. In these conditions, the position of manufacturers in the market and their possibilities of expansion were largely determined by the degree of technical progress and innovation, so that competition in the field of R&D was extremely important. The Commission found that the agreement appreciably restricted competition by preventing the parties from gaining competitive advantages over each other and granted individual exemption only after having ensured that the agreement enabled both parties to have access and to use the results of the joint R&D without limitation and did not lead to market sharing or to concerting the production and sales policies.[294] The Commission's further case law is based on Regulation 417/85,[295] as amended by Regulation 2236/97,[296] which fixed a combined market share threshold of 20% and, in the case of joint marketing, 10%,[297] extended by Regulation 151/93[298] and now replaced by Regulation 2659/2000, with a single market share threshold of 25% for joint R&D and joint marketing.

(b) Scope of Regulation 2659/2000

Definition of R&D.

R&D means the acquisition of know-how relating to products or processes and the carrying out of theoretical analysis, systematic study or experimentation, including experimental production, technical testing of products or processes, the establishment of the necessary facilities and the obtaining of intellectual property rights.[299] Accordingly, any joint exploitation must relate to results which are protected by intellectual property rights or constitute valuable know-how, and the results must be decisive for the manufacture of the contract products or the application of the contract processes.[300] Under these conditions it may be assumed that R&D agreements enable the parties to achieve better and more rapid results than by proceeding individually,[301] thereby leading to significant cross fertilisation of

294. The Commission reconsidered the agreement after expiration of the exemption and objected to the clause according to which the parties had to agree before a licence could be issued to third parties, which lead to the termination of the agreement: Eighth Report on Competition Policy, points 89–91.
295. 1985 OJ L 53/14. *See Beecham/Parke Davis*, D.Comm. Jan. 17, 1979, 1979 OJ L 70/11.
296. 1997 OJ L 306/12.
297. Higher market shares do not exclude individual clearance in cases where the new products are still subject to competition from the 'classical' products: *Asahi/Saint Gobain*, D.Comm. Dec. 16, 1994, 1994 OJ L 354/87.
298. 1993 OJ L 21/8.
299. Article 2 (4).
300. Article 3 (4).
301. Within the group of companies or by way of outsourcing: Guidelines on Horizontal Cooperation, point 39.

ideas and experience reducing duplicative, unnecessary costs and substantially contributing to technical or economic progress.[302]

Types of R&D Agreements Covered by the Block Exemption.
Regulation 2659/2000 applies, as did its predecessor:

(i) to mere *joint R&D* without joint exploitation of the results,
(ii) to *joint R&D and joint exploitation of the results*, and
(iii) to *joint exploitation of the results* of previous joint R&D.[303]

In most cases, joint R&D does not start at the very beginning of a research effort but only when the individual efforts fail or prove unsuccessful or too expensive. Most cases therefore concern *further* joint research or development of the results of individual research on which the parties base their further joint programme. However, the regulation no longer requires that the R&D be carried out in the framework of a pre-defined program, as was the case under Article 2 (a) of the previous regulation. This gives the parties more flexibility to adapt R&D according to new and unforeseeable developments. The *joint R&D* may be carried out by all the participants by contributing equally and exchanging their individual results, by way of specialization, by a joint team or by a jointly entrusted third party.[304] Unequal contributions may be compensated by royalties or services.[305] Joint R&D must be distinguished from the bundling of the results of the parties' previous *individual* research. Patent pools between competitors are likely to infringe Article 81 (1).[306] They are not block exempted under the transfer of technology regulation but may have meet the criteria for exemption if the foreclosure effect is outweighted by the positive effects of the agreement.[307]

Combination of Joint R&D with Joint Production, Joint Marketing and Joint Licensing.
The R&D agreement may provide for *joint production* of the contract products: by each of the parties, by one of the parties by way of specialisation,[308] by a joint

---

302. *Ibid.*, points 39–42.
303. Article 1 (1).
304. Article 2 (11).
305. Such a clause used to be white-listed under Article 5 (1) (f) of the previous Regulation 417/85; now it is included in the general exemption provision of Article 1 (1).
306. Except in cases where competitors owing 'blocking' patents grant each other non-exclusive licenses with no restrictions, which would not restrict competition at all and would only facilitate competition that was otherwise impossible; *see Iridium*, D.Comm. Dec. 18, 1996, 1997 OJ L 16/87 (negative clearance).
307. *See DVD Technology*, D.Comm. Oct. 9, 2000, IP/00/1135, 2000–5 CMLR 785 (comfort letter for *Digital Versatile Disc* patent pool; single non-exclusive licence program administered by one of the parents).
308. Articles 2 (11) (c) and 3 (5).

venture or by a third party, such as – this is new – by way of subcontracting agreements.[309] The R&D agreement may also provide for *joint distribution* of the contract products: by each party, by one party in the case of specialisation[310] (such party must be required to fulfill orders from all the parties[311]) or by a joint venture.[312] Joint production and distribution is no longer limited to 10% but is exempted up to a 25% combined market share of the relevant market for the products capable of being improved or replaced by the contract products.[313] Finally, the R&D agreement may provide for the assignment or *licensing* of the results.[314]

Types of Agreements Excluded from the Block Exemption.
The block exemption does not apply in particular:

- To the *mere exchange of existing technology* by way of reciprocal licence agreements, which must be assessed under the technology transfer regulation, which provides for a lower market share threshold of 20% for agreements between competitors.[315]
- To agreements which aim at *promoting* the application of products in new fields, without implying any R&D activities. However, they are not necessarily restrictive of competition if the parties are not prevented from carrying out R&D individually and third party competitors are not affected.[316]
- To agreements where R&D is only a *secondary* or long-term goal. In the *Siemens/Fanuc*[317] case, R&D played too small a part in the arrangements to justify the wide-ranging cooperation between the parties which had anticompetitive effects at the distribution level;
- Technology pools, i.e., pooling existing technology between competitors with a view of joint exploitation;[318]
- To *full-function joint ventures* which are entrusted with all the functions (R&D, production and distribution) of an autnomous economic entity. Such joint ventures are subject to the merger control regulation (and not Regulation 2659/2000), provided they have a Community dimension.[319] Full or partial func-

309. Article 2 (11) (b).
310. Article 2 (11) (c).
311. Article 3 (5).
312. *See* Articles 1 (1), 2 (8) and 2 (11) (a).
313. Article 4. The reason probably is that joint distribution is mostly entrusted to a joint venture which fulfills all the function of an autonomous economic entity and is subject to the merger control and to its minimum threshold of 25% (provided it has a Community dimension).
314. Article 2 (8) and Article 1 (1) (b) .
315. Article 3 (1) of the new Regulation 772/2004 on technology transfer agreements. E.g. *Concast/Mannesman*, Eleventh Report on Competition Policy, point 93.
316. *Eurogypsum*, D.Comm. Feb. 26, 1968, 1968 OJ L 57/9.
317. *Siemens/Fanuc*, D.Comm. Dec. 18, 1985, 1985 OJ L 376/29.
318. *DVD Standard*, D.Comm. Oct. 9, 2000, IP/00/1135. *See also IGR Television I*, Eleventh Report on Competition Policy, point 94.
319. Article 21 (1) of Regulation 139/2004.

tion joint ventures that do *not* have a Community dimension must be assessed under Article 81 and Regulation 2659/2000.

Market Share Threshold of 25%.

The application of the block exemption is subject to a market share threshold of 25% depending on whether or not the parties are competitors.

- Mere R&D agreements between firms that are *neither actual nor potential competitors*[320] are, as under the previous regulation, exempted without any market share limitation for the duration of the R&D[321] and for seven years (previously five years) from the time the contract products are first put on the market within the Community in order to guarantee a minimum period of return on the investments involved by the introduction of an entirely new product.[322] After that period the exemption continues to apply, provided the parties' aggregate market shares do not exceed 25%.[323] The market share threshold may be exceeded up to 30% for temporary periods without the benefit of the exemption being lost.[324]
- R&D agreements *between actual or potential competitors* are exempted if, at the time the agreement is entered into, the combined market share of the participating firms does not exceed 25% (not only 20% as under the predecessor regulation) of the relevant markets for the products capable of being improved or replaced by the contract products.[325] Since, at the time the R&D agreement is entered into, the products of the R&D do not yet have a market, the relevant market is for products *capable* of being improved or replaced (substituted) by the R&D.[326] The regulation therefore requires a difficult comparison of the actual existing market shares and the potential future market shares and an assessment of whether the parties already exert a significant constraining influence or whether there is a significant likelihood that they would grow into an effective competitive force.[327] The market share threshold of 25% also applies

320. Article 2 (12).
321. Recital 20.
322. Recital 16.
323. Article 4 (1) and (3).
324. Article 6 (2) and (3): The exemption continues for two additional calender years following the year in which the 25% threshold was exceeded but failed to exceed 30%; once the 30% market share threshold is exceeded, the exemption applies for only one additional calender year following the year in which the 30% threshold was first exceeded.
325. Article 4 (2). Under the new transfer of technology block exemption the relevant market may be the technology market (which is difficult to determine) and the product market including the products *capable* of being improved or replaced (substituted) by the R&D.
326. Guidelines on Horizontal Cooperation, points 43 and 53. Example: DCD's replacing CD's and records, *see DVD*, D.Comm. Oct. 9, 2000, IP/00/1135.
327. *Cf.* under the Commission Notice on the appraisal of horizontal mergers, 2002 OJ C 331/18, point 73.

to R&D agreements that provide for joint distribution, which was limited to 10% under the previous regulation.[328] R&D agreements between parties with market shares below this threshold are presumed to fulfill the conditions of Article 81 (3) (safe harbor principle). However, in the exceptional case where the conditions of the block exemption are met but the joint R&D agreement still has effects which are incompatible with Article 81 (3), the Commission may withdraw the benefit of the block exemption.[329]

Definition of the Relevant Market and Calculation of Market Shares. The calculation of market shares greatly depends on the point of time when they are to be determined by the regulation. Market shares have to be defined at the time the agreement is entered into for determining whether the 25% market share limitation is met at the stage of joint R&D and for the first seven years of joint exploitation of the results. According to the Commission's Guidelines on horizontal cooperation,[330] the key to defining the relevant market is to identify those products, technologies or R&D efforts that will act as a competitive constraint on the parties, and, 'if possible', to assess the effects of the cooperation on innovation over time. [331] This implies practical difficulties when calculating market shares.[332] In the case where the subject of the R&D is a component of other products, the market shares were based, under the previous regulation,[333] on the market for final products for which the component represents a significant part. The new block exemption does not include this market definition, probably because of cases such as *Commercial Solvents*, which demonstrate that competition on the market for intermediate or upstream products may be significantly restricted by cooperation between major market players even if there is effective competition on the market for final products.[334]

***De Minimis* Market Shares Precluding the Applicability of Article 81 (1).** Where the parties market shares do not exceed the limits of the Commission's *de minimis* notice (which are 10% in the case of horizontal and 15% in the case of vertical agreements) the agreements normally do not infringe Article 81 (1).[335] Furthermore, R&D cooperation between small and medium-sized undertakings[336]

328. Article 3 (3a) of Regulation 418/85.
329. Article 7 (unchanged).
330. 2001 OJ C 3/2, point 43.
331. The new technology transfer regulation distinguishes more clearly between the relevant technology or the relevant product market (Article 3).
332. Examples: Guidelines on Horizontal Cooperation, points 75–77. These practical difficulties are the reason why under the merger control regulation potential competition is disregarded when defining the relevant market.
333. Article 3 (3) of Regulation 418/85.
334. *Commercial Solvents*, ECJ March 14, 1973, 1973 ECR 357, para. 22.
335. 2001 OJ C 368/13.
336. New definition in the Commission's Recommendation 2003/361/EC, 2003 OJ L 124/36.

may be the only way of increasing overall R&D and innovation activities and of competing more vigorously with the stronger market players and therefore not fall under Article 81 (1).[337]

(c) Joint R&D without Joint Exploitation

Mere Joint R&D.
According to Article 2 (11) of Regulation 2659/2000 joint R&D may be:

- carried out by a joint team, organization or undertaking, including a subcontractor or a joint venture created to this effect,[338]
- jointly entrusted to a third party, including research institutes, academic bodies or undertakings which supply R&D as a commercial service without normally being active in the exploitation of the results, or
- allocated between the parties by way of specialization, whereby unequal contributions may be compensated.[339]

Joint R&D means the acquisition of secret, substantial and identified know-how[340] and the carrying-out of theoretical analysis, systematic study or experimentation, including experimental production, technical testing of products or processes, the establishment of the necessary facilitites and the obtaining of (jointly owned) intellectual property rights for the results.[341] Experimental production or testing of products is therefore not deemed to be joint exploitation and is therefore not subject to the market share limitation of 25%.[342]

Conditions for the Block Exemption to Apply.
- *Free access to the results of joint R&D*: The parties must have free access to the results for the purposes of further R&D, including pre-existing know-how which is necessary to the joint R&D.[343]
- *Free exploitation of the results of joint R&D*: The parties must be free independently to exploit the results, including any pre-existing know-how which

337. First Report on Competition Policy, point 32; Guidelines on Horizontal Cooperation, points 41. Examples: *Elopak/Metalbox*, D.Comm. July 13, 1990, 1990 OJ L 209/15; *Konsortium ECR 900*, D.Comm. July 27, 1990, 1990 OJ L 228/31.
338. The *Tetra Pak I* case concerned the development of a new technology by the British Technology Group, a UK public corporation having the object of licensing the results of public research and the grant of an exclusive licence to a licensee which became, following a takeover, a dominant firm, subject to Article 82: CFI July 10, 1990, 1990 ECR II-309.
339. *Cf.* Article 5 (1) (f) of Regulation 418/85.
340. Article 2 (10).
341. Article 2 (4).
342. Article 2 (4) and Article 4 (1).
343. Article 3 (2). Research bodies may be restricted to applying the results solely for the purposes of further research.

forms part of the new technology and is therefore necessary to its exploitation, including for their own use and for licensing to third parties.[344] This presupposes co-ownership of the results and, in the case of individual contributions by the parties, the right to grant a licence to third parties on the bundle of new technology and the pre-existing know-how necessary to its exploitation. However, the parties may agree among themselves to limit the free exploitation of the results to one or more technical fields of use[345] (but not to separate product markets as under the technology transfer regulation[346]), provided the parties are not competitors at the time the agreement is entered into.[347] If they are competitors the agreements need individual assessment under Article 81. The requirement not to grant licences to third parties where the exploitation by at least one of the parties is not provided for or does not take place is blacklisted.[348] This means that the parties must have the choice between exploiting the results themselves or granting licences to third parties, including subcontractors, in order to avoid the results of joint R&D not being exploited at all or only by one party, except when there is an 'objectively valid reason'.[349] The *joint* licensing of the results to third parties is a form of joint exploitation of the results.[350]

– *Non-compete clauses*: The parties may be prevented from carrying out R&D independently in the same or a *closely connected field* by themselves or with third parties during the execution of the program in order to ensure that the parties concentrate their efforts on the joint R&D programme.[351] However, non-compete clauses relating to *unconnected fields* of the joint R&D, or, after its completion, in the field to which the joint R&D relates or in a connected field are blacklisted.[352] Where the R&D agreement substantially restricts the scope for third parties to carry out research the Commission may withdraw the benefit of the exemption.[353] Parties may not be prohibited from challenging, after completion of the R&D, the validity of intellectual property rights which the parties hold in the Common Market and which protect the results of the R&D or, after the expiry of the R&D agreement, the validity of intellectual property rights which the parties hold and which are relevant for the R&D without prejudice to the possibility of terminating the agreement.[354] This means that parties

344. Article 3 (3).
345. Article 3 (3).
346. Article Article 4 (1) (c) (i) of Regulation 772/2004.
347. Article 3 (3).
348. Article 5 (1) (h).
349. *See* Article 7 (c) which provides for withdrawing the benefit of the block exemption where, without any objectively valid reason, the parties do not exploit the results of the joint R&D.
350. *See* Section B.3.d. below.
351. Such a clause used to be white-listed under Article 4 (1) (a) and (b) of the previous regulation; now it is included in the general exemption provision of Article 1 (2).
352. Article 5 (1) (a).
353. Article 7 (a).
354. Hardcore restriction: Article 5 (1) (b).

are not precluded from including no-challenge obligations *during the period of the joint R&D activity* with respect to (i) the results of the joint R&D and (ii) rights to which the joint venture is given access by the parties; and *during the period that the joint venture agreement remains in force after completion of the joint R&D activity* with respect to only those rights to which the joint venture is given access by the parties. Furthermore, the agreement may provide for the possibility to terminate the R&D agreement in the event of one of the parties challenging the validity of such intellectual property rights.[355]

– *Free use of the results of joint R&D after completion.* The parties must be free to use the results of joint R&D after completion of the R&D.[356] However, if the results of the joint R&D are not severable from the original technological contributions the agreement may impose a limited post-term use ban of, say, five years, in order to solve the practical problems of maintaining confidentiality of the (still secret) original know-how which one party contributed to the joint R&D.[357]

Obligations with respect to the exchange of technical knowledge and experience, including grant back obligations relating to improvements or new applications of the results,[358] and to maintaining confidentiality of know-how, even after expiration of the agreement, are normally not restrictive of competition or at least covered by the general exemption provision of Article 1 of Regulation 2659/2000.

Restrictions in the Framework of Individual Exploitation Infringing Article 81 (1).

In the case of individual, independent exploitation of the results of the joint R&D the parties are supposed to compete fully; any restriction agreed in addition or subsequent to the R&D agreement on prices, customers or markets would be infringements of Article 81 (1) and are, if agreed in the context of the R&D agreement, black listed by Article 5 (c)–(j) of Regulation 2659/2000 anyway. In particular, the parties may not limit output or sales, fix prices or agree on territorial restrictions, except active sales bans which are accepted up to seven years from the time the contract products are first put on the market within the EEA.[359] Restrictions solely on marketing outside the EEA do not ordinarily affect trade between member states and are generally not caught by Article 81 (1).[360] However, agreements between competitors sharing markets between third countries and the EEA is are normally prohibited.[361]

355. Article 5 (1) (b), last subparagraph.
356. Article 5 (1) (a).
357. *See BBC Brown Boveri/NGK*, D.Comm. Oct. 11, 1988, 1988 OJ L 301/68.
358. *See* 4 (1) (g) of the previous Regulation 418/85.
359. Article 5 (1) (e).
360. E.g., *Fujitsu AMD Semiconductor*, D.Comm. Dec. 12, 1994, 1994 OJ L 341/66, point 39.
361. *See Siemens/Fanuc*, D.Comm. Dec. 18, 1985, 1985 OJ L 376/29 (however, R&D played in this case only a secondary role).

(d) Joint R&D including Joint Exploitation

Various Types of Joint Exploitation.
Joint exploitation may consist of:

- production and/or distribution of the contract products or the application of the contract processes, or
- the assignment or licensing of intellectual property rights or the communication of know-how required for such manufacture or application.[362]

However, any joint exploitation must relate to the results of the joint R&D, which substantially contribute to technical or economic progress, and the result must be decisive for the manufacture of the contract products or the contract processes.[363] Any anticompetitive cooperation going beyond these limits does not justify the conditions of the block exemption and is subject to an individual assessment under Article 81 (3).[364]

Joint Production Excluding Joint Distribution.
Joint production of the contract products may be carried out in the following ways:

- the parties jointly entrust the manufacture to a third party, in particular a joint venture, or
- the parties allocate production between them by way of specialization.[365]

In the case of joint production the parties may set production 'targets', but may not 'limit' their output.[366] In the case of production by way of specialization the parties must produce such quantities as are necessary to comply with their obligation to fulfil orders for supplies from all parties.[367]

However, the *individual distribution* of the products which are manufactured in one of these ways must not be subject to the following hardcore restrictions:

- *Fixing of prices.* The parties may *not* fix prices when selling the contract products to third parties, either directly nor indirectly, in particular by way of exchanges of pricing information.[368] It may be argued that maximum and

362. Article 2 (8).
363. Article 3 (4).
364. E.g., *CSV*, D.Comm. July 20, 1978, 1978 OJ L 242/15.
365. Article 2 (11).
366. Article 5 (1) (c).
367. Article 3 (5).
368. Article 5 (1) (d). *See* the decision imposing a fine of EUR 110 million in *ADM, Ajinomoto (Amino Acids)*, D.Comm. June 7, 2000, 2001 OJ L 152/14.

recommended prices are not hardcore restrictions by analogy to Article 4 (a) of Regulation 2790/1999 on vertical restraints.

- *Limitation of output or sales*. Exchanges of information on output and sales may lead to a control of output or sales and possibly to an indirect limitation.[369]
- *Territorial and customer restrictions*. The parties may not be prevented from pursuing an *active* sales policy in territories that are reserved to other parties after seven (previously, five) years after the contract products are first put on the market within the Community or EEA countries.[370] No restriction for any period of time is permitted for *passively* selling in those territories, including by impeding parallel exports or imports.[371] The differentiation between active and passive sales is maintained although the (permitted) passive sales may increase substantially by way of e-commerce.[372] The parties may also not be prevented from serving certain *customers* after seven years,[373] whereas customer limitations according to *different fields of use* for the entire duration of the agreement are accepted, provided the parties are not competing manufacturers (neither actual nor potential competitors) at the time the agreement was entered into.[374] In the case of joint production by way of specialization the parties must be required to fulfill orders for supplies from all parties,[375] which may indirectly imply that certain customers are supplied by only one party with its products, thereby excluding direct shipments by the other party to those customers. Parallel trade within the EEA may also not be prevented: clauses which require the parties to refuse to meet demand from users or resellers in their respective territories who would market the contract products in other territories within the EEA or to make it difficult for users or resellers to obtain the contract products from other resellers within the EEA (including by using intellectual property rights) are blacklisted.[376] In the case of specialization the parties may accept exclusive purchase and/or exclusive supply obligations, which are covered by Article 3 (a) of the block exemption Regulation 2658/2000 on specialization agreements, subject to the market share threshold of 20% (not 25% as under the R&D block exemption), although they may be tantamount to a market sharing between the parties.
- *Non-compete clauses* are accepted to the same extent as in the case of joint R&D without joint exploitation.[377]

---

369. Article 5 (1) (c).
370. Article 5 (1) (g).
371. Article 5 (1) (f), (g), (i) and (j).
372. This is not mentioned in the Guidelines on Horizontal Cooperation, but in the Guidelines on vertical restraints under point 51.
373. Article 5 (1) (e).
374. Article 3 (3).
375. Article 3 (5).
376. Article 5 (1) (i) and (j).
377. *See* section 3.(c) *supra*.

Joint Production including Joint Distribution.
The block exemption of Regulation 2659/2000 applies to *joint distribution* up to the 25% market share threshold, which considerably extends its scope beyond the threshold of the previous Regulation 418/85 (which was limited to 10%).[378] Joint distribution includes allocating distribution:

- to one party,[379]
- to one joint undertaking or to a third undertaking,[380] or
- to several joint undertakings or third undertakings.[381]

The allocation of R&D, production and distribution among the parties to a joint undertaking implies the creation of a joint venture which normally fulfills all the functions of an autonomous economic entity and is therefore subject to the merger control regulation, provided it has a Community dimension.[382] In the absence of a Community dimension R&D agreements must be assessed under Article 81 and Regulation 2659/2000. For the block exemption to apply, the agreement must satisfy the following conditions:

- The *fixing of prices* when selling to third parties is blacklisted,[383] except in the case of joint distribution which justifies the joint setting of sales targets and the fixing of prices charged to the immediate customers.[384]
- The *limitation of output or sales* is also blacklisted,[385] except in the case of joint distribution.[386] This exception is justified by the fact that the parties to the joint venture are capable of influencing, by way of exercising their right of joint control, the joint venture's commercial activity.
- *Active sales bans* are block exempted up to seven years from the time the contract products are first put on the market within the EEA, whereas *passive sales bans* are blacklisted.[387] Parallel trade within the EEA may also not be prevented: clauses which require the parties to refuse to meet demand from users or resellers in their respective territories who would market the contract products in other territories within the EEA or to make it difficult for users or resellers

378. Article 3 (3a) of Regulation 418/85.
379. *See* Article 4 (1) (fa) of Regulation 418/85.
380. *See* Article 4 (1) (fb) of Regulation 418/85. E.g., *Pasteur Mérieux*, D.Comm. Oct. 6, 1994, 1994 OJ L 309/1, point 94 (joint distribution necessary for the implementation of cooperation in R&D).
381. *See* Article 4 (1) (fc) of Regulation 418/85.
382. Article 21 (1) of the merger control Regulation 139/2004.
383. Article 5 (1) (d) of Regulation 2659/2000.
384. Article 5 (2) (b).
385. Article 5 (1) (c).
386. Article 5 (2) (a)–(b).
387. Article 5 (1) (e) and (f).

to obtain the contract products from other resellers within the EEA (including by using intellectual property rights) are blacklisted.[388] In the case of several joint ventures it must be ensured that there is no market or customer sharing between the different joint ventures,[389] that they are not prevented from actively selling beyond seven years and from passively selling without time limit into territories reserved to others,[390] that they do not refuse to meet demand from other territories,[391] and that customers are free to obtain the contract products from different sources.[392]
- *Non-compete clauses* are accepted if they are directly related to and necessary for the implementation of the agreement in order to introduce and promote the new products.[393] However, they are not covered by the block exemption if the products concerned are unconnected with the field of joint R&D.[394]

Joint Assignment or Licensing.
Joint licensing implies the obligation on the parties to assign or grant licences of intellectual property rights (such as patents, know-how and copyrights) to third parties only with each other's approval and to agree on the sharing of licence royalties,[395] whereby unequal contributions of the parties to the joint R&D may be compensated.[396] If the parties decide to grant a licence to a third party this licence agreement is not covered by the block exemption but must satisfy the technology transfer Regulation 772/2004. In particular, the licence agreements may not contain hardcore restrictions, and they may not be limited to one or more technical fields of use or one or more separate product markets where the licensing parties and the licensees are competitors having a combined market share of more than 20%.[397]

Where at least one of the parties does not exploit the results of the joint R&D itself, the agreement may not prohibit the parties from granting licences to third parties.[398] In this case the party may not be prevented from granting a licence to a third party in order to ensure that the dissemination of the new technology cannot be completely blocked or limited to a single operator. However, it may be

388. Article 5 (1) (i) and (j).
389. Article 5 (1) (c).
390. Article 5 (1) (f).
391. Article 5 (1) (i).
392. Article 5 (1) (j).
393. Article 1 (2).
394. Article 5 (1) (a).
395. This was unclear under Regulation 418/85 which blacklisted the obligation not to grant licences to third parties even though the exploitation by the parties themselves is not provided for or does not take place (Article 6 (g)).
396. Such a clause used to be white-listed under Article 5 (1) (f) of the previous Regulation 417/85; now it is included in the general exemption provision of Article 1 (1).
397. Article 4 (1) (c) (i) of Regulation 772/2004.
398. Article 5 (1) (h).

argued that the co-owership of the results of the joint R&D entitles the parties to veto the grant of such a licence, subject to the application of Article 82.[399] Where the parties jointly exploit the results of their joint R&D by granting an exclusive licence to a third party that has a dominant position, the application of the block exemption is not necessarily excluded, provided the parties' combined market shares do not exceed 25%, but the Commission may withdraw the benefit of the block exemption according to Article 7 of Regulation 2659/2000, and the exclusive licence would constitute an infringement of Article 82 anyway, without a prior withdrawal being required.[400] Where the parties to the joint R&D *acquire* a dominant position in the technology market and proceed to a joint exploitation by granting an exclusive licence the block exemption does not apply; instead, the licence is likely to constitute an abuse infringing Article 82 because it substantially restricts the access of third parties to the new market and virually eliminates any competition on the relevant market.[401]

(e) Withdrawal of the Block Exemption

The Commission may withdraw, on its own initiative or upon request of a member state, a natural or legal person, the benefit of the block exemption pursuant to Article 7 of Regulation 2659/2000 if it finds that an R&D agreement, although fulfilling the conditions of the block exemption, nevertheless has effects incompatible with Article 81 (3),[402] in particular where the agreement:

- substantially restricts third parties from carrying out concurrent R&D in the relevant field because of the limited R&D capacity available elsewhere, which may occur when the parties have or acquire a high degree of market power;[403]
- substantially restricts the access of third parties to the market (possibly as a result of the non-compete clauses imposed on the parties);[404]
- is not followed, without any objective reason, by the appropriate exploitation of the results to the disadvantage of customers;[405]

399. Recital 22 to Regulation 2659/2000.
400. *Tetra Pak I*, CFI July 10, 1990, 1990 ECR II-309, paras 21–38.
401. *See* Article 7 (b) of Regulation 2659/2000.
402. Article 7 of Regulation 2659/2000, which corresponds to Article 10 of Regulation 418/85.
403. Example: the two major competitors combine the main existing poles of reasearch: Guidelines on Horizontal Cooperation, points 71 and 75. Article 82 applies in any event without prior withdrawal: Recital 22 and *Tetra Pak I*, CFI July 10, 1990, 1990 ECR II-309, para. 30.
404. A licensee having a dominant position abuses its position by requiring the licensor not to grant licences to third parties: *Tetra Pak I*, CFI July 10, 1990, 1990 ECR II-309, para. 23.
405. Blocking rather than promoting technical progress, *see also* Article 6 (1) (c) of the new regulation on technology transfer agreements.

- is not subject, in the whole or a substantial part of the Common Market, to effective competition from substitutes on the market (in particular in cases where the parties' market shares are likely to lead to a paramount market position).[406]

4. INDIVIDUAL ASSESSMENT OF AGREEMENTS THAT ARE *NOT* COVERED BY THE BLOCK EXEMPTION REGULATIONS

Assessment of Market Shares Exceeding the Thresholds of the Block Exemptions.
Agreements between undertakings whose market shares collectively exceed the thresholds of the block exemption require individual assessment, provided they contain restrictions of competition that infringe Article 81 (1). They may satisfy the conditions for exemption under Article 81 (3) if competition is protected not only in the short term but also in the long term. The magnitude of remaining sources of competition cannot be assessed purely on the basis of market share; more intensive qualitative and quantitative analysis of the market structure in the relevant market (in particular the existence of an oligopolistic market structure), market entry barriers and potential competition need to be assessed.[407] In cases of an oligopolistic market structure cooperation between large market operators may not satisfy the conditions of Article 81 (3) at all[408] or only if it is strictly limited to R&D, thereby ensuring effective competition between them on the production and distribution level.[409] However, joint marketing is commonly accepted where the agreement concerns a 'relatively minor input' of a final product or 'entirely new' products.[410]

Hardcore Restrictions Satisfying the Conditions of Article 81 (3) under Exceptional Circumstances.
Hardcore restrictions are generally considered to have an *object* that infringes Article 81 (1) without needing to prove that they may have *effects* that are incompatible with Article 81 (3).[411] However, there may be exceptional circumstances under which some hardcore restrictions nevertheless fulfill the criteria for exemption under Article 81 (3). For example, active sales bans may be necessary for a longer period than seven years (if necessary to guarantee an adequate return on

406. However, Article 82 may be applied directly, no prior withdrawal of the block exemption being required: Recital 22 and *Tetra Pak I*, CFI July 10, 1990, 1990 ECR II-309, para. 30.
407. Commission's Notice on Article 81 (3), points 96–107.
408. Example in point 75 of the Guidelines on Horizontal Cooperation.
409. Specialization agreement: *Ford/Volkswagen*, D.Comm. Dec. 23, 1992, 1993 OJ L 20/14; R&D agreement: *Henkel/Colgate*, D.Comm. Dec. 23, 1971, 1972 OJ L 14/14.
410. Guidelines on Horizontal Cooperation, points 64 and 65. Even higher market shares may still justify an individual exemption: Guidelines, example under point 77.
411. Commission's Guidelines on Article 81 (3), points 21 and 24.

the investments involved)[412] and passive sales bans which are normally black-listed may satisfy the conditions of Article 81 (3) if they are limited to the period necessary for penetrating a new market (say, 2–3 years).[413]

C. Individual Assessment of Various Forms of Horizontal Cooperation under Article 81 (3) in the Light of the New Guidelines and Complementary Case Law

1. Issues Addressed by the Guidelines

Horizontal Cooperation.
In 2001 the Commission issued Guidelines for the assessment of horizontal agreements under Article 81, in particular agreements not covered by the new block exemption regulations.[414] These Guidelines relate to the assessment of horizontal cooperation, i.e., agreements between companies operating at the same level in the market, e.g., at the same level of R&D, production or distribution. They are complemented by the Commission's Guidelines on the application of Article 81 (3) and must therefore be read in parallel (which is quite difficult and leads in some cases to different conclusions). The Guidelines on horizontal cooperation address the following issues:

- *Classification of Firms as 'Potential' Competitors*: The Guidelines suggest that the classification of firms as 'potential' competitors normally requires that market entry would occur so that the threat of potential entry is a constraint on the market participants' behavior, which normally means that that entry has to occur within a short period, usually within 2–3 years.[415]
- *Assessment of Horizontal Cooperation under Article 81 (1) in the Economic Context*: The Guidelines clarify that the assessment of negative market effects as to process, output, innovation or the variety or quality of goods and services

412. Guidelines on Horizontal Cooperation, point 73. Ten years: *Asahi/St. Gobain*, D.Comm. Dec. 16, 1994, 1994 OJ L 354/87, points 30–31; more than ten years: *Pasteur Mérieux/Merck*, D.Comm. Oct. 6, 1994, 1994 OJ L 309/1, point 106.
413. *See*, in the case of a reciprocal licence agreement: *IFPI Simulcasting*, D.Comm. Oct. 8, 2002, 2003 OJ L 107/58 (2 ½ years). *See also* Article 1 (3) of Regulation 240/96 on technology transfer agreements (five years).
414. 2001 OJ C 3/2. The Guidelines therefore complement the Guidelines on vertical restraints which address vertical agreements between companies that operate at a different level of the production or distribution chain (2000 OJ C 291/1, point 23). They replace those on cooperation between enterprises (1968 OJ C 75/3), and on assessment of cooperative joint ventures (1993 OJ C 43/2). *See supra* Section I.1. *See also* Guidelines on the Application of Article 81 (3), 2004 OJ C 101/97.
415. Guidelines on Horizontal Cooperation, note 9 and *Elopak/Metalbox*, D.Comm. July 13, 1990, 1990 OJ L 209/15.

for Article 81 (1) to be infringed, depends on the economic context taking into account both the nature of the agreement and the parties' combined market power which determines – together with other structural factors – the capability of the cooperation to affect overall competition to such a significant extent.[416] However, in the case where the agreements contain *hardcore* restrictions, i.e., price fixing, output limitation or sharing of markets or customers, it is not necessary to examine their actual effects on competition and the market in order to establish that they fall within Article 81 (1).[417] The Commission states that horizontal cooperation does not imply anticompetitive behavior in markets where the parties are not competitors, where they cannot independently carry out the project or activity covered by the cooperation,[418] or when the cooperation concerns an activity far removed from the marketing level, which therefore does not influence the relevant parameters of competition.[419]

- *Confirmation of the de minimis Rule*: Normally there is no restrictive effect where both parties have market shares that do not exceed 10%[420] or where one party is big but the other has only insignificant market shares.[421]
- *General Criteria for Assessing Agreements between Companies*: The Guidelines discuss the economic benefits and potential efficiencies generated by such agreements, in particular those which exceed the market share thresholds and need assessment under Article 81 (3).[422]
- *Particulars with Regard to Certain Types of Cooperation Agreements*: The Guidelines analyse the particulars of R&D, production, purchasing, commercialization, standardization, environmental agreements as well as strategic alliances,[423] except where sector-specific rules apply.[424]

---

416. Guidelines, point 20. *See* the complementing Guidelines on the Application of Article 81 (3), points 28–31, in particular with respect to ancillary restraints.
417. Guidelines on Horizontal Cooperation, point 18.
418. An agreement between competitors to set up a joint venture does not in itself constitute a restriction of competition: *Indentrus*, D.Comm. July 31, 2001, 2001 OJ L 249/12, point 41; *see also BT-MCI*, D.Comm. July 27, 1994, 1994 OJ L 223/36, point 44. This coincides with the interpretation of the 'risk of coordination' within the meaning of Article 2 (4) of the merger regulation which does not exist where the parties have small market shares and hence there are no adverse effects: *Scandia/Storebrand/Pohjola*, D.Comm. Aug. 17, 1999, JV.21, point 39–40; *Electrabel/Totalfinaelf/Photovoltech*, D.Comm. April 18, 2002, M.2712, point 25.
419. Guidelines, point 24.
420. The Guidelines are without prejudice to the application of the *De Minimis* Notice (point 15 of the Guidelines).
421. Guidelines, point 29.
422. Guidelines, points 31–36. The Guidelines on the application of Article 81 (3) provide for a more comprehensive analysis of the criteria to be considered under Article 81 (3), points 38–116; these guidelines are discussed in greater detail in Chapter II.C.
423. Discussed under point 12 of the Guidelines on Horizontal Cooperation.
424. Guidelines, point 13.

However, the Guidelines do not address other types of agreements between competitors, such as the exchange of information or on minority shareholdings,[425] and the delineation between cooperative joint ventures which must be assessed under Article 81 (and are likely to be covered by the block exemptions) and joint ventures that perform on a lasting basis all the functions of an autonomous entity, which must be assessed under the merger control regulation, provided they have a Community dimension (*see infra* section 10). The Notice on the concept of full-function joint ventures[426] and the Information on the Assessment of Full-Function Joint Ventures[427] have not been updated yet in the light of the Commission's extensive recent practice under both Article 81 and the merger control regulation.

Economic Analysis v. Legal Certainty.
The general rule is that agreements must be evaluated in their economic context.[428] This economic analysis should lead to more horizontal cooperation agreements falling outside the scope of Article 81 (1) than before but they will remain subject to national competition rules.[429] The self-assessment of agreements that are not covered by the block exemption remains difficult, in particular because of the risks with regard to the accurate definition of the relevant market and evaluation of economic efficiencies.[430] The companies faced with such uncertainty because there are novel or unresolved questions will probably request clearance by the Commission[431] or national authorities, in particular where their cooperation involves important long-term investments. With respect to *vertical* agreements the Commission stated that it will not give priority to clearances unless there is litigation in national courts[432] but the Commission has not made any similar statement with respect to *horizontal* agreements.[433] In any event, clearance of *horizontal* agreements will be difficult to obtain from national authorities because a com-

425. They will be addressed separately: Guidelines, point 10.
426. 1998 OJ C 66/1.
427. 1998 OJ C 66/6.
428. The Commission's assessment is fully reviewed by the Court of Justice, *see M6, Antena 3, Gestévision, SIC/Eurovision II*, CFI Oct. 8, 2002, T-216/00 a.o. (annulling the Commission's exemption decision).
429. National law is only preempted by block exemptions and by Commission decisions finding that the conditions of Article 81(3) are fulfilled pursuant to Article 10 of Regulation 1/2003. *See* Chapter I.F.2.
430. *See* Griffith and Nüesch, *Modernising the treatment of horizontal agreements – an analysis of the Commission's proposals*, 2000 ECLR 452.
431. In such cases the Commission may be more inclined to issue guidance stating that the criteria of Article 81 (3) are met if the parties also offer commitments, which need to be submitted to, discussed with, and approved by the Commission.
432. Guidelines on Vertical Restraints, points 64–65.
433. The Commission intends to issue informal guidance only in cases of genuine uncertainty which present novel and unresolved questions: Recital 38 to Regulation 1/2003.

prehensive economic analysis of an agreement between companies operating on different national markets may go beyond the administrative means of a national authority to assess its impact, even when taking into account cooperation between national authorities and the Commission.[434]

2. Joint R&D Agreements

The Safe Harbor of Regulation 2659/2000.
R&D agreements are difficult to assess: they may reduce duplicative, unnecessary cost and result in new products or technologies more rapidly than would otherwise be the case, but they may also have anticompetitive effects on prices, output or innovation. Regulation 2659/2000 therefore provides for a safe harbor without prejudging the applicability of Article 81 (1),[435] provided the market share thresholds are not exceeded and the conditions (in particular the absence of hardcore restrictions) are fulfilled.[436] In the *IFPI Simulcasting* case the Commission affirmed the applicability of Article 81 (1) with respect to a model reciprocal agreement between record producers' rights administration societies for the licensing of 'simulcasting', i.e. the simultaneous transmission by radio and TV stations via the Internet of sound recordings included in their broadcasts of radio and/or TV signals in order to facilitate the grant of international licenses to radio and TV broadcasters who wish to engage in simulcasting. However, although not expressly presented as an R&D case, the Commission stated with respect to Article 81 (3) that

> 'in certain circumstances co-operation may be justified and can lead lead to substantial economic benefits, namely where companies need to respond to increasing competitive pressure and to a changing market driven by globalisation, the speed of technological progress and the generally more dynamic nature of the market'.[437]

The Commission exempted the agreement for these reasons but limited to an experimental phase of 2 ½ years.

Need for Careful Analysis of Agreements not Covered by the Block Exemption.
R&D agreements may merit positive assessment in new (innovative) markets even if the participants are actual or potential competitors and the market share

434. Commission Notice on Cooperation between National Competition Authorities and the Commission, 1997 OJ C 313/3.
435. *Ibid.*, point 63.
436. *Ibid.*, points 39–42.
437. *IFPI Simulcasting*, D.Comm. Oct. 8, 2002, 2003 OJ L 107/58, point 84.

threshold of 25% in Regulation 2659/2000 is exceeded, without reaching the level of dominance.[438] However, the effects on competition must be analysed in detail,[439] in particular with respect to the indispensability of the restrictions and their likely effect on competition. In cases of market shares considerably exceeding the threshold of the block exemption, the clearance by the Commission or a national competition authority may have to be subject to conditions or commitments[440] to ensure competition between the parties and to differentiate themselves in terms of efficiency, quality of service, costs and commercial terms[441] and limited to a relatively short period (i.e., three years).[442] Normally the parties will prefer to implement such procompetitive obligations into the original agreement, thereby alleviating the need for a review and the probable delay associated with a clearance by the Commission or a national competition authority. Absent extraordinary circumstances, the arrangement probably will fail to meet the criteria of exemption under Article 81 (3) where it combines the only main existing poles of research, even if the parties enter into a commitment to license key elements of the results of their joint R&D to third parties because it eliminates very meaningful competition at the R&D level.[443]

3. Joint Production Agreements

The Safe Harbor of Regulation 2658/2000.
Joint production agreements do not infringe Article 81 (1) if they are concluded between non-competitors, including companies which manufacture only for internal use or where joint production represents only a small part of total output of final products.[444] Even production agreements between competitors may not infringe Article 81 (1), in particular where the output is marketed through the parties' own distribution networks[445] or where the cooperation is the only commercially justifiable way to enter a new market, to launch a new product or to carry out a specific

438. Guidelines on Horizontal Cooperation, points 50–52 (innovative v. stagnant markets).
439. Examples: *Pasteur Mérieux/Merck*, D.Comm. Oct. 6, 1994 OJ L 309/1; *Asahi/St. Gobain*, D.Comm. Dec. 16, 1994, 1994 OJ L 354/87.
440. Regulation 1/2003 introduces 'commitments' as a means to meet the competitive concerns of the Commission in a way similar to the merger control regulation.
441. *IFPI Simulcasting*, D.Comm. Oct. 8, 2002, 2003 OJ L 107/58, points 119–120.
442. *KSB/Goulds/Lowara*, D.Comm. Dec. 12, 1990, 1991 OJ L 19/25. *See* Guidelines on Horizontal Cooperation, points 72–74.
443. *Ibid.*, point 71 and the example under point 75. Extraordinary circumstances that may nevertheless justify such cooperation might be if the cooperation is the only commercially justifiable way to enter a new market, to launch a new product or to carry out a specific project.
444. Guidelines on Horizontal Cooperation, point 86.
445. *See Scanlube*, Commission comfort letter, Twenty-seventh Report on competition Policy, p. 131 (after removal of the territorial exclusivity); *Solvay/Sisecam*, D.Comm. Sept. 25, 1999, 1999 OJ C 272/144 (comfort letter).

project.[446] In order to avoid legal uncertainty, Regulation 2658/2000 constitutes a safe harbor for specialization agreements between non-competitors and agreements between competitors with market shares that do not exceed 20%, provided the agreement does not contain hardcore restrictions.

Specialization Agreements that Need Individual Assessment.
Specialization agreements between undertakings with a combined market share exceeding 20% are not covered by the block exemption and fall almost always within Article 81 (1) because of the exclusivity granted by the parents to each other.[447] A different analysis applies if specialized production is conferred on a joint venture whereas the distribution function is reserved to the parents' individual networks; in this case the Commission tends to consider such joint ventures as not infringing Article 81 (1) in the same way as mere joint production agreements. Specialization agreements which are not covered by the block exemption and infringe Article 81 (1) must be analysed under Article 81 (3) on the market to which the specialized products belong and on possible spill-over (related) markets,[448] the absolute limit for exemption being the elimination of effective competition, i.e., where the parties would be likely to become dominant (acquiring a sole or collective dominant position).[449] In the light of the Commission's administrative practice, combined market shares up to 50% may still qualify for exemption, except in cases of a firm dominating its much smaller competitors or of collective dominance.[450] Higher market shares normally raise serious doubts and may need commitments in order to remove these doubts, e.g. by granting market or network access or removing exclusive supply or purchasing obligations.[451] Agreements containing hardcore restrictions are presumed to have negative market effects and will normally not be granted clearance.[452]

Specialization Joint Ventures.
Specialization agreements by which the parties entrust a joint venture with joint production and joint distribution constitute a 'full-function joint venture' fulfilling all the functions of an autonomous economic entity (even if the parents remain independent with respect to the use and distribution of its output)[453] and must be assessed under the merger control regulation, provided the criteria of a Community dimension are met. In the absence of a Community dimension specialization

446. Guidelines, point 87. *See* the examples under points 107–114.
447. Guidelines, point 90.
448. *See* Guidelines, examples points 106–114.
449. Guidelines, point 36.
450. *See* example under point 105.
451. *See Bayer/Gist*, D.Comm. Dec. 15, 1975, 1976 OJ L 30/13; *Ford/Volkswagen*, D.Comm. Dec. 22, 1987, 1988 OJ L 50/18.
452. Guidelines, points 18 and 90.
453. Article 3 (4) of Regulation 139/2004 on Merger Control.

joint ventures between parties having a combined market share of more than 20% must be assessed individually under Article 81 and need careful evaluation of the pro- and anti-competitive effects,[454] in particular of the spill-over effects on neighbouring markets. In the case of higher market shares of more than 50% the exemption may be made subject to conditions in order to maintain a certain independence of the parties (by establishing Chinese walls between them) and by limiting the scope of the cooperation.[455]

Outsourcing and Subcontracting Agreements.
Outsourcing agreements and subcontracting agreements are normally not concluded between competitors.[456] However, in cases where the parties are actual or potential competitors the Commission's Guidelines on Horizontal Cooperation suggest an assessment by analogy to other types of joint production agreements: they do not necessarily infringe Article 81 (1), in particular where the cooperation is the only commercially justifiable way to enter a new market,[457] or where the agreements are limited to individual sales and purchases on the merchant market without any further obligations and without forming part of a wider commercial relationship between the parties.[458] However, subcontracting agreements may also constitute unilateral specialization which must be assessed under Regulation 2658/2000.[459] Where subcontracting agreements involve the transfer of substantial know-how the new Regulation 772/2004 on technology transfer agreements applies, including its thresholds of 20% (if the parties are competitors) or 30% (if they are not competitors). Thus, there is a broad spectrum of how to assess subcontracting agreements, in particular in cases where the parties' market share exceeds the thresholds.

Standardization Agreements.
Standardization agreements define the technical or quality requirements with respect to a product or a service.[460] The Commission is authorized to issue a block exemption under Article 1 (1) (a) of Regulation 2821/71[461] for agreements on standards or types.[462] However, because of limited experience in this field, it has not made use of this authority. They therefore need individual assessment under

---

454. Examples: *BASF/Bayer/Hoechst/Dystar*, D.Comm. Sept. 5, 2000, M.1987 (market shares between 40 and 60%).
455. E.g., *GEAE/P&W (Engine Alliance)*, D.Comm. Sept. 14, 1999, 2000 OJ L 58/16; *Powertrain – GM/Fiat*, D.Comm. Aug. 16, 2000, IP/00/932.
456. Guidelines on technology transfer agreements, point 44.
457. Guidelines on Horizontal Cooperation, point 87.
458. *Ibid.*, point 89.
459. *Ibid.*, point 86.
460. *Ibid.*, point 159.
461. 1971 OJ L 285/46.
462. They used to be exempt from notification under Article 4 (2) (a) of Regulation 17.

Article 81. Standardization may hold great advantages not only for manufacturers because it rationalizes production, but also for consumers because it simplifies choice, improves intercompatibility[463] and makes for easier repair services. On the other hand, standardization can reduce competition between producers, restrict procompetitive differentiation and development and limit consumer choice.[464] If the majority of suppliers in a market take part in a standardization scheme, it may serve to foreclose the market to outsiders or to introduce a new technology.[465] The Commission has therefore often taken a critical stance towards such agreements, especially if the parties undertake not to manufacture or distribute products conforming to another standard[466] or if the standardization agreement makes market entry more difficult for third parties,[467] unless third parties have access to technical information on a non-discriminatory basis and reasonable terms.[468] The administrative practice includes exemptions for agreements establishing standards for computer software,[469] quality standards for paints,[470] environment-friendly washing machines,[471] standards for certain banking services,[472] for tendering procedures,[473] and for an agreement between major competing suppliers of DVD systems to develop standards for their competing technologies, subject to the condition that licences be granted in a non-exclusive and non-discriminatory way.[474] On the other hand, fines were imposed in cases where the development of quality standards for industrial copper tubes was used as a pretext for price fixing and market sharing.[475] The conclusion is that even higher market shares do not preclude an exemption under Article 81 (3), provided the agreements are limited to what is necessary to comply with objective production standards and do not extend to sales or marketing restrictions.[476]

---

463. Divergence between national standards does not justify monitoring of exports: *Cement*, CFI March 15, 2000, 2000 ECR II-491, para. 2082.
464. *Belasco*, D.Comm. July 10, 1986, 1986 OJ L 232/15, 23–24, *aff'd* ECJ July 11, 1989, 1989 ECR 2117, paras 29–30.
465. *Pre-insulated Pipes*, D.Comm. Oct. 21, 1998, 1999 OJ L 24/1, point 147 (*aff'd* CFI March 20, 2002, 2002 ECR II-1647). Under Article 82: *Eurofima*, Third Report on Competition Policy, points 68–69.
466. *Video Cassette Recorders*, D.Comm. Dec. 20, 1977, 1978 OJ L 47/42.
467. *See Mineral Water*, Seventeenth Report on Competition Policy, point 75.
468. Guidelines on Horizontal Cooperation, point 178.
469. *X-Open*, D.Comm. Dec. 15, 1986, 1987 OJ L 35/36 (exemption).
470. *VVVF*, D.Comm. June 25, 1969, 1969 OJ L 168/22 (negative clearance).
471. *CECED*, D.Comm. Feb. 11, 2000, 2000 OJ L 187/47.
472. *Irish Banks*, D.Comm. Sept. 30, 1986, 1986 OJ L 295/28; *Dutch Banks*, July 19, 1989, 1989 OJ L 253/1, 8–11 (negative clearances).
473. *FIEC/CEETB*, Eighteenth Report on Competition Policy, point 60 (comfort letter).
474. *DVD Standard*, D.Comm. Oct. 9, 2000, IP/00/1135; *MPEG-2 Standard* (moving pictures expert group), D.Comm. Dec. 18, 1998, IP/98/1155.
475. *Industrial Copper Tubes Cartel*, D.Comm. Dec. 16, 2003, IP/03/1746 (fines of EUR 79 million).
476. E.g. *General Motors, Fiat – Powertrains*, D.Comm. Aug. 16, 2000 (comfort letter), IP/00/932 (agreement between two car manufacturers to purchase certain standardized car parts (power-

4. Environmental Agreements

Environmental agreements are generally not restrictive,[477] except where they result in significant foreclosure effects.[478] Agreements between competing manufacturers of washing machines to phase out production of machines that do not meet industry efficency standards restrict competition but bring about advantages and considerable savings for consumers, thereby satisfying the conditions of Article 81 (3).[479] However, if they do not concern truly environmental objectives or if they are used as a tool to disguise a cartel, they may infringe Article 81 (1).[480] Agreements that allocate 'pollution quotas' or which appoint an exclusive recycling service collector or provider may fall under Article 81 (1).[481] National collecting societies may abuse their dominant position and infringe Article 82 if they require a flat fee for the collection of waste packaging irrespective of whether these services will be carried out by the collecting society or by its competitors.[482] However, the Commission takes a positive stance on the use of environmental agreements as a policy instrument to achieve the goals of Articles 2 and 174 of the EC Treaty, provided they do not contain non-indispensable restrictions, in particular any exclusivity obligations.[483]

5. Joint Purchasing Agreements

Various Forms of Joint Purchasing.
Joint purchasing agreements aim at combining demand in order to obtain better prices and at rationalizing ordering and the use of transport and storage facilities. Unlike joint sales organizations, a joint purchasing agreement does not necessitate the creation of a joint venture, in particular in cases of a limited number of

---

train) through a joint venture while allowing each parent to concentrate its individual efforts in powertrain customization).

477. Guidelines on Horizontal Cooperation, points 184–187.
478. *Ibid.*, point 189. *See Anseau*, D.Comm. Dec. 17, 1981, 1982 OJ L 167/39 (fines imposed because of foreclosure effect preventing parallel imports of washing machines) (*aff'd* ECJ Nov. 11, 1983, 1983 ECR 3369).
479. *CECED*, D.Comm. Feb. 11, 2000, 2000 OJ L 187/47.
480. Guidelines on Horizontal Cooperation, point 188.
481. *Ibid.*, points 189–191.
482. *FFAD*, ECJ May 23, 2001, C-209/98, para. 74; *Duales System ('Green Dot')*, D.Comm. April 20, 2001, 2001 OJ L 16/1 (prohibition decision without fines).
483. Guidelines, points 192 – 196. Examples: *CECED*, D.Comm. Feb. 11, 2000, 2000 OJ L 187/47; *Eco Emballage*, D.Comm. June 15, 2001, 2001 OJ L 233/37 (French packaging collection); *DSD*, D.Comm. Sept. 17, 2001, 2001 OJ L 319/1 (German packaging collection), which were cleared after assurance of free and unimpeded access to the collection infrastructure for competitors. *See* the previous cases *Michelin/Continental (recycling)*, Commission comfort letter, Twenty-seventh Report on Competition Policy, pp. 129–130, and the cases referred to in Chapter II, pp. 123–124.

participants. The anticompetitive risks of joint purchasing result from the setting of uniform prices (influencing the resale price and disadvantaging outsiders which do not benefit from the joint purchasing), fixing quotas and, by creating buying power, distorting competition on the demand side.[484]

Applicability of Article 81 (1).

Joint purchasing agreements do not fall within Article 81 (1) where the parties' combined market shares do not exceed the de minimis threshold (10%)[485] or where they are concluded between small and medium-sized enterprises ('SMEs').[486] However, joint purchasing infringes Article 81 (1) where it involves companies with market power (i.e., with a combined market share significantly above 15%[487]) and leads to buyer power, thereby discriminating against third parties,[488] to uniform purchase prices, and to similar costs and similar prices of the goods when they are resold or processed into other goods.[489] Anticompetitive coordination among joint purchasers is unlikely where the proportion of the joint purchases represent only a minor part (25–40%) of their total requirements.[490]

Exclusive v. Non-Exclusive Purchasing Arrangements.

The Commission has challenged joint purchasing agreements mostly where they cover a high percentage of the relevant market (usually exceeding 25–40% of the total purchases of the relevant goods or services[491]) and include *exclusive* purchasing obligations[492] or oblige the parties to purchase exclusively a fixed percentage of their supplies from a particular source.[493] In the *Rennet* case the Commission intervened against a joint exclusive purchasing agreement between the major suppliers of rennet (used in the fermentation of cheese) because the parties' combined market shares exceeded 90% of the relevant Dutch market and therefore afforded them the possibility of eliminating competition.[494] The Court

484. *Stora Enso/Assi Domän*, D.Comm. Dec. 22, 2000, M.2243.
485. *De minimis* Notice, 2001 OJ C 149/18, point 8 (a).
486. Guidelines on Horizontal Cooperation, point 116 and example under point 136. *See ORPHE*, D.Comm. Dec. 6, 1990, Twentieth Report on Competition Policy, point 102 (comfort letter for joint purchasing by medium-sized pharmaceutical wholesalers who were to distribute the products individually but under a common trademark).
487. Guidelines, point 131. Examples: *SOCEMAS*, D.Comm. July 17, 1968, 1968 OJ 201/4; *Intergroup Trading (SPAR)*, D.Comm. July 14, 1975, 1975 OJ L 212/23.
488. Guidelines, point 128; *M6/Eurovision II*, CFI Oct. Oct. 8, 2002, 2002 ECR II-3805, para. 68.
489. Example in Guidelines, point 135.
499. Under Article 81: *National Sulphuric Acid Association*, D.Comm. July 9, 1980, 1980 OJ L 260/24 (exclusive purchasing obligation reduced to 25%); under the the merger control regulation: *Stora Enso/Assi Domän*, D.Comm. Dec. 22, 2000, M.2243 (15–40%).
491. Guidelines, point 128 and example under point 137.
492. Leading case: *Rennet*, D.Comm. Dec. 5, 1979, 1980 OJ L 51/19, *aff'd* ECJ March 25, 1981, 1981 ECR 851.
493. E.g., *GISA*, D.Comm. Dec. 22, 1972, 1972 OJ L 303/45, 48.
494. *Rennet*, D.Comm. Dec. 5, 1979, 1980 OJ L 51/19.

of Justice affirmed the decision.[495] However, even *non-exclusive* joint purchasing may, depending on its factual and legal context, affect the competitive structure (i) of the upstream market by eliminating competition between the participants which, by creating a system of solidarity, bind themselves to jointly acquire goods or rights[496] and (ii) of the downstream market by creating an incentive for the participants to coordinate their competitive market behaviour, in particular where the costs of the upstream product represent a 'significant' proportion of total costs of the downstream product,[497] or by restricting or eliminating competition from non-members, in particular where the rights, which are jointly acquired, are used by priority or exclusively by the members themselves.[498] Although the parties to a non-exclusive purchasing arrangement are more flexible, they may be induced to acquire their total requirements through the joint purchasing scheme in order to fully benefit from its advantages.

Applicability of Article 81 (3).

Clearance under Article 81 (3) may be granted if the agreement leads to economic benefits, in particular transport cost savings or quantity discounts.[499] Negative effects prevail where the agreement is the tool of a disguised cartel[500] or leads to buyer power, thereby discriminating against third parties,[501] to uniform purchase prices and, if significant, to similar costs and similar prices of the processed goods.[502] Joint purchasing agreements are unlikely to be cleared where the products that are jointly purchased account for 50% of the total costs and the parties in the joint purchasing arrangement have market shares between 25 and 40% of the relevant downstream market,[503] unless it concerns only a small purchase volume[504]

495. *Rennet*, ECJ March 25, 1981, 1981 ECR 851, paras 17–18.
496. Instead of bidding against each other, members participate in joint negotiations and agree (or are bound to agree) among themselves on the financial and other conditions for the joint acquisition: *Eurovision II*, D.Comm. May 10, 2000, 2000 OJ L 151/18, point 73 (in this respect confirmed by CFI Oct. 8, 2002, 2002 ECR II-3805, para. 64, which annulled, however, the exemption decision because of the risk of eliminating competition in the sense of Article 81 (3) (b), *see* para. 86) .
497. This may be difficult to evaluate, *see* Guidelines on Horizontal Cooperation, points 127–131.
498. In cases such as joint acquisition of television rights to sporting events: *M6/Eurovision II*, CFI Oct. 8, 2002, 2002 ECR II-3805, paras 64–68.
499. *Powertrain – GM/Fiat*, D.Comm. Aug. 16, 2000, IP/00/932. However, cost savings that are caused by the mere exercise of power and which do not benefit customers cannot be taken into account: Guidelines, point 132.
500. Guidelines on Horizontal Cooperation, point 124. *See Industrial Timber*, Fifth Report on Competition Policy, points 36–37.
501. *See Eurovision*, CFI July 11, 1996, 1996 ECR II-649, paras 117–121 (overruling the Commission's decision June 11, 1993, 1993 OJ L 179/23).
502. Example in Guidelines, point 135.
503. Guidelines, point 128 and example under point 137.
504. *National Sulphuric Acid Association I*, D.Comm. July 9, 1980, 1980 OJ L 260/24, 29, 31; and *National Sulphuric Acid Association II*, D.Comm. June 9, 1989, 1989 OJ L 190/22, 24 (pur-

or sufficient guarantees are provided in order to permit third parties equal access to the jointly purchased goods or rights (e.g. television rights).[505] In the EBU Eurovision System case the Commission first prohibited the joint purchasing of broadcasting rights for international sports events by the national TV broadcasters[506] but exempted under Article 81 (3) the amended arrangement after having obtained certain improvements for purely commercial broadcasters.[507] However, the Court of First Instance annulled the exemption decision because of discriminatory treatment by the Eurovision system when accepting certain commercial broadcasters as members and excluding others.[508] The same Court later also reversed the amended exemption decision[509] because the grant of sublicenses did not guarantee reasonable access by third parties.[510] In cases of higher combined market shares the Commission has granted exemption only after reduction of the degree of exclusivity. For instance, in the case *Film Purchases by German Television Stations*[511] the Commission exempted the joint purchasing arrangement only under the condition that the parties conceded a large number of 'windows' lifting exclusivity for a relatively short period (2–6 years) and permitting the grant of broadcast licences to third parties. If the joint purchasing is conferred on a joint venture, it is still unclear whether such an operation must be assessed under Article 81 rather than under the merger control regulation.[512]

chasing obligation limited to 25%, although the members did not in fact fully exercise their right to purchase the remaining 75% individually). However, under the merger control regulation the Commission stated that coordination is unlikely where the products that are jointly purchased represent only 15–40% of the parties' total purchases: *Stora Enso/Assi Domän*, D.Comm. Dec. 22, 2000, M.2243.

505. This was denied in *M6/Eurovision II*, CFI Oct. 6, 2002, 2002 ECR II-3805, annulling D.Comm. May 10, 2000, 2000 OJ L 151/18; *Téléfonica/Sogécable/Prisa Es*, D.Comm. Nov. 23, 2000, Thirtieth Report on Competition Policy, point 220 (Article 15 (6) decision). Both cases concerned television rights to sports events.
506. *Screensport/EBU Member (Eurosport)*, D.Comm. Feb. 19, 1991, 1991 OJ L 63/32.
507. *EBU/Eurovision I*, D.Comm. June 11, 1993, 1993 OJ L 179/23. However, the improvements consisted only in the possibilities of deferred transmissions and live transmissions of sports events which the EBU do not themselves broadcast live. In *ARD/MGM*, D.Comm. Sept. 15, 1989, 1989 OJ L 284/36, the Commission exempted joint purchasing of exclusive television broadcasting rights for films after 'windows' allowing broadcasting by third parties during certain periods had been agreed.
508. *Eurovision*, CFI July 11, 1996, 1996 ECR II-649, paras 117–121.
509. *EBU/Eurovision II*, D.Comm. May 10, 2000, 2000 OJ L 151/18.
510. *M6, Antena 3, Gestévision/Eurovision*, CFI Oct. 10, 2002, T-185/00, paras 71–75.
511. *Film Purchases by German Television Stations*, D.Comm. Sept. 15, 1989, 1989 OJ L 284/36.
512. Under Article 81: *Powertrain – GM/Fiat*, Comfort letter of Aug. 16, 2000, IP/00/932; under the merger control regulation: *BSkyB/KirchPayTV*, D.Comm. March 21, 2000, JV.37.

Joint Purchasing via the Internet.

The guidelines do not deal with joint purchasing via the internet (e-commerce business-to-business – 'B2B–platform').[513] The few Commission decisions adopted so far concerned the creation of B2B-platforms between non-competitors on behalf of independent clients, which did not raise any competition problems because of the very dynamic and competitive markets.[514] In the absence of administrative experience on the use and implementation of such platforms it is still an open question to what extent competitors may cooperate via the internet in order to jointly use internet information to coordinate purchasing conditions among the joint purchasers and then to proceed to joint purchasing from third parties via the internet.[515] It is generally accepted that joint purchasing may lead to economies of transport and storage costs and to greater efficiency and lower prices.[516] Such a joint platform may be cleared under particular economic circumstances, provided the members have non-discriminatory access to the platform, are not prevented from establishing, or participating in, competing platforms, that the joint use of the platform does not impair the competitive position of third parties, in particular hindering their market access through exclusive or preferential arrangements,[517] and that the platform acts to the greatest possible extent in an autonomous way without exchanging commercially sensitive information between the (competing)

513. *See* FTC Report of Oct. 26, 2000, *Entering the 21st Century: Competition Policy in the World of B2B Electronic Marketplaces*, htpp://www.ftc.gor/bc/b2b/index.htm; Miezitis and Batchelor, *Issues for B2B Exchanges under EU Competition Law*, Antitrust Fall 2000, p. 39; Tack, *Commerce électronique et droit de la concurrence*, Journal des tribunaux, droit européen, Janvier 2001, 1.

514. *See Arrow Electronics/Tekelec*, D.Comm. April 14, 2000, IP/00/386; *Deutsche Bank/SAP – emaro*, D.Comm. July 13, 2000, M.2027, IP/00/783 (supply of office equipment); *Bayer/Deutsche Telekom/Infraserv Hoechst – Chemplorer*, D.Comm. Oct. 6, 2000, IP/00/1131 (procurement of technical and administrative goods and services)

515. *See*, under U.S. antitrust law, the Covisint B2B-platform created by Daimler and Chrysler which was investigated by the FTC. The FTC closed its investigation on Sept. 11, 2000, reserving, however, the possibility to take the appropriate measures according to the later development and the implementation of the platform (www.ftc.gov/os/2000/09/covisintchrysler.htm). Under European law joint purchasing internet platforms were cleared under Article 81: *General Motors/Fiat*, D.Comm. Aug. 16, 2000, IP/00/932; *Covisint*, D.Comm. July 31, 2001, IP/01/1155, and under the merger control provisions by the German Antitrust Authority, Sept. 25, 2000, WuW 2000–12, 1237 (conditional clearance of the e-commerce joint venture as an internet platform for trade in auto components between Daimler-Chrysler, Ford and General Motors which hold one third of the European and half of the worldwide car production, each of which have 27% in the internet platform), in particular because the joint venture would face competition from other industry-specific B2B exchanges of other car producers and component suppliers.

516. However, purchasing costs resulting from the exercise of buying power cannot be seen as pro-competitive: Guidelines, point 128.

517. *Telia/Oracle*, D.Comm. Sept. 12, 2000, IP/00/991; *M6/Eurovision II*, CFI Oct. 8, 2002, T-185/00, paras 64–68.

parents, in particular on prices and discounts.[518] However, the use of the joint platform may effectively (even if limited to a short duration[519]) lead to a factual exclusivity ('solidarity') between the parent companies and their preferred supplier(s)[520] and to anticompetitive coordination of the market behaviour on the downstream market, when the cost of the jointly purchased (upstream) product is the critical component or a sizeable percentage of the cost of the final manufactured or processed (downstream) product.[521] Furthermore, on oligopolistic markets a joint internet platform may be the incentive to similar joint purchasing cooperation between other competitors or to cooperation or concentration on the suppliers' side,[522] thereby increasing market and price transparency.[523]

6. Joint Commercialization Agreements

Different Forms of Joint Selling.
Joint commercialization agreements involve cooperation between actual or potential competitors in the selling, distribution or promotion of their products, which can have a widely varying scope, ranging from joint advertising to the joint determination of all commercial aspects related to the sale of the product including price.[524] Suppliers may entrust a single third party,[525] including an

518. Under the merger control regulation: *Newhouse/Jupiter/Scudder/M&G – Cofunds*, D.Comm. Sept. 1, 2000, M.207, point 20; under Article 81: *Volbroker*, D.Comm. July 31, 2000, IP/00/896 (comfort letter in the framework of the accelerated procedure for structural joint ventures); this case concerned a joint venture established by six competing banks for developing an electronic brokerage service for trading amongst themselves in foreign currency options.
519. 18 months in *Covisint*, D.Comm. July 31, 2001, IP/01/1155.
520. Because of such a possible anti-competitive risk Volkswagen, BMW and Toyota each established individual platforms for spare parts.
521. *See M6/Eurovision II*, CFI Oct. 6, 2002, 2002 ECR II-3805, para. 68.
522. Guidelines on Horizontal Cooperation, point 135.
523. *See Volbroker*, D.Comm. July 31, 2000, IP/00/896.
524. Guidelines, point 139. *See* Chapter III, pp. 186–189. *See Enterprise Oil, Statoil, Marathon*, D.Comm. April 20, 2001, IP/01/578 (settlement following commitment to sell independently).
525. Joint ventures, such as *CSV* (the Dutch fertilizer common sales organization), D.Comm. July 20, 1978, 1978 OJ L 242/15. Joint ventures may be responsible for any infringement of Article 81 (1), including fines, if they are created to run the members' marketing activities (*see Eurofer*, CFI March 11, 1999, 1999 ECR II-263, paras 167–180), except where its function is limited to purely organizational activities (*Woodpulp I*, ECJ Sept. 27, 1988, 1988 ECR 193, paras 24–27). An individual who acts as an agent on behalf of the members of the joint sales organization is not an independent operator and therefore does not itself commit a separate infringement (*SCPA/Kali + Salz (Potassium salts)*, D.Comm. May 11, 1973, 1973 OJ L 217/3), except where the individual (e.g. an auditor) is helping to run the cartel. *See Italian Glass Cast*, D.Comm. Dec. 17, 1980, 1980 OJ L 383/19, 23–24, 26; *IFTRA Aluminium*, D.Comm. July 15, 1975, 1975 OJ L 228/38; *Organic Peroxides Cartel*, D.Comm. Dec. 10, 2003, IP/03/1700 (fining *Treuhand*, a Swiss based consultancy company, for its key role in the cartel).

agent,[526] or one of themselves[527] or each other[528] with the distribution and sale of their products or they may create a joint venture for this purpose.[529] This joint venture may have the status of an agent[530] or distributor acting in its own name which is the usual form. Joint sales organizations are motivated by the need to avoid duplication of individual sales outlets and to economize on distribution, logistic and marketing costs. A joint sales organization may also, but not necessarily, be a vehicle for joint price fixing because it centralizes decisions on pricing in a single organization and it may be unrealistic to expect a single seller to offer the same or substitutable product at different prices, discounts or terms.[531]

Applicability of Article 81 and not of Merger Control Regulation. A joint venture created for joint sales activities is limited to the distribution of its parents' products and is therefore a partial-function venture which, unlike a full-function venture, is not subject to the merger control regulation. Therefore, Article 81 remains fully applicable.[532] However, in clearing the *Texaco/North Hydro* case,[533] the Commission concluded that the transfer of all the business activities (mainly marketing) to a joint venture resulted in the complete withdrawal of the parent firms from that market and therefore should be considered a concentrative operation. This decision does not seem to be consistent with the Commission's practice with respect to joint sales organizations and may not be regarded as a fundamental change. However, in the light of the merger control regulation the

---

526. Likely to be a disguised cartel (no investment): Guidelines on Horizontal Cooperation, point 153. *See SCPA/Kali+Salz*, D.Comm. May 11, 1973, 1973 OJ L 217/3; *CNSD*, ECJ June 18, 1998, 1998 ECR I-3851, para. 44.
527. *ASTRA*, D.Comm. Dec. 23, 1992, 1993 OJ L 20/23.
528. *SCPA/Kali + Salz (Potassium salts)*, D.Comm. May 11, 1973, 1973 OJ L 217/3; *SACEM III*, ECJ July 13, 1989, 1989 ECR 2811 para. 14 (reciprocal exercise of copyrights by the copyrights collecting societies of different member states); *Banque Nationale de Paris/Dresdner Bank*, D.Comm. June 24, 1996, 1996 OJ L 188/37 (entrusting each other with offering the services of both to their reciprocal clients in their home markets, however, after objection, without exclusivity); *Nederlandse Federatieve Vereniging voor de Groothandel op Elektrotechnisch Gebied*, CFI Dec. 16, 2003, T-5/00, para. 342 (collective system of exclusivity aiming at fixing prices and foreclosing competitors).
529. *See CSV*, D.Comm. July 20, 1978, 1978 OJ L 242/15; *Floral*, D.Comm. Nov. 28, 1979, 1980 OJ L 39/51.
530. *SCPA/Kali + Salz (Potassium salts)*, D.Comm. May 11, 1973, 1973 OJ L 217/3.
531. The possibility of the joint sales organization acting as a joint price fixing scheme is highest between competitors, especially close competitors, such as those supplying agricultural products or basic materials. *See Telecommunication Directive Terminal Equipment*, ECJ March 19, 1991, 1991 ECR I-1223 paras 40–43; *Greek Television Monopoly*, ECJ June 18, 1991, 1991 ECR I-2925, paras 22–23.
532. Commission Notice on the assessment of cooperative joint ventures under Article 81 (1993 OJ C 43/2), para. 11.
533. *Texaco/North Hydro*, D.Comm. Jan. 9, 1995, M.511. Similarly: *Advent International/EMI*, D.Comm. March 24, 1998, M.1112.

approach towards joint sales organizations has slightly changed insofar as the Commission accepts certain contractual obligations as 'ancillary', provided that their duration, geographic scope and subject matter are directly related and necessary to the formation and operation of the joint venture.[534] However, this does not mean that joint sales ventures which normally include joint price fixing will be authorized by the Commission under Article 81 (3). On the contrary, the Commission remains very critical and considers carefully whether the size and market position of the parent companies justify joint selling, as explained below.[535]

Applicability of Article 81 (1): Cooperation between Non-Competitors v. Cooperation between Competitors.

Agreements between *non-competitors* do not fall under Article 81 (1), except where they contain vertical restraints, which may, however, be exempted under Regulation 2790/1999. Likewise, cooperation that is objectively necessary to allow one party to enter a market it could not have entered individually, in particular because of the costs involved or in the case of consortia where companies would not be able to mount a credible tender individually, is unlikely to fall within Article 81.[536] This also applies to joint marketing arrangements between firms supplying complementary products.[537] However, companies which compete on their traditional market may be considered as *potential competitors* with respect to other geographic markets where they were not operating yet. In cases such as *Floral*[538] and *ANSAC*[539] the Commission prohibited commercialization joint ventures despite the non-existing or relatively low market shares of the participants because they were major players on a neighbouring geographic market, held sufficient skills and resources and could bear the financial and economic risks required to launch their products or services individually.[540]

Agreements between *competitors* to sell products or commercial rights jointly are most likely to infringe Article 81 (1) even if the combined market shares are

534. Commission Notice on Cooperative Joint Ventures, 1990 OJ C 43/2, paras 52, 60 and 65–76. This reasoning was confirmed, although not expressly referring to this notice, in *Gottrup Klim*, ECJ Dec. 15, 1994, 1994 ECR I-5641.

535. E.g., *GFU Gas Norway*, D.Comm. June 21, 2001, IP/01/830; *Enterprise Oil/Statoil/Marathon*, D.Comm. April 20, 2001, IP/01/578.

536. Guidelines on Horizontal Cooperation, point 143. With respect to shipping consortia *see* Regulation 823/2000, 2000 OJ L 100/24, as amended by Regulation 463/2004, 2004 OJ L 77/23.

537. *See Siemens/Yazaki Automotive Components JV*, D.Comm. Aug. 6, 2001, IP/01/1194 (clearance under the merger control regulation).

538. *Floral*, D.Comm. Nov. 28, 1979, 1980 OJ L 39/51.

539. *Ansac*, D.Comm. Dec. 19, 1990, 1991 OJ L 152/54.

540. Other joint marketing to which the Commission has objected includes: *Enterprise Oil, Statoil, Marathon (Irish gas)*, D.Comm. April 20, 2001, IP/01/578; *GFU (Norwegian gas producers)*, D.Comm. July 17, 2002, IP/02/1084.

relatively low (e.g., 10%[541]) because they prevent the parties from individually marketing such products or such rights.[542] They may have as their object or effect[543] not only fixing or coordinating prices, thereby eliminating price competition between the parties, but also to restrict the volume of the products to be delivered by the participants (including a joint venture) within the framework of the system for allocating orders.[544]

A '*consortium*' between competitors making anticompetitive joint or coordinated bids or proposals to public or private purchasers (bid-rigging) clearly infringes Article 81 (1) and is likely to be heavily fined.[545] However, joint bidding between smaller companies which is pre-approved and/or provided for by private or governmental agencies does not infringe Article 81 (1), in particular where several firms combine to compete for a very large, risky or difficult project.[546]

Exclusive v. Non-Exclusive Joint Marketing Arrangements.
Exclusive joint marketing arrangements between competitors are likely to eliminate virtually all competition between the parties on prices and other terms of sale, thereby reducing the customers' choice. *Non-exclusive* arrangements may also lead to the fixing of identical or similar prices for the parties' products and to market sharing or customer allocation because the parties will, even in the absence of any contractual exclusivity, be induced to sell through their joint marketing scheme and to refrain from selling directly themselves, or at least from actively selling, in the others' territory or to the others' customers in order to fully benefit from the advantages from the joint marketing.[547]

Exchange of Pricing Information Likely to Infringe Article 81 (1).
Even in the absence of an express pricing agreement, joint commercialization may infringe Article 81 (1) because it provides a clear opportunity for exchanges of sensitive commercial information on marketing strategy and pricing.[548]

541. Guidelines, example point 157. Joint marketing agreed between smaller competitors with market shares not exceeding 10% do not qualify for the application of the *De Minimis* Notice because it implies joint price fixing which is a hardcore restriction. *See ANSAC*, D.Comm. Dec. 19, 1990, 1991 OJ L 152/54.
542. *UEFA Champions League*, D.Comm. July 23, 2003, 2003 OJ L 291/25, points 113–124 (joint selling the media rights relating to matches in the UEFA Champions League, which are jointly owned by the participating clubs and the UEFA).
543. Where price fixing is the object of an agreement the anti-competitive effects do not need to be demonstrated: *LR af 1998 A/S*, CFI March 20, 2002, 2002 ECR II-1705, para. 47.
544. Guidelines on Horizontal Cooperation, point 144.
545. *See Pre-insulated Pipes*, D.Comm. Oct. 21, 1998, 1999 OJ L 24/1, *aff'd Ke Kelit*, CFI March 20, 2002, 2002 ECR II-1647.
546. *See Konsortium*, D.Comm. July 27, 1990, 1990 OJ L 228/31 (negative clearance).
547. Guidelines on Horizontal Cooperation, point 147. For this reason arrangements between competitors are excluded from block exemption Regulation 2790/99 (Article 2 (4)).
548. *Ibid.*, points 146–147.

Although an exchange of information between competitors is not as such restrictive of competition it may infringe Article 81 (1) if the information exchanged is commercially sensitive and precise.[549] Such an exchange is likely to be challenged because it may, depending on the structure of the market, reduce or remove the degree of uncertainty as to the parties' conduct on the market and thereby impede competition.[550] This also applies where the information exchange is used to implement or complement production or commercialization agreements between competitors.[551] The risk of anticompetitive collusion between the parents may be reduced by establishing a 'Chinese wall' on the exchange of such competitively sensitive information.[552]

Applicability of Article 81 (3) only in Exceptional Cases.
Joint commercialization agreements may meet the criteria for individual exemption under Article 81 (3) if they lead to substantial efficiencies, in particular cost reduction,[553] which compensate the disadvantages[554] or increase the available choice to customers.[555] Exemption depends in particular on the efficiency of third parties' competition. Agreements between companies having combined market shares below 15–30%, but exposed to effective competition from larger competitors, are likely to meet the criteria for exemption.[556] However, in the case of higher market shares (more than 30%) an exemption is unlikely or can only be granted if the joint marketing is limited to a short initial period of 2–3 years[557] or market

549. *Wirtschaftsvereinigung Stahl*, CFI April 5, 2001, 2001 ECR II-1217, para. 44.
550. *See UK Agricultural Registration Exchange*, ECJ May 28, 1998, 1998 ECR I-3175, para. 90.
551. *Pasteur/Mérieux*, D.Comm. Oct. 6, 1994, 1994 OJ L 309/1; *Ford/VW*, D.Comm. Dec, 23, 1992, 1993 OJ L 20/14; *ADM, Ajinomoto*, D.Comm. June 7, 2000 (fine of EUR 110 million for breach of Article 81).
552. Under Article 81: *Exxon/Shell*, D.Comm. May 18, 1994, 1994 OJ L 144/20; under the merger control regulation: *British Telecommunications/AT&T*, D.Comm. March 30, 1999, JV.15; *GF-X Freight Trading Platform between several European airlines*, D.Comm. Oct. 28, 2002, IP/02/1560.
553. Not only cost reductions that derive from eliminating competition between the parties: Guidelines, point 157.
554. *See P&O/Stena Line*, D.Comm. Jan. 26, 1999, 1999 OJ L 163/21 (exemption for 3 years, but extended by comfort letter of March 8, 2001, IP/01/333); *UEFA Champions League*, D.Comm Aug. 17, 2002, 2002 OJ C 196/3 (joint selling of television broadcasting rights on an exclusive basis, but clubs retain life radio broadcasting rights).
555. Examples in Guidelines, points 156–158. Example: network sharing for the third generation of GSM mobile telecommunications *BT Cellnet & BT3G/One2One*, D.Comm. Sept. 10, 2002, 2002 OJ C 53/18.
556. *See* Guidelines, example point 158.
557. Under Article 81: *IFTI Simulcasting*, D.Comm. Oct. 8, 2002, 2003 OJ L 107/58 (joint licensing to authorize simulcasting of sound recordings at agreed fees, exempted for a duration of 2 ½ years); under the merger control regulation: *GF-X Air Freight Trading*, D.Comm. Oct. 28, 2002, IP/02/1560 (B2B trading platform for selling air freight capacity, cleared for a two-year starting-up period); *UIP* (joint marketing of films by MCA and MGM/UA), D.Comm. July 13, 1989, 1989 OJ L 226/25.

access is not unduly restricted or sufficient guarantees have been given by way of commitments.[558] In the *UEFA Champions League* case,[559] which concerned joint selling of media rights to football matches of the Champions League, an exemption was granted under Article 81 (3) because of the interest of media operators and consumers in an overview of the *whole* UEFA Champions League, provided it was limited in time (e.g., seven years) and subject to conditions in order to ensure that the restrictions were limited to what is indispensable for achieving the advantages of joint selling (e.g., by reserving the right of the members to sell individually certain live TV rights to free-TV broadcasters). However, the general tendency of the Commission is to object to joint marketing arrangements between competitors,[560] except where the joint marketing is non-exclusive,[561] limited to a short initial period necessary for penetrating a new market,[562] or justified by exceptional (sector-specific) circumstances, in particular in the transport sector.[563] In the fertilizer sector the Commission prohibited joint marketing,[564] even if it was limited to sales outside the Community,[565] and in the energy sector the Commission has repeatedly intervened against joint marketing.[566]

Applicability of Block Exemptions.
Where competitors agree on joint commercialization by a third party (which is not a competitor) of products which are jointly developed and/or manufactured, the agreements are covered by the block exemptions up to their respective market

558. Under Article 81: *British Interactive Broadcasting (BiB)*, D.Comm. Sept. 15, 1999, 1999 OJ L 312/1, points 141 and 173–187; similarly under the merger control regulation: *BSkyB/Kirch-PayTV*, D.Comm. March 21, 2000 JV.37; *Cap Gemini/Vodafone*, D.Comm. Nov. 30, 2000, M.2195, IP/00/1383.
559. *UEFA Champions League*, D.Comm. July 23, 2003, 2003 OJ L 291/25, points 147, 158 and 201. *See also Football Association Premier League*, D.Comm. April 3, 2004, 2004 OJ C 115/3.
560. *See FLORAL*, *supra* note 538, and *ANSAC*, *supra* note 539.
561. Less restrictive than exclusive joint marketing, despite the possibility that non-exclusive joint marketing may lead to actual coordination. *See* Guidelines, points 144–145.
562. *P&O/Stena Line*, D.Comm. Jan. 26, 1999, 1999 OJ L 163/21 (exeption for three years, but extended by comfort letter of March 8, 2001, IP/01/333; *GF-X Air Freight Trading*, D.Comm. Oct. 28, 2002, IP/02/1560 (B2B trading platform for selling air freight capacity, cleared for a starting-up period).
563. Guidelines, points 151–153. E.g. *Austrian Airlines/Lufthansa*, D.Comm. July 15, 2002, 2002 OJ L 242/25 (exemption subject to amendments in order to reduce market barriers); in the maritime sector: *TACA II*, D.Comm. Nov. 14, 2002, IP/02/1677 (clearance subject to commitments to reduce coordination on capacity and exchange of information).
564. *See NCH*, D.Comm. Dec. 23, 1971, 1972 OJ L 22/16.
565. Because of its probable repercussions inside the Community: *CSV*, D.Comm. July 20, 1978, 1978 OJ L 242/15.
566. E.g., *Statoil/North Hydro*, D.Comm. July 17, 2002, IP/02/1084; *Enterprise Oil/Statoil/Marathon (Caribean Gas)*, D.Comm. April 20, 2001, IP/01/578; *Shell/Maersk/Chevron-Texaco (DONG/DUC)*, D.Comm. April 24, 2003, IP/03/91.

share thresholds, 25% in the case of R&D agreements and 20% in the case of specialization agreements. Agreements between parties with higher market shares need to be evaluated under Article 81 (3), whose criteria may be met provided the market shares are not indicative of a (sole or collective) dominant position.[567] Where competitors confer production and commercialization of certain products on a *joint venture*, its assessment under the merger control regulation instead of under Article 81 depends on the degree of autonomy and independence that it will have from its parents and whether it has a Community dimension.[568]

Joint Marketing via the Internet.
Joint marketing may also result from the creation of a joint e-commerce platform between competitors (business-to-customers – B2C), which may lead to a joint or coordinated marketing policy by the members.[569] However, the Commission tends to consider internet sales as a distinct market from traditional distribution channels to the extent that the participants are unlikely to engage in anticompetitive coordination on other markets, provided the internet platform is open to third undertakings (no foreclosure effects) and does not lead to the exchange of commercially sensitive information.[570] Internet platforms established by non-competitors and working like a traditional (strictly neutral) auction normally do not raise antitrust concerns.[571]

7. Information Exchange without Joint Marketing

Case-by-Case Evaluation.[572]
Information exchange agreements require careful scrutiny, because the distinction between competitively neutral exchanges of information and anticompetitive conduct in the form of notification systems on orders, sales, investment and prices is difficult. It is impossible to say without a close study of the facts that agreements of this type – particularly as to prices or other competitively sensitive data in an

---

567. Guidelines, point 155.
568. *See infra* section 10.
569. *See TruckXchange*, created as an internet platform for producers, customers, distributors and subcontractors of trucks as mentioned in *Covisint*, D.Comm. July 31, 2001, IP/01/1155.
570. Under the merger control regulation: *GF-X Air Freight Trading Platform* between several European airlines, D.Comm. Oct. 22, 2002, IP/02/1560. This separation may appear artificial, *see* text at notes 518–523 *supra*.
571. *See Newhouse/Jupiter/Scudder/M&G – Cofunds*, D.Comm. Sept. 1, 2000, M.2075 (independent online supermarket for sale of retail mutual funds via independent intermediaries); *Telia/Oracle – Drutt*, D.Comm. Sept. 12, 2000, IP/00/991 (wireless internet portal for mobile phone users); *Siemens/SAP – Governet*, D.Comm. Oct. 3, 2000, IP/00/1102 (provision of information technology services); *Cap Gemini/Vodafone*, D.Comm. Nov. 30, 2000, IP/00/1383 (provision of information technology services).
572. Information exchange systems are not addressed in the Guidelines on Horizontal Cooperation but may be the subject of future specific guidelines (point 10).

oligopolistic market with homogeneous products – do not or could not restrict competition. The regular exchange of information by competitors can be part of a pattern of conduct which consciously substitutes practical cooperation for the risks of competition and leads to competitive conditions unlike those normally obtaining on the open market by disclosing to each other the course of conduct which competitors decided to adopt or contemplate adopting on the market.[573]

Information Exchange not as such Restrictive but Dependent on its Extent and the Market Structure.
Exchange of information is not *as such* restrictive, even if agreed between competitors, but only in its factual and legal context, in particular depending on its extent and the market structure.[574] Article 81 (1) is based on the principle that every trader must determine independently the policy it intends to follow on the market. This independent decision-making may not be distorted or undermined by exchanges of information that substitute practical cooperation for the normal risks of competition.[575] In the leading case, *UK Agricultural Tractor Registration Exchange*,[576] the Commission prohibited an agreement between the main tractor suppliers in the UK to exchange information identifying the origin of tractors imported, sold and registered in the UK. The Court of First Instance[577] confirmed the Commission prohibition by stating:

> 'that … on a truly competitive market transparency between traders is in principle likely to lead to the intensification of competition between the suppliers, since in such a situation, the fact that a trader takes into account information made available to him in order to adjust conduct on the market is not likely, having regard to the atomized nature of supply, to reduce or remove for the other traders any uncertainty about the foreseeable nature of its competitors' conduct. On the other hand … general use, as between suppliers, of exchanges of precise information at short intervals, identifying registered vehicles and the place of registration is, on a highly concentrated oligopolistic market on which competition is already greatly reduced and

573. *ICI-Dyestuffs*, ECJ July 14, 1972, 1972 ECR 619, paras 99–119; *Sugar*, ECJ Dec. 16, 1975, 1975 ECR 1663, paras 172–175; reconfirmed in *Polypropylene – Rhône-Poulenc*, CFI Oct. 24, 1991, 1991 ECR I-867 para. 121; *aff'd Polypropylene-Montecatini*, ECJ July 8, 1999, 1999 ECR I-4539, para. 162; *SPO (Dutch Construction Works)*, CFI Feb. 21, 1995, 1995 ECR I-289 paras 173–174.
574. *Steel Beams Eurofer*, CFI March 11, 1999, 1999 ECR II-263, paras 167–174; *Wirtschaftsvereinigung Stahl*, CFI April 5, 2001, 2001 ECR II-1217, para. 44.
575. With respect to Article 65 (1) of the ECSC Treaty: *Thyssen Stahl*, CFI March 11, 1999, 1999 ECR II-347, paras 393 and 406, *aff'd* ECJ Oct. 2, 2003, C-194/99 P, paras 82–83 and 410.
576. *UK Agricultural Tractor Registration Exchange*, D.Comm. Feb. 17, 1992, 1992 OJ L 68/19.
577. *UK Agricultural Tractor Registration Exchange – John Deere*, CFI Oct. 27, 1994, 1994 ECR I-957, paras 51–52; *idem Fiatagri and New Holland Ford*, CFI Oct. 27, 1994, 1994 ECR I-905, para. 91.

exchange of information facilitated, likely to impair considerably the competition which exists between traders. In such circumstances, the sharing, upon a regular and frequent basis, of information concerning the operation of the market has the effect of periodically revealing to all competitors the market positions and strategies of the various individual competitors. Furthermore, provision of the information in question to all suppliers presupposes an agreement, or at any rate a tacit agreement, between the traders to define the boundaries of dealers sales territories by reference to the United Kingdom postcode system, as well an institutional framework enabling information to be exchanged between the traders through the trade association to which they belong and, secondly, having regard to the frequency of such information and its systematic nature, it also enables a given trader to forecast more precisely the conduct of its competitors, so reducing or removing the degree of uncertainty about the operation of the market which would have existed in the absence of such an exchange of information.'

The Court of Justice affirmed this assessment of the Court of First Instance and concluded:

> 'that the information exchange system reduces or removes the degree of uncertainty as to the operation of the market and that the system is therefore liable to have an adverse influence on competition between manufacturers.'[578]

The Court of Justice enlarged this approach in the *Steel Beams* case[579] by stressing that an information exchange system may constitute a separate breach of competition rules not only in a highly concentrated oligopolistic market, as in the *UK Agricultural Tractors Registration Exchange* case, but also in less concentrated market structures.[580]

Various Forms of Information Exchanges.

Agreements on the exchange of commercially sensitive information may serve as a control mechanism to reinforce other restraints of competition such as agreements on investments, capacity and output,[581] market sharing and quotas,[582] sales

578. ECJ May 28, 1998, 1998 ECR I-3175, para. 90.

579. *Steel Beams – Thyssen Stahl*, ECJ Oct. 2, 2003, C-194/99 P, paras 77–89.

580. Also to other market structures, 'the only general principle applied in relation to the market structure being that supply must not be atomized': *Steel Beams – Thyssen Stahl*, ECJ Oct. 2, 2003, C-194/99P, para. 86.

581. *Welded Steel Mesh*, D.Comm. D.Comm. Aug. 2, 1989, 1989 OJ L 260/1; *aff'd* CFI April 6, 1995, 1995 ECR I-145/89; *aff'd* ECJ July 17, 1997, 1997 ECR I-4411.

582. *Potassium Salts*, D.Comm. May 11, 1973, 1973 OJ L 217/3; *Vegetable Parchment*, D.Comm. Dec. 23, 1977, 1978 OJ L 70/54, 61–63; *CSV*, D.Comm. July 20, 1978, 1978 OJ L 242/15, 27–29; *White Lead*, D.Comm. Dec. 12, 1978, 1979 OJ L 21/16, 21; *Italian Cast Glass*, D.Comm. Dec. 17, 1980, 1980 OJ L 383/19, 25; *Benelux Flat Glass*, July 23, 1984, 1984 OJ L 212/13, 19–20.

and purchases[583] or coordination of prices[584] or other terms of sale.[585] However, information exchange agreements may have anticompetitive effects quite apart from any related agreements, particularly in oligopolistic markets for fungible (non-differentiated) products; in such cases the exchange of information constitutes an independent infringement of Article 81 (1)[586] so that a decision of the Commission may be upheld in this respect even if the anticompetitive collusion on prices or markets is not proved.[587] Exchange of commercially sensitive information may take place directly between competitors (and in this case hardly disguise its anticompetitive object)[588] or through a trade association,[589] an auditor or a fiduciary agency[590] entrusted to collect, to aggregate, disseminate and to monitor the information.[591] Exchange of information normally leads to regular discussions

---

583. *COBELPA*, D.Comm. Sept. 8, 1977, 1977 OJ L 242/10, 15.
584. *Plasterboard*, D.Comm. Nov. 27, 2002, IP/02/1744; *Food flavour enhancer*, D.Comm. Dec. 17, 2002, IP/02/1907. Mostly both sales prices and volume, *see Carton*, D.Comm. July 13, 1994, 1994 OJ L 243/1; *aff'd Stora*, CFI May 14, 1998, 1998 ECR I-2111, para. 111; *Pre-insulated Pipes*, D.Comm. Oct. 21, 1998, 1999 OJ L 24/1, point 147 (*aff'd* CFI March 20, 2002, 2002 ECR II-1647); *Methionine*, D.Comm. July 2, 2002, 2003 OJ L 255/1, points 215–217.
585. *Industrial Timber*, Fifth Report on Competition Policy, points 36–37; *OFITOMEP*, Sixth Report on Competition Policy, points 134–136; *IFTRA Glass*, D.Comm. May 15, 1974, 1974 OJ L 160/1, 13; *IFTRA Aluminium*, D.Comm. July 15, 1975, 1975 OJ L 228/3, 10–11; *Vimpoltu*, D.Comm. July 13, 1983, 1983 OJ L 200/44, 48; *Wood Pulp*, D.Comm. 1984, 1985 OJ L 85/1, 20, *aff'd* ECJ March 31, 1993, 1993 ECR I-1307, paras 131–132, 154–163. Under Article 65 ECSC Treaty: *Steel Stockholders*, D.Comm. Feb. 8, 1980, 1980 OJ L 62/28, 35–36; *Wirtschaftsvereinigung Stahl*, D.Comm. Nov. 26, 1997, 1998 OJ L 1/10, point 40.
586. Twenty-fourth Report on Competition Policy, p. 642.
587. Examples: *Wood Pulp*, D.Comm. Dec. 19, 1984, 1985 OJ L 85/1, 20; (in this respect upheld ECJ March 31, 1993, 1993 ECR I-1307, paras 131–132, 154–163); *Italian Flat Glass*, D.Comm. Dec. 8, 1988, 1989 OJ L 33/44 (in this respect *aff'd* CFI March 10, 1992, 1992 ECR I-1403, paras 334–335). In *Carton*, D.Comm. July 13, 1994, 1994 OJ L 243/1, para. 136, the parties submitted, without awaiting the result of their appeals, amendments to their information exchange system for clearance by the Commission: Twenty-sixth Report on Competition Policy, p. 127. The Court of First Instance upheld the Commission's ruling on the restrictive nature of the information exchange system (*Carton – Stora*, CFI May 14, 1998, 1998 ECR II-2111, paras 111–112), which was affirmed by the Court of Justice, which reduced, however, the degree of Stora's responsibility (ECJ Nov. 16, 2000, 2000 ECR I-9925), which led to a reduction of the fine by the Court of First Instance (CFI Feb. 28, 2002, 2002 ECR I-843).
588. E.g. *Fatty Acid*, D.Comm. Dec. 2, 1986, 1987 OJ L 3/17 (prohibition of an information exchange between the three major suppliers on an oligopolistic market with fines of ECU 150,000 each).
589. E.g., *Wirtschaftsvereinigung Stahl*, D.Comm. Nov. 26, 1997, 1998 OJ L 1/10.
590. For example a fiduciary agency such as IFTRA in *IFTRA Aluminium*, D.Comm. July 15, 1975, 1975 OJ L 228/3, 8; or as Fides in *Woodpulp*, ECJ March 31, 1993, 1993 ECR I-1307, para. 154; or Eurofer in the case *Steel Beams*, D.Comm. Feb. 16, 1994, 1994 OJ L 116/1; and *Wirtschaftsvereinigung Stahl*, D.Comm. Nov. 26, 1997, 1998 OJ L 1/10, paras 39–54 (under Article 65 of the ECSC Treaty).
591. This monitoring may be part of, or a substitute for, a cartel: *Belasco*, D.Comm. July 10, 1986, 1986 OJ L 232/15, paras 20 and 75, *aff'd* ECJ July 11, 1989, 1989 ECR 2117. Consequently,

between the parties aiming at correcting or updating the information exchanged ('monitoring'[592]) and is therefore likely to be used as platform for anticompetitive coordination.[593] The dissemination of the collected data is normally limited to the parties, thereby confining the benefit of the system to the participating parties alone, thereby excluding competing companies, traders and consumers.[594]

Complex Evaluation.
The line between competitively neutral and anticompetitive exchanges of information is difficult to draw and depends, in particular, on the nature of the information exchanged, on the frequency with which it was disseminated[595] and on the persons to whom it is disclosed.[596] This evaluation becomes particularly complex if the data exchanged is of a non-public, confidential character. In this case the data of individual firms should be aggregated in a manner so that individual firm data cannot be ascertained. Such information-collecting systems do not in themselves affect competition.[597] Exchange of aggregate industry-wide statistical data on past production or sales is normally unobjectionable, even if they are more precise and current than government statistics, and provided that individual firms' figures are not identifiable.[598] For instance, the exchange of information the essential terms of which are published by a governmental body (even in a non-EC country, such as the United States) does not infringe Article 81 (1).[599] On the other hand, an

information exchange systems may constitute *separate* infringements of the competition rules: *Steel Beams – Thyssen Stahl*, CFI March 11, 1999, 1999 ECR II-347, para. 392.

592. *Steel Beams – Thyssen Stahl*, ECJ Oct. 2, 2003, C-194/99 P, para. 113.

593. *Steel Beams – Thyssen Stahl*, CFI March 11, 1999, 1999 ECR II-347, paras 402–410.

594. *Ibid.*, para. 408.

595. E.g., less than three weeks: *Steel Beams – Thyssen Stahl*, CFI March 11, 1999, 1999 ECR II-347, para. 396.

596. *UK Tractor Registration Exchange – John Deere*, ECJ May 28, 1998, 1998 ECR I-3175, para. 89.

597. Example: market studies established by an independent body based on sharing aggregate (not company-specific) data. Studies carried out by specialist organizations on the basis of surveys at the point of sale do not represent an anticompetitive exchange of information between competitors but are rather sold by the organizations: *Wirtschaftsvereinigung Stahl*, Nov. 26, 1997; 1998 OJ L 1/10, para. 58. Examples of such studies are those of *Nielsen*, Twenty-sixth Report on Competition Policy, pp. 144–148. Nielsen statistics were used in *Kesko/Tuco*, D.Comm. Nov. 20, 1996, 1997 OJ L 110/53, points 93–103.

598. *Carton – Sarrio*, CFI May 14, 1998, 1998 ECR I-2111, paras 111–112. *See Cobelpa*, D.Comm. Sept. 8, 1977, 1977 OJ L 276/19; *Fatty Acids*, D.Comm. Dec. 2, 1986, 1987 OJ L 3/17, 22; *CEPI Cartonboard*, Twenty-sixth report on Competition Policy, point 127. However, the exchange of individual data which are twelve months old are normally accepted: *UK Agricultural Tractor Registration Exchange*, D.Comm. Feb. 17, 1992, 1992, 1992 OJ L 68/19, point 61, *aff'd* CFI Oct. 27, 1994, 1994 ECR II-905, and IP/99/690 of Sept. 20, 1999 (final clearance). Under Article 65 of the ECSC Treaty: *Wirtschaftsvereinigung Stahl*, D.Comm. Nov. 26, 1997, 1998 OJ L 1/10, para. 52.

599. *TACA I*, CFI Sept. 30, 2003, T-191/98, para. 1154.

exchange of information about future output levels is highly likely to infringe Article 81 (1) and to be unacceptable;[600] it is designed to eliminate uncertainty about future market conduct, and it is therefore not necessary to demonstrate that the exchange of information led to a *specific* result or were put into effect on the market in question.[601] Information systems which include commercially sensitive and sufficiently current (e.g., monthly) information which competitors normally keep secret and do not reveal to other competitors, such as capacity utilization, output, orders received and order backlog, selling prices, price announcements, costs and marketing plans,[602] may have as their object[603] or effect a distortion or restraint of competition by increasing market transparency and allowing one competitor to detect in advance another competitor's strategy[604] or to identify competitive behavior such as parallel imports.[605] An anticompetitive exchange of information may lead to the imposition of fines[606] even if the exchange is encouraged by a public authority.[607] However, the line between competitively neutral and anticompetitive exchanges of information is difficult to draw,[608] and prior clearance by the Commission or national authorities may be difficult to obtain in the absence of any notification and clearance procedure.[609]

---

600. *See Steel Beams – Thyssen Stahl*, ECJ Oct. 2, 2003, C-194/99 P, para. 130.
601. *Steel Beams – Thyssen Stahl*, ECJ Oct. 2, 2003, C-194/9 P, para. 271.
602. *Carton – Sarrio*, CFI May 14, 1998, 1998 ECR II-1439, paras 264–281; *aff'd* ECJ Nov. 16, 2000, 2000 ECR I-9991. *See also Woodpulp*, ECJ March 31, 1993, 1993 ECR I-1307, para. 131 (in particular where the members of the exchange system are committed to communicate, to explain or to discuss, deviations from the announced prices, paras 149, 160–161); *Steel Beams – Eurofer*, CFI March 11, 1999, 1999 ECR II-263, paras 180–208).
603. Without need to prove the actual effect: *UK Agricultural Tractor Registration Exchange – John Deere*, CFI Oct. 27, 1994, 1994 ECR I-957, paras 61 and 92; *aff'd* ECJ May 28, 1998, 1998 ECR I-3111, para. 98. *See Fatty Acids*, D.Comm. Dec. 2, 1986, 1987 OJ L 3/17, 23, where the Commission stated: 'The Commission considers that an agreement concluded between, and subsequently implemented by, the three major producers in a market in recession, and based on an exchange of confidential information on the one hand about traditional market positions and on the other hand providing a means of monitoring their future performance, has inherent restrictive effects upon competition although these may not be measurable or even apparent to an observer of the market unaware of the existence of such an agreement'.
604. *UK Agricultural Tractor Registration Exchange – Fiatagri*, CFI Oct. 27, 1994, 1994 ECR I-905 paras 49–54. *See Whitelead*, D.Comm. Dec. 12, 1978, 1979 OJ L 21/16.
605. *UK Agricultural Tractor Registration Exchange – John Deere*, CFI Oct. 27, 1994, 1994 ECR I-957 para. 101; *aff'd* ECJ May 28, 1998, 1998 ECR I-3111, paras 88–90. *See IMA*, D.Comm. Sept. 18, 1980, 1980 OJ L 318/1.
606. As in *Food flavour enhancer*, D.Comm. Dec. 17, 2002, IP/02/1907.
607. *Steel Beams – Thyssen Stahl*, ECJ Oct. 2, 2003, C-194/99P, para. 103.
608. *See* e.g. the discussion in *Polypropylene – Atochem*, CFI Oct. 24, 1991, 1991 ECR I-1177, paras 95–96, 187.
609. The Commission may issue 'informal guidance' 'where cases give rise to genuine uncertainty': Recital 38 to Regulation 1/2003.

Code of Practice for Information Exchange.
A study commissioned by the Commission[610] suggests the following guidelines for information exchange and reflects the Court's and Commission's practice:

'1. The exchange of individual price and quantity data will be considered a restriction of competition in itself and is therefore an independent infringement of Article 85 (1). An exemption under Article 85 (3) will be granted only if the firms demonstrate that there are business reasons (other than collusion) that require this type of information exchange and that it cannot be achieved otherwise. In addition, the exemption will be granted only if the structural features of the industry make collusive outcomes unlikely.
2. The exchange of other individualized data will not be considered a restriction of competition in itself, but it will give cause to investigate a possible infringement of Article 85 (1). Particularly when the exchange of data is frequent and detailed, and when markets are concentrated and barriers to entry are high, information exchange may be admitted as supplementary evidence in a collusion case.
3. The exchange of aggregate data (through independent trade associations) will not be challenged unless there is independent evidence of collusion in the industry.
4. Communications about intended future price-setting behaviour not combined with commitments to maximum prices for consumers should be considered a restriction of competition. Information exchange through public price announcements (in particular in the trade press) to customers should not be challenged.'

The Study notes with regard to the exchange of aggregate data through trade associations:

'1. There should be exemptions in information sharing on individualized customer information (possibly in form of a block exemption) in markets like banking and insurance when these can be justified by problems of adverse selection or moral hazard. These agreements should not include agreements on prices.
2. The bypassing of trade associations by a coalition of firms in the industry may be grounds for the competition policy authority to investigate whether there exists a collusive agreement in the industry.[611]
3. Trade associations should be allowed to collect verifiable information or to conduct auditing procedures on firms to compile their aggregate statistics.

610. Twenty-fourth Report on Competition Policy, Annex IV p. 642.
611. *Wirtschaftsvereinigung Stahl*, D.Comm. Nov. 26, 1997, 1998 OJ L 1/10, paras 57–58.

4. Trade association programmes on joint research on demand or cost should generally not raise policy concerns.
5. Trade associations should not be run by managers of participating firms'.[612]

The Commission's Administrative Practice.
The Commission's experience in cases such as *Polypropylene*[613] shows the practical dilemma of exchanging data which are, although aggregate, as recent and exact as possible and which need a control mechanism through bilateral or multilateral consultations. Such meetings may be used for a permanent updating and detailing of the provisional data communicated to the trade association or auditing firm and in this case turn out as a platform of anticompetitive collusion. In the *Carton* case[614] the Commission tried to overcome this dilemma by obliging the parties:

> 'to refrain in relation to their cartonboard activities from any agreement or concerted practice ... including any exchange of commercial information:
> (a) by which the participants are directly or indirectly informed of the production, sales, order backlog, machine utilization rates, selling prices or marketing plans of other individual producers; or
> (b) by which, even if no individual information is disclosed, a common industry response to economic conditions as regards price or control of production is promoted, facilitated or encouraged; or
> (c) by which they might be able to monitor adherence to or compliance with any express or tacit agreement regarding prices or market sharing in the Community.
> Any scheme for the exchange of general information to which they subscribe, such as the Fides system or its successor, shall be so conducted as to exclude not only any information from which the behavior of individual producers can be identified but also any data concerning the present state of the order inflow and backlog, the forecast utilization rate of production capacity (in both cases, even if aggregated) or the production capacity of each machine'.

The Court of First Instance affirmed the obligation under (a)[615] but annulled the obligations under (b) and (c) stating that those prohibitions exceeded what is necessary to bring the infringement to an end because it seeks to prevent the

612. *See CEPI Cartonboard*, Twenty-sixth Report on Competition Policy, p. 127 (exchange of information amended in this sense in order to comply with the Commission's requirements in its decision of July 13, 1994, 1994 OJ L 243/1).
613. *Polypropylene*, D.Comm. April 23, 1986, 1986, 1983 OJ L 230/36, paras 80–92, *aff'd* CFI Oct. 24, 1991, 1991 ECR I-1177, paras 166–173, 182; *aff'd* ECJ July 8, 1999, 1999 ECR I-4539.
614. *Carton*, D.Comm. July 13, 1994, 1994 OJ L 243/1 (Article 2 of the operative part of the decision).
615. Similarly *Steel Beams – Thyssen Stahl*, ECJ Oct. 2, 2003, C-194/99P, para. 89.

exchange of purely statistical information and that the mere fact that the exchange of statistical information might be used for anticompetitive purposes does not make it contrary to Article 81 (1), 'since in such circumstances it is necessary to establish its actual anticompetitive effect'.[616]

8. Consortia and Strategic Alliances

Still Undeveloped Tools.[617]
The terms consortia and strategic alliances are used to describe a form of cooperation between firms – commonly with competing or complementary skills – which do not establish a separate business entity, but which instead provides for a legally structured framework designed to promote synergy and closer cooperation for the purpose of rationalizing their operations by means of technical, operational and/or commercial means. These forms of cooperation may be competitively neutral, they may restrict competition but nevertheless satisfy the conditions of Article 81 (3) or they may mask anticompetitive, cartel-like practices that do not qualify for exemption.

Consortia.
The term 'consortium' is, apart from the special form of agreements between liner shipping companies,[618] used for describing agreements on the joint execution of orders where the participating firms do not compete with each other as regards the work to be done or where each of them by itself is unable to execute the orders. Such a 'consortium' does not restrict competition.[619] This applies not only to firms belonging to different industries, but also to firms in the same industry but with different, complementary skills having as their sole object carrying out different complementary tasks, even if the participating firms might nevertheless be qualified as potential competitors. Even in cases when the participating firms normally compete with each other, there may be no restriction of competition if they are unable to execute a specific order individually for reasons of technical knowledge, capacity or financial resources, provided that non-compete clauses are limited to the strict minimum and the cooperation is limited to a specific project and therefore will not affect competition between the consortium partners on other projects in which they can individually compete.[620] In certain cases of public procurement

---

616. *Carton – Stora*, CFI May 14, 1998, 1998 ECR I-2111, paras 111-112; similarly *Carton – Sarrio*, CFI May 14, 1998, 1998 ECR II-1439, paras 265–280, *aff'd* ECJ Nov. 16, 2000, 2000 ECR II-9991.

617. Consortia and strategic alliances are not addressed in the Guidelines on Horizontal Cooperation, *see* point 12.

618. Article 2 of Regulation 823/2000, 2000 OJ L 100/24, amended by Regulation 463/2004, 2004 OJ L 77/23.

619. Previously Commission's 1968 Notice on cooperation, under 11.5.

620. *Konsortium ECR 900*, D.Comm. July 27, 1990, 1990 OJ L 228; *International Private Satellite Partners*, D.Comm. Dec. 15, 1994, 1994 OJ L 354/75 (negative clearance decisions); *General*

the purchaser may even expressly request a joint bid between different firms with complementary technical and manufacturing skills.[621] However, a strategic alliance between major competitors can only be cleared if the conditions of Article 81 (3) are satisfied,[622] and a 'consortium' between competitors masking an anti-competitive joint or coordinated bidding to public or private tenders (bid-rigging) is clearly prohibited and likely to be heavily fined.[623]

Strategic Alliances.

Strategic alliances are cooperative arrangements of varying scope involving the creation of several contractual or structural links, such as the creation of a joint venture, specialization in certain markets, joint R&D, technology transfer, cross-supply arrangements, commitments to cooperate in other fields in the future and the acquisition of shareholdings.[624] Strategic alliances are usually limited to very specific fields of the parties' activities, such as the development and introduction of a new technology or cooperation on the frequency and modalities of services (i.e., flights and telecommunication services) in order to bundle synergies and to avoid overlapping. Strategic alliances are often concluded between actual or potential competitors in order to compete with other, similar alliances, in particular in liberalized markets such as telecommunications[625] or transport,[626] as a result of growing integration of world markets.[627] They may include certain exclusive license, purchase, distribution or non-compete obligations (choosing one partner and thereby excluding alliances with other competing partners) so that they restrict competition between them and, possibly, between them and third parties and are therefore likely to be caught by Article 81 (1). However, they may satisfy

---

Electric Aircraft/Pratt & Whitney, 1998 OJ C 339/3 (comfort letters for engine alliance); *DVD Technology*, D.Comm. Oct 9, 2000, IP/00/242/5 ('open' patent pool without any exclusivity and discrimination).

621. The Commission issued comfort letters in cases of cooperation designed to improve safety in the East-European reactors: *Independent Power Generators*, 1992 OJ C 92/4; *Twining Program Engineering Group*, 1992 OJ C 148/8; *ENAC*, 1993 OJ C 175/12. However, in order to be considered competitively neutral the cooperation may have to be limited to the project in question and not extend to other projects where the purchaser does not request, and is not interested in, joint bidding.
622. *British Airways/Sabena* D.Comm. March 10, 2003, IP/03/350.
623. *SPO – Dutch Construction Works*, D.Comm. Feb. 5, 1992, 1992 OJ L 92/1, *aff'd* CFI Feb. 21, 1995, 1995 ECR II-289; *aff'd* ECJ March 25, 1996, 1996 ECR I-1611.
624. Strategic alliances are often difficult to assess as long as they lack a precise scope of activities: Guidelines on Horizontal Cooperation, point 12.
625. *See Atlas/Phoenix*, Twenty-fifth Report on Competition Policy, point 57 and p. 121 (comfort letter); *Global Satellite Systems*, Twenty-fifth Report on Competition Policy, point 58.
626. *Lufthansa/SAS*, D.Comm. Jan. 16, 1996, 1996 OJ L 54/28; *Austrian Airlines/Lufthansa*, D.Comm. July 15, 2002, 2002 OJ L 242/25. *See also* Twenty-seventh Report on Competition Policy, point 92.
627. 'Market driven by globalization': *IFPI Simulcasting*, D.Comm. Oct. 8, 2002, 2003 OJ L 107/58; Guidelines on Horizontal Cooperation, point 3.

the conditions for clearance under Article 81 (3) because of their rationalization effects enabling them to compete with other alliances, provided the cooperation is limited in scope and time and that the access of third parties to the market is not unduly impaired.[628] The Commission's main competitive concern is ensuring independence and effective competition between the different strategic alliances in the market.[629]

Various Types of Strategic Alliances as Mergers.
Strategic alliances may involve several lasting contractual or structural links between competitors, such as the creation of a joint venture, specialization in certain markets, joint R&D, technology transfer, cross-supply arrangements, commitments to cooperate in other fields, including commercialization,[630] and the joint acquisition of shareholdings.[631] Therefore, a strategic alliance may also turn, sooner or later, into a merger, performing on a lasting basis all the functions of an autonomous economic entity,[632] which must be assessed under the merger control regulation if the criteria for a Community dimension are fulfilled.[633]

---

628. Examples: *BT/MCI* D.Comm. July 27, 1994, 1994 OJ L 223/36 (telecommunication, reciprocal exclusive licenses and exclusive distribution exemption). Examples of strategic alliances which, in a later phase, turned into mergers: *Olivetti/Digital*, D.Comm. Nov. 11, 1994, 1994 OJ L 309/24 (computer systems; exclusive purchase obligations, exemption granted); *Lufthansa/SAS*, D.Comm. Jan. 16, 1996, 1996 OJ L 54/28 (air transport; joint network planning, joint frequent flyer programs, exemption granted under conditions).
629. In particular in the telecommunication sector: *ATLAS*, D.Comm. July 17, 1996, 1996 OJ L 239/23 and *Phoenix/Global One*, D.Comm. July 17, 1996, 1996 OJ L 239/57 (telecommunication; exclusive distribution, exemptions granted under conditions); *Uniworld and Unisource*, D.Comm. March 19, 1997, 1997 OJ L 318/24 and L 318/1 (telecommunication, exemptions granted); *GEN (Global European Network)*, Twenty-seventh Report on Competition Policy, point 73. *See also* the critical remarks with regard to the air alliances because of the risk of market foreclosure: Twenty-seventh Report on Competition Policy, points 86–91, and *KLM/Alitalia*, D.Comm. Aug. 11, 1999, JV. 19 (clearance of an air alliance, treated as a merger, following commitments to facilitate the market entrance of potential competitors); *Air Austria/Lufthansa*, Thirtieth Report on Competition Policy, point 240; *Air France / Alitalia*, D.Comm. April 7, 2004, IV/38.284, points 164–169.
630. *See EUCAR*, Twenty-seventh Report on Competition Policy, p. 138.
631. Guidelines, point 12.
632. Article 3 (4) Regulation 139/2004.
633. Assessment of a strategic alliance under the merger control regulation: *KLM/Alitalia*, D.Comm. Aug. 11, 1999, JV.19 (clearance of the joint venture subject to the commitment to surrender up to 16 slots); under Article 81: *Austrian Airlines/Lufthansa*, D.Comm. July 15, 2002, 2002 OJ L 242/25 (40% of the slots to be left to competitors); *Air France/Alitalia*, D.Comm. April 7, 2004.

9. Other Forms of Marketing Cooperation

(a) Quality Labels

Article 81 Usually not Infringed.
Agreement on the use of a common quality label or certification mark by competing firms does not infringe Article 81 if other competitors whose products objectively meet the stipulated quality requirements may use the label on non-discriminatory terms, the participating firms are not prevented from advertising individually and their freedom in other fields, such as production, distribution or prices, is not restricted.[634] If the manufacture and sale of products which do not meet the minimum standards of the quality mark are restricted or prohibited, care must be taken to ensure that the scheme does not discriminate against parallel importers selling products that meet the standards.[635]Associations with the primary purpose of promoting a quality standard may also be the cover for a price-fixing and market-sharing cartel of its members, thereby constituting a serious infringement of Article 81 (1) and leading to high fines.[636]

(b) Joint Debt Collection

Article 81 (1) Normally not Infringed.
Joint debt collecting ('factoring') associations whose activities are strictly limited to this function are unobjectionable unless they influence the members' pricing, for example by leading to the exchange of information on prices and discounts or to price comparisons.[637] Because of these dangers, it is often advisable to entrust a neural third party, such as a professional factoring agency or an accounting firm, with such duties.

---

634. *CECED*, D.Comm. Jan. 24, 1999, 2000 OJ L 187/47. Previously Commission Notice on Cooperation Agreements, section II.8 (not expressly addressed in the Guidelines on Horizontal Cooperation); *Transocean Marine Paint Association I*, D.Comm. June 27, 1967, 1967 OJ L 163/10 (exemption extended: *Transocean Marine Paint Association V*, D.Comm. Dec. 2, 1988, 1988 OJ L 351/40); *Welded Pipe Manufacturers Association*, D.Comm. June 29, 1970, 1970 OJ L 153/14; *Belgian Pharmaceutical Association*, D.Comm. Dec. 14, 1989, 1990 OJ L 18/35.
635. Discrimination against parallel imports was found in *Anseau*, ECJ Nov. 8, 1983, 1983 ECR 3369, paras 22–28; *Poroton*, Tenth Report on Competition Policy, point 130.
636. *Industrial Copper Tubes Cartel*, D.Comm. Dec. 16, 2003, IP/03/1746 (fine of EUR 79 million).
637. *See* Commission's 1968 Notice on Cooperation Agreements, section II.2.(c); not explicitly repeated in the current Guidelines on Horizontal Cooperation but still unobjectionable.

(c) Joint Trademarks

Likely to Infringe Article 81 if they Isolate Markets.
If two competitors use their own trademarks within their own national territories, but jointly use a different mark in another national market within the Community, this may constitute a restraint of competition affecting trade between member states. The Commission objected to such a scheme by two firms that were already established in certain countries of the Community and wished to improve their market share in France, where more powerful competitors were already present, through the establishment of a joint venture employing a common trademark different from those they used elsewhere in the Community. The scheme was abandoned when the Commission concluded that the firms were capable of expanding their sales in France independently, and that use of a new joint trademark in France would prevent the partners from selling throughout the Community under their own respective trademarks. The common trademark scheme would have tended to isolate the French market from the other markets served by the partners.[638] Agreements with regard to the use of a common industry trademark ('Green Dot') for collective collecting and recovery of household packaging are therefore accepted, provided they are not discriminatory[639] and foreign suppliers may also enjoy the full benefits of the collection system associated with the trademark.[640] Agreements between two companies owning different, confusingly similar trademarks on the use of these trademarks in their respective countries may be justified by the pre-existence of original trade mark rights in the hands of different owners,[641] such as part of an overall trademark de-limitation agreement that is likely to satisfy conditions of Article 81 (3),[642] or they may also be tantamount to market sharing that infringes Article 81 (1).[643]

(d) Joint Advertising

Can be Easily Structured so as not to Infringe Article 81.
Agreements whose sole object is to carry out joint advertising do not normally restrict competition. For example, the Commission cleared agreements to pro-

---

638. Sixth Report on Competition Policy, point 178.
639. *Duales System ('Green Dot')*, D.Comm. April 20, 2001, 2001 OJ L 16/1, points 114–115 and 136 (prohibition decision without fines because of discriminatory application); amended system cleared in *DSD*, D.Comm. Sept. 17, 2001, 2001 OJ L 319/1.
640. *Eco-Emballages*, D.Comm. June 15, 2001, 2001 OJ L 233/37 (negative clearance); *DSD*, D.Comm. Sept. 17, 2001, 2001 OJ L 319/1 (negative clearance); *ORPHE*, D.Comm. Dec. 6, 1990, Twentieth Report on Competition Policy, point 102 (comfort letter for agreement for the use of a common trade mark among medium-sized pharmaceutical wholesalers).
641. *Ideal Standard*, ECJ June 22, 1994, 1994 ECR I-2789.
642. *Michelin/Continental*, 1996 OJ C 236/9 (comfort letter).
643. *EMI/CBS*, ECJ June 15, 1976, 1976 ECR 811, 871 and 913.

mote plasterboard and other plaster products as a construction materia1[644] and to improve publicity for environment-friendly products.[645] On the other hand, a prohibition of individual advertising or other restrictions on individual conduct under such an agreement would bring a joint advertising agreement within Article 81 (l), and before granting exemption the Commission has had to be satisfied that the agreement achieved rationalization and cost savings and presented advantages to consumers that objectively outweighed the restrictive elements involved.[646]

(e) Auctions and Commodity Markets

Auctions.

Agreements relating to auctions may restrict competition if the members are committed to deal exclusively through the auction or if third party manufacturers or importers are denied free and non-discriminatory access to the auction. The Commission has intervened in several cases against exclusive dealing obligations in auction agreements which prevented competitors in other member states from supplying the market,[647] and against obligations to deal through only specific auctions.[648]

Commodity Markets.

The Commission has granted negative clearance for the rules of commodity markets after satisfying itself that the conditions of membership were based on objective criteria and did not lead to a closed shop or prescribe minimum commissions.[649]

---

644. *Eurogypsum*, D.Comm. Feb. 26, 1968, 1968 OJ L 57/9.

645. *EUCAR*, Twenty-seventh Report on Competition Policy, p. 138 (comfort letter for cooperation agreement between car manufacturers in the ecological field); *European Wastepaper InformationService*, 1987 OJ C 339/7 and Eighteenth Report on Competition Policy, point 63 (comfort letter); *DSD – Dual System*, 1997 OJ C 100/4 (comfort letter). *See also Europages*, 1982 OJ C 343/5; IFCO II, News Letter 1998–3, p. 48 (packaging system).

646. *See also Milk Promotion Fund*, D.Comm. Dec. 7, 1984, 1985 OJ L 35/35; *EPI Code of Conduct*, D.Comm. April 7, 1999, 1999 OJ L 106/14 (restriction on comparative advertising imposed on patent agents by their association).

647. *Frubo*, D.Comm. July 25, 1974, 1974 OJ L 237/16, 18–19; *British Dental Trade Association*, D.Comm. July 13, 1988, 1988 OJ L 233/15 (fines); *Flower Auctions Aalsmeer l*, D.Comm. July 26, 1988, 1988 OJ L 262/27, 37–38; *Hudson's Bay I*, D.Comm. Oct. 28, 1988, 1988 OJ L 316/43, 46–47 (fines).

648. *Cauliflowers I*, D.Comm. Dec. 2, 1977, 1978 OJ L 21/23, 28.

649. *Terminal Markets I (Sugar, Cocoa, Coffee, Rubber)*, D.Comm. Dec. 13, 1985, 1985 OJ L 369/25, 28, 31, 34; *Terminal Markets II (International Petroleum of London Ltd.)*, D.Comm. Dec. 4, 1986, 1987 OJ L 3/27; *Terminal Markets III (Soya, Grain, Potatoes, Meat)*, D.Comm. Dec. 10, 1986, 1987 OJ L 19/18, 22, 26, 30.

(f) Trade Fair Agreements

Key Issues are Admission Criteria and Non-Competition Restrictions. Agreements on trade fairs may restrict competition if they exclude certain manufacturers or importers from exhibiting or make their access more difficult, or if they affect the organization of other trade fairs for the same products. The Commission has intervened in numerous cases[650] in order to:

- Ensure that importers from other member states are admitted on an objective basis.[651] But charging a higher entrance fee to non-members may be justifiable on cost grounds and not be discriminatory.[652]
- Improve the procedures for admitting exhibitors and settling disputes about admission.
- Reasonably limit the duration of any obligation imposed on exhibitors not to participate in other rival trade fairs. 'Closed' periods of several months on either side of an exhibition are accepted in order to realize the rationalization benefits of a reasonable spacing of such events.[653] However, the Commission has challenged efforts by one trade fair to veto the organization of a competing trade fair[654] and in one case fined an organizer for discriminating against foreign exhibitors.[655]

650. *EMO-CECIMO I* (machine tools), D.Comm. March 13, 1969, 1969 OJ L 69/13; *EMO-CECIMO II*, D.Comm. Dec. 7, 1978, 1979 OJ L 11/16; *EMO-CECIMO III*, D.Comm. Dec. 20, 1988, 1989 OJ L 37/11; *CEMATEX I* (textile machinery), D.Comm. Sept. 24, 1971, 1971 OJ L 227/26; *CEMATEX II*, D.Comm. May 24, 1983, 1983 OJ L 140/27; *UNIDI I* (dental supplies), D.Comm. July 17, 1975, 1975 OJ L 228/14; *UNIDI II*, D.Comm. Nov. 23, 1984, 1984 OJ L 322/10 (upheld by the Court of Justice in *ANCIDES*, ECJ July 9, 1987, 1987 ECR 3131); *BPICA I* (motor vehicles), D.Comm. Nov. 7, 1977, 1977 OJ L 299/18; *BPICA II*, D.Comm. April 30, 1982, 1982 OJ L 156/16; *SMM&T* (motor vehicles), D.Comm. Dec. 5, 1983, 1983 OJ L 376/1; *Vifka* (office equipment), D.Comm. Sept. 30, 1986, 1986 OJ L 291/46; *British Dental Trade Association I*, D.Comm. July 11, 1988, 1988 OJ L 233/15; *British Dental Association II*, Twenty-seventh Report on Competition Policy, p. 134 (extension of exemption by comfort letter); *International Dental Exhibition*, D.Comm. Sept. 18, 1987, 1987 OJ L 293/58; *LIBS* (boats), 1985 OJ C 253/2 (comfort letter); *SIPPA* (paper industry), D.Comm. Feb. 15, 1991, 1991 OJ L 60/19.
651. *See*, e.g., *UNIDI I*, D.Comm. July 17, 1975, 1975 OJ L 228/14, 17; *British Dental Trade Association*, D.Comm. July 11, 1988, 1988 OJ L 233/15, 16–17, 22–23.
652. *SMM&T*, D.Comm. Dec. 5, 1983, 1983 OJ L 376/1.
653. *ANCIDES*, ECJ July 9, 1987, 1987 ECR 3131, paras 19–20.
654. *SMM&T*, D.Comm. Dec. 5, 1983, 1983 OJ L 376/1, 2–4.
655. *British Dental Trade Association*, D.Comm. July 11, 1988, 1988 OJ L 233/15 (symbolic fine because of the legal novelty).

10. Assessing Joint Ventures under Article 81 or the Merger Control Regulation

Applicability of Both Article 81 and the Merger Control Regulation. The creation of joint ventures between competitors for the purposes of R&D, production and commercialization may fall within Article 81 (1) but are block exempted under Regulation 2658/2000 on Specialization Agreements or Regulation 2659/2000 on R&D Agreements, provided the agreements do not include hardcore restrictions and the parties' combined market share does not exceed the applicable thresholds of 20% and 25% respectively. Agreements between parties with a combined market share exceeding the applicable thresholds, which contain restrictions of competition, need individual assessment under Article 81 (3) without requiring prior notification or clearance. However, hardcore restrictions are generally forbidden regardless of whether or not the market share thresholds are exceeded.

The merger control Regulation 139/2004 applies to the creation of a joint venture which is jointly controlled by the parent companies and is a full-function company, i.e. performs on a lasting basis all the functions of an autonomous entity,[656] provided the operation has a Community dimension but irrespective of the parties' market shares. Such a joint venture may not be put into effect without having been notified to and cleared by the Commission. The Commission's assessment includes ancillary restrictions[657] and the effects of any anticompetitive coordination between the parties.[658] The application of Regulation 139/2004 precludes the application of Article 81.[659] However, joint ventures that lead to anticompetitive coordination but do *not* have a Community dimension must be assessed under Article 81, including the applicable block exemptions.

Commission's Tendency to Apply the Merger Control Regulation Broadly. In its most recent decisions the Commission tends broadly to apply the merger control regulation to joint ventures, assuming that a large number of joint ventures are autonomous economic entities in the sense of Article 3 (4) of the merger control regulation when they have their own premises, own capital, own staff and (as the case may be) own technology and own sales forces[660] and when the

656. Notice on the Concept of Concentration, point 14; *MyAircraft,* IP/00/912 of Aug. 4, 2000. However, this demonstrates a certain contradiction: for a joint venture to be considered a 'concentration' it must be autonomous but at the same time its strategic decisions must be subject to joint control by its parent companies.
657. Article 6 (1) (b) and Article 8 (2) of Regulation 139/2004.
658. Article 2 (4) of Regulation 139/2004.
659. Article 21 (1) of Regulation 139/2004.
660. *Brambles/Ermewa/JV,* D.Comm. Aug. 4, 2000, M.2023, points 8–9; *Blackstone/CDPQ/Kabel Nordrhein-Westfalen*, D.Comm. June 19, 2000, JV.46, points 18–19.

joint venture determines its own commercial policy with only strategic decisions involving the parent companies.[661]

Similar Substantive Criteria to be Applied to Joint Ventures under Both Regulation 139/2004 and Article 81.
The creation of a joint venture may be prohibited under both Regulation 139/2004 and Article 81 where:

- it significantly impedes effective competition (Article 2 (3) of Regulation 139/2004) or affords the parties the possibility of eliminating competition in respect of a substantial part of the market (Article 81 (3) (b));
- the agreement contains certain restraints which are not directly related to or not necessary for the implementation of the joint venture (Article 6 (1) (b) and 8 (2) of Regulation 139/2004) or are not indispensible (Article 81 (3) (a));
- the agreement leads to anticompetitive coordination which does not satisfy the conditions of Article 81 (3) (which is the same assessment under Article 2 (4) of Regulation 139/2004 and under Article 81 proceedings); and
- the negative effects on competition are *not* counterbalanced by sufficient economic efficiencies (Article 2 (1) of Regulation 139/2004 and the first two conditions of Article 81 (3)).

The substantive criteria for assessing joint ventures under Regulation 139/2004 and Article 81 are therefore similar and should be applied in a similar way.

Need for Legal Certainty.
Whereas clearance under Regulation 139/2004 ensures legal certainty (except for clauses which are *not* considered ancillary and which are therefore left to a subsequent individual assessment under Article 81), an assessment of Article 81 must be made by the parties themselves without prejudice to the possibility of the Commission and the national competition authorities:

- to withdraw the benefit of the block exemption where a joint venture is covered by this block exemption but has effects that are incompatible with Article 81 (3), or
- to initiate proceedings where a joint venture is *not* covered by a block exemption and does not satisfy the conditions of Article 81 (3).

The parties to a joint venture that does not have a Community dimension (in particular smaller firms) may request informal guidance from the Commission

---

661. *TXU Europe/EDF London/London Investment,* D.Comm. Feb. 2, 2000, JV.36, point 18. *See Haniel/Fels,* D.Comm. Feb. 21, 2002, M.2495, points 62–70, where the Commission accepts 'joint control' although the JV's statutes confer 'autonomy' on the JV because it depends on its parents with respect to strategic policy decisions.

where the case gives rise to 'genuine uncertainty' and needs clearance in the light of their longterm investment strategies.[662] Where the Commission does not respond to such a request, e.g., by stating that the case does not present novel or unresolved questions, the parties may be able to rely on the principle of legitimate expectations where they have submitted such a request in good faith and in the form as requested in the Notice on Guidance Letters so that the Commission may be prevented from taking action with respect to past conduct that was described in the parties' request for informal guidance which is incompatible with Article 81.[663]

662. Recital 38 to Regulation 1/2003; Commission Notice on Guidance Letters, 2004 OJ C 101/78.
663. This would correspond to Article 11 (5) of Regulation 17 which provided for immunity from fines with respect to agreements which had been duly notified to the Commission.

Chapter IV

Vertical Restraints of Competition in Distribution and Purchasing Agreements

CONTENTS

A. Introduction

1. The Principle of Free Choice of Distribution and Freedom of Intergroup Allocation of Tasks

Distribution Alternatives.
A manufacturer is free to determine the means of distributing its products according to its own preferences,[1] except where it constitutes an abuse of a dominant position.[2] It may distribute products via its own network of affiliates by allocating specific distribution tasks for that purpose,[3] or via agents or exclusive distributors. It may sell to wholesalers or via retailers or sell itself directly to customers. It may sell via dealers reselling only its brands ('one-brand dealer' – exclusive purchasing), or via dealers reselling also brands of competing suppliers ('multi-brand dealers'). It may also promise to sell to only a single dealer in a particular territory ('exclusive dealers' or franchisees) or only to certain dealers meeting objective criteria ('selective' distribution). It may also combine different sales channels, selling in one member state via its own sales outlets, in another member state via an exclusive distributor and in a third member state by means of a selective distribution system. However, the system the manufacturer chooses must conform to Article 81 once it employs agreements or concerted practices that are likely to restrict competition. This corresponds to the objective of Article 81 (1) which is – irrespective of whether the restriction is the result of a horizontal or a vertical agreement – to safeguard market integration and effective competition in the Community.

2. Applicability of Article 81 to Vertical Restraints

No Explicit Distinction between Horizontal and Vertical Agreements.
Unlike some national antitrust laws[4] but similar to the antitrust laws of of the United States,[5] the Community's competition rules do not explicitly distinguish

1. *Yves Saint Laurent*, D.Comm. Dec. 16, 1991, 1992 OJ L 12/24, 29. *See* draft guidelines on vertical restraints, 1999 OJ C 270/12, points 131 *et seq.*
2. *Viho/Parker Pen*, CFI Jan. 12, 1995, 1995 ECR II-17, paras 48–50, *aff'd* ECJ Oct. 24, 1996, 1996 ECR I-5457, para. 16.
3. *Grundig/Consten*, ECJ July 13, 1966, 1966 ECR 299, para. 16; *Viho/Parker Pen*, ECJ Oct. 24, 1996, 1996 ECR I-5457, para. 16. In such cases Article 81 is excluded but Article 82 remains applicable: *Italy/Commission*, ECJ July 13, 1966, 1966 ECR 389, 407, para. 23; *Volkswagen/Audi*, D.Comm. Jan. 28, 1998, 1998 OJ L 124/60, point 128 (*aff'd* CFI July 6, 2000, 2000 ECR II-2707); *Novalliance/Systemform*, D.Comm. Dec. 4, 1996, 1997 OJ L 47/11.
4. *See* section 16 of the German antitrust law. Some other national laws, although copying Article 81, distinguish, in practice, between horizontal and vertical restrictions, in particular Italy, Spain and Portugal.
5. With certain exceptions, such as section 3 of the Clayton Act which governs tying arrange-

between horizontal and vertical restraints of competition. Article 81 applies to vertical agreements between firms at different levels in the production and distribution chain no less than it applies to horizontal agreements between competitors. From the very beginning the Court of Justice rejected the view that Article 81 could only apply to horizontal agreements and that vertical arrangements were only subject to Article 82:

> 'Article 85 [*now Article 81*] refers in a general way to all agreements which distort competition within the Common Market and does not lay down any distinction between those agreements based on whether they are made between competitors operating at the same level in the economic process or between non-competing persons operating at different levels. In principle, no distinction can be made where the Treaty does not make any distinction.'[6]

Concerted v. Unilateral Conduct.

The vertical restraint must be the object or effect of an agreement or concerted practice. This means that it must be an integral part of an 'agreement' in the broadest sense, which is characterized by a 'concurrence of wills',[7] 'joint intention'[8] or some form of taking account of each other's interests and submitting oneself to economic, social or moral pressure.[9] Circular letters may lead to concertation of the competitive behaviour of the parties to a distribution system, provided they form part of a set of continuous business relations governed by a general agreement drawn up in advance.[10] Tacit acceptance may suffice[11] but there is no acquiescence where the dealer does not give the impression to agree with the supplier's restrictive policy[12] or manifests its wish to achieve the anticompetitive goal jointly, all the more where such an agreement is not in the interest of the other

---

ments and exclusive dealing, the United States antitrust statutes can generally be applied to both horizontal and vertical restraints.

6. *Grundig/Consten*, ECJ July 13, 1966 ECR 299, 399. *See also Italy/Commission*, ECJ July 13, 1966, 1966 ECR 389, 407, para. 22.
7. *See Volkswagen*, CFI July 6, 2000, 2000 ECR II-2713, paras 48–49, *aff'd* ECJ Sept. 18, 2003, C-338/00, paras 60–67; *Opel*, D.Comm. Sept. 20, 2000, 2001 OJ L 59/1; *Volkswagen II*, D.Comm. June 29, 2001, 2001 OJ L 262/14; *rev'd* CFI Dec. 3, 2003, T-208/01.
8. *Jaeger/Opel Norge*, EFTA Court of Justice April 1, 1998, 1998 EFTACR 38, para. 35; *Bayer*, CFI Oct. 26, 2000, 2000 ECR II-3383, paras 66–71; *Nintendo*, D.Comm. Oct. 30, 2002, 2003 OJ L 255/33, points 442–447.
9. 'Creating a visible and psychological climate': *Hasselblad*, ECJ Feb. 21, 1984, 1984 ECR 883, para. 46; *Parker Pen*, CFI July 14, 1994, 1994 ECR II-549, para. 55; *BASF Coatings*, CFI May 19, 1999, 1999 ECR II-1581, para. 156.
10. *BMW Belgium*, ECJ July 12, 1979, 1979 ECR 2435, paras 26–36; *Opel*, CFI Oct. 21, 2003, T-368/00, para. 53; *Volkswagen I*, ECJ Sept. 18, 2003, C-338/00P, para. 60; *Yamaha*, D.Comm. July 16, 2003, IP/03/1028.
11. E.g., *Nintendo*, D.Comm. Oct. 30, 2002, 2003 OJ L 255/33, point 251.
12. *Bundesverband der Arzneimittelimporteure – Bayer*, ECJ Jan. 6, 2004, C-2/01, paras 54 (reduction of orders in the case of exports).

party.[13] By contrast, merely unilateral conduct without express or implied acquiescence by the other partners is not covered by Article 81[14] and is only prohibited if it constitutes an abuse of a dominant position, thereby infringing Article 82.[15] In the *Volkswagen II* case the Court of First Instance annulled the Commission decision by stating that the mere signature by the dealers of the dealership agreement does not involve acceptance in advance on their part of a later unlawful variation of that contract, in particular where the contract could not enable the dealer to foresee such a variation.[16]

A Leading Case: *Grundig/Consten.*

This case[17] related to an agreement between Grundig, a major German manufacturer of consumer electronics equipment, such as stereos and televisions, and its exclusive distributor in France, Consten. Grundig ensured this exclusivity by prohibiting its distributors in Germany and elsewhere from making sales into France. Consten also undertook not to sell competing goods, thus entering into an exclusive purchasing obligation, and undertook not to supply Grundig products, either directly or indirectly, from France into other countries. The Commission ruled that such absolute territorial protection of distributors infringed Article 81, and noted that the arrangement reinforced price disparities. The Commission had found prices of Grundig products in France to be as much as 23% higher than in Germany. The Court of Justice upheld the Commission's ruling and stated that

> '… an agreement between producer and distributor which might tend to restore the national divisions in trade between Member States might be such as to frustrate the most fundamental objectives of the Community. …
>
> The situation as ascertained above results in the isolation of the French market and makes it possible to charge for the products in question prices which are sheltered from all effective competition. In addition, the more producers succeed in their efforts to render their own makes of product individually distinct in the eyes of the consumer, the more the effectiveness of competition between producers tends to diminish. Because of the considerable impact of distribution costs on the aggregate cost price, it seems important that competition between dealers should also be stimulated. The efforts of the dealer are stimulated by competition between distributors of products of the same make. Since the agreement thus aims at isolating the

---

13. *Ibid.*, paras 85–86, 102–108 and 140–146; *Nintendo II*, D.Comm. Oct. 30, 2002, 2003 OJ L 255/33, points 246–330.
14. *See Bayer*, CFI, Oct. 26, 2000, 2000 ECR II-3383, paras 66–72, 114–124 and 173; *Volkswagen II*, CFI Dec. 32, 2003, T-208/01, paras 43–45; *Opel*, CFI Oct. 21, 2003, T-368/00, paras 58 and 79.
15. *Bayer*, CFI, Oct. 26, 2000, 2000 ECR II-3383, para. 180.
16. *Volkswagen II*, CFI Dec. 3, 2003, T-208/01, paras 43–46.
17. *Grundig/Consten*, ECJ July 13, 1966, 1966 ECR 299.

French market for Grundig products and maintaining artificially, for products of a very well-known brand, separate national markets within the Community, it is therefore such as to distort competition in the Common Market.'[18]

No exemption could be granted under Article 81 (3) because absolute territorial protection was not a necessary element for establishing an effective distribution system for Grundig products in the French market.

No Explicit Distinction between Restriction of Inter-Brand and Intra-Brand Competition.

Vertical restrictions often have procompetitive effects on the marketing of different *brands* of products produced by competing manufacturers (*inter*-brand competition). Yet those very same vertical restrictions usually have anticompetitive effects amongst the dealers that handle the *same brand* of products (*intra*-brand competition). For instance, when a manufacturer grants each of its dealers an exclusive sales territory, this may strengthen inter-brand competition. The exclusive sales territory gives each dealer a greater incentive to promote the brand through advertising and service targeted at a specific territory, and thereby to increase its market share against competing brands, than would be the case if other local dealers selling the same brand were likely to benefit from its efforts. On the other hand, exclusive sales territories may virtually eliminate *intra*-brand competition among dealers for that particular brand of product. This is because dealers do not face direct local competition from other dealers selling the same brand, but only that from dealers located in other areas who are often bound by contract to confine their sales efforts to their own territories and not to 'poach' on those of other dealers. Other forms of vertical arrangement may simultaneously restrict intra-brand competition and inter-brand competition. This is often true, for instance, of agreements providing for resale price maintenance or restricting the categories of outlets through which goods may be sold. In an oligopolistic market such restraints may significantly diminish *inter*brand price competition when competing manufacturers or wholesalers adopt similar restrictions in their contracts.[19] Finally, vertical agreements requiring the purchaser to deal exclusively in the supplier's products or to purchase all or a high proportion of its requirements from a single supplier may primarily restrict *inter*-brand competition. Such restrictions prevent dealers from dealing in other competing brands of products and may have a 'foreclosure' effect: excluding competing manufacturers from access to distribution channels which may be critical to the effective marketing of their products.[20] Therefore, Article 81 (1) applies to both restrictions of inter-brand competition and restrictions

18. *Grundig/Consten*, ECJ July 13, 1966, 1966 ECR 299, 339–343.
19. *SABA II*, ECJ Oct. 22, 1986, 1986 ECR 3021, paras 60–66; *Hesbignonne*, ECJ April 19, 1988, 1988 ECR 1919, paras 12–15.
20. *Haecht I*, ECJ Dec. 12, 1967, 1967 ECR 407, 415–416; *Concordia*, ECJ Feb. 1, 1977, 1977 ECR 65, paras 25–33; *Delimitis/Henninger Bräu*, ECJ Feb. 28, 1991, 1991 ECR I-935, paras 11–15.

of intra-brand competition. As the Court of Justice stated in *Grundig/Consten:*

> 'Although competition between producers is generally more noticeable than that between distributors of products of the same make, it does not thereby follow that an agreement tending to restrict the latter kind of competition should escape the prohibition of Article 85 (1) merely because it might increase the former.'[21]

Vertical Restrictions may Retard Market Integration.
The basic approach expressed in the *Grundig/Consten* case has been repeatedly followed by both the Court of Justice[22] and the Commission:[23] the process of market integration must not be impeded by either government or private restrictions on the distribution of goods and services. This is the principal reason why vertical restrictions are judged more strictly under EC competition law than under that of the United States or some European countries. The markets of the member states of the Community have not yet been completely integrated into one large market. The federal character of the Community leaves the member states considerable control over economic policy. This, together with different languages, different currencies (despite the introduction of the single currency, the Euro, in the majority of member states),[24] consumer preferences, tax systems and technical regulations, helps preserve varying market conditions in the different countries. The result is that the price for the same brand of products may differ substantially from one member state to the next. Consumers and dealers often attempt to take advantage of the price differences by making their purchases in the member state with the lowest prices rather than in their home market. In order to protect the local dealer network in high-priced countries and to maximize profits in each member state, the manufacturer is tempted to respond by requiring his distributors and dealers to sell only to local residents and not to dealers whom they suspect of buying for export, so as to stop such 'parallel imports.'[25] The dual prohibitions of absolute territorial protection and resale price maintenance – another common way of supporting artificial price differences for the same brand of goods in dif-

21. *Grundig/Consten*, ECJ July 13, 1966, 1966 ECR 299, 342.
22. *See Ford II*, ECJ Sept. 17, 1985, 1985 ECR 2725, para. 46; *Langnese-Iglo*, CFI June 8, 1995, 1995 ECR II-1533, para. 150; *aff'd* ECJ Oct. 1, 1998, 1998 ECR I-5609.
23. *See Volkswagen/Audi*, D.Comm. Jan. 28, 1998, 1998 OJ L 124/60, points 111–152, *aff'd* CFI July 6, 2000, 2000 ECR II-2707 and ECJ Sept. 18, 2003, C-338/00P.
24. The UK, Denmark and Sweden have not yet joined the Monetary Union.
25. A typical example is the car industry where significant differences in sales taxes and annual road taxes on cars in different member states have led to substantial price differences for some models between neighbouring countries (which still exist today, *see* press release of March 2, 2004, IP/04/285) and where in a number of cases car manufacturers and dealers were found to be imposing restrictions to prevent this trade: E.g. *VW/Audi*. D.Comm. Jan. 28, 1998, 1998 OJ L 124/60 (*aff'd* CFI July 6, 2000, 2000 ECR II-2707 and ECJ Sept. 18, 2003, C-338/00 P); *General Motors – Opel*, CFI Oct. 21, 2003, T-368/00.

ferent member states – form a common thread that runs through the decisions of the Commission[26] and the Court of Justice.[27]

Development of the Commission's Enforcement Policy.
From the very beginning, the Commission has placed a high priority on strict enforcement of Article 81 against vertical restraints of competition that isolate national markets. Consequently, in 1962 at the Commission's proposal the Council adopted Regulation 17, which provides (with minor exceptions) that all types of restrictive agreements – horizontal or vertical – can only be cleared if they are notified to and exempted by the Commission.[28] Subsequently, the Commission received notification of thousands of vertical (in particular exclusive distribution) agreements. In order to overcome the 'mass problem', the Commission asked the Council to delegate power to issue block exemption regulations,[29] which make individual notification and clearance superfluous. Accordingly, in 1967 the Commission adopted Regulation 67/67,[30] which was replaced by Regulations 1983/83 on exclusive distribution and 1984/83 on exclusive purchasing[31] and Regulation 4087/88 on franchising,[32] which are now replaced by a single block exemption Regulation 2790/1999 on vertical restraints[33] (except the motor vehicle and spare parts sector, which are subject to Regulation 1400/2002[34]). These regulations will be discussed in Sections B and C. On the other hand, the Commission has always sought to avoid an overly broad interpretation and application of Article 81 (1) by excluding cases in which it need not intervene:

i. by delimiting the scope of Article 81 (1) with regard to certain types of vertical arrangements, in particular agency agreements by the Commission's Notice on exclusive dealing contracts with commercial agents (1962),[35] which is superseded (without substantial changes) by the Commission's Guidelines on Vertical Restraints (hereafter 'Guidelines');[36]
ii. by establishing qualitative criteria in order to define the appreciability of vertical agreements with regard to certain normally pro-competitive clauses in exclusive dealing agreements (case law) and vertical license agreements

26. *See VW/Audi*. D.Comm. Jan. 28, 1998, 1998 OJ L 124/60 (*aff'd* CFI July 6, 2000, 2000 ECR II-2707); *Daimler Chrysler*, D.Comm. Oct. 10, 2001, 2002 OJ L 257/1.
27. *See Dunlop/Slazenger*, CFI July 7, 1994, 1994 ECR II-441, para. 52.
28. From May 1, 2004 Regulation 1/2003 (2003 OJ L 1/1) abolishes the Commission's exclusive competence for applying Article 81 (3) and the system of notification.
29. Regulation 19/65, 1965 OJ L 533.
30. 1967 OJ 849.
31. 1983 OJ L 173/1 and L 173/5.
32. 1988 OJ L 359/46.
33. 1999 OJ L 336/21.
34. 2002 OJ L 203/30.
35. 1962 OJ 2921.
36. Guidelines (2000 OJ C 291/1), points 12–20.

(Commission's 1962 Notice, the predecessor of the subsequent block exemption regulations[37]); and

iii. by establishing quantitative criteria in order to define the appreciability of vertical restrictions by fixing certain minimum market share thresholds (*De Minimis* Notices beginning in 1977,[38] the most recent in 2001[39]).

3. Inappreciability of Certain Types of Vertical Arrangements under Article 81 (1)

(a) Inapplicability of Article 81 (1) to Agency Agreements

New Guidelines But Similar Assessment to Previous Commission Practice. Agreements between a supplier of goods or services and a person with the power to negotiate and to conclude contracts in the supplier's name or on its behalf may not be covered by the block exemption. The conditions defined in the Commission's Guidelines on Vertical Restraints with respect to agency agreements[40] replace those of the Commission's 1962 Notice[41] but are, in fact, not dissimilar. The determinative factor is that the financial and commercial risk is not borne by the agent,[42] which is in accordance with the Commission's 1962 Notice.[43] The new Guidelines state that an agency agreement falls outside Article 81 (1) if the agent does not bear any, or only insignificant, risks in relation to the contracts concluded on the behalf of the principal(s)[44] and/or negotiated on behalf of the principal(s) and in relation to market-specific investments for that field of activity,[45] for which the Guidelines contain a non-exhaustive list of examples.[46] However, unlike the Commission's 1962 Notice, the new Guidelines distinguish more clearly between intra-brand and inter-brand restrictions: limitations on the price to be applied and the territory and the clients to be served may be justified by the economic dependence of the agent as well as limitations on the principal from appointing other agents (exclusive agency provisions), whereas provisions preventing the agent from acting as an agent or distributing for competing firms (non-compete provisions) and post-term non-compete provisions may lead to foreclosure of the

37. 1962 OJ 2922; Regulation 772/2004.
38. 1977 OJ C 313/3.
39. 2001 OJ C 368/13 (minimum threshold for vertical agreements: 15%).
40. Guidelines, points 12–20, in particular fn. 7.
41. 1962 OJ 2921.
42. Guidelines, points 15–16. *See CNSD (Consiglio Nationale degli Spedizioneri Doganali)*, CFI March 30, 2000, 2000 ECR II-1807, para. 37.
43. Commission's 1962 Notice, point 1. *See also British Airways*, D.Comm. July 14, 1999, 1999–5 CMLR 581 and the Guidelines annexed to that decision.
44. It is not material for the assessment whether the agent acts for one or several principals, except where this leads to anticompetitive collusion: Guidelines, points 13 and 20.
45. Guidelines, point 15.
46. Guidelines, point 16.

market where the goods[47] or services[48] are sold or purchased when the principal holds a powerful position.[49] If an agent is acting for several competing suppliers or operators the agency agreement falls within the scope of Article 81 (1) where it facilitates collusion,[50] in particular when the principals use the same agents collectively while excluding others from using these agents, or when they use the agents to collude on marketing strategy[51] or to exchange commercially sensitive information.[52] In the *Flemish Travel Agencies* case the Court stated that although an agent acting for numerous principals obviously had to conclude the contract in the name and on the terms fixed by those different principals, any restriction against the agent passing on a part of its commission to the client constituted a restriction of competition contrary to Article 81 (1).[53] This has become the ongoing practice of the Commission.[54] Agreements fixing minimum prices between agents providing services linked to custom clearance operations[55] or patent agents[56] are horizontal restraints and clearly infringements of Article 81.

Agency Agreements Falling within the Scope of Articles 81 (1) and 82. Agreements with 'agents' that exercise in fact an independent economic activity ('non-genuine agency agreements') may infringe Article 81 (1) but are in this case covered by the block exemption, if and insofar as its conditions are fulfilled.[57] For instance, if a sales agent makes substantial sales for his principal[58] but also acts as an independent trader with respect to the same or a similar commodity for other manufacturers, then any restriction on his independent trading activities remains subject to Article 81.[59] The Guidelines are without prejudice to the applicability

47. *See*, *Sugar*, ECJ Dec. 16, 1975, 1975 ECR 1663, paras 459–468.
48. *See Virgin/British Airways*, D.Comm. July 14, 1999, 2000 OJ L 30/1, points 97–107.
49. Guidelines, point 19.
50. *Flemish Travel Agents*, ECJ Oct. 1, 1987, 1987 ECR 3801, 3828, paras 19–21; *UIC – Distribution of Railway Tickets*, D.Comm. Nov. 25, 1992, 1992 OJ L 366/47; *rev'd* on procedural grounds (application of Regulation 17 instead of Regulation 1017/68) CFI June 6, 1995, 1995 ECR II-1503 and CFI March 11, 1997, 1997 ECR I-1287.
51. *See Potassium Salts*: *SCPA/Kali+Salz*, D.Comm. May 11, 1973, 1973 OJ L 217/3.
52. Guidelines, point 20. *CSND*, D.Comm. June 30, 1993, 1993 OJ L 203/27, *aff'd* CFI March 30, 2000, 2000 ECR II-1807; *COAPI*, D.Comm. Jan. 30, 1995, 1995 OJ L 122/37.
53. *Flemish Travel Agencies*, ECJ Oct. 1, 1987, 1987 ECR 3801, paras 19–21.
54. *Distribution of Railway Tickets*, D.Comm. Nov. 25, 1992, 1992 OJ L 366/47; *IATA Passenger Agency Programme*, Nineteenth Report on Competition Policy, point 58; *Center Parcs* and *Halifax/Standard Life*, Twenty-first Report on Competition Policy, pp. 421–422; *Daimler-Chrysler*, D.Comm. Oct. 10, 2001, 2002 OJ L 257/1, points 153–168.
55. *CSND*, D.Comm. June 30, 1993, 1993 OJ L 203/27 (*aff'd* CFI March 30, 2000, 2000 ECR II-1807). *See also Italian Custom Agents*, ECJ Feb. 9, 1994, 1994 ECR I-393.
56. *COAPI*, D.Comm. Jan. 30, 1995, 1995 OJ L 122/37.
57. Guidelines, point 13.
58. Therefore the amount of sales is not decisive for determining the qualification as an 'agent': *Sugar*, ECJ Dec 16, 1975, 1975 ECR 1663, para. 544.
59. *Sugar*, ECJ Dec. 16, 1975, 1975 ECR 1663, paras 544–553.

of Article 82, e.g. in the case of loyalty rebate schemes tying travel agents to a dominant airline.[60]

(b) Qualitative Criteria for the Appreciability of Vertical Restraints

The Appreciability Concept of the Court of Justice.
The Court of Justice requires a restraint of competition to be 'appreciable' to infringe Article 81 (1). It judges appreciability in the light of the economic and legal setting of the agreement and its objects and effects. The Court of Justice has never quantified appreciability and has affirmed the application of Article 81 (1) even in cases involving relatively small market shares and turnovers, without specifying any specific threshold of appreciability.[61] The Court has also held that Article 81 (1) does not require proof that the agreement in question has in fact appreciably affected trade between the member states since in many cases that would be too difficult to establish. Rather, it must only be shown that the agreement is *capable* of appreciably affecting trade.[62] In the *Ford* case the Commission challenged the decision of Ford's German subsidiary to discontinue supplies of right-hand-drive cars to its German dealers in order to prevent low priced car imports from being purchased in Germany for export to the high-priced United Kingdom market. The Court stated:

> '... the Commission is not obliged to carry out a detailed examination of all the advantages and disadvantages likely to flow from a selective distribution system when it has good reason to believe that a manufacturer has used such a system to prevent parallel imports and thus artificially to partition the common market.'[63]

Restrictions of a critical form of competition (for example price competition) may be 'so important that it can never be eliminated'[64] and must therefore be regarded as 'hardcore' or '*per se*' restrictions or so 'obvious' that they 'may be weighed against their claimed procompetitive effects only in the context of Article 85 (3).[65] On the other hand, in a case in which the parties' market position was very weak the Court held that even an exclusive distributorship that conferred absolute territorial

60. *Virgin Airlines/British Airways*, D.Comm. July 14, 1999, 2000 OJ L 5/55 (fine of EUR 6.8 million). The agent commissions may, however, reflect cost savings and relate to sales in a period not exceeding six months.
61. *Ciment Kerpen*, ECJ Dec. 14, 1983, 1983 ECR 4173, para. 9.
62. *Miller International*, ECJ Feb. 1, 1978, 1978 ECR 131, para. 15.
63. *Ford II*, ECJ Sept. 17, 1985, 1985 ECR 2725, para. 46. The Court of Justice ruled that these actions to protect the UK dealers infringed Article 81.
64. *SABA I*, ECJ Oct 23, 1977, 1977 ECR 1875, para. 21.
65. *European Night Services*, CFI Sept. 15, 1998, 1998 ECR II-3141, para. 136.

protection did not have an appreciable effect on competition.[66] Thus, the question of 'appreciability' depends very much on the facts of each case. The same vertical restraint can have different effects depending on the market structure and the market power of the company applying the vertical restraint. The risk that the Court will find a restriction to have appreciable effects on trade and competitive conditions rises in direct proportion to the anticompetitive nature of the restriction.[67]

The Qualitative Appreciability Test as Precursor of a More General *De Minimis* Rule.
Irrespective of market share and turnovers both the Court of Justice and the Commission have found certain vertical restrictions to be non-appreciable on qualitative grounds. Indeed, there is an example in Article 81 (1) itself: subparagraph (e) prohibits tying only insofar as it is not 'according to commercial usage'. Other vertical restraints that the Commission or the Commission have recognized as non-appreciable include:

- the grant of an exclusive licence without exclusive territorial protection,[68]
- restrictions to sell only to selected licensees,[69] dealers[70] or final customers,[71]
- restrictions essential to the orderly functioning of a franchising system, [72]
- obligations necessary to protect intellectual property rights,[73] and
- more generally, ancillary restrictions.[74]

(c) Quantitative Criteria for the Appreciability of Vertical Restraints

The Commission's *De Minimis* Notices – Rules of Thumb.
The Commission has issued two different notices with respect to when vertical restraints become appreciable and therefore can infringe Article 81 (1): a notice on the appreciability of the effect on competition and a notice on the effect on the trade between member states.

---

66. *Völk/Vervaecke*, ECJ July 9, 1969, 1969 ECR 295, 302. *See* Commission Notice on agreements of minor importance, 2001 OJ C 368/13, point 12.
67. For example, in *Delimitis/Henninger Bäu*, ECJ Feb. 28, 1991, 1991 ECR I-935, paras 11–13.
68. Patent: Commission Notice 1962 OJ 2922; *Maize Seed*, ECJ June 8, 1982, 1982 ECR 2015, paras 53–58. Copyrights: *Coditel II*, Oct. 6, 1982, 1982 ECR 3381, paras 15–16.
69. Plant variety rights: *Hesbignonne*, ECJ April 19, 1988, 1988 ECR 1919, para. 10.
70. Qualitative selective distribution systems: *SABA I*, ECJ Oct. 25, 1977, 1977 ECR 1875, paras 20 and 26–27.
71. Prohibition on wholesalers from reselling to final customers: Article 4 (b) of Regulation 2790/1999; *SABA I*, ECJ Oct. 25, 1977, 1977 ECR 1875, paras 28–29.
72. *Pronuptia*, Jan. 28, 1986, 1986 ECR 353, paras 15–22.
73. The Guidelines aim at defining obligations which may not fall within Article 81 (1) and those which are likely to be covered by Regulation 2790/1999: points 30–45.
74. Non-compete obligations strictly necessary for the proper functioning of a joint venture: leading case: *Mitchell Cotts/Sofiltra*, D.Comm. Dec. 17, 1986, 1987 OJ L 41/31, 36.

- *Notice on the appreciability of the restriction*: The Commission introduced in its 1977 Notice[75] quantitative criteria for assessing the appreciablity of restrictions. In this notice ('Notice on Agreements of Minor Importance') and its 1986 successor[76] the Commission fixed a minimum 5% market share threshold in conjunction with a minimum aggregate annual turnover. In its 1997 Notice[77] the Commission abolished the turnover threshold and increased the minimum market share threshold for vertical agreements to 10% and in its 2001 Notice[78] to 15% or, in cases which are difficult to classify as either vertical or horizontal agreements, to 10%.[79] These limits refer to the aggregate market sharees of the parties to the agreement and their connected undertakings.[80] Unlike the previous notice, the 2001 Notice does not establish turnover criteria to determine whether there is an actual or potential effect on trade between member states.[81]
- *Notice on the appreciability of the effect on trade between member states*: In its 2003 Notice on the Effect on Trade Concept, the Commission introduced quantitative criteria for assessing the appreciability of the effect on trade between member states which are different from those for assessing the appreciability of the effect on competition. The Commission holds the view that in principle agreements are *not* capable of appreciably affecting trade between member states when the aggregate market shares of the parties on any relevant market within the Community affected by the agreement does not exceed 5% and, in the case of vertical agreements, the aggregate annual Community turnover of the supplier in the products covered by the agreement does not exceed EUR 40 million.[82] In the case of vertical agreements the turnover limit applies to the supplier and, in the case of purchasing agreements giving rise to buyer power, to the buyer. This means that agreements may be capable of affecting trade between member states, *irrespective* of whether they contain appreciable restrictions of competition. The notice is therefore rather a rule determining the relationship between the EC competition rules and national competition laws. According to Article 3 of Regulation 1/2003 national competition authorities must apply EC competition law (and are prevented from applying stricter national law) when an agreement is likely to affect trade between member states.
- *Rules of thumb*: Both *De Minimis* Notices establish a rebuttable presumption and are therefore a rule of thumb:[83] Agreements which are below the quantita-

75. 1977 OJ C 313/3.
76. 1986 OJ C 231/2.
77. 1997 OJ C 372/4.
78. 2001 OJ C 368/13 ('*De Minimis* Notice').
79. The market share may be exceeded by 1% during two successive calendar years: *De Minimis* Notice, point 10.
80. Point 12 (2) of the *De Minimis* Notice.
81. *De Minimis* Notice, point 3.
82. Notice on the Effect on Trade Concept, point 52.
83. *Ibid.*, point 50.

tive limits are normally not caught by Article 81 (1). However, such agreements may still be held restrictive of competition and likely to affect trade between member states even though the Commission does not intend to institute proceedings (thereby creating legitimate expectations). Agreements which exceed those limits do not automatically have an appreciable effect on competition and trade such that they would be prohibited under Article 81 (1).[84] Unlike the Notice on Agreements of Minor Importance, the Notice on the Effect on Trade Concept does not make an exception for agreements which contain hardcore restrictions, such as fixing resale prices or territorial and customer restrictions, so that such agreements normally do not infringe Article 81 (1) (because they are unlikely to affect trade between member states), without prejudice to the application of national law.[85]

***De Minimis* Restrictions v. Community Interest.**
Agreements below the *de minimis* thresholds are supposed to have only a negligible effect on competition and normally do not give rise to proceedings either upon application (complaint) or on the Commission's own initiative, and therefore will not result in fines.[86] The Commission's notices do not legally bind the Court of Justice and national authorities and courts (which have, however, a duty to take them into account as guidance)[87] and are without prejudice to the application of national competition law.[88] They bind only the Commission itself to regard agreements as not having an appreciable effect on competition or trade. However, even agreements between undertakings which exceed the set limits may not be caught by Article 81 (1), in particular if they have an exclusively favorable impact on competition.[89] In general, the Commission may see reason for taking action only in cases of a 'Community interest', which is recognized by the Court as a selection criteria at the Commission's discretion, provided the Commission considers duly the factual and legal circumstances of the case.[90] A 'Community interest' should be found when the restriction significantly restricts trade between member states and restrains competition, in particular by the cumulative effect of similar

84. E.g. *Ciment Kerpen*, ECJ Dec. 14, 1983, 1983 ECR 4173 (10% market share); *SSI*, ECJ Dec. 10, 1985, 1985 ECR 2831, para. 48; *Cement*, CFI March 15, 2000, 2000 ECR II-491, para. 3930.
85. *De Minimis* Notice, point 12.2. as compared to the Notice on the Effect on Trade Concept, point 50 (contradicting, however, point 48, which states that agreements concerning imports and exports are 'by their very nature' likely to affect trade between member states).
86. *De Minimis* Notice, point 4.
87. *Ibid.*, points 4 and 6.
88. *Ibid.*, point 7.
89. *Ibid.*, point 3.
90. Longstanding practice: *Automec II*, Sept. 18, 1992, 1992 ECR II-2223, para. 72; *Asia Motors*, CFI June 29, 1993, 1993 ECR II-669, paras 34–35; *IECC*, ECJ May 17, 2001, 2001 ECR I-3247, paras 42–45.

agreements to such an extent that it threatens the realization of effective competition and open markets in the relevant sector.[91]

Judging Cumulative Effects of Parallel Agreements.
The Court of Justice held that where the individual effects of vertical agreements are not appreciable from the standpoint of market share and sales volume competition may nonetheless be restricted by the cumulative effects of parallel networks of similar agreements, thereby increasing significantly the barriers to entry to the market by potential new entrants.[92] The *De Minimis* Notice states that in cases of networks with a cumulative effect on competition the market share threshold is reduced to 5%.[93] Individual suppliers or distributors with a market share not exceeding 5% are in general not considered to contribute significantly to a cumulative foreclosure effect, and a cumulative foreclosure effect is unlikely to exist if less than 30% of the relevant market is covered by parallel networks of similar agreements.[94]

Uncertainty of Assessing the Cumulative Effect.
Whether a supplier's agreements with his dealers fall foul of Article 81 (1) on account of the cumulative foreclosure effect of networks of similar agreements depends on an economic analysis, which includes the degree of foreclosure effect of the network of similar agreements, the number of resellers tied, the duration of the exclusivity, the opportunities of access, the competitive forces on the market and whether the individual agreements contribute 'significantly' or 'insignificantly' to the cumulative anticompetitive effect of the network and consequently infringe Article 81 (1).[95] The degree of the foreclosure effect is assessed on the basis of the 'coverage rate', i.e., the percentage of resellers tied. The Commission's adminis-

---

91. *De Minimis* Notice, point 8.
92. Significant foreclosure effect in the order of 40%: *Van den Bergh Foods (HB Ice Cream)*, CFI Oct. 23, 2003, T-65/98, para. 140. *See Haecht I*, Dec. 12, 1967, 1967 ECR 407, 415; *Béguelin*, ECJ Nov. 25, 1971, 1971 ECR 949, para. 18; *Delimitis/Henninger Bräu*, ECJ Feb. 28, 1991, 1991 ECR I-935, paras 11–13; *Langnese-Iglo*, CFI June 8, 1995, 1995 ECR II-1533, paras 98–99, *aff'd* ECJ Oct. 1, 1998, 1998 ECR I-5609.
93. *De Minimis* Notice, point 8; Guidelines, point 142. The principle of 'significant' contribution (based on a minimum market share rather than the number of outlets) was applied in *Delimitis/Henninger Bräu*, ECJ Feb. 28, 1991, 1991 ECR I-935, para. 24; *Neste Markkinointi/Yötuuli Ky*, ECJ Dec. 7, 2000, 2000 ECR I-11121, paras 36–38; *Whitbread*, D.Comm. Feb. 24, 1999, 1999 OJ L 88/26, *aff'd Shaw, Falla/Whitbread*, CFI March 21, 2002, 2002 ECR II-2033; *Van den Bergh Foods (HB Ice Cream)*, CFI Oct. 23, 2003, T-65/98, para. 118 (significant); *Roberts/Greene*, D.Comm. Nov. 12, 1998, IP/98/967 (*aff'd* CFI July 5, 2001, 2001 ECR II-1881), and *Inntrepreneur and Spring*, D.Comm. June 29, 2000, 2000 OJ L 195/49 (insignificant).
94. In the case *Van den Bergh Foods*, which concerned a freezer exclusivity (obligation on the dealer to stock in the supplier's cabinet only the supplier's ice creams), the coverage was 40%: CFI Oct. 23, 2003, T-65/98, para. 140.
95. *Delimitis/Henninger Bräu*, ECJ Feb. 28, 1991, 1991 ECR I-935, paras 19–33; *Whitbread*, D.Comm. Feb. 24, 1999, 1999 OJ L 88/26, points 107–138 (*aff'd* CFI March 21, 2002, 2002 ECR II-2033).

trative practice is based on a 'coverage rate' of 50–60%.[96] Individual agreements may not significantly contribute to the cumulative effects of a network where the parties' market shares are not more than 1–5% and the duration of the exclusivity is not excessive, e.g., in the beer sector not longer than 15 years.[97] Such an economic analysis (definition of the relevant market and the determination of the cumulative effect and the individual contribution to this effect) may be beyond the means of the parties and even of a national court;[98] it may be only the Commission which is able to undertake the necessary investigations. Regulation 2790/1999 brings this uncertainty to an end by extending its benefit to parallel networks of restrictive agreements that have a cumulative anticompetitive effect, unless (i) one of the suppliers or distributors has an *individual* market share exceeding 30% of the relevant market or (ii) the parallel network covers more than 50% of the relevant market *and* the Commission withdraws with prospective (*ex nunc*) effect the benefit of the block exemption.

B. New Block Exemption Regulation 2790/1999 on Vertical Restraints and Commission Guidelines

1. Main Characteristics

Follow-up to Commission's Green Paper.

Following its Green Paper on vertical restraints, the Commission adopted a new block exemption regulation, Regulation 2790/1999, on December 22, 1999[99] replacing Regulations 1983/83 on exclusive distribution, 1984/83 on exclusive purchasing and 4088/87 on franchising agreements which were scheduled to expire on December 31, 1999. The new regulation does not apply to vertical

---

96. Examples of agreements which constituted a network that infringed Article 81 (1): *Langnese-Iglo*, CFI June 8, 1995, 1995 ECR II-1533, paras 94–113; *Van der Bergh Foods*, D.Comm. March 11, 1998, 1998 OJ L 246/1, points 202–210 (combined market shares of approximately 60% of the impulse ice cream market); *Whitbread*, D.Comm. Feb. 24, 1999, 1999 OJ L 88/26, points 106–118 (*aff'd* CFI March 21, 2002, 2002 ECR II-2033); *Scottish and Newcastle*, D.Comm June 16, 1999, 1999 OJ L 186/28, point 140; *Bass*, D.Comm. June 16, 1999, 1999 OJ L 186/1, point 135 (between 50 and 70% of the beer market).

97. *Whitbread*, D.Comm. Feb. 24, 1999, 1999 OJ L 88/26, points 130–138 (*aff'd* CFI March 21, 2002, 2002 ECR II-2033); *Roberts/Greene King*, D.Comm. Nov. 30, 1998 (not published), points 95–107, *aff'd* CFI July 5, 2001, 2001 ECR II-1881 (insignificant contribution – 'considerably less than 5%', namely 1.3% – to the network of tying agreements existing on the UK market).

98. The difficulties of assessing the cumulative effect of networks by national courts are highlighted in the cases referred to in the Twenty-first Report on Competition Policy, point 444; Twenty-sixth Report on Competition Policy, point 338; Twenty-seventh Report on Competition Policy, point 350.

99. 2003 OJ L 1/1.

agreements which are subject to specific regulations, such as vertical restraints in motor vehicle distribution agreements[100] or in transfer of technology agreements.[101] The application of the new regulation is subject, as from May 1, 2004, to the new procedural rules of Regulation 1/2003 replacing Regulation 17 on the basis of its White Paper on modernization of the EC competition rules.[102] These procedural rules create a new system of enforcement of Article 81 (3) constituting a directly applicable exception system. Nevertheless, it will maintain the possibility of block exemptions[103] but will no longer provide for individual notification of agreements between companies with market shares exceeding the thresholds fixed in such block exemptions. However, the Commission may, at the parties' request, issue informal guidance, in particular where cases give rise to genuine legal uncertainty because of novel or unresolved questions.[104]

Entry into Force of the New Rules.
The new rules on vertical restraints entered into force on June 1, 2000 (Article 13); the previous regulations continued to apply until May 31, 2000 (Article 12 (1)). The prohibition of Article 81 (1) does not apply during the period from June 1, 2000 to December 31, 2001 in respect of agreements already in force on May 31, 2000 which do not satisfy the conditions for exemption provided for in the new regulation but which satisfy the conditions of the previous regulations (Article 12 (2)). Agreements which are already in force, not covered by the previous block exemptions but cleared by individual decision or comfort letter of the Commission, continue to be exempt from the prohibition of Article 81 (1) as long as the decision or comfort letter remains applicable.[105] Agreements which were concluded before June 1, 2000, but not covered by the previous block exemptions and not individually cleared (clearance refused or not requested) must be reconsidered under the new rules.[106]

The Main Issues.
The main features of the new Regulation 2790/1999 on vertical restraints are:

100. Regulation 1400/2002, *see* Section C *infra*.
101. Article 2 (3) and (5) of Regulation 2790/1999. Restraints in transfer of technology agreements which are ancillary to vertical agreements are covered by the block exemption; restraints which constitute the *primary object* of such agreements are subject to Regulation 772/2004 on technology transfer agreements.
102. Commission Program No 99/027, 1999 OJ C 132/1.
103. Article 29 of Regulation 1/2003. Block exemption regulations adopted prior to the date of application of the new regulation (May 1, 2004) continue to apply up to the date of their expiration (with respect to exemption decisions: Article 43 (1) of the new regulation).
104. Recital 38 of Regulation 1/2003.
105. Even after the date of application of Regulation 1/2003 (May 1, 2004): Article 43 (1).
106. *See Audi/Volkswagen*, D.Comm. Jan. 20, 2003, IP/03/80.

(i) *More Flexible Economic Approach*: The regulation provides for a broad exemption of vertical restraints which is based on a more economic rather than a 'legalistic' evaluation of the different forms of vertical restraints.[107] The regulation aims at facilitating a more tolerant policy on vertical restraints, at simplifying supervision by the Commission and at stimulating the decentralized application of the EC competition rules by national authorities and courts.
(ii) *30% Market Share Cap*. The new regulation grants the benefit of the block exemption only if the supplier's market share does not exceed 30% of the relevant market in which it sells the contract goods or services. In the case of an exclusive supply obligation, the 30% market share limitation applies to the buyer. (Articles 3 and 9.)
(iii) *Application Also to Selective Distribution, Component Supply Agreements and to Services*: The regulation extends the benefit of the block exemption to selective distribution agreements,[108] component supply agreements and agreements for providing services.[109] (Articles 2 and 4.)
(iv) *Safe Harbour Principle*: The regulation creates a presumption of legality of vertical restrictions without listing the exempted clauses ('safe harbour principle')[110] whereas the previous regulations did not apply to agreements which contained restrictions other than those expressly 'white-listed'. (Article 2.)
(v) *No Exemption if 'Hardcore' Restrictions Are Present*: Agreements that contain 'hardcore' restrictions (i.e., minimum resale price maintenance and certain forms of customer and territorial restrictions) do not benefit from the block exemption,[111] whereas other non-hardcore restrictions, i.e., non-compete clauses, may as such not be exempted but do not preclude the application of the block exemption to other restrictive clauses in the agreements.[112] (Articles 4 and 5.)
(vi) *Cumulative Effect of Parallel Agreements*: The regulation contains specific provisions on the cumulative effects resulting from parallel networks of similar agreements. (Article 8.)

---

107. There are indications that the Court of Justice has favored a more flexible economic approach towards vertical restraints since the very beginning of its case law. *See Haecht*, ECJ Dec. 12, 1967, 1967 ECR 407; *Grundig/Consten*, ECJ July 13, 1966, 1966 ECR 299; *Pronuptia*, ECJ Jan. 28, 1986, 1986 ECR 353, paras 14–15; *Delimitis/Henninger Bräu*, ECJ Feb. 28, 1991, 1991 ECR I-935, paras 11–12, 24–27.
108. Previously selective distribution agreements were not covered by any block exemption regulation because they did not contain any exclusive obligations.
109. The Commission's powers were extended by Regulation 1215/99.
110. Guidelines, point 21.
111. Inapplicability of the exemptions to *agreements* containing hardcore restrictions.
112. Inapplicability of the exemption to *obligations* – this by contrast to the 'all or nothing' approach under the previous regulations. With regard to the severability of restrictions, *see* Guidelines, points 66–67.

(vii) *Withdrawal by National Authorities*: Not only the Commission but also national authorities are entitled to withdraw the benefit of the block exemption regulation. (Article 7.)

The new regulation is intended to grant a 'safe harbour' of legal certainty over a broader range of vertical restrictions and to empower national competition authorities to play a far more active role than ever before in evaluating and clearing agreements under Article 81.[113] However, a relatively large number of agreements will still need individual clearance, in particular because of the difficulty in distinguishing certain hardcore restrictions from their exceptions, assessing non-compete clauses agreed for a longer duration than five years, defining the relevant market to determine compliance with the 30% market share threshold, and unavoidable uncertainty about the criteria for the individual assessment of agreements entered into by companies having a market share exceeding the 30% market share threshold. The 'safe harbour' may therefore be illusory for firms whose agreements are for the time being covered by the old block exemptions (which applied without market share limitation). Such firms will now encounter stormy seas when applying to the Commission to obtain individual clearance[114] or awaiting a challenge at a later time.

2. STRUCTURE AND SCOPE OF EXEMPTION

Structure of the Regulation.

Under the previous regulations exclusive distribution, purchasing and franchise agreements received the benefit of the relevant block exemption without any market share limit, the only exceptions being (i) the possibility of withdrawing the benefit of exemption in the absence of effective competition and (ii) the applicability of Article 82 in the case of a dominant position held by the supplier[115] or distributor.[116] Under the new regulation, vertical agreements are block exempted only if the supplier's market share does not exceed 30% of the relevant market.[117] In the case of an exclusive supply obligation, the 30% market share limitation

113. The complexity of the EC competition rules and the difficulty of assessing the factual context of a case (definition of the relevant market, cumulative effect of networks, appreciability of restraints on parties and third parties) may hinder national courts in playing a more active role, *see* Mestmäcker, WuW 2000–7/8, 683.

114. *See* Recital 38 to Regulation 1/2003.

115. *See Franzen/Swedish Alcohol Monopoly*, ECJ Oct. 23, 1997, 1997 ECR I-5909, paras 38–40.

116. *See AAMS*, D.Comm. June 17, 1998, 1998 OJ L 252/47; *Italian Electricity Monopoly*, ECJ Oct. 23, 1997, 1997 ECR I-5789, paras 23–28.

117. The main reason being the risk of market partitioning between supplier and buyer (reduction of intra-brand competition), *see* Guidelines points 103 and 161, and of anticompetitive collusion between competing suppliers or buyers (reduction of inter-brand competition), *see* Guidelines, point 114.

applies to the buyer. Agreements between companies having a market share that exceeds the 30% market share threshold[118] need, unlike under the previous block exemption regulations, individual evaluation.

Broader Scope of the New Regulation.
The new regulation has a broader scope than the previous regulations in that it

(i) includes agreements and concerted practices[119] between two or more[120] parties operating on different market levels ('vertical agreements'), thereby covering exclusive distribution, exclusive purchasing, selective distribution and franchise agreements (excluding, however, rent and lease agreements),
(ii) extends to services,[121]
(iii) extends to incorporation of goods (subcontracting agreements),[122]
(iv) applies to agreements without genuine exclusivity,
(v) includes agreements between an association of retailers and its members, provided no individual member has a turnover exceeding EUR 50 million,[123] and
(vi) includes agreements containing provisions which relate to the assignment or licence of intellectual property rights,[124] provided those provisions do not constitute the primary object and are ancillary (not containing hardcore restrictions[125]).

---

118. Under Article 9 the block exemption continues to apply for two years when the market share does not exceed 35% and for one year if it exceeds 35%.
119. The decisive criteria being the joint intention: *Bayer*, CFI Oct. 26, 2000, 2000 ECR II-3383, paras 66–71. With respect to circular letters: *Volkswagen II*, D.Comm. June 29, 2001, 2001 OJ L 262/14; *rev'd* CFI Dec. 3, 2003, T-208/01, points 56–69; *Daimler/Chrysler*, D.Comm. Oct. 10, 2001, 2002 OJ L 257/1 point 125.
120. Included by Regulation 1215/99. However, Regulation 1983/83 did already apply by analogy to agreements between one supplier and different dealers, *see* Notice on Regulations 1983/83 and 1984/83, 1984 OJ C 101/2, point 14.
121. Included expressly in Regulation 1215/99. *See* Guidelines, point 2.
122. Renting/leasing may be assimilated to purchasing: point 25.
123. Article 2 (2). This provision is, however, ambiguous in applying to arrangements between an association and its members (which are supposed to be vertical) but not to arrangements between members of that association (which are supposed to be horizontal). Furthermore, this provision may apply to an arrangement between an association and its members not to supply non-members (collective boycott) which was, however, prohibited and fined in *FEG*, D.Comm. Oct. 26, 1999, 2000 OJ L 39/1, points 103 and 127. Only in the framework of selective distribution systems are restrictions of sales to unauthorized distributors permitted: Article 4 (b), third indent.
124. Article 2 (3). This applies in particular to franchise agreements and exclusive distribution agreements including the exclusive use of a trade mark but without absolute territorial protection (which was prohibited in *Grundig/Consten*, ECJ July 13, 1966, 1966 ECR 322).
125. *E.g.* fixing or recommending prices by an association: *FEG*, D.Comm. Oct. 26, 1999, 2000 OJ L 39/1, point 111 (only strictly *vertical* price recommendations are accepted under Article 4 (a)). *See also Belasco*, ECJ July 11, 1989, 1989 ECR 2181, para. 15.

The regulation does not apply to vertical agreements the subject matter of which is regulated by other block exemption regulations (Article 2 (5)), in particular on technology transfer (Regulation 240/96) and on motor vehicle distribution and service agreements (Regulation 1400/2002).

Severability v. All-or-Nothing-Approach.
The previous block exemption regulations did not apply when the agreement in question contained clauses which were blacklisted or not expressly white-listed ('all-or-nothing approach'). The new block exemption regulation applies on condition that no hardcore restrictions are contained or exercised in the vertical agreement; in such a case, the benefit of the block exemption is lost for the *entire* agreement.[126] However, non-compete clauses, which were, to a certain extent, blacklisted under the previous regulations, do not preclude the application of the block exemption in relation to that part of the agreement which does not comply with the conditions of the regulation.[127] Similarly, in the case of a distribution network used for several products or services ('portfolio'), the block exemption applies to that part for which its conditions, in particular the market share threshold, are fulfilled.[128]

Agreements or Concerted Practices between only Two Firms.
Regulation 2790/1999 applies to agreements and concerted practices between two or more non-competing firms.[129] Moreover, the parties' obligation to ensure that obligations they have accepted are respected by affiliated firms, referred to as 'connected undertakings,' i.e., firms that are legally independent but form one economic unit with one of the parties, is authorized by the regulation.[130] The term 'agreements' must be interpreted in the sense of 'concurrence of wills' without needing a detailed and finalized agreement.[131] In *BMW Belgium* the Court stated that a circular which was sent to dealers to halt exports to Germany and which obtained the consent of the dealers constituted an agreement which supplemented their contractual relationship.[132] Any concertation may therefore be caught by

---

126. Article 4 of Regulation 2790/99; Guidelines, point 66.
127. Article 5 of Regulation 2790/99; Guidelines, point 67.
128. Guidelines, point 69.
129. The previous regulations applied only to agreements between two firms, which unnecessarily limited the scope of the regulation although a single supplier was allowed to conclude separate agreements with multiple purchasers, i.e., parallel agreements constituting the supplier's distribution network.
130. Article 11 (2) (e).
131. *Cement*, CFI March 15, 2000, 2000 ECR II-491, para. 2061; *CEWAL*, CFI Aug. 16, 2000, 2000 ECR II-1365, paras 54–57.
132. *BMW Belgium*, ECJ July 12, 1979, 1979 ECR 2435, paras 28–36. *See Volkswagen*, CFI July 6, 2000, 2000 ECR II-2707, paras 48–49; *Mercedes Benz*, D.Comm. Oct. 10, 2001, 2002 OJ L 257/1, point 125.

Article 81 (1) whereas unilateral conduct falls outside its scope.[133]

Methodology of Analysis.
The assessment of vertical restraints involves the following steps:[134]

- the evaluation of whether hardcore restrictions are present that are not covered by the block exemption irrespective of the parties' market share: if one or more hardcore restrictions are included in the agreement, the agreement infringes Article 81 (1) and the block exemption does not apply, and it probably does not fulfill the conditions of an exemption under Article 81 (3);
- definition of the relevant market, namely evaluation of the parties' market share in order to assess whether the agreement may receive the benefit of the block exemption (section 4 below);
- if the supplier's market share does *not* exceed the 30% threshold (and if the buyer's market share does not exceed 30% in the case of an exclusive supply obligation): assessment of whether the conditions of the regulation are fulfilled with respect to the various types of vertical restrictions (sections 5–8 below), subject to the possibility of withdrawing the benefit of the exemption (section 9 below);
- if the conditions of the block exemption are not fulfilled, in particular if the supplier's market share exceeds 30% (or the buyer's market share exceeds 30% in the case of an exclusive supply obligation): evaluation of whether the agreement infringes Article 81 (1) at all[135] and, if so, whether it meets the conditions for individual exemption under Article 81 (3) (section 10 below).

3. Hardcore Restrictions outside the Scope of the Regulation

Inapplicability of the Block Exemption.
Pursuant to Article 4, the block exemption does not apply to vertical agreements which, directly or indirectly, in isolation or in combination with other factors under the control of the parties, provide for hardcore restrictions. Hardcore restrictions may be expressly agreed or result from the behaviour of the parties themselves or of connected undertakings under their 'control', which, in the case of 'implicit acquiescence' by the other parties ('concurrence of wills'[136]), may become an integral part of their contractual relations.[137] Hardcore restrictions normally

133. *Bayer*, CFI Oct. 26, 2000, 2000 ECR II-383, paras 66–71.
134. Guidelines, point 120.
135. The regulation dispenses with such evaluation because it applies, up to 30% market share, to vertical agreements provided they fall within the scope of Article 81 (1): Article 1 (1).
136. In a horizontal context: *Cement*, CFI March 15, 2001, 2001 ECR II-491, para. 2061
137. Affirmed in *Volkswagen*, CFI July 6, 2000, 2000 ECR II-2713, para. 237; denied in *Bayer*, CFI Oct. 26, 2000, 2000 ECR II-3383, paras 66–72 and 114 *et seq.*, *aff'd* ECJ Jan. 6, 2004, C-2/01P, *see* Guidelines, point 66; circular letters may suffice: *Bayer*, CFI Oct. 26, 2000, 2000 ECR II-3383, para. 134, and *Volkswagen II*, D.Comm. June 29, 2001, 2001 OJ 262/14, points 56–69.

infringe Article 81 (1) even if the parties' market share does not exceed the 15% *de minimis* threshold.[138] They preclude the applicability of the block exemption (even if they are not systematically applied[139]) and normally do not qualify for individual clearance.[140]

Restrictions on Prices.

Pursuant to Article 4 (a), minimum resale price maintenance is listed as a hardcore restriction. It is defined as 'a restriction on the buyer to determine its sale price, without prejudice to the possibility of the supplier's imposing a maximum sale price or recommending a sale price,[141] provided that they do not amount to a fixed minimum sale price as a result of indirect means, such as pressure from, or incentives offered by, any of the parties'[142] or exchange of price information.[143] Resale price maintenance leads to a total elimination of intra-brand price competition and increases transparency on price, thereby facilitating horizontal collusion between competing manufacturers or distributors.[144] This applies to resale price maintenance for books insofar as it extends to intra-Community trade,[145] whereas mere national price maintenance systems are normally unlikely to affect trade between member states.[146] However, maximum[147] and recommended

---

In the horizontal context: *see Cement*, CFI March 15, 2000, 2000 ECR II-491, paras 1849, 4114 and 4020, *rev'd* CFI Dec 3, 2003, T-208/01. Article 4 should be read as extending to the 'effect' (not only object) of the agreements.

138. *De Minimis* Notice 2001 OJ C 149/18, point 8 (b); Guidelines, points 7–11. Examples: *Editions Nathan*, D.Comm. July 5, 2000, 2001 OJ L 54/1; *Triumph*, D.Comm. Sept. 15, 2000, IP/00/1014. Market partitioning is by its very nature likely to affect trade between member states and therefore does not depend on the definition of the relevant geographic market: *Volkswagen*, CFI July 6, 2000, 2000 ECR II-2713, para. 231.
139. 'Guidelines' not to apply a hardcore restriction are 'irrelevant'; a legally binding agreement can only be changed by another formal agreement: *Anheuser-Busch*, D.Comm. Dec. 14, 1999, 2000 OJ L 49/17, point 67.
140. Guidelines, point 46. *See Nintendo II*, D.Comm. Oct. 30, 2002, 2003 OJ L 255/33, point 341.
141. A prohibition to apply a price substantially below the recommended prices is tantamount to resale price maintenance: *Volkswagen II*, D.Comm. June 29, 2001, 2001 OJ L 262/14.
142. Guidelines, point 47.
143. *British Sugar, Tate & Lyle*, CFI July 12, 2001, 2001 ECR II-2035, paras 58–59.
144. This corresponds to the case law under Regulation 1983/83, *see Net Book Agreement*, ECJ Jan. 17, 1995, 1995 ECR I-23, para. 34 (although there may be reasons for applying Article 81 (3) in specific cases).
145. *German Books: Sammelrevers I*, IP/00/651 of June 22, 2000, and *Sammelrevers II*, IP/01/1035 of July 19, 2001; *Deutsche Buchpreisbindung*, March 22, 2002, IP/02/461 and MEMO O2/63; *Proxis/KNO*, March 22, 2002, IP/02/461, Thirty-second Report on Competition Policy, point 151.
146. *Echirolles/Association du Dauphiné*, ECJ Oct. 3, 2000, C-9/99; *Dutch Books*, IP/99/668 of Sept. 9, 1999; *German-Austrian Book Price Maintenance*, IP/00/651 of June 22, 2000. *See Nehl and Nuijten*, DG IV Newsletter 2002–2, 35.
147. *See* Guidelines, point 225. However, maximum prices may work as a focal point for the resellers and may be followed by them or lead to price collusion. Normally merely recommending

prices[148] may be applied.[149] Since these practices do not prevent the buyer from reselling below a certain price, such clauses normally do not have the negative impact of resale price maintenance on consumers, unless used as an indirect means to implement a minimum resale price.[150]

Restriction of Territories or Customers.

Article 4 (b) blacklists restrictions on the territory into which, or of customers to whom, the buyer may sell the contract goods or services,[151] including limitations of parallel trade,[152] exports via the internet[153] and indirect restrictions, such as arrangements to contact the dealer in the country of destination[154] or to identify parallel suppliers,[155] to pay that dealer a support fee in the case of export,[156] or to exclude exports from a bonus scheme.[157] However, the following restrictions are exempt:

- restrictions of active sales (including active sales via the internet such as by sending unsolicited e-mails to potential customers[158]) into the exclusive territory or to an exclusive customer group insofar as the allocation of territories or customers is itself block exempted (up to a 30% market share);[159]
- restrictions on wholesalers not to sell directly to end users;[160]

---

a maximum price should suffice in order to prevent dealers from charging high prices. A non-discrimination rule preventing dealers or merchants from (sur)charging was accepted by the Commission under exceptional circumstances (VISA card use): *VISA International*, D.Comm. Aug. 9, 2001, 2001 OJ L 293/24, points 54–58.

148. *See Pronuptia*, ECJ Jan. 28, 1986, 1986 ECR 353, para. 25. The provision of a list of recommended prices is not considered in itself as leading to a resale price maintenance: Guidelines, point 47.
149. Article 4 (a); Guidelines, points 47 and 225.
150. Guidelines, point 111.
151. Both the ban of passive sales to other dealers of the selective distribution network and the other side of the coin, the obligation on the dealers not to purchase from other dealers, are hardcore restrictions: *JCB Service*, CFI Jan. 13, 2004, T-67/01, paras 85 and 111.
152. *Nintendo II*, D.Comm. Oct. 30, 2002, 2003 OJ L 255/33, points 331–333.
153. *Yamaha*, D.Comm. July 16, 2003, IP/03/1028.
154. *Yamaha*, D.Comm. July 16, 2003, IP/03/1028.
155. *Nintendo II*, D.Comm. D.Comm. Oct. 30, 2002, 2003 OJ L 255/33, points 276–277. *See Van Doren + Q v. Lifestyle sports*, ECJ April 8, 2003, C-244/00, para. 21 (identifying the parallel exporter would be liable to dry out immediately the supply source).
156. *JCB Service*, CFI Jan. 13, 2004, T-67/01, para. 13.
157. *Opel*, CFI Oct. 21, 2003, T-368/00, paras 97–104.
158. Guidelines, point 51 and Section B.5(e) *infra*.
159. Guidelines, points 50, 161, 178. In the case of higher market shares active sales bans are unlikely to be exempted: Guidelines, points 166, 180, unless they are limited in time: Guidelines, point 183.
160. *SABA I*, ECJ Oct. 25, 1977, 1977 ECR 1875, paras 28–29. *See* Article 4 (1) (b) (ii) of Regulation 1400/2002 on motor vehicles.

- restrictions of sales to non-authorized dealers by members of a selective distribution system;[161]
- field-of-use restrictions, i.e. restrictions of the buyer's ability to sell components, supplied for the purposes of incorporation, to customers who could use them to manufacture the same type of goods.[162]

The blacklisted territorial restrictions imposed on the *buyer* include their substitutes, such as refusal to supply,[163] reduction or limitation of supplied volumes,[164] application of lower rebates,[165] e.g. by excluding export sales from the bonus system,[166] or of higher prices in the case of export ('dual pricing'),[167] threat of termination,[168] or tracing sources of parallel trade.[169] However, these means must be an integral part of an agreement ('concurrence of wills' or 'joint intention'[170]) and not a merely unilateral conduct without express or implied acquiescence by the other partners.[171]

161. These obligations on selected dealers were held the corollary of the requirement that only dealers with the appropriate technical qualifications were admitted to the network and therefore did not infringe Article 81 (1) (*SABA I*, ECJ Oct. 25, 1977, 1977 ECR 1875, paras 26–27). However, under Regulation 2790/1999 they are exempted up to a market share of 30%, which implies the need of an individual clearance in cases exceeding this market share threshold: Guidelines, point 188.
162. E.g. in the motor vehicle sector, *see* Article 4 (1) (b) (iv) of Regulation 1400/2002.
163. *Tretorn*, D.Comm. Dec. 22, 1994, 1994 OJ L 378/45.
164. *Volkswagen*, CFI July 6, 2000, 2000 ECR II-2707, paras 79–89, *aff'd* ECJ Sept. 18, 2003, C-338/00, para. 67; *Sandoz*, D.Comm. July 13, 1987, 1987 OJ L 222/28, 32; *Opel*, D.Com. Sept. 9, 2000, 2001 OJ L 59/1, point 112; *Daimler/Chrysler*, D.Comm. Oct. 10, 2001, 2002 OJ L 257/1.
165. *Volkswagen*, CFI July 6, 2000, 2000 ECR II-2707, paras 48–49, *aff'd* ECJ Sept. 18, 2003, C-338/00, paras 44–49; *JCB*, D.Comm. Dec. 21, 2000, 2002 OJ L 69/1.
166. *Opel*, D.Comm. Sept. 20, 2000, 2001 OJ L 59/1, points 113–115, *aff'd* CFI Oct. 21, 2003, T-368/00, paras 97–105; *Volkswagen*, ECJ Sept. 18, 2003, C-338/00P, para. 66 ('15% rule', under which, for the calculation of the bonus, all sales were to be taken into account but those made outside the contract territory would be taken into account only up to a maximum of 15% of total sales achieved by the dealer).
167. *Glaxo Wellcome*, D.Comm. May 8, 2001, 2001 OJ L 302/1, points 119–125.
168. Guidelines, point 49. *See* in greater detail Section B.10.(b).
169. *Nintendo*, D.Comm. Oct. 30, 2002, 2003 OJ L 255/33, points 276–277 (although not sufficiently proved in this case). However, numbering the products was held ancillary to the implementation of a selective distribution system in *SABA I*, ECJ Oct. 25, 1977, 1977 ECR 1875, para. 20.
170. *Bayer*, CFI Oct. 26, 2000, 2000 ECR II-3383, paras 66–71. *See also Volkswagen*, CFI July 6, 2000, 2000 ECR II-2713, paras 48–49, *aff'd* ECJ Sept. 18, 2003, C-338/00, paras 60–67; *Opel*, D.Comm. Sept. 20, 2000, 2001 OJ L 59/1; *Volkswagen II*, D.Comm. June 29, 2001, 2001 OJ L 262/14; *rev'd* CFI Dec. 3, 2003, T-208/01.
171. *Bayer*, fn. 170, paras 66–72 and 114–124; *Nintendo II*, D.Comm. Oct. 30, 2002, 2003 OJ L 255/33, point 251; unilateral conduct being only prohibited if it constitutes an abuse of a dominant position in the sense of Article 82: *ibid.* para. 180.

By contrast, territorial restrictions imposed on the *supplier* are covered by the general exemption provision of Article 2 (1).

4. Evaluation of the Parties' Market Shares

(a) Market Share Thresholds

***De Minimis* Notice Unaffected.**

According to the Commission's 2001 Notice on Agreements of Minor Importance,[172] vertical agreements entered into by companies whose market share do not exceed 15% and which do not include 'hardcore' restrictions are generally considered as falling outside the scope of Article 81 (1). This notice is not affected by Regulation 2790/1999.[173]

New Maximum Thresholds: 30%.

According to Article 3, the block exemption applies on the condition that the market share held by the supplier does not exceed 30% of the relevant market on which it sells the contract goods or services, whereas in the case of vertical agreements containing exclusive supply obligations the market share threshold of 30% may not be exceeded on the market on which the buyer (within the meaning of Article 1 (g)) purchases the contract goods or services.[174] The Guidelines define the relevant geographic market as the market on which the supplier sells 'to his buyers',[175] which is, according to the *Michelin* case to which the Guidelines refer, the market on which buyers are subject to restrictive practices, thereby excluding other markets on which the same supplier sells to other distinct buyers.[176] In the case of an agreement which contains exclusive distribution *and* exclusive purchasing obligations the exemption only applies when neither the supplier nor the buyer has a market share exceeding 30%. However, the block exemption *continues* to apply:

- if the market share exceeds 30% but not 35% for a period of two consecutive calendar years (Article 9 (2) (c));

172. 2001 OJ C 368/13, thereby increasing the vertical threshold of the 1986 notice (5%) and of the 1999 Notice (10%).
173. Guidelines, points 8–11.
174. A higher market share of the other party who is *not* subject to the 30% market share threshold (even a dominant position) does not preclude the applicability of the regulation, without prejudice, however, to the application of Article 82 (recital 16).
175. Guidelines, point 91.
176. *Michelin I*, ECJ Nov. 9, 1983, 1983 ECR 3461, where the relevant geographic market was the Dutch market on which the buyers were subject to abusive practices although Michelin sold the same products to other buyers Community-wide. *See* Guidelines, points 91 and 92.

– if the market share exceeds 35% for a period of one calendar year (Article 9 (2) (d)). These exceptions presuppose that the agreement was *originally* covered by the block exemption and the parties *acquired* higher market shares in the course of the implementation of the agreement.

(b) Definition of the Relevant Market

Applicability of the Commission Notice on the Definition of the Relevant Market.

The definitions of the relevant product/service market[177] and of the relevant geographic market are based on the criteria developed in the Commission's 1997 Notice.[178] The definition of the relevant product/service market depends primarly on substitutability from the buyer's perspective,[179] which may be based on consumer preferences and lead to narrowly defined markets.[180]

Portfolio of Products.

Where a supplier uses the same distribution agreement to distribute several goods/services ('portfolio of products') the entire portfolio may determine the relevant market when the portfolios, and not the individual products or services, are regarded as substitutes by the buyers and, in view of the market share threshold, be covered by the block exemption; in other cases the block exemption applies only to those goods and services for which its conditions are fulfilled.[181] Under the merger control regulation, the Court of First Instance affirmed that a merger may have anticompetitive effects by combining several brands and that the Commission was therefore right in taking account of portfolio effects.[182] This judgment may be interpreted as confirming the relevance of a portfolio of products for defining the relevant market.

Original Equipment and Spare Parts.

Where a supplier produces original equipment and the repair or replacement parts for this equipment, the relevant market may be the original equipment market

177. In the case of franchising agreements the relevant market is that of the franchisee's services to the consumers since the franchisor (e.g. McDonald's) normally does not sell any product to its franchisees.
178. Notice on the definition of the relevant market, 1997 OJ C 372/3. *See* Guidelines, point 88.
179. Guidelines, points 88, 91. The relevant product market may therefore be limited to intermediate goods or services or to the original equipment market, Guidelines, point 96, or the primary or secondary market: *see Pelikan/Kyocera*, Twenty-fifth Report on Competition Policy, point 87 (interrelation between the primary and secondary market for printers and cartridges).
180. *See* Guidelines, point 91. E.g., whisky is distinct from gin and other drinks: *Distillers*, D.Comm. Dec. 13, 1985, 1985 OJ L 369/19.
181. Guidelines, points 68–69 and 91.
182. *BaByliss/SEB-Moulinex*, CFI April 3, 2003, T-114/02, paras 376–377.

including the spare parts. There may also be a separate original equipment market and an after-sales market depending on the circumstances of the case, in particular as the lifetime of the original equipment and repair costs increase.[183] Vertical agreements concluded by a manufacturer of original equipment having a market share exceeding 30% may not be covered by Regulation 2790/1999 or, in the case of spare parts for motor vehicles, by Regulation 1400/2002[184] and need indivividual clearance even if the manufacturer is exposed to considerable potential competition.[185]

(c) Calculation of Market Shares

Criteria for Calculating Market Shares.
The parties' position on the relevant market is reflected not only by their market shares and the market structure, but also by other circumstances, such as the number of outlets tied by restrictive agreements.[186] Article 9 sets out how to calculate market shares. The definition of the relevant market follows the Commission's general Notice on the definition of the relevant market[187] and is explained in greater detail in the Guidelines.[188] The market share is calculated on sales value figures or estimates of the companies concerned, including affiliated companies, which are defined in Article 11, but excluding any in-house production of intermediate goods or services that are used or consumed internally.[189] Normally it is the supplier's market share that is decisive,[190] even if the supplier sells only a small part of its output through tied retailers.[191] In the case of exclusive supply agreements that protect the buyer against the supplier dealing with other buyers, thereby foreclosing the supplier from dealing with other buyers,[192] the application of the exemption depends on the market share of the buyer.[193] Captive production

183. Guidelines, point 94.
184. *See* section B.10.(c) *infra.*
185. Potential competition and in-house production of a component for internal use is not taken into account when *defining* the relevant market but may be important in a competitive analysis of one of the competitive constraints. *See* Notice on the definition of the relevant market, 1997 OJ C 372/3, point 24, and Guidelines, point 98.
186. *De Limitis/Henninger Bräu*, ECJ Feb. 28, 1991, 1991 ECR I-935, para. 21; *Neste Markkinointi/Yötuuli*, ECJ Dec. 7, 2000, 2000 ECR I-11121, paras 25–27; *Inntrepreneur and Spring*, D.Comm. June 29, 2000, 2000 OJ L 195/49, points 61–62.
187. 1997 OJ C 372/3.
188. Guidelines, points 89–95.
189. Guidelines, points 97–99.
190. Article 3 (1). With respect to tying and tied goods and services, *see* Guidelines, point 218–220.
191. An agreement concluded by a supplier having a market share of more than 30% needs individual clearance but the smaller use of a tied dealer network would be an important criterion for granting clearance: Guidelines, points 160, 219–222.
192. Article 1 (c).
193. Article 3 (2).

is not taken into account when calculating market shares but only when assessing the individual merits of a case.[194]

Market Share in the Case of Parallel Networks of Similar Vertical Agreements.
In the case of parallel networks of similar vertical agreements the individual market shares must normally be added up because access to the relevant market may be significantly restricted by their cumulative effect.[195] The parallel existence of similar non-compete agreements 'facilitates' collusion between competing suppliers, and creates entry barriers,[196] thereby leading to the nullity of all similar agreements.[197] However, the individual agreement must contribute *significantly* to the cumulative restrictive effect, the threshold being 5%.[198] Both the existence of a network and the extent of the contribution of an individual agreement are very difficult to prove,[199] leading to legal uncertainty.[200] The new block exemption ends this legal uncertainty by including agreements having a cumulative foreclosure effect, except where the Commission withdraws, by *decision*, in particular cases where the cumulative effects are incompatible with Article 81 (3)[201] or, by *regulation*, where the cumulative market share exceeds 50% of the relevant market.[202] Both the decision and the regulation have a prospective (*ex nunc*) effect and do not affect the past validity of the agreements.

(d) Evaluation of Market Shares

Market Shares as the Most Important but not only Criteria for Measuring Market Power.
If sales are usually the reference to calculate market shares, there are nevertheless

194. Guidelines, point 98.
195. *See* section A.3.(a).
196. Guidelines, point 142.
197. The exemption granted by the Commission to all agreements concluded by a beer supplier with numerous retailers can be appealed individually by one retailer even if this would lead to the prohibition and nullity of the whole system: *see Bass*, D.Comm. June 16, 1999, 1999 OJ L 186/1; *aff'd* CFI March 21, 2002, 2002 ECR II-2085, paras 32–34.
198. New *De Minimis* Notice, point 9 (2001 OJ C 149/18); Guidelines, point 142. *See* Section A.3.(c) *supra*.
199. Guidelines, points 71–79.
200. *See* Oberlandesgericht (Higher Court) Karlsruhe, Jan. 30, 1990, WuWE OLG 4575.
201. Article 6 of Regulation 2790/99. National authorities have similar powers: Article 7 of Regulation 2790/99.
202. Article 8 of Regulation 2790/99. Example: *Shaw, Falla/Whitbread*, CFI March 21, 2002, 2002 ECR II-2033 (58%). A cumulative foreclosure effect is unlikely to exist if less than 30% of the relevant market is covered by the network of parallel agreements: *De Minimis* Notice, 2001 OJ C 368/13, point II.8.

other indications such as, in particular, capacity and the number of market players, both on the supply and the demand side.[203]

Potential Competitors.
Potential competition is not taken into account when *defining* the relevant market but only when *evaluating* the position of the parties on the narrowly defined relevant market, which is required where the parties' market shares are so high as to raise concerns from a competition point of view.[204] This makes the block exemption difficult to apply where vertical restraints are agreed on a *new* market, e.g. on the internet market on which the parties have substantial market shares but are subject to potential competition by similar e-commerce platforms.[205]

Buyers' Power.
The importance of the buyer on the downstream market is a factor which determines whether negative anticompetitive effects may be expected. The anticompetitive effects may increase in cases where the buyer holds a share which exceeds 30% on the downstream market and all the more where the buyer holds a dominant position.[206]

5. Distribution Agreements

(a) Distribution through Exclusive Distributors

Single Branding Agreements.
Under the heading of single branding come those agreements that have as their main element that the buyer is obliged or induced to concentrate his orders for a particular type of good or service with one supplier,[207] usually limited to a sales area which has been assigned exclusively to that buyer.[208] The supplier is usually subject to the obligation to supply certain goods or services only to the other party[209] and not to other distributors or users. The supplier may reserve to itself

203. Notice on the relevant market, 1997 OJ C 372/3, point 54.
204. Notice on the Definition of the Relevant Market, point 24. Example under the merger control regulation: *Tetra Laval/Sidel*, D.Comm. Oct. 30, 2001, M.2416, points 291, 325–331 (prohibition decision, however annulled by CFI Oct. 24, 2002, 2002 ECR II-4091, paras 321–33, in particular 325).
205. *See* under the merger control regulation: *Babcock Borsig/mg technologies and SAB*, D.Comm. Nov. 8, 2000, M.2172, IP/00/1266. These problems could be avoided it the relevant market included, as under Article 4 (2) of Regulation 2659/2000 on R&D agreements, the products and services 'capable of being improved or replaced' by the contract products or services.
206. Guidelines, point 204.
207. Guidelines, point 106
208. Guidelines, point 161.
209. Article 2 (1). *Cf.* Article 1 of Regulation 1983/83. Article 1 (c).

certain territories and certain groups of customers,[210] or allocate them to other distributors.[211] The buyer is usually subject to an obligation to concentrate his orders for a particular type of good or service on one supplier and to purchase this good or service only from the supplier.[212] This obligation is, in the new terminology of the Regulation, a specific form of, and generally backed by, a non-compete obligation[213] which is exempted for only five years.[214] This five-year limitation does not apply where the contract goods or services are sold by the buyer from premises owned or leased by the supplier from third parties not connected with the buyer, provided that the non-compete obligation does not exceed the period of occupancy of the premises by the buyer. It is permissible for the buyer to be expressly obliged to purchase the totality or more than 80% of the contract goods from the supplier directly or from a third party designated by the supplier,[215] such as:

- by the obligation to purchase his requirements *mainly* from the other party ('quantity forcing'[216]);
- by preferential placement of the contract goods in the dealer's premises as compared to competing goods;[217]
- by the requirement to purchase subject to the condition to purchase another product or service ('tying'[218]); or
- by obligations which have the same economic effect, in particular by exclusionary rebate schemes ('incentive schemes')[219] or 'English clauses', requiring the buyer to report any better offer and allowing it only to accept such an offer when the supplier does not match it.[220]

---

210. Article 4 (b). *Cf.* under Regulation 772/2004 on technology transfer agreements, the compatibility of field-of-use restrictions and similar product market restrictions in the vertical context (Article 4 (1) (i)).
211. This is new, *see* Guidelines, points 178–182. Under the previous regulations individual exemption was necessary and even unlikely as in *BP Kemi/DDSF*, D.Comm. Sept. 5, 1979, 1979 OJ L 286/32 (cease and desist order).
212. Article 1 (c) specifies that the obligation must concern the supply to one buyer *inside the Community*. An obligation not to purchase the goods from a supplier in a third country normally does not infringe Article 81(1)) and therefore does not preclude the applicability of the block exemption; *see Javico/Yves St. Laurent*, ECJ April 28, 1998, 1998 ECR I-1983.
213. *See* in particular *Inntrepreneur and Spring*, D.Comm. June 29, 2000, 2000 OJ L 195/49, points 47–50.
214. Article 5 (a). Under Article 2 (2) (b) of Regulation 1983/83 the exemption of this exclusive purchasing obligation was unlimited in time.
215. Article 1 (b). In practice it will be difficult for the supplier to calculate the buyer's total purchases without knowing the 'purchases of the preceding calendar year' nor the origin of such purchases.
216. Guidelines, points 154–159.
217. *Liebig*, D.Comm. Dec. 21, 1977, 1978 OJ L 53/20.
218. Guidelines, point 106; *see* Section B.10 (g) *infra*.
219. Guidelines, points 138 and 152.
220. Guidelines, point 152.

Multiple Branding Agreements.
Under the heading of multiple branding come those agreements by which various competing suppliers appoint the same retailer, often centrally located[221] and rather specialized in the product.[222] The block exemption applies, provided the suppliers have market shares below the 30% threshold. This corresponds to the Commission's general intention to avoid exclusive ('monopolistic') positions of the exclusive dealer as under Regulation 1400/2002 on Motor Vehicle Distribution and Servicing Agreements.[223] However, in an oligopolistic market there is a risk of collusion between competing suppliers using the same distributor, thereby restricting competition between them and possibly precluding access by other competitors.[224] In the case of such an arrangement with horizontal anticompetitive effects, the block exemption does not apply, in particular in cases in which the majority of suppliers appoint the same dealer in a given area or country. This may be tantamount to joint selling between competitors which clearly infringes Article 81 (1) and is likely to meet the conditions of Article 81 (3) only under exceptional circumstances.[225]

Single Buyer Agreements.
The block exemption applies to exclusive supply agreements, provided that the buyer's market share does not exceed 30%.[226] An exclusive supply obligation means 'any direct or indirect obligation causing the supplier to sell the goods or services specified in the agreement only to one buyer inside the Community ... for resale'.[227] The previous Regulation 1983/83 exempted exclusive supply obligations for resale *within the whole or a defined area of the Common Market*. It may be assumed that the new regulation must be interpreted in the same sense because otherwise the exemption would be limited to very rare cases in which a supplier of a third country assigns one distributor for the whole Community, typically with regard to a new product.[228] The block exemption applies without time limitation, unless the buyer is expressly subject to a non-compete clause in which case the non-compete obligation must not exceed five years.

---

221. *See*, however, *Ivoclar*, D.Comm. Nov. 27, 1985, 1985 OJ L 369/1, 4.
222. Guidelines, points 164 and 176.
223. Although the competing distribution activity of the dealer is conditional upon separate sales premises, a distinct legal entity and separate management may be sufficient.
224. This explains why the block exemption does not apply to the obligation on members of a selective distribution system not to sell brands of *particular* competing suppliers (Article 5 (c)).
225. *See SCPA/Kali+Salz*, D.Comm. May 11, 1973, 1973 OJ L 217/3 (prohibition decision).
226. Article 3 (2). The applicability of the block exemption therefore depends on the degree of foreclosure of other buyers on the upstream market: Guidelines, point 214.
227. Article 1 (c). The draft regulation did not contain the wording 'inside the Community'.
228. *See* the Commission's negative clearance in *Mertens/Bendix*, June 1, 1964, 1964 OJ 1426.

Assessment of the Most Common Restrictions.

(i) *Territorial and customer restrictions on the supplier*: The obligation to supply goods or services, within the area assigned to the exclusive distributor, only to that distributor and not to other distributors or customers[229] (either actively or passively) is exempted.[230] The obligation on the supplier to sell the goods or services only to one buyer inside the Community[231] is block exempted without time limitation,[232] provided the buyer's market share does not exceed 30%.[233]

(ii) *Territorial and customer restrictions on the buyer*: The obligation on the buyer not to sell actively into the territory or to customers[234] reserved to the supplier or attributed to other buyers (dealers)[235] and the obligation imposed on wholesalers not to sell directly to final customers (which are reserved to the retail dealers)[236] are exempted, whereas bans on passive sales constitute a hardcore restriction and are likely to be heavily fined.[237] An active sales ban may be interpreted in the same sense as under the previous Regulation 1983/83 as an 'obligation to refrain, outside the contract territory and in relation to the contract goods, from seeking customers, from establishing any branch and from maintaining any distribution depot'.[238] Passive sales include sales via the Internet,[239] except sending unsolicited e-mails to individual customers or groups of customers.[240] Other impermissible forms of export prohibitions likely to carve out national markets and to prevent customers from profiting from parallel trade and more attractive prices in other member states[241] include:

229. Including certain groups of customers, *see* Article 4 (b) first indent.
230. Article 2 (1); *cf.* Article 1 of Regulation 1983/83.
231. Article 1 (c).
232. Article 2 (1).
233. Article 3 (2).
234. The term 'customers' refers mainly to 'classes' of customers (Guidelines, point 178) without excluding particular customers. *See*, however, *BP Kemi/DDSF*, D.Comm. Sept. 5, 1979, 1979 OJ L 286/32 (cease and desist order).
235. Article 4 (b), first indent ('free rider problem' Guidelines, point 116).
236. Article 4 (b), second indent. This obligation used to be considered as not falling within the scope of Article 81 (1): *SABA*, ECJ Oct. 25, 1977, 1977 ECR 1875, paras 28–30; *Grundig II*, D.Comm. July 10, 1985, 1985 OJ L 233/1, 5.
237. Article 4 (b). *Cf.* Article 2 (2) (c) of Regulation 1983/83. *See Volkswagen*, CFI July 6, 2000, 2000 ECR II-2713, para. 241; *Editions Nathan*, D.Comm. July 5, 2000, 2001 OJ L 54/1; *Daimler/Chrysler*, D.Comm. Oct. 10, 2001, IP/01/1394 (fine of EUR 72 million).
238. Article 2 (2) (c) of the previous Regulation 1983/83 on exclusive distribution agreements.
239. *See German/Austrian Book Price Maintenance*, IP/00/651 of June, 22, 2000. Passive sales will therefore increase substantially and may blur the fundamental distinction between 'active' and 'passive' sales.
240. Guidelines, point 51. *See*, in greater detail, section 5 (e) *infra*.
241. *See Nintendo II*, D.Comm. Oct. 30, 2002, 2003 OJ L 255/33 (collusion between a supplier and seven distributors of video games intended to prevent parallel trade and to keep prices artificially high).

- any measure preventing dealers or users from obtaining properly marketed contract goods outside the contract territory, in particular by applying higher prices in the case of export[242] or by preventing the exclusive dealer from advertising its goods or services;[243]
- by applying loyalty discounts,[244]
- by excluding export sales from a bonus system,[245]
- by limiting the quantities supplied,[246]
- by controlling systematically the dealer's sales,[247] or
- by abusively asserting intellectual property rights.[248]

(iii) *Territorial and customer restrictions on sales outside the EU* are normally unlikely appreciably to affect trade between member states.[249] This applies to obligations on dealers not to export into third countries, thereby preventing the re-importation into the Common Market,[250] except in the case of an oligopolistic market structure within the Common Market and appreciable price differences[251] and in the context of a broader horizontal concertation.[252]

---

242. *See Bayer/Adalat*, D.Comm. Jan. 10, 1996, 1996 OJ L 201/1, points 29–31 (*rev'd* because of lacking 'agreement': CFI Oct. 26, 2000, 2000 ECR II-3383).
243. *Inntrepreneur and Spring*, D.Comm. June 29, 2000, 2000 OJ L 195/49, points 65–70.
244. *See VW/Audi*, D.Comm. Jan. 28, 1998, 1998 OJ L 124/60; *aff'd* CFI July 6, 2000, 2000 ECR II-2713, at paras 48–49. *See*, however, *Solvay/Sisecam*, Comfort letter (point 22), 1999 OJ C 272/14; 1999–5 CMLR 1444 ('commercial rebates' accepted in the context of a production joint venture).
245. *Opel*, CFI Oct. 21, 2003, T-368/00, paras 97–105; *Volkswagen*, ECJ Sept. 18, 2003, C-38/00P, para. 66.
246. *Daimler/Chrysler*, D.Comm. Oct. 10, 2001, 2002 OJ L 257/1. *See Johnson & Johnson*, D.Comm. Nov. 25, 1980, 1980 OJ L 377/16; *Sandoz*, D.Comm. July 13, 1987, 1987 OJ L 222/28; *Volkswagen*, CFI July 6, 2000, 2000 ECR II-2713, paras 79–89. However, unilaterally limiting quantities is not prohibited under Article 81 (1): *Bayer*, CFI Oct. 26, 2000, 2000 ECR II-3383, paras 66–70; *Opel*, CFI Oct. 21, 2003, T-368/00, paras 78–88 (because of lacking an 'agreement'); or limiting quantities by governmental intervention: *Asia Motors*, CFI Oct. 26, 2000, 2000 ECR II-3456 (because of lacking an agreement 'between enterprises').
247. *Volkswagen*, CFI July 6, 2000, 2000 ECR II-2713, para. 178.
248. *See Grundig/Consten*, ECJ July 13, 1966, 1966 ECR 299; *Upjohn/Paranova*, ECJ Oct. 12, 1999, 1999 ECR I-6927 (incompatibility with Articles 28 and 30 of asserting intellectual property rights in order to prevent parallel imports of legally re-branded goods); *Texaco/Preem*, Twenty-seventh Report on Competition Policy, pp. 131–132.
249. *Javico/Yves St. Laurent ECJ*, April 28, 1998, 1998 ECR I-1983; *Iqbal*, Twenty-first Report on Competition Policy, p. 334. *See*, however, *Solvay/Sisecam*, D.Comm. Sept. 25, 1999, 1999–5 CMLR 1444, point 21.
250. *Grosfillex/Fillistorf*, D.Comm. March 11, 1964, 1964 OJ 915; *Distillers*, D.Comm. Dec. 20, 1977, 1978 OJ L 50/16 (negative clearance).
251. *Yves St. Javico/Yves St. Laurent*, ECJ April 28, 1998, 1998 ECR I-1983, point 1 of the operative part. However, in the case of an oligopolistic structure (characterized by market shares exceeding 30%) the block exemption does not apply anyway.
252. *Sugar*, ECJ Dec. 16, 1975, 1975 ECR 1663, paras 558–602; *Solvay/Sisecam*, D.Comm. Sept. 25, 1999, 1999–5 CMLR 1444, point 21 (clearance of a joint venture after removal of the

However, import into the Common Market may constitute an infringement of industrial property rights, in particular trademarks, provided the product in question has not been put on one of the EEA markets by the owner itself or with its consent.[253]

(iv) *Territorial and customer restrictions imposed on the customers of the buyer* (second hand export bans) constitute a hardcore restriction.[254]

(v) *Non-compete clauses*: Non-compete clauses imposed on the buyer[255] are exempted only for five years, except where the goods or services are sold by the buyer from premises owned or leased by the supplier; in this case the non-compete clause may be imposed for the entire period of the occupancy.[256] After the termination of the agreement, a non-compete clause may be imposed for one year with respect to competing goods or services, provided it is limited to the premises of the dealer's activity;[257] a longer duration is permitted if it is indispensable to protect know-how which is still secret and substantial.[258] Non-compete clauses, including exclusive purchasing obligations that are agreed for a longer period need individual exemption, even if the parties' market share does not exceed 30%.

(vi) *Resale price maintenance* constitutes a hardcore restriction. However, the supplier may impose a maximum sale price or supply a recommended resale

---

obligation imposed on the distributor outside the Common Market not to resell the product (soda) within the Common Market).

253. *Phyteron International/Jean Bourdon*, ECJ March 20, 1997, 1997 ECR I-1729, para. 24; *Silhouette International/Hartlauer*, ECJ June 16, 1998, 1998 ECR I-4799, paras 25–29 (principle of Community exhaustion but no exhaustion if imported from a non-Community country). The consent of the right holder to the marketing within the EEA of products which have previously been placed on the market outside the EEA by the proprietor or with his consent may be implied only if it is unequivocally demonstrated that the proprietor has renounced his right to oppose placing the goods on the market within the EEA: *Davidoff/Levi Strauss*, ECJ Nov. 20, 2001, 2001 ECR I-8691, operative part point 1. However, the EFTA Court of Justice ruled in the case *Maglite* Dec. 3, 1997, E-2/97) that the Council Trade Mark Directive 89/104/EEC is to be interpreted as leaving it up to the EEA countries (such as Norway) to introduce or maintain the principle of international exhaustion of trade mark rights.

254. Article 4 (b), first indent: 'where such a restriction does not limit sales by the customers of the buyer'.

255. With regard to wholesalers, *see* Guidelines, point 175.

256. Article 5 (a). This corresponds to the exceptions provided for under the previous Regulation 1984/83 for beer and service-station agreements (Articles 8 (2) and 12 (2)). *See Inntrepreneur and Spring*, D.Comm. June 29, 2000, 2000 OJ L 195/49, point 33.

257. Regulation 1983/83 did not exempt any post-term non-compete obligation (*see* German Supreme Court, March 28, 2001, WuWE 2001–10, 979), just as Regulation 1400/2002 (Article 5 (1) (d)).

258. Article 5 (b). An obligation not to divulge know-how which is still secret is generally considered as ancillary and does not infringe Article 81 (1). *See Yves Rocher*, D.Comm. Dec. 17, 1986, 1987 OJ L 8/49, point 48.

price, provided that they do not amount to a fixed or minimum resale price as a result of pressure from, or incentives offered by, any of the parties.[259]

(b) Distribution through Selected Dealers

Supplier's Freedom of Choice.
A supplier is basically free to select the distribution channels and distributors it considers best for its products and services including implementing in one member state of a distribution system different from that used in another member state.[260] A supplier is also not prohibited – as long as it does not hold a dominant position – from treating similarly-placed consumers differently and is under no obligation to supply. Many manufacturers, especially of consumer products, prefer to have their products distributed by selected specialist wholesalers and retailers who employ trained sales staff, provide customer services and who are prepared to undertake certain sales commitments, in terms of carrying a full range, maintaining sufficient inventories and promoting and displaying the product.[261] In contrast to exclusive distribution and exclusive purchasing arrangements, such a 'selective distribution' or dealership system does not assign an exclusive territory to the dealer or prevent him from dealing in competing products. However, it results in a series of contractual relationships between the supplier and his dealers whereby only a selected group of dealers gain the right to distribute a certain brand of product, the latter being prohibited from reselling the goods to dealers outside the system. The Commission's practice was based on established case law.[262] The new regulation takes account of this case law. Its applicability is, however, limited to the general market share thresholds.

Qualitative v. Quantitative Selective Distribution Systems.
Under the heading of selective distribution systems come those agreements by which a supplier selects his distributors on the basis of 'qualitative' criteria linked to the nature of the product or service, such as the training of sales personnel, the service provided at the point of sale and a certain range of products being sold (*qualitative selective distribution system*). Selective distribution systems may also be established on the basis of 'quantitative' criteria that limit the number of dealers according to the density in terms of population or to quantitative commitments in terms of the proportion of the range to be carried,

---

259. Article 4 (a).
260. *Vichy*, D.Comm. Jan. 11, 1991, 1991 OJ L 75/57, *aff'd* CFI Feb. 27, 1992, 1992 ECR II-415 (distribution of cosmetics).
261. Rather than through non-specialist outlets, such as department stores, supermarkets, self-service-convenience stores and 'cash-and-carry' wholesalers.
262. Leading cases: *SABA II*, ECJ Oct. 22, 1986, 1986 ECR 3021, paras 40–42; *Grundig II*, D.Comm. July 10, 1985, 1985 OJ L 233/1.

the level of stocks to be held and minimum purchase quantities (*quantitative selective distribution system*).[263]

Application of the Block Exemption to Qualitative *and* Quantitative Distribution Systems.

Qualitative selective distribution systems have long been held compatible with Article 81 (1) where the nature of the product or service requires a specialized shop, technical skills[264] or high standing (luxurious).[265] However, the criteria for selecting dealers must be applied uniformly and without discrimination, and admission to the network must not be linked to any criteria other than objective selection based on qualitative criteria, in particular without implementation of a resale price maintenance scheme.[266]

Quantitative selective distribution systems have been held to infringe Article 81 (1), and formerly were much less likely to be considered as fulfilling the exemption conditions of Article 81 (3).[267] The new block exemption regulation exempts *both* forms irrespective of the nature of the goods or services,[268] provided the supplier's market share does not exceed 30% of the relevant market.[269] However, where the nature of the product does *not* require selective distribution, such a distribution system does not generally bring about sufficient efficiency and may have appreciable anticompetitive effects, in which case the Commission has to withdraw (*ex nunc*) the benefit of the block exemption.[270]

---

263. Guidelines, points 184–186.
264. Examples include consumer electronics equipment (*Grundig II*, D.Comm. July 10, 1985, 1985 OJ L 233/1), photographic products (*DuPont/Adox*, D.Comm. June 14, 1973, 1973 OJ L 194/27), household appliances (*Krups*, D.Comm. April 17, 1980, 1980 OJ L 120/26), personal computers (*IBM Personal Computer*, D.Comm. April 18, 1984, 1984 OJ L 118/24), pharmaceutical but not paramedical products (*Bomee Stichting*, D.Comm. Nov. 21, 1975, 1975 OJ L 329/30), shoes (*Charles Jourdan*, D.Comm. Dec. 2, 1988, 1989 OJ L 35/31), tableware (*Villeroy & Boch*, D.Comm. Dec. 16, 1985, 1985 OJ L 376/15), and plant varieties (*Sicosov*, D.Comm. Dec. 14, 1998, 1999 OJ L 4/27).
265. Examples of luxurious products include jewelery (*Murat*, D.Comm. Dec. 5, 1983, 1983 OJ L 348/20), and perfumes (*Yves St. Laurent*, CFI Dec. 12, 1986, 1986 ECR II-1851, para 179).
266. *See L'Oréal*, ECJ Dec. 11, 1980, 1980 ECR 3775, para. 16.
267. Guidelines, point 73. Examples of products which justified quantitative selective distribution include clocks and watches (*Omega*, D.Comm. Oct. 28, 1970, 1970 OJ L 242/22; *Junghans*, D.Comm. Dec. 21, 1976, 1977 OJ L 30/10), motor vehicles (*BMW*, D.Comm. Dec. 13, 1974, 1975 OJ L 29/1), dental supplies (*Ivoclar*, D.Comm. Nov. 27, 1985, 1985 OJ L 369/1), and newspaper and magazines (*Binon/AMP*, ECJ July 3, 1985, 1985 ECR 2015, paras 27–35).
268. The selection criteria related to the nature of the goods or services remain decisive for the individual assessment of a selective distribution system.
269. Guidelines, point 187. *See Leclerc/Yves St.Laurent*, CFI Dec. 12, 1996, 1996 ECR II-1851, paras 71–78 and 106; *Yves Rocher*, D.Comm. Dec. 17, 1986, 1987 OJ L 8/49.
270. Guidelines, point 186. In *De Beers* Supplier of Choice Agreement, D.Comm. Jan. 16, 2003, IP/03/64, the block exemption did not apply because of market shares exceeding the maximum thresholds of the regulation.

This ends a formerly controversial discussion of whether a qualitative selective distribution system infringes Article 81 (1) only because it includes certain minimum quantity obligations ('quantity forcing').[271] A qualitative selective distribution system combined with minimum sales obligations is now considered equivalent to a 'quantitative' selective distribution system because it *indirectly* reduces the number of the selected dealers. When applied by one supplier whose market share does not exceed the 30% threshold, a quantitative selective distribution system is exempted under the regulation.[272] In the case of parallel selective distribution systems based on qualitative *or* quantitative selection criteria that are entered into by suppliers with individual market shares not exceeding 30%, the block exemption still applies regardless the nature of the product concerned.[273] The question whether the nature of the product or services justifies a qualitative or quantitative selective distribution system is therefore relevant only in those cases where the market share limit of 30% is exceeded and individual assessment is required.[274]

Common Issues.

Both qualitative and quantitative selective distribution systems normally provide for obligations on the supplier not to appoint other dealers who do not fulfil the selection criteria and to refrain from any of its own marketing or sales activity in the area assigned to the selected dealer. These restrictions on the supplier receive the benefit of the block exemption.[275] Both forms of selective distribution system normally imply the obligation not to resell to dealers who are not admitted to the supplier's network (an ancillary restriction considered not to infringe Article 81 (1)),[276] whereas restrictions on active and passive resales to other members of the network and to end users have long been prohibited and now belong to the hardcore restrictions under Article 4 (c) and (d) of the new regulation.

Assessment of the Most Common Restrictions in Selective Distribution Systems.

(i) *Territorial restrictions on the supplier*: The obligation on the supplier to refrain from any of its own marketing or sales activity in the dealer's assigned area is covered by the block exemption.[277]

---

271. *Grundig II*, D.Comm. July 10, 1985, 1985 OJ L 233/1; *Leclerc/Yves St. Laurent*, CFI Dec. 12, 1996, 1996 ECR II-1961.
272. Guidelines, points 186–187.
273. Guidelines, point 186. However, the benefit of the exemption may be withdrawn where the cumulative application of selective distribution systems impedes access of competing suppliers (i.e., general price discounters): Guidelines, point 198. *See also Yves St. Laurent*, CFI Dec. 12, 1996, 1996 ECR II-2109, paras 40–42.
274. *See* section B.10.(e) *infra*.
275. Article 2 (1). *See Yves Rocher*, D.Comm. Dec. 17, 1986, 1987 OJ L 8/49, point 54.
276. *SABA I*, ECJ Oct. 25, 1977, 1977 ECR 1875, paras 26–27.
277. Article 2 (1).

(ii) *Territorial and customer restrictions on the selected dealers*: The restriction of active or passive sales to end users by the selected dealers operating at the retail level constitutes a hardcore restriction.[278] A ban on internet sales is a restraint of sales to customers and not covered by Regulation 2790/1999.[279] However, the selected dealer may be obliged to operate only from the authorized place of business[280] and not to sell to non-authorized dealers;[281] parallel trade within the franchise 'family' must not be restricted.[282] A dealer at the wholesale level may be subject to the obligation not to sell to end users.[283]

(iii) *Territorial and customer restrictions on sales outside the EU* are unlikely to infringe Article 81 (1), unless they have an appreciable effect on the pattern of trade between member states. Therefore, obligations on dealers not to export into third countries, thereby preventing the re-importation into the Common Market,[284] do not infringe Article 81 (1) except in the case of an oligopolistic market structure within the Common Market supported by territorial restrictions that preserve appreciable price differences which are not the result of transport costs and import taxes.[285] However, import into the Common Market may constitute an infringement of industrial property rights, in particular trademarks, provided the product in question has not been put on one of the EEA markets by the owner itself or with its consent.[286]

---

278. Article 4 (c). *See Volkswagen*, CFI July 6, 2000, 2000 ECR II-2713, para. 241; *JCB*, D.Comm. Dec. 21, 2000, 2002 OJ L 69/1; *Yamaha*, D.Comm. July 16, 2003, IP/03/1028 (obligation on official dealers to sell only to final customers and to purchase exclusively from Yamaha subsidiaries, thereby precluding parallel trade).
279. *Yamaha*, D.Comm. July 16, 2003, IP/03/1028 (obligation on the official dealers to contact Yamaha before exporting via the Internet). *See Yves St. Laurent II*, May 17, 2001, IP/01/713 (comfort letter following amendment). *See Martinez-Lopez*, DG IV Comp. News Letter, 2001–2, p. 7.
280. *JCB*, D.Comm. Dec. 21, 2000, 2002 OJ L 69/1.
281. Article 4 (b), third sub-paragraph.
282. *Volkswagen*, CFI July 6, 2000, 2000 ECR II-2713, para. 241; *Tretorn*, D.Comm. Dec. 22, 1994, 1994 OJ L 378/45, points 57–58; *B&W Loudspeakers*, IP/00/1418; *JCB*, D.Comm. Dec. 21, 2000, 2002 OJ L 69/1.
283. Article 4 (b), second sub-paragraph.
284. *Grosfillex/Fillistorf*, D.Comm. March 11, 1964, 1964 OJ 915; *Distillers*, D.Comm. Dec. 20, 1977, 1978 OJ L 50/16 (negative clearance).
285. *Yves St. Javico/Yves St. Laurent*, ECJ April 28, 1998, 1998 ECR I-1983, point 1 of the operative part.
286. *Phyteron International/Jean Bourdon*, ECJ March 20, 1997, 1997 ECR I-1729, para. 24; *Silhouette International/Hartlauer*, ECJ June 16, 1998, 1998 ECR I-4799, paras 25–29 (principle of Community exhaustion but no exhaustion if imported from a non-Community country). The consent of the right holder to the marketing within the EEA of products which have previously been placed on the market outside the EEA by the proprietor or with his consent may be implied only if it is unequivocally demonstrated that the proprietor has renounced his right to oppose placing the goods on the market within the EEA: *Davidoff/Levi Strauss*, ECJ Nov. 20, 2001, 2001 ECR I-8691, paras 60 and 66; *see Nintendo II*, D.Comm. Oct. 30, 2002, 2003 OJ L 255/33, para. 62. However, the EFTA Court of Justice ruled in the case *Maglite* Dec. 3, 1997,

(iv) *Non-compete clauses*: An obligation imposed on the selected dealer not to engage in any competing activities has been held necessary to protect the supplier's commercial know-how that has been disclosed to the dealer and is therefore ancillary.[287] Any direct or indirect obligation causing the members of a selective distribution system not to sell the brands of *particular* competing suppliers does not receive the benefit of the block exemption.[288]

(v) *Resale price maintenance* constitutes a hardcore restriction,[289] including regulating bonuses and discounts across different territories.[290] However, the supplier may impose a *maximum* resale price or supply a recommended resale price, provided they do not amount to a fixed or minimum sale price as a result of pressure from, or incentives offered by, any of the parties.[291]

(c) Distribution through Franchisees

Franchising.

Franchising entails a system of contracts through which the franchisor furnishes know-how about the operation of a business to a number of independent firms called franchisees, and the franchisees sell goods or services under the franchisor's trade name using the franchisor's distinctive business format and promotional methods.[292] Franchise agreements therefore combine elements of selective distribution with elements of a know-how and trademark license. Most of the obligations contained in franchise agreements can be assessed as ancillary and necessary to protect the franchisor's intellectual property rights or to maintain the common identity and reputation of the franchised network and therefore do not infringe Article 81 (1). However, the inclusion of franchise agreements in the block exemption was necessary with respect to the restrictions on sales by the franchisee, in particular location and non-compete clauses.[293] The

---

E-2/97 that the Council Trade Mark Directive 89/104/EEC is to be interpreted as leaving it up to the EEA countries (such as Norway) to introduce or maintain the principle of international exhaustion of trade mark rights. With respect to the burden of proof *see Van Doren + Q v. Lifestyle sports*, ECJ April 8, 2003, C-244/00, paras 25–42.

287. *See Yves Rocher*, D.Comm. Dec. 17, 1986, 1987 OJ L 8/49, point 47.

288. Article 5 (c). The reason may be that such a non-compete clause that is limited to *particular* suppliers may indicate a collusion between the contract supplier and these 'particular' competitors.

289. Article 4 (a). *See B&W Loudspeakers*, IP/00/1418 of Dec. 6, 2000; *Volkswagen II*, D.Comm. June 29, 2001, 2001 OJ L 262/14; *rev'd* CFI Dec. 3, 2003, T-208/01.

290. *JCB*, D.Comm. Dec. 21, 2000, 2002 OJ L 69/1.

291. *See* in the similar case of franchising agreements: *Pronuptia*, ECJ Jan. 28, 1986, 1986 ECR 353, para. 25.

292. *See Pronuptia*, ECJ Jan. 28, 1986, 1986 ECR 353, and Guidelines, point 199.

293. Article 4 (b) and Article 5 (a) and (c) and Guidelines, point 201 (the Commission's interpretation in the Guidelines goes further than the regulation itself).

franchisor may be subject to the obligation not to appoint other franchisees and not to engage in any of its own marketing activity in the franchisee's area. The franchisee may be obliged to purchase the contract goods or services only from members of the franchise 'family' (franchisor and other franchisees) or other companies designated by the franchisor.[294] The Commission's practice was based on case law[295] and the former block exemption Regulation 4087/88.[296] The new regulation integrates this regulation without substantial amendments, except that the maximum market share thresholds also apply to franchise agreements. Manufacturing franchise agreements (agreements under which the franchisee manufactures goods in accordance with the franchisor's instructions and know-how and resells the goods under the franchisor's trademark) are not covered by Regulation 2790/1999 (which is limited to distribution) but may come within Regulation 772/2004.[297]

Assessment of the Most Common Restrictions.

(i) *Territorial and customer restrictions on the franchisor*: The obligation on the franchisor not to compete against the franchisee within a specific area is exempted.[298]

(ii) *Territorial and customer restrictions on the franchisee*: The obligation on the franchisee to operate only out of an authorized place of business (location clause) is block exempted,[299] whereas restrictions on active or passive sales by the franchisee to other franchisees, including other dealers authorized by the franchisor,[300] and to any end user are hardcore restrictions.[301]

(iii) *Non-compete clauses*: The obligation on the franchisee to purchase and sell goods or services which are necessary to protect the franchisor's property rights or 'to maintain the common identity and reputation of the franchised network' falls outside Article 81 (1)[302] and therefore does not need to be limited to five years as provided under Article 5 (a) because no exemption is required for such a non-compete obligation irrespective of the parties' market share. The new block exemption exempts tied goods or services and,

294. Articles 1 (b) and 2 (1).
295. Leading cases: *Pronuptia*, ECJ Jan. 28, 1986, 1986 ECR 353; *Charles Jourdan*, D.Comm. Dec. 2, 1988, 1989 OJ L 35/21.
296. 1988 OJ L 359/46.
297. Leading case *Campari*, D.Comm. Dec. 23, 1977, 1978 OJ L 70/69.
298. Article 2 (1).
299. Article 2 (1). *See* Article 2 (c) of Regulation 4087/88.
300. Sales to other dealers outside the franchisor's authorized network (non-franchisees or other dealers) may be prohibited: Article 4 (b) third indent, read in the light of Article 4 (a) of Regulation 4087/88.
301. Article 4 (b).
302. Guidelines, point 200. *See* Article 3 (1) (a) of Regulation 4087/88; *Pronuptia*, ECJ Jan. 28, 1986, 1986 ECR 353, para. 21.

unlike Regulation 4087/88,[303] even provisions preventing the franchisee from obtaining supplies of goods or services from third parties of a quality equivalent (or superior) to those offered by the franchisor. The obligation on the franchisee not to change the location of the contract premises may be imposed while the franchise agreement is in force and for one year after the termination of the agreement, provided it is limited to the contract premises and necessary for protecting the know-how transferred to it.[304]

(iv) *Resale price maintenance* constitutes a hardcore restriction, except that the supplier may impose a *maximum* resale price or supply a *recommended* resale price, [305] provided they do not amount to a fixed or minimum sale price as a result of pressure from, or incentives offered by, any of the parties.

(d) Exclusive Supply Arrangements

Any direct or indirect obligation causing the supplier to sell the goods or services specified in the agreement only to one buyer for the purposes of a specific use is block exempted, provided the buyer's market share does not exceed 30%.[306] Only where the buyer is also committed to a non-compete clause (an obligation not to purchase the contract goods from competing suppliers) must the term of that obligation be limited to five years.[307] This provision does *not* concern most intermediary or components supply agreements since the supplier normally reserves the possibility to supply other buyers. Furthermore, subcontracting agreements that include an exclusive supply obligation may be justified in order to avoid the risk that any supply to third parties of products manufactured using the technology and equipment provided by the principal reveals the know-how or confidential information. Accordingly, such agreements are normally considered as not giving grounds for objection under Article 81 (1).[308]

(e) Distribution through E-Commerce[309]

No Distinct Rules.

As a general rule, e-commerce is not different from any other kind of transaction: it simply is a special electronic means of commercial communication in the

303. *Cf.* Article 5 (b) of Regulation 4087/88.
304. Article 5 (b) and Guidelines, point 116 (5) ('hold-up problem'). *See* Article 3 (1) (c) of Regulation 4087/88, and *Pronuptia*, ECJ Jan. 28, 1986, 1986 ECR 353, para. 16.
305. Article 4 (a). *See Pronuptia*, ECJ Jan. 28, 1986, 1986 ECR 353, para. 25.
306. Articles 1 (c), 2 (1) and 3 (2).
307. Article 5 (a).
308. Commission Notice on subcontracting agreements, point 3, which is replaced by the Guidelines on technology transfer agreements, point 36, however, without changing the basic approach (*see* Guidelines on horizontal cooperation, points 86–89).
309. *See* Thirtieth Report on Competition Policy, Box 4, p. 55, and Directive 2000/31/EC on Certain Legal Aspects of Information Society Services, 2000 OJ L 178/1.

framework of a sales contract. Therefore, the existing rules apply both to e-commerce[310] and to traditional commerce since agreements, however reached, are to be analysed in their legal and economic context anyway.[311] For instance, in the *B&W Loudspeaker* case, the Commission challenged an agreement by which a supplier prohibited, without objective reasons, its authorized dealers from engaging in distance sales, including sales via the internet, which aimed at protecting their traditional distribution channel and was tantamount to an export ban.[312] In the *Yves St.Laurent* case[313] the Commission clarified that a ban on internet publicity and sale normally constitutes a hardcore restriction preventing the application of the former block exemption.[314] However, the Commission's case law is still scarce[315] and the existing regulations are silent, whereas the guidelines contain only marginal references to e-commerce.[316]

E-commerce – A Specific Relevant Market?

In merger cases the Commission tends to consider internet sales as a *distinct product market* from mail order, sales in stores or in supermarkets, or sales through clubs (book clubs).[317] However, it may be argued that a communication on a website targets all potential customers who also have access to all sales channels and

310. E.g., *Yamaha*, D.Comm. July 16, 2003, IP/03/1028. The electronic commerce has been promoted by the European Council of Lisbon, March 23 and 24, 2000, Conclusions of the Presidency, point 10.
311. Guidelines, point 7.
312. *B&W Loudspeakers Ltd*, Thirtieth Report on Competition Policy, point 215.
313. *Yves St. Laurent II*, IP/01/713 of May 17, 2001.
314. In the *Yves St. Laurent I* case, the Court of First Instance annulled part of the Commission's exemption decision, which raised indirect obstacles to sales in supermarkets: *Leclerc*, CFI Dec. 12, 1996, 1996 ECR II-1851, para. 157.
315. *See*, however, the extensive commentary, in particular Ruttley, *EC Competition Law in Cyberspace: An Overview of Recent Developments*, 1998 ECLR 186; Lange, *Unternehmenskooperation im Internet und EG-Kartellrecht*, 2000 EWS 291; Vajda/Gahnström, *Competition Law and the Internet*, 2000 ECLR 94; Seeliger, *EG-kartellrechtliche Probleme in Vertikalverhältnissen beim Vertrieb über das Internet*, WuW 2000–12, 1174; OFTEL/OFT Study, *Competition in E-commerce*, http://www.oftel; Dietrich/Menais, *Réseau de distribution et vente sur internet*, http://www.juriscom.net/espace2/2/ce0602.htm; Urrutia, *Internet and its effect on competition*, Paper delivered to the Universidad International Menendez Pelayo, Barcelona, July 10, 2000; Burrichter, *Vertical Restraints and E-Commerce*, 2001 Fordham Corporate Law Institute (B. Hawk, ed. 2000), pp. 131–150.
316. Guidelines, point 51.
317. *Bertelsmann/Mondadori*, D.Comm. April 22, 1999, M.1407; *Bertelsmann/Havas/BOL*, D.Comm. May 6, 1999, M.1459; *Time Warner/EMI*, D.Comm. June 14, 2000, M.1852, IP/00/617; *BOL Italia/Bertelsmann*, D.Comm. Sept. 1, 2000, JV 51; *Babcock Borsig, mg technologies and SAP*, D.Comm. Nov. 8, 2000, M.2172, IP/00/1266; *Otto Versand/Sabre*, D.Comm. Dec. 20, 2001, IP/01/1881; *GF-X Air Freight Trading*, D.Comm. Oct. 28, 2002, IP/02/1560 (in this case the Commission stated that the participants (competing European airlines) were unlikely to enter into anticompetitive coordination although electronic and traditional distribution channels were considered as constituting one single market).

can freely choose according to their preferences (direct contact with sales staff, consulting a catalogue or dialoging via the internet).[318] Since the internet can reach customers anywhere, the *geographic market* may be the world market, e.g. in a case where two companies operating worldwide establish an e-commerce market place for aerospace products (B2B exchange).[319] In the case of a B2C website the world market may reasonably be relevant only if a large proportion of customers is used to worldwide shopping.[320] However, access to the website may be effectively limited to customers within a certain territory on account of transport costs or the specificity of the product (freshness, durability, national regulations[321]) or of the language used.[322] In such a case, the relevant geographic market may be limited to a member state or, at the most, the Community.

Possible Restrictions Related to the Use of the Internet.
An obligation imposed on the distributor not to use the internet for promotion purposes (which the supplier reserves to itself) may be tantamount to a passive sales ban and to a hardcore restriction.[323] If a customer visits the supplier's website but instead contacts its local distributor, and if this contact leads to a sale, including delivery, that is considered (permitted) passive selling.[324] However, it is probably permissible for the supplier to prohibit distributors from targeting customers in territories which are allocated to other distributors via *unsolicited* e-mails, as this would be considered (prohibited) active selling outside the distributor's assigned territory. The consequence will, however, be that passive selling which was once rather rare increases substantially due to internet websites, and this in turn makes exclusive distribution systems increasingly unworkable.[325] On the other hand, the supplier is not prevented from requiring quality standards for the presentation of

318. *See*, in particular, Vajda/Gahnström, 2000 ECLR 94, 97–98. If the internet market constituted a new distinct market the parties would have substantial market shares (exceeding the block exemption threshold and preventing its application) despite the fact that there is potential competition from similar (future) platforms and therefore no possibility of creating a dominant position: *Babcock Borsig, mg technologies and SAP*, D.Comm. Nov. 8, 2000, M.2172, IP/00/1266. The Commission tries to avoid this consequence by considering the competitive pressures of the conventional means of distributing: *Newhouse/Jupiter/Scudder/M&G – Cofunds*, D.Comm. Sept. 1, 2000, M.2075, point 16.
319. *MyAircraft*, D.Comm. Aug. 4, 2000, M.1969, point 15.
320. *See* Seeliger, WuW 2000–12, 1174, 1185.
321. *See Worldcom/MCI*, D.Comm. July 8, 1998, 1999 OJ L 116/1, point 80.
322. E.g., a website message in Finland targets only Finnish speaking customers.
323. Guidelines, point 51. A prohibition not to sell to 'internet customers' would be a hardcore restriction in the sense of Article 4 (b). However, if e-commerce and traditional sales constitute distinct product markets (as suggested by the Commission), it may be argued that distributors can be prohibited from selling on that distinct market.
324. A supplier may not prevent a distributor from using its trademark rights for promotional purposes: *see BMW/Deenik*, ECJ Feb. 23, 1999, 1999 ECR I-1341. This may also apply for promotional purposes via the internet.
325. Seeliger, WuW 2000–12, 1174, 1182.

its products or services via the internet just as it may impose quality standards for a shop or advertising in general,[326] in particular in the case of franchise systems[327] or in selective distribution systems,[328] provided they are not tantamount to (indirect) quantitative selection.[329] It is not inconceivable that both the supplier and its distributors use the internet, the supplier to present the product and to refer customers to the appropriate local retailer or distributor, and the distributor to present the product and to offer pricing and terms of sale, provided they do not collude on pricing and terms of sale which would be contrary to Article 4 (a).

Creating Purchasing or Marketing E-Mail Platforms in a Horizontal Context.
Joint purchasing and joint marketing is generally accepted within the (very narrow) limits of Article 2 (2) of Regulation 2790/1999, which provides that the block exemption applies to an association and its members, or between an association and its suppliers only 'if all its members are retailers of goods and if no individual member of the association, together with its connected undertakings, has a total annual turnover exceeding EUR 50 million …'. The block exemption does not permit the association members to collude on pricing or terms of sale, as this would infringe Article 81. The same applies in the case of joint purchasing or joint marketing between competitors, including where an association and its members jointly establish e-mail platforms for joint purchasing or marketing. The Commission distinguishes web-site business-to-business (B2B) and business-to-consumer (B2C) services.[330] Both must be looked at under Article 81, unless the parties jointly create and control a new company performing on a lasting basis all the functions of an autonomous entity, in which case the merger control regulation applies.[331] However, the Commission accepts that B2B and B2C platforms both have the potential to increase competition and boost efficiencies and are normally likely to qualify for clearance under Article 81 (3), if they are within the scope of Article 81 (1) but not covered by any block exemption regulation.[332]

326. Including the requirement to sell products under the condition to provide for the necessary after-sales services.
327. Guidelines, point 51.
328. *Grundig II*, D.Comm. Dec. 21, 1993, 1994 OJ L 20/15 (prohibition on the selective distributor to sell products by mail order); Court d'Appel de Versailles, Dec. 2, 1999, http://www.juriscom.net:jurisfr/fabre2.htm. 3f. *See* Martinez-Lopez, 'Distribution sélective et Internet', DG IV Comp. NewsLetter, 2001–2, p. 7.
329. Martinez-Lopez, DG IV Comp. NewsLetter, 2001–2, p. 10.
330. Thirtieth Report on Competition Policy, point 214 and Box 4.
331. Article 3 (2) of Regulation 4064/89. Examples for clearances of joint purchasing: *Babcock Borsig/MG technologies/SAP Markets/ec4ec*, D.Comm. Nov. 7, 2000, M.2172; examples for clearances of joint marketing: *Accor Forte/Hilton*, D.Comm. Feb. 19, 2001, M.2197; *Getronics/Hagemeyer*, D.Comm. April 4, 2001, M.2223.
332. Thirtieth Report on Competition Policy, point 214.

- E-mail platforms for joint purchasing: In the *Covisint* case[333] the Commission concluded that the creation by five major vehicle manufacturers of a B2B internet marketplace intended to serve the procurement needs of major carmakers and suppliers was likely to create more transparency and to reduce search and information costs and to lead ultimately to lower prices for consumers.[334]
- E-mail platforms for joint marketing: In the *Angelini/Phoenix* case[335] the Commission cleared a wholesale JV which combined both parents' wholesale activities: although the parties were competitors their market share on the relevant south-Italian market (18%) was low enough to prevent them from 'exercising undue market power'.[336] In the case of substantial market power, however, the Commission continues its critical approach to joint sales arrangements.[337]

In cases which are not covered by the block exemption individual clearance has been granted in particular cases[338] but there is no clear guidance yet as to whether this will become a general rule under the new Regulation 1/2003 which provides only in cases of genuine uncertainty for the possibility of 'informal clearance' (comparable to comfort letters).[339]

(f) Mixed Distribution Systems

A supplier is entitled to choose the distribution system according to the specific conditions of the markets concerned. A supplier may establish selective distribution systems in certain countries whereas he may prefer to appoint exclusive distributors or sell through its own subsidiaries in other countries. The Guidelines on vertical restraints state that a supplier cannot combine the advantages of two distribution systems, in particular not impose an active sales ban on a selective

333. *Covisint*, D.Comm. July 31, 2001, IP/01/1155 (comfort letter).
334. *See also* the clearance of the creation of a joint network for e-commerce for establishing a global, interoperatable network between financial institutions: *Identrus*, D.Comm. Aug. 11, 2000, 2000 OJ C 227/6 (comfort letter), and the joint purchasing of components by two major car manufacturers: *GM/Fiat*, D.Comm. Aug. 16, 2000, DG Newsletter 2000–3, p. 54.
335. *Angelini/Phoenix*, D.Comm. July 9, 2001, IP/01/973 (comfort letter).
336. *See also* the clearance of the creation of joint ventures for establishing a cross-border exchange for electronic trading in derivatives: *Eurex*, D.Comm. Aug. 11, 2000, 2000 OJ C 231/2 (comfort letter).
337. *See Joint Gas Sales in Norway*, IP/01/830 of June 13, 2001.
338. Under Article 81 (because of lacking 'joint' control by the parents on the joint venture): *Volbroker*, D.Comm. July 31, 2000, IP/00/896; *SKF*, 2001 OJ C 122/7 of April 24, 2001; *Internet Platform Linde*, D.Comm. April 25, 2001, WuW 2001–6, 577; *Covisint*, IP/01/1155 of July 31, 2001; under the merger control regulation (because of 'joint' control by the parents): *MyAircraft*, D.Comm. Aug. 4, 2000, M.1969, point 15. Similarly under German law: *Rubber Network*, German Antitrust Authority, Jan. 21, 2001, WuW 2001–6, 611.
339. Recital 38 to Regulation 1/2003.

distributor with respect to the territory allocated to another selective distributor.[340] However, an exclusive distributor may need a certain territorial protection against active sales, including from selective dealers appointed in the 'traditional' markets, in order to establish an efficient distribution system in a new geographic market and to compensate its promotional efforts as long as the market share threshold of 30% is not exceeded.[341]

6. Exclusive Purchasing Agreements

(a) Exclusivity and its Substitutes

No Genuine Exclusivity Required.
The new Regulation 2790/1999 exempts a considerably larger number of restrictive purchasing obligations, including non-compete obligations imposed on the dealer not to manufacture, to purchase,[342] to sell or resell other goods or services than the contract goods or services or their substitutes or not to purchase such goods or services from third parties for the purpose of reprocessing or incorporation. It also includes purchasing arrangements which concern only a substantial part of the dealer's requirements.[343] However, these agreements are covered by the block exemption on the condition that the supplier's market share does not exceed 30%.[344]

Quantity Forcing – 'Tying'.
Quantity forcing may constitute an indirect non-competition obligation.[345] The regulation exempts direct or indirect non-compete obligations (Article 5 (a)). Non-compete obligations are defined in Article 1 (b) as any direct or indirect obligation causing the buyer not to manufacture, purchase, sell or resell goods or services which compete with the contract goods or services, or any direct or indirect obligation on the buyer to purchase from the supplier or a third party designated by the supplier more than 80% of the buyer's total purchases of the contract goods or services and their substitutes, calculated on the basis of the value of its purchases

340. Guidelines on Vertical Restraints, points 55 and 177.
341. With respect to oligopolistic markets *see* Guidelines on Vertical Restraints, point 176.
342. Including by way of freezer exclusivity (the obligation on the dealer to stock in the supplier's cabinets only the supplier's ice creams): *Van den Bergh Foods*, CFI Oct. 23, 2003, T-65/98, paras 135–144.
343. Under Regulation 2790/1999 a 80% coverage is tantamount to exclusivity whereas under Regulation 1400/2002 a 30% coverage may already be tantamount to exclusivity. A lower coverage leads to a market foreclosure only where the parties' market share exceeds considerably the limits of the block exemption or is close to a dominant position.
344. Article 3 (1). The exception of Article 3 (2) concerns the case of exclusive supply obligations as defined in Article 1 (c).
345. Guidelines, point 152.

in the previous calendar year.[346] The regulation therefore fills a gap in the previous regulation which applied only to a traditional obligation to buy all of the buyer's needs, thereby excluding agreements for the purchase of 90% of the buyer's needs, which often had the same effect as a 100% requirement, but which required an individual clearance ('partial requirement contracts').[347] However, it remains difficult for the supplier to verify the implementation of a partial requirements clause without requesting the buyer to reveal his total requirement and the quantities supplied by third parties. Quantity forcing is generally considered less restrictive since it leaves the buyer some scope to purchase competing products[348] but it is doubtful whether obligations to purchase *less* than 80% lead to an anticompetitive market foreclosure so that they may be held compatible with Article 81. *Tying* is when the supplier makes the sale of one good or service conditional upon the purchase of another distinct[349] good or service from the supplier or a third party designated by the supplier and therefore constitutes a specific form of quantity forcing on the buyer in respect of the tied good or service.[350] Tying is also block exempted under Article 2 (1), subject to the five-year limitation of Article 5 (a).[351] Where the market share thresholds are exceeded tying may have an appreciable market foreclosure effect and is therefore unlikely to merit an Article 81 (3) exemption.[352]

(b) Exclusive Purchasing Agreements for Reselling

Restating the Principles of Regulation 1984/83.
If the supplier has a market share of 30% or less, the obligation on the reseller to purchase the contract goods or services only from the supplier is exempted, provided the duration of the obligation does not exceed five years and is not tacitly renewable.[353] The exclusive purchasing obligation (or its substitute) is considered as a type of non-compete clause committing the buyer not to purchase the contract goods or services from other sources and also not to manufacture or purchase competing goods or services. The main competitive risk of exclusive purchasing agreements is that of foreclosing the market for other suppliers. This risk exists in particular in cases of exclusive purchasing agreements between companies with a market share exceeding 30%. Such agreements are excluded from the block exemption and need individual evaluation.[354]

---

346. Example of quantity forcing: Guidelines, point 160.
347. Commission's Notice on Regulations 1983/83 and 1984/84, point 35.
348. Guidelines, point 119 (4).
349. Combinations of goods (e.g., shoes supplied with laces) are not distinct goods, Guidelines, point 216.
350. Guidelines, point 217.
351. *See*, in greater detail, Section 10 (g), *infra*.
352. Guidelines, point 223.
353. Articles 3 (2) and 5 (a).
354. Individual exemption was rejected in *Langnese/Iglo*, CFI June 8, 1995, 1995 ECR II-1533; *aff'd* ECJ Oct. 1, 1998, 1998 ECR I-5609. Such agreements will only be accepted if the

Assessment of the Most Common Restrictions.

(i) *Territorial restrictions on the reseller* are hardcore restrictions (Article 4 (b)).[355] However, active sales bans are block exempted up to the market share limit of 30%, provided it aims at protecting a dealer to which a territory or a customer group has been allocated exclusively because of specific efforts or investments in promoting the goods or services (Article 4 (b), first indent). Passive sales are impermissible, including restrictions on use of the internet to advertise or sell products.[356]

(ii) *Exclusive purchasing obligations* are exempted so long as the supplier's market share does not exceed 30%, provided they are limited to five years and not automatically renewable. The obligation must be limited to the 'contract' goods or services[357] but may include tied goods or services.[358] Such tied products were previously excluded from exclusive purchasing. However, in order to be enforceable, the agreements must, similarly to the Commission's previous practice,[359] identify the tied products or services.

(iii) *Special provisions in the case of premises and land owned or leased by the supplier*: In cases when the contract goods or services are sold by the buyer from premises or land owned by the supplier or leased by the supplier from third parties not connected with the buyer, the exclusive purchasing obligation may extend to the entire period of occupancy of the premises and land and for one year after termination of the agreement.[360]

---

exclusivity is relaxed and the duration of the agreements is reduced to 1–2 years. Individual clearance was granted in *Interbrew*, D.Comm. Nov. 20, 2002, 2002 OJ C 283/14, despite Interbrew's nearly dominant position.

355. Guidelines, points 46–56.

356. *Ibid.*, point 51.

357. 'Contract' goods or services may be interpreted as requiring a 'specification' in the agreement (*see* Article 1 (c)) because the buyer must know which goods or services it is bound to purchase from the supplier or from a party designated by the supplier and which it is free to purchase from third parties. Such requirement of 'specification' would prevent the supplier from unilaterally adding goods or services on the list of tied goods or services, without prejudice to the lessor's right to control the lessee's premises with respect to the installation of amusement machines: *Whitbread*, D.Comm. Feb. 24, 1999, 1999 OJ L 88/26, points 147–148 (*aff'd* CFI March 21, 2002, T-131/99); *Inntrepreneur and Spring*, D.Comm. June 29, 2000, 2000 OJ L 195/49, points 36–39.

358. Guidelines, point 106. Under the previous Regulation 1984/83 on exclusive purchasing agreements the block exemption did not extend to products other goods than beers or drinks in beer agreements or other goods than fuels or services in service station agreements (Articles 8 (1) (a) and 12 (1) (a) of this regulation). *See*, however, *Inntrepreneur and Spring*, D.Comm. June 29, 2000, 2000 OJ L 195/49, point 66.

359. *See* Notice on Regulation 1983/83 and 1984/83, point 40, and *Whitbread*, D.Comm. Feb. 24, 1999, 1999 OJ 88/26, points 147–148, *aff'd* CFI March 21, 2002, T-131/99.

360. Article 5 (a) and (b). Similarly Article 3 (d) of Regulation 1984/83 on exclusive purchasing agreements. *See Inntrepreneur and Spring*, D.Comm. June 29, 2000, 2000 OJ L 195/49, point 33.

(iv) *Obligation on the buyer not to manufacture, purchase, sell or resell goods or services which compete with the contract goods or services*: Such an obligation is also exempted, provided the duration does not exceed five years and the supplier's market share does not exceed 30%.[361] Obligations agreed for a longer duration need individual assessment, which depends in particular on whether specific investments to be made by either the supplier or the buyer, such as special equipment or training, justify a longer duration.[362] The obligation may extend to tied goods or services. The regulation exempts the resulting restriction, which consists in a foreclosure on the market of the tied product, provided it is limited to five years and the supplier's market share does not exceed 30%.[363] The extension to tied products differs from the previous Regulation 1984/83.[364] However, the Commission recognizes that tying can pose a competitive risk in the case of buyers which do not hold significant buying power[365] and may in fact lead to greater economic dependence of the dealers and by the cumulative effect of similar agreements to greater foreclosure of competing suppliers which are prevented from offering their products to the tied dealers.[366]

(c) Component Supply Agreements[367]

Extended Powers Conferred to the Commission by Regulation 1215/99. Regulation 1215/99 refers in its recital 7 to agreements for the purposes of processing or incorporation, thereby conferring to the Commission the power to adopt block exemptions with regard to such agreements. Article 1 (c) of Regulation 2790/1999 relates to exclusive supply obligations 'for the purposes of a specific use or for resale' without any further characterization, whereas Article 4 (b) and (e) refer only to 'incorporation' of components and spare parts. However, components supplied for the purpose of incorporation[368] are not dissimilar from intermediate goods for the purpose of processing,[369] the main difference being that components remain identifiable and separable, whereas the processing of

361. Articles 1 (a) and 5 (a).
362. Guidelines, point 116 (4).
363. Guidelines, points 215–218.
364. *See* Articles 8 (1) (a) and 12 (1) (a) of Regulation 1984/83 on exclusive purchasing agreements.
365. Guidelines, points 218–222.
366. Under the new block exemption regulation the Commission would have to withdraw the benefit of the block exemption. Such a withdrawal would have an effect only *ex nunc* (prospectively) preventing the tied buyer from invoking the nullity sanction under Article 81 (2) for the exclusive purchasing obligation retroactively and its legal consequences such as termination of the agreement without notice (*See* Guidelines, point 75).
367. The Commission uses the term 'industrial supply agreements': Guidelines, points 202 and 208.
368. *E.g.*, batteries supplied to a car manufacturer.
369. *See* example discussed in Guidelines, point 213

intermediate goods results in a change of identity. It may therefore be assumed that the new block exemption exempts exclusive supply obligations as well as exclusive purchasing obligations for the purposes of any specific use, including incorporation or processing, and original equipment manufacturer (OEM) agreements, provided the exclusive purchasing obligations are agreed for not more than five years and the supplier's share in the component market does not exceed 30%.[370] This interpretation would end the uncertainty as to the assessment of such agreements.[371]

Assessment of the Most Common Restrictions.

(i) *Customer Restrictions on the Supplier*: In some exceptional cases the supplier may be committed not to supply the same goods for the purposes of incorporation into *other buyers' products* who may compete with the contract buyer[372] or for the purposes of distribution by competitors in the buyer's territory.[373] Such an obligation is normally a restriction of competition but exempted, provided the purchaser's market share does not exceed 30%. A restriction agreed between the supplier of components and a buyer who incorporates those components, which prevents the supplier from selling the components as *spare parts* to end users or to repairers or other service providers not entrusted by the buyer with the repair or servicing of its goods is however a hardcore restriction.[374]

(ii) *Customer Restrictions on the Buyer*: Restricting the buyer from using the product for other purposes,[375] in other premises or reselling[376] the components, supplied for the purposes of processing or incorporation, to other customers who would use them to manufacture the same type of goods as those produced by the supplier are excepted from hardcore restrictions.[377] This should apply by analogy to similar restrictions imposed on the buyer of intermediate goods[378] or services or original equipment for the purposes

370. However, even suppliers which have a dominant position are not obliged to supply products adapted to the specific needs of a customer: *Industrie des poudres sphériques*, CFI Nov. 30, 2000, 2000 ECR II-3755, para. 77.

371. However, when the agreement contains provisions on the use of industrial property rights which constitute its primary object, it would not be covered by Regulation 2790/1999 (Article 2 (3) and Guidelines, point 30) and instead be assessed under Regulation 772/2004 on transfer of technology agreements, which likewise exempts such obligations up to a 30% market share.

372. *See Siemens/Fanuc*, D.Comm. Dec. 18, 1985, 1985 OJ L 376/29, point 24.

373. Objected to by the Commission in *Wingas/EDF Trading*, D.Comm. Sept. 12, 2002, IP/02/1293.

374. Article 4 (e).

375. However, gas for electricity generation is not a distinct field-of-use and does not justify an obligation on the buyer (the electricity generator) not to resell gas to final gas consumers: *Gas Natural/Endesa*, D.Comm. March 27, 2000, IP/00/297.

376. Including exporting, thereby being tantamount to a blacklisted export ban.

377. Article 4 (b) fourth indent.

378. E.g., basic vitamins or natural gas.

of processing into the end product[379] if their effect is similar to a field-of-use restriction which is generally held ancillary in license agreements.[380] In case the supplier has a dominant market position, however, the effect of such a clause may (i) foreclose the market to competitors and therefore preclude application of the block exemption and any individual clearance and (ii) be subject to objections under Article 82.[381]

(iii) *Exclusive Purchasing Obligations*: The obligation on the buyer not to purchase the contract goods from other suppliers or to purchase more than 80% of the total requirement from the contract supplier is block exempted, provided it does not exceed five years.[382] However, longer-term purchasing agreements are common in the energy sector and are, as the Commission stated in the *Wingas/EDF Trading* case,[383] not necessarily incompatible with Articles 81 and 82, in particular in respect to the security of supply. Longer-term obligations need individual clearance by balancing duration and extent of the supply obligations in the light of the efficiencies necessary to outweigh the cumulative foreclosure effect of such obligations.[384] Longer-term exclusive supply obligations may be justified to open up or enter new markets[385] or to depreciate client-specific investments, such as for building new machines, tools or networks, provided the investment cannot be used after termination of the contract to supply other customers.[386] Substantial investments made on the upstream market (e.g., long-term pay-or-take obligations to import gas via co-financed pipelines) justify longer-term supply obligations on the downstream market only if they are limited or reduced[387] to 8–12 years and

379. *E.g.*, pharmaceutical end-products or generation of electricity.

380. *See* Article 4 (1) (c) (i) of Regulation 772/2004 on technology transfer agreements.

381. *See Soda Ash*,, D.Comm. Dec. 13, 2000, IP/00/449, restating the decision of Dec. 19, 1990, 1991 OJ L 152/21 and 40, *rev'd*, on procedural grounds, ECJ April 6, 2000, C-286/95 P and C-287/95 P.

382. Article 5 (a) and 1 (b).

383. D.Comm. Sept. 12, 2002, IP/02/1293.

384. Guidelines, points 205–206. In the gas sector, the assessment of such a cumulative effect must take into account the interdependence of parallel supply agreements applied by operators acting on different national markets (which are still the relevant geographic markets) and having thereon substantially different market positions to the extent that any evaluation must be compatible with both Article 81 *and* 82, as in the *Industrial Gases* case, Nineteenth Report on Competition Policy, point 62.

385. Guidelines, point 116 (2), e.g., *ISAB/ENEL*, 1996 OJ C 138/3) and *REN/Turbogas*, 1996 OJ C 118/7 (20 year exclusivity reduced to 15 years).

386. Guidelines, point 116 (4), e.g., building a pipeline between the gas production unit and the gas consumption steel work: *Industrial Gases*, Nineteenth Report on Competition Policy, point 62; *Pego*, Thirteenth report on Competition Policy, point 222 (15 year supply obligations within a minimum/maximum range accepted). Non-refundable loans for furbishing pubs: *Interbrew*, 2002 OJ C 283/14.

387. By way of curative interpretation in order to maintain the validity of the remaining (acceptable) part of the agreement, thereby guaranteeing with immediate effect both continuing traditional

to quantities or parts of the total requirements which leave sufficient possibilities of alternative purchasing (varying between 50%[388] and to 75–80% of the total requirements[389]) or are relaxed by an 'English clause'.[390] However, as a rule, exclusive purchasing obligations lasting longer than five years are for most types of investments not considered necessary to achieve claimed efficiencies.[391]

(iv) *Resale Prices and Territorial Restrictions*: Any form of minimum resale price arrangements, whether agreed with respect to the intermediate product or not, would constitute a hardcore restriction, provided that the supplier may impose a *maximum* sale price or supply a *recommended* resale price.[392] Restrictions as to territories or to down-stream buyers on the sale of the processed good or end product are also hardcore restrictions.[393]

7. Applicability of the Block Exemption to License, Franchise and Subcontracting Agreements

General Applicability of the Block Exemption.

Pursuant to Article 2 (3) the block exemption regulation[394] applies to provisions contained in vertical agreements concerning the assignment or use of intellectual property rights for the purpose of using or reselling the goods or services supplied, on the condition that these licensing provisions (i) do *not* constitute the *primary object*[395] of, but are directly related to, the implementation of such agreements (i.e., they are 'ancillary' licensing provisions), and (ii) do not contain restrictions of competition having the same object or effect as vertical restraints not exempted under the block exemption. This Article 2 (3) provision fills a gap since license agreements entered into solely for the purposes of resale, including repackaging and bottling,[396] are precluded from the applicability of Regulation 772/2004 on

---

supply relationships and opening the market for competitors; e.g., *Gas Natural*, D.Comm. March 27, 2000, IP/00/297.

388. *Olivetti/Digital*, D.Comm. Nov. 11, 1994, 1994 OJ L 309/24, point 20.
389. *Gas Natural*, D.Comm. March 27, 2000, IP/00/297.
390. However, the contract supplier may not be entitled to be informed of confidential details of the client's alternative purchases in order to identify the competitors' strategy, *see Hoffmann-La Roche*, ECJ Feb. 13, 1979, 1979 ECR 461, paras 102–107.
391. Guidelines, point 205.
392. Article 4 (a).
393. Article 4 (b) seems to cover such a restriction.
394. *See* Guidelines, point 30.
395. For applying Regulation 772/2004 on technology transfer agreements the licensed know-how must be '*secret, substantial and identified*' (Article 1 (1) (i)).
396. Cases such as *Campari* (D.Comm. Dec. 23, 1977, 1978 OJ L 70/69) or *Carlsberg* (D.Comm. July 12, 1984, 1984 OJ L 207/26) might be covered by the new block exemption, provided the supplier's market share does not exceed the 30% threshold.

transfer of technology agreements,[397] and agreements for the purposes of incorporation were not covered by the preceding block exemption regulations. Article 2 (3) of Regulation 2790/1999 applies to all vertical agreements that include ancillary assignment or license provisions, including, but not limited to, provisions concerning trademarks,[398] copyrights[399] and commercial know-how[400] which are not concluded for the purpose of manufacturing but directly related to the use or resale of goods or services by the buyer or its customers. This includes franchising agreements which are no longer subject to the specific Regulation 4087/88[401] but to the general Regulation 2790/1999.[402]

Applicability of Regulation 772/2004 on Transfer of Technology Agreements.
Regulation 772/2004 on transfer of technology agreements remains applicable to agreements containing licensing provisions which *do* constitute the primary object, in particular involving the transfer of technology (substantial, secret and identifiable know-how[403]) to a manufacturer of drinks (not only bottlers).[404]

Particularities of Subcontracting Agreements.
Whereas subcontracting agreements between actual or potential competitors are subject to the general rules on horizontal agreements, in particular on specialization agreements,[405] subcontracting agreements between non-competitors are vertical agreements and must be assessed under Regulation 2790/1999[406] or, if they involve the transfer of know-how to the subcontractor, under the transfer of technology regulation.[407]

Hardcore Restrictions Always Blacklisted, Ancillary Restrictions Always Exempt.
Hardcore restrictions are always blacklisted whichever specific rule applies: Regulation 2790/1999 on vertical agreements, Commission Notice on franchis-

397. The block exemption on technology transfer agreements does not apply to agreements entered into solely for the purpose of sale nor to license agreements containing provisions relating to intellectual property rights other than patents which are not ancillary (Article 1 (1) (b) of Regulation 772/2004).
398. Pure trademark licenses (without any element of distribution) are, however, excluded: Guidelines, point 321.
399. Including agreements for the incorporation of software protected by copyright: Guidelines, points 32–34.
400. *See Moosehead/Whitbread*, D.Comm. March 23, 1990, 1990 OJ L 100/32.
401. Except manufacturing franchises which remain subject to Regulation 240/96.
402. Article 12 (2) of Regulation 2790/1999.
403. However, agreements under which the buyer provides only specifications to the supplier are covered by Regulation 2790/99: Guidelines, point 33
404. *See Campari*, D.Comm. Dec. 23, 1977, 1978 OJ L 70/69.
405. Guidelines on horizontal cooperation, points 79 and 100.
406. *Ibid.*, point 80.
407. *Ibid.*, points 81, 86–89.

ing agreements, Regulation 772/2004 on transfer of technology agreements, the rules on horizontal cooperation (if the horizontal aspect prevails), or the Notice on *de minimis* agreements.[408] Ancillary restrictions are normally not within the scope of Article 81 (1),[409] provided they are directly related and necessary to the implementation of the agreement, which is, as such, compatible with the EC competition rules.[410]

8. Applicability of the Block Exemption in a Horizontal Context

(a) Multiple Exclusive Distribution Dealerships

Block Exemption Applicable but Likely to be Withdrawn.
If a dealer is granted the exclusive right to distribute two or more competing products to the same customer group, inter-brand competition is likely to be substantially restricted for those brands, in particular in the event the relevant products hold higher cumulative market shares.[411] This could constitute grounds for withdrawing the benefit of the block exemption under Article 6.[412] Further, any agreement *between competitors* on the quantities to be supplied to certain distributors or customers, including reprocessors, are hardcore restrictions that infringe Article 81 (1).[413]

(b) Vertical Agreements Entered into between an Association of Retailers and its Members

Vertical v. Horizontal Nature of the Agreements.
Article 2 (2)[414] provides that the block exemption applies to vertical agreements entered into between an association of undertakings and its members, or between an association and its suppliers, provided all members are retailers of goods and no member has a total annual turnover exceeding EUR 50 million. However, horizontal agreements directly between the members of the association or decisions adopted by the association remain subject to Article 81. Accordingly, joint

---

408. *See* Article 2 (3) of Regulation 2790/1999.
409. Article 2 (1), second subparagraph, e.g., the obligation on the licensor/supplier not to grant licenses to other parties (*see Maize Seed*, ECJ June 8, 1982, 1982 ECR 2015, para. 57) or non-compete clauses in know-how agreements, effective after the term of the agreement (Article 5 (b) of Regulation 2790/1999).
410. They may, for the sake of legal certainty, be included in a block exemption, as in the case of an open exclusive license (*see* Article 1 (1) and (2) of Regulation 240/96).
411. *See* Guidelines, point 164.
412. *Ibid.*, point 176.
413. *Italian Flat glass*, D.Comm. Sept. 28, 1981, 1981 OJ L 326/32; annulled, however, for lack of proof: CFI March 10, 1992, 1992 ECR II-1403.
414. The provision refers to recital 10 of Regulation 1215/99 amending Regulation 19/65.

purchasing and joint sales arrangements through an association of smaller or medium-sized undertakings are permissible,[415] provided each member's annual turnover does not exceed EUR 50 million[416] and their aggregate market share does not exceed 30%.[417] Any direct restrictive coordination among the member retailers is not covered by the block exemption.[418] *A fortiori*, the block exemption does not apply to joint sales arrangements between competing suppliers, which normally infringe Article 81 (1) and normally are unlikely to fulfill the conditions for exemption under Article 81 (3). Similarly, the Commission objected to (and fined) a collective dealing arrangement of an association intended to prevent supplies to non-members.[419]

(c) Vertical Non-Reciprocal Agreements between Competitors

Covered by the Block Exemption Only to a Limited Extent.
Article 2 (4) provides that the benefit of the block exemption does not apply to vertical agreements between competitors,[420] except where competing companies enter into non-reciprocal vertical agreements and:

– the buyer has a total annual turnover not exceeding EUR 100 million,[421] or

415. *See* the Commission's negative clearance in *SOCEMAS*, D.Comm. July 17, 1968, 1968 OJ L 201/4. The Notice on Agreements of Minor Importance may also apply.
416. In the Guidelines, point 28, the Commission states that this provision applies even when certain members have a turnover of more than EUR 50 million. It is however questionable whether national courts will take the same lenient attitude.
417. This is similar to the US antitrust practice. With regard to health care the U.S. Department of Justice has stated the agencies will not challenge any joint purchasing arrangement among health care providers, provided the joint purchases account for less than 35% of the total sales of the purchased product or service in the relevant market and the cost of the jointly purchased products or services accounts for less than 20% of the total revenues from all products or services sold by each competing participant in the joint purchasing arrangement: U.S. Department of Justice and Federal Trade Commission, 'Statement of Antitrust Enforcement Policy in Health Care' (1996), 4 Trade Reg. Rep. (CCH) at p. 410.
418. A coordination through the association 'can be a substitute for an agreement or a concerted practice as a means to coordinate market conduct': Twenty-fourth Report on Competition Policy, point 149, or even a precondition for implementing a scheme of collective exclusivity: *FEG Nederlandse Federative Vereniging voor de Groothandel op Electrotechnisch Gebied*, CFI Dec. 16, 2003, T-5/00, paras 319–328.
419. *FEG Nederlandse Federative Vereniging voor de Groothandel op Electrotechnisch Gebied*, D.Comm. Oct. 26, 1999, 2000 OJ L 39/1, point 127, *aff'd* CFI Dec. 16, 2003, T-5/00, paras 342–367.
420. E.g., *Tate & Lyle*, CFI July 12, 2001, 2001 ECR II-2035, paras 55–56.
421. Article 3 (b) of the previous Regulation declared the exemption applicable where *one* of the parties had a total annual turnover of no more than EUR 100 million.

- the supplier is a manufacturer *and* a distributor of goods, while the buyer is a distributor but not a manufacturer of competing goods,[422] or
- similarly, with respect to services, the supplier is a provider of services at several levels of trade, whereas the buyer does not provide competing services at the level of trade where it purchases the contract services.[423]

This provision does not deal with agreements between a supplier of goods, which it manufacturers and reprocesses or incorporates, and a buyer, which does not manufacture the basic products but competes on the level of the reprocessed or final products. However, it may be argued that the provision applies by analogy.[424] A typical case of a horizontal agreement between competitors which is *not* covered by the block exemption is the case *German Book Price Fixing* where the Commission prosecuted the concerted embargo (collective boycott) by the German publishers and booksellers at the expense of foreign internet booksellers that served to block cross-border internet trade in books at reduced prices to German consumers (at prices far below the fixed prices).[425]

9. Inapplicability of the Block Exemption in the Case of Withdrawal by the Commission or National Authorities

Withdrawal by the Commission.

Pursuant to Article 6 of Regulation 2790/1999, the Commission may withdraw the benefit of the block exemption where it finds that vertical agreements have effects that are incompatible with the conditions laid down in Article 81 (3), and in particular where access to the relevant market or competition therein is significantly restricted. This provision will not have much practical importance with regard to individual agreements that are below the 30% market share threshold, which must not be exceeded in order for the block exemption to apply. The only vertical case where the Commission withdrew the benefit of a block exemption, Langnese-Iglo,[426] would not have necessitated a withdrawal under the new regula-

422. *See* Article 3 (4) of Regulation 240/96 on technology transfer agreements, which prohibits customer restrictions in license agreements between parties which 'were already competing manufacturers'.
423. This is new due to the inclusion of services in the regulation.
424. *See* section 6 (c) *supra*.
425. IP/02/461 of March 22, 2002. *See also Iqbal*, Twenty-first Report on Competition Policy, p. 334, concerning the obligation, by the British manufacturers of pharmaceuticals, on the resellers residing within the Common Market to sell the products only to a certain country of destination outside the Common Market, thereby restricting the freedom to resell the product within the Common Market.
426. *Langnese-Iglo*, D.Comm. Dec. 23, 1992, 1993 OJ L 183/19, point 115; *aff'd* CFI June 8, 1995, 1995 ECR II-1611 and ECJ Oct. 1, 1998, 1998 ECR I-5606, without, however, taking a position on the application of the withdrawal provision, Article 14 of Regulation 1984/83.

tion since it concerned parties with market shares well beyond the limit of 30%. However, the new provision does have a significant impact with regard to parallel networks of similar agreements employed by competing firms whose cumulative impact may be a significant market foreclosure.[427] Under the previous system it was difficult to assess a vertical agreement which alone did not have any appreciable effect on competition or trade between member states but which together with agreements that included similar vertical restraints employed by competing firms led to a cumulative restrictive effect. The new regulation creates a presumption of legality for parallel vertical agreements constituting a network[428] unless the Commission finds that access to the relevant market is significantly restricted. In such a case the Commission may withdraw the benefit of the block exemption by formal decision with respect to certain individual agreements (Article 6) or adopt a new regulation declaring Regulation 2970/1999 inapplicable to an indefinite number of vertical agreements constituting a parallel network and containing specific restraints covering more than 50% of a relevant market (Article 8).[429] These rules, when read together, indicate that parallel restrictive agreements having a cumulative restrictive effect but that are within the scope of the regulation can only be objected to once the Commission has taken the appropriate action, i.e. a withdrawal decision or adoption of a regulation. Both of these forms of Commission action apply prospectively (*ex nunc*).[430]

Withdrawal by National Authorities.
Pursuant to Article 7 (2) of Regulation 19/65 as amended by Regulation 1215/99[431] and Article 7 of the new Regulation 2790/1999, national competition law authorities may, on their own initiative or at the request of the Commission or persons having a legitimate interest, withdraw the benefit of the block exemption when agreements have effects incompatible with the conditions of Article 81 (3) in their national territory or in a part thereof which has all the characteristics of a *distinct geographic market*.[432] The national authorities are free to apply their national law, provided that this does not prejudice the uniform application of

---

427. E.g., multiple exclusive dealerships applied by four market leaders having each about 20% of the market: Guidelines, point 176.
428. This presupposes that Article 2 applies to parallel networks of similar agreements and similar buyers although the text refers to 'the supplier' or 'the buyer'.
429. *See* Guidelines, points 80–87.
430. *Ibid.*, point 75. A regulation adopted pursuant to Article 8 cannot enter into effect earlier than six months following its adoption (Article 8 (2)).
431. Article 7 of Regulation 19/65 is repealed by Article 40 of the new regulation replacing Regulation 17, which contains a specific withdrawal provision (Article 29 (2)).
432. The same right is conferred as a general rule by Article 29 (2) of the new regulation replacing Regulation 17. The provision is apparently influenced by the distinct market concept of Article 9 (2) (a) of the merger control regulation.

the Community competition rules throughout the Community[433] or the full effect of any measures adopted in implementation of those rules, including the block exemption regulation.

10. Individual Assessment of Obligations outside the Scope of the Block Exemption

(a) Introduction

Hardcore Restrictions Generally Prohibited and Normally Heavily Fined. Hardcore restrictions such as fixing resale prices and allocation of territories or customers are not covered by the *de minimis* rules and block exemption Regulation 2790/1999, except certain forms which are expressly accepted by the regulation. Hardcore restrictions comprise price fixing and allocation of territories or customers as well as their substitutes, such as fixing or limiting price discounts or rebates or regulating quantities sold in a particular territory to what is usual to local demand. They are generally prohibited irrespective of the parties' market share and are unlikely to obtain individual exemption under Article 81 (3). The Commission's new more flexible approach toward vertical restraints does not lead to a fundamental change of its enforcement policy which is in accord with the Green Paper to stay 'as close as possible' to its administrative practice and the Court's case law.[434] Since the *Pioneer* decision[435] hardcore restrictions have frequently resulted in the imposition of high fines.[436] Lower fines have been imposed in cases where the parties did not implement in full the vertical restrictions,[437] where the parties held market shares below the 15% threshold[438] or where the

433. Recital 17. With respect to the parallel application of Community competition law by national courts/authorities and the Commission, *see Van der Bergh Foods*, D.Comm. March 11, 1998, 1998 OJ L 246/1, points 276–279.

434. 1998 OJ C 365/3, 22.

435. *Pioneer*, D.Comm. Dec. 14, 1979, 1980 OJ L 60/21 (start of Commission's policy of higher fines to deter hardcore infringements: total fines of ECU 6.9 million reduced by ECJ on appeal to ECU 3.2 million because of insufficient evidence of infringement for part of period but high-fine policy as such upheld: *Pioneer*, ECJ June 7, 1983, 1983 ECR 1825, paras 101–110).

436. *See* most recently *Opel*, D.Comm. Sept. 20, 2000, 2001 OJ L 59/1 (fines of EUR 43 million, however reduced to EUR 35.5 million by CFI Oct. 21, 2003, T-368/00); *Bramford*, D.Comm. Dec. 21, 2000, 2001 OJ L 69/1 (fines of EUR 39.6 million); *Volkswagen I*, D.Comm. Jan. 28, 1998, 1998 OJ L 124/60 (fine of EUR 102 million, however reduced to EUR 90 million by CFI July 6, 2000, 2000 ECR II-2707, *aff'd* ECJ Sept. 18, 2003, C-338/00 P); *Volkswagen II*, D.Comm. June 29, 2001, 2001 OJ L 262/14; *rev'd* CFI Dec. 3, 2003, T-208/01, points 75–80 (fines of EUR 30.96 million); *Daimler Chrysler*, D.Comm. Oct. 10, 2001, 2002 OJ L 257/1 (fine of EUR 72 million); *Nintendo*, D.Comm. Oct. 30, 2002, IP/02/1584 (fines of EUR 167.8 million).

437. *Yamaha*, D.Comm. July 16, 2003, IP/03/1028 (fine of EUR 2.56 million).

438. *Editions Nathan*, D.Comm. July 5, 2000, 2001 OJ L 54/1. *See also Miller International*, D.Comm. Dec. 1, 1976, 1976 OJ L 357140; *aff'd* ECJ Feb. 1, 1978, 1978 ECR 131; *Theal/*

prices were subject to government regulation in different countries, which caused large price differences and hence parallel imports and efforts of manufacturers to stop them.[439] The Commission does not impose fines or imposes only low fines if the infringement is minor and is terminated prior to the Commission procedure[440] or if the dealer was compelled to submit to an anticompetitive agreement[441] or unwillingly participated in the violation[442] rather than instigating the arrangement in order to eliminate troublesome competitors.[443]

No Presumption of Illegality.

Agreements that are not covered by Regulation 2790/1999 are not automatically presumed to be illegal but require individual examination under Article 81. They may not come within Article 81 (1) at all:

- if they do not contain any restriction of competition falling within the scope of Article 81 (1),[444]
- if they are unlikely to affect trade between member states,[445]
- if they are necessary for the performance of particular tasks assigned under Article 86 (2),[446]
- if they are ancillary to the implementation of a joint venture, or
- if they do not *appreciably* restrict competition because certain *qualitative* criteria are not met or the market share held by each of the parties does not

Watts, D.Comm. Dec. 21, 1976, 1977 OJ L 39/19; *aff'd Tepea*, ECJ June 20, 1978, 1978 ECR 138; *Hasselblad*, D.Comm. Dec. 2, 1981, 1982 OJ L 161/18; *aff'd* ECJ Feb. 21, 1984, 1984 ECR 883; *Polistil/Arbois*, D.Comm. May 16, 1984, 1984 OJ L 136/9; *Konica*, D.Comm. Dec. 18, 1987, 1988 OJ L 78/34.

439. *Johnson & Johnson*, D.Comm. Nov. 25, 1980, 1980 OJ L 377/16; *Sandoz*, D.Comm. July 13, 1987, 1987 OJ L 222/28 (pharmaceuticals).

440. Commission Notice 1996 OJ C 207/4 and *Novalliance/Systemform*, D.Comm. Dec. 4, 1996, 1997 OJ L 47/11 (symbolic fine of ECU 100,000). This conforms to the Commission's previous practice in cases terminated without fines such as *Caterpillar*, Fifteenth Report on Competition Policy, point 57; *Spectacle Frames*, Fifteenth Report on Competition Policy, points 64–66; *Mitsui/Bridgestone*, Fifteenth Report on Competition Policy, point 60.

441. *See Volkswagen/Audi*, D.Comm. Jan. 28, 1998, 1998 OJ L 124/60, para. 202 (*aff'd* CFI July 6, 2000, 2000 ECR II-2707).

442. *BMW Belgium*, D.Comm. Dec. 23, 1977, 1978 OJ L 46/33, 42 (*aff'd* July 12, 1979, 1979 ECR 2435, paras 53–54); *Tipp-Ex*, D.Comm. July 10, 1987, 1987 OJ L 222/1, 10 (*aff'd* Feb. 8, 1990, 1990 ECR II-261); *Daimler Chrysler*, D.Comm. Oct. 10, 2001, 2002 OJ L 257/1, point 233.

443. *Pioneer*, ECJ June 7, 1983, 1983 ECR 1825, 1912, para. 133; *British Sugar – Tate & Lyle*, D.Comm. Oct. 14, 1998, 1999 OJ L 76/1, *aff'd* CFI July 12, 2001, 2001 ECR II-2035; the parties were in this case competitors: para. 103.

444. *See* Article 2 (1), second subparagraph of Regulation 2790/1999.

445. E.g. in the case of a mere national resale price maintenance system: *German/Austrian Books*, IP/00/651 of June 22, 2000; *Deutsche Buchpreisbindung*, D.Comm. March 22, 2002, IP/02/461.

446. *FFSA*, CFI Feb. 27, 1997, 1997 ECR II-229, paras 176–177.

exceed the *quantitative* limits which are set in the new Commission Notice on Agreements of Minor Importance at 15% and do not constitute hardcore restrictions.[447]

Where agreements contain appreciable restrictions of competition that are not exempted by the regulation (in particular between companies with a market share exceeding 30% or non-compete obligations agreed for a longer duration than five years) they necessitate individual assessment under Article 81 (3), which requires clear and substantial efficiency effects.[448] Companies are asked to do a *self-assessment* of the possible consequences of their vertical agreements under the law; the Guidelines assist them in carrying out such an assessment under the EC competition rules.[449]

No Need for Precautionary Notification.
The new Regulation 1/2003 adopted on November 26, 2002,[450] which replaces Regulation 17, abandons notification with effect from May 1, 2004. Article 81 (3) may be applied directly, as the case may be, by the Commission, the national competition authorities or the national courts in the framework of a close cooperation between them, designed to avoid conflicts. Only where cases give rise to genuine uncertainty does the Commission intend, when requested, to issue informal guidance.[451]

(b) Hardcore Restrictions

(i) Resale Price Maintenance and Substitutes

Minimum Prices.
Obliging a purchaser to resell at not less than a particular price is an obvious restraint of competition that is expressly prohibited by Article 81 (1) (a) and is not exempted by Regulation 2790/1999[452] because of the two main negative effects: a reduction in intra-brand price competition and increased pricing transparency.[453] The prohibition applies not only at retail level but also at higher levels of trade,[454]

447. *De Minimis* Notice, 2001 OJ C 149, points 8 and 12. There is a 5% threshold for a contribution to a cumulative effect to be deemed 'significant' (point 9).
448. *See* Guidelines, point 180. Hardcore restrictions are normally unlikely to obtain clearance under Article 81 (3): *Nintendo II*, D.Comm. Oct. 30, 2002, 2003 OJ L 255/3, point 341.
449. IP/00/520 of May 24, 2000.
450. 2003 OJ L 1/1.
451. Recital 38 of Regulation 1/2003.
452. Article 4 (a).
453. Guidelines, 2000 OJ C 291/1, point 112.
454. *Editions Nathan*, D.Comm. July 5, 2000, 2001 OJ L 54/1.

and not only to setting minimum *final* price[455] but also to laying down a minimum profit margin to be retained by the dealer[456] or the maximum discount to be granted to its customers,[457] which are tantamount to setting minimum final prices. Minimum resale price provisions at the wholesale level may restrain or prevent competition between wholesalers and retailers even if retail prices are controlled, and, therefore, also infringe Article 81 (1).[458]

Maximum and Recommended Prices.
Setting *maximum* prices – despite appearing at first glance to be beneficial to consumers – may interfere with the dealer's freedom to set its own prices and may, in practice, mostly be understood as fixing the final price. A manufacturer may have an interest in preventing dealers from charging high prices for short periods while it is promoting a new product, but normally merely recommending a maximum price should suffice in such circumstances; this is permitted, [459] provided that there is no agreement or concerted practice that the dealer will observe the recommended price.[460] Accordingly, Article 4 (a) permits imposing a maximum or recommending a sale price, provided they do not amount to a fixed or minimum sale price even indirectly a result of pressure from, or incentives offered to, any of the parties.[461] However, the exemption of maximum or recommended prices is limited to the block exemption's market share threshold of 30%. In cases where this threshold is exceeded Article 81 (1) may be infringed if the maximum or recommended price is uniformly implemented by resellers and, especially in a narrow oligopoly, facilitates collusion between suppliers by exchanging information on the preferred price level and by reducing the likelihood of lower prices.[462] In such a case Article 81 (3) is unlikely to be applied.

---

455. *Vichy*, D.Comm. Jan. 11, 1991, 1991 OJ L 75/57; *aff'd* CFI Feb. 27, 1992, 1992 ECR II-415, para. 111.
456. *See* in an horizontal context *Centraal Bureau voor de Rijwielhandel*, D.Comm. Dec. 2, 1977, 1978 OJ L 20/18, 24.
457. *Distillers*, D.Comm. Dec. 20, 1977, 1978 OJ L 50/16; or prohibiting discounts altogether: *Flemish Travel Agents*, ECJ Oct. 10, 1987, 1987 ECR 3801, para. 17; *Editions Nathan*, D.Comm. July 5, 2000, 2001 OJ L 54/1, point 87 (fixing price margins).
458. *See FEDETAB*, ECJ Oct. 29, 1980, 1980 ECR 3125, 3263–3264, paras 131–134.
459. *Editions Nathan*, D.Comm. July 5, 2000, 2001 OJ L 54/1, point 87. *See Yves Rocher*, D.Comm. Dec. 17, 1986, 1987 OJ L 8/49, 56; *Pronuptia*, ECJ Jan 29, 1986, 1986 ECR 353, para. 25; *Pronuptia*, D.Comm. Dec. 17, 1986, 1987 OJ L 13/39, 44.
460. Agreements to prevent price concertation may be a condition for clearance: *VISA International*, D.Comm. D.Comm. July 24, 2002, 2002 OJ L 318/17, point 106.
461. The U.S. Supreme Court decided in 1997 that setting *maximum* resale prices is not *per se* unlawful, but instead must be judged under the so-called 'rule of reason' since this form of vertical price setting may restrain pricing to the final consumer: *State Oil v. Khan*, 118 S. Ct. 275 (1997).
462. Guidelines, points 225–228.

Commission's Enforcement Practice toward National Resale Price Maintenance.
Faced with the legality and even official encouragement of resale price maintenance in the member states, an attitude which has only recently changed in most countries and still prevails in some sectors (notably, books), the Commission has traditionally been reluctant to take action against national resale price maintenance arrangements unless they exhibited other anticompetitive features and clearly affected trade between member states;[463] if not, resale price maintenance was considered a matter for national law.[464] The Commission has intervened in national resale price maintenance arrangements only where they:

– are supported by prohibitions on exports[465] or reimports,[466]
– are applied also to exports[467] or imports,[468]
– form part of a selective distribution system,[469] or
– are practised in connection with an exclusive distribution or purchasing agreement.[470]

These examples show how difficult it is to establish and enforce a resale price maintenance scheme in different member states with different price levels unless

---

463. *GERO-fabriek*, D.Comm. Dec. 22, 1976, 1977 OJ L 16/8, 10.
464. E.g. in the case of a mere national resale price maintenance system: *German/Austrian Books*, IP/00/651 of June 22, 2000; *Deutsche Buchpreisbindung*, D.Comm. March 22, 2002, IP/02/461.
465. *Glaxo Wellcome*, D.Comm. May 8, 2001, 2001 OJ L 302/1, points 116–118 (no fine because of notification immunity); *Volkswagen II*, D.Comm. June 29, 2001, 2001 OJ L 262/14, points 85–91 (high fine).
466. *Agfa-Gevaert*, First Report on Competition Policy, point 55; *Deutsche Philips*, D.Comm. Oct. 5, 1973, 1973 OJ L 293/40, 41; *GERO-fabriek*, D.Comm. Dec. 22, 1976, 1977 OJ L 16/8, 11; *AEG-Telefunken*, ECJ Oct. 25, 1983, 1983 ECR 3151, paras 71–76.
467. *Italian Spectacles*, Fifteenth Report on Competition Policy, point 66; *Junghans*, D.Comm. Dec. 21, 1976, 1977 OJ L 30/10, 12–13; *Net Book Agreements*, CFI July 9, 1992, 1992 ECR II-1995 paras 57, 83–84, 98.
468. *Agfa-Gevaert*, First Report on Competition Policy, point 55; *Deutsche Philips*, D.Comm. Oct. 5, 1973, 1973 OJ L 293/40, 42; *SABA I*, D.Comm. Dec. 15, 1975, 1976 OJ L 28/19, 24; *Dutch Books*, IP/99/668 of Sept. 9, 1999 (clearance following commitment to abolish resale price maintenance on imported books). But *cf. French Book Prices I*, ECJ Jan. 10, 1985, 1985 ECR 1, paras 26–27 (applying resale price maintenance to reimports of books not contrary to free trade rules of Article 28 if the books were exported for the *purpose* of avoiding French resale price maintenance legislation)
469. *SABA I*, D.Comm. Dec. 15, 1975, 1976 OJ L 28/19, 24; *Hasselblad*, D.Comm. Dec. 2, 1981, 1982 OJ L 161/18, 25, 29; *AEG-Telefunken*, ECJ Oct. 25, 1983, 1983 ECR 3151, paras 71–76; *Spanish Car Prices*, Commission Press Release No. IP/89/639; *Yamaha*, D.Comm. July 16, 2003, IP/03/1028 (fining concerted practices aimed at partitioning markets and fixing resale prices even if the restrictions are limited to certain dealers).
470. *Hennessey/Henkell*, D.Comm. Dec. 11, 1980, 1980 OJ L 383/11, 15; *Liebig (Spices)*, D.Comm. Dec. 21, 1977, 1978 OJ L 53/20, 23.

it is associated with further restrictions of competition. In such cases the fact that national law permits resale price maintenance does not preclude the application of Article 81 to the aspects of the arrangement that affect intra-Community trade, even if this leads to the practical difficulties in enforcing the resale price maintenance scheme. The Commission intervened against the resale price maintenance in the book sector insofar as the system extended to exports and imports between member states, except where the books in question are exported and reimported with the sole purpose of circumventing the national resale price maintenance tolerated by the Commission.[471] The result of the Commission's enforcement action was the abolition of national resale price maintenance schemes with the exception of books, newpapers and magazines.[472]

Threats or Inducements to Maintain Prices.
Resale prices may be set directly by agreement or indirectly by other means, such as by offering inducements (e.g., annual bonuses or fidelity rebates)[473] or threatening detriments (e.g., refusal to supply). A systematic refusal to supply or threats to that effect in retaliation for undercutting a particular resale price may make it apparent to other dealers that following the manufacturer's pricing policy is a condition of being supplied.[474] The danger of resale price maintenance being indirectly enforced by these means is especially great in a selective distribution system, which can be implemented so as to exclude price-conscious dealers.[475] Although there is an inherent tendency for selective distribution to weaken intrabrand price competition in return for benefits such as quality of service – one of several other forms of intra-brand competition – this does not warrant the total elimination of price competition or the establishment of a rigid price structure among distributors.[476] An effect similar to resale price maintenance may be obtained indirectly by prohibiting dealers from engaging in certain forms of allegedly unfair competition, such as aggressive cut-price sales promotions.[477] This policy may be enforced by

471. *German/Austrian Books*, IP/00/651 of June 22, 2000; *Deutsche Buchpreisbindung*, IP/00/651 of June 22, 2000 and IP/02/461 of March 22, 2002; *Editions Nathan*, D.Comm. July 5, 2000, 2001 OJ L 54/1 (imposing a moderate fine of EUR 60,000).
472. The Court suggested in the *AMP/Binon* case that there might well be good reasons for exempting the resale price maintenance scheme, and referred in particular to the need for publishers to take back unsold copies: *AMP/Binon*, ECJ July 3, 1985, 1985 ECR 2015, 2045–2046, paras 39–47; *Net Book Agreement*, ECJ Jan. 17, 1995, 1995 ECR I-23, paras 45–48. *See also Echirolles/Association du Dauphiné*, ECJ Oct. 3, 2000, 2000 ECR I-8207.
473. *Liebig (Spices)*, D.Comm. Dec. 21, 1977, 1978 OJ L 53/20, 23.
474. *Johnson & Johnson*, D.Comm. Nov. 25, 1980, 1980 OJ L 377/16, 24.
475. *AEG-Telefunken*, ECJ Oct. 25, 1983, 1983 ECR 3151, paras 67–78; *Hasselblad*, ECJ Feb. 21, 1984, 1984 ECR 883, paras 44–52.
476. *SABA I*, ECJ Oct. 25, 1977, 1977 ECR 1875, paras 21–22; *FEDETAB*, ECJ Oct. 29, 1980, 1980 ECR 3125, para. 139; *SABA II*, D.Comm. Dec. 21, 1983, 1983 OJ L 376/41, 47; *Grundig II*, D.Comm. July 10, 1985, 1985 OJ L 233/1, 8.
477. *Hasselblad*, ECJ Feb. 21, 1984, 1984 ECR 883, paras 24–29.

cutting off offending dealers' supplies or threatening to do so, and by threatening legal action under national laws on unfair competition that prohibit 'loss-leading,' if dealers fail to observe the supplier's desired resale price level.[478] A similar form of indirect influence over resale prices occurs when a dealer is required to give an undertaking to follow the supplier's general pricing policy.[479]

Collective Resale Price Maintenance Prohibited.
An agreement among competitors to set the retail price at which the goods will be sold to consumers violates Article 81 (1) and is not exempted by Regulation 2790/1999,[480] even if the retail prices charged by dealers are not identical and there is inter-brand competition.[481] If competitors collectively set *recommended* resale prices, this will also infringe Article 81 even if dealers do not follow the recommended price.[482]

Government Action to Enforce Resale Price Maintenance.
The Court of Justice has ruled that Belgian legislation making legally binding a collective resale price maintenance scheme agreed between travel agents, under which agents were not allowed to pass on any of the commission they received from tour operators to their customers, was a breach of Article 10 of the EC Treaty which forbids member states to enact or maintain in force legislation contrary to the specific requirements of the Treaty, namely Articles 3 (g) and 81.[483] On the other hand, the Court found that French legislation requiring resale price maintenance for books did not necessarily infringe Article 10 in conjunction with Articles 3 (g) and 81 since no clearly developed Community policy had been established in this sector and because the Commission had not yet taken enforcement action against purely national resale price maintenance schemes.[484]

---

478. *See VBVB/VBBB*, ECJ Jan. 17, 1984, 1984 ECR 19, 63, paras 35–37.
479. *AEG-Telefinken*, ECJ Oct. 25, 1983, 1983 ECR 3151, para. 43. *See also British Sugar – Tate & Lyle*, D.Comm. Oct. 14, 1998, 1999 OJ L 76/1, points 66–78 (mutual information on resale prices), *aff'd* CFI July 12, 2001, 2001 ECR II-2035, paras 58–59 and 66.
480. Article 2 (4).
481. *FEDETAB*, ECJ Oct. 29, 1980, 1980 ECR 3125, paras 129–134; *VBVB/VBBB*, ECJ Jan. 17, 1984, 1984 ECR 19, paras 44–46; *SSI*, ECJ Dec. 10, 1985, 1985 ECR 3831, paras 29–32; *Flemish Travel Agents*, ECJ Oct. 1, 1987, 1987 ECR 3801, paras 17–21.
482. *VCH*, ECJ Oct. 17, 1972, 1972 ECR 977, paras 15–25; *Fire Insurance*, ECJ Jan. 27, 1987, 1987 ECR 405, paras 39–43; *FENEX*, D.Comm. June 5, 1996, 1996 OJ L 181/28.
483. *Flemish Travel Agents*, ECJ Oct. 1, 1987, 1987 ECR 3801, paras 22–24. Where both the government and undertakings or associations infringed Community law (respectively Article 10 and Article 81) the Commission must take action against both, as in the *CSND* case against the government (ECJ June 18, 1998, 1998 ECR I-3851) and against the association (D.Comm. June 30, 1993, 1993 OJ L 203/27, *aff'd* CFI March 30, 2000, 2000 ECR II-1807). *See* in greater detail Chapter IX.F.
484. *French Book Prices I*, ECJ Jan. 10, 1985, 1985 ECR 1, para. 31.

(ii) Territorial Restrictions and Substitutes

Allocation of Territories or Customers.

Export and import prohibitions are usually designed to protect dealers from parallel imports and reinforce artificially different price levels between member states.[485] Therefore, a prohibition on exports to other member states will be found to infringe Article 81 (1) even if it was imposed by pressure or threats[486] or as a means of self-defense against growing parallel imports[487] and regardless of whether it was strictly enforced,[488] because even then it will have a psychological effect on potential exporters.[489] This accords with the equal status of anticompetitive *object* and *effect* in Article 81 (1); however, export bans that were not strictly enforced, were ineffective or were quickly abandoned may incur lower fines.[490] Even an additional clause in the agreement providing that the export prohibition does not apply where it is illegal or unenforceable will still infringe Article 81 (1) since this conveys the impression to uninformed dealers that they may not export when they have the right to do so.[491]

Disguised Export Restrictions.

An export prohibition need not necessarily be expressed in those terms. The following restrictions also amount to export prohibitions:

– limiting quantities to be exported,[492] e.g. by imposing supply quotas (obligation

485. *See Editions Nathan*, D.Comm. May 16, 2000, 2001 OJ L 54/1; *Opel*, D.Comm. Sept. 20, 2000, 2001 OJ L 59/1; *JC Bamford*, D.Comm. Dec. 21, 2000, 2002 OJ L 69/1; *Volkswagen II*, D.Comm. June 29, 2001, 2001 OJ L 262/14; *rev'd* CFI Dec. 3, 2003, T-208/01; *Daimler Chrysler*, D.Comm. Oct. 10, 2001, 2002 OJ L 257/1; *Nintendo*, D.Comm. Oct. 30, 2002, 2003 OJ L 255/33, points 262–282.
486. *Tipp-Ex*, D.Comm. July 10, 1987, 1987 OJ L 222/1, 7.
487. *Pioneer*, ECJ June 7, 1983, 1983 ECR 1825, paras 88–90; *BASF Coatings*, CFI May 19, 1999, 1999 ECR II-1581, para. 109.
488. *Hasselblad*, ECJ Feb. 21, 1984, 1984 ECR 883, paras 45–46; *BASF Coatings*, CFI May 19, 1999, 1999 ECR II-1581, para. 139. However, it may be an attenuating factor when imposing fines, *see Yamaha*, D.Comm. July 16, 2003, IP/03/1028.
489. *Miller International*, ECJ Feb. 1, 1978, 1978 ECR 131, 148, paras 6–7; *Herlitz*, CFI July 14, 1994, 1994 ECR II-53 1, para. 40; *BASF Coatings*, CFI May 19, 1999, 1999 ECR II-1581, para. 156.
490. *JCB Service*, CFI Jan. 13, 2004, T-67/01, para. 117. *See also Miller International*, D.Comm. Dec. 1, 1976, 1976 OJ L 357/40, 43; *Polistil/Arbois*, D.Comm. May 16, 1984, 1984 OJ L 136/9, 15; *Konica*, D.Comm. Dec. 23, 1987, 1988 OJ L 78/34, 42; *Novalliance/Systemform*, D.Comm. Dec. 4, 1996, 1997 OJ 47/11.
491. *Kodak*, D.Comm. June 30, 1970, 1970 OJ L 147/24, 25; *John Deere*, D.Comm. Dec. 14, 1984, 1985 OJ L 35/58, 62.
492. *See* the discussion of the case law in *Bundesverband der Arzneimittel-Importeure – Bayer*, CFI Jan. 6, 2004, C-2/01 P, paras 78–89.

on the dealers to sell at least 85% of available vehicles within their contract territory);[493]

- subjecting exports to prior approval of the supplier[494] or to prior contact with the dealer in the country of destination;[495]
- subjecting export to compensatory payments[496] or splitting the profit when selling in another country ('profit splitting mechanism');[497]
- prohibiting or controlling sales to dealers which are identified as exporters[498] or applying different prices or rebates according to the destination,[499]
- excluding export sales from a bonus scheme;[500]
- obliging the dealer to pass on orders from customers in other territories to the distributor to whom that territory is allocated,[501]
- restricting exports by dealers to a particular member state by enforcement or threatened enforcement of industrial property rights or other rights against imports to that member state,[502] or by initiating systematic control of parallel imports,[503]

---

493. *Volkswagen*, CFI July 6, 2000, 2000 ECR II-2707, paras 49, 79–89, 189, 236 and 343, *aff'd* ECJ Sept. 18, 2003, C-338/00P, paras 44, 60–67.
494. *Ciment/Kerpen*, ECJ Dec. 14, 1983, 1983 ECR 4173, paras 6–9; *Hasselblad*, ECJ Feb. 21, 1984, 1984 ECR 883, paras 41–46; *Yamaha*, D.Comm. July 16, 2003, IP/03/1028.
495. *Yamaha*, D.Comm. July 16, 2003, IP/03/1028.
496. *JCB Service*, CFI Jan. 13, 2004, T-67/01, para. 136. *See also Gosme/Martell-DMP*, D.Comm. May 15, 1991, 199 1 OJ L 185/23.
497. *Volkswagen*, CFI July 6, 2000, 2000 ECR II-2707, para. 236, *aff'd* ECJ Sept. 18, 2003, C-338/00P, para. 44. *Nigeria LNG*, IP/02/1869.
498. *Novalliance/Systemform*, D.Comm. Dec. 4, 1996, 1997 OJ L 47/11; *Volkswagen*, CFI July 6, 2000, 2000 ECR II-2707, para.178; *Nintendo II*, D.Comm. Oct. 30, 2002, 2003 OJ L 255/33, points 276–277. *See General Motors – Opel*, CFI Oct. 21, 2003, T-368/00, paras 78–88 (however, annulling the Commission decision in this respect because it was a unilateral act rather than part of an agreement). *See also Van Doren + Q v. Lifestyle sports*, ECJ April 8, 2003, C-244/00, paras 25–42 (with respect to the risks of identifying parallel exporters).
499. *Pittsburgh Corning*, D.Comm. Nov. 23, 1972, 1972 OJ 272/35; *Moët et Chandon*, D.Comm. Nov. 27, 1981, 1982 OJ L 94/7; *Gosme/Martell-DMP*, D.Comm. May 15, 1991, 1991 OJ L 185/21; *Glaxo Wellcome*, D.Comm. May 8, 2001, 2001 OJ L 302/1, point 119 (cease and desist orders); *JCB*, D.Comm. Dec. 21, 2000, 2002 OJ L 69/1.
500. *JCB*, D.Comm. Dec. 21, 2000, 2002 OJ L 69/1, *aff'd* CFI Jan. 13, 2004, T-67/01, paras 97–104; *General Motors – Opel*, CFI Oct. 21, 2003, T-368/00, paras 97–105.
501. This obligation is tantamount to a passive sales ban: *BASF*, D.Comm. July 12, 1995, 1995 OJ L 272/16 (fine of ECU 2.6 million); *aff'd* CFI May 19, 1999, 1999 ECR II-1581, paras 80–90; *Volkswagen*, ECJ Sept. 18, 2003, C-338/00P, para. 66.
502. *Dalle Crode*, ECJ Oct. 1, 1975, 1975 ECR 1103, paras 6–18; *Hydrotherm/Compact*, ECJ July 12, 1984, 1984 ECR 2999, paras 21–22; *Bayer Dental*, D.Comm. Nov. 28, 1990, 1990 OJ L 351/46, 49 (warning customers against exporting because of possible damages claims for infringement of (unspecified) industrial property rights in the country of destination); *VIHO/Parker Pen*, D.Comm. July 15, 1992, 1992 OJ L 233/27 (fine reduced by CFI July 14, 1994, 1994 ECR II-549 from ECU 700,000 to 400,000).
503. *See John Deere Agricultural Tractor Registration Exchange*, CFI Oct. 27, 1994, 1994 ECR II-957, paras 47–50.

- obliging the dealer not to purchase from other dealers in other member states;[504]
- making parallel imports more difficult by delaying or raising the cost of the necessary conformity certificate necessary for importing the products,[505] or by not granting the usual warranty,[506]
- making parallel imports more difficult by exercising industrial[507] or intellectual property rights,[508]
- discontinuing shipments to exporters,[509] and
- reducing shipments to dealers to what is considered their 'normal' demand, i.e. for satisfying the demand in their contractual territory, when the practice is a well known and systematically applied policy in a market with active parallel trade.[510]

Prohibitions on Exports to Non-EC Countries and of Reimportation into the EC.
Prohibiting exports from the EC and/or reimportation into the Community infringes Article 81 only if it may appreciably restrict competition and trade within the Community, which depends – according to the Court of Justice – in particular on the structure of the market (whether characterized by a large or small number of competitors) and on the existence of substantial price differences (which cannot be explained by duties, taxes or transport costs).[511] Obligations to export goods to countries outside the Community and EEA and not to sell them within the EC and EEA countries do not as such infringe Article 81 (1) and Article 58 of

504. *JCB Service*, CFI Jan. 13, 2004, T-67/01, para. 111.
505. *General Motors*, ECJ Nov. 13, 1975, 1975 ECR 1367, para. 12; *British Leyland*, ECJ Nov. 11, 1986, 1986 ECR 3263, paras 30–34; *Montedison/Stähler*, D.Comm. June 24, 1993, 1993 OJ L 272/28.
506. *Zanussi*, D.Comm. Oct. 23, 1978, 1978 OJ L 322/28; *Sperry New Holland*, D.Comm. Dec. 16, 1985, 1985 OJ L 376/21, 26. However, providing additional national warranty services for locally purchased products is permissible: *Hasselblad*, ECJ Feb. 21, 1984, 1984 ECR 883, paras 32–34. After the *MetroCartier* decision of the Court of Justice (Jan. 13, 1995, 1995 ECR I-15) the supplier may, however, oblige the dealer to limit the warranty services to the products supplied by authorized dealers.
507. *Beguélin*, ECJ Nov. 25, 1971, 1971 ECR 949, paras 19–24.
508. *Norway/Astra Norge*, EFTA Court of Justice, Nov. 24, 1998, E-1/98 (claimed copyright on description of medical properties of a pharmaceutical product).
509. *Tretorn*, D.Comm. Dec. 22, 1994, 1994 OJ L 378/45 (fine of ECU 600,000).
510. *Sandoz*, D.Comm. July 13, 1987, 1987 OJ L 222/28, 32; *Volkswagen/Audi*, D.Comm. Jan. 28, 1998, 1998 OJ L 124/60 (*aff'd* CFI July 6, 2000, 2000 ECR II-2707 and ECJ Sept. 18, 2003, C-338/00 P); *Daimler Chrysler*, D.Comm. Oct. 10, 2001, 2002 OJ L 257/1; *EdF/Wingas*, IP/02/1293. In the *Opel* case the Court of First Instance annulled the Commission decision with regard to Opel's policy to limit the delivery volumes in the case of exports because this practice did not enter into the field of contractual relations between the supplier and the dealers identified as exporters (unilateral act): *Opel*, CFI Oct. 21, 2003, T-368/00, paras 78–88.
511. *Javico/Yves St. Laurent*, ECJ April 28, 1998, 1998 ECR I-1983, paras 17–28.

the EEA Agreement[512] but may do so in the context of other, broader horizontal restrictions.[513]

Partitioning Markets by Way of Dual Pricing Systems: Usually Anticompetitive.
If prices vary from one member state to the next for the same product, the supplier may try to maintain those price differences by selling the product to exporters at different prices or different rates of discount depending on the product's ultimate destination.[514] The Commission considers such practices to be tantamount to an export restriction that infringes Article 81 (1).[515] The basic concern is that it is incompatible with a common market to require an exporter to report where the product will ultimately be delivered, to set the price accordingly and thereby to influence the exporter's sales activities.[516] In one exceptional case, however, the Commission considered exempting for a limited period a dual pricing system planned by Distillers in order to reintroduce Johnny Walker Red Label whisky into the United Kingdom.[517] In the end, the Commission reiterated its objections to the dual pricing system and Distillers abandoned it.[518] Another question is whether a supplier may charge some of his dealers lower prices in order to meet lower priced competition. The Commission has not challenged this practice on competitive local markets such as petrol (gasoline) retailing,[519] but did so in the *Polistil/Arbois* case where the lower prices were charged to enable an exclusive distributor to compete with parallel imports into its territory.[520]

Dual Pricing Induced by Government Price Controls.
Manufacturers may be obliged to charge different prices in different national markets because in some markets prices are kept artificially low or high owing to government price regulation. In such cases manufacturers may not impose

---

512. *Zanussi*, D.Comm. Dec. 23, 1977, 1978 OJ L 322/36; *Iqbal*, Twenty-first Report on Competition Policy, p. 334.
513. *Sugar*, ECJ Dec. 16, 1975, 1975 ECR 1663, paras 558–602; *Asturienne-Zinc*, ECJ March 28, 1984, 1984 ECR 1679, paras 24–30; *Steel Mesh*, CFI April 6, 1995, 1995 ECR II-987, paras 115–116.
514. *Javico/Yves St. Laurent*, ECJ April 28, 1998, 1998 ECR I-1983, paras 17–28.
515. *Bayer-Adalat*, D.Comm. Jan. 10, 1996, 1996 OJ L 201/1, paras 29–31 (*rev'd* CFI Oct. 26, 2000, 2000 ECR II-3383 because no 'concurrence of wills' was proved); *Pittsburgh Coming*, D.Comm. Nov. 23, 1972, 1972 OJ L 272/35, 38; *Sperry New Holland*, D.Comm. Dec. 16, 1985, 1985 OJ L 376/21, 26.
516. *Glaxo Wellcome*, D.Comm. May 8, 2001, 2001 OJ L 302/1, points 119–143; *Moët et Chandon*, D.Comm. Nov. 27, 1981, 1982 OJ L 94/7, point 11; *Gosme/Martell*, D.Comm. May 15, 1991, 1991 OJ L 185/23, points 19 and 22.
517. *Distillers I*, D.Comm. Dec. 20, 1977, 1978 OJ L 50/16.
518. *Distillers III*, Seventeenth Report on Competition Policy, point 65.
519. *VEB/Shell*, Sixteenth Report on Competition Policy, point 55.
520. *Polistil/Arbois*, D.Comm. May 16, 1984, 1984 OJ L 136/9, 12.

export restrictions or restrict supplies to low-price markets in order to prevent parallel imports.[521] Distortions caused by government regulation do not justify private self-help measures to restrict trade.[522] However, a manufacturer cannot be realistically expected to increase supplies at low prices that are set by government regulation in order to meet increased demand from dealers that are engaged in systematic and massive exports to other member states. On the other hand, a strict and carefully monitored prohibition against any export activity would infringe Article 81 (1) because it would be a disproportionate remedy for the evil to be avoided.[523] When goods are scarce in a low-price market as a result of increased demand it may be sufficient to limit supplies *pro rata* to all customers (and not only those who are likely to export to other member states) to normal quantities, without attempting to control exports to other member states.

Partitioning Product Markets by Way of Field-of-Use Restrictions. Field-of-use restrictions are not hardcore restrictions and are therefore exempted up to a market share of 30%. However, restrictions on the use of goods supplied may be tantamount to partitioning of markets and maintaining artificial price differences according to the use of the goods, thereby infringing Article 81 (1).[524] Examples are exclusive customer allocation,[525] the obligation to use the goods only for internal consumption,[526] to sell white sugar only for denaturing and not for consumption,[527] not to resell green bananas[528] or green (unroasted) coffee[529] and to resell pharmaceutical raw materials only as finished, packaged medicines and not in bulk or by category of end use, e.g., human or veterinary medicines.[530] However, the Commission and the Court have found that certain use and customer restrictions do not infringe Article 81 (1). Examples are restrictions obliging dealers that distribute goods in large quantities to particular categories of customers, such as to hotels and restaurants, not to sell to others[531] or limiting wholesalers to resell to dealers and not end users on the ground that the wholesale and retail trade

---

521. *Gosme/Martell*, D.Comm. May 15, 1991, 1991 OJ L 185/23 (fine of ECU 300,000).
522. *Glaxo Wellcome*, D.Comm. May 8, 2001, 2001 OJ L 302/1, point 132. *See FEDETAB*, ECJ Oct. 29, 1980, 1980 ECR 3125, paras 150–156.
523. *Johnson & Johnson*, D.Comm. Nov. 25, 1980, 1980 OJ L 377/36.
524. Article 4 (a) and (b) of Regulation 2790/1999.
525. *BP Kemi/DDSF*, D.Comm. Sept. 5, 1979, 1979 OJ L 286/32, 45.
526. *Ciment/Kerpen*, ECJ Dec. 14, 1983, 1983 ECR 4173, paras 6–9.
527. *Sugar*, ECJ, Dec. 16, 1975, 1975 ECR 1663, paras 241–308; *British Sugar*, D.Comm. Oct. 14, 1998, 1999 OJ L 76/1, points 163–168 (*aff'd* CFI July 12, 2001, 2001 ECR II-2035).
528. *United Brands*, ECJ. Feb. 14, 1978, 1978 ECR 207, paras 130–162 (infringement of Article 82).
529. *Cafeteros de Colombia*, D.Comm. Dec. 10, 1982, 1982 OJ L 360/31, 34; *Brazilian Coffee*, Fifth Report in Competition Policy, point 33; Sixteenth Report on Competition Policy, point 54.
530. *Beecham Pharma/Hoechst*, Sixth Report on Competition Policy, points 129–133.
531. *Villeroy & Boch*, D.Comm. Dec. 16, 1985, 1985 OJ L 376/15, 19–20.

perform different functions.[532] Restrictions on the sale of alcoholic beverages by special duty-free wholesalers other than for duty-free consumption have been upheld.[533] Field-of-use restrictions in patent or know-how license agreements that restrict use to one or more technical fields of application or to one or more product markets (but not to particular classes of customer within the same technological field or the same product market) are not considered as restricting competition.[534]

(iii) Exceptions to Hardcore Resale Restrictions.

Certain resale restrictions may be covered by the block exemption or not lead to an appreciable restriction of competition:[535]

- restrictions on active sales into the exclusive territory[536] or to an exclusive customer group reserved to the supplier or allocated by the supplier to another buyer,[537] where such a restriction does not limit sales by the customers of the buyer,
- restrictions on wholesalers not to sell directly to consumers;[538]
- restrictions on resales to unauthorized distributors by members of a selective distribution system;[539]
- restrictions against a buyer's reselling components, supplied for the purposes of incorporation, to customers who would use them to manufacture the same types of goods as those produced by the supplier;[540]
- restrictions not to sell outside the franchisee's business premises (location clause).[541]

(c) Exclusive Distribution Agreements

Possible Anticompetitive Effects on Intra-Brand Competition.
Even a supplier in an overall strong position may need the assistance of an exclusive distributor for introducing and marketing its products in a certain national

---

532. *SABA I*, ECJ Oct. 25, 1977, 1977 ECR 1875, paras 28–30.
533. *Distillers (Victuallers)*, D.Comm. July 22, 1980, 1980 OJ L 233/43, 44–45.
534. Article 4 (1) (c) (i) of Regulation 772/2004 on technology transfer agreements.
535. Article 4 (b) of Regulation 2790/1999.
536. Commission's practice since *Grundig*, ECJ July 13, 1966, 1966 ECR 322; *Kodak*, D.Comm. June 30, 1970, 1970 OJ L 147/24; *Computerland*, D.Comm. July 13, 1987, 1987 OJ L 222/12.
537. Article 4 (b), first indent, of Regulation 2790/1999; *see* Guidelines, points 178–183.
538. Article 4 (b), second indent, of Regulation 2790/1999; *SABA I*, ECJ Oct. 25, 1977, 1977 ECR 1875, paras 28–30.
539. Article 4 (b), third indent, of Regulation 2790/1999; *De Beers*, D.Comm. Jan. 16, 2003, IP/09/64 (clearance following amendment of the selective distribution scheme).
540. Article 4 (b), fourth indent, of Regulation 2790/1999; *see* Article 4 (1) (b) (iv) of Regulation 1400/2002 on motor vehicles.
541. Article 4 (c) of Regulation 2790/1999.

market. Supposing that the relevant geographic market has to be defined as national,[542] a significant market share in certain national markets does not seem to preclude an individual exemption of the exclusive distribution arrangement (which only prevents the supplier from entering into other dealership agreements and from competing actively with the exclusive dealer in its territory). The possible negative effect of parallel exclusive distribution agreements entered into by several large competing suppliers is the reduction of *inter-brand* competition between those competitors, facilitating collusion between suppliers or buyers,[543] in particular in cases of multiple exclusive dealerships.[544] This anti-competitive risk is minor when a supplier with a market share of 50% or more sells only a small amount of its output (say, 5%) through tied retailers and the rest of its production is sold through dealers without any non-compete or quantity forcing obligations.[545]

Possible Negative Effects on Inter-Brand Competition.
The major competitive concern is, however, the risk of a significant market foreclosure effect which results from an exclusionary or non-compete clause imposed on the dealer.[546] In cases where the *supplier* has a dominant position, it may be necessary to give exclusive distributors more independence from the contract supplier in order to enable them to compete independently.[547] In cases where the *buyer* (dealer) has a dominant position, i.e. where a commercial monopoly is not fully liberalized yet according to Article 31, future competition may be restricted by long-term exclusive distribution agreements concluded between a foreign supplier and the dealer-monopolist that are likely to reinforce the dealer's dominant position during and after the liberalization.[548] Therefore such arrangements are

542. *See* under the merger regulation *Fiat-New Holland/Case*, D.Comm. Oct. 28, 1999, M.1571, point 33 (serious doubts as to the compatibility of the merger because, *inter alia*, of the high market share in Denmark and Iceland).
543. Guidelines, point 103 ('collusion' includes, according to the Commission, conscious parallel behaviour, which is not in conformity with the Court's interpretation, *see Bayer*, CFI Oct. 26, 2000, 2000 ECR II-3383, paras 66–72).
544. Guidelines, point 176.
545. *Ibid.*, point 160.
546. Example: Guidelines, point 177.
547. Under the merger control regulation: *Imperial Tobacco Reemtsma*, D.Comm. May 8, 2002, M.2779, points 61–63.
548. *Philip Morris/Tabacalera* (the Spanish tobacco ex-monopolist), D.Comm. Feb. 23, 2001, IP/01/249 (shortening the duration of the exclusivity and progressively reducing the quantities). Further examples of exclusive customer allocation (obligation of a supplier to sell only to one particular distributor for resale of its products to a particular class of customers): Guidelines, point 183. *See Franzen/Swedish Alcohol Monopoly*, ECJ Oct. 23, 1997, 1997 ECR I-5909 (exclusive distribution for resale only through selected dealers restrictive but compatible with Article 31 on grounds of public health).

unlikely to qualify for exemption under Article 81 (3).[549] More generally, intra-brand competition (including price discrimination) may be a serious problem in *mature* markets but less in a market with growing demand, changing technologies and changing market positions.[550] In case a supplier wants to enter a *new market* this may involve special first time investment to establish the brand in the market. In order to convince a local distributor to make these investments it may be necessary to provide territorial protection even if the supplier has a market share in other markets or in the entire Community exceeding 30%, e.g., 50%, provided that such an exclusive distribution relationship combined with territorial protection is of a limited duration,[551] probably less than five years. However, the Guidelines do not explain how to calculate and to evaluate whether 50% of the distribution is affected, but it may be assumed that it normally requires the evaluation of the number of outlets, the past sales volumes and the capacity of those outlets.[552]

(d) Long-Term Purchasing Agreements

Evualuation of the Foreclosure Effect.
Exclusive purchasing agreements which are not covered by the block exemption are not *per se* illegal[553] but need careful evaluation of the eventual foreclosure effect, which may result from contractual obligations. Exclusive or preferential purchasing obligations relate to the *freedom* of the buyer to choose its supplier. The buyer is not prevented from choosing freely a single supplier although this leads to a foreclosure of the market to competing suppliers with respect to this buyer.[554] The foreclosure effect resulting from exclusive or preferential purchasing obligations, i.e. the impact on the competitors' market access, must be measured on the basis of the supplier's market share, the buyer's market position (including its countervailing power), the number, past sales volumes and capacity of the tied, as compared to the un-tied, outlets.[555] The higher the tied supply share, and the longer the duration, the more significant the foreclosure is likely to be. Normally, agreements lasting longer than 5 years are not considered likely to achieve efficiencies that outweigh the foreclosure effect (proportionality test).[556] This is the reason why the block exemption is limited to a market share of 30% and a duration of 5 years.

---

549. *AAMS*, D.Comm. June 17, 1998, 1998 OJ L 252/47; *Swedish Matches*, Twenty-seventh Report on Competition Policy, p. 138 (both cases concern tobacco products).
550. Guidelines, points 168 and 194.
551. *Ibid.*, point 116 (2)–(4).
552. *See* example in Guidelines, point 160.
553. *Wingas/EDF-Trading*, IP/02/1293 of Sept. 12, 2002.
554. Brochure to Motor Vehicle Regulation 1400/2002, question 13.
555. Guidelines, points 204–205.
556. Guidelines, point 205.

Assessment of Exclusive Purchasing Obligations Where Market Shares Exceed 30%.

In the *Liebig* case[557] the Commission prohibited an exclusive purchasing agreement between one of the four major suppliers of spices and three large distributors having a market share of more than 30%.[558] In the *Ice Cream* cases[559] the Commission prohibited a non-compete clause (i) in the form of a long-term (2 ½ year) exclusive obligation on the resellers to purchase single-item ice cream exclusively from the two major suppliers Unilever and Schöller and (ii) in the form of freezer exclusivity, by which a freezer cabinet was put at the disposal of the retailers free of charge but subject to the condition that the cabinet be used exclusively for the storage of Unilever's or Schöller's products (and not of competitors, in particular the complainant Mars). The Commission and the European Court acknowledged that the network of agreements constituted a major barrier to the entry of other competitors into the market, the level of the foreclosure effect being excessive, namely on the order of 40% (whereas a coverage of 30% may be accepted),[560] and that a duration of 2 ½ years was too long in the light of the parties' very large market shares (more than 70%).[561] On the other hand, the block exemption may be declared inapplicable by the Commission regulation to parallel networks of similar exclusive purchasing agreements if they cover more than 50% of the relevant market, the assumption being that the cumulative effect leads to a significant foreclosure of the market.[562] Since the extent of market foreclosure does not depend on whether it is the effect of a network or a single agreement, it may be argued that even single agreements which do not cover more than 50% of the market may still qualify for exemption under Article 81 (3).[563] However, exclusive purchasing agreements covering more than 50% of distribution in the relevant market are likely to be opposed, in particular in the case of a dominant posi-

557. *Liebig*, D.Comm. Dec. 21, 1977, 1978 OJ L 53/20.

558. Similarly, the Commission intervened against exclusivity arrangements between VISA and a group of financial institutions imposing non-compete clauses with respect to other credit cards: *VISA*, IP/96/585 of July 3, 1996. *See also IRI/Nielsen*, Twenty-sixth Report on Competition Policy, pp. 144–146 (the Commission objected to an obligation imposed by a company of retail tracking services on its multinational customers not to call upon any competitors' services).

559. *Langnese* and *Iglo*, D.Comm. Dec. 23, 1992, 1993 OJ L 183/1 and 19 (German market), *aff'd* CFI June 8, 1995, 1995 ECR II-1533 and 1611, ECJ Oct. 1, 1998, 1998 ECR I-5609; *Van den Bergh Foods (Unilever)*, D.Comm. March 11, 1998, 1998 OJ L 246/1 (Irish market), CFI Oct. 23, 2003, T-65/98.

560. *Langnese-Iglo*, CFI June 8, 1995, 1995 ECR II-1533, paras 94–105; *Van den Bergh Foods*, CFI Oct. 23, 2003, T-65/98, para. 140.

561. *Langnese-Iglo*, CFI June 8, 1995, 1995 ECR II-1533, para. 111.

562. Article 8. *See* Guidelines, point 222.

563. Even undertakings having a dominant position are not precluded from the benefit of an individual exemption: *Interbrew*, 2002 OJ C 283/14.

tion.[564] However, even in the case of a dominant position exclusive purchasing agreements limited to one year may not be restrictive at all[565] whereas exclusive purchasing agreements between one and five years in duration require a proper balancing of pro- and anti-competitive effects[566] while a duration of more than five years or an automatic renewal is normally considered unnecessarily long to obtain efficiencies for most types of investments.[567]

Economic Justifications and Limits of Longer-Term Purchasing Obligations.

The criteria of Article 81 (3) are normally met where the agreement aims at opening up or enabling the parties to enter a new market,[568] permits the amortization of considerable customer-specific investments,[569] or fulfills missions of general economic interest.[570] Examples of customer-specific investments include the building or leasing of new machines, tools or equipment to satisfy a particular requirement of customers,[571] the joint construction of a pipeline for supplying gas to an electricity generator or a steel works[572] or long-term purchasing obligations on the up-stream market for reasons of security of supply.[573] In the Commission's

564. *See AAMS*, D.Comm. June 17, 1998, 1998 OJ L 252/47; *Van den Bergh Foods (HB Ice Cream)*, CFI Oct. 23, 2003, T-65/98, paras 154–162.
565. *Solvay (Soda Ash) II*, D.Comm. Dec. 19, 2000, IP/00/1449, point 68. *See Neste Markkinointi/ Yötuuli*, ECJ Dec. 7, 2000, C-214/99, paras 35–36.
566. Most types of investments are not considered necessary to achieve the claimed efficiencies or efficiencies are not sufficient to outweigh the foreclosure effect: Guidelines, point 205. *See TPS*, D.Comm. March 3, 1999, 1999 OJ L 90/6, points 102–109.
567. *Soda Ash – Solvay*, D.Comm. Dec. 19, 1990, 1991 OJ L 152/21; *rev'd* on procedural grounds CFI June 29, 1995, 1995 ECR II-1775 (dominant position); *Langnese-Iglo*, CFI June 8, 1995, 1995 ECR II-1533, para. 111 (dominant duopoly). Under the merger control regulation the joint acquisition by two competing suppliers of a regional gas wholesaler was cleared under the condition that local gas distributors be granted the right to terminate long-term gas supply agreements with the acquirers on a six-month notice: *EnBW, ENI/GVS*, D.Comm. Dec. 17, 2002, IP/02/1905.
568. Guidelines, point 116 (2). Under point 119 (10) the Commission states that vertical restraints linked to opening up *new* markets 'in general, do not restrict competition', which would lead to a general inapplicability of Article 81 (1) (and of the block exemption) irrespective the parties' market share which is, however, contradicted by other statements, in particular in point 109, which declare such restraints exemptible only if they are limited to the period necessary for introducing the new product. *See Olivetti/Canon*, Dec. 22, 1987, 1988 OJ L 52/51 (exemption).
569. Guidelines, point 116 (4). However, the isolated examination of elements of depreciation is not a sufficient standard: Monti, answer to written question 2002 OJ C 309E/11.
570. The Commission seems to interpret Article 86 (2) in a rather wide sense in the light of Article 16, *see* Report from the Commission of December 13, 2002 on the state of play in the work on the guidelines for state aid and services of general economic interest.
571. 'Hold-up problems', Guidelines, point 116 (4).
572. Industrial Gases, Nineteenth Report on Competition Policy, point 62.
573. *Wingas/EDF-Trading*, IP/02/1293 of Sept. 12, 2002. However, the duration of these long-term obligations do not necessarily justify the same duration of the purchasing obligations

practice even considerable investments justify long-term purchasing obligations only for a maximum duration of 15 years and for limited quantity requirements which leave sufficient possibilities for realistic purchasing alternatives.[574] Market shares of 30–50% may necessitate relaxation by an English clause[575] or by a reduction of the extent and duration of the purchasing obligations,[576] provided the agreements do not contain hardcore restrictions such as territorial resale and use restrictions.[577] In the absence of substantial investments, high market shares, in particular when approaching a dominant position, normally justify only minimum and maximum quantity commitments limited to 1–3 years. Examples include ice cream,[578] soda ash[579] and bulk deliveries of industrial gases.[580]

(e) Selective Distribution Agreements

Qualitative Selective Distributions Agreements.
Selective distribution agreements based on objective and qualitative criteria and applied in a non-discriminatory manner do not infringe Article 81 (1) irrespective of the parties' market shares. Article 81 (1) applies only if there are hardcore restrictions, such as resale price maintenance or the restriction of active or passive resales to users by, or of cross-supplies between, members of the selective

---

on the down-stream market, *see Gas Natural/Endesa*, IP/00/297 of March 27, 2000 (duration reduced by one third from eighteen to twelve years).

574. *Industrial Gases*, Nineteenth Report on Competition Policy, point 62; *Pego*, Twenty-third Report on Competition Policy, point 222; *ISAB/ENEL*, Twenty-sixth Report on Competition Policy, p. 133; *REN/Turbogas*, 1996 OJ C 118/7; *Gas Natural/Endesa*, IP/00/297 of March 27, 2000. *See* Guidelines, point 205 (without, however, fixing a maximum duration).
575. Accepted when requested by the buyer and provided that the alternative sources of supply are not identified: Industrial Gases, Nineteenth Report on Competition Policy, point 62.
576. Less than five years (two to three years) in the absence of investments: *see MD Foods Ambra – FDB*, Twenty-fifth Report on competition Policy, p. 136. Customer-specific investments justify a longer duration: *Electrabel*, Twenty-seventh Report on Competition Policy, point 169 (ten years – 75%); *Gas Natural/Endesa*, IP/00/297 of March 27, 2000 and Newsletter DG IV 2000–258 (twelve years – 75%); *Wingas/EDF-Trading*, IP/02/1293 of Sept. 12, 2002 (fifteen years –respectively 20% and 80% (two suppliers). *See*, under the merger control regulation, *Danish Crown/Vestjyske Slagterier*, D.Comm. March 9, 1999, 2000 OJ L 20/1, point 236. The modalities should be such as to be applicable to all (dominant and non-dominant) suppliers in order to avoid an unequal treatment, as in *Industrial Gases supra*, note 574. *See*, with respect to the regulatory framework for electronic communications networks, Guidelines 2002 OJ C 165/6, point 124.
577. *Nigerian gas company (NLNG)*, D.Comm. Dec. 12, 2002, IP/02/1869 (settlement following commitment to delete a clause preventing customers to re-sell the gas supplied by NLNG outside its national borders or to use the gas for a different purpose than that agreed upon).
578. 2 ½ years too long: *Langnese-Iglo*, CFI June 8, 1995, 1995 ECR II-1533, para. 111.
579. One to two years: *Soda Ash – Solvay II*, D.Comm. Dec. 13, 2000, IP/00/1449, point 68.
580. Three years: Industrial Gases, Nineteenth Report on Competition Policy, point 62 (in this case the limitation to three years was applied to all suppliers on the market in question independently of their size) in order to avoid an unequal treatment).

distribution system.[581] Even large and powerful firms, such as IBM, may establish a qualitative selective distribution system, provided it is based on objective criteria.[582] In the case of national commercial monopolies (e.g., tobacco) it is not contrary to Article 31 to distribute the products through dealers who are selected, for reasons of public health, according to objective qualitative criteria.[583] However, the selection criteria may not imply any control by the dominant supplier over the distributors' purchasing and selling policy, as in the case of 'Supplier of Choice Agreements' concluded by the dominant supplier of rough diamonds De Beers.[584] If the implementation of a qualitative selective distribution system raises competition concerns, it is rather more likely to be the nature of the products themselves that may not justify the qualitative selection criteria of dealers that constitutes the problem.[585] In the absence of hardcore restrictions a qualitative selective distribution system does not need individual exemption, unless it includes minimum quantity obligations. In the latter case, individual exemption depends on the degree of foreclosure effect of such 'quantity forcing', which will be difficult to establish.[586]

Quantitative Selective Distribution Agreements.

A selective distribution system based on quantitative criteria (distance from other distributors, density of population, minimum quantity obligations) normally does infringe Article 81 (1) but is not necessarily incompatible with Article 81 (3) even if the market share exceeds 30%, depending in particular on the quality of the

581. Article 4 (c) and (d) of Regulation 2790/1999. Furthermore, the resale by parallel traders which are not members of the system cannot be restricted: *BMW/ALD*, ECJ Oct. 24, 1985, 1985 ECR I-3459, para. 30; *Nissan France*, ECJ Feb. 15, 1996, 1996 ECR I-677, para. 20.
582. Negative clearance, D.Comm. April 18, 1984, 1984 OJ L 118/24 (IBM has not been dominant in the sector of personal computers but its market share probably exceeded 30%).
583. Under Article 31: *Franzen/Swedish Alcohol Monopoly*, ECJ Oct. 23, 1997, 1997 ECR I-5909, paras 43–51.
584. *DTC 'Supplier of Choice' (De Beers)*, D.Comm. Jan. 16, 2003, IP/03/64 (clearance of the selective distribution system after substantial amendments: relaxation of minimum purchasing requirements, dispute resolution by Ombudsman).
585. Guidelines, point 199. Examples where the nature of the product or service did not justify exemption under Article 81 (3) include cosmetics (*Vichy*, CFI Feb. 27, 1992, 1992 ECR II-415; cosmetic products not justifying exclusive distribution through pharmacies), tobacco (*FEDETAB*, ECJ Oct. 29, 1980, 1980 ECR 3125), windsurfing equipment (*Windsurfing*, D.Comm. July 11, 1983, 1983 OJ L 229/1, *aff'd* ECJ Feb. 25, 1986, 1986 ECR 611), sanitary fixtures (*Ideal Standard* and *Grohe*, D.Comm. Dec. 10, 1984, 1985 OJ L 20/38 and 17), furniture (*Interlübke*, Fifteenth Report on Competition Policy, point 61), power tools (*Hilti*, D.Comm. Dec. 22, 1987, 1988 1989 OJ L 65/19, 38–41, *aff'd* ECJ March 2 1994, 1994 ECR I-667), bananas (*United Brands*, ECJ Feb. 14, 1978, 1978 ECR 207, paras 157–160), and coffee (*Cafeteros de Colombia*, D.Comm. Dec. 10, 1982, 1982 OJ L 360/31).
586. *See Liebig*, D.Comm. Dec. 21, 1977, 1978 OJ L 53/20 (indirect non-compete obligation by forcing the dealer to display its own-brand spices separately from Liebig's spices).

service which only a limited number of dealers are able to supply.[587] However, the restrictive clause must be limited to the 'necessary' standard: minimum quantity obligations are usually regarded as less restrictive of competition than a limitation of the number of the selected dealers.

(f) Franchise Agreements

Franchise agreements entered into by companies with a market share exceeding 30% are to be evaluated by analogy to exclusive purchasing agreements, depending on the nature of the goods or services[588] and the degree of the individual or – mainly – cumulative market foreclosure effect.[589] Possible examples are service stations and restaurants with a uniform shop sign on restricted highways (motorways), for which the owner, having a natural monopoly, grants concessions based on qualitative and quantitative criteria similar to a franchise agreement. The principal competitive risks in cases of higher market shares are discrimination and excessive duration. Individual exemption will therefore depend on a structure which would be likely to eliminate or to reduce these risks.[590]

(g) Tying Practices

The Commission's assessment of tying under Article 81 (1) is not entirely clear.[591] Article 81 (1) (e) applies undoubtedly to *horizontal* agreements between competitors which are conditional on the acceptance by the other party of supplementary obligations, which, by their nature or according to commercial usage,[592] have no connection with the subject of the contract.[593] Such horizontal agreements between competing suppliers are separate and apart from any *vertical* contract concluded

---

587. *Franzen/Swedish Alcohol Monopoly*, ECJ Oct. 23, 1997, 1997 ECR I-5909, paras 53–57 (justified by public health considerations).
588. E.g., sweets sold in 'fun shops' may justify a franchise distribution system: Guidelines, point 201.
589. In the latter case, the block exemption still applies but the benefit of the block exemption may be withdrawn: Guidelines, point 201.
590. However, it may be argued, following the Commission's statement in its Guidelines, point 200, that non-compete obligations fall outside Article 81 (1) if they are necessary to maintain the common identity and reputation of the franchised network and do not need any assessment under Article 81 (3).
591. Guidelines, points 215–224. Article 3 (c) of the previous Regulation 1984/83 was not clear either: the block exemption does not apply where the exclusive purchasing obligation is agreed for more than one type of goods where these are neither by their nature nor according to commercial usage connected to each other.
592. As a complete range of products (Article 2 (3) (a) of the previous Regulation 1984/83) or the Commission's example of shoes and laces (Guidelines, point 216). However, commercial usage is, according to the Court of Justice, no absolute justification: *Tetra Pak*, ECJ Nov. 14, 1996, 1996 ECR I-5951, paras 34–37.
593. Guidelines, point 215.

between one of the suppliers and its buyer(s). In the absence of any horizontal agreement, it seems misleading to state that 'tying may also constitute a vertical restraint'.[594] The vertical tying agreement contains the obligation on the buyer to purchase one product (A) and another distinct product (B) from the contracting supplier and may be restrictive because the purchasing obligation is exclusive and long-term, thereby hindering the access of competitors to the market for the tied product.[595] This restriction (not the tying as such) is block exempted when the market share of the supplier on both the market of product A (the 'tying' product) and the market share of product B (the 'tied'product) does not exceed 30%; the application of the block exemption is, however, excluded and the criteria of Article 81 (3) are unlikely to be met when the supplier has significant market power in the market of product A. The main question is whether the supplier is able to impose the *conclusion* of such contract on the customer, i.e. whether the supplier can effectively threaten to refuse to supply product A without supplying product B. Such refusal may be unlawful when the seller has a powerful but not yet so dominant position as to be obliged to supply (but nevertheless obliged not to engage in tying) under Article 82.[596]

C. New Block Exemption Regulation 1400/2002 in the Motor Vehicle Sector

1. Reasons for and Main Objectives of the New Block Exemption Regulation

The New Regulation and the Explanatory Brochure.
On July 31, 2002 the Commission adopted a new motor vehicle block exemption, Regulation 1400/2002,[597] which enters into force on October 1, 2002 (a first transitional period ending on October 1, 2003 and a second on October 1, 2005[598]) and replaces Regulation 1475/95 expiring on September 30, 2002.[599] The regulation is explained in an Explanatory Brochure ('Brochure')[600] the volume of which indicates the complexity of the matter. The main reasons for a new specific regime

594. *Ibid.*, point 215.
595. *Ibid.*, point 217. *See Check Point Technologies/Stonesoft*, D.Comm. April 9, 2002 (settlement), IP/02/521.
596. Examples of prohibited tying practices under Article 82: *Tetra Pak*, ECJ Nov. 14, 1996, 1996 ECR I-5951, paras 34–37; *Belgian Post*, D.Comm. Dec. 5, 2001, 2002 OJ L 61/32, point 73; *Microsoft*, IP/00/906 and IP/01/1232.
597. 2002 OJ L 203/30.
598. IP/03/1318.
599. *See also* the document 'Frequently Asked Questions' referred to in IP/03/1318.
600. IP/02/1392 of Sept. 30, 2002.

that deviates from the more general block exemption rules on vertical restraints of Regulation 2790/1999 are:

- strengthening competition between dealers of the same brand;
- facilitating cross-border sales;
- increasing competition in after-sales servicing;
- strengthening the dealers' position *vis-à-vis* manufacturers,
- promoting competition in distribution agreements for spare parts (which are now included in the regulation), and more generally
- safeguarding the consumers' interests.

According to the Commission's findings, the previous regulation did not ensure that the Single Market operates fully to allow customers to take advantage of the often extraordinarily high price differentials between member states.[601] The Commission's survey shows that price differences are more than 20% within the Euro-zone.[602] These price differences are largely due to manufacturers' pricing policies and, to a lesser extent, in response to high taxes. Most car manufacturers determine their list prices before tax at a low level in countries with high car purchase taxes, arguing that it is necessary for selling their cars in those countries at affordable after-tax prices.[603] The consequence is that customers in countries with a low tax level but higher before-tax prices are trying to purchase cars from a dealer (or even buyer) in a country with a higher tax level but at a lower before-tax price. Because the tax is refunded on export sales, the tax *and* the price differentials make parallel imports attractive.[604] Restrictions of such parallel imports by agreement or concerted practices have repeatedly resulted in heavy fines insofar as they resulted from concerted conduct between a manufacturer and its dealers.[605] More

601. This was already the objective of substituting Regulation 123/85 with Regulation 1475/95, *see* Notice on Regulation 1475/95 under IV.

602. *Car prices in the EU: still substantial prices differences, especially in the mass market segments*, IP/02/1109 of July 22, 2002. With respect to heavy vehicles *see Volvo/Scania*, D.Comm. March 15, 2000, M.1672, pt. 38–49.

603. *See Car prices in the EU: price differentials remain high*, IP/04/285 of March 2, 2004.

604. *See*, however, the study 'Customer Preferences for Existing and Potential Sales and Servicing Alternatives in Automotive Distribution' undertaken by Dr. Lademann & Partner on behalf of the Commission, which questions the price comparisons of the Commission and concludes that consumers prefer more direct sales opportunities and the multi-brand dealerships but consider other new sales forms to be of secondary importance.

605. *Volkswagen I*, D.Comm. Jan. 28, 1998, 1998 OJ L 124/60, *aff'd* ECJ Sept. 18, 2003, C-338/00P; *Opel*, D.Comm. Sept. 20, 2000, 2001 OJ L 59/1, *aff'd* CFI Oct. 21, 2003, T-368/00; *Volkswagen II*, D.Comm. June 29, 2001, 2001 OJ L 262/14; *rev'd* CFI Dec. 3, 2003, T-208/01; *Daimler Chrysler*, D.Comm. Oct. 10, 2001, 2002 OJ L 257/1. Governmental measures requiring immediate payment of registration taxes on parallel imported cars backed by heavy and disproportionate fines may be incompatible with the principle of free movement of goods (Directive 83/182/EEC) and lead to proceedings under Article 226, as in the cases *Commission/Greece*, ECJ July 12, 2001, 2001 ECR I-5547, para. 71.

intra-brand and inter-brand competition is likely to reduce these price differences although the regulation is not aimed at bringing about price harmonisation.[606]

Enlarged Scope of the Regulation.
Whereas the previous regulation applied only to combined motor vehicle distribution and servicing agreements, the new regulation covers agreements with respect to distribution of new motor vehicles, distribution of spare parts and use of spare parts for after-sales servicing and maintenance. Its scope is therefore much broader than the previous regulation and extends, e.g., to agreements on the distribution of lubricants (as spare parts) which used to be exempted under Regulation 1984/83 that are now, up to the end of the transitionary period on September 30, 2003,[607] covered by Regulation 2790/1999.

Main Objectives of the New Regulation: More Intra-Brand and More Inter-Brand Competition.
The new regulation is stricter than both the previous Regulation 1475/95 and the general Regulation 2790/1999 on vertical restraints. The regulation is designed to ensure more intra-brand and more inter-brand competition for both new motor vehicles and spare parts:

– *More intra-brand competition by permitting more sales activities*: (i) more *passive* sales within the supplier's distribution system, including sales via intermediaries (which were formerly limited) and internet sales, whereas a prohibition against sales to unauthorized dealers is still permitted; and (ii) more *active* sales by permitting active sales bans only within an exclusive distribution system whereas selective distributors may no longer be limited to their original location ('location clause'), but must be free, from October 1, 2005, to establish additional sales or delivery outlets at other locations within the Common Market for selling new motor vehicles.[608] An authorized distributor may also expand its business by acquiring the business of another authorized dealer in which case the supplier must transfer the rights and obligations to the acquiror.[609]

606. Brochure, under 5.1.

607. Article 10. However, this provision refers only to agreements which satisfied the conditions of the previous Regulation 1475/95, but should be applied, by analogy, to agreements satisfying Regulation 2790/1999 (*see* Article 2 (5) of that regulation).

608. Article 5 (2) (b) and Article 12 (2). Additional outlets established for multi-branding activities no longer require separate premises, a separate company, separate management and separate sales forces as under the previous regulation. *See* (under Regulation 1475/95) *Jaeger/Opel Norge*, EFTA Court of Justice, April 1, 1998, E-3/97, 1998–4 ECL 158.

609. Article 3 (3); Brochure, under 5.3.7. This may, however, lead to more concentration in motor vehicle distribution; the Commission is therefore committed to monitor the structure and level of concentration (Article 11).

- *More intra-brand competition by separating distribution and after-sales servicing of motor vehicles*, which permits the existence of parallel – competing – networks of motor vehicle distributors assuring after-sales servicing themselves or through authorized repairers.[610]
- *More inter-brand competition* by permitting dealers to engage in *multi-branding* activities by purchasing and selling competing goods (motor vehicles or spare parts), and to sell in their sales outlets new motor vehicles of different makes, without prejudice to the obligation on the distributor to sell motor vehicles from competing suppliers in separate areas of the showroom in order to avoid confusion between the makes.[611] Dealers and repairers thereby become more independent from a particular motor vehicle manufacturer since they are free to purchase and use spare parts also from competing suppliers, without prejudice to the ability of the supplier of new motor vehicles to require the use of original spare parts supplied by it for repairs carried out under warranty, free servicing and vehicle recall work.[612]
- *Advantages for the end user* by enabling them to purchase a new motor vehicle wherever they want throughout the Common Market and to benefit from the supplier's Community-wide network of warranty, repair and maintenance services.[613] They may also resell freely motor vehicles to other end users within the Common Market.

The Products and Services Concerned.
The products and services concerned are:

- new vehicles with three or more wheels for use on public roads, which *include*, (as under the previous regulation) (i) passenger cars and light commercial vehicles (including trucks, buses and coaches up to 3.5 tonnes) and (ii) heavier motor vehicles (versions thereof exceeding 3.5 tonnes); but the regulation *excludes* used cars, motorcycles (with two wheels) and vehicles which are not self-propelled;[614] agricultural vehicles such as tractors are not subject to the regulation, as their main use is not on public roads;[615]
- spare parts, which are to be installed in or upon a motor vehicle so as to replace components of that vehicle, including goods such as lubricants which are nec-

610. Article 4 (1) (g). The parallel existence of distribution and after-sales servicing systems was incompatible with the previous regulation, *see Cicra/Fiat Auto*, Twenty-fourth report on Competition Policy, point 361.
611. Article 1 (1) (b).
612. Article 4 (1) (k).
613. Recital 17 and Article 4 (1) (b) (i). *See* Brochure, Question 29.
614. Article 1 (1) (n).
615. *See* Notice on Regulation 1475/95, under I.1. Cases such as *John Deere* (D.Comm. Dec. 14, 1984, 1985 OJ L 35/58) and *Sperry New Holland* (D.Comm. Dec. 16, 1985, 1985 OJ L 376/21) were not assessed under the car regulation.

essary for the use of a motor vehicle,[616] whereas accessories, such as radios and navigation systems, are not covered;[617] and

- repair and maintenance services.[618] Distribution agreements on products which are excluded from the specific car regulation are subject to the general block exemption on vertical restraints, Regulation 2790/1999. Distribution agreements on products which are covered by Regulation 1400/2002 (in particular spare parts) are excluded from Regulation 2790/1999.[619]

Vertical Agreements Covered by the Regulation.
Whereas the previous regulation was limited to agreements concerning the distribution *and* servicing of motor vehicles, the new regulation applies to *all* vertical agreements[620] concluded between the following undertakings:

- Between manufacturers/importers of new motor vehicles and their dealers within an exclusive or selective distribution system, whereas 'genuine' agency agreements are not prohibited under Article 81 (1) and do not need to be exempted under the regulation;[621]
- Between dealers of new motor vehicles (on the wholesale or retail level);
- Between manufacturers of spare parts and manufacturers of motor vehicles which use spare parts as components and (re)sell spare parts for after-sales servicing and maintenance;
- Between manufacturers of original spare parts or of spare parts of matching quality and dealers or repairers;
- Between dealers of spare parts (on the wholesale or retail level); and
- Between dealers of spare parts and repairers, to the extent that they contain vertical restraints.[622]

The agreements may contain ancillary licence provisions,[623] thereby including subcontracting[624] and franchising provisions.[625]

---

616. Article 1 (1) (s).
617. Brochure, Question 95.
618. Authorized repairers and independent repairers: Article 1 (1) (l) and (m).
619. Article 2 (5) of Regulation 2790/1999.
620. Including concerted practices: Article 1 (1) (c). Circulars and instructions become part of the agreement, *see Mercedes-Benz*, D.Comm. Oct. 10, 2001, 2002 OJ L 257/1, point 125; *AEG-Telefunken*, ECJ Oct 25, 1983, 1983 ECR 31651, 3195.
621. Brochure, Question 5.
622. Article 2 (1), second subparagraph.
623. The license provisions must not constitute the primary object of such agreements: Article 2 (2) (b).
624. Brochure, under 7.
625. Not expressly stated in the Brochure, but *see* Guidelines on Vertical Restraints (2000 OJ C 291/1), points 42–44.

Agreements between Competitors Normally not Covered.
Vertical agreements involving *competing* undertakings are not covered by the regulation, except:

- agreements between an association of distributors or repairers and its members or suppliers if no member has a total annual turnover exceeding EUR 50 million,[626]
- agreements between a manufacturer which also distributes its new motor vehicles[627] and its buyer which distributes in competition with the supplier,[628]
- agreements between a supplier providing services at different levels of trade and a buyer which does not provide competing services at the level of trade where it purchases the contract goods,[629] and
- non-reciprocal vertical agreements entered into between competing undertakings when the buyer has a turnover not exceeding EUR 100 million,[630] whereas other vertical agreements between competitors are excluded and subject to the general provisions of Article 81.[631]

Therefore the regulation excludes in particular collective exclusive dealing agreements between competing dealers or set up by their organizations.[632]

Market Share Thresholds.
In line with the Commission's new approach on vertical restraints, the block exemption is limited to market share thresholds. According to Article 3 (1) the benefit of the block exemption does not apply to agreements between companies with market shares that exceed:

- 30% in the case of exclusive distribution, and
- 40% in the case of *quantitative* selective distribution for new motor vehicles[633] the relevant market being that on which the supplier sells new motor vehicles, spare parts or repair and maintenance services.[634]

---

626. Article 2 (2) (a). This is without prejudice to the applicability of Article 81 to any horizontal agreements concluded between the members, which makes the provision of Article 2 (2) (a) highly unlikely to apply at all.
627. In particular through an own subsidiary.
628. Article 2 (3) (b). These agreements are classified as 'non-reciprocal agreements' although they provide for a reciprocal protection of each other's territory.
629. Article 2 (3) (c)
630. Article 2 (3) (a).
631. E.g. agreements between dealers not to compete for each other's customers.
632. Recent example: *FEG*, D.Comm. Oct. 26, 1999, 2000 OJ L 39/1; fines imposed on the association (EUR 4.4 million) and on its largest members (EUR 2.15 million).
633. In the case of quantitative selective distribution for spare parts the 30% threshold applies.
634. Article 3 (1). The market shares are calculated for new motor vehicles on the basis of the

In both cases the regulation tolerates a certain margin: if the market share is initially not more than 30% or 40% respectively but consequently rises above that level without exceeding 35% or 45% respectively, the exemption continues to apply for a period of two calendar years and, if it exceeds 35% or 45%, for a period of one calendar year.[635] *Qualitative* selective distribution agreements are permitted without market share limit.[636] However, *hardcore restrictions* are prohibited irrespective of market share limits, and the benefit of the block exemption is lost for the entire agreement (not just the blacklisted clause).[637]

Agreements between companies with *higher* market shares are not covered by the regulation. They do not imply illegality, but they are normally not supposed to meet the individual exemption criteria of Article 81 (3).[638] Under specific circumstances they may meet the criteria for clearance under Article 81, except where they contain blacklisted clauses.[639] In the case of a dominant position, the regulation is without prejudice to the overlapping application of Article 82.[640] However, market shares exceeding substantially the limits of the regulation may lead to a parallel application of Articles 81 and 82 anyway.

Definition of the Relevant Market.[641]
The relevant *product* market of motor vehicles is to be divided into passenger cars and commercial vehicles of different types (light, medium, heavy, buses, coaches, etc.); whether the passenger car market must be subdivided (e.g. according to engine size and car type) has been left open in the Commission's decisions.[642] With respect to trucks the Commission determined three categotires: light trucks up to 7 tonnes, medium trucks between 7 and 16 tonnes and trucks above 16 tonnes.[643] Different types of heavy trucks (more than 16 tons) do not constitute separate

---

volume, for spare parts and services on the basis of the value or estimates of the preceeding calender year: Article 8 (1).

635. Article 8 (2) (c) and (d).
636. Article 3 (1) third subparagraph; recital 8.
637. Article 4 (1)–(2); Recital 12.
638. Recital 8.
639. E.g. the BMW distribution system was cleared despite the higher (national) market shares: *BMW*, D.Comm. Dec. 13, 1974, 1975 OJ L 29/1, point 31.
640. Recital 35.
641. *See* Brochure, under 6.2.
642. With respect to the possible (but undecided) segmentation of passenger cars, *see Mercedes Benz*, D.Comm. Oct. 10, 2001, 2002 OJ L 257/1, points 143–149. The narrowest segmentation is the following: mini cars, small cars, medium cars, large cars, executive cars, luxury cars, sport coupes, multi purpose cars, sport utility cars, *see Daimler-Benz/Chrysler*, D.Comm. July 22, 1998, M.1204, points 7–10; *General Motors/Daewoo Motors*, D.Comm. July 22, 2002, M.2832, points 13–15.
643. *Volvo/Renault*, D.Comm. Sept. 1, 2000, M.1980; *General Motors*, D.Comm. July 22, 2002, M.2832.

product markets.[644] However, this market definition based on previous merger decisions may have to be reviewed in the light of the regulation which distinguishes clearly between light commercial vehicles with a maximum weight not exceeding 3.5 tonnes and heavy commercial verhicles above 3.5 tonnes, which are subject to different rules.[645] As to after-sales servicing and spare parts the vertical agreement between a supplier of motor vehicles and its authorized repairers often covers a bundle of goods and services, support and licensing rights, which enables the repairer to provide repair services for the vehicles of the brand in question. In such cases, the relevant market comprises both the products (original spare parts and their substitutes assessed from the perspective of the buyer/end-user) and services. [646] However, spare parts supplied at no profit for the purposes of honouring legal obligations of warranty may not be included in the calculation of market shares.[647]

The relevant *geographic* market for motor vehicles is possibly still today the national market because of the remaining differences with regard to, *inter alia*, prices and vehicle taxation.[648] The narrow market definition may cause problems and lead to legal uncertainty. The Commission's *New Holland/Case* decision shows that a motor vehicle manufacturer that has implemented the same distribution system within all EEA countries, may, although not dominant in the entire territory of the EEA, have a substantial or even dominant position on certain national markets by exceeding the 30 or 40% thresholds.[649] Such a manufacturer is prevented from enforcing its agreements throughout its entire EU distribution system as long as parts of it are not covered by the block exemption.[650]

The relevant geographic market for components and spare parts may be European-wide with respect to the original equipment market and the independent

644. *Volvo/Scania*, D.Comm. March 15, 2000, M.1672, points 24–30.
645. *See*, however, Brochure, under 6.1.
646. Brochure, under 6.1. and note 187. *See* Commission's Notice on the relevant market, 1997 OJ C 372/3, point 56; Commission's Guidelines on vertical restraints, 2000 OJ C 291/1, points 94–95. *See Pelican/Kyocera*, Twenty-fifth report on Competition Policy, point 87 (under Article 81); *Varta/Bosch*, D.Comm. July 31, 1991, 1991 OJ L 320/26; *Lucas/Varity*, D.Comm. March 11, 1996, M.728; *SOGEFI/FILTRAUTO*, D.Comm. Oct. 29, 2001, M.2535, point 8; *Donellyagna International*, D.Comm. Sept. 17, 2002, IP/02/1313 (under the merger control regulation). The German Supreme Court held that original spare parts was a distinct market: *BGH Feuerwehrgeräte*, April 27, 1999, WuW 1999–11, 1111.
647. Brochure, 6.1. example (c).
648. *Volkswagen II, D.Comm.* June 29, 2001, 2001 OJ L 262/14; *rev'd* CFI Dec. 3, 2003, T-208/01, point 80; *Mercedes-Benz*, D.Comm. Oct. 10, 2001, 2002 OJ L 257/1, point 151 (under Article 81); *Daimler-Benz/Chrysler*, D.Comm. July 22, 1998, M.1204, point 13 (under the merger control regulation).
649. *New Holland/Case Corporation*, D.Comm. Oct. 28, 1999, M.1571, where the merging parties were held dominant on certain national markets such as UK, Belgium, Austria, Iceland and Denmark, and had to submit commitments in order to remove the Commission's concerns.
650. Brochure, Question 6.

after sales market for operators with a wide-spread activity[651] whereas distribution at the retail level and repair services may require a narrower delineation of the relevant geographic market.[652]

'Technique' of the New Regulation.

The previous regulation was seen as a straightjacket because it prescribed clauses which had to be inserted in motor vehicle agreements. This approach was already modified in Regulation 2790/1999. Accordingly, the new regulation applies to all vertical restraints, subject to a large number of obligations which may *not* be inserted and other obligations which *must* be inserted. The technique of the new regulation is as follows:

- *General exemption provision*: Articles 2 (1) and 3 (1) provide a general exemption up to the market share limits of respectively 30% for vertical restraints generally and 40% for quantitative selective distribution systems for new vehicles, except those which are expressly excepted.
- *Application of this general provision to vertical agreements in a horizontal context*: Article 2 (2) and (3) define the categories of agreements between competing companies to which the regulation extends.
- *Hardcore restrictions*: Article 4 blacklists hardcore restrictions: resale price fixing,[653] territorial and customer restrictions[654] irrespective of the parties' market shares, subject to exceptions. Hardcore restrictions are even prohibited where the parties market shares are *de minimis* and are unlikely to gain individual clearance.[655]
- *Non-compete clauses*: According to Article 5 the block exemption does *not* exempt certain restrictive non-compete obligations, including obligations to purchase more than 30% of the total purchases from a single supplier or from an undertaking designated by the supplier, post-term non-compete obligations, any prohibition against selling leasing services, and (from October 1, 2005) location clauses, except for heavier motor vehicles. It is unclear (and legally

651. *E.g*, *SOGEFI/FILTRAUTO*, D.Comm. Oct. 29, 2001, M.2535, point 24; *Lucas/Varity*, D.Comm. March 11, 1996, M.728, point 12 (under the merger control regulation).
652. Brochure, under 6.2., in particular note 189.
653. Price fixing include discount fixing. Dual price systems (application of different prices in different member states) has been prohibited even if the price differences are partly due to national regulations or measures: *see Glaxo Wellcome*, D.Comm. May 8, 2001, 2001 OJ L 302/1, points 117–125 and 148. Maximum prices and recommended prices are accepted as under Regulation 2790/1999. However, the obligation on the dealer not to sell substantially below the recommended price infringes Article 81: *Volkswagen II*, D.Comm. June 29, 2001, 2001 OJ L 262/14; *rev'd* CFI Dec. 3, 2003, T-208/01, points 71 and 77.
654. Including indirect restrictions, such as incentives not to sell in other countries, e.g. by way of limiting the quantities (Brochure, under 5.3.) or by way of fidelity rebates, which must be distinguished from (admissible) quantity rebates (Brochure, Question 12).
655. Commission's *De Minimis* Notice, point 11 (1).

doubtful) whether the supplier is entitled to require that the dealer disclose its total purchases of all vehicle brands (including confidential data on purchases from competitors) in order to calculate the 30% limit. Obligations to purchase less than 30% are accepted (no anticompetitive foreclosure effect); obligations to purchase more than 30% raise 'serious competition concerns that can only be assessed in an individual examination' (by the parties themselves rather than by way of notification).[656] The dealer must therefore be able to choose freely (without any obligation or constraint) between buying and selling goods from at least four competing suppliers[657] and selling goods from a single supplier. Freely negotiated long-term supply arrangements on quantities which cover more than 30% are therefore not precluded from the regulation although they may have a factual foreclosure effect.[658]

- *Obligations*: Article 3 declares the block exemption inapplicable to agreements which do not provide certain rights and obligations, concerning the transfer of the business,[659] duration, termination, formalities for the notice of termination[660] and the possibility to refer a dispute to an expert or arbitrator.[661] In the absence of these provisions the distribution system in question is not exempted and cannot be enforced, unless the system is below the *de minimis* thresholds:[662] 15% if it is purely vertical, 10% in a horizontal context and 5% if there are cumulative effects.[663]

The clauses which may not be, and those which must be, inserted in an agreement are different according to the system of distribution chosen by the supplier and according to the market function of the parties, and are therefore commented upon when discussing the relevant types of agreements.

Prohibition of Supply and Sale Restrictions on the Distributor v. Supply and Sale Obligations on the Supplier.
One of the main objectives of the new regulation is to permit the dealers more purchasing and sales possibilities in order to facilitate cross-border sales in the interest of consumers. In particular, a dealer of new motor vehicles may not be restricted from selling any new motor vehicle which corresponds to a model within its contract range (including right-hand drive cars),[664] and a dealer of spare

656. Brochure, Question 17.
657. Which seems, however, rather unrealistic.
658. Brochure, Question 13.
659. The possibility to acquire another distributors' business with all rights and obligations allows to seize additional opportunities and increases the value of the business.
660. Article 3 (5).
661. Article 3 (6); Brochure, Question 61.
662. Commission's Notice, 2001 OJ C 368/13 (provided there are no hardcore restrictions).
663. Brochure, Question 7.
664. Article 4 (1) (f).

parts may not be restricted from obtaining spare parts from a third undertaking of its choice.[665] The Brochure states that suppliers must provide dealers with motor vehicles built to specifications current in other member states.[666] With respect to the manufacturer's obligation to supply additional sales outlets, the Commission states that the supplier 'will have to make the necessary arrangements to ensure that a dealer can buy sufficient quantities of new motor vehicles to satisfy both the demand at his initial (main) outlet and any additional outlet(s). Any supply restriction would amount to an indirect restriction of the dealer's right to open additional outlets in other areas of the Common Market.'[667] However, the Brochure also recognizes that although a manufacturer must honour orders for new vehicles (e.g. of right hand drive vehicles) for supply to customers from other areas of the Common Market in the same way as for sales to local customers (according to the principle 'first come first served'), the manufacturer is not prevented from limiting product output where overall demand is higher than output, provided the available vehicles are not allocated in a discriminatory way.[668] It may therefore be argued that the distributor's freedom to purchase (which may not be restricted) does not necessarily imply the supplier's *obligation* to supply beyond the contracted quantities,[669] unless the refusal is part of a distribution system aiming at protecting national markets, thereby infringing Article 81 (1),[670] or constitutes an abuse of the supplier's dominant position, thereby infringing Article 82[671] (in which case the regulation does not apply anyway).

Duration and Termination of Agreements.

The exemption applies on the condition that the agreement is concluded by the supplier of new motor vehicles:

- for at least five years[672] with at least six months' prior notice in the case of non-renewal, or

665. Article 4 (1) (k).
666. Brochure, Question 30.
667. Brochure, Question 57.
668. Brochure, Question 41. A manufacturer of right hand drive vehicles can not be forced to sell a major part of its production to dealers outside UK in order to facilitate UK customers' purchases from countries where these vehicles are cheaper. *See* in the pharmaceutical sector, which is also characterized by considerable price differences from country to country: *Sandoz*, D.Comm. July 13, 1987, 1987 OJ L 222/28, 32 (limitation of supply to 'normal demand', however, without discriminating between dealers selling mostly 'national' and dealers engaged in parallel trade).
669. The quantities agreed at the moment when the additional outlet(s) were approved by the manufacturer on the basis of its selective criteria (the quantities *may* take into account the prospective additional output if the manufacturer has the capacity to supply).
670. *Ford*, ECJ Sept. 17, 1985, 1985 ECR 2725, para. 21.
671. *See Ford* (interim measure), ECJ Feb. 28, 1984, 1984 ECR 1129, para. 16.
672. The four years of the previous regulation have been extended in order to increase the independence of the dealers. Regulation 2790/1999 provides for a maximum duration of five years (without any tacit renewal): Article 5 (a).

- for an indefinite period with at least two years' prior notice in the case of regular termination.[673]

Any notice of termination must be in writing and include detailed, objective and transparent reasons,[674] which may be reviewed by an expert or arbitrator.[675] There is no similar provision for the distribution of spare parts.[676] After termination a dealer may remain in the business as an unauthorized distributor or independent repairer.

Territorial Scope of the New Regulation.
The new block exemption applies in the Common Market and will extend to the whole EEA area once an EEA Committee has decided to amend Annex XIV (Competition) to the EEA Agreement.[677] The regulation may apply to agreements entered into by undertakings located outside the EEA area. The prohibition of Article 4 (the blacklist) against territorial restrictions imposed on dealers fails to limit its territorial scope to dealers inside the EU or EEA (unlike the definition of 'exclusive supply obligation' in Article 1 (1) (e), which expressly refers to the Common Market). However, prohibitions imposed on dealers located outside the EU or EEA against re-exporting back into the EU or EEA countries are caught by Article 81 (1) or Article 58 of the EEA Treaty only if they have appreciable anticompetitive effects on trade within the EEA area,[678] except where they represent a broader horizontal cooperation, including territorial restrictions on dealers in the EU or EEA.[679] A supplier may normally extend its exclusive or selective distribution system to third countries and include the same kind of territorial restrictions on its distributors inside and outside the Common Market, i.e., not only restrictions on exports to third countries but also restrictions on imports from third countries,[680] provided, of course, those restrictions do not offend the local laws of the third countries. For instance, in the *Jacivo/Yves St. Laurent* case, which

---

673. Article 3 (5).
674. Article 3 (4).
675. Article 3 (6) (g). *See* Brochure, Questions 67–72.
676. It is therefore of utmost importance whether a spare parts distribution agreement falls under Regulation 2790/1999 (possibility of exclusive purchasing up to 30% market share, but limited to five years) or Regulation 1400/2002 (the agreement may be concluded for an undefinite duration but must not contain exclusive purchasing or even obligations to purchase more than 30% of the total purchases). *See* Brochure, Question 79.
677. Regulation 1475/95 was applicable in the EEA countries according to EEA Joint Committee Decision 46/96 of July 19, 1996 (1996 OJ L 291/39).
678. *Grosfillex/Fillistorf*, D.Comm. March 11, 1964, 1964 OJ 915; with respect to trade mark license agreements: *Campari*, D.Comm. Dec, 23, 1977, 1978 OJ L 70/69, 74. *See also* Chapter I at pp. 58–59.
679. *Iqbal*, Twenty-first Report on Competition Policy, p. 334.
680. Example: *Jaeger/Opel Norge*, EFTA Court of Justice, April 1, 1998, E-3/97, ECL 1998–4, 158.

concerned the European-wide distribution of perfumes (including Ukraine and Slovenia), the Court of Justice stated that restrictions on imports from third countries may have appreciable effects on trade within the Common Market where the market structure in the Common Market is oligopolistic and where substantial price differences exist between the third country and the Common Market which cannot be explained by customs duties and transport costs.[681] Otherwise the block exemption applies to the same extent as it would apply to agreements that apply within the Common Market. This means that restrictions of active sales into the exclusive territory reserved to one or more distributors within the Common Market are exempted, except for selective distribution systems,[682] whereas restrictions of passive sales are blacklisted.[683] However, in case the products in question are covered by industrial property rights, e.g. trademarks, even passive sales into the Common Market may constitute an infringement of industrial property rights which are not exhausted because the products have not been put on the market within the EEA area by the owner or with its consent.[684] Regulation 1983/83 tried to overcome this discrepancy by declaring the block exemption inapplicable where the parties to an exclusive distribution agreement exercise industrial property rights so as to prevent dealers or users from obtaining outside the contract territory properly marked or otherwise properly marketed contract goods.[685] However, this provision is overruled by the Court of Justice's decision not to recognize the international exhaustion of industrial property rights, except where international agreements provide for further extension of the exhaustion principle, as under the EEA[686] or the TRIPs Agreements.[687]

Entry into Force of the New Regulation and Transitional Provisions.
The regulation entered into force on October 1, 2002 and will expire on May 31, 2010 (in order to coincide with Regulation 2790/1999).[688] The regulation provides for a one year transition period (up to September 30, 2003) allowing for

681. *Javico/Yves St. Laurent*, ECJ April 28, 1998 ECR I-1983. This may be the case in particular for certain spare parts where the manufacturer has a dominant position.
682. Article 4 (1) (b) (i).
683. Article 4 (1) (b). However, it may be argued, with respect to imports from third countries, that this prohibition does not apply *irrespective* of the market shares but only if the market share within the Common Market is substantial, i.e. non-*de minimis*.
684. *Polydor*, ECJ Feb. 9, 1982, 1982 ECR 329, para. 22 (copyrighted products); *Phyteron International/Jean Bourdon*, ECJ March 20, 1997, 1997 ECR I-1729, para. 24 (trademark); *Silhouette*, ECJ July 18, 1998, 1998 ECR I-4799, paras 25–29 (trademark). The consent must be unequivocal and explicit: *Davidoff/Levi Strauss*, ECJ Nov. 20, 2001, C-414–416/99, paras 47–54.
685. Article 3 (d) of Regulation 1983/83.
686. *Silhouette*, ECJ July 18, 1998, 1998 ECR I-4799, paras 25–26.
687. *Maglite Mag Instrument/California*, EFTA Court of Justice, Dec. 3, 1997, E-3/97, ELR 1998–1, 2.
688. Article 12.

the adaptation of existing contracts[689] which satisfied on October 1, 2002,[690] and continue to satisfy, the conditions of Regulation 1475/95 (without market share limitation).[691] The provision does not expressly include agreements which satisfy the conditions of Regulation 2790/1999 (which may be the case for agreements on the distribution of spare parts such as lubricants,[692] tires, batteries, etc.), but should be applied by analogy.[693] A longer adaptation period until September 30, 2005 applies for the phasing-out of location clauses in selective distribution agreements for passenger cars and light commercial vehicles, which limit the selective dealer's ability to establish additional sales or delivery outlets at other locations within the Common Market where the selective distribution system is applied.[694] The regulation does not deal expressly with the question whether a dealer (which assures the after-sales servicing itself) is entitled to invoke its rights under its exclusive distribution agreement against the appointment of a new repairer within its allocated territory, but the answer is most probably affirmative because it constitutes an infringement of the agreement which still is provisionally valid.[695]

2. Distribution of New Motor Vehicles

(a) Exclusive Distribution of New Motor Vehicles

Definition.

In an exclusive distribution system the supplier may reserve to itself[696] or allocate to exclusive distributors a certain territory or an exclusive customer group.[697] The

689. Article 10. Brochure, Question 20, states that notices on termination should be given two years in advance to comply with Regulation 1475/95 and thus, to benefit from the transitional period (but this would lead to a nullity of the agreement during the second year).
690. This was not the case in *Audi/Volkswagen*, D.Comm. Jan. 20, 2003, IP/03/80: settlement after conversion of pure service agreements (which were not covered by Regulation 1475/75) into an objective qualitative selective distribution system.
691. Therefore, third parties may not complain if a distribution system that fulfilled the conditions of Regulation 1475/95 on Oct. 1, 2002 remains unchanged up to Oct. 1, 2003.
692. It remains a problem how to assess filling station agreements which are, with respect to fuel, subject to Regulation 2790/1999, and with respect to lubricants to Regulation 1400/2002 (*see* 'lubricants' as part of the definition of 'spare parts' in Article 1 (1) (s); *see also* Article 2 (5) of Regulation 2790/1999), the conditions of which are different, in particular concerning the non-compete clauses and the provisions on the duration of the agreement.
693. *See* Brochure Question 24 which concludes that an agreement covered by Regulation 2790/1999 does not constitute 'a priority' for Commission enforcement but does not exclude individual clearance (which is however difficult to obtain for one year).
694. Article 12 (2). The transitional period of Regulation 1475/95 was also of seven years. The extension of this transitional period was the compromise accepted by the Commission in order to match the Parliament's and industry's objections, *see* IP/02/1073.
695. Brochure, Questions 20–23.
696. By establishing an own sales network, in particular through an affiliate.
697. Article 4 (1) (b) (i) and Article 2 (3) (b) (the block exemption applies to this market sharing between the supplier and its distributors which are insofar competitors on the distribution level).

supplier may select its exclusive distributors according to its own strategy on the kind of territorial coverage and on the basis of certain qualitative criteria (qualification of the dealer and its personnel). The exclusive distributor is protected against

- competition from the *supplier* (who is prevented from selling to other dealers and to end users in the exclusive distributor's territory or to the exclusive customer group),[698] and
- active competition from other (exclusive or selected) *dealers*,[699] including new or additional outlets.[700]

The territory or customer group reserved to the supplier[701] is also protected against active competition from other dealers.

Relevance of Market Shares.
Exclusive distribution agreements are exempted up to a market share of 30%.[702]

Accepted and Prohibited Territorial and Customer Restrictions.
Within its sales territory the exclusive dealer may sell actively and passively to customers of its choice, including:

- to unauthorized operators,[703]
- to supermarkets; [704] however, studies undertaken on behalf of the Commission[705] revealed that no supermarket or association speaking on their behalf expressed the desire to sell cars on a regular basis;
- to internet operators or via internet referral sites,[706] provided the distributor complies with the qualitative requirements regarding the promotion of the relevant brand of the motor vehicle,[707]

---

698. This obligation is exempted under the general provision of Article 2 (1).
699. Article 4 (1) (b) (i).
700. A location clause is only prohibited within a selective distribution system for passenger cars and light commercial vehicles (Article 5 (1) (e) and from Oct. 1, 2005 (Article 12 (2)).
701. The supplier may distribute its products on reserved markets through its own subsidiaries: *General Motors/Daewoo*, D.Comm. July 22, 2002, M.2832, point 36.
702. Article 3 (1), first subparagraph.
703. Article 4 (1) (b) (i); Brochure, under 5.3. and Question 40. By contrast, within a selective distribution system a dealer may be prevented from selling to unauthorized distributors: Article 4 (1) (b) (iii).
704. Recitals 14 and 15.
705. Lademann study on potential sales and servicing alternatives in automobile distribution, p. 41.
706. Recital 15; Brochure, Question 44. By contrast, within a selective distribution system sales to unauthorized distributors may be prohibited and sales to and by supermarkets are only admitted if they meet the qualitative criteria and are authorized by the manufacturer or importer.
707. Brochure, Question 44.

- to any end user, including leasing companies,[708] even if the cars are leased to customers outside the territory[709] and even if they purchase a large number of vehicles for leasing, [710] provided that the leasing contracts do not provide for a transfer of ownership or an option to purchase the vehicle prior to the expiry of the contract[711] and that the leasing company does not resell a motor vehicle while it is new;[712] the exclusive dealer may not be prevented from selling leasing services itself;[713]
- to intermediaries or agents, provided there is a valid mandate from an individual customer.[714]

The exclusive dealer may use e-mail or personalized letters to contact potential customers, even if these are allocated exclusively to other dealers.[715]

Outside its sales territory the exclusive dealer may not *actively* sell into the exclusive territory or to an exclusive customer group allocated to another exclusive dealer or reserved to the supplier itself, i.e. not actively advertise or seek customers nor establish any branch, except for solicitation via the general (not targeted or personalized) use of the internet.[716] However, the exclusive dealer may not be prevented from selling actively in those areas where selective distribution is applied. [717]

The dealer may not be prevented from *passively* selling in all areas of the Community, irrespective of whether exclusive or selective distribution is applied in those areas. The dealer may sell to customers who contact him from outside its territory either directly or via an intermediary or a purchasing agent,[718] including the right to use the internet[719] or internet referral sites, such as *Autobytel.*[720] The

708. Brochure, Questions 46–48. *See Mercedes-Benz*, D.Comm. Oct. 10, 2001, 2002 OJ L 257/1, points 138, 176, 196 and 204.
709. *BMW/ALD AutoLeasing*, ECJ Oct. 24, 1995, 1995 ECR I-3459, para. 16–19.
710. Brochure, under 5.3.1.
711. Article 5 (2) (a) and Article 1 (1) (w).
712. Brochure, Question 47.
713. Recital 30.
714. Recital 14, Brochure, under 5.2. and Question 48. Under the previous situation a dealer was prevented from selling more than 10% of its cars through intermediaries. Under the new regulation (which abolishes the previous Notice on intermediaries, 1991 OJ C 329/20), no such limit exists to the extent that dealers are now free to establish active partnerships with all kinds of intermediaries.
715. Brochure, Question 45.
716. Article 4 (1) (b). This provision corresponds to Article 4 (b), first indent, of Regulation 2790/1999.
717. Article 4 (1) (b) and (d).
718. Recital 14. *See* Guidelines on Vertical Restraints, point 51. However, in merger decisions the Commission considered e-commerce and traditional sales as constituting distinct markets.
719. Provided the internet is not used in a *personalized* way: Brochure, Question 45.
720. Recital 15.

prohibition of passive sales bans includes any *indirect* restrictions, in particular where the dealer's remuneration or a bonus scheme is made dependent on the destination of the vehicles, where sales quotas based on sales territory are applied[721] or where shipments are limited, thereby limiting the dealer's capacity to passively sell outside its territory.[722] Although the regulation provides manufacturers with substantial means by which to protect their distribution system, it does not authorize the adoption of measures which contribute to a partitioning of the market.[723]

The exclusive dealer may not operate out of an *unauthorized place of establishment*, in particular not establish additional sales outlets; location clauses are exempted with respect to exclusive distributors.[724] However, the exclusive dealer cannot be prevented from outsourcing the after-sales servicing to an authorized repairer in the vicinity of its sales outlet, provided the end user is duly informed before the conclusion of the sales contract.[725]

Non-Compete Clauses Normally Blacklisted.
Article 5 (1) (a) blacklists any direct or indirect non-compete clause, including any direct or indirect[726] obligation on the dealer to purchase *more than 30%* of its total purchases of the contract goods from a single supplier.[727] The exclusive dealer may not be prevented from selling one or more additional brands ('multi-branding') and from selling motor vehicles from a *particular* competing supplier.[728] However, the dealer may be obliged to sell vehicles from a competing suppliers in separate areas of the same showroom[729] and to comply with requirements relating to the showroom decoration (which may be different between the Champs Elisée and a rural location). The dealer may also be obliged to purchase *up to 30%* of its total purchases of the contract goods from the contract supplier, thereby limiting purchases from competing suppliers.

721. Recital 16; Brochure, Question 43.
722. Direct or indirect restrictions on passive sales outside the dealer's territory are the most frequent infringements likely to lead to heavy fines in cases such as *BMW*, D.Comm. Dec. 23, 1977, 1978 OJ 46/33; *Volkswagen I*, D.Comm. Jan. 28, 1998, 1998 OJ L 124/60; *Volkswagen II*, D.Comm. June 29, 2001, 2001 OJ L 262/14; *rev'd* CFI Dec. 3, 2003, T-208/01; *Opel*, D.Comm. Sept. 20, 2000, 2001 OJ L 59/1; and *Daimler Chrysler*, D.Comm. Oct. 10, 2001, 2002 OJ L 257/1.
723. *Volkswagen*, ECJ Sept. 18, 2003, C-338/00P, para. 49.
724. Brochure, under 5.3.3. This restriction is exempted by the general provision of Article 2 (1), the provision of Article 4 (1) (e) being limited to selective distributors of new passenger cars and light commercial vehicles.
725. Article 4 (1) (g); Brochure, under 5.3.6.
726. E.g., by applying higher margins or a bonus if the dealer only sells the vehicles of one supplier, Brochure, Question 50.
727. Article 1 (1) (b); Article 5 (1) (a).
728. Article 5 (1) (c).
729. Separate legal entity and separate management are no longer required.

(b) Qualitative Selective Distribution of New Motor Vehicles

Definition.
A selective distribution system means a distribution system where the supplier selects dealers according to qualitative criteria which must be objective and justified by the nature of the goods. A selective distribution system implies:

- the supplier is obliged to sell the contract goods or services only to the selected ('authorized') dealers, not to unauthorized dealers and not directly to end users,[730] and
- the selected dealer has the right to sell actively or passively to end users within the Common Market where selective distribution is applied and to other selected dealers, including (from October 1, 2005) from the selected dealer's additional sales outlets, but not to unauthorized dealers.[731]

Irrelevance of Market Shares.
In the case of qualitative selective distribution no market share threshold applies because it is not restrictive of competition, provided the criteria are *purely* qualitative, laid down uniformly for all distributors and applied in a non-discriminatory manner.[732] This corresponds to the case law of the Commission and the Court.[733]

Qualitative Selection Criteria.
Qualitative criteria may include:[734]
(i) technical qualification of personnel;[735] if brand-specific sales personnel is necessary the supplier must pay all the additional costs involved;[736]
(ii) qualification of after-sales personnel, unless the distributor decides to subcontract the after-sales servicing to an authorized repairer, which must meet the qualification criteria; however, the manufacturer may not require the dealer to assure after-sales servicing if the dealer prefers to subcontract the provision of repair and maintenance services;[737]
(iii) requirements on product display,[738] in particular the obligation to display the full range of motor vehicles in the showroom;[739] this quality standard also ap-

730. Article 1 (1) (f).
731. Article 4 (1) (d) and Article 4 (1) (b) (iii).
732. Article 3 (1), third subparagraph.
733. *SABA I*, ECJ Oct. 25, 1977, 1977 ECR 1875, para. 20.
734. Article 3 (6) of the new regulation and Article 4 of Regulation 1475/95 (*see BMW*, D.Comm. Dec. 13, 1974, 1975 OJ L 29/1, point 13).
735. *See* Article 4 (1) (1) (b) of the previous Regulation 1495/75.
736. Article 1 (1) (b); Recital 27.
737. Article 4 (1) (g).
738. This also applies to additional sales outlets. However, the standards may differ according to, e.g., rural or urban areas: Brochure, Question 54.
739. Recital 27 and Brochure, Question 14.

plies to additional sales outlets (which a dealer is free to establish but which must comply with the quality standards);[740]

(iv) size and quality of showroom; motor vehicles of competing suppliers may have to be sold in separate areas of the showroom where it is necessary to avoid confusion between the makes;[741]

(v) the obligation to provide or use demonstration vehicles;

(vi) the obligation to use franchising elements, such as a distinctive business format and promotional methods. However, such franchising is frequently combined with a location clause (the obligation to operate only out of an authorized place of business), which in this case is precluded under the block exemption beginning on October 1, 2005;[742]

(vii) the obligation to agree with the evolving sales policy of the manufacturer, in particular concerning changes to the range of vehicles and services supplied;[743]

(viii) more generally, any objective criteria required by the nature of the product;[744] however, minimum purchasing obligations constitute quantitative criteria[745] and are exempted only up to a the market share limit of 40%.[746] The location clause (obligation to operate only from an authorized place of establishment) limits the number of establishments or outlets and is therefore a prohibited quantitative criteria beginning on October 1, 2005.[747]

Refusal of Admission to a 'Qualitative' Selective Distribution System. The regulation is based on the assumption that the selective distribution system must be applied in an objective and non-discriminatory way.[748] This implies that the car manufacturer is constrained to admit all dealers or repairers which meet the qualitative criteria, including supermarkets which meet the qualitative criteria, in particular have a showroom, demonstration vehicles and trained sales

740. Brochure, Question 56.
741. Article 1 (1) (b).
742. Article 5 (2) (b) and Article 12 (2).
743. Such commitments are frequent in agreements which exist for several decades; obviously, they may not include hardcore restrictions.
744. Commission's Notice on Vertical Restraints, points 184–196; *Leclerc/Givenchy*, CFI Dec. 12, 1996, 1996 ECR II-1961, paras 106, 116 and 139.
745. This was the reason why the modified *Grundig* selective distribution system constituted an infringement of Article 81 (1) and therefore needed exemption under Article 81 (3): *Grundig II*, D.Comm. July 10, 1985, 1985 OJ L 233/1, 5.
746. Article 3 (1). However, it may be argued that an obligation to purchase not more than 30% of the total purchases from a single supplier is not restrictive of competition (Article 1 (1) (b)) and is therefore not subject to a market share threshold.
747. Article 5 (2) (b) and Article 12 (2).
748. Article 1 (1) (h). *See Leclerc/Givenchy*, CFI Dec. 12, 1996, 1996 ECR II-1851, paras 111–117.

staff.[749] Thus, all operators who meet the qualitative criteria must be admitted to the manufacturer's network and may be supplied directly by the manufacturer or by other authorized dealers.[750]

Criteria for Refusing Admission.

Qualitative selection criteria may include undetermined criteria such as 'appropriate' sales facilities and 'adequate' inventories which involve the exercise of discretion.[751] Past experience shows that such a system may give rise to abuse to exclude unwelcome operators or to delay their admission. This was the reason why the Commission imposed in its *SABA II* decision a time limit of four weeks for deciding on admission of new dealers and the obligation to give reasons for any refusal.[752] The refusal to admit dealers is therefore subject to judicial review.[753] A dealer who is refused although it fulfils the selection criteria can challenge the refusal before the national courts.[754] A single refusal does not automatically lead to a loss of the benefit of the exemption, as is the case where a supplier refuses to give independent repairers access to technical information.[755] However, the dealer may complain to the Commission where a car manufacturer *systematically* refuses the admission of a certain group of distributors,[756] arguing that the system is applied in a discriminatory way or that the criteria are in fact not purely qualitative, thereby infringing Article 81[757] and producing effects which are incompatible with Article 81 (3).[758] Such disputes are not subject to the regula-

---

749. This is the reason why department stores were admitted to the selective distribution systems, such as Givenchy (luxury perfumes): *Leclerc/Givenchy*, CFI Dec. 12, 1993, 1996 ECR II-1851, paras 18 and 111–117. Supermarkets and pure internet dealers which do not meet these criteria could, however, be excluded because of the risk of free-riding on other distributors, unless they act as agent or intermediaries.

750. The prohibition against dealers not selling to unauthorized dealers is block exempted (Article 4 (1) (b) (iii)).

751. Article 1 (1) (h).

752. *SABA II*, D.Comm. Dec. 21, 1983, 1983 OJ L 376/41, 47–49.

753. Although cases such as selective distribution systems for luxury goods (perfumes) show how difficult it is for a national judge to assess a dealer's qualification, *see Leclerc/Yves St. Laurent*, CFI Dec. 12, 1996, 1996 ECR II-1851, paras124–192, it seems highly likely that a national court may try to avoid the application of this very complex regulation by stating that the selective distribution system does not appreciably affect trade between member states. A national judge would not have the procedural means to evaluate a Community-wide foreclosure effect resulting from a cumulative effect of parallel networks, which under Regulation 2790/1999 is reserved to a Commission withdrawal proceeding anyway (Article 8 of that regulation) whereas the new regulation is silent on this point.

754. *Leclerc/Yves St. Laurent*, CFI Dec. 12, 1996, 1996 ECR II-1851, para. 129.

755. Article 4 (2).

756. *Leclerc/Yves St. Laurent*, CFI Dec. 12, 1996, 1996 ECR II-1851, para. 130.

757. *See Leclerc/Yves St. Laurent*, CFI Dec. 12, 1996, 1996 ECR II-1851, para. 130; *Dalmasso*, CFI Jan. 21, 1999, 1999 ECR II-93, para. 68.

758. This may lead to a withdrawal of the benefit of the block exemption according to Article 6, which is not limited to the examples mentioned therein ('in particular').

tion's mandatory dispute resolution mechanism as provided by Article 3 because there is no agreement yet which must provide for the right to refer the matter to an expert or arbitrator;[759] however, the parties are obviously not prevented from calling upon an expert or arbitrator in order to settle their conflict.[760] If the supplier has a dominant position its refusal would infringe Article 82, but in this case the block exemption is inapplicable anyway.

Appointment of Distributors does not Imply Supply.
The appointment of a dealer means that the dealer is admitted to the supplier's distribution network and can be supplied by any other member of that network.[761] However, appointment does not imply direct supply by the manufacturer, except where the refusal to supply would amount to an indirect means of restricting parallel trade[762] or where the supplier has a dominant position. Normally, the appointment of a selected (authorized) distributor is combined with a sales contract which determines the quantities and prices to be applied. Additional quantities must be renegotiated (in particular in the case where the dealer establishes an additional sales outlet in order to increase the number of motor vehicles to be sold); the supplier is not obliged to sell such additional quantities, except in cases where the supplier holds a dominant position.[763] It is questionable whether a manufacturer of right hand drive vehicles can be held obliged to satisfy without limits the demand of a continental distributor which wants to sell such cars from its additional sales outlets to UK customers at lower prices than the distributors located in that area.[764]

Exempted and Prohibited Territorial and Customer Restrictions.
Territorial restrictions on the selected distributors are generally blacklisted.[765] The selected dealer may sell new passenger cars and light commercial vehicles actively and passively within all EEA countries where a selective distribution system is applied, including from additional sales outlets which selected dealers are entitled to establish from October 1, 2005 for all but for heavier vehicles. The selected dealer may sell to authorized dealers which are members of the supplier's

---

759. Article 3 (6).
760. *See* Article 5 (3) of the previous Regulation 1475/95.
761. Only reselling to unauthorized distributors and independent repairers is prohibited: Article 1 (1) (f).
762. The Commission states in its Brochure, Question 57, that the supplier 'will have to make the necessary arrangements that a dealer can buy sufficient quantities' without, however, being *obliged* to do so. *See Ford*, ECJ Sept. 17, 1985, 1985 ECR 2725, para. 33.
763. *See Jaeger/Opel Norge*, EFTA Court of Justice, April 1, 1998, E-3/97, paras 45–51; ECL 1998–4, 158.
764. *See* the difficulties of defining the 'normal demand' in the pharmaceutical sector, which is also characterized by important price differences and increasing parallel trade between member states: *Sandoz*, D.Comm. July 13, 1987, 1987 OJ L 222/28, 32.
765. Article 4 (1) (b).

selective distribution network (but not to non-authorized dealers and independent repairers) and to all end users, [766] except where the end user is a disguised independent reseller.[767] With respect to *spare parts*, however, the dealers may not be restricted from reselling spare parts to independent repairers which do not operate within the supplier's distribution system[768] but use these parts for the repair or maintenance for the supplier's motor vehicles.[769] On the other hand, the selected dealer may not resell components, supplied for the purposes of incorporation, to customers who would use them to manufacture the same type of goods as those produced by the supplier, in order to prevent counterfeiting.[770]

Non-Compete Obligations Normally Blacklisted.
The general provision of Article 5 (1) (a), which blacklists non-compete clauses as defined in Article 1 (1) (b), thereby including obligations to purchase more than 30% of the dealer's purchases from the contract supplier (thereby limiting purchases from competing suppliers), fully applies to selective distribution systems. The selected dealer may not be prevented from purchasing from other authorized distributors within the supplier's network[771] and from selling (in separate areas of their showroom) competing goods (motor vehicles or spare parts) or services. However, this 'location clause' is no longer applicable from October 1, 2005.[772]

Unlike an exclusive dealer, a selected dealer is normally engaged in multi-brand activities to a considerable extent. In particular in low sales or remote areas the viability of selected dealerships depends largely on their multi-branding ability.[773]

(c) Quantitative Selective Distribution of New Motor Vehicles

Definition.
Quantitative selection directly or indirectly limits the number of dealers according to the supplier's strategy and gives the supplier a wider discretionary power: a dealer may be refused admission even if it fulfils the selection criteria.

Relevance of Market Shares.
Quantitative selective distribution is exempted up to a market share of 40%.[774]

766. Article 1 (f); Article 4 (1) (b) (iii); Article 4 (1) (c).
767. Brochure, Question 29.
768. Article 1 (1) (m).
769. Article 4 (1) (i), which is an exception of Article 4 (1) (b) (iii).
770. Article 4 (1) (b) (iv). It may be difficult to control the implementation of this provision (how can a supplier suspect a repairer to use the spare parts for counterfeiting purposes?).
771. *See* Brochure, Question 58.
772. Article 1 (1) (b).
773. MEMO/02/174 p. 11.
774. Article 3 (1), second subparagraph. *See*, however, Section C.4. *infra*.

Quantitative Criteria.
Quantitative criteria may include:

(i) a maximum number of dealers per sales area[775] (but not a maximum number of sales outlets of a dealer[776]);
(ii) obligations to purchase complete ranges or minimum quantities of contract goods;[777]
(iii) obligations to purchase up to 30% of the total purchases from a single supplier;[778]
(iv) minimum turnover;
(v) quantitative stocking requirements.

Unacceptable Direct or Indirect Territorial Limitations.
The supplier may not include in its selection criteria any reference as to where the dealer is reselling (destination clause)[779] and to whom the dealer is reselling.[780] The dealer's selection cannot depend on any limitation of active or passive reselling within the Common Market where selective distribution is applied.[781] Location clauses (the obligation to operate only from an authorized place of establishment) are prohibited beginning on October 1, 2005: from that day forward an authorized distributor of new passenger cars and light commercial vehicles may not (unlike dealers of new heavy vehicles[782]) be prevented from establishing additional sales or delivery outlets within the Common Market where selective distribution is applied,[783] whereas a prohibition against establishing additional sales outlets in areas where exclusive distribution is applied remains permitted.

The prohibition against location clauses negates the supplier's right to control the distributor's locations although the supplier may still include in its selection criteria the requirement that any such additional sales outlet fulfil the selection

775. Limiting the number in an inadequate manner may lead to a withdrawal of the block exemption: Brochure, Question 19.
776. *See* discussion of the 'location clause' hereafter.
777. Under Regulation 2790/1999 purchasing obligations are exempted up to 80% of the buyer's total purchase: Article 1 (b).
778. Obligations to purchase more than 30% would constitute an unacceptable non-compete clause and preclude the application of the regulation.
779. Including discounts depending on the destination of sales, *see Mercedes-Benz*, D.Comm. Oct. 10, 2001, 2002 OJ L 257/1, points 177–190; *Irish Sugar*, CFI Oct. 7, 1999, 1999 ECR II-2969, paras 140–145.
780. The dealer may not be prevented from selling to any end user (including leasing companies, internet providers, etc.) and to other distributors within the selective distribution system, including between distributors operating at different levels of trade (thereby preserving the possibility of cross-supplies): Article 4 (1) (c) and (d).
781. Article 4 (1) (d).
782. Article 4 (1) (e).
783. Article 4 (1) (d), Article 5 (2) (b), Article 12 (2), except in *de minimis* cases such as *Porsche*, D.Comm. May 3, 2004, IP/04/585.

criteria. However, the authorized distributor may not be prevented from expanding its business at the authorized place in order to allow increases in sales volumes.[784]

Non-Compete Clauses.
Non-compete clauses are blacklisted to the same extent as under a qualitative selective distribution system.

(d) Distribution of New Motor Vehicles by Unauthorized Dealers and Intermediaries

Definition.
Unauthorized dealers are dealers which operate outside the supplier's network. A dealer authorized by a supplier is deemed to be an unauthorized dealer for the purposes of selling motor vehicles of another supplier if he is not a member of that supplier's distribution system.[785] An intermediary or purchase agent is a person or undertaking who purchases a new motor vehicle on behalf of an individual consumer on the basis of a valid mandate[786] without being a member of the distribution network.[787] No further requirements may be imposed, in particular with respect to quantitative limitation of this activity.[788]

Rights and Obligations.
Unauthorized dealers may be supplied with new motor vehicles by members of an exclusive distribution system but not by members of a selective distribution network.[789] Their principal activity therefore is to act for individual customers on the basis of a valid mandate. They may, however, be supplied with spare parts from manufacturers and authorized distributors of spare parts.[790] Obviously, an unauthorized dealer is free to purchase spare parts from any third undertaking.

(e) Juxtaposition of Exclusive and Selective Distribution

Carmakers may choose between an exclusive distribution and a selective distribution system. They may choose to apply an exclusive distribution system in certain

784. Recital 18.
785. By analogy to Article 1 (1) (m).
786. Recital 14.
787. Brochure under 5.2.
788. The Commission abolished its previous notices on motor vehicle intermediaries according to which a dealer could be requested not to sell more than 10% through a given intermediary (1991 OJ C 329/20).
789. Article 4 (1) (b) (iii).
790. Article 4 (1) (j).

territories within the EEA and a selective distribution system in others.[791] In such a case, the exclusive dealer is protected against active sales by the selected dealers, whereas the selected dealers are *not* protected against active sales by exclusive dealers who may actively seek customers, establish sales outlets or maintain a depot in countries with a selective distribution system (except for heavier commercial vehicles). In view of this differentiated treatment, it will be difficult for the carmaker to find dealers willing to enter into a combined exclusive/selective distribution system. This may be a reason for choosing an exclusive *or* selective distribution system for *all* dealers across the entire EEA.

Smaller motor vehicle manufacturers (in particular importers) may prefer exclusive distribution systems in order to allow a solid control and a territorial coverage by fewer and more dispersed dealers, which normally do not wish to establish additional sales outlets but rather wish and need protection against active sales of other exclusive dealers. Such manufacturers may appoint exclusive dealers who are authorized dealers of competing manufacturers that may display the vehicles in a separate area of their showroom without any risk of confusion between the different makes. Given their limited market position these manufacturers may have to accept the dealers' right to sell within their allocated territory to all (authorized and unauthorized) distributors, including supermarkets, and to all end users, including via intermediaries. An exclusive distribution system allows the manufacturer to reserve certain markets and customers to itself (and to be protected against active sales of other dealers) and to supply those customers directly or through affiliate companies.[792]

Bigger manufacturers may prefer selective distribution systems based on criteria which still allow them to control the network by way of qualitative selection of the dealers and their initial and additional outlets (following the prohibition of the location clauses in 2005) and by the requirement that the motor vehicles supplied to those dealers be resold within the closed circuit of the selected dealers (which may also operate for competing manufacturers). However, the manufacturer cannot prevent the selected dealers from selling actively and passively within the entire selective distribution system.

3. Restrictions with Respect to the Distribution and Use of Spare Parts

(a) Definition of Spare Parts

Spare Parts v. Accessories.

Spare parts are parts which are installed in or upon a motor vehicle so as to replace components of that vehicle, including batteries, tires and lubricants (but

791. Recital 13.
792. Article 4 (1) (b) (i).

not fuel),[793] whereas accessories such as radios, navigation systems, luggage racks etc. are not covered.[794]

Original Spare Parts.
Original spare parts are parts manufactured according to the specifications and production standards of a car manufacturer and used for the assembly of a motor vehicle. These parts include parts which are manufactured on the same production line, and they are presumed to have the same quality as the components used for the assembly of the motor vehicle.[795]

Spare Parts of Matching Quality.
Spare parts of matching quality are parts which are not produced according to the specifications and production standards of the motor vehicle manufacturer and for which the part manufacturer can certify[796] that the parts in question match the quality of the components used for the assembly of the motor vehicle in question.[797]

(b) Manufacturers of Spare Parts

Original spare parts are produced by the car manufacturer (20% of the total spare parts production) or by a third undertaking according to the specifications and production standards and with the manufacturer's consent (80% of the total spare parts production).[798] Original spare parts may be supplied:[799]

- by the *motor vehicle manufacturer* under its trade mark and logo (whether or not they are produced by the car manufacturer itself or produced and supplied by the part manufacturer) to any authorized or independent wholesaler or retailer or directly to any authorized or independent repairer,[800] or
- or by the *part manufacturer* under its own trade mark and logo[801] (whether or not they are supplied to the car manufacturer), who is guaranteed the right under

793. Article 1 (1) (s).
794. The distribution of accessories is subject to Regulation 2790/1999: Brochure, Question 95.
795. Article 1 (1) (t), Brochure under point 7. This is new in order to avoid any confusion which currently exists among consumers which may still believe that parts supplied by the motor vehicle manufacturer are better than parts that come from the part manufacturer on the same production line.
796. As to the details of such certificates *see* Brochure, Questions 101–103.
797. Article 1 (1) (u); Brochure, Question 102.
798. The specifications and standards may have been developed by the car manufacturer or by the parts manufacturer or by means of a joint development programme: Brochure, under point 7.
799. The sale of original spare parts includes the right of the buyer (authorized distributor or official repairer) to use the trademark and the logo under which they are supplied.
800. Article 4 (1) (j), Brochure, Question 97.
801. They may be placed effectively and in an easily visible manner on those parts and on the packaging: Article 4 (1) (l); Brochure, Question 97.

the regulation to sell to *any* distributor or repairer, including *un*authorized ('independent') dealers and repairers.[802] This right to sell directly to unauthorized undertakings products that are manufactured according to the specifications and production standards provided by, or developed with the consent of, the car manufacturer deviates from the previous Notice on Subcontracting Agreements, which provided that the obligation on the subcontractor (the supplier) to supply goods resulting from the use of this technology *only* to the contractor (the carmaker) or performed on its behalf was held compatible with Article 81 (1).[803]

(c) Authorized and Unauthorized Distributors of Spare Parts

Definition.
Authorized distributors of spare parts are distributors operating at the wholesale or retail level which the motor vehicle manufacturer or the parts manufacturer has selected (authorized) to distribute those parts.

Unauthorized distributors are distributors who operate outside the distribution system set up by the car or the parts manufacturer, even if they are authorized by other competing suppliers.

Selection of Distributors and Relevance of Market Shares.
Car and parts manufacturers are not obliged to select their distributors according to certain criteria; they may supply distributors whether or not they are authorized.[804] However, they may decide to establish an exclusive, a quantitative or qualitative selective distribution system.[805] In cases of exclusive and quantitative selective distribution, the market share limit of 30% applies, whereas qualitative selective distribution is not subject to market share limits.[806]

The definition of the relevant *product* market depends on the substitutability of the goods supplied which is large with respect to unsophisticated spare parts likely to be used in different car models but limited with respect to brand-specific spare parts for which no readily alternative source of supply exists.[807] The assessment of demand substitution entails a determination of the range of products ('portfolio') which are viewed as substitutes by the buyer, repairer and

802. Article 4 (1) (j) and (k) and Brochure, under point 7. Even if intellectual property rights developed by the part manufacturer are transferred to the vehicle manufacturer these rights may not be used to restrict the parts manufacturer to sell parts only to authorized or independent repairers: Brochure, Question 104.
803. Notice on Subcontracting Agreements, 1979 OJ C 1/2, point 2. *See* Guidelines on Horizontal Cooperation, 2001 OJ C 3/2, point 81.
804. Article 4 (1) (j).
805. Brochure, Question 100.
806. Article 3 (1).
807. Brochure, under 6.1 notes 186 and 187.

end-user.[808] The relevant product market may be subdivided into original equipment and aftermarket.[809] This narrow market definition may lead to a multitude of relevant markets on some of which the parties' market share may exceed 30%, thereby necessitating an individual assessment of the agreement. The definition of the relevant *geographic* market depends on the geographic scope of activity of the distributors, which may be different for wholesalers (European-wide)[810] and for smaller distributors (national or regional).[811]

Exclusive Distribution.
If the manufacturer decides to allocate exclusive territories for the distribution of its spare parts,[812] the exclusive dealers cannot be prevented from selling within the allocated territory freely to any dealer, repairer and user, and from passively selling outside the territory, whereas active sales in territories of other exclusive dealers may be prohibited.[813]

Qualitative and Quantitative Selection.
A qualitative selective distribution system may be based on criteria such as technical qualification of personnel,[814] stocking requirements, use of computerized systems and requirements regarding promotion (e.g., via the internet). The qualitative selection must be applied in a non-discriminatory manner: the manufacturers are constrained to make the selection criteria public in order to enable interested distributors to verify whether they meet the criteria,[815] and they must make the selected dealers known to suppliers of spare parts and other dealers which are only permitted to sell to authorized, and not to non-authorized dealers.[816] A distribution system based on criteria such as obliging the dealer to respect certain sales

---

808. The Commission privileges demand substitubility over supply substitubility for the purposes of market definition and requires an assessment as to the extent to which demand would react to small and lasting price increases of, say, 5–10% ('SSNIP test'): Brochure, under point 6.1. *See* Guidelines on Vertical Restraints, point 95.
809. However, this question of subdividing the market into OEM and IAM submarkets has been left open in *ZF Friedrichshafen/Mannesmann Sachs*, D.Comm. Sept. 14, 1998, M.1291, point 15.
810. *Bosch/ZF Friedrichshafen*, D.Comm. Nov. 19, 2001, M.2603, point 20; *TMD/MENETA/MAST*, D.Comm. Jan. 25, 2002, M.2696.
811. *See* Brochure, note 189.
812. A smaller manufacturer may wish to allocate exclusive territories for the distribution of both motor vehicles and spare parts to the same dealers.
813. *See* Brochure, Question 100.
814. If manufacturers require brand-specific personnel they must pay all the additional costs involved: Article 1 (1) (b).
815. *See* Brochure, Question 73. Example: *Volkswagen/Audi*, IP/03/80 of Jan. 20, 2003.
816. Article 4 (1) (b) (iii). The authorized dealer's ability to transfer its business is also limited to other authorized dealers: Article 3 (3) and Brochure, Question 83. The interest of a dealer to enter into an authorized dealership agreement is to obtain rebates (on the basis of the dealer's total sales within the Common Market and without any fidelity element), which he would not get as unauthorized dealer.

targets[817] or to purchase minimum quantities must be qualified as quantitative selection and is only permitted up to a 30% market share.[818] Under a selective distribution agreement the supplier may be obliged not to sell to unauthorized distributors.[819] No direct or indirect territory or customer restrictions may be imposed on the selected dealers of spare parts. They can actively and passively resell the spare parts (including from additional sales outlets[820]):

- to authorized distributors in the supplier's distribution system, and not to unauthorized distributors[821] (possibility of cross-supplies even on different levels of trade[822]), and
- to authorized or unauthorized ('independent') repairers which use these parts for repair and maintenance of any motor vehicle.[823] However, spare parts supplied for the purposes of incorporation (components), may not be sold to customers who would use them to manufacture the same type of goods as those produced by the supplier.[824]

A distributor operating on the wholesale level may, however, be prohibited from selling to end users (bypassing the retailer).[825]

Non-Compete Obligations Blacklisted.
Non-compete obligations as defined in Article 1 (1) (b) are normally blacklisted.[826] The distributor may only be obliged to purchase up to 30% of its total purchases from a single supplier; exclusive purchasing is prohibited.[827] However, the dealer is not prevented from purchasing freely (without being obliged) quantities which exceed the 30% market share limit.[828]

---

817. Sales targets are only accepted when they refer to *all* sales within the Common Market and not to a part of it in order to avoid any indirect territorial restriction, *see* recital 16.
818. Article 3 (1), first subparagraph.
819. Article 1 (1) (f).
820. Brochure, Question 75. The prohibition of location clauses is not expressly stated (as for official repairers in Article 5 (3)), but the general provision of Article 4 (1) (b) applies which bans any territorial restriction.
821. Article 4 (1) (b) (iii). The distributor may also transfer its business to an authorized dealer (without the manufacturer's consent): Article 3 (3).
822. Article 4 (1) (c).
823. Article 4 (1) (i).
824. Article 4 (1) (b) (iv). However, it seems difficult for a dealer to foresee that the spare parts supplied would be used for counterfeiting purposes.
825. Article 4 (1) (b) (ii).
826. Article 5 (1) (a) and (b).
827. Article 1 (1) (b). Under Regulation 2790/1999 the limit is 80% (Article 1 (b)). As for selective distribution systems relating to new motor vehicles, it remains questionable how this provision can be enforced, in particular how to calculate the 30% limit without knowing the dealer's total purchases, including substitutable goods purchased from a competitor.
828. Brochure, Question 13.

Regulation 1400/2002 v. Regulation 2790/1999.
Unlike the previous regulation, the new regulation applies to agreements relating to the supply, distribution and use of spare parts (including lubricants) *irrespective* of whether they are linked to the supply of new motor vehicles. This raises the question whether Regulation 1400/2002 supercedes Regulation 2790/1999. Article 2 (5) of Regulation 2790/1999 precludes the application of that block exemption to agreements the 'subject matter' of which falls within the scope of any other regulation. The 'subject matter' of Regulation 1400/2002 may be defined as supply and/or distribution of new motor vehicles and/or spare parts; in this case the distribution of spare parts would be covered by Regulation 1400/2002.[829]

The differences between the two regulations are important:

- Regulation 2790/1999 allows exclusive purchasing agreements with a duration up to five years. Exceptionally the agreements may be concluded for the whole duration of occupancy of the buyer's premises owned or leased by the supplier (which is the case for beer and filling station agreements) in order to honour the supplier's investment in such premises.[830]
- By contrast, Regulation 1400/2002 exempts only agreements which include an obligation to purchase from a single supplier not more than 30% of the buyer's total purchases of the contract goods and substitutable goods, but these agreements may be concluded, as a rule, for an indefinite period.[831] Exclusive purchasing obligations are precluded by the regulation, even if they are motivated by investments or trade loans granted by the supplier.[832] If filling station agreements were to fall within this regulation, there would not be a transitional period up to September 30, 2003, which is only granted with respect to agreements which satisfy the conditions of Regulation 1475/95 (and not those of Regulation 2790/1999).[833]

According to the Commission's Brochure,[834] the distribution of spare parts is only covered by Regulation 1400/2002 if there is certainty that 'such goods will be used *only* for installation in or upon a motor vehicle which falls under the regulation'; distribution of lubricants are, according to this criteria, not covered since they are also sold to filling stations, supermarkets and do-it-yourself stores.[835] However,

829. Although the transitional provision of Article 7 is limited to agreements which satisfy the conditions of Regulation 1475/95 (and not those of Regulation 2790/1999), it could be applied by analogy.
830. Article 5 (a) of Regulation 2790/1999.
831. Article 3 (5); Brochure, Question 79.
832. Brochure, Question 15.
833. Article 7 of Regulation 1400/2002. This transitional provision could, however, be applied by analogy.
834. Brochure, Question 2.
835. The sale of lubricants for sale to filling stations remain therefore subject to Regulation 2790/1999.

this narrow interpretation would exclude a majority of spare parts which are used also on or upon agricultural vehicles and motor-cycles (at least those spare parts which are not brand-specific). In order to avoid a conflict between the two regulations, it may be argued that the new regulation does not cover the distribution of spare parts which are not the *primary* object of the agreement (i.e., *ancillary* to the distribution of fuel) and therefore remain subject to Regulation 2790/1999, whereas agreements the primary object of which is the distribution of spare parts may well be covered by Regulation 1400/2002. In any event, the new regulation needs further clarification in order to reduce legal uncertainty.[836]

(d) Authorized and Independent Repairers

Authorized Repairers.
Authorized repairers are providers of repair and maintenance services for motor vehicles[837] which are authorized by a motor vehicle manufacturer and operate within that manufacturer's distribution system.[838] The distribution system may be an *exclusive* distribution, a *quantitative* or *qualitative* selective distribution system, all of which must allow the authorized repairer to honour warranties, perform free warranty service and carry out recall work for all motor vehicles of the brand in question sold in the Common Market.[839] The motor vehicle manufacturer may confer the repair and maintenance services to the distributors of its vehicles who are prepared to provide repair and maintenance services themselves, to repairers who, after termination of their dealership agreement, continue after-sales servicing,[840] or to other repairers in order to increase the density of its after-sales serving, to which a car dealer who does not like to provide repair and maintenance services itself may subcontract these services.[841] However, a motor vehicle dealer may be interested to maintain (and not to subcontract) the servicing activities because the cost of after-sales servicing for a car accounts for 40% of the total cost of ownership (the sales price accounts for 40% and the remaining 20% being for financing, insurance and other costs) and because good quality after-sales service frequently

836. E.g. by way of a preliminary ruling of the Court of Justice or a notification or negative clearance requesting confirmation that filling station agreements are entirely covered by Regulation 2790/1999 (also with respect to lubricants).
837. The spare parts may be used in the repairer's workshop or for the provision of roadside assistance services: Brochure, Question 97.
838. Article 1 (1) (l).
839. Brochure, Question 74. Motor vehicles manufactured outside the Common Market are included once they are put on the market within the Community.
840. Brochure, Question 72.
841. The authorized repairer must, however, be in the dealer's vicinity because customers do not like to travel far for having the car repaired, ideally 15 minutes, but in no case more than 30 minutes, and may therefore continue to prefer a one-stop shop which combines both services. *Cf.* Lademann Study, p. 46.

brings customer loyalty and leads to future new car purchases. Subcontracting the after-sales servicing may be interesting for multi-branding dealers which continue to assure after sales servicing for their principal make but subcontract this service for other makes to an authorized repairer of those vehicles.

Selection of Repairers and Relevance of Market Shares.
The supplier of spare parts may select its repairers on the basis of qualitative or quantitative selective distribution criteria or under traditional exclusive distribution in basically the same manner as the regulation applies to the supply of motor vehicles, with some exceptions.[842]

Qualitative selection criteria may include:

- technical qualification of the personnel;
- stocking requirements;
- use of computerized systems;
- the requirement to honour the warranty, perform free warranty service and to carry out recall work which the manufacturer is obliged to ensure in respect to any motor vehicle sold in the Common Market;[843] and
- the requirement to erect brand-related signage.[844]

Selection criteria may *not* include:

- any obligation as to the place of establishment of an authorized repairer where selective distribution is applied[845] (which precludes any control of the density of the system and reduces the practical importance of quantitative selection[846]), or
- any restriction of its ability to limit its activities to the provision of repair and maintenance services, in particular the prohibition to sell new or used motor vehicles.[847]

A qualitative selective distribution system must be applied in a non-discriminatory manner; refusal must be reasoned;[848] disputes may be referred to an expert or arbitrator.[849] The authorization of a repairer does not imply supply, except where

842. Article 1 (1) (f); Article 4 (1) (h)–(l).
843. Recital 17.
844. Brochure, Question 52.
845. Article 5 (3), beginning on 1 Oct. 1, 2005.
846. Spare part distribution agreements may exceed the market share threshold of 30% on the relevant markets (*see* section II.3 (c) *supra*), and will therefore be covered by the regulation only if the selection is based on *qualitative* criteria (the market share limit of 40% only applies for the sale of new motor vehicles).
847. Article 4 (1) (h).
848. *See SABA II*, D.Comm. Dec. 21, 1983, 1983 OJ L 376/41, 47–49.
849. Article 3 (6).

the supplier has a dominant position; the advantage of an authorized rapairer is to be supplied by other authorized repairers and intermediaries and to be allowed to honour warranties, perform free servicing and carry out recall work in respect to all motor vehicles of the brand in question.[850]

Quantitative selection criteria may include:

- limitation on the number of repairers in a geographic area;
- respect of sales targets; and
- minimum purchasing obligations.

In the case of quantitative and exclusive distribution the market share limit of 30% applies. According to Article 8 (1) (c), the market share must be calculated on the basis of the value of the contract services sold by the members of the supplier's distribution network together with any other services sold by these members which are regarded as interchangeable or substitutable, the national market being relevant.[851] The market share limit of 30% may therefore be exceeded in many cases, thereby making quantitative selection unlikely.

Multiple Authorizations.
A repairer may be authorized by different competing motor vehicle manufacturers or parts manufacturers.[852] A repairer may also be appointed by one supplier but not by another supplier who applies different criteria. A motor vehicle manufacturer may authorize several repairers for its different models requiring specialized after-sales servicing.

Use Restrictions Blacklisted.
The authorized repairer has the right to use the spare parts freely for any motor vehicle, without prejudice to the manufacturer's ability to require the use of original spare parts for repairs under warranty, free servicing and vehicle recall work.[853] However, this implies that the authorized repairer may not resell original spare parts over the counter to an end user, unless the repairer is expressly authorized by the supplier to do so.

Non-Compete Clauses.
Non-compete clauses preclude the the application of the block exemption, except obligations on the authorized repairer to purchase up to 30% of its total purchases

850. Brochure, Question 74. A dealer whose contract has been terminated may continue as an authorized repairer (without a supply contract): Question 72.
851. Brochure, under 6.1. example (c).
852. The existing diagnostic systems which are available to the repairers cover already the majority of car models.
853. Article 4 (1) (k).

of the contract goods from the authorizing manufacturer or from another undertaking designated by the manufacturer (which includes purchases from an authorized parts dealer).[854] Authorized repairers are free to obtain original spare parts or spare parts of matching quality from any third undertaking of their choice.[855]

Authorized repairers may not be limited to the provision of repair and maintenance services and the distribution of spare parts;[856] in particular they may not be prevented from selling new motor vehicles (e.g. as an intermediary[857]) or used motor vehicles. Any restriction as to the place of establishment of an authorized repairer in the area where selective distribution is applied is blacklisted.[858] The Commission policy is to open up the repair market in order to maintain or even increase the density of the official repair network to the benefit of the consumer at a time where many manufacturers are considering a major reduction in dealership coverage.[859]

However, the car manufacturer may require the authorized repairers to use only original spare parts for repairs carried out under warranty, free servicing and vehicle recall work.[860]

Repairers which fulfil the qualitative selection criteria must be authorized (but not necessarily directly supplied) by the motor vehicle manufacturer. Authorized car dealers may therefore, after termination of their car distribution agreement, become authorized repairers and even continue to sell new motor vehicles, in particular as an intermediary.[861]

Independent Repairers.
Independent repairers are undertakings directly or indirectly involved in the repair and maintenance of motor vehicles[862] but are not authorized ('selected') by a motor vehicle manufacturer of new motor vehicles or a spare part manufacturer.[863] They operate outside the supplier's distribution network and must be given access

854. Article 5 (1) (a) and Article 1 (1) (b). Obligations to purchase more than 30% of the total purchases from a single supplier preclude, however, the application of the regulation and cannot be justified by investments of the supplier in the repairer's premises; only trade loans which can be repaid at any moment are accepted, provided they do not directly or indirectly hinder the buyer from selling competing goods. *See* Brochure, Question 15.
855. Article 4 (1) (k).
856. Article 4 (1) (h).
857. This is an alternative for a dealer whose distribution contract is terminated by the motor vehicle manufacturer.
858. Article 5 (3). Exclusive distribution systems may, however, include location clauses.
859. This is the reason why the Commission is obliged to monitor the structure and level of concentration of motor vehicle distribution and the resulting effects on competition (Article 11 (1) (b)).
860. Article 4 (1) (k).
861. Brochure, Questions 72 and 74.
862. Brochure, Question 84.
863. An authorized dealer of new motor vehicles may not be prevented from being an independent repairer of that brand: Brochure, under 5.5.2. and Question 62.

to the technical information for providing after-sales servicing.[864] Independent repairers typically include independent garages, fast-fit chains, autocenters and body repairers.[865] An authorized repairer within the distribution system of a given supplier is deemed to be an independent repairer to the extent he provides repair and maintenance services for motor vehicles of a competing supplier.[866] Independent repairers are important operators since they currently carry out about 50% of all repairs to motor vehicles.[867]

Non-Discriminatory Access to Technical Information.
The independent repairer must have *access* to the necessary technical information to the same extent as the authorized repairer. This now includes software and re-programming, tools, diagnostic equipment, garage equipment and training.[868] The access must be granted by the supplier of the spare parts or the supplier or importer of motor vehicle and spare parts,[869] the principle being that the repairer should get both the spare parts and the technical information from the same source.[870] The supplier may charge a fee but must not discriminate between authorized and independent repairers; [871] any refusal to give independent operators access makes the regulation inapplicable.[872] This may create the risk of legal uncertainty, because the reasons for such a refusal may not be transparent, in particular with respect to the price to be paid for a specific software[873] and to the extent access is granted, including subsequent updating (e.g. training courses), and because of the uncertain consequences of a single refusal for the entire distribution system.[874]

Free Purchasing and Free Use of Spare Parts.
Independent repairers are free to obtain original spare parts or spare parts of matching quality from any undertaking of their choice who will supply them.[875] They are free to use those parts for repairing vehicles of all makes in their workshop or for roadside assistance services.[876] They may use original spare parts, even

864. Article 1 (1) (m); Article 4 (2).
865. Article 3 (2) fourth subparagraph; Brochure, Question 84.
866. Article 1 (l) and (m).
867. Brochure, under 3.2.
868. Article 4 (1) (j) and Article 4 (2) (only information on anti-theft devices being excluded for security reasons).
869. Brochure, Question 85.
870. Brochure, Question 93.
871. Discrimination includes undue delay and charging unjustified prices: recital 26 and Brochure, Questions 90 and 91.
872. Article 4 (2), *see* recital 26.
873. *See* MEMO/02/174, p. 7.
874. It may be argued that a single refusal does not lead to loosing the benefit of the block exemption for ever but can be renewed when the manufacturer complies with this requirement.
875. Article 4 (1) (k).
876. Brochure, Question 97.

for repairs carried out under warranty[877] but as an independent repairer have no right to remuneration from the manufacturer for such repair works.[878] Independent repairers are obviously free to sell any new or used motor vehicle.

4. Agreements Precluded from the Block Exemption

Agreements between Parties with Market Shares of Minor Importance (*De Minimis*).
Agreements between parties with market shares that are within the *de minimis* thresholds do not fall within Article 81 (1) unless the agreements contain hardcore restrictions. This applies to:

- agreements between parties which have a market share of less than 15%;[879] and
- agreements which contribute insignificantly (i.e. less than 5%) to the cumulative effect of a parallel network of similar agreements.[880]

Agreements between Parties with Market Shares Exceeding the Limits of the Block Exemption.
Agreements between parties with market shares exceeding respectively 30% (i.e., for exclusive distribution) and 40% (i.e., for quantitative selective distribution) are not covered by the block exemption. There can be no presumption that such agreements give rise to objective advantages of such a character and magnitude as to compensate for the anticompetitive disadvantages.[881] This seems to apply, at first glance, not only where the parties' *individual* market shares exceed the limits of the block exemption but also where the agreements are part of a parallel network of similar agreements that have a *cumulative* anticompetitive (foreclosure) effect exceeding respectively the 30% or the 40% market shareholds. In the *Porsche* case[882] the Commission found that in Europe nearly all new motor vehicles are distributed by means of quantitative selective distribution systems, but that Porsche with a market share of less than 5% did not contribute to a significant extent to the cumulative effect of this network. Therefore the Commission decided that Porsche could continue to apply the 'location clause' beyond the normal time limit of October 1, 2005. However, it may be concluded that the block exemption

877. Article 4 (1) (i).
878. Brochure, Question 62.
879. Commission's *de minimis* Notice, point 7.
880. *Ibid.*, point 8. *See Neste Markkinointi/Yötuuli,* ECJ Dec. 7, 2000, 2000 ECR I-11121, para. 39; *Shaw, Falla/Whitbread,* CFI March 21, 2002, 2002 ECR II-2023.
881. Recital 8 to Regulation 1400/2002.
882. *Porsche,* D.Comm. May 3, 2004, IP/04/585. In this case the Commission granted clearance to the quantitative selective distribution of new motor vehicles established by Porsche including – because of the low market share – the continued application of the 'location clause' (which is not a hardcore restriction) beyond the normal limit of October 1, 2005.

does not apply to quantitative selective distribution systems applied by the larger motor vehicle manufacturers based on the cumulative foreclosure effect covering more than 50% of the relevant market because the parties' individual market shares exceed the 5% threshold. Since competitors are not supposed to know or inquire directly about commercially sensitive details of each other's distribution agreements it seems more appropriate for the Commission or the competent national authority to withdraw (with prospective effect) the benefit of the block exemption pursuant to Article 7, provided that parallel networks cover more than 50% of a relevant market.[883]

Agreements Containing Restrictions which are not Covered by the Block Exemption.

Agreements which contain restrictions that are not covered by Regulation 1400/2002 cannot be saved under the block exemption Regulation 2790/1999 which does not apply, according to Article 2 (5), to vertical agreements the subject matter of which falls within the scope of any other block exemption regulation. Such agreements require an individual assessment and normally do not justify clearance, unless it is clearly demonstrated that the agreement in question is likely to bring about substantial efficiencies which counterbalance the anticompetitive disadvantages.

Hardcore restrictions (Article 4) are normally unlikely to get any individual clearance, unless under very exceptional circumstances.[884] Such restrictions are null and void in their entirety (Article 81 (2)). Agreements which contravene the conditions of Article 3 or 5 are not covered by the block exemption but lead only to the nullity of the clauses directly affected, in particular with respect to non-compete clauses, whereas the remainder of the agreement can operate independently[885] and can be enforced if it is severable (which is wholly a matter of national law).[886] Agreements which are concluded between parties with market shares exceeding the 30% or 40% limits must be analyzed to determine whether they meet the clearance criteria of Article 81 (3). In cases where the distribution network established by a carmaker for the whole EEA area generally complies with the market share thresholds but exceeds them in only limited parts of that area, the parties may not have the benefits of the regulation but nevertheless meet the conditions for an exemption under Article 81 (3).

Agreements between Competitors.

According to Article 2 (1) and (3) the benefit of the block exemption only applies to vertical restraints in agreements between companies operating at different

883. This provision corresponds to Article 8 of Regulation 2790/1999. *See* Section A.3.(c) *supra*.
884. Brochure, 3.1.
885. Brochure, 3.1.
886. *Delimitis/Henninger Bräu*, ECJ Feb. 28, 1991, 1991 ECR I-935, para. 40.

levels.[887] However, the block exemption nevertheless applies to agreements between members of or suppliers to an association of distributors of motor vehicles or spare part or repairers whose members each individually have a total turnover not exceeding EUR 100 million (Article 2 (2) (a)), non-reciprocal vertical agreements between competitors when the buyer's turnover does not exceed EUR 100 million (Article 2 (3) (a)), where the supplier is a manufacturer and distributor, while the buyer is a distributor not manufacturing goods competing with the contract goods (Article 2 (3) (b)), and between suppliers of services at several levels of trade, such as between a wholesaler and a retailer (Article 2 (3) c)).[888] Other forms of vertical agreements between competing.firms may only be cleared individually.

Examples of horizontal agreements that are excluded from the block exemption but which have been found not to infringe Article 81 (1) or to meet the exemption criteria of Article 81 (3) are:

- agreements between car importers resulting from governmentally imposed restrictions on imported car sales to a certain quota and to divide up this quota among themselves;[889] and
- agreements between competing carmakers creating a B2B marketplace joint venture intended to provide the automotive industry with procurement and collaborative development of automotive components; although the cooperation may be tantamount to joint purchasing and joint selling, the few cases decided up to now have been cleared following commitments for data protection through the use of firewalls and security rules.[890]

---

887. The fact that the manufacturer is also a distributor and therefore a competitor of the contractual dealer does not preclude the application of the block exemption: Article 2 (3) (b).

888. *See* Commission Explanatory Brochure, 4.2.

889. *Asia Motor France*, ECJ Sept. 20, 2001, 2001 ECR I-6349. This judgment was favourable to the Commission, which had rejected complaints inasmuch as the problems complained of resulted directly from the policy of public authorities and not from an agreement between undertakings. This settlement brings to an end a long series of legal conflicts between the complainant and the Commission which resulted in numerous Court decisions concerning the Commission's right to reject a complaint because of a lack of Community interest.

890. *General Motors/Fiat*, Commission clearance, IP/00/932 of Aug. 16, 2000; *Covisint*, Commission clearance, IP/01/1155 of July 31, 2001; Thirty-first Report on Competition Policy, Box 4. One may have doubts with respect to the efficiency of such firewall provisions since the joint use of the market place by the carmakers (which represent 63% of the worldwide car production) as well as by the manufacturers of the components (most suppliers are willing to join) necessarily implies a certain cooperation between them even if they are formally free to use other market places.

Withdrawal of the Benefit of the Block Exemption.
According to Article 6 (1) the benefit of the block exemption may be withdrawn by the Commission where agreements, although covered by the regulation, have effects incompatible with Article 81 (3), *in particular*:

- where access to the market is significantly restricted by the cumulative effect of parallel networks;[891]
- where the contract supplier is not exposed to effective competition;[892]
- where prices or conditions differ significantly between geographic areas,[893] in particular where discriminatory prices or sales conditions, or unjustifiably high supplements are charged for right hand drive vehicles;[894] or where discriminatory prices or sales conditions are applied.

Another example not set forth in Regulation 1400/2002 but referred to in the Brochure is setting the total number of distributors in a quantitative selection system at a level which is inadequate for the distribution of the products in question.[895]

In cases where the agreements produce negative effects in the territory of a member state or a part thereof, which has all the characteristics of a distinct market, the competent national competition authority has the same power in respect to that territory (Article 6 (2)). Article 7 entitles the Commission to declare, by regulation, the regulation inapplicable where parallel networks cover more than 50% of a relevant market.[896]

891. Article 6 (1) (a). In the absence of a withdrawal decision of the Commission, vertical agreements are covered by the regulation, provided the *individual* market shares do not exceed the thresholds, even if the agreements have the *cumulative* foreclosure effect, which is probably to be assumed where parallel networks cover more than 50% of a relevant market. *See* Article 7 (1). *Cf.* Article 8 of Regulation 2790/1999.
892. Article 6 (1) (b). This provision is unlikely to be applied since agreements of a supplier having market shares which exceed respectively 30 and 40% are excluded from the block exemption anyway or may give rise to the (parallel) application of Article 82, as in *Van den Bergh Foods*, D.Comm. March 11, 1998, 1998 OJ L 246/1, points 276–279.
893. Article 6 (1) (c). *Cf.* Article 8 (2) of Regulation 1475/95, which required that price differences should be chiefly due to obligations exempted under the Regulation and Recital 31 clarified that the Commission should take into account any price differentials which do not principally result from the imposition of national fiscal measures. Under the regime of the first car Regulation 123/75, 12% price differences were supposed to give rise to a withdrawal of the block exemption (Commission Notice 1985 OJ C 17/4). However, in fact they did not result in any withdrawal proceedings.
894. Article 6 (1) (d); Recital 32.
895. Brochure, Question 19.
896. This corresponds to Article 8 of Regulation 2790/1999. However, there is no case law yet in order to evaluate the meaning and efficiency of this provision. The provision could be interpreted as ending the uncertainty of how to ascertain the cumulative effect of parallel networks. It seems more appropriate to consider individual distribution systems covered by the block exemption, provided that the parties to those agreements individually do not exceed respectively 30% or 40%, and to leave it up to the Commission to initiate withdrawal proceedings where it identifies a cumulative anticompetitive effect. *See* Brochure, Question 18.

Chapter V

Article 82: Abuse of Dominant Position

CONTENTS

A. Scheme of Article 82

Common Aim of Articles 81 and 82: Maintaining Effective Competition.
Article 82 prohibits any abuse of a dominant position by one or more firms in a substantial part of the Common Market that may affect trade between member states. Article 82 is to be applied and construed – like Article 81 – in the light of the task assigned to the Community by Article 3 (g) of the Treaty of instituting a system ensuring the maintenance of effective competition in the Common Market.[1] Article 81 prohibits the prevention, restriction or distortion of competition by means of an agreement or concerted practice between firms, regardless of whether they have market power. By contrast, Article 82 applies only to firms that have market power and seeks to prevent the abuse of such power for anticompetitive ends. It prohibits the abuse of market power both by the unilateral conduct of a single firm, and by the interdependent action of several oligopolists. In the latter case, no agreement or concerted action between multiple actors must be proved as under Article 81. However, where the conditions of both provisions are fulfilled both Articles 81 and 82 may be applied in parallel.[2]

Unchanged Application of Article 82 in the Framework of the Commission's Modernization.
The modernization of the EC competition rules does not bring significant changes with respect to Article 82. In particular, there is no change to the basic approach, which is the existence and abuse of a dominant position.[3] Article 82 was and remains directly applicable in parallel by the Commission, the national competition authorities and the national courts (subject to close cooperation[4]). Where national authorities or national courts apply national law to any abuse prohibited by Article 82 (because it is likely to affect trade between member states), they must also apply Article 82, thereby reducing the risk of conflicting decisions.[5]

1. *Continental Can*, ECJ Feb. 12, 1973, 1973 ECR 215, paras 22–25; *Hoffmann-La Roche*, ECJ Feb. 13, 1979, 1979 ECR 461, 520, para. 38; *Michelin*, ECJ Nov. 9, 1983, 1983 ECR 3461, paras 29–30.
2. *See infra* Section F.
3. There is no application of the new standard of 'significantly impeding effective competition' as applies under Article 2 (2) of Regulation 139/2004 on the control of concentrations, 2004 OJ L 24/1.
4. Articles 11 and 15 of Regulation 1/2003 and the Commission's notices.
5. Article 3 of Regulation 1/2003. *See* Chapter I.F.

Existence or Acquisition of Dominant Position Unobjectionable under Article 82.
Article 82 covers only the abuse of an already existing dominant position. The existence or attainment of a dominant position[6] is in itself unobjectionable. This applies however the dominant position was obtained, whether by internal growth, resulting from superior performance or technological prowess,[7] by the acquisition of exclusive rights,[8] or by merger.[9] Mergers or acquisitions which have a Community dimension must be assessed under a stricter standard. Regulation 139/2004 provides that mergers may be declared incompatible with the Common Market where they significantly impede effective competition in the Common Market or a substantial part of it, in particular as a result of the creation or strengthening of a dominant position. Mergers and acquisitions that do not have a Community dimension may be assessed:

- under Article 82 where they constitute an abuse of a dominant firm *already holding* a dominant position within the terms of the Continental Can doctrine,[10] and
- under the merger provisions of national competition law by national competition authorities, unless the case is referred to the Commission according to Article 22 of Regulation 139/2004.

Different Types of Abuse.
Article 82 enumerates certain types of abuses without being exhaustive. The general concept of 'abuse' is broad and comprises any type of conduct that runs counter to the principle of Article 3 (g).[11] The main categories of abuse are:

- *Exploitative Abuses*: Exploiting market power in trading relationships with customers or suppliers by such practices as unfair purchase or selling prices, tying arrangements, price discrimination, etc.

---

6. *Michelin*, ECJ Nov. 9, 1983, 1983 ECR 3461, 3511, para. 57: 'A finding that an undertaking has a dominant position is not in itself a recrimination but simply means that, irrespective of the reasons for which it has such a dominant position, the undertaking concerned has a special *responsibility* not to allow its conduct to impair genuine undistorted competition on the Common Market.' *See Telecommunication Directive Services*, ECJ Nov. 17, 1992, 1992 ECR I-5833, para. 35.
7. *Hoffmann-La Roche*, ECJ Feb. 13, 1979, 1979 ECR 461, 524, para. 48.
8. *British Leyland*, ECJ Nov. 11, 1986, 1986 ECR 3263, paras 3–10; *Renault*, ECJ Oct. 5, 1988, 1988 ECR 6039, para. 15; *Crespelle*, ECJ Oct. 5, 1994, 1994 ECR I-5077, paras 17, 22; *Magill*, ECJ April 6, 1995, 1995 ECR I-743, para. 46; *Banchero*, ECJ Dec. 14, 1995, 1995 ECR I-4663, para. 55.10: *UPS Europe*, CFI March 20, 2002, 2002 ECR II-1915, para. 51.
9. *Continental Can*, ECJ Feb. 21, 1973, 1973 ECR 215, paras 18–27.
10. *Ibid.*
11. *See Continental Can*, ECJ Feb. 21, 1973, 1973 ECR 215, 244–245, paras 24–25.

- *Exclusionary Abuses*: Abusing market power to harm a competitor by anticompetitive means such as refusal to deal, predatory pricing, or other predatory actions.
- *Structural Abuses*: Eliminating a competitor by merger or acquisition. This can also be regarded as a subcategory of exclusionary abuses.

Elements to be Proved.
The elements that must be proved to establish an abuse of a dominant position which infringes Article 82 are that:

- one or more *undertakings*
- that hold a *dominant position* conferring market power
- within a *relevant product and geographic market*
- within the *Common Market* or in a *substantial part* thereof
- commit an *abuse* of the dominant position
- that may *affect trade* between member states.

This Chapter will discuss the various forms of abuse under Article 82, with the exception of 'structural abuses', i.e., creating or strengthening a dominant position by takeover of a competitor, which are covered in Chapter VI dealing with the evaluation of mergers and joint ventures under the merger control regulation.

B. Undertaking

Definition.
The meaning of 'undertaking' was discussed in Chapter I.[12] It refers to any entity engaged in business activities, regardless of its legal status and the way it is financed.[13] Thus both private and state-owned or controlled firms and public bodies that engage in industrial or commercial activities may be subject to Article 82.[14]

---

12. *See* Chapter I.D.
13. *Telecommunication Directive Services*, ECJ Nov. 17, 1992, 1992 ECR I-5833, para. 24. This may include associations or cooperatives provided they have the legal status of an undertaking: *Milk Marketing Board*, Comm. comfort letter, Twenty-second Report on Competition Policy, points 161–167; *CEWAL*, D.Comm. Dec. 23, 1992, 1993 OJ L 34/20, upheld in substance by CFI Oct. 8, 1996, 1996 ECR II-1201 (arguing that CEWAL, the association composed by four members, acted on the market autonomously as one single unit), *aff'd* ECJ March 16, 2000, 2000 ECR I-1365. *Aéroports de Paris*, CFI Dec. 12, 2000, 2000 ECR II-3929, para. 107, *aff'd* ECJ Oct. 24, 2002, 2002 ECR I-9297, para. 79; *Deutsche Bahn (German Railways)*, CFI Oct. 21, 1997, 1997 ECR II-1689; *aff'd* ECJ April 27, 1999, 1999 ECR I-2387.
14. *Commission/Italy*, ECJ June 16, 1987, 1987 ECR 2599, para. 7; *Höfner/Macrotron*, ECJ April 23, 1991, 1991 ECR I-979 para. 26; *Greek Television*, ECJ June 23, 1991, 1991 ECR I-2925, para. 38; *Diego Cali & Figli/Porto di Geneva*, ECJ March 18, 1997, 1997 ECR I-1547, para. 16. Article 82 applies directly to any enterpreneurial behavior whereas governmental behavior

The fact that a firm owes its dominant position to government measures such as the grant of monopoly rights is irrelevant.[15] By contrast, entities to which a member state has conferred a task of public interest which forms part of the essential functions of the state are not subject to Article 82,[16] whereas those parts of the activities of such an entity that can be separated from those in which it engages as a public authority (exercising sovereign powers) are subject to Articles 81 and 82.[17] The decisive criteria is whether the undertaking acts autonomously and at its own initiative or whether national measures require, reinforce or encourage the undertaking's anti-competitive conduct[18] (creating a situation 'where that body (*Deutsche Post*) may be led, to the detriment of users of postal service, to abuse its dominant position resulting from the exclusive right'[19]).

Examples.
Examples of 'undertakings' to which Article 82 has been applied are:

- The UK national telecommunications authority, British Telecommunications, which refused to allow private message-forwarding agencies to use its network to relay telex messages between foreign countries.[20]

---

is subject to a combined application of Articles 82 and 86 (because the decision has to be addressed to a member state): *GT-Link A/S v. De Dansk Statsbaner*, ECJ July 17, 1997, 1997 ECR I-4449; *Telecommunication Directive Terminal Equipment*, ECJ March 19, 1991, 1991 ECR I-1223, paras 53–57; *Ilmailulaitos/Luftfartsverket*, D.Comm. Feb. 10, 1999, 1999 OJ L 69/24, points 21–23.

15. *Télémarketing*, ECJ Oct. 3, 1985, 1985 ECR 3261, paras 17–18; *General Motors*, ECJ Nov. 13, 1975, 1975 ECR 1367, para. 9; *INNO/ATAB*, ECJ Nov.16, 1977, 1977 ECR 2115, paras 24–38; *British Telecommunications*, ECJ March 20, 1985, 1985 ECR 873, paras 16–20. *See also supra* Chapter I.D. and *infra*, section D.1 (Article 86 (2) exception) of this chapter.
16. *AOK Bundesverband/Ichthyol-esellschaft Kordes*, ECJ March 16, 2004, C-264/01, paras. 55–57. *See also Eurocontrol*, ECJ Jan. 19, 1994, 1994 ECR I-43, paras 28–32; *Diego Cali & Figli/Porto di Genova*, ECJ March 18, 1997, 1997 ECR I-1547, paras 23–25; *French Post*, D.Comm. Oct. 23, 2001, 2002 OJ L 120/19, point 29.
17. *SAT/Eurocontrol*, ECJ Jan. 19, 1994, 1994 ECR I-43; *Portuguese Airport*, D.Comm. Feb. 10, 1999, 1999 OJ L 69/31 (under Article 86 (3)), *aff'd* ECJ March 29, 2001, 2001 ECR I-2613; *Aéroports de Paris*, CFI Dec. 2000, 2000 ECR II-3929, paras 100 and 108–130 (distinction between State fees for supervisory activities and commercial fees for purely commercial activities such as groundhandling), *aff'd* ECJ Oct. 24, 2002, 2002 ECR I-9297, para. 75.
18. *Irish Sugar*, CFI Oct. 7, 1999, 1999 ECR II-2969, para. 130; *Arduino*, ECJ Feb. 19, 2002, 2002 ECR I-1529, paras 34–43; *German Post*, D.Comm. July 25, 2001, 2001 OJ L 331/40, points 99–102.
19. *Deutsche Post/GVS*, *Citicorp*, ECJ Feb. 10, 2000, 2000 ECR I-825, para. 48.
20. *British Telecommunications*, ECJ Oct. 3, 1985, 1985 ECR 3261, paras 17–18. *See* the *Telecommunication Directives* judgments where the Court confirmed the application of Article 86 (1) and (3) to the obligations imposed by the government (responsibility of the government) but considered Article 82 directly applicable to restrictive agreements concluded by the telecommunication body (responsibility of this entity): ECJ March 19, 1991, 1991 ECR I-1223, paras 53–57 and Nov. 17, 1992, 1992 ECR I-5833, para. 24.

- The monopoly Luxemburg television network which refused to sell TV advertising time to a private 'tele-sales' agency.[21]
- National posts and telecommunications administrations which wanted to extend their monopoly to courier services,[22] the supply of telecommunications terminals, to the marketing and maintenance of equipment to be connected to the network,[23] or to unfair trading conditions[24] or discriminatory (predatory) practices.[25]
- The national railway administrations, which engaged in joint marketing of combined land and sea transport of containers and abusive practices by applying discriminatory tariffs.[26]
- The UK central bank, the Bank of England, which sponsored agreements restricting admission to the London foreign exchange market.[27]
- The state-owned British automobile manufacturer, British Leyland, which among other measures charged excessive fees for issuing conformity certificates for imported cars in order to curb parallel imports.[28]
- State-owned airlines, which refused to grant a competitor access to its computerized reservation system[29] or applied exclusionary royalty rebates.[30]
- The state-owned airport administrations, which reserved the new terminal at Orly to national airlines whereas the other airlines were left with the old terminal,[31] or which at Frankfurt refused groundhandling services.[32]
- Port authorities which granted preferential rights to national persons or firms.[33]

---

21. *Télémarketing*, ECJ Oct. 3, 1985, 1985 ECR 3261, 3275–3276, paras 17–18.
22. *Bundespost I*, Fifteenth Report on Competition Policy, point 259. *An Post (Irish Postal Company)*, Sixteenth Report on Competition Policy, point 298; *French Postal Monopoly*, Bull. EC 12–1985, point 2.1.79; *Italian International Courier Services*, Nineteenth Report on Competition Policy, point 228; *Dutch Express Mail Service*, D.Comm. Dec. 20, 1989, 1990 OJ L 10/47.
23. *RTT/GB-INNO-BM*, ECJ Dec. 13, 1991, 1991 ECR I-5941, paras 17–19.
24. *German Post II*, D.Comm. July 25, 2001, 2001 OJ L 331/40.
25. *German Post I*, D.Comm. March 20, 2001, 2001 OJ L 125/27.
26. *HOV-SVZ/Deutsche Bahn*, D.Comm. March 29, 1994, 1994 OJ L 104/34, para. 47, *aff'd* CFI Oct. 21, 1997, 1997 ECR II-1689.
27. *Sarabex*, Eighth Report on Competition Policy, points 35–37.
28. *British Leyland*, ECJ Nov. 11, 1986, 1986 ECR 3263, para. 9. *See also General Motors*, ECJ Nov. 13, 1975, 1975 ECR 1367, para. 9.
29. *Sabena*, D.Comm. Nov. 4, 1988, 1988 OJ L 317/47.
30. *Virgin Airlines/British Airways*, D.Comm. July 14, 1999, 2000 OJ L 30/1, points 108–111.
31. *Aéroports de Paris*, D.Comm. June 11, 1998, 1998 OJ L 230/10, *aff'd* ECJ Oct. 24, 2002, 2002 ECR I-9297, para. 116.
32. *Airport of Frankfurt*, D.Comm. Jan. 14, 1998, 1998 OJ L 72/30.
33. *Porto di Geneva*, ECJ Dec. 10, 1991, 1991 ECR I-5889 (application of Article 82) confirmed by Corto di Appello of Florence, Italy, of 9 Oct. 1993, Twenty-fourth Report on Competition Policy, point 102); *Harbour of Roscoff (ICG/CCI Morlaix)*, D.Comm. May 16, 1995,Twenty-fifth Report on Competition Policy, p. 120. However, a port authority entrusted with the compulsory surveillance and rapid interrvention service designed to protect the maritime

- Maritime conferences applying exclusionary practices and predatory tariffs.[34]
- The German monopoly over recruitment services which is part of the public administration and which used its exclusive rights in order to prevent others from furnishing these services.[35]
- A privately-owned funeral services firm which was able to charge excessive prices thanks to the monopoly granted to it by the local authority.[36]

C. Dominant Position

1. Definition and Criteria

Definition.
In the *Hoffmann-La Roche* judgment the Court of Justice defined a dominant position as:

> '... a position of economic strength enjoyed by an undertaking which enables it to prevent effective competition being maintained on the relevant market by affording it the power to behave to an appreciable extent independently of its competitors, its customers and ultimately of the consumers. Such a position does not preclude some competition, which it does where there is a monopoly or a quasi-monopoly, but enables the undertaking which profits by it, if not to determine, at least to have an appreciable influence on the conditions under which that competition will develop, and in any case to act largely in disregard of it so long as such conduct does not operate to its detriment.'[37]

The existence of a dominant position may derive from several factors, which, taken separately, are not necessarily decisive; however, extremely large market shares are in themselves, save exceptional circumstances, evidence of the existence of a dominant position:[38] 'The market definition makes it possible to calculate market

---

environment does not exercise a commercial activity even where port users must pay fees to finance that activity: *Diego Cali & Figli/Porto di Genova*, ECJ March 18, 1997, 1997 ECR I-1547.

34. *CEWAL*, D.Comm. Dec. 23, 1992, 1993 OJ L 34/20, *aff'd* in substance by CFI Oct. 8, 1996, 1996 ECR II-1201.
35. *Höfner/Macrotron*, ECJ April 23, 1991, 1991 ECR I-1979, paras 25–31.
36. *Bodson – Funeral Services*, ECJ May 4, 1988, 1988 ECR 2479, paras 26–29.
37. *Hoffmann-La Roche*, ECJ Feb. 13, 1979, 1979 ECR 461, paras 38–39. *See also Michelin*, ECJ Nov. 9, 1983, 1983 ECR 3461, para. 30; *Alsatel/Novasam*, ECJ Oct. 5, 1988, 1988 ECR 5987, para. 12; *AKZO*, ECJ July 3, 1991, 1991 ECR I-3359, para. 69; *Irish Sugar*, Oct. 7, 1999, 1999 ECR II-2969, para. 70.
38. *Irish Sugar*, CFI Oct. 7, 1999, 1999 ECR II-2969, para. 70.

shares that would convey meaningful information regarding market power'.[39] Thus, in determining whether a firm has a dominant position on a market, the first – but often most difficult – step is to define the market concerned, the 'relevant market,' both in terms of products and geography. Indeed, Article 82 presupposes a link (but not necessarily a causal connection[40]) between the dominant position and the alleged abusive conduct, which must produce its effects on the dominated market or, under special circumstances, on a distinct, but associated, market.[41] This process of determining the relevant market is described in section 2 below and is based upon the general description of the relevant market which is common to any application of the EC competition rules, and therefore is explained as one of the 'fundamentals' in Chapter I.C. above. Only after the 'relevant market' has been properly defined is it possible to apply the various criteria suggested by the Court's definition of dominant position.

Criteria of Dominant Position.
These can be summarized under three main headings in order of decreasing importance: market structure, firm structure and market conduct.

- The *structure* of the *relevant market* must be such as to give the firm the ability to act in a largely unconstrained manner because of the absence of effective competition. The main elements are the firm's market share, its lead in terms of market share over its rivals, the degree of dependence of its customers or suppliers, and its ability to set its prices and terms and conditions of sale without serious regard to the competitive response of smaller competitors. The evaluation of market structure is the most important in determining whether a firm holds a dominant position.
- The *structure* and characteristics of the *firm* itself may give it the ability to prevent effective competition due to its internal strength. Relevant factors are the firm's technological resources, production capacity, access to raw materials, financial strength and other commercial advantages over its rivals.
- The *conduct* of the firm on the *market*, such as overpricing or predatory acts against competitors, may indicate that the firm is behaving in a manner largely unconstrained by competition and therefore holds a dominant position. However, caution must be exercised in drawing conclusions from market behaviour, as most types of behaviour can be practised both by dominant and non-dominant firms.

The criteria for evaluating dominance are described in section 3 below. Section 4 deals with the concept of collective dominance, i.e., a dominant position held collectively by several firms, while section 5 is devoted to dominant purchasers.

---

39. Commission Notice on the definition of the relevant market, 1997 OJ C 372/3, point 2.
40. *Continental Can*, ECJ Feb. 21, 1973, 1973 ECR 215, para. 27.
41. *Tetra Pak II*, ECJ Nov. 14, 1996, 1996 ECR I-5951, para. 27.

2. Relevant Market

Uniform Parameters for Defining the Relevant Market.
The definition of the relevant market or markets is the first step in the evaluation of any alleged abuse of a dominant position under Article 82. The question of how to define the relevant market was answered by the Court of Justice in the *Michelin* case as follows:

> '... the determination of the relevant market is useful in assessing whether the undertaking concerned is in a position to prevent effective competition from being maintained and behave to an appreciable extent independently of its competitors and customers and consumers. For this purpose, therefore, an examination limited to the objective characteristics only of the relevant products cannot be sufficient; the competitive conditions and the structure of supply and demand on the market must also be taken into consideration.'[42]

The possibilities of competition must be judged in the context of the market comprising the totality of the products or services which, with respect to their characteristics, are particularly suitable for satisfying constant needs and are only to a limited extent interchangeable with other products or services.[43] This approach has been further developed by the Commission in its 'Guidelines on the Definition of the Relevant Market for the Purposes of Community Competition Law',[44] which provide guidance on its concept of relevant product and geographic market in its ongoing enforcement of Articles 81, 82 and the merger control regulation. The parameters for defining the relevant market are basically the same under each of these provisions, and have therefore been discussed in Chapter I under section C. This section is limited to highlighting certain particulars when applying Article 82.

Relevant Product Market: Narrow Definitions Predominate.
The relevant product market includes those products, which are actually or potentially substitutable,[45] thereby including short-term and medium and long-term substitutability[46] on both the demand and the supply side.[47] The Court of Justice and the Commission tend to define the relevant product market rather narrowly, including sub-markets, as may be shown by the following examples:

---

42. *Michelin*, ECJ Nov. 9, 1983, 1983 ECR 3461, para. 37.
43. *British Airways*, CFI Dec . 17, 2003, T-219/99, para. 91.
44. Commission Notice, 1997 OJ C 372/3.
45. *RTE(Magill)*, ECJ April 6, 1995, 1995 ECR I-743, paras 53–54; *Tierce Ladbroke*, CFI June 12, 1997 ECR II-923, para. 131; *European Night Services*, CFI Sept. 15, 1998, 1998 ECR II-3141, para. 208; *Belgian Post*, D.Comm. Dec. 5, 2001, 2002 OJ L 61/32, points 39–51.
46. *Tetra Pak II*, ECJ Nov. 14, 1996, 1996 ECR I-5951, para. 19.
47. E.g. *DSD ('Green Dot')*, D.Comm. April 20, 2001, 2001 OJ L 166/1, points 65–86.

- pharmaceuticals according to their therapeutic effect[48] and, even if chemically identical, distinguishing markets based on different end-uses,[49]
- chemicals as raw materials as distinct from the finished products,[50]
- products supplied to reprocessors from products supplied on the merchant market,[51]
- natural sugar as distinct from sugar substitutes,[52]
- impulse ice cream, consisting of single-wrapped items, as distinct from other ice cream, such as take-home and catering ice cream,[53]
- natural beet or cane sugar in granulated form (as distinct from speciality sugars, liquid sugars and syrups) sold in two sub-markets, namely to retail and industrial customers,[54]
- cola-flavoured carbonated soft drinks from other soft drinks,[55]
- bananas as distinct from other fresh fruit,[56]
- aseptic milk filling machines from fresh milk filling machines,[57]
- plasterboard as distinct from wet plastering,[58]
- flat glass as distinct from hollow glass containers which are in competition with cans and plastic bottles,[59]

---

48. Vitamin A to be distinct from vitamin B, etc.: *Hoffmann-La Roche*, ECJ 13 Feb. 1979, 1979 ECR 461, paras 21–30, and *Vitamins*, D.Comm. Nov. 21, 2001, 2003 OJ L 6/1, points 22–73.
49. Human v. veterinary use or cosmetics in pharmacies v. cosmetics which are freely marketed: *Vichy*, CFI Feb. 27, 1992, 1992 ECR II-415, para. 63 (under Article 81).
50. *Commercial Solvents*, ECJ March 6, 1974, 1974 ECR 223, paras 19–22; *Aminobutanol*, Sixteenth Report on Competition Policy, point 76. *See*, however, Article 4 (2) of the R&D block exemption regulation, Regulation 2659/2000, which requires products in which the newly developed products are integrated as components to be considered when calculating the market share limit of 25%.
51. *See*, under Article 81, *Philips/Osram*, D.Comm. Dec. 21, 1994, 1994 OJ L 378/37, points 7–8.
52. Assumed in *Sugar*, D.Comm. Jan. 2, 1973, 1973 OJ L 140/17, 18; *Aspartame*, Eighteenth Report on Competition Policy, point 53; *British Sugar*, D.Comm. July 18, 1988, 1988 OJ L 284/41; *Irish Sugar*, D.Comm. May 14, 1997, 1997 OJ L 258/1, points 86–90.
53. *Van den Bergh Foods*, D.Comm. March 11, 1998, 1998 OJ L 246/1, point 255. *See under* Article 81: *Langnese-Iglo*, CFI June 8, 1995, 1995 ECR II-1533, paras 60–72; *aff'd* ECJ Oct. 1, 1998, 1998 ECR I-5609.
54. *British Sugar*, D.Comm. July 18, 1988, 1988 OJ L 284/41, 50; *Irish Sugar*, D.Comm. May 14, 1997, 1997 OJ L 258/1, paras 86–90 (*aff'd* CFI Oct. 7, 1999, 1999 ECR II-2969).
55. *Coca Cola I*, D.Comm. IP (88)615. *See also* under the merger control regulation *Coca Cola/ Carlsberg*, D.Comm. Sept. 11, 1997, Twenty-seventh Report on Competition Policy, p. 193.
56. *United Brands*, ECJ Feb. 14, 1978, 1978 ECR 207, paras 12–35.
57. *Tetra Pak I*, D.Comm. July 26, 1988, 1988 OJ L 272/27, 33–38; *aff'd* CFI July 10, 1990, 1990 ECR II-309; *aff'd* ECJ Oct. 6, 1994, 1994 ECR I-5951.
58. *British Plasterboard*, D.Comm. Dec. 5, 1988, 1989 OJ L 10/50, 51–52, 64–65, *aff'd* ECJ April 6, 1995, 1995 ECR I-865.
59. *Italian Flat Glass II*, D.Comm. Dec. 7, 1988, 1989 OJ L 33/44, 65; *rev'd* CFI March 10, 1992, 1992 ECR II- 1403 (for lack of evidence for anticompetitive coordination).

- tyres: original equipment market as distinct from replacement market tyres,[60] replacement truck tyres as distinct from truck retreads,[61]
- nail guns as a specific fastening system from other fastening systems, to be separated from the market of cartridges and nails,[62]
- different sizes and capacities of computers,[63] motors[64] and aircraft,[65]
- computerized airline reservation systems from non-computerized systems,[66]
- postal universal services from specific services, such as collection and distribution of business mail,[67]
- advanced weekly listings of all TV programmes in TV guides from daily listings,[68]
- mobile telephone from voice telephone,[69]
- spare parts for particular makes of cash registers or particular car models from the 'primary product',[70]
- deliveries of industrial gases (oxygen, hydrogen, nitrogen) in pipelines from deliveries in bulk or in bottles,[71]
- scheduled airline flights from charter flights and other means of transport,[72] i.e., means of transport for time-sensitive passengers (business travellers) from transport means of price-sensitive leisure passengers,[73] and
- services of air travel agencies distinct from the air transport market.[74]

---

60. *Michelin I*, ECJ Nov. 9, 1983, 1983 ECR 3461, paras 38 *et seq.*
61. *Michelin II*, D.Comm. June 20, 2001, 2002 OJ L 143/1, points 109–118; *aff'd* CFI Sept. 30, 2003, T-203/01.
62. *Hilti*, D.Comm. Dec. 22, 1987, 1988 OJ L 65/19, 31–33; *aff'd* CFI Dec. 12, 1991, 1991 ECR II-1439, paras 66–78, and ECJ March 2, 1994, 1994 ECR I-667.
63. *IBM*, Fourteenth Report on Competition Policy, point 94.
64. *UTC/MTU*, Twenty-second Report on Competition Policy, p. 415.
65. *Aerospatiale Alenia/DeHavilland*, D.Comm. Oct. 2, 1991, 1991 OJ L 334/42; *Boeing/McDonnell Douglas*, D.Comm. July 30, 1997, 1997 OJ L 336/16; *ATR/Alenia/British Aerospace II*, Twenty-fifth Report on Competition Policy, pp. 128–131 (comfort letter).
66. *Sabena*, D.Comm. Nov. 4, 1988, 1988 OJ L 317/47, 49–50.
67. *Italian Post*, D.Comm. Dec. 21, 2000, 2001 OJ L 63/59, point 17; *German Post*, D.Comm. July 25, 2001, 2001 OJ L 331/40, point 84; *Belgian Post*, D.Comm. Dec. 5, 2001, 2002 OJ L 61/32, points 43–51.
68. *Magill TV Guide*, D.Comm. Dec. 21, 1988, 1989 OJ L 78/43, 48.
69. *Omnitel Pronto Italia*, D.Comm. Oct. 4, 1995, 1995 OJ L 280/49, point 16.
70. *Hugin/Liptons*, ECJ May 31, 1979, 1979 ECR 1869, paras 3–10; *Renault*, ECJ Oct. 5, 1988, 1988 ECR 6039, paras 15–16.
71. *Industrial Gases*, Nineteenth Report on Competition Policy, point 62; *Dutch Industrial and Medical Gases*, D.Comm. July 24, 2002, 2003 OJ L 84/1, points 55–63.
72. *Ahmed Saeed*, ECJ April 11, 1989, 1989 ECR 803, paras 39–41; *European Night Services*, CFI Sept. 15, 1998, 1998 ECR II-3141, para. 90.
73. *See* the air alliances, Twenty-seventh Report on Competition Policy, point 92; *European Night Services*, CFI Sept. 15, 1998, 1998 ECR II-3141, para. 90
74. *British Airways*, CFI Dec. 17, 2003, T-219/99, para. 100.

Relevant Geographic Market: Difference between Analysis under Article 82 and Analysis under Merger Control Regulation.
The principal purpose of Article 82 is to halt abuses of a single or a collective dominant position that are likely to harm competitors, customers and ultimately consumers, whereas the objective of the merger control regulation is to control anticompetitive structural changes in the supply of a product or service. Therefore, the methodologies of applying Article 82 and of applying the merger control regulation may lead to different results: the analysis of abuse of a dominant position concerns essentially past and present behaviour,[75] whereas the analysis of a merger or a joint venture calls for an evaluation of prospective anticompetitive effects and may therefore include, to a greater extent, potential competition arising from the ongoing process of market integration.[76] For example, the *Michelin I* case[77] under Article 82 concerned the abusive application of exclusive supply obligations imposed on Dutch distributors. Similarly, the *Michelin II* case[78] concerned the abusive application of loyalty-inducing rebates to new replacement tyres and retreaded tyres in France. The relevant geographic market was the Netherlands because that was the market in which Michelin employed abusive practices when distributing a whole range of tyres to dealers for replacement purposes. On the other hand, in the *Continental/Michelin* joint venture case dealt with under Article 81,[79] the relevant geographic market was held to be that of the whole Community because the joint venture would produce a new tyre for purposes of both replacement and original equipment for distribution Community-wide. This accords with the determination of the relevant geographic market in merger cases where the Commission tends to a wider market definition in order to take into account the growing 'Europeanization',[80] except in cases of 'distinct markets', i.e. where the competitive conditions on the market are still appreciably different in view of the nature and the characteristics of the products or services concerned, the existence of entry barriers, consumer preferences and the existence of appreciable differences in market shares and prices between territories.[81] The distinct market concept as applied by the Commission in merger cases may sustain the tendency of a rather narrow definition of the relevant geographic market under Article 82.[82]

75. *UFEX*, CFI May 25, 2000, 2000 ECR II-2167, para. 49.
76. Commission Notice on the definition of the relevant market, point 32. *See Airtours*, CFI June 6, 2002, 2002 ECR II-2585, para. 210.
77. *Michelin I*, D.Comm. Oct. 7, 1981, 1981 OJ L 353/33, *aff'd* ECJ Nov. 9, 1983, 1983 ECR 346.
78. *Michelin II*, D.Comm. June 20, 2001, 2002 OJ L 143/1, points 119–171.
79. D.Comm. Oct. 11, 1988, 1988 OJ L 305/33.
80. *See Procter & Gamble/Schickedanz*, D.Comm. June 21, 1994, 1994 OJ L 354/32, point 104.
81. Article 9 (7) of Regulation 139/2004. *See Royal Philips Electronics*, CFI April 3, 2003, T-119/02, paras 335–337.
82. *See* Chapter VI.C.4.(b)(iii) and VI.D.1.

Examples of Geographic Market Definitions.
The relevant geographic market may be:

- the whole Community,[83] possibly including the EEA countries[84] or even extending to the whole world market;[85]
- several member states;[86]
- one single member state,[87] in particular because of high costs of transport[88] or the nation-wide coverage of a fixed telecommunications network (local loop);[89]
- a part (region) of a member state;[90]
- an 'essential facility' within a member state such as ports[91] or airports;[92] and

---

83. *See Hoffmann-La Roche*, ECJ Feb. 13, 1979, 1979 ECR 461, para. 22; *Hilti*, ECJ Dec. 12, 1991, 1991 ECR II-14339, paras 80–81; *Tetra Pak II*, CFI Oct. 6, 1994, 1994 ECR II-755, paras 92–99.
84. Commission Notice on the definition of the relevant market, point 28.
85. *Commercial Solvents*, D.Comm. Dec. 14, 1972, 1972 OJ L 299/51; *aff'd* ECJ March 6, 1974, 1974 ECR 223 (world monopoly). *See under* Article 81 *British Telecommunications/MCI I*, D.Comm. July 27, 1994, 1994 OJ L 223/36; under the merger control regulation *British Telecommunications/MCI II*, D.Comm. Jan. 30, 1997 M.856; *Boeing/McDonnell Douglas*, D.Comm. July 30, 1997, 1997 OJ L 336/16, para. 20.
86. *Sugar*, ECJ Dec. 16, 1975, 1975 ECR 1663, paras 370–375 (Belgium and Luxembourg); *United Brands*, ECJ Feb. 14, 1978, 1978 ECR 207, paras 36–38 (Germany, Benelux-countries, Denmark and Ireland); *Magill*, CFI July 10, 1991, 1991 ECR II-485, para. 64 (Ireland and Northern Ireland).
87. *British Leyland*, ECJ Nov. 11, 1986, 1986 ECR 3263, paras 4–9; *British Telecommunications*, ECJ March 20, 1985, 1985 ECR 873, paras 21–22; *RTB/SABAM II*, ECJ March 27, 1974, 1974 ECR 313, para. 5; *Michelin I*, ECJ Nov. 9, 1983, 1983 ECR 3461, paras 32–61; *Michelin II*, D.Comm. June 20, 2001, 2002 OJ L 143/1, points 119–168, *aff'd* CFI Sept. 30, 2003, T-203/01; *BPB*, CFI April 1, 1993, 1993 ECR II-389, para. 66; *aff'd* ECJ April 6, 1995, 1995 ECR I-865; *Deutsche Bahn* (combined container traffic by rail and boat), D.Comm. March 29, 1994, 1994 OJ L 104/34, paras 191–250; *aff'd* CFI Oct. 21, 1997, 1997 ECR II-1689, para. 58.
88. *Irish Sugar*, CFI Oct. 7, 1999, 1999 ECR II-2969, paras 86–88.
89. *Deutsche Telekom*, D.Comm. May 21, 2003, IP/03/717; *Wanadoo*, D.Comm. July 16, 2003, IP/03/1025.
90. Southern part of Germany: *Sugar*, ECJ Dec. 16, 1975, 1975 ECR 1663, paras 441–448; Northern part of Ireland: *Irish Sugar*, D.Comm. May 14, 1997, 1997 OJ L 258/1, paras 99–113 (*aff'd* CFI Oct. 7, 1999, 1999 ECR II-2969, paras 87–92). Under the merger control regulation: *Promodes/S21/Gruppo GS*, D.Comm. March 10, 1998, M.1086 (partial referral with respect to the retail activities in certain Italian provinces whereas the other activities were dealt with by the Commission itself).
91. *Porto di Genova I*, ECJ Dec. 10, 1991, 1991 ECR I-5889; *Silvano Raso (Porto di Genova II)*, ECJ Feb. 12, 1998, 1998 ECR I-593, para. 26; *Port of Rodby*, D.Comm. Dec. 21, 1993, 1994 OJ L 55/52; *Porto di Genova (employment)*, D.Comm. Oct. 21, 1997, 1997 OJ L 301/17, point 20.
92. *Aéroports de Paris*, CFI Dec. 12, 2000, 2000 ECR II-3929, paras 137–143; *aff'd* ECJ Oct. 24, 2002, 2002 ECR I-9297, paras 91–96; *Airport of Frankfurt*, D.Comm. Jan. 14, 1998, 1998 OJ L 72/30, point 56.

– transport connections between two different destinations,[93]

provided the challenged conduct has appreciable effects on trade between member states.[94]

Definition of the Relevant Time Period.
A position of market power may arise from an emergency like an oil shortage which temporarily increases the customer's dependence on its traditional supplier.[95] Under normal conditions, however, the market must be considered over a longer period.[96] Seasonal variations in demand were not accepted by the Court of Justice in the *United Brands* case as sufficient to consider bananas as belonging temporarily to a larger fresh fruit market.[97] Such temporary changes in market shares are nevertheless relevant considerations when evaluating the existence of a dominant position.

Definition of the Relevant Market in Cases of Buying Power.
In the case of an abuse of buying power by a dominant purchaser, the relevant product market is judged by similar criteria but based primarily upon the standpoint of the seller, i.e. whether the seller has realistic alternatives for distributing its products or to offer its services via other outlets.[98] Examples of applying the concept of buying power include:

– the supply of railway rolling stock material by independent manufacturers to dominant railways,[99]
– the licensing of films by film distributors to television stations,[100]

---

93. *French-West-African Shipowners Committee*, D.Comm. April 1, 1992, 1992 OJ L 134/1; *British Midland/Aer Lingus*, D.Comm. April 10, 1992, 1992 OJ L 96/34; *CEWAL*, D.Comm. Dec. 23, 1992, 1993 OJ L 34/20, *aff'd* CFI Oct. 8, 1996, 1996 ECR II-1201, para. 75; under Article 81: *Lufthansa/SAS*, D.Comm. Jan 16, 1996, 1996 OJ L 54/28; *Transatlantic Air Agreements*, Twenty-seventh Report on Competition Policy, point 92.
94. *See*, in particular, *Sea Containers/Stena Sealink*, D.Comm. 21 Dec. 1993, 1994 OJ L15/8, point 77.
95. *BP*, ECJ June 29, 1978, 1978 ECR 1513, paras 16–18, although the Court neither confirmed nor rejected the Commission's holding on this issue.
96. *See infra* section C.3 (a).
97. *United Brands*, ECJ Feb. 14, 1978, 1978 ECR 207, paras 12–35.
98. Twenty-sixth Report on Competition Policy, point 147. *See* with respect to countervailing effects of buying power: Commission Notice on horizontal mergers, points 64–67.
99. *Eurofima*, Third Report on Competition Policy, points 68–69.
100. *CICCE*, ECJ March 28, 1985, 1985 ECR 1105 (however, in this case, the question of dominant position was not discussed by the Court since it agreed with the Commission that the alleged abuse of imposing unfair prices was not proven).

- the collective purchasing of copyrights by a single copyright collecting society,[101]
- procuring products, services or licences by dominant, mostly state-owned telecommunication operators,[102] and
- procurement of services by ports[103] or airports.[104]

Calculation of Market Shares – The Merchant Market Rule.
The total market size and market shares of each supplier are calculated on the basis of their sales of the relevant products on the relevant market.[105] The calculation must include all of the important competitive constraints and exclude all those products that are irrelevant to the analysis of the parties' market power. Therefore, the calculation must include those products made to independent third parties ('merchant market sales') and exclude sales made by the suppliers to customers to whom the suppliers are linked by full or partial ownership and swaps between suppliers ('captive sales').[106]

3. Dominant Position

Criteria for Dominant Position.
The Court of Justice has defined a dominant position as 'a position of economic strength enjoyed by an undertaking which enables it to prevent effective competition being maintained on the relevant market by affording it the power to behave to an appreciable extent independently of its competitors, its customers and ultimately of the consumers'.[107]As noted above, the main criteria by which a dominant position is judged are (a) the structure of the market, (b) the structure of the firm and (c) the firm's conduct.

---

101. *GEMA*, D.Comm. June 2, 1971, 1971 OJ L 134/15; *BRT/SABAM*, ECJ March 27, 1974, 1974 ECR 313, paras 3–5.
102. Commission Guidelines on the Application of EC Competition Rules in the Telecommunication Sector, 1991 OJ C 233/2, points 116–120.
103. *Porto di Geneva*, ECJ Dec. 10, 1991, 1991 ECR I-5889, paras 13–15.
104. *Airport of Frankfurt*, D.Comm. Jan. 14, 1998, 1998 OJ L 72/30, points 61–68; *Aeroports de Paris II*, D.Comm. June 11, 1998, 1998 OJ L 230/10, points 56–58; *Portuguese Airports*, D.Comm. Feb. 10, 1999, 1999 OJ L 69/3 1, point 21 (*aff'd* ECJ March 29, 2001, 2001 ECR I-2613). *See* Directive 96/67/EC on ground-handling services, 1996 OJ L 272/36.
105. Commission Notice on the definition of the relevant market, 1997 OJ C 372/3, point 53.
106. *See* in particular, under the merger control regulation: *BP/Erdölchemie*, D.Comm. March 22, 2001, M.2345, point 40; *Shell/DEA*, D.Comm. Dec. 20, 2001, M.2389, points 22–23.
107. *United Brands*, ECJ Feb. 14, 1978, 1978 ECR 207, para. 65; *Hoffmann-La Roche*, ECJ Feb. 13, 1979, 1979 ECR 461, paras 38, 41; *Alpha Flight/Aeroports de Paris*, D.Comm. June 11, 1998, 1998 OJ L 230/10, point 72; *aff'd* CFI Dec. 12, 2000, 2000 ECR II-3929, para. 147–150 and ECJ Oct. 24, 2002, 2002 ECR I-9297, para. 105; *British Airways*, CFI Dec. 17, 2003, T-219/99, para. 189.

(a) Market Structure

Monopoly as Dominant Position.
A monopolist who does not face any competition at all is dominant by definition.[108] The monopoly may be based on exclusive rights, granted by government ('statutary monopoly'),[109] or may be held as a result of economic or technical factors. Examples include:

- National copyright collecting societies, which have monopolies on their territory, owing either to reciprocal exclusive agreements with other national societies or to the economics of managing the exploitation of copyright abroad. This means that copyright holders cannot turn to foreign collecting societies to manage their copyrights.[110]
- Undertakings to which a member state grants exclusive rights in each of its departments or states, thereby establishing a contiguous series of monopolies territorially limited but together covering the entire territory of a member state that create a collective dominant position in a substantial part of the Common Market.[111]
- Undertakings to which member states grant exclusive rights enjoy a dominant position[112] and are subject to Article 82 insofar as its application does not obstruct the performance, in law or in fact, of the particular tasks assigned to them (Article 86 (1) and (2) of the EC Treaty). Even after formal abolition of the exclusive rights (liberalization) such undertakings may, in the absence of any realistic alternatives, continue to occupy a dominant position for a certain time period.[113]

---

108. *BRT/SABAM II*, ECJ March 27, 1974, 1974 ECR 313, paras 3–5.
109. *German Post/GZS, Citicorp*, ECJ Feb. 10, 2001, 2001 ECR I-825, para. 38; *French Post*, D.Comm. Oct. 23, 2001, 2002 OJ L 120/19, point 60 (with further references). *See also INNO/ATAB*, ECJ Nov. 16, 1977, 1977 ECR 2115, 2145, para. 35; *British Telecommunications*, ECJ March 20, 1985, 1985 ECR 873, paras 21–22; *SACEM I*, ECJ April 9, 1987, 1987 ECR 1747, para. 5; *SACEM II*, ECJ July 13, 1989, 1989 ECR 2811, paras 10–20; *SACEM III*, ECJ July 13, 1989, 1989 ECR 2521, paras 16–26; *Deutsche Post*, D.Comm. July 25, 2001, 2001 OJ L 331/40, points 88–96.
110. *GEMA I*, D.Comm. June 2, 1971, 1971 OJ L 134/15, 20; *GVL*, ECJ March 2, 1983, 1983 ECR 483, para. 44; *SACEM II*, ECJ July 13, 1989, 1989 ECR 2811, paras 10–20; *SACEM III*, ECJ July 13, 1989, 1989 ECR 2521, paras 16–26.
111. *Bodson – Funeral Services* ECJ May 4, 1988, 1988 ECR 2479, para. 13 (funeral services enjoying exclusive rights limited to communes); *Crespelle*, ECJ Nov. 5, 1994, 1994 ECR I-5077, para. 17 (approved bovine insemination centers); *Almelo*, ECJ April 27, 1994, 1994 ECR I-1477, para. 42 (regional electricity distributors even if vested with non-exclusive rights); *Porto di Genova (employment)*, D.Comm. Oct. 21, 1997, 1997 OJ L 301/17, points 20–21.
112. *General Motors*, ECJ Nov. 13, 1975, 1975 ECR 1367, paras 5–10; *British Leyland*, ECJ Nov. 11, 1986, 1986 ECR 3263, paras 3–10; *Deutsche Bahn*, CFI Oct. 21, 1997, 1997 ECR II-1689, para. 57; *ITT/Promedia*, CFI July 17, 1998, 1998 ECR II-2937, paras 92–98.
113. Commission Notice on Access in Telecommunications, 1997 OJ C 76/9, para. 71.

– Factual monopolies, such as *essential facilities* that may be defined as 'a facility or infrastructure which is essential for reaching customers and/or enabling competitors to carry on their business and which cannot be duplicated by any reasonable means.'[114] Examples have included electricity grids, telecommunications networks, harbours and airports.[115]

Importance of Market Share.
A high market share is necessary, though rarely sufficient alone, to prove the existence of a dominant position.[116] In the *Hilti* case, the Court of First Instance held that

> 'in this it is established that Hilti holds a share of between 70 and 80% in the relevant market. Such a share is, in itself, a clear indication of the existence of a dominant position.'[117]

Market share is therefore always an important factor in assessing dominance.[118] In *Hoffmann-La Roche* the Court of Justice explicitly accepted a very high market share of 75% or more maintained over a relatively long period as such strong evidence of dominance that no further investigation is necessary.[119] Strong evidence

114. Commission Notice on Access in Telecommunications, 1997 OJ C 76/9, para. 68.
115. *See infra* section D.6 (e) and Chapter VIII.C., E and F.
116. *United Brands*, ECJ Feb. 14, 1978, 1978 ECR 207, para. 107: 'A trader can only be in a dominant position on the market for a product if he has succeeded in winning a large part of this market.'
117. *Hilti*, CFI Dec. 12, 1991, 1991 ECR II-1439, para. 92, *aff'd* ECJ March 2, 1994, 1994 ECR I-667; reaffirmed in *Van den Bergh Foods*, CFI Oct. 23, 2003, T-65/98, paras 90 and 154 (market share of 89%, the remainder being shared between several small suppliers).
118. *Hoffmann-La Roche*, ECJ Feb. 13, 1979, 1979 ECR 461, paras 39–41: 'The existence of a dominant position may derive from several factors which, taken separately, are not necessarily determinative but among these factors a highly important one is the existence of very large market shares. An undertaking which has a very large market share and holds it for some time, by means of the volume of production and the scale of the supply which it stands for – without those having much smaller market shares being able to meet rapidly the demand from those who would like to break away from the undertaking which has the largest market share – is by virtue of that share in a position of strength which makes it an unavoidable trading partner and which, already because of this secures for it, at the very least during relatively long periods, that freedom of action which is the special feature of a dominant position.' On the other hand, a decline in market shares cannot in itself prove the absence of dominance: *TACA II*, D.Comm. Sept. 16, 1998, 1999 OJ L 95/1, point 533; *see*, however, *CEWAL*, CFI 8 Oct. 1996, 1996 ECR II-1201, para. 103–104 (progressive erosion of market shares does not exclude dominance).
119. *Hoffmann-La Roche*, ECJ Feb. 13, 1979, 1979 ECR 461, paras 41, 53–56, 59–60 and 67. *See British Plasterboard*, D.Comm. Dec. 5, 1988, 1989 OJ L 10/50, 64, *aff'd* ECJ April 6, 1995, 1995 ECR I-865, and ECJ April 6, 1995, 1995 ECR I-865. However, it has to be noted that under the merger regulation high market shares may, unlike the short-term view on behavioral abuses under Article 82, be compensated or attenuated by a longer-term evaluation of potential competition. *See* e.g. *Mannesmann-Hoesch*, D.Comm. Nov. 12, 1992, 1993 OJ L 114/34;

of a dominant position is also provided by market shares of between 40% and 55%, but this must be confirmed by data on the relative market shares of competitors and other evidence of competitive conditions on the market and the firm's own structure, resources and conduct.[120] Further evidence is especially necessary if the definition of the relevant market is complex.[121] In *Hoffmann-La Roche*, the Court found that in one vitamin market a market share varying from year to year between 20 and 50%, with a Japanese competitor accounting for 30% in one year, was insufficient evidence of a dominant position in the absence of other confirmatory data.[122] Under the merger control regulation the Commission tends to use the Herfindahl-Hirschman Index (HHI) as a first indication of the competitive pressure in the relevant market, in particular for evaluating the relative size of the leading firm compared to its nearest rivals.[123]

Dominance Unlikely at Market Shares under 25%.
A firm with a market share below 25% is unlikely to have a dominant position.[124] In *SABA II* the Court of Justice found such a position virtually impossible with a market share of only 10%.[125] This is confirmed by the combined market share limit of 20–30% which the Commission has laid down for exemption under some of the block exemption regulations, although it is a condition that the parties do not eliminate all competition between them at the marketing level but remain as independent sellers.[126]

Procter & Gamble/Schickedanz, .*Comm.* June 21, 1994, 1994 OJ L 354/34; *Siemens/Italtel*, D.Comm. Feb. 12, 1995, 1995 OJ L 161; *Nestle/Dalgety*, D.Comm. April 2, 1998, M.1127.

120. *Hoffmann-La Roche*, ECJ Feb. 13, 1979, 1979 ECR 461, paras 50–52 and 61–63 (vitamins A and C, market shares of 47% and 63–66%); *United Brands*, ECJ Feb. 14, 1978, 1978 ECR 207, 282–285, paras 108–129 (market share of 40–45%); *AKZO*, ECJ July 3, 1991 ECR I-3359, para. 60 (50% market share); *Sabena*, D.Comm. Nov. 4, 1988, 1988 OJ L 317/47, 52 (50% market share); Commission Notice on the Application of the Competition Rules to Access Agreements in the Telecommunications Sector, 1998 OJ C 365/2, point 73 (50%); *Irish Sugar*, CFI Oct. 7, 1999, 1999 ECR II-2969, para. 70 (50%); *DSD*, D.Comm. April 20, 2001, 2001 OJ L 166/1, point 94.
121. *Michelin I*, ECJ Nov. 9, 1983, 1983 ECR 3461, paras 32–52.
122. *Hoffmann-La Roche*, ECJ 13 Feb. 1979, 1979 ECR 461, 527–528, paras 57–58, vitamin B_3.
123. Commission Notice on horizontal mergers, points 19–21. *See* Chapter VI. at pp. 577–578.
124. *See* recital 32 to Regulation 139/2004 on merger control.
125. *SABA II*, ECJ Oct. 22, 1986, 1986 ECR 3021, paras 85–86. In *Grundig*, D.Comm. July 10, 1985, 1985 OJ L 233/1, 7, the Commission considered that market shares of 23% of the German color TV market held by the Thomson-Brandt group and 33% by Philips-Grundig did not indicate dominance. In *Alsatel/Novasam*, ECJ Oct. 5, 1988, 1988 ECR 5987, paras 11 and 18–19, Alsatel held a market share of one third on a regional market which did not constitute a dominant position within the Common Market or in a substantial part of it.
126. *See* Article 3 (3) of Regulation 2659/2000 on R&D cooperation agreements (2000 OJ L 304/7).

Further Market Structure Criteria.
Other market structure variables relevant to the question of whether the leading firm on a market has a dominant position are:

- The relative size of the market shares of the leading firm's nearest rivals, or, in other words, the size of its lead over them.[127]
- Competition from surplus production capacity: Low market shares held by competitors are not necessarily indicative of a lack of competition if there is substantial surplus production capacity in the industry.[128]
- Stability of the leader's market share over a period of time: Although the ability to retain a large market share over long periods despite intermittent fierce competition from smaller rivals is not conclusive evidence of dominance because a stable market may reflect competition as well as lack of competition,[129] fluctuating market shares are rather an indication of the lack of a dominant position.[130]
- Vertical integration both upstream and downstream.[131]
- Existence of well-known trademarks[132] and a powerful distribution network.[133]
- Barriers to entry, such as prohibitive transport costs,[134] government regulation,[135] technological advantages leading to high technical entry barriers,[136] and high capital cost of entry.[137]

127. *United Brands*, ECJ Feb. 14, 1978, 1978 ECR 207, paras 108–129; *Hoffmann-La Roche*, ECJ Feb. 13, 1979, 1979 ECR 461, paras 57–58; *Hilti*, D.Comm. Dec. 22, 1987, 1988 OJ L 65/19, 34; *aff'd* CFI Dec. 12, 1991, 1991 ECR II- 1439; *British Sugar*, D.Comm. July 18, 1988, 1988 OJ L 284/41, 52–53.
128. *Hoffmann-La Roche*, ECJ Feb. 13, 1979, 1979 ECR 461, paras 33–34, 48. *Cf. Commercial Solvents*, ECJ March 6, 1974, 1974 ECR 223, paras 13–15 (pilot plants for other processes not genuine potential competition).
129. *United Brands*, ECJ Feb. 14, 1978, 1978 ECR 207, paras 113–121; *Hoffmann-La Roche*, ECJ Feb. 13, 1979, 1979 ECR 461, paras 42–44; *ECS/Akzo II*, D.Comm. Dec. 14, 1985, 1985 OJ L 374/1, 18.
130. *Hoffmann-La Roche*, ECJ Feb. 13, 1979, 1979 ECR 461, paras 57–58.
131. *United Brands*, ECJ Feb. 14, 1978, 1978 ECR 207, paras 94–96.
132. *United Brands*, ECJ Feb. 14, 1978, 1978 ECR 207, paras 88–93.
133. *Omnitel Pronto Italiana*, D.Comm. Oct. 4, 1995, 1995 OJ L 270/49, point 16; *Michelin II*, D.Comm. June 20, 2001, 2002 OJ L 143/1, points 193–196, *aff'd* CFI Sept. 30, 2003, T-203/01.
134. *See supra* pp. 393–395.
135. *British Sugar*, D.Comm. July 18, 1988, 1988 OJ L 284/41, 52–53; *British Telecommunications*, ECJ March 20, 1985, 1985 ECR 873, paras 21–22. *See also supra* sections 2 (a) and (b).
136. *Tetra Pak I*, CFI July 10, 1990, 1990 ECR II-309, para. 23; *Hilti*, CFI Dec. 12, 1991, 1991 ECR II-1439, para. 93; *British Sugar*, D.Comm. July 18, 1988, 1988 OJ L 284/41, 52–53.
137. *Hoffmann-La Roche*, ECJ Feb. 13, 1979, 1979 ECR 461, para. 48; *DSD ('Green Dot')*, D.Comm. April 20, 2001, 2001 OJ L 166/1, point 96.

– Mature v. dynamic, rapidly changing markets: On mature markets firms may be better able and more determined to protect a dominant position than on dynamic, rapidly changing markets.[138]
– Countervailing buying power, i.e. the ability of large and sophisticated customers within a reasonable timeframe to resort to credible alternatives if the supplier decides to increase prices or deteriorate the conditions of delivery.[139] The commercial strength of such customers is capable of counterbalancing the dominant position, provided they absorb an substantial part of the supply.[140]
– Product characteristics that tie customers to a particular supplier.[141]

Relevance of Potential Competition.
Potential competition, although not measurable in terms of market share and therefore not a criterion for defining the relevant market,[142] is likely to reduce market power.[143] However, the assessment of the abuse of a dominant position under Article 82 must consider the competitive constraints at the time the alleged abuse was committed which includes future competition only if there are relatively short-term effects which are likely to reduce the alleged firm's ability to abuse its market position,[144] whereas the assessment under the merger control regulation includes a prospective analysis of the foreseeable reactions of current and futur competitors and consumers.[145] The Commission's prohibition decision in the case *Continental Can* was reversed by the Court of Justice, *inter alia*, because it had not been proved 'that competitors from other sectors of the market for light metal containers are not in a position to enter this market, by simple adaptation, with sufficient strength to create a serious counterweight.'[146]

Concept of 'Obligatory Trading Partner'.
A dominant position can be inferred if the supply conditions on the relevant market indicate that a firm is an 'obligatory trading partner' for its customers because they depend closely on the supplier and do not have sufficient or reasonable alternative sources of supply.[147] The concept of 'obligatory trading partner' was developed under French law ('*partenaire obligatoire*'). Under Article 8 of Ordon-

138. *Hilti*, CFI Dec. 12, 1991, 1991 ECR II-1439, para. 93.
139. Commission Notice on horizontal mergers, points 64–67.
140. *Tetra Pak II*, CFI Oct. 7, 1999, 1999 ECR II-2969, paras 97–100.
141. *E.g.*, the need for constant quality in plaster deliveries: *British Plasterboard*, D.Comm. Dec. 5, 1988, 1989 OJ L 10/50, 68.
142. *See* Chapter I.C.
143. *See* Commission Notice on horizontal mergers, points 58–60.
144. *UFEX*, CFI May 25, 2000, 2000 ECR II-2167, para. 49.
145. *Airtours*, CFI June 6, 2002, 2002 ECR II-2585, para. 210.
146. *Continental Can*, ECJ Feb. 21, 1973, 1973 ECR 215, para. 33.
147. *Hoffmann-La Roche*, ECJ Feb. 13, 1979, 1979 ECR 461, paras 57–58; *GVL*, ECJ March 2, 1983, 1983 ECR 483, para. 42. *Cf.* section 20 (2) of the German Act Against Restraints of Competition (GWB): 'relative dominance' of firm for dependent trading partners.

nance No. 86–1243 on Freedom in Pricing and Competition, which is succeded by Article L.420–2 du Code de Commerce, a dominant position is tantamount to a situation where a client or supplier is economically dependent upon it and which has no equivalent alternative. It is in this sense that the Court of First Instance has applied the 'obligatory trading partner' concept. The *Deutsche Bahn* case[148] concerned the application, by the German Railways having a statutory monopoly on the sub-market for rail transport services, of discriminatorily low prices for combined rail and sea transport services if the ports of origin or destination were located in Germany (and not in Belgium or the Netherlands), thereby favouring the German ports. The Court of First Instance stated:

> 'that where, as in the present case, the services covered by the sub-market are the subject of a statutory monopoly, placing those seeking the services in a *position of economic dependence on the supplier*, the existence of a dominant position on a distinct market cannot be denied, even if the services provided under a monopoly are linked to a product which is in itself in competition with other products.' (emphasis added).

The concept of an 'obligatory trading partner' is therefore only a means of defining the dominant position in a vertical or conglomerate context. The Commission studied the possibility of employing the concept of 'obligatory trading partner' as 'a supplementary tool' when considering dominant positions of a vertical or conglomerate nature.[149] In its Guidelines on the Application of the EC Competition Rules in the Telecommunications Sector,[150] the Commission referred to the dependence which 'could exist when the supplier cannot sell to other customers a substantial part of its production or change a production.'[151] However, the Commission has not expressly used the term 'obligatory trading partner' in its decisions even when dealing with long-term economic dependence of customers on a supplier. Examples include:

- A monopoly supplier of a raw material needed by a processor.[152]
- A manufacturer of soda ash that concludes long-term exclusive supply contracts with its most important customers.[153]

---

148. *Deutsche Bahn (German Railways)*, CFI Oct. 21, 1997, 1997 ECR II-1689, para. 57; *aff'd* ECJ April 27, 1999, 1999 ECR I-2387.
149. Sixteenth Report on Competition Policy, point 340.
150. 1991 OJ C 233/2, point 82.
151. 'Change a production' probably means shifting production to produce other products.
152. *Commercial Solvents*, ECJ March 6, 1974, 1974 ECR 223, paras 9–18.
153. *Soda Ash – Solvay*, D.Comm. Dec. 19, 1990, 1991 OJ L 152/21, points 56–59, *rev'd* on procedural grounds CFI June 29, 1995, 1995 ECR II-1825 (although the Commission decision does not use the term 'economic dependence'), and restated in the Commission decision Dec. 13, 2000, 2003 OJ L 10/10.

- A purchaser of non-interruptible gas supplies[154] who depends on regular deliveries.
- A car importer that depends on a car manufacturer that has been assigned the function of issuing conformity certificates stating that a car meets the importing country's regulatory requirements.[155]
- Service providers that may depend on lines leased from a telecommunications monopoly.[156]
- A cash register or car manufacturer, for service or repair firms dependent on supplies of its spare parts to carry on their business.[157]
- An already established ferry service operator that depends on the continuing access to the port facilities.[158]
- Owners of technical interface information needed to permit competitive products to be used with the owner's system.[159]
- A subcontractor or materials processor that has undertaken substantial investment in order to meet the specific needs of his principal (e.g., a car manufacturer) or the specifications of his supplier. [160]

Dependence on an 'obligatory trading partner' and, consequently, a dominant position has been *denied* under the following circumstances:

- An occasional customer does not 'depend' on a particular supplier even during a severe shortage, and therefore Article 82 does not require this supplier to allocate an equitable portion of the available supplies to it, whereas a longstanding

154. *Industrial Gases*, Nineteenth Report on Competition Policy, point 62.
155. *General Motors*, ECJ Nov. 13, 1975, 1975 ECR 1367, paras 4–10; *British Leyland*, ECJ Nov.11, 1986, 1986 ECR 3263, paras 3–10.
156. *British Telecommunications*, ECJ March 20, 1985, 1985 ECR 873, paras 21–22.
157. *Hugin/Liptons*, ECJ May 31, 1979, 1979 ECR 1869, paras 9–10; *Renault*, ECJ Oct. 5, 1988, 1988 ECR 6039, paras 15–16; *Volvo/Veng*, ECJ Oct. 5, 1988, 1988 ECR 6211, para. 9; *Boosey & Hawkes*, D.Comm. July 29, 1987, 1987 OJ L 286/36,40. *See also United Brands*, ECJ Feb. 14, 1978, 1978 ECR 207, para. 182 (withdrawal of supplies to Olesen, a Danish ripener of bananas).
158. *B&I/Sealink*, D.Comm. (interim measure) June 11, 1992, Twenty-second Report on Competition Policy, point 219. The Commission rejected, however, an interim measure in *Sea Containers/Stena Sealink*, D.Comm. Dec. 21, 1993, 1994 OJ L 15/8.
159. *IBM*, Fourteenth Report on Competition Policy, point 94; *Microsoft*, Twenty-fourth Report on Competition Policy, p. 417.
160. *EUROFIMA*, Third Report on Competition Policy, points 68–69. *See Filtrona/Tabacalera*, Nineteenth Report on Competition Policy, point 61, in which the Commission rejected a complaint by a cigarette filter manufacturer against the monopoly of the Spanish cigarette manufacturer which had begun making all its own filters and had therefore stopped buying from the filter manufacturer. The issue was not reviewed in the appeal as this was judged to be beyond the statute of limitations: *Filtrona*, CFI July 10, 1990, 1990 ECR II-393.

ongoing customer may hold such a right to continued supply of the scarce product, such as in the case of an oil shortage.[161]

- An exhibitor does not depend on a major trade fair organizer if there are alternatives (parallel trade fairs).[162]
- Where the economic dependence of customers is the result of long-term exclusive purchasing agreements, the Commission acts against these restraints on turning to alternative supplies under Article 81 in order to reduce the duration and the exclusivity of the agreements and thereby the degree of dependence.[163]

The examples show that the concept of 'obligatory trading partner' is only the other side of the coin of dominance and is not intended to extend the scope of Article 82[164] but rather to corroborate the evidence of a dominant position.[165] The concept should not be used to expand the concept of dominance, but rather to explain it in a specific factual context where a dominant position exists *vis-à-vis* a purchaser that does not have viable alternative sources of supply reasonably available.[166]

(b) Firm Structure and Performance

Corroborative Value.

Data on the structure and resources of the firm in question is not sufficient on its own to establish a dominant position, but may corroborate evidence of a dominant position indicated by an analysis of market structure.[167] Relevant factors for assessing the commercial strength of a firm,[168] i.e. its structure and resources, include:

- technological lead over competitors, [169]

---

161. *BP*, ECJ June 29, 1978, 1978 ECR 1513, paras 18–34. *See also Lederle-Praxis Biological*, Twenty-fourth Report on Competition Policy, p. 353.
162. *ANCIDES*, ECJ July 9, 1987, 1987 ECR 3131, paras 12–14.
163. E.g., *Industrial Gases*, Nineteenth Report on Competition Policy, point 62. *See also* Chapter IV.B. and C.
164. §20 (2) of the German Law on Restraints of Competition is different to the extent that it adds to the provision on abuse of a dominant position (§19) a prohibition that addresses to enterprises on which small or medium-sized suppliers or purchasers depend 'to the extent that sufficient and reasonable possibilities to deal with other enterprises do not exist.'
165. *Michelin II*, D.Comm. June 20, 2001, 2002 OJ L 143/1, points 200–208.
166. However, under national competition laws, such as the French and the German law, the concept of an 'obligatory trading partner' may be broader than the concept of dominance.
167. *Hoffmann-La Roche*, ECJ Feb. 13, 1979, 1979 ECR 461, paras 42–49; *Michelin*, ECJ Nov. 9, 1983, 1983 ECR 3461, paras 53–60.
168. *Irish Sugar*, CFI Oct. 7, 1999, 1999 ECR II-2969, para. 100.
169. *United Brands*, ECJ Feb. 14, 1978, 1978 ECR 207, paras 82–84: 'In the field of technical knowledge, ... UBC keeps on improving the productivity and yield of its plantations ... That is another factor to be borne in mind when considering UBC's position since competing firms

- large production capacity and long-term security of supply that are effectively unattainable by competitors,[170]
- management of premises and services which are indispensable to the marketing[171] or the exercise of groundhandling services,[172]
- superior access to raw materials,[173]
- diversification of production,[174]
- strong presence on adjacient markets,[175]portfolio of products capable of accentuating the market position to the disadvantage of competitors,[176]
- vertical integration both upstream and downstream,[177]
- existence of well-known trademarks[178] and a powerful distribution network,[179] thereby creating customer preferences,[180] or even dependence,[181]
- decisive commercial advantages, for example, a well-known trademark,[182] a very strong and well-organized distribution network,[183] or an integrated transport infrastructure,[184]

---

cannot develop research at a comparable level and are in this respect at a disadvantage compared with the applicant.' *See also Michelin*, ECJ Nov. 9, 1983, 1983 ECR 3461, para. 55; *Tetra Pak I*, D.Comm. July 26, 1988, 1988 OJ L 272/27, 39, *aff' d* CFI Oct. 6, 1994, 1994 ECR II-755; *Hilti*, D.Comm. Dec. 22, 1987, 1988 OJ L 65/19, 34; *aff'd* CFI Dec. 12, 1991, 1991 ECR II-1439; *Michelin II*, D.Comm. June 20, 2001, 2002 OJ L 143/1, points 182–183. Even after the expiration of a patent the patentee may keep a decisive technological advantage: *Racal Decca*, D.Comm. Dec. 21, 1988, 1989 OJ L 43/27, 41.

170. *United Brands*, ECJ Feb. 14, 1978, 1978 ECR 207, paras 69–77.
171. *British Leyland*, ECJ Nov. 11, 1996, 1996 ECR 3263, para. 5.
172. *Aéroports de Paris*, CFI Dec. 12, 2000, 2000 ECR II-3929, para. 138.
173. *United Brands*, ECJ Feb. 14, 1978, 1978 ECR 207, paras 69–77; *British Sugar*, D.Comm. July 18, 1988, 1988 OJ L 284/41, 53; *Soda Ash II*, D.Comm. Dec. 13, 2000, 2003 OJ L 10/10 and 33.
174. *Michelin I*, ECJ Nov. 9, 1983, 1983 ECR 3461, para. 59.
175. *Michelin II*, D.Comm. June 20, 2001, 2002 OJ L 143/1, points 186–190, *aff'd* CFI Sept. 30, 2003, T-203/01.
176. *Michelin I*, Nov. 9, 1983, 1983 ECR 3461, paras 127–151. Under the merger control regulation: *BaByliss*, CFI April 3, 2003, T-114/02, paras 354.
177. *United Brands*, ECJ Feb. 14, 1978, 1978 ECR 207, paras 94–96.
178. *Ibid.*, paras 88–93.
179. *Omnitel Pronto Italia*, D.Comm. Oct. 4, 1995, 1995 OJ L 280/49, para. 16; *AAMS*, CFI Nov. 22, 2001, 2001 ECR II-3413, para. 52; 191–196.
180. *British Sugar*, D.Comm. July 18, 1988, 1988 OJ L 284/41, point 44.
181. *Michelin II*, D.Comm. June 20, 2001, 2001 OJ L 143/1, points 200–208.
182. *United Brands*, ECJ Feb. 14, 1978, 1978 ECR 207, paras 88–93.
183. *Ibid.*, para. 93; *Hilti*, D.Comm. Dec. 22, 1987, 1988 OJ L 65/19, 34; *aff'd* CFI Dec. 12, 1991, 1991 ECR II-1439. *See* Commission Guidelines on the Application of the EC Competition Rules in the Telecommunications Sector, 1991 OJ C 233/2, para. 80.
184. *United Brands*, ECJ Feb. 14, 1978, 1978 ECR 207, paras 69–96; *United Brands*, D.Comm. Dec. 17, 1975, 1976 OJ L 95/1, 13; *British Sugar*, D.Comm. July 18, 1988, 1988 OJ L 284/41, 53.

- presence in other key markets through subsidiaries, [185]
- financial resources ('deep pockets'),[186] or funds or income obtained from activities in reserved markets enabling cross-subsidiation in other markets,[187]
- possibility of spreading risks over other lines of business.[188]

Firm Size and Financial Performance not Decisive.
A firm's range of products and overall size and sales volume are not in themselves an indicator of market dominance.[189] Nor is profitability a reliable criterion. Poor profitability or even short-term losses are not incompatible with the existence of a dominant position, just as large profits may be compatible with effective competition. [190] Likewise, periods of intense competition limited in time and space that do not cover the whole of the relevant market are not inconsistent with the existence of a dominant position.[191]

(c) Firm Conduct

Ability to Pursue Abusive Courses of Conduct as Evidence of Dominance.
Finally, conduct that shows that a firm can act largely in disregard of competitors on the market may confirm that a firm holds a dominant position.[192] The ability to set or control market prices is of great significance.[193] For example, in *United Brands* the firm's ability to adapt its prices to competitive conditions in the various national markets was evidence of its dominant position.[194] Practices by which

---

185. *Michelin I*, ECJ Nov. 9, 1983, 1983 ECR 3461, para. 55; *ECS/Akzo II*, D.Comm. Dec. 14, 1985, 1985 OJ L 374/1, 18. But *see Hoffmann-La Roche*, ECJ Feb. 13, 1979, 1979 ECR 461, para. 47.
186. *Continental Can*, D.Comm. Dec. 9, 1971, 1972 OJ L 7/25, 35; *United Brands*, D.Comm. Dec. 17, 1975, 1976 OJ L 95/1,13; *British Plasterboard*, D.Comm. Dec. 5, 1988, 1989 OJ L 10/50, 64.
187. *UPS Europe*, CFI March 20, 2002, 2002 ECR II-1915, paras 51–64. *See* Commission Notice on the application of the competition rules to the postal sector and on the assessment of certain State measures relating to postal services, 1998 OJ C 39/2, point 3.3.
188. *Hoffmann-La Roche*, ECJ Feb. 13, 1979, 1979 ECR 461, para. 47.
189. *Ibid.*, paras 42–49.
190. *United Brands*, ECJ Feb.14, 1978, 1978 ECR 207, paras 125–128; *Michelin*, ECJ Nov. 9, 1983, 1983 ECR 3461, para. 59; *Irish Sugar*, CFI Oct. 7, 1999, 1999 ECR II-2969, para. 102.
191. *United Brands*, ECJ Feb. 14, 1978, 1978 ECR 207, paras 113–121; *Hoffmann-La Roche*, ECJ Feb. 13, 1979, 1979 ECR 461, paras 39, 69–78.
192. *United Brands*, ECJ Feb. 14, 1978, 1978 ECR 207, para. 68; *Hoffmann-La Roche*, ECJ Feb. 13, 1979, 1979 ECR 461, para. 49; *Michelin I*, ECJ Nov. 9, 1983 ECR 3461, paras 26–27; *Hilti*, D.Comm. Dec. 22, 1987, 1988 OJ L 65/19, 34–35; *aff'd* CFI Dec. 12, 1991 ECR II-1439; *Michelin II*, D.Comm. June 20, 2001, 2002 OJ L 143/1, point 197, *aff'd* CFI Sept. 30, 2003, T-203/01.
193. *Continental Can*, D.Comm. Dec. 9, 1971, 1972 OJ L 7/25, 35; *British Sugar*, D.Comm. July 18, 1988, 1988 OJ L 284/41, 53.
194. *United Brands*, ECJ Feb. 14, 1978, 1978 ECR 207, paras 204–234; an even stronger indication was in this case its discriminatory pricing between national markets.

a powerful firm seeks to contain or limit the number of competitors may also indicate dominance, especially predatory tactics against competitors,[195] such as tying practices.[196] However, conduct that is normally pro-competitive, such as cutting prices in order to defend market share (provided it is not clearly predatory), innovation, improvements in quality and the like cannot be interpreted to a firm's disadvantage simply because it may strengthen the firm's competitive position.[197] Also, there is an obvious danger of circular reasoning in inferring dominance from conduct and then going on to infer that because the firm is dominant the conduct is an abuse.[198]

4. Collective Dominance

Different Approach with Respect to Collective Dominance under Article 82 and the Merger Control Regulation.
Article 82 applies not only to abuse of a dominant position by a single firm, but also to abuses by 'one or more' firms. Although neither single nor collective dominance is as such objectionable, the members of the oligopoly have a special responsibility and are therefore prevented from abusing their position.[199] The Court of Justice confirmed the application of both Article 82 and the merger control regulation (although it does not expressly refer to 'one or more' dominant firms) to cases of collective dominance in basically similar terms.[200] Under Article 82 the Court of Justice held in the *CEWAL* case[201] that, in order for a collective dominant position to exist, two or more undertakings legally independent of each other must be linked in such a way that they adopt the same conduct on the market, thereby presenting themselves or acting together as a collective entity *vis-à-vis*

---

195. *ECS/Akzo II*, D.Comm. Dec. 14, 1985, 1985 OJ L 374/1, 18.
196. 'Typical' of a company in a dominant position: *Michelin II*, D.Comm. June 20, 2001, 2002 OJ L 143/1, points 173 and 197.
197. *Hoffmann-La Roche*, ECJ Feb. 13, 1979, 1979 ECR 461, paras 42–48; *Michelin I*, ECJ Nov. 9, 1983, 1983 ECR 3462, paras 53–59.
198. The Court does not require a causal link between the dominant position and the alleged abuse, *see Continental Can*, ECJ Feb. 21, 1973, 1973 ECR 215, para. 27.
199. *Cewal*, ECJ March 16, 2000, 2000 ECR I-1365, para. 37. The actual approach to collective dominance is resumed in the Commission's guidelines on market analysis and assessment of significant market power under the Community regulatory framework for electronic communication networks and services, 2002 C 165/6, points 86–106.
200. The possibility of following the same approach under Article 82 and the merger control regulation seems to be accepted in *Irish Sugar*, ECJ July 10, 2001, 2001 ECR I-5333, paras. 44–45. Obviously, Article 82 differs from the merger control regulation in that Article 82 requires the abuse of an *existing* dominant position whereas the merger control regulation applies to the mere *creating or strengthening* of a collective dominant position: *CEWAL*, CFI Oct. 8, 1996, 1996 ECR II-1201, para. 60.
201. *CEWAL*, ECJ March 16, 2000, 2000 ECR I-1365.

their competitors, trading partners and consumers.[202] Under the merger control Regulation 1310/97 the Court of First Instance stated in the *Airtours* case:[203]

> 'A collective dominant position significantly impeding effective competition in the Common Market or a substantial part of it may thus arise as the result of a concentration where, in view of the actual characteristics of the relevant market and of the alteration in its structure that the transaction would entail, the latter would make each member of the dominant oligopoly, as it becomes aware of common interests, consider it possible, economically rational, and hence preferable, to adopt on a lasting basis a common policy on the market with the aim of selling above competitive prices, without having to enter into an agreement or resort to a concerted practice within the meaning of Article 81 (1) and without any actual or potential competitors, let alone customers or consumers, being able to react effectively.'[204]

Under Article 2 of the amended merger Regulation 139/2004[205] the Commission may declare a merger incompatible with the Common Market where it would significantly impede effective competition, *in particular* as a result of the creation or strengthening of a dominant position, which allows the Commission to act against oligopolies irrespective of whether or not they have coordinating effects,[206] i.e., also where a merger is likely to make coordination between the remaining firms more likely.[207] However, this broader concept which may applied under the amended merger regulation does not affect the scope of Article 82, which remains limited to cases of abuse of an *existing* single or collective dominant position. The interpretation of this dominance concept by the Commission and the Court of Justice remains therefore relevant.

Development of the Case Law under Article 82.
The Commission's administrative practice is characterized by a cautious application of the collective dominance concept. The Commission started with cases which concerned both restrictive practices infringing Article 81 (1) and abuses of a collective dominant position infringing Article 82, the collective dominance being demonstrated by the restrictive arrangements between the members of the oligopoly.

202. *Ibid.* paras 36–42.
203. *Airtours*, CFI June 6, 2002, 2002 ECR II-2585.
204. *Ibid.* para. 61, referring to *Gencor*, CFI March 25, 1999, 1999 ECR II-753, para. 277. *See also SCPA/Kali+Salz-MdK*, ECJ March 31, 1998, 1998 ECR I-1375, para. 221.
205. 2004 OJ L 24/1.
206. Commission Notice on horizontal mergers, point 22.
207. 2003/IP/1744.

- In *Commercial Solvents*[208] the Commission considered the collective economic strength of a group of companies which although legally distinct were run as a single economic unit. The Court of Justice confirmed the abuse of a dominant position but stated that the companies in question formed in fact a single economic unit and that their joint conduct had to be assessed as a single unit rather than a shared dominance.[209] Similarly, in the *SABA* case,[210] which concerned only the application of Article 81 to a selective distribution system, the Court of Justice considered also the concept of a collective dominant position but denied any dominance likely to give rise to the application of Article 82.[211]
- In *Binon/AMP*[212] the Advocate General argued that the mere parallel behaviour of oligopolists concluding identical contracts is not in itself an indication of collective dominance, but the Court of Justice did not rule on the matter.
- In *Alsatel/Novasam*[213] the Court of Justice did not rule on the issue either, but appeared to accept parallel behaviour as a valid indicator of collective dominance if it is sufficiently proved by the Commission. In the relatively few cases decided by the Commission under the collective dominance theory either this aspect of the decision was not appealed to the Court of Justice or the Court's decision was rendered on grounds other than the concept of collective dominance.
- In *Sugar*[214] the Commission proceeded under the collective dominance theory against identical abusive conduct by the only two firms present on the Dutch market based on their close cooperation in the fields of purchasing, research, production and sales promotion, their common identity in the marketplace, and in particular their threat to cut off supplies to distributors who were importing sugar from other member states or selling imported sugar at cut-rate prices. However, the charge of bringing undue pressure to bear on the importers was reversed by the Court of Justice on appeal because of insufficient evidence that the alleged abusive conduct had taken place.' [215]
- In *ABG/BP*[216] the Commission found that during the oil crisis competition between the oil companies at the distribution level was so reduced that they were collectively dominant, each *vis-à-vis* its own customers, and that BP had abused this dominance by curtailing supplies disproportionately to a distribu-

208. *Commercial Solvents*, D.Comm. Dec. 14, 1972, 1972 OJ L 299/51.
209. *Commercial Solvents*, ECJ March 6, 1974, 1974 ECR 223, paras 36–41.
210. *SABA II*, Dec. 21, 1983, 1983 OJ L 376/41.
211. *SABA II*, Oct. 22, 1986, 1986 ECR 3021, paras 79–82.
212. *Binon/AMP*, ECJ July 3, 1985; 1985 ECR 2015, 2028 and 2042, para. 25.
213. *Alsatel/Novasam*, ECJ Oct. 5, 1988, 1988 ECR 5987, paras 21–22.
214. *Sugar*, D.Comm. Jan. 2, 1973, 1973 OJ L 140/17, 38–39.
215. *Sugar*, ECJ Dec. 16, 1975, 1975 ECR 1663, paras 403–420.
216. *ABG/BP*, D.Comm. April 19, 1977, 1997 OJ L 117/1.

tors' group. The Court of Justice, however, overruled the decision because the group was not a regular customer and on other grounds.[217]

- In *Italian Flatglass*[218] the Commission proceeded to a parallel application of Articles 81 and 82 to price fixing and market sharing between the members of an oligopoly. However, the Court of First Instance anulled the decision with respect to the collective dominance because the Commission failed to prove the 'unitary presence' on the relevant market.[219]
- In *CEWAL*[220] the Court affirmed the Commission's statement that Article 82 applied to the collective predatory practices (tariffs and fidelity rebates) and Article 81 applied to the market-sharing agreement between the members of a maritime association. In such cases both Articles 81 and 82 apply and point to the same conclusion: The parallel behaviour (if sufficiently proved) is a violation of Article 82 and the supply agreements between each manufacturer and its customers or other anticompetitive agreements between them are also caught by Article 81 (1) and are ineligible for exemption because, together with the parallel conduct of other firms, they give the collectively dominant firms the ability to eliminate competition. This commission decision was upheld by the Court of First Instance.[221]
- In the *Magill* case[222] the Commission found parallel behaviour without restrictive collusion. This case concerned the three Irish broadcasting organizations publishing separate television programme guides. Each held a dominant position with respect to the weekly advance listing of their programmes thanks to their inside knowledge of programme planning and the copyright they claimed for the listings. The Commission ruled that the parallel refusal to grant a copyright licence to a weekly magazine providing a comprehensive weekly TV guide constituted an abuse of their dominant position. The Court of Justice

---

217. *BP*, ECJ June 29, 1978, 1978 ECR 1513. The particularity of this case was the economic dependence of the traditional customers on their traditional supplier (obligatory trading partner) to such an extent that *each* member of the oligopoly was considered by the Commission as having a dominant position.
218. *Italian Flatglass*, D.Comm. Dec. 7, 1988, 1989 OJ L 33/44.
219. *Italian Flatglass*, CFI March 10, 1992, 1992 ECR II-1403, paras 358–366 (in this case the Court of First Instance accepted the Commission's concept of 'unitary presence', but annulled the Commission's decision with respect to the collective dominance because of lack of evidence); *CEWAL*, CFI Oct. 8, 1996, 1996 ECR II-1201, paras 60–62; *French-West African Shipowners' Committee*, D.Comm. April 1, 1992, 1992 OJ L 134/1; *TACA II*, D.Comm. Sept. 16, 1998, 1999 OJ L 95/1, points 522–531; *P&I Clubs*, D.Comm. April 12, 1999, 1999 OJ L 125/12, point 127. In *Irish Sugar*, D.Comm. May 14, 1997, 1997 OJ L 258/1, point 117, the Commission applied the concept of collective dominance to joint anticompetitive practices of the dominant producer Irish Sugar and its main distributors in Ireland.
220. *CEWAL*, D.Comm. Dec. 23, 1992, 1993 OJ L 34/20. Similarly *French-West-African Shipowners Committee*, D.Comm. April 1, 1992, 1992 OJ L 134/1.
221. *CEWAL*, CFI Oct. 8, 1996, 1996 ECR II-1201, in particular paras 64–66
222. *Magill TV Guide*, D.Comm. Dec. 21, 1988, 1989 OJ L 78/43, 48–49, *aff'd* CFI July 10, 1991, 1991 ECR II-485, 535 and 575.

upheld the Commission' decision affirming the dominant position of each of the broadcasting organizations with respect to their respective copyrights and the dependence of Magill as the weekly magazine provider without explicitly addressing the issue of collective dominance.[223]

– In the *Irish Sugar* case[224] the Commission fined the leading Irish sugar producer for having abused its dominant position which it held at its own or at least – during a certain period – collectively with its main distributor in Ireland. The Court of First Instance[225] and the Court of Justice[226] upheld this approach of collective dominance because of the economic links which existed between them and enabled them to adopt a Common Market policy and to act together independently of their competitors, their customers and consumers.
– In *TACA*[227] the Commission again applied Article 82 in parallel with Article 81. The case concerned an agreement between the members of the maritime association TACA (Transatlantic Conference Agreement) relating to transatlantic liner services between northern Europe and the United States. The Commissions stated (i) that the TACA members collectively fixed the transport rates and conditions relating to the maritime transport and to inland transport services as part of a multimodal transport operation, thereby infringing Article 81 (1), and (ii) that the members abused their collective dominant position by entering into an agreement to place restrictions on the availability and content of services contracts and by altering the competitive structure of the market so as to reinforce TACA's dominant position to the disadvantage of potential competitiors, thereby infringing Article 82. The Commission imposed fines only with respect to Article 82. The Court of First Instance[228] upheld the Commission's conclusions with respect to Article 81 but annulled the decision (and the fines) with respect to Article 82. In this respect the Court affirmed that the members of TACA held a collective dominant position because of 'factors of economic correlation' enabling the members to adopt the same line of action on the market,[229] but found that the Commission had not shown that the specific measures adopted by the TACA members, rather than particular economic considerations, had induced two outsiders (from Korea and China) to become members of the association and did not abusively alter the competitive structure of the market.[230]

223. *Magill*, ECJ April 6, 1995, 1995 ECR I-743, paras 47–56. By contrast, in the *Tierce/Ladbroke* case the Court denied the applicability of Article 82 to the refusal of different horse race organisators to license sound and pictures of the races to bookmakers, because such a licence was useful but not indispensable to their business (no 'economic dependence'), but it applied Article 81 to their possible anticompetitive collusion: CFI June 12, 1997, 1997 ECR II-923.
224. *Irish Sugar*, D.Comm. May 14, 1997, 1997 OJ L 258/1, point 113.
225. *Irish Sugar*, CFI Oct. 7, 1999, 1999 ECR II-2969, paras 46–49.
226. *Irish Sugar*, ECJ Jule 10, 2001, 2001 ECR I-5333, paras 46–47.
227. *TACA*, D.Comm. Sept. 16, 1998, 1999 OJ L 95/1, points 522–531.
228. *TACA – Atlantic Container Line AB,* CFI Sept. 30, 2003, T-191/98.
229. *Ibid.*, paras 594–595 and 694–757.
230. *Ibid.*, para. 1368.

Conditions for Finding a Collective Dominant Position – Collusive v. Non-Collusive Oligopolies.
The conditions for which the Commission must produce convincing evidence when finding a collective dominant position under the merger control regulation are defined by the Court of Justice in the *SCPA/Kali + Salz-MdK* case[231] and were reconfirmed in the *Airtours* case,[232] which was decided under the dominance concept of the former Regulation 1310/97, as follows:

- 'first, each member of the dominant oligopoly must have the ability to know how the other members are behaving in order to monitor whether or not they are adopting the common policy … [I]t is not enough for each member of the dominant oligopoly to be aware that independent market conduct is profitable for all of them[233] but each member must also have a means of knowing whether the other operators are adopting the same strategy and whether they are maintaining it. There must, therefore, be sufficient market teransparency for all members of the dominant oligopoly to be aware, sufficiently precisely and quickly, of the way in which the other members' market conduct is evolving';
- 'second, the situation of tacit coordination must be sustainable over time, that is to say, there must be an incentive not to depart from the common policy on the market. … [I]t is only if all the members of the dominant oligopoly maintain the parallel conduct that all can benefit. The notion of retaliation in respect of conduct deviating from the common policy is thus inherent in this condition. … [T]here must be adequate deterrents to ensure that there is a long-term incentive in not departing from the common policy, which means that each member of the dominant oligopoly must be aware that highly competitive action on its part designed to increase its market share would provoke identical action by the others, so that it would derive no benefit from its initiative';[234]
- 'third, to prove the existence of a collective dominant position to the requisite legal standard, the Commission must also establish that the foreseeable

231. *SCPA/Kali + Salz-MDK*, ECJ March 31, 1998, 1998 ECR I-1375, para. 221. In the *Gencor/Lonrho* case, D.Comm. 24 April 1996, 1997 OJ L 11/30; *aff'd* CFI 25 March 1999, 1999 ECR II-753, paras 205–206 and 273–276; the Court of First Instance affirmed the Commission's findings (under the merger control regulation) of a duopolistic dominance in a highly concentrated supply side with high transparency for a homogeneous product, mature production technology, high entry barriers (including high sunk costs) and producers with financial links and multimarket contacts. *See also Airtours*, CFI June 6, 2002,2002 ECR II-2585, para. 59.
232. *Airtours*, CFI June 6, 2002, 2002 ECR II-2585, para. 62.
233. On the contrary, losses are irrelevant, as stated in *Irish Sugar*, D.Comm. May 14, 1997, 1997 OJ L 258/1, point 103.
234. *See Gencor/Lonrho*, CFI March 25, 1999, 1999 ECR II-753, para. 276.

> reaction of current and future competitors, as well as of consumers, would not jeopardise the results expected from the common policy.'[235]

Although this interpretation does not anticipate the interpretation of the broader oligopoly concept of Regulation 139/2004, it remains relevant with respect to finding a collective dominant position under Article 82: The members of an oligopoly must be linked in such a way that they adopt the same conduct on the market,[236] thereby presenting themselves on the market as a collective entity and holding together a dominant position on the relevant market, without being subject to effective *external* actual or potential competition.[237] However, a collective dominant position does not require the elimination of *all* internal competition between the members of the oligopoly, as stated by the Court of First Instance in the *TACA* case:[238]

> 'the possibility to align competitive conduct in no way implies that competition between the undertakings concerned is completely eliminated. Furthermore, the existence of a dominant position within the meaning of Article 86 (*now 82*) of the Treaty presupposes the existence of economic links between two or more economic entities which are, by definition, independent and, accordingly, capable of competitng with one another.'

Accordingly, the Commission tends to extend the concept of collective dominance to non-collusive oligopolies. The Commission tried to apply this concept in the *Magill* case.[239] The Court of First Instance did not find a collective dominant position of the three Irish broadcasting organizations but rather the existence of *individual* dominant positions of each of them because of their respective exclusive rights without focusing on the concept of collective dominance.[240] In its Notice on access agreements in the telecommunications sector the Commission considers that in case of joint dominance behaviour of one of several jointly dominant firms may be abusive even if they are not engaged in restrictive collusion and are not behaving in the same way.[241] It depends on further case law developments as to whether, under Article 82, a collective dominant position may exist where its members adopt on a lasting basis a common policy on the market *without* any

235. *Airtours*, CFI June 6, 2002, 2002 ECR II-2585, para. 62. *See also*, with respect to coordinated effects of a collective dominant position: Commission Notice on horizontal mergers, points 39–57.
236. *CEWAL*, CFI Oct. 8, 1996, 1996 ECR II-1201, para. 62.
237. *CEWAL*, ECJ March 16, 2000, 2000 ECR I-1365, paras 36 and 54.
238. *TACA – Atlantic Container Line AB*, CFI Sept. 30, 2003, T-191/98, paras 653–656.
239. *Magill*, D.Comm. Dec. 21, 1988, 1989 OJ L 78/43. *See also* Telecommunications Guidelines, 2002 OJ C 165/6, points 86–106; Commission Notice on the appraisal of horizontal mergers, Dec. 11, 2002, point 25.
240. *Magill*, ECJ April 6, 1995, 1995 ECR I-743, paras 47–56.
241. 1998 OJ C 365/2, point 129.

collusion, in particular without having to enter into an agreement or concerted practice,[242] but already where the likelihood of such coordination exists.[243]

Symmetric v. Asymmetric Oligopolies.
The requirement of market transparency and retaliation implies the existence of a small number of companies with comparable market power holding collectively a high market share so that they jointly 'dominate' their smaller competitors outside the oligopoly. An oligopoly must comprise firms each holding approximately the same market shares[244] and a similar degree of vertical integration[245] (*symmetric* oligopoly) in order to allow them to adopt a common policy on the market.[246] An oligopoly comprising firms with disparate market shares, i.e. different firm size and financial resources (*asymmetric* oligopoly), is less likely to lead to tacit collusion.[247] The market shares must be rather constant; fluctuations over time or progressive decline in the market shares would indicate a level of competition on the market.[248]

Sufficient Links between the Members of the Oligopoly.
There must be sufficient links between the members of the oligopoly, giving them the possibility to influence one another's competitive conduct on the market and

---

242. *Ibid.*, para. 61. Obviously, any actual collusion between the members of the oligopoly would have constituted an infringement of Article 81. In the second *Soda Ash* case both Solvay and ICI were found guilty of abuse of their individual dominant positions by means of requirements contracts and exclusionary rebates, but were also found to have infringed Article 81 by market sharing: *Soda Ash – Solvay II* and *Soda Ash – ICI II* (Article 82), D.Comm. Dec. 13, 2000, 2003 OJ L 10/10 and 33. The effect of the parallel behaviour of tacitly colluding oligopolists would be the same as that of oligopolists colluding overtly to exploit a collective dominant position (*Sugar*, ECJ Dec. 16, 1975, 1975 ECR 1663, paras 172–175). But the market structure criteria only indicate a likelihood of tacit collusion and would have to be supported by further evidence showing that the parallel behaviour was not in fact autonomous. A possible further criterion might be the pattern of the behaviour over time. One-off parallel decisions of firms adapting 'intelligently' to the actions of competitors (*Soda Ash I*, *supra* note 153; *Industrial Gases*, *ibid.*; *Aminobutanol*, Sixteenth Report on Competition Policy, point 76) would have to be distinguished from a long-term tacitly collusive strategy to eliminate actual or potential competitors from the market.
243. With respect to the broader approach under Regulation 139/2004: Recital 25.
244. The market shares may not be volatile, dynamic and fluctuating: *Airtours*, CFI June 6, 2002, 2002 ECR II-2585, paras 109–119.
245. *Airtours*, CFI June 6, 2002, 2002 ECR II-2585, paras 105–108.
246. Under the merger control regulation: symmetric oligopoly affirmed in *Gencor/Lonrho*, CFI March 25, 1999, 1999 ECR II-753, paras 293–298 (duopoly of 35% and 35%); symmetric oligopoly denied in *Airtours*, CFI June June 6, 2002, 2002 ECR II-2585, paras 74–77 (three-party oligopoly of 32%, 27% and 20%, which did not allow the Commission to conclude that the parties would have had the ability, which they previously did not have, to adopt a common policy on the market). *See* Commission Notice on horizontal mergers, point 48.
247. Under the merger control regulation: 37% and 23% (*Renault/Iveco*, D.Comm. Oct. 22, 1998, M.1202).
248. *Airtours*, CFI June 6, 2002, 2002 ECR II-2585, para. 118.

thereby jeopardize their independence. The links may consist of contractual or structural links.

- Contractual links are established by the nature and terms of an agreement and by the way in which it is implemented and, consequently, by the links or factors which give rise to a connection between the undertakings.[249] Contractual links include agreements on horizontal cooperation,[250] vertical supply[251] and distribution relationships,[252] strategic alliances,[253] the systematic exchange of information,[254] or distribution.[255] It is true that the mere fact that two or more undertakings are linked by an agreement does not, of itself, constitute a sufficient basis but the way it is implemented may lead to conduct as a collective entity; however, the implementation of such contractual links may lead to joint uniform conduct. [256] The cases of collective dominance under Article 82 mostly concern agreements between the members of the oligopoly.[257]
- Structural links are links or factors which give rise to a connection between undertakings which might be characterized as a collective entity vis-à-vis both users and competitors.[258] Structural links include horizontal and vertical links, such as shareholdings,[259] personal links 'interlocking directorates',[260] joint ventures,[261] and network interconnection which commit their owners to act as collective entity.[262] The assessment of structural oligopolies must be based on the parties' and their competitors' market shares and their fluctuations over

249. *CEWAL*, ECJ March 16, 2000, 2000 ECR I-1365, paras 45 and 54.
250. E.g. liner conferences: *TACA*, D.Comm. June 17, 1998, 1998 OJ L 252/47; *CEWAL*, ECJ March 16, 2000, 2000 ECR I-1365, paras 48–52.
251. *Almelo*, ECJ April 27, 1994, 1994 ECR I-1477, para. 42.
252. *Irish Sugar*, D.Comm. May 14, 1997, 1997 OJ L 258/1, point 117 (*aff'd* ECJ July 12, 2001, 2001 ECR I-5333).
253. E.g. *Air Alliances*, D.Comm. Oct. 29, 2002, IP/02/1569.
254. *Flatglass*, CFI March 10, 1992, 1992 ECR II-1403, para. 358.
255. In *Irish Sugar* the Court of First Instance confirmed that the economic links between a supplier of sugar and its main distributor (both providing competing services on the same market) enabled them to act together independently of their other competitors and therefore constituted a collective entity: CFI July 10, 2001, 2001 ECR II-5333, para. 46.
256. *CEWAL*, ECJ March 16, 2000, 2000 ECR I-1365, paras 43–44.
257. *See* in particular, *French-West-African Shipowners Committee*, D.Comm. April 1, 1992, 1992 OJ L 134/1.
258. *CEWAL*, ECJ March 16, 2000, 2000 ECR I-1365, paras 45–48.
259. Including minority shareholding: Commission Notice on Access to Telecommunications, 1998 OJ C 365/2, point 79; *Gencor/Lonrho*, CFI March 25, 1999, 1999 ECR II-753, paras 169–180.
260. Refraining from interlocking directorates may be a condition for clearance under the merger control regulation: *Generali/INA*, D.Comm. Jan. 17, 2000, M.1712.
261. Under the merger control regulation *Gencor/Lonrho*, CFI March 25, 1999, 1999 ECR II-753, paras 94–100.
262. *Marathon/Gasunie*, D.Comm. April 16, 2003, IP/03/547 (joint refusal to grant access to continental European gas pipelines).

time, and the characteristics of the market in question, which include, according to a study carried out for the Commission,[263] low price elasticity, stable market conditions and structure, and barriers to entry and to exit, whether of an economic nature (e.g. economies of scale) or due to governmental action (e.g. import restrictions), which limit the effect of potential competition.

Difficult Prospective Analysis.
The assessment of whether the structure of oligopolistic markets is conducive to coordinated effects on those markets must be based on the appropriate characteristics, in particular in terms of market concentration, transparency and other characteristics. The Commission established the following a check list for its decision-making practice in Annex II of the ONP framework Directive:[264]

- mature market,
- stagnant or moderate growth on the demand side,
- low elasticity of demand,
- homogeneous product,
- similar cost structures,
- similar market shares,
- lack of technical innovation, mature technology,
- absence of excess capacity,
- high barriers to entry,
- lack of countervailing buying power,
- lack of potential competition,
- various kinds of informal or other links between the undertakings concerned,
- retaliatory mechanisms,
- lack or reduced scope for price competition.

This assessment implies a difficult prospective evaluation of the 'foreseeable reactions'.[265] However, the Court tends to examine rather strictly whether the

263. As described in the Sixteenth Report on Competition Policy, points 331–333.
264. 1990 OJ L 192/1. *See also* Guidelines on market analysis and the assessment of significant market power for electronic telecommunications networks and services, 2002 OJ C 165/6, point 97, and the study carried out for the Commission in 1986 whose results are described in the Sixteenth Report on Competition Policy, points 331–333, suggested that tacit collusion between oligopolists was likely on certain kinds of markets, namely those characterized by:
    - low price elasticity,
    - stable market conditions and structure, and
    - barriers to entry and to exit, whether of an economic nature (i.e., economies of scale) or due to government action (e.g., import restrictions), which limited the effect of potential competition.
265. Such a perspective analysis is particularly difficult in cases where the companies did not enjoy a collective dominant position (because of lack of collusion) but *create* a collective dominant position, as in the case *Airtours*, ECJ CFI June 6, 2002, 2002 ECR II-2585, para. 210.

Commission's prospective analysis complies with the requisite legal standards.[266] It is still an open question how the Commission is going to comply with these high legal standards.

5. Dominant Purchasers

Limited Experience.
The dominance of purchasers is to be determined by analogy to the definition of dominant suppliers.[267] A purchaser's dominant position is thus a position of economic strength enjoyed by a firm which enables it to prevent effective competition being maintained on the relevant market by affording it the power to behave to an appreciable extent independently of its competitors and its suppliers. A purchaser's buying power depends largely on the ability of suppliers to switch to other trading partners. If the purchaser is an 'obligatory trading partner' for its suppliers but is itself capable of switching easily to other suppliers or starting its own production, it enjoys a dominant position. There have been relatively few such cases decided by the Community antitrust authorities, because the effects of such practices are typically dealt with by national competition authorities under their national law.[268] Thus far the cases decided by the Commission and the European Court of Justice have mainly concerned the buying power of copyright association and broadcasting monopolies.[269]

D. Abuse

1. Introduction

Protecting Commercial Interests v. Abusing a Dominant Position.
Competition on the merits alone does not infringe Article 82, even when pursued by a dominant firm. Only conduct that may be classified as an exploitative, exclusionary, predatory or structural abuse infringes Article 82. Even an undertaking in

266. *Airtours*, ECJ CFI June 6, 2002, 2002 ECR II-2585, para. 294.
267. Twenty-sixth Report on Competition Policy, point 147. *See EUROFIMA*, Third Report on Competition Policy, points 68–69; Commission's Memorandum to railway companies: Twentieth Report on Competition Policy, point 115 (railway companies in their capacity as purchasers of railway carriage).
268. *See*, e.g., the German Monopoly Commission's study on abuse of buying power, Sondergutachten 7 (1977), and the UK Monopolies and Mergers Commission's Report on Discounts to Retailers, 1981.
269. *See* the examples given in the Commission's Telecommunication Guidelines, 1991 OJ C 233/2, points 116–120; *EUROFIMA*, Third Report on Competition Policy, points 68–69; *Filtrona/Tabacalera*, Nineteenth Report on Competition Policy, point 61.

a dominant position is entitled to take reasonable steps to defend its position on the market and to compete on the merits,[270] including:

- asserting its exclusive industrial property right;[271]
- refusing to grant a licence;[272] and
- taking recourse to legal instruments established in the interest of the Community, such as an antidumping procedure.[273]

However, on a market where competition is already weakened by the very presence of a limited number of powerful undertakings, a dominant position implies a 'special responsibility', irrespective of the cause of that position, not to allow its conduct to impair genuine undistorted competition on the market.[274] It may be difficult to distinguish practices that amount to competition on the merits, which should be encouraged, from practices that go beyond 'normal' competition, and so are regarded as abusive. The actual scope of the special responsibility imposed on a dominant firm must be considered in the light of the specific circumstances of each case.[275]

The Court of First Instance held in the *British Plaster Board* case:

> '... although the fact that an undertaking is in a dominant position cannot disentitle it from protecting its commercial interests if they are attacked and that such an undertaking must be conceded the right to take such reasonable steps as it deems appropriate to protect its said interests, such behaviour cannot be countenanced if its actual purpose is to strengthen this dominant position and abuse it.'[276]

---

270. *British Airways*, CFI Dec. 17, 2003, T-219/99, para 243. *See UPS*, CFI March 20, 2002, 2002 ECR II-1915, para. 62. Including recourse to a legitimate legal instrument such as the anti-dumping procedure: *IPS*, Twenty-sixth Report on Competition Policy, pp. 138–139; *Deutsche Bahn*, CFI Oct. 21, 1997, 1997 ECR II-1689, para. 78 ('on the basis of quality').
271. *Magill*, CFI April 6, 1995, 1995 ECR II-743, para. 50.
272. *Renault*, ECJ Oct. 5, 1988, 1988 ECR 6039, para. 16; Opinion of Advocate General Tizzano in *IMS Health*, C-418/03 of Oct. 2, 2003, paras 77–86.
273. *Industrie des poudres sphériques*, CFI Nov. 30, 2000, 2000 ECR II-3755, paras 213–217.
274. *British Airways*, CFI Dec. 17, 2003, T-219/99, para. 242. *See AKZO*, ECJ July 3, 1991, 1991 ECR I-3359, para. 70; *Hilti*, CFI Dec. 12, 1991, 1991 ECR II-1439, paras 99–101; *Deutsche Bahn*, CFI Oct. 21, 1997, 1997 ECR II-1689, para. 78; *Michelin II*, D.Comm. June 20, 2001, 2002 OJ L 143/1, point 211, *aff'd* CFI Sept. 30, 2003, T-203/01. *Michelin*, ECJ Nov. 9, 1983, 1983 ECR 3461, para. 57; *CEWAL*, ECJ March 16, 2000, 2000 ECR I-1365, para. 85.
275. *CEWAL*, ECJ March 16, 2000, 2000 ECR I-1365, para. 114.
276. *BPB*, CFI April 1, 1993, 1993 ECR II-389, para. 117; *aff'd* ECJ April 6, 1995, 1995 ECR I-865; *Irish Sugar*, CFI Oct. 7, 1999, 1999 ECR II-2969, paras 112 and 189; *CEWAL*, CFI Oct. 8, 1996, 1996 ECR II-1201, para. 146.

Thus, even a dominant firm may take measures of defensive nature based on criteria of economic efficiency, provided it is consistent with the interest of consumers.[277] On the other hand, firms in a dominant position may commit an abuse by adopting a course of conduct or taking measures which would not be objectionable if adopted or taken by non-dominant firms because the conclusion of a contractual obligation or the acquisition of a right by a dominant firm has a more severe or wide-ranging anticompetitive effect than by a non-dominant firm.[278]

Classification of Abuses Covered by Article 82.
Article 82 does not define 'abuse' in general terms, but gives four examples, all of which happen to fall mainly into the 'exploitative' category, i.e., exploiting market power in trading relationships with customers or suppliers in order to earn excessive profits or gain other advantages.[279] However, the Court of Justice has held that the four examples given are not exhaustive and that other forms of abuse are covered. These are to be determined by the general principles and objectives of the Treaty, especially Article 3 (g) which calls for maintenance of effective competition in the Common Market.[280] Consequently, Article 82 also prohibits 'exclusionary' or 'predatory' abuses, i.e., abusing market power to eliminate a competitor or restrict or impede its activities, because such conduct imperils the competition remaining in the market. The different forms of abuse may overlap; a exploitative abusive may be only a means for a predatory purpose. For instance, a selective application of unfair prices or rebates may be a discrimination aiming at eliminating a competitor,[281] fidelity rebates are likely or even designed to affect the market access of competitors,[282] and tying practices are by their very nature a mainly predatory abuse.[283] Finally, another form of abuse covered by Article 82 but not explicitly referred to in it, which is called a 'structural abuse' because of its immediate radical effect on market structure, is the takeover of a competitor likely to create or to strengthen a dominant position, which is discussed in Chapter VI.

---

277. *Irish Sugar*, CFI Oct. 7, 1999, 1999 ECR II-2969, paras 187–189.
278. *ITT/Promedia*, CFI July 17, 1998, 1998 ECR II-2937, paras 139–140. *See Michelin I*, ECJ Nov. 9, 1983, 1983 ECR 3461, para. 57; *Tetra Pak I*, CFI July 10, 1990, 1990 ECR II-309, para. 23.
279. *Cf.* the anti-monopolization provision of the ECSC Treaty, Article 66 (7), which concerns the abuse of a dominant position 'for purposes contrary to the objectives of this Treaty'.
280. *Continental Can*, ECJ Feb. 21, 1973, 1973 ECR 215, paras 23–26; *Commercial Solvents*, ECJ March 6, 1974, 1974 ECR 223, para. 25; *CEWAL* ECJ March 16, 2000, 2000 ECR I-1365, para. 112. In *Hoffmann-La Roche* the Court of Justice held that, interpreted in the light of Article 3 (g), the concepts of 'dominant position' and 'abuse' were not too vague to justify the imposition of fines: ECJ Feb. 13, 1979, 1979 ECR 461, paras 128–136.
281. *Irish Sugar*, CFI Oct. 7, 1999, 1999 ECR II-2969, para. 224.
282. *Sugar*, ECJ Dec. 16, 1975, 1975 ECR 1663, paras 523–527.
283. *Tetra Pak II*, ECJ Nov. 14, 1996, 1996 ECR I-5951, paras 34–37.

Definitions and Main Categories of Abuse.
The most general definition of 'abuse of dominant position is found in the Court's judgment in the *Hoffmann-La Roche* case:

> 'The concept of abuse is an objective concept relating to the behaviour of an undertaking in a dominant position which is such as to influence the structure of a market where, as a result of the very presence of the undertaking in question, the degree of competition is weakened and which, through recourse to methods different from those which condition normal competition in products or services on the basis of the transactions of commercial operators, has the effect of hindering the maintenance of the degree of competition still existing in the market or the growth of that competition.'[284]

This definition, however, fits exclusionary abuses more than exploitative ones and does not mention the fact that normal competitive conduct (e.g., price-cutting, takeovers) by a non-dominant firm may constitute an abuse when engaged in by a dominant one. Other judgments have given definitions and set forth the main characteristics of the various categories of abuse:

- An *exploitative abuse* was characterized in *United Brands* as conduct by a dominant firm that 'made use of the opportunities arising out of its dominant position in such a way as to reap trading benefits which it would not have reaped if there had been normal and sufficiently effective competition.'[285] The alleged abuse was the charging of excessive prices, which the Court found unproved, although it upheld the Commission on other abuses (a resale ban and price discrimination) that were designed to divide national markets so as to enable the dominant firm to better exploit its control over those markets. An exploitative abuse mainly harms parties with whom the dominant firm deals, i.e., its customers or suppliers. Hence, such abuses can also occur in an absolute monopoly where there is no competition.[286] In some cases, however, exploitative abuses harm both vertical trading partners and competitors. An example is tying: the customer is forced to buy products from the dominant firm that he could buy from a competitor and the competitor is prevented from selling them to that customer. In such a case the exploitative abuse is also exclusionary.

---

284. *Hoffmann-La Roche*, ECJ Feb. 13, 1979, 1979 ECR 461, para. 91. Quoted in, *inter alia*, *ITT/Promedia*, CFI July 17, 1998, 1998 ECR II-2937, para. 138; *L'Oréal*, ECJ Dec. 11, 1980, 1980 ECR 3775, para. 27; *ECS/Akzo II*, D.Comm. Dec. 14, 1985, 1985 OJ L 374/1, 19.
285. *United Brands*, ECJ Feb. 14, 1978, 1978 ECR 207, para. 249.
286. *BRT/SABAM II*, ECJ March 27, 1974, 1974 ECR 313, para. 15: 'The fact that an undertaking entrusted with the exploitation of copyrights and occupying a dominant position within the meaning of Article 82 imposes on its members obligations which are not absolutely necessary for the attainment of its object and which thus encroach unfairly upon a member's freedom to exercise his copyright can constitute an abuse.'

- *Exclusionary abuses* are chiefly referred to in the general definition quoted above from the *Hoffmann-La Roche* case, which concerned fidelity rebates. Another typical exclusionary abuse is refusal to supply by a firm that is the sole or a dominant source of supplies of a product. In the *Commercial Solvents* case, the Court held that

  '... an undertaking which has a dominant position in the market in raw materials and which, with the object of reserving such raw material for manufacturing its own derivatives, refuses to supply a customer, which is itself a manufacturer of these derivatives, and therefore risks eliminating all competition on the part of this customer, is abusing its dominant position within the meaning of Article 82.'[287]

  Exclusionary abuses involve direct or indirect injury to competitors. A *direct* injury occurs if a firm that has a dominant position in the supply of an input for a product – as in the *Commercial Solvents* case – or that controls access to a technology necessary for manufacturing the product refuses to supply the input to a competitor in the product market or to grant it a licence to the technology. Competitors are harmed *indirectly* for example by predatory pricing, where a dominant firm cuts its prices or improves its conditions of sale to selected customers in order to freeze out a competitor. Thus, unlike an exploitative abuse, exclusionary abuses need not be immediately detrimental to the dominant firm's trading partners, although the long-term result is likely to be so.
- *A structural abuse* of a dominant position is a radical form of exclusionary conduct whereby the dominant firm acquires or merges with a competitor and thereby immediately reduces the degree of competition in the market and strengthens its dominant position. In the *Continental Can* case the Court of Justice held that Article 82 applied to mergers and acquisitions involving a dominant firm because they eliminated the competition that previously came from the acquired firm just as effectively as (if not more effectively than) an anticompetitive agreement with the firm would do:

  'The restraint of competition which is prohibited if it is the result of behaviour falling under Article 81, cannot become permissible by the fact that such behaviour succeeds under the influence of a dominant undertaking and results in the merger of the undertakings concerned. In the absence of explicit provisions one cannot assume that the Treaty, which prohibits in Article 81 certain decisions of ordinary associations of undertakings restricting competition without eliminating it, permits in Article 82 that undertakings, after merging into an organic unity, should reach such a dominant position that any serious chance of competition is practically rendered impossible ...

  Abuse may therefore occur if an undertaking in a dominant position strengthens such position or enlarges such position on related markets in

287. *Commercial Solvents*, ECJ March 6, 1974, 1974 ECR 223, para. 25.

> such a way that the degree of dominance reached substantially fetters competition, i.e. that only undertakings remain in the market whose behaviour depends on the dominant one.'[288]

Abuse by Unilateral Action or by Contractual Means.
A dominant firm may commit an abuse by unilaterally imposing abusive prices, conditions or conduct. However, as the Court of First Instance ruled in the *Deutsche Bahn* case:

> 'the existence of a dominant position cannot be ruled out by the fact that the undertaking which holds the dominant position has formally entered into an agreement the object of which is the joint fixing of tariffs and therefore falls within the scope of the prohibition of restrictive agreements.'[289]

Therefore, both Articles 81 and 82 may be applied in parallel to the same set of facts.[290] However, the abuse of a dominant position may infringe Article 82 even if the anticompetitive arrangement that is the basis of the dominance is notified and cleared under Article 81 (3)[291] or covered by a block exemption regulation.[292]

No Need for Causal Link between Dominant Position and Abuse.
The existence of a dominant position is a necessary condition for application of Article 82, but it is not necessary for there to be a causal link between the dominant position and the abuse, or for the dominant position to be the means of the abuse. Thus, a dominant firm can abuse its dominant position without using the market power which the dominant position confers, but by ordinary commercial practices also engaged in by non-dominant firms.[293] While some kinds of conduct, such as excessive pricing, are easier to practice for a firm in a dominant position, others may be not only perfectly compatible with but indeed a normal expression of competition, such as undercutting a competitor's prices in order to win custom-

288. *Continental Can*, ECJ Feb. 21, 1973, 1973 ECR 215, paras 25–26. *Cf.* Article 2 (2) of the merger control Regulation 139/2004: significantly impede effective competition, *in particular* as a result of the creation or strengthening of a dominant position.
289. *Deutsche Bahn*, CFI Oct. 21, 1997, 1997 ECR II-1689, para. 79, *aff'd* ECJ April 27, 1999, 1999 ECR I-2387. *See Ahmed Saaed*, ECJ April 11, 1989, 1989 ECR 803, paras 34–37.
290. *Hoffmann-La Roche*, ECJ Feb. 13, 1979, 1979 ECR 461, para. 116.
291. *BPB*, ECJ April 6, 1995, 1995 ECR I-865, para. 11; *CEWAL*, ECJ March 16, 2000, 2000 ECR I-1365, para. 130; *TACA II*, D.Comm. Sept. 16, 1998, 1999 OJ L 95/1, points 585–587.
292. *Tetra Pak I*, CFI July 10, 1990, 1990 ECR II-309, para. 21; *TACA II*, D.Comm. Sept. 16, 1998, 1999 OJ L 95/1, point 550.
293. *Continental Can*, ECJ Feb. 21, 1973, 1973 ECR 215, para. 27; *Hoffmann-La Roche*, ECJ Feb. 13, 1979, 1979 ECR 461, paras 91 and 120; *ECS/Akzo II*, D.Comm. Dec. 14, 1985, 1985 OJ L 374/1, points 73–74; *aff'd* ECJ July 3, 1991, 1991 ECR I-3359.

ers from it and gain market share.[294] However, such conduct may become abusive if engaged in by a dominant enterprise with the effect of appreciably restricting or distorting competition in the marketplace. This is not to be seen as penalizing the dominant firm for the superior quality of its products which may have contributed to its achieving dominance, but merely reflects the special responsibility incumbent on it not to reduce competition on the market even further from the reduced level remaining, as a result of its position of dominance.[295] Just as the means used need not involve the exercise of market power, the market on which the abusive conduct takes place need not be the same as that on which the dominant position is held.[296] The alleged abusive conduct is normally found on the dominated market but may also be found on other than the dominated market, i.e. distinct, but closely associated markets, likely to strengthen the position on the dominated market,[297] such as in cases of abusive tying practices where a firm uses its dominant position in one market as a 'leverage' on a distinct, but closely associated market.[298]

No Need for Intent or Practical Action.

As abuse is a question of fact, an 'objective' concept; it is not normally necessary to prove any intent or 'fault'[299] nor any direct effect.[300] It is not necessary that the

294. *British Plasterboard*, CFI April 1, 1993, 1993 ECR II-389, paras 106, 117, *aff'd* ECJ April 6, 1995, 1995 ECR I-865; *CEWAL*, CFI Oct. 8, 1996, 1996 ECR II-1201, para. 146; *Van den Bergh Foods*, D.Comm. March 11, 1998, 1998 OJ L 246/1, point 267, *aff'd* CFI Oct. 23, 2003, T-65/98, paras 157–158.
295. *Michelin*, ECJ Nov. 9, 1983, 1983 ECR 3461, 3511, para. 57; *Tetra Pak I*, CFI July 10, 1990, 1990 ECR II-309, para. 37; *Tetra Pak II*, CFI Oct. 6, 1996, 1996 ECR II-755, para. 114; *CEWAL*, CFI Oct. 8, 1996, 1996 ECR II-1201, para. 106. *See also ECS/Akzo II*, D.Comm. Dec. 14, 1985, 1985 OJ L 374/1, 21, *aff'd* ECJ July 3, 1991, 1991 ECR I-3359.
296. *Commercial Solvents*, ECJ March 6, 1974, 1974 ECR 223, para. 21; *ECS/Akzo II*, ECJ July 3, 1991, 1991 ECR I-3359, para. 37; *Tetra Pak*, ECJ Oct. 6, 1996, 1996 ECR I-755, para. 25; *Aéroports de Paris*, CFI Dec. 12, 2000, 2000 ECR II-3929, para. 164.
297. *Tetra Pak II*, CFI Nov. 14, 1996, 1996 ECR II-5951, paras 23–28; *Irish Sugar*, CFI Oct. 7, 1999, 1999 ECR II-2969, paras 166–167; *Aéroport de Paris*, CFI Dec. 12, 2000, 2000 ECR II-3929, para. 164, *aff'd* ECJ Oct. 24, 2002, 2002 ECR I-9297. Other examples of abuses having effects on markets other than the dominated markets include *Commercial Solvents*, *Hoffmann-LaRoche*, ECJ March 6, 1974, 1974 ECR 223, and *Télémarketing (CBEM)*, ECJ Oct. 3, 1985, 1985 ECR 3261.
298. Commission Guidelines on market analysis and the assessment of significant market power for electronic communications networks and services, 2002 OJ C 165/6, point 84. *See infra* Section D.6.(e).
299. *Hoffmann-La Roche*, ECJ Feb. 13, 1979, 1979 ECR 461, para. 91; *British Plaster Board*, CFI April 1, 1993, 1993 ECR II-389, para. 70, *aff'd* ECJ April 6, 1995, 1995 ECR I-865. An exception must be made in the case of conduct such as predatory pricing which may be explainable as normal competitive behavior in the absence of evidence of a deliberate strategy to eliminate the competitor without, however, the need to prove that the dominant firm achieved the intended elimination of its competitor: *CEWAL*, CFI Oct. 8, 1996, 1996 ECR II-1201, para. 149; *ECS/Akzo II*, D.Comm. Dec. 14, 1985, 1985 OJ L 374/1, 21.
300. *Michelin II*, CFI Sept. 30, 2003, T-203/01, para. 258.

dominant firm take practical action to obtain the desired behaviour by other firms. The threat of action may suffice to achieve the anticompetitive effect.[301]

Exceptions.

Unlike Article 81 (3), which allows the Commission to exempt restrictive practices that on balance are pro-competitive, Article 82 does not provide exceptions for conduct found to be an abuse of a dominant position. Thus, for example, it is no defence that a practice, such as tying or fidelity rebates, is of benefit to the dominant firm's customers, at least in the short term, if it harms the firm's competitors to the extent they may be shut out of the market.[302] However, in certain circumstances conduct that would normally be regarded as an abuse of dominance may escape Article 82:

- *Trivial Cases.* A trivial case, in which the abuse lasts only for a short period and is terminated soon after discovery, may not justify fines or even not infringe Article 82 at all, as the Court of Justice held in the General Motors case.[303] However, unlike under Article 81, there is no general threshold of appreciability, in terms of the size of the firm or firms concerned, below which Article 82 is considered not to apply.[304]
- *Exceptional Trading Conditions.* During periods of exceptional trading conditions, conduct that would ordinarily be regarded as an abuse of dominance may not be so, especially if the national government or EC authorities have failed to take measures to deal with the situation. In the BP case, an above-average cut in supplies of oil products to a customer at the height of the first oil crisis when no guidance on the allocation of supplies had been forthcoming from the EC or national authorities was judged not to infringe Article 82.[305]
- *Article 86 (2)*: Under Article 86 (2), firms performing public service obligations or operating a 'revenue-producing monopoly' may not be infringing Article 82 when they engage in conduct that would normally be an abuse of a dominant position, if the application of Article 82 would obstruct the performance of the special tasks assigned to them and the development of trade is not affected

301. *IMI/Heilmann*, Commission Press Release No. IP/78/111 (the account in the Seventh Report on Competition Policy, points 31–32, did not deal with this aspect); *Payne/Molins*, Commission Press Release No. IP/87/415.
302. *Hoffmann-La Roche*, ECJ Feb. 13, 1979, 1979 ECR 461, paras 120–121.
303. *General Motors*, ECJ Nov. 13, 1975, 1975 ECR 1367, paras 15–24. *But see British Leyland*, ECJ Nov. 11, 1986, 1986 ECR 3263, paras 11–34.
304. The Commission's *De Minimis* Notice and the Guidelines on the effect on trade do not establish quantitative criteria for abusive practices likely to come within Article 82, *see supra* Chapter I.E.2 and Chapter II.B.7. However, any infringement of Article 82 presupposes dominance and hence large market shares.
305. BP, ECJ June 29, 1978, 1978 ECR 1513, paras 29–34. *See also Almelo*, ECJ April 27, 1994, 1994 ECR I-1477, para. 46 (referring to *Corbeau*, ECJ May 19, 1993, 1993 ECR I-2533, para. 14).

to an extent contrary to the Community interest. Article 86 (2) may apply to certain activities of public utilities.[306]

On the other hand, the existence of an abuse cannot be justified by the fact that it is the result of a restrictive agreement, which is formally covered by a block exemption regulation; the application of a block exemption regulation is without prejudice to the application of Article 82.[307]

The following more detailed discussion of the various kinds of abuse will first deal with the four examples given in Article 82 (a)-(d), which are mainly of the exploitative type, and then with exclusionary practices and discrimination on grounds of nationality which are not explicitly referred to in Article 82. The abuse of a dominant position by merger with a competitor ('structural abuse') is addressed in Chapter VI, which deals with the application of Articles 81 and 82 and the merger control regulation to mergers and joint ventures.

2. Imposition of Unfair Purchase or Selling Prices or Conditions (Article 82 (a))

The Different Forms.

A firm abuses its dominant position if it charges its customers unfairly high prices or extorts unfairly low prices from its suppliers, or if it imposes other unfair terms or conditions on its customers or suppliers. This is a typical form of exploitative abuse. It is to be distinguished from the exclusionary abuse of predatory pricing, i.e., price-cutting to injure or remove a competitor, which is discussed together with other exclusionary practices in section 6 below. However, the Court of Justice also considers predatory pricing as a form of unfair pricing falling within Article 82 (a).[308] Hence, the application of unfair prices may in some cases constitute both an exploitative and a predatory abuse.[309]

(a) Unfairly High Prices Charged by a Dominant Seller

Definition, Proof of Overpricing.

A firm that holds a dominant position may have sufficient market power to charge its customers unfairly high prices. Often the overpricing may be selective, i.e.,

---

306. *Corbeau*, ECJ May 19, 1993, 1993 ECR I-2533, para. 21; *Almelo*, ECJ April 27, 1994, 1994 ECR I-1477, para. 46; *FFSA*, CFI Feb. 27, 1997, 1997 ECR II-229, para. 175. Article 86 (2) has been held to be potentially applicable to, for example, the operation of telecommunications networks and loss-making air services. *See infra* Chapter VIII.

307. *Tetra Pak I*, CFI July 10, 1990, 1990 ECR II-309, para. 30.

308. *Ahmed Saeed*, ECJ April 11, 1989, 1989 ECR 803, para. 42. *Cf.* generally the protection given by the law to private consumers against unfair terms in contracts, draft EC directive to harmonize member states' law on unfair terms in consumer contracts, 1990 OJ C 243/2.

309. E.g. *DSD ('Green Dot')*, D.Comm. April 20, 2001, 2001 OJ L 166/1, points 111 and 114.

it may involve price discrimination between different customers or geographic markets. Multinational companies that practice discriminatory pricing to different national markets are particularly susceptible to the charge of excessive pricing.[310] Overpricing has been defined by the Court of Justice as charging a price which is excessive (unfair or disproportionate) because it has no reasonable relation to the economic value of the product or service supplied[311] or, in other terms, which fails to comply with the principle of proportionality.[312] The Commission ruled in the *Deutsche Post* case[313] that a dominant firm may not impose a price that exceeds the average economic value of a service (exploiting customers). The Court has also said that the onus of proof of overpricing rests on the Commission or other persons alleging it.[314] To prove overpricing conclusively requires a comparison of the selling price of the product in question with its costs of production.[315] However, costs can be extraordinarily difficult to determine, especially for multi-product (e.g., pharmaceutical) firms where fixed costs such as capital investment, R&D and administrative and selling costs have to be allocated between many products, and for firms that may use differing methodology for charging costs associated with major investments or infrastructure, such as for access to a telecommunication or energy network.[316] In the case of multinational firms the picture may be complicated by discriminatory intra-company transfer prices which do not always

310. *See infra* section D.4. *See also United Brands*, ECJ Feb. 14, 1978, 1978 ECR 207, paras 120–122 and 235–240; *Tetra Pak II*, CFI Oct. 6, 1994, 1994 ECR II-755, para. 160; Fifth Report on Competition Policy, point 9.3 (oil prices).
311. *TNT*, ECJ May 17, 2001, 2001 ECR I-4109, para. 46; *United Brands*, ECJ Feb. 14, 1978, 1978 ECR 207, para. 250; *General Motors*, ECJ Nov. 13, 1975, 1975 ECR 1367, para. 12. *Cf. also* under Article 81: *Coditel II*, ECJ Oct. 6, 1982, 1982 ECR 3381, para. 19; *Deutsche Bahn*, CFI Oct. 21, 1997, 1997 ECR II-1689, paras 70–86. The Court of Justice did not address the impact of distribution costs and different marketing conditions, which also were not discussed in the Commission decision.
312. *United Brands*, ECJ Feb. 14, 1978, 1978 ECR 207, para. 190. *See DSD ('Green Dot')*, D.Comm. April 20, 2001, 2001 OJ L 166/1, point 112.
313. *Deutsche Post*, D.Comm. July 25, 2001, 2001 OJ L 331/40, points 155–167. The 25% limit corresponds to the conclusions of the Commission in the *United Brands* case, D.Comm. Dec. 17, 1975, 1976 OJ L 95/1, 15–16 (when assessing price discrimination).
314. *United Brands*, ECJ Feb. 14, 1978, 1978 ECR 207, para. 264.
315. In the *United Brands* case the Court considered the Commission's investigation of the cost structure as insufficient: ECJ Feb. 14, 1978, 1978 ECR 207, paras 251–257. The *ITT/Belgacom* case was settled by replacing a price exceeding unfairly the costs by a 'cost + price', i.e. a price comprising the costs and a reasonable profit margin: IP/97/292 of 11 April 1997. *See also Belgacom/ITT Promedia*, Twenty-seventh Report on Competition Policy, point 67, *aff'd* CFI July 17, 1998, 1998 ECR II-2937, and *Deutsche Telekom*, Twenty-seventh Report on Competition Policy, points 76–78.
316. However, cost allocation may, in the future, be facilitated by the cost accounting requirement set out in the Community directives: *see* Article 7 of Directive 97/33/EC on telecommunications open network provision (ONP), 1997 OJ L 199/32, and Articles 13–15 of Directive 96/92/EC on the internal market in electricity, 1996 OJ L 27/20.

reflect costs[317] or by internal cross-subsidization.[318] In the absence of complete cost data, evidence of overpricing may be provided by the very marked price differences for the same or similar products in different geographic markets, provided that these markets are objectively comparable and are not significantly affected by regulatory measures; such marked differences must be regarded as indicative of an abuse with the consequence of shifting of the burden of proof to the alleged dominant firm.[319]

The *United Brands* ('Chiquita' Bananas) Case – The Cost Approach.
In the *United Brands* case,[320] the Commission accused United Brands of selling 'Chiquita' bananas at unfairly high prices to its German, Danish, Dutch, Belgian and Luxembourg customers, which it alleged were sometimes double the prices charged to comparable customers in Ireland. In addition it claimed that 'Chiquita' brand bananas were sold at prices 20 to 40% higher than unbranded bananas of similar quality. The Commission therefore found that United Brands had abused its dominant position in violation of Article 82 and ordered it to reduce its prices except in Ireland, recommending a cut to at least 15% below the prices then charged in Germany and Denmark. On appeal, the Court of Justice found that the Commission had failed to prove its case. Conclusive proof of overpricing could be furnished by comparing the selling price of the product and its production costs. But the Commission had failed to analyse United Brands' cost structure, although the difficulties of doing so with an agricultural commodity like bananas were not insuperable. Instead, it had based its allegations on a comparison of the high prices charged on the Continent with those charged in Ireland, which accounted for only 1.6% of its European imports and had made losses. Further, United Brands produced evidence that banana prices had not risen in real terms

317. Fifth Report on Competition Policy, point 9.3 (oil prices).
318. *See infra* Section D.6.(b).
319. *United Brands*, ECJ Feb. 14, 1978, 1978 ECR 207, paras 258–267; *SACEM II*, ECJ July 13, 1989, 1989 ECR 2521, paras 38 and 46. *See also Parke Davis*, ECJ Feb. 29, 1968, 1968 ECR 55, 72–73 (higher sale price for patented product as compared to imported non-patented product does not necessarily constitute an abuse); *Sirena*, ECJ Feb. 18, 1971, 1971 ECR 69, para. 17 (a particularly high price charged for a branded product as compared with the same product imported from another member state may, if unjustified by any objective criteria, indicate an abuse); *Deutsche Grammophon*, ECJ June 8, 1971, 1971 ECR 487, para. 19 (difference between price controlled by manufacturer and price of the same product re-imported from another member state may be evidence of an abuse if it is large and not explained on any objective grounds); *Funeral Services*, ECJ May 4, 1988, 1988 ECR 2479, para. 31 (comparison of prices of firms holding concessions and prices charged elsewhere); and esp. *SACEM II*, ECJ July 13, 1989, 1989 ECR 2811, paras 24–25 (discussed *below* – reversal of burden of proof where price differences are extremely marked).
320. *United Brands*, ECJ Feb.14, 1978, 1978 ECR 207, paras 235–268. *Cf. United Brands*, D.Comm. Dec. 17, 1975, 1976 OJ L 95/1, 15–16. *See also Ahmed Saeed*, ECJ April 11, 1989, 1989 ECR 803, para. 43.

for nearly 20 years, and that the price difference between 'Chiquita' bananas and those of its principal competitors was in fact only 'about 7 per cent, a percentage which has not been challenged and which cannot automatically be regarded as excessive and consequently unfair.'[321] Accordingly, the Court annulled the part of the Commission's decision relating to unfair pricing while upholding its other findings of abuse of United Brands' dominant position by restrictions on resale, refusal to supply and price discrimination. However, the Court did not dispute that substantial price differences between member states could indicate overpricing.

The *SACEM II* and *SACEM III* Cases – The Market Comparison Approach. The market comparaison approach was confirmed by the Court in two cases concerning alleged overcharging of discotheques by the French performing rights society SACEM.[322] Discotheques in France were charged a flat-rate royalty of 8.25% of their turnover for the right to play French and foreign records from SACEM's repertoire. Because of reciprocal agreements between SACEM and other national performing rights societies, discotheques could not obtain rights for the mainly American and British records they played directly from the foreign societies concerned. Also, SACEM would not license the American and British part of its repertoire to them separately, but insisted on their taking the full repertoire. The Court left it to the national courts to decide on the facts whether the reciprocal agreements between SACEM and the other national societies amounted to a concerted practice[323] and whether the refusal to license part of the repertoire separately was an abuse of SACEM's dominant position.[324] On the question of the alleged overcharging, however, it ruled that significant differences in the levels of royalties charged to discotheques in different member states were *prima facie* evidence of an abuse of dominant position.[325] The Commission had established, by a comprehensive survey that took into account the different ways royalties were calculated and differences in legislation,[326] that the royalties charged to French discotheques were indeed several times higher than in other EC countries. In these circumstances, the Court held that the onus was on the society charging the higher prices to prove that it was not abusing its position. It suspected, however, that

321. *United Brands*, ECJ Feb. 14, 1978, 1978 ECR 207, para. 266. The same applies to comparisons with product markets, e.g., unbranded bananas.

322. *SACEM II*, ECJ July 13, 1989, 1989 ECR 2811; *SACEM III*, ECJ July 13, 1989, 1989 ECR 2521.

323. *SACEM II*, ECJ July 13, 1989, 1989 ECR 2811, paras 10–20; *SACEM III*, ECJ July 13, 1989, 1989 ECR 2521, paras 16–26.

324. *SACEM III*, ECJ July 13, 1989, 1989 ECR 2521, paras 27–33.

325. *SACEM II*, ECJ July 13, 1989, 1989 ECR 2811, paras 24–25; *SACEM III*, ECJ July 13, 1989, 1989 ECR 2521, paras 37–38.

326. Including the fact that an additional royalty was chargeable that did not exist in most other member states (at issue in *SACEM I*, ECJ 9, April 1987, 1987 ECR 1747, and *SACEM IV*, ECJ Dec. 12, 1990, 1990 ECR I-4607).

the higher prices were due to excessive administrative costs which SACEM's dominant position allowed it to pass on to its captive customers.[327]

Other Overpricing Abuses Based on Exclusive Rights.
The *SACEM* cases are typical of many others in which it has been established that the charging of exorbitant prices on the basis of exclusive rights, particularly intellectual property rights or monopolies granted by government, can constitute an abuse of dominant position under Article 82.

- The *ITT Promedia/Belgacom* case[328] concerned the alleged excessive prices charged by the Belgian telecommunications operator for access to subscriber data for the publication of telephone directories. The Commission, on the basis of the expertise of an auditing firm, insisted on fully implementing the cost-oriented principle. The case was settled after a substantial reduction (by more than 90%) of the prices by dropping any variable component in relation to the turnover or profit of directory publishers.
- The *Deutsche Telekom I* case[329] concerned DT's excessive fees for the provision of carrier-preselection and number portability. The Commission proceeded to a comparative market analysis which led DT to reduce substantially (by almost 50%) the fees concerned.
- Other examples include the overpricing of products protected by copyright (car spare parts, records) or trademarks (cosmetics)[330] and overcharging for services (funeral services, leasing of telecommunications equipment) provided under a local monopoly.[331]

In a number of cases the overpricing has been aimed at preventing market entry by potential competitors, and thus falls into the exclusionary rather than the exploitative category.[332] Instances have included overcharging for leased telephone

327. *SACEM II*, ECJ July 13, 1989, 1989 ECR 2811, para. 25; *SACEM III*, ECJ July 13, 1989, 1989 ECR 2521, para. 38. With respect to unfair air fares: *see* Article 5 (2) of Regulation 868/2004, 2004 OJ L 162/1.

328. *ITT Promedia/Belgacom*, IP/97/292; Twenty-seventh Report on Competition Policy, pp. 152–153 (rejection of a complaint), *aff'd* CFI July 17, 1998, 1998 ECR II-2937, paras 68–76.

329. *Deutsche Telekom*, IP/98/430; M. Haag and R. Klotz, 'Commission Practice concerning excessive pricing in telecommunications, ' DG IV Newsletter 1998–2, pp. 35, 37.

330. *Renault*, ECJ Oct. 5, 1988, 1988 ECR 6039, paras 16–17; *Volvo/Veng*, ECJ Oct. 5, 1988, 1988 ECR 6211, para. 9; *Deutsche Grammophon*, ECJ June 8, 1971, 1971 ECR 487, paras 14–19; *Sirena*, ECJ Feb. 18, 1971, 1971 ECR 69, paras 14–17.

331. *Funeral Services*, ECJ May 5, 1988, 1988 ECR 2479, paras 30–34; *Alsatel/Novasam*, ECJ Oct. 5, 1988, 1988 ECR 5987, 6008, paras 9–10 (but no infringement of Article 82 found because there was no dominant position in a substantial part of the Common Market).

332. E.g., *Corporate Network Services Providers/Deutsche Telekom*, IP/96/975; K. van Miert, 'Issues arising in connection with the opening up to competition of markets with network structures', WuW 1998–1, 7 (application, by DT, of tariffs more than 100% higher than those applied on comparable competitive markets leading to an abusive price-cost squeeze on competitors).

lines and motor vehicle type approval certificates and demanding prohibitively high royalties for patent licences.[333]

Price and Margin Squeezing.
Applying higher prices (or lower rebates) to customers with which the supplier competes (e.g. wholesalers or reprocessors) whereas other customers are supplied at lower prices (or higher rebates) constitutes a clear case of abusive (predatory) pricing.[334] In the *Deutsche Telekom II* case[335] the Commission fined the German dominant provider of local loop access on the wholesale and retail level for having applied higher prices for wholesale access to new entrants than it charges its own subscribers for access at the retail level. Both markets are closely linked to each other. In the absence of any sufficiently developed alternative network this constitutes an abusive form of margin squeeze because the price difference is insufficient to cover the specific costs for the supply of the end-users services and therefore leaves new entrants no margin to compete for downstream retail subscribers.

Commission not a Price Control Agency.
The Commission has stated that in controlling price abuses it is not attempting to play the role of a price control agency or to interfere in internal pricing policies of enterprises. Its aims are to prevent dominant firms from exploiting their market power against consumers or other firms and to create open EC-wide markets and increase opportunities of market entry.[336] This underlines the difficulty of establishing the 'right' or 'fair' price. The better methodology is maintaining or restoring a competitive market structure which prevents the application of prices which are not 'market prices'.

(b) Imposition of Unfairly Low Prices by a Dominant Purchaser: Abuse of Buying Power

The CICCE Case.
The Court of Justice confirmed in the *CICCE* case[337] that a dominant purchaser (in the extreme case of only one buyer in a market, a monopsonist) or a group of

---

333. *British Telecommunications*, D.Comm. Dec. 10, 1982, 1982 OJ L 360/36, 37; *British Telecommunications*, ECJ March 20, 1985, 1985 ECR 873, paras 24–27; *General Motors*, ECJ Nov. 13, 1975, 1975 ECR 1367, paras 11–12; *British Leyland*, ECJ Nov. 11, 1986, 1986 ECR 3263, paras 25–33; *Hilti*, D.Comm. Dec. 22, 1987, 1988 OJ L 65/19, 36–37, *aff'd* ECJ March 2, 1994, 1994 ECR I-667.
334. *Commercial Solvents*, ECJ March 14, 1974, 1974 ECR 223, para. 25; *British Sugar*, D.Comm. July 18, 1988, 1988 OJ L 284/41, point 66.
335. *Deutsche Telekom II*, D.Comm. May 21, 2003, IP/03/717.
336. Fifth Report on Competition Policy, points 3–7 and 76.
337. *CICCE*, ECJ March 28, 1985, 1985 ECR 1105. *See also* Sixteenth Report on Competition Policy, points 346–348 (buying power of large retailers).

dominant purchasers could abuse their position by extracting unfairly low prices from their suppliers. In this case, the European film industry trade association *CICCE* had complained to the Commission that the fees three French television stations paid distributors for the rights to broadcast movies were unreasonably low. The Commission determined that there was insufficient evidence that the television companies were abusing their undisputed buying power as the only potential purchasers of broadcasting rights for French television. To establish whether or not the prices the companies offered were unfair required an analysis of the relationship between the price and the economic value of the broadcasting rights. The value depended on many factors and was different for each individual movie, as the varying licence fees for different movies showed. In the absence of detailed information about these various factors for individual films, the Commission found the allegations of abuse unproven, and its decision was upheld by the Court. Evidence of average higher film licence fees paid by television companies in some other member states was not regarded as conclusive.[338]

(c) Applying Unfairly Low Prices through Cross-Subsidization

Artificial Cost-Allocation.
Cross-subsidization means, according to the Commission's definition in its Notice on the Application of the Competition Rules in the Postal Sector:[339]

> '… that an undertaking bears or allocates all or part of the costs of its activity in one geographic or product market to its activity in another geographic or product market. Under certain circumstances, cross-subsidization … can distort competition and lead to competitors being beaten by offers which are made possible not by effciency (including economies of scope) and performance but by cross-subsidies.'

Applying cross-subsidized prices may therefore constitute a predeatory abuse.[340] However, a certain cost-allocation system[341] or cross-subsidization may be justified in order to allow the dominant firm to offset its losses in one sector of activity by profits in another and thereby fulfill a task of general economic interest assigned to it (Article 86 (2)).[342]

338. *CICCE*, ECJ March 28, 1985, 1985 ECR 1105, paras 22–25.
339. 1998 OJ C 39/2, point 3.1.
340. *See infra* Section D.6.(a)–(b).
341. Commission recommendation on accounting liberalization in a liberalized telecommunications market, 1998 OJ L 141/6, point 3.
342. *Corbeau*, ECJ May 19, 1993, 1993 ECR I-2533, paras 15–21; *IECC*, CFI Sept. 16, 1998, 1998 ECR II-3645, paras 94–106; *UPS/Deutsche Post*, March 20, 2002, 2002 ECR II-1915, paras 51 and 61.

(d) Imposition of Other Unfair Trading Conditions

Dominant Sellers.
A dominant firm may be in a position to impose unfair terms and conditions of sale on its customers that they would not accept if there were effective competition. For instance, it is an abuse for copyright collecting societies to demand royalties from record manufacturers also for works whose copyright has expired.[343] Other common examples are export prohibitions and restrictions on use contained in dominant firms' terms of sale. These also infringe Article 82 (b) (abuse of a dominant position to limit markets) and are dealt with below.[344]

Dominant Purchasers.
Dominant purchasers may dictate unfair terms and conditions of sale to sellers, such as when a copyright collecting society requires members to assign the copyright in their works to it for an unreasonably long period and to assign the rights in future works as well.[345] Another example was when national railroad administrations that had established a company for the joint purchase of rolling stock required the successful bidder for a contract for developing and supplying a new type of passenger carriage to assign to them all the patents and other proprietary rights arising out of the development work, although the value of such rights could not be estimated in advance.[346]

3. Limiting Production, Markets or Technical Development to the Prejudice of Consumers (Article 82 (b))

Introduction.
A dominant firm that limits production, markets or technical development to the prejudice of consumers may infringe Article 82 (b). These forms of abuse require that consumers be directly or indirectly prejudiced. Proof is difficult, particularly in cases where the conduct can also be explained by commercial or technical reasons.

---

343. *GEMA I*, D.Comm. June 2, 1971, 1971 OJ L134/15, 25. *See also TACA II*, D.Comm. Sept. 16, 1998, 1999 OJL 95/1, point 551 (restrictions on the content of service contracts concluded by the members of an oligopoly).
344. *Infra* section D.3.(b).
345. *GEMA I*, D.Comm. June 2, 1971, 1971 OJ L134/15, 24; *BRT/SABAM II*, ECJ March 27, 1974, 1974 ECR 313, paras 6–12; *SACEM/SABAM*, Fourth Report on Competition Policy, points 112–113.
346. *Eurofima*, Third Report on Competition Policy, point 68; Commission's Telecommunication Guidelines, 1991 OJ C 233/2, points 116–120.

(a) Limitation of Production

Scarce Case Law.
There is as yet little case law on abuse of a dominant position by restricting output. However, both restrictions of output by the dominant firm itself and restrictions imposed by it on third parties have been identified by the Court and the Commission as possible abuses.

- *Restriction of the Dominant Firm's Output.* A reduction or complete halting of output of a product in order to raise its price or to increase sales of another product may infringe Article 82. An example is the discontinuance of production of spare parts for a car model that is no longer in production.[347] However, a dominant firm is not committed to adapt its production to satisfy specific customers' needs.[348]
- *Restriction of Third Parties' Output.* Restricting the output of third parties, such as licensees or suppliers, through contract terms that limit them to producing for an overly narrow field of use or territory or in unduly small quantities may also constitute an abuse.[349] Such restrictions may serve exploitative purposes, as when the dominant firm restricts its own output, or exclusionary ones. Examples of mainly exclusionary abuses of this type are changes in the specifications of equipment – such as navigation systems – so that competing manufacturers' receivers cannot be used with them,[350] and exploiting a monopoly for supplying telecommunications terminals to restrict the range supplied and hence the output of excluded manufacturers.[351] However, a cigarette manufacturer holding a dominant position as a purchaser of cigarette filters does not necessarily abuse its position by increasing its own production of filters (to the disadvantage of third filter producers) since a company's production of its own requirements is not in itself an abnormal act of competition and is based on economic grounds to achieve economies of scale and to reduce its production costs.[352]

---

347. *Renault*, ECJ Oct. 5, 1988, 1988 ECR 6039, paras 16–17; *Volvo/Veng*, ECJ Oct. 5, 1988 ECR 6211, para. 9. *See also P&I Clubs*, D.Comm. April 12, 1999, 1999 OJ L 125/12, points 128–131 (limitation of products offered on the market).
348. *Industrie des Poudres Sphériques*, CFI Nov. 30, 2000, 2000 ECR II-3755, para. 77.
349. In the *IGR Stereo Television* case the Commission objected to an agreement between Community television manufacturers who jointly held the patents for stereo TV only to grant licences to competitors from non-EC countries with a time lag and subject to a restriction on their output: Eleventh Report on Competition Policy, point 94.
350. *Racal Decca*, D.Comm. 21, Dec. 1988, 1989 OJ L 43/27, 43. A similar case was *IBM* where IBM refused to give interface information in advance of product launches in order to delay the appearance of IBM-compatible equipment: Fourteenth Report on Competition Policy, points 94–95.
351. *Telecommunications Directive (Terminal Equipment)*, para. 13 of preamble.
352. *Filtrona/Tabacalera*, Nineteenth Report on Competition Policy, point 61.

(b) Limitation of Markets

Through Horizontal Agreements between Competitors.
Competing manufacturers of identical or substitutable goods may infringe Article 81 and are not covered by Regulation 2790/2000 (Article 2 (4)) if they enter into exclusive distribution agreements unless one of them has *de minimis* turnover of no more than EUR 100 million. It seems obvious that a dominant manufacturer who obtains exclusive distribution rights or the exclusive licence of a smaller competitor or a competitor having an important position on other markets that is also trying to enter the market served by the dominant firm[353] infringes Article 82 because of the inherent tendency of the dominant firm to give priority to the sale of its own products, thereby creating a conflict of interest that is prone to restrain vigorous competition from the smaller competitors' offerings.[354]

Through Vertical Contract Terms.
Contractual restrictions on the geographic markets or customers to which a firm may sell or the suppliers from which it may buy ordinarily infringe Article 81 unless exempted under Article 81 (3). If such restrictive agreements infringe Article 81 when made by non-dominant firms, it is clear that they constitute a serious infringement of Article 82 when they are, or may be, imposed by a dominant firm.[355] Hence, a dominant firm may not impose the following restrictive contract terms on its customers:

- restrictions on export to other member states,[356]
- contractual obligations equivalent to export restrictions, such as a prohibition on selling green bananas[357] or unroasted coffee,[358]

353. *Carlsberg/Interbrew*, Twenty-fourth Report on Competition Policy, p. 35 1; *Swedish Match Sverige/Skandinavisk Tobakskompagni*, Twenty-seventh Report on Competition Policy, point 66 (parallel proceedings under Articles 81 and 82 halted after amendment of the exclusive licence agreement concluded between the Swedish monopolist and the Danish competitor for the manufacture and distribution of the Prince brand of cigarette, whereby the exclusivity is abandoned and most of the marketing of the Prince brand is now placed under the supervision of the Danish company).

354. *Telecommunication Directive Terminal Equipment*, ECJ March 19, 1991, 1991 ECR I-1223, paras 40–43 and 48–52; *Greek Television*, ECJ June 23, 1991, 1991 ECR I-2925, paras 22–23; *RTT/GB-INNO*, ECJ Dec. 13, 1991, 1991 ECR I-5941, para. 25; *Decoster*, ECJ Oct. 27, 1993, 1993 ECR I-5335, para. 18.

355. *Deutsche Bahn*, CFI Oct. 21, 1997, 1997 ECR II-1689, para. 79; *TACA II*, D.Comm. Sept. 16, 1998, 1999 OJ L 95/1, points 551–558 (restrictions on the availability and content of service contracts concluded by the members of an oligopoly).

356. *United Brands*, ECJ Feb. 14, 1978, 1978 ECR 207, 288, para. 154.

357. *Ibid.*, para. 159.

358. *Brazilian Coffee I and II*, Fifth Report on Competition Policy, point 33; Sixteenth Report on Competition Policy, point 54. Similarly under Article 81: *Cafeteros de Colombia*, D.Comm. Dec. 10, 1982, 1982 OJ L 360/31, 34.

- restrictions on the uses for which a product may be resold, e.g., sugar for direct human consumption, confectionery or denaturing an intermediate metal product for processing,[359] or 'leveraging' or tying services over which a telecommunications organization does not have a regulated monopoly (i.e. long-distance service) with the provision of the regulated services over which it holds a monopoly (i.e. local services),[360]
- restrictions on markets or customers in a selective distribution system although such restrictions are not necessary for a proper distribution of the products,[361]
- customer restrictions in licence agreements,[362]
- exclusive purchasing obligations,[363]
- fidelity rebate schemes which may have effects similar to an exclusive purchase obligation,[364] and
- an arrangement between the former Italian state monopoly and importers of tobacco products to resell the imported product through the state monopoly's outlets, thereby eliminating any competition between national and imported products (tantamount to an import monopoly).[365]

By Unilateral Action – Refusal to supply.
Unilateral action by a dominant firm to restrict the markets or customers supplied by distributors or to cut off supplies to certain purchasers may also infringe Article 82.

Unlike refusal of access to a technology, network or facility which aims at eliminating competitors of the dominant firm in the dominated market (which will be discussed under 6.(e) below), a refusal of supply usually impacts a secondary market on which the dominant firm competes with the customer which it has refused to supply. A refusal of supply can take many forms: an outright refusal, a refusal otherwise than on the terms which the supplier knows are acceptable ('constructive refusal') or refusal otherwise than on the basis of fair conditions,[366]

---

359. *Sugar*, ECJ Dec. 16, 1975, 1975 ECR 1663, paras 396–401; *Billiton/M&T*, Seventh Report on Competition Policy, point 131.
360. Commission's Telecommunication Guidelines, 1991 OJ C 233/2, points 89, 95–97.
361. *United Brands*, ECJ Feb. 14, 1978, 1978 ECR 207, para. 159; *Salonia*, ECJ June 16, 1981, 1981 ECR 1563, 1581, para. 27. *Cf.* under Article 81 (3): *FEDETAB*, ECJ Oct. 29, 1980, 1980 ECR 3125, paras 183–185. *See*, however, under Articles 28 and 30: *Franzen/Swedish Alcohol Monopoly*, ECJ Oct. 23, 1997, 1997 ECR I-5909, paras 53–57 and 75–76.
362. *Racal Decca*, D.Comm. Dec. 21, 1988, 1989 OJ L 43/27, 42.
363. *British Plasterboard*, CFI April 1, 1993, 1993 ECR II-389, paras 68, 120; *Soda Ash I*, Eleventh Report on Competition Policy, points 73–76; *Industrial Gases*, Nineteenth Report on Competition Policy, point 62. *See also infra* section D.6.
364. *See infra* section D.6.(c).
365. *AAMS*, D.Comm. June 17, 1998, 1998 OJ L 252/47. *See also Irish Sugar*, D.Comm. May 14, 1997, 1997 OJ L 258/1, paras 124–126.
366. *TACA II*, D.Comm. Sept. 16, 1998, 1999 OJ L 95/1, point 553. Commission Notice on the application of the competition rules to the postal sector, 1998 OJ C 39/2, points 2.8. and 2.9.

in particular by making the delivery subject to abusive surcharges,[367] discriminatory prices[368] or lengthy delays.[369]

The *Commercial Solvents* and the *Télémarketing* Cases.
In both cases the Court of Justice confirmed that a dominant firm's refusal to supply a customer with whom it competed in a secondary market was an abuse aimed at eliminating its competitor, thereby strengthening its dominant position in the secondary market. In the *Commercial Solvents* case[370] the Italian subsidiary of a U.S. corporation was found to have abused its dominant position as the sole EC supplier of an essential raw material for the anti-tuberculosis drug, ethambutol, when it stopped supplying the raw material to an Italian drug manufacturer. The raw material supplier had started manufacturing the finished product itself, and so wanted to halt competition from its Italian customer in this market. In the *Télémarketing* case,[371] which concerned the refusal to grant television advertising rights in order to exclude potential competitors, the Court of Justice ruled:

> 'that an abuse within the meaning of Article 82 is committed where, without any objective necessity, an undertaking holding a dominant position on a particular market reserves to itself or to an undertaking belonging to the same group an ancillary activity which might be carried out by another undertaking as part of its activities on a neighbouring but separate market, with the possibility of eliminating all competition from such undertaking.'

Further Examples.
Refusal to supply by a dominant firm was also held abusive in the following cases:

- putting pressure on dealers not to export,[372]
- restricting supplies to quantities sufficient to meet local demand so as to prevent the purchaser from exporting,[373]

---

367. *Volvo/Veng*, ECJ Oct. 5, 1988, 1988 ECR 6211, para. 16; *CICRA/Renault*, ECJ Oct. 5, 1988, 1988 ECR 6039, para. 9; *British Sugar*, D.Comm. July 18, 1988, 1988 OJ L 284/41, 54–55; *Napier Brown/British Sugar*, Sixteenth Report on Competition Policy, point 74.
368. *British Leyland*, ECJ Nov. 11, 1986, 1986 ECR 3263 (conformity certificates for imported cars); *Irish Sugar*, D.Comm. May 14, 1997, 1997 OJ L 258/1, paras 145–150.
369. *Deutsche Post*, D.Comm. July 25, 2001, 2001 OJ L 331/40, points 135–154 and 175; *Belgian Post*, D.Comm. Dec. 5, 2001, 2002 OJ L 61/32, point 55.
370. *Commercial Solvents*, ECJ March 6, 1974, 1974 ECR 223.
371. *Télémarketing*, ECJ Oct. 3, 1985, 1985 ECR 3261, paras 19–27.
372. *Hilti*, D.Comm. Dec. 22, 1987, 1988 OJ L 65/14, 36; *aff'd* CFI Dec. 12, 1991, 1991 ECR II-1439, paras 99–101. *See also Sugar*, ECJ Dec. 16, 1975, 1975 ECR 1663, paras 396–399; *United Brands*, ECJ Feb. 14, 1978, 1978 ECR 207, paras 151–161.
373. *Polaroid/SSI Europe*, Thirteenth Report on Competition Policy, points 155–157. Under Article 81: *Sandoz (Adalat)*, D.Comm. July 13, 1987, 1987 OJ L 222/28, 32; *aff'd* ECJ Jan. 11, 1990, 1990 ECR I-45.

- reducing supplies disproportionately to certain customers during a shortage,[374]
- cutting off supplies to distributors who refuse to comply with the supplier's sales policies or who promote competing brands, in order to deter other distributors from those practices,[375]
- cutting off supplies to a purchaser in order to remove him as a competitor from a market, whether this is the market for the product supplied[376] or a related market,[377]
- refusing to grant a licence to manufacture and market spare parts to independent repairers where the supplier demands unfairly high prices or terminates production for a certain model even though vehicles of that model are still in circulation,[378]
- refusal to continue to supply a dealer because of advertising activities for competing products;[379]
- refusal to supply spare parts for a particular make of cash registers[380] or music instruments[381] in order to remove a competitor from the secondary market;
- refusal to supply spare parts for cars in order to eliminate independent car repairers;[382]
- refusal by the dominant UK sugar producer to supply industrial (i.e., bulk) sugar to a merchant who intended to package it for retail sale in order to prevent the customer from competing with it on the retail market;[383]
- withdrawal of access to a telecommunications network in order to eliminate an existing competitor.[384]

---

374. *BP*, ECJ June 29, 1978, 1978 ECR 1513, paras 18–34. (The Commission's decision was annulled, however, because the distributor had stopped being a regular customer of BP before the oil crisis and therefore did not have to be treated the same as regular customers.)
375. *United Brands*, ECJ Feb. 14, 1978, 1978 ECR 207, paras 163–203.
376. *Boosey & Hawkes*, D.Comm. July 29, 1987, 1987 OJ L 286/36, 40–41 (interim order, case later closed after Boosey & Hawkes had given an undertaking: Eighteenth Report on Competition Policy, point 71); *British Sugar*, D.Comm. July 18, 1998, 1998 OJ L 284/41, points 61–64.
377. *Commercial Solvents*, ECJ March 6, 1974, 1974 ECR 223, paras 23–28; *British Sugar*, D.Comm. July 18, 1998, 1998 OJ L 284/41, points 65–66 (the market for the finished product manufactured with the raw material supplied); *aff'd* CFI July 12, 2001, 23001 ECR II-2035; *Hugin/Liptons*, ECJ May 31, 1979, 1979 ECR 1869, paras 11–13 (the market for servicing cash registers for which supplies of spare parts were required).
378. *Renault*, ECJ Oct. 5, 1988, 1988 ECR 6039, para. 16; *Volvo/Veng*, ECJ Oct. 5, 1988, 1988 ECR 6211, para. 9; *cf. Magill -RTE*, CFI July 10, 1991, 1991 ECR II-485, para. 74.
379. *United Brands*, ECJ Feb. 14, 1978, 1978 ECR 207, paras 189–202.
380. *Hugin/Liptons*, ECJ May 31, 1979, 1979 ECR 1869, paras 11–13.
381. *Boosey & Hawkes*, D.Comm. July 29, 1987, 1987 OJ L 286/36, 41.
382. *Volvo/Veng*, ECJ Oct. 5, 1988, 1988 ECR 6211, para. 9; *CICRA/Renault*, ECJ Oct. 5, 1988, 1988 ECR 6067, para. 18.
383. *British Sugar*, D.Comm. July 18, 1988, 1988 OJ L 284/41, points 65–68. *See also Building Materials*, Commission Press Release No. IP/89/884. Regarding refusal to provide the services of a copyright collecting society to foreign authors and artists, *see infra* section D.7.
384. Commission Notice on Access Agreements in the Telecommunications Sector, 1998 OJ C 265/2, points 99–100.

Legitimate and Illegitimate Reasons for a Refusal to Supply.
Although even a firm in a dominant position is free to determine its marketing policy and to select its customers based on objective criteria such as technical skills,[385] it has to take into account the particular degree of dependence of its customers owing to the fact that they have few alternative suppliers. This may justify a minimum duration of certain distribution agreements.[386] A dominant firm is, however, free to renew or terminate the agreement at the end of its term,[387] and is entitled to review its entire distribution system and to phase out certain customers even without having objective reasons over time, provided that it respects a reasonable notice period.[388] But it may infringe Article 82 if it withdraws supplies suddenly or without notice. Thus, a refusal to supply may constitute an abuse of a dominant position if it is not justified by objective reasons and proportional (in particular unlikely to oblige the customer to cease its business).[389] In any case, a dominant firm may not use its position in a repressive manner in order to enforce its marketing policy[390] or to remove an actual or potential competitor.[391] However, even a dominant firm is entitled to select its distributors on the basis of strictly qualitative criteria,[392] whereas a quantitative selection is only admissible if it is justified on grounds of the protection of public health.[393]

Refusal as a Means of Restricting Existing Customers v. Impeding New Customers.
A refusal by a dominant firm to supply may concern *existing* or *new* customers and may be a means of enforcing its marketing policy and thereby 'limiting markets' in the sense of Article 82 (b). There are three relevant scenarios:[394]

---

385. *United Brands*, ECJ Feb. 14, 1978, 1978 ECR 207, paras 152–160.
386. Article 5 (2) (2) of Regulation 1475/95 on Car Vehicle Distribution and Servicing Agreements (Appendix 19) provides for a minimum duration of the agreement of five years or, if for an indefinite period, for a period of notice of at least two years for both parties (exceptionally one year).
387. A refusal to do so does not necessarily constitute an abuse: *Automec*, D.Comm. Feb. 28, 1990 (not published); *aff'd* CFI Sept. 18, 1992, 1992 ECR II-2223.
388. Article 5 (3) of Regulation 1475/95.
389. *Boosey & Hawkes*, D.Comm. July 29, 1987, 1987 OJ L 286/36, 41.
390. *United Brands*, ECJ Feb. 14, 1978, 1978 ECR 207, paras 183–194.
391. *See Hugin/Liptons*, D.Comm. Dec. 8, 1978, 1978 OJ L 22/23, 31, where the refusal to supply spare parts had the result of removing a major competitor in the matter of service, repair and supply of reconditioned cash registers *(rev'd* ECJ May 31, 1979, 1979 ECR 1869 because the necessary effect on trade between member states was lacking).
392. *Franzen/Swedish Alcohol Monopoly*, ECJ Oct. 23, 1997, 1997 ECR I-5909, paras 43–51.
393. *Franzen/Swedish Alcohol Monopoly*, ECJ Oct. 23, 1997, 1997 ECR I-5909, paras 53–57. Under Article 86: *FFAD*, ECJ May 23, 2000, 2000 ECR I-3743, paras 75–79.
394. *See* Commission's Notice on the Application of the Competition Rules to Access Agreements in the Telecommunication Sector, 1998 OJ C 265/2, point 84.

– A refusal of supply to an *existing* customer will usually be abusive. In *Commercial Solvents* the Court of Justice held that:

> '... an undertaking which has a dominant position on the market in raw materials and which, with the object of reserving such raw material for manufacturing its own derivatives, refuses to supply a customer, which is itself a manufacturer of these derivatives, and therefore risks eliminating all competition on the part of this customer, is abusing its dominant position within the meaning of Article 82.'[395]

A refusal to supply existing customers may also be a sanction for past and/or a means of compelling future behaviour.[396] A sanction for the past behaviour may be justified in case of breach of contract by the distributor if the breach is evident, admitted by the dealer or confirmed by a national court[397] or in case of crisis and scarcity of production obliging a dominant firm to allocate the available quantities amongst the old and traditional customers as opposed to the occasional customers.[398] A refusal in order to compel future behaviour is abusive if it aims at inducing anticompetitive behaviour, such as respecting certain minimum prices (resale price maintenance),[399] certain destinations (resale bans)[400] or a limitation of competitive activities (non-compete clauses).[401]

– A refusal to supply a *new* customer while supplying other customers operating in the same downstream market may constitute a discriminatory abuse if it would restrict competition on that market,[402] unless it is objectively justified, such as by selecting customers according to objective qualitative criteria.[403] In the *BP* case[404] the Court of Justice clarified the limits of the requirement of

395. *Commercial Solvents*, ECJ March 6, 1974, 1974 ECR 223, para. 25.
396. In practice, both cases are difficult to distinguish although compelling future anticompetitive behaviour may be considered as more serious. Often the refusal is aimed at both past and future behaviour.
397. *See* the Commission's practice in cases of selective distribution where the withdrawal of the admission as a selected dealer (leading to or combined with a refusal of supply) is only accepted if the dealer objectively no longer fulfils the selection criteria: *Grundig II*, D.Comm. Dec. 21, 1993, 1994 OJ L 20/15, para. 33.
398. *ABG/BP*, D.Comm. April 19, 1977, 1977 OJ L 1, 9, *rev'd* ECJ June 29, 1978, 1978 ECR 1513, paras 32–43, because the refusal to supply concerned an occasional customer meriting a less favourable treatment during the crisis and who also could obtain supplies from other sources.
399. *British Sugar*, D.Comm. July 18, 1988, 1988 OJ L 284/41, 55.
400. *United Brands*, ECJ Feb. 14, 1978, 1978 ECR 207, paras 152–160; *Polaroid/SSI*, Thirteenth Report on Competition Policy, point 155 (dealer refused to indicate the final destination of the – abnormally large – order of films)
401. *Boosey & Hawkes*, D.Comm. July 29, 1987, 1987 OJ L 286/36, 41; *British Sugar*, D.Comm. July 18, 1988, 1988 OJ L 284/41, points 61–64 (refusal to supply an existing customer with sugar for industrial purposes).
402. *IGR I (Stereo Television)*, Eleventh Report on Competition Policy, point 94; *DISMA*, Twenty-third Report on Competition Policy, point 223.
403. *See* the application of a selective distribution system for personal computers by *IBM*, D.Comm. 18 April 1984, 1984 OJ L 118/24 (negative clearance).
404. *BP*, ECJ June 29, 1978, 1978 ECR 1513.

Article 82 to treat like transactions alike. The Court acquitted BP of abusive discrimination when it discontinued supplies to an occasional customer while continuing limited supplies to regular customers during the 1974–1975 oil crisis. Sales to occasional and regular customers were not equivalent transactions.[405]

- A refusal to supply a customer in order to thwart that customer from penetrating a *new market* may be held abusive under similar conditions as a refusal of access to a facility[406] (i) if access to the product or service is essential for the customer, i.e., if the refusal would block the emergence of a potential new product or service or make the new activities either impossible or seriously and unavoidably uneconomic, (ii) if there is sufficient capacity available to provide access, (iii) if the customer is prepared to pay a reasonable price and to take the necessary technical precautions,[407] and (iv) if there is no objective justification for the refusal to supply.[408] Likewise, a dominant firm's refusal to supply a new potential customer that aims at preventing competition can be a form of exclusionary abuse.[409]

(c) Limitation of Technical Development

Control over Technology not Necessarily Source of Dominant Position. A dominant firm may fall foul of Article 82 by restricting access to or the use or development of a new technology to the detriment of consumers. The dominant position may be based on control over access to the technology, for example through the ownership of intellectual property rights.[410] In other cases the dominant position may result from market power accumulated through longstanding commercial and technological success in a related market or from a government

405. *BP*, ECJ June 29, 1978, 1978 ECR 1513, paras 24–34. However, it is arguable that in other circumstances discriminating against occasional customers could increase a dominant firm's power in the distribution of its products and so constitute an abuse. *See also Lederle-Praxis Biological*, Twenty-fourth Report on Competition Policy, p. 353. With respect to interim measures, however, the Commission stated in *Sea Container/Stena Sealink* (D.Comm. Dec. 21, 1993, 1994 OJ L 15/8, point 67): 'A decision on interim measures may be just as necessary, to ensure that any final decision of the Commission is effective, in a case of a complainant who is a new entrant as it is in the case of an already established competitor.'

406. *See infra* section D.6 (e).

407. *See DISMA*, Twenty-third Report on Competition Policy, points 223–224.

408. Commission's Notice on Access Agreements, 1998 OJ C 265/2, point 91.

409. *British Sugar*, D.Comm. July 18, 1988, 1988 OJ L 284/41, point 63. *See infra* section D.6.

410. However, the ownership or acquisition of intellectual property rights does not in itself establish a dominant position: *Deutsche Grammophon*, ECJ June 8, 1971, 1971 ECR 487, para. 16 (copyrighted products); *Parke Davis*, ECJ Feb. 29, 1968, 1968 ECR 55, 72 (patents); *Sirena*, ECJ Feb. 18, 1971, 1971 ECR 69 (trademarks); *Renault*, ECJ Oct. 5, 1988, 1988 ECR 6039, para. 15 (ornamental models).

monopoly. In each case a careful analysis must be made of the relevant market and, in particular, of substitute products or processes.[411]

Examples of Abuses.

There have been few decisions by the Commission or the Court of Justice on abuse of a dominant position solely through restriction of technical development. However, such a restriction has formed part of the finding of abuse in the following cases:

- The *British Telecommunications* case[412] concerned a ban imposed by the formerly state-owned UK telecommunications monopoly on private message-forwarding agencies relaying telex messages between foreign countries over the British network. The ban clearly operated to the detriment of telex users in those countries, because direct transmission was more expensive, and it restricted the use of a technology against the public interest.[413] The Court of Justice ruled that the application of Article 82 to the case was not limited by the principle of non-interference in member states' systems of property ownership (including nationalized industries and state monopolies) guaranteed by Article 295 (*ex 222*), because the statutory network monopoly did not extend to ancillary services such as the retransmission of messages on behalf of third parties. The practice was therefore not justifiable by the need to preserve the monopoly.[414]
- The *Télémarketing* case[415] concerned a restriction on the advertising agency that 'tele-sales' advertisers could use on a Luxembourg television station. 'Telesales' or 'telemarketing' is an advertising technique whereby the TV viewer can ring a number to obtain further information about the advertised product. The TV station refused to sell advertising time to a private telemarketing agency but restricted such advertising to an agency belonging to the same group as itself. The Court of Justice held that it was an abuse of the TV station's broadcasting monopoly to reserve for itself or a firm belonging to the same group, without any objective necessity, an ancillary activity on a neighbouring but separate market that might be carried out by another firm, if the result might be to eliminate competition from the second firm.[416]

---

411. *IBM*, Fourteenth Report on Competition Policy, points 94–95; *Racal Decca*, D.Comm. Dec. 21, 1988, 1989 OJ L 43/27, 40–41.
412. *British Telecommunications*, ECJ March 20, 1985, 1985 ECR 873.
413. *Ibid.*, para. 26. Similarly, *Telecommunications Directive Terminal Equipment*, 1988 OJ L 131/73, para. 13 of preamble; *Telecommunications Directive Services*, 1990 OJ L 192/10, recital 14.
414. *British Telecommunications*, ECJ March 20, 1985, 1985 ECR 873, paras 21–22. *See also* Telecommunication Guidelines, 1991 OJ C 233/2, points 89–94; *Dutch Express Mail Services*, D.Comm. Dec. 20, 1989, 1990 OJ L 10/47.
415. *Télémarketing*, ECJ Oct. 3, 1985, 1985 ECR 3261.
416. *Télémarketing*, ECJ Oct. 3, 1985, 1985 ECR 3261, paras 19–27. *See also IECC (Express Post)*, CFI Sept. 16, 1998, 1998 ECR II-3605.

- In the *IBM* case,[417] the Commission found that IBM had abused its dominant position to the detriment of consumers by withholding certain critical information from competitors which made it difficult for them to offer IBM-compatible computer equipment in time to compete with IBM products following new system launches.
- In the *Microsoft* case,[418] the Commission objected to the structure of Microsoft's standard agreements for licensing software to PC manufacturers holding that the use of 'per processor' and 'per system' licences, the requirements to pay a minimum royalty and the duration of the licence agreements had the effect of foreclosing the European market to other software producers. The Commission closed the case after having obtained Microsoft's commitments not to impose minimum requirements, to allow the freedom to purchase non-Microsoft products, to avoid payment of royalties in such cases and to limit the duration of the licences to one year.[419]
- In the *Tetra Pak* case,[420] a firm holding a dominant position in aseptic milk cartons and carton-filling machinery and technology took over a competitor and acquired thereby an exclusive licence for a new filling process. Following a complaint by a smaller competitor, the Commission decision that the concentration of technology in the hands of a dominant firm without the licensor of one of the processes being entitled to grant further licences constituted an infringement of Article 82.
- In the *Magill TV Guide* case[421] the Commission ordered two television stations and a commercial television publications company operating in Ireland to licence another company to publish their copyrighted advance programme listings in a comprehensive weekly TV guide. The three television organizations previously published three separate guides containing only their own programme listings. They were also ordered to supply each other with the listings.
- The *Sabena* case[422] concerned the refusal by the Belgian state-owned airline Sabena to grant a fare-cutting competitor, London European, access to its

---

417. *IBM*, Fourteenth Report on Competition Policy, points 94–95, and Twenty-fourth Report on Competition Policy, p. 365.
418. *Microsoft*, Twenty-fourth Report on Competition Policy, pp. 364–365. In *Microsoft II* the Commission objected to the refusal to disclose information for the development of interoperable products: D.Comm. March 24, 2004, IP/04/382, points 999–1004.
419. *See also Santa Cruz/Microsoft*, Twenty-seventh Report on Competition Policy, point 79 (abusive contractual clause obliging Santa Cruz to use the outdated technology of Microsoft, thereby limiting the innovative capacity of a competitor).
420. *Tetra Pak I*, D.Comm. July 26, 1988, 1988 OJ L 272/27; *aff'd* CFI July 10, 1990, 1990 ECR II-309.
421. *Magill TV Guide*, D.Comm. Dec. 21, 1988, 1989 OJ L 78/43; *aff'd* CFI May 10, 1991, 1991 ECR II-485, 535 and 575; *aff'd* ECJ April 6, 1995, 1995 ECR I-743.
422. *Sabena*, D.Comm. Nov. 4, 1988, 1988 OJ L 317/47.

computer reservation system. London European, which operated on the London-Brussels route, had sought access to the reservation system so that it would be listed on the terminals of Belgian travel agencies, which made almost 80% of their reservations through this system. The refusal was held to be an abuse.[423] Similarly, the Commission held the refusal by *British Midland* to continue interlining with its competitor *AER Lingus* between British and Irish airports to be an abuse.[424]

4. Applying Dissimilar Conditions to Equivalent Transactions (Article 82 (c))

Introduction.

The third example of abuse of dominance given in Article 82 is 'applying dissimilar conditions to equivalent transactions with other trading parties, thereby placing them at a competitive disadvantage.'[425] Discrimination may also represent the application of similar conditions to unequal transactions.[426] This prohibition aims at guaranteeing the equality of opportunity for all economic operators in the various member states in order to institute 'a system ensuring that competition in the Common Market is not distorted' (Article 3 (g)).[427] A dominant firm can abuse its dominant position by discriminating between different trading partners (customers or suppliers) in its terms and conditions of trading with them, with the result that some are disadvantaged. Article 82 (c) has been found applicable most often in cases of price discrimination. The wording of the provision suggests that it is mainly directed at exploitative discrimination, such as overcharging customers who do not have alternative sources of supply in order to maximize profits. But in many cases discrimination is practised not solely or even mainly to maximize short-term profits, but is part of a wider pattern of monopolizing conduct designed to divide markets or exclude competitors in order to be better able to exploit

---

423. Access to such systems is now guaranteed by Article 3 of the block exemption regulation for computer reservation systems, Regulation 83/91.

424. *British Midland/AER Lingus*, D.Comm. April 10, 1992, 1992 OJ L 96/34. In this case a fine of ECU 750,000 was imposed.

425. *See Tetra Pak II*, CFI Oct. 6, 1994, 1994 ECR II-755, para. 160; *aff'd* ECJ Nov. 14, 1996, 1996 ECR I-5951; *Deutsche Bahn*, CFI Oct. 21, 1997, 1997 ECR II-1689, paras 78–93. However, since the list of abuses is not exhaustive, Article 82 may be applied even in the absence of a direct effect on competition between undertakings in any given market, in particular in situations where the dominant firm's conduct causes damage directly to consumers: *Deutsche Post*, D.Comm. July 25, 2001, 2001 OJ L 331/40, point 133.

426. Under Article 60 of the ECSC Treaty: *Imports of Refrigerators*, ECJ July 17, 1963, 1963 ECR 105.

427. *Telecommunications Directive Terminal Equipment*, ECJ March 19, 1991, 1991 ECR I-1223, para. 51; *Tetra Pak II*, CFI Oct. 6, 1994, 1994 ECR II-755, para. 160; *aff'd* ECJ Nov. 14, 1996, 1996 ECR I-5951; *Alpha Flight/Aeroports de Paris*, D.Comm. June 11, 1998, 1998 OJ L 230/10, point 83.

market power in the longer term.[428] Price discrimination may constitute selective unfair pricing, falling under Article 82 (a), if some of the prices are unfair, but, as the *United Brands* case showed, unfair pricing is difficult to prove.[429]

Equivalent Transactions.

Failing to treat like cases alike and treating unlike cases alike are both discriminatory.[430] To show discrimination it is necessary to determine whether or not transactions are alike, or rather 'equivalent' in the words of Article 82 (c). This requires a comparison of the transactions, taking into account relevant differences such as marketing and transport costs,[431] the size of the customer's purchases and any promotional, warehousing, servicing or other functions that it performs.[432]

Identical Treatment not Required.

Given that transactions are rarely exactly alike, Article 82 (c) does not require a dominant firm to offer identical prices and conditions throughout the Community, but the prices or fees applied to different customers may not be arbitrary.[433] Different prices or fees may be justified on the basis of objective criteria, i.e. the existence of objectively different situations or circumstances capable of justifying any disparity in treatment.[434] Price differences are regarded as abusive once a certain tolerance level is exceeded and they become disproportionate and unjustifiable.[435] The tolerance level is less in cases where the discrimination is part of a clear policy of dividing markets or excluding competitors. On the other hand, the application of identical prices to large individual customers and joint sales

428. *Irish Sugar*, D.Comm. May 14, 1997, 1997 OJ L 258/1, points 123 and 151–154.

429. *See supra* section D.2 (a).

430. *See Italy v. Commission*, ECJ July 17, 1963, 1963 ECR 165, 177–178; *Corsica Ferries*, ECJ May 17, 1994 ECR 1994 I-1783, paras 43–44. On discrimination under Article 81, *see supra* Chapter III.A.5. An example of treating unlike cases alike is uniform delivered prices: *see supra* Chapter III.E and *British Sugar*, D.Comm. July 18, 1988, 1988 OJ L 284/41, 55.

431. *Deutsche Bahn*, CFI Oct. 21, 1997, 1997 ECR II-1689, para. 86.

432. *Corsica Ferries*, ECJ May 17, 1994, 1994 ECR I-1783, para. 43; *HOV-SVZ/Deutsche Bahn*, D.Comm. March 29, 1994, 1994 OJ L 104/34, points 191–248; *aff'd* CFI Oct. 21, 1997, 1997 ECR II-1689, para. 86.

433. *Aéroports de Paris*, CFI Dec. 12, 2000, 2000 ECR II-3929, para. 202.

434. This is not considered as reversal of the burden of proof: *Aéroports de Paris*, CFI Dec. 12, 2000, 2000 ECR II-3929, paras 202–203.

435. *Deutsche Bahn*, CFI Oct. 21, 1997, 1997 ECR II-1689, para. 86. There are, for example, limits on the degree to which a dominant supplier may charge what the market will bear: *United Brands*, ECJ Feb. 14, 1978, 1978 ECR 207, 298, para. 227. *See also* the UK Monopolies and Mergers Commission report on gas supplies, Cm 500, 1988, p. 98 *et seq.* (discrimination between the prices for firm and interruptible supplies, exploiting the dependence of customers unable to switch to alternatives). In the insurance sector: *P&I Clubs*, D.Comm. April 12, 1999, 1999 OJ L 125/12, points 134–136.

cooperatives is not necessarily abusive.[436] Nor does the owner of a network discriminate when applying different fees to customers depending on whether they contributed to the construction and maintenance costs.[437]

Examples.
In most decided cases in which an Article 82 (c) abuse has been found, discrimination has also been associated with other wider abuses:

- In the *United Brands* case[438] the dominant banana importer to the EC market charged its national distributors widely differing prices for identical bananas collected at the same ports. The price discrimination was part of a strategy of dividing national markets in order to better exploit the firm's market power and keep out competitors.
- In *GEMA*[439] the German performing rights society was found to have abused its dominant position by discriminating between German and foreign-made tape recorders and between records imported by manufacturers and by dealers in the rates of royalties and licence fees it charged on these items. The practice was associated with a policy of protecting the German market from parallel imports.
- In *Hoffmann-La Roche*[440] the world's leading producer of vitamins practised discrimination in the rebates it offered to customers, which were set at a level sufficient to retain the customer's business. The highest rebates were granted to a firm capable of switching to supplies produced within its own group. The main abuse, however, consisted not in discrimination, but in the exclusion of competitors through the rebate system.[441] Discriminatory discounts were also found to be an abuse of a dominant position in the *Sugar*,[442] *TACA*,[443] *Hilti*[444] and *Deutsche Telekom*[445] cases, in the latter cases associated with tying (Article 82 (d)).
- In the *British Sugar* case[446] the Commission held it to be an abuse for a sugar producer in a dominant position to offer industrial (i.e., bulk) sugar to a firm

---

436. *AKZO*, ECJ July 3, 1991, 1991 ECR I-3359, para. 120.
437. *DISMA*, Twenty-third Report on Competition Policy, point 223. The right-owner may, in particular, 'lawfully call for a return on the amounts which he has invested in order to perfect the protected design': *CICRA/Renault*, ECJ Oct. 5, 1988, 1988 ECR 6039, para. 17.
438. *United Brands*, ECJ Feb. 14, 1978, 1978 ECR 207, paras 204–234. *See also British Leyland*, ECJ Nov.11, 1986, 1986 ECR 3263, paras 25–33 (charging higher prices for conformity certificates for left-hand-drive cars than for right-hand-drive ones, to discourage parallel imports; *British Sugar*, D.Comm. July 18, 1988, 1988 OJ L 284/41, points 73–76.
439. *GEMA I*, D.Comm. June 2, 1971, 1971 OJ L 134/15, 25–26.
440. *Hoffmann-La Roche*, ECJ Feb. 13, 1979, 1979 ECR 461, paras 80–121.
441. *See infra* section D.6 (c) (iv) at pp. 465–470.
442. *Sugar*, ECJ Dec. 16, 1975, 1975 ECR 1663, paras 499–528.
443. *TACA*, D.Comm. Sept. 16, 1998, 1999 OJ L 95/1, point 535.
444. *Hilti*, D.Comm. Dec. 22, 1987, 1988 OJ L 65/19, 36–38; *aff'd* CFI Dec. 12, 1991, 1991 ECR I-1439; *aff'd* ECJ March 2, 1994, 1994 ECR I-667.
445. Twenty-sixth Report on Competition Policy, point 71.
446. *British Sugar*, D.Comm. July 18, 1988, 1988 OJ L 284/41, 54–55 and 65–68.

packaging the sugar for retail sales at a price that did not allow it a sufficient margin after packaging costs to compete with the producer in the retail market. Here price discrimination was found between customers for a bulk and a packaged product. The discrimination was part of a strategy to eliminate a competitor, as was the selective price-cutting in the *ECS/Akzo* case.[447]

- In the *Irish Sugar* case[448] the Commission found that the Irish sugar producer applied discriminatory practices by offering selectively low prices to customers of a competitor (an importer of French sugar) and by offering selective 'border' rebates to customers who were located close to the border with Northern Ireland. Customers who did not receive selective low prices and rebates were placed at a competitive disadvantage in the retail sugar market. Selective pricing and fidelity rebates constitute not only a discrimination but also a predatory practice aiming at precluding competitors.[449]
- In the *BP* case[450] the Court of Justice clarified the limits of the requirement of Article 82 to treat like transactions alike. The Court acquitted BP of abusive discrimination when it cut supplies to an occasional customer by more than to regular customers during the 1974–1975 oil crisis. Sales to occasional and regular customers were not equivalent transactions.[451]
- In the *Belgacom* case[452] the Commission ruled that Belgacom, the Belgian telecommunication operator, had applied discriminatory and excessive prices to the Belgian subsidiary of the US telephone directory publisher ITT Promedia for access to Belgacom's data on its subscribers for voice telephone services by calculating prices on the basis of the operator's turnover rather than on the ratio of the operator's own costs.[453]
- In the *Airport of Brussels* case[454] the Commission held that the airport administration abused its dominant position by granting discounts on landing fees that

447. *ECS/Akzo II*, D.Comm. Dec.14, 1985, 1985 OJ L 374/1, 21–22.

448. *Irish Sugar*, D.Comm. May 14, 1997, 1997 OJ L 258/1; *aff'd* CFI Oct. 7, 1999, 1999 ECR II-2969 and ECJ, July 10, 2001, 2001 ECR I-5333.

449. *See infra* Section D.6.

450. *BP*, ECJ June 29, 1978, 1978 ECR 1513.

451. *Ibid.*, paras 24–34. However, it is arguable that in other circumstances discriminating against occasional customers could increase a dominant firm's power in the distribution of its products and so constitute an abuse.

452. *Belgacom/ITT Promedia*, Twenty-seventh Report on Competition Policy, point 67; *aff'd* CFI July 17, 1998, 1998 ECR II-2937.

453. Similarly, the Commission held in *British Telecommunications* (D.Comm. Dec. 10, 1982, 1982 OJ L 360/36; *aff'd* ECJ March 20, 1985, 1985 ECR 873) that restrictions imposed by British Telecom on the usage of telex and telephone networks by third parties discriminated against these operators, thereby placing them at a competitive disadvantage *vis-à-vis* operators not bound by these restrictions.

454. *Airport of Brussels*, D.Comm. June 28, 1995, 1995 OJ L 216/8; *see also Ismalulaitos/Luftfartsverket*, D.Comm. Feb. 10, 1999, 1999 OJ L 69/24, point 42; *Portuguese Airports*, D.Comm. Feb. 10, 1999, 1999 OJ L 69/31, points 25–35 (under Article 86). With respect to discrimina-

varied substantially according to the user, to the detriment of airlines *not* based at Brussels.

- In the *Aéroports de Paris* case[455] the Commission held that the application of commercial fees varying individually according to supplier or users of the same groundhandling services (catering and cleaning) at the same airport constituted a discrimination contrary to Article 82, in particular because of the favourable treatment of self-servicing companies against whom no commercial fees were imposed. Both the Court of First Instance and the Court of Justice affirmed that the Commission was correct to make a comparaison between third party and self-handling services providers in order to evaluate the discriminatory effect of the groundhandling fee.[456]
- In the *Deutsche Bahn* case[457] the Court of First Instance affirmed the Commission's statement that the application of substantially dissimilar transport fees (amounting up to 50%) depending on whether the ports of origin or destination were located in Germany or Belgium/Netherlands in order to favour the transport of sea containers through German ports constituted an abuse.[458]
- In the *German Post* cases[459] a discrimination was found in the different treatment between the normal domestic mail and the domestic mail which was incorrectly considered as circumvented (A-B-A remail) by intercepting, delaying and surcharging A-B-A remail, thereby applying different prices for equivalent transactions. In both cases the German Post performed exactly the same delivery service but charged customers differently, depending *inter alia* on whether or not the foreign senders had indicated a reference to an entity residing in Germany.[460]

Conflict of Interest Leading to Discriminatory Practices.
Under Article 86 (1) the Court of Justice acknowledged that a measure by which a member state confers on an undertaking the power to lay down rules with which

---

tory discounts granted by port administrations: *Tariffs for Piloting in the Port of Genova*, D.Comm. Oct. 21, 1998, 1998 OJ L 301/27, points 14–15.

455. *Alpha Flight/Aeroports de Paris*, D.Comm. June 11, 1998 OJ L 230/10, points 85–127, *aff'd* CFI Dec. 12, 2000, 2000 ECR II-3929, paras 200–202. *See also Airport of Frankfurt*, D.Comm. Jan 14, 1998, 1998 OJ L 72/30; Commission's guidelines on the application of the EC competition rules in the telecommunications sector, 1991 OJ C 233/2, point 86.
456. *Aéroports de Paris*, CFI Dec. 12, 2000, 2000 ECR II-3929, para. 85; ECJ Oct. 24, 2002, 2002 ECR I-9297, para. 116.
457. *Deutsche Bahn*, CFI 21 Oct. 1997, 1997 ECR I-1689.
458. *Ibid.*, paras 77–93. *See also TACA II*, D.Comm. Sept. 16, 1998, 1999 OJ L 95/1, points 535–544.
459. *Deutsche Post*, D.Comm. July 25, 2001, 2001 OJ L 331/40, points 126–134; *Deutsche Post/GZS, Citicorp*, ECJ Feb. 10, 2000, 2000 ECR I-825, para. 61.
460. Subsequent to the Commission's decision in the *German Post* case the national postal operators within the Community agreed on the remuneration that public postal operators pay each other for the delivery of incoming cross-border mail (terminal dues): Publication Article 19 (3) Regulation 17 in the case *Reims II*, April 23, 2003, IP/03/557.

its competitors must comply results in a conflict of interest by giving preference directly or indirectly to its own subsidiaries, thereby leading to a violation of the principle of equal opportunity (discrimination); therefore, a conflict of interest constitutes an abuse in itself and the mere grant of such powers may be contrary to Article 86 (1), no evidence of actual abuse being required.[461]

Article 82, however, is not infringed by the mere existence of a conflict of interest situation but only if it leads effectively to an abusive discrimination. In cases where such a discrimination has been found the Commission may, however, when requiring to bring such infringement to an end, ensure to prevent fresh abuses, for instance, by creating an independent legal entity for the purpose of full transparency, thereby ending the conflict of interest itself.[462]

5. Tying Practices (Article 82 (d))

Nature of Tying.

The final example of abuse of dominance given in Article 82 is tying, i.e., 'making the conclusion of contracts subject to acceptance by the other parties of supplementary obligations which, by their nature or according to their commercial usage, have no connection with the subject of such contracts.' Tying is the most typical form of an exclusionary abuse, involving direct or indirect injury to competitors.[463] Tying in agreements made by non-dominant firms is prohibited by Article 81.[464] For a dominant firm it is especially easy to use the leverage created by its dominant position in one product (the 'tying' or 'leveraging' product) to induce customers to purchase from it other goods and services that they might obtain from other suppliers on better terms or conditions (the 'tied' product).[465] Illegal tying can occur only where the two products by their nature or according to commercial usage need not be sourced from the same supplier, although they may be closely related.[466] The illegal conduct does not necessarily enable the firm

---

461. *GM-Inno-BM*, ECJ Dec. 13, 1991, 1991 ECR I-5941, para. 25 (with further references); *Silvano Raso*, ECJ Feb. 12, 1998, 1998 ECR I-593, paras 30–31; *Deutsche Post/ZVS*, *Citicorp*, ECJ Feb. 2000, 2000 ECR I-825, para. 48; *French Post*, D.Comm. Oct. 23, 2001, 2002 OJ L 120/19, point 64 (Article 86 (3) decision). *See also* Commission Notice on the application of the competition rules to the postal sector, 1998 OJ C 39/2, point 6.4.

462. E.g. *Deutsche Post*, D.Comm. March 2001, 2001 OJ L 125/27, point 47: in order to bring the infringement of Article 82 to an end, *Deutsche Post* undertook to provide full transparency by creating independent legal entities.

463. *Belgian Post*, D.Comm. Dec. 5, 2001, 2002 OJ L 61/32, point 73; *ATLAS*, D.Comm. July 17, 1996, 1996 OJ L 239/23, point 60.

464. *See supra* Chapter III.A.6 and Chapter IV.B.10.(g).

465. *See Microsoft*, D.Comm. March 24, 2004, IP/04/382 (Microsoft abused its near monopoly in the market for PC operating systems by tying its Windows Media Player, a product, where it faced competition, with its Windows operating system).

466. *Hoffmann-La Roche*, ECJ Feb. 13, 1979, 1979 ECR 461, 547, para. 111 (different vitamins): *IBM*, Fourteenth Report on Competition Policy, points 94–95, and *Microsoft*, Twenty-fourth

which holds a dominant position on the market of the tying product to acquire a dominant position on the market of the tied product; it infringes Aricle 82 by significantly weakening competition on this market.[467]

Justification for Tying.

Tying obligations may be justified by the nature of the products concerned. A supplier may impose on its exclusive reseller the obligation to purchase a complete range of goods.[468] A licensor may impose on its licensee the obligation to procure goods or services which are necessary for a technically satisfactory exploitation of the licensed technology or for ensuring conformity with certain quality standards.[469] Similarly the licensor may impose the obligation to accept further licences provided they are necessary for a technically satisfactory exploitation.[470] Article 82 (d) seems to indicate that commercial usage may justify tying practices. While common commercial usage may not distort competition, the commercial usage as to some products may have the likely effect of unduly excluding competitors, and thus constitute an abuse within the general meaning of Article 82 of which the practice described under (d) is only one example.[471]

Examples.

Illegal tying practices were found in the following cases:

- In the *IBM* case[472] the Commission challenged IBM's practice of tying the sale of main memory capacity or basic software to that of its large System 370 computers. Because of IBM's dominance in these mainframes, the practice harmed competing suppliers of IBM-compatible equipment and software. The case was settled when the Commission accepted undertakings from IBM to change the practices. IBM had already unbundled software. It now undertook to supply the computers either without any memory capacity or with only such memory

Report on Competition Policy, p. 364 (bundling copyrighted software with computer hardware); *Digital*, Twenty-seventh Report on Competition Policy, point 69 (tying after-sales software with Digital hardare); *Fidicine*, ECJ May 4, 1993, 1993 ECR I-2239 (under Article 28) (tying the licence to American films with the distribution of Spanish films). *See* draft Commission Notice on Open Network Provision, 1997 OJ C 76/9, point 90.

467. *See Microsoft*, D.Comm. March 24, 2004, IP/04/382.
468. *Cf.* The former Article 2 (3) (a) of Regulation 1983/83 and Article 2 (2) (a) of Regulation 1984/83. However, the goods must belong to the same relevant product market; applying full-range rebates including other goods can be tantamount to an exclusionary practice: *Coca Cola*, Comm. Memo 99/42 of 22 July 1999.
469. Article 2 (1) (5) of the former Regulation 240/96.
470. 'Package licensing' is not exempted but subject to the opposition procedure: Article 4 (2) a of Regulation 240/96. Prohibited as abusive in *GEMA I*, D.Comm. June 2, 1971, 1971 OJ L 134/15, 24.
471. *Tetra Pak II*, ECJ Nov. 14, 1996, 1996 ECR I-5951, paras 34–37.
472. *IBM*, Fourteenth Report on Competition Policy, points 94–95.

capacity as was strictly required for testing. The Commission also secured undertakings from IBM to disclose interface information for new computer models in advance so as to shorten the lead-time for manufacturers of IBM-compatible products to design equipment to work with new IBM systems.[473]

- Similarly, in *Microsoft I* the Commission intervened against Microsoft's tying personal computer operating systems to services for low-end server operating systems, by withholding technical interface information which alternative server software suppliers needed to compete with Microsoft's products.[474]
- In the *Microsoft II* case[475] the Commission imposed a heavy fine on Microsoft for having tied its Windows Media Player, a product where it faced competition, with its Windows operating system, a product where it holds a near monopoly, and ordered Microsoft to offer to PC manufacturers a version of its Windows operating system *without* its own Windows Media Player, thereby un-tying the two products.
- In the *Hilti* case[476] the world leader in the supply of nail guns (used in the construction industry) and consumables for use with them was found to have abused its dominant position by tying the purchase of unpatented Hilti nails to the sale of its patented cartridge strips, thus injuring competing nail manufacturers. This represented the abuse of an industrial property right, namely the Hilti patents for cartridge strips.
- In the *Oliofiat* case[477] the Italian car maker Fiat obliged dealers and repair shops to use 'Oliofiat' lubricants which were produced by a Fiat company. After the Commission intervened, the obligation was dropped so that other lubricants could be used so long as they were of like quality.
- In the *British Sugar* case[478] British Sugar was charged with tying the supply of a service (delivery) to supply of a product (sugar) in which it held a dominant position. The company had refused to supply sugar to customers unless they agreed to have it delivered by British Sugar itself or by firms acting for British Sugar. The Commission held that British Sugar had abused its dominant position on the sugar market by refusing to give its customers the option of purchasing sugar on an ex-factory or delivered price basis. The practice also damaged potential competitors for the haulage business.

---

473. *See* Commission's Telecommunication Guidelines, 1991 OJ C 233/2, points 99–101.
474. *Microsoft I*, D.Comm. Aug. 30, 2001, IP/01/1232, and Twenty-fourth Report on Competition Policy, pp. 364–365; *Microsoft/Santa Cruz*, Twenty-seventh Report on Competition Policy, pp. 140–141.
475. *Microsoft II*, D.Comm. March 24, 2004, IP/04/382, points 1061–1067.
476. *Hilti*, D.Comm. Dec. 22, 1987, 1988 OJ L 65/19, 36; *aff'd* CFI March 2, 1994, 1994 ECR II-667; *aff'd* ECJ Nov. 14, 1996, 1996 ECR I-5951.
477. *Oliofiat*, Seventeenth Report on Competition Policy, point 84. *See also* (under Article 81) *D'Ieteren*, D.Comm. Dec. 19, 1990, 1991 OJ L 20/42; (under Article 82) *Industrial Gases*, Nineteenth Report on Competition Policy, point 62.
478. *British Sugar*, D.Comm. July 18, 1988, 1988 OJ L 284/41, points 69–73.

- In the *Alsatel/Novasam* case[479] the Court of Justice found that it was not illegal for a dominant supplier of telecommunications equipment which leased the equipment to its customers to require any modifications of the equipment to be carried out by the supplier. On the other hand, if the equipment were sold to the customer, such tying would be an abuse.
- In the *Tetra Pak II* case[480] the Court of Justice affirmed the Commission's decision that Tetra Pak, the largest supplier for the packaging of liquid foods in cartons, abused its dominant position by unduly obliging users to use only Tetra Pak cartons with licensed Tetra Pak filling machines.
- In the *Novo Nordisk* case[481] the Commission objected to the refusal, by a firm holding a dominant position on the insulin market and on the markets for various components of insulin self-injection ('pen') delivery systems, to guarantee pen products when they are used in conjunction with the compatible components of other manufacturers.[482]
- In the *IRI/Nielsen* case,[483] which concerned the sale by A.C. Nielsen Company of retail tracking services to multinational customers, the Commission objected to contracts with substantial discounts in exchange for commitments from customers to call upon Nielsen's services in a wide range of countries.
- In the *Belgian Post* case,[484] the Commission found that the Belgian Post's grant of preferential tariffs to business-to-private mail (which is covered by the postal monopoly) only if its customers also accepted its business-to-business mail service constituted an abusive tying practice; the Belgian Post had unfairly used discounts in reserved markets in order to gain advantages in activities open to competition.[485]
- In its Notice on Access Agreements in the Telecommunications Sector[486] the Commission states that an abuse occurs when the vertically integrated dominant network operator obliges the party requesting access to purchase one or more services[487] without adequate justification, thereby excluding rivals of the dominant access provider from offering those elements of the package independently.

479. *Alsatel/Novasam*, ECJ Oct. 5, 1988, 1988 ECR 5987, para. 10.
480. *Tetra Pak II*, ECJ Nov. 14, 1996, 1996 ECR I-5951, paras 34–37.
481. Twenty-sixth Report on Competition Policy, pp. 142–143.
482. This example shows that tying is a specific type of exclusionary practice.
483. *IRI/Nielsen*, Twenty-sixth Report on Competition Policy, pp. 144–146.
484. *Belgian Post*, D.Comm. Dec. 5, 2001, 2002 OJ L 61/32, points 54–62 and 73.
485. *See ATLAS*, D.Comm. July 17, 1996, 1996 OJ L 239/23, point 60.
486. 1998 OJ C 265/2, para. 103. In order to prevent such an abuse, the Council adopted Directive 1999/64/EC (1999 OJ L 175/39) ordering the member states to ensure that no telecommunications organization operates its cable TV network using the same legal entity as it uses for its telecommunications network.
487. Including those which are superfluous to the party requesting access, or indeed those which may constitute services which that party itself would like to provide for its customers.

– The Commission intervened in several cases against tying practices by applying discriminatory prices or rebates. In the *Digital* case[488] the Commission intervened against the supply of logistical services by a dominant firm (Digital) at discriminatory prices depending on whether the user was prepared to buy computer hardware from the same supplier. Similarly, the Commission ordered Microsoft to refrain from using any commercial, technological or contractual terms that would have the effect of rendering the unbundled version (its PC operating system without its own media players) less attractive.[489] Aggregated rebate schemes, i.e., arrangements under which the supplier grants a rebate based on the customer's total purchases from it of different products, may have the same effect as direct tying clauses and be caught by Article 82 (d).[490] Applying a licence fee calculated on the sale of both patented and unpatented parts of a product (a windsurfing rig only together with an unpatented sailboard) may also constitute anticompetitive tying.[491] Tying is often imposed by agreement, pressure or an offer of special prices or conditions for the dominant firm's tied goods or services.[492]

6. Exclusionary Abuses not Directly Covered by the Examples in Article 82 (a)–(d)

Legitimate Competition v. Exclusionary Abuse of Market Power.
As mentioned above,[493] even a firm in a dominant position is entitled to defend that position by competing with rivals in its markets, provided it competes on the merits.[494] This also applies with respect to conduct that is likely to exert vigorous

488. *Digital*, Twenty-fourth Report on Competition Policy, pp. 364–365 and Twenty-seventh Report on Competition Policy, point 69.

489. *Microsoft II*, D.Comm. March 24, 2004, IP/04/382 points 1011–1014 (fine of EUR 497.2 million).

490. *Hoffmann-La Roche*, ECJ Feb. 13, 1979, 1979 ECR 461, para. 111. *See also infra* section D.6. (c) (iv).

491. *Windsurfing*, ECJ Feb. 25, 1986, 1986 ECR 611, para. 67.

492. Commission Guidelines on the application of the EC competition rules in the telecommunications sector, 1991 OJ C 233/2, points 84–115; *Belgian Post*, D.Comm. Dec. 5, 2001, 2002 OJ L 61/32, point 58.

493. Section D.I.

494. *AKZO*, ECJ July 3, 1991, 1991 ECR I-3359, para, 70; *Deutsche Bahn*, CFI Oct. 21, 1997, 1997 ECR II-1689, para. 78. The Commission emphasized in its *AKZO* decision 'that it does not consider an intention even by a dominant firm to prevail over its rivals as unlawful. A dominant firm is entitled to compete on the merits. Nor does the Commission suggest that large producers should be under any obligation to refrain from competing vigorously with smaller competitors or new entrants. The maintenance of a system of effective competition does however require that a small competitor be protected against behaviour by dominant undertakings designed to exclude it from the market not by virtue of greater efficiency or superior performance but by an abuse of market power. *ECS/Akzo*, D.Comm. Dec. 14, 1985, 1985 OJ L 374/1, 21 (*aff'd* ECJ July 3, 1991, 1991 ECR I-3359). *See also Boosey & Hawkes*,

competitive pressure on other, probably smaller competitors unable to respond to such competition. However, as the Court of First Instance stated in the *British Plaster Board* case:[495]

> '... such behaviour cannot be countenanced if its actual purpose is strengthen this dominant position and abuse it ...
>
> The Court considers that it is not appropriate for an undertaking in a dominant position to take, at its own initiative, measures intended as a retaliation against commercial practices which it considers unlawful or unfair. Accordingly it is irrelevant whether the measures referred to in the Decision were adopted in response to "appeal" prices applied by certain competitors or ... to forestall "appeal" prices which certain merchants intended applying to imported products. The only important issue is whether, through recourse to methods differing from those governing normal competition in products based on traders' performance, the conduct at issue was intended or likely to affect the structure of a market where, as a direct result of the presence of the undertaking in question, competition had already been weakened.'

Thus, the dominant firm has a 'special responsibility' not to allow its conduct to impair genuine undistorted competition in the Common Market[496] or – in the terms of the Court of Justice in the *British Airways* – 'to influence the structure of a market where, as a result of the very presence of the undertaking in question, the degree of competition is already weakened and which, through recourse to methods different from those governing normal competition in products or services on the basis of the transactions of commercial operators, has the effect of hindering the maintenance of the degree of competition still existing in the market or the growth of that competition.'[497]

Predatory Intent.
Although the concept of abuse is an objective one and does not require any 'fault',[498] exclusionary practices are normally directed at damaging or eliminating

---

D. Comm. July 29, 1987, 1987 OJ L 286/36, 40–41; Eighteenth Report on Competition Policy, point 71; Commission Notice on the application of the competition rules in the postal sector, 1998 OJ C 39/2, point 2.9.

495. *British Plaster Board*, CFI April 1, 1993, 1993 ECR II-389, paras 117–118; *see also Tetra Pak II*, CFI Oct. 6, 1994, 1994 ECR II-755, para. 147.

496. *Michelin*, ECJ Nov. 9 1983, 1983 ECR 3461, para. 57; *British Plaster Board*, CFI April 1, 1993, 1993 ECR II-389, para. 67; *Irish Sugar*, D.Comm. May 14, 1997, 1997 OJ L 258/1, point 134.

497. *British Airways*, CFI Dec. 17, 2003, T-219/99, para. 241. *See also Hoffmann-La Roche*, ECJ Feb. 13, 1979, 1979 ECR 461, para. 91.

498. *Ibid.*, para. 207. *See British Plaster Board*, CFI April 1, 1993, 1993 ECR II-389, para. 70.

a competitor and therefore are often part of a predatory 'plan' or 'intent' which can be sufficiently proven.[499]

The Court of First Instance ruled in the *ITT Promedia* case that pricing practices can be characterized as an abuse, within the meaning of Article 82,

> '... only if they cannot reasonably be considered to be an attempt to assert the rights of the undertaking concerned and can therefore only serve to harass the opposing party.'[500]

However, the intent of behaviour which cannot reflect any economic rationale other than ousting a competitor[501] may be apparent from its very nature, in particular from the duration, the continuity[502] and, in the case of predatory pricing, the scale of the sales at a loss.[503] This section will discuss the most characteristic types of exclusionary conduct that are prohibited by Article 82, but which are not in all cases covered by the examples given in the Article. The conduct may be aimed directly at the actual or potential competitor, i.e. directed against existing competitors on the market or against new entrants. Examples of such abusive behaviour directed at an actual or potential competitor are (a) refusal to supply and (b) refusal of access to a market, or aimed at the competitor via its actual or potential customers or suppliers, as in the cases of (c) exclusionary pricing and (d) exclusionary dealing arrangements.

(a) Exclusionary or Predatory Pricing

Introduction.
While it is normal competitive conduct for a firm to seek to win business and gain market share from its rivals by offering lower prices or better service, a dominant firm will abuse its position if it wages a long-term, systematic price war against smaller competitors for the express purpose of driving them from the market. Predatory pricing may comprise systematically undercutting the competitor's price or selectively aligning price to the competitor's prices without extending those prices to the dominant firm's own customers. The predatory intent is evident where the dominant firm deliberately applies selective price cuts to customers who otherwise were likely to purchase from a competitor or competitors in order

499. *Tetra Pak II*, CFI Oct. 6, 1994, 1994 ECR II-755, para. 149. *See also* Twenty-sixth Report on Competition Policy, points 59–64.
500. *ITT Promedia*, CFI July 17, 1998, 1998 ECR II-2937, para. 72.
501. *CEWAL*, ECJ March 16, 2000, 2000 ECR I-1365, para 101.
502. E.g., by refusing deliberately – as part of a broader strategy – interface information which would enable competitors to develop products which are fully interoperable with the dominant firm's products in order to compete on an equal footing in the market: *Microsoft*, D.Comm. March 24, 2004, IP/04/382.
503. *Tetra Pak II* CFI Oct. 6, 1994, 1994 ECR II-755, para. 150. *See also Hilti*, CFI Dec. 12, 1991, 1991 ECR II-1439, paras 99–101. *See* in greater detail section 6 (a) *infra*.

to drive them from the market or to signal them to adopt higher prices in line with those charged by the dominant firm.[504] If the predatory purpose is not self-evident, documentary evidence of intent may be required.[505]

Commission Study on Predatory Pricing.

In 1986 the Commission had a study of predatory pricing carried out and reported on its main findings in the Sixteenth Report on Competition Policy[506] which may still be helpful. The study found that predatory pricing would be rational behaviour in certain circumstances, namely where:

(i) the aggressor was a multi-product firm able to make up for the losses incurred in the market in which the aggression took place in one or more other markets,
(ii) the predatory price reduced the present value of the entrant's future profits below its fixed ('sunk') entry costs so that it would not be able to survive in the long run, and
(iii) the victim was unsure that the price cut was predatory; it might then come to the conclusion that there was no room for it in the market under normal competitive conditions.

Commenting on the study, the Commission reiterated the approach it had applied in *ECS/Akzo* and rejected both a purely cost-based rule[507] and a policy of doing nothing. The latter has been advocated by some commentators on the ground that punishing predatory pricing could discourage fair competition.[508]

The *ECS/Akzo* Case.

In this case,[509] although the Commission investigated whether Akzo's selling prices were below full cost, it refused to adopt an exclusively cost-based test for determining the limits of legal pricing conduct. This is in contrast to the rule

504. *CEWAL*, ECJ March 16, 2000, 2000 ECR I-1365, paras 101 and 117. The predatory intent was also evident in the *AKZO* case (D.Comm. Dec. 14, 1985, 1985 OJ L 374/1, 19–22) where the Commission was able to prove that the dominant firm had made direct threats with the aim of eliminating its competitor.

505. E.g. in the *Industrie des Poudres Sphériques/Pechiney* case (Twenty-sixth Report on Competition Policy, p. 138) the Commission did not find evidence of predatory pricing, *aff'd* CFI Nov. 30, 2000, 2000 ECR II-3755.

506. Sixteenth Report on Competition Policy, points 334–336.

507. Areeda and Turner, 'Predatory Pricing and Related Practices under Section 2 of The Sherman Act', 88 *Harv. L. Rev.* 697 (1975).

508. Brodley and Hay, 'Predatory Pricing: Competing Economic Theories and the Evolution of Legal Standards', *Cornell L. Rev.* 738 (1981); V. Korah, *EC Competition Law and Practice*, 5th ed. (1994), pp. 91–92; P. Areeda and H. Hovenkamp, *Antitrust Law: An Analysis of Antitrust Principles and Their Application*, §§ 723–748 (1996).

509. *ECS/Akzo II*, D.Comm. Dec. 14 1985, 1985 OJ L 374/1, 19–22; *aff'd* ECJ July 3, 1991, 1991 ECR I-3359.

followed by some U.S. courts that a price at or above marginal cost (or average variable cost, which is a close approximation) is presumed to be lawful, while a price below it may be abusive.[510] In addition to evidence of selling below full cost, the Commission based its case on many other factors which indicated a systematic plan to drive the competitor, ECS, from the market. These factors included the selective nature of the price cuts to regular customers of the competitor while maintaining higher levels to its own established customers, the departure from its previous pattern of full cost recovery, and subsidizing[511] price cuts by below-cost transfer prices from other divisions. The fact that in some cases Akzo was apparently only matching the prices quoted by another competitor was no defence, as the prices in question were artificial and Akzo knew or should have known this,[512] The Court of Justice, confirming these conclusions, stated:[513]

> 'Prices below average costs (that is to say, those which vary depending on the quantities produced) by means of which a dominant undertaking seeks to eliminate a competitor must be regarded as abusive. A dominant undertaking has no interest in applying such prices except that of eliminating competitors so as to enable it subsequently to raise its prices by taking advantage of its monopolistic position, since each sale generates a loss, namely the total amount of the fixed cost (that is to say, those which remain constant regardless of the quantities produced) and, at least, part of the variable cost relating to the unit produced.
>
> Moreover, prices below average total cost, that is to say, fixed costs plus variable costs, but above average variable costs, must be regarded as abusive if they are determined as part of a plan for eliminating a competitor. Such prices can drive from the market undertakings which are perhaps as efficient as the dominant undertaking but which, because of their smaller resources, are incapable of withstanding the competition waged against them.'

In the *Tetra Pak* case[514] the Court of Justice confirmed this approach by emphasizing that it does not need to be proved that the dominant firm has in fact a real

510. Areeda and Turner, 'Predatory Pricing and Related Practices Under Section 2 of the Sherman Act', 88 *Harv. L. Rev.* 697 (1975); *see also* P. Areeda and H. Hovenkamp, *Antitrust Law: An Analysis of Antitrust Principles and Their Application*, §§ 723–748 (1996); ABA, *Antitrust Law Developments* (Fourth) 252–270 (1997).
511. *See infra*, Section D.6.(b). Cross-subsidization may be abusive in the telecommunication sector: Commission's Guidelines, 1991 OJ C 233/2, points 102–110.
512. *ECS/Akzo*, D.Comm. Dec. 14, 1985, 1985 OJ L 374/1, 22.
513. *AKZO II*, ECJ July 3, 1991, 1991 ECR I-3359, paras 71–72.
514. *Tetra Pak II*, ECJ Nov. 14, 1996, 1996 ECR I-5951, para. 44. The exclusionary practices in this case included the buying up of competitors' machines, despite the various financial sacrifices involved, in order to eliminate them from the market: *Tetra Pak II*, D.Comm. July 24, 1991, 1992 OJ L 72/1, point 165. *See also AKZO*, ECJ July 3, 1991, 1991 ECR I-3359, para. 108.

chance of compensating its losses. In the *Deutsche Post I* case,[515] the Commission held that offering very low prices to customers for mail-order parcel services (which was open to competition) was predatory on the basis of the relationship between the costs of maintaining capacity and the incremental costs of providing these services.

The *Hilti* Case.
The Commission followed a similar approach in the *Hilti* case, in which predatory pricing was only one of the abuses of dominance that it found:

> 'The abuse in this case does not hinge on whether the prices were below costs (however defined – and in any case certain products were given away free). Rather it depends on the fact that, because of its dominance, Hilti was able to offer special discriminatory prices to its competitors' customers with the view to damaging their business, while maintaining higher prices to its own equivalent customers.'[516]

The *Wanadoo* Case.
In the *Wanadoo* case[517] the Commission imposed fines on the French high-speed internet provider Wanadoo, a subsidiary of Telecom France, for having applied predatory prices in ADLS-based[518] internet access services. The Commission found that the retail prices were below its average costs (leading to substantial losses) and restricted the market entry and development potential for competitors with the effect that the market share of Wanadoo's main competitors tumbled and Wanadoo's market share rose from 46% to 72%.[519]

Exclusionary Price Squeezing.
A firm which is dominant in the markets for both a raw material and a derived product may commit an abuse by charging an inflated price for the raw material to companies which compete with the dominant firm in the production of the derived product. Such a price squeeze applied by a dominant firm with the result

515. *Deutsche Post I*, D.Comm. March 20, 2001, 2001 OJ L 125/27, points 35–36.
516. *Hilti*, D.Comm. Dec. 22, 1987, 1988 OJ L 63/19, 37; *aff' d* CFI Dec. 12, 1991, 1991 ECR II-1439 and ECJ March 2, 1994, 1994 ECR I-667. The *Macron/Angus* case concerned also a complaint of predatory pricing against a smaller competitor by a producer of fire hoses who held 70% of the UK market; however, the case was settled and no details were published: Seventeenth Report on Competition Policy, point 81. *See also supra* section D.5 (tying).
517. *Wanadoo*, D.Comm. July 16, 2003, IP/03/1025.
518. Assymetric digital subscriber line.
519. *See also Deutsche Telekom II*, D.Comm. July 16, 2003, IP/03/717 (imposition of fines in order to prevent the application of exclusionary prices for access to the local loop).

that competition in the market of the derived 'product is restricted is a form of predatory pricing and constitutes an abuse within the meaning of Article 82.[520]

(b) Exclusionary Pricing by Means of Cross-Subsidization [521]

Artificial Cost-Allocation.

Cross-subsidization may lead to abusive predatory pricing by selling a service below cost with the intention to eliminating competitors or deterring entry, enabling it to further increase its market power. Cross-subsidization practised by a dominant firm means that it distorts competition by allocating all or part of its costs in one product or one geographic market (which it dominates) to another product or geographic market, thereby enabling it to beat other competitors with offers which are made possible not by efficiency and performance but by artificial means of internal subsidies. Cross subsidization can, according to the Commission's definition in its Notice on the Application of the Competition Rules in the Postal Sector, 'distort competition and lead to competitors being beaten by offers which are made possible not by efficiency (including economies of scale) and performance but by cross-subsidies.'[522] However, cross-subsidization is not an abuse in itself[523] although the Commission's Telecommunications Notice on the Application of the Competition Rules in the Telecommunications Sector may be read in this sense.[524] For instance, a state may finance the provision of services of general interest, provided it does not exceed the additional costs actually incurred in providing services in the general interest. In this case state financing ceases to be a real advantage within the meaning of Article 87 (1) and may be regarded as reasonable compensation for the discharge of public service obligations,[525] in

520. *British Sugar*, D.Comm. July 18, 1988, 1988 OJ L 284/41, para. 66; *Deutsche Telekom II*, D.Comm. May 21, 2003, IP/03/717. Under Article 66 of the ECSC Treaty: *National Carbonizing*, ECJ 22 Oct. 1975, 1975 ECR 1193. *See* Commission's Notice on the Application of the Competition Rules to Access Agreements in the Telecommunications Sector, 1998 OJ C 265/2, point 117.
521. *See* D. Geradin, *The Opening to Competition of State Monopolies: An Overview of the Main Issues of the Liberalization Process*, Liege, 5–6 November 1998, pp. 9–16; Abbamonte, *Cross-Subsidization and Community Competition Rules: Efficient Pricing v. Equity?* 23 ELRev 414 (1999)
522. 1998 OJ C 39/2, point 3.1.
523. *UPS/Deutsche Post*, CFI March 20, 2002, 2002 ECR II-1915, para. 61.
524. Guidelines on the Application of the Competition Rules in the Telecommunications Sector, 1991 OJ C 233/2, points 102–110. However, the Court appears to interpret these Guidelines in such a way as not to contradict the Commission
525. *Cf.* Commission Recommendation on Accounting Liberalization in a Liberalized Telecommunications Market, 1998 OJ L 141/6, point 3; Commission Notice on Postal Services, 1998 OJ C 329/2, points 3.1.–3.4. Commission Directive 1999/64/EC on Separation of Telecommunications Networks and Cable TV Networks, 1999 OJ L 175/39, recital 2.

particular of the universal service reserved to postal monopolies.[526] Assessing cross-subsidization is therefore rather a specific issue of identifying and allocating costs in order to evaluate predatory pricing.[527] The qualification of cross-subsidization as a means of predatory pricing therefore depends on the funds used and the purpose pursued.

Funds Used for Cross-Subsidization.
The funds used for cross-subsidization may result from revenues obtained from commercial activities in the dominated market or from funds received from the state to finance the dominant firm's public mission in that market.[528]

- With regard to funds received from activities in the reserved market, the Court of First Instance stated in the *UPS/Deutsche Post* case[529] the mere fact that an exclusive right is granted in order to guarantee a universal service does not preclude the owner of such rights from earning profits from those reserved activities and does not in itself raise any problem from the standpoint of the competition rules. However, competition problems could arise (i) where such funds derived from excessive or discriminatory prices or from other unfair practices in the reserved market and are used for predatory purposes in markets open to competition, and (ii) where such funds are used for predatory purposes in a market open to competition.[530]
- With regard to funds received from the state, the Commission stated in its *Deutsche Post III* decision[531] that funds received from the state to compensate losses and to discharge its public service mission but used ('misused'[532]) for financing a predatory pricing policy towards its private rivals in the markets

526. *Corbeau*, ECJ May 19, 1993, 1993 ECR I-2533, paras 15–21; *IECC*, CFI Sept. 16, 1998, 1998 ECR II-3645, paras 94–106; *TNT/Poste Italiana*, ECJ May 17, 2001, 2001 ECR I-4109, paras 57–62. *See also* the Commission's Communication on Services of General Interest in Europe (2001 OJ C 17/4) where the Commission stated that 'the experience gained so far also confirms the full compatibility of the Treaty rules on competition and the internal market with high standards in the provision of services of general interest. In certain circumstances, in particular where market forces alone do not result in a satisfactory provision of services, public authorities may entrust certain operators of services with obligations of general interest and where necessary grant them special or exclusive rights *and/or devise a funding mechanism for their provision*' (emphasis added).
527. *See Cost Allocation in Competition Policy*, Oxford Economic Research Associates (OXERA), Competing Ideas, May 2003, pp. 1–3.
528. *See* the definition of 'subsidy' in Article 4 of Regulation 868/2004, 2004 OJ L 162/1.
529. *UPS/Deutsche Post*, CFI March 20, 2002, 2002 ECR II-1915, paras 51 and 61.
530. *Ibid.* paras 55 and 62.
531. *Deutsche Post III*, D.Comm. June 19, 2002, 2002 OJ L 247/27 (by this decision the Commission ordered the government to recover those funds).
532. *See* Article 88 (2).

open to competition constituted an illegal state aid.[533] Such funds may only be received and used for financing the public service itself.[534]

Unjustified Cost Advantages.
The greatest practical difficulty is to identify and allocate costs of the firm's activities in related but distinct markets (in particular reserved markets and markets open to competition) in order to assess any predatory pricing. In its *Deutsche Post* case[535] the Commission stated:

> 'According to the case law of the European Court of Justice, pricing below average variable costs must be regarded as abusive.[536] This principle was established in *AKZO*, where the Court defined average variable costs as 'costs which vary depending on the quantities produced'. In determining which costs vary depending on the quantities produced, the division between common fixed costs and costs attributable to a specific service ... must be borne in mind... Given the public universal service obligation, only the additional costs of providing a particular service vary with the volume produced.'

The *German Post III* decision gives an example of how difficult it is to divide up cost and to calculate the *net additional costs* to the specific service on a market open to competition, in particular due to the rebate policy with respect to the Post's door-to-door services.[537] For instance, the comparison of the cost-price relationship in such a case must include the provision of logistical and commercial assistance.[538] In the case of products and services provided between companies belonging to the same group, the internal price must not involve any financial advantage whatsoever, i.e. must be full-cost prices (total costs plus a mark-up to

533. Accordingly, the Commission examines the legality of state aid when assessing a cooperation agreement (*Unisource*, D.Comm. Oct. 29, 1997, 1997 OJ L 381/1, exemption subject to the condition not to cross-subsidize), the creation of a joint venture (*Matra*, ECJ June 15, 1993, 1993 ECR I-3250) or the acquisition of a company (*RJB Mining*, CFI Jan. 31, 2001, 2001 ECR II-337); in this case the Court found that a state aid (in the present case the possibility to acquire a state-owned company at a symbolic price of 1 DM, which did not reflect the real value) constituted a risk of distorting competition likely to strengthen the financial power of the merged entities). The merger *Deutsche Post/DHL* was cleared by the Commission on June 26, 1998, M.1168, 'without prejudice to any decision the Commission may take on the basis of the EC competition rules ...' (in particular Article 82).
534. *UFEX*, CFI Dec. 14, 2000, 2000 ECR II-4055, annulling Commission decision of Oct. 1, 1997, 1998 OJ L 164/37 (which erroneously stated that no state aid was involved); *TNT/Italian Post*, ECJ May 17, 2002, 2002 ECR I-4109.
535. *Deutsche Post*, D.Comm. March 20, 2001, 2001 OJ L 125/27, point 35.
536. *AKZO II*, ECJ July, 3, 1991, 1991 ECR I-3359, paras 71–72; *BPB*, CFI April 1, 1993, 1993 ECR II-389, para. 68 (*aff'd* ECJ April 6, 1995, 1995 ECR I-865).
537. *German Post III*, D.Comm. June 19, 2002, 2002 OJ L 247/27, points 86–91.
538. *UFEX*, CFI Dec. 14, 2000, 2000 ECR II-4055, para. 68.

remunerate equity capital investment), which would be obtained under normal market conditions.[539]

(c) Exclusionary Dealing Arrangements

Introduction.
A dominant firm may also infringe Article 82 by certain types of dealing arrangements with its customers that tend to exclude competitors. Such arrangements include long-term requirements (exclusive dealing) or part-requirements contracts and equivalent informal relationships secured by pressure or threats, clauses requiring customers to disclose more favourable offers received from competitors, supply contracts associated with the leasing of equipment, and exclusionary rebate schemes.

(i) Requirements Contracts (Exclusive Dealing)

General.
Requirements contracts – i.e., vertical agreements that tie the purchaser to obtaining all or most of its requirements of a good or service from the supplier over a certain period – are more likely to violate the competition rules when the supplier holds a dominant position.[540] A dominant supplier who enters into long-term exclusive dealing relationships with its customers is likely to infringe Article 82. The anticompetitive abuses lie in precluding the customer from switching to alternative suppliers and conversely foreclosing competing suppliers from the opportunity to make sales to the customers bound by the exclusive dealing relationship.[541] This applies to agreements a dominant firm enters into with processors[542] as well as with distributors[543] or customers.[544]

---

539. *Ibid.*, paras 68–72 (with further references).
540. For the treatment of similar agreements under Article 81, *see supra* Chapter IV.B.5 and F.5.
541. *Hoffmann-La Roche*, ECJ Feb. 13, 1979, 1979 ECR 461, paras 89–90; *AKZO*, ECJ July 3, 1991, 1991 ECR I-3359, para. 149; *Almelo*, ECJ April 27, 1994, 1994 ECR 3359, para. 44.
542. *Hoffmann-La Roche*, ECJ Feb. 13, 1979, 1979 ECR 461, paras 89–90 (exclusive use of HLR's basic vitamine for further treatment); *Billiton/M&T*, Seventh Report on Competition Policy, point 13 1 (exclusive use of an intermediate chemical for reprocessing); *Aspartame*, Eighteenth Report on Competition Policy, point 53 (exclusive use of sweetener Aspartame in Coca Cola); *Soda Ash Z*, Eleventh Report on Competition Policy, points 73–76; *Soda Ash I – Solvay*, D.Comm. Dec. 13, 1999, 2003 OJ L 10/10 (exclusive use of Solvay's soda ash for glass production).
543. *Sugar*, ECJ Dec. 16, 1975, 1975 ECR 1663, paras 459–468 (exlusive dealing imposed on dealers of sugar); *Oliofiat*, Seventeenth Report on Competition Policy point 84 (exclusive dealing of lubricants imposed on Fiat dealers); *Coca Cola II*, Nineteenth Report on Competition Policy, point 50 (exclusivity of cola-flavored soft drinks imposed on Coca Cola distributors); *Van den Bergh Foods*, D.Comm. March 11, 1998, 1998 OJ L 246/1, points 263–264 (provision of deepfreezer cabinets on exclusive terms); *aff'd* CFI Oct. 23, 2003, T-65/98; *TACA II*, D.Comm. Sept. 16, 1998, 1999 OJ L 95/1, points 493–494 (ban on multiple service contracts

Equivalent Relationships Secured by Pressure or Threats.
A dominant supplier may be able to keep its customers 'loyal' by threatening to withdraw supplies in case they purchase from a competitor or by giving an exclusive or preferential status to customers that deal with it.[545] In the *British Plasterboard* case[546] the dominant supplier, British Plasterboard's subsidiary British Gypsum, made it clear to its customers that those who did not deal in imported plasterboard would be given priority for deliveries of plaster when plaster was in short supply. As the customers were dependent on regular deliveries of plaster from a single source (because of differences of quality), this policy would have strongly discouraged them from purchasing their plasterboard from the only competitors of British Plasterboard, namely importers. It was therefore considered to be an abuse of the supplier's dominant position.

Part-Requirements Contracts.
Long-term supply contracts with a dominant supplier covering less than the customer's total requirements may also be contrary to Article 82 if they impose unreasonable conditions on the customer or give the supplier a decisive competitive advantage over other suppliers or lead to collusion with them. Such effects may arise where:

- The customer has contracted to obtain a fixed percentage of its requirements, or a fixed quantity that is close to its total requirements, from the dominant supplier, even if this percentage is declining over a period of years.[547]
- The contractual arrangements enable the supplier to find out the customer's total requirements, including the quantities purchased from competitors, to identify competing suppliers and to obtain information about their prices, etc., thus gaining a competitive advantage over them.[548]

---

with any particular shipper), in this respect *aff'd Atlantic Container Line AB*, CFI Sept. 30, 2003, T-191/98, paras 560–577.

544. *Pelikan/RAY*, Twenty-sixth Report on Competition Policy, point 61 and p. 140 (cartridges for printers); *Sega/Nintendo*, Twenty-seventh Report on Competition Policy, point 80 (amusement machines); *IRE/Nordion*, Twenty-eighth Report on Competition Policy, point 74.
545. *United Brands*, ECJ Feb. 14, 1978, 1978 ECR 207, para. 155; *AKZO II*, ECJ 3 July 1991, 1991 ECR I-3359, para. 147; *Irish Sugar*, D.Comm. May 14, 1997, 1997 OJ L 258/1, points 120–123.
546. *British Plasterboard*, D.Comm. Dec. 5, 1988, 1989 OJ L 10/50, 67–68; *aff'd* CFI April 1, 1993, 193 ECR I-389 and ECJ April 6, 1995, 1995 ECR I-865, paras 69–72 (security of supply does not justify long-term exclusivity).
547. *Hoffmann-La Roche*, ECJ Feb. 13, 1979, 1979 ECR 461, paras 82–87; *British Plasterboard*, CFI April 1, 1993, 1993 ECR I-389, paras 68, 120: *aff'd* ECJ April 6, 1995, 1995 ECR I-865. *See also UCB-Almirall*, Twenty-fourth Report on Competition Policy, p. 362 (clearance of the amended agreement which consisted in a three-year 50% purchasing obligation together with UCB's commitment to fulfill the customer's complete demand, if requested).
548. *See also infra* section 6 (c) (ii), 'English Clauses'.

– The supply arrangements are such – for example, the customer is buying 50% of its requirements from the dominant supplier and 50% from an outsider – that they lead to collusion between the suppliers and possibly to the allocation of other customers between them.[549]

Permissible Types and Duration of Supply Contracts.
On the basis of the few decisions taken so far on supply contracts with dominant suppliers, it may be concluded that fixed-term contracts under which the supplier undertakes to supply certain purchase quantities (but not certain percentages of the purchaser's requirements, or quantities directly related to requirements) at agreed prices, may be made for between six months and two years if this is reasonable given the supplier's interest in stability for planning purposes and the customer's interest in flexibility in choosing its source of supply.[550] Similar contracts concluded for an indefinite duration, but allowing a right of termination at reasonable notice (which may be laid down in national law, e.g. six months under Italian law), are also permissible. Longer-term supply contracts can only be justified by major investments in licence agreements,[551] in storage facilities or pipeline or network links between supplier and customer.[552] Safety reasons[553] or technical

549. *Italian Flat Glass II*, D.Comm. Dec. 7, 1988, 1989 OJ L 33/44, 66; *aff'd* in part and *rev'd* in part (for lack of proof) CFI March 10, 1992, 1992 ECR II-1403, paras 260–267.

550. Under Article 81 the Court of First Instance found that exclusive supply agreements between the two major manufacturers having a joint market share of respectively 45 and 25% of the relevant market and binding more than 30% of the customers may not be concluded for a period exceeding 2½ years: *Langnese/Iglo*, CFI June 8, 1995, 1995 ECR II-1533, para. 94; *aff'd* ECJ Oct. 1, 1998, 1998 ECR I-5609. Six-month contracts covering a minimum of 25% of requirements have been accepted under arrangements with a buying pool: *National Sulphuric Acid Association I*, D.Comm. July 9, 1980, 1980 OJ L 260/24, 27. Two years has been accepted in cases where industrial customers required longer-term security of supply and regular deliveries in order to avoid storage costs: *Soda Ash I*, Eleventh Report on Competition Policy, points 73–76; *Aspartame*, Eighteenth Report on Competition Policy, point 53. *Cf.*, however, the second *Soda Ash* case, where two-year contracts covering the bulk of the customer's requirements were considered too long and Solvay was required to reduce them to one year and to reduce the period of notice on indefinite contracts from two years to six months: *Soda Ash II – Solvay*, D.Comm. Dec. 13, 2000, 2003 OJ L 10/10, (the *Soda Ash I* decision of Dec. 19, 1990, 1991 OJ L 152/21, was annulled on procedural grounds, CFI June 29, 1995, 1995 ECR I-1825). Five-year contracts with a dominant supplier have also been challenged under Article 82 (*Soda Ash I* and *Aspartame*, *supra*) but are permitted under Regulation 2790/1999. In longer-term contracts the price should be fixed in order to prevent the supplier's unilaterally dictating price increases: *Alsatel/Novasam*, ECJ 5 Oct. 1988, 1988 ECR 5987, para. 10.

551. *See* under the merger control regulation the merger between *SEB* and *Moulinex* which was likely to lead to a dominant position and was only cleared subject to the commitment to licence the acquired trademark Moulinex for 5 years (which corresponded to the life cycle of the products concerned: CFI April 3, 2003, T-119/02, para. 127.

552. Supplies of liquid gas, three years; supplies of gas by pipeline, fifteen years: *Industrial Gases*, Nineteenth Report on Competition Policy, point 62; Commission Press Release No. (89) 426. *See also Pego*, Twenty-third Report on Competition Policy, points 133a and 222; *Isar Energy*

requirements[554] may justify longer-term supply contracts.[555]

(ii) 'English Clauses'

The *Hoffmann-La Roche* and *Industrial Gases* Cases.
Exclusive dealing contracts may contain a so-called 'English clause' which slightly relaxes the exclusive purchase requirement. Under this type of clause the purchaser may accept lower-priced quotations from competitors of the supplier if, after being informed of them by the purchaser, the supplier declines to match the quoted prices. In the *Hoffmann-La Roche* case[556] the Court of Justice held that in practice such clauses provided little more scope for competition than simple requirements contracts because they tended to be hedged with restrictions, and that moreover they allowed the dominant firm to find out the prices offered by its competitors and to identify those competitors. They were therefore just as much an abuse of dominance as simple exclusive dealing contracts or exclusionary rebate schemes. In the *Industrial Gases* case[557] the Commission got the suppliers to amend their 'English clauses' into a form that mitigated the danger of their serving to inform the dominant supplier of competitors' prices. Under such clauses, which would be included in the contract only at the customer's request, the customer would inform a third party confidentially of a competing offer, so that the detailed information of price and identity did not reach the dominant firm. This type of 'English clause' would guarantee the advantages to the purchaser of dealing with third parties, thereby relaxing a purchase obligation, while avoiding the anticompetitive effect of passing on detailed information about competitors' prices directly to the dominant firm.

Possible Justifications of Longer-Term Exclusive Dealing.
A dominant firm may be able to justify exclusive dealing where use of a particular product or service is objectively necessary for a technically satisfactory exploitation of a licensed technology or for ensuring respect of a quality standard,[558] for ensuring

---

and *Transgas/Turbogas*, Twenty-sixth Report on Competition Policy, pp. 133–135 (supply of electricity by high voltage network or gas by pipeline; duration of 20–30 years reduced to 15 years).

553. *Industrial Gases*, Nineteenth Report on Competition Policy, point 62 (exclusive right to fill a particular storage facility).

554. Rejected in *Hilti*, CFI Dec. 12, 1991, 1991 ECR II-1439, paras 115–119, 135; *Novo Nordisk*, Twenty-sixth Report on Competition Policy, point 62 and p. 142.

555. The maximum duration of an exclusive supply agreement for the resale of goods that is accepted under block exemption Regulation 2790/1999 is five years: Article 5 (a).

556. *Hoffmann-La Roche*, ECJ Feb. 13, 1979, 1979 ECR 461, paras 102–108.

557. *Industrial Gases*, Nineteenth Report on Competition Policy, point 62.

558. Rejected in *Hilti*, CFI Dec. 12, 1991, 1991 ECR II-1439, paras 115–119, 135; *Novo Nordisk*, Twenty-sixth Report on Competition Policy, point 62 and p. 142.

the performance of particular tasks assigned by a governmental measure[559] or for permitting the phasing-in of a new competitor in a recently liberalized sector such as energy.[560]

(iii) Supply Contracts Associated with the Leasing of Equipment

Necessarily Long-Term.
Another way a dominant supplier can abusively lock its customers into a long-term exclusive dealing relationship is to require them to rent necessary equipment from it. In the *Industrial Gases* case[561] the Commission objected to storage tank rental contracts, which were necessarily long-term, being incorporated in the gas supply contract. This tied the customer to the gas supplier. Instead, customers should be free to rent their equipment from any firm of their choice.

(iv) Exclusionary Rebate Schemes – Fidelity Rebates

Introduction.
Certain kinds of price discounts can tie customers to a supplier just as effectively as requirements contracts or can reinforce the effect of such contracts. This is especially the case with rebates, i.e., discounts paid retrospectively in respect of past purchases. Rebate schemes, whether in conjunction with requirements contracts or by themselves, are likely to infringe Article 82 when practised by a dominant supplier. As the Court of Justice stated in *Hoffmann-La Roche:*

> 'An undertaking which is in a dominant position on a market and ties purchasers – even if it does so at their request – by an obligation or promise on their part to obtain all or most or their requirements exclusively from the said undertaking abuses its dominant position within the meaning of Article 82 of the Treaty, whether the obligation in question is stipulated without

559. Article 86 (2) of the EC Treaty; *Almelo*, ECJ April 27, 1994, 1994 ECR I-1477, paras 47–49. Justification rejected in: *British Telecommunication*, ECJ March 20, 1985, 1985 ECR 873, para. 33; *Porto di Genova*, ECJ Dec. 10, 1991, 1991 ECR I-5889.
560. Commission's Notice on access agreements in the telecommunications sector, 1998 OJ C 265/2, point 91. The Commission was opposed to 20–30 years, but accepted a duration of 15 years: *Pego*, Twenty-third Report on Competition Policy, points 133a and 222 (electricity in Portugal); *Isar Energy*, Twenty-sixth Report on Competition Policy, p. 133 (electricity in Italy); *Electrabel*, IP/97/351 (electricity in Belgium); *REN/Turbogas*, Twenty-sixth Report on Competition Policy, p. 135 (importation of Algerian natural gas by pipeline to Portugal).
561. *Industrial Gases*, Nineteenth Report on Competition Policy, point 62. *See also Total*, Commission Press Release No. IP/88/503; Eighteenth Report on Competition Policy, point 140; *Tetra Pak II*, CFI Oct. 6, 1994, 1994 ECR II-755, para. 82 (purchasing or leasing of milk filling machines); *Van den Bergh Foods*, D.Comm. March 11, 1998, 1998 OJ L 246/1, points 263–264 (provision of deep-freezer cabinets on exclusive terms), *aff'd* CFI Oct. 23, 2003, T-65/98.

further qualification or whether it is undertaken in consideration of the grant of a rebate.

The same applies if the said undertaking, without tying the purchasers by a formal obligation, applies, either under the terms of agreements concluded with these purchasers or unilaterally, a system of fidelity rebates, that is to say discounts conditional on the customer's obtaining all or most of its requirements – whether the quantity of its purchases be large or small – from the undertaking in a dominant position.'[562]

Types of Discount Arrangements.

The types of discount arrangements practised by a dominant supplier that are likely to infringe Article 82 are, first, so-called 'fidelity' or 'loyalty rebates, as in the *Hoffmann-La Roche* case, i.e., rebates conditional on the customer purchasing all or a large proportion of its requirements from the supplier over a certain period, and, secondly, aggregated rebates which are paid in respect of the customer's total purchases of all products from the supplier over a period. Their aim is, by granting financial advatages which are not justified by any economic service, to prevent customers from obtaining their supplies from competing producers and so consolidate and entrench the supplier's dominant position,[563] even if the amount of the fidelity rebate seems, in absolute figures, rather small, e.g. 1% or less.[564] They are not related to genuine cost savings achieved by the supplier, as is the case with quantity discounts for large orders, discounts related to the distance of the destination to which the goods are delivered, or cash discounts for prompt payment; nor are they a consideration for services performed by the customer, such as special promotional efforts.[565] The fact that such rebates may nevertheless be compatible with national law is irrelevant, given the supremacy of Community law, except where the national provisions require the firm to act in that way.[566]

Fidelity and Minimum Purchases Rebates.

Fidelity rebates can be stipulated in contracts or granted unilaterally at the supplier's discretion. They usually involve price (rebate) discrimination in the sense of Article 82 (c) between different customers, i.e. between the customers which are induced to loyalty and those which are willing to bear the disadvantages, including the loss of a service bonus.[567] A particularly abusive form of fidelity rebates

562. *Hoffmann-La Roche*, ECJ Feb. 13, 1979, 1979 ECR 461, para. 89.
563. *Irish Sugar*, CFI Oct. 7, 1999, 1999 ECR II-2969, para. 197.
564. *Ibid.* paras 226–239.
565. *Sugar*, ECJ Dec. 16, 1975, 1975 ECR 1663, paras 517–518; *Hoffmann-La Roche*, ECJ Feb. 13, 1979, 1979 ECR 461, para. 90; *Michelin I*, ECJ Nov. 9, 1983, 1983 ECR 3461, paras 73 and 85; *Irish Sugar*, CFI Oct. 7, 1999, 1999 ECR II-2969, para. 214.
566. *Irish Sugar*, CFI Oct. 7, 1999, 1999 ECR II-2969, para. 211; *Ladbroke Racing*, ECJ Nov. 11, 1997, 1997 ECR I-6265, paras 33–34.
567. *Michelin II*, D.Comm. June 20, 2001, 2002 OJ L 143/1, points 248–249 and 256–258, *aff'd* CFI Sept. 30, 2003, T-203/01, paras 213–220.

is the *progress bonus* by which the dealer has to commit himself to a minimum amount of purchases corresponding either to the previous year's purchases or to the average of the last two or three years depending on the initial basis rather than on the quantities effectively purchased.[568]

- *Contractual Arrangements.* A contractual fidelity rebate scheme was practised by *Hoffmann-La Roche*.[569] Its contracts with vitamin purchasers that contained an exclusive, or virtually exclusive, dealing obligation stipulated a fixed rate of rebate conditional on the purchase requirement being fulfilled, and so underpinning the exclusivity obligation. In contracts without a fixed purchase obligation, on the other hand, a progressive rate of rebate was offered which rose with the proportion of the customer's requirements obtained from La Roche, for instance a 1% rebate for purchasing 60% of requirements, 1.5% for 70% and 2% for 80%. The progressive rebates thus acted as a substitute for a contractual purchase requirement in such contracts. In *British Sugar*,[570] fidelity rebates were offered to a group of buyers if all of them purchased exclusively from British Sugar. The supplier used peer pressure[571] as well as the financial inducement of the rebate to gain all the group's business. Even quite small fidelity rebates can represent a strong incentive to remain loyal to the supplier, because the amount lost, should the rebate be forfeited, may add up to a substantial sum so that major savings would be required on deliveries from other suppliers to compensate.[572] The incentive effect is greater still if the supplies obtainable elsewhere are uncertain, which allows the dominant supplier to exploit customers' fears of being left short.[573] Fidelity rebates often also lead to the dominant supplier receiving commercially valuable information about the customer and other suppliers which it can exploit to tighten its control of the market.[574] The commercial agreements between the dominant firm and its distributors are likely to aggravate the abusive nature of the fidelity rebate system.[575] In the *Deutsche Post I* case,[576] the Commission stated that a provi-

---

568. *Ibid.*, paras 260–266.
569. *Hoffmann-La Roche*, ECJ Feb. 13, 1979, 1979 ECR 461, paras 80–121.
570. *British Sugar*, D.Comm. July 18, 1988, 1988 OJ L 284/41, point 74.
571. *See also Irish Sugar*, D.Comm. May 14, 1997, 1997 OJ L 258/1, point 120 (pressure on transporters not to transport competitor's products).
572. *Michelin I*, ECJ Nov. 9, 1983, 1983 ECR 3461, paras 79–82.
573. *Sugar*, ECJ Dec. 16, 1975, 1975 ECR 1663, para. 503; *Michelin II*, D.Comm. June 20, 2001, 2002 OJ L 143/1, point 220, *aff'd* CFI Sept. 30, 2003, T-203/01, paras 204–212. Fidelity rebates were also used in *British Sugar*, D.Comm. Oct. 14, 1998, 1999 OJ L 76/1, and *Coca Cola I*, Commission Press Release No. IP/88/615; similarly, *Coca Cola II*, Nineteenth Report on Competition Policy, point 50; *British Airways*, D.Comm. July 14, 1999, 2000 OJ L 30/1 (fine of EUR 6.8 million), *aff'd* CFI Dec. 17, 2003, T-219/99, paras 270–299.
574. As in the case of part-requirements contracts and 'English clauses': *see infra* section D.6 (c) (i) and (ii) and Guidelines on Vertical Restraints, 1999 OJ C 270/12, point 152.
575. *Michelin II*, D.Comm. June 20, 2001, 2002 OJ L 143/1, points 272–280 and 315–331 (concerning the 'Michelin Friends Club'), *aff'd* CFI Sept. 30, 2003, T-203/01, para. 228.
576. *Deutsche Post I*, D.Comm. March 20, 2001, 2001 OJ L 125/27, points 33–34.

sion whereby the special price stipulated therein is dependent on the customer adding the quantity it dispatched the previous year via a competitor in addition to the quantity already dispatched via the Deutsche Post infringed Article 82. Such a tying practice tends to extend the statutary monopoly into neighbouring and competitive markets which is contrary to Article 82.[577]

- *Unilateral or Selective Rebate Policies*. In the *Michelin I* case, the Dutch subsidiary of the French tyre company set rebates individually for different dealers conditional on their reaching a sales target for Michelin tyres based on their previous years' sales. The rates of rebate to be granted and the sales targets were not communicated in writing to the dealers so that they were kept in a state of uncertainty, especially towards the end of the year, as to whether they would meet their target and earn the rebate. This uncertainty made them especially reluctant to purchase from outsiders. The fact that the rebates were dependent on meeting volume targets did not make them into quantity discounts, which are normally unobjectionable, because (i) quantity discounts are normally paid in respect of individual orders and in return for cost savings achieved by the supplier, and (ii) the volume targets in question were closely related to the customers' total requirements.[578] The *Michelin II* case concerned similar fidelity practices on the French market.[579] In the second *Soda Ash* case[580] the Commission held that both Solvay and ICI applied in their respective territories where they held a dominant position a system of exclusionary 'top slice' rebates whereby they charged the ordinary price for a customer's core requirements that it was accustomed and prepared to take from the dominant producer, but offered deep discounts on marginal quantities (the 'top slice') in excess of those core requirements in order to ensure that the customer took these, too, from the dominant supplier. Discretionary loyalty payments were also a feature of the dominant supplier's abuse of its position in the *British Plasterboard* case. In this case, selected merchants who undertook to take all their requirements of plasterboard from British Plasterboard received regular extra payments, and the company withdrew rebates from Northern Irish merchants who were planning to import plasterboard from Spain and introduced new rebates precisely on those sizes of board that were to be imported.[581] Similarly, in the *Hilti* case

577. *Italian Post*, D.Comm. Dec. 21, 2000, 2001 OJ L 63/59 (Article 86 (3) decision), points 24–28.
578. *Michelin I*, ECJ Nov. 9, 1983, 1983 ECR 3461, paras 62–86. *See also Hoffmann-La Roche*, ECJ Feb. 13, 1979, 1979 ECR 461, para. 90; *British Airways*, D.Comm. July 14, 1999, 2000 OJ L 30/1, *aff'd* CFI Dec. 17, 2003, T-3219/99; *Coca Cola*, D.Comm. Memo 99/42 of July 22, 1999 (pending investigation on target/growth rebates, full range rebates, and de-listing payments).
579. *Michelin II*, D.Comm. June 20, 2001, 2002 OJ L 143/1, points 215 *et seq*, *aff'd* CFI Sept. 30, 2003, T-203/01.
580. *Soda Ash – Solvay II*, D.Comm. Dec. 13, 2000, 2003 OJ L 10, 10, points 149–176.
581. *British Plasterboard*, D.Comm. Dec. 5, 1988, 1989 OJ L 10/50, 65–66, 68–69; *aff'd* CFI April 1, 1993, 1993 ECR II-389; *aff'd* ECJ April 6, 1995, 1995 ECR I-865.

discretionary discounts were reduced for firms that did not buy Hilti nails, showing that the discounts were in fact a reward for loyalty.[582]

Aggregated Rebate Schemes.

Rebate schemes in which the amount of rebate depends on the customer's aggregate purchases of all products from the supplier are a form of tying, a practice expressly referred to in Article 82 (d).[583] Fidelity rebates are often based on aggregate purchases. The aggregation increases the exclusionary effect of the rebate scheme because it induces the customer also to obtain products from the supplier which the latter would otherwise not be able to sell to the customer because adequate competitively priced supplies are available from other suppliers. The effect is further increased if the rate of rebate rises with the aggregate purchase volume, as in the *Michelin* cases.[584] Here, the rebate was paid on total purchases of tyres during a period of one year (largely exceeding a reasonable period of three months), including the purchases of tyres in market segments where Michelin was *not* dominant, thereby leveraging its dominant position in one market segment into other market segments.

Discount Schemes that are not Abusive.

As noted above, the granting of a rebate is abusive where such a rebate has the effect, through the granting of financial advantages, of preventing customers from obtaining supplies from rival producers. By contrast, quantitative rebate schemes that are linked exclusively to the volume of purchases made from a dominant producer are generally regarded as not having such an exclusionary effect because they are deemed to reflect gains in efficiencies and economies of scale.[585] This is true, for example, of automatic quantity discounts deducted directly from the invoiced price (i.e., unrelated to the customer's purchases over a period of time), discounts dependent on the distance of the destination to which the goods are delivered, and cash discounts for prompt payment. In the Italian *Coca Cola* case,[586]

582. *Hilti*, D.Comm. Dec. 22, 1987, 1988 OJ L 65/19, 38; *aff'd* CFI Dec. 12, 1991, 1991 ECR II-1439; *aff'd* ECJ March 2, 1994, 1994 ECR I-667. This policy was pursued by the practice of granting smaller discounts for orders for cartridge strips without nails which was prohibited on similar grounds. *See also Irish Sugar*, D.Comm. 14 May 1997, 1997 OJ L 258/1, points 127–135 and points 151–154 ('target rebates').

583. *See supra* section D.5. For aggregated rebate schemes by non-dominant firms and collective aggregated rebate arrangements, *see also supra* Chapter IV.F.6 and Chapter II.E.3.

584. *Michelin I*, ECJ Nov. 9, 1983, 1983 ECR 3461, para. 66; *Michelin II*, D.Comm. June 20, 2001, 2002 OJ L 143/1, points 216–220, *aff'd* CFI Sept. 30, 2003, T-203/01. Purchases of all vitamins were aggregated in *Hoffmann-La Roche*, ECJ Feb. 13, 1979, 1979 ECR 461, para. 87; similarly, *Coca Cola I*, IP/88/615; *Coca Cola II*, Nineteenth Report on Competition Policy, point 50.

585. *British Airways*, CFI Dec. 17, 2003, T-219/99, paras 244–246.

586. *Coca Cola I*, IP/88/615; *see also Michelin I*, ECJ Nov. 9, 1983, 1983 ECR 3461, para. 66 and the amended rebate scheme in the *British Plaster Board* case, Twenty-second report on Competition Policy, p. 443.

the Commission found that offering discounts for taking a full range of sizes of the same product and for promotional efforts on behalf of the supplier was acceptable, but required fidelity and aggregated rebates to be discontinued. In *British Plaster Board II*[587] the Commission accepted discounts that are economically justified on the basis of cost savings, such as quantities supplied, promotion and transport costs, provided they are applied in a non-discriminatory way.[588]

Product Swap Agreements.
Fidelity rebates may be combined with product swaps. In *Irish Sugar* the Court of First Instance ruled that it was an infringement of Article 82 for the dominant firm to agree with one wholesaler and one retailer to swap competing retail sugar products for its own products under the threat of a withdrawal of the preferential discounts hitherto granted to them, thereby preventing new products being resold at competitive conditions and consolidating its dominant position.[589]

(d) Abusive (Predatory) Use of Industrial or Intellectual Property Rights

Dominance and Abuse not Automatic – Existence v. Exercise.
The mere existence of industrial or intellectual property rights does not constitute a dominant position, unless there are no substitutable products or technologies on the relevant market,[590] nor does the exercise of such rights constitute, as such, an abuse but under exceptional circumstances – even by a dominant firm.[591] In each case concerning refusal of access to a technology the Court of Justice has repeatedly stated that the application of Community law shall not prejudice the rules in member states governing the system of property ownership as long as these rights are not harmonized, but that the *exercise* of these rights may conflict with Community law, in particular Articles 81 and 82.[592] Thus, the exercise of an industrial

---

587. Discount schemes notified in the context of the Commission's proceedings under Article 82 (Twenty-second Report on Competition Policy, p. 443) and accepted by way of comfort letters: *Super Stockist Scheme* (1992 OJ C 321/9), *Buying Societies Plasterboard Rebate Scheme* (1992 OJ C 321/10), *Efficiency Rebate Scheme* (1992 OJ C 321/11) and *Accessories and Do-it-yourself Promotion Schemes* (1992 OJ C 321/12).
588. *See also Irish Sugar*, CFI Oct. 7, 1999, 1999 ECR II-2969, paras 203–224.
589. *Irish Sugar*, CFI Oct. 7, 1999, 1999 ECR II-2969, paras 226–234. *See Tetra Pak II*, D.Comm. July 24, 1991, 1992 OJ L 72/1, point 165.
590. *Deutsche Grammophon*, ECJ June 8, 1971, 1971, ECR 487, para. 16.
591. *Magill*, ECJ April 6, 1995, 1995 ECR I-743, para. 50; *Micro Leader*, CFI Dec. 16, 1999, 1999 ECR II-3989, para. 56; *IMS Health*, ECJ April 11, 2002, 2002 ECR I-3401, paras 64–65. However, Article 86 may be infringed if the grant of an exclusive right leads to an abuse (*Deutsche Post*, ECJ Feb. 10, 2000, 2000 ECR I-825, para. 48) or creates a situation in which the owner of exclusive rights cannot avoid abusing its dominant position (*TNT*, ECJ May 17, 2001, 2001 ECR I-4109, para. 44).
592. *Grundig/Consten*, ECJ July 13, 1966, 1966 ECR 299, 344–346 (trademarks); *Deutsche Grammophon*, ECJ June 8, 1971, 1971 ECR 487, paras 11–12 (copyrighted products); *Parke Davis*,

or intellectual property right may give rise to abusive conduct which goes beyond what is necessary to fulfil the essential function of the exclusive right as permitted in Community law.[593] Accordingly, the exercise of such rights may in particular constitute an abuse of a dominant position if the dominant firm unreasonably denies other firms' access to the relevant market,[594] In the *Volvo/Veng* case, which concerned the refusal by the holder of a registered design on replacement parts to license other parties to supply such parts, the Court of Justice ruled:

> '... the exercise of the exclusive right of the proprietor of a protected design to prevent third parties from manufacturing and selling or importing, without its consent, products incorporating the design constitutes the very subject-matter of his exclusive right. It follows that an obligation imposed upon the proprietor of the protected design to grant to third parties, even in return for a reasonable royalty, a licence for the supply of products incorporating the design would lead to the proprietor thereof being deprived of the substance of his exclusive right, and that a refusal to grant such a licence cannot in itself constitute an abuse of a dominant position.
>
> It must however be noted that the exercise of an exclusive right by the proprietor of a registered design in respect of car body panels may be prohibited by Article 82 if it involves, on the part of the undertaking holding a dominant position, certain abusive conduct such as an arbitrary refusal to supply spare parts to independent repairers, the fixing of prices for spare parts at an unfair level or a decision no longer to produce spare parts for a particular model even though many cars of that model are still in circulation, provided that such conduct is liable to affect trade between member states.'[595]

The *Magill* Case.

The circumstances under which the exercise of an exclusive right may be held abusive were further elaborated in the *Magill* case.[596] This case concerned the refusal, by three Irish television stations, to grant copyright licences on their advanced weekly listings for television and radio programmes to an independent editor of a general comprehensive television magazine in order to preserve these rights for their own separate publications. The Court of First Instance affirmed that the right to prevent the marketing of products manufactured without the con-

---

ECJ Feb. 29, 1968, 1968 ECR 55, 72 (patents); *Sirena*, ECJ Feb. 18, 1971, 1971 ECR 69 (trademarks); *Volvo/Veng*, ECJ Oct. 5, 1988, 1988 ECR 6211 (registered design).

593. *Magill – BBC*, CFI July 10, 1991, 1991 ECR II-535, para. 61; *DSD ('Green Dot')*, D.Comm. April 20, 2001, 2001 OJ L 166/1, point 109.

594. *Magill – RTE and ITP*, ECJ April 6, 1995, 1995 ECR I-743, paras 49–50.

595. *Volvo/Veng*, ECJ Oct. 5, 1988, 1988 ECR 6211, paras 8–9.

596. *Magill – RTE*, CFI July 10, 1991, 1991 ECR II-485; *aff'd* ECJ April 6, 1995, 1995 ECR I-743.

sent of the right-owner belongs to the essence of the right which must not be frustrated, but:

> '... that does not apply when, in the light of the details of each individual case, it is apparent that the right is exercised in such ways and circumstances as in fact to pursue an aim manifestly contrary to the objectives of Article 86.'[597]

The Court of First Instance found in this case that there was a potential consumer demand for the new product – a comprehensive TV magazine – and that there was no objective justification for the refusal, in particular because the same applicant was authorized, free of charge, to publish the television stations' daily listings in both Ireland and the United Kingdom and – even more importantly – also to publish the weekly listings in other member states without payment of royalties. Similarly, the Court of Justice ruled in the *Télémarketing* case[598] that a television station abused its dominant position by reserving for an affiliated company the market for 'tele-sales' advertising on the station and refusing access to other parties.

Tendencies of a More Cautious Approach.
In other cases the case law tends to culminate in a more cautious approach.

- In the *Tiercé Ladbroke* case[599] the Commission rejected the complainant's allegation that the refusal, by a French company holding exclusive rights to exploit televised pictures of, and information about, horse races organized in France, to grant to a Belgian bookmaker the right to retransmit the French sound and pictures in Belgium was abusive. The Court of Justice affirmed the Commission's assessment that Article 82 was not infringed because the mere transmission of pictures and information – unlike the situation in the *Magill* case – was not indispensable to the bookmaker's business and did not constitute a discrimination between businesses operating in the Belgian market.
- The *Bronner/Mediaprint* case[600] concerned the alleged abuse of a dominant position held by Mediaprint on the market of home-delivery services for daily

597. *Ibid.*, para. 71.
598. *Télémarketing*, ECJ Oct. 3, 1985, 1985 ECR 3261, paras 25–27; *Airport of Frankfurt*, D.Comm. Jan. 14, 1998, 1998 OJ L 72/30, point 71.
599. *Tiercé Ladbroke*, CFI June 12, 1997, 1997 ECR II-923, paras 123–134. Similarly, the Court of Justice held the refusal of access non-abusive because the access was not necessary for the applicant's business: *Bronner/Mediaprint*, ECJ Nov. 26, 1998, 1998 ECR I-7791. This discrimination was the main reason for accepting compulsory licences, although the Court of Justice did not use expressly the term 'discrimination': *Magill*, ECJ April 6, 1995, 1995 ECR I-743, paras 52–55. However, the Court of First Instance did use this term in *Tierce Ladbroke*, CFI June 12, 1997, 1997 ECR II-923, paras 131–132, when comparing the merits of this case with those *of Magill*.
600. *Bronner/Mediaprint*, ECJ Nov. 26, 1998, 1998 ECR I-1779.

newspapers published by itself by refusing to include another daily newspaper published by a competing editor who claimed to be unable to organize its own home-delivery service or an equivalent alternative because of its small number of subscribers. In this case the Court of Justice interpreted its *Magill* judgment as follows:

> '... even if that case law on the exercise of an intellectual property right were applicable to the exercise of any property right whatever, it would still be necessary, for the *Magill* judgment to be effectively relied upon in order to plead the existence of an abuse within the meaning of Article 82 of the Treaty in a situation such as that which forms the subject-matter of the first question, not only that the refusal of service comprised in home delivery be likely to eliminate all competition in the daily newspaper market on the part of the person requesting the service and that such refusal be incapable of being objectively justified, but also that the service in itself be indispensable to carrying on that person's business, inasmuch as there is no actual or potential substitute in existence for that home-delivery scheme.'[601]

– In *IMS Health*[602] the Court of Justice, although accepting the principle of the essential facilities doctrine, denied an urgent need for an interim measure. The case concerned a complaint by NDC, a data collector on pharmaceutical sales, against the leading data collector in Germany, IMS Health, for abusive refusal to license its copyright to the '1860 brick structure', which segments Germany into 1860 zones or 'bricks'. IMS developed this structure (protected under copyright) which had become a national standard in the pharmaceutical industry and the access to which the Commission concluded was necessary to compete on the pharmaceutical sales data market.[603] The interim measure ordering a compulsory license was suspended by order[604] and by interim relief of the Court of First Instance,[605] which was confirmed by the Court of Justice.[606] Although the Court grants the Commission broad discretion and accepts that the refusal to license may, under exceptional circumstances, prevent the appearance of a new product on a market separate from that on which the undertaking in question has a dominant position and justify, under the essential facilities doctrine, the imposition of a compulsory license obligation the Court denied a sufficient degree of probability of serious and irreparable damage, and therefore found inadequate urgency to require an interim measure.[607] The refusal to

601. *Ibid.*, para. 40. *See also Info Lab/Ricoh*, D.Comm. Jan. 27, 1999, DG IV Newsletter, 1999–1, 35.
602. *IMS Health*, Interim measure, July 3, 2001, 2001 OJ L 59/18; CFI Oct. 26, 2001, 2001 ECR II-3193 (suspension of the interim measure); ECJ April 11, 2002, 2002 ECR I-3401 (suspension affirmed).
603. *NDC/IMS Health*, interim measure. July 3, 2001, 2001 OJ L 59/18.
604. *IMS*, CFI Aug. 10, 2001, 2001 ECR II-2349.
605. *IMS Health*, CFI Oct. 26, 2001, 2001 ECR II-3193.
606. *IMS Health*, ECJ April 11, 2002, 2002 ECR I-3401.
607. *IMS Health*, CFI Oct. 26, 2001, 2001 ECR II-3198, paras 120, 140–149.

license question then became the subject of proceedings before a German court (Landgericht Frankfurt[608]) which it in turn referred to the Court of Justice. On 29 April 2004 the Court of Justice ruled,[609] in line with its *Bronner/Mediaprint* approach, that

> 'The refusal by an undertaking which holds a dominant position and owns a copyright of a brick structure indispensable to the presentation of regional sales data on pharmaceutical products in a member state to grant a licence to use that structure to another undertaking which also wishes to provide such data in the same member state, constitutes an abuse of a dominant position within the meaning of Article 82 EC where the following conditions are fulfilled:
> - the undertaking which requested the licence intends to offer, on the market for the supply of the data in question, new products or services not offered by the rightowner and for which there is a potential consumer demand;[610]
> - the refusal is not justified by objective considerations;
> - the refusal is such as to reserve to the copyright owner the market for supply of data on sales of pharmaceutical products in the Member State concerned by eliminating all competition on that market.'

Insofar as NDC could adopt a different structure for its data in order to compete without infringing the IMS copyright, the copyrighted IMS Health 'brick structure' was not the only means of organizing pharmaceutical sales data. Under this premise, IMS did not infringe Article 82 by refusing to licence its copyrighted 'brick structure' to NDC.

Examples of Exceptional Circumstances.
A refusal to grant a licence may be justified on grounds that the refusal is within the specific subject matter of the applicable individual right.[611] The right-owner cannot be deprived of the substance of his right, which includes the free choice of exploiting the right itself or of granting a licence and, if so, to whom.[612] However, a right-owner having a dominant position may abuse this position under exceptional circumstances, i.e. when a refusal would be 'manifestly' contrary to the objectives of Article 82.[613]

---

608. Judgment of July 12, 2001 (not published).
609. *IMS Health,* ECJ April 29, 2004, C-418/01, para. 52; *see also* opinion Advocate General Tesauro of Oct. 2, 2003, paras. 55-66.
610. This accords with the 'fallow field doctrine', *see* Chapter IX.B.3.(b).
611. *See also* Chapter VII.F.
612. Even a dominant firm is normally under no obligation to share its rights with third parties to allow them to develop or to use the same products or services: *Lederle-Praxis Biologicals*, Twenty-fourth Report on Competition Policy, p. 353.
613. *Magill – RTE,* CFI July 10, 1991, 1991 ECR II-485, para. 71. *See also Volvo/Veng*, ECJ Oct. 5, 1988, 1988 ECR 6211 (examples of arbitrary refusal, section D.3.(b) *supra)* and in greater detail

Examples of *exceptional circumstances* under which the exercise of an exclusive property right involves abuse include:

- *Arbitrary refusal of access: forfeiting the exclusive right.* The refusal of a licence may constitute an abuse if the right-owner does not use the right itself or through licensees at all or insufficiently. This corresponds to the conditions under which the Court of Justice held that the exercise of an exclusive right granted by the government constitutes an abuse of a dominant position within the terms of Article 82[614] and under which a compulsory licence may be imposed under patent and plant variety rights law.[615] In *Hoffmann-LaRoche/Boehringer* the Commission made the approval of the merger subject, *inter alia*, to the condition of granting a further licence to a competitor in order to avoid a dominant position.[616] The Court of Justice ruled that refusal to grant a licence to registered designs would be abusive if the right-owner no longer produces spare parts for a particular car model even though many cars of that model remain in circulation, thereby preventing any producer from supplying the spare parts.[617]
- *Predatory refusal of access.* The refusal to grant a licence may be abusive if it aims at eliminating or substantially damaging market access of competitors. Examples include:
  - the practice of *IBM* to withhold from competitors certain critical information necessary for offering IBM-compatible products,[618]
  - the refusal of *Microsoft* to provide interface information necessary for competitors to be able to develop fully interoperable products[619] or to

---

Chapter VII.F. (abuse of industrial property rights) and Chapter IX.C.2. (limits of the exception of Article 86 (2)). Under U.S. antitrust law, the Supreme Court seems to require a complainant to present strong evidence of *intent*, such as evidence that the monopolist sacrified short-term profits in order to eliminate or harm a competitor: *Verizon Communications Inc. v. Law Offices of Curtis V. Trinko*, U.S., No. 02–682, 1/13/04.

614. *Höfner/Macrotron*, ECJ April 23, 1991, 1991 ECR I-1979, paras 25–26 ('fallow field doctrine'). *See* in greater detail Chapter IX.B.3 (b).
615. A compulsory licence is provided for by Articles 21–22 of the Community Patent Convention Proposal on the ground of lack or insufficiency of exploitation' (8539/03); by Article 29 of Regulation 2100/94 on Community plant variety rights (1994 OJ L 227/1) 'on grounds of public interest' and by Article 17 of the EAEC Treaty where, in the absence of an amicable agreement, the granting of a compulsory licences to joint undertakings 'is necessary for the continuance of their own research or indispensable to the operation of their installations'. On the other hand, under national (UK) law a licence of right may be granted if the national demand for the licensed product fails to be satisfied. No licence of right may be granted if the national demand could be satisfied by imports from other member states: *Commission/UK and Ireland*, ECJ Feb. 18, 1992, 1992 ECR I-829; *Generics, Harris/Smith Kline*, ECJ Oct. 27, 1992 ECR I-5335.
616. *Hoffmann-La Roche/Boehringer*, D.Comm. Feb. 4, 1998, WuW 1998–11, 1120, points 157–161.
617. *CICRA/Renault*, ECJ Oct. 5, 1988, 1988 ECR 6039, para. 16.
618. *IBM*, Fourteenth Report on Competition Policy, points 94–95.
619. *Microsoft II*, D.Comm. March 24, 2004, IP/04/382 (fine of EUR 497.2 million and cease and desist order).

grant licences to other PC manufacturers in such a way as to foreclose the European market to other software producers,[620]

- the refusal of a licence by the group of stereo television manufacturers collectively holding a dominant position in order to prevent competitors from operating within the Common Market,[621]
- the acquisition of an exclusive licence for a new product by a dominant firm, thereby preventing the licensor from granting licences to other smaller competitors[622] and
- the refusal by three television stations to license their copyrighted advance programme to the editor of a new comprehensive weekly TV guide.[623]

However, the refusal by a dominant firm probably does not infringe Article 82 if access to the technology in question is *not necessary* to carrying on that person's business in the relevant market.[624]

– *Discriminatory licensing*. If the refusal of a licence discriminates against a third party as compared to other third parties to which a licence has been granted or to the dominant firm's own activities, this '*discrimination*' may indicate the lack of an objective justification.[625] A dominant firm would expose itself to the claim of 'arbitrary discrimination' if it selects licensees on the basis of objective criteria but discriminates against potential licensees that have the same or similar qualifications,[626] In the absence of such objective criteria the right-owner's refusal of a licence may be held abusive only if it is discriminatory or predatory, i.e. directed at eliminating a competitor.[627] Discriminatory licensing

620. *Microsoft I*, Twenty-fourth report on Competition Policy, pp. 364–365 (settlement following commitments). *See* the Commission's proposal for a Council Directive on the legal protection of computer programs, 1989 OJ C 91/16, and recital 27 of Council Directive on the legal protection of computer programs, 1991 OJ L 122/42.
621. *IGR I*, Eleventh Report on Competition Policy, point 94 (however investigated under Article 81). The equivalent to a refusal was the application of excessively high licence fees: *IGR II*, Fourteenth Report on Competition Policy, point 92.
622. *Tetra Pak I*, CFI July 10, 1991, 1990 ECR II-309.
623. *Magill*, CFI July 10, 1991, 1991 ECR II-485, 535, 575, *aff'd* ECJ April 6, 1995, 1995 ECR I-743. This ruling, which concerns the grant of a copyright licence, does not necessarily prejudge the rights of a patentee under Article 82 because of the different subject matter.
624. *Tierce/Ladbroke*, CFI June 12, 1997, 1997 ECR II-923; paras 123–124; *Bronner/Mediaprint*, ECJ Nov. 26, 1998, 1998 ECR II-7791, paras 36–47.
625. E.g. in *DSD ('Green Dot')* (D.Comm. April 20, 2001, 2001 OJ L 166/1) where the fees for granting a licence corresponded to the volume of packaging bearing the Green Dot trademark rather than fees corresponding to the volume of packaging for which DSD is actually providing a take-back and recycling service (instead, the 'no service, no fee' principle should apply).
626. The *Magill* case may be understood as a discriminatory refusal of a licence: *Magill*, ECJ April 6, 1995, 1995 ECR I-743, paras 52–55; as compared to *Tiercé Ladbroke*, CFI June 12, 1997, 1997 ECR II-923, paras 123–124, where the refusal of a licence was not held abusive in the absence of any discrimination.
627. *IGR II (Stereo Television)*, Fourteenth report on Competition Policy, point 92. With regard to the refusal of access to an essential facility: *French Post/SWIFT*, Twenty-seventh Report on Competition Policy, point 68 and pp. 143–154.

must be distinguished from the application of *discriminatory licensing conditions*. The application of discriminatory licence fees or conditions may place certain licensees at a competitive disadvantage and constitute an abuse within Article 82 (c) if the difference is so substantial or disproportionate as to place them at a significant competitive advantage and not otherwise be objectively justified by a corresponding cost difference.[628]

(e) Abusive Refusal of Access to an Essential Facility or Network

Balance of Interests.
A firm whose dominant position in a market allows it to control access to the same or another market abuses its position if it unreasonably denies other firms access to the market. The qualification of a refusal as 'unreasonable' and therefore 'abusive' depends on a balancing of the legitimate individual interests resulting from investments, property and industrial property rights, and public interests in 'ensuring that competition in the Common Market is not distorted.'[629] The mere existence and recognition by the Community legal order of such rights does not prevent the exercise of those rights, in certain circumstances, from conflicting with the public interest and the application of Article 82.[630] A dominant firm is under no general obligation to offer access to its facility, network or technology.[631] However, according to *Bronner/Mediaprint*,[632] Article 82 may apply if three conditions are fulfilled:

(i) the refusal of access to a facility must be likely to prevent any competition at all on the applicant's market,
(ii) the access must be *indispensable or essential* for carrying out the applicant's business, and
(iii) the access must be denied *without any objective justification*, as may be demonstrated by arbitrary, discriminatory or predatory conduct or decision.[633]

---

628. *See SACEM II*, ECJ Sept. 13, 1989, 1989 ECR 2811, paras 21–33, and Chapter VII.F.
629. Article 3 (g) of the EC Treaty. *See Airport of Frankfurt*, D.Comm. Jan. 14, 1998, 1998 OJ L 72/30, point 90.
630. *Hauer*, ECJ Dec. 13, 1979, 1979 ECR 3727, para. 17; *Airport of Frankfurt*, D.Comm. Jan. 14, 1998, 1998 OJ L 72/30, paras 89–92. With regard to tangible industrial property rights, *see* Chapter VII.A.3. With regard to tangible property rights, *see Van der Bergh Foods*, D.Comm. March 11, 1998, 1998 OJ L 246/1, points 211–220.
631. *See Lederle-Praxis Biologicals*, Twenty-fourth Report on Competition Policy, p. 353.
632. *Bronner/Mediaprint*, ECJ Nov. 26, 1998, 1998 ECR I-7791, para. 40.
633. *See*, under U.S. law, *Verizon Communications Inc. v. Law Offices of Curtis V. Trinko, LLP*, U.S., No. 02–682, 72 U.S.L.W. 4114 (Jan. 13, 2004); 124 S.Ct. 872(2004). (casting doubts on the viability of the essential facilities doctrine because likely to lessen the incentive of the monopolist to create superior facilities). Membership in an association may be a condition to market access, and therefore refusal of membership may be abusive: *French- West-African Shipowners Committee*, D.Comm. April 1, 1992, 1992 OJ L 134/1.

This case concerned the refusal by the Austrian newspaper group Mediaprint to grant a competing newspaper access to its delivery network. The Court gave a preliminary ruling under Article 234 of the EC Treaty that Mediaprint had not engaged in an abuse that infringes Article 82 because there are alternative means of distributing newspapers, such as by post and sale in shops and kiosks; finally, it was not enough to argue that is was not economically viable to establish a stand-alone nationwide home-delivery scheme by reason of the small circulation of the daily newspapers which the complainant wished to distribute. The *Bronner/Mediaprint* decision emphasizes that each case requires a careful examination of the legal and economic context and a balancing of individual and public interests.[634] This applies to both the refusal of intellectual property rights (as discussed above) and the refusal of access to an essential facility.

Refusal of Access to an Essential Facility: Common Features.
The Commission has defined its approach to essential facilities under Article 82 as follows:

> 'An undertaking which occupies a dominant position in the provision of an essential facility and itself uses that facility (i.e., a facility or infrastructure, without access to which competitors cannot provide services to their customers), and which refuses other companies access to that facility without objective justification or grants access to competitors only on terms less favourable than those which it gives its own services, infringes Article 82 if the other conditions of Article 82 are met.'[635]

'*Essential*' means that there must not be any realistic alternative ('no actual or potential substitute') to the use of the infrastructure concerned.[636] This limits the cases of abusive refusal to companies having a 'factual monopoly'[637] or a quasi-monopoly. Such an undertaking may not, in order to strengthen its own position without objective justification, (i) discriminate in favour of its own activities in a related market by refusing access or granting access to competitors on less favourable terms, (ii) withdraw access to a competitor to whom access had been previously given, or (iii) refuse access to a new entrant seeking access to the market. In the absence of an objective justification such behaviour is likely to infringe Article 82.[638] This basic approach applies also to the refusal of access to a network, provided there is no realistic alternative to the use of the network

---

634. *Bronner/Mediaprint*, ECJ Nov. 26, 1998, 1998 ECR I-7791, paras 37–47. *See infra* at pp. 472–474.
635. *Sea Containers – Stena Sealink*, D.Comm. Dec. 21, 1993, 1994 OJ L 15/8, para. 66, with further references to the case law of the Court of Justice and the Commission.
636. *Magill*, ECJ April 6, 1995, 1995 ECR I-743, para. 52.
637. Term 'borrowed' from U.S. law: *See United States v. Terminal Railroad Association*, 224 U.S. 383, 406–409 (1912).
638. *See* Commission Draft Guidelines on Open Network Provision, 1997 OJ C 76/9, para. 72.

concerned as noted in the *French Post/SWIFT* case.[639] In this case SWIFT, the operator of an international payment message transfer network, refused access by the French Post Office to its network arguing that this network was reserved to its members which were financial institutions around the world and that the applicant did not satisfy the admission criteria because the French Post did not carry on an activity identical to that of credit institutions in a similar competitive environment and under equivalent regulatory conditions. The Commission objected under Article 82 stating that the refusal of access was tantamount to a *de facto* exclusion from the market for international payment transfers and that SWIFT had abused its dominant position by laying down unjustified admission criteria and applying these criteria in a discriminatory way. The case was settled following SWIFT's undertaking to grant full access to any institution in the European Union which provides cross-border payment services to the public and fulfils the criteria laid down by the European Monetary Institute.

Refusal of Access to Essential Facilities in the Commission's Practice. The application of Article 82 against refusal of access to an essential facility includes telecommunications networks,[640] postal networks,[641] electricity networks,[642] gas[643] or fuel pipelines and storages,[644] ports,[645] airports,[646] interlining,[647] ground-

639. *French Post/SWIFT*, Twenty-seventh Report on Competition Policy, point 68 and pp. 141–145.

640. *British Telecommunications*, ECJ March 20, 1985, 1985 ECR 873, para. 26 (affirming the Commission's cease and desist order of 10 Dec. 1982, 1982 OJ L 360/36); *Eirpage*, D.Comm. Oct. 18, 1991, 1991 OJ L 306/22 (exemption following improvement of access to network); GSM *Italy*, D.Comm. Oct. 4, 1995, 1995 OJ L 280/49; *GSM Spain*, D.Comm. Dec. 18, 1996, 1997 OJ L 76/19.

641. Article 9 of Directive 97/67/EC on postal services, 1998 OJ L 15/14.

642. Articles 16–22 of Directive 96/92/EC, 1997 OJ L 27/20.

643. *Marathon/Gasunie*, D.Comm. April 16, 2003, IP/03/547 (joint refusal to grant access to continental European gas pipelines).

644. Articles 14–23 of Directive 98/30/EC, 1998 OJ L 204/1; *DISMA*, Twenty-third Report on Competition Policy, point 223; *REN/Turbogas*, Twenty-sixth Report on Competition Policy, p. 134 (comfort letter after reduction of duration of exclusive supply to the Portuguese grid operator from 25 to 15 years).

645. *Porto di Genova I*, ECJ Dec. 10, 1991, 1991 ECR I-5889; *Porto di Genova II (Silvano Raso)*, ECJ Feb. 12, 1998, 1998 ECR I-593; *Porto di Genova III*, D.Comm. Oct. 21, 1998, 1998 OJ L 301/27; *GT-Link/Dansk Statsbaner*, ECJ July 17, 1997, 1997 ECR I-4449; *Port of Rodby*, D.Comm. Dec. 21, 1993, 1994 OJ L 55/52; *Sea Containers/Stena Sealink*, D.Comm. Dec. 21, 1993, 1994 OJ L 15/8, points 57–59; *Tariffs for Piloting in the Port of Genova*, D.Comm. Feb. 10, 1999, 1999 OJ L 301/27.

646. Regulation 95/93/EC on the allocation of slots at airports; *Lufthansa*, Twenty-fifth Report on Competition Policy, point 106; *British Midland/Aer Lingus*, D.Comm. Feb. 26, 1992, 1992 OJ L 96/34; *Lufthansa/SAS*, D.Comm. Jan. 16, 1996, 1996 OJ L 54/28 (clearances following undertakings); *Brussels Airport*, D.Comm. June 28, 1995, 1995 OJ L 216/8.

647. *Air Europe/Lufthansa*, Twentieth Report on Competition Policy, point 107; *CRS Galileo and Coria*, 1993 OJ C 107/4 (comfort letter following undertaking); *TAT/Air Inter*, IP of 27 April 1994.

handling services,[648] computer reservation systems,[649] rail network,[650] and national waste collection systems.[651] The difficulty of ensuring undistorted competition in network industries may be overcome by obliging the undertaking enjoying exclusive rights in the reserved area to offer access to their networks to any competitor in the open market on the same conditions that access or services are offered to its own subsidiary.[652] The Commission has intervened in cases of arbitrary or discriminatory refusal of access:

- if the third party depends on use of the infrastructure or facilities for supplying his customers and building his own infrastructure is not a realistic alternative;[653]
- if the third party satisfies objectively justified criteria for admission;[654]
- if the admission is subject to discriminatory conditions;[655]
- if the capacity of the infrastructure is adequate to carry the additional traffic, having due regard to space and capacity constraints[656] and to the infrastructure operator's own requirements to provide supplies during periods of peak demand and its other long-term commitments,[657] without recognizing, however, any 'grandfathered' or 'historical' rights;[658]
- if the traffic for which a licence to use the infrastructure is sought satisfies the relevant technical standards and is in sufficient quantity to meet the operating

---

648. Regulation 97/67/EC on access to the groundhandling market at Community airports, 1996 OJ L 272/36; *Airport of Frankfurt*, D.Comm. Jan. 14, 1998, 1998 OJ L 72/30; *Aéroports de Paris*, CFI Dec. 12, 2000, 2000 ECR II-3929, para. 122 *(aff'd* ECJ Oct. 24, 2002, 2002 ECR I-9297); *Athens Airport*, Twenty-seventh Report on Competition Policy, p. 165; *Ilmailulaitos/Luftfartverket*, D.Comm. Feb. 10, 1999, 1999 OJ L 69/24.
649. Regulation 3652/93 on access to computerized reservation systems, 1993 OJ L 333/37. *See* Commission's Notice on access agreements in the telecommunications sector, 1998 OJ C 265/2, points 83.
650. *GVG/FS*, D.Comm. Aug. 27, 2003, 2004 OJ L 11/7, point 153 (refusal by the Italian dominant rail traction provider to enter into an international grouping with a German railway undertaking for the purposes of providing an international rail passenger service between Germany and Italy).
651. *Duales System*, D.Comm. April 20, 2001, 2001 OJ L 166/1, points 114–155 and 136.
652. Nicolaides, *Effective competition in network industries*, 2001–9 ECLR 390, 393.
653. *Tiercé/Ladbroke*, CFI June 12, 1997, 1997 ECR II-923, paras 123–134; but *see Bronner/Media-print*, ECJ Nov. 26, 1998, 1998 ECR I-7791, paras 41–47.
654. *French Post/SWIFT*, Twenty-seventh Report on Competition Policy, point 68 and pp. 143–145; Article 15 of Council Directive 96/67/EC on access to ground handling services, 1996 OJ L 272/36.
655. *Duales System*, D.Comm. April 20, 2001, 2001 OJ L 166/1, points 114–115 (discriminatory fee for using the 'green dot' trademark for collecting and recycling services).
656. *Airport of Frankfurt*, D.Comm. Jan. 14, 1998, 1998 OJ L 72/30, points 75–88.
657. *See* the electrticity and gas directives 2003/54/EC and 2003/55/EC (2003 OJ L 176/37 and 57).
658. *Airport of Frankfurt*, D.Comm. Jan. 14, 1998, 1998 OJ L 72/30, points 97–98.

requirements of the infrastructure;[659]

- if the party seeking access is prepared to pay the operator adequate compensation,[660] and
- if the request is reasonable – which requires a balancing of the interests of the operator, security of supply and the public interest in competition and free trade of goods and services within the Common Market.[661]

7. Abusive Discrimination by Nationality

No Discrimination on National Lines Permitted

A dominant firm that discriminates against nationals of other member states infringes Article 12 of the EC Treaty as well as Article 82, in particular sub-paragraphs (b) and (c). Article 12 prohibits discrimination on grounds of nationality by national governments, the EC authorities or businesses. The refusal of a German copyright collecting society – which held a *de facto* monopoly in its member state – to provide its full services to foreign composers and artists was found to violate Article 12 in the *GVL* case.[662] In the *Porto di Genova* case[663] the Court of Justice considered the grant of an exclusive right to the port administration for loading and unloading services reserved only to nationals as an infringement of Article 86 (1).[664] Discrimination on national lines with regard to prices or other terms and conditions of sale would also do so.[665]

---

659. Abuse of an 'essential facility': *Port of Rodby*, D.Comm. Dec. 21, 1993, 1994 OJ L 55/52; *Sea Containers/Stena Sealink*, D.Comm. Dec. 12, 1993, 1994 OJ L 15/8; *B&I*, D.Comm. June 11, 1992, Twenty-second Report on Competition Policy, point 219; *Harbour of Roscoff (IGC/CCI Morlaix)*, D.Comm. May 16, 1995, Twenty-fifth Report on Competition Policy, point 43. *See* Article 3 (2) of Council Directive on the Internal Market in Electricity, 1997 OJ L 27/20.
660. *See* Article 6 of Regulation 3652/93, 1993 OJ L 333/37; Article 9 (4) of Directive 97/67/EC on postal services, 1998 OJ L 15/14; Article 18 (2) of Directive 96/92/EC on electricity, 1997 OJ L 27/20; Article 15 (2) of Directive 98/30/EC on natural gas, 1998 OJ L 204/1.
661. *See* in greater detail *infra* Chapter VIII.A and E.2.
662. *GVL*, ECJ March 2, 1983, 1983 ECR 483, paras 46–56. *See also GEMA I*, D.Comm. June 2, 1971, 1971 OJL 134/15, 21; *IGR Stereo Television I*, Eleventh Report on Competition Policy, point 94.
663. *Porto di Genova*, ECJ Dec. 10, 1991 ECR I-5889.
664. However, without expressly referring to Article 82 or Article 12. The application of Article 82 was confirmed by Corto di Apello (Florence, Italy), Oct. 9, 1993, Twenty-fourth Report on Competition Policy, point 102.
665. Commission's Guidelines on the application of the EC competition rules in the telecommunications sector, 1991 OJ C 233/2, points 117–120. Such conduct is also a clear breach of Article 82 (c), *see also 1998 Football Word Cup Finals*, D.Comm. July 20, 1999, IP/99/541.

E. Effect on Trade between Member States

Effect on Trade Determines whether Community or only National Law is Applicable.

Only an abuse of dominant position that is likely to affect trade between member states is prohibited by Article 82. The concept of effect on trade is interpreted in principle in the same manner as under Article 81.[666] The Court of Justice stated in the *Hugin/Liptons* case:

> 'The interpretation and application of the condition relating to effects on trade between Member States contained in Articles 81 and 82 of the Treaty must be based on the purpose or that condition which is to define, in the context of the law governing competition, the boundary between the areas respectively covered by Community law and the law of the Member States. Thus Community law covers any agreement or any practice which is capable of constituting a threat to freedom of trade between Member States in a manner which might harm the attainment of the objectives of a single market between the Member States, in particular by partitioning the national markets or by affecting the structure of competition within the Common Market. On the other hand conduct the effects of which are confined to the territory of a single Member State is governed by the national legal order.'[667]

Accordingly, an abusive practice carried on in a single member state[668] or only part of a state, provided it constitutes a substantial part of the Common Market,[669] may affect trade between member states if it serves to protect the national or regional market against competition from other parts of the Community. In *Michelin I*, which concerned the application of fidelity rebates to Dutch dealers, the Court of Justice stated:

666. *See supra* Chapter I.E. 1–3.
667. *Hugin/Liptons*, ECJ May 31, 1979, 1979 ECR 1869, para. 17. *See also Commercial Solvents*, ECJ March 6, 1974, 1974 ECR 223, paras 30–33; *Funeral Services*, ECJ May 4, 1988, 1988 ECR 2479, para. 24; *CEWAL*, CFI 8, Oct. 1996, 1996 ECR II-1201, para. 203.
668. Guidelines on the Effect on Trade Concept, points 93–96, *Michelin I*, ECJ Nov. 11, 1983, 1983 ECR 3461, paras 102–104 ('... when the holder of a dominant position obstructs access to the market by competitors it makes no difference whether such conduct is confined to a single member state as long as it is capable of affecting patterns of trade and competition in the Common Market ... It must also be remembered that Article 82 does not require it to be proved that the abusive conduct has in fact appreciably affected trade between member states but that it is capable of having that effect.'). E.g., *ECS/Akzo II*, D.Comm. Dec. 14, 1985, 1985 OJ L 374/1, 23, *aff'd* ECJ July 3, 1991, 1991 ECR I-3359; *Irish Sugar*, D.Comm. May 14, 1997, 1997 OJ L 258/1, paras 155–158; *Michelin II*, D.Comm. June 20, 2001, 2002 OJ L 143/1, points 312 and 344–347, *aff'd* CFI Sept. 30, 2003, T-203/01.
669. *Sugar*, ECJ Dec. 16, 1975, 1975 ECR 1663, paras 514–516, 521; *Silvano Raso (Porto di Genova II)*, ECJ Feb. 12, 1998, 1998 ECR I-593, para. 26. *See* Guidelines on the Effect on Trade Concept, points 97–99.

> 'when the holder of a dominant position obstructs access to the market by competitors it makes no difference whether such conduct is confined to a single Member State as long as it is capable of affecting patterns of trade and competition in the common market.'[670]

Proof of Actual Appreciable Effect not Required.
Article 82 does not require it to be proved that the abusive conduct has actually appreciably affected trade between member states but only that it is capable of having that effect.[671] A firm that holds a dominant position for the purposes of Article 82 is likely to affect interstate trade if it abuses that position. The Commission's Guidelines on the Effect on Trade Concept establish criteria for indicating when agreements are normally not capable of appreciably affecting trade between member states, namely a market share not exceeding 5% and a turnover of less than EUR 40 million, but state, with respect to Article 82, that when a dominant firm engages in exclusionary conduct, such abuse is 'normally by its very nature' capable of having such effects, including in cases the abuse covers a single member state.[673] However, the situation is more complex in the case of price discrimination between domestic customers, which may not be used to prevent or disadvantage imports. In the *Hugin/Liptons* case the Court of Justice overruled the Commission on the question of an effect on trade because the British repair shop which had been refused supplies of spare parts had no intention of extending its business outside of the UK and there was no genuine interstate trade in spare parts.[673]

Effect on Trade via Effect on Market Structure.
An effect on trade can usually be assumed in the case of exclusionary abuses because these seek to affect market structure which is bound, at least in the long term, to have repercussions on trade.[674] Thus, attempts to eliminate a competitor are almost certain to affect interstate trade, even if the competitor imports the products from outside the Community or exports the bulk of its output to non-EC

670. *Michelin I*, ECJ Nov. 11, 1983, 1983 ECR 3461, para. 103.
671. *Michelin II*, CFI Sept. 30, 2003, T-203/01, paras 238 and 258. *See also British Leyland*, ECJ Nov. 11, 1986, 1986 ECR 3263, para. 20; *CEWAL*, CFI Oct. 8, 1996, 1996 ECR II-1201, para. 149.
672. Guidelines on the effect on trade concept, points 50, 75 and 93-96.
673. *Hugin/Liptons*, ECJ May 31, 1979, 1979 ECR 1869, paras 15–26. *See also Irish Sugar*, CFI Oct. 7, 1999, 1999 ECR II-2969, para. 170, *aff'd* ECJ July 10, 2001, 2001 ECR I-5333, and Guidelines on the Effect on Trade Doctrine, point 95.
674. *Commercial Solvents*, ECJ March 6, 1974, 1974 ECR 223, paras 30–33; *United Brands*, ECJ Feb. 14, 1978, 1978 ECR 207, para. 201; *Akzo II*, D.Comm. Dec. 14, 1985, 1985 OJ L 374/1, 23; *aff'd* ECJ July 3, 1991, 1991 ECR I-3359; *Boosey & Hawkes*, D.Comm. July 29, 1987, 1987 OJ 286/36, 41.

countries,[675] and even if the abuse concerns an intermediate product that is not traded and only affects the producer's costs of producing the finished product.[676]

F. Parallel Application of Articles 81 and 82

Principle of Parallel Application.
The same agreement or practice may infringe both Article 82 and Article 81. For instance, in *Hoffmann-La Roche* the Court considered that La Roche's agreement with Merck, by which La Roche violated Article 82 because of the exclusive dealing obligation in its favour and the fidelity rebates underpinning the obligation, possibly also infringed Article 81 on account of the reciprocal exclusive dealing obligations undertaken by both parties. The Court said:

> '... the fact that agreements of this kind might fall within Article 81 and in particular within paragraph 3 thereof does not preclude the application of Article 82, since this latter article is expressly aimed in fact at situations which clearly originate in contractual relations so that in such cases the Commission is entitled, taking into account the nature of the reciprocal undertakings entered into and to the competitive position of the various contracting parties on the market or markets in which they operate to proceed on the basis of Article 81 or Article 82.[677]

Similarly, in the *Racal Decca* case,[678] that company's contracts with two competitors infringed Article 82 because they were secured by an abuse of its dominant position that went beyond normal competitive behaviour, and also violated Article 81 because they provided for market and customer sharing. Breaches of both Articles are also sometimes found in different aspects of complex anticompetitive arrangements such as cartels. In the *Sugar* case, for example, the dominant positions that several producers or producer groups abused on their home markets were based on a concerted practice by which the producers agreed to concentrate their activity on the home market and not to export directly to others' markets (the

675. *United Brands*, ECJ Feb. 14, 1978, 1978 ECR 207, paras 197–202.
676. *Commercial Solvents*, ECJ March 6, 1974, 1974 ECR 223, para. 34. Similarly, the Court of Justice has ruled that restrictive practices and government subsidies concerning untraded inputs can affect trade for the purposes of Article 81 and Article 87: *BNIC II*, ECJ Dec. 3 1987, 1987 ECR 4789, para. 18; *Dutch Natural Gas Prices I*, ECJ Feb. 2, 1988, 1988 ECR 219, para. 59.
677. *Hoffmann-La Roche*, ECJ Feb. 13, 1979, 1979 ECR 461, para. 116. *See Ahmed Saeed*, ECJ April 11, 1989, 1989 ECR 803, para. 32; *Tetra Pak I*, CFI July 10, 1990, 1990 ECR II-309, para. 21; *Match Sverige/Skaninavisk Tobakskompagni*, Twenty-seventh Report on Competition Policy, point 66.
678. *Racal Decca*, D.Comm. Dec. 21, 1988, 1989 OJ L 43/27, 39–45.

'*chacun chez soi*' – each stays out of the other's backyard – policy).[679] In cases of a collective dominant position, which are based on anticompetitive agreements contrary to Article 81, there may well be breaches of both Articles.[680]

Implications of Parallel Application.
In cases where Articles 81 and 82 may both apply, the Commission can take action under either provision, as the Court of Justice stated in *Hoffmann-La Roche*.[681] There is nothing to prevent it evaluating an agreement under both provisions in a single set of proceedings.[682] Notification will protect an agreement from fines for an infringement of Article 81, but not usually for a breach of Article 82.[683] Nor is the application of Article 82 ruled out by the fact that an agreement appears to meet the conditions of a block exemption regulation. In the *Tetra Pak I* case,[684] the Commission found that Tetra Pak had abused its dominant position by acquiring an exclusive licence when it took over a smaller competitor. The licence agreement was formally covered by the patent licensing block exemption then in effect, Regulation 2349/84, but a block exemption regulation, unlike an individual exemption, does not imply a positive evaluation of the individual case and is therefore without prejudice to the application of Article 82. No fine was imposed, however, because of possible doubts about whether the agreement was a violation.[685]

---

679. *Sugar*, ECJ Dec. 16, 1975, 1975 ECR 1663, paras 311–364 and 421–528. The Commission's allegation of a concerted practice to protect the South German market was, however, held not to be proven.
680. *Italian Flat Glass II*, D.Comm. Dec. 7, 1988, 1989 OJ L 33/44, 60–66; *CEWAL*, ECJ March 16, 2000, 2000 ECR I-1365, para. 130.
681. *Hoffman-LaRoche*, ECJ Feb. 13, 1979, 1979 ECR 461, para. 116.
682. *BPB*, ECJ April 6, 1995, 1995 ECR I-865, para. 11; *CEWAL*, ECJ March 16, 2000, 2000 ECR I-1365, para. 130.
683. Except if linked to an agreement notified under Article 81: *United Brands*, D.Comm. Dec. 17, 1975, 1976 OJ L 95/1, 18.
684. *Tetra Pak I*, CFI July 10, 1990, 1990 ECR II-309, paras 21–30, affirming the Commission decision of July 26, 1988, 1988 OJ L 272/27. Block exemption regulations usually indicate that the exemption is without prejudice to the application of Article 82, *see* e.g. Recital 16 to Regulation 2790/2000.
685. *Tetra Pak I*, D.Comm. July 26, 1988, 1988 OJ L 272/27, point 62.

G. Legal Consequences of Infringement of Article 82

Clearance.
Formerly, conduct of a dominant or possibly dominant firm could be submitted to the Commission for clearance under Article 2 of Regulation 17 by using form A/B.[686]

Under Article 10 of the new Regulation 1/2003 the Commission may, when the Community public interest so requires, take a decision finding that Article 82 is not applicable to particular conduct. In cases that give rise to genuine uncertainty because they present novel or unresolved questions firms may wish to seek informal guidance from the Commission and the Commission may issue such informal guidance (guidance letters comparable to the former comfort letters).[687]

Cease and Desist Orders.
Under Article 7 of Regulation 1/2003[688] the Commission may issue a decision finding that a violation of Article 82 has occurred[689] and ordering it to be terminated, if it has not already been so,[690] e.g. to put an end to the application of unfairly high or low prices or of a discriminatory scheme of commercial fees,[691] including measures having equivalent effect.[692] Details of how the infringement should be put to an end may be explained in the reasoning of the decision.[693] In cases requiring some positive act to heal an infringement like refusal to supply, the Commission may order the offending party:

- to resume deliveries,[694]
- to grant a license,[695]

---

686. Rarely used, but *see Metaleurope,* D.Comm. June 26, 1990, 1990 OJ L 179/41 (decision); *British Plasterboard II,* Twenty-second Report on Competition Policy, p. 422; *Deutsche Telecom,* Twenty-sixth Report on Competition Policy, points 69-71 (comfort letters).
687. Recital 38 to Regulation 1/2003; Notice on informal guidance, in particular point 13.
688. Similar to Article 3 of Regulation 17.
689. The order may be rather detailed as in *DSD ('Green Dot'),* D.Comm. April 20, 2001, 2001 OJ L 166/1, 23.
690. Purely declaratory orders were approved by the Court in *GVL*, ECJ March 2, 1983, 1983 ECR 483, paras 16–28.
691. *Aéroports de Paris*, CFI Dec. 12, 2000, 2000 ECR II-3929, para. 83.
692. *Michelin II*, D.Comm. June 20, 2001, 2002 OJ L 143/1, point 349. However, such an order is rather declaratory and does not have any direct effect since the Commission would have to initiate new proceedings and to communicate objections anyway, stating that the new measures do have an equivalent effect before adopting any sanction.
693. *United Brands*, D.Comm. Dec. 17, 1975, 1976 OJ L 95/1, point 19 (indicating that a reduction of the price differences of 30–40% by 15% would be sufficient to eliminate the discrimination); *Aéroports de Paris*, CFI Dec. 12, 2000, 2000 ECR II-3929, para.238; *DSD ('Green Dot')*, D.Comm. April 20, 2001, 2001 OJ L 166/1, points 165–167.
694. E.g. *Commercial Solvents*, ECJ March 6, 1974, 1974 ECR 223, paras 42–46.
695. E.g. *Magill TV Guide*, ECJ April 6, 1995, 1995 ECR I-743, para. 90.

- in cases of access to networks (e.g. in the postal sector): to provide full transparency of the financial relationship between the reserved area and the market open to competition (e.g. parcel service),[696] or
- in cases of doubt: to submit proposals in order to bring the infringement to an end.[697]

To prevent a violation causing irreparable injury to the victim, the Commission also has the power to issue an interim order – similar to a preliminary injunction – to preserve the status quo.[698] In cases involving price abuses, the Commission confines itself to providing guidance as to how the abuse should be cured. It is not a price control agency.[699]

Fines.

Infringements of Article 82 may result in the imposition of fines even if they have been terminated.[700] No fines[701] or only moderate ones[702] may be imposed if it was unclear whether the conduct was a violation. The size of fines for clear breaches of Article 82 are often quite large and, like those for Article 81 infringements, have shown a rising trend in recent years.[703]

696. E.g. *Deutsche Post II*, D.Comm. July 25, 2001, 2001 OJ L 331/40, point 47: The German Post undertook to provide full transparency by creating independent legal entities in order to facilitate access to the network.
697. *Commercial Solvents*, D.Comm. Dec. 14, 1972, 1972 OJ L 299/51, 57; *aff'd* ECJ March 6, 1974, 1974 ECR 223, paras 45–46; *ECS/Akzo I*, D.Comm. July 29, 1983, 1983 OJ L 252/13; *ECS/Akzo II*, D.Comm. Dec. 14, 1985, 1985 OJ L 374/1; *Boosey & Hawkes*, D.Comm. July 29, 1987, 1987 OJ L 286/36. The addressee can apply to the Court of Justice for a preliminary injunction setting aside the order: *Continental Can* (injunction), ECJ March 21, 1972, 1972 ECR 157; *Commercial Solvents* (injunction), ECJ March 14, 1973, 1973 ECR 357 (in this case an injunction against the order of immediate resumption of supplies was granted but not against the order to submit proposals); *Peugeot (injunction)*, CFI May 21, 1991, 1991 ECR II-653.
698. E.g. *Commercial Solvents*, ECJ March 14, 1973, 1973 ECR 357 (this order was not appealed); *ECS/Akzo I*, D.Comm. July 29, 1983, 1983 OJ L 252/13; *Boosey & Hawkes*, D.Comm. July 29, 1987, 1987 OJ L 286/36.
699. *United Brands*, D.Comm. Dec. 17, 1975, 1976 OJ L 95/1, 19. *See also supra* D.2 (a).
700. E.g., *Italian Flat Glass II*, D.Comm. 7 Dec. 1988, 1989 OJ L 33/44.
701. E.g., *Tetra Pak I*, D.Comm. July 26, 1988, 1988 OJ L 272/27; *Racal Decca*, D.Comm. Dec. 21, 1988, 1989 OJ L 43/27; *Magill TV Guide*, D.Comm. Dec. 21, 1988, 1989 OJ L 78/43; *Ilmailulaitos/Luftfartverket*, D.Comm. Feb. 10, 1999, 1999 OJ L 69/24.
702. E.g. *Sabena*, D.Comm. Nov. 4, 1988, 1988 OJ L 317/47, 53. A symbolic fine of EUR 1,000 was imposed because of the novelty of the legal issue in *German Post*, D.Comm. July 25, 2001, 2001 OJ L 331/40.
703. *See* list of fines at the end of Chapter X.

Civil Remedies.

Unlike Article 81 (2), which provides that agreements contrary to Article 81 (1) are automatically void, Article 82 does not specify the civil consequences of violations of the Article. However, agreements that constitute an abuse of a dominant position may also infringe Article 81 with the consequence of nullity under Article 81 (2).[704] Furthermore, the Court of Justice has made it clear that breaches of Article 82, too, are illegal under national law and hence actionable in national civil courts and are likely to lead to damage and restitution claims.[705]

704. *See TACA II*, D.Comm. Sept. 16, 1998, 1999 OJ L 95/1, points 580–582.

705. *BRT/SABAM I*, ECJ Jan. 30, 1974, 1974 ECR 51, paras 15–20; *GT-Link A/S/De Dansk Statsbaner*, ECJ July 17, 1997, 1997 ECR I-4449, para. 61. *See* in greater detail *infra* Chapter X.G.

Chapter VI

Mergers, Joint Ventures and Shareholdings under the Merger Control Regulation and Articles 81 and 82

CONTENTS

A. Introduction

Layout of Chapter.
This chapter is devoted to an appraisal of mergers, joint ventures and shareholding links under the EC competition rules, in particular Regulation 139/2004, the merger control regulation. The chapter first reviews the application of Articles 81 and 82 to mergers prior to the adoption of the merger control regulation. The prior case law under Articles 81 and 82 has clearly influenced the practice under the regulation; it is also relevant to transactions that are not governed by the merger control regulation because they fail to meet the high sales thresholds that are a precondition of its application. This discussion is followed by a detailed description of the contents and application of the merger control regulation to mergers and to 'full-function' joint ventures that are governed by the regulation. The discussion then turns to the treatment under Article 81 of minority shareholdings and joint ventures that are beyond the scope of the merger control regulation.

Both Pro- and Anticompetitive Effects.
The effects on competition of mergers and joint ventures are as varied as are the types and structures of such transactions. They may bring about substantial competitive benefits or severely restrict competition, or they may be neutral in their overall effects. The principal benefits are in promoting investment, developing new product or geographic markets, diversification, assuring supplies or outlets, promoting innovation and transfers of technology, achieving economies of scale and cost reductions, restructuring or rationalization of businesses, and establishing countervailing market power. The detriments include the reinforcement of oligopolistic market structures, the raising of barriers to market entry, sharing markets, and strengthening market power which can be exploited against competitors, suppliers or customers.

Complex Evaluation.
The evaluation of mergers and joint ventures requires a detailed study of the facts of each case. The Court of Justice gives the Commission a certain discretionary margin, subject to judicial review of errors of assessment and misuse of powers, without wishing to substitute the Court's evaluation for that of the Commission.[1] Article 2 of Regulation 139/2004 requires an often more complex evaluation than of other restrictive practices for several reasons. The evaluation calls for a prediction of the long-term effects of the transaction, which may in complex cases be assessed somewhat differently by the Commission than by the Court of Justice, as

1. *Airtours*, CFI June 6, 2002, 2002 ECR II-2585, paras 64–65; *Petrolessence*, *SG2R*, CFI April 3, 2003, T-342/00, para. 101.

shown in cases such as *First Choice/Airtours*,[2] *Schneider/Legrand*,[3] *Tetra Laval/Sidel*[4] and *SEB/Moulinex*.[5] Finally, there has been a rapid development of the case law (250–350 decisions per year), and of the merger rules, including substantive amendments and guidelines, and a new test for the evaluation of mergers and joint ventures under Regulation 139/2004: will the transaction 'significantly impede effective competition (in lieu of the former 'create or strengthen a dominant position'). Consequently, the views expressed in this chapter must be regarded as tentative and subject to review as the law develops in this field.

B. Background to Adoption of the Merger Control Regulation

1. The 1966 Memorandum on Mergers

Fundamental Distinction between Mergers and Restrictive Practices. In the mid-1960s the Commission engaged academics to study the question of whether Article 81 ought to be applied to mergers. After considering their reports, it published a memorandum to discuss the findings and announce its conclusions as to future policy.[6] The Commission found that, although the dividing line was often blurred, a fundamental distinction could be drawn between restrictive practices and mergers. Whereas a restrictive practice regulated or influenced the *conduct* of firms that remained independent, a merger brought about a lasting change in the *structure* of the merging firms in which they gave up their economic independence and were brought under common management.

Majority Favored Applying Article 81 to Mergers. The majority of the academics who gave their opinion before issuance of the Commission's memorandum believed that Article 81 should be applied to mergers so long as two legal entities continued in existence after the merger and competition was appreciably restricted. They considered that only two categories of mergers should escape Article 81: first, those whereby one firm was completely

2. *Airtours*, CFI June 6, 2002, 2002 ECR II-2585 (finding of collective dominance reversed).
3. *Schneider*, CFI Oct. 22, 2002, 2002 ECR II-4201 (finding of conglomerate dominant position reversed).
4. *Tetra Laval*, CFI Oct. 25, 2002, 2002 ECR II-4519 (finding of conglomerate dominant position reversed).
5. *Royal Philips Electronics – SEB Moulinex*, CFI April 3, 2003, T-119/02 (finding that the merger did not create a dominant position on certain geographic markets reversed, thereby necessitating a new assessment by the Commission, D.Comm. Nov. 11, 2003, which granted unconditional approval for these markets).
6. Memorandum on the problem of mergers in the Common Market, Competition Series Study No. 3, Brussels 1966.

absorbed into another and the acquired firm ceased to exist as a separate entity; and secondly, mergers which did not involve an agreement between the merging firms, for example, those effected by the purchase of shares on the stock market.

Commission's Conclusions: Primarily Application of Article 82 and Limited Application of Article 81.

The Commission rejected the advice of the academics to apply Article 81 to mergers by agreement. First, the prohibition of Article 81 (1) was too harsh on mergers because they were beneficial in a greater number of instances than restrictive agreements. Secondly, the conditions for exemption under Article 81 (3) were too restrictive, especially the indispensability criterion. Thirdly, it was impracticable in a permanent arrangement such as a merger to reevaluate at a later time under Article 81 (3) whether its benefits subsisted. Finally, application of Article 81 would lead to unequal treatment of mergers that were agreed between the parties and economically equivalent transactions effected by unilateral action. The Commission therefore decided against applying Article 81 generally to mergers. Instead, the Commission declared that it would apply Article 81 only if several economically independent businesses continued in existence after the transaction, as in the case of a joint venture, and apart from any change in ownership, the parties entered into agreements or concerted practices that led to coordination of their market behavior. The principal rule for assessing mergers therefore became Article 82, which the Commission has applied only to prohibit mergers that strengthen a dominant position.

The 1966 Memorandum.

In essential respects the approach set forth in the 1966 memorandum continues to represent the Commission's general thinking on the application of Articles 81 and 82 to mergers. The current merger control regulation prohibits large mergers and full-function joint ventures that significantly impede effective competition. Other transactions, such as non-full function joint ventures and other forms of cooperation between enterprises that may coordinate the competitive behavior of the business entities concerned which remain independent afterwards, are left to assessment under Articles 81 and 82.[7] Transactions that are too small to be subject to the merger control regulation also remain subject to member state competition laws, including member state merger control rules.

---

7. The *Philip Morris* judgment, however, affirmed the application of Article 81 to the acquisition of minority shareholdings in other companies that allow the acquirer to influence their conduct, and so appeared to extend the possibilities of applying Article 81 to mergers: ECJ Nov. 17, 1987, 1987 ECR 4487.

2. Application of Article 82: *Continental Can*

Strengthening of Dominant Position.
The Commission's first attempt to apply Article 82 to a merger was in the *Continental Can* case[8] decided by the Court of Justice in 1973.[9] The case concerned the acquisition of a Dutch meat and fish can manufacturer, Thomassen & Drijver-Verblifa NV, by Continental Can, a United States food can manufacturer which operated in the Community through various subsidiaries. The Commission found that Continental Can held a dominant position in the German market through its affiliate Schmalbach-Lubeca, which was also a strong potential competitor in the Benelux countries. The Commission concluded that the elimination of a strong Dutch competitor, Thomassen, in the relevant market which comprised the northwestern part of Germany and the Benelux countries constituted an abuse prohibited under Article 82 because it consolidated Continental Can's dominant position in that market. The Commission ordered Continental Can to submit proposals for reversing the transaction.

Applicability of Article 82 Confirmed.
The Court of Justice affirmed the Commission's contention that Article 82 prohibited 'structural' abuses of a dominant position by merger or takeover, yet it reversed the decision because of shortcomings in the Commission's definition of the relevant product market. The Court held:

> 'Articles 85 and 86 [*now 81 and 82*] seek to achieve the same aim on different levels, *viz*. the maintenance of effective competition within the Common Market. The restraint of competition which is prohibited if it is the result of behavior falling under Article 85 cannot become permissible by the fact that such behavior succeeds under the influence of a dominant undertaking and results in the merger of the undertakings concerned. In the absence of explicit provisions one cannot assume that the Treaty, which prohibits in Article 85 certain decisions of ordinary associations of undertakings restricting competition without eliminating it, permits in Article 86 that undertakings, after merging into an organic unity, should reach such a dominant position that any serious chance of competition is practically rendered impossible. Such a diverse legal treatment would make a breach in the entire competition law which could jeopardize the proper functioning of the Common Market ….
>
> It is in the light of these considerations that the condition imposed by Article 86 is to be interpreted whereby in order to come within the prohibition a dominant position must have been abused. The provision states a certain number of abusive practices which it prohibits. The list merely gives

8. *Continental Can*, D.Comm. Dec. 9, 1971, 1972 OJ L 7/25.
9. *Continental Can*, ECJ Feb. 21, 1973, 1973 ECR 215.

examples, not an exhaustive enumeration of the sort of abuses of a dominant position prohibited by the Treaty. As may further be seen from letters (c) and (d) of Article 86 (2), the provision is not only aimed at practices which may cause damage to consumers directly, but also at those which are detrimental to them through their impact on an effective competition structure, such as is mentioned in Article 3 (g) [now 3 (f)] of the Treaty. *Abuse may therefore occur if an undertaking in a dominant position strengthens such position in such a way that the degree of dominance reached substantially fetters competition, i.e. that only undertakings remain in the market whose behaviour depends on the dominant one.*' [Emphasis added.] [10]

But only to Mergers that Strengthen an Existing Dominant Position.
Thus, the Court of Justice confirmed that mergers that strengthened an *existing* dominant position were caught by Article 82. On the other hand, the Court has never addressed the issue of whether a merger between non-dominant firms that *creates* a dominant position is prohibited by Article 82. The Commission has taken the view that Article 82 does not apply in these circumstances and that therefore a specific regulation would be needed to block such mergers.

Application of the *Continental Can* Doctrine by the Commission.
In 1988, prior to the Regulation 4064/89 on merger control, the Commission applied the *Continental Can* doctrine in the *Tetra Pak I (BTG licence)* case.[11] This case concerned the acquisition by Tetra Pak, a large Swiss-headquartered packaging company, of Liquipak, a company specialized in filling equipment for fresh and aseptic (UHT-treated) liquid food products, which was accompanied by the transfer of Liquipak's exclusive licence of a sterilization process granted by British Technology Group (BTG). Quoting the *Continental Can* case, the Commission held that Tetra Pak strengthened, and therefore abused, its dominant position in the EC market for UHT packages and their filling machines by acquiring an exclusive license, which had not been previously exploited but created a legal barrier to third companies wishing to enter the market. The Court of First Instance upheld the decision confirming the applicability of the *Continental Can* doctrine.[12] In *Gillette/Wilkinson*[13] the Commission ordered Gillette, the U.S. razor

10. *Ibid.*, paras 25–26.
11. *Tetra Pak I*, D.Comm. 26 July 1988, 1988 OJ L 272/27, 40. The proposed acquisition by *Douwe Egberts*, the leading Dutch coffee producer, of *Van Nelle*, a major Belgian coffee producer, was another case in which the Commission proceeded to an application of the *Continental Can* doctrine but abandoned the case because of lack of consensus on the question whether the Benelux countries constituted a substantial part of the Common Market: *European Report* (Nov. 24, 1990), Part II, at 12; Fine, *Mergers and Joint Ventures in Europe*, 2nd ed., 1994, p. 104.
12. *Tetra Pak I*, CFI July 10, 1990, 1990 ECR II-309, paras 22–23.
13. *Gillette/Wilkinson*, D.Comm. Nov. 11, 1992, 1993 OJ L 116/21.

group, to dispose of its interest in its main competitor, Wilkinson, and to retransfer it to Wilkinson's parent company Eemland. Both companies held a combined market share of 85% in the Community's wet shaving market. The Commission concluded that Gillette's shareholding in Wilkinson, which was acquired before the merger control regulation entered into force, constituted an abuse of its dominant position under Article 82.

3. APPLICATION OF ARTICLE 81: *PHILIP MORRIS/ROTHMANS*

Commission's Clearance of the Philip Morris Stake in Rothmans.
In 1981 the cigarette manufacturer Philip Morris acquired 50% of the shares in the holding company of a competitor, Rothmans Holdings, from the South African company, Rembrandt. Rembrandt retained its remaining 50% shareholding in Rothmans Holdings. Philip Morris and Rembrandt each had the right to appoint an equal number of members to the holding company's board, but Rembrandt was to retain management control. The Commission challenged this arrangement under both Articles 81 and 82. After negotiations with the Commission, the parties replaced it with new arrangements which the Commission approved.[14]

Under the revised agreements, Philip Morris gave up its shareholding in Rothmans Holdings in exchange for a direct shareholding in Rothmans International, the cigarette manufacturing subsidiary. The shareholding was the same as Rembrandt's (30.8%) but commanded only 24.9% of the voting rights, against Rembrandt's 43.6%. The parties had given the Commission undertakings that Philip Morris would not be represented on Rothmans' board and that information concerning the Rothmans business that might influence the behaviour of the Philip Morris group would not be made available to Philip Morris. Philip Morris also promised to inform the Commission of any amendments to the agreements and of any increase in its shareholding.

The Court's Ruling.
British-American Tobacco (BAT) and R.J. Reynolds, competitors of Philip Morris and Rothmans, brought actions under Article 230 of the EC Treaty for annulment of the Commission's decision not to object to the revised agreements. The Court of Justice upheld the Commission's assessment of the revised agreements under both Articles 81 and 82. The main significance of the judgment was the Court's holding that Article 81 may prohibit the acquisition of a minority shareholding in a competitor:

14. *See Philip Morris/Rembrandt/Rothmans*, Fourteenth Report on Competition Policy, points 98–100. However, Article 81 may be applied to anticompetitive cooperation preceding a merger, especially if the parties' intentions are not clear: *Philip Morris/Rothmans*, ECJ Nov. 17, 1987, 1987 ECR 4487, paras 3–4.

'*Although the acquisition by one company of an equity interest in a competitor does not in itself constitute conduct restricting competition, such an acquisition may nevertheless serve as an instrument for influencing the commercial conduct of the companies in question so as to restrict or distort competition on the market on which they carry on business.*

That will be true in particular where, by the acquisition of a shareholding or through subsidiary clauses in the agreement, the investing company obtains legal or de facto control of the commercial conduct of the other company or where the agreement provides for commercial cooperation between the companies or creates a structure likely to be used for such cooperation.

That may also be the case where the agreement gives the investing company the possibility of reinforcing its position at a later stage and taking effective control of the other company. Account must be taken not only of the immediate effects of the agreement, but also of its potential effects and of the possibility that the agreement may be part of a long-term plan.

Finally, every agreement must be assessed in its economic context and in particular in the light of the situation on the relevant market. Moreover, where the companies concerned are multinational corporations which carry on business on a worldwide scale, their relationships outside the Community cannot be ignored. It is necessary in particular to consider the possibility that the agreement in question may be part of a policy of global cooperation between the companies which are party to it.

...

The Commission considers that on the market for cigarettes, which is stagnant and oligopolistic and on which there is no real competition on prices or in research, advertising and corporate acquisition are the principal means of increasing market share. Furthermore, since the market is dominated by large companies with considerable resources and expertise, and advertising is of great importance, barriers to entry are very high.

In the market situation described by the Commission, a description which was not disputed in any substantial respects by the other parties to the proceedings, any company wishing to increase its market share will be strongly tempted, where the opportunity arises, to take control of a competitor. In such circumstances, any attempted takeover and any agreement likely to promote commercial cooperation between two or more of those dominant companies is liable to result in restriction of competition.

In such a market situation the Commission must display particular vigilance. It must consider in particular whether an agreement which at first sight provides only for a passive investment in a competitor is not in fact intended to result in a takeover of that company, perhaps at a later stage, or to establish cooperation between the companies with a view to sharing the market. Nevertheless, *in order for the Commission to hold that an infringement of Article 81 has been committed, it must be able to show that the agreement has the object or effect of influencing the competitive behaviour of the companies on the relevant market.*

...

[I]t must also be considered whether, in the circumstances of this case, Philip Morris's shareholding in Rothmans International requires the companies involved to take into consideration the other party's interest when determining their commercial policy, as the applicants argue.'[15] [Emphasis added.]

The Court recognized that the Commission had considerable discretion and declined to overturn its assessment that the revised agreements did not appreciably restrict competition. The Court also refused to find an abuse of a dominant position. The question of abuse of a dominant position could only arise when 'the shareholding in question results in effective control of the other company or at least in some influence over its commercial policy', and no such effect was found in this case.[16] Uncertainty about the possible wide-ranging scope of application of Article 81 to mergers brought about by the *Philip Morris/Rothmans* judgment gave a powerful impetus to adoption of a merger control regulation.[17]

Application of the *Philip Morris* Doctrine by the Commission.
The Commission tested the *Philip Morris* doctrine in *BT/MCI*.[18] This case concerned the creation of a joint venture to develop and market new international value-added telecommunication services, including British Telecom's acquisition of a minority shareholding of 20% in MCI. The Commission decided that this acquisition did not lead to control by British Telecom over MCI and therefore was not subject to the merger control regulation. Subsequently the Commission examined the case under Article 81 in the light of the *Philip Morris* doctrine and stated that the minority shareholding did not lead to an anticompetitive coordination of the commercial conduct between British Telecom and MCI, such as via access to, and exchange of, commercially sensitive information, and issued a negative clearance in this respect.[19] The Commission is applying the *Philip Morris* doctrine in cases of minority shareholdings which do not lead to control (and therefore are not within the merger control regulation) but are likely to amount to anticompetitive coordination (and therefore may come within Article 81), and is discussed in section F of this Chapter.

---

15. *Philip Morris/Rothmans*, ECJ Nov. 17, 1987, 1987 ECR 4487, paras 37–40, 43–45, 48.
16. *Philip Morris/Rothmans*, ECJ Nov. 17, 1987, 1987 ECR 4487, para. 65.
17. The more recent merger between *BAT* and *Rothmans* was cleared by the Commission in view of their relatively small market shares (around 15%): D.Comm. March 17, 1999, M.1415.
18. *BT/MCI I*, D.Comm. Sept. 13, 1993, M.353.
19. *BT/MCI II*, D.Comm. July 27, 1994, 1994 OJ L 223/36, point 44.

4. The 1989 Merger Control Regulation and its Amendments

Long Gestation Period.
The Commission first made a proposal to the Council of Ministers to give it the power to prohibit large mergers outside of the coal and steel industries in 1973 after the *Continental Can* judgment.[20] However, the Council did not get down to serious consideration of the proposal until 1986–1987, when the cause of European merger control was given fresh impetus by the Single Market program and the rush of industry to restructure on a European basis to take advantage of the new market opportunities. By then it had become widely recognized in the member states that while most mergers did not pose any problem, there could be a threat to competition when large firms operating in several states merged their businesses. On 21 December 1989, after more than two years of intensive negotiations on successive drafts of the Commission's proposal, the Council of Ministers finally adopted a merger control regulation.[21] The regulation entered into force nine months later, on 21 September 1990.

The 1997 Amendment.
On 30 June 1997, the Council adopted Regulation 1310/97 amending the merger control regulation which entered into force on 1 March 1998.[22] These amendments extended the application of the regulation to a wider range of mergers and joint venture transactions. Article 57 of the EEA Agreement[23] contains similar merger control rules with respect to the territory covered by that Agreement.

The 2003 Amendment.
Following its Green Paper on the Review of Council Regulation 4064/89,[24] on 16 December 2003 the Commission adopted Regulation 139/2004,[25] which constitutes the new compehensive reform of merger control in the EU. In order to implement and clarify the terms and application of the merger control regulation the Commission has issued the following regulations, notices and guidelines:

- Regulation 802/2004 implementing Council Regulation 139/2004, replacing Regulation 447/97;[26]

20. 1973 OJ C 92/1.
21. 1989 OJ L 395/1, as corrected by 1990 OJ L 257/13 and as amended by the Act of Adhesion of Austria, Finland and Sweden, in particular Article 8 (2) thereof.
22. *See* consolidated version at 1997 OJ C 180/1.
23. Article 57 of the EEA Agreement. The EEA includes the 25 member states of the EU plus Norway, Iceland and Liechtenstein.
24. COM(2001) 745/6 final of 11 December 2001.
25. 2004 OJ L 24/1.
26. 2004 OJ L 133/1.

- Guidelines on the Assessment of Horizontal Mergers,[27] which deals with the possible anti-competitive effects of horizontal mergers, in particular in the light of market shares and concentration thresholds,[28] with the evaluation of the increased risk of co-ordination on oligopolistic markets,[29] countervailing buyer power,[30] potential competition,[31] efficiencies,[32] and the failing company defense;[33]
- Notice on the Definition of the Relevant Market;[34]
- Notice on a Simplified Procedure for Treatment of Certain Concentrations;[35]
- Notice on the Concept of Concentration;[36]
- Notice on the Concept of Full-Function Joint Ventures;[37]
- Notice on the Concept of Undertakings Concerned;[38]
- Notice on the Calculation of Turnover;[39]
- Paper on the Competitive Effects of Efficiencies in European Merger Control.[40]
- Notice on Remedies;[41]
- Notice on Restrictions Directly Related and Necessary to Concentrations ('Ancillary');[42]
- Best Practices on the Conduct of EC Merger Control Proceedings.[43]
- Best Practices Guidelines: The Commission's Model Texts for Divestiture Commitments and the Trusteee Mandate under the Merger Regulation;[44]
- Draft 2004 Notices on case allocation (case referral), ancillary restraints (amending the 2001 Notice) and simplified procedures (amending the 2000 Notice), available on the Commission's website: http://europa.eu.int/comm/competition/mergers/legislation/consultation.

The Main Issues of the Amended Merger Control Regulation 139/2004. The main issues addressed in the new merger control regulation are the following:

---

27. 2004 OJ C 31/5.
28. By applying, as a first indication, the Herfindahl-Hirshman Index (HHI), *ibid.*, point 16.
29. *Ibid.*, points 40–69, following *Airtours*, CFI June 6, 2002, 2002 ECR II-2585.
30. Guidelines on Horizontal Mergers, points 75–77.
31. *Ibid.*, points 78–86.
32. Points 87–95.
33. Points 96–98.
34. 1997 OJ C 372/3.
35. 2000 OJ C 217/32.
36. 1998 OJ C 66/5.
37. 1998 OJ C 66/1.
38. 1998 OJ C 66/14.
39. 1998 OJ C 66/25.
40. Elaborated by the Commission's Enterprise Directorate-General, Enterprise Paper No. 11, 2002.
41. 2001 OJ C 68/3, replacing the previous Notice, 1990 OJ C 203/5.
42. 2001 OJ C 188/5.
43. Commission's website: http://europa.eu.int/comm/competition/mergers/legislation/best_practices.pdf
44. IP/03/614.

- defining the new standards for mergers that are likely to 'significantly impede effective competition', irrespective of whether they create or strengthen a dominant position in the Common Market (which broadens the standards applied under the previous Regulation 1310/97), in particular by extending the scope of the merger control to 'non-collusive oligopolies';
- rationalizing timing of the notification, by allowing notication *prior* to the conclusion of a binding agreement;
- amending the referral procedure both from and to the Commission in order to simplify and to render more flexible the current provisions, in particular to apply the referral procedure at the pre-notification stage, to simplify the referral criteria and to give both the Commission and the parties a right of initiative;[45]
- introducing extra time for the proper consideration of proposed remedies; and
- improving the fact-finding procedure, in particular by increasing the amount of fines for failure to comply with information requests (in alignment with the new Regulation 1/2003 replacing Regulation 17).

The new regulation does *not* include changes to the actual turnover thresholds for a Community dimension which shall, however, be reviewed in 2009 in the light of statistical data to be supplied by the member states.[46]

Better Decision-Making Process.
The non-legislative measures to be implemented under the new regulation are the following:

- creating a post of Chief Competition Economist;
- appointing a peer review panel for all in-depth merger investigations;
- strengthening the Hearing Officers;
- appointing a Consumer Liaison Officer;
- granting earlier access to the file;
- giving early opportunity to review and discuss third party submissions; and
- keeping the merging parties informed of the progress of in-depth investigations.

Plan of this Chapter.
This Chapter will deal with the transactions covered by the merger control regulation and those which are excluded, in particular minority shareholdings (under C.), with the assessment of mergers likely to significantly impede effective competition, ancillary restrictions and commitments in order to facilitate clearance (under D.), the procedural rules (under E.), and the assessment of transactions which are not covered by the merger control regulation, in particular minority

45. Amendments of Articles 4, 9 and 22.
46. Article 1 (4) of Regulation 139/2004.

shareholdings and joint ventures that are not full-function or do not have a Community dimension (under F).

C. Transactions Covered by the Merger Control Regulation

1. Overview of Main Principles

Legal Basis.
The merger control regulation, Regulation 139/2004, is based on both Articles 83 and 308 of the EEC Treaty. Article 83 by itself would have been insufficient because it only enables the Council to legislate on conduct caught by Articles 81 or 82, which is not the case with some mergers: for example, a merger that strengthened an existing dominant position clearly fell within Article 82 under the *Continental Can* doctrine, but it was not clear that a merger that creates a dominant position or significantly impedes effective competition does so. Consequently, the Council also took the precaution of basing the merger control regulation on Article 308, which allows the Council to take action not provided for in the Treaty where the action is necessary to attain the objectives of the Treaty, including the maintenance of effective competition in the Common Market (Article 3 (g)).[47]

Industry-Wide Application.
The regulation applies to all industries, including – since July 20, 2002 – to the coal and steel sectors.[48]

Scope Limited to Transactions with a 'Community Dimension'.
The regulation covers only mergers and 'full-function' joint ventures with a 'Community dimension', defined as those involving firms with either (i) combined worldwide sales of at least EUR 5 billion, a minimum of EUR 250 million sales each within the Community and not more than two-thirds of each firm's sales in the Community coming from within the same member state, or (ii) combined worldwide sales of at least EUR 2.5 billion, a combined minimum of EUR 100 million within each of at least three member states with at least two of the undertakings having sales of more than EUR 25 million within each of those three

47. Recital 7 to Regulation 139/2004.
48. After the expiry of the ECSC Treaty the EC rules apply; mergers in the coal and steel industries are no longer subject to Article 6 (1)–(6) but to the EC merger control regulation. *See* Commission's Communication, 2002 OJ C 152/5. The procedures for processing mergers under the ECSC and EC Treaties were already aligned by the Commission Notice on the Alignment of Procedures for Processing Mergers under the ECSC and EC Treaties, 1998 OJ C 66/36, e.g. *Usinor/Arbed/Aceralia*, D.Comm. Nov. 2, 2001, 2003 OJ L 88/1. Example of applying both the ECSC and the EC merger rules in parallel, *see Verband freier Rohrwerke*, CFI July 8, 2003, T-374/00.

member states, and the Community-wide sales of at least two of the undertakings being more than EUR 100 million with not more than two-thirds of each firm's sales in the Community coming from the same member state.

Compulsory Notification.
Mergers and full-function joint ventures having a 'Community dimension' must be notified to the Commission in advance of their implementation. Community dimension is based on turnover, not on market share thresholds. Transactions may not be implemented until the Commission has given clearance or the time limit for Commission action has expired.

Fast Processing.
The regulation takes into account the need for speedy clearance of transactions. Difficult cases will normally be decided within 90 working days and straightforward cases will be cleared within only 25 working days from notification. Simple cases may be decided in a simplified procedure.

Principal Criterion: Significantly Impeding Effective Competition.
The criteria the Commission must apply in appraising transactions are competition-orientated. The principal criterion is whether the transaction would significantly impede effective competition in the Common Market or a substantial part of it, in particular as a result of the creation or strengthening of a dominant position. The 'development of technical and economic progress' which is included in the appraisal according to Article 2 (1) (b) must also be interpreted in the light of Article 3 (g) in a competition-orientated way, namely as ensuring that competition in the Common Market is not distorted.

One-Stop Shop and Referral to and from Member States.
In order to avoid overlapping review of transactions by the Commission and national authorities, the regulation in principle gives the Commission exclusive jurisdiction over transactions covered by the regulation. However, the Commission may also refer transactions to national authorities in certain cases with a view to the application of national competition law, and member states may refer cases that do not have a Community dimension to the Commission with a view to the application of EC merger rules, for the purpose of avoiding multi-filings at the national level. Accordingly, the regulation provides for a mechanism of referrals to and from member states which ensures that a case is dealt with by the most appropriate authority in the light of the principle of subsidiarity and with a view to ensuring that multiple notifications of a given concentration and 'fragmentations' of cases are avoided to the greatest possible extent.[49]

---

49. Recital 14 to Regulation 139/2004 and Draft Commission Notice on Case Allocation, in particular point 12.

Mergers without a Community Dimension and Non-Merger Type Transactions.
Because of the high sales thresholds required to meet the regulation's 'Community dimension' criterion, a large number of transactions will, even under the lower thresholds of the amended regulation, escape Community control and will be subject mainly to control by national authorities, unless they refer the case to the Commission for decision. Article 81 and Regulation 1/2003 are still applicable to cooperation arrangements that are not mergers or full-function joint ventures, such as partial-function joint ventures and minority shareholdings that do not confer control.

Transactions with EEA Relevance.
Article 57 of the EEA Agreement provides that mergers and full-function joint ventures which create or strengthen a dominant position as a result of which effective competition would be significantly impeded within the territory covered by the Agreement shall be declared incompatible with the functioning of the Agreement. The Commission has sole competence to take decisions on concentrations with a Community dimension[50] in cooperation with the EFTA Surveillance Authority.[51] The EFTA Surveillance Authority is competent where the relevant thresholds are met in the territory of the EEA Agreement, but without prejudice to the competence of EC member states (Article 57(2)).[52] The Commission and the EFTA Surveillance Authority have established rules for cooperation in cases where the parties have a combined turnover in the EEA countries that equals 25% or more of their total turnover or at least two parties achieve a turnover of EUR 250 million in the territory of the EEA Agreement and the transaction is likely to impede effective competition, in particular as a result of the creation or strengthening a dominant position in the EEA territory or a substantial part thereof.[53]

Statistics.
Up to April 30, 2004, 2489 transactions were notified to the Commission.[54]

(i) In Phase 1 review:
- 61 notifications were withdrawn prior to a Phase 1 decision;

---

50. This is normally the case, even where the relevant geographical market is limited to one member state, *see Bertelsmann/Kirch/Première*, D.Comm. May 27, 1998, 1999 OJ L 53/1, point 22.
51. Protocol 24 to the EEA Agreement; *Orkla/Volvo*, D.Comm. Sept. 20, 1995, 1996 OJ L 66/17, points 7–9.
52. There are no cases decided by the EFTA Surveillance Authority, and it is unlikely that a merger will fulfill the thresholds in the EEA countries (Norway, Iceland and Liechtenstein).
53. Article 2 of Protocol 24 to the EEA Agreement. *See Multimedia/Telenor Nextel/Telia*, D.Comm. May 27, 1998, JV.I.
54. Commission's website statistics: http://europa.eu.int/comm/competition/mergers/cases/stats.html. The figures do not add up, probably because of still pending cases

- *54* transactions were held not be within the scope of Regulation 139/2004 (Article 6 (1) (a) decisons stating that the notified transaction was not a merger or a full-function joint venture or did not have a Community dimension);
- *2192* transactions were declared compatible with the Common Market, out of which 2081 were without (Article 6 (1) (b) decisions) and 111 with commitments (Article 6 (2) decisions);
- *24* transactions were fully[55] referred to member states (Article 9 (3) decisions);
- *134* transactions were subjected to an Article 6 (1) (c) decision (initiating Phase 2).

(ii) In Phase 2 proceedings:
- *23* transactions were withdrawn prior to a Phase 2 decision;
- *86* transactions were declared compatible with the Common Market (Article 8 (2) decisions), out of which 24 were without and 62 with commitments;
- *18* transactions were declared incompatible with the Common Market (Article 8 (3) decisions);
- *4* mergers which were already implemented were ordered to be dissolved (Article 8 (4) decisions).

(iii) *7* transactions were referred from member states to the Commission, out of which 4 were declared compatible (2 subject to commitments) and 3 incompatible with the Common Market (Article 22 (3) decisions).[56]

The Commission's statistics are – unfortunately – silent on the number of transactions which were abandoned in the pre-notification phase, mostly following the Commission's objections, which are, however, significant for assessing the effectiveness of the merger control regulation. It may be assumed that the number is considerably higher than the number of cases withdrawn following their notification.

2. Companies Covered by the Merger Control Regulation

No Discrimination between Public and Private Sector Firms.
The regulation applies not only to private-sector (including acquisition by individual persons[57]) but also to state-owned firms[58] – however constituted, financed and administered – unless application of the regulation would jeopardize public

55. 32 transactions have been partially referred to member states but are also cleared by the Commission.
56. These 3 prohibition decisions are included in the 18 decisions mentioned above.
57. Commission Notice on the Concept of Undertakings Concerned, 1998 OJ C 6/14, points 51–52.
58. Commission Notice on the Concept of Undertakings Concerned, 1998 OJ C 6/14, point 55.

service obligations (Article 86 (2)). In the case of state-owned enterprises, only the sales of businesses making up an economic unit with independent power of decision are taken into account for the purposes of the turnover thresholds.[59]

No Merger between Firms Already Forming an Economic Unit.
A merger presupposes the disappearance of, or acquisition of control ('exercising decisive influence') over, one or more economically independent business unit(s); a business controlled by another firm is already economically dependent on that firm, so that a strengthening of the pre-existing control is not a new merger but rather an internal restructuring within a group of companies.[60] The existence of shareholding links is not, however, conclusive of dependence.[61] Hence, a merger of two state-owned firms in the same country may fall within the regulation if they were separately run economic units prior to the transaction.[62]

Transactions Involving Firms from Non-EC Countries – Immediate and Substantial Effects within the Community.
The regulation may apply, as do Articles 81 and 82,[63] to transactions involving operations of firms from non-EC countries.[64] However, any enforcement measures that the Commission takes must be limited to what is necessary to safeguard or restore effective competition within the Common Market.[65] In *Gencor/Lonrho*[66] the Commission declared incompatible with the Common Market the proposed merger in the platinum sector between Impala Platinum, controlled by the South

59. Recital 12 of the preamble to Regulation 4064/89. *See Neste/IVO*, D.Comm. June 2, 1998, M.931.
60. *Fortis/Generale*, D.Comm. June 24, 1998, M.1172. *See also* under Article 66 of the ECSC Treaty: *Arbed/Neunkirchener/Rodange*, D.Comm. June 6, 1978, 1978 OJ L 164/14, 18 (increase of Arbed' s shareholding in Rochling-Burbach from 50% to 100%); *Dillinger Hütte-Saarstahl*, Nineteenth Report on Competition Policy, point 78 (increase in Usinor/Sacilor's shareholding in Dillinger from 58% to 70%). However, the buying out by one partner of the other partner's share in a joint venture does constitute a merger as the first partner is assuming *sole* control: *ICI/Tioxide*, D.Comm. Nov. 28, 1990, M.23; *AXA/Royale Beige*, D.Comm. June 12, 1998, M.1193.
61. *Gencor/Lonrho*, CFI 25 March 1999, 1999 ECR II-753, paras 169–193.
62. Para. 12 of preamble; Notice on Concept of Concentration, point 8. *See Pechiney/Usinor*, D.Comm. June 24, 1991, M.97; *CEA Industrie/France Telecom/SGS-Thomson*, D.Comm. Feb. 22, 1993, M.216. Under Article 66 (2) of the ECSC Treaty: *VEBA/Gelsenberg*, D.Comm. Dec. 16, 1974, 1975 OJ L 65/16; Fourth Report on Competition Policy, points 128–131. *See also* generally *supra* Chapter I.D.1.
63. *Wood Pulp*, ECJ Sept. 27, 1988, 1988 ECR 5193, paras 11–18. The applicability of the EC competition rules was not disputed in *Philip Morris/Rothmans* which concerned the EC business of the South African company Rembrandt: ECJ Nov. 17, 1987, 1987 ECR 4487.
64. *See* Recital 10 to Regulation 139/2004.
65. *See* generally *supra* Chapter I.E.5. *See also* under Article 81 the possible impact of third country cooperation in *Philip Morris/Rothmans*, ECJ Nov. 17, 1987, 1987 ECR 4487, para. 40; and, under Article 82, *Tetra Pak I*, D.Comm. July 26, 1988, 1988 OJ L 272/27, 44; *aff'd* ECJ Nov. 14, 1996, 1996 ECR I-5951.
66. *Gencor/Lonrho*, D.Comm. April 24, 1996, M.619, 1997 OJ L 11/30.

African company Gencor, and the Lonrho platinum division, a South African subsidiary of the British Company Lonrho, both having substantial operations in the Community. The Commission considered that the merger would lead to the creation of a duopoly dominating the world market for platinum and rhodium. The Court of First Instance affirmed this decision by stating that the merger control regulation applies to *all* mergers with a Community dimension:

> 'Article 1 does not require that, in order for a concentration to be regarded as having a Community dimension, the undertakings in question must be established in the Community or that the production activities covered by the concentration must be carried out within the Community territory .... The Regulation does not, for the purpose of defining its territorial scope, ascribe greater importance to production operations than to sales operations. On the contrary, by setting quantitative thresholds in Article 1 which are based on the worldwide and Community turnover of the undertakings concerned, it rather ascribes greater importance to sales operations within the Common Market as a factor linking the concentration to the Community.'[67]

The Court of First Instance affirmed the compatibility of this interpretation with public international law:

> 'Application of the Regulation is justified under public international law when it is foreseeable that a proposed concentration will have an immediate and substantial effect in the Community.'[68]

The Commission has applied the merger control regulation in various cases to mergers involving firms established in third countries. For example, in *Boeing/McDonnell Douglas*[69] the Commission announced that it was prepared to block a United States-based transaction, namely the acquisition of McDonnell Douglas by Boeing. The matter was ultimately resolved after Boeing gave commitments to the Commission designed to preserve competitive conditions in the Community. However, the same was not true in the *GE/Honeywell* case,[70] which ultimately was blocked by the the Commission although it had already been cleared by the U.S. authorities.

Non-Discriminatory Treatment of Non-EC and EC Firms by the Respective Authorities.

The Commission will monitor the treatment accorded to EC firms undertaking mergers in non-EC countries, and if they are treated less favorably than non-EC

67. *Gencor/Lonrho*, CFI March 25, 1999, 1999 ECR II-753, paras 79, 85.
68. *Gencor/Lonrho*, CFI March 25, 1999, 1999 ECR II-753, para. 90.
69. *Boeing/McDonnell Douglas*, D.Comm. July 30, 1997, 1997 OJ L 336/16.
70. *GE/Honeywell*, D.Comm. July 3, 2001, M.2220, IP/01/939.

firms are treated in the Community, it will ask the Council for a negotiating mandate to secure non-discriminatory treatment from the non-EC country (Article 24 and recital 44). However, the international cooperation established by bilateral agreements[71] and within the multilateral framework of the Organization for Economic Cooperation and Development (OECD) and the World Trade Organization (WTO) provide means of avoiding conflicts over enforcement activities.[72]

3. Types of Transactions Covered by the Merger Control Regulation

(a) General

Scope: 'Concentrations'.
The merger control regulation applies to 'concentrations', which are defined in Article 3 and commented upon in the Commission Notice on the Concept of Concentration.[73] 'Concentration' comprises two main categories of transactions. First, it applies to transactions whereby *two* companies legally merge into *one* (Article 3 (1) (a)) or *one* firm takes *sole* control of the whole or part of another (Article 3 (1) (b)).[74] Such transactions are commonly referred to as mergers, acquisitions or takeovers, or more generally as 'mergers'. Secondly, 'concentration' covers transactions whereby *two* or *more* firms acquire *joint* control of another firm, i.e., joint ventures (Article 3 (1) (b)). The regulation applies, however, only to joint ventures that are of a 'full-function' nature. A joint venture is 'full-function', and hence falls within the regulation, if it '[performs] on a lasting basis all the functions of an autonomous economic entity' (Article 3 (4)). In the event that a full-function joint venture 'has as its object or effect the coordination of the competitive behavior of undertakings which remain independent', such coordination shall be appraised in accordance with the criteria of Article 81 (1) and (3), with a view of establishing whether or not the operation is compatible with the Common Market (Article 2 (4)).

---

71. Agreement between the European Communities and the Government of the United States (1995 OJ L 95/47), Canada (1999 OJ L 175/50) and Japan (July 10, 2003). *See* the Commission's Reports on the application of these agreements in merger cases, COM(2002)505 final.
72. *See* Twenty-seventh Report on Competition Policy, points 330–348.
73. 1998 OJ C 66/5.
74. Internal reorganization within a group is not a merger: *Fortis AG/Generale Bank*, D.Comm. June 24, 1998, M.1172. However, where both the acquiring and the acquired company are owned by the same state or the same public body but have an independent power of decision, in particular where they were formerly part of different economic units, the operation will be deemed to constitute a merger: Notice on the Concept of Concentration, point 8; Notice on Turnover, points 43–44. *See Pechiney/Usinor*, D.Comm. June 24, 1991, M.97; *CEA Industrie/France Telecom/SOS Thomson*, D.Comm. Feb. 22, 1993, M.216.

(b) Mergers – Sole Control

Definition of Merger.
The regulation applies to mergers in the following cases:

- *Absorption – Legal Merger.* The acquired business is completely absorbed and loses its separate legal identity or when two businesses are absorbed into a new company and both lose their previous legal identities (Article 3 (1) (a)).[75]
- *Acquisition of Control over a Whole Business.* One firm acquires direct or indirect control over the whole of another firm's business through the purchase of shares or assets, by contract or by any other means (Article 3 (1) (b)).
- *Acquisition of Control over Part of a Business.* One firm acquires control over part of another firm's business by one of the above means, a transaction traditionally known as a 'partial merger' (Article 3 (1) (b) and Article 5 (2)). Examples are where only part of the physical production and marketing operations – separable from the rest of the selling firm's activities in technical and organizational respects – are acquired[76] or where a subsidiary operating in a particular geographic market is acquired leaving the seller active in the same product market but a different geographic market.[77] The Commission tends to consider the transfer of certain customers as acquisition of a part of an undertaking.[78] The reciprocal acquisition of the other party's business, in particular asset swaps, normally constitutes two separate operations although the reciprocal transfer is usually considered by the parties as interdependent.[79]

75. Referred to as 'fusion' in French and as 'legal merger' in English: *see* UK House of Lords Select Committee on the European Communities, *International Mergers*, 28th Report, 1977–78 Session, pp. 3–4. 'Legal mergers' are rare in the UK and U.S. where the acquisition ('takeover') or exchange of shares or purchase of assets is the usual merger route. However, they are not uncommon in Japan: *Kyowa/Saitama Banks*, D.Comm. March 7, 1991, M.69. *See also Price Waterhouse/Coopers & Lybrand*, D.Comm. May 20, 1998, 1999 OJ L 50/27, point 8.
76. *Agfa-Gevaert/Du Pont*, D.Comm. Feb. 11, 1998, 1998 OJ L 211/22, paras 6–7. *See Promodes/Dirsa*, D.Comm. Dec. 17, 1990, M.27 (acquisition of Tabacalera's food retailing business); *Cargill/Unilever*, D.Comm. Dec. 20, 1990, M.26 (acquisition of Unilever's UK agricultural merchanting business); *Fiat/Ford New Holland*, D.Comm. Feb. 8, 1991, M.9 (acquisition of Ford's agricultural machinery business).
77. *Pilkington/BSN-Gervais-Danone*, Tenth Report on Competition Policy, points 152–155 (first sale of parts of BSN's flat glass business).
78. *ECS/Sibelga*, D.Comm. Dec. 19, 2003, M.3318, point 10 (transfer of eligible customers in the electricity and natural gas sector). However, such an agreement could be held infringing Article 81 irrespective of the parties' market share because it contains a hard-core restriction (allocation of customers).
79. Notice on Undertakings Concerned, points 49–50; *Dupont/ICI*, D.Comm. Sept. 30, 1992, 1992 OJ L 7/13 (the acquisition of ICI's worldwide nylon operations by Dupont was granted conditional clearance by the Commission, whereas the acquisition of Dupont's worldwide acryl operations by ICI was considered as a separate transaction which did, however, not fulfill the thresholds of the Community dimension: IP/92/765). *See also Renault/Volvo*, D.Comm.

However, the joint acquisition of a company with a view to immediate sharing of the assets acquired constitutes two concentrations, by means of which each undertaking acquires part of that company.[80]

Identity and Competitive Relationship of Parties.
The acquirer may be a company or companies or an individual or group of individuals controlling a firm (Article 3 (1) (b)). The merging firms may be competitors (a horizontal merger) or supplier and customer (a vertical merger) or they may operate in different, unrelated markets (a conglomerate merger). The merger may take place by agreement between the parties or by takeover bid which may be agreed[81] or contested.[82]

Key Criterion: Control.
The key criterion for a merger (except in the rare cases where the acquired business ceases to exist as a separate legal entity) is the acquisition of direct or indirect 'control' by one firm over another.[83] Regulation 139/2004 amends Article 3 (1) so as to explicitly recite that a concentration requires a 'change in control on a lasting basis'. 'Control' is defined in Article 3 (2) as rights (ownership or the right to use all or part[84] of the assets), contracts[85] or any other means[86] which, either separately or jointly and having regard to the considerations of fact or law involved, confer

Nov. 7, 1990, M.4 (reciprocal acquisition of 45% of each company's truck and bus businesses amounting to a merger, but exchange of only 25% cross-shareholdings in their car businesses, not a merger).

80. *Portugal – Secil/Holderbank/Cimpor*, ECJ June 22, 2004, C-42/01, para. 27.
81. *See Framatome/Berg Electronics*, Oct. 8, 1998, M.1314.
82. *See*, e.g., *Arjomari/WigginsTeape*, D.Comm. Dec. 10, 1990, M.25 (horizontal merger); *ICI/Tioxide*, D.Comm. Nov. 28, 1990, M.23 (vertical merger); *AT&T/NCR*, D.Comm. Jan. 18, 1991, M.50 (conglomerate merger though including some same or related businesses).
83. Control may be acquired indirectly via a holding company: *Normura/Blueslate*, D.Comm. Nov. 17, 1997, M.1037.
84. The acquisition of part of a business is deemed a partial merger whether or not the part is a separate legal entity: Article 5 (2), first subparagraph. The 'right to use' parts of a business's assets may refer to arrangements such as the leasing of a production facility which remains integrated in the lessor's plant. The reciprocal grant of such rights is common in cooperative specialization arrangements which have traditionally been evaluated under Article 81, *see BP-Chemicals/ICI*, D.Comm. July 19, 1984, 1984 OJ L 212/1; *ENI/Montedison*, D.Comm. Dec. 4, 1986, 1987 OJ L 5/13. It appears that this position will continue to be taken under the merger regulation.
85. *See Fortis/CGER*, D.Comm. Nov. 15, 1993, M.342. Contractual arrangements providing for joint management and risk spreading ('*Gleichordnungskonzern*' under German law) are considered equivalent to a merger: *see RTZ/CRA*, D.Comm. Dec. 7, 1995, M.660. *See* under Articles 81, 82 *IMI/Heilmann I*, Seventh Report on Competition Policy, points 29–32; Notice on the Concept of Concentration, point 7.
86. In particular interlocking directorates; *see* under the ECSC Treaty: *Thyssen/Röchling-Burbach* and *Dillingen/Arbed*, Eleventh Report on Competition Policy, points 108–110.

the possibility of exercising 'decisive influence'[87] on a firm. Temporary holdings by banks and insurance companies, holdings by financial holding companies and control by office holders in bankruptcy and liquidation proceedings are not deemed to be a merger (Article 3 (5)).[88] The influence is almost certainly 'decisive' if a firm owns more than half the share capital,[89] holds more than half the voting rights,[90] is able to appoint more than half of the members of the board of another firm,[91] or has the power to manage the undertakings' affairs.[92] However, even with under 50% of the shares, voting rights or board representation, the influence of a firm may be decisive, especially if the ownership of the rest of the shares or rights is scattered over many different persons or firms.[93] But a minority shareholding does not in itself confer control, especially if other firms hold larger shares, except where the other firms are dispersed and hold minor shares. Contracts made with a firm concerning the calculation or allocation of profits or supply or distribution contracts covering all or a major proportion of its supplies or output and exceeding the normal term of such contracts were considered to indicate control under ECSC law, but are not considered to do so by themselves under Regulation 139/2004.[94]

Acquisition of a Minority Shareholding.
Minority shareholdings normally do not confer *control*, which is decisive influence on the target company. However, a minority shareholder may be the largest shareholder of a company whose shares are split up in small portions, thereby conferring *de facto* control, in particular where the minority shareholding is linked

87. *Cf*, the use of this term or 'dominant influence' in some of the company law harmonization directives, e.g., Article 1 (2) of the Seventh Directive (consolidated accounts), 1983 OJ L 193/1. *See*, generally, Article 1 of the Seventh Directive for the definition of a control relationship.
88. Mergers between banks and insurance companies are, however, treated in the same way as other mergers; *see Eagle Star/Allianz*, Twelfth Report on Competition Policy, point 103.
89. Even 50.1% of the share capital can be sufficient ('Golden Share'): *Magneti-MarelliCEAC*, D.Comm. May 29, 1997, 1997 OJ L 222/38; *Credit Lyonnaise/BFG*, D.Comm. Jan. 11, 1993, M.296; *Tractebel/Distrigas*, D.Comm. Sept. 1, 1994, M.493.
90. *Eurocom*, D.Comm. Dec. 18, 1991, M.147. The majority of votes at shareholders' meeting suffices: *see Coca Cola/Amalgamated Beverages GB*, D.Comm. Jan. 22, 1997, 1997 OJ L 218/15, points 5–13; *Mannesmann/Vallourec*, D.Comm. June 3, 1997, M.906, points 11–20.
91. *IFINT/Exor*, D.Comm. March 2, 1992, M.187.
92. *Accor/Wagons Lits*, D.Comm. April 28, 1992, 1992 OJ L 204/1.
93. *Arjomari/Wiggins Teape*, D.Comm. Dec. 10, 1990, M.25 (acquisition of 39% giving control); *Mannesmann/Vallourec*, D.Comm. June 3, 1997, M.906 (21%); *Anglo American Corpor-ation/Lonrho*, D.Comm. April 23, 1997, 1998 OJ L 149/21 (27.5%); *Pirelli/Edizione Olivetti/Telecom Italia*, D.Comm. Sept. 20, 2001, M.2574 (27%). Under Article 66 (2) of the ECSC Treaty: *Arbed/Neunkirchener/Rodange*, D.Comm. June 6, 1978, 1978 OJ L 164/14,15 (25.09% with management control, all other shareholders having less than 16%).
94. *See* Article 1 (4) and (5) of High Authority (Commission) Decision 24/54 defining 'control' for the purposes of Article 66 (1) of the ECSC Treaty, which is the model for the definition of 'control' in Article 3 (2)–(3) of Regulation 139/2004, except the inclusion of long-term contracts concerning the whole or an important part of the parties' supplies or outlets.

with representation in the management. Similarly, the acquisition of a minority shareholding may lead to *joint control* of the target company, which is exercised together with one or more other undertakings, thereby creating a joint venture.[95] Finally, minority shareholdings may serve as instrument for assuring preferential treatment of the minority shareholder and therefore strengthen its market position, likely to significantly impede effective competition between the minority shareholder and its competitors.[96] In these cases the acquisition or the change of a minority shareholding is subject to the merger control mechanism (notification and clearance), provided the thresholds of Community dimension are met.

In the absence of any 'control' or a Community dimension minority shareholdings are not subject to EC merger control[97] but to applicable national merger control rules.[98] Article 81 may be applicable where the acquisition of the minority shareholding is used as 'an instrument for *influencing* the commercial conduct of the companies in question so as to restrict or distort competition on the market on which they carry on business'.[99] Competition concerns normally do not arise where the minority shareholding is limited to what is necessary to protect the investors' *financial interests*.[100] Minority shareholdings that are not covered by the EC merger control regulation are discussed in section F.1. below.

(c) Full-Function Joint Ventures – Joint Control

Different Ways of Forming a Joint Venture.
A joint venture may be a new company created by the parents in order to pool all or part of their existing businesses[101] or to carry on a new business.[102] A joint

95. E.g. *Electrabel/Totalfina Elf/Photovoltech*, D.Comm. April 18, 2002, M.2712 (42.5% : 34% : 8.5%, but ¾ majority required). In the case of shifting majorities Article 81 applies: *see Eureko*, D.Comm. April 27, 1992, M.207; *Channel Five*, D.Comm. Dec. 22, 1995, M.673, points 8–14. However, in *Newscorp/Telepiù*, D.Comm. Nov. 29, 2002 (Art. 6 (1) (c)) M.2876, the Commission examined the likely anticompetitive coordination between the minority shareholder Telecom Italia holding 20% and Newscorp holding 80% in Stream, which is therefore, according to the Commission, solely (and not jointly) controlled.
96. Accordingly, the Commission may make the approval of a merger subject to the minority shareholder's withdrawing from representation on the board, *see Pilkington/BSN*, Tenth Report on Competition Policy, points 152–155; *Gencor/Lonrho*, CFI March 25, 1999, 1999 ECR II-753, paras 205–206; under the ECSC Treaty: *CLIF/Marine*, D.Comm. March 5, 1975, 1975 OJ L 196/27.
97. The Commission does not intend to extend the merger control to such minority shareholdings: Green Paper of Dec. 11, 2001, COM(2001)745/6 final, points 106–110.
98. *See* Article 21 (1) of Regulation 139/2004. Certain national merger provisions (such as the French and the German laws) apply to the acquisition of shareholding exceeding 25% irrespective of whether or not they confer control.
99. *Philip Morris/Rothmans*, ECJ Nov. 17, 1987, 1987 ECR 4487, para. 37.
100. *Ibid.*, point 22.
101. *AG/Amev*, D.Comm. Nov. 21, 1990, M.18; *Aérospatiale/MBB*, D.Comm. Feb. 25, 1991, M.17; *UPM-Kymene/April*, D.Comm. June 11, 1998, M.1006; *Shell/Exxon II*, D.Comm. July 8, 1998, M.1137.

venture can also be an existing company that used to be under one parent's sole control until a third company acquired an ownership stake in it.[103] Thus, a joint venture can be formed in different ways. The key characteristic is joint control by the parents.

Joint Control.
A preliminary question that must be answered is whether the transaction constitutes a joint venture at all – which necessitates joint control – or rather constitutes a merger with one of the parents which is in sole control, or falls into some other category to be judged under Article 81, such as a specialization or a joint R&D agreement. Joint control implies that neither parent can determine the joint venture's activities on its own and that major decisions can only be taken if the parent companies agree.[104] The Commission has commented in its Notice on the Concept of Concentration that joint control exists where two or more undertakings have the possibility of exercising 'decisive influence' over another undertaking.[105] Decisive influence normally means the power to block actions which determine the strategic commercial behavior of the undertaking.[106] The parents are bound, in order to avoid reciprocal blocking votes, to reach agreement on decisions concerning the joint venture and to take each other's interests into account.[107] This does not, however, require them to have exactly equal shareholdings or voting rights or equal numbers of representatives on the joint venture's governing bodies. Joint control can be exercised through a wide variety of contractual arrangements.[108]

Equal Shareholdings or Voting Rights.
Joint control is clearly present if two or more companies have exactly equal shares of the capital or assets of another company or exactly equal voting rights on its board. In such circumstances the parents are obliged, even in the absence of any express agreement, to cooperate on a permanent basis if they are to avoid reciprocal blocking votes.[109] However, even with equal shareholding rights one parent

---

102. *Dresdner Bank/Banque Nationale de Paris*, D.Comm. Feb. 4, 1991, M.21; *Thomson/Daimler Benz*, D.Comm. May 21, 1996, M.744.
103. *Mitsubishi/UCAR*, D.Comm. Jan. 4, 1991, M.24; *Baxter/Nestlé/Salvia*, D.Comm. Feb. 6, 1991, M.58; *Generali/Banca Intesa/Intesa Vita*, D.Comm. Dec. 15, 2003, M.2768.
104. *Air France/British Airways – TAT*, CFI May 19, 1994, 1994 ECR II-323, paras 62–65.
105. 1998 OJ C 66/5, point 19. Holding jointly the majority of votes present at the shareholders' meeting is joint control: *EDFI/Graninge*, D.Comm. May 25, 1998, M.1169.
106. *Endemol*, CFI April 28, 1999, 1999 ECR II-1299, para. 161. Option rights may suffice: *Thyssen/Krupp*, D.Comm. June 2, 1998, M.1080; *Newhouse/Jupiter*, D.Comm. Sept. 1, 2000, M.2075.
107. Even if the joint control leads to such an permanent or occasional (*Hermes/Sampo/FGB-FCIC*, D.Comm. May 19, 1998, M.1101) anticompetitive 'group effect' it does not preclude the applicability of the merger regulation; it may only necessitate an additional assessment under Article 2 (4), *see* section D.2(g) *infra*.
108. *See GEAUCREA/CGE*, D.Comm. June 18, 1998, M.1186.
109. Joint control accepted: *Sextant/BGT/VDO*, D.Comm. Dec. 21, 1992, M.290 (50.5% : 49.5%); *Continental/Kaliko/DGBank/Benecke*, D.Comm. Nov. 29, 1993, M.363 (50.1% : 49.9%).

company may have the power to determine the strategic decisions of the joint venture and the composition of the board. Mere 'management control' or 'day-today management' may, but does not necessarily, indicate sole control.[110]

Unequal Shareholdings or Voting Rights.
If one of the companies alone has 'the possibility of exercising decisive influence' over a jointly-owned undertaking because it owns more than half the capital or assets, has more than half the voting rights or the power to appoint more than half the board or is in a position to manage the company's business, it may control the company alone, in which case the transaction would constitute a merger.[111] However, joint control may exist even where there is no equality between the two parent companies in votes or representation in decision-making bodies or where there are more than two parent companies.[112] The joint venture agreement or articles[113] or actual conduct[114] may lead to the conclusion that, despite unequal shareholdings or rights in the joint venture company, the parent companies are mutually dependent on each other, at least with respect to major decisions, and

110. *Continental/Kaliko/DG Bank/Benecke*, D.Comm. Nov. 29, 1993, M.363.
111. This follows the standard definition of a parent-subsidiary relationship used in block exemption regulations and the merger control regulation (Article 5 (4)) to determine which businesses are to be included in the aggregate (group) turnover. *See Commercial Solvents*, ECJ March 6, 1974, 1974 ECR 223, para. 37.
112. *BT/ESB/AIG*, D.Comm. May 19, 1998, M.1132; *SAir/LTU*, D.Comm. Dec. 21, 1998, M.1354. However, the possibility of shifting majorities and hanging alliances between the parents contradicts 'joint' control: Notice on Concept of Concentration, point 35; *Eureka*, D.Comm. April 27, 1992, M.207; *Philips/Thompson/SAGEM*, D.Comm. Jan. 18, 1993, M.293, points 8–11; *Channel Five*, D.Comm. Dec. 22, 1995, M.673, points 8–14; *Koipe-Tabacalera/Elosua*, D.Comm. July 28, 1992, M.160; *Wintershall/ENBW/MW/MV/DEO*, D.Comm. Dec. 11, 1998, JV. 13; *Ericsson/Nokia/Psion/Motorola*, D.Comm. Dec. 22, 1998, JV. 12. *See* Notice on the Concept of Concentration, point 32: 'Very exceptionally, collective action can occur on a *de facto* basis where strong common interests exist between minority shareholders to the effect that they would not act against each other in exercising their rights in relation to the joint venture.' Joint ventures constituted by various parent companies with unequal participations and different interests may therefore normally not be regarded as a 'merger' (*ibid.*, point 35).
113. E.g., a requirement for unanimity of all shareholders (*Aérospatiale/MBB*, D.Comm. Feb. 25, 1991, M.17; *UIP*, D.Comm. July 12, 1989, 1989 OJ L 226/25; *Optical Fibers*, D.Comm. July 14, 1986, 1986 OJ L 236/30, 34) or for a certain majority (e.g., 70 or 80%) to be obtained for certain decisions which exceeds the voting power of the majority shareholder (*Olivetti/Canon*, D.Comm. Dec. 22, 1987, 1988 OJ L 52/51, 56; *Cekacan*, D.Comm. Oct. 15, 1990, 1990 OJ L 299/64, 66); or a requirement for decisions concerning the joint venture to be taken jointly or only with the other's consent, as through the joint committee arrangements in *Renault/Volvo*, D.Comm. Nov. 7, 1990, M.4.
114. For example, the plans to integrate the parties' truck and bus businesses in *Renault/Volvo*, D.Comm. Nov. 7, 1990, M.4.

are obliged to agree on a common policy for the joint venture.[115] This may apply even if one partner only has veto power over important decisions since the other partners will be forced to take its interests into account, resulting in *de facto* joint control.[116] Two companies with unequal shareholdings in a third company may likewise be in a position of jointly controlling it if they are also the parents of another company in which the majority/minority relationship is reversed (e.g., 60:40 in one joint venture and 40:60 in the other).[117] However, in order for veto rights to confer a 'decisive influence', the veto rights must be related to strategic decisions on the business policy of the joint venture, such as in relation to adoption of the budget or business plan,[118] to making major investments or the appointment of senior management.[119] Call options do not normally confer joint control; however, the exercise of the option may lead to sole or joint control and must be notified.[120] Veto rights normally accorded to minority shareholders which do not affect strategic decisions on the joint venture's business policy, such as changes in the joint venture articles or bylaws, capital increases or decreases, or relating to sale or winding up the joint venture, do not confer control or a decisive influence on the minority shareholder.[121] Likewise, no control is conferred when a financial institution acquires a shareholding as part of its regular business operations on a temporary basis, by the appointment of a liquidator or similar office-holder, or a financial holding company under the Fourth Council Directive 78/660/EC. However, a rescue operation involving a restructuring program normally confers control within the meaning of the merger control regulation because

115. Agreement on joint control may be ensured by consortium or share pooling arrangements: *Gaz de France/BEWAG/GASAG*, D.Comm. Jan. 20, 1999, M.1402, points 6–9. *See* Notice on the Concept of Concentration, points 30–35.

116. E.g., *Degussa/Ciba-Geigy*, D.Comm. April 5, 1993, M.317 (70:30); *Air France/Sabena*, D.Comm. Oct. 5, 1992, M.157 (37.5% : 62.5%); *TNT/GD Net*, D.Comm. Dec. 2, 1991, M.102 (30% : 25% : 18% : 15% : 12%), but decisions to be taken with a 60% majority); *RTL/Veronica/Endemol*, D.Comm. Sept. 20, 1995, 1995 OJ L 134/21, points 10–13. However, changing alliances between parent companies fall short of 'joint' control (*see Channel Five*, D.Comm. Dec. 22, 1995, M.673).

117. *UPM/Kymmene/April*, D.Comm. June 11, 1998, M.1006 (two joint ventures set up simultaneously, the one being conditioned upon completion of the other). *See BSN/St. Gobain*, Fifth Report on Competition Policy, point 34.

118. *See Air France/British Airways – TAT*, CFI May 19, 1994, 1994 ECR II-323, paras 62–65; *Endemol*, CFI April 28, 1999, 1999 ECR II-1299, para. 161.

119. *Wintershall/ENBW/MW/WV/DEO*, D.Comm. Dec. 11, 1998, JV. 13, point 14 (requirement of a 4/5 majority). *See CPC/McCormick/Rabobank*, D.Comm. Oct. 29, 1993, M.330; *PanAgora/DG Bank*, D.Comm. Nov. 26, 1998, JV. 14, points 8–10; *Mannesmann/Olivetti/Infostrada*, D.Comm. Jan. 15, 1998, M.1025; *Pirelli/Edizione/Olivetti/Telecom Italia*, D.Comm. Sept. 20, 2001, M.2574, point 23 (deadlock situation because of right to sell).

120. Notice on the Concept of Concentration, point 16; *Promodes/S21/Gruppo GS*, D.Comm. March 10, 1998, M.1086; *Dow/Buna*, D.Comm. July 4, 1995, M.591.

121. Notice on the Concept of Concentration, points 21–24. *See Wintershall/ENBW/DEO*, D.Comm. Dec. 11, 1998, JV. 13, points 9–17.

the controlling financial institutions determine the strategic commercial behavior of the rescued undertaking.[122]

Full-Function v. Partial-Function Joint Ventures.
Once the fact of joint control has been established, it is necessary to examine whether the joint venture is an operation governed by the merger control regulation or it is a partial-function joint venture governed by Article 81. The transaction is deemed as '*full function*' whenever two or more firms set up a joint venture that performs 'on a lasting basis all the functions of an autonomous economic entity' (Article 3 (4)). Joint ventures which satisfy this requirement bring about a lasting change in the structure of the undertaking concerned. Insofar as a joint venture 'has as its object or effect the coordination of the competitive behaviour of undertakings which remain independent', such coordination will be appraised in accordance with the criteria of Article 81 (1) and (3) within the same procedure (Article 2 (4)). A joint venture is '*partial function*' if it only assumes limited functions within the parent companies' business activities, such as a joint venture limited *only* to R&D, production, distribution or sales.[123] However, the fact that an otherwise full-function joint venture makes use of the distribution network of one or more of its parents will not disqualify it as full-function as long as the parents are only acting as agents of the joint venture.[124] If the joint venture makes sales to the parents the essential question is whether, regardless of those sales, the joint venture is geared to play an active role on the market. In this respect the relative proportion of these sales compared with the joint venture's total production and whether sales to the parent companies are made on the basis of normal commercial relations are important factors.[125]

Criteria for Distinguishing Full-Function from Partial-Function Joint Ventures.
In order to be 'full-function' the joint venture must have a secure long-term basis.[126] The joint venture must carry on all the normal functions of an independent

122. Notice on the Concept of Concentration, points 41–45.
123. Notice on the Concept of Full-Function Joint Ventures (1998 OJ C 66/1), point 13. *See Pasteur-Merieux/Merck*, D.Comm. July 5, 1993, M.285.
124. *Ibid.*, points 11–13. *See TWD/AKZO Nobel*, D.Comm. Feb. 10, 1995, M.533; *Behringwerke/Armour Pharmaceuticals*, D.Comm. April 3, 1995, M.495. *See also Cultalia/Banca delle Marche/JV*, D.Comm. Sept. 13, 1999, M.1627 (where the joint ventures, active in the bank insurance sector in Italy, would distribute its insurance policies through the distribution channels of the parent companies (banks, branches, promoters) but remain free to use other modes of distinction) and *Generali/Banca Intesa/Intesa Vita*, D.Comm. Dec. 15, 2003, M.2768.
125. *Ibid.*, point 14. *See Teksid/Norsk Hydro/Meridian*, D.Comm. July 17, 1998, M.1189.
126. *See UPM-Kymmene*, D.Comm. June 11, 1998, M.1006; *Krauss-Maffei/Wegmann*, D.Comm. June 19, 1998, M.1153 (indefinite period).

business.[127] If the parent companies commit the resources to operate as a full-function joint venture on a lasting basis, provisions that permit dissolution or withdrawal of a partner in the event of failure of the joint venture or fundamental disagreement between the parent companies will not prevent the joint venture from being considered as operating on a lasting basis. However, a short-term joint venture agreement, such as to construct a power plant without ongoing operational responsibility once construction has been completed[128] or one that can be terminated by the parties in the short term, e.g. at regular intervals or upon notice without cause, or provision for intellectual property rights, technology and production skills to revert to the parents after termination of the agreement,[129] are indications of a partial-function joint venture. The Commission has issued a Notice on the Concept of Full-Function Joint Ventures.[130] Key indicia for classifying a joint venture as a full-function or partial-function operation are summarized in the following checklist:

(i) *Stability.*
Is the joint venture a separate legal entity and a viable business in its own right? In particular, does it have:
– a secure long-term basis?
– its own capital?
– its own technology?
– its own production facilities?
– its own sales or distribution functions?
– its own trade name, trademark or other designation to distinguish it from its parents?

(ii) *Dependence on Parents.*
Substantial dependence of the joint venture on one or more of the parents is a factor against finding a full-function joint venture. The joint venture may be dependent on one or more parents for:
– personnel,[131]

---

127. *See Renault/Iveco*, D.Comm. Oct. 22, 1998, M.1202; *Elf/Texaco/Antifreeze*, D.Comm. Aug. 18, 1998, M.1135; *Volvo Aero/ABB/Turbogen*, D.Comm. Nov. 17, 1998, M.1334.
128. Notice on the Concept of Full-Function Joint Ventures, point 15. Five years sufficient: *Enichem/ICI*, D.Comm. Dec. 22, 1987, 1988 OJ L 50/18. Under ECSC law, however, the acquisition of 13.9% of a majority government-owned company together with a contract giving management control for five years was held to be a merger: *Cockerill/Jemappes*, Eighth Report on Competition Policy, point 143.
129. *Baxter/Nestlé/Salvia*, D.Comm. Feb. 6, 1991, M.58. *See* under Article 81: *De Laval/Stork I*, D.Comm. July 25, 1977, 1977 OJ L 215/11, 15–16; *GEC/Weir*, D.Comm. Nov. 23, 1977, 1977 OJ L 327/26, 29; *Rockwell/Iveco*, D.Comm. July 13, 1983, 1983 OJ L 224/19, 22–23; *Olivetti/Canon*, D.Comm. Dec. 22, 1987, 1988 OJ L 52/51, 55; *BBC Brown Boveri*, D.Comm. Oct. 11, 1988, 1988 OJ L 301/68, 69.
130. Notice on the Concept of Full-Function Joint Ventures, 1998 OJ C 66/1.
131. *ENW/Eastern*, D.Comm. Oct. 15, 1998, M.1315. However, although the staff of the joint

- supply of inputs,[132]
- production, e.g., the integration of its production facilities with one or more of the parents[133] or use of technology belonging to the parents,[134] or
- distribution, i.e., the joint venture sells principally or exclusively to the parents for processing or resale.[135]

Tendency for a Broad Application of the Full-Function Concept by the Commission.

The Commission tends to apply the full-function concept generously with the effect that the majority of joint ventures are now subject to the merger control regulation, provided they have a Community dimension.[136] In *Multimedia/Telenor Textel/Telia*[137] the Commission found that the joint venture performed on a lasting basis all the functions of an autonomous economic entity because (i) the two companies, previously operating as independent business entities, contributed most of their own assets and activities to the joint venture (for internet gateway services and website production for third parties), (ii) the joint venture had its own organization and staff and, after a start up period, its own financial resources, (iii) the joint venture was expected to sell less than 10% of its output to its parent companies and was to use the parent companies' services without exclusivity on a arms' length basis, and (iv) the joint venture was automatically renewable once its term had run and the parties were prohibited from transferring their shares to third parties. However, in *ENW/Eastern*[138] the Commission categorized a joint venture as only partial-function because (i) the joint venture did not have access to sufficient resources, including finance, staff and assets, (ii) its limited staff was supplemented by personnel from the parent companies, and (iii) the parent companies were to provide various services, such as marketing, tendering and

venture is seconded by the parent companies it may be placed under the control of the joint venture's own management: *Elf/Texaco/Antifreeze*, D.Comm. Aug. 18, 1998, M.1135.

132. *Preussag/Voest Alpine*, D.Comm. Oct. 1, 1997, M.979, points 9–10 (the joint venture's exclusive purchase obligation reduces its price autonomy); *ENW/Eastern*, D.Comm. Oct. 15, 1998, M.13 15. *See*, however, *Mannesmann/Hoesch*, D.Comm. Nov. 12, 1992, 1993 OJ L 114/34, point 10.

133. However, the fact that the joint venture's business is integrated in one of the parent companies' facilities does not disqualify the joint venture as full-function: *BASF/Shell II*, D.Comm. Oct. 23, 1997, M.1041; *Hitachi/DuPont*, D.Comm. Oct. 24, 1997, M.994; *Exxon/Shell II*, D.Comm. July 8, 1998, M.1137 (*Exxon/Shell I*, D.Comm. May 18, 1994, 1994 OJ L 144/20, concerned the exemption granted for a production joint venture without distribution function).

134. *Baxter/Nestlé/Salvia*, D.Comm. Feb. 6, 1991, M.58.

135. *ENW/Eastern*, D.Comm. Oct. 15, 1998, M.1315.

136. Even if the joint venture's business and turnover is insignificant (in particular in case of a joint venture entering a new market) the Community dimension is based on the parent companies' turnover and more often likely to exceed the thresholds than in case of the acquisition of a part of a business (Article 5 (2)).

137. *Multimedia/Telenor Textel/Telia*, D.Comm. May 27, 1998, JV. 1.

138. *ENW/Eastern*, D.Comm. Oct. 15, 1998, M.1315.

information technology.[139] In *Haniel/Cementbouw*[140] the Commission cleared the take-over of a joint sales company by two of its members, thereby transforming it into a single, full-fledged company, subject to the commitment to terminate the joint sales activities via the jointly acquired company, thereby creating two independent market players.[141] In *Accor/Hilton/Six Continents*[142] the Commission cleared the creation of an internet hotel bookings joint venture by three competing hotel chains because the joint venture was equipped to act to a large extent for third parties (other than the parents) and did not lead, given the built-in safeguards (Chinese wall), to an anticompetitive exchange of sensitive information between the parents nor to a foreclosure of the market.

Joint Ventures Providing Services Often Full-Function.
It is common that joint ventures in service businesses are more readily able to perform on a permanent basis all the functions of an autonomous economic entity and therefore be considered as full-function,[143] unless the service is auxiliary to the parent companies' activities.[144] For instance, services of a joint venture which merely consist of marketing the parents' products in a single member state cannot be separated from the production and the marketing of those products in other member states so that it does not seem justified to consider a joint venture limited to providing these services as performing 'all the functions of an autonomous entity'.[145] However, more recently the Commission decided that the joint venture to be created by De Agostini and Holding di Partecipazioni, two groups active among others in the publishing sector, for the distribution to local outlets of newspapers and magazines and a range of other products was to be considered as being full function. The Commission justified its position on two grounds: first, the joint venture would not merely distribute the print media produced by the parent companies but was to enter in the future into agreements with other publishers with a view to distributing their products. Second, the joint venture would generate

139. *Cf.* under Article 3 of Regulation 4064/89 before its amendment: *Generali/Unicredito*, D.Comm. March 26, 1996, M.711; *aff'd* CFI March 4, 1999, 1999 ECR II-203, paras 69–83.

140. *Haniel/Cementbouw*, D.Comm. June 26, 2002, M.2650.

141. In fact, the operation consisted of a joint acquisition and a subsequent break-up of the acquired company ('demerger'), *see* Notice on the concept of undertakings concerned, points 46–48; *Solvay-Laporte/Interox*, D.Comm. April 30, 1997, M.197.

142. *Accor/Hilton/Six Continents*, D.Comm. May 19, 2003, M.3101.

143. *Bertelsmann/Kirch/Première*, D.Comm. May 27, 1998, 1999 OJ L 53/1, point 14; *Multimedia/Telenor Nextel/Telia*, D.Comm. May 27, 1998, JV. 1; *PanAgora/DG Bank*, D.Comm. Nov. 26, 1998, JV. 14, points 18–21.

144. Examples: *Bertelsmann/Havas*, D.Comm. May 7, 1999, M.1275 (joint venture created for the purpose of selling consumer books via the internet); *Rolls-Royce*, *HAESL*, D.Comm. May 11, 1999, M.1506 (joint venture for repairing and overhauling large commercial aircraft engines).

145. The Commission, however, considered the creation by *Texaco* and *Norsk Hydro* of a joint venture for marketing their products in Denmark as a full-function transaction which it cleared under Article 6 (1) (b) of Regulation 4064/89 (D.Comm. Jan. 9, 1995, M.511).

a significant proportion of its turnover from the distribution of other products, such as mobile phone cards, batteries and razors.[146] Other examples include joint ventures in the bank insurance sector which are considered as full-function.[147]

(d) Transactions Regarded as Mergers

Examples.
The following transactions are regarded as a concentration subject to the merger control regulation:

- changing sole control into joint control;[148]
- changing partners to an existing joint venture[149] or increasing the number of shareholders;[150]
- changes in the structure of control,[151] including the change from joint to sole control because decisive influence exercised alone is substantially different from decisive influence exercised jointly,[152]
- joint control preceded by cooperation during the phase-in period;[153]

---

146. *De Agostini/Holding di Partecipazioni/RCS Diffusione/JV*, D. Comm. May 12, 2003, M.3063.
147. *See Cultalia/Banca delle Marche/JV*, D.Comm. Sept. 13, 1999, M.1627; *Generali/Banca Intesa/Intesa Vita*, D.Comm. Dec. 15, 2003, M.2768 (change from sole to joint control of a pre-existing company which was able to independently provide insurance policies).
148. Notice on the Concept of Concentration, point 18. The reason given is that decisive influence exercised alone is substantially different from decisive influence exercised jointly. *See Mannesmann Demag/De Laval Stork*, D.Comm. Dec. 21, 1994, M.535.
149. Notice on undertakings concerned, points 33–45. *See Warner Brothers/Lusomundo/Sogecable*, D.Comm. May 12, 1997, M.902, points 6–13.
150. Notice on the Concept of Concentration, point 17 and Notice on Undertakings Concerned, points 30–32. *See ICI/Tioxide*, D.Comm. Nov. 28, 1990, M.23, paras 2–47; *AXA/Royale Beige*, D.Comm. June 12, 1998, M.1193; *British Steel/Europipe*, D.Comm. Feb. 26, 1998, M.1014, point 61.
151. Notice on the Concept of Concentration, point 40. *See Bertelsmann/Kirch/Première*, D.Comm. May 27, 1998, 1999 OJ L 53/1, point 12; *BSCH/Champalimaud*, D.Comm. July 20, 1999, M.1616, point 7–13. The structure of control would not be changed by the creation of a holding company as a vehicle in order to facilitate decision-making, *see* Notice on the Concept of Undertakings Concerned, point 29.
152. Notice on the Concept of Concentration, point 16. *See McDermott/EPTM*, D.Comm. June 4, 1998, M.1157; *AXA/Royale Belge*, D.Comm. June 12, 1998, M.1193; *Philips/Lucent Technologies*, D.Comm. Jan. 6, 1999, M.1358 (increase from 50 to 100%); *NEC/PBN*, D.Comm. Sept. 3, 1998, M.1276 (increase from 49% to 52.8%); *Cargill/Continental*, D.Comm. Feb. 3, 1999, M.1376. However, such a 'deconcentration' may improve the competitive structure and therefore not pose any problem: *Daimler*, D.Comm. March 15, 1999, M.1446; *VW/Autoeurope*, D.Comm. Feb. 2, 1999, M.1375.
153. Notice on the Concept of Full-Function Joint Ventures (1998 OJ C 66/1), point 14. However, Article 81 may be applied to anticompetitive cooperation preceding a merger: *Philip Morris/Rothmans*, ECJ Nov. 17, 1987, 1987 ECR 4487, para. 45, including by abusing the due diligence process, in particular by allowing managers to have access to commercially sensitive information of the competing target company.

- exchange of assets,[154] and
- 'deconcentrations': the break-up of a joint venture by splitting the assets between the parent companies.[155]

(e) Transactions not Regarded as Mergers

Examples.
The following transactions are not regarded as a concentration subject to the merger control regulation:

- joint ventures that do not perform all the functions of an autonomous economic entity, in particular where the joint venture does not have access to sufficient resources and depends on various services provided by its parent companies (partial-function joint ventures), which are discussed in Section F.2.;
- the acquisition of shareholdings below the level required to exercise control (Article 3 (1) (b)), which is discussed in Section F.1. hereafter.
- temporary holdings by banks and insurance companies, holdings by financial holding companies and control by office holders in bankruptcy and liquidation proceedings (Article 3 (5));[156] and
- short-term joint venture agreements, such as to construct a power plant without ongoing operational responsibility once construction has been completed or one that can be terminated by the parties in the short-term.[157]

(f) Assessment of Transactions not *Covered by the Regulation*

Applicability of the EC Competition Rules by the Commission.
The merger control regulation applies only to transactions that have a Community dimension; the Commission is prevented from using the powers conferred by Regulation 17 or Regulation 1/2003 with respect of transactions that do not have a Community dimension. However, the Commission may take action against such transactions at the request of a member state, provided the transaction significantly impedes effective competition within the territory of that member state and is likely to affect trade between member states.[158] According to the statement of the

154. Notice on the Concept of Undertakings Concerned (1998 OJ C 66/14), point 49.
155. Notice on the Concept of Undertakings Concerned, points 46–48. *See Solvay/Laporte/Interox*, D.Comm. April 30, 1992, 197, points 14–19; *McDermott/EPTM*, D.Comm. June 4, 1998, M.1157; *Philips/Lucent Technologies*, D.Comm. Jan. 6, 1999, M.1358; *Siemens/Italtel*, D.Comm. Dec. 15, 1999, M.1717.
156. Mergers between banks and insurance companies are, however, treated in the same way as other mergers: *see Eagle Star/Alliance*, Twelfth Report on Competition Policy, point 103.
157. Notice on Full-Function Joint Ventures, point 15 (they are not joint ventures 'on a lasting basis' as required by Article 3 (1) of the merger control regulation).
158. Article 22.

Commission and the Council concerning the prior Regulation 4064/89 (*re* Article 22), the Commission reserves the right to take action against transactions with a lower turnover in accordance with the (limited) powers conferred by Article 84 of the EC Treaty. This statement refers to the possibiliy of applying the *Continental Can* doctrine in such cases.[159]

On the other hand, the merger control regulation does not preclude the application of Article 81:

- to restrictions which are not directly related and necessary to the implementation of the transaction (and therefore not covered by a clearance under the merger control regulation);[160]
- to partial function joint ventures (which are excluded from the merger control regulation);[161]
- to full-function joint ventures which do not have a Community dimension and have as their object or effect the coordination of the competitive behavior of undertakings which remain independent ('spill-over effect'), provided that this behaviour has an appreciable effect on trade between member states;[162] and
- to minority shareholdings which do not confer control and remain subject to Article 81 according to the *Philip Morris* doctrine.[163]

Applicability of the National Competition Rules by National Authorities. The exclusive competence conferred to the Commission precludes member states from applying their national legislation to transactions that have a Community dimension.[164] Transactions that do *not* have a Community dimension are therefore subject to national merger control[165] and may require multiple notification and clearance if their effects extend to different member states. However, one or more member states may request the Commission to examine any concentration that does not have a Community dimension but affects trade between member states and threatens to significantly affect competition within the territory of the member state(s) making the request.[166] In the absence of such a referral one and the same transaction may be assessed by different national competition authorities under their respective laws, thereby unavoidably leading to the risk of contradictory decisions.[167] A conflict may in particular arise where a national authority

---

159. *See* Section B.2. *supra*.
160. *See Lagadère*, CFI Nov. 20, 2002, 2002 ECR II-4825, para. 104.
161. Article 3 (2).
162. Article 22 (1).
163. *See* Section B.3. *supra*. Certain national merger control rules extend to minority shareholdings, e.g. § 37 (3) of the German Law Against Restraints of Trade (acquisition of 25% or more).
164. Article 21 (1) and (2).
165. *See* Article 3 (3) of Regulation 1/2003.
166. Article 22 (1).
167. In the case of a partial referral the Court of First Instance recognizes the possibility of conflicts as 'inherent': *Philips, DeLonghi/SEB-Moulinex*, CFI April 3, 2002, T-119/02, paras 367, 380.

takes measures to protect legitimate interests (public security, plurality of media and prudential rules).[168] Any other public interest must be communicated to the Commission in advance[169] which shall decide whether or not the contemplated measures are compatible with the general principles of Community law.[170] However, the risk of conflicting decisions may be reduced by the close cooperation between the national authorities and the Commission according to Article 19 of Regulation 139/2004 and Article 11 of Regulation 1/2003.

4. Transactions with and without a Community Dimension

(a) Distinction According to Turnover Thresholds

Introduction.
The merger control regulation distinguishes between transactions (mergers and full-function joint ventures) with and transactions without a Community dimension on the basis of sales (also called 'turnover') thresholds. Transactions with a Community dimension, whose impact on the market extends beyond the national borders of any one member state,[171] are subject, with certain exceptions, to the exclusive competence of the Commission (one-stop shop principle). Transactions without a Community dimension are subject to the national legislation of member states. However, the Commission may also act in these cases if the national authorities refer the case to the Commission for a decision. The Commission may also take action in *any* case irrespective of turnover threshold insofar as the conduct of the parties leads to anticompetitive coordination contrary to Article 81.

'Accounting' Calculation of Turnover in the Case of Group of Companies.
Article 5 of the regulation lays down rules for calculating turnover (sales) for the purpose of determining whether a transaction meets the 'Community dimension' sales thresholds, which are further explained by the Commission Notice on Calculation of Turnover.[172] The 'aggregate turnover' of each party must include:

- *Subsidiaries*. The sales revenues of firms that the party controls directly or indirectly, i.e., itself or via another subsidiary (Article 5 (4) (b)),
- *Parents*. The sales revenues of firms by which the party is controlled directly or

168. Article 21 (4).
169. In the *Secil/Holderbank/Cimpor* case the member state concerned failed to communicate the measure to the Commission, *see Portugal*, ECJ June 22, 2004, C-42/01.
170. *See* Section C.4.(b)(ii), *infra*.
171. Recital 9 to Regulation 4064/89. The concept of 'Community dimension' focuses on transborder effects without referring to the criterion of likely effect on interstate trade in Articles 81 and 82.
172. Notice on the Calculation of Turnover (1998 OJ C 66/25).

indirectly, i.e., parents and grandparents[173] (Article 5 (4) (c)),
- *Sister Firms.* The sales revenues of controlled subsidiaries of parents and grandparents, i.e., sister companies controlled by parents and grandparents (Article 5 (4) (d)), and
- *Jointly Controlled Firms.* The sales revenues of firms controlled jointly by any two or more of the firms listed above, i.e., by companies in the party's group (Article 5 (4) (e)). This principle applies, by analogy, in the case of joint ventures between one of the parties and third parties; however, the turnover shared equally by all the controlling companies must be allocated to each of them in order to avoid unreasonable results.[174]

Two Calculations of Turnover Thresholds.
The 'Community dimension' criterion, expressed in euro (€),[175] is fulfilled when either of the following two multi-part turnover threshold calculations are met.

Calculation No. 1. The first multi-part turnover threshold calculations were the original criteria set forth when the regulation was adopted in 1989. All of the following criteria must be met for the regulation to apply:
- *EUR 5 billion turnover worldwide.* The combined worldwide turnover of all the firms concerned, including their parents, subsidiaries and sister companies – i.e., the combination of all the firms' 'aggregate' turnover[176] (while applying the exception for parts of a firm being sold[177]) – must exceed EUR 5 billion (indicating the overall size of the firms involved);
- *EUR 250 million turnover Community-wide by firms concerned with the transaction.* At least two of the firms concerned with the transaction must each have an aggregate Community-wide turnover of ECU 250 million (indicating a substantial presence in the Community); and

---

173. Article 5 (4) (c) must be understood as including grandparents and companies further up in the ascending line, because the powers of control to which Article 5 (4) (c) refers can, according to Article 5 (4) (b), be direct or indirect. This also means that under Article 5 (4) (d) the subsidiaries of grandparents and of other companies in the ascending line are to be included. The precondition is actual control, which in the case of a minority shareholding may be demonstrated by the exercise of voting rights: *see Arjomari/Wiggins Teape*, D.Comm. Dec. 10, 1990, M.25.
174. Notice on the calculation of turnover, point 40. *See* the similar rules for calculating market shares of 'connected companies' in Article 11 of Regulation 2790/1999, Article 2 of Regulation 2659/2000 (R&D agreements block exemption), Article 2 of Regulation 2658/2000 (specialization block exemption) and Commission's Notice on agreements of minor importance, 2001 OJ C 368/13, under point 12.
175. Regulation 2866/98, 1998 OJ L 359/1. With respect to the conversion of turnover figures into ECU/EUR, *see* Notice on the calculation of turnover, points 49–50.
176. The sales of a given firm plus those of its parent company and its subsidiaries and sister companies, if any, are its 'aggregate' turnover. Thus, 'aggregate' refers to the total sales of a party's group.
177. *See infra* this section 'Exception for Sale of Parts of a Business'.

- *Less than two-thirds of Community-wide turnover in any single member state.* Each of the firms concerned must *not* earn more than two-thirds of its aggregate Community-wide turnover within one and the same member state (which would indicate the transaction's lack of transnational implications) (Article 1 (2)).

Calculation No. 2. If the criteria set forth in Calculation No. 1 are not met, then a second multi-part calculation must be made. This calculation, added by the 1997 amendment to the merger control regulation, effectively reduces the turnover thresholds if each of five tests are met.[178] All of the following criteria must be met for the regulation to apply:

- *EUR 2.5 billion turnover worldwide.* The combined worldwide turnover of all the firms concerned, including their parents, subsidiaries and sister companies – i.e., the combination of all the firms' 'aggregate' turnover (while applying the exception for parts of a firm being sold) – must exceed EUR 2.5 billion;
- *EUR 100 million turnover in three member states.* The combined aggregate turnover of *all* the firms concerned, including their parents, subsidiaries and sister companies, must exceed EUR 100 million in each of at least three member states;
- *EUR 25 million turnover by at least two firms concerned with the transaction in same three member states.* The combined aggregate turnover of each of at least two of the firms concerned, including their parents, subsidiaries and sister companies, must also exceed EUR 25 million in each of the same three member states as met the EUR 100 million turnover calculation noted above;
- *EUR 100 million Community-wide turnover by at least two firms concerned with the transaction.* The aggregate Community-wide turnover of *each* of at least *two* of the firms concerned, including their parents, subsidiaries and sister companies, must also exceed EUR 100 million; and
- *Less than two-thirds of Community-wide turnover in any single member state.* Each of the firms concerned must *not* earn more than two-thirds of its aggregate Community-wide turnover within one and the same member state (which would indicate the transaction's lack of transnational implications) (Article 1 (3)).

'National' Mergers.

A Community dimension is absent where each of the firms concerned earns more than two-thirds of its aggregate Community-wide turnover within one and the same member state.[179] These 'national' mergers are subject to national law

178. *See Valmet/Rauma*, D.Comm. Feb. 8, 1999, M.1379, point 5.
179. Thus, mergers involving a company with a strong international presence outside the Community but with an EC presence substantially confined to the same home member state of the other party which makes over two-thirds of its turnover there will fall outside the regulation. The same applies to mergers involving two non-EC multinationals which both have EC operations that are largely confined to one member state, but not when the EC operations of only one of them are largely confined to one state.

(Article 1 (2) and (3) in conjunction with Article 21), unless the member state concerned specifically asks the Commission to act against a merger which significantly impedes effective competition within that member state's territory and affects trade between member states (Article 22 (3) and Recital 29).[180]

Deduction of 'Internal' Turnover.

According to Article 5(1), first subparagraph, the aggregate turnover shall not include the sale of products or the provision of services between any of the undertakings within the commonly controlled group to which the undertaking concerned belongs (essentially parent companies and subsidiaries). Therefore only the transactions between its group of undertakings and third persons are taken into account.[181] In the case of state-owned firms, only the turnover of enterprises forming part of the same economic unit with an independent power of decision are included so as to avoid all commercial enterprises controlled by the same government from automatically being considered as part of a single entity (recital 12).[182] The sales of existing joint ventures in which one of the firms concerned has a 50% stake or less are taken into account only if the joint venture is with another firm concerned in the merger or members of the groups to which they belong (Article 5 (5)). When the sales of a joint venture are taken into account, the rule is that sales between the joint venture and its parents or members of their respective groups are not counted and that sales to third parties are apportioned equally between the parties to the joint venture.[183] The same applies in the case of a joint venture between one of the parties and a third party.[184]

180. *See Blokker/Toys 'R' Us*, D.Comm. June 26, 1997, 1998 OJ L 316/1, point 1.
181. Notice on the Calculation of Turnover, points 22–23; *Endemol*, CFI 28 April 1999, 1999 ECR II-1299, para. 109; *Mannesmann/Boge*, D.Comm. Sept. 23, 1991, M.134, point 19. With respect to franchising activities *see Accor/Wagons Lits*, D.Comm. April 28, 1992, 1992 OJ L 204/1, point 15.a; *Kali + Salz/MdK*, D.Comm. Dec. 14, 1993, 1994 OJ L 186/30, point 46; *Cable & Wireless/Schlumberger*, D.Comm. Dec. 22, 1994, M.532; *UBS/Mister Minit*, D.Comm. July 9, 1997, M.940; *British Airways/Air Liberté*, D.Comm. Feb. 28, 1997, M.857; *Mitsui/CVRD/Caemi*, D.Comm. Oct. 30, 2001, M.2420, point 172.
182. *Alcan/Inespal/Palco* D.Comm. April 14, 1993, M.322; Twenty-third Report on Competition Policy, point 250.
183. *See* section 3 of the 'CO' notification form attached to Regulation 802/2004.
184. Notice on the Calculation of Turnover, point 40. However, joint ventures excluded from the calculation of a merging firm's turnover can be taken into account when considering the parties' economic and financial power and the access of third parties to supplies or markets under Article 2 (1) (b). *See AG/Amev*, D.Comm. Nov. 21, 1990 (AG's joint venture with Royale Beige in France). In cases where the joint venture is created for the purposes of the acquisition the Commission considers the joint venture as a 'transparent vehicle' and includes the turnover of the indirectly acquired business: *BSN-Nestlé/Chokoladovny*, D.Comm. Feb. 17, 1992; *Eucom/Digital*, D.Comm. May 18, 1992 M.218. Calculation of turnover in the case of

Calculation of Turnover for Air Transport, Banking and Insurance Sectors. Special rules are applied for calculation of turnover in the air transport, banking and insurance sectors.

- To calculate turnover in *air transport* the Commission bases the geographic allocation of turnover on the 50–50 method (the turnover on each route is allocated on a 50–50 basis to the country of origin and the country of final destination) or on the point-of-sale method (the turnover resulting from the air transport service allocated to the country where the ticket was sold). In addition, even if an airline has ceased operations definitively or for a long period on a particular route, the turnover attributable to the route will be preserved if the airline has kept the corresponding slots in order to pursue operations elsewhere.[185]
- For *credit and other financial institutions*, the following shall be used in place of turnover: the sum of interest income and similar income, income from securities, commissions receivable, net profit on financial operations and other operating income, after deduction of value added tax and other taxes directly related to those items.[186]
- For *insurance undertakings*, the following shall be used in place of turnover: the value of gross premiums written which shall comprise all amounts received and receivable in respect to insurance contracts issued by or on behalf of the insurance undertakings, including also outgoing reinsurance premiums, after deduction of taxes and parafiscal contributions or levies.[187]

Exception for Sale of Part of a Business.
The most important exception from the turnover calculation rules concerns acquisitions of parts of a business. If the transaction involves the acquisition of parts of a business, whether or not they are constituted as legal entitles, i.e.

- a subsidiary, or
- some of the assets of one or more companies,

only the turnover relating to the parts that are the subject of the transaction are taken into account when calculating the turnover of the *sellers* (Article 5 (2)). Thus

transfer of joint control into sole control: *British Airways/TAT II*, D.Comm. Aug. 26, 1996, M.806, Twenty-sixth Report on Competition Policy, p. 169.

185. Notice on the Calculation of Turnover, points 45–48 and Twenty-seventh Report on Competition Policy, p. 171. *See British Airways/Air Liberté*, D.Comm. Feb. 28, 1997, M.857.

186. Article 5 (3) (a). With respect to operating leasing and financial leasing *see GECC/Avis Lease*, D.Comm. July 15, 1992, M.234.

187. Article 5 (3) (b) and Notice on the Calculation of Turnover, points 51–61. *See Mediobanca/Generali*, D.Comm. Dec. 19, 1991, M.159; *AG/AMEV*, D.Comm. Nov. 21, 1990, M.18; *Eureka*, April 27, 1992, M.207; *Allianz/DKV*, D.Comm. Sept. 10, 1992, M.251.

the turnover of parents and sister firms (and even subsidiaries) that are not being sold are not included in the calculation.[188] As a result, a large multinational group which is selling one of its operations includes only the sales of the operation being sold in its turnover; other sales made by members of the group are excluded from the calculation. Therefore, an acquisition of part of a business has a Community dimension and is subject to EC merger control if the turnover attributed to that part of business being sold exceeds (i) EUR 250 million within the Community, or (ii) EUR 100 million within the Community *and* EUR 25 million within at least three member states. However, two or more such transactions within a two-year period between the same parties will be treated as the same transaction (Article 5 (2), second subparagraph). This is to prevent evasion of the rules by spreading out a merger over a number of step-transactions.[189] The exception does not apply, however, to bilateral exchanges or swaps of assets in which two competitors sell each other part of their business in different, but usually related, product markets. In such cases, as each party is seller *and* buyer, their total turnover has to be taken into account for the purposes of the merger regulation. Finally, the exception does not apply to transactions by which two or more parties transfer all of their business that serves the same product market to a joint venture. In such a case, both parties continue to play a role in the relevant market once the operation has been implemented.[190] Therefore the total aggregate turnover of both parties has to be included.

(b) Transactions with a Community Dimension

(i) The One-Stop Shop Principle

Introduction.

The Commission has exclusive jurisdiction over mergers with a 'Community dimension' (Article 21 (2)), even if they only involve firms based in the same member state, provided that at least one party earns more than a third of its Community turnover in other member states. No member state may apply its national legislation on its own initiative to such a merger (Article 21 (3))[191] In merger cases, there is, as a rule, no parallel application of Community and national competition law. Parallel scrutiny by national authorities according to national law

188. *See ICI/Tioxide*, D.Comm. Nov. 28, 1990, M.23.
189. In case of the sale of a beverage business the turnover resulting from the bottling activities may have to be included: *Cadbury/Coke*, Commission request for information April 23, 1999.
190. *See* Notice on the Calculation of Turnover, point 31.
191. When the Commission clears an operation having a Community dimension the member state is precluded from opposing the operation, including provisional measures, such as the suspension of voting rights: *BSCH/Champalimaud*, D.Comm. July 20, 1999, M.1616, points 14 and 22.

is precluded by this 'one-stop shop' principle, subject to the 'legitimate interest' and 'distinct market' exceptions. Cases of referrals *from* the Commission to national competition authorities are subject to exclusive review under their national law,[192] limited, however, to the parts of the operation referred to them,[193] whereas cases referred *to* the Commission are reviewed exclusively under the Community merger regulation, as described below.

(ii) The 'Legitimate Interest' Exception

Principles.
Notwithstanding the principle of exclusive jurisdiction of the Commission over mergers with a Community dimension, a member state may take the 'appropriate measures' to challenge a merger under national legislation to protect legitimate national interests, in particular public security,[194] defence,[195] media pluralism[196] and prudential rules for financial services firms,[197] and such other 'legitimate interests' as may be recognized by the Commission.[198] Any 'legitimate interest'

192. *Royal Philips*, April 3, 2003, T-119/02, paras 280–288.
193. Article 9 (3) (b) of Regulation 139/2004.
194. *See Lyonnaise des Eaux/Northumbrian Water*, D.Comm. Dec. 21, 1995, M.567; *London Electricity/EdF*, D.Comm. Jan. 27, 1999, M.1346 (energy). Defense interests were invoked in the *Plessey/GEC-Siemens* takeover case, 1990 OJ C 239/2; Nineteenth Report on Competition Policy, point 66; UK Monopolies and Mergers Commission, *The General Electric Company plc and the Plessey Company plc. A Report on the proposed merger*, London, August 1986, paras 10.48–10.83; UK Monopolies and Mergers Commission, *The General Electric Company plc, Siemens AG and The Plessey Company plc. A Report on the proposed merger*, London, April 1989, paras 6.21–6.57. §42 of the German Law Against Restraints of Competition allows the Minister of Economic Affairs to overrule a prohibition decision of the German competition authority for reasons of public interest, but this may also conflict with Community law. *See* Fritzsche, WuW 2003–11, 1153.
195. Articles 296 and 298: *see GEC/Marconi/Alenia*, D.Comm. 28 Aug. 1998, M.1258. In *Boeing/McDonnell Douglas*, D.Comm. July 30, 1997, 1997 OJ L 336/16, the Commission considered whether Boeing's dominant position on the market in commercial aircraft would be significantly strengthened through the addition of McDonnell's defence and space business; Twenty-seventh Report on Competition Policy, p. 192.
196. *See Newspaper Publishing*, D.Comm. March 14, 1994, M.423; *Bertelsmann/Kirch/Première*, D.Comm. May 27, 1998, 1999 OJ L 53/1, point 118. The member states' right to plead the 'plurality of the media' recognizes the legitimate concern to maintain diversified sources of information for the sake of plurality of opinion and multiplicity of views: Council Statements in Minutes to Regulation 4064/89, 1990–4 CMLR 314, re Article 21 (3). Statements of the Commission relating to Regulation 1310/97, re Article 21 (3).
197. *See Sun Alliance/Royale Insurance*, D.Comm. June 18, 1996, M.759.
198. The application of such rales is normally confined to national bodies for surveillance of banks, stockholding firms and insurance companies. They concern, for example, the good repute of individuals, the honesty of transactions and the rules of solvency: Statements, re Article 21 (3). *See Allianz/AGF*, D.Comm. May 8, 1998, M.970 (exemption subject to compliance with commitments). In *Commission v. Germany (Insurance)*, ECJ Dec. 4, 1986, 1986 ECR 3755,

other than those specified above may be invoked only if it is compatible with the general principles and other provisions of Community law, the member state has communicated it to the Commission and the Commission has agreed that it is consistent with Community law (Article 21 (4)).

Legitimate Interests v. National Interests.
The 'legitimate interest' exception may not be of great practical importance. First, legitimate national interests will be taken into account by the Commission, which is required to make its assessment in the overall context of the achievement of the fundamental aims of the Community. Secondly, Article 21 (4) merely affirms the residual powers of member states to block a merger or to make it subject to conditions and obligations 'to protect legitimate interests other than taken into consideration by this Regulation and compatible with the general principles and other provisions of Community law'. However, a member state is not entitled to authorize a merger that the Commission has prohibited.[199] Thirdly, action taken to protect national interests must be limited to the essential minimum and may not constitute a form of arbitrary discrimination or a disguised restriction on trade.[200] In its administrative practice the Commission has carefully considered 'legitimate interests' which member states may have invoked, in particular when prohibiting proposed mergers in the military[201] and media sectors.[202] National provisions which allow a government to prohibit a merger because it interferes with national interests in 'strategic' sectors which are essential to the member state's economy

---

paras 25–41, the Court of Justice held that restrictions on the cross-frontier provision of insurance services were justified for prudential reasons (i.e., protection of policy holders) in the present unharmonized state of Community law. However, prudential rales are now being harmonized: *see infra* Chapter VIII.D.

199. Accordingly, where a transaction is authorized by a national authority on grounds of public interest (e.g., §42 of the German Law Against Restraints of Competition – 'Ministererlaubnis'), this authorization may conflict with Community law and the Commission's exclusive competence accorded by Article 21 (1) of Regulation 139/2004, provided the transaction has a Community dimension. However, there is no case law yet. *See* Fritzsche, WuW 2003–11, 1153.

200. Statements re Article 21 (3) of Regulation 1310/97. *Cf.* Article 36 of the EC Treaty which similarly qualifies national interest exceptions from the free trade rules.

201. *British Aerospace/Lagardère*, D.Comm. Sept. 23, 1996, M.820; *Engines for Missiles*, D.Comm. Oct. 29, 1993, Twenty-third Report on Competition Policy, points 324–326. In *Boeing/McDonnell Douglas* the Commission made the approval of the merger subject to commitments concerning the military (defense) activities of Boeing: D.Comm. July 30, 1997, 1997 OJ L 336/16, points 122–123. The *Daimler/MBB* merger was also considered fully by the German Economics Ministry for its military implications before being allowed, against the advice of the Federal Cartel Office (April 17, 1989, WuW/E BKartA 2335; Sept. 6, 1989, WuW/E BWM 191, 204–205).

202. *See MSG Media Sendee*, D.Comm. Nov. 9, 1994, 1994 OJ L 364/1; *Bertelsmann/Kirch/Première*, D.Comm. May 27, 1998, 1999 OJ L 53/1, point 118; *Blokker/Toys 'R' Us*, D.Comm. June 26, 1997, 1998 OJ L 316/1.

and financial system have not been recognized by the Commission as legitimate public interests compatible with the general principles of Community law.[203] In *BSCH/Champalinaud* which concerned a merger between a Portuguese and a Spanish bank having a Community dimension and which was prohibited by the Portuguese government[204] the Commission cleared the merger under its merger control regulation[205] and declared the national interests on which the Portuguese government relied incompatible with the general principles of Community law.[206] Subsequently, the prohibition decision was revoked and the notification of the merger in its amended version withdrawn.[207] Similarly, in *Secil/Holderbank/Cimpor* which concerned the proposed joint acquisition of more than 10% (including special voting rights) in Cimpor, a privatized Portuguese cement producer, by a Swiss bank and another Portuguese cement producer, the Commission declared the national provisions, which were the basis of the Portuguese government's prohibition decision, incompatible with the general principles of Community law and ordered the Portuguese government to withdraw its decisions.[208] The Court of Justice dismissed the action of the Portuguese government and confirmed the Commission's decision.[209] Without waiting the outcome of the Court's procedure, the Portuguese government decided to fully liberalize Cimpor including the abdication of its 10% in the company.[210] Another way of protecting national interests is to reserve special powers for the state or public bodies including a right to veto certain decisions, in particular the sale of shares ('golden share'), which may be used in an arbitrary manner, likely to hinder or to make less attractive the exercise of fundamental rights, such as the freedom of establishment and the movement of capital. Such rights have been held by the Court of Justice as incompatible with Articles 43 and 56, unless they are justified by overriding considerations of public interest, appropriate for ensuring that the pursued objective is achieved and necessary to achieve that objective.[211] The Commission tends to limit this exception to interests likely to be assimilated to the general principles of Community law, and has opposed the holding of 'golden shares' in cases of telecommunications privatization.[212]

---

203. Article 21 (4) of Regulation 139/2004, which corresponds to Article 21 (3) of Regulation 1310/97.
204. Decision of June 18, 1999 (without prior communication to the Commission according to Article 21 (4), first subparagraph).
205. Decision of July 20, 1999, M.1616.
206. Decision of Oct. 20, 1999.
207. IP/00/21 of Jan. 12, 2000, M.1724.
208. *Secil/Holderbank/Cimpor,* D.Comm. Nov. 22, 2000, M.2054.
209. *Portuguese Republic – Secil/Holderbank/Cimpor,* ECJ June 22, 2004, C-42/01, in particular paras 59–60.
210. IP/00/1338. *See also* Chapter VIII. at p. 880.
211. *Commission/Italy*, ECJ May 23, 2000, 2000 ECR I –3811, para. 13. *See also Commission/Portugal, France and Belgium*, ECJ June 4, 2002, 2002 ECR I-4731.
212. *KPN and TPG*, D.Comm. Feb. 5, 2003, IP/03/180.

(iii) The 'Distinct Market' Exception – Referral from the Commission to Member States

Principles.
The Commission may waive its exclusive competence ('one-stop shop' principle) by referring a case, in whole or in part, to a national competition authority, provided the merger significantly affects a market within a member state which presents all the characteristics of a distinct market. The term 'distinct market' is defined in Article 9 (7) as the area in which the conditions of competition are sufficiently homogeneous and which can be distinguished from neighbouring areas because, in particular, of appreciably different conditions of competition. The referral corresponds to the principle of subsidiarity,[213] which means that a case should be handled by that authority which is capable of taking the most appropriate action for effective protection of competition.[214] A referral may be suggested:

- by the parties to a transaction, including persons[215] according to Article 4 (4); or
- by a member state according to Article 9.

In both cases the parties may discuss the possibility of referrals to or from national jurisdictions and parallel proceedings in other non-EU jurisdictions with the Commission prior to the notification. Such pre-notification contacts must be initiated with the Commission at least two weeks before the expected date of notification.[216]

Referral Suggested by the Parties.
The parties may inform the Commission during their pre-notification contacts[217] by means of a reasoned submission[218] that a transaction may significantly affect competition in a market within a member state which presents all the characteristics of a distinct market and should therefore be examined, in whole or in part, by that member state. The Commission transmits this submission to all member states without delay. Where the member state referred to in the reasoned submission disagrees the case will not be transferred but dealt with by the Commission. Where the competent member state agrees or is deemed to agree (if no disagreement is expressed within 15 working days)[219] the Commission must decide within

213. Article 5 (2) of the EC Treaty, recital 12 to Regulation 139/2004.
214. *See* Recital 18 to Regulation 1/2003; Draft Notice on Case Allocation, points 33–45.
215. Article 3 (1) (b) of Regulation 139/2004.
216. Best Practices, points 10 and 25.
217. *Ibid.* point 25; Draft Notice on Case Allocation, points 15–18.
218. Article 4 (4), first subparagraph. *See* Form RS (reasoned submission) in Annex III of Regulation 802/2004.
219. Article 4 (4), second subparagraph.

25 working days from the receipt of the reasoned submission whether or not to refer the case, in whole or in part. If the Commission does not take a decision within this time limit it is deemed to have referred the case in accordance to the submission.[220] Where the case is referred to the competent national authority the case shall not be notified to the Commission and instead assessed under national competition law.[221] The application of national law is limited to those meassures which are strictly necessary to safeguard or to restore competition on the market concerned (the 'distinct market').[222]

Referral Suggested by Member States or the Commission.
Within 15 working days after the receipt of the copy of the notification to the Commission a member state may, at its own initiative or upon invitation of the Commission, inform the Commission (which informs the parties) that a transaction:

– *threatens to affect* significantly competition in a market within that member state, which presents all the characteristics of a distinct market, or
– *affects* competition in a market within that member state which does not constitute a substantial part of the Common Market.[223]

In the first case the Commission *may*, if it considers that there is such a market and that such a threat exists, refer the whole or part of the case to the competent national authority[224] or deal itself with the whole case or with that part which is not referred.[225] A referral is precluded where the Commission concludes that there is no distinct market or that a threat of impeding competition significantly does not exist.[226]

The Commission is *obliged* to refer the case to the competent national authority if it concludes that a distinct market is affected that does not form a substantial

220. Article 4 (4), fourth subparagraph.
221. Article 4 (4), fifth subparagraph.
222. Article 4 (4), fifth paragraph and Article 9 (8).
223. Article 9 (2).
224. Referrals were requested in 57 cases. Examples for referring the entire transaction: *BAT/ETI*, D.Comm. Oct. 23, 2003, IP/03/1441; partial referral: *Compass/Restorama*, D.Comm. Feb. 26, 2002, M.2639; for rejecting a referral: *EdF/London Electricity*, D.Comm. Jan. 27, 1999, M.1346; *Tarmac/Steetley*, D.Comm. Jan. 24, 1992, M.180, *and CPC/McCormick/Rabobank/ Ostmann*, D.Comm. Oct. 29, 1993, M.330 (in both latter cases the parties abandoned the proposed acquisition).
225. E.g., *SEB/Moulinex*, D.Comm. Nov. 11, 2003, M.2621 (Article 8 (2) decision subject to commitments where that part which was referred to the French competition authority was cleared without commitments, leading to an appeal and the annulment by the Conseil d'Etat on Feb. 6, 2004).
226. Article 9 (3). The refusal of referral is carefully reasoned, *see Lagardère/Natexis/VUP*, D.Comm. July 23, 2003, M.2978 (decision of 54 pages).

part of the Common Market.[227] The Commission would not even have the competence to assess such a case itself because its powers are limited to transactions that are likely to significantly impede effective competition in the Common Market *or in a substantial part* of it.[228]

The Commission must take its decision[229] to refer or not to refer within the time limit imposed for the first phase (35 working days) or the second phase (65 working days at most of the notification).[230] Where the case is referred to the competent national authority the case must be assessed under national competition law. However, the application of national law is limited to those meassures which are strictly necessary to safeguard or to restore competition on the market concerned (the 'distinct market').[231]

Commission's Discretion Whether or not to Refer.
The Court of Justice agrees that the Commission enjoys a broad discretion[232] in deciding whether or not a distinct market and a competitive threat exist, although the provision should be interpreted restrictively and applied only in exceptional cases.[233] However, the parties to the merger and third parties[234] are entitled to appeal the Commission's referral decision because it has a direct and automatic effect by depriving them of the opportunity to have the Commission review the lawfulness of the merger.[235]

The Distinct Market Concept – The *Royal Philips Electronics – SEB/ Moulinex* Case.
According to Article 9 (3), first subparagraph, the Commission must determine whether there is a distinct market 'having regard to the market for the products or services in question and to the geographic reference market within the meaning of Article 9 (7)' which relate, in particular, to the nature and characteristics of the products or services concerned, the existence of entry barriers, consumer preferences

227. Article 9 (3) third subparagraph.
228. Article 2 (2) and (3).
229. Article 9 (1).
230. Article 9 (4) in conjunction with Article 10 (1), second subparagraph. Decision to refer a case during the second phase may only be adopted on the Commission's own initiative since the member state's right to request a referral is limited to 15 working days following the receipt of the copy of the notification.
231. Article 9 (8).
232. Except with respect to market which is not a substantial part of the Common Market: in this case the Commission is bound to refer it.
233. *Royal Philips Electronics – SEB/Moulinex*, CFI April 3, 2003, T-119/02, paras 343–354. A referral may be appropriate in particular where a case requires coordinated investigation and/or remedial action, *see* Draft Notice on Case Allocation, point 22.
234. *See ARD/BskyB-KirchPayTV*, CFI Sept. 30, 2003, T-158/00, paras 58–95.
235. *Ibid.*, paras 277–282. However, it seems unlikely that a Commission decision rejecting the referral request may be successfully appealed by the applicant member state.

and the existence of appreciable differences in market shares or prices between the territories. In the *Royal Philips Electronics* case[236] the Court of First Instance clarified the criteria for considering a national market as a distinct market. This case concerned the merger between two French companies, *SEB* and *Moulinex*. Both are manufacturers of small electrical household appliances throughout the Community. On 8 January 2002 the Commission adopted two decisions, one accepting the application of the French authorities to refer the French aspects of the case to France, where the effects of the operation were primarily felt,[237] and another decision approving the transaction with respect to all other member states but France, which was made subject to commitments in nine member states and without commitments in Finland, Ireland, Italy, Spain and the United Kingdom. On 3 April 2003 the Court of First Instance annulled the substantive decision with respect to those member states for which the Commission granted unconditional approval, by holding that the Commission had not given sufficient reasons for finding that no competition problems arose in those countries.[238] After reconsidering the case the Commission gave its final unconditional approval with respect to these countries because its fresh analysis confirmed that the consumer benefitted from sufficient competition on those markets even after the transaction.[239] The referral decision to France was affirmed by the Court of First Instance.[240] The Court agreed with the criteria which led the Commission to consider France as a distinct market:

- The market shares varied between member states and were particularly large in France;
- Market penetration differed greatly according to the market;
- Prices were significantly different and followed different trends;
- Commercial and marketing policies were set nationally in order to take account of the particularities and preferences of consumers;
- Logistic structures were different;
- Distribution structures contrasted with those in other member states; and
- Customer/supplier relationships were forged on a national basis, even where internationally established supermarkets are concerned, in particular due to the new entity's unrivalled portfolio of trade marks.[241]

---

236. *Royal Philips Electronics*, CFI April 3, 2003, T-119/02, paras 335–337.
237. *SEB/Moulinex I*, D.Comm. Jan. 8, 2002, M.2621. Following the referral decision, the French authorities approved unconditionally the case with respect of the French market. However, this decision has been annulled by the Conseil d'Etat (Supreme Court) Feb. 6, 2004, No. 249267, so that the part of the case which has been transferred by the Commission to the French authority must be reconsidered by the French competition authority.
238. *BaByliss – SEB/Moulinex*, CFI April 3, 2003, T-114/02, para. 410.
239. *SEB/Moulinex II*, D.Comm. Nov. 11, 2003, IP/03/1531.
240. *Royal Philips Electronics*, CFI April 3, 2003, T-119/02.
241. *Ibid.*, paras 327–340.

Examples of Distinct Markets Considered by the Commission.
The following examples illustrate typical situations in which a local or national market may be a relevant 'distinct' geographic market:

- First, a local or national market may have all the features of a relevant geographic market as defined in Article 9 (7), i.e., competitive conditions on the market may be appreciably different from other areas because of the nature and characteristics of the goods or services concerned, the existence of entry barriers, consumer preferences, appreciable differences in the firms' market shares between the area concerned and neighboring areas or substantial price differences. Examples of such markets can be found in retailing[242] and in industries such as energy and telecommunications equipment where there are high regulatory barriers between national markets.[243]
- Secondly, a national market may still be relevant while an industry is in transition from closed national markets to more open EC-wide markets, as in banking, insurance and public procurement. In these cases a national market may no longer have all the features of a relevant geographic market as defined in Article 9 (7), in view of the emergence of an EC-wide market, but may still require an evaluation of possible competitive implications on the national market in parallel to the wider market examination. The lack of entry barriers and the growing potential competition from other member states have been the main reasons for the Commission not to refer such a case but to deal with the case itself.[244] However, the ongoing market integration process tends to be taken into account more consistently since the analysis of mergers is prospective and normally not limited to past or current market conditions.[245]

Total or Partial Referral.
The Commission may refer the *whole or part* of the case to the competent national authority.[246] This rule seems to be a compromise between the Commission's inter-

---

242. *Promodes/Dirsa*, D.Comm. Dec. 17, 1990, M.27.
243. *See Alcatel/AEG Kabel*, D.Comm. Dec. 18, 1991, M.165 (request by the German antitrust authority rejected because there was no distinct market for telecoms cables and no threat to significantly affect competition in the market of power cables). *See also Aerospatiale/MBB*, D.Comm. Feb. 25, 1991 (national military helicopter markets totally isolated because of 'buy national' defence procurement practices); *Deutsche Telekom/France Télécom/Energis*, D.Comm. March 31, 1999 (construction of an optical fibre network in certain local areas within the UK, starting with London).
244. E.g., in the cable sector where the Commission considered the national markets progressively opening to competition from other member states following the liberalization of the former national telecommunications monopolies: *Alcatel/AEG* (Germany), D.Comm. Dec. 18, 1991, M.165.
245. *See* Commission Notice on the Relevant Market, point 12.
246. There are 62 decisions pursuant to Article 9 of Regulation 1139/2004. Example of a referral requested by two member states: *Lafarge/Redland*, D.Comm. Dec. 16, 1997, M.1030; by three

est to deal itself with one significant aspect of the case and the member state's interest to deal with the other aspects of the case and to protect the competitive structure of that market, thereby avoiding an 'all or nothing' approach. In theory, a single merger may concern severable assets and severable markets, which is more likely with respect to unrelated product or service markets[247] but much less likely with respect to different regional or local markets. In *Promodes/S21/Gruppo GS* the Commission referred the case to the Italian authority with respect to the retail activities in the provinces of Torino, Vercelli and Aosta whereas the other activities were dealt with by the Commission itself.[248] However, in most cases it may be assumed that the activities concerned by the merger are a non-severable part of the deal and that the fact of multiple proceedings with respect to the same transaction 'increases legal uncertainty, effort and cost for companies and may lead to conflicting assessments'.[249]

Risk of Conflicting Decisions.

In the case of a partial referral there is a risk of conflicting decisions taken by the Commission under Community law and by the national authority(ies) under national law. First, the applicable substantive and procedural rules are different.[250] Secondly, the impact of the operation on the structure of competition may be assessed in a different way.[251] However, when adopting the amendment of Article 9 providing for partial referrals to member states, both the Council and the Commission were conscious that fragmented assessments undermining the one-stop-shop principle are inherent to a partial referral, which should therefore be limited to exceptional cases.[252] The Court of First Instance realized the risks of contradic-

---

member states: *Leroy Merlin/Brico*, D.Comm. Dec. 13, 2002, M.2898 (clearance decision and three separate decisions of referral to France, Portugal and Spain); *AREVA/URENCO/ETC JV*, request of May 25, 2004, 2004 OJ C 141/6, M.3099; *see* IP/04/777; by seven member states: *GE/Unisa*, M.2738.

247. *See Krauss-Maffei/Wegmann*, D.Comm. June 19, 1998, M.1153 (military and non-military activities); *Vendex/Bijenkorf*, D.Comm. May 26, 1998, M.1060 (food and non-food activities).

248. *Promodes/S21/Gruppo GS*, D.Comm. March 10, 1998, M.1086.

249. The better solution would be to leave a case 'in one hand', as the Commission stated in *Preussag/Hapag – Lloyd/TUI*, D.Comm. Nov. 10, 1997, M.1019.

250. *See Royal Philips Electronics – SEB/Moulinex*, CFI April 3, 2003, T-119/02, paras 283–286.

251. E.g. *IEH/EC*, D.Comm. Dec. 20, 2002, IP/02/1962: referral of the whole issue of a dozen transactions involving Intercommunale d'Electricité du Hainaut and Electrabel on the supply of electricity to eligible customers, half of which were, because of the lack of a Community dimension, the responsibility of the Belgian authorities (which prohibited three transactions) whereas the other transactions were notified to the Commission and referred to the Belgian authorities in order to avoid contradictory decisions. *See also Enel/Wind/Infostrada*, D.Comm. Jan. 19, 2001, M.2216 (referred to the Italian competition authority which authorized the operation subject to commitments).

252. Statement of the Council and the Commission when adopting Regulation 1310/97 and Green Paper of the Commission on the review of the merger regulation, COM(96)19 final of Jan. 31, 1996, point 94. *See Royal Philips Electronics*, CFI April 3, 2003, T-119/02, paras 349–356.

tory decisions adopted by the Commission and the national authority, which are likely to jeopardize a coherent assessment of the merger, in particular because the Commission is not obliged to consult the national authority beforehand on the substance of the case, e.g. the application of the failing company doctrine.[253] However, the Court of First Instance upheld the possibility of a partial referral decision despite the risk of irreconcilable decisisons.[254] A possible solution may be a referral decision which contains a more detailed reasoning likely to prepare the way for a coherent assessment by the Commission and the national authority(ies), as in *Sogecable/Canalsatellite Digital/Via Digital*, where the Commission substantiated the reasons why the 'failing company doctrine' did not apply.[255] However, risks of fragmented assessment may arise in the case of a partial referral when the Commission and national authorities decide on the same transaction with respect to the same products but in different *geographic* markets, in particular when the clearance is made subject to commitments. For instance, a commitment requiring the grant of exclusive territorial licences on different national markets to different independent companies could run counter to the principle of free circulation of the licensed products.[256] A more appropriate (because single-market friendly) solution consists in the full transfer of production and R&D capacity, including intellectual property rights, as in *DSM/La Roche*.[257] The risk of jeopardizing a coherent assessment is less likely where the partial referral concerns products or services that represent different relevant *product* markets.[258] In the *Carnival Corporation/P&O Princess* case, which raised competition concerns in various member states, the Commission considered 'that it is under these circumstances more appropriate not to fragment the case and not to conduct parallel investigations in Europe' and, accordingly, not to refer the case (even if the national authority already started a

253. *Royal Philips Electronics*, CFI April 3, 2003, T-119/02, para. 372. In the referral decision *Sogecable/Canalsatellite* the Commission substantiated in detail its view on the failing company defense: D.Comm. Aug. 14, 2002, M.2845.

254. *Ibid.* para. 380.

255. D.Comm. Aug. 14, 2002, M.2845, points 110–117.

256. Examples: *Ciba-Geigy/Sandoz*, D.Comm. July 17, 1996, 1996 OJ L 201/1; *Pfizer/Warner-Lambert*, D.Comm. May 22, 2000, M.1878, *SEB/Moulinex*, D.Comm. Jan. 8, 2002, M.2621, *aff'd* April 3, 2003, T-119/02, para. 172 (referring to the consequence of granting exclusive territorial licences, which is to prevent direct competition between licensor and licensees within the Common Market).

257. E.g., *DSM/La Roche*, D.Comm. July 23, 2003, M.2972.

258. Example: *Arla/Express Dairies*, D.Comm. June 10, 2003, M.3130, a merger between the Danish-based dairy products company Arla Foods and Britain's Express Dairies, where the Commission referred that part to the UK authority which concerned the supply of fresh milk in Britain, a clearly distinct market, whereas it assessed the remaining product markets because of their Community-wide implication. On the other hand, the Commission rejected the request of partial referral in *Lagardère/Natexis/VUP* (D.Comm. July 23, 2003, M.2978), the planned merger between two largest publishers in France, because the French-speaking area in Europe had a supranational geographic dimension.

preliminary investigation) but to review the transaction exclusively under Community rules.[259] The referral procedure must thus be seen in the light of the most appropriate allocation of tasks between the Commission and national authority aiming at the most efficient application of the merger rules, likely to lead to a coherent, and to avoid any fragmented, assessment.[260] Obviously, the risk of conflicting decisions can be reduced by the close cooperation between national competition authorities and the Commission according to Article 19 of Regulation 139/2004 and the ECN (European Competition Network established in the framework of Regulation 1/2003).

Consideration of Member States' Legitimate Interests.
According to Article 21 (4) member states may take appropriate measures to protect legitimate interests, such as public security, plurality of the media and prudential rules, subject to their compatibility with the general principles, which must be decided by the Commission. A request for referral might be motivated with the view of protecting such interests, e.g. in cases which involve security of electricity supply in a national or local market or mergers between national publishers; however, this issue has not been expressly addressed in the administrative practice so far.[261]

(iv) Transactions without a Community Dimension – Referral to the Commission upon Request by the Parties or from Member States

Principle.
In order to avoid multiple notifications to and clearances of the same transaction by different national competition authorities with the inherent risk of conflicting decisions[262] the Commission may be requested to examine a transaction that does not have a Community dimension upon:

- a request made by the *parties* before *any* notification to the competent national competition authorities that a concentration, which is capable of being reviewed

259. *Carnival Corporation/P&O Princess I*, D.Comm. July 24, 2002, M.2706 (Article 8 (2) decision), points 8–10 and 196 (no competition concerns on the UK market for which referral was requested despite 'relatively high market shares') and, more explicitly, IP/02/552.

260. *See Anglo American/Tarmac*, D.Comm. Jan. 13, 2000, M.1779; *Hanson/Pioneer*, D.Comm. March 24, 2000, M.1827; *Interbrew/BASS*, D.Comm. Aug. 22, 2000, M.2044; *C3D/Rhône/Go Ahead*, D.Comm. Oct. 20, 2000, M.2154.

261. Mergers in the electricity sector: *EdF/London Electricity*, D.Comm. Jan. 27, 1999, M.1346 (referral rejected); *Electrabel*, D.Comm. Feb. 13, 2003, IP/03/230 (request for referral accepted); publishers: *VUP/Lagardère*, D.Comm. July 23, 2003, IP/03/1078 (request for referral accepted); *Bertelsmann/Kirch/Première*, D.Comm. May 27, 1998, 1999 OJ L 53/1 (merger prohibited; however, the German authorities relied on the distinct market concept without formally requesting a referral).

262. Recital 12 to Regulation 139/2004.

under national competitions laws by at least three member states,[263] should be examined by the Commission (Article 4 (5)), or
- a request by one or more *member states* that a concentration, which affects trade between member states and threatens to significantly affect competition within the territory of the member state(s) making the request, should be examined by the Commission (Article 22).[264]

Referral at the Request of the Parties.
Any request by the *parties* must be made during the pre-notification stage in their reasoned submission. The parties must indicate that the concentration may significantly affect competition in a market within a member state which presents all the characteristics of a distinct market, which is, in particular, the case where the effects of the concentration or their main economic impact is confined to a single member state, whereas in a case with effects beyond national boundaries the Commission is in the best position to carry out the investigation. The parties may also submit that a case should be treated by the Commission having regard in particular to factors such as the cost and time delay involved in submitting multiple member state filings.[265] The Commission transmits a copy of the reasoned submission to all member states. Any member state competent to examine the concentration under its national law[266] may, within 15 days of receiving the reasoned submission, express its disagreement. Where at least one of such member states expresses its disagreement, the case shall not be referred. If there is no disagreement the case is deemed to be referred to the Commission and shall be notified to the Commission (Article 4 (5)).

Referral Request by Member States.
One or more member states (not necessarily three member states) may request the Commission to examine a transaction that does not have a Community dimension but affects trade between member states and threatens to significantly affect competition in a market of the member state(s) in question. The request must be made within 15 working days after receipt of a copy of the notification. The

263. *See* Draft Notice on Case Allocation, points 20–32 and 70–78 (*supra* p. 502).
264. The member states' competition authorities have issued a recommendation designed to provide guidance as to the principles upon which national competition authorities should deal with cases eligible for joint referrals under Article 22: *Principles on the Application, by National Competition Authorities within the ECA Network, of Article 21* (Draft Notice on Case Allocation, fn. 5 and 30).
265. Draft Notice on Case Allocation, point 32. *See* Recital 14 to Regulation 139/2004.
266. The Commission states in its Draft Notice on Case Allocation (fn. 41), that a member state can request the referral even where the operation does not fall at all within the scope of its national competition law, which, however, does not conform with the overall objective of the referral mechanism (application of the competition rules by the most appropriate authority rather than the possibility to preclude the application by another authority).

Commission informs the parties to the transaction of the request and transmits a copy of the request to all other member states, which may join the request within 15 working days during which they must suspend any time limits for national proceedings. As soon as a member state informs the Commission that it does not wish to joint the request, the suspension of its national time limits ends. The Commission must take a decision to examine the transaction under Community law within 10 further working days. If the Commission does not take a decision within this time limit the case is to be examined in accordance with the request, thereby precluding the application of national competition law by the member state(s) which made the request.[267]

The Commission may also invite member states to make such a request.

Unlike Article 22 (5) of the former Regulation 1310/97, Article 22 does not limit the decisional powers of the Commission to the measures which are strictly necessary to maintain or restore competition in the territory(ies) of the requesting member state(s). Through the end of 2003 12 decisions had been adopted by the Commission pursuant to Article 22 (4) of the former Regulation 1310/97,[268] which include three prohibition decisions.[269]

(v) Limited Powers of the Commission in Other Cases not Covered by the Merger Regulation

Transactions without a Community dimension are, regardless of the degree of market dominance acquired, not generally subject to Regulation 139/2004 nor to Regulation 1/2003 nor the special procedural regulations for transport. However, the Commission may take action in four cases:

- *Referral from a National Authority to the Commission.* As described above, upon a request by a member state or a joint request by several member states the Commission may investigate a transaction that falls below the 'Community dimension' thresholds.
- *Application of Article 82 under the Transitional Enforcement Powers of Article 85.* The Commission is in principle entitled to intervene against a transaction

267. Article 22 (3) third subparagraph.
268. Example of a clearance decision with commitments: *GE/Agfa NDT*, D.Comm. Dec. 5, 2003, M.3136.
269. Examples of Article 8 (3) prohibition decisions: *RTL/Veronica/Endemol*, D.Comm. Sept. 20, 1995, 1996 OJ L 34/21, *aff'd* CFI April 28, 1999, 1999 ECR II-1199 (the prohibition decision was followed by the conditional clearance of the amended agreement, D.Comm. July 17, 1996, 1998 OJ L 294); *Blokker/Toys 'R' Us*, D.Comm. June 26, 1997, 1998 OJ L 316/1; *Kesko/Tuco*, D.Comm. July 26, 1996, 1997 OJ L 110/53 and April 18, 1997 (Article 8 (4) decision because the prohibited transaction was already implemented and had to be divested). Article 8 (2) decisions: *Promatec/Sulzer*, D.Comm. April 16, 2002, M.2638; Article 6 (1) (b) decisions: *British Airways*, D.Comm. Feb. 17, 1993, M.278; *GEC/Unison*, D.Comm. April 17, 2002, M.2738.

without a Community dimension under Article 82 in conjunction with Article 89 if the merger fulfils the criteria of the *Continental Can* doctrine, i.e., if it is likely to strengthen an already existing dominant position. However, the Commission has stated that it does not intend to take action against transactions falling below one of these thresholds as they will normally not significantly affect trade between member states.[270]

- *Application of Article 82 under Regulation 1/2003 to Predatory Practices Preceding a Takeover.* The Commission could intervene under Article 82 and Regulation 1/2003 against abusive practices by a firm holding a dominant position aimed at preparing the way for the takeover of another firm, such as by price-squeezing or predatory pricing *vis-à-vis* a competitor. In this event the Commission could take action against the practices preparing the way for the takeover – though not against the takeover itself – even if the firms concerned fell below the 'Community dimension' thresholds.[271]
- *Application of Article 81 under Regulation 1/2003 to Non-Ancillary Restrictions.* Article 22 (1) does not prevent the Commission from applying Article 81 and Regulation 1/2003 to restrictions that are not ancillary, i.e., not 'directly related and necessary' to implementation of a transaction without a 'Community dimension', for example to non-compete clauses that are excessive in duration or scope and which amount to market sharing between the parties to the merger.[272]

Unrestricted Powers of National Authorities and National Courts. National authorities and national courts are entitled to apply national law to transactions without a Community dimension which are not likely to affect trade between member states. Article 82 can also be applied insofar as it can be enforced by national authorities and by national courts as directly effective Community law.[273] However, the Commission is empowered to block the application of national law by initiating proceedings and dealing with the case itself under Community law,[274] provided trade between member states is likely to be affected and its jurisdiction is therefore ensured.

---

270. With respect to the creation of full-function joint ventures below these thresholds which a national authority intends to prohibit, the Commission intends not to grant an exemption under Article 81 (3) and to leave the assessment of any anticompetitive spill-over effect to the national authorities 'as far as possible': Statements on Regulation 4064/89 and Statements on Regulation 1310/97, re Article 22.
271. *See also supra* Chapter V.D.6.
272. Notice on the Concept of Full-Function Joint Ventures, point 16; Notice on Ancillary Restraints, point 6. *See Reuter/BASF*, D.Comm. July 29, 1976, 1976 OJ L 254/40; *Remia/Nutricia*, ECJ July 11, 1985, 1985 ECR 2545, para. 20; *Quantel Continuum*, D.Comm. July 27, 1992, 1992 OJ L 235/9; *BT/MCI II*, D.Comm. July 27, 1994, 1994 OJ L 223/36, point 48.
273. *Ahmed Saeed*, ECJ April 11, 1989, 1989 ECR 803, paras 20 and 33.
274. Article 22 (3), third subparagraph which corresponds to Article 11 (6) of Regulation 1/2003.

D. Assessment of Mergers, Joint Ventures, Ancillary Restraints and Remedies

1. Defining the Relevant Market as Precondition for any Assessment of 'Significantly Impeding Effective Competition'

(a) Need for Defining the Relevant Market

Market Shares as Main but not only Indicator of Significantly Impeding Effective Competition.
Article 2 of Regulation 139/2004 empowers the Commission to act against mergers and full-function joint ventures that would significantly impede effective competition in the Common Market or a substantial part of it, in particular as a result ot the creation or strengthening of a dominant position. The definition of a 'dominant position' corresponds to the Court of Justice's definition as 'a position of economic strength enjoyed by an undertaking which enables it to prevent effective competition from being maintained on the relevant market by affording it the power to behave to an appreciable extent independently of its competitors, its customers and ultimately of its consumers'.[275] However, the substantive test is broader than that of the former Regulation 1310/97, which required the creation or strengthening of a dominant position as a result of which effective competition would significantly impeded.[276] Under the new regulation the creation or strengthening of a dominant position is only an example of significantly impeding effective competition. Therefore, the firms involved in a merger must not necessarily 'dominate' the market but must be likely to eliminate important competitive constraints which consequently would increase market power or are significantly more likely to harm effective competition on the relevant market. The first step when assessing a merger is to define the relevant product and geographic market. The second step is the calculation of the parties' and their competitors' market shares on the relevant market(s).[277] The third step is to evaluate the impact of

---

275. Under Article 82: *United Brands*, ECJ Feb. 14, 1978, 1978 ECR 207, para. 65. Under the merger control regulation: *Gencor/Lonrho*, CFI March 25, 1999, 1999 ECR II-753, para. 200.
276. However, under the former Regulation 1310/97 the Commission found in some cases a dominant position which would *not* result in significantly impeding effective competition: *Mannesmann/Vallourec/Ilva*, D.Comm. Jan. 31, 1994, 1994 OJ L 102/15, points 131–133 (because of potential competition); *Knorr Bremse/Rexroth*, D.Comm. August 23, 1999 (because of buyer power). A dominant position which *would* significantly impede effective competition was found in: *Endemol*, CFI April 28, 1999, 1999 ECR II-1299, paras 167–170 (because of structural links between the merging companies impeding effective competition of third companies). *See also SCPA/Kali + Salz-MdK*, ECJ March 31, 1998, 1998 ECR I-1375, para. 219.
277. In the case of multiple relevant markets the parties' position must be assessed in respect of each of these markets, *see BaByliss*, CFI April 3, 2003, T-114/02, paras. 308–314.

any increase in market shares in the light of the market setting of each case, in particular in the light of the market structure and the efficiencies associated with the transaction.

The Commission Notice on Definition of the Relevant Market.
A proper definition of the relevant market is a necessary precondition for any assessment of the effect on competition of a merger or full-function joint venture.[278] The approach is basically the same as under Article 81 or 82 and is harmonized in the Commission's Notice on the Definition of the Relevant Market for the Purposes of Community Competition Law:[279] The relevant market is established by the combination of the product and the geographic market according to the basic principles of competitive constraints, which are demand substitutability, supply substitutability and potential competition. Demand substitutability constitues the most immediate and effective disciplinary force on the suppliers of a given product. Supply-side substitutability is in general less immediate and in any case requires additional factors. *Potential competition* is not taken into account when defining markets but only at a subsequent stage, in order to assess whether the transaction between the companies significantly impedes effective competition in the relevant market.[280]

(b) Relevant Product Market

Narrow Market Definition Predominates.
The Commission has defined the relevant product market as follows:

> 'A relevant market comprises all those products and/or services which are regarded as interchangeable or substitutable by the consumer, by reason of the products' characteristics, their prices and their intended use.'[281]

The Commission tends to favor a narrow definition of the relevant product market. Sometimes the Commission finds it appropriate to distinguish separate markets (sub-markets) for the same product group, which correspond to different categories of customers having distinct demand characteristics.[282] However,

---

278. *SCPA/Kali + Salz-MdK*, ECJ March 31, 1998, 1998 ECR I-1375, para. 143.
279. 1997 OJ C 372/3,.
280. Notice on the definition of the relevant market, points 13, 14 and 24.
281. Notice on the definition of the relevant market, point 7.
282. The Commission may, for example, define separate markets according to whether supplies to certain customers are subject to governmental regulation, in particular state aids, whereas supplies to other customers are subject to competition: *Ruhrkohle AG/Saarbergwerke/Preussag Anthrazit*, D.Comm. 29 July 1998, ECSC 1252, points 22–23, 32. The Commission will not consider there to be a competitive overlap when the products are imperfect substitutes for one another and they are based on different technologies and traditions: *Johnson & Johnson/Depuy*, D.Comm. Oct. 28, 1998, M.1286.

the Commission may also investigate whether it is appropriate that supply-side substitutability (the ability of other manufacturers to switch production to the merging parties' products) should be integrated into the product market definition. Finally, the Commission may examine price evidence (levels, elasticity and correlations) to determine to what extent such evidence may complement findings based on other criteria.[283] The Commission takes into account any *portfolio effect*, i.e. products which are normally supplied to, and purchased by, customers as a package.[284] However, products which overlap only to an insignificant extent (e.g., 5%) are not considered as substitutable.[285] The Commission leaves the precise definition of the relevant market open where the parties aggregate market shares do not appear to indicate dominance on the narrowest possible market.

Examples in Alphabetical Order.

– *Accounting Services*
  Price Waterhouse/Coopers & Lybrand, May 20, 1998, 1999 OJ L 50/27.

– *Advertising*
  Vodafone/Vivendi/Canal+, D.Comm. July 20, 2000, JV. 48, points 42–44.

– *Aircraft*
  Commercial aircraft, subdivided (according to the number of seats) into large, medium-sized and small aircrafts: *Boeing/McDonnell Douglas*, D. Comm. July 30, 1997, M.877, OJ L 336/16, point 9; *Aerospatiale-Alenia/de Havilland*, D. Comm. October 2, 1991, M.53, OJ L 334/42.
  Aircraft landing gear: *SNECMA/TI*, D. Comm. January 17, 1994, M.368.
  Aircraft engines: large and small; civil and military; repair and overhaul services: *Rolls Royce, SIA, HAESL*, D.Comm. May 10, 1999, M.1506.
  Military – missiles: *Matra Bae Dynamics/Dasa/LFK*, D.Comm. January 27, 1998, M.945.

– *Airports*
  Airport services – groundhandling services: *Birmingham International Airport*, D.Comm. March 25, 1997, M.786; *Hochtief/AerRianta/Düsseldorf Airport*, D.Comm. December 22, 1997, M.1035; *Maersk Air/LFV Holdings*, D.Comm. July 6, 1998, M.1124.
  Automatic transport systems at airports: *Siemens/Lagardere (Matra)*, D.Comm. February 8, 1996, M.685.

---

283. Twenty-third Report on Competition Policy, point 273.
284. *BaByliss/SEB-Moulinex*, CFI April 3, 2003, T-114/02, paras 346–347.
285. *Ibid.*, para 325.

Cargo handling in sheds: *Lufthansa/Menzies/LCC*, D.Comm. June 30, 1998, M.1165.

– *Air Transport*
Connections between destinations: *Swissair/Sabena*, D.Comm. July 20, 1995, M.616; *Air France/KLM*, D.Comm. Feb. 11, 2004, M.3280.
Air Traffic Management: *Alcatel/Thomson SA-ThomsonCSF*, D.Comm. May 25, 1998, M.1121.

– *Audit and Accounting Services*
Price Waterhouse/Cooper & Lybrand, D.Comm. May 20, 1998, 1999 OJ L 50/27, points 21–35.

– *Automobiles*
Passenger cars (small, medium-sized, large, luxury) *Toyota/Daihatsu*, D.Comm. November 6, 1998, M.1326; *Volkswagen/Rolls-Royce/Cosworth*, D.Comm. August 24, 1998, *M.1283*; *Daimler Benz/Chrysler*, D.Comm. July 22, 1998, M.1204; *Ford/Volvo*, D.Comm. March 26, 1999, M.1452.
Passenger – commercial vehicles: *Ford/Mazda*, D.Comm. May 24, 1996, M.741.
Buses (city buses – coaches): *Mercedes Benz/Kässbohrer*, D.Comm. Feb. 14, 1995, M.477, 1995 OJ L 211/1; *RenauMveco*, D.Comm. October 22, 1998, M.1202.
Trucks (light, middle, heavy)'; *Renault/Volvo*, D.Comm. November 7, 1990, M.4.
Tractors, escavators, dredgers: *New Holland/Orenstein & Koppel*, D.Comm. December 18, 1998, M.1235.
Services of assistance and security for car drivers: *Securior Datatrak*, D.Comm. March 20, 1995, M.561; *Magnetti Marelli/Telespazio*, D.Comm. 2 July 1998, M.1211.
Car components (OE market distinct from replacement market): *Mannesmann/Boge*, D.Comm. September 23, 1991, M.134; *Arvin/Sogefi*, D.Comm. September 23, 1993, M.360; *BMW/Rover*, D.Comm. March 14, 1994, M.416; *Bosch/Allied Signal*, D.Comm. April 9, 1996, M.726; *Lucas/Varity*, D.Comm. July 11, 1996, M.768.

– *Automobile Equipment*
Automobile equipment (airbags, wheels, batteries, door panels): *TRW/Magna*, D.Comm. January 28, 1997, M.872; *Siemens/HUF*, D.Comm. April 29, 1997, M.912; *Lear Keiper*, D.Comm. July 22, 1997, M.937; *Johnson Controls/Becker*, D.Comm. June 24, 1998, M.1196.
Automobile parts: *Valeo/ITT Industries*, D.Comm. July 30, 1998, M.1245; *Dana/Echlin*, D.Comm. July 6, 1998, M.1207.

Automatic transmission: *Ford/ZF*, D.Comm. December 21, 1998, M.1368, point 12.
Body panels: *Thyssen/Krupp*, D.Comm. June 2, 1998, M.1080; *Johnson Controls/Becker*, D.Comm. June 24, 1998, M.1196.
Brakes: *Knorr Bremse/Bosch*, D.Comm. December 14, 1998, M.1342.
Pumps: *SKF/INA/WPB*, D.Comm. February 19, 1996, M.694.
Seats: *ECIA/Bertrand Faure*, D.Comm. January 28, 1998, M.1093.
Shock absorbers: *Mannesmann/Boge*, D.Comm. September 23, 1991, M.134, para. 8.
Sun visors: *Johnson Controls/Becker*, D.Comm. June 24, 1998, M.1196.
Steering systems: *Bosch/Friedrichshafen*, D.Comm. September 14, 1998, M.1291.
Tires: *Nokia Corporation/SP Tyres*, D.Comm. March 14, 1995, M.548.
Transmissions: *Ford/ZF*, D.Comm. December 21, 1998, M.1368, point 12.

– *Banking*

Retail banking – corporate banking – financial markets: *Fortis/CGER*, D.Comm. November 15, 1993, M.342.
Wholesale or corporate banking: *Credit Suisse/Winterthur*, D.Comm. October 10, 1997, M.985; *Fortis AG/Generale Bank*, D.Comm. June 24, 1998, M.1172; *BNP/Dresdner Bank – Austrian JV*, D.Comm. December 21, 1998, M.1340, point 9.
Financial markets: *Crédit Suisse/Winterthur*, D.Comm. October 15, 1997, M.985; *Fortis/CGER*, November 15, 1993, M.342; *Fortis AG/Generale Bank*, D.Comm. June 24, 1998, M.1172.
Real estate financing: *CDE/LaHenin*, D.Comm. September 3, 1998, M.1254.
Payment systems (cards – cheques): *Eurocard/Eurocheque-Europay*, D.Comm. July 13, 1992, M.241; *BAI/Banca Populare di Lecco*, D.Comm. December 20, 1993, M.391.
Retail banking: *Credit Suisse/Winterthur*, D.Comm. October 10, 1997, M.985; *Fortis/CGER, M.342*; *Fortis AG/Generale Bank*, D.Comm. June 24, 1998, M.1172.

– *Beverages*

Bottled water – mineral water: *Nestlé/Perrier*, D.Comm. July 22, 1992, M.190, OJ L 356/1, point 19; *Nestlé/San Pellegrino*, D.Comm. February 16, 1998, M.1065.
Carbonated soft drinks – cola: *Coca Cola/Amalgated Beverages*, D.Comm. January 22, 1997, 1997 OJ L 218115; *Coca Cola/Carlsberg*, D.Comm. September 11, 1997, M.833. *See Coca Cola/Pernod*, French Ministry of Financial and Economic Affairs (prohibition of the proposed acquisition of Pernod's brand 'Orangina' because it was likely to lead to a dominant position on the away-from-home market for carbonated soft drinks other than colas), WuW 1999–3, 260.

Spirits (genever, gin, whisky, brandy and rum as distinct markets): *Guinness/Grand Met.*, D.Comm. October 15, 1997, M.938.
Beer: *Orkla/Volvo*, D.Comm. September 20, 1995, 1996 OJ L 66/17.

- *Books*
  Academic journals; professional books on law and taxation; educational publishing; business publications; dictionaries: *Wolters Kluwer/Reed Elsevier*, Twenty-eighth Report on Competition Policy, point 154; *Bertelsman/Kooperativa Förbundet*, D.Comm. May 12, 2000, JV. 45.
  School books separate from others: *Legardère/Natexis,VUP*, D.Comm. July 23, 2003, M.2978, points 26–140.

- *Butanol*
  Celanese/Degussa/JV, June 11, 2003, 2004 OJ L 38/47, points 80–85.

- *Cables*
  General wiring – power cables – components of power transmission: *GEC Alsthom/AEG*, D.Comm. September 3, 1996, M.706; *Pirelli/Siemens*, D.Comm. September 30, 1998, M.1271; *Pirelli/BICC*, D.Comm. July 19, 2000, M.1822, points 11–32 (high – medium – low voltage cables).

- *Cans*
  Tinplate aerosol cans: *Crown Cork and Seal/Carnaud MetalBox*, D.Comm. November 14, 1995, 1996 OJ L 75/38.
  Bottles and cans one beverage container market, but not necessarily cans for meat and fish: *Continental Can*, ECJ February 21, 1973, 1973 ECR 215, paras. 32–35.

- *Catering services*
  Accor/Wagons-Lits, D.Comm. April 28, 1992, M.126, OJ 1992 L204/1.

- *Chemicals*
  Additives and adjuvants: *Harrisons & Crosfield/Akzo*, D.Comm. April 29, 1993, M.310; *Veba/Degussa*, D.Comm. December 3, 1997, M.942; *Akzo Nobel/Courtaulds*, D.Comm. June 30, 1998, M.1182.
  Distribution of chemicals: *Metallgesellschaft AFT/Klockner Chemiehandel*, D.Comm. January 29, 1998, M.1073.
  Fibers: *Akzo Nobel/Courtaulds*, D.Comm. June 30, 1998, M.1182; *Koch Industries/Saba/Hoechst'*, D.Comm. November 24, 1998, M.1337 (polyester).
  PET: *Dupont/ICI*, D.Comm. October 2, 1997, M.984.
  Polyamide: *Hitachi/DuPont*, D.Comm. October 24, 1997, M.994; *Hoechst/Clariant*, D.Comm. June 10, 1997, M.911.
  Polyethylene: *BASF/Shell*, D.Comm. December 23, 1997, M.1041; *Elenac/Hoechst*, D.Comm. November 24, 1998, M.1287; *Borealis/IPIC/OMV/PCD*,

D.Comm. July 24, 1998, M.1163; *Shell/DEA*, D.Comm. December 20, 2001, M.2839.
Polypropylene: *Shell/Montecatini I*, D.Comm. June 8, 1994, 1994 OJ L 332/48; *Shell/Montecatini II*, D.Comm. April 24, 1996, M.269; *Hoechst/BASF*, D.Comm. June 17, 1997, M.845; *Shell/Montell*, D.Comm. October 23, 1997, M.1007.
Potash: *Kali+Salz/MDK/Treuhand I*, D.Comm. December 14, 1993, M.308, 1994 OJL 186/38; *Kali+Salz/MDK/TreuhandII*, D.Comm. July 9, 1998, M.308, 1998 OJ L 275.
Pulp dryers: *Valmet/Rauma*, D.Comm. February 8, 1999, M.1379.
Silicones: *Saint Gobain/Wacker Chemie*, D.Comm. December 4, 1996, 1997 OJ L 247/1, points 19–39; *GE/Bayer*, D.Comm. June 11, 1998, M.1162.
Speciality chemicals to the paper and pulp industry: *Hercules/Betzdeaborn*, D.Comm. October 5, 1998, M.1304.
Toluene, *Shell/DEA*, D.Comm. December 20, 2001, M.2839, points 159–165.
Vinyl acetate monomer: *Wacker/Air Products*, D.Comm. August 4, 1998.

– *Coal*
Pit coal – brown coal: submarkets according to industrial and private customers: *Raab Karcher/Ruhrkohle*, D.Comm. February 28, 1996, 1996 OJ L 193; RAG/*Saarbergwerke/Preussag*, D.Comm. July 29, 1998, ECSC 1252, points 18–21.

– *Coatings*
13 segments as submarkets: *AKZO Nobel/Courtaulds*, D.Comm. June 30, 1998, M.1182; *Degussa/Ciba-Geigy*, D.Comm. April 5, 1993, M.317.
Decorative coatings: *ICI/Williams*, D.Comm. April 29, 1998, M.1167.

– *Computers*
Personal computers, low end servers, workstations and disk storage subsystems: *Compaq/Digital*, D.Comm. March 23, 1998, M.1120; *AT&T/NCR*, D.Comm. January 18, 1991, M.50; *Digital/Philips*, D.Comm. September 2, 1991, M.129.
Software: *IBM France/CGI*, D.Comm. May 19, 1993, M.336; *Philips/Origin*, D.Comm. December 22, 1995, M.668; *Deutsche Telekom/SAP-S*, D.Comm. March 29, 1996, M.705.
Marketing and servicing: *KNP BT/Société Générale*, D.Comm. October 3, 1995, M.640.
Wholesale distribution and related services: *Tech Data/Computer 2000*, D.Comm. June 3, 1998, M.1179; *Otto Versand/Actebis*, D.Comm. February 26, 1998, M.1099; *Ingram/Macroton*, D.Comm. July 17, 1998, M.1232; *NEC/PEN*, D.Comm. September 3, 1998, M.1276.

– *Construction*
Bricks: *Creditanstalt/Kommic/Wienerberger*, D.Comm. June 28, 1996, M.755.
Cement: *Lafarge/Redland*, D.Comm. December 16, 1997, M.1030; *Holdercim/Cedest*, D.Comm. July 6, 1994, M.460; *Skanska/Scancem*, D.Comm. October 23, 1998, M.1157; *Haniel/Cementbouw/JV*, D.Comm. June 26, 2002, M.2650, points 61–80.
Storage and materials handling systems (commercial – industrial): *Constructor/Dexion*, October 30, 1998, M.1318.
Building control and security systems: *Elektrowatt/Landis & Gyr*, D.Comm. February 12, 1996, M.692; *Siemens/Elektrowatt*, D.Comm. November 18, 1998, 1998 L 88/1, point 68.
Escalators: *Thyssen/Krupp*, D.Comm. June 2, 1998, M.1080.
Equipment (heavy – light), escavators, dredgers: *New Holland/Orenstein & Koppel*, D.Comm. December 18 1998, M.1235, points 8–9.

– *Consumer Goods*
Stationery, small electrical and electronic appliances, batteries *Gillette/Duracell*, D.Comm. November 8, 1996, M.836.
Matches – lighters: *Swedish Match/KAV*, D.Comm. December 18, 1997, M.997.

– *Containers*
Glass containers: *Owens-Illinois/BTR Packaging*, D.Comm. April 21, 1998, M.1109. Marine containers: *GE Capital/Sea Containers*, April 28, 1998, M.1020.

– *Corrugated Case Materials and Corrugated Cases: Jefferson Smurfit/Stone Containers*, D.Comm. July 8, 1998, M.1208.

– *Electrical Household Appliances*
Fryers, toasters, coffee makers, food processors etc. – distinct markets: *BaByliss*, CFI April 3, 2003, T-114/02, paras. 307–310.

– *Electricity*
Distinction between gas and electricity (except heating and cooking): *Tractebel/Distrigaz II*, September 1, 1994, M.493; *Neste/IVO*, D.Comm. June 2, 1998, M.931; *EDFI/ESTAG*, D.Comm. March 17, 1998, M.1107; *Gaz de France/BEWWG/GASAG*, D.Comm. January 20, 1999, M.1402.
Space heating: *Neste/TVO*, D.Comm. June 2, 1998, M.931.
Distinction between wholesale and retail market (sales to eligible customers): *Grupo Vilar Mir/EnBW/Cantabrico*, D.Comm. September 26, 2001, 2004 OJ L 48/86, points 18–23.
Power plants: *Amoco/Repsol/Iberdrola/Ente Vasco de la Energia*, August 11, 1998, M.1190.

- *Electronics*
  Consumer electronics: *Philips/Grundig*, D.Comm. December 3, 1993, M.382; *Philips/Lucent Technologies*, D.Comm. January 6, 1999, M.1358.
  Photocopiers, cameras, faxes: *Ricoh/Gerstner*, D.Comm. September 12, 1995, M.622.
  Microprocessors: *Schneider/AEG*, August 1, 1994, M.447.
  Defense electronics: *Alcatel/Thomson SA-Thomson CSF*, D.Comm. May 25, 1998, M.1121.
  Processing electronics: *Philips/Origin*, D.Comm. December 22, 1995, M.668; *ABB/Elsag Bailey*, D.Comm. December 16, 1998, M.1339.

- *Electronic Data Transmission*
  Bertelsmann/Burda/Springer-HOS-MM, D.Comm. September 15, 1997, M.972; *Bertelsmann/Burda-HOS Lifeline*, D.Comm. September 15, 1997, M.973.

- *Engines for large, regional and corporate aircraft*
  General Electric/Honeywell, D.Comm. July 3, 2001, 2004 OJ L 48/1, points 14–34.

- *Fibers*
  Fibers for textile, industrial purposes and for use in carpets: *DuPont/ICI*, D.Comm. September 30, 1992, 1993 OJ L 7/13, points 10–28.

- *Films*
  Graphic art films: *Eastman Kodak/Sun Chemical*, D.Comm. January 15, 1998, M.1042.
  Offset printing plates: *Agfa-Gevaert/DuPont*, D.Comm. February 11, 1998, 1998 OJ L 211/22, points 9–42.

- *Food*
  Ice cream (impulse, take-home, catering): *Nestlé/Italgel*, D.Comm. September 15, 1993, M.362; D.Comm. *Unilever France/Ortiz Miko*, D.Comm. March 15, 1994, M.422.
  Edible oils – olive oils: *Cargill/Vandemoortele-JV*, D.Comm. July 20, 1998, M.1227, points 15–16; *Medeol/Elosua*, D.Comm. June 6, 1994, M.431.
  Pet food (dog and cat food): *Dalgety PLC/The Quaker Oats Company*, D.Comm. March 13, 1995, M.554; *Nestlé/Dalgety*, D.Comm. April 2, 1998, M.1127 (distinction between the two markets), *Masterfood/Royal Canin*, D.Comm. February 15, 2002, M.2544, points 9–24.
  Snack food: *PepsiCo/General Mills*, D.Comm. August 5, 1982, M.232.
  Spices (full range): *McCormick/CPC/Ostmann*, D.Comm. October 29, 1993, M.330.
  Sugar (end consumers – industrial use): *Eridania/ISI*, D.Comm. July 30, 1991, M.62.

– *Fuels and Lubricants*
Retail motor fuels – lubricants: *BP/Mobil*, D.Comm. August 7, 1996, M.727; *Texaco/Chevron*, D.Comm. October 30, 1998, M.1301; *BP/Amoco*, D.Comm. December 11, 1998, M.1293; *Total/Petrofina*, D.Comm. March 26, 1999, M.1464.
Motorway service stations: *Rust- und Tankstation AG*, D.Comm. December 7, 1998, M.1361.
Lubricating, oil additives, antifreeze: *Exxon/Shell*, D.Comm. July 8, 1998, M.1137, points 9–16; *RWE-DEA/Fuchs Petrolube*, D.Comm. August 11, 1998, M.1239.

– *Gas*
Natural gas: *Neste/IVO*, D.Comm. June 2, 1998, M.93 1.
Regasification plant (liquid natural gas) *Amoco/Repsol/Iberdrola/Ente Vasco de la Energia*, August 11, 1998, M.1190.
Industrial gas turbine overhaul and repair: *TPM/Wood Group*, D.Comm. July 20, 1998, M.1224.

– *Glass*
Raw float glass: *Glaverbel/PPG*, 7 August 1998, D.Comm. August 7, 1998, M.1230.
Glass – transparent plastic: *Italian Flat Glass II*, D.Comm. December 7, 1988, 1989 OJ L 33/44, point 76; *Veba/Degussa*, D.Comm. December 3, 1997, M.942, 1998 OJ L 201/102; *GE/Bayer*, D.Comm. June 11, 1998, M.1162.

– *Hotel Services*
'Upscale' and 'midscale' hotel services: *Bass PLC/Saison Holdings B.V.*, D.Comm. March 23, 1998, M.1133.
Human Resources Consulting: ASKO/Omni, D.Comm. February 21, 1991, M.65; *ASKO/Jacobs/ADIA*, D.Comm. May 16, 1991, M.82; *ADDIA/ECCO*, D.Comm. June 24, 1996, M.765; *Marsh & McLennan/Sedgwick*, D.Comm. October 23, 1998, M.1307.

– *Household appliances*
Royal Philips Electronics, CFI April 3, 2003, T-119/02, paras. 89–93 (separate submarkets).

– *Insurance*
Insurance – banking activities: *Crédit Suisse/Winterthur*, D.Comm. October 10, 1997, M.985.
Life – non-life insurance (with submarkets according to the risk insured) – Re-insurance – financial services: *Allianz/Vereinte*, D.Comm. November 11, 1996, M.812; *AXA/UAP*, D.Comm. December 20, 1996, M.862; *Bank Austria/Cred-it-anstalt*, D.Comm. March 11, 1997, M.873; *AXA/UAP*, D.Comm. December

20, 1996, M.862; *BAT/Zurich*, D.Comm. February 16, 1998, Case IV/M.1043; *Allianz/AGF*, D.Comm. May 8, 1998, M.1082; *Berkshire Hathaway/General Re*, D.Comm. September 18, 1998, M.1306; *Schweizer Rück/NCM*, D.Comm. June 26, 1998, M.1150.
Life insurance: *AEGON/Scottish Equitable*, D.Comm. June 25, 1993, M.349.
Transport insurance: *Zurich/MMI*, D.Comm. April 2, 1993, M.286.
Reinsurance: *BAT/Zurich*, D.Comm. February 16, 1998, M.1043.
Credit insurance: *Allianz/AGF*, May 8, 1998, M.1082; *Hermes/Sampo/FGB-FCIC*, D.Comm. May 19, 1998, M.1101 *(del credere* insurance).
Insurance brokerage: *KKR/Willis Conoon*, D.Comm. 24 August 1998, M.1280; *Schweizer Ruck/NCM*, D.Comm. June 26, 1998, M.1150; *Marsh & McLennan/Sedgwick*, D.Comm. October 23, 1998, M.1307.

– *Media*
Production of films and films distribution: *Seagram/Polygram*, D.Comm. August 21, 1998, M.1219.
Independent production of Dutch-language television programmes (distinct from programmes produced by public broadcasters): *RTL/Veronica/Endemol*, D.Comm. September 20, 1995, 1996 OJ L 134/21; *aff'd Endemol*, CFI April 28, 1999, 1999 ECR II-1299, paras. 106–112.
Free access TV: *Bertelsmann/CLT*, D.Comm. October 7, 1996, M.779.
Free TV – Pay TV: *Bertelsmann/Kirch/Première*, D.Comm. May 27, 1998, 1999 OJ L 53/1; *Canal+/CDPQ/Bank America*, December 3, 1998, M.1327.
Administrative and technical services for pay-TV operators: *MSG Media Service*, D.Comm. November 9, 1994, 1994 OJ L 364/1.

– *Medical equipment*
Siemens/Drägerwerke, D.Comm. April 30, 2003, 2003 OJ L 291/1, points 12–34.

– *Metals*
Aluminium: *Alcoa/Alumax*, D.Comm. May 28, 1998, M.1161.
Platinum, rhodium: *Gencor/Lonrho*, D.Comm. April 24, 1996, 1997 OJ L 11/30; *aff'd* 25 March 1999, 1999 ECR II-753; *Anglo American Corporation/Lonrho*, D.Comm. April 23, 1997, M.754.
Magnesium; aluminium: *Teksid/Vorsk Hydro Produksjon/Meridian*, D.Comm. July 17, 1998, M.1189.

– *Music*
Music recording and distribution, music retailing and music publishing: *Seagram/Poly gram*, D.Comm. August 21, 1998, M.1219.

– *Newspapers*
Editing, publishing and distributing newspapers – selling advertising space: *Recoletos/Unedisa*, D.Comm. February 1, 1999, M.1401.

– *Oilfield Services*
Drilling services and completion products and services: *Halliburton/Dresser*, D.Comm. July 6, 1998, M.1140.

– *Orthopaedic Industry*
Seven segments: *Johnson & Johnson/Depuy*, D.Comm. October 10, 1998, M.1286.

– *Packaging*
Different materials (aluminium, carton, glass, metal, plastic): *Alcan/Inespal/Palco*, D.Comm. April 14, 1993, M.322; *Crown Cork & Seal/Carnaud Metalbox*, D.Comm. November 14, 1995, 1996 OJ L 96/38.
Septic and aseptic packaging: *Tetra Pak/Alfa-Laval*, D.Comm. July 19, 1991, 1991 OJ L 290/35; *Tetra Laval*, CFI April 3, 2003, T-5/02 (actual v. potential competition para. 325).
Recipients (glass, carton, can, plastic): *VIAG/Continental Can*, D.Comm. June 6, 1991, M.81.

– *Paper*
Fine paper; newsprint paper; cartons: *KNP/BT/VRG*, D.Comm. May 4, 1993, 1993 OJ L 217/35; *Enso/Stora*, D.Comm. November 25, 1998, M.1225.
Fine paper – woodpulp: *Mondi/Frantschach*, D.Comm. May 12, 1992, M.210; *UPM-Kymmene*, D.Comm. D.Comm. June 11, 1998, M.1006.
Printing paper: *Repola/Kymmene*, D.Comm. October 30, 1995, M.646.
Household paper and sanitary protection products: *Procter & Gamble/Schickedanz*, D.Comm. June 21, 1994, 1994 OJ L 354/32; *Kimberley Clark/Scott Paper*, D.Comm. January 16, 1996, 1996 OJ L 183/1.
Packaging products: *Viag/Continental Can*, D.Comm. June 6, 1991, M.081, para. 14.

– *Perfume*
Sanofi/Yves Saint Laurent, D.Comm. March 15, 1993, M.312.

– *Pharmaceuticals*
Submarkets according to their therapeutical effect: *Pfizer/Pharmacia*, D.Comm. Feb. 27, 2003, M.2922, point 15; *Procordia/Erbamont*, D.Comm. April 29, 1993, M.323; *Glaxo/Wellcome*, D.Comm. February 28, 1995, M.555; *Sanofi/Kodak*, D.Comm. August 12, 1994, M.480; *Hoffman La Roche/Boehringer Mannheim*, D.Comm. February 4, 1998, 1998 OJ L 234/1; *Ciba-Geigy/Sandoz*, D.Comm. July 17, 1996, 1996 OJ L 201/1.

Antibiotics: *DSM/Koninklijke Gist-Brocades*, D.Comm. May 7, 1998, M.1143.
Plasma derivatives: *Behringwerke/Armour Pharmaceuticals*, D.Comm. April 3, 1995, M.495.
Vaccine products: *Pasteur/Merieux*, D.Comm. July 5, 1993, M.285.
Wound closure products: *TYCO International/US Surgical Corp.*, D.Comm. August 7, 1998, M.1223.
Surgical drapes, swabs and gowns: *Nordic Capital/Mölnlycke Clinical/Kolmi*, D.Comm. January 20, 1998, M.1075.
Wound care products: *Smith & Nephew/Beiersdorf*, D.Comm. January 30, 2001, JV. 54, points 13–22.
Pharmaceutical full-line wholesale: *Alliance Unichem PLC/Safa Galenica SA*, July 27, 1998, M.1243.
Diagnostics: *Bayer/Chiron Diagnostics*, D.Comm. November 17, 1998, M.1325.
Medical imaging: *Kodak/Imation*, D.Comm. October 23, 1998, M.1298.

– *Postal and Telecommunications Services*
International mail; remail; express deliveries: *TNT/GD Net*, D.Comm. December 2, 1991, M.102; *PTT Post/TNT/GD Express Worldwide*, D.Comm. November 8, 1996, M.843; *DHL/Deutsche Post*, D.Comm. June 26, 1998, M.1168.
Pay phones: *Siemens/Elektrowatt*, D.Comm. November 18, 1997, 1999 OJ L 88/1, points 34–38, 113.
Fixed telephony (leased lines, data services): *UTA Telekom AG/Swisscom*, D.Comm. July 13, 1998, M.1199.
International voice telephony services: *British Telecom/MCI*, D.Comm. May 14, 1997, 1997 OJ L 336/1.
Corded, cordless and cellular telephones, answering machines, pagers: *Philips/Lucent Technologies*, D.Comm. January 6, 1999, M.1358, points 11–12.
Mobile telephony – GSM digital telephony: *PTA/STET/Mobilkom*, D.Comm. June 11, 1997, M.908; *Cegetel/Vodafone/SFR*, D.Comm. December 19, 1997, M.1055; *BT/AirTouch, Airtel*, D.Comm. July 8, 1998, JV. 3.

– *Printing Presses*
Omnigraph/Roland, D.Comm. May 5, 1999, M.1448.

– *Publicity: Eurocom/RSCG*, D.Comm. December 18, 1991, M.147.

– *Pumps (industrial – mobile pumps)*
Bosch/Rexroth, D.Comm. January 12, 2001, 2004 OJ L 43/1, points 21–57.

– *Rail Transport*
Railway vehicles (submarkets according to local or cross-country traffic): *ABB/Brel*, D.Comm. May 26, 1992, M.221.
Magnetic railways: *Adtranz/Siemens/Thyssen/Transrapid*, D.Comm. March 9, 1998, M.987.
Railway vehicles (maintenance, design, assembly and sale): *Babcock/Siemens/ BSRailcare*, D.Comm. June 30, 1995, M.542.
Rail transport material: *Voest Alpine Stahl/Vossloh*, D.Comm. October 10, 1998, M.1259.
Components (brakes; wheels, aftermarket): *Cardo/Thyssen*, D.Comm. December 2, 1996, M.818.
Railroad forwarding services: *Dan Transport/Inter Forward*, D.Comm. May 25, 1998, M.1170.

– *Retail Trade*
Wholesale – cash-and-carry: *Kesko/Tuko*, D.Comm. November 20, 1996, OJ 1997 L110/53, points 14–20.
Different forms of distribution (hyper, super, discount): *Tengelmann/GrupepoPAM*, D.Comm. March 10, 1998, M.1105; *Promodes/S21/Gruppo GS*, D.Comm. March 10, 1998, M.1086; *Promodes/Casino*, D.Comm. October 30, 1997, M.991; *Intermarché/Spar*, D.Comm. June 30, 1997, M.946; *SPAR/Pro*, D.Comm. 15 January 1998, M.1071.
Mail-order: *Otto/Grattan*, D.Comm. March 21, 1991, M.070; *LaRedoute/Empire*, D.Comm. April 25, 1991, M.80.
Food retailing: *Rewe/Billa*, D.Comm. 27 August 1996, M.803; *Rewe/Meinl*, D.Comm. February 3, 1999, M.1221.
Full line of products: *McCormick/CPC/Rabobank/Ostmann*, D.Comm. October 29, 1993, M.330, point 40 (spices).
Specialized retailing: *ADEG/EDEKA*, D.Comm. November 9, 1998, M.1303; *Blokker/Toys 'R' Us*, D.Comm. June 26, 1997, 1998 OJ L 316/1, points 27–42 (toys).
Retailing of Books: *Advent InternationaVEMI/WH Smith*, D.Comm. March 24, 1998, M.1112.
Electrical retailing: *Kingfisher/BUT*, D.Comm. August 21, 1998, M.1248.

– *Satellites*
Military – civil: *Alcatel/Thomson CSF-SCS*, D.Comm. June 4, 1998, M.1185.
Simulation technologies: *Krauss-Maffei/Wegmann*, D.Comm. June 19, 1998, M.1153.

– *Seeds*
Basic seed – certified seed: *BASF/Svalof Weibull*, D.Comm. March 3, 1999, M.1420.

– *Steel Products*
  Cold-rolled stainless steel, electrical sheets: *Thyssen/Krupp/Riva/Falck/Tadfin/AST*, D.Comm. December 21, 1994, 1995 OJ L 251; *Krupp II*, D.Comm. May 2, 1996, M.740; *Thyssen/Krupp*, D.Comm. June 2, 1998, M.1080.
  Flat steel products: *Krupp Hoesch/Thyssen*, D.Comm. August 11, 1997, M.925/ECSC.1243. Sheets: *Usinor/Finarvedi*, D.Comm. September 29, 1998, M.1203.
  Tubes: *Mannesmann/Hoesch*, D.Comm. November 12, 1992, M.222, OJ L 114/34; *Mannesmann/Vallourec/Ilva*, D.Comm. January 31, 1994, 1994 OJ L 102; *Mannesmann/Vallourec*, D.Comm. June 3, 1997, M.906; *British Steel/Europipe*, D.Comm. February 26, 1998, M.1014; *Usinor/Finarvedi*, D.Comm. September 29, 1998, M.1203.
  Steel raw products to be separated from processed products which are not covered by the ECSC Treaty but by the EC Treaty: *Premsag/Voest-Alpine*, D.Comm. October 1, 1997, M.979.

– *Telecommunications*
  Digital power line products: *Nortel/Norweb*, D.Comm. March 18, 1998, M.1113.
  Data networking products: *Nortel/Bay*, D.Comm. August 21, 1998, M.1263.
  Domestic and international voice and data telecommunications services: *Tele-nordic/BT/Teledanmark/Telenor*, D.Comm. April 24, 1995, M.570; *Mannesmann/Olivetti/Infostrada*, D.Comm. January 15, 1998, M.1025.
  Global telecommunication services for multinational corporate customers: *BT/AT&T*, D.Comm. March 30, 1999, JV. 15.
  GSM connection – voice telephony: *Telecom Eireann*, D.Comm. December 18, 1996, M.802.
  Internet services: *Worldcom/MCI*, D.Comm. July 8, 1998, M.1069.
  Telecommunications equipment: *Siemens/Italtel*, D.Comm. February 17, 1995, 1995 OJ L 1161/27.
  Network – terminal equipment – services: *Bell Cablemedia/Cable & Wireless/Videotron*, D.Comm. December 11, 1996, M.853; *Cable & Wireless/Nynex/Bell Canada*, D.Comm. December 11, 1996, M.865; *Deutsche Telekom/Beta-Research*, D.Comm. May 27, 1998, M.1027.
  TV networks (terrestrial, satellite, cable): *MSG Media Service*, D.Comm. November 9, 1994, 1994 OJ L 364/1; *Hermes Europe Railtel*, D.Comm. March 5, 1996, M.683 (pan-European telecommunications network along the rights of way of railway undertakings and telecommunications operators).
  Pay-TV; technical services for pay-TV: *Bertelsmann/Kirch/Première*, D.Comm. May 27, 1998, 1999 OJ L 53/1, points 18–25.
  Satellite TV: *Nordic Satellite Distribution*, D.Comm. July 19, 1995, 1996 OJ L 53/20.
  Pay television: *TPS*, D.Comm. April 30, 2002, JV. 57, points 14–15.

TV broadcasting – TV advertising: *RTL/Veronica/Endemol I*, D.Comm. September 20, 1995, 1996 OJ L 134121; *RTL/Veronica/Endemol II*, D.Comm. July 17, 1996, 1998 OJ L 294.
Transmission equipment and public switching: *GEC/GPTH*, D.Comm. July 27, 1998, M.1226; *VoestAlpineStahl/Vossloh*, D.Comm. October 10, 1998, M.1259.

– *Tourism*
Distinction between business and leasure trips: *West L.B./Thomas Cook/LTU*, D.Comm. June 30, 1993, M.350; *Havas Voyage/American Express*, D.Comm. April 6, 1995, M.564; *Wagons-Lits/Carlson*, D.Comm. March 7, 1997, M.867; *BBL/American Express*, D.Comm. April 29, 1998, M.1102.
Package holiday market – cruise market: *Costa Crociere/Chargeurs/Accor*, D.Comm. July 19, 1993, M.334; cruises: *Carnval Corporation/P&O Princess*, D.Comm. July 24, 2002, M.2706, points 100–112.

– *Track Fastening Systems*
Voest Alpine Stahl/Vossloh, D.Comm. October 10, 1998, M.1259.

– *Transport*
International land transport: *Stinnes/BTL*, D.Comm. February 4, 1998, M.1056.
Transshipment traffic: *Hutchinson/ECT*, D.Comm. November 29, 2001, JV. 56, points 12–16.
See air transport, rail transport.

– *Waste Management*
Ordinary waste – industrial waste: *Waste Management International*, D.Comm. December 21, 1992, M.283; *Rhone Poulenc/Lyonnaise des Eaux*, D.Comm. November 26, 1992, M.266; *Lyonnaise des Earn/Suez*, D.Comm. June 5, 1997, M.916.
Hazardous – non-hazardous waste: *GKN/Brambles/SKP*, D.Comm. May 26, 1998, M.1160.
Recycling services: *GKN/Brambles*, D.Comm. June 9, 1994, M.448.

– *Water*
Collection, purification and distribution of water: *Lyonnaise des Eaux/Northumbrian Water*, D.Comm. December 21, 1995, M.567; *FCC/Vivendi*, March 4, 1999, M.1365.

(c) Relevant Geographic Market

Need of Sufficiently Homogeneous Market Conditions.
The relevant geographic market is described in Article 9 (7) of the Regulation 139/2004 as:

> 'the area in which the undertakings concerned are involved in the supply and demand of products or services, in which the conditions of competition are sufficiently homogeneous and which can be distinguished from neighbouring areas because, in particular, conditions of competition are appreciably different in those areas. This assessment should take account in particular of the nature and characteristics of the products or services concerned, of the existence of entry barriers or of consumer preferences, of appreciable differences of the undertakings' market shares between the area concerned and neighbouring areas or of substantial price differences.'[286]

Still National Markets but Trend to a Wider Geographic Market Definition.
The Commission used to define the relevant geographic market mainly on a country-by-country basis because of the tendency of suppliers to organize their distribution network within each national market and of the consumer preference to buy 'national' (for linguistic and other reasons). Now national markets are becoming more and more integrated into a single European market. The Commission stated in its Notice on the Definition of the Relevant Market[287] that it will take into account the continuing process of market integration. The measures adopted and implemented in the internal market program to remove barriers of trade and further integrate the Community markets cannot be ignored when assessing the effects of a transaction. Accordingly, the Commission tends to define the geographic market more broadly than in its past administrative practice in order to take into account the growing 'europeanization'[288] or 'globalization' of the markets.[289] Examples include markets which used to be separated by government

---

286. *See* Notice on the definition of the relevant market, point 8, and *SCPA/Kali + Salz – MdK*, ECJ March 31, 1998, 1998 ECR I-1375 para. 143. Although the definition is given in the context of the referral of cases to member states because of a 'distinct market' problem and is termed the 'geographical reference market', it is repeated word for word in section 5 of the 'CO' merger notification form under the heading 'relevant geographic market'. The wording is clearly reminiscent of the definition of relevant geographic market as developed in the Court's case law (*see*, in particular, *United Brands*, ECJ Feb. 14, 1978, 1978 ECR 207, paras 10–11 and 44).
287. 1997 OJ C 372/3, point 32; Guidelines on the Assessment of Horizontal Mergers, 2004 OJ L 31, point 10.
288. *Procter & Gamble/Schickedanz*, D.Comm. June 21, 1994, 1994 OJ L 354/32, point 104; *Pirelli/BICC*, D.Comm. July 19, 2000, M.1882.
289. Twenty-eighth Report on Competition Policy, point 134 (insert 5).

regulatory measures and consumer preferences that have become increasingly open to competitors from other countries.[290] However, in various cases the Commission still proceeds to an alternative evaluation of the parties' aggregate market shares on a narrower (national or regional) and a wider (European) market.[291]

Examples.
The determination of the relevant geographic market within which suppliers compete is an economic and factual assessment. The Commission has found world, European (including EEA countries), Community, national, regional and local markets. Examples include:

– *World Market:*
Fungible products that can be easily transported, are refined to the same purity standards throughout the world and readily traded without trade barriers, such as platinum and rhodium: *Gencor/Lonrho*, D.Comm. April 24, 1996, 1997 OJ L 11/30, points 68–73, *aff'd* CFI March 25, 1999, T-1021/96; *Anglo American Corporation/Lonrho*, D.Comm. April 23, 1997, 1998 OJ L 149/21, points 94–99;
Aircraft: *Aerospatiale-Alenia/DeHavilland*, D.Comm. October 2, 1991, 1991 OJ L 334142, point 20; *Boeing/McDonnell Douglas*, D.Comm. July 30, 1997, 1997 OJ L 336/16, para. 20;
Aircraft components: *Rolls Royce, SIA, HAESL*, D.Comm. May 11, 1999 (engines); *SNECMA/TI*, D.Comm. January 17, 1994, M.368 (landing gears);
Production of passenger cars is international or even global in its outlook, but the exact definition of the geographic market has been left open until now: *Ford/Mazda*, D.Comm. 24 May 1996, M.741; *Daimler-Benz/Chrysler*, D.Comm. July 22, 1998, M.1204; *Toyota/Daihatsu*, D.Comm. November 6, 1998, M.1326;
Global telecommunications services for multinational corporate customers: *Worldcom/MCI*, D.Comm. July 8, 1998, M.1137; *BT/AT&T*, D.Comm. March 30, 1999, JV. 15;
Spatial telecommunications (satellites): *Alcatel/Thomson CSF-SCS*, D.Comm. June 4, 1998, M.1185, points 23–24;
Reinsurance and asset management because of the need to pool risks on an international basis: *BAT/Zürich*, D.Comm. February 16, 1998, M.1043, point 10.

– *Third Country – European Country Links:*
International voice telephony: *British Telecom/MCI*, D.Comm. May 14, 1997, 1997 OJ L 336/1.

---

290. *See Siemens/Elektrowatt*, D.Comm. Nov. 18, 1997, 1999 OJ L 88/1, points 40–44; *TNT Post Group/Jet Services*, D.Comm. Feb. 15, 1999, M.1405.
291. *See AT&T/Philips*, D.Comm. Feb. 5, 1996, M.651.

– *West-European Market, including the EEA Countries*:
  Easily traded products of a similar standard with a European-wide marketing strategy by manufacturers and low transport costs: *Celanese/Degussa/JV*, D.Comm. June 11, 2003, 2004 OJ L 38/47, points 86–91 (chemical intermediates); *Philips/Lucent Technologies*, D.Comm. January 6, 1998, M.1358 (electronic consumer communications terminal devices): *International Paper/Union Camp*, D.Comm. February 5, 1999, M.1391, points 30–31 (resins); *DuPont/Hoechst/Herberts*, D.Comm. February 5, 1999, M.1363, point V (coatings); *Mannesmann/Demag/DeLaval Stork*, D.Comm. December 21, 1994, M.535 (compressors); *Pirelli/BICC*, D.Comm. July 19, 2000, M.1822, point 33 (cables).
  Automotive lubricants specified according to international standards: despite national governments' price influences the relevant market tends to be broader than national markets: *BP/Mobil*, D.Comm. August 7, 1996, M.727; *Total/Petrofina*, D.Comm. March 26, 1999, M.1464; Services provided to multinational clients requiring professional services in several countries: *Price Waterhouse/Coopers & Lybrand*, D.Comm. May 20, 1998, 1999 OJ L 50/27, point 57 (audit and accounting services); Substantial trade flows between countries (customers buying directly from different suppliers): *Agfa-Gevaert/DuPont*, D.Comm. February 11, 1998, 1998 OJ L 211/22, points 37–41 (offset printing plates); *SCPA/Kali + Salz-MdK*, ECJ March 31, 1998, 1998 ECR I-1375, paras 127–151 (potash) (with respect to the European market outside Germany); *Shell/Montecatini*, D.Comm. June 8, 1994, 1994 OJ L 332/48 (polypropylene); EEA markets despite imports from third countries without, however, having an impact on the price-setting of the products in question: *Saint Gobain/Wacker*, D.Comm. December 4, 1996, 1997 OJ L 247/1, points 99–136 (silicones).
  Electricity: gradual liberalization of electricity markets has led the markets for production and sales of power cables to evolve as Community-wide (even if not yet reflected in market shares): *Pirelli/BICC*, D.Comm. July 19, 2000, M.1882.

– *EEA markets including eastern countries* (the new member states): *BASF/Eurodiol/Pantochim*, D.Comm. July 11, 2001, M.2314, point 42; *Celanese/Degussa/JV (Euroepan Oxo-Chemicals)*, D.Comm. June 11, 2003, 2004 OJ L 38/47, points 86 and 141.

– *National Markets:*
  Countries which are isolated because of particularly high cost of imports: *SCPA/Kali + Salz-MdK*, ECJ March 31, 1998, 1998 ECR I-1375 *Kali/Salz/MdK II*, D.Comm. July 9, 1998, M.308, point 17 (potash) (with respect to the German market);
  Countries which are isolated because of high transport costs: *Haniel/Cementbouw/JV*, D.Comm. June 26, 2002, M.2650, points 82–84 (cement).

Countries which are isolated because of existing state aids preventing imports: *RAG/Saarbergwerke/Preussag Anthrazit*, D.Comm. July 29, 1998, ECSC 1252, point 23 (coal);
Markets which are isolated from each other because of regulatory barriers, such as administrative procedures for pharmaceuticals: *Pfizer/Pharmacia*, D.Comm. February 27, 2003, M.2922, point 62–64, or insurance: *AXA/UAP*, D.Comm. December 20, 1996, M.862; *Allianz/AGF*, D.Comm. May 8, 1998, M.1082; however, these regulatory differences are becoming smaller, and there is a trend towards Europeanization of former national markets: *Siemens/Elektrowatt*, D.Comm. November 18, 1997, 1999 OJ L88/1, points 40–44; *TNT Post Group/Jet Services*, D.Comm. February 15, 1999, M.1405;
Markets which are not yet liberalized, such as telecommunication networks: *Nordic Satellite Distribution*, D.Comm. July 19, 1995, 1996 OJ L 53/20, point 73; *Mannesmann/Olivetti/Infostrada*, D.Comm. January 15, 1998, M.1025; *Telecom UTA/TelecomAG/Swisscom*, D.Comm. July 13, 1998, M.1199;
Electricity wholesale market: *Vilar Mir/EnBW/Cantabrico*, D.Comm. September 26, 2001, 2004 OJ L 48/86, points 24–26;
Preferences to buy 'national': *ABB/Daimler Benz*, D.Comm. October 18, 1995, 1997 OJ L 11/29 (railway equipment); *Mercedes-Benz/Kässbohrer*, D.Comm. February 14, 1995, 1995 OJ L 211/1 (transit buses and intercity coaches); *Renault/Iveco*, D.Comm. October 22, 1998, M.1202 (buses); *British Aerospace/Saab*, D.Comm. July 3, 1998, M.1198 (aircraft and components for defence purposes);
Consumer preferences and habits differ from one national market to the other, necessitating national sales policies and distinct economic operators without substantial parallel trade: *Royal Philips Electronics*, CFI April 3, 2003, T-119/02, paras. 94–103; *Blokker/Toys 'R'Us*, D.Comm. June 26, 1997, 1998 OJ L 316/1, points 39–42 (toys); *Siemens/Drägerwerk*, D.Comm. April 30, 2003, 2003 OJ L 291/1, point 69 (conservative nature of customer preferences); *SEB/Moulinex*, D.Comm. January 8, 2002, M.2621, point 13 (Article 9 (3) decision) (household appliances).
Supply of goods to retail and to cash-and-carry customers: *Kesko/Tuco*, D.Comm. November 20, 1996, 1997 OJ L 110/53, points 36–37; *Procter &Gamble/VB Schickedanz*, D.Comm. June 21, 1994, 1994 OJ L 354/32, points 76–104 (however, with a trend towards a possible Europeanization of national and regional markets); *CHS/Vobis*, D.Comm. August 21, 1998, M.1265; *Danish Crown*, D.Comm. March 9, 1999, M.1313;
Deliveries of refined products by truck: *Texaco/Norsk Hydro*, D.Comm. January 9, 1995, M.511;
National express delivery: *DHL/Deutsche Post*, D.Comm. June 26, 1998, M.1168, points 22–25;
TV broadcasting: *RTL/Veronica/Endemol*, D.Comm. September 20, 1995, 1996 OJ L 134/21;

Banking and insurance services supplied to national clients: *Insecurazioni/Banca di Roma*, D.Comm. March 3, 1996, M.707;
Technical assistance services provided to national customers: *Siemens/Elektrowatt*, D.Comm. November 18, 1997, 1999 OJ L 88/1, point 42.

- *Regional Markets Crossing National Borders*
  Special characteristics and prohibitive transport costs beyond a reasonable distance (e.g. 300 km): *Cargill/Vandemoortele*, D.Comm. July 20, 1998, M.1227, point 24 (oilseeds); *REWE/Meinl*, D.Comm. February 3, 1999, M.1221; *MMP/AFP*, D.Comm. March 3, 1999, M.1442;
  Cultural and linguistic frontiers: *Thorn EMI/Virgin Music*, D.Comm. April 27, 1992, M.202, point 58 (records and compact discs); *MSG Media Service*, D.Comm. November 9, 1994, 1994 OJ L 364/1, point 47 (pay TV); *Bertelsmann/Kirch/Première*, D.Comm. May 27, 1998, 1999 OJ L 53/1, point 22 (pay TV).

- *Local Markets* (provided they are a substantial part of the Common Market):
  Retail trade in consumer goods (however, various local markets may be combined into a national market): *Delhaize/PG*, D.Comm. August 22, 1994, M.47; *Kesko/Tuko*, D.Comm. November 20, 1996, M.784; *Promodes/S21/Gruppo GS*, D.Comm. March 10, 1998, M.1086; *Rewe/Meinl*, D.Comm. February 3, 1999, M.1221 (groceries);
  Distribution of gas: *Gaz de France/BEWAG/GASAG*, D.Comm. January 20, 1999, M.1402; *ECS/Sibelga*, D.Comm. December 19, 2003, M.3318.
  Dependence of gas consumers on short-term delivery contracts with regional suppliers: *EnBW/ENI/GVS*, D.Comm. December 17, 2002, M.2822.
  Distribution of electricity (unlike the generation of electricity which is a national market): *EOF/London Electricity*, D.Comm. January 27, 1999, M.1346, points 18–25; *EDFI/ESTAG*, D.Comm. March 17, 1998, M.1107.
  Pipeline networks: *Shell/DEA*, D.Comm. December 20, 2001, M.2839, point 17.
  Airport management services: *Birmingham International Airport*, D.Comm. March 25, 1997, M.785; *Hochtief/Aer Rianta/Düsseldorf Airport*, D.Comm. December 22, 1997, M.1035;
  Harbour operation services: *Pakhoed/Van Ommeren*, M.1145, Twenty-eighth Report on Competition Policy, point 162;
  Provision of credits for local entities: *Dexia/Argentaria/Credito local*, D.Comm. October 28, 1998, M.1279).

2. General Criteria for Assessing Mergers Likely to Significantly Impede Effective Competiton

(a) The Scope of the Merger Control Regulation

Application to All Types of Transactions.
Regulation 139/2004 applies to all types of transactions having a Community dimension which would significantly impede effective competition in the Common Market, in particular as a result of the creation or strengthening of a dominant position, irrespective of the economic sector concerned, the horizontal, vertical or conglomerate nature of the transaction and the involvement of the merging or other parties (single or collective 'dominance').

Industry-Wide Application.
The merger control regulation applies to all industries, including – since July 20, 2002 – to the coal and steel sectors, thereby replacing the sector-specific merger control under Article 6 of the ECSC Treaty.[292]

Horizontal v. Vertical and Conglomerate Mergers.
The merger control regulation applies to:

- *horizontal* mergers, i.e. mergers between companies which are active on the same relevant market(s) or are potential competitors on such market(s) and where the merger gives rise to horizontal overlaps between the activities of the parties, such as a merger between companies operating in the same mineral resources field,[293]
- *vertical* mergers, i.e. mergers between companies which operate at a different level of the production, transformation or distribution chain, such as a merger between a manufacturer of packaging equipment and a supplier of cartons for filling machines,[294]
- *conglomerate* mergers, i.e. mergers between companies which are not in a direct horizontal or vertical relationship, either as direct competitors or as suppliers and customers, such as a merger between suppliers of products which are not directly substitutable but belong to a portfolio of products all of which are

292. *See* Commission Communication 2002 OJ C 152/5. The procedures for processing mergers under the ECSC and EC Treaty were already aligned by Notice 1998 OJ C 66/36, e.g. *Usinor, Arbed, Aceralia*, D.Comm. Nov. 2, 2001, 2003 OJ L 88/1.

293. *Gencor*, CFI March 25, 1999, 1999 ECR II-753. *See* Guidelines on Horizontal Mergers, point 5: 'when the undertakings concerned are actual or potential competitors on the same relevant markets'.

294. *Tetra Laval*, CFI Oct. 25, 2002, 2002 ECR II-4519.

normally demanded by the same customers, to the disadvantage of competitors supplying only some products.[295]

A merger may simultaneously have horizontal, vertical and conglomerate dimensions, as in the case *General Electric/Honeywell*[296] where the Commission based its prohibition decision mostly on conglomerate and vertical integration: foreclosure of Honeywell's competitors as independent suppliers of engine controls to jet engine manufacturers competing with General Electric (GE) and leverage ability to foster the placement of GE's products through the extension of its GE product assortment to include Honeywell products.[297]

Single and Collective Market Power Subject to Merger Control.
Although neither Regulation 1310/97 nor Regulation 139/2004 expressly says so, the merger control regulation applies to single firm and collective market power that creates or strengthens a dominant position (Regulation 1310/97) or significantly impedes effective competition (Regulation 139/2004). Not only transactions which create or strengthen an individual firm's market power – that is to say a position held by the *parties* to the transaction – may be prohibited under the regulation, but also the creation or strengthening of a *collective* position, that is to say one held by the parties to the transaction together with one or more undertakings not parties thereto. The Commission held in *Nestlé/Perrier*[298] and *Gencor/Lonrho*,[299] and the Court of Justice[300] and the Court of First Instance[301] confirmed, that the merger control regulation applies to the creation or strengthening of a *collective* dominant position as a result of which effective competition would be significantly impeded even if some members of the dominant group are not party to the transaction in question. The Court concluded that a failure to apply the merger control prohibition under such circumstances would be liable to prove incompatible with the system of undistorted competition laid down by Article 3 (g) of the EC Treaty. In *Airtours*,[302] which concerned the *creation* of a collective dominant position (which did not exist prior to the merger), the Court of First Instance confirmed the applicability of the merger control regulation to the creation of a collective dominant position but overturned the Commission's findings for lack of adequate proof that the members of the resulting oligopoly were likely to adopt on a lasting basis a common policy ('tacit coordination sustainable over time').

295. *BaByliss*, CFI April 3, 2003, T-114/02, paras. 309–354.
296. *General Electric/Honeywell*, D.Comm. July 3, 2001, M.2220 (appeal still pending).
297. *See also YLE/TDF (France Telecom)/Digita/JV*, D.Comm. June 26, 2001, M.2300.
298. *Nestlé/Perrier*, D.Comm. July 22, 1992, 1992 OJ L 356/1.
299. *Genco/Lonrho*, D.Comm. April 24, 1996, 1997 OJ L 11/30.
300. *SCPA/Kali* + Salz – *MdK*, ECJ March 31, 1998, 1998 ECR I-1375, para. 166.
301. *Gencor/Lonrho*, CFI March 25, 1999, 1999 ECR II-753, para. 125.
302. *Airtours*, CFI June 6, 2002, 2002 ECR II-2585, paras 57–64, 294–295.

Plan of the Following Sections.
The following sections deal with:

- the new concept of Regulation 139/2004 (under (b));
- the calculation and evaluation of market shares (under (c));
- the assessment of corroborating and countervailing factors (under (d));
- the particulars when assessing oligopolies (under (e));
- the particulars when assessing vertical and conglomerate mergers (under (f)), and
- the assessment of anticompetitive coordination in the framework of joint ventures (under (g)).

(b) The New Concept of Regulation 139/2004

New Basic Approach.
Article 2 of Regulation 139/2004 empowers the Commission to act against mergers and full-function joint ventures that would significantly impede effective competition in the Common Market[303] or the EEA[304] or a substantial part of it, in particular as a result of creating or strenghtening a dominant position.[305] In Regulation 1310/97 the order of the two criteria was reversed: Article 2 of Regulation 1310/97 empowered the Commission to act against the creation or strengthening of a dominant position as a result of which effective competition would be significantly impeded in the Common Market or a substantial part of it. The difference seems evident: Under Regulation 1310/97 a dominant position was not prohibited where it did not significantly impede effective competition, whereas under Regulation 139/2004 effective competition can be significantly impeded even where a dominant position is neither created nor strengthened.[306] The new concept is intended to widen the scope for intervention under the merger control. Recital 25 states:

> 'The notion of 'significant impediment of effective competition' in Article 2 (2) and (3) should be interpreted as extending, beyond the concept of

---

303. Article 2 (2) and (3) of Regulation 139/2004.
304. Article 57 of the EEA Agreement.
305. A dominant position is, according to the Court of Justice's well established definition, 'a position of economic strength enjoyed by an undertaking which enables it to prevent effective competion from being maintained on the relevant market by affording it the power to behave to an appreciable extent independently of its competitors, its customers and ultimately of its consumers': Under Article 82: *United Brands*, ECJ Feb. 14, 1978, 1978 ECR 207, para. 65; under the merger control regulation: *SCPA/Kali* + Salz – *MdK*, ECJ March 31, 1998, 1998 ECR I-1375, para. 170; *Gencor/Lonrho*, CFI March 25, 1999, 1999 ECR II-753, para. 200; Guidelines on the Assessment of Horizontal Mergers, point 2.
306. *ARD/BSkyB –Kirch Pay TV*, CFI Sept. 30, 2003, T-158/00, para. 130. *See also Mannesmann/ Hoesch*, D.Comm. Nov. 12, 1992, 1993 OJ L 114/34, points 103–104.

dominance, only to the anti-competitive effects of a concentration resulting from the non-coordinated behaviour of undertakings which would not have a dominant position on the market concerned.'

The Commission's Guidelines on the Assessment of Horizontal Mergers read in conjunction with the new Regulation 139/2004 clearly extend its reach in a new approach to single and collective market power positions by stating that effective competition can be significantly impeded in two ways:

- By eliminating important competitive constraints on one or more firms (i.e., single or collective dominance), which consequently would have increased market power, without resorting to coordinated behaviour (*non-coordinated effects*);
- By changing the nature of competition in such a way that firms that previously were not coordinating their behaviour, are now significantly more likely to coordinate and raise prices or otherwise harm effective competition. A merger may also make coordination easier, more stable or more effective for firms which were coordinating prior to the merger (*coordinated effects*).[307]

Non-Coordinated Effects – Unilateral Effects.
The 'non-coordinated effects' concept concerns a single firm which is able to increase its prices regardless of the response of its remaining competitors, thereby enjoying a position which gives rise to *unilateral effects*.[308] This new concept will allow the Commission to challenge mergers at levels of market share *below* the traditional thresholds for finding single firm dominance and to cover cases which were previously pursued under the collective dominance test. Under the well established case law,[309] a *single* firm's dominance may be found in cases where the firm has a very large post-merger market share (of at least 40–50%), which is appreciably larger than the next competitors and therefore in itself is evidence of the existence of a dominant position.[310] According to the new concept, a firm with a lower post-merger market share may, by its *unilateral effects*, significantly impede effective competition, provided the following conditions are fulfilled:

307. Guidelines on the Assessment of Horizontal Mergers, 2004 OJ C 31/5, point 22. *See* Derek Ridyard, The Commission's new horizontal merger guidelines – an economic commentary, paper prepared by Université libre de Bruxelles on 17 February 2004 for The DGCOMP.
308. This term is used in the Commission's Guidelines on the Assessment of Horizontal Mergers in fn. 27.
309. Under Article 82: *Hilti*, CFI Dec. 12, 1991, 1991 ECR II-1439, para. 92, *aff'd* ECJ March 2, 1994, 1994 ECR I-667 (70–80%).Under the merger control regulation: *Blokker/Toys 'R' Us*, D.Comm. June 26, 1997, 1998 OJ L 316/1 (55%); *Endemol*, CFI April 28, 1999, 1999 ECR II-1299, para. 134.
310. Guidelines on the Assessment of Horizontal Mergers, points 4, 17 and 25.

(i) The merger eliminates an important competitive force;[311]
(ii) The merging firms have a combined market share exceeding 25%, and the transaction results in a firm that is appreciably larger than its next competitor;[312]
(iii) The merging firms are close competitors supplying goods with a high degree of substitutability;[313]
(iv) The customers have limited possibilities of switching suppliers[314] because the competitors are unlikely to increase supply if prices increase (lack of retaliatory reactions);[315] and
(v) The merged entity is able to hinder expansion by competitors, in particular because of its technological, economic and financial advatages.[316]

By contrast, where the merged entity has a market share larger than, but close to, those of its next competitors the merger would have to be assessed under the *collective* dominance concept and need evaluation of the '*coordinated effects*'.

Coordinated Effects – Tacit Collusion.
With respect to oligopolies the new 'significantly impede effective competition' standard goes *beyond* the definition of dominance.[317] On a concentrated market characterized by the existence of a few players, symmetry of market shares,[318] homogeneous products and a stable economic environment[319] there is a likelihood of common conduct ('coordinated effects') if the following conditions are fulfilled:[320]

311. *Ibid.*, points 37–38.
312. Recital 32 to Regulation 139/2004; Guidelines on the Assessment of Horizontal Mergers, point 18. The UK competition authority held in *LloydsTSB/Abbey National* that the post-merger entity would become the leader (acquiring a market share of 27%) on a market shared with three smaller competitors (a 'paramount' market position compared to its next rivals), although the UK competition authority also examined the coordinated effects between the members of the oligopoly: *Abbey National/Lloyds TSB Bank*, UK Office of Fair Trading, Report under Section 125 (4) of the Fair Trading Act 1973 of 18 June 2001.
313. *Ibid.*, points 28–30.
314. *Ibid.*, point 31.
315. *Ibid.*, points 32–35.
316. *Ibid.*, point 36.
317. Recital 25 to Regulation 139/2004; Guidelines on the Assessment of Horizontal Mergers, point 39.
318. E.g., *Exxon/Mobil*, D.Comm. Sept. 29, 1999, M.1383, point 477.
319. Guidelines on the Assessment of Horizontal Mergers, points 15, 39 and 45 (in particular stable (non-volatile) market shares).
320. *Ibid.*, points 39–57, focusing in particular on the ability to monitor the credible deterrent mechanism and the reactions of outsiders.

(i) The operators have similar views regarding which actions would be considered to be in accordance with the aligned behaviour and are able to adopt coordinated conduct, in particular because they are relatively symmetric in terms of market shares, cost structures, capacity levels and levels of vertical integration;[321]
(ii) The operators are able to monitor deviations, the predicate of which is sufficient transparency;[322]
(iii) There is sufficient certainty that the deterrent mechanism could be activated (credible threat to timely and sufficient retaliation);[323] and
(iv) Competitors and customers are unable to jeopardize the common conduct.[324]

These criteria for assessing coordinated effects overlap with those which predicate unilateral effects and conform with those established and examined by the Court of First Instance in its *Airtours* judgment,[325] as may be more apparent if the merger eliminates an important actual or potential competitor or creates or strengthens market power in upstream markets.[326] They are necessary for assessing whether a transaction significantly impedes effective competition in the two different scenarios: the creation or strengthening of single or collective market power. The 'non-coordinated effects' may therefore be described as the unilateral effects of single market power, whereas 'coordinated effects' may be misleading (because it still presupposes a certain action and not a mere passive reaction) and therefore is better described as 'tacit coordination', a term which was already used by the Court of Justice in the *Airtours* case,[327] or 'tacit collusion', as used in the IDEI, Toulouse, final report for DGCOMP of March 2003 entitled 'The Economics of Tacit Collusion', which was the basis for the Commission's Guidelines on the Assessment of Horizontal Mergers.[328]

Two Main Scenarios.
Two main scenarios arise:

- The merger *strengthens* collective dominance which already existed prior to the merger: in this case the members of the oligopoly were probably already coordinating or aligning their conduct in the market prior to the merger without

321. *Ibid.*, points 44–51.
322. *Ibid.*, points 49–51.
323. *Ibid.*, points 52–55.
324. *Ibid.*, points 56–57.
325. *Airtours*, CFI June 6, 2002, 2002 ECR II-2585, paras. 61–62.
326. Guidelines on the Assessment of Horizontal Mergers, points 61–63.
327. *Airtours*, CFI June 6, 2002, 2002 ECR II-2585, para. 83.
328. Authors: Marc Ivaldi, Bruno Jullien, Patrick Rey, Paul Seabright and Jean Tirole. Available on the Commission's website.

necessarily infringing Article 81.[329] The merger is in this case likely to significantly impede effective competition by making coordination or aligment 'easier, more stable or more effective'.[330] This was the scenario in the *Gencor/Lonrho* case.[331] In such a case it is rather up to the parties to show that the merger will *not* make coordination easier or more effective or will even *disrupt* that coordination.[332]

- The merger *creates* collective dominance which did not exist prior to the merger: in this case the merging parties were not coordinating or aligning their conduct prior to the merger. The merger is likely to significantly impede effective competition by eliminating the competitive constraints that the parties exerted previously on each other and by increasing its market power over the remaining competitors.[333] In other terms, the merging parties and their competitors are more likely to act in an anticompetitive manner (loss of competitive constraints) 'without resorting to coordinated behaviour'.[334] This was the scenario in the *Airtours* case, which is more difficult to prove because of the uncertainty of reasonably predicting future changes to the market.

This implies a very complex prospective analysis which may, despite the broader approach of Regulation 139/2004, lead to different conclusions by the Commission and the Court of Justice as shown in the *Airtours* case.

Conclusions.
In sum, the new merger control Regulation 139/2004 extends the prohibition to transactions that do not create a dominant postion but that are nevertheless likely to result in non-coordinated anticompetitive consequences that may not have infringed previous versions of the merger control regulation. The objective of the new concept is to maintain effective competition on oligopolistic markets and to act against mergers which significantly impede effective competition by eliminating important competitive constraints that the merging firms had exerted on each other or by reducing competitive pressure on the remaining competitors, even in the absence of the likelihood of coordination between the members of the oligopoly.[335] The merger is to be prohibited even though anticompetitive behaviour may be *non-coordinated* and therefore not infringe Article 81, but nevertheless results from an alignment of common interests to adopt on a lasting basis a common policy with the aim of selling at above competitive prices and without any

329. *Gencor/Lonrho*, CFI March 25, 1999, 1999 ECR II-753, para. 276.
330. Guidelines on the Assessment of Horizontal Mergers, point 22.
331. *Gencor/Lonrho*, CFI March 25, 1999, 1999 ECR II-753.
332. *See* Derek Ridyard, *op.cit.*, page 5.
333. Guidelines on the Assessment of Horizontal Mergers, point 25.
334. *Ibid.*, point 22.
335. Recital 25 to Regulation 139/2004.

actual or potential competitors, let alone customers or consumers, being able to react effectively.[336]

The new concept brings the EC law closer to the U.S. antitrust law, to which the IDEI Study expressly refers.[337] It is therefore not surprising that EC and U.S. competition law arrive at similar conclusions:

- a reduction from 4 to 3 independent companies within an oligopoly raises serious doubts under U.S. law[338] and has been considered by the Court of First Instance in the *Airtours* case as necessitating specific proofs (which the Commission failed to supply);
- a reduction from 3 to 2 is, as a rule, prohibited under U.S. antitrust law and was also prohibited under EC antitrust law in the *Gencor/Lonrho* case because it strengthened an already existing collective dominant position.[339]

(c) Importance of Market Shares

Market Shares as Primary Indication of Market Power.
In the case of horizontal mergers market shares held by the parties are the primary indication of the competitive importance of both the parties and their competitors. They may be corroborated by customer preference information in order to evaluate potential changes of market shares in the near future as well as by an analysis of entry barriers, buying power or efficiencies likely to enhance the incentive of the merged entity to act pro-competitively for the benefit of consumers, thereby counteracting the negative effects on competition which the merger would otherwise have.[340] The market shares of the merging parties are cumulated and compared with the market shares of the competitors in the market, using the Herfindahl/Hirschman Index (HHI), explained below, which presents a better method of balancing the importance of market shares and establishing market share thresholds.

Calculation of Market Shares.
The Commission mostly calculates market shares on the basis of turnover in the relevant market(s) on which the merging parties are present,[341] and only occasion-

336. *Airtours*, CFI June 6, 2002, 2002 ECR II-2585, para. 61.
337. *See* Monti, Convergence in EU-US antitrust policy regarding mergers and acquisitions: an EU perspective, Los Angeles, Feb. 28, 2004, SPEECH/04/107.
338. *See* the Department of Justice and Federal Trade Commission Horizontal Merger Guidelines (1992), especially the discussion of the Herfindahl-Hirschman Index ('HHI') at point 1.51.
339. *Gencor/Lonrho*, CFI March 25, 1999, 1999 ECR II-753.
340. Guidelines on the Assessment of Horizontal Mergers, points 14–15, 76–84.
341. *See Thyssen/Krupp*, D.Comm. June 2, 1998, M.1080; *BaByliss*, CFI April 3, 2003, T-114/02, para. 354.

ally on the basis of unit sales when it gives a fairer reading of market shares.[342] Affiliated companies are to be included to the same extent as for the purpose of calculating the turnover.[343] However, market shares of companies which the parties do not control (mere financial participations) are normally not included in the calculation of the parties' market shares.[344] Sales among firms under common control within the same group are not taken into account because they do not appear on the market.[345] The same applies to delivery for captive use within the same group of companies.[346] Captive production refers to that part of a firm's output that is used internally and therefore does not appear on the market.[347] In the case of a joint venture, the turnover resulting from the sale of products or services to the parent companies must not be taken into account, whereas the turnover resulting from sales to third parties must be included but apportioned equally between the parent companies (Article 5 (5)).

In some cases it may be more appropriate to base the calculation on other measures, such as production capacity,[348] fleet capacity,[349] orders firmly booked[350] or advertising revenue of TV broadcasters.[351]

Market Shares on New Product Markets.
The calculation of market shares is particularly difficult in the case of establishing a joint venture on a new product market without any actual turnover and

---

342. *Procter & Gamble/Schickedanz*, D.Comm. June 21, 1994, 1994 OJ L 354/32, point 118.
343. Article 5 (4) of Regulation 139/2004 and Commission Notice on the Concept of Undertakings Concerned (1998 OJ C 66/14).
344. *Fortis/CGER*, D.Comm. Nov. 15, 1993, M.342, point 31; *UAP.VINCI*, D.Comm. Dec. 1, 1993, M.384, point 10. *See Anglo American Corp./Lonrho*, D.Comm. April 23, 1997, 1998 OJ L 149/21 (minority participation reduced to 9.99%).
345. Article 5 (1) of Regulation 139/2004 and Notice on the Calculation of Turnover, point 22. *See Mannesmann/Boge*, D.Comm. Sept. 23, 1991, M.134; *Exxon/Mobil*, D.Comm. Sept. 29, 1999, M.1383, point 363.
346. *Lucas/Eaton*, D.Comm. Dec. 9, 1991, M.149; *Elf/BC/CEPSA*, D.Comm. June 18, 1991, M.98.
347. However, such internal sales may be taken into account with respect to supply substitutability and more generally in the overall competitive assessment (*see Mannesmann/Boge*, D.Comm. Sept. 23, 1991, M.134, point 19), in particular where such quantities are likely to be supplied (or resold) on the free market (e.g., *Lucas/Eaton*, D.Comm. Dec. 9, 1991, M.149; *DuPont/ICI*, D.Comm. Sept. 30, 1992, 1993 OJ L 7/13).
348. *See EDF/EnBW*, D.Comm. Feb. 7, 2001, M.1853, points 34–36.
349. *Delta Airlines/PanAm*, D.Comm. Sept. 13, 1991, M.130; *Air France/Sabena*, D.Comm. Oct. 5, 1992, M.157.
350. *Aérospatiale-Alenia/DeHavilland*, D.Comm. Oct. 2, 1991, 1991 OJ L 334/42, points 21–25; *Ericson/Kolbe*, D.Comm. Jan. 22, 1992, point 23; *Voith/Sulzer II*, D.Comm. July 29, 1994, points 28–29; *Marconi/Finnmeccanica*, D.Comm. Sept. 5, 1994, point 18. However, mere options are not taken into account.
351. *Bertelsmann/News International/VOX*, D.Comm. Sept. 6, 1994, point 22; *RTL/Veronica/Endemol*, D.Comm. Sept. 20, 1995, points 30, 69.

where in the short term the parties may have a factual monopoly. By analogy to Article 4 (2) of Regulation 2659/2000 on R&D agreements, the relevant product market must include products capable of being improved or replaced by the new products, e.g., in the case of 'pipeline products', i.e. pharmaceutical compounds which are not yet on the market but are at an advanced stage of development and therefore potentially substitutable.[352]

Market Share Thresholds as General Indicators of Dominance.
The aggregate market shares of the parties to the transaction are usually assessed by cumulating the individual shares on the relevant markets. There are basically three key market share thresholds:

(i) A minimum threshold of 25%. The regulation itself does not specify a minimum market share from which a threat to competition is perceived; however, the preamble states that a market share not exceeding 25% either in the Community as a whole or in a substantial part of it is an indication that no such threat exists (Recital 32).[353]
(ii) Market shares of 40% or 50% create a serious risk of dominance but call for an in-depth assessment of the particular circumstances of the case,[354] whereas market shares between 25% and 35% normally do not indicate a dominant position.[355]
(iii) Very high market shares of more than 50% may be taken as *prima facie*

352. *Glaxo Wellcome/SmithKline Beecham*, D.Comm. May 8, 2000, M.1846, points 70–73; *Pfizer/Pharmacia*, D.Comm. Feb. 27, 2003, M.2922, point 22.
353. Guidelines on the Assessment of Horizontal Mergers, point 18. *See Tetra Laval*, CFI Oct. 25, 2002, 2002 ECR II-4519, para. 232.
354. Guidelines on the Assessment of Horizontal Mergers, point 17. Examples of mergers involving market shares of more than 40%: *BaByliss*, CFI April 3, 2003, T-114/02, paras. 315–365; *Pirelli/BICC*, D.Comm. July 19, 2000, M.1882 (between 45 and 55% at Community level for power cables but unlikely that Pirelli would be able to sustain the high combined market share, among others because of buyer power of utilities in the framework of bidding process and the ongoing structural change in the electricity industry). *See DuPont/ICI*, D.Comm. Sept. 30, 1992, 1993 OJ L 7/13, point 32 (43% which, compared with much smaller market shares of the competitors, were likely to lead to a dominant position); *Shell/Montecatini*, D.Comm. June 8, 1994, 1994 OJ L 332/48, points 102–105 (market shares based on sales of 35–40%, based on own production capacity of 50% and own and licensed production capacity of between 50 and 75% constitute a dominant position the effects of which have been attenuated by commitments); *Worldcom/MCI*, D.Comm. July 8, 1998, 1999 OJ L 116/1 (conditional clearance of a merger holding 50%). Examples of cases involving market shares of around 50%: *Endemol*, CFI April 28, 1999, 1999 ECR II-1299, para. 134; *Gencor*, CFI March 25, 1999, 1999 ECR II-753, para. 205; *Blokker Toys 'R' Us*, D.Comm. June 26, 1997, 1998 OJ L 316/1, point 74.
355. Guidelines on the Assessment of Horizontal Mergers, points 17–18. *See Codan/Hafnia*, D.Comm. May 28, 1993, M.344, point 12 (33%); *Mitsubishi/UCAR*, D.Comm. Jan. 4, 1991, M.24, points 12–14 (35–40%).

evidence of a dominant position,[356] unless it is rebutted by effective competition from the rest of the market or by significant potential competition.[357]

Comparison with Competitors' Market Shares.
The parties' market shares have to be evaluated in the context of the market shares of their competitors.[358] If they have a clear lead over their competitors who form a 'competitive fringe' with considerably smaller market shares ('fragmentation of competitors'), the merger may reinforce that lead.[359] On the other hand, the merger may not significantly impede effective competition if it merely counterbalances a similar market position held by competitors[360] or considerable buying power of customers.[361] A comparison with the market shares of competitors is particularly

356. Under Article 82: *Hilti*, CFI Dec. 12, 1991, 1991 ECR II-1439, para. 92, *aff'd* ECJ March 2, 1994, 1994 ECR I-667 (70–80%).Under the merger control regulation: *Blokker/Toys 'R' Us*, D.Comm. June 26, 1997, 1998 OJ L 316/1 (55%). *Gencor/Lonrho*, CFI March 25, 1999, 1999 ECR II-753, paras. 205, 297 (duopoly of 35–40% each prohibited); *Endemol*, CFI April 28, 1999, 1999 ECR II-1299, para. 134; *Kesko/Tuko*, D.Comm. Nov. 20, 1996, 1997 OJ L 110/53, point 106 (55% on the local, regional or national level creates a 'presumption' of dominance; merger declared incompatible with the Common Market and the functioning of the EEA Agreement).

357. *Mannesmann/Hoesch*, D.Comm. Nov. 12, 1992, 1993 OJ L 114/34, points 103–104 (70% but significant potential competition); *Schering/Gehe-Jenapharm*, D.Comm. Sept. 23, 1996, M.781 (despite a market share of 60% the Commission did not find dominance because of innovative products and demand mobility); *Pirelli/BICC*, D.Comm. July 19, 2000, M.1882 (45–55%). *See also* the Court of Justice's discussion of market shares in *Hoffmann-La Roche*, ECJ Feb. 13, 1979, 1979 ECR 461, paras 39–68. Significant potential competition denied in: *St. Gobain/Wacker Chemie*, D.Comm. Dec. 4, 1996, 1997 OJ L 247/1, points 188–211.

358. *See Renault/Volvo*, D.Comm. Nov. 7, 1990, M.4; *AG/Amev*, D.Comm. Nov. 21, 1990, M.18; *AT&T/NCR*, D.Comm. Jan. 18, 1991, M.50. In the statements in the Council's minutes when the prior Regulation 1310/97 was adopted, re Article 2, the Commission announced its intention of taking into account the competitiveness of firms located in regions that are greatly in need of restructuring; *cf.* the discretionary exceptions from the prohibition on government subsidies made in Article 92 (3) of the EC Treaty for regional policy reasons.

359. In *Bosch/Rexroth* the merger between the leading firm with a market share of 30–40% with its nearest competitor having a market share of 5–15% clearly created a dominant position giving the new entity an aggregate market share that would be 3–4 times more than any of the biggest remaining competitors: D.Comm. Jan. 12, 2001, 2004 OJ L 43/1, point 62. *See also DuPont/ICI*, D.Comm. Sept. 30, 1992, 1993 OJ L 7/13, point 32; *Blokker/Toys 'R' Us*, D.Comm. June 26, 1997, 1999 OJ L 53/1, points 59–70; *Amicon/Fortia*, Eleventh Report on Competition Policy, point 112.

360. *Pilkington/BSN*, Tenth Report on Competition Policy, points 152–155; *Finsider/Tehid*, Twelfth Report on Competition Policy, point 99.

361. *Renault/Volvo*, D.Comm. Nov. 7, 1990, M.4 (buses); *Alcatel/Telettra*, D.Comm. April 12, 1991, 1992 OJ L 122/48, point 38; *Lucas/Eaton*, Dec. 9, 1991, M.149, point 37; *AKZO/Nobel*, D.Comm. Jan. 17, 1994, M.396, point 18; *ABB/Daimler Benz*, D.Comm. Oct. 18, 1995, 1997 OJ L 11/1, point 101; *Kodak/Imation*, D.Comm. Oct. 23, 1998, M.1298; *Enso/Stora*, D.Comm. Nov. 25, 1998, 1999 OJ L 254/9, points 84–97. However, the countervailing buying power argument does not hold for public purchasers who are disinclined to seek further afield than

important in oligopolistic markets where the positions of a few roughly equal competitors may be finely balanced. The merger between two members of such an oligopoly or the merger of a member of the oligopoly with an important supplier or customer may disturb this balance, giving them a dominant position or triggering a series of mergers in which other members of the oligopoly attempt to maintain their position and which result in a tightening of the oligopoly and a significant diminution of competition.[362]

Additional Evaluation of the Aggregate Market Shares by Using the Herfindahl-Hirschman Index ('HHI').

The Commission uses the HHI test for balancing the merging parties' market shares and those of their competitors.[363] The HHI is calculated by summing the squares of the individual market shares of *all* the firms in the market and by doubling the product of the market shares of the *merging firms*. Competition concerns[364] are *unlikely* to exist:

- when the HHI is less than 2000 but would be increased by the merger by less than 250 points (the 'delta'), or
- when the HHI is more than 2000 but would be increased by less than 150 points.

However, competition concerns are *likely* to exist where the 'delta' is more than respectively 250 and 150 points. For instance, a market containing six firms with market shares of 30%, 20%, 15%, 15%, 10%, 5% and 5% respectively has a HHI of 1.900. If the firm with a 20% market share merges with the firm with a 5% market share, the HHI will increase by 200 points without raising competition concerns. If the firm with a 20% market share merges with the firm with a 10% market share the HHI would increase by 400 points, thereby raising competition concerns.[365] On a market with a higher HHI (e.g., 30%, 30%, 20%, 15% and 5%) a merger between the firms with 15 and 5% market shares would bring the HHI from 2,450 to 2,600, a 'delta' of 150 points (15 x 5 x 2), which confirms that in cases where the merger strengthens a collective dominant position a combined market share of less than 25% may raise competition concerns.[366] The HHI is, more generally,

their established national manufacturers: *Alcatel/Telettra*, D.Comm. April 12, 1991, 1991 OJ L 122/48. Under Article 82: *British Sugar/Berisford*, Twelfth Report on Competition Policy, points 104–106.

362. *See Price Waterhouse/Coopers & Lybrand*, D.Comm. May 2, 1998, 1999 OJ L 50/27, points 95–119 (however, no conclusive proof of collective dominance).
363. Guidelines on the Assessment of Horizontal Mergers, point 20.
364. 'Serious doubts' in the sense of Article 6 (1) (c) of Regulation 139/2004.
365. 20 x 5 x 2 = 200, thereby increasing the HHI from the sum of the squares of their *individual* market shares $20^2 + 5^2 = 425$ up to the square of the joint market share $25^2 = 625$.
366. *See Kali + Salz*, ECJ March 31, 1998, 1998 ECR I-1375, para. 171; *Gencor/Lonrho*, CFI March 25, 1999, 1999 ECR II-753, para. 134.

a good indicator for assessing the acquisition of smaller competitors by companies with larger market shares. The HHI identifies competition concerns when a firm that already holds a strong position in an oligopolistic market acquires a direct competitor with even a small market share. For instance, the addition of an insignificant increase of market shares, e.g., 1–2%, normally does not contribute significantly to impeding effective competition, provided the independence and competitive vigor of the remaining competitors is not affected.[367]

The HHI Test as a Rule of Thumb.
The HHI is purely indicative. Mergers with a 'delta' of more than respectively 150 and 250 points do not give rise to a presumption of the existence of competitive concerns. Mergers with a 'delta' below these thresholds may, under special circumstances, give rise to competitive concerns,[368] in particular where:

- one of the parties has a pre-merger market share of 50% or more;
- a merger involves a potential entrant or a recent entrant with a (still) small market share;
- one or more merging parties are important innovators;
- there are significant cross-shareholdings among the market participants;[369]
- one of the merging firms is a firm with a high likelihood of disrupting coordinated conduct (a 'maverick' firm); and/or
- there are indications of past or ongoing oligopolistic coordination.

The new notification Form CO requires an estimate of the HHI index pre- and post-merger, and the difference between the two (Section 7.3).

Evaluation of Market Shares in the Light of Market Development.
The development of market shares is looked at over time;[370] the analysis is not limited to immediate or short-term effects.[371] Instability and volatility of market shares over time is a sign of effective competition even if the historic market

367. *Pepsi/KAS*, D.Comm. Dec. 21, 1992, M.289, point 65; *Ciba-Geigy/Degussa*, D.Comm. April 5, 1993, M.317, point 25; *Crown Cork & Seal/Carnaud Metalbox*, D.Comm. Nov. 14, 1995, 1996 OJ L 75/38, point 86; *Deutsche Post/DHL*, D.Comm. June 26, 1998, M.1168; *Gaz de France/Bewag/Gasag*, D.Comm. Jan. 20, 1999, M.1402; *Haniel/Fels*, D.Comm. Feb. 21, 2002, M.2475.

368. Guidelines on the Assessment of Horizontal Mergers, point 20.

369. Such links may be included in the HHI test: *Exxon/Mobil*, D.Comm. Sept. 29, 1999, M.1383, point 256. A merger may be cleared only under the condition that such links be removed: *Allianz/AGF*, D.Comm. May 8, 1998, M.1082; *Thyssen/Krupp*, D.Comm. June 2, 1998, M.1080.

370. Guidelines on the Assessment of Horizontal Mergers, point 15. *See Gencor/Lonrho*, CFI March 25, 1999, 1999 ECR II-753, para. 295, Twenty-second Report on Competition Policy, point 249.

371. *See* Guidelines on the Assessment of Horizontal Mergers, points 87–95.

shares are rather high,[372] while stability is ambivalent and may indicate market dominance as well as effective competition.[373] Steadily decreasing market shares are a strong indication of effective competition resulting, for example, from the market entry of competitors from outside the EC[374] or from the expiration of patent protection.[375] The evaluation has to be made separately for the various relevant markets affected by the merger, including upstream and downstream markets,[376] regardless of the proportion of the parties' turnover they represent.[377] Thus, even if a merger significantly impedes effective competition only in a market that accounts for a relatively minor part of the firms' activities, it is likely to be prohibited if the firm has, despite its relatively small market share, promising 'pipeline' products, i.e. pharmaceutical compounds which are not yet on the market but are at an advanced stage of development and therefore potentially substitutable.[378] However, such a transaction may be cleared if the entry of a potential competitor in the relevant market is likely, timely and sufficient,[379] or if the parties agree to divest certain of the assets serving that market or take other steps to mitigate the anticompetitive features of the transaction.[380]

Historic Market Shares and Past Performance.
Historic market shares and past performance of the market operators often provide a useful indication of the anticompetitive effects of a merger, depending on whether the past market shares are stable or volatile.[381] However, the evaluation of dominance is inevitably prospective and requires an examination of the reasonably foreseeable effects,[382] in particular of potential competition in the case

372. Guidelines on the Assessment of Horizontal Mergers, point 15. *See Airtours*, June 6, 2002, 2002 ECR II-2585, paras. 109–119; *ELF Aquitaine-Thyssen/Minol*, D.Comm. Sept. 4, 1992, M.235, point 11; *Bosch/Allied Signal*, D.Comm. April 9, 1996, M.726, points 25, 44. Under Article 82: *Hoffmann-La Roche*, ECJ Feb. 13, 1979, 1979 ECR 461, paras 57–58.
373. *Hoffmann-La Roche*, ECJ Feb. 13, 1979, 1979 ECR 461, para. 44.
374. *IMI/Heilmann I*, Seventh Report on Competition Policy, points 29–32.
375. *Rhône Poulenc/Monsanto*, Nineteenth Report on Competition Policy, point 67.
376. Guidelines on the Assessment of Horizontal Mergers, point 61; *Exxon/Mobil*, D.Comm. Sept. 29, 1999, M.1383, points 478 and 769.
377. *BaByliss/SEB-Moulinex*, CFI April 3, 2003, T-114/02, paras. 309–310.
378. Guidelines on the Assessment of Horizontal Mergers, point 38; *Glaxo/Wellcome/Smith Kline Beecham*, D.Comm. May 8, 2000, M.1846, points 70–73 and 188; *Pfizer/Pharmacia*, D.Comm. Feb. 27, 2003, M.2922, point 22.
379. Guidelines on the Assessment of Horizontal Mergers, points 58–60; *Akzo Nobel/Hoechst Roussel*, D.Comm. Nov. 22, 1999, M.1681 point 64 (evidence that a potential competitor had *plans* to enter a market). *See also Pirelli/BICC*, D.Comm. July 19, 2000, M.1882 ('competitive pressure is nevertheless exerted by foreign competitors').
380. As, e.g., in *AT&T/NCR*, D.Comm. Jan. 18, 1991, M.50; *TWIL/Bridon*, Nineteenth Report on Competition Policy, point 64; *Johnson & Firth Brown/British Steel*, Fourth Report on Competition Policy, points 125–127.
381. Guidelines on the Assessment of Horizontal Mergers, point 15.
382. Guidelines on the Assessment of Horizontal Mergers, point 9. *See Hoffmann-La Roche/Boeh-*

of horizontal mergers and of the foreclosure and leveraging effects in the case of vertical and conglomerate mergers, for which the burden of proof is on the Commission 'to the requisite legal standard'.[383] The prospective analysis must allow an assessment of the anticompetitive effects of a merger with a sufficiently high degree of probability. The period of time to be considered when proceeding to such a prospective analysis must have due regard to the gradual development of market structures, thereby excluding short-term changes as well as long-term evolution, which would be tantamount to speculation. The Commission seems to consider a period of two or three years when assessing potential competition.[384] Differences in this prospective analysis and the legal standards to be applied were the main reasons for the Court of First Instance reversing the Commission prohibition decisions in *Airtours*[385] (with respect of potential competition) and *Tetra Laval*[386] (in respect of the foreseeable effects of a conglomerate merger).

Dominant Positions Held by Third Parties.

Article 2 (3) applies to the creation or strengthening of a dominant position without expressly stating whether this position is held by the parties or by one of them and a third party or whether the operation contributes to creating or strengthening a dominant position held by one or more third parties. The Commission has stated that Article 2 (3) of the merger regulation is 'in terms, *not* limited to the prohibition of a dominant position *on the part of one or more of the parties to the concentration*'.[387] The Commission has applied this concept in cases where the parties and a third party jointly control a joint venture[388] or are linked through a strategic alliance[389] or a shareholding,[390] thereby likely to create[391] or to strengthen[392] a

ringer, D.Comm. 1998 OJ L 14, Feb. 4, 1998, M.850, point 13; *Glaxo/Wellcome/Smith Kline*, D.Comm. May 8, 2000, M.1846, points 70–72; *Bayer/Aventis*, D.Comm. April 17, 2002, M.2547, point 324.

383. *Tetra Laval*, CFI Oct. 25, 2002, 2002 ECR II-4519, paras. 225, 307 and 333.

384. *Procter & Gamble/Schickedanz*, D.Comm. June 21, 1994, 1994 OJ L 354/32, points 175–180. The German Supreme Court accepts longer-term perspectives, such as for five to eight years: *Kfz-Kupplungen*, BGH WuWE BGH 1501, 1507.

385. *Airtours*, CFI June 6, 2002, 2002 ECR II-2585, para. 59.

386. *Tetra Laval*, CFI Oct. 25, 2002, 2002 ECR II-4519, para. 307.

387. *Exxon/Mobil*, D.Comm. Sept. 29, 1999, M.1383, point 225. The parties' allegation that there is no precedent for this application has been held by the Commission as 'correct, but irrelevant' (point 229).

388. *Exxon/Mobil*, D.Comm. Sept. 29, 1999, M.1383; *Mitsui/CVRD/Caemi*, D.Comm. Oct. 30, 2001, M.2420, point 252.

389. *DSM/Roche*, D.Comm. July 23, 2003, M.2972.

390. Shareholding in a competing third party: *France Telecom/Orange*, D.Comm. Aug. 11, 2000, M.2016; minority shareholding of a third party in one of the merging parties: *Newscorp/Telepiù*, D.Comm. April 2, 2003, M.2876.

391. *Sogecable/Canal Satellite/Digital/via Digital*, D.Comm. Aug. 14, 2002, M.2845 (Article 9 (3) decision).

392. *Group Villar, EnBW/Hidroeléctrica de Cantabrico*, D.Comm. Sept. 26, 2001, M.2434; *EnBW, EDP, Cajastur/Hidrocantabrico*, D.Comm. March 19, 2002, M.2684.

collective dominant position held together with third parties.[393] In the *EnBW/EDP/Cajastur* case the Commission found that the acquisition of the fourth Spanish electricity generator by a Portuguese and a German generator (with a 50% participation of EDF which owns the interconnector between France and Spain and therefore controls the Spanish imports) would have strengthened the duopoly of the two largest Spanish generators Endesa (44%) and Iberdrola (34%) on the Spanish wholesale market. Therefore, the Commission made its clearance subject to commitments of EDF to increase substantially the commercial capacity of the interconnector.[394] However, the merger control regulation does not seem to be conceived for including the creation or strengthening of a dominant position held by a third party. First, for the purposes of notification the application of the merger control regulation does not depend on the Community dimension based on the turnover of that third party. Secondly, the third party must be held responsible for impeding effective competition in the relevant market. Such responsibility may exist where the third party is linked with the parties to the operation by a shareholding ensuring sole or joint control or by economic links constituting an oligopoly. In any event, the application of the merger control regulation to third parties requires the proper hearing of third parties,[395] and the decision must be addressed to third parties that are directly concerned by the merger proceedings, and any commitments to be implemented by the third party must be with its active or passive cooperation.[396] In the *Newscorp/Telepiù* case the Commission tried to overcome these problems by accepting commitments from the (dominant) third party without making the clearance decision subject to the implementation of this commitment.[397] However, the implementation of such commitments are not enforceable because they are not integrated into the operative part of the decision and therefore not subject to sanctions.[398]

(d) Assessment of Corroborating and Countervailing Factors

The Requirements of Article 2 (1) of Regulation 139/2004.
According to Article 2 (1) of Regulation 139/2004 (which does not differ from Regulation 1310/97), any appraisal of mergers must take into account:

---

393. In the case *Newscorp/Telepiù*, D.Comm. April 2, 2003, M.2876, the thorough investigation did not reveal sufficient evidence to show that the minority shareholding of Telecom Italia in the merged entity would strengthen its pre-merger dominant position in some telecom services markets in Italy.
394. *EnBW/EDP/Cajastur*, D.Comm. March 19, 2002, M.2684.
395. Article 11 (b) of Regulation 447/98. *See Kali + Salz*, ECJ May 14, 1975, 1975 ECR 499, para. 175; *Gencor*, CFI March 25, 1999, 1999 ECR II-753, paras. 142–146.
396. *See Haniel/Cementbouw/JV CVK*, D.Comm. June 26, 2002, M.2650.
397. *Newscorp/Telepiù*, D.Comm. April 2, 2003, M.2876, point 324.
398. The German antitrust authority, too, tried to apply its merger control mechanism to the creation or strengthening of dominant position held by third parties but its decision was reversed on appeal: *Siegländer Transportbeton*, Kammergericht (Appeals Court), Oct. 24, 1979, WuWE OLG 2256, 2261.

- the anticompetitive effects on the competitive structure in the relevant market(s) and actual or potential competition from companies located either within or outside the EEA countries;
- the market position of the companies concerned and their economic or financial power, the alternatives available to suppliers and users, their access to supplies or markets, any legal and other barriers to entry, supply and demand trends for the relevant goods and services, the interests of the intermediate and ultimate customers, and the development of technical and economic progress, provided that it is to the consumers' advantage and does not form an obstacle to competition.

A further analysis of corroborating and countervailing factors is required even in cases where the aggregate market share suggests the existence of a dominant position unless the market shares are extremely high (e.g., more than 85%). This analysis depends on a multitude of issues which partially overlap. If, however, there is no indication of the likelihood of significantly impeding effective competition the transaction must be authorized.[399]

Economic Power.

The strong market position of a firm relative to its rivals can be based on a technological lead, advantages in investment and research,[400] surplus capacity,[401] a wider product range ('portfolio power'),[402] industrial property rights[403] including trademarks[404] and fidelity of customers to well-known trademarks,[405] presence on a large number of markets,[406] possibility of more efficient advertising,[407] possibility of offering multinational services,[408] or exclusive distribution and exclusive

399. *Tetra Laval*, CFI Oct. 25, 2002, 2002 ECR II-4519, para. 120.
400. *Shell/Montedison*, D.Comm. June 8, 1994, 1994 OJ L 332/48, point 103. Similarly: *United Brands*, ECJ Feb. 14, 1978, 1978 ECR 207, paras 82–84.
401. *Carnival/P&O Princess*, D.Comm. July 24, 2002, M.2706, points 238–240; *Celanese/Degussa/JV*, D.Comm. June 11, 2003, 2004 OJ L 38/47, point 73.
402. Guidelines on the Assessment of Horizontal Mergers, point 30. *See Schneider Electric*, CFI Oct. 22, 2002, 2002 ECR II-4201, paras. 234–249; *BaByliss*, CFI Oct. 25, 2002, 2002 ECR II-4519, para. 354; *Guinness/Grand Metropolitan*, D.Comm. Oct. 15, 1997, M.938; *Boeing/McDonnell Douglas*, D.Comm. July 30, 1997, 1997 OJ L 336/16, points 40–42.
403. *Boeing/McDonnell Douglas*, D.Comm. July 30, 1997 OJ L 336/16, point 102.
404. *See* under Article 82: *Tetra Pak I*, D.Comm. July 26, 1988, 1988 OJ L 272/27, 39; *aff'd* CFI July 10, 1990, 1990 ECR II-309, para. 23.
405. *Nestlé/Perrier*, D.Comm. July 22, 1992, 1992 OJ L 356/1, point 60; *Procter & Gamble/VP Schickedanz*, D.Comm. June 21, 1994, 1994 OJ L 354/32, point 125; *Kimberly-Clark/Scott*, D.Comm. Jan. 16, 1996, 1996 OJ L 183/1, points 200–205.
406. *AT&T/NCR*, D.Comm. Jan. 18, 1991, M.50. Under Article 82: *Michelin*, ECJ Nov. 9, 1983, 1983 ECR 3461, para. 55; *ECS/Akzo II*, D.Comm. Dec. 14, 1985, 1985 OJ L 374/1, 18; *aff'd* ECJ July 3, 1991, 1991 ECR I-3187, paras 58 and 61.
407. *Kimberly-Clark/Scott*, D.Comm. Jan. 16, 1996, 1996 OJ L 183/1, points 139–153.
408. *Price Waterhouse/Coopers & Lybrand*, D.Comm. May 20, 1998, 1999 OJ L 50/27, point 57.

purchase agreements that prevent competitors from successfully entering the market.[409] Such factors are especially relevant in vertical or conglomerate mergers.[410] The addition of greater financial resources as a result of a merger can lead to the creation or strengthening of a dominant position.[411] However, large market shares of the merging companies may be counterbalanced by the economic and financial strength of their competitors and partners,[412] including their market shares and their buying power.[413] Buying power may have a countervailing effect likely to reduce the risk of preventing effective competition despite high market shares.[414] However, it may be difficult to evaluate the strength of the different buyers and to differentiate according to their individual or joint buying power.[415]

Factors Likely to Strengthen the Market Power.
The parties' market position may be strengthened by economic advantages, such as state aid, or indirect links with third competitors, such as the acquisition of joint control of, or minority shareholdings in, companies operating in the same sector or even by the conclusion of anticompetitive agreements, which constitute breaches of the EC competition rules other than the merger control provisions. The question arises whether such factors must be included in the overall assessment of the operation under the merger control regulation or lead to separate, although parallel, proceedings. It is settled cased law of the Court of Justice that the Commission must, as a matter of principle, avoid inconsistencies that might arise in the implementation of the various provisions of Community law.[416] This

---

409. *Bertelsmann/Kirch/Première*, D.Comm. May 27, 1998, 1999 OJ L 53/1, point 122; *Boeing/McDonnell Douglas*, D.Comm. July 30, 1997, 1997 OJ L 336/16, points 43–46 and 68–71. With respect to the possibility of offering package deals: *Agfa-Gevaert/DuPont*, D.Comm. Feb. 11, 1998, 1998 OJ L 211/22, points 112–114.
410. *See* the mergers in financial services involving banking services on the one hand and insurance on the other: *Fortis/Mees Pierson*, D.Comm. Feb. 6, 1997, M.850; *Fortis/ASLK-CGER*, D.Comm. Oct. 2, 1997, M.981; *Credit Suisse/Wintherthur*, D.Comm. Oct. 15, 1997, M.985; *Merita/Nord-banken*, D.Comm. Dec. 10, 1997, M.1029. Under Article 82: *British Sugar/Berisford*, Twelfth Report on Competition Policy, points 104–106. Under Article 66 of the ECSC Treaty: *GKN/Miles Druce*, D.Comm. March 14, 1974, 1974 OJ L 132/28; *Special Products Lemförder*, Nineteenth Report on Competition Policy, point 77.
411. *BSkyB/Kirch Pay TV*, D.Comm. March 21, 2000, JV.37, point 50.
412. *See Matsushita/MCA*, D.Comm. Jan. 10, 1991, M.37.
413. *See Agfa-Gevaert/DuPont*, D.Comm. Feb. 11, 1998, 1998 OJ L 211/22, points 102–103; *Pirelli/BICC*, D.Comm. July 19, 2000, M.1882. Buying power of supermarkets denied in *Kimberley-Clark/Scott*, D.Comm. Jan. 16, 1996, 1996 OJ L 183/1, points 185–189.
414. *Alcatel/Telettra*, D.Comm. April 12, 1991, 1991 OJ L 122/48, point 38; *SNECMA/TI*, D.Comm. Jan. 17, 1994, M.368, point 38; *ABB/Daimler Benz*, D.Comm. Oct. 18, 1995, 1997 OJ L 11/1, point 101; *Ensor/Stora*, D.Comm. Nov. 25, 1991, M.1225 (buying power examined but countervailing power denied).
415. The case *Nestlé/Perrier*, D.Comm. July 22, 1992, 1992 OJ L 356/1, point 78, highlights these difficulties.
416. *Matra*, ECJ June 15, 1993, 1993 ECR I-3203, paras. 41–47; *DIR International Film*, ECJ Jan.

implies that the Commission must maintain consistency between the provisions of the Treaty on state aid and the competition rules, which both have undistorted competition in the Common Market as their aim.[417] In the case of a joint venture the Commission must examine whether the joint control leads to anticompetitive conduct between the parent companies infringing Article 81[418] or has negative implications on the competitive structure of the relevant market which must be included in the overall merger assessment.[419] Mere minority participations in another competing company normally do not suffice because they do not confer decisive influence over the other company's conduct and are therefore, as such, not subject to the merger control regulation, as the Commission stated in its Green Paper.[420] However, the clearance of a merger may be subject to commitments to remove or reduce minority shareholdings[421] or interlocking directorates[422] with the view of removing any anticompetitive effect.[423]

Financial Power.

As under Article 82,[424] financial power may corroborate market dominance under the merger control regulation ('deep pockets'), in particular where the financial resources of the parties to the transaction are predominant compared to those of their competitors.[425] Financial resources, combined with know-how, are important

---

27, 2000 ECR I-447, paras. 21 and 30; *RJB Mining*, CFI Jan. 31, 2001, 2001 ECR II-337, para. 112; *Verband der freien Rohrwerke*, CFI July 8, 2003, T-374/00, para. 169.

417. In the case *RJB Mining*, CFI Jan. 31, 2001, 2001 ECR II-337, para. 112, the Court of First Instance annuled the Commission decision, which did not take into account the state aid granted to the merging German coal producers, which led to separate proceedings, the first declaring the state aid and the second declaring the merger compatible with the Common Market: *RAG/Saarbergwerke/Anthrazit*, D.Comm. May 7, 2002, IP/02/674.
418. *Verband der freien Rohrwerke*, CFI July 8, 2003, T-374/00, paras. 167–171 (denied because of lack of evidence).
419. *Verband der freien Rohrwerke*, CFI July 8, 2003, T-374/00, paras. 172–180 (appreciable impact denied because of low market shares).
420. Green Paper on the Review of Council Regulation 4064/89, COM(2001) 745/6 final, point 109, suggesting that minority shareholdings and interlocking directorates can be satisfactorily addressed under Articles 81 and 82.
421. E.g., *Alcatel/Telettra*, D.Comm. April 12, 1991, 1991 OJ L 122/45, points 44–46.
422. E.g., *Varta/Bosch*, July 31, 1991, 1991 OJ L 320/26, point 63; *Thyssen/Krupp*, D.Comm. June 2, 1998, M.1080; *Generali/INA*, D.Comm. Jan. 12, 2000, M.1712.
423. According to the *Philip Morris* doctrine, *see* Section B.3.
424. *Continental Can*, D.Comm. Dec. 9, 1971, 1972 OJ L 7/25, 35; *British Plaster Board*, D.Comm. Dec. 5, 1988, 1989 OJ L 10/50, 64, without, however, being confirmed expressly by the Court of Justice, except in cases of predatory pricing, *see AKZO*, ECJ July 3, 1991, 1991 ECR I-3439, paras 72 and 146.
425. *Matsushita/MCA*, D.Comm. Jan. 10, 1991, M.37, point 6; *Mannesmann/VDO*, D.Comm. Dec. 13, 1991, point 28; *Pirelli/Siemens*, D.Comm. Sept. 30, 1998, M.1271; *Boeing/McDonnell Douglas*, D.Comm. July 30, 1997, 1997 OJ L 336/16, points 73–82. *See also* the various mergers in financial services between banks and insurance companies, Twenty-seventh Report on Competition Policy, pp. 183–184.

criteria for assessing conglomerate effects of a merger.[426]

Alternatives Available to Suppliers and Users – Countervailing Power on the Demand Side.

In the case of a horizontal transaction, which eliminates one of the direct competitors operating on the market, the limitation of alternatives available to suppliers and users[427] is inherent.[428] However, the criterion is also the major indicator of anti-competitive effects of vertical and conglomerate transactions.[429] The Commission considers the effects of a merger on the free choice of customers between the merging firms and competing companies by way of exclusive or preferential links, thereby creating market access barriers.[430] The Commission may therefore subject its clearance to the parties' commitment to cease such exclusive or preferential links.[431] However, the existence of alternatives may also counterbalance the parties' market position, depending on their own market power,[432] including the possibility of buyers to start their own production.[433]

---

426. *BSkyB/Kirch Pay TV*, March 21, 2000, JV.37, point 50; *Wolters Kluwer/Reed Elsevier*, Twenty-eighth Report on Competition Policy, point 154. *See* in particular in cases of mergers between banks and insurance companies, thereby pooling their financial resources and their respective techniques and know-how and sharing their distribution channels; *Credit Suisse/Winterthur*, D.Comm. Oct. 15, 1997, M.985, points 16–20; *Fortis/Mees Pierson*, D.Comm. Feb. 6, 1997, M.850; *Fortis/ASLK-CGER*, D.Comm. Oct. 2, 1997, M.981; *Merita/Nordbanken*. D.Comm. Dec. 10, 1997, M.1029.
427. In particular by exclusive distribution and purchase arrangements: *see Agfa-Gevaert/DuPont*, D.Comm. Dec. 11, 1998, 1998 OJ L 211/22, point 68.
428. *Gencor/Lonrho*, CFI 25 March 1999, 1999 ECR II-753, paras 255–262.
429. *See VIAG/Continental Can*, D.Comm. June 6, 1991, M.81, point 46; *Nordic Satellite Distribution*, D.Comm. July 19, 1995, 1996 OJ L 53/20, point 74; *Guinness/Grand Metropolitan*, D.Comm. Oct. 15, 1997, M.938; Twenty-seventh Report on Competition Policy, pp. 194–196; *Skanska/Scancem*, D.Comm. Nov. 11, 1998, M.1157. In *General Electric/Honeywell*, D.Comm. July 3, 2001, 2004 OJ L 48/1, points 224–228, the Commission rejected the argument of countervailing power.
430. *Eurocom/RSCG*, D.Comm. Dec. 18, 1991, M.147, points 19–20; *KTL/Veronica/Endemol*, D.Comm. Sept. 20, 1995, 1996 OJ L 134/32, point 92; *Aérospatiale-Alenia/De Havilland*, D.Comm. Oct. 2, 1991, 1991 OJ L 334/42, points 33–35; *MSG Media Service*, D.Comm. Nov. 9, 1994, 1994 OJ L 364/1, points 75–84; *Boeing/McDonnell Douglas*, D.Comm. July 30, 1997, 1997 OJ L 334/16, points 68–71; *Bertelsmann/Kirch/Première*, D.Comm. May 27, 1998, 1999 OJ L 53/1, points 62–65.
431. *Generali/INA*, D.Comm. Jan. 12, 2000, M.1712. *See also Alcatel/Telettra*, D.Comm. April 12, 1991, 1991 OJ L 122/48, point 44; *Fiat/Geotech*, D.Comm. Feb. 8, 1991, M.9, points 25–30; *TNT/GD NET*, D.Comm. Dec. 2, 1991, M.102, points 46–56; *Elf Aquitaine-Thyssen/Minol*, D.Comm. Sept. 4, 1992, M.235, point 13; *Boeing/McDonnell Douglas*, D.Comm. July 30, 1997, 1997 OJ L 334/16.
432. *Continental Can*, D.Comm. Dec. 9, 1971, 1972 OJ L 7/25, 38; *see* ECJ Feb. 21, 1973, 1973 ECR 215, para. 36.
433. *Lucas/Eaton*, D.Comm. Dec. 9, 1991, M.149; *Rhône Poulenc/SNIA*, D.Comm. Aug. 10, 1992, M.206.

Possibilities of Market Entry – Potential Competition.
Potential competition, though not measurable in terms of market share and therefore not a criterion for defining the relevant market,[434] reduces market power[435] and must be included in the assessment of the prospective longer-term effects and efficiencies of a merger.[436] Even potential customers may exert demand-side power, thereby countervailing the parties' market power.[437] This prospective analysis of the future anticompetitive effects of a merger differs from the assessment of a past abuse of a dominant position under Article 82, which must consider past and current rather than future competition:[438] According to the Commission's statement in *Procter & Gamble/Schickedanz*,[439] for market entry or the potential for such entry to constrain a dominant firm's behaviour, it is necessary to examine whether such entry:

- is probable (which depends on the nature of the product, commodity or innovative product; ability to establish an effective distribution network),
- is competitively meaningful and effective (which requires a meaningful market presence), and
- could take place within a time frame short enough to deter the dominant firm from exploiting its market power (i.e. within two to three years).[440]

Therefore, the potential competitor must already exert a significant constraining influence or there must be a significant likelihood that it would grow into an effective competitive force.[441] For example, a pharmaceutical firm manufacturing products which are not yet on the market but which are at an advanced stage of development ('pipeline products') may be capable of entering the market of the dominant firm and making a timely response to excessive pricing in the market.[442] Similarly, a firm in the same product line but operating in another geographic

---

434. *See* Chapter I.C.
435. E.g. *Mannesmann/Vallourec/Ilva*, D.Comm. Jan. 31, 1994, 1994 OJ L 102/15; *Nestlé/Dalgety*, D.Comm. April 2, 1998, M.1127; *Enso/Stora*, D.Comm. Nov. 25, 1998, M.1225.
436. Notice on the definition of the relevant market, points 13, 14 and 24. *See*, in particular, *Ciba-Geigy/Sandoz*, D.Comm. July 17, 1996, 1996 OJ L 200/1, points 295–302.
437. *Celanese/Degussa/JV*, D.Comm. June 11, 2003, 2004 OJ L 38/47, point 111.
438. *UFEX*, CFI May 25, 2000, 2000 ECR II-2167, para. 49.
439. *Procter & Gamble/Schickedanz*, D.Comm. June 21, 1994, 1994 OJ L 354/32, points 175–180.
440. Guidelines on the Assessment of Horizontal Mergers, point 68 ('likely, timely and sufficient to deter or defeat any potential anti-competitive effect of the merger'). Example for a case where market entry by the other merging firm was *not* sufficiently likely in the short to medium term: *ARD*, CFI Sept. 30, 2003, T-158/00, paras. 115–127.
441. Guidelines on the Assessment of Horizontal Mergers, points 60 and 68–75.
442. *Ciba-Geigy/Sandoz*, D.Comm. July 16, 1996, 1997 OJ L 201/1, point 42; *Glaxo Wellcome/SmithKline Beecham*, D.Comm. May 8, 2000, M.1846, points 70–73; *Pfizer/Pharmacia*, D.Comm. Feb. 27, 2000, M.2922, point 22.

market or a customer may be in a position to start supplying the market in question, provided they possess the technical capabilities, production capacity and quality requirements to supply on that other market in sufficient quantities.[443] Likewise, a producer of related or complementary products may be able to switch manufacturing capacity to producing the relevant product.[444] Such potential competition may be removed by a merger with the potential competitor.[445] The evaluation of such a merger will depend on the actual competitor's market position and on the potential competitor's proximity to the relevant market in terms of geography and product offerings[446] and in access to the necessary technology.[447] The greater the ability of the potential competitor to become an actual competitor within a relatively short period of time, the greater is the likelihood that the merger does not impede effective competition.[448] On the other hand, the existence of potential competition from several firms not involved in the merger will be a factor in favor of allowing the merger to proceed. For example, a firm that appears at first glance to hold a dominant position in a geographic market that consists of only one member state may in fact not be dominant if producers of the same or similar products in nearby member states could quickly commence sales operations in the alleged dominant firm's market. These potential competitors might so reduce the alleged firm's ability to abuse its local market position as to make its acquisition of a smaller rival unlikely to strengthen its largely illusory dominant position.

Market Entry Barriers.

This criteria overlaps with that of potential competition.[449] Legal or other barriers to entry may exist, in particular where market access depends on the granting of

443. *Continental Can*, ECJ Feb. 21, 1973, 1973 ECR 215; *ICI/Tioxide*, D.Comm. Nov. 28, 1990, M.23; *Pirelli/BICC*, D.Comm. July 19, 2000, M.1882, point 73 (Article 8 (2) decision without commitments). Under Article 82: *Eagle Star/Allianz*, Twelfth Report on Competition Policy, point 103; *Ibercobre/Outokumpu*, Nineteenth Report on Competition Policy, point 65. Potential competition denied in *Special Products Lemförder*, Nineteenth Report on Competition Policy, point 77. *Cf. Mitsubishi/UCAR*, D.Comm. Jan. 4, 1991.

444. *Digital/Kienzle*, D.Comm. Feb. 25, 1991, M.57. Under Article 82: *Continental Can*, ECJ Feb. 21, 1973, 1973 ECR 215, para. 33. Under Article 66 of the ECSC Treaty: *Cockerill/Sambre*, Twelfth Report on Competition Policy, point 96 (producers of complementary ranges of products may be potential competitors).

445. Guidelines on the Assessment of Horizontal Mergers, point 58–60. *See Continental Can*, ECJ Feb. 21, 1973, 1973 ECR 215.

446. Potential entrants may encounter barriers to entry because of the impact of risks and costs on the profitability of entry: Guidelines on the Assessment of Horizontal Mergers, point 70.

447. *See GE/ENI/Nuovo Pignone*, D.Comm. May 6, 1994, M.440, point 27.

448. *St. Gobain/Wacker*, D.Comm. Dec. 4, 1996, 1997 OJ L 247/1, points 188–219.

449. *See Agfa-Gevaert/DuPont*, D.Comm. Feb. 11, 1998, 1998 OJ L 211/22, point 104; *Blokker/Toys 'R' Us*, D.Comm. June 26, 1998, 1998 OJ L 316/1, points 105–107.

licenses by one of the merging firms,[450] requires economies of scale,[451] high investment[452] or high advertising costs,[453] access to distribution or service networks[454] or where access is impeded by national or EC regulations,[455] technical standards which are not yet harmonized,[456] or antidumping measures,[457] or where access is restricted by long-term exclusive purchasing arrangements.[458]

The impact of potential competition is highlighted in the *Agfa/Dupont* case.[459] This case concerned the acquisition by Agfa-Gevaert of DuPont's worldwide graphics and press room business by which Agfa-Gevaert would acquire a market share 2.5 times greater than the next largest competitor, thereby leading to the creation of a dominant position on the EEA market for negative offset printing plates. However, the Commission arrived at the conclusion that producers already present in this market could rapidly develop additional production capacity and that new competitors could readily enter the EEA market. The Commission declared the acquisition compatible with the Common Market and the functioning of the EEA Agreement subject to, *inter alia*, the condition that Agfa-Gevaert release its dealers and distributors from their exclusive dealing obligations.[460] Similarly, the Commission cleared the *TKS/Signode/Titan* case[461] in the second phase after having found that the parties' combined market share of 40% in the market of steel and plastic strapping was counterbalanced by adequate safeguards to competition by the likelihood of new entry in the plastic strapping sector, which was not found to be difficult (by contrast to that for the steel variety). In the *Pfizer/Pharmacia*

450. *Tetra Pak/Alfa Laval*, D.Comm. July 19, 1991, 1991 OJ L 290/35; *CUE/GTE*, D.Comm. Sept. 25, 1992, M.258, point 25; *Crown Cork & Seal/Carnaud Metalbox*, D.Comm. Nov. 14, 1995, 1996 OJ L 75/38, point 76.

451. *See Procter & Gamble/VP Schickedanz*, D.Comm. June 21, 1994, 1994 OJ L 354/32, points 132–147.

452. *Mitsubishi/WAR*, D.Comm. Jan. 4, 1991, M.24. Under Article 82: *United Brands*, ECJ Feb. 14, 1978, 1978 ECR 207, paras 69–77.

453. *Nestlé/Perrier*, D.Comm. July 22, 1992, 1992 OJ L 356/1.

454. *Volvo/Lex*, D.Comm. May 21, 1992, M.224; *TNT/GD*, D.Comm. Dec. 12, 1991, M.102.

455. Governmental grant of landing rights: *Air France/Sabena*, D.Comm. Oct. 5, 1992, M.157; *British Airways/TAT*, D.Comm. Nov. 27, 1992, M.259.

456. *Mannesmann/Hoesch*, D.Comm. Nov. 12, 1992, 1993 OJ L 114/34, point 107.

457. *ICI/Tioxide*, D.Comm. Nov. 28, 1990, M.23; *Alcatel/Telettra*, D.Comm. April 12, 1991, 1991 OJ L 122/48. Under Article 82: *British Sugar*, D.Comm. July 18, 1988, 1988 OJ L 284/41, 52–53; *British Telecommunications*, ECJ March 20, 1985, 1985 ECR 873, paras 21–22.

458. Guidelines on the Assessment of Horizontal Mergers, point 71. *See Ensor/Stora*, D.Comm. Nov. 25, 1998, 1999 OJ L 254/9.

459. *Agfa/DuPont*, D.Comm. Feb. 11, 1998, 1998 OJ L 211/22.

460. *Ibid.*, points 57 and 113–116. *See*, however, *Aerospatiale-Alenia/DeHavilland*, D.Comm. Oct. 14, 1991, 1991 OJ L 334/42, points 53–64. *See also Procter & Gamble/VP Schickedanz*, D.Comm. June 21, 1994, 1994 OJ L 354/32, points 175–182.

461. *TKS/Signode/Titan*, D.Comm. May 6, 1998, M.970; Twenty-eighth Report on Competition Policy, point 158. *See also Enso/Stora*, D.Comm. Nov. 25, 1998, 1999 OJ L 254/9, points 75–83.

case[462] the Commission granted clearance to a merger leading to aggregate market shares between 65% and 85% in certain markets because of the potential impact of new products ('pipeline products' which are not yet on the market but at an advanced stage of development). In the *Daimler Chrysler/Deutsche Telecom* case[463] the Commission granted clearance to the acquisition of joint control of the newly created joint venture Toll Collect to establish and operate a system of the collection of road tolls from heavy trucks which, at the same time, can be used as a platform to provide telematic services, which could control access to third parties' telematic services providers to the toll collect onboard units. The clearance was made subject to the commitment to create an independent Telematics Gateways company and to develop an interface for the toll collect open to third party peripherals.

Buying Power.

The merged entity may *create* for itself buying power and impede effective competition by imposing vertical restraints on suppliers, such as an obligation to supply the merged entity exclusively, thus foreclosing competitors from access to an essential output. However, it may also lead to lower input costs without restricting downstream competition, and cost reductions may be passed onto consumers in the form of lower prices.[464] On the other hand, the merged entity may be *subject* to buying power of its customers, which is likely to counter the increase in market power that a merger is expected to create (countervailing buying power).[465] Even firms with very high market shares may not be in a position, post merger, to significantly impede effective competition, if their customers possess countervailing buying power.[466] This applies in particular in public procurement markets or when buying power can be exercised by large and sophisticated customers.[467] The degree of buying power depends on the customers' ability to resort to credible alternatives[468] or to threaten to vertically integrate into the upstream market.[469]

---

462. *Pfizer/Pharmacia*, D.Comm. Feb. 27, 2003, M.2922, point 154 (Article 6 (2) decision). *See Ciba-Geigy/Sandoz*, July 16, 1996, 1997 OJ L 201/1, points 214–217 (Article 8 (2) decision).
463. *Daimler Chrysler/Deutsche Telecom*, D.Comm. April 30, 2003, M.2903.
464. Guidelines on the Assessment of Horizontal Mergers, points 61–62.
465. E.g., *Knorr Bremse/Rexrodt*, D.Comm. June 10, 1999, M.1293; *Hutchinson/ECT*, D.Comm. Nov. 29, 2001, JV. 56, points 42–45.
466. Guidelines on the Assessment of Horizontal Mergers, points 64–67.
467. *Pirelli/BICC*, D.Comm. July 19, 2000, M.1882, points 73–80.
468. *Danish Crown/Vestiyske Slagerier*, D.Comm. March 9, 1999, 2000 OJ L 20/1, point 171–173.
469. *See Continental Can*, ECJ Feb. 21, 1973, 1973 ECR 215, para. 33; *Enso/Stora*, D.Comm. Nov. 25, 1998, 1999 OJ L 254/9, point 89 and 95–96.

Supply and Demand Trends.
Supply and demand trends[470] include market entry after the expiration of patents or the development of substitutes, which erodes a dominant position.[471] Declining demand and over-capacity are likely to hamper any effort of the merging companies, even having significant market shares, to raise prices.[472] On the other hand, saturation of the market reduces the scope for new entry.[473] Developing markets may not indicate market dominance where the market remains open to future competition and where high market shares are only temporary,[474] but they do not justify such a market to be sealed off already in the development phase by the establishment of a joint venture as a vehicle of a long-term monopoly.[475]

Interests of Intermediates and Ultimate Consumers.
This criterion does not have any significance in itself and mostly coincides with the criterion of 'alternatives available to suppliers and users'. Normally, a merger that leads to high concentration in a market adversely affects the interests of consumers and therefore corroborates the conclusion drawn from the high market shares.[476] Occasionally the conclusions drawn from the market share assessment may be counterbalanced by the customers being sufficiently sophisticated purchasers who pay special attention to controlling costs and creating efficiencies.[477]

Efficiencies Contributing to the Development of Technical or Economic Progress.
According to Article 2 (1) (b), the Commission takes into account 'the development of technical and economic progress provided that it is to consumers' advantage and does not form an obstacle to competition'.[478] There are no grounds

470. In some sectors detailed statistics are available showing supply and demand trends, *see Kesko/Tusco*, D.Comm. Nov. 20, 1996, 1997 OJ L 110/76, points 94–104 (Nielsen statistics in the retail market). *See also Gencor/Lonrho*, D.Comm. April 24, 1996, 1997 OJ L 11/30, points 48–55.
471. *Rhône Poulenc/Monsanto*, Nineteenth Report on Competition Policy, point 67.
472. *Kodak/Imation*, D.Comm. Oct. 23, 1998, M.1298.
473. *Fiat/Ford New Holland*, D.Comm. Feb. 8, 1991, M.9.
474. *See Digital/Kienzle*, D.Comm. Feb. 22, 1991, M.57, point 22; *American Home Products/Monsanto*, D.Comm. Sept. 28, 1998, M.1229, point 17.
475. *MSG Media Service*, D.Comm. Nov. 9, 1994, 1994 OJ L 364/1, point 55.
476. *Orkla/Volvo*, D.Comm. Sept. 20, 1995, 1996 OJ L 66/17, points 94–99; *Kesko/Tuko*, D.Comm. Nov. 20, 1996, 1997 OJ L 110/53, points 106–115 (concentration of the markets for beer or daily consumer goods respectively). The fact that some customers take a positive or neutral reaction to the proposed merger does not bind the Commission when it makes its own assessment of the impact of the merger: *Gencor/Lonrho*, CFI March 25, 1999, 1999 ECR II-753, paras 290–291.
477. *Johnson & Johnson/Depuy*, D.Comm. Oct. 28, 1998, M.1286.
478. Guidelines on the Assessment of Horizontal Mergers, point 76.

for declaring a merger incompatible with the Common Market where there is sufficient evidence[479] that the efficiencies generated by the merger are likely to enhance the ability and incentive of the merged entity to act pro-competitively for the benefit of consumers, thereby counteracting the adverse effects on competition which the merger would otherwise have.[480] The efficiencies must be substantiated and likely to counteract the harm to consumers or, in other words, 'benefit' the consumers.[481] The definition of a transaction 'which would significantly impede effective competition' (Article 2 (2) and (3)) implies the existence of 'an obstacle to competition'. Therefore, a dominant position cannot be justified only by benefits of technical or economic progress, in particular in cases where the aggregate market shares are so high that they are *prima facie* evidence of dominance:[482] A monopoly cannot be declared compatible with the Common Market on mere efficiency grounds.[483] The Commission examines this criterion with care in cases where market shares and other criteria are not yet a clear indication of dominance. The effects on competition which result from the first indication of dominance may be counteracted by the benefits resulting from the development of technical and economic progress, likely to enhance the incentive of the merged entity to act pro-competitively,[484] or may be corroborated in the absence of substantial efficiencies.[485] In order to take account of efficiencies claims in the assessment of a transaction, the efficiencies 'have to benefit consumers, be merger-specific and be verifiable. These conditions are cumulative.'[486] This requires a balancing of efficiencies and anti-competitive effects: the greater the possible negative effects on competition, the more the claimed efficiencies must be substantial and likely to be realized to the direct benefit of the consumer. It is for the notifying parties to provide evidence necessary to show why the efficiencies will counteract any adverse effects on competition.[487] The practical problem is, however, to quantify

479. To be demonstrated by the merging parties, *see* Form CO, Section 9.3.
480. Recital 29 to Regulation 139/2004; Guidelines on the Assessment of Horizontal Mergers, point 77.
481. Recital 29 to Regulation 139/2004, which is similar to the requirement of Article 81 (3) (a).
482. Technical progress is not 'a legitimate defence for a merger which creates a dominant position': Sir Leon Brittan, 'The Law and Practice of Merger Control in the EEC', 1990 ELR 351, 353. The claimed economic or technical benefits of the merger must be substantiated with studies or reports sent with the notification (*see* 'CO' merger notification form).
483. The efficiencies must be merger-specific: Guidelines on the Assessment of Horizontal Mergers, point 85.
484. *See Aérospatiale-Alenia/De Havilland*, D.Comm. Oct. 2, 1991, 1991 OJ L 334142, point 65; MSG *Media Service*, D.Comm. Nov. 9, 1994, 1994 OJ L 364/1, points 100–101; *Nordic Sellite*, D.Comm. July 19, 1995, 1996 OJ L 53/20, points 145–152; *Bertelsmann/Kirch/Première*, D.Comm. May 27, 1998, 1999 OJ L 53/1, points 119–122.
485. *Delta Airlines/Pan Am*, D.Comm. Sept. 13, 1991, M.130, point 21. *See also Gencor/Lonrho*, CFI March 25, 1999, 1999 ECR II-753, para. 287.
486. Guidelines on the Assessment of Horizontal Mergers, point 78.
487. Guidelines on the Assessment of Horizontal Mergers, points 76–88, Form CO Section 9. 'The efficiencies must be substantial enough to counteract the merger's potential harm to consumers

and to verify dynamic and cost efficiencies and 'to foresee a clearly identifiable positive impact on consumers, not a marginal one'.[488] Similarly high standards of proof apply for assessing agreements under Article 81 (3).[489] There is no exhaustive case law yet but the following types of efficiencies may be pertinent:[490]

- Rationalization, in particular cost savings that may be realized from shifting output from one plant with high marginal costs of production to another lower-cost plant, or improving coordination of joint operations and product interoperability;[491] however, with respect to Article 81 (3) the Commission stated that it does not take into account cost savings that arise from the mere exercise of market power or from anticompetitive reductions in output;[492]
- Specialization to achieve economies of scale; the weight to be attached to such arguments depends on whether (i) market forces would remedy the overcapacity by themselves, (ii) there is a precise plan and timetable for cutting capacity or carrying out the rationalization, and (iii) there is no danger of new overcapacity being created;[493]
- Development of new or improved products or services;[494]
- Combining complementary assets, technology, knowledge or skills; a frequent argument advanced in favor of mergers is that they enable the parties to improve efficiencies of production or infrastructure, which must, however, be weighted against the possibilities of market access by third parties.[495]

---

and should therefore be quantified where reasonably possible': Guidelines on the Assessment of Horizontal Mergers, point 77.

488. *Ibid.*, point 86.

489. Guidelines on the Application of Article 81 (3), points 44–45, 64–68 and 102–104. Some critique has been voiced in relation to the treatment of efficiencies under Article 81 (3), *see* Lugard and Hancher, 'Honey, I shrunk the Article! A Critical Assessment of the Commission's Notice on Article 81 (3)', 2004 ECLR 410, 419, and under the U.S. Merger Guidelines, *see* Gerard, 'Merger Control Policy: How to give meaningful consideration to efficiency claims?', 2003 CMLR 1367.

490. *See* Annex 1 of Enterprise Papers No. 11 (2002) '*For the customer's sake: The competitive effects of efficiencies in European merger control*', elaborated by the Enterprise Directorate General of the Commission (which does not necessarily reflect the views of the Competition Directorate General).

491. Guidelines on the Assessment of Horizontal Mergers, point 80 (efficiencies in variable or marginal costs v. efficiencies in fixed costs). *See*, under Article 81 (3), Commission Notice on Horizontal Cooperation, points 151–155.

492. *See*, under Article 81 (3): Commission Notice on Horizontal Cooperation, points 33 and 152.

493. The existence of overcapacity may indicate effective competition (*Kodak/Imation*, D.Comm. Oct. 23, 1998, M.1298) and does not justify anticompetitive arrangements: *Welded Steel Mesh – Baustahlgewerbe*, CFI April 6, 1995, 1995 ECR II-987, paras 55–56 and 121 (only a mitigating factor when imposing fines).

494. Guidelines on the Assessment of Horizontal Mergers, point 81, which follows the case law under Article 81 (3). However, mere assertions to this effect do not suffice, point 94.

495. *Nordic Satellite Distribution*, D.Comm. July 19, 1995, 1996 OJ L 53/20, point 151. In *Aérospatiale-Alenia/De Havilland*, D.Comm. Oct. 2, 1991, 1991 OJ L 334142, point 65, the

Importance of Innovation.

A likely contribution to 'the development of technical or economic progress' may be an important benefit from a merger. In some markets innovation is the main competitive force.[496] The Commission must therefore examine how a merger will affect the competitive pressure to innovate in the market,[497] which depends on existing technology barriers.[498] The Commission has stated that the concept of technical and economic progress must be understood in the light of the principles of Article 81 (3) as interpreted by the case law of the Court of Justice.[499] The reference to Article 81 (3) is probably intended to refer to the Court's rulings that the advantages of a transaction must be appreciable from an objective point of view and not only from the subjective point of view of the parties and that they must clearly outweigh the harm to competition.[500] Thus, the contribution to technical or economic progress will be discounted if the merger could put the parties in a position to eliminate competition in respect of a substantial part of the products in question. In *MSG Media Services* the bundling of technologies was considered as preventing potential competition and strengthening a dominant position rather than improving technical progress.[501] While alleged contributions to technical progress will not be accepted as justification for anticompetitive transactions, rapid technical change throughout an industry will make the Commission less sceptical about allowing mergers that create substantial market shares.[502]

Economic and Social Cohesion.

The preamble to the original Merger Regulation 4064/89[503] stated that mergers are to be appraised within the general framework of the achievement of the fundamental objectives of the Community referred to in Article 2 of the EC Treaty, including that of strengthening the Community's economic and social cohesion

---

Commission held that, without prejudice as to whether cost savings are relevant for assessing a merger under Article 2, such cost savings would have in the present case a negligible impact and would not arise as the consequence of the merger but could be achieved by De Havilland's existing owner.

496. E.g. *Sanofi – Synthilabo/Aventis*, D.Comm. April 26, 2004, IP/04/545. *See* under Article 81: *Henkel/Colgate*, D.Comm. Dec. 23, 1971, 1972 OJ L 14/14.
497. Guidelines on the Assessment of Horizontal Mergers, point 81.
498. *Tetra Laval*, CFI Oct. 25, 2002, 2002 ECR II-4519, paras. 229–235.
499. Statements of the Commission, re Article 2; *see* Commission's Notice on Horizontal Cooperation, points 68–71.
500. General principle, *see* under Article 81 (3): *Grundig/Consten*, ECJ July 13, 1966, 1966 ECR 299, 347–348. Similarly under the state aid rules (Article 87), *Deufil*, ECJ Feb. 24, 1987, 1987 ECR 901, para. 8: That article does not therefore distinguish between the measures of state intervention concerned by reference to their causes or their aims but defines them in relation to their effects.
501. *MSG Media Services*, D.Comm. Nov. 9, 1994, 1994 OJ L 364/1, point 55.
502. *See Digital/Kienzle*, D.Comm. Feb. 25, 1991, M.57; *Nordic Satellite Distribution*, D.Comm. July 19, 1995, 1996 OJ L 53/20, points 145–152.
503. Recital 13 to Regulation 4064/89 and Statements of the Commission, re Article 21 (3).

referred to in Article 158, which aims in particular at reducing disparities between the various regions and the backwardness of the least favored regions.[504] However, considerations of economic and social cohesion cannot override the specific criteria laid down in the regulation and thus have only the status of interpretative guidance.[505] The reference to economic and social cohesion was dropped from the recitals to the present Regulation 139/2004. Under Regulation 1310/97 these criteria have only been applied in the context of the failing firm defense,[506] and may no longer be relevant.

Failing Firm Defence.
The 'failing firm' doctrine is not explicitly recognized in the merger control regulation.[507] However, a merger which would otherwise be considered as leading to the creation or strengthening of a dominant position may be regarded as not doing so when the target is a truly failing firm. The basic requirement is that the deterioration of the competitive structure that follows the merger cannot be said to be caused by the merger, or, in other words, that the disappearance of the failing firm is unavoidable whether or not the merger takes place.[508] However, the takeover of a failing firm by a strong and even dominant competitor may weaken the competitive position of the remaining smaller competitors and possibly cause them to react by seeking out their own merger partners, which brings about further market concentration. Accordingly, the takeover of a failing firm by a competitor is probably best limited to the willing buyers that are the least likely to gain market share through the transaction. A dominant firm should be a permissible acquirer only where there is an imminent danger of liquidation of the failing firm and no other less anticompetitive purchaser is available.

Criteria for Evaluating a 'Failing Firm' Defence.
The practical problem in applying a failing company defence is to define how severe the financial difficulties must be before determining whether the merger is likely to reduce or preserve competition. Just temporary problems are not sufficient. It has to be shown that the failing firm faces a longer-term serious

504. *See* Commission notice on regional and competition policy, 1998 OJ C 90/3.
505. In a case involving financial assistance to Philip Morris to build a factory in the Netherlands, the Court of Justice ruled that the Commission must make the economic and social assessments involved against the background of the interests of the Community as a whole: *Philip Morris*, ECJ Sept. 17, 1980, 1980 ECR 2671, paras 24–26.
506. *Kali + Salz/MdK*, D.Comm. Dec. 14, 1993, 1994 OJ L 186/30, point 95.
507. Monti/Russeva, *Failing Firms in the Framework of the EC Merger Control Regulation*, 1999–4 ELRev 38; Claudio Tesauro, *Crisi dell 'impresa e posizione dominante collettiva nella disciplina delle concentrazioni*, 11 Foro Italiano, 183. The 'failing company' concept under EC law does not entirely coincide with U.S. law, *see SCPA/Kali + Salz-MdK*, ECJ March 31, 1998, 1998 ECR I-1375, para. 112, and opinion of Advocate General Tesauro in this case, 1998 ECR I-1375, paras 49–60.
508. Guidelines on the Assessment of Horizontal Mergers, points 89–91.

economic deterioration and consistently incurs considerable losses due to, *inter alia*, obsolete production facilities, high production and labour costs, the lack of an efficient distribution system or the collapse of its traditional markets. Furthermore, it has to be shown by the parties[509] that restructuring the failing firm by other means than a takeover (reducing overcapacity, modernization of production and management structure) will be unable to make it operate more efficiently and to survive as an independent entity and would force the company to withdraw from the market as an independent competitor.[510] The financial difficulties must concern the entire company, not only part of its business.[511]

The *Kali + Salz/MdK* Case.

The Commission found in this case[512] that the proposed acquisition of a smaller competitor by the dominant firm Kali + Salz would increase the market shares in Germany from 80% to 98% in the market for potash products. However, the Commission also found that the target company continued to make losses due to its obsolete operating structure and the collapse of markets in eastern Europe, that it was no longer economically viable and would inevitably have been forced out of the market if it were not taken over by a private company. The Treuhand, established under public law for restructuring the former state-owned enterprises of the German Democratic Republic, covered the losses but would be prevented from doing so in the long term because continued state aids would, according to the Commission decisions adopted in 1991 and 1992, be incompatible with the state aid provisions of the EC Treaty. Therefore the Commission concluded that there was no causal link between the merger and the deterioration of the competitive market structure, and decided not to oppose it under the merger control regulation. The Court of Justice affirmed this part of the decision by stating that the absence of a causal link between the merger and the deterioration of the competitive market structure was not effectively called into question by the applicant companies and that the merger satisfied the criterion referred to in Article 2 (2).[513] However, the Court of Justice annulled the Commission decision in its entirety because the Commission had made erroneous findings with respect to the collective dominant

509. The burden of proof is on the parties to the transaction: *Blokker/Toys 'R' Us*, D.Comm. June 26, 1997, 1998 OJ L 316/1, point 110; *Bertelsmann/Kirch/Première*, D.Comm. May 27, 1998, 1999 OJ L 53/1, point 70.

510. *SCPA/Kali + Salz-MdK*, ECJ March 31, 1998, 1998 ECR I-1375 paras 117–120.

511. *Bertelsmann/Kirch/Première*, D.Comm. May 27, 1998, 1999 OJ L 53/1, point 71; *REWE/Meinl*, D.Comm. Feb. 3, 1999, M.1221. Accordingly, the Commission does not seem to accept a 'failing division' defence.

512. *Kali + Salz/MdK/Treuhand*, D.Comm. Dec. 14, 1993, 1994 OJ L 186/30, points 73–76. *See LSG/Onexcorp/Sky Chefs/Caterair*, D.Comm. Nov. 9, 1998, M.1269, point 14 (no anticompetitive effect of a merger because of preexisting links, which the Commission considered tantamount to a mere intra-group restructuring operation).

513. *SCPA/Kali + Salz-MdK/Treuhand*, ECJ March 31, 1998, 1998 ECR I-1375, paras 112–124.

position on the non-German markets within the Community. The Commission was therefore required to issue a new decision. With respect to the German market the Commission repeated its conclusions that:

- the acquired company would have been forced out of the market if not taken over by another company;
- the acquiring company would have gained the market share of the acquired company if it were forced out of the market, and
- there was no less anticompetitive alternative purchaser.[514]

On the basis of further observation of the market after the merger had been completed, the Commission affirmed that the merger was not the cause of a deterioration of the competitive market structure, that the market position of the parties had in any event declined in the five-year period since the Commission's original decision, and that MdK had effectively merged into a new inseparable unit with Kali + Salz which could not be 'unscrambled' anyway.[515]

Revised, but not Substantially Different Approach in the *BASF/Eurodiol/ Pantochim* Case.

In this case[516] the Commission granted regulatory approval to the proposed takeover of Eurodiol and Pantochim, two Belgian companies active in the chemical sector, by the German company BASF. The Commission stated that BASF will achieve high market shares on certain base chemical products but concluded that the operation would have a less harmful impact on the market than if the Belgian companies were closed down. For applying the failing company doctrine the Commission accepts that 'particular and exceptional circumstances' are present where:

- the acquired company could have been forced out of the market if it were not taken over by another company;
- there is no less anticompetitive alternative purchaser, and
- the assets to be purchased would inevitably disappear from the market in the absence of the merger.[517]

In addition, however, the Commission examined the competitive structure of the market and the likelihood of price increases (which the Commission considered unlikely because the transaction would not trigger a sharp shortfall of capacity). The case may therefore still be seen as an exceptional case rather than to a relaxation of the failing company doctrine.

---

514. *See also* Guidelines on the Assessment of Horizontal Mergers, points 89–91.
515. *Kali + Salz-MdK II*, D.Comm. July 9, 1998, M.308, points 19–24.
516. *BASF/Eurodiol/Pantochim*, D.Comm. July 11, 2001, M.2314 (Article 8 (2) decision).
517. *Ibid.*, point 141; *Newscorp/Telepiù*, D.Comm. April 2, 2003, M.2876, points 207–208.

Cases not Meeting 'Failing Firm' Criteria.
In *Saint Gobain/Wacker Chemie*,[518] *Blokker/Toys 'R' Us*[519] and *Bertelsmann/Kirch/Première*[520] the Commission found, in applying the same criteria as in the *Kali + Salz/MdK* case, that a lack of causality between the merger and its effects on the market had *not* been established and declared the transaction incompatible with the common market in each case. In *REWE/Meinl*[521] the Commission also rejected the 'failing firm' defence and declared the merger compatible with the Common Market only after the takeover was limited to part of the business. These examples show that the Commission accepts the 'failing firm' defence only in exceptional cases.[522] The argument that the target company will not survive as an independent entity or that jobs will be lost if the merger is not consummated will rarely be the principal reason for clearance, but revitalization of the target company to make it operate more efficiently may be a reason to be considered under Article 1 (b), which calls for an evaluation of 'the development of technical and economic progress' possibly in the light of 'economic and social cohesion' as referred to in recital 13 to Regulation 4064/89 and Article 158;[523] however, the reference to 'economic and social cohesion' was dropped from the recitals to the present Regulation 139/2004. In *Newscorp/Telepiù*[524] the Commission concluded that there was no causal link between the merger of the two existing satellite pay-TV platforms in Italy and the effect on competition because an authorization of the merger subject to appropriate commitments would be more beneficial to consumers that a disruption caused by a potential closure.[525] Where the 'failing' company is revitalized by means of state aid one might expect that the assessment of the transaction extends to the question whether the state aid is compatible with the Common Market.[526] However, the state aid granted to the acquired company is

518. *Saint Gobain/WackerChemie*, D.Comm. Dec. 4, 1996, 1997 OJ L 247/1, point 247.
519. *Blokker/Toys 'R' Us*, D.Comm. June 26, 1997, 1998 OJ L 316/1, points 109–112.
520. *Bertelsmann/Kirch/Première*, D.Comm. May 27, 1998, 1999 OJ L 53/1, points 69–76.
521. *REWE/Meinl*, D.Comm. Feb. 3, 1999, 1999 OJ L 274/1, points 62–69 and 116.
522. *See also Bertelsmann/Kirch/Première*, D.Comm. May 27, 1998, 1999 OJ L 53/1, point 71; *Deloitte & Touche/Andersen*, D.Comm. July 1, 2002, M.2816; *Ernst & Young/Andersen*, D.Comm. Aug. 27, 2002, M.2824.
523. *See infra* at section (c) (viii). Under Article 66 of the ECSC Treaty: *Neue Maxhütte Stahlwerke*, D.Comm. June 27, 1989, Nineteenth Report on Competition Policy, point 75 (takeover of a company which had been declared bankrupt but for which a restructuring plan providing for production cuts and closures had been submitted, thereby contributing to the restructuring of the Community steel industry).
524. *Newscorp/Telepiù*, D.Comm. April 2, 2003, M.2876, points 205–221.
525. *Ibid.* point 221
526. *See*, under ECSC law: *Riva/Ilva Laminati Piani*, D.Comm. April 3, 1995, Twenty-fifth Report on Competition Policy, p. 178 (two decisions, but coordinated); Commission Guidelines on State Aid for Rescueing and Restructuring Firms in Difficulty, 1994 OJ C 368/12, in particular under 3.2.2.(ii) (restructuring preferable to selling the production capacities to a competitor). *See United Kingdom, Industry Scheme*, D.Comm. Feb. 13, 1985, 1985 OJ L 155/55, 58, Fourteenth Report on Competition Policy, point 224, and Chapter IX.G.2.

not taken into account when assessing a merger[527] or a joint venture.[528] Similarly, the assessment of the state aid granted to a joint venture under Article 88 does not include or anticipate the compatibility of the joint venture itself; both procedures are independent of one another.[529]

(e) Particulars when Assessing Olipopolies

(i) Characteristics of Oligopolistic Market Structure

General.
Not only may transactions which significantly impede effective competition, in particular as a result of creating or strengthening an individual dominant position – that is to say a dominant position held by the *parties* to the transaction – be prohibited under the regulation, but also the creation or strengthening of a *collective* dominant position, that is to say one held by the parties to the transaction together with one or more undertakings not parties thereto. Companies may have, *as a group*, the ability to act to an considerable extent independently of their competitors, their customers and, ultimately, of consumers, as a result of which effective competition would be significantly impeded in the Common Market or a substantial part thereof. The reduction of the small number of similarly powerful companies may diminish the degree of competition by removing important competitive constraints that the merging firms exerted on each other and non-merging firms can also benefit from the reduction of competitive pressure that results from the merger.[530]

Small Number of Similarly Powerful Companies.
An oligopolistic market structure presupposes a small number of similarly powerful companies that collectively dominate their smaller competitors.[531] These companies must be unlikely to compete effectively with one another and not be faced with any effective competition from other, usually minor, competitors outside the oligopoly group. The intensity of internal and external competition is, in fact, interconnected as stated by the Commission in the *ABB/Daimler-Benz* case with respect to a duopoly:

> 'The intensity of competition inside the duopoly will also be affected by the intensity of competition outside it: if there is a structural basis for signifi-

527. Under the merger control regulation: *SCPA/Kali + Salz-MdK*, ECJ March 31, 1998, 1998 ECR I-1375, para. 119. Under Article 66 of the ECSC Treaty: *RAG/Saarbergwerke/Preussag Anthrazit*, D.Comm. July 29, 1998, ECSC. 1252, point 40.
528. Under Article 81: *Ford/Volkswagen*, D.Comm. Dec. 23, 1992, 1993 OJ L 20/14; *Kali + Salz/MdK*, D.Comm. Dec. 14, 1993, 1994 OJ L 186/30, point 6.
529. *Matra/Volkswagen-Ford*, ECJ June 15, 1993, 1993 ECR I-3250, para. 44.
530. Guidelines on the Assessment of Horizontal Mergers, point 25.
531. Guidelines on the Assessment of Horizontal Mergers, fn. 29. *See Exxon/Mobil*, D.Comm. Sept. 29, 1999, M.1383, point 477.

cant internal competition, that competition may be strengthened by outside competition which would not itself be considered significant, making anticompetitive parallel conduct on the part of the duopolists economically impossible, or at least so unlikely that a lack of competition inside the duopoly can no longer be predicted with the requisite degree of probability.'[532]

Symmetric v. Asymmetric Oligopolies.
The most frequent form of an oligopoly comprises two, three or four companies holding an aggregated market share of 60–80%.[533] The oligopolists' individual market shares are substantially higher than the market share of their other competitors. A larger group of companies is less likely to engage in tacit coordination of their competitive conduct. An oligopoly comprising firms each holding approximately the same market share (symmetric oligopoly) may be strong evidence of the existence of a collective dominant position.[534] An oligopoly comprising firms with disparate market shares, i.e. different firm size and financial resources (asymmetric oligopoly), is less likely to lead to tacit collusion.[535] The market shares of the members of the oligopoly must be rather constant; fluctuations over time or the progressive decline in the market shares would indicate a level of competition in the market.[536] The Commission found symmetric oligopolies to be present in the following cases:

---

532. *ABB/Daimler-Benz*, D.Comm. Oct. 18, 1995, 1997 OJ L 11/1, point 87.
533. Oligopolistic markets in which one of its members has a market share of less than 25% are 'relatively rare' according to the Commission and the Court of First Instance: *Gencor/Lonrho*, CFI March 25, 1999, 1999 ECR II-753, para. 134.
534. Examples: duopolies with 'relatively similar' individual market shares and an aggregated market share of 60–80%: *Gencor/Lonrho*, CFI March 25, 1999, 1999 ECR II-753, paras 293–298 (35% + 35% = 70%; transaction prohibited); *Nestlé/Perrier*, D.Comm. July 22, 1992, 1992 OJ L 356/1, points 117–131 (48% + 34% = 82%; transaction declared compatible following commitments); *Mannesmann/Vallourec/Ilva*, D.Comm. Jan. 31, 1994, 1994 OJ L 102/15, points 131–133 (36% + 33% = 69%; transaction declared compatible in view of significant potential competition); *New Holland/Case*, D.Comm. Oct. 28, 1999, M.1571, point 73 (35% + 37% = 72%). Example of an oligopoly constituted by three members with similarly high market shares: *Renault/Iveco*, D.Comm. Oct. 22, 1998, M.1202, point 54.
535. *In Danish Crown*, D.Comm. March 9, 1999, M.1313 (two companies with dissimilar market shares and an aggregated market share of 75%) the Commission declared the transaction compatible in view of commitments; in *SCPA/Kali + Salz-MdK* (ECJ March 31, 1998, 1998 ECR I-1375, para. 226 (duopoly with companies having within the Community 23% and 37% respectively) the Court of Justice considered such a duopoly as not of itself indicating a collective dominant position and annulled the Commission decision which was made subject to a condition. In other cases of asymmetric oligopolies the Commission did not find evidence of a collective dominant position: *Renault/Iveco*, D.Comm. Oct. 22, 1998, M.1202, point 55 (asymmetric oligopoly between companies of different size and involving different companies in different member states); *Kodak/Imation*, D.Comm. Oct. 23, 1998, M.1298, point 59.
536. *Gencor/Lonrho*, CFI March 25, 1999, 1999 ECR II-753, para. 293–295. Therefore, previous developments in the conditions of competition in the market must be examined: *SCPA/Kali + Salz-MdK*, ECJ March 31, 1998, 1998 ECR I-1375, para. 262.

- *Nestlé/Perrier:* the merging firms had an aggregate market share of 48–50%, together with a third company they held an 82% share;[537]
- *ABB/Daimler Benz:* the new entity and its major competitor held 65%;[538]
- *Varta/Bosch:* duopoly, each party holding 45%;[539]
- *Danish Crown/Vestijske Slagterier:* duopoly, the merged entity and a third competitor holding 70%;[540]
- *Mannesmann/Vallourec/Ilva:* duopoly, the new entity holding 36% and the strongest competitor 33%, while the next two smaller competitors had market shares of only 13% and 11%;[541]
- *VEBA/VIAG:* duopoly, the merged entity holding 31%, while its competitor RWE/VEW held 27% of the German electricity market;[542]
- *Shell/DEA* and *BP/E.ON:* joint dominant position on the market for the supply of ethylene on their pipeline network;[543]
- *EnBW/EDP and Cajastur:* strengthening of the duopoly held by Endesa (44%) and Ibendrola (34%) on the Spanish electricity wholesale market by the acquisition of joint control of the fourth largest Spanish utility company by a strong German generator and the French competitor EDF, which owned the interconnector between France and Spain and therefore controlled the Spanish electricity imports structure.[544]

All these cases were ultimately cleared by the Commission, subject to appropriate commitments to divest assets likely to remove anticompetitive overlaps and any incentive to coordination.

Criteria for Assessing Oligopolies Developed under Regulation 1310/97 Remain Valid.
The criteria developed under Regulation 1310/97 remain as good indicators for assessing oligopolies under Regulation 139/2004. According to the traditional case law any assessment of a collective dominant position must include an evaluation of structural or economic links between the members of the oligopoly in order to ascertain whether they 'align their conduct in the market'.[545] Often the same

537. *Nestlé/Perrier*, D.Comm. July 22, 1992, 1992 OJ L 356/1 (appeal of trade union rejected by CFI April 27, 1995, 1995 ECR II-1213 and 1247.
538. *ABB/Daimler Benz*, D.Comm. Oct. 18, 1995, 1997 OJ L 11/1.
539. *Varta/Bosch*, D.Comm. July 31, 1991, 1991 OJ L 320/26.
540. *Danish Crown/Vestijske Slagterier*, D.Comm. March 9, 1999, M.1313.
541. *Mannesmann/Vallourec/Ilva*, D.Comm. Jan. 31, 1994, 1994 OJ L 102/15.
542. *VEBA/VIAG*, D.Comm. June 13, 2000, M.1673.
543. *Shell/DEA* and *BP/E.ON*, D.Comm. Dec. 20, 2001, 2003 OJ L 15/35, points 52–62.
544. *EnBW/EDP* and *Cajastur*, D.Comm. March 19, 2002, M.2684.
545. *Gencor/Lonrho*, CFI March 25, 1999, 1999 ECR II-753, para. 276. *See also Bodson – Funeral Services*, ECJ May 4, 1988, 1988 ECR 2479, para. 22; *Almelo*, ECJ April 27, 1994, 1994 ECR I-1477, para. 42; *Centro Sevizio Spediporto*, ECJ Oct. 5, 1995, 1995 ECR I-2883, para. 33.

categories of structural or economic links were required to be dissolved in order to reduce the anticompetitive impact and therefore render the notified transaction compatible with the Common Market.[546]

- *Structural links* include:
  - shareholdings;[547]
  - personal links, including interlocking directorates;[548]
  - joint production;[549]
  - marketing arrangements, in particular joint marketing;[550]
  - joint ventures in the relevant market or in a closely related product or services market[551] or pipeline networks.[552]
- *Economic links* include:
  - product homogeneity, in particular commodity products,[553] and similar product lines, whereas heterogeneous (differentiated) products make alignment of conduct less likely;[554]
  - production capacity:[555] significant overcapacity may allow retaliation more easily;[556]

---

546. *See* section D.4.(b) *infra*. The Commission's broad assessment of structural or economic links likely to lead to tacit coordination in oligopolistic markets contrasts with the application of much stricter standards when assessing coordination effects (group or spill-over effects) within a joint venture according to Article 2 (4) of the merger control regulation: *see* Section D.2.(g) *infra* and *Mannesmann/Bell Atlantic/Omnitel*, D.Comm. May 21, 1999, JV. 17.
547. *See Alcatel/Telettra*, D.Comm. April 12, 1991, 1991 OJ L 122/48, points 44–46. However, a mere financial shareholding of 9.99% may not suffice: *Anglo American Corp/Lonrho*, D.Comm. April 23, 1997, 1998 OJ L 149/27. In *Blokker/Toys 'R' Us*, D.Comm. June 26, 1997, 1998 OJ L 316/1, points 132–133, the Commission accepted, at least for a certain period of time, the continued presence of Blokker in the form of a 20% minority shareholding in the company to be divested and transferred to an independent third party.
548. *See Varta/Bosch*, D.Comm. July 31, 1991, 1991 OJ L 320/26, point 63.
549. Including exchange of products. *See Nestlé/Perrier*, D.Comm. July 22, 1992, 1992 OJ L 356/1, points 136–138.
550. *See Kali + Salz/MdK*, ECJ March 31, 1998, 1998 ECR I-1375, where the Commission made the declaration of compatibility subject to the dissolution of a joint marketing organization with its French competitor but the Court annulled the decision. However, distribution links concerning products which are *not* forming part of the relevant product market are irrelevant. *Ibid.*, para. 230.
551. *See Veba/Degussa*, D.Comm. Dec. 3, 1997, M.942.
552. *Shell/DEA* and *BP/E.ON*, D.Comm. Dec. 20, 2001, 2003 OJ L 15/35.
553. *Gencor/Lonrho*, CFI March 25, 1999, 1999 ECR II-753, para. 159; *Mannesmann/Vallourec/Ilva*, D.Comm. Jan. 31, 1994, 1994 OJ L 102/15, point 92.
554. *SCPA/Kali + Salz-MdK*, ECJ March 31, 1998, 1998 ECR I-1375, para. 240; *SNECMA/TI*, D.Comm. Jan. 17, 1994, M.368; *Voith/Sulzer*, D.Comm. July 29, 1994, M.478 (heterogeneity because of customer specifications); *Ciba-Geigy/Sandoz*, D.Comm. July 17, 1996, 1996 OJ L 201/1, point 304.
555. *See Mitsui/CVRD/Caemi*, D.Comm. Oct. 30, 2001, M.2420, point 238.
556. *Mannesmann/Vallourec/Ilva*, D.Comm. Jan. 31, 1994, 1994 OJ L 102/15, points 62–67; *Kodak/Imation*, D.Comm. Oct. 23, 1998, M.1298, point 57.

- similarity of production cost structures[557] (whereas substantially different marginal costs make coordination more difficult to achieve[558]);
- absence of supply alternatives;[559]
- high market access barriers,[560] including barriers to growth (as opposed to innovation potential);[561]
- inelasticity of demand; stagnant demand or low demand growth;[562] absence of demand alternatives,[563] possibly due to a geographic split (protection of home markets);[564]
- absence of countervailing buyer power;[565]
- market maturity (low rate of innovation);[566]
- market transparency (transparency may be limited to the industry on the basis of an information exchange system established by the members of the oligopoly and their competitors);[567]
- absence of price competition over time;[568]

---

557. *Gencor/Lonrho*, CFI March 25, 1999, 1999 ECR II-753, paras. 218–222. *See Mannesmann/Vallourec/Ilva*, D.Comm. Jan. 31, 1994, 1994 OJ L 102/15, points 68–69.
558. *Celanese/Degussa/JV (European Oxo Chemicals)*, D.Comm. June 11, 2003, M.3056, point 161.
559. *Price Waterhouse/Coopers & Lybrand*, D.Comm. May 20, 1998, 1999 OJ L 50/27, point 101; *Gencor/Lonrho*, CFI March 25, 1999, 1999 ECR II-753, paras 247–263.
560. *See ENSO/Stora*, D.Comm. Nov. 25, 1998, 1999 OJ L 254/9.
561. *Price Waterhouse/Coopers & Lybrand*, D.Comm. May 20, 1998, 1999 OJ L 50/27, point 100; *Procter & Gamble/VP Schickedanz*, D.Comm. June 21, 1994, 1994 OJ L 354/32, points 125–130 (brand fidelity as market barrier). *See Dow Chemicals/Shell*, German Federal Cartel Office, April 28, 1999, WuW DE-V 109.
562. *See ENSO/Stora*, D.Comm. Nov. 25, 1998, 1999 OJ L 254/9.
563. *SCPA/Kali + Salz-MdK*, ECJ March 31, 1998, 1998 ECR I-1375, paras 23 1–245; *Gencor/Lonrho*, CFI March 25, 1999, 1999 ECR II-753, paras 231–237; *Mannesmann/Vallourec/Ilva*, D.Comm. Jan. 31, 1994, 1994 OJ L 102/15, point 55; *Price Waterhouse/Coopers & Lybrand*, D.Comm. May 20, 1998, 1999 OJ L 50/27, points 98–99. *See* Twenty-fourth Report on Competition Policy, point 306.
564. *Mitsui/CVRD/Caemi*, D.Comm. Oct. 30, 2001, M.2420, point 236.
565. *AKZO/Nobel Industries* D.Comm. Jan 14, 1994, M.390, point 18; *Procter & Gamble/VP Schickedanz*, D.Comm. June 21, 1994, 1994 OJ L 354/32, points 166–171; *Kodak/Imation*, D.Comm. Oct. 23, 1998, M.1298. *See* Twenty-fourth Report on Competition Policy, points 309–310.
566. *SCPA/Kali + Salz-MdK*, ECJ March 31, 1998, 1998 ECR I-1375, para. 240. *Gencor/Lonrho*, CFI March 25, 1999, 1999 ECR II-753, para. 287; *Mannesmann/Vallourec/Ilva*, D.Comm. Jan. 31, 1994, 1994 OJ L 102/15, points 78 and 129; *Price Waterhouse/Coopers & Lybrand*, D.Comm. May 20, 1998, 1999 OJ L 50/27, point 100; *ENSO/Stora*, D.Comm. Nov. 25, 1998, 1999 OJ L 254/9.
567. *Mannesmann/Vallourec/Ilva*, D.Comm. Jan. 31, 1994, 1994 OJ L 102/15, points 80 and 91–96; *CVC/Danone/Gerresheimer*, D.Comm. July 5, 1999, M.1539. *See RWE-DEA/Huls*, D.Comm. June 11, 1998, M.1174; *Kodak/Imation*, D.Comm. Oct. 23, 1998, M.1298, point 58.
568. *See Dow Chemicals/Shell*, German Federal Cartel Office, 28 April 1999, WuW DE-V 109.

- similar cost structures;[569]
- price stability or parallelism[570] and low price sensitivity;[571]
- similar sales channels;[572]
- vertical integration likely to prevent dealers from switching to other sources of supply, thereby making collusion easier to achieve;[573]
- anticompetitive cooperation, in particular exchange of information on prices, quantities or destinations,[574] and ability to monitor to a sufficient degree each other's conduct and to adopt retaliatory measures where deviation is taking place[575]).

(ii) Development of the Case Law

The Development of the Commission's Case Law Prior to the *Gencor/ Lonrho* Case.
The cases examined by the Commission in view of the existence of a collective dominant position include:

– *Nestlé/Perrier*:[576] The case concerned the merger between two major French producers of mineral water which would lead to an aggregate market share of 48–50% and together with a third company to combined market share of 82% on the French market. The Commission concluded that the reduction of three to two suppliers would lead to a dominant duopoly and declared the merger compatible with the Common Market only under the condition that

569. *ENSO/Stora*, D.Comm. Nov. 25, 1998, 1999 OJ L 254/9; *Danish Crown/Vestijske Slagterier*, D.Comm. March 9, 1999, M.1313.
570. *Mitsui/CVRD/Caemi*, D.Comm. Oct. 30, 2001, M.2420, point 233.
571. Including the absence of secret rebates: *Mannesmann/Vallourec/Ilva*, D.Comm. Jan. 31, 1994, 1994 OJ L 102/15, points 55 and 89. Twenty-fourth Report on Competition Policy, point 306.
572. *Danish Crown/Vestijske Slagterier*, D.Comm. March 9, 1999, M.1313.
573. *Mannesmann/Vallourec/Ilva*, D.Comm. Jan. 31, 1994, 1994 OJ L 102/15, points 70–75; *SCPA/ Kali + Salz – MdK*, ECJ March 31, 1998, 1998 ECR I-1375, paras 228–231; *American Home Products/Monsanto*, D.Comm. Sept. 28, 1998, M.1229, points 24 and 53–54. *See* Twenty-fourth Report on Competition Policy, point 310.
574. *See American Home Products/Monsanto*, D.Comm. Sept. 28, 1998, M.1229, point 24; *BT/ AT&T*, D.Comm. March 30, 1999, JV. 15. Anticompetitive arrangements between the members of the oligopoly which in themselves infringe Article 81 constitute evidence for a collective dominant position. *See also* the cases decided under both Article 81 and Article 82: *CEWAL*, CFI Oct. 8, 1996, 1996 ECR II-1201, paras 60–62; *French-West-African Shipowners' Committee*, D.Comm. April 1, 1992 OJ L 134/1 (with fines); *TACA II*, D.Comm. Sept. 16, 1998, 1999 OJ L 95/1 (with fines); *P&I Clubs*, D.Comm. April 12, 1999, 1999 OJ L 125/12, points 120–123 (links between insurance associations by way of anticompetitive pooling arrangement).
575. Guidelines on the Assessment of Horizontal Mergers, point 55.
576. *Nestlé/Perrier*, D.Comm. July 22, 1992, 1992 OJ L 356/1; appeal of trade union rejected, CFI April 27, 1995, 1995 ECR II-1213 and 1247.

the parties complied with an undertaking to divest certain businesses in the relevant sector.

- *Kali + Salz/MdK/Treuhand:*[577] The case concerned the joint acquisition of MdK, a potash producer in the former East Germany, by one of the two major potash suppliers within the Community, the German Kali + Salz, and the Treuhand, established under public law for restructuring the former state-owned enterprises of the German Democratic Republic. The Commission distinguished two geographic markets: (i) the German market, which was not easily penetrable by imports, and (ii) the rest of the Community with considerable and increasing import activity. The Commission found that the merger increased the market shares in Germany but that the acquired company was a '*failing company*' and therefore the merger was not the cause for the deterioration of the competitive structure. In the Community outside of Germany the Commission found that the merger led to a dominant duopoly held by the new unit and its major competitor, the French SCPA, increasing their aggregated market share from 50% to 60% (Kali+ Salz 15%, MdK 10% and SCPA 35%). The Commission declared the transaction compatible with the Common Market only under the condition that Kali + Salz/MdK withdrew from a joint export organization held together with SCPA. However, the Court of Justice[578] annulled the decision. While it confirmed that a collective dominant position does not fall outside the scope of the merger control regulation, it concluded that the Commission misapplied the concept of a collective dominant position in the present case because of the insignificant accretion of market shares (7%), the falling demand, the considerable imports and the lack of structural and economic links between the major competitors. Subsequently, the Commission issued a decision clearing the transaction without being subject to any condition because the market position of the parties had declined over the five-year period since the Commission had issued its original decision.[579]
- *ABB/Daimler Benz:*[580] The Commission declared the proposed joint venture compatible with the Common Market only after the parties offered a divestiture of their affiliate Kiepe, an electrical supplier of rail equipment, to remedy the competitive problem that resulted from the creation of a duopoly in the sectors of trams and metro systems (the new entity and its major competitor Siemens would have held combined market shares of 65%).
- *Varta/Bosch:*[581] Despite the creation of a duopoly in Spain (each party holding a 45% market share in Spain) the Commission declared the merger compatible with the Common Market because of effective competition from others within the entire Community.

---

577. *Kali + Salz/MdK/Treuhand*, D.Comm. Dec. 14, 1993, 1994 OJ L 186/30.
578. *SCPA/Kali + Salz-MdK/Treuhand*, ECJ March 31, 1998, 1998 ECR I-1375.
579. *Kali + Salz/MdK II*, D.Comm. July 9, 1998, M.1069.
580. *ABB/Daimler Benz*, D.Comm. Oct. 18, 1995, 1997 OJ L 11/1.
581. *Varta/Bosch*, D.Comm. July 31, 1991, 1991 OJ L 320/26.

- *Danish Crown/Vestjyske Slagterier*:[582] The Commission found that the proposed merger between two Danish slaughter-houses would have led to the creation of a duopolistic dominant position between the parties together with another large Danish cooperative slaughter-house, accounting collectively for about 70% of the Danish market for fresh pork sold through supermarkets. The Commission found structural and economic links (similar cost structures and sales channels and price transparency) likely to remove any incentive to compete with each other. Following commitments to dissolve important structural links and to make the market less transparent the Commission declared the transaction compatible with the Common Market, and therefore cleared the transaction.

The *Gencor/Lonrho* Case.
This case[583] concerned the proposed merger of the platinum and rhodium interests of the South African company Gencor, and of the South African subsidiary of the British company Lonrho. Prior to the transaction Gencor exercised sole control over the company Implats by holding 46.5%, while the remaining 53.5% was held by the public. Lonrho held 73% of LPD (Lonrho Platinum Division), the holding company of Eastplats and Westplats, whereas 27% were held by Implats. The operation involved two steps: (i) the acquisition of joint control by Gencor and Lonrho of Implats and (ii) the acquisition of sole control by Implats of the two companies Eastplats and Westplats. Implats, Eastplats and Westplats represented the entire interests of Gencor and Lonrho in the platinum and rhodium sector. The main other supplier of platinum and rhodium was Amplats, whose major shareholder was the South African company Anglo-American Corporation of South Africa (AAC). The Commission found that the proposed transaction would have enabled the two companies to reach roughly the same market shares of approximately 35% of the world market each, whereas the other major supplier was Russia with a market share of 25%. In view of the similarity of cost structures, the inelasticity of demand and the control of 90% of world reserves by the two South African groups (the remaining 10% being located in Russia) the Commission concluded that the transaction would lead to a dominant duopoly likely to impede effective competition within the Common Market. The Commission issued a decision prohibiting the proposed transaction under Article 8 (3) of Regulation 4064/89.[584] The Court of First Instance affirmed the Commission's decision. The

582. D.Comm. March 9, 1999, M.1313. Similarly *Group Villar Mir/EnBW/Hidroeléctrica del Cantábrico*, D.Comm. Sept. 26, 2001, M.2434, points 32–48

583. *Gencor/Lonrho*, D.Comm. April 24, 1996, 1997 OJ L 11/30.

584. *See Anglo American Corporation/Lonrho*, D.Comm. April 23, 1997, 1998 OJ L 149/21. In this case the Commission declared the acquisition of a minority shareholding compatible with the Common Market following the commitment to reduce AAC's shareholding from 24.13% to 9.99% and to assure that AAC's nominee on Lonrho's board of directors would not be party to any commercially sensitive information (points 124–138).

Court confirmed the applicability of the merger control regulation to collective dominant positions by ruling:

> 'Since the interpretations of the Regulation, in particular Article 2 thereof, based on their wording and history and the scheme of the Regulation do not permit their precise scope to be assessed as regards the type of dominant position concerned, the legislation in question must be interpreted by reference to its purpose .... As is apparent from the first five recitals in its preamble, the principal objective set for the Regulation, with a view to achieving the aims of the Treaty and especially of Article 3 (f) thereof [*now Article 3 (g)*] following the entry into force of the Treaty of the European Union], is to ensure that the process of reorganising undertakings as a result in particular of the completion of the internal market does not inflict lasting damage on competition .... Furthermore, it follows from the sixth, seventh, tenth and eleventh recitals in the preamble to the Regulation that it, unlike Articles 85 and 86 [*now 81 and 82*] of the Treaty, is intended to apply to all concentrations with a Community dimension in so far as, because of their effect on the structure of competition within the Community, they may prove incompatible with the system of undistorted competition envisaged by the Treaty.'[585]

The *Airtours* Case: Stronger Proof of Collective Dominance Required by the Court of First Instance.

The *Airtours* case concerned the merger of two major suppliers of leisure travel services in the UK. The Commission prohibited the proposed acquisition of First Choice by Airtours, both vertically integrated companies with upstream charter airline operations and downstream businesses. Prior to the transaction there were four independent operators in the short-haul foreign package holidays market in the UK: Airtours with 21%, First Choice with 11%, Thomson with 27% and Thomas Cook with 20% market shares. The Commission prohibited the acquisition because it would reduce the number of substantial, integrated suppliers from four to three. Prior to the transaction the four suppliers did not coordinate their market conduct (although there was a tendency to do so). According to the Commission the transaction was likely to *create*[586] a collective dominant position: (i) the market would become highly concentrated, the three leading operators assuming about 80% of the market (the merged entity 32%, Thomson 27% and Cook 20%), (ii) the merger would increase the interdependency and transparency, and (iii) the merger would further weaken the ability of the 'fringe' players to compete with

585. *Gencor/Lonrho*, CFI March 25, 1999, 1999 ECR II-753, paras 148–151; referring to *SCPA/Kali + Salz/MdK*, ECJ March 31, 1998, 1998 ECR I-1375, paras 168–171.

586. The fact that the four operators competed with each other prior to the transaction (which is demonstrated by the volatility of their market shares) increased the difficulty of proving the prospective *creation* of a collective dominant position, *see Airtours*, CFI June 6, 2002, 2002 ECR II-2585, paras 109–119 and 134–147.

the majors.[587] The Court of First Instance annulled the Commission prohibition decision.[588] The Court ruled that the Commission failed to prove that, following the merger, the three operators, the new entity Airtours/First Choice, Thomson and Thomas Cook, 'would have had the ability, which they did not previously have, to adopt a common policy on the market…',[589] and therefore the transaction did not give rise to the creation (rather than the strengthening) of dominant position. The Court identified three conditions necessary for a finding of collective dominance:

- each member of the dominant position must have the ability to know how the other members are behaving in order to monitor whether or not they are adopting the common policy;
- the situation of tacit coordination must be sustained over time, i.e. there must be an incentive not to depart from the common policy on the market (credible threat of retaliation); and
- to prove the existence of a collective dominant position to the requisite legal standard, the Commission must also establish that the foreseeable reaction of current and future competitors, as well as of consumers, would not jeopardize the results expected from the common policy.[590]

On the basis of these reformulated criteria, the Court of First Instance found that the Commission erred when assessing the vertical integration (which was rather pro-competitive), the volatility of historic market shares, the low demand growth, demand volatility, and market transparency. In particular, the Court observed that the Commission should have established 'that the foreseeable reactions of current and future competitors and consumers would not jeopardize the results expected from the large tour operators' common policy'.[591]

Subsequent Case Law on Collective Dominance.
The Commission applies the criteria developed by the Court of First Instance when assessing cases involving a collective dominant position.[592] A recent case is *Air Liquide/Messer*[593] which concerned the acquisition of Messer's German industrial gases activities by the French industrial gas producer Air Liquide. The

587. *Airtours/First Choice*, D.Comm. Sept. 22, 1999, 2000 OJ L 93/1, points 168–171 and 194.
588. *Airtours*, CFI June 6, 2002, 2002 ECR II-2585.
589. *Ibid.*, para. 77.
590. *Airtours*, CFI June 6, 2002, 2002 ECR II-2585, para. 62.
591. *Ibid.*, paras 106, 118, 133, 142, 180 and 210.
592. Guidelines on the Assessment of Horizontal Mergers, point 4; Guidelines on Market Analysis and the Assessment of Significant Market Power under the Community Regulatory Framework Framework for Electronic Communications Networks and Services, 2002 OJ C 165/6, points 86–106.
593. *Air Liquide/Messer,* D.Comm. March 15, 2004, M.3314, points 92–100.

Commission found that on the national level for gases supplied both in bulk and in cylinders the merger might create a collective dominant position between the merged entity and their major competitor Linde, in particular on the following grounds:

- Both parties would have relatively symmetric positions (40–50% – 30–40%);[594]
- the products are 'very' homogeneous;
- the market transparency is higly increased;[595]
- post-merger coordination would be sustainable because of the possibility for the duopoly to present an effective threat of future retaliation against smaller competitors; and
- customers would not be in a position to jeopardize the coordination.[596]

Accordingly, the Commission cleared the operation only after having obtained significant divestiture commitments.

(iii) The New Approach under Regulation 139/2004

Significantly Impeding Effective Competition.
The new concept of Regulation 139/2004 has been explained in general in Section D.2.(b) above. Article 2 of Regulation 139/2004 empowers the Commission to act against mergers on an olipolistic market that would significantly impede effective competition in the Common Market or a substantial part of it, in particular as a result of the creation or strengthening of a dominant position. Mergers may have such effects according to the Commission's interpretation in its Guidelines on horizontal mergers:[597]

- by eliminating important competitive constraints on one or more firms even without resorting to coordinated behavior (*non-coordinated or unilateral effects*)[598] or
- by changing the nature of competition in such a way that firms that previously were not coordinating their behavior become significantly more likely to coordinate their competitive behavior, or that the merger makes such coordination

594. A symmetric market position was denied in *Price Waterhouse/Coopers & Lybrand*, D.Comm. May 20, 1998, 1999 OJ L 50/27, points 95–111 (31.7% as compared to 25.9 and 15.7%).
595. This factor was denied in *Mannesmann/Vallourec/ILVA*, D.Comm. Jan. 31, 1994, 1994 OJ L 102/15, and in *Sony/Bertelsmann*, D.Comm. July 20, 2004, M.3333, IP/04/959.
596. However, potential competition from imports (*Mannesmann/Vallourec/Ilva*, D.Comm. Jan. 31, 1994, 1994 OJ L 102/15) and significant buying power (*Enso/Stora*, D.Comm. Nov. 25, 1998, 1999 OJ L 254/9) could jeopardize any anticompetitive coordination between the oligopolists.
597. Guidelines on the Assessment of Horizontal Mergers, points 22–57.
598. *See* Guidelines on the Assessment of Horizontal Mergers, points 24–38.

easier, more stable and more effective for firms which were coordinating prior to the merger (*coordinated effects or tacit collusion*).[599]

Accordingly, the merger control regulation applies to collective dominant positions irrespective of whether or not the members were coordinating prior to the merger and even in the absence of the likelihood of actual coordination between the members of the oligopoly after the transaction is completed.[600] However, the new approach of extending the prohibition of mergers to non-coordinated effects – namely the mere change in competitive market structure[601] – is not substantially different from the requirements of the Court of First Instance in the *Airtours* case. A prospective assessment must be made of the future changes to the market caused by the merger with a view of evaluating whether it would significantly impede effective competition by eliminating competitive constraints which existed prior to the merger or by making coordination easier, more stable or more efficient. The Commission's Guidelines on horizontal mergers identify quite similar criteria for 'tacit collusion',[602] incentive to reduce competition with each other,[603] and non-coordinated effects within an oligopoly:[604]

- The merging firms must have large market shares;
- Their market shares must be relatively symmetric;[605]
- They must be close competitors, supplying close substitutes;[606]
- The members must have enough capacity to expand output sufficiently,[607] which presupposes the possibility of monitoring and retaliating against deviations;[608]
- The members of the oligopoly must be able to monitor the market and the competitors (which presupposes market transparency);[609]

---

599. *See* Guidelines on the Assessment of Horizontal Mergers, points 39–57.
600. Recitals 25–26 to Regulation 139/2004.
601. This is the basic approach under U.S. antitrust law, which, based on economic experience, considers a change within an oligopoly from 4 to 3 players raises serious doubts as to its compatibility whereas a change from 3 to 2 players is, as a rule, prohibited. As to the result of the merger assessment U.S. law and EC merger rules accord: the *Gencor/Lonrho* merger which concerned a change from 3 to 2 players was held incompatible by the Court of First Instance wherease the prohibition of the *Airtours/First Choice* merger which concerned a reduction from 4 to 3 players was annulled because of lack of sufficient proof.
602. *Airtours*, CFI June 6, 2002, 2002 ECR II-2585, para. 83.
603. *Ibid.*, paras 79 and 207.
604. Guidelines on the Assessment of Horizontal Mergers, points 24–38 and 41 (which refers to the *Airtours* judgment).
605. Guidelines on the Assessment of Horizontal Mergers, point 48 and fn 29.
606. Guidelines on the Assessment of Horizontal Mergers, points 28–30.
607. Guidelines on the Assessment of Horizontal Mergers, point 54.
608. These criteria are mentioned in the Guidelines on the Assessment of Horizontal Mergers, points 49–55, as making 'coordination' (or parallel market conduct) easier or more likely, which is similar to the findings in *Airtours*, CFI June 6, 2002, 2002 ECR II-2585, paras 171 and 183–206.
609. *Airtours*, CFI June 6, 2002, 2002 ECR II-2585, para. 148.

- The merger must eliminate an important competitive force in a market which is already concentrated,[610] so that competitors are not be able to jeopardize the outcome expected from the parallel conduct.[611]

Significance of the 25% Market Share Limit.
It is recognized that the reference in Recital 32 of the merger regulation to the 25% minimum threshold for a transaction to be unlawful does not preclude the applicability of the regulation to oligopolistic dominance.[612] However, the regulation has been held not to apply to an oligopolistic market structure in which the parties to the transaction have *themselves* a combined market share of less than 25%,[613] whereas the regulation may, under exceptional circumstances, apply to oligopolies in which the parties to the transaction collectively have 25% or more whereas the other members of the oligopoly that are *not* involved in the transaction have lower market shares (although this may be 'relatively rare').[614]

However, the HHI test as described above is a more accurate indicator for identifying competition concerns on oligopolistic markets[615] or the absence of such concerns,[616] thereby allowing actions against mergers between members of an oligopoly below the 25% threshold.

610. Guidelines on the Assessment of Horizontal Mergers, point 37.

611. Guidelines on the Assessment of Horizontal Mergers, point 36, which conforms with *Airtours*, CFI June 6, 2002, 2002 ECR II-2585, para. 62.

612. *Gencor/Lonrho*, CFI March 25, 1999, 1999 ECR II-753, paras 132–136. This 25% market share minimum does not apply to the assessment of collective dominant positions under Article 82: *see P&I Clubs*, D.Comm. April 12, 1999, 1999 OJ L 125/12, point 10: collective dominance by fourteen insurance companies holding individual market shares between 1 and 16% and an aggregated market share of 89%, which were linked by an anticompetitive pooling arrangement.

613. *See SCPA/Kali + Salz-MdK*, ECJ March 31, 1998, 1998 ECR I-1375, paras 176–177. In *Price Waterhouse/Coopers & Lybrand* (D.Comm. May 20, 1998, 1999 OJ L 50/27, point 113) the Commission stated that 'collective dominance involving more than three or four suppliers is too complex and unstable to persist over time'.

614. *See Enso/Stora*, D.Comm. Nov. 25, 1998, M.1225, where the Commission examined an oligopolistic dominant position between one big company and two smaller competitors that held a combined market share of 20% but concluded that no such dominant position existed.

615. For instance, a market gap of less than 10% between the 'oligopoly family' and its smaller competitors makes an effective anticompetitive coordination unlikely (*Cf. Price Waterhouse/Cooper & Lybrand*, D.Comm. May 20, 1998, 1999 OJ L 50/27, point 117) whereas a market lead of 20% precludes the smaller competitor from effectively competing (*Mannesmann/Vallourec/Ilva*, D.Comm. Jan. 31, 1994, 1994 OJ L 102/15, points 55–56).

616. An accretion of 7% has been held insignificant (*SCPA/Kali + Salz-MDK*, ECJ March 31, 1998, 1998 ECR I-1375, para. 226), although it would normally (in the absence of exceptional circumstances) go largely beyond the acceptable limits when applying the HHI test.

(f) Particulars when Assessing Vertical and Conglomerate Mergers

Generally Neutral Effects of Vertical and Conglomerate Mergers.
The effects of vertical and conglomerate mergers are generally considered to be neutral, or even beneficial, for competition on the markets concerned; however, they may be incompatible with the Common Market if there is convincing evidence that they would lead in the relatively near future to effective competition on the market being significantly impeded, in particular to the creation or strengthening of a dominant position.[617] Vertical integration may be necessary in order to compete with large competitors which are already vertically integrated.[618] On the other hand it may have significant negative effects if it leads to the disappearance of the integrated company as a potential customer of the other operators active on that market.[619] In the absence of such evidence, the mere general strengthening effect does not in itself suffice to prohibit the transaction.[620]

Dominance Through Vertical Links.
A dominant position may be created or strengthened by vertical links (competitive risk of creating a vertically-integrated structure). Examples are the German digital pay-TV cases *Bertelsmann/Kirch/Première*[621] and *Deutsche Telekom/BetaResearch*,[622] which gave rise to concerns over the creation of dominance through vertical links rather than through horizontal overlaps. The parties were able to supply consumers with a complete package of digital pay-TV services, including a specific technology, access to cable and/or satellite networks and programming resources. Alternative technologies were unlikely to be developed, so the transaction risked foreclosing the market to competitors. In both cases the Commission declared the proposed transaction incompatible with the Common Market.[623]

Dominance through Conglomerate Links.
A dominant position may be created or strengthened by conglomerate links, namely a merger between companies which are basicly active on different markets and which do not compete directly with each other. Anti-competitive repercussions may result from leveraging, elimination of potential competition and strengthening of the merged entity's overall position.[624] In *Wolters Kluwer/Reed*

617. *Airtours*, CFI June 6, 2002, 2002 ECR II-2585, paras 63 and 106; *Tetra Laval*, CFI Oct. 25, 2002, 2002 ECR II-4519, paras 153–155.
618. *Airtours*, CFI June 6, 2002, 2002 ECR II-2585, para. 105.
619. *Tetra Laval*, CFI Oct. 25, 2002, 2002 ECR II-4519, paras 135–140.
620. *Tetra Laval*, CFI Oct. 25, 2002, 2002 ECR II-4519, paras 334–336.
621. *Bertelsmann/Kirch/Première*, D.Comm. May 27, 1998, 1999 OJ L 53/1.
622. *Deutsche Telekom/BetaResearch*, D.Comm. May 27, 1998, 1999 OJ L 53/31.
623. *See* Twenty-eighth Report on Competition Policy, point 155.
624. *Tetra Laval*, CFI Oct. 25, 2002, 2002 ECR II-4519, paras 154 *et seq.*

Elsevier[625] the Commission found that the proposed merger between two of the world's largest publishers was likely to create a dominant position through the parties' strength across a wide-ranging series of closely related markets, their financial resources and their ownership of copyrighted material which could impede effective competition from their much smaller competitors. Following the initiation of second phase proceedings the parties abandoned their merger plans and withdrew the notification. In *Guinness/Grand Metropolitan*[626] the Commission examined the 'portfolio power' of the parties to a merger in the sector of spirits and brands. The Commission stated that the holder of a wide portfolio of products will have greater flexibility to structure its prices, promotions and discounts, have greater potential for tying, and be able to realize economies of scale and scope in its sales and marketing activities ('portfolio effect').[627] Although the parties' products were largely complementary and the transaction was found to create a troublesome overlap in only a few countries and product markets, the Commission made its clearance subject to selling off certain whisky brands and to terminating certain exclusionary distribution arrangements. However, the Commission did not clearly state whether such 'portfolio power' may be considered as a component of a conglomerate dominance, thereby indicating that product range extensions may harm competition, or only as one criteria among others for evaluating the economic strength of the parties to the transaction.[628] In *General Electric/Honeywell*[629] the Commission prohibited the merger between General Electric, which already had a dominant position in the markets for jet engines for large commercial and large regional aircrafts, and Honeywell, a supplier of avionics, non-avionics and corporate jet engines, because it would have resulted in the creation of a dominant position as a result of some horizontal overlaps and, in particular, in the strengthening of a dominant position as a result of GE's financial power and vertical integration which would enable the new entity to leverage the respective market power of the merging parties into products of one another, thereby foreclosing competitors.[630]

625. Twenty-eighth Report on Competition Policy, point 154.
626. *Guinness/Grand Metropolitan*, D.Comm. Oct. 15, 1997, M.938, point 40.
627. *See* Guidelines on the Assessment of Horizontal Mergers, point 30. However, the Guidelines do not cover vertical and conglomerate effects (fn. 6).
628. *See* Baker and Ridyard, 'Portfolio Power: A Rum Deal?' 1999 ECLR 181. *See also Boeing/McDonnell Douglas*, D.Comm. July 30, 1997, 1997 OJ L 336/16, points 40–42.
629. *General Electric/Honeywell*, D.Comm. July 3, 2001, M.2220 (appeal still pending).
630. The remedies proposed by GE were rejected as insufficient to resolve the EC competition concerns. The case was cleared by the U.S. Department of Justice. The dissenting views were regretted by Commissioner Monti (IP/01/939) and criticized by Kolasky, 'Conglomerate Mergers and Range Effects: It's a long way from Chicago to Brussels', Nov. 9, 2001. The case is still pending before the CFF.

Critical View of the Court on Dominance through Vertical and Conglomerate Links.

In its prohibition decision *Schneider/Legrand* the Commission based its assessment of the economic power of the group on potential portfolio effects ('panoply' effects).[631] The Court, however, found that the Commission overestimated the importance of a complete range of brands which was also offered by competitors and did not constitute a substantial competitive advantage in the present case.[632] Similarly, the Court overruled the Commission's analysis of the conglomerate effects in the *Tetra Laval/Sidel* case.[633] This case concerned a merger in the liquid food sector where Sidel held a dominant position in PET packaging machines and Tetra Laval in aseptic machines and aseptic carton packaging. According to the Commission, Tetra Laval would have strengthened its already strong position in the aseptic carton sector by extending it into the plastic sector, although the Commission acknowledged that little additional market power was created as a result since any future substitution by plastic cartons would be in substitution to its sister Sidel. The decision was appealed to the Court of First Instance. The Court accepted that, in exceptional cases, conglomerate mergers may create or strengthen a dominant position and therefore did not prevent the Commission opposing future conglomerate mergers, but the Court overruled the Commission decision and placed the clear burden of economic and factual proof on the Commission. The Court found that the Commission did not prove that the merged entity would have put pressure on its current carton and packaging equipment customers wishing to switch over to PET packaging to use equipment produced by Sidel when they make that switch (no proved risk of leveraging)[634] and that the Commission overestimated the possibility of strong growth of the PET market.[635] The Court's decision shows that the anticompetitive effects of a conglomerate merger are more difficult to predict than in the case of a horizontal merger and that the Court's new criteria of 'reasonably predicting future changes to the market' will be and remain subject to critical evaluation by the Court of Justice, despite the broader approach in Article 2 of Regulation 139/2004 ('significantly impeding effective competition' v. creation or strengthening of a dominant position).

---

631. *Schneider/Legrand*, D.Comm. Oct. 10, 2001, M.2283.
632. *Schneider Electric*, CFI Oct. 22, 2002, 2002 ECR II-4201, paras. 234–249.
633. *Tetra Laval/Sidel*, D.Comm. Oct. 30, 2001, M.2416.
634. The mere *possibility* of leveraging is inherently more difficult and speculative than prosecuting a firm *after* bundling and leveraging has already occurred in the market place (abusively, i.e. in violation of Article 82).
635. *Tetra Laval*, CFI Oct. 25, 2002, 2002 ECR II-4519, paras. 321–335.

(g) Particulars When Assessing Joint Ventures

(i) The Basic Criteria[636]

Separate Assessment of Anticompetitive Coordination. Regulation 4064/89 in its original form applied to full-function joint ventures with a Community dimension only insofar as they did *not* give rise to a coordination of the competitive behavior amongst themselves or between them and the joint venture (Article 3 (2) para 2). When the Commission found that a notified joint venture *did* give rise to such anticompetitive coordination and therefore did *not* fall under the merger control regulation, it had to issue a decision under Article 6 (1) (a) with the consequence that the joint venture needed clearance under Article 81 and Regulation 17 and – as the case may be – under parallel national competition law.[637] The amended regulation applies to full-function joint ventures independently of whether or not they give rise to anticompetitive coordination (Article 3 (4) and Article 2 (4) of Regulation 139/2004) and extends the competitive appraisal of the transaction to any coordination object or effect 'in accordance' with the criteria of Article 81 (1) and (3) (Article 2 (4)).[638] The amendment means that full-function joint ventures can now benefit from the 'one-stop shop' principle (excluding parallel proceedings under national law) and the fixed time tables of the merger control regulation. Article 2 (4) therefore avoids parallel proceedings which may increase legal uncertainty, effort and cost for companies and are likely to lead to conflicting assessments. On the other hand, full-function joint ventures that do not have a Community dimension continue to be assessed under Article 81 and Regulation 1/2003 (Article 21 (1) of Regulation 139/2004).[639] The assessment of such joint ventures is not subject to legally fixed time tables[640] and may, in case the Commission issues a non-binding guidance letter, need additional clearance under national law.

---

636. *See* Kemp, 'Recent Developments and Important Decisions', DG IV Newsletter 1999–1, 40, 42.

637. *See STRABAG/Bank Austria/STUAG*, D.Comm. Jan. 15, 1996, M.661 (notification converted to an application under Regulation 17 and comfort letter granted on May 29, 1997, Twenty-seventh report on Competition Policy, p. 160); *General/Unicredito*, D.Comm. March 25, 1996, M.711 (subsequently partly authorised, partly – in certain provinces – prohibited by decision of the Italian antitrust authority of May 28, 1997).

638. The parties' notification must contain information on the likely coordination effects: Form CO, section 10.

639. *See* Commission Notice on the Concept of Full-Function Joint Ventures under EC Competition Rules (1998 OJ C 66/1). In substance, however, the assessment of a cooperative full-function venture would not be different irrespective of whether it is assessed under the merger control regulation (in the case of a Community dimension) or under Regulation 17 or Regulation 1/2003 (in the absence of a Community dimension; *see P&I Clubs II*, D.Comm. April 12, 1999, 1999 OJ L 125/12 (clearance under the merger control regulation); *Télévision par Satellite*, 1998 OJ C 65 (comfort letter under Regulation 17).

640. Normally within two months according to the Commission administrative guidelines, Twenty-third Report on Competition Policy, point 193.

Relation between Article 2 (1)–(3) and Article 2 (4).
Under Article 2 (l)–(3) of Regulation 139/2004 the Commission must assess whether the creation of a joint venture in itself would significantly impede effective competition, in particular as a result of the creation or strengthening of a dominant position; Article 2 (4) concerns objects or effects of the joint venture on the coordination of competitive behaviour of parent firms or third parties, referred to in this provision as 'undertakings that remain independent'. If the Commission concludes that the transaction would significantly impede effective competition, in particular as a result of the creation or strengthening of a dominant position, it declares its incompatibility with the Common Market without needing to assess additional anticompetitive coordination effects under Article 81.[641] If the Commission concludes that the joint venture would not in itself have such prohibited effects it must also appraise anticompetitive effects resulting from the parties' coordination of their competitive behavior. The Commission may clear such effects in accordance with the criteria of Article 81 (1) and (3) and declare the transaction compatible with the Common Market, and may make a declaration of compatibility subject to conditions or obligations to comply with commitments likely to settle the Commission's concerns[642] or, in exceptional cases, declare the transaction incompatible when one of the three first conditions of Article 81 (3) is not fulfilled, even if it passed the dominance test (which corresponds to the fourth condition of Article 81 (3)).[643]

Coordination as Object or Effect of the Joint Venture Agreement – Spillover or Group Effect.
The coordination of the parents' competitive behaviour may be the *object*, resulting from express agreements, or *effect* of the creation and functioning of the joint venture, resulting from joint management or control over the joint venture, likely to lead to coordination of the parties' competitive behaviour outside the joint venture, namely on the same market or on a upstream, downstream or closely related

641. This is the new element in Article 2 (4); in its decision *SCPA/Kali + Salz-MdK*, ECJ March 31, 1998, 1998 ECR I-1375, para. 68, the Court of Justice criticized the mixing up of elements of the merger control regulation and Article 81 *prior* to the amendment of the merger control regulation.

642. *Canal+/CDPQ/BankAmerica*, D.Comm. Dec. 3, 1998, M.1327 (first phase proceeding); *BT/AT&T*, D.Comm. March 30, 1999, JV. 15 (second phase proceeding). *See* Twenty-eighth Report on Competition Policy, point 180 (insert 7).

643. There is no case law yet under the EC competition rules. However, under German antitrust law the German Federal Cartel Office cleared under its merger control regulation the creation by three publishers of a joint venture for publishing applications for employment because it was unlikely to lead to a dominant position, but the Office reserved its rights to examine the anticompetitive coordination between the parent companies, resulting from their equal rights in the joint venture, under the cartel prohibition of the German antitrust law: *Stellenmarkt für Deutschland GmbH*, German Federal Cartel Office 26 Jan. 1999, WuW 1999–5, 528.

product or geographic market.[644] These 'automatic' effects resulting from joint management or joint control may be compared with the 'spillover effects'[645] or the 'group effect' which developed under the ECSC Treaty in the *SIDMAR* case.[646]

This accords with the statement of the Court of Justice in *BAT/Philip Morris-Rothmans*[647] that the acquisition of an equity stake in a competitor 'may … serve as an instrument for influencing the commercial conduct of companies in question so as to restrict or distort competition on the market on which they carry on business'. That is especially likely if the agreement 'provides for commercial cooperation between the companies or creates a structure likely to be used for such coordination'.[648] Under the merger control regulation, the Commission provides for a separate assessment of such a 'likelihood of coordination' or the 'commercial incentives and, thus, the risk of coordination'.[649]

Coordination between Parent Companies v. Coordination between One Parent Company and the Joint Venture.

Article 2 (4) and (5) contain the main criteria for assessing the coordination effects resulting from the creation of a joint venture: The coordination effect depends in particular on:

- whether two or more parent companies retain, to a significant extent, activities in the same market as the joint venture or in a downstream or upstream or

644. Under Regulation 4064/89: *STRABAG/Bank Austria/STUAG*. D.Comm. Jan. 15, 1996, M.661, point 12. Under Regulation 1310/97: *Telia/Telenor/Schibsted*, D.Comm. May 27, 1998, JV. 1, points 38–39; *PanAgora/DG Bank*, D.Comm. Nov. 26, 1998, JV. 14, point 29; *Hitachi/NEC-Dram/JV*, D.Comm. May 3, 2000, JV. 44, points 36–37; *Asahi Glass/Mitsubishi/F2Chemicals*, D.Comm. March 21, 2000, JV. 42, point 18.
645. *See* Twenty-eighth Report on Competition Policy, point 180 (insert 7).
646. *SIDMAR*, High Authority 25 April 1962, Eleventh ECSC General Report, points 346–349. In this case the High Authority held: '… where the controlling enterprises produce the same or much the same products as the enterprise controlled, competition among all the participating enterprises in respect of the products in question is bound to be affected by the group control, since in the exercise of joint control, e.g. in fixing the prices of the enterprise controlled, the controlling enterprises will inevitably take into account their own prices for the same or similar products, and very possibly agree all prices ("group effect").' Thus, under the ECSC competition rules the Commission considered the 'group effect' an inherent consequence of joint control over a joint venture and is therefore not assessed as a separate restriction of competition but rather as part of the overall evaluation of the transaction. Under Article 81 of the EC Treaty the Commission, although not using the term 'group effect', took into account the 'opportunities and inducements' to restrict competition when evaluating the grant of an exemption. *See Blackpowder*, D.Comm. Oct. 20, 1978, 1978 OJ L 322/26, 31; *Olivetti/Canon*, D.Comm. Dec. 22, 1987, 1988 OJL 52/51, 58.
647. *BAT/Philip Morris-Rothmans*, ECJ Nov. 17, 1987, 1987 ECR 4487, paras 37–38.
648. *Sugar*, ECJ Dec. 16, 1975, 1975 ECR 1663, para. 174 (so-called 'requirement of independence'). *See UK Agricultural Tractor Registration Exchange – John Deere*, CFI Oct. 27, 1994, 1994 ECR II-957, paras 50–52.
649. *BT/AT&T*, D.Comm. March 30, 1999, JV. 15.

closely related neighbouring market.[650] Coordination is therefore unlikely to exist where the parent companies merge their entire (production and distribution) activities into the joint venture and abandon any activity in this field.[651] However, the question arises whether this refers to coordination between the parent companies or extends to coordination between the parent companies and the joint venture. Article 3 (2) of the original Regulation 4064/89 expressly provided: 'coordination of the competitive behavior between the parties themselves or between them and the joint venture', which differs from the wording of Article 2 (4) of Regulation 139/2004 'coordination of the competitive behavior of undertakings which remain independent' and may call for a narrower interpretation of the new provision.

- The coordination effect must be the *direct* consequence of the creation of the joint venture. This raises the question whether *inherent* effects may be considered. It must be noted that an anticompetitive 'incentive' or 'group effect' is inherent in horizontal joint ventures where the parent companies are competitors and the joint venture is to operate in the same or a closely related market, and that no such effect generally exists if the parties are not competitors. However, in both horizontal and vertical cases competition may be restricted by additional restrictions, such as non-compete clauses in a horizontal context and exclusive supply or purchasing agreements in a vertical context. Additional restrictions that are not ancillary justify an assessment under Article 2 (4) in order to avoid the prior practice, which declared the restriction non-ancillary and reserved its assessment to a separate proceeding under Article 81 and Regulation 17.[652]

Relevance of Restrictions between One Parent Company and the Joint Venture.

Restrictions between one parent company and the joint venture cannot be regarded as mere allocation of tasks within one economic entity ('*intra-enterprise doctrine*')[653] but rather as concluded 'between undertakings that remain independent'. A full-function joint venture is by definition 'autonomous', which means it must be capable of performing all the functions of an autonomous economic entity similar to other operators on the market. A full-function joint venture differs from a subsidiary, which is controlled by its parent company, is considered as an integral part of that company, and follows the instructions given by the parent company. This would accord with the Commission's practice to examine carefully exclusive supply or purchase agreements between one parent company

650. *PanAgora/DG Bank*, D.Comm. Nov. 26, 1998, JV. 14, point 28.
651. E.g., *Celanese/Degussa/JV*, D.Comm. June 11, 2003, 2004 OJ L 38/47, points 5–7.
652. *See Saudi Amoco/MOH*, D.Comm. May 23, 1995, M.574; *Dow/Buna*, D.Comm. July 4, 1995, M.591; *Alcatel/Thomson-CSF-SCS*, D.Comm. May 25, 1998, M.1121.
653. Chapter I.D.3. *See ICI – Dyestuffs*, ECJ July 14, 1972, 1972 ECR 619, para. 132; *Viho – Parker Pen*, ECJ Oct. 24, 1996, 1996 ECR I-987, para. 107; *PVC II*, CFI April 20, 1999, 1999 ECR II-931, para. 960, *aff'd* ECJ Oct. 15, 2002, 2002 ECR I-8375.

and the joint venture under Article 81 and to oppose those which go beyond the necessary standard.[654] It seems therefore consistent to include restrictions resulting from coordination between one parent company and the joint venture in the Commission's assessment under Article 2 (4). This may in particular be the case where the joint venture is obliged to purchase certain products exclusively from one parent company for a longer duration than necessary (e.g. ten years). Such a contractual obligation prevents the joint venture from using alternative sources of supply and other companies from competing with the parent company. Provided the parent company's market share is considerable and the exclusive purchasing obligation cannot be justified by technical reasons ('necessary for a technically proper exploitation of the licensed technology' within the meaning of Article 2 (1) (5) of the former Regulation 240/96 on technology transfer agreements) the restriction is likely to result in an objection under Article 2 (4), unless it meets the criteria of Article 81 (3). The fact that the Commission has made its clearance of a transaction subject to the removal of exclusive purchasing obligations demonstrates that it is not only concerned with restrictions of competition between the parent companies but also between the joint venture and a parent company.[655] However, in more recent decisions, the Commission tends to disregard restrictions between one parent company and the joint venture.[656]

Important Differences of Assessment under the Merger Control Regulation and Article 81.

The substantive criteria to be applied when assessing joint ventures are those of Article 81 (1) and (3), irrespective of whether they are to be qualified as full-function or partial-function joint ventures. The Commission's notice indicates[657] that these criteria should be interpreted in the same way in both cases.[658] However, the procedural differences are important:[659]

654. Under the merger control regulation: *Herba/IRR*, D.Comm. April 28, 1992, M.188; *Montedison/Group Vernes*, D.Comm. Dec. 8, 1995, M.639. Under Article 81: *BT/MCI*, D.Comm. July 27, 1994, 1994 OJ L 223/36, points 33–40; *TPS*, D.Comm. March 3, 1999, 1999 OJ L 90/6 (*aff'd* CFI Sept. 18, 2001, 2001 ECR II-2459).

655. *See Agfa-Gevaert/DuPont*, D.Comm. Feb. 11, 1998, 1998 OJ L 211/22, points 113–116.

656. E.g., *Celanese/Degussa/JV*, D.Comm. June 11, 2003, 2004 OJ L 38/47. It is significative that their are no recent cases enregistered under a 'JV' number (which indicates the need of an assessment under Article 2 (4) of Regulation 139/2004).

657. Commission Notice on the Concept of Full-Function Joint Ventures, point 16.

658. The Commission's Communication on the Assessment of Full-Function Joint Ventures Under the Competition Rules (1998 OJ C 66/38) confirms that there is no change in the provisions applicable to cooperative full-function joint ventures. In particular, the Commission Notice on the Assessment of Cooperative Joint Ventures is still relevant. Examples of similar evaluation: under Article 81: *Television Par Satellite*, D.Comm. March 3, 1999, 1999 OJ L 90/6; under the merger control regulation: *BT/AT&T*, D.Comm. March 30, 1999, JV. 15.

659. *See* Chapter III.C.10.

- *Assessment under the Merger Regulation.* If a joint venture falls under the merger control regulation it must be notified to and cleared by the Commission, irrespective of the parties' market shares (even if they are *de minimis*, i.e. less than 10%).[660] The one-stop-shop principle applies. According to Article 7 (1) a joint venture operation may *not* be put into effect before its notification and clearance; a breach can be fined (Article 14 (2) (b)), irrespective of whether the operation fulfills the conditions for clearance.[661] Where the Community merger control regulation is not applicable (in particular because of the lack of a Community dimension) the joint venture is subject to Article 81 (provided is has a cooperative effect) and, possibly, national law.[662]
- *Assessment under Article 81 and Regulation 1/2003:* Joint ventures that are not subject to the merger control regulation (because they do not have a Community dimension and have a cooperative object or effect) must be assessed individually under Article 81, unless they are block exempted under Regulation 2658/2000 on specialization agreements or Regulation 2659/2000 on R&D agreements. From 1 May 2004 there is no need for notification under Community law but the transaction may have to be assessed in parallel under Community law and national law(s), and national law may provide for notification(s). The Commission may oppose joint venture agreements even below any market dominance and even below the market share limits fixed by the block exemption regulations.[663] Such a joint venture may be put into effect at the parties' own risk without having obtained prior clearance.[664] The agreements remain, however, subject to civil actions or fines if the conditions of Article 81 (3) are not fulfilled.[665] However, the Commission does not intend to impose fines where the parties assumed, in good faith, that the agreements were covered by a block exemption.[666]

Commission's Tendency to Apply the Full-Function Concept Broadly. In its most recent decisions the Commission tends broadly to apply the merger control regulation to joint ventures, assuming that a large number of joint ventures are autonomous economic entities in the sense of Article 3 (4) of the merger control

660. In some cases, however, clearance can be expected under the simplified merger procedure: Commission Notice on simplified procedure for treatment of certain concentrations, 2000 OJ C 217/32, to be amended upon finalization of the Commission's 2004 Draft Notice.
661. *See Moller*, D.Comm. Feb. 10, 2000, 1999 OJ L 183/29. Implementation may even be fined when the operation was (erroneously) notified under Regulation 17: *Hutchinson Atlantic*, Commission's statement of objections of Nov. 9, 2000, IP/00/1199.
662. Article 21 (1) (no sole jurisdiction of the Commission).
663. *See Floral*, D.Comm. Nov. 28, 1979, 1980 OJ L 39/51; *ANSAC*, D.Comm. Dec. 19, 1990, 1991 OJ L 152/54.
664. *MyAircraft*, D.Comm. Aug. 4, 2000, M.1969, in particular IP/00/912.
665. *See SSI*, ECJ Dec. 10, 1985, 1985 ECR 3831, paras. 73–78.
666. *See* Guidelines on Vertical Restraints, point 65.

regulation when they have their own premises, own capital, own staff and (as the case may be) own technology and own sales forces[667] and when the joint venture determines its own commercial policy without involving the parent companies' responsibility.[668] However, the Commission does *not* require that the joint venture operate at all levels of an economic activity for the merger control regulation to apply; a joint venture may be limited to a particular function, such as production,[669] purchasing[670] *or* distributing[671] and to a particular geographic market,[672] provided that the parents are not, or no longer, active on the joint venture's market[673] and that the joint venture has a secure long-term basis.[674] The consequence is that, e.g., a distribution joint venture may be assessed on the basis of different criteria according to its degree of autonomy and independence depending on whether the assessment is carried out under the merger control regulation or under Article 81. In addition, distribution joint ventures that are given by the parents the status of an autonomous economic entity may be cleared under the merger control regulation without a thorough analysis of their economic efficiencies and without the indispensability test as applied under Article 81 (3).[675]

---

667. *Brambles/Ermewa/JV*, D.Comm. Aug. 4, 2000, M.2023, points 8–9; *Blackstone/CDPQ/Kabel Nordrhein-Westfalen*, D.Comm. June 19, 2000, JV. 46, points 18–19.
668. *TXU Europe/EDF London/London Investment*, D.Comm. Feb. 2, 2000, JV. 36, point 18. *See*, however, *Haniel/Fels*, D.Comm. Feb. 21, 2002, M.2495, points 62–70, where the Commission rejects the argument that the JV's autonomy excludes the parents' joint control; even if the JV's statutes confer autonomy to the JV the parents may retain control of important strategic decisions.
669. *See Asahi Glass/Mitsubishi/F2 Chemicals*, D.Comm. March 21, 2000, JV. 42. *See* White Paper, Commission Program No. 99/027, 1999 OJ C 132/1, point 14 of the executive summary and points 79–81.
670. *See BSkyB/KirchPayTV*, D.Comm. March 21, 2000, JV. 37. *See*, however, the *Powertrain* joint venture between GM and Fiat (both remaining independent), which was assessed and cleared under Article 81 (3): D.Comm. Aug. 16, 2000, IP/00/932
671. *See Bertelsmann/Kooperativa Förbundet/BOL Nordic*, D.Comm. May 18, 2000, JV. 45, point 13; *MyAircraft*, D.Comm. Aug. 4, 2000, M.1969; *BOL Italia/Bertelsmann*, D.Comm. Sept. 1, 2000, JV. 51; *Beiselen/BayWA/MG Chemag*, D.Comm. Feb. 1, 2000, JV. 35, point 6 (JV for joint imports from third countries without risk of restrictive coordination between the competing parents, even in the light of the sales/purchasing relations between the JV and both parents); *De Agostini/Holding di Participazioni/RCS Diffusione/JV*, D.Comm. May 12, 2003, M.3063, point 11.
672. *See BOL Italia/Bertelsmann*, D.Comm. Sept. 1, 2000, JV. 51; *Bertelsmann/Kooperativa Förbundet/BOL Nordic*, D.Comm. May 18, 2000, JV. 45.
673. *See Norsk Hydro/Texaco*, D.Comm. Jan. 9, 1995, M.511 (according to which joint commercialisation of petrochemical products in Denmark does not affect the parents' competitive position on other markets).
674. *See UPM-Kymmene*, D.Comm. Oct. 22, 1998, M.1202; *Krauss-Maffei/Wegmann*, D.Comm. June 19, 1998, M.1135.
675. Example: *GEAE/P&W*, D.Comm. Sept. 14, 1999, 2000 OJ L 58/16.

Commission's Tendency to Interpret the Coordination Criterion Narrowly. Even though a joint venture may perform all the functions of an autonomous economic entity on a lasting basis, Article 2 (4) mandates that any 'coordination' of competitive behaviour between undertakings that remain independent must be appraised under Article 81 (1) and (3). The Commission seems to interpret the coordination criterion rather narrowly,[676] in particular:

- by finding that the remaining competition on the relevant market prevents any anticompetitive coordination between the parties[677] or that the parties together or separately did not have sufficient market power to make coordination 'worthwhile';[678]
- by finding no[679] or non-appreciable restrictive coordination where the parent companies' activities overlap only partly;[680] or where the parents are and remain active on a closely related market (e.g. on the market for mail order books) but do not have, taking account of their market position, any incentive for coordinating the publishing of books;[681] the Court of First Instance seems to have followed the Commission by stating that coordination may be a consequence of the right to adapt intelligently to existing or anticipated conduct (individual

676. *AT&T/TCI*, D.Comm. Dec. 4, 1998, M.1252; *Skanska/Scancem*, D.Comm. Nov. 11, 1998, M.1157, DG IV Newsletter 1999–1, 40. *See*, on the other hand, the broader assessment of structural or economic links likely to lead to a tacit collusion between the members of an oligopoly, section D.2.(e) *supra*.

677. *BSkyB/Kirch Pay/TV*, D.Comm. March 21, 2000, JV. 37, point 91; *Chemag/Beiselen/BayWa*, D.Comm. Feb. 1, 2000, JV. 35, point 30; *Electrabel/Totalfina/Elf/Photovoltech*, D.Comm. April 18, 2002, M.2712, point 26 (arguing that a coordination is unlikely between a company with a national market share of 60–70% and its smaller competitor with an market share of 10%); *TPS*, D.Comm. April 20, 2002, JV. 57, point 30.

678. *Electrabel/Totalfina/Elf/Photovoltech*, D.Comm. April 18, 2002, M.2712, point 25; *Hitachi/NEC-Dram/JV*, D.Comm. May 3, 2000, JV. 44, points 37–39 (no appreciable coordination effect if parties' market shares do not exceed 15%); *Asahi Glass/Mitsubishi/F2Chemicals*, D.Comm. March 21; 2000, JV. 42, point 23 (coordination 'unlikely'); *Canal+/Lagardère/Liberty Media*, D.Comm. June 22, 2000, JV. 40; *Newhouse/Jupiter/Scudder/M&G – Cofunds*, D.Comm. Sept. 1, 2000, M.2075, point 19. However, if this reasoning is correct it could also apply when assessing the effects of hard-core restrictions, such as joint price fixing as effect of creating a joint marketing company.

679. *See BASF/Shell*, D.Comm. Dec. 23, 1997, M.1041, point 30; *Game Channel*, D.Comm. May 6, 1999, IP/99/308; *Mannesmann/BellAtlantic/Omnitel*, D.Comm. May 21, 1999, JV. 17.

680. *Telenor/Telia/Schibsted*, D.Comm. May 27, 1998, JV. 1; *Deutsche Telekom/Springer/Holtzbrink, Infoseek*, D.Comm. Sept. 28, 1998, JV. 8; *Cegetel/AOL/Bertelsmann*, D.Comm. Aug. 4, 1998, JV. 5; *PanAgora*, D.Comm. Nov. 26, 1998, JV. 14, points 28–32 (no incentive to anticompetitive coordination when combined market shares are 5–10%); *Skandia/Storebrand/Pohjola*, D.Comm. Aug. 17, 1999, JV. 21 (clearance after commitments); *Smith Nephew/Beiersdorf/JV*, D.Comm. Jan. 30, 2001, JV. 54, point 86; *Hitachi/NEC-Dram/JV*, D.Comm. May 3, 2000, JV. 44, points 37–39 (no appreciable coordination effect if parties' market shares do not exceed 15%).

681. *Bertelsmann/Planeta/BOL Spain*, D.Comm. Dec. 3, 1999, JV. 24, points 23–26.

'reaction' rather joint 'action');[682]
- by stating that there is no causal link between the transaction and any anti-competitive coordination, in particular where the incentive to cooperate exists separately from the transaction.[683]

In the very few cases where the Commission finds an anticompetitive coordination effect it tends to request the notifying parties to remove such coordination or to reduce the coordination effect[684] rather than finding that the transaction as such raises serious doubts as to its compatibility with the Common Market.[685] Examples of commitments include the non-use of veto rights to prevent competing activities,[686] prohibiting the exchange of commercially sensitive information,[687] the non-discriminatory treatment of third parties impeding their market access,[688] lowering the barriers to entry in order to prevent the dominant firm from leveraging its dominance,[689] the removal of excessive exclusive supply obligations that hinder third parties from entering the market,[690] or even of the joint control itself, which is the cause of potential coordination.[691] The clearance of the joint venture extends to restrictions which are necessary to its implementation. However, the Commission no longer makes an assessment in its clearance decision,[692] thereby

682. *Airtours*, CFI June 6, 2002, 2002 ECR II-2585, paras. 61, 86, 105.
683. *BskyB/Kirch Pay/TV*, D.Comm. March 21, 2000, JV. 37, point 91. *See also Canal+/Lagardière/Liberty Media*, D.Comm. June 22, 2000, JV. 40; *Newhouse/Jupiter/Scudder/M&G – Cofunds*, D.Comm. Sept. 1, 2000, M.2075, point 19; *Electrabel/Totalfina/Elf/Photovoltech*, D.Comm. April 18, 2002, M.2712, point 25; *TPS*, D.Comm. April 20, 2002, JV. 57, point 30.
684. *BT/AT&T*, D.Comm. March 30, 1999, JV. 15; *KLM/Alitalia*, D.Comm. Aug. 11, 1999, JV. 19, IP/99/628.
685. *BT/AT&T*, D.Comm. March 30, 1999, JV. 15.
686. *Hutchinson/RCPM/ECT*, D.Comm. July 3, 2001, JV. 55.
687. *BT/AT&T*, D.Comm. March 30, 1999, JV. 15. This conforms to the Commission's practice under Article 81. *See Exxon/Shell*, D.Comm. May 18, 1994, 1994 OJ L 144/20, points 72–77 (aggregate market shares of about 20%).
688. *Canal+/CDPQ/Bank America*, D.Comm. Dec. 3, 1998, M.1327. In *Enso/Stora*, D.Comm. Nov. 25, 1998, 1999 OJ L254/9, the Commission accepted as a remedy a 'price protection arrangement' precluding any changes in the prices charged to three major customers, which was designed to ensure that smaller competitors were not subject to unjustified price discrimination. However, such an arrangement may be tantamount to price fixing. *See* Twenty-eighth Report on Competition Policy, point 166.
689. *BskyB/Kirch Pay/TV*, D.Comm. March 21, 2000, JV. 37, point 94; *Vodafone/Vivendi/Canal+*, D.Comm. July 20, 2000, JV. 48, point 88.
690. In *Danish Crown/Vestjyske Slagterier*, D.Comm. March 9, 1999 (Article 8 (2) decision) the Commission requested a reduction of the exclusivity to a 85% supply obligation (although the oversight of this obligation may, again, lead to an anticompetitive coordination).
691. *Yoplait/Valio*, D.Comm. June 23, 1999, IP/99/420 (50:50 control of a joint venture between competitors transferred into a 51:49 sole control in order to ensure the joint venture's independent competitive force and to avoid anticompetitive coordination between the parents and the joint venture).
692. Commission Notice on Ancillary Restrictions, point 2.

requiring (unnecessarily) a separate evaluation under Article 81.[693] If the Commission stated the non-ancillarity of a clause because the conditions of Article 81 (3) are not fulfilled – as in the case of a post-term non-compete clause or a non-compete clause of an excessively long duration (e.g, more than five years)[694] – its finding would lead, although not legally binding, to legal certainty so that the parties would know within which limits their agreement is enforceable before national courts. However, according to the Court of First Instance's judgment in *Canal+/Lagardère*,[695] the Commission cannot be relieved from assessing ancillary clauses, which are duly communicated to the Commission in the parties' notification or a separate letter.

Horizontal v. Vertical and Conglomerate Joint Ventures.
The assessment of coordination of competitive behavior within a joint venture under both the merger control regulation and Article 81 depends on whether the parties thereto are actual or potential competitors or non-competitors, including companies with complementary skills.[696] In its Notice Concerning the Assessment of Cooperative Joint Ventures[697] which is, although integrated in the Notice on Horizontal Cooperation,[698] still of useful informative value, the Commission gave a checklist for determining whether firms are potential competitors, which is still a valid source of information.[699] Even if the parties are not competitors there may be anticompetitive coordination between them likely to affect the market position of third companies, in particular in the case of exclusive supply arrangements the effect of which increases with the market shares and the economic strength of the parties to the joint venture.[700]

693. E.g. *Blackstone/CDPQ/Kabel Nordrhein-Westfalen*, D.Comm. June 19, 2000, JV. 46, points 53–58; *Bertelsman/Montadori/BOL Italia*, D.Comm. Sept. 1, 2000, JV. 51, points 51–53; *Canal+/Lagadère/Canalsatellite*, D.Comm. June 22, 2000, JV. 40, points 61–70. Comfort letters which may have been granted subsequently are, however, scarcely reported. In *Asahi Glass/Mitsubishi/F2Chemicals*, D.Comm. March 21, 2000, JV. 42, point 28, the clearance did not cover restrictions because the parties did not provide adequate reasons for considering them ancillary. In *Alcatel/Thomson SA-Thomson CSF*, D.Comm. May 25, 1998, M.1121, the Commission considered an exclusive supply arrangement as not ancillary, leaving the assessment to an individual application of Article 81.
694. *Fujitsu/Siemens*, D.Comm. Sept. 30, 1999, JV. 22, point 81; *Bertelsmann/Planeta/NEB*, D.Comm. Feb. 28, 2000, JV. 39, point 30.
695. *Canal+/Lagardère*, CFI Nov. 20, 2002 ECR II-4825, paras 83–87 and 106–113.
696. *See Blackstone/CDPQ/Kabel Würtemberg*, D.Comm. Aug. 1, 2000, JV. 50, points 31–38; *TPS*, D.Comm. April 30, 2002, JV. 57, points 23–30.
697. 1993 OJ C 43/2.
698. Guidelines on Horizontal Cooperation, point 5.
699. E.g., *Vopak/Van der Sluis/JV*, D.Comm. Feb. 25, 2002, point 33.
700. E.g., *Shell Chemie/Elf Atochem*, D.Comm. Dec. 22, 1994, M.475, point 54; *Blackstone/CDPQ/Kabel Würtemberg*, D.Comm. Aug. 1, 2000, JV. 50, point 44 (clearance subject to a reduction of the duration of non-compete supply obligations to 3–5 years).

The Importance of Market Shares in the Commission's Practice. The assessment of anticompetitive coordination depends on the facts of each case, in particular on the parties' position on the joint venture's and closely related markets and the structural change resulting from the creation of the joint venture.[701] The Commission tends to evaluate the strength of the joint venture's and the parent companies' businesses on those markets and to find no appreciable anticompetitive impact or incentive if the parent companies' activities overlap only insignificantly,[702] represent less than a 10 or 15% market share[703] or are subject to effective competition in a growing market.[704] Another approach is to weigh the relative size of the joint venture's sub-market against to the total market.[705] The Commission will almost certainly consider a coordination effect insignificant if the parties to a horizontal joint venture hold combined market shares of less than 10% or, if they are parties to a vertical or conglomerate joint venture, of less than 15%.[706] This accords with the Commission's 2001 *de minimis* rule.[707] Market shares up to 20–25% are generally accepted in horizontal[708] and up to 30% in vertical cases.[709] According to recital 32 of Regulation 139/2004, market shares that do not exceed 25% indicate that a transaction is not likely to impede effective competition. However, the *BT/AT&T* case[710] shows that combined market shares of 20% in the joint venture's market and between 30 and 50% in a closely related market may require appropriate remedies. On the other hand, the Commission concluded in the *Electrabel/TotafinaElf/Photovoltec* case[711] that coordination was unlikely between a company with a national market share of 60–70% and its smaller competitor with a market share of 10%. In general terms, it may be concluded that market shares of more than 40% require a more critical evaluation (because 40% is considered by the Commission as the level 'where single market dominance may start'[712]) and that market shares of 50–55% or more are unlikely

701. *Hitachi/NEC – Dram/JV*, D.Comm. May 3, 2000, JV. 44, point 37.
702. *See Game Channel*, D.Comm. May 6, 1999; *PanAgora/DG Bank*, D.Comm. Nov. 26, 1998, JV. 14 (however, market shares omitted).
703. *See Telia/Teknor/Schibsted*, D.Comm. Aug. 14, 1998, JV. 7 (less than 10%); *ENEL/FT/DT*, D.Comm. June 22, 1998, JV. 2; *Hitachi/NEC – Dram/JV*, D.Comm. May 3, 2000, JV. 44, point 38 (less than 15%).
704. *Telia/Telenor/Schibsted*, D.Comm. Aug. 14, 1998, JV. 7.
705. *Ibid.*; Twenty-eighth Report on Competition Policy, point 180 (insert 7).
706. In *BNP/Dresdner Bank/Austrian*, D.Comm. Dec. 21, 1998, M.1340, the Commission did not consider anticompetitive coordination effects because any coordination would be part of a more general coordination which had already been exempted under Article 81 (3): *BNP/Dresdner Bank*, D.Comm. June 24, 1996, 1996 OJ L 188/37.
707. 2001 OJ C 368/13, point 7.
708. Regulations 2658/2000 and 2659/2000 on specialization and R&D agreements.
709. Regulation 2790/1999 on vertical restraints.
710. *BT/AT&T*, D.Comm. March 30, 1999, JV. 15.
711. D.Comm. April 18, 2002, M.2712, point 26.
712. Twenty-eighth Report on Competition Policy, point 40. However, market shares are of limited

to justify clearance under Article 2 (4), unless appropriate remedies are proposed by the parties and accepted by the Commission.

The Importance of Efficiencies.
When assessing a full-function joint venture the Commission takes into account the development of technical and economic progress, in particular any substantiated efficiencies. The efficiencies generated by the transaction[713] must benefit consumers, be merger-specific and be verifiable[714] and be likely to enhance continuing incentives of the merged entity to act pro-competitively for the benefit of consumers and to counteract any adverse effect of the merger on competition.[715] This presupposes sufficient competitive pressure from the remaining competitors and from potential entry; it is therefore unlikely that a market position approaching that of a monopoly can be declared compatible with the Common Market on efficiency grounds.[716]

(ii) Product/Service Market Extension Joint Ventures.

Mostly Full-Function Joint Ventures – Application of the Merger Control Regulation.
The most typical case is a joint venture associated with *new investment* to enter a new product market (product or service market extension joint venture). Experience shows that a company usually does not decide to enter a promising new product or service market by setting up a joint venture with another company, unless they both have some basic expertise in the sector or in related fields which can be transferred to and developed by the joint venture. Although both may have the necessary organizational, technical and financial resources to enter the new market independently, they decide to pool the risks involved in launching the project, often with the intention of continuing the new business independently after a certain period of cooperation. The companies are therefore usually actual or potential competitors and consequently the arrangement may restrict competition.[717] New product/service joint ventures which include joint marketing

---

significance on a growing market: *Telia/Sonera/Lithuanian Telecommunications*, D.Comm. Aug. 14, 1998, JV. 7, point 43.

713. Not cost reductions that merely result from anticompetitive reductions in output: Guidelines on the Assessment of Horizontal Mergers, point 80.
714. Guidelines on the Assessment of Horizontal Mergers, points 76–88. Similarly, under Article 81 (3), Commission Guidelines on Horizontal Cooperation, point 152.
715. Guidelines on the Assessment of Horizontal Mergers, point 86.
716. *Ibid.*, point 84.
717. In *FT/DT/ENEL*, D.Comm. June 22, 1998, JV. 2, the Commission argued, however, that the major German and French telecommunications operators, although considered as potential competitors, were not coordinating their competitive behaviour because their absence from the other's markets was a 'deliberate decision' and not the result of the creation of the joint venture.

normally are full-function joint ventures and must be assessed under the merger control regulation, provided they have a Community dimension.[718] The *Television Par Satellite (TPS)* case[719] demonstrates that one of the major problems of assessing product/service extension joint ventures is the evaluation of the non-compete clause imposed on the parent companies in favour of the joint venture. This case concerned the creation of a joint venture by five companies, each active in the audiovisual and telecommunications sector, including cable networks, with a view to establishing a new satellite pay-TV operator. The joint venture's object was to receive, develop and market a range of programmes and services by satellite to be received directly by satellite dishes and cable networks. The Commission issued a negative clearance with respect to the creation of the joint venture in itself and the non-compete clause insofar as it prevented the parent companies from competing against the joint venture for a three-year phase-in period in order to permit the joint venture to enter the pay-TV market. The Commission also granted an exemption under Article 81 with respect to joint venture's exclusive right to broadcast the parties' TV programmes via satellite, which prevented the parent companies from broadcasting these programmes via cable. However, the Commission limited this exemption to three years instead of ten years as agreed between the parties because of the rapid development of the satellite TV and the rapid return on investment in this industry.[720]

Subsidiary Application of the Block Exemption Regulation 2659/2000.
A joint venture that involves R&D, production *and* distribution and is therefore a full-function joint venture must be notified and cleared under the merger control regulation even if it fulfills the conditions of Regulation 2659/2000, including the market share limit of 25%. However, joint ventures that are limited to R&D and production (non-full function joint venture because distribution is carried out by the parents) must be assessed under Regulation 2659/2000.

Normally Favorable Attitude.
Joint ventures set up in order to develop a new product normally produce substantial efficiencies to the benefit of consumers and competition.[721] Joint ventures which are a means for the parents to share a substantial investment risk in connection with extending their business activities into a new product or service market, are viewed favourably by the Commission because they permit the parent companies to renounce manufacturing the new product or service individually and instead share the risk by establishing a joint venture with a direct competitor or a company with complementary skills on a related market (in product or

718. *See Nortel/Norweb*, D.Comm. March 18, 1998, M.1113.
719. *Television Par Satellite (TPS)*, D.Comm. March 3, 1999, 1999 OJ L 90/6.
720. *Ibid.*, point 134.
721. Under the merger control regulation: Guidelines on the Assessment of Horizontal Mergers, points 79–84; under Article 81: Guidelines on horizontal cooperation, points 68–77.

territory). The creation of a joint venture may be the most efficient means to bring new innovations to the market and to increase the competitive pressure.[722] The *Volkswagen/Ford* joint venture for producing a new van was mainly exempted because it was likely to increase competition with the major competitor Renault.[723]

Significance of Market Shares.
If such a joint venture is concluded between companies with market shares which do not exceed the *de minimis* limit of 10% they may not even give rise to any appreciable anticompetitive coordination effects.[724] If they do not exceed the 25%-share limit of Regulation 2659/2000 they are likely to be cleared, provided the duration does not exceed the period of time necessary to guarantee an adequate return of the investment involved, which may vary widely by industry[725] which is measured under Regulation 139/2004 beginning at the time the newly developed products are first put on the market within the EEA.[726] However, joint ventures between companies having market shares of 40% or more may still be cleared.[727]

Conditional Clearance in Cases of Higher Market Shares.
Where the parties are dominant in related markets, the joint venture is likely to produce substantial anticompetitive effects, in particular where the agreement combines two leading technologies, thereby foreclosing the market to weaker competitors[728] However, higher market shares may be counterbalanced by effective potential competition, in particular by 'pipeline products', i.e. pharmaceutical products which are not yet marketed but in an advanced phase of development.[729] In other cases the Commission granted conditional clearance:

722. Guidelines on the Assessment of Horizontal Mergers, point 81.
723. *Ford/Volkswagen*, D.Comm. Dec. 23, 1992, 1993 OJ L 20/14, *aff'd Matra/Volkswagen-Ford*, CFI July 15, 1994, 1994 ECR 11–595. *See also Philips/Osram*, D.Comm. Dec. 23, 1994, 1994 OJ L 378/37.
724. *Ericsson/Nokia/Psion*, D.Comm. Aug. 11, 1998, JV. 6.
725. Not necessarily seven years as accepted by Article 4 of Regulation 2659/2000 in cases of agreements between undertakings with limited market power.
726. *See* Article 4 (1) of Regulation 2659/2000 and Guidelines on Horizontal Cooperation, point 73.
727. R&D agreements under Article 81: BBC *Brown Boveri/NGK*, D.Comm. Oct. 11, 1988, 1988 OJ L 301/68; *Asahi/St. Gobain*, D.Comm. Dec. 16, 1994, 1994 OJ L 354/87. Specialization agreements under Article 81: *Fiat/Hitachi*, D.Comm. Dec. 21, 1992, 1993 OJ L 20/10; *Philips/Osram*, D.Comm. Dec. 23, 1994, 1994 OJ L378/37. Under the merger control regulation: *see Adtrans/Siemens/Thyssen*, D.Comm. March 9, 1998, M.987; *Nortel/Norweb*, D.Comm. March 18, 1998, M.1113; *Bosch/ZF Friedrichshafen*, D.Comm. Sept. 14, 1998, M.1291.
728. *See* Guidelines on Horizontal Cooperation, point 71.
729. *Pfizer/Farmacia*, D.Comm. Feb. 27, 2000, M.2922, point 22.

- Under the *merger control regulation* the Commission granted conditional clearance in the *BT/AT&T* case.[730] This case concerned the creation of a joint venture between British Telecommunications and the AT&T group to provide global telecommunications services to multinational companies and international carrier services on the US-UK route and certain international voice telephony services in the UK. The Commission acknowledged that the transaction was likely to improve competition in these international markets and that the parties, although having a combined market share of between 30 and 50% on the global telecommunications market and about 20% of the total international bilateral traffic, were subject to vigorous competition from actual competitors such as MCI WorldCom, GlobalOne, Equant and Cable & Wireless, from other potential competitors, and that the market was dynamic. Therefore, the Commission concluded that the transaction did not create or strengthen a dominant position. However, the Commission was concerned by anticompetitive effects in regard to the distribution of AT&T/Unisource Communications services on the UK market resulting from a coordination involving ACC, a wholly-owned subsidiary of AT&T, British Telecommunications and Telewest, a UK cable company offering television channels, data communications services and Internet access, in which AT&T held a 22% stake. In the course of the second phase investigation the parties submitted commitments to divest ACC, to create a greater structural separation between AT&T and Telewest and to provide the possibility for another distributor to be appointed to distribute the AT&T/Unisource services in the UK. Subject to compliance with these commitments, the Commission declared the transaction compatible with the Common Market.
- Under *Article 81* the Commission granted conditional clearance in the *General Electric Aircraft Engines/Pratt & Whitney* case.[731] This case concerned a joint venture for producing a new powerful engine designed for Boeing's 'growth 747' project which necessitated the synergy of both partners and was strictly limited in scope, thereby maintaining competition between the three engine manufacturers operating on this highly oligopolistic market. In this case the Commission imposed the following conditions:
    - the parent companies must market the new product separately,[732] and in particular the joint venture must not be granted exclusive distribution rights,[733]
    - the joint venture must keep separate accounting;[734]

730. *BT/AT&T*, D.Comm. March 30, 1999, JV. 15; IP/99/209.
731. *General Electric Aircraft Engines/Pratt & Whitney*, D.Comm. Sept. 14, 1999, 2000 OJ L 58/16.
732. *See also Volkswagen/Ford*, D.Comm. Dec. 23, 1992, 1993 OJ L 20/14.
733. *See also CEGETEL*, 1998 OJ C 238 (comfort letter after amendment of the agreement); *T-mobile/MMO2*, D.Comm. Sept. 10, 2002, IP/02/1277.
734. *General Electric Aircraft Engines/Pratt & Whitney*, D. Comm. Sept. 14, 1999, 2000 OJ L 58/16, points 95–96.

- the parents must abstain from any exchange of commercially sensitive information;[735] and
- the parent companies must regain independence and have access to the joint venture's new product and related technology after losing joint control or after a limited period (up to two years) following the termination of the joint venture.[736]

Risk of Market Foreclosure.
Joint ventures which risk foreclosing the market to competitors are likely to be opposed[737] or to be cleared subject to conditions and/or obligations, such as that licences be granted to third parties on non-discriminatory conditions,[738] as shown in the Nordic Satellite Distribution (NSD) case. [739] This case concerned the creation of a joint venture between Norsk Telekom, the largest cable TV operator in Norway, TeleDenmark (TD), the largest cable TV operator in Denmark, and Kinnevik, a Swedish conglomerate with interests in TV programming. The joint venture was designed to transmit satellite TV programmes to cable TV operators and households receiving satellite TV on their own dish ('direct-to-home' market). The Commission found that the joint venture constituted a highly vertically integrated operation which would reinforce the parties' market positions on the downstream market of TV operations and pay-TV as well as on their upstream market positions, namely satellite transponders and provision of TV programmes, with the likely effect of foreclosing the Nordic market for satellite TV. The Commission found that the creation of NSD would (i) lead to a dominant position on the market for satellite transponder services and provision of programmes suitable for Nordic viewers, (ii) strengthen TD's dominant position on the Danish market for operation of cable TV networks, and (iii) create a dominant position on the market for distribution of satellite pay-TV and other encrypted channels to direct-to-home households (TD controlled approximately 50% of the cable connections in Denmark). The Commission therefore declared the transaction incompatible with the Common Market and the EEA Agreement, but invited the parties to present a modified project because it recognized that transnational joint ventures could be instrumental in developing the media and telecommunications sector to their full potential, provided potential competitors are not discriminated against and foreclosed from these future markets.[740]

---

735. *See also Exxon/Shell I*, D.Comm. May 18, 1994, 1994 OJ L 144/20.
736. *See also BIB (British Interactive Broadcasting)*, 1998 OJ C 322/6.
737. *MSG Media Services*, D.Comm. Nov. 9, 1994, 1994 OJ L 364/1.
738. *Canal+/CDPQ/Bank America*, D.Comm. Dec. 3, 1998, M.1327.
739. *Nordic Satellite Distribution*, D.Comm. July 19, 1995, 1996 OJ L 53/20.
740. Twenty-fifth Report on Competition Policy, pp. 173–174; however, no new project was presented. *See also MSG Media Services*, D.Comm. Nov. 9, 1994, 1994 OJ L 364/1, *Bertelsmann/Kirch/Première*, D.Comm. May 27, 1998, 1999 OJ L 53/1, and *Deutsche Telekom/BetaResearch*, D.Comm. May 27, 1998, 1999 OJ L 53/31. Under Article 81 *see ASTRA*,

Ancillary Restrictions.
Ancillary restrictions must be assessed in the light of Regulation 2659/2000 in non-full-function joint ventures, which means that clauses which are black-listed under that Regulation (Article 5) may not be considered ancillary.[741] If the joint venture is full-function, the ancillary restrictions are evaluated under the merger control regulation to the extent they are directly related and necessary to implementing the joint venture.[742]

(iii) Geographic Market Extension Joint Ventures.

Differentiated Attitude of the Commission According to the Parties' Market Position.
Whenever two or more competitors in a particular product market in part of the Community with a combined market share of 25–40% set up a joint venture to extend their activities to a new part of the Community, the likely long-term anticompetitive coordination of the parties' behavior will tend to prevail over any short-term benefits to competition if each of the firms has the necessary resources to enter the new geographic market independently. The Commission has therefore regularly challenged such arrangements between major Community producers.[743] Similar objections have been raised in cases where competitors

---

D.Comm. Dec. 23, 1992, 1993 OJ L 2023 (cease and desist order with respect to the joint use of satellite capacities by certain competitors, which would today have to be assessed under the merger control regulation).

741. However, a joint venture commercializing the parents' (homogeneous) products necessarily leads to joint price fixing (which would be black-listed). Even if the JV's statutes confer autonomy to the JV the parents still exercise joint control and must be held co-responsible: *Haniel/Fels*, D.Comm. Feb. 21, 2002, M.2495, points 62–70. However, in *TXU Europe/EDF London/London Investment*, D.Comm. Feb. 2, 2000, JV. 36, point 18, the Commission argued that an autonomous joint venture determines the price policy without involving the parents' responsibility.
742. Article 6 (1) (b) and Article 8 (2) of Regulation 139/2004.
743. Guidelines on Horizontal Cooperation, points 144–150. *See Floral*, D.Comm. Nov. 28, 1979, 1980 OJ L 39/51; *ANSAC*, D.Comm. Dec. 19, 1990, 1991 OJ L 152/54; *Tarmac/Steetley*, D.Comm. Jan. 24, 1992, M.180 (joint venture created by two competitors for cement products in the South-East of England, referred to the national authority but abandoned by the parties); *Sächsische Asphaltmischwerke*, D.Comm. April 2, 1998, M.1079 (joint venture considered by the Commission 'partial function'). Under Article 81 *see Industrial Gases*, Nineteenth Report on Competition Policy, point 62 (joint ventures in France, Benelux and Germany between major producers of industrial gases disbanded); *Cotelle*, 1989 OJ C 208/11 (joint venture in France between major washing powder producers, Henkel and Colgate, abandoned and bought up by Colgate); *Sofreb II*, Seventeenth Report on Competition Policy, point 70 (joint interests in French can manufacturer by leading can producer in the Community, Continental Can, and biggest producer in France, Carnaud, terminated with buy-out of Continental Can's interest by Carnaud); *BSN/St. Gobain*, Fifth Report on Competition Policy, point 34 (separation of flat glass producers' safety glass interests in common distribution organizations and joint ventures); *Astra*, D.Comm. Dec. 23, 1992, 1993 OJ L 20/23. Under the merger control

have planned not to set up a new company in another member state, but jointly to take over another competitor there with the intention of operating it as a joint venture.[744] However, if a smaller competitor operating on a national market and a larger competitor operating primarily on another national market establish a joint venture on this market in order to strengthen the former's position, and if these national markets are subject to different competitive conditions, the joint venture is likely to improve the competitive structure, unless there are indications of predatory pricing (in particular by cross-subsidization).[745] Joint ventures between EC companies for production and marketing outside the Community will normally not have anticompetitive repercussions in the Common Market[746] unless the coordination also extends to their activities in the Common Market.[747]

Geographic Market Extension by One Partner and Product Market Extension by the Other.

A firm may decide not to enter a new geographic market on its own, but to go into partnership with a firm that is established in the area or country of interest though not in the same line of business. The foreign partner(s) may have valuable technological and marketing expertise and knowledge of national buying habits. Notwithstanding the fact that the one of the partners is entering a new geographic market and the other a new product/service market, the partners may be considered to be potential competitors,[748] so that a joint venture may lead to coordination of competitive behavior between the parent firms. However, such coordination is unlikely where the relevant geographic market is that of the joint venture's business and where the partner operating on that market is not active on the other partner's market. In *PanAgora/DG Bank*,[749] a joint venture was set

regulation *see Microsoft/Liberty Media/Telewest*, D.Comm. March 22, 2000, JV. 27 (Article 6 (1) (c) decision because of the risk of strengthening Telewest's existing dominant position as an exclusive supplier of cable services in its franchised area; notification withdrawn: IP/00/287).

744. *Irish Distillers Group*, Eighteenth Report on Competition Policy, point 80 (attempted takeover of only Irish whisky producer by three of the EC's largest spirits producers).

745. *See* in the electricity sector: *EdF/London Electricity*, D.Comm. Jan. 27, 1999, M.1346; *EDF/ESTAG*, D.Comm. March 17, 1998, M.1107; in the market of internet sales of books: *Bertelsmann/Kooperativa Förbundet/BOL Nordic*, D.Comm. May 12, 2000, JV. 45, points 21–24.

746. *BNP/Dresdner Bank*, D.Comm. Feb. 4, 1991, M.21; *BNP/Dresdner Bank – Austrian JV*, D.Comm. Dec. 21, 1998, M.1340. Under Article 81: *BNP/Dresdner Bank*, D.Comm. June 24, 1996, 1996 OJ L 188/37 (exemption).

747. *Philip Morris/Rothmans*, ECJ Nov. 17, 1987, 1987 ECR 4487, para. 40.

748. *See* under Article 81: *SNCF/Cégétel (Télécom Développement)*, 1998 OJ C 293/4; Twenty-eighth Report on Competition Policy, points 88–89. The Commission issued a formal negative clearance decision on 27 July 1999, 1999 OJ L 218/24, and, with respect to the related agreements with four telecommunications companies, a negative clearance and exemption on 20 May 1999 ('*Cégétel + 4*', 1999 OJ L 218/14).

749. *PanAgora/DG Bank*, D.Comm. Nov. 26, 1998, JV. 14.

up by a provider of investment management and advisory services and a bank for providing asset management services to institutions in the agreed territory, including to the bank, which was located in the agreed territory and also a party to the transaction. The Commission concluded that the market for asset management services provided to institutions is very competitive in the joint venture's territory without service market entry barriers, that the parent companies' market shares were relatively small and that the joint venture would therefore not lead to any coordination of competitive behavior.[750] In *Canal+/CDPQ/Bank America*,[751] a joint venture was set up to operate pay-TV services in France by Canal+, which held a strong position on the pay-TV market in Spain and on the upstream market for content, and two other companies (CDPQ and Bank America) which jointly controlled Cableuropa, a company wholesaling TV rights in Spain. The Commission did not object to the joint venture as such but found that the transaction gave Canal+, through the balance of power in the joint venture, a strong incentive to favour Cableuropa in the purchase of Spanish TV rights. The Commission granted clearance after the parties adopted remedies designed to eliminate the possibility of discrimination against other competitors on the Spanish pay-TV market. The *Telia/Telenor/Schibsted* case[752] concerned the creation of a joint venture to provide Internet gateway services by Telia and Telenor, both telecommunications operators in Sweden and Norway respectively and active in the production of web sites, as well as Schibsted, a Norwegian publishing and broadcasting company. The Commission stated that there was no appreciable anticompetitive coordination effect in the web site production market because the combined market share of the parent companies and the joint venture was less than 10%. On the dial-up Internet access market the Commission found that Telia and Telenor enjoyed market shares of 25–40% and 10–25% respectively but that these shares were of limited significance in the growing market in question and that there would be no likelihood of the parent companies coordinating their market behaviour.[753]

(iv) Production Joint Ventures

Production as Partial Function.

Production joint ventures that do not provide for joint distribution are not considered as 'full-function' because they do *not* perform *all* the functions of an

---

750. *See* under Article 81: *Rockwell/Iveco*, D.Comm. July 13, 1983, 1983 OJ L 224/19 (joint production of truck axles); *De Laval/Stork I*, D.Comm. July 25, 1977, 1977 OJ L 215/11; *De Laval/Stork II*, D.Comm. Dec. 22, 1987, 1988 OJ L 59/32 (joint manufacturing, marketing and servicing of power turbines and compressors in Europe).
751. *Canal+/CDPQ/Bank America*, D.Comm. Dec. 3, 1998, M.1327.
752. *Telia, Telenor/Schibsted*, D.Comm. May 27, 1998, JV.1.
753. Twenty-eighth Report on Competition Policy, point 180 (insert 7). In *Farland Network*, a joint venture between BT, Sunrise, Telfort, Albacom and Viag for cross-border transmission networks, the Commission issued a comfort letter under Article 81: 1999 OJ C 77/2.

autonomous economic entity. They depend on their parent companies' technological inputs and supplies of raw material, are not independently active on the market, and sell their products to, or at the request of, the parent companies. They are therefore auxiliary to the parent companies' businesses.[754] Under the present administrative law, mere production joint ventures must be assessed under Article 81.[755] The Commission has held that the creation of a production joint venture whose output was marketed independently through the parents' own distribution networks may not infringe Article 81 at all.[756] In its White Paper on Modernization of the competition rules,[757] the Commission proposed to submit production joint ventures to the procedural rules of the merger control regulation although a joint venture limited to production activities (excluding in particular any sales activities) does not perform 'on a lasting basis all the functions of an autonomous economic entity' as required by Article 3 (4). The Commission has granted clearances under the merger control regulation to production joint ventures even if the joint venture sells its products to the parents and only exceptionally to third parties.[758]

(v) Distribution Joint Ventures

Distribution Joint Ventures Exceptionally Full-Function.
Distribution joint ventures are normally not full-function and subject to Article 81. In the case of major operators they are opposed,[759] in the case of smaller operators cleared by the Commission,[760] as discussed in greater detail in Chapter III. C.6. However, in exceptional cases the Commission has ruled that a joint venture, although limited to distribution, performed on a lasting basis all the functions of an autonomous entity, thereby falling within the merger control regulation. The common issue of these cases is that the joint venture was acting on a product or geographic market which was distinct from those of the parents and that the joint venture exercised on this distinct market all the functions of an autonomous entity with an independent power of decision separate from its parents. The Commission can be convinced that such a joint venture will not lead to coordination of the parents' commercial strategies where there is no correlation between the joint venture's and the parents' markets, provided the parents do not have access

754. *See E.ON/Verbund*, D.Comm. Jan. 15, 2002, IP/02/62.
755. E.g., *Solvay/Sisecam*, D.Comm. Sept. 25, 1999, 1999 OJ C 272/14 (applicability of Article 81 (1) denied).
756. *Solvay-Sisecam*, 1999 OJ C 272/14.
757. White Paper of 28 April 1999 on Modernization of the Rules Implementing Articles 85 and 86 *[81 and 82]* of the EC Treaty, 1999 OJ C132/1, point 14.
758. *Hitachi/NEC-DRAM/JV*, D.Comm. May 3, 2000, JV. 44, points 9–10.
759. E.g., *Enterprises Oil/Statoil/Marathon*, D.Comm. April 20, 2001, IP/01/578; *Joint Gas Sales in Norway*, D.Comm. June 13, 2001, IP/01/830 and July 17, 2002, IP/02/1084.
760. E.g., *Angelini/Phoenix*, D.Comm. July 9, 2001, IP/01/973.

to commercially sensitive information given that there are built-in safeguards ('Chinese walls') and competing suppliers are not foreclosed.[761] The *Bertelsman/Mondadori/BOL Italia* case[762] concerned the creation of a joint venture by two competing publishers for the purpose of setting up an online sales business in the Italian language which is to be separated from the book retail market on which the parents remain competitors.[763] The *Texaco/North Hydro* case[764] concerned the creation of a joint venture operating in the business of distribution of refined oil products in Denmark, whereas the parents were and remained active on other markets. In the *KLM/Alitalia* case[765] the Commission qualified as a full function joint venture a long-term alliance (without legal personality), as a result of which the parties would progressively integrate their scheduled passenger and cargo business, maintenance, ground handling services and revenue management, based on the principle of sharing the corresponding costs and revenues. Since the joint venture was likely to create a dominant position on certain routes the Commission's clearance was made subject to commitments aiming at removing the barriers to entry and facilitating the effective entry of competitors into those markets.[766] In any event, these cases seem to be exceptional.

761. *See also Bertelsmann/Mondadori*, D.Comm. April 22, 1999, M.1407; (in this case the Commission stated that the participants – competing European airlines – were unlikely to enter into anticompetitive coordination although electronic and traditional distribution channels were considered as constituting one single market).
762. *Bertelsman/Mondadori/BOL Italia*, D.Comm. Sept. 1, 2000, JV. 51. *See also Bertelsmann/Havas/BOL*, D.Comm. May 6, 1999, M.1459; *Time Warner/EMI*, D.Comm. June 14, 2000, M.1852, IP/00/617; *Babcock Borsig, MG technologies and SAP*, D.Comm. Nov. 8, 2000, M.2172, IP/00/1266; *Otto Versand/Sabre*, D.Comm. Dec. 20, 2001, IP/01/1881; *GF-X Air Freight Trading*, D.Comm. Oct. 28, 2002, IP/02/1560; *Angilini/Phoenix*, D.Comm. July 9, 2001, M.2432; *De Agostini/Holding di Participazioni/RCS Diffusione/JV*, D. Comm. May 12, 2003, M.3063, point 11.
763. Because of the heterogeneous nature of the products there was no risk of joint price fixing (although the Commission did not deal expressly with this aspect).
764. *Texaco/North Hydro*, D.Comm. Jan. 9, 1995, M.511.
765. *KLM/Alitalia*, D.Comm. Aug. 11, 1999, JV. 19.
766. However, this decision contrasts with other decisions concerning alliances which the Commission assessed under Article 81, *See British/Airways/Brussels Airlines*, D.Comm. March 10, 2003, IP/03/350. The fact that the KLM/Alitalia alliance broke up shortly after the decision and is being replaced by other alliances demonstrates that alliances are often unlikely to perform 'on a lasting basis' all the functions of an autonomous economic entity as required by Article 3 (4) of the merger control regulation.

3. Assessment of Ancillary Restrictions

(a) The Development of the 'Ancillary' Concept

The Relevant Case Law.

The concept of an 'ancillary' restriction developed with regard to the *transfer of businesses* in the *Reuter/BASF* case.[767] This case concerned the assignment of Mr. Reuter's entire business in a specific chemical sector to his competitor BASF. The agreement included a non-competition provision on Mr. Reuter which the Commission ruled was necessary to the acquirer and compatible with the competition rules because 'technical knowledge … constitut[ed] an important part of the value of [the] transferred undertaking'. If Mr. Reuter could compete, this would severely impair the value of the business transferred to the acquirer. However, under the particular circumstances of the case the non-compete clause was held contrary to Article 81 insofar as it granted BASF special protection beyond an initial period of five years and extended to independent research and development.[768] In *Remia/Nutricia*[769] the Court of Justice affirmed the Commission's decision applying the 'ancillary' concept to a transfer of a part of a business, including a trademark, by stating that a non-competition clause imposed on the seller is necessary to the transfer and does not infringe Article 81, provided its duration and scope is strictly limited to that purpose. In this case a duration of four years was held necessary for ensuring the transfer of technical know-how, whereas the transfer of commercial know-how justified a non-competition clause of only two years. The Commission also applied this approach to a joint venture in the *Elopak/Metal Box* case.[770] The case concerned setting up a joint venture to carry out research and development of a container with a carton base and a separate closure intended for packaging UHT processed food. The joint venture obtained an exclusive licence to exploit the intellectual property rights (patented and unpatented) of the two parent companies anywhere in the world. The Commission found that the parents were neither actual nor potential competitors, but companies with complementary skills aiming at combining their experience and resources necessary for the new product. The Commission issued a negative clearance stating that ancillary restraints in a joint venture to develop a new technology, such as non-competition provisions limited to five years, were 'no more than … necessary to ensure the starting up and the proper functioning of the joint venture'.[771] The Commission also applied the ancillary restraints concept to the dissolution or break-up of the joint venture, i.e. the transfer of the entire shareholding of one parent to the other stating that the limitation of the licensed technology to the business transferred was necessary

---

767. *Reuter/BASF*, D.Comm. July 26, 1976, 1976 OJ L 254/40.
768. *Ibid.*, pp. 46–48.
769. *Remia/Nutricia*, ECJ July 11, 1985, 1985 ECR 2545, paras 19–20.
770. *Elopak/Metal Box*, D.Comm. July 13, 1990, 1990 OJ L 209/15.
771. *Ibid.*, point 36.

because 'this provision does no more than ensure that such an eventuality (dissolution or break-up) will not be used as a pretext by one party to obtain the other party's know-how outside the highly specific field of the agreement'.[772]

(b) Commission Notices on Ancillary Restrictions

The 2001 Notice on Ancillary Restraints.
On 4 July 2001 the Commission published a new Notice on restrictions directly related and necessary to concentrations (ancillary restraints).[773] It replaces its previous 1990 Notice[774] and further develops the draft notice of 18 August 1999, without changing substantially the Commission's administrative practice but trying to make it more transparent. It should be viewed in the context of the Commission's current efforts to simplify and modernize the procedural aspects of European competition law. The Notice is based on the assumption that clearance of a concentration under Article 6 (1) (b) and Article 8 (2), third subparagraph, automatically covers ancillary restraints, *whether or not* explicitly assessed in the Commission's decision. The position of the Commission is clearly that it does not need and no longer intends to make such an assessment in its merger decisions.[775] This approach is consistent with its administrative practice introduced for cases qualifying for simplified treatment.[776] The most important consequence is that the notification form CO does not need to identify ancillary restraints or to explain why they are directly related and necessary to the implementation of the concentration.[777] Instead, companies and their lawyers have to assess themselves whether the ancillary restraints are implicitly covered by the merger decision as 'directly related and necessary to the implementation of the concentration' or by a relevant block exemption regulation or may otherwise be held compatible with Article 81.[778] Clauses which cannot be considered 'ancillary' as defined in the Notice are

---

772. *Ibid.*, point 33.
773. 2001 OJ C 188/5 (hereafter 'Notice on Ancillary Restrictions').
774. 1990 OJ C 203/5.
775. *See*, however, *De Beers/LVMH*, D.Comm. July 25, 2001, M.2333 (Article 8 (2) decision) where the Commission did not deal expressly with 'ancillary' restrictions but issued a *separate* statement of objection under Article 81 relating to 'Supplier of Choice Agreements' between the newly created joint venture and its customers ('Sightholders') for the purchasing and selling of rough diamonds (IP/01/1069). *See*, however, *Canal+/Lagardère*, CFI Nov. 20, 2002, 2002 ECR II-4825.
776. 2000 OJ C 217/32. In cases qualifying for a simplified procedure the Commission does not assess the ancillarity of restrictions. *See HVB/Commerzbank/DB/Dresdner/JV Trust Center*, D.Comm. Oct. 4, 2000, M.2039. However, the CFI stated that ancillary restraints must be assessed by the Commission even in the simplified procedure *Canal+/Lagardère*, CFI Nov. 20, 2002, 2002 ECR II-4825, para. 113.
777. This information was only necessary for the Commission's evaluation of the parties' *request* to assess ancillary restraints in the merger decision.
778. *See* IP/01/908.

not *per se* illegal; they are just not automatically covered by a merger clearance but may be 'justified' under Article 81 or under a block exemption regulation. In the case of a dispute, this 'justification' must be assessed by national courts.[779] The Notice is designed to give guidance in the light of past Commission practice and experience.

The Court of First Instance's Objection: Assessment of Ancillary Restraints as an Inseparable Part of Any Merger Decision Clearance.

In its decision of November 20, 2002 in the case *Canal+/Lagardère*,[780] the Court of First Instance annulled the Commission's decision of July 10, 2000, which modified an earlier decision of June 22, 2000, granting unconditional clearance of the creation of joint ventures for the production of interactive television services and the development of new thematic channels. The notified agreements contained ancillary restraints, notably pre-emptive rights and non-compete clauses, which the Commission in its June decision considered directly related and necessary to the implementation of the operation. The decision of July 10, 2000 did not affect the result of the earlier decision (the declaration of compatibility with the Common Market) but affected its substance, since it declared the majority of the notified restrictions were *not* directly related and necessary to the implementation of the concentration. On the question of admissibility of an appeal against the July decision, rejecting the Commission's argument, the Court ruled *inter alia* that where, in a clearance decision, the Commission declares that notified restrictions are ancillary or not ancillary, such a declaration is not merely a non-binding opinion. The Court further held that to oblige parties to a concentration to notify under Regulation 17 restrictions which they consider to be economically inseparable from the operation (in parallel with the notification under the Merger Regulation) or to submit such restrictions to a national court for clearance was contrary to the principles of efficient control of concentrations with a Community dimension and legal certitude. The Court expressly rejected the Commission's reference to its recent notices on simplified merger procedures and ancillary restraints by ruling that administrative difficulties, however great, could not be invoked to avoid the legal constraints resulting from the merger regulation.[781] The consequence is that the Commission cannot decline to make an assessment of ancillary restraints. It would also appear that it cannot declare a merger compatible with the Common Market where the merger agreement contains restraints which *cannot* be held ancillary, thereby leaving the non-ancillary restraints to an application of Regulation 17 or Regulation 1/2003 or by the national courts.[782]

---

779. *See* IP/01/908 and Notice on Ancillary Restrictions, point 3. This raises the question whether the parties are prevented from notifying their agreement for the sake of legal certainty.

780. CFI Nov. 20, 2002, 2002 ECR II-4825.

781. *Ibid.*, paras 108–113.

782. The Court did not accept the Commission's argument that its assessment in the decision of June 22, 2000 was compatible with its previous administrative practice (*see TPS*, D.Comm.

The 2004 Draft Notice on Ancillary Restrictions.
In its 2004 Draft Notice on Ancillary Restrictions, which shall replace the 2001 Notice on Ancillary Restrictions, the Commission interprets Article 6 (1) (b), second subparagraph, and 8 (2) (a decision declaring a concentration compatible with the Common Market 'shall be deemed to cover' ancillary restrictions) as reflecting the intention of the legislator not to oblige the Commission to assess and individually to address ancillary restrictions. According to Recital 21 to Regulation 139/2004 the Commission should, at the request of the parties, expressly assess the ancillarity of restrictions if a case presents novel or unresolved questions giving rise to genuine uncertainty, i.e. questions which are not covered by the relevant Commission notice in force or a published Commission decision. The 2004 Draft Notice provides guidance for the self-assessment by the parties and states that restrictions that are not ancillary to the concentration remain subject to Articles 81 and 82 but are 'not, as such, prejudicial to the legal status thereof' (point 7). However, the Commission adds that its interpretation is without prejudice to the interpretation by the Court of Justice and the Court of First Instance, which had been given in the *Canal+/Lagardère,* referred to above,[783] and which remains relevant. The Commission may include ancillary restrictions in its overall assessment of the merger in order to establish or corroborate a position likely to significantly impede effective competition, and may make its clearance subject to the amendment or termination of such restrictions.[784] It follows that the parties cannot be prevented from expressly referring, in their notification or reasoned submission, to ancillary restrictions, and the Commission cannot be relieved from assessing such restrictions in order to ascertain whether they are not prejudicial to the compatibility of the merger or need to be eliminated or amended by way of commitments. The large spectrum of the Commission's administrative practice and the need to assess ancillary restrictions 'in the light of the circumstances of the case in question' can rarely provide legal certainty, in particular with respect to scope and duration of non-compete clauses and supply and purchase obligations, and avoid future conflicts before national courts. It may therefore be argued that non-ancillary restrictions are automatically included in the Commission's clearance if the Commission remains undecided, provided they are duly disclosed in the notification.[785]

March 3, 1999, 1999 OJ L 90/6, *aff'd* CFI Sept. 8, 2001, 2001 ECR II-2459), however, without any further detail.

783. CFI Nov. 20, 2002, 2002 ECR II-4825.

784. *See Danish Crown/Verstjyske Slagterier,* D.Comm. March 9, 1999, M.1313, point 200 (commitment to terminate exclusive supply arrangement). *See also Quantel/Continuum,* D.Comm. July 27, 1992, 1992 OJ L 235/9.

785. *See* Article 10 (6) of Regulation 139/2004, which may be interpreted as also applying to the assessment of ancillary restrictions as an inseparable part of the merger and integral part of the Commission's merger clearance decision, which would accord with the Court of First Instance's judgment in *Canal+/Lagardère,* CFI Nov. 20, 2002, 2002 ECR II-4825, paras 83–87 and 106–113.

(c) Definition of Ancillary Restraints

With regard to the substance, the Commission's new approach remains largely unchanged. An 'ancillary' restraint must be:

- 'Directly related' to the implementation of the concentration, meaning that an agreement on such restraints must normally be entered into at the same time or in the same context of the concentration.[786] Agreements relating to stages before the establishment of control cannot be considered directly related, except where they serve to facilitate the acquisition of control.[787]
- 'Necessary' to the implementation of the concentration, meaning that in the absence of those agreements, the concentration could not be implemented or could only be implemented under more uncertain conditions, at substantially higher cost, over an appreciably longer period or with considerably greater difficulty.[788] This proportionality test requires taking account of the nature of the restriction, its duration, subject matter and geographic field of application.[789] If equally effective alternatives are available for attaining the legitimate aim pursued, the undertakings must choose the one which is objectively the least restrictive.[790]

(d) Restrictions Agreed in the Context of the Transfer of Companies or Assets

Protection of the Assets Transferred.
Restrictions agreed in the context of the transfer or companies or business assets are usually ancillary if they aim at protecting the value transferred, maintaining the continuity of supply after the break-up of a former economic entity, or enabling the start-up of a new entity.[791] As it is the acquirer who needs to be assured about acquiring the full value of the business, restrictions which benefit the seller of the business are considered either not directly related and necessary to the implementation of the concentration at all, or their scope and/or duration need to be more limited than clauses which benefit the acquirer.[792]

786. They must not aim at implementing agreements concluded with third parties: *Blackstone/CDPQ/Kabel Nordrhein*, D.Comm. June 19, 2000, JV. 46; *Blackstone/CDPQ/Kabel Nordrhein*, D.Comm. Aug. 1, 2000, JV. 50, point 53.
787. 2001 Notice on Ancillary Restrictions, points 7 and 10; 2004 Draft Notice, point 14. *See Ericson/Nokia*, D.Comm. Aug. 11, 1999, JV. 6.
788. *See Vodafone/BT/Airtel JV*, D.Comm. Dec. 18, 2000, M.1863, point 20.
789. Notice on Ancillary Restraints, points 8–9.
790. *Ibid.*, point 9.
791. *Ibid.*, point 8.
792. *Ibid.*, point 12.

Non-Competition Clauses.
Non-competition clauses (including non-solicitation and confidentiality clauses[793]) must be limited to:

- *Goodwill only*
  two years for cases involving the protection of goodwill only, in particular customer relationships and customer loyalty;[794]
- *Goodwill and Know-How*
  three years for cases involving both elements of goodwill and technical know-how.[795]

Non-competition clauses agreed for a longer period may be held ancillary only if they are sufficiently 'justified'.[796] In the absence of sufficient justification they are not covered by the merger clearance decision[797] and need individual clearance under Article 81 (3).[798]

Territorial and Product Limitation of Non-Competition Clauses.
The scope of a non-competition clause must normally be limited:[799]

- to the *area* in which the seller offered the relevant products or services before the transfer, including markets the seller was planning to enter at the time of the transaction,[800] and

793. *Ibid.*, point 20. Example of a non-solicitation clause: *Bayer/Lyondell*, D.Comm. Feb. 21, 2000, M.1796.
794. Notice on Ancillary Restrictions, point 15; Draft 2004 Notice on Ancillary Restrictions, point 20. *See also Bayer/Lyondell*, D.Comm. Feb. 21, 2000, M.1796, point 26. *See* under the merger control regulation: *Vodafone plc/Eircell*, D.Comm. March 2001, M.2305, points 21–22; under Article 81: *Remia/Nutricia*, ECJ July 11, 1985, 1985 ECR 2545. The transfer of physical assets (land, machinery) does not justify any non-competitions clause: 2004 Draft Notice, point 21.
795. Notice on Ancillary Restrictions, point 15; 2004 Draft Notice, point 20. This is new. Under the 1990 Notice (under III.A.2.) the protection could be granted for five years, according to the Commission's *Reuter/BASF* doctrine: D.Comm. July 26, 1976, 1976 OJ L 254/40.
796. A duration of five years has been accepted in several cases: under the merger control regulation, *Fiat/Ford New Holland*, D.Comm. Feb. 8, 1991, M.9; *Digital/Kienzle*, D.Comm. Feb. 25, 1991, M.17; under Article 81: *Reuter/BASF*, D.Comm. July 26, 1976, 1976 OJ L 254/40, points 47–48.
797. *Bayer/Lyonell*, D.Comm. Feb. 21, 2000, M.1796, point 25.
798. The same principles apply to non-competition obligations that restrict the seller's right to purchase or hold shares in a company competing with the business transferred, except where the shares are purchased or held for investment purposes without granting the seller management functions or a material influence in the competing company: Notice on Ancillary Restrictions, point 19.
799. *See* 2004 Draft Notice on Ancillary Restrictions, point 22.
800. Notice on Ancillary Restrictions, point 16, referring to various Comission decisions.

- to the *relevant* products or services, offered by the seller before the transfer, including improved versions, updates and successor models as well as products that are already fully developed but not yet marketed.[801] However, the seller may not be prevented from researching and developing *new*, although substitutable, products.[803]

Non-competition clauses which go beyond these limits may be justified 'by particular circumstances of the case'.[803]

(e) Ancillary Restraints in License Agreements

Field-of-Use Licenses.

The transfer of assets normally includes the transfer of intellectual property rights which may constitute an important part of their value. However, in cases where the rights can also be used in fields of activity other than those transferred, the seller may want to keep the full use of the rights in those fields and to grant a license limited to the specific field of the transferred business. Such field-of-use licenses are normally not restrictive of competition,[804] and ancillary to the implementation of the operation.[805] Such licences of patents, of similar rights, of know-how or trademarks can be considered necessary to the implementation of the concentration and need not be limited in time.[806] Any evaluation of restrictions in licence agreements calls for application of Regulation 772/2004 on Technology Transfer Agreements.[807]

Territorial Protection.

Territorial limitations on manufacture reflecting the territory of the transferred activity are normally *not* necessary to the implementation of the operation.[808] They may reflect, or lead to, market sharing between seller and buyer, which may, however, be covered by the Article 2 of Regulation 772/2004 on Transfer of Technology Agreements.[809] Under particular circumstances they may constitute an undue protection of the buyer if they are not limited to a provisional period.[810]

---

801. *Ibid.*, point 17, referring to various Comission decisions.
802. *Reuter/BASF*, D.Comm. July 26, 1976, 1976 OJ L 254/40, point II.4 (a).
803. Notice on Ancillary Restrictions, point 16 with reference to the Commission's established practice.
804. *See* Article 2 (1) (8) of the former Regulation 240/96 on Technology Transfer Agreements.
805. Notice on Ancillary Restrictions, points 21–23. *See Quantel/Continuum*, D.Comm. July 27, 1992, 1992 OJ L 235/9.
806. Notice on Ancillary Restrictions, points 22–23; Draft 2004 Notice on Ancillary Restrictions, points 27–31.
807. *See* Chapter VII.E.
808. Notice on Ancillary Restrictions, point 22.
809. *Ibid.*, point 22.
810. *Philip Morris/Altadis (ex Tabacalera)*, D.Comm. Feb. 23, 2001, IP/01/249 (closure of procedure following the limitation of the territorial exclusivity to 3 years).

(f) Ancillary Purchase, Supply and Resale Obligations

Purchase and supply obligations may be necessary, at least for a transitional period, which is normally up to five years,[811] in order to maintain the continuity of supply after the break-up of the former entity,[812] enabling the start-up of a new entity,[813] or in cases of vertical integration of a new entity.[814] There is no general justification for *exclusive* purchase and supply obligations in unlimited quantities,[815] but even exclusive purchase and supply obligations may be covered, in a vertical context, by Regulation 2790/1999 up to five years,[816] provided the parties market share does not exceed 30%.[817] In the context of a specialization[818] or R&D agreement[819] such obligations are exempted by the respective block exemption for the entire duration of the agreement, provided the parties' market share do not exceed the market share limits of these regulations (respectively 20 and 25%). Cases where these market shares are exceeded justifiy individual clearance under Article 81 (3) only under exceptional circumstances.[820]

Restrictions against exports or imports to or from other EU or EEA countries imposed on resellers are never ancillary;[821] they are hardcore restrictions und unlikely to qualify for individual clearance.[822]

(g) Ancillary Restraints in Cases of Joint Acquisitions

Arrangements to acquire joint control or to divide up the acquired assets among the parties[823] are ancillary, including joint bidding.[824] Non-competition clauses

811. 2004 Draft Notice on Ancillary Restrictions, point 33 (transfer of business) and 44 (joint ventures); *see BT/AT&T,* D.Comm. March 30, 1999, JV.15, point 209. The 2001 Notice accepted such obligations, as a rule, only up to three years: point 30.
812. *See BP/JV Dissolution,* D.Comm. Feb. 2, 2000, M.1820.
813. 2001 Notice on Ancillary Restrictions, points 25–31. *See Dow/Enichem,* D.Comm. April 6, 2001, M.2355, point 28.
814. *See Shell/Halliburton,* D.Comm. March 15, 2001, M.1976, point 54.
815. Draft 2004 Notice on Ancillary Restrictions, point 34; 2001 Notice, points 28–29. *See Valeo/ITT,* D.Comm. July 30, 1998, M.1245, points 63–64.
816. Article 5 (a) of Regulation 2790/1999.
817. Article 3 of Regulation 2790/1999.
818. Article 3 of Regulation 2658/2000.
819. Article 1 of Regulation 2659/2000.
820. 2001 Notice on Ancillary Restrictions, point 29.
821. 2004 Draft Notice on Ancillary Restrictions, point 24; 2001 Notice, point 18.
822. *See* Guidelines on Vertical Restrictions, points 46–56.
823. 2004 Draft Notice on Ancillary Restrictions, points 15–16. Example: *Solvay/Laporte/Interox,* D.Comm. April 30, 1992, M.197.
824. 2004 Draft Notice on Ancillary Restrictions, point 14 with further references to the relevant case law; 2001 Notice, points 32–34.

must be limited to the necessary standard, which is normally three years.[825]

(h) Ancillary Restraints in the Context of Joint Ventures

Non-compete obligations between the parents and the joint venture are justified if and insofar as they reflect the *need to fully utilize the joint venture's assets*, to enable the joint venture to assimilate know-how and goodwill provided by its parents and to secure the parents' investment and the future economic success of the joint venture. Such non-compete clauses are, according to the 2004 Draft Notice on Ancillary Restrictions, justified for the lifetime (but not beyond the lifetime) of the joint venture.[826]

However, the non-compete clause must be *limited to the products, services and territories covered by the joint venture agreement*.[827] If the parents remain present in a market upstream or downstream of the joint venture, any purchase and supply agreements, including service and distribution agreements, are recognized as ancillary if they do not provide for legal or factual exclusivity or a preferential status and are limited to five years.[828] Non-compete clauses are therefore not justified insofar as they relate or extend directly or indirectly to the parents' businesses *outside* the product and territorial market of their joint venture.[829]

In addition, the joint venture must be[830] and remain[831] under the *joint control* of the parents so that the parents and the joint venture are operative parts in a closely aligned business. Non-compete clauses are therefore *not* ancillary where

825. 2004 Draft Notice on Ancilllary Restrictions, point 13 with further references to the relevant case law; 2001 Notice, points 32–34.
826. Point 36. The 2001 Notice accepted non-compete clauses, as a rule, only for three or, if duly justified , for five years: point 36. Post-term non-compete clauses up to one year may be considered ancillary only under exceptional circumstances: *Bertelsmann/Kooperativa Förbundet/ BOL Nordic,* D.Comm. May 12, 2000, JV. 45, point 26.
827. 2004 Draft Notice on Ancillary Restrictions, points 37–38; 2001 Notice, point 17; *see Stora Enso/AssiDomän,* D.Comm. Dec. 22, 2000, M.2243, point 49, last sentence.
828. 2004 Draft Notice on Ancillary Restrictions, points 43 and 33, whereas the 2001 Notice, points 45 and 30, accepted, as a rule, only three-year obligations.
829. However, the non-compete clause may extend to territories which the parents were planning to enter at the time of the transaction and to products and services at an advanced stage of development at the time of the transaction: 2004 Draft Notice on Ancillary Restrictions, points 37-38.
830. *Ibid.*, point 40. Where parents do not have 'joint' control because of the possibility of shifting majorities and hanging alliances between the parents: Notice of the Concept of Concentration, point 35 (normally not to be regarded as a 'merger' and therefore to be assessed under Article 81 (1)), *see Eureko,* D.Comm. April 27, 1992, M.207*; Ericson/Nokia/Psion/Motorola,* D.Comm. Dec. 22, 1998, JV.12.
831. The parents no longer have joint control because of the termination or dissolution of the joint venture, *see Framatome/Siemens,* D.Comm. Dec. 6, 2000, M. 1940, point 147.

companies transfer part of their business completely and definitely to another company in which they do not retain any ownership interest or only a financial interest.[832] In this case non-compete clauses are only justified if and insofar as they are necessary to ensure that the acquiror can exploit the full value of the business transferred, namely normally up to three years when the transfer includes both goodwill and know-how, and up to two years when only goodwill is included.[833] However, where the companies retain joint control over the joint venture the general rule of a longer duration applies.[834] The transfer may include the grant of an exclusive licence and and of licences limited to a particular field of use or a particular site.[835]

Non-compete clauses are not ancillary if they lead to anticompetitive coordination *between* the controlling parents, in particular in the case where two competitors establish a joint venture in a new geographic market, except where such coordination satisfies the conditions of Article 81 (3).[836] As a rule, non-compete clauses may not extend to import or export *restrictions imposed on resellers or users*.[837]

4. Merger Remedies – Commitments

(a) The New Commission Notice on Merger Remedies

The Legal Basis.

The Commission may attach to its clearance decision conditions and obligations intended to ensure that the undertakings concerned comply with the commitments

832. 2004 Draft Notice on Ancillary Restrictions, points 39–40.
833. *Ibid.,* point 20, whereas the 2001 Notice, point 36, accepted restrictions for more than three years if duly justified. Two years: *Kingfisher/Grosslabor,* April 12, 1999, M.1482, point 33. Three years: *Smith & Nephew/Beiersdorf/JV,* D.Comm. Jan. 30, 2001, JV.54, points 88–89. Five years: *Stora Enso/AssiDomänJV,* D.Comm. Dec. 22, 2000, M.2243, point 49 (reduced to five years); *SLDE/INTL/MSCP/NOOS,* D.Comm. Oct. 16, 2000, M.2137, point 41 (3–10 years).
834. *See Unicarbide/Enichem,* D.Comm. March 13, 1995, M.550, point 90; *Framatome/Siemens,* D.Comm. Dec. 6, 2000, M. 1940, points 147–148; *Sony/Bertelsmann,* D.Comm. July 20, 2004, M.3333, IP/04/959 (however, no details published yet).
835. 2004 Draft Notice on Ancillary Restrictions, points 42–43. *See Elopak/Metalbox-Odin,* D.Comm. July 13, 1990, 1990 OJ L 209/15 (site licence accepted); *Repsol/Arco,* Commission's Evaluation Report on Regulation 240/96, FN 49 (opposed).
836. Under Article 2 (4) of Regulation 139/2004: *Canal+/Lagardère/Canalsatellite,* D.Comm. June 22, 2000, JV. 40, points 44–70; under Article 81 (3): *BNP/Dresdner Bank,* D.Comm. June 24, 1996, 1996 OJ L 188/37, and. *BNP/Dresner Bank – Austrian JV,* D.Comm. Dec. 21, 1998, M.1340, point 12. Strategic partnerships are not considered ancillary: *ENI/GALP,* D.Comm. June 29, 2000, M.1859, point 21.
837. 2004 Draft Notice on Ancillary Restrictions, point 24; 2001 Notice, point 18.

they have entered into *vis-à-vis* the Commission with a view of rendering the concentration compatible with the Common Market. The Commission may do so:

- in the first phase (Article 6 (2)) if the proposed commitments are *prima facie* likely to remove the Commission's competition concerns, i.e., where the competition problem is 'readily identifiable and can easily be remedied',[838] without necessitating a market investigation (market inquiry) by the Commission,[839] or
- in the second phase (Article 8 (2) second paragraph) if the commitments need a more comprehensive evaluation.

The Commission enjoys discretion as to whether to accept commitments in the first phase or to initiate the second phase with a view to making a more comprehensive evaluation.[840] In both cases the Commission decision contains first the statement why and in which respects the notified operation raises serious doubts as to its compatibility with the Common Market, and secondly an assessment of the commitments submitted by the parties as to whether and why they are likely to remove the competition concerns. Evaluating the Commission's administrative practice is difficult because its serious doubts are generally sufficiently reasoned whereas the assessment of the commitments is often quite summary and does not clearly indicate why the commitments are likely to remove the serious doubts.

The New Commission Notice on Merger Remedies.
On December 21, 2000 the Commission finalized its Notice on Remedies.[841] The Notice focuses on the general principles under which remedies, i.e. commitments to restore effective competition, can be proposed and implemented in merger proceedings. The Notice describes the main types of remedies, the procedural requirements, the major elements for implementing divestiture commitments and – however only incidentally – the legal consequences for failure to comply with commitments. The Notice also applies to the assessment of joint ventures under Article 81 (1) and (3) in the framework of Article 2 (4) of the merger control regulation. The Notice is supplemented by Best Practices on Merger Control Proceedings Guidelines on the substance and implementation of commitments ('Standard Model Divestiture Commitments', 'Standard Model for Trustee Mandates' and 'Explanatory Note').[842] These models are intended to make negotiation and implementation of commitments more effective and more efficient for both

838. Recital 30 to Regulation 139/2004.
839. Notice on Remedies, 2001 OJ C 68/3, fn 11. Such a market investigation is normally reserved for the second phase, *see Siemens/Dematic/Sachs VDO*, D.Comm. Aug. 29, 2000, M.2059, point 80.
840. *ARD/BskyB-Kirch PayTV*, CFI Sept. 30, 2003, T-158/00, paras 329 and 362–366.
841. Commission Notice on Remedies, 2001 OJ C 68/3.
842. Explanatory Note, available on the Commission's website (no publication in the Official Journal).

the merging parties and the European Commission. While the models are useful, the major difficulties encountered by parties in first phase proceedings relate more to the substantive issue of identifying remedies that remove the serious doubts raised by the Commission (when it is not required to justify its position), than to the procedural matters dealt with in the standard models. Furthermore, the Best Practices on Merger Control Proceedings should be read in conjunction with the '*stop the clock*' mechanism proposed in the Green Paper on the Review of Council Regulation 4064/89 relating to the Commitments procedure.

The defined objective of the standard models is to relieve both the merging parties and the Commission of some of the burden – both in terms of time and resources – of negotiating the standard terms and provisions for commitments and trustee mandates within very strict time limits. '*The use of the standardized models will expedite the proceedings and allow the merging parties to concentrate more on the actual substance and implementation of the commitments.*'[843] While it is true that when evaluating commitments the Commission must look at their substance and form, once agreement has been reached by the parties and the Commission on the nature and scope of the remedy, the parties and their counsel should be allowed the freedom to draft such commitments in the manner which they deem fit, provided of course that the text of the commitments reflects what was agreed in the negotiations and contains all the elements required to ensure their correct implementation.

(b) Types of Commitments

Objective of Reducing the Parties Market Power.

Commitments must be capable of removing the Commission's competitive concerns, i.e., reducing the parties' market power and re-establishing conditions of effective competition, thereby rendering the operation compatible with the Common Market.[844] They may concern the transfer of a viable part of the merged assets (including assets held jointly with a third company) capable of being operated autonomously, i.e., independently of the parties to the merger, except for a transitional period.[845] The prospective buyer must be 'a viable existing or prospective competitor, independent of and unconnected to the parties and possessing the financial resources and proven expertise enabling it to maintain and develop the divested business as an active competitive force in competition with the parties'.[846]

---

843. Best Practices: The Commission's Modfelm Texts for Divestiture Commitments and Trustee Mandate under EC Merger Regulation, available on the Commission's website, point 5.
844. Notice on Remedies, points 26–30.
845. *Ibid.*, points 14–15.
846. *Ibid.*, point 49. *See Sanitec/Sphinx*, D.Comm. Dec. 1, 1999, 2000 OJ L 294/1, points 252–259.

Alternative Remedies.
Where the competitive concern cannot be removed by a transfer of assets, alternative remedies (second-best or 'suboptimal' remedies) may be considered, in particular commitments to facilitate the access of other operators to the market by granting access to a network or licenses to a basic technology.[847] Where remedies are difficult or impossible to find, the Commission has no choice but to prohibit the merger.[848]

Structural v. Behavioral Commitments.
The commitments must be of such a nature as to guarantee effective competitive market structures and to rule out 'serious doubts' in the sense of Article 6 (1) (c) of Regulation 139/2004. Preferably, the commitments should be of a *structural* nature, but certain behavioral commitments may also be capable of removing entirely the competitive problems, provided they do not require medium or long-term monitoring measures.[849] However, a mere commitment to behave in a certain way, e.g., not to enter into anticompetitive agreements or not to abuse a dominant position, is unsuitable because such a commitment only restates what the parties are obliged to do under Articles 81 and 82 anyway.[850] In practice, structural and behavioral commitments often overlap.

– *Structural Commitments.* Structural commitments may concern:
  - the sale of parts of the entity arising from the concentration to a third party that, if operated by a suitable purchaser, can compete effectively with the merged entity'[851]

847. Notice on Remedies, point 28. *See Boeing/McDonnell Douglas*, D.Comm. June 30, 1997, 1997 OJ L 336/16; *ARD/Commission*, CFI Sept. 30, 2003, T-158/00, para. 193.

848. Notice on Remedies, points 31–32. *See Volvo/Scania*, D.Comm. March 14, 2000, M.1672; *Worldcom/Sprint*, D.Comm. June 28, 2000, M.1741; *Honeywell/GE*, D.Comm. July 3, 2001, IP/01/939.

849. *Gencor/Lonrho*, CFI March 25, 1999, 1999 ECR II-753, paras 316–319.

850. Notice on Remedies, point 9. *See Bosch/Rexroth*, D.Comm. Jan. 12, 2001, 2004 OJ L 43/1, point 81. *See also Hoechst/Rhône Poulenc*, D.Comm. Jan. 30, 2004, M.1378: 'The Commission has a clear policy not to accept undertakings in merger control which are purely behavioural and equate to a mere promise to respect the law' (point 32).

851. *Air Liquide/Messer*, D.Comm. March 15, 2004. M.3314: 'Divested entity will be in a position to exercise competitive pressure on Linde and Air Liquide similar to Messer prior to the mergers' (point 203). *See Sara Lee/Courtaulds*, D.Comm. May 8, 2000, M.1892; *Alcoa/Reynolds*, D.Comm. May 9, 2000, M.1693; *Dyno/Industri Capital*, D.Comm. July 12, 2000, M.1813; *Preussag/Thomson*, D.Comm. July 26, 2000, M.2002; *Industri Kapital/Perstorp*, D.Comm. May 14, 2001, IP/01/686; *Masterfood/Royal Canin*, D.Comm. Feb. 15, 2002, M.2544, point 103. Where two parallel mergers are likely to lead to a dominant duopoly the commitments may consist in a divestiture of parts of the merging entities to a company which is independent from the merging companies with the view of creating a third effective competitor, as in the parallel merger proceedings against the two mergers in the German electricity market: *VEBA/VIAG*, D.Comm. June 13, 2000, M.1673, and *RWE/VEW*, Decision of the German antitrust authority, July 3, 2000, WuW 2000–11, 1117.

- the sale, the winding-up or reduction of shareholdings in a major competitor,[852]
- the divestiture of minority shareholdings,[853] or, only as second-best solution, the obligation of a minority shareholder not to use its shareholding to influence the market behavior of the operator in which it holds the stake.[854]
- termination of vertical alliances,[855]
- commitments not to exercise voting rights,[856]
- withdrawal from the board,[857]
- refraining from interlocking directorates,[858]
- the removal of co-ownership,[859]
- legal separation in order to ensure the independence of the separated entities,[860]
- the transfer or license of industrial or intellectual property rights,[861]
- the grant of non-exclusive licences for manufacturing intermediate products,[862] or
- commitments which aim at facilitating market entry by ensuring that competitors will have non-discriminatory access to the necessary infra-

852. Notice on Remedies, point 24. Shareholdings in a competitor: *VEBA/VIAG*, D.Comm. June 13, 2000, M.1673; *Preussag/Thomson*, D.Comm. July 26, 2000, M.2002; shareholdings in a joint venture with a competitor: *Alcoa/Reynolds Metals*, D.Comm. May 3, 2000, M.1671; *France Telecom/Orange*, D.Comm. Aug. 11, 2000, M.2029; shareholdings in a downstream company: *Coca Cola Beverages*, D.Comm. Feb. 9, 2000, M.1683. Exceptionally, the Commission accepts the maintenance of minority shareholdings that do not allow participation in management and thus to have access to confidential information: *see Blokker/Toys 'R'*, D.Comm. June 26, 1997, 1998 OJ L 316/1, points 132–133; *VEBA/VIAG*, D.Comm. June 13, 2000, M.1673, point 241; *Konica/Minolta*, D.Comm. July 11, 2003, M.3091; *Tejin/Zeon*, D.Comm. Aug. 13, 2003, M.3235.

853. Notice on Remedies, point 25. *See Hutchinson/IRCM/ECT*, D.Comm. July 3, 2001, JV. 55, point 132; *Hutchinson/ECT*, D.Comm. Nov. 29, 2001, JV. 56, point 48.

854. *Microsoft*, IP/00/569 of April 18, 2000. Not accepted in *Hoechst/Rhône-Poulenc*, D.Comm. Jan. 30, 2004, M.1378, point 30.

855. *DSM/Roche*, D.Comm. July 23, 2003, M.2972.

856. *Skanska/Scancem*, D.Comm. Nov. 11, 1998, 1999 OJ L 183/1, point 213; *Verbund/Energie Allianz*, D.Comm. June 11, 2003, M.2947.

857. *EDF/EnBW*, D.Comm. Feb. 7, 2001, IP/01/1853.

858. *See Generali/INA*, D.Comm. Jan. 12, 2000, M.1712.

859. *Danish Crown/Vestjyske Slagterier*, D.Comm. March 9, 1999, 2000 OJ L 20/1, point 236; *Haniel/Ytong*, D.Comm. April 9, 2002, M.2568, points 149–152.

860. By creating a Chinese wall: *Telia/Sonera*, D.Comm. July 10, 2002, M.2803 or by 'unbundling', *see* Commission Note on the Unbundling Regime under the energy liberalization directives: http://europa.eu.int/comm/energy/electricity/legislation/notes_for_implementation_en.htm.

861. *Ciba-Geigy/Sandoz*, D.Comm. July 17, 1996, 1996 OJ L 201/1; *EADS*, D.Comm. May 11, 2000, M.1745; *Sanofi-Synthilabo/Aventis*, D.Comm. April 26, 2004, M.3354, IP/04/545.

862. *Ciba-Geigy/Sandoz*, D.Comm. July 17, 1996, 1996 OJ L 201/1, points 275–280.

structure,[863] including networks[864] and slots[865] or to key technology,[866] or access to electricity generation capacity via auctions over five years.[867]
'Parts of the entity' include a subsidiary[868] or assets, provided they are severable and viable,[869] such as plants,[870] trademark and design licenses, service contracts, technical assistance and personnel to run the plant,[871] business lines,[872] patents and know-how,[873] trademarks,[874] retail outlets,[875] and supply contracts together

863. Notice on Remedies, point 28. Network: *VEBA/VIAG*, D.Comm. June 13, 2000, M.1673; airport slots: *KLM/Alitalia*, D.Comm. Aug. 11, 1999, JV. 19; postal services: *Deutsche Post/DHL*, D.Comm. June 26, 1998, M.1168.
864. *Kirch/BSkyB*, D.Comm. March 21, 2000, JV. 37 (pay-TV); *BVEBA/VIAG*, D.Comm. June 13, 2000, M.1673 (energy).
865. *United Airlines/US Airways*, D.Comm. Jan. 15, 2001, IP/01/48 and *Air France/KLM*, D.Comm. Feb. 11, 2004, M.3314, point 162 (allocation of slots as structural commitment because of its indefinite nature).
866. Notice on Remedies, point 24. *See Glaxo/SmithKline*, D.Comm. May 8, 2000, M.1846; *ASTRA Zeneca/Novartis*, D.Comm. July 26, 2000, M.1806; *ADtrans/Bombardier*, D.Comm. April 3, 2001, M.2139, IP/01/501. In *Tetra Laval/Sidel*, the Commission held that the grant of a license 'may actually introduce complex mechanisms in the market resulting in artificial regulation' and was insufficient to solve the concerns arising from the structure of the market following the merger: D.Comm. Jan. 30, 2002, M.2416, point 424; *see* CFI Oct. 25, 2002, 2002 ECR II-4381, para. 59.
867. *EDF/EnBW*, D.Comm. Feb. 7, 2001, M.1853, points 106–112; *Verbund/Energie Allianz*, D.Comm. June 11, 2003, M.2947.
868. *See Metsä-Serla/Modo*, D.Comm. Aug. 4, 2000, M.2020.
869. Notice on Remedies, point 14. 'Distinct and saleable business': *Telia/Telenor*, D.Comm. Oct. 13, 1999, 2001 OJ L 40/1, points 383–385; *SCA Packaging/Metsä*, D.Comm. Aug. 25, 2000, M.2032.
870. *Dyno/Industri Kapital*, D.Comm. July 12, 2000, M.1813; *Rexam/American National Can*, D.Comm. July 19, 2000, M.1939; Aug. 29, 2000, M.2059; *Promatech/Sultzer*, D.Comm. July 24, 2002, M.2698.
871. *See Hoffmann La Roche/Boehringer Mannheim*, D.Comm. Feb. 4, 1998, 1998 OJ L 234/14; *Dow Chemicals/Union Carbide*, D.Comm. May 3, 2000, M.1671; *EADS*, D.Comm. May 11, 2000, M.1745; *Unilever/Bestfood*, D.Comm. Sept. 28, 2000, M.1990.
872. *AGA/Linde*, D.Comm. Feb. 9, 2000, M.1641; *Dow Chemicals/Union Carbide*, D.Comm. May 3, 2000, M.1671.
873. *Dow Chemicals/Union Carbide*, D.Comm. May 3, 2000, M.1671. Divestiture by way of licensing ('license divestment'): *Monsanto/Pharmacia & Upjohn*, D.Comm. March 30, 2000, M.1835; *Glaxo/SmithKline*, D.Comm. May 8, 2000, M.1846.
874. *Ciba-Geigy/Sandoz*, D.Comm. July 27, 1996, 1997 OJ L 201/1; *Unilever France/Amora Maille*, D.Comm. March 8, 2000, M.1802; *Sara Lee/Courtaulds*, D.Comm. May 8, 2000, M.1892; *Unilever/Bestfoods*, D.Comm. Sept. 28, 2000, M.1990. However, the mere license of trademarks in certain countries (where the parties are dominant) seems a doubtful effective remedy, since it is likely to lead to a separation of markets within the Community leaving only the possibility of passive sales: *see Monsanto/Pharmacia & Upjohn*, D.Comm. March 30, 2000, M.1835, point 96; *Smith Nephew/Beiersdorf*, D.Comm. Jan. 30, 2001, JV. 54; under Article 81: *Orangina/Coca Cola*, Twenty-ninth Report on Competition Policy, Box 2 after point 42. However, the Court of First Instance accepted in *BaByliss/SEB-Moulinex* the grant of territorial trademark licences because it seemed unlikely to lead to an absolute market partitioning: CFI April 3, 2003, T-114/02, paras 421–424. The grant or divestiture of trademarks

with appropriate distribution infrastructure, such as transfill facilities.[876] In the exceptional case where there is no suitable candidate found for buying the assets to be divested, the Commission accepts hold-separate obligations as a (sub-optimal) remedy to cure the competitive concerns.[877] The parties may propose alternative commitments for negotiation with the Commission[878] or submit amended or new proposals, provided they are submitted within the time limits.[879]

- *Behavioural Commitments*. As a second-best solution the Commission sometimes accepts commitments of a *behavioural* nature designed to remove on a lasting basis the competitive concerns arising from the operation, in particular the emergence or strengthening of a dominant position by vertical links.[880] The commitments must be proportionate and capable of removing entirely the serious doubts expressed by the Commission; they must be compatible with Article 81[881] and likely to be implemented speedily and effectively[882] without requiring medium or long-term monitoring.[883] Behavioural commitments include obligations:
    - to terminate contractual links with a competitor,[884]
    - to terminate exclusive supply and/or distribution agreements,[885] or to

---

for the entire Community is, however, acceptable: *Masterfoods/Royal Canin*, D.Comm. Feb. 15, 2002, M.2544, point 103.

875. *See Rewe/Meinl*, D.Comm. Feb. 3, 1999, 1999 OJ L 274/1; *Total Fina/Elf Aquitaine*, D.Comm. Feb. 9, 2000, M.1628.
876. *Air Liquide/BOC/Japan Air Gases*, D.Comm. Oct. 10, 2002, M.2871, point 296.
877. Accepted: *Boeing/McDonnell Douglas*, D.Comm. July 30, 1997, 1997 OJ L 336/16, point 123; *Air Liquide/BOC*, D.Comm. Jan. 18, 2000, M.1630 (obligation to nominate a third person for managing a joint venture constituted with a competitor); *AOL/Time Warner*, D.Comm. Oct. 11, 2000, M.1845 (obligation to keep relationships at arms' length). Rejected: *Microsoft/Liberty Media/Telewest*, D.Comm. March 22, 2000 (Article 6 (1) (c) decision following which the parties withdrew their notification).
878. *Dyno/Industri Kapital*, D.Comm. July 12, 2000, M.1813.
879. *Dow Chemicals/Union Carbide*, D.Comm. May 3, 2000, M.1671. Modifications to the original remedies may be submitted without time-limit: *Air Liquide/Messer*, D.Comm. March 15, 2004, M.3314, point 165.
880. Notice on Remedies, points 11 and 13. Rejected in *Volvo/Scandia*, D.Comm. March 14, 2000, M.1672. Commitment to create a 'Chinese wall' or a 'firewall arrangement' in order to ensure independence accepted in *BT/AT&T*, D.Comm. March 30, 1999, JV. 15 points 187 and 192.
881. *BaByliss/SEB-Moulinex*, CFI April 3, 2003, T-114/02, para. 421.
882. Recital 8 of Regulation 1310/97. *See ARD*'s appeal T-158/00 against the *BSkyB/Kirch Pay TV* clearance (D.Comm. March 21, 2000, JV. 37).
883. Notice on Remedies, point 9.
884. *See VEBA/VIAG*, D.Comm. June 13, 2000, M.1673; *AOL/Time Warner*, D.Comm. Oct. 11, 2000, M.1845.
885. Notice on Remedies, points 26–27. *See BT/Esat*, D.Comm. March 27, 2000, M.1838; *VEBA/VIAG*, D.Comm. June 13, 2000, M.1673; *GVS/EnBW/ENI*, D.Comm. Dec. 17, 2002, IP/02/1905, M. 2822, point 75.

reduce exclusive supply arrangements,[886]
- to grant a special right of early termination of long-term supply contracts with the dominant supplier(s),[887]
- not to enter into new distribution agreements for a certain period,[888]
- to enter into supply arrangements only if they are limited to an initial start-up period necessary for ensuring the effective continuation of the divested business,[889] or
- not to use certain contractual or industrial property rights.[890]

– *Long-Term Behavioural Commitments*. Examples include obligations, entered into for a longer period[891] or unlimited in time:[892]
- to maintain,[893] reduce[894] or to enlarge capacity,[895] e.g., to increase in electricity interconnection in order to facilitate third parties' access to the enlarged network,[896]
- to grant non-exclusive licences (with no right to sub-license) of a new technology, which may be limited to a market entry period;[897]
- to license trademarks,[898] accompanied with an obligation on the licensor

886. E.g. by permitting to supply 15% to competitors: *Danish Crown/Vestjyske Slagterier*, D.Comm. March 9, 1999, 2000 OJ L 20/1, points 200 and 236.
887. *EnBW/ENI/GVS*, D.Comm. Dec. 17, 2002, M.2822, points 64–72.
888. *Generali/INA*, D.Comm. Jan. 12, 2000, M.1712.
889. *See BP/Amoco*, D.Comm. Dec. 11, 1998, M.1293 (five years); *DuPont/Tejin*, D.Comm. Nov. 24, 1999, M.1599 (3–5 years); *BP JV Dissolution*, D.Comm. Feb. 2, 2000, M.1820 (five years).
890. *SEB Moulinex*, Jan. 8, 2002, M.2621; *Masterfoods/Royal Canin*, D.Comm. Feb. 15, 2002, M.2544.
891. *See Ciba-Geigy/Sandoz*, D.Comm. July 17, 1996, 1996 OJ L 201/1; *Akzo Nobel/Hoechst Roussel*, D.Comm. Nov. 22, 1999, M.1681.
892. *Boeing/McDonnell Douglas*, D.Comm. July 30, 1997, 1997 OJ L 336/16, points 120–124.
893. *Gencor/Lonrho*, CFI March 25, 1999, 1999 ECR II-753, para. 322.
894. Reducing capacity by granting access, for a limited period of five years, to competitors: *EDF/EnBW*, D.Comm. Feb. 7, 2001, M.1853, points 106–112. However, the obligation to make part of the production capacity available to third parties does normally not provide a long-lasting remedy.
895. Clearances of mergers in the electricity sector were made subject to commitments to enlarge the interstate transmission capacity in order to open the network for any new entrant: *Gruppo Villar/Mir/EnBW/Hidroelectrica del Cantabrio*, D.Comm. Article 8 (2), Sept. 26, 2001, M.2434, 2004 OJ L 48/86, points 123–127 and 133; *EnBW/Cajastur/Hidrocantabrico*, D.Comm. Article 8 (2), March 19, 2002, M.2684.
896. *Grupo Villar Mir/EnBW/Hidroeléctrica del catabrico*, D.Comm. Sept. 26, 2001, 2004 OJ L 48/86, points 133–135.
897. *Alcan/Pechiney*, D.Comm. Sept. 29, 2003, M.3225, point 150; *Tetra Laval II*, D.Comm. Jan. 13, 2003, M.2416 (even if the technology to be licensed is still being developed); *Sanofi – Synthélabo/Aventis*, D.Comm. April 26, 2004, M.3354.
898. *SEB/Moulinex*, D.Comm. Jan. 8, 2002, M.2621, *aff'd* CFI April 3, 2003, T-114/02, paras 417–424. This operation was cleared by the Commission following commitments to grant exclusive trademark licenses to independent third companies (competitors) in certain countries where the operation leads to a dominant position whereas the parties remained entitled to

not to compete against the future licensee for a start-up period, of, say, 3–5 years;[899]
- to ensure price protection to smaller customers,[900]
- to refrain from cross-subsidizing,[901]
- to guarantee the independence and autonomy of a gateway company for granting non-discriminatory access to third parties,[902] or
- 'Chinese wall' obligations in order to prevent the exchange of commercially sensitive information between competitors.[903]

However, commitments which require long-term monitoring by the Commission[904] may not constitute a sufficient remedy with a view of making the transaction compatible with the Common Market. For instance, it may be argued that non-compliance with a commitment to grant access to a network for an undefined period may not be directly enforceable by means of the merger control regulation (fines, penalty payments or withdrawal of clearance decision) but requires a fresh analysis under Article 81 or 82 in order to assess the actual market conditions and the parties' market position, which may be substantially different from those which were the basis for the Commission's decision.[905]

– *Voluntary Commitments.* In cases where commitments are not strictly necessary to remove competition concerns the Commission may nevertheless take

---

use the same trademarks on other markets for similar products themselves, including on the French market (for which the French authority granted unconditional clearance following the Commission's partial referral decision but is reconsidering its decision which was anulled by the Conseil d'Etat on Feb. 6, 2004). According to this commitment, licences have been granted to two independent companies, one for Greece and another for eight other member states (IP/03/1531).

899. *SEB/Moulinex*, D.Comm. Jan. 8, 2002, M.2621, point 146, *aff'd* CFI April 3, 2003, T-114/02; *Bosch/Rexroth*, D.Comm. Jan. 12, 2001, 2004 OJ L 43/1, point 91; *Procter & Gamble/Wella*, D.Comm. July 30, 2003, M.3149 (grant of an exclusive 5 year licence, followed by a 3 year black-out (non-use) period).

900. *Enso/Stora*, D.Comm. Nov. 25, 1998, 1999 OJ L 254/9.

901. *See PTT Post/TNT/GD Express*, D.Comm. Nov. 8, 1996, M.843; *DHL/Deutsche Post*, D.Comm. June 26, 1998, M.1168 (rejection of a competitor's complaint *aff'd* CFI March 20, 2002, T-175/99; acquisition of sole control cleared D.Comm. Oct. 22, 2002, IP/02/1312). State aid v. cross-subsidization: *Deutsche Post*, D.Comm. June 19, 2002, 2002 OJ L 247/27.

902. *See Daimler Chrysler/Deutsche Telecom (Tollcollect)*, D.Comm. April 30, 2003, M.2903.

903. *See also Boeing/Hughes Electronics*, D.Comm. Sept. 27, 2000, M.1879. No 'Chinese wall' commitments are necessary where the creation of a joint venture does not lead to any anticompetitive coordination between the parents because the operation does not confer 'undue power power' or sufficient market power for making coordination 'worthwhile': *see TXU Europe/EDF London Investment*, D.Comm. Feb. 3, 2000, JV. 36; *Hilton/Accor/Forte/Travel Services/JV*, D.Comm. Feb. 16, 2001, M.2197; *Angilini/Phoenix*, D.Comm. July 9, 2001, IP/01/973.

904. The Commission accepted the need for a constant monitoring in some cases by establishing a new administrative entity within the Merger Task Force.

905. This may be concluded from *Coca Cola*, CFI March 22, 2000, 2000 ECR II-1733, para. 82.

note without making them a condition of approval. In this case the commitments rather stress the parties' readiness to cooperate and may, by way of the publication of the decision, give third parties certain assurances.[906]

(c) Procedural Requirements

Time Limits for Submitting Commitment Proposals.
Where a proposed concentration threatens to significantly impede effective competition, in particular as a result from the creation or strengthening of a dominant position, the parties may seek to resolve the competitive problem either in the pre-notification phase or after notification by modifying the originally notified concentration and implementing the modification *before* the adoption of the clearance decision[907] or by renotifying the amended operation.[908] However, parties usually enter into commitments to modify the concentration within a specified period *after* clearance.[909] The parties must respect the following time limits:

- During the first phase remedy proposals must be submitted within not more than 20 working days;[910] the Commission must adopt its decision within 35 working days (instead of the normal 25 working days).[911]
- During the second phase commitments must be submitted within not more than 65 working days from the date on which proceedings were initiated by an Article 6 (1) (c) decision;[912] the Commission must adopt its decision within 105 days (instead of the normal 90 working days).[913] Where the proposals are submitted immediately after this date the Commission may take the final decision 'as soon as it appears that the serious doubts … have been removed', and at the latest by the deadline of the second phase.[914]

The Commission may reject *belated proposals*;[915] it accepts late proposals only

906. E.g., *Boeing/Hughes*, D.Comm. Sept. 29, 2000, 2004 OJ L 63/53, point 102; *Boeing/McDonnell Douglas*, D.Comm. July 30, 1997, 1997 OJ L 336/16; *Celanese/Degussa/JV*, D.Comm. June 11, 2003, 2004 OJ L 38/47, point 79.
907. *See Ferrovie dello Stato/Schweizerische Bundesbahnen/JV*, D.Comm. Nov. 26, 2000, M.1805.
908. *See Procter & Gamble/Schickedanz I*, M.398, and *Procter&Gamble/Schickedanz II*, D.Comm. June 21, 1994, 1994 OJ L 354/32.
909. Notice, point 5.
910. Article 19 (1) of Regulation 882/2004.
911. Article 10 (1) of Regulation 139/2004.
912. Article 19 (2) of Regulation 882/2004.
913. Article 10 (3) of Regulation 139/2004.
914. *See BP Amoco/Arco*, D.Comm. Sept. 29, 1999, M.1532.
915. *See Volvo/Scandia*, D.Comm. March 14, 2000, M.1672; *General Electric/Honeywell*, D.Comm. July 3, 2001, 2004 OJ L 48/1, points 546–549.

in exceptional circumstances[916] and where it is able to duly consult third parties and the Advisory Committee.[917] Of 2,419 final merger decisions issued as of April 30, 2004, 111 mergers were cleared with commitments during the first phase and 62 mergers during the second phase, whereas 18 mergers were prohibited, some of which because commitments were submitted belatedly[918] or considered insufficient by the Commission to remove the competition problems.[919]

Assessment and Acceptance of Commitments by the Commission. The Commission consults the national authorities on the proposed commitments and also third parties in the form of a market test.[920] If the Commission accepts the proposals, it makes its clearance decision *subject to compliance* with the commitments.[921] If the Commission considers the proposals as insufficient for removing its competitive concerns, the Commission informs the parties accordingly. The parties may submit *amended proposals*, provided that there are alternative remedies for removing the competitive concern, that they can be assessed by the Commission on the basis of prior market testing and that the Commission has sufficient time for proper consultation of the national authorities.[922] In the first phase the Commission accepts, because of the time constraints, only limited modifications.

916. E.g., *Schneider/Legrand*, D.Comm. Oct. 10, 2001, *rev'd* CFI Oct. 22, 2002, 2002 ECR II-4091 (the fact that the last minute proposals had to be rejected was possibly a reason for adopting a prohibition decision which did not conform to the legal standards required by the Court of First Instance). The Commission reserves its right to refuse late proposals (Notice on Remedies, point 12) but may also accept late proposals under exceptional circumstances, *see Alcoa/Reynolds*, D.Comm. May 9, 2000, M.1693. The merger *First Choice/Airtours* was prohibited by the Commission because of insufficient commitment proposals (D.Comm. Sept. 21, 1999, M.1524) but the Court of First Instance annulled the decision because of manifest errors when analyzing the impact on the market structure (CFI Oct. 8, 2002, 2002 ECR II-3805, para. 86).

917. Notice on Remedies, point 35. *See General Electric/Honeywell*, D.Comm. July 3, 2001, M.2220, points 546–566 (on appeal); *Totalfina/Elf Aquitaine*, D.Comm. Feb. 9, 2000, M.1628, point 345; *BSkyB/Kirch*, D.Comm. March 21, 2000, JV. 37, *aff'd* CFI Sept. 30, 2003, T-158/00. In appropriate cases the Commission also consults third countries' antitrust authorities in the framework of bilateral agreements, such as the Agreement between the European Community and the U.S. (1995 OJ L 95/45), Canada (June 17, 1999, Nineteenth Report on Competition Policy, points 342–345) and Japan (IP/00/739 of July 19, 2000).

918. However, under exceptional circumstances the Commission may also accept late proposals, *see Alcoa/Reynolds*, D.Comm. May 9, 2000, M.1693.

919. *See SCA/Metsä*, D.Comm. Sept. 26, 2000, M.2097 (first phase Article 6 (1) (c) decision); *Blokker/Toys 'R' Us*, D.Comm. June 26, 1997, 1998 OJ L 316/1; *MCI Worldcom/Sprint*, D.Comm. June 28, 2000, M.1741; *Metsä Tissue/Mölnlycke*, D.Comm. Jan. 31, 2001, IP/00/147 (second phase decisions).

920. Notice on Remedies, point 35.

921. Article 6 (2) and Article 8 (2) of Regulation 139/2004. *See Nabisco/United Biscuits*, D.Comm. May 5, 2000, M.1920 (first phase proceedings); *Dow Chemical/Union Carbide*, D.Comm. May 3, 2000, M.1671 (second phase proceedings).

922. Notice on Remedies, point 35. *See ARD/Commission*, CFI Sept. 30, 2003, T-158/00, paras 405–407.

If there is not sufficient time for assessing the modified commitments without proceeding to any other market investigation[923] the Commission takes a decision initiating the second phase pursuant to Article 6 (1) (c)[924] or, if the second phase is already initiated, a prohibition decision pursuant to Article 8 (3).[925] Where the Commission concludes that there are no competitive problems or no need for the proposed commitments the parties may withdraw their commitments.

In its Green Paper the Commission suggested a '*stop the clock provision*' for both the first and the second phase proceedings in order to solve the problem of the current tight time limits available to itself and the member states when proposed amendments are submitted towards the end of the period allowed or amended after this deadline.[926]

Modalities.
The Notice on Remedies clarifies the modalities for submitting commitments.[927] The parties must submit,[928] and the Commission must approve, a precise and exhaustive definition of the 'divestiture package' in order to allow an unambiguous identification of all relevant assets and a strict and legally binding timetable (which is not disclosed to third parties) for carrying out structural commitments:

- a first time limit for entering into a binding contract with a suitable purchaser approved by the Commission, which must be independent, unconnected with the parties and possess the financial resources and proven expertise enabling it to maintain and develop the divested business as an active competitive force in competition with the parties ('divestiture period'),[929] and

923. *Ibid.*, point 37.
924. *See SCA/Metsä*, D.Comm. Sept. 26, 2000, M.2097.
925. Notice on Remedies, points 31–32. *See General Electric/Honeywell*, D.Comm. July 3, 2001, M.2220 IP/01/939 (on appeal). In several cases the Commission prohibited the merger because the assessment and the market investigation of the proposed amended commitments would have belayed the proper preparation of the decision with the risk of it being annulled by the Court of First Instance: e.g., *Schneider/Legrand*, D.Comm. Oct. 10, 2001, M.2223 (annulled for lack of reasoning by CFI Oct. 22, 2002, 2002 ECR II-4091); *First Choice/Airtours*, D.Comm. Sept. 21, 1999, M.1524 (annulled because of manifest errors when analyzing the impact on the market structure by CFI Oct. 8, 2002, 2002 ECR II-3805, para. 86).
926. COM(2001)745/6 final, points 212–221. Under the present regulation the period can only be extended by not more than 20 working days (Article 10 (3), second subparagraph of Regulation 139/2004), and suspended where the Commission had to proceed to – time consuming – requests for information or investigations, owing to circumstances for which the parties are responsible, in particular when they provided insufficient information in the notification (Article 10 (4)).
927. Notice on Remedies, points 44–45. *See* Best Practices on Merger Control Proceedings, point 40.
928. 1 original and 10 copies: Article 20 of Regulation 882/2004. The original must be signed by the mandatory of the company. An electronic copy must also be provided.
929. Notice on Remedies, points 46–49.

– a second time limit during which an independent and experienced institution is irrevocably appointed (with the Commission's approval) as trustee (divestiture trustee) entrusted to identify and propose a suitable purchaser should the parties fail to do so within the first time limit (or any extension thereof – 'extended divestiture period').[930] The parties must normally propose within one week the name of a monitoring trustee and submit a draft mandate to the Commission, which has discretion to approve or reject the proposal. The divestiture trustee (to be proposed not later than one month before the end of the divestiture period) must conduct negotiations in accordance with the parties' commitments with a view to concluding a binding contract for the divestiture and submit appropriate proposals to the Commission for approval. The trustee will be discharged as soon as the commitments have been implemented.

Obligation to Preserve the Value of Assets to be Divested.
Until completion of the divestiture the parties must undertake to continue the business to be divested as a viable business and not take any measures which would have a material adverse effect on the business.[931] Pending divestiture, the parties must appoint, and a trustee (which may be the divestiture trustee or another person or institution, the 'hold-separate manager')[932] must ensure the independence, economic viability, marketability and competitiveness of the divestiture package. This includes holding separate and managing the assets as a distinct, viable and saleable entity with its own management[933] and refraining from 'ring-fencing' (hiring away) of key personel.[934] Generally, the Commission requires the trustee to monitor the fulfillment of the parties' obligations, and to provide the Commission with a monthly report on the management of the assets or companies to be sold.[935] The Commission may not clear the transaction unless the parties undertake not to complete the notified transaction before having entered into a binding agreement with a purchaser for the divested business ('upfront buyer') in order to prevent the business being sold from being weakened in the meantime.[936]

930. *Ibid.*, points 53–57. Examples: *Sara Lee/Courtaulds*, D.Comm. May 8, 2000, M.1892; *VEBA/VIAG*, D.Comm. June 13, 2000, M.1673; *Preussag/Thomson*, D.Comm. July 26, 2000, M.2002.
931. Notice, points 50–52. Example: *Dow Chemical/Union Carbide*, D.Comm. May 3, 2000, M.1671, point 53 of the commitment.
932. Notice on Remedies, points 52 and 55. Both the divestiture trustee and the hold-separate trustee must report to the Commission: *see VEBA/VIAG*, D.Comm. June 13, 2000, M.1673.
933. Notice on Remedies, points 50–52. *See Preussag/Thomson*, D.Comm. July 26, 2000, M.2002.
934. *See Metsä-Serla/Modo*, D.Comm. Aug. 4, 2000, M.2020, point 13 of the commitment.
935. Best Practices on Merger Control Proceedings Guidelines on Divestiture Commitments, points 19–24. *See Generali/INA*, D.Comm. Jan. 12, 2000, M.1712; *Dow Chemical/Union Carbide*, D.Comm. May 3, 2000, M.1671, point 14 of the commitment.
936. Notice on Remedies, point 20. E.g., *Rexrodt/Bosch*, D.Comm. Dec. 13, 2000, M.2060, IP/00/1457.

Deadlines for the Implementation.
Where the commitment consists of the divestiture of companies or assets, the divestiture, whether by the parties or the trustee,[937] must take place within a fixed time period[938] which is normally not disclosed to third parties. Normally the parties are given six months in which to sign a binding sale agreement and an additional period in which to close. However, the period may vary from case to case.[939] Normally, there is an express provision that after the expiry of a certain period the responsibility for effecting the divestiture passes to the trustee.[940] In the *New Holland* case[941] the undertakings provided that 'in the event that the Divestments have not been effected within (...) months of the Decision ... New Holland undertakes to give the Trustee an irrevocable mandate to find a purchaser for those Divestments which have not been effected ... within a further (...) months (or within such longer period as the Commission, upon request of the Trustee, agrees)'.[942] The Commission has in these cases insisted that the undertaking given by the merging parties must be an absolute commitment to divest the required asset (by the parties or the trustee) within a given time period.

Evaluation of Commitments by the Commission.
The Commission has broad discretion when evaluating the parties' proposals. According to the Commission, it is up to the parties to demonstrate that the commitments are likely to resolve its competitive concerns.[943] The Commission is not required to take a reasoned decision for rejecting proposals when it considers the proposals as insufficient. The parties can only appeal the final decision if they are directly and individually concerned,[944] i.e., if the clearance decision is subject to

937. Notice on Remedies, point 54.
938. Notice on Remedies, point 48.
939. The divestiture may be realized within 4–6 months, as in *BT/AT&T*, cleared March 30, 1999, JV. 15, followed by divestiture of Telewest cleared July 23, 1999, M.1551; *BP/Amoco*, cleared Sept. 29, 1999, M.1532, followed by transfer divestiture *BP/Mobil* cleared Feb. 3, 2000; but divestiture may require much more time as in *DuPont/ICI*, D.Comm. Sept. 30, 1992, 1992 OJ L 7/13 and IP/94/1179 of Dec. 9, 1994 (more than two years), and *Totalfina/Elf Aquitaine*, D.Comm. Feb. 9, 2000, M.1628 (decision objecting to the proposed sell-off because the candidate was not a 'suitable purchaser' capable of becoming an efficient competitor, which was affirmed in *SG2R (Totalfina/Elf)*, CFI Jan. 17, 2001, 2001 ECR II-67, para. 38).
940. This period may be extended upon written request.
941. *Fiat New Holland*, D.Comm. Oct. 28, 1999, M.1571.
942. Models 'Trustee Divestiture Period' Notice on Commitments, point 24. *See* however *Metsä-Serla/Modo*, D.Comm. Aug. 4, 2000, M.2020 where the undertakings expressly provided that the trustee had the power to effect the divestiture within a prescribed period from the date of the decision. However, this period was not disclosed in the public version of the decision. *See also Preussag/Thomson*, D.Comm. July 26, 2000, M.2002.
943. Notice on Remedies, points 6–7.
944. Article 230 (4) of the EC Treaty.

a condition or obligation[945] or if the decision declares the incompatibility of the merger with the Common Market.[946]

Approval of the Buyer by the Commission.
The parties or the trustee can only proceed to the sale if the Commission approves the proposed purchaser within any time limit expressly prescribed in the commitments.[947] In the case where a suitable buyer has already been found during the proceedings, the Commission includes its approval in the clearance decision.[948] The Commission may disqualify the proposed purchaser as a suitable buyer if it does not satisfy the 'suitable purchaser' standard.[949] In this case the Commission must formally communicate its reasoned view to the parties, which constitutes a decision likely to be appealed only in the case of a manifest error in its appraisal.[950] Such a decision may have direct legal effects because it may prevent the parties from selling the business at a reasonable price[951] to the buyer of their choice although this buyer satisfies (contrary to the Commission's findings) the objective criteria of the decision.[952] The Commission may have a certain discretionary power but the abuse of this discretion may be a ground for appeal.[953]

Need to Notify the Divestiture as Fresh Merger Operation.
The final sale of the company or of the assets may constitute a separate transaction, which has to be notified to and approved by the Commission[954] if the thresholds of

945. *Coca Cola*, CFI March 22, 2000, 2000 ECR II-1733.
946. *Endemol*, CFI April 28, 1999, 1999 ECR II-1299.
947. Notice on Remedies, point 58–60. *See Dow Chemicals/Union Carbide*, D.Comm. May 3, 2000, M.1671. In the event that the Commission does not give its approval within any such prescribed period the purchaser will be deemed implicitly approved by the Commission: *ibid.* point 54.
948. *See SCA Packaging/Metsä Corrugated*, D.Comm. Aug. 28, 2000, IP/00/948.
949. Notice on Remedies, points 19–21.
950. *SG2R (Totalfina/Elf)*, CFI Jan. 17, 2001, 2001 ECR II-67, para. 38 and CFI April 3, 2003, T-342/00, para. 100.
951. *See BT/MCI II*, D.Comm. May 14, 1997, 1997 OJ L 336/1, point 76 (h) where the Commission accepted the parties' proposal to obtain a 'reasonable price'. *See Faull/Nikpay*, 'The EC Law of Competition' (1999), 4.170 at p. 251.
952. E.g., possessing independent sources of supply, thereby excluding free station networks depending on third sources of supply, as in the case *Totalfina/Elf Aquitaine*, D.Comm. Feb. 9, 2000, M.1628; *SG2R*, CFI Jan. 17, 2001 ECR II-67. However, the Commission's assessment may be based on subjective criteria, e.g. the probability that the prospective buyer would become an 'aggressive' competitor (which is in fact highly speculative), as demonstrated in the same case when the Commission disqualified the proposed buyer: D.Comm. Sept. 13, 2000, referred to in *SG2R (Totalfina/Elf)*, CFI Jan. 17, 2001, 2001 ECR II-67, para. 5.
953. *See Endemol*, CFI April 28, 1999, 1999 ECR II-1299, para. 169.
954. *See AT&T/BT*, D.Comm. March 30, 1999, JV. 15; *Enichem/Polimeri*, D.Comm. April 6, 2001, M.2354.

the merger control regulation are met.[955] However, the simplified procedure may apply if the market shares do not exceed 15% for horizontal and 25% for vertical relationships.[956]

Re-Acquisition Prohibition.
The divestiture commitment normally includes the commitment not to re-acquire direct or indirect influence over the divested business. This re-acquisition prohibition is limited to ten years after the date of the decision and serves to maintain the structural effects of the commitments.[957] The Commission may grant a waiver if the structure of the market has substantially changed.[958] However, any re-acquisition must be re-notified and assessed in the light of the new market structure anyway.

(d) Administrative Consequences of the Non-Fulfilment of Commitments

Legal Obligation to Comply with Commitments.
Parties are legally bound to comply with their commitments; non-compliance may lead to the invalidity of the clearance decision and to sanctions, as explained in greater detail below.[959] It may be necessary to include in a divestiture assets which are related to markets where the Commission did *not* raise competition concerns if this would be the only possible way to find a suitable buyer which would become an effective competitor in the affected markets.[960] However, when it is objectively impossible[961] to comply with their commitments, i.e., when neither the parties nor the trustee succeed in selling-off the assets to a suitable buyer, the parties must make proposals to the Commission, and it seems that it is for the Commission to re-enter into negotiations in order to find the second-best remedy to cure the competitive problem ('sub-optimal remedies'), including behavioral commitments prior to the adoption of the decision as in the case *Boeing/McDonnell Douglas*.[962] The commitments may expressly provide that they may be substituted by other commitments of

955. E.g. *Siemens/Fujitsu*, D.Comm. Sept. 30, 1999, JV. 22: clearance subject to the condition to sell-off the retail and banking system, which was cleared in the subsequent Commission decision of Dec. 12, 1999. However, in many cases, the assets to be sold do not exceed the thresholds of Article 5 (2), *see Bellsouth/VRT/E-plus*, D.Comm. Jan. 26, 2000, M.1821; *Blu*, D.Comm. Sept. 12, 2002, M.2958, IP/02/1295 (approval of divestiture which was the condition of the approval of *Pirelli/Edizione/Olivetti*, D.Comm. Sept. 20, 2001, M.2574.
956. Commission Notice on a simplified procedure, point 4.
957. *See GE/AGFA NDT*, D.Comm. Dec. 5, 2003, M.3136, point B.2. of the commitments; Best Practices Guidelines, point 17.
958. *Ibid.*
959. Article 23 (2) (c) of Regulation 1/2003 and Article 14 (2) (d) of Regulation 139/2004.
960. Notice on Remedies, points 17 and 21.
961. *See* the concept of 'objective impossibility' under the rules on state aid: *Commission/Belgium*, ECJ Jan. 15, 1986, 1986 ECR 89, para. 14.
962. Example: *Boeing/McDonnell Douglas*, D.Comm. June 30, 1997, 1997 OJ L 336/16 (impossibility of finding a buyer for the aeronautic division of Douglas).

equal effect.[963] If no suitable purchaser can be found the Commission may authorize the separate sale of business assets to other operators in the sector.[964]

Non-Compliance with a Commitment.
Decisions may be the subject of conditions or obligations attached to the clearance decision.[965] The legal consequences are different, in particular with respect to the validity of the clearance decision.

(i) *Non-compliance with a condition.*
Where a *condition* is not fulfilled, the situation rendering the merger compatible 'does not materialize'[966] and the decision 'no longer stands'.[967] A merger implemented without complying with a condition should be treated in the same way as a non-notified transaction implemented without authorization and entitles the Commission to directly order the dissolution of the transaction, so as to restore the situation prevailing prior to the implementation.[968] Furthermore, the Commission may:
- impose fines,[969]
- enforce the compliance by imposing penalty payments,[970] or
- take interim measures appropriate to restore or maintain conditions of effective competition.[971]

However, it seems doubtful whether the non-compliance with a condition always and automatically leads to the incompatibility of the transaction. First,

963. Standard Model of Commitments, Notice on Remedies, point 34 (review clause). *See Fiat/New Holland*, D.Comm. Oct. 28, 1999, M.1571, point 27.
964. *Pirelli/Edizione Holding/Blu*, D.Comm. Aug. 5, 2002, IP/02/1183. The transaction whereby Pirelli and Edizione Holding acquired joint control of Telecom Italia was approved by the Commission on Sept. 20, 2001, M.2574, on the basis of the commitment to sell Edizione's stake in Blu to a suitable purchaser. In the absence of a suitable purchaser Edizione requested, and the Commission agreed to, the modification of the original commitmemt.
965. Article 6 (2) and Article 8 (2) of Regulation 139/2004.
966. Recital 31 to Regulation 139/2004.
967. Notice on Remedies, point 12. *See Haniel/Ytong*, D.Comm. April 9, 2002, M.2568, point 154; *Imperial Tobacco/Reemtsma*, D.Comm. May 8, 2002, M.2779, point 65 ('Where a *condition* is not fulfilled, the Commission's decision … no longer stands; where the undertakings commit a breach of an *obligation*, the Commission may revoke'); *ENBW/ENI/GVS*, D.Comm. Dec. 17, 2002, M.2822, point 74.
968. Recital 31; Article 8 (4) (b) of Regulation 139/2004.
969. Article 14 (2) (c) and (d) of Regulation 139/2004. This is new. According to Article 14 (2) (a) of Regulation 1310/97 fines could be imposed only where the parties failed to comply with an *obligation*. Where the parties failed to fulfill a *condition* (in particular the condition to comply with the parties' commitments) the Commission was obliged to initiate fresh proceedings for having put into effect a merger without valid authorization (Articles 14 (2) (b) and 7 (1) of Regulation 1310/97). Applying Article 14 (2) (a) by analogy would have contravened the principle of '*nulla poena sine lege*'.
970. Article 15 (1) (c) of Regulation 139/2004.
971. Article 8 (5) of Regulation 139/2004.

compliance with a condition may presuppose the implementation of the transaction, e.g., in cases where the transaction aims at establishing a new network or infrastructure access to which must be granted at the future request of third parties.[972] Secondly, non-compliance with minor structural commitments or a partial non-compliance with commitments (e.g., divestiture of one out of ten plants to divest in different countries) cannot affect the entire transaction.[973] The only way is to impose sanctions and to review (not necessarily revoke) the decision, e.g., amend the conditions attached to the prior decision. It is true that these provisions apply, strictly interpreted, only where the parties commit a breach of an *obligation*. However, they should apply by analogy so that non-compliance with minor conditions cannot affect the clearance decision as such and must therefore be considered equivalent to an obligation.

(ii) *Non-compliance with an obligation.*
In the case of non-compliance with an *obligation* (e.g., to nominate a trustee) the compatibility decision is not directly affected and 'still stands'.[974] However, the Commission may:
- impose fines,[975]
- enforce the compliance by imposing penalty payments,[976] or
- revoke the authorization decision adopted in accordance with Article 6 (3) (b) or Article 8 (6) (b).[977] By analogy to Article 8 (3) of the former Regulation 17 the right to revoke may include less stringent means, such as the amendment of conditions.

In any event, commitments which require long-term monitoring cannot be enforced without a fresh analysis of the facts and the market structure which may have changed substantially in the meantime, as stated by the Court of First Instance in *Coca Cola*.[978] It may therefore be appropriate to initiate new proceedings on the basis of Article 82 in order to evaluate whether there is an infringement and to order it to be brought to an end.[979]

Postponing the Effect of the Authorization Decision.
In the case of divestiture commitments the parties may commit themselves not to implement the operation before the conditions are fulfilled ('*Up-front Buyer solution*'). The parties may accept that the ban on putting the transaction into effect as set forth in Article 7 of Regulation 139/2004 will continue to apply up to the

---

972. *See Daimler Chrysler/Deutsche Telekom*, D.Comm. April 30, 2003, M.2903, IP/03/594.
973. *See Unilever/Bestfood*, D.Comm. Sept. 28, 2000, M.1990, points 178–180.
974. Notice on Remedies, point 12.
975. Article 14 (2) (d) of Regulation 139/2004.
976. Article 15 (1) (c) of Regulation 139/2004.
977. *Haniel/Ytong*, D.Comm. April 9, 2002, M.2568, point 154.t
978. *Coca Cola*, CFI March 22, 2000, 2000 ECR II-1733, para. 82.
979. Article 7 of Regulation 1/2003.

implementation of the commitment. This avoids the danger that if the transaction were to be completed before the business to be divested was effectively disposed of, the added market shares would in time automatically accrue to the parties.[980] If the Commission wishes the commitments to be fully complied with *before* its decision takes effect it should state so in its decision, i.e. state that the authorization will enter into its (full) effect only if and when the parties comply with their commitments.[981] If in such a case the parties implement the operation before complying with their commitments prior to final clearance, the parties clearly infringe Article 7 (1).

Amendment of Conditions.

Where the implementation of a divestiture commitment meets serious problems, such as deterioration of the financial situation of the company to be divested or restructured, the Commission may adopt a decision agreeing with the parties' proposal to modify their original commitments, and replace them by other means.[982] The clearance decision and/or the commitment may provide for a 'review clause' (possibility to modify the commitment under exceptional circumstances).[983]

Particulars in the Case of Commitment Packages.

Commitments can be part of a package, i.e. of several commitments of the same type in the same sector or different commitments of different types concerning different product or geographic markets, the sum of which are able to remedy the Commission's competitive concerns.[984] The Commission's Notice on Remedies does not indicate the consequences of a *partial* compliance with commitments that form part of a package. In principle, the condition which is attached to a clearance decision is only fulfiled if *all* commitments are complied with ('subject

980. *Bosch/Rexroth*, D.Comm. Jan. 12, 2001, 2004 OJ L 43/1, points 92–94; *Masterfoods/Royal Canin*, D.Comm. Feb. 5, 2002, M.2544; *The Post Office/TPG/SPPL*, D.Comm. March 13, 2001, M.1915, point 135.
981. Similarly under the state aid provisions: *Alitalia*, D.Comm. July 15, 1997, 1997 OJ L 322/44 (obligation imposed on the member state not to pay the aid or part of the aid before the member state's compliance with commitments, in the case at issue the implementation of restructuring plan and achievement of the expected results).
982. *See Edizione/Blu*, D.Comm. Aug. 5, 2002, IP/02/1183 (where the commitments have been modified on the basis of a review clause because the committed divestment appeared impossible); *Shell/Montecatini*, D.Comm. April 24, 1996, M.269 (where the commitment was 'annulled' following other commitments given in the U.S. which covered the commitments given to the Commission); *Hoechst/Rhône Poulenc (Aventis)*, D.Comm. Jan. 30, 2004, IP/04/135 (where the clearance decision of Aug. 9, 1999, M.1378, was amended to the extent that the parties were committed to divest a remaining 15% participation in Rhodia, *see Rhodia/Donau Chemie*, D.Comm. July 13, 1999, M.1517).
983. *See* Standard Model of Commitments.
984. Notice on Remedies, point 30.

to the full compliance with the undertakings').[985] By analogy to partial nullity,[986] a partial compliance with a 'bundle' of commitments is tantamount to a total non-fulfilment justifying a revocation of the conditional clearance if they cannot be severed, whereas the non-fulfilment of a commitment concerning a particular product or a particular market may only justify a revocation of that part of the decision, thereby leaving the clearance of the other part(s) intact.

(e) Civil Consequences of Non-Fulfilment of Commitments

Insofar as non-compliance with a condition leads to the incompatibility of the clearance decision (which 'no longer stands') the agreement on which the (illegal) transaction is based is null and void. The nullity can be invoked before national courts. However, third parties cannot rely on commitments which are entered into *vis-à-vis* the Commission. Non-compliance entitles the Commission to take the appropriate measures under administrative law,[987] but, unlike Article 9 of Regulation 1/2003 which empowers the Commission to make the commitments 'binding on the undertakings',[988] commitments do not create rights which may be enforced before the national courts with the means of national civil law. Third parties may appeal a conditional clearance decision[989] and initiate action for harm caused by the breach of the obligation not to put the merger into effect before compliance with the commitments,[990] provided the decision provides expressly for such an obligation.[991] However, transactions in publicly traded securities remain valid, unless the buyer *and* the seller knew or ought to have known that the transaction was carried out in contravention of the suspension obligation.[992]

985. *See Boeing/McDonnell Douglas*, D.Comm. July 30, 1997, 1997 OJ L 336/16, point 123.
986. *See Delimitis/Henninger Bräu*, ECJ Feb. 28, 1991, 1991 ECR I-935, para. 40; *Automec II*, CFI Sept. 18, 1992, 1992 ECR II-2223, paras 92–95.
987. Including fines according to Article 14 (2) (d) of Regulation 139/2004.
988. *See also* under German law the construction of commitments as a legally enforceable contract of public law ('*Öffentlichrechtlicher Vertrag*'), *see* Wiedemann/Richter, *Handbuch des Kartellrechts* (Beck, 1999), §21, point 58.
989. *See Coca Cola*, CFI March 22, 2000, 2000 ECR II-1733, paras 97 and 106; *ARD/BSkyB/Kirch*, CFI Sept. 30, 2003, T-158/00.
990. Such an action was successful in *Global One* (D.Comm. July 17, 1996, 1996 OJ L 239/57) where the Commission's exemption under Article 81 (3) was made subject to a condition and the parties put the operation into effect before that condition was fulfilled: Oberlandesgericht Düsseldorf (High Court), June 16, 1998, WuW 1998–7/8, 713.
991. As, for the first time, in *Rexrodt/Bosch*, D.Comm. Dec. 13, 2000, IP/00/1457.
992. Article 7 (4), second subparagraph of Regulation 139/2004.

E. Merger Control Regulation – Procedural Rules

1. Notification

Transactions Subject to Notification.
Mergers with a Community dimension *must* be notified to the Commission prior to their implementation; failure to notify is subject to substantial fines.[993] They *may* be notified where the parties demonstrate a good faith intention to conclude an agreement or, in the case of a public bid, where they have publicly announced an intention to make such a bid,[994] whereas under Regulation 1310/97 a notification could only be submitted *after* (but not later than one week after) the conclusion of the agreement.[995] The plan to merge must be sufficiently concrete, e.g., on the basis of a memorandum of understanding or a letter of intent signed by the parties concerned.[996]

Parties to Notify.
A merger must be notified by the parties to the transaction. In the event of the acquisition of joint control the transaction must be notified jointly by the parties acquiring joint control, in all other cases by the person or undertaking acquiring control.[997] The creation of several joint ventures by the same parent companies constitute different transactions and requires different notifications.[998] The same applies to the break-up of a joint venture between the parent companies.[999]

Several Transactions.
Normally each transaction must be notified separately. A transaction involving the acquisition of joint control by one company and of sole control of another part is normally regarded as two separate transactions.[1000] In the case of the acquisition of a controlling interest in a company by another and in the case of a public bid,

993. Article 14 (2) (a) of Regulation 139/2004.
994. Article 4 (1) of Regulation 139/2004.
995. Article 4 (1) of Regulation 1310/97.
996. Recital 34 to Regulation 139/2004.
997. Article 4 (2) of Regulation 139/2004; Article 2 of Regulation 802/2004.
998. In *Renault/Volvo*, D.Comm. Nov. 7, 1990, M.4, the Commission evaluated the two transactions within one decision. In *DuPont/ICI* the Commission declared the acquisition of ICI's worldwide nylon operations by DuPont compatible with the Common Market whereas the acquisition of Dupont's acryl operations by ICI was considered as a separate transaction which did not, however, fulfill the threshold of Community dimension: D.Comm. Sept. 30, 1992, 1993 OJ L 7/13, and IP/92/765.
999. *Solvay/Laporte/Interox*, D.Comm. April 30, 1992, M.197; *Portugal – Secil/Holderbank/Cimport*, ECJ June 22, 2004, C-42/01, para.27. Notice on the Concept of Undertakings Concerned, 1998 OJ C 66/14, points 46–48.
1000. Notice on Concept of Concentration, point 16; *ABB/Renault Automation*, D.Comm. March 9, 1994, M.409.

the person or firm acquiring control must notify.[1001] However – and this is new – transactions which are closely connected in that they are linked by condition or take the form of a series of transactions in securities taking place within a reasonably short period of time may form part of one single notification.[1002] When a clearance is made subject to a commitment to sell off assets or to divest shareholdings the acquisition of those assets or shareholdings by a third company must be communicated to, and accepted by, the Commission and normally constitutes a separate transaction which has to be notified to and approved by the Commission if the thresholds of the merger control regulation are met.[1003] However, the simplified procedure may apply if the market shares do not exceed 15% for horizontal and 25% for vertical relationships.

Pre-Notification Contacts.

The Commission favors pre-notification contacts even in seemingly non-problematic cases.[1004] Such contacts should be launched with a reasoned submission, which contains a brief description of the relevant sector(s) and market(s) involved and the likely impact of the transaction similar to Form CO.[1005] The purpose is to discuss an intended transaction, to identify possible competition concerns at an early stage and to proceed to a first market test, even by using the means of a formal request for investigation (which normally presupposes a formal notification).[1006] The parties may seek DGCOMP's informal guidance on procedural and substantive matters. The matters to be discussed may include the amount of information to be provided (in order to avoid incompleteness and to obtain waivers) and the possibility of referral to national competition authorities where the operation affects competition within a distinct market of a member state.[1007] In this case the Commission transmits the submission to all member states. The member state referred to in the reasoned submission may, within 15 working days, express their agreement or disagreement, and the Commission will decide, within 25 working days from the receipt of the reasoned submission, whether or not to refer the case to the national authority of that member state.[1008] Where the Commission decides to refer the case no official notification shall be made to the Commission.[1009] The

1001. Article 4 (2) and Form CO, section 1.2.
1002. Recital 20 to Regulation 139/2004.
1003. E.g. *Siemens/Fujitsu*, D.Comm. Sept. 30, 1999, JV. 22: clearance subject to the condition to sell-off the retail and banking system, which was cleared in the subsequent Commission decision of Dec. 12, 1999. However, in many cases, the assets to be sold do not exceed the thresholds of Article 5 (2), *see Bellsouth/VRT/E-plus*, D.Comm. Jan. 26, 2000, M.1821.
1004. Best Practices on the Conduct of Merger Control Proceedings, point 5; Form CO, Section 1.1.
1005. Annex III to Regulation 802/2004; Best Practices on the Conduct of Merger Control Proceedings, point 14.
1006. Best Practices, point 26.
1007. *Ibid.*, point 25; Article 4 (4) Regulation 139/2004; Draft Notice on Case Allocation.
1008. Article 4 (4), second and fourth subparagraph, of Regulation 139/2004.
1009. This is new: Article 4 (4), fifth subparagraph.

pre-notification discussions may also concern the question whether or not a transaction that lacks a Community dimension but is capable of being reviewed under the national competition laws of at least three member states should be referred to the Commission for disposition under Community law. In such a case the Commission transmits the submission to all national authorities which may express their agreement or disagreement within 15 working days. Where no disagreement has been expressed the transaction is deemed to have a Community dimension and must be notified to the Commission, thereby precluding national competition authorities from applying national competition law.[1010] Pre-notification contacts allow better coordination not only with the competition authorities of the member states but also with the competition authorities of third countries.[1011] The Commission may even use its fact-finding powers during the pre-notification phase if the existence of the transaction is in the public domain and once the parties have had the opportunity to express their views on such enquiries.[1012]

Notification Formalities: The Form CO.
The notification formalities are laid down in Form CO, which is annexed to Regulation 802/2004. The information that must be provided includes numerous facts and circumstances which are relevant for taking a decision on the notified merger:

- an executive summary explaining the merger, the markets affected and the rationale for the merger;
- information on the parties, in particular on the undertakings belonging to the same group and turnover in each country, Community-wide and worldwide;
- definitions of the affected markets, including neighbouring markets,[1013]
- estimates of the HHI levels before and after the merger, as well as market shares for each of the affected markets and each of the competitors;
- estimates of the market shares of all competitors having at least 5% of the relevant geographic market;
- identification and e-mail addresses of the five largest suppliers and the five largest independent customers of the parties;

1010. This is also new: Article 4 (5) of Regulation 139/2004.
1011. *See* EU-US Best Practices on Merger Control Proceedings on cooperation in merger investigations, of Jan. 12, 2004, available at the Commission's website.
1012. Best Practices on the Conduct of Merger Control Proceedings, points 26–27. The Commission does not intend to publish the fact that a reasoned submission has been lodged: Draft Notice on Case Allocation, point 61.
1013. Neighbouring markets are defined as ones where the products are complementary to each other or where they belong to a range of products that is usually purchased by the same set of customers for the same end use; Section 6.3.(c) of Form CO.

– description of the overall market context and efficiencies;[1014] and
– cooperative effects of a joint venture for the purpose of Article 2 (4) of Regulation 139/2004.

The Form CO no longer contains a section with respect to ancillary clauses because the Commission normally does not intend to proceed to an express assessment, except in cases of novel and unresolved questions.[1015] Where the parties request such an express assessment, thereby referring to the Court of First Instance's judgment in *Canal+/Lagardère*,[1016] they must do so in a separate letter annexed to the Form CO. A short form may be used for notification of certain transactions that do not raise competition concerns[1017] as specified in the Commission's Notice on a Simplified Procedure.[1018] Where parties request a pre-notification referral under Article 4 (4) and (5) of Regulation 139/2004 they must make a reasoned submission in the form RS (reasoned submission).[1019] Incorrect or misleading information in a submission, notification or supplement thereto is subject to procedural fines, even if they are supplied by natural persons.[1020]

Need for Complete Notification.
The information must be correct and complete in order to be effective. One original and 35 copies must be submitted to the Commission by post or by hand (notification[1021]), letter, fax, telex or electronic mail (other documents).[1022] Where the notification is incomplete in a material respect, the Commission shall inform the notifying parties and set an appropriate time limit for completion of the information. In such cases, the notification becomes effective on the date on which the complete information is received by the Commission.[1023] However, the Commission may accept an incomplete notification, provided the parties give reasons for the unavailability and provide their best estimates.[1024] The Commission may waive particular items of information required by the 'CO' form if it considers

1014. For any efficiency claim the parties must provide a detailed explanation of how the efficiency will be achieved, a quantification of the efficiencies and the customer benefits. *See* Guidelines on Horizontal Mergers (2004 OJ C 31/5), points 76–88; *see* Form CO, Section 9.3.
1015. Commission's Notice on Ancillary Restrictions, 2001 OJ C 188/5, point 2. *See* Section D.3.(h) *supra*. *See* Recital 21 to Regulation 139/2004.
1016. *Canal+/Lagardère*, CFI Nov. 20, 2002, 2002 ECR II-4825, paras 83–87, 106–113.
1017. Annex II to Regulation 802/2004.
1018. 2000 OJ C 217/32. *See* Section E.2. *supra*.
1019. Annex III to Regulation 802/2004.
1020. Article 14 (1) (a) of Regulation 139/2004.
1021. Article 3 (1) of Regulation 802/2004.
1022. Article 21 (1) of Regulation 802/2004; Best Practices, point 21.
1023. A notification which has been declared incomplete must be re-notified and re-published: Article 5 (4) of Regulation 802/2004. *See Blohm+Voss/Lisnave*, D.Comm. June 18, 1998, M.1004; *BP/Amoco*, D.Comm. Dec. 11, 1998, M.1293 (Article 6 (1) (b) decisions).
1024. Form CO, point 1.3.(f).

that such information is not necessary for the examination of the case in question.[1025] This is usually agreed in informal contacts prior to notification.

Consequences of Incomplete Notification.
A procedural fine may be imposed where the parties supply incorrect or misleading information in a submission (including a pre-notification reasoned submission), notification or supplement thereto.[1026] Even natural persons – i.e., persons that are already controlling at least one undertaking and acquire another undertaking – are subject to fines if they supply incorrect or misleading information.[1027] Moreover, if the Commission orders the parties to disclose information or to submit to an on-the-spot investigation owing to incorrect or incomplete information being supplied in the notification, it is not bound by the normal time limit of 90 working days after opening proceedings for making the final decision.[1028] It may also revoke a decision based on incorrect information.[1029]

Language.
The notification must be completed in one of the official languages of the Community which will be thereafter the language of the proceedings. The rules of the EEA Agreement provide for the alternative use of any language of an EEA country. Form CO requires a translation into an official language of the Community.[1030]

No Fee.
Unlike other competition laws, notifications to the Commission are not subject to any administrative fee.

Privileged and Confidential Information.
Article 214 of the EC Treaty, Article 17 (2) of Regulation 139/2004 and the corresponding provisions of the EEA Agreement[1031] provide for the non-disclosure of information covered by the obligation of professional secrecy, which includes the protection of confidential information between the notifying parties. Parties who believe they might be harmed by the publication or disclosure of any confidential

1025. Article 4 (2) of Regulation 802/2004. The completeness of the notification and waivers may be discussed in pre-notification contacts with the Commission: Best Practices on the Conduct of Merger Control Proceedings, points 20–23.
1026. Article 14 (1) of Regulation 139/2004.
1027. Article 14 (1) and Article 3 (1) (b) of Regulation 139/2004.
1028. Article 10 (4) of Regulation 139/2004.
1029. Article 6 (3) and Article 8 (6) of Regulation 139/2004. *See Sanofi/Synthelabo*, D.Comm. March 15, 1999, M.1397; clearance withdrawn: D.Comm. April 21, 1999, M.1542.
1030. Regulation 1/58 on languages, 1958 OJ 385; Article 3 (4) of Regulation 802/2004; Form CO, Section 14.
1031. Article 122 of the EEA Agreement, Article 9 of Protocol 24 and Article 17 (2) of Protocol 4 to the Agreement on the establishment of a Surveillance Authority and a Court of Justice.

business information may submit such information separately with each page clearly marked 'Business Secrets'.[1032]

Publication.
When the Commission finds that a notified transaction falls within the scope of the merger regulation, it publishes the fact of the notification, the names of the notifying parties, the nature of the concentration and the economic sectors concerned in the Official Journal, which gives third parties the opportunity to submit comments (Article 4 (3) of Regulation 139/2004).

Withdrawal of Notification.
A second phase proceeding must be closed by formal decision under Article 8 of Regulation 139/2004, unless the notifying parties have demonstrated to the satisfaction of the Commission that they have abandoned the concentration.[1033] This provision should apply by analogy to first phase proceedings.[1034] However, in pre-notification contacts the parties are free to to withdraw their submission (i.e., not to proceed to a formal notification).

2. Simplified Procedure for the Treatment of Certain Concentrations

(a) New Commission Notice on a Simplified Procedure

The Commission has published a Notice on a Simplified Procedure for the Treatment of Certain Merger Cases. The notice applies since September 1, 2000; it will be amended upon finalization of the 2004 Draft Notice.[1035] The notice provides for a simplified procedure suitable for certain mergers consisting of simplified notification requirements and a short-form decision.[1036]

(b) Categories of Mergers Qualifying for a Simplified Procedure

The Notice on a Simplified Procedure provides for a streamlined procedure suitable for the following categories of mergers:[1037]

1032. Form CO Section 1.5.

1033. This is new: Article 6 (1) (c) of Regulation 139/2004 accords with the prior practice of the Commission, which adopted a prohibition decision in *MCI WorldCom/Sprint* although the parties withdrew the notification a few hours before adoption: D.Comm. June 28, 2000, 2003 OJ L 300/1 (on appeal: T-310/00).

1034. Dittert, WuW 2004–2, 148, 153.

1035. 2000 OJ C 217/32 and Commission's website.

1036. The Tribunal of First Instance introduced an expedited procedure for mergers, pursuant to Article 76a of the Rules of Procedure, which was applied in two recent merger cases: *Schneider*, CFI Oct. 22, 2002, 2002 ECR II-4091; and *Tetra Laval*, CFI Oct. 25, 2002, 2002 ECR II-4381, reducing the procedure from several years to less than one year.

1037. Notice on a Simplified Procedure, point 4 (a)–(c).

(i) Mergers with a *negligible effect within the area of the EEA*: Two or more companies acquire joint control of a joint venture, provided that the joint venture has no, or negligible, actual or foreseen activities within the territory of the EEA, which occurs where:
  - the turnover of the joint venture and/or the turnover of the contributed activites is less that than EUR 100 million in the EEA territory; and
  - the total value of assets transferred to the joint venture is less than EUR 100 million in the EEA territory.[1038]

(ii) Mergers between *companies without any overlapping activities*: Two or more companies merge, or one or more companies acquire sole or joint control of another company, provided that none of the parties to the merger are engaged in business activities in the same product and geographical market, or in a product market which is upstream or downstream of a product market in which any other party to the merger is engaged.[1039] Mergers involving conglomerate aspects may, however, be excluded from the simplified procedure, in particular where the parties hold individually a market share of 25% or more because of the risk of increasing the parties' market power.[1040]

(iii) Mergers between parties with *modest market shares*: Two or more companies merge, or one or more companies acquire sole or joint control of another company and:
  - and two or more of the parties to the merger are engaged in business activies in the same product or geographical market (*horizontal* relationships) whose combined market share is not more than 15%; or
  - one or more of the parties to the merger are engaged in business activities in a product market which is upstream or downstream of the product market in which any other party to the merger is engaged (*vertical* relationships) whose combined market share is not more than 25%;[1041] or
  - a party is to acquire sole control of an undertaking over which it already has joint control.

It can normally be assumed that such operations will not raise serious doubts as to their compatibility with the Common Market.[1042] However, exceptional situations may require a closer investigation and a full decision.

1038. *See* under the previous procedural rules: *BNP/Dresdner Bank/Szecho-Slovakia*, D.Comm. Aug. 26, 1991, M.124 (clearance of the creation of a joint venture in a third country). Under the new simplified procedure: *see BHP/Mitsubishi/QCT*, D.Comm. Sept. 28, 2000, M.2153.

1039. *See Techint/Stella/James Jones/Sirti*, D.Comm. Nov. 22, 2000, M.2215.

1040. Notice on a Simplified Procedure, point 8.

1041. *See RWE/Thames Water*, D.Comm. Oct. 27, 2000, M.2181; *Kohlberg Kravis Roberts/Laporte*, D.Comm. Nov. 13, 2000, M.2184.

1042. Notice on a Simplified Procedure, point 7. Possible example (however, decided before the notice entered into force): *Lafarge/Titan/Amereyah*, D.Comm. March 8, 2000, M.1862 (objection against joint acquisition of a competitor in a third country by two leading firms).

(c) Product and Geographical Market Definitions

The parties are required during the pre-notification phase to identify alternative product and geographical markets on which the transaction may have an impact. The Commission will apply the simplified procedure only in those cases where the markets can be clearly determined (otherwise, the normal procedure applies, at the discretion of the Commission).[1043] In the case of incorrect information the decision may be revoked according to Article 6 (3) (a) of the merger control regulation.

(d) Procedural Provisions

The simplified procedure provides for the following:

- Pre-notification contacts are beneficial because such contacts allow the Commission and the parties to determine the amount of information to be provided in a notification.[1044] According to the Best Practices on the Conduct of Merger Control Proceedings,[1045] in most of the cases where the notification was declared incomplete, it was *not* preceded by a pre-notification contact. It seems therefore generally advisable to enter into pre-notification talks in *all* cases, including those which qualify for a simplified procedure.
- There is a short-form notification.[1046]
- There is a short-form publication in the Official Journal of the *fact* of notification in order to allow interested third parties to submit observations.[1047]
- If the Commission is satisfied that the operation qualifies for the simplified procedure it will normally issue a short-form decision as soon as possible after the 15 working days' period during which member states may request referral. The decision only includes the names of the parties, a very brief description of the nature of the merger and the economic sectors involved.[1048] If third parties, in particular competitors, object to the merger they should make their views known immediately after the publication of the notification. Although third parties have no procedural rights during the first phase of the Commission

1043. Notice on a Simplified Procedure, point 6.
1044. Article 4 of Regulation 802/2004; Notice on a Simplified Procedure, point 10, and Draft Notice on the Simplified Procedure; *see* in greater detail: Best Practices on Merger Control Proceedings Guidelines issued by the European Competition Lawyers Forum, http://europa.eu.int/comm/competition/mergers/others/best_practices.pdf.
1045. The Best Practices are reviewed from time to time.
1046. Annex II to Regulation 802/2004.
1047. Notice on a Simplified Procedure, point 11.
1048. Notice on a Simplified Procedure, point 12; Draft Notice, point 17. The Commission could have used the possibility of clearance by silence as provided for in Article 10 (6) but preferred an express, although short-form, decision.

proceedings this does, by analogy to the state aid rules, not release the Commission from the duty to examine third parties' objections[1049] and third parties (i.e., competitors) would have the right to appeal a Commission decision that does not take due account of their objections.[1050]
- If the Commission judges the merger unsuitable for the simplified procedure (in particular in the light of a complaint), the Commission may revert to the normal procedure.[1051]
- The *fact* of the clearance is published in the Official Journal, whereas a public version of the decision will be available only on the Internet (for a limited period).

(e) Appraisal of Ancillary Restrictions

According to the Commission's notices the simplified procedure also applies to ancillary restrictions, i.e., restrictions directly related and necessary to the implementation of the merger, provided they are specified by the parties in their notification.[1052] A simplified procedure is not suited where the parties request an express assessment of ancillary restrictions.[1053]

3. SUSPENSION AND WAIVERS OF SUSPENSION

Automatic Suspension – Exceptional Derogation.
No merger may be put into effect either before notification nor until it has been declared compatible with the Common Market.[1054] However, most mergers are conditional on antitrust approval anyway.[1055] As an exception, a public bid, duly notified, may be implemented, provided that the acquirer does not exercise the voting rights attached to the securities or only does so to maintain the full value of those investments on the basis of a derogation granted upon request to the

1049. Notice on a Simplified Procedure, point 11.
1050. *See CIRFS*, ECJ March 24, 1993, 1993 ECR I-1125, paras 19–30.
1051. Notice on a Simplified Procedure, point 12.
1052. Notice on a Simplified Procedure, point 14.
1053. 2004 Draft Notice, point 19. However, the Court of First Instance stated that the Commission cannot be relieved, even in a simplified procedure, from assessing ancillary restrictions: It is questionable whether the parties to a merger that fulfills the criteria for a simplified procedure can be 'punished' by withholding the benefit of an assessment of ancillary restrictions even in cases where they give rise to 'novel or unresolved questions', *see Canal+/Lagardère*, CFI Nov. 20, 2002, 2002 ECR II-4825, para. 113.
1054. Article 7 (1) of Article 139/2004. Exceptions apply for the implementation of a public bid or a series of transactions in securities according to Article 7 (2) of Regulation 139/2004.
1055. Under the rules of the French stock exchange, the acquisition cannot be conditional on antitrust approval.

Commission.[1056] The Commission also has discretion to grant a derogation from the suspensive effect notification under other circumstances on request, even before notification, and subject to conditions or obligations on the parties, such as enjoining the parties from exercising voting rights, from acquiring further shares or assets of the targeted company or from exchanging competitively sensitive commercial information.[1057] Where such derogation is likely to affect one or more of the parties, in particular in cases of acquisition of joint control, the Commission must give the parties the opportunity to comment in writing before its decision or, if a provisional decision is necessary for reasons of urgency, after such provisional decision.[1058] A decision rejecting such a waiver may be appealed to the Court of First Instance, but the appeal does not have the effect of suspending enforcement of the order unless the Court of First Instance itself so orders.[1059]

Provisional Suspension Decision under Article 18 (2).
The Commission may take a suspension decision provisionally under Article 18 (2) without first having given the notifying parties and other involved parties the opportunity to make known their views;[1060] however it shall send them without delay the text of the provisional decision and, once the parties have made known their views within the time limit set by the Commission, take the final decision, which may annul, amend or confirm the provisional decision.[1061]

No Publication of a Provisional Suspension Decision.
A provisional suspension decision is not published nor available on internet. However, the final decision refers to the suspension decision.[1062]

1056. Article 7 (2) (b) of Regulation 139/2004. In *Tetra Laval* (M.2416) and *Schneider Legrand* (M.2283) the merger had been implemented (public bid), and the Commission ordered separation by decision of Jan. 30, 2002 on the basis of Article 8 (4). Both decisions were appealed and reversed (T-80/02 and 76/02); the requests for interim measures were withdrawn following the Commission's decision to extend the time-limit for divestment.

1057. Article 7 (3) of Regulation 139/2004. *See Group Cofinga/BNP*, D.Comm. Feb. 19, 1999, M.1419 (because there was no overlap of the parties' activities and the transaction therefore did not raise serious doubts); *Sanofi/Synthélabo*, D.Comm. April 21, 1999, M.1397 (based, however, on incorrect information in the notification which led to withdrawing the clearance decision, to reconsidering the case and a new clearance decision (May 17, 1999) but also to imposing fines for supplying incorrect information (fine of EUR 40.000, decision of July 28, 1999).

1058. Article 18 (2) of the Regulation 139/2004. *See* Article 12 of Regulation 802/2004.

1059. *Cf.* interim and other orders under Article 8 of Regulation 1/2003.

1060. E.g., *Group Cofinga/BNP*, D.Comm. Jan. 15, 1999, M.1419.

1061. Article 18 (2) of Regulation 139/2004 and Article 12 (2) of Regulation 802/2004.

1062. E.g., *Group Cofinga/BNP*, D.Comm. Feb. 19, 1999, M.1419, referring to the suspension decision of Jan. 15, 1999.

Penalties for Failure to Observe the Suspension Obligation or Order.
If the notifying parties implement a merger before its notification or disregard a decision under Article 7 (1) or an obligation[1063] imposed under Article 7 (3), they may be fined up to 10% of aggregate turnover.[1064]

Civil Consequences.
The validity of any transaction carried out in disregard of the suspension of a merger or other order depends on the final decision, i.e., whether the Commission allows the merger (and, if so, subject to what conditions or obligations), disallows it, or the merger goes through without a decision (Articles 7 (4) and 10 (6)). Consequently, the implementation of transactions is undertaken at the parties' own risk. If the merger is disallowed or if it is allowed subject to conditions or obligations, any transactions carried out while the suspension or other order was in force which run counter to the final decision will be invalid and will have to be reversed.[1065] The prohibition on putting the merger into effect during the suspension and on taking action in breach of a specific order is absolute and therefore has direct effect in national law, so that parties (such as the target of a hostile takeover bid) or third parties would probably be able to ask national courts to enforce the ban, as in the case of breaches of the prohibition on governments granting subsidies before the Commission has authorized them.[1066] The remedies obtainable from national courts could include injunctions, declarations of nullity and damages for injury sustained as a result of breach of the ban.[1067] Injunctions

---

1063. Conditions have the direct effect of invalidity of the transaction. Under Article 7 (1) and Article 10 (1) of Regulation 139/2004 a merger can be put into effect after 25 working days following its notification, unless the Commission decides to continue the suspension by initiating proceedings. The obligation of suspension does not apply under Article 22 (4) to transactions which are referred to the Commission by the competent national antitrust authority and which may already be implemented: *RTL/Veronica/Endemol*, D.Comm. Sept. 20, 1995, M.553; *aff'd* CFI April 28, 1999, 1999 ECR II-1299, para. 21, and therefore necessitate a divestiture: *Blokker/Toys 'R' Us*, D.Comm. June 26, 1997, 1998 OJ L 316/1.

1064. Article 14 (2) (a) and (b) of Regulation 139/2004. E.g. under the similar provision of Regulation 1310/97: *Samsung*, D.Comm. Feb. 11, 1998 (symbolic fine of ECU 33,000); *A.P.Moller*, D.Comm. Oct. 12, 1998, M.969 (fine of ECU 219,000).

1065. Article 8 (4). *See*, with respect to transactions referred to the Commission by a member state, Article 21 (4) and *Blokker/Toys 'R' Us*, D.Comm. June 26, 1997, 1998 OJ L 316/1. *Cf.* the position with government subsidies granted without the Commission having authorized them, which the Commission can order the government to recover from the recipient: policy announced in 1983 OJ C 3 18/3; *see also* Seventeenth Report on Competition Policy, point 173; *France v. Commission*, ECJ Feb. 14, 1990, 1990 ECR I-307, para. 22.

1066. *See* Düsseldorf Higher Regional Court, April 16, 1997, WuW 1998–7/8, 713: obligation to compensate the loss and injury resulting from the implmentation of the telecommunications joint venture before the conditions attached to the Commission's exemption decision (*Phoenix/Global One*, D.Comm. July 17, 1996, 1996 OJ L 239/23) were fulfilled.

1067. *Ibid.* Such remedies would be available irrespective of whether the merger were allowed or disallowed, as in the case of breaches of Article 82 (*BRT/SABAM I*, ECJ Jan. 30, 1974, 1974

have already been granted.[1068]

Validity of Purchases and Sales of Shares during Takeover Bids.
Purchases and sales of shares during a public tender offer are valid, provided the acquirer does not exercise its voting rights. However, a simple purchase of shares listed on a public exchange (without a public tender offer for them) would be invalid if both the buyer and seller knew or ought to have known that the transaction was carried out in contravention of the ban.[1069]

Special Situation of Joint Ventures.
If the parties went ahead with setting up a joint venture in disregard of a suspension or other order, the joint venture company would remain valid until compulsorily dissolved.[1070]

4. FACT-FINDING

Requests for Information and Investigation.
The Commission's fact-finding powers are adapted to those under Regulation 1/2003 (Articles 11–13 of Regulation 139/2004) and include the right to request information and/or to proceed to investigations (by simple warrant or by decision at the Commission's choice[1071]). The Commission may use these powers in particular towards third parties (requesting replies to questionnaires), whereas the parties to the merger are normally requested to submit the relevant information when checking the completeness of the parties' submission during the pre-notification contacts or in the first phase without delay after the notification.[1072] The Commission may proceed to oral requests;[1073] however, the parties are not subject to sanctions if they supply incorrect or incomplete information following such

ECR 51, para. 16; *Ahmed Saeed*, ECJ 11 April 1989, 1989 ECR 803, para. 32; *Nouvelles Frontières*, ECJ April 30, 1986, 1986 ECR 1425, para. 65).

1068. For example, by a French court in *Sofreb II* (joint venture between Schmalbach-Lubeca (Continental Can) and Carnaud), Seventeenth Report on Competition Policy, point 70; 1988–4 CMLR 262.

1069. Article 7 (2) and (4), second sub-paragraph.

1070. Articles 11 and 12 of the First Directive on company law harmonization, 1968 OJ L 65/8 (Special Edition 1968 41), in particular Article 12 (2) which requires member states to provide for the compulsory winding up of companies that have been formed unlawfully. This provision would also apply to a new company formed by the legal merger of two existing companies.

1071. *Schneider*, CFI Oct. 22, 2002, 2002 ECR II-4201, para. 77.

1072. Best Practices on the Conduct of Merger Control Proceedings, points 20–23. The parties are allowed to rectify or complete their notification within one or two days before a formal declaration of incompleteness.

1073. The Commission is entitled to proceed to oral requests for information (by telephone): *Endemol*, CFI April 28, 1999, 1999 ECR II-1299, paras 83–91. *See* Best Practices on Merger Control Proceedings, point 27 ('mainly in writing').

oral requests.[1074] The Commission's inspection powers include the right to examine books and records, irrespective of the medium on which they are stored (except documents enjoying legal privilege), and to seal any business premises,[1075] excluding, however (unlike Regulation 1/2003), inspection of private homes.

Use and Disclosure of Information.
Information acquired using the Commission's fact-finding powers or from submissions by parties or third parties may only be used for the purpose of the relevant proceedings (Article 17 (1)). This means that information acquired in this way may not be used for other purposes than enforcement of the competition rules (such as for tax offenses, prevention of fraud, or insider dealing prosecutions) or for proceedings in relation to other antitrust cases at the EC or national levels. However, the Commission may use evidence of infringements of Articles 81 and 82 disclosed in the notification to initiate enforcement proceedings under those provisions. Examples might include a joint venture notified under the regulation that is in fact an anticompetitive partial function joint venture or ancillary restraints not directly related or necessary to the implementation of the transaction. The regulation prohibits the Commission and the member state authorities from disclosing or publishing confidential information coming into their possession.[1076] Disagreements on confidential information must be finally decided by Commission decision.[1077]

'State-of-Play Meetings'.
The Commission endeavours to maintain close contact with the *notifying parties* by inviting them to attend 'State-of-Play meetings' at key stages of the investigation and to discuss the case with senior officials, which includes the possibility of reviewing documents in the Commission's file and confronting the concerns of third parties at the earliest possible stage of the proceedings. State-of-play meetings[1078] take place:

- within three weeks in the first phase where it appears that 'serious doubts' are likely to be present or are already raised,
- within two weeks following the adoption of the Article 6 (1) (c) decision to go to second-phase proceedings in order to address the Commission's competitive concerns in an early stage,

1074. Only incorrect or misleading answers given during an inspection may be fined: Article 14 (1) (e) of Regulation 139/2004.
1075. Article 13 (2) of Regulation 139/2004. However, the period for sealing must normally not exceed 48 hours (Recital 39 to Regulation 139/2004) (72 hours under Regulation 1/2003).
1076. *Cf.* Article 17 of Regulation 4064/89. For more details on the rules concerning the official use and the disclosure of information, *see infra* Chapter X.D.7.
1077. Article 19 of Regulation 802/2004.
1078. Alternatively, by telephone or video conference: Best Practices on the Conduct of Merger Control Proceedings, point 31.

– before issuing of a Statement of Objections,
– following the reply to the Statement of Objections and the oral hearing, and
– before the meeting of the Advisory Committee.[1079]

Third parties are also involved in the proceedings and invited to put forward views on key market data and any 'complaint'. The parties to the merger and third parties may be invited to a 'triangular' meeting on a voluntary basis in order to hear the views of both in a single forum to discuss the submissions made.[1080] To this effect third parties receive a non-confidential version of the Statement of Objections.[1081] However, access to the file is granted to the parties only after the sending of the Statement of Objections.[1082] In order to preserve confidentiality, the parties are invited to provide non-confidential versions.[1083]

5. First Phase Proceedings

Overview.
Decisions on a notified transaction may be taken within the first phase proceedings, which is limited to 25 working days (35 working days where the parties offer commitments) from the day following the notification or, in the cases of a request for referral by a member state, following the day after the Commission decision to examine the merger.[1084] If the transaction raises serious doubts as to its compatibility with the Common Market and therefore needs a more comprehensive evaluation, second phase proceedings are initiated which may take 90 working days (105 working days where the parties offer commitments, likely to be extended at the parties' request by 15–20 additional working days, unless the commitments are offered less than 55 days after the initiation of proceedings).[1085] The Commission's statistics reveal that the large majority of cases (about 90%) are cleared in the first phase by a decision stating that the transaction is compatible with the Common Market (Article 6 (1) (b)), a small proportion (about 2%) by a decision stating that the notified operation is not a 'merger' within the meaning of the regulation[1086] or not a merger with a Community dimension, and another

1079. Best Practices on the Conduct of Merger Control Proceedings, point 33.
1080. *Ibid.*, points 34–37.
1081. This is new: Best Practices on the Conduct of Merger Control Proceedings, point 33 (e).
1082. Article 18 (2) of Regulation 139/2004; Article 17 of Regulation 802/2004; Best Practices on the Conduct of Merger Control Proceedings, points 42–44. In pre-notification contacts the Commission may accept, but is not obliged, to grant access to, and discuss, key documents in order to facilitate further proceedings.
1083. Best Practices on the Conduct of Merger Control Proceedings, points 38–39.
1084. Articles 9 (2) and 22 (4) of Regulation 139/2004.
1085. Article 10 (1) and (3) of Regulation 139/2004.
1086. Commission's statistics on merger cases: http://europa.eu.int/comm/competition/mergers/cases/stats.html.

small proportion (about 5%) passes into the second phase proceedings leading to a clearance decision, more than half of them subject to conditions and obligations, or a prohibition decision (about 1%). Some 61 notifications have been withdrawn in the first phase and 23 in the second phase. There are (unfortunately) no statistics on the cases which have been abandoned following doubts raised during the pre-notification phase.[1087]

Fact Finding during the First Phase.
The Commission may obtain all necessary information by written (Article 11 of Regulation 139/2004) or oral requests. Market contacts may also be initiated informally prior to the notification.[1088]

Due Process during the First Phase.
Due process is ensured during the first phase by giving the parties and third parties the opportunity of making their views known in the State-of-Play meetings, which include the opportunity of commenting on 'key documents', on substantiated submissions of third parties,[1089] on 'serious doubts' which may be raised, and on possible remedies.[1090] In complex cases such a State-of-Play meeting may not be sufficient for a compehensive discussion of the key points in the procedure within the time limits of the first phase so that there may be no other solution but to initiate the second phase and to address a formal Statement of Objections, which is preceded and followed by further State-of-Play meetings.[1091]

Decisions at the End of the First Phase: Clearance or Opening of Second Phase Proceedings.
At the end of the first phase the Commission has to decide, by way of a letter to the parties, whether the notified transaction:

- Falls *outside* the scope of the regulation because it does not constitute a merger as defined in Article 3 or lacks a 'Community dimension' as defined in Article 1 (Article 6 (1) (a));[1092]
- Falls *within* the scope of the regulation but *does not raise serious doubts* as to its compatibility with the Common Market (Article 6 (1) (b)). Such a clearance may be subject to conditions and obligations intended to ensure that the parties

1087. Examples: *Telefonica/Sogecable/Cablevision*, M.709; *KPMG/Ernst & Young*, M.1044; *Wienerberger und Breuer*, M.1047; *Wolters Kluwer/Reed Elsevier*, M.1040; *Pakhoed/Van Ommeren*, M.1454;
1088. Best Practices on the Conduct of Merger Control Proceedings, points 26–28.
1089. Best Practices, points 38–39.
1090. Best Practices, point 33.
1091. *Ibid.*
1092. Example of a joint venture that is not considered 'full-function' and therefore not subject to the merger control: *ENW/Eastern*, D.Comm. Oct. 15, 1998, M.1315.

comply with the commitments they have entered into vis-a-vis the Commission (Article 6 (2)). In this case the commitments must be submitted to the Commission not later than 20 working days from the date of the notification (one original and ten copies).[1093] The commitments must include a precise plan of how and when to comply with commitments, such as the sale of a business, and they are described in, or annexed to, the Commission decision.[1094] The clearance also covers restrictions directly related and necessary to the implementation of the transaction, so-called ‘ancillary restraints’ (Article 6 (1) (b)). In addition, restraints that are *not* ancillary and coordinate the competitive behavior of firms that remain independent may still be cleared under the new Article 2 (4) if they satisfy the criteria of Article 81 (3).[1095] A clearance under Article 2 (4) is granted within the framework of Regulation 139/2004, including the time constraint of Article 10 (1) and (6);[1096]
- Falls *within* the scope of the regulation and *raises serious doubts* as to its compatibility with the Common Market, in which case the Commission initiates second phase proceedings (Article 6 (1) (c)). Serious doubts may also result from the coordination of the competitive behaviour between the parent companies that is contrary to Article 81 (1) and (3) and *therefore* renders the operation incompatible with the Common Market. In order to avoid second phase proceedings, the notifying parties may submit commitments which are intended to permit the Commission to take a decision stating that the notified transaction no longer raises serious doubts and may be declared compatible with the Common Market.[1097] However, such a decision must be taken ‘as soon as it appears that the serious doubts … have been removed’;[1098] this means that commitments must be submitted without delay after the notification of the Article 6 (1) (c) decision.[1099] If no commitments are submitted the final decision will be taken at the end of the second phase of the proceedings according to Article 8 (2) or (3).

If the Commission fails to take a decision within the time limits, the merger is deemed automatically to have been authorized (‘clearance by silence’).[1100]

1093. Article 19 (1) of Regulation 802/2004.

1094. *See Deutsche Post/DHL*, D.Comm. June 26, 1998, M.1168; *Usinor/Cockerill*, D.Comm. Feb. 4, 1999, M.1329; *Alcatel/Thomson-SCF-SCS*, D.Comm. June 4, 1998, M.1185 (however, confidential information will be deleted).

1095. *See* Form CO, Section 10.

1096. This is because the appraisal ‘in accordance with the criteria of Article 81 (1) and (3)’ is part to ‘establishing whether or not the operation is compatible with the Common Market’.

1097. Article 8 (2) of Regulation 139/2004.

1098. Article 10 (2) of Regulation 139/2004. Examples: *Siemens/Drägerwerk/JV*, D.Comm. April 30, 2003, M.2861, point 4; *Bombardier/Adtrans*, D.Comm. April 3, 2001, M.2139.

1099. E.g. *British Telecom/AT&T*, 1998 OJ C 390/21, cleared on March 30, 1999, JV. 15.

1100. Article 10 (6) of Regulation 139/2004.

Cooperation with National Antitrust Authorities.
The Commission must transmit to the national antitrust authorities copies of the notification and the most important documents, which include commitments by the parties in order to gain clearance pursuant to Article 6 (1) (b).[1101] The national authorities may express their views[1102] but the Advisory Committee is not consulted during the initial scrutiny phase, including waivers of suspension.[1103]

No Publication but Availability via Internet.
Decisions under Article 6 are not published in the Official Journal. However, after deletion of confidential information a public version, including commitments,[1104] is made available via the Internet, except for decisions under Article 6 (1) (c) because of their provisional nature. The Commission lists all cases decided within the first phase and summarizes the more important ones in its Report on Competition Policy.

6. SECOND PHASE PROCEEDINGS

More Comprehensive Examination.
Second phase proceedings are devoted to a comprehensive examination of the transaction because the Commission has serious doubts as to its compatibility with the Common Market. This comprehensive evaluation includes a wider use of the Commission's fact-finding powers, including discovery in the form of requests for information or for documents and on-the-spot investigations. Both discovery and on-the-spot investigations may be directed to parties to the transaction and to third parties. The powers may be exercised both in the form of a voluntary request and a compulsory order.[1105]

Time Limits.
The second phase must be concluded:

- within 90 working days, or
- within 105 working days, where commitments are submitted, unless they are submitted within 55 days of the opening of proceedings, or
- within a further 15 (not more than 20) working days in complex cases where the parties anticipate the need of a more comprehensive assessment.[1106]

1101. Article 19 (1) of Regulation 139/2004.
1102. Article 19 (2) of Regulation 139/2004.
1103. Article 19 (3) and Article 18 (2) of Regulation 139/2004.
1104. *See Exxon/Shell*, D.Comm. July 8, 1998, M.1137.
1105. The Commission is entitled to proceed to oral requests of information (by telephone): *Endemol*, CFI April 28, 1999, 1999 ECR II-1299, paras 83–91.
1106. Article 10 (3) of Regulation 139/2004.

The periods are extended where the Commission, owing to circumstances for which the parties are responsible, proceeds to investigations.[1107] The period may be shorter where the competitive concerns have been removed by the parties, in particular as a result of amendments.[1108]

Due Process.
Before the Commission takes a decision under Article 8(2), second subparagraph (exemption subject to conditions or obligations), under Article 8 (3) (declaration of incompatibility) or under Article 8 (4) (decision ordering the divestiture of the notified merger), it must hear the notifying parties and grant third parties involved in the proceedings the opportunity, at every stage of the procedure, up to the consultation of the Advisory Committee, of making known their views on the objections against them.[1109] Normally, the Commission issues a Statement of Objections in writing to the notifying parties, inviting them to comment[1110] within a time limit, which the Commission sets, thereby having regard to the time required for the preparation of statements and the urgency of the case.[1111]

(i) *Hearing of the Notifying Parties.*
The notifying parties may make known their views on the objections raised against them within the the time limit set by the Commission.[1112] Before doing so, they may request access to the file, which does not extend, however, to confidential information or internal documents of the Commission, including the correspondence between the Commission and the competent national authorities.[1113] They may request in their written comments the opportunity to develop their arguments in an Oral Hearing.[1114] In addition, the Commission may offer the parties the opportunity of attending a State-of-Play meeting before issuing the Statement of Objections, following the reply to the Statement of Objections, following the Oral Hearing and before the Advisory Committee meets.[1115]

1107. Article 10 (4) of Regulation 139/2004.
1108. Article 10 (2) of Regulation 139/2004. E.g., *Siemens/Drägerwerk/JV*, D.Comm. April 30, 2003, M.2861 point 4; *Bombardier/Adtranz*, D.Comm. April 3, 2001, M.2139.
1109. Article 18 (1) of Regulation 139/2004; Article 13 (1) of Regulation 802/2004; Best Practices on the Conduct of Merger Control Proceedings, point 29.
1110. Article 13 (2) of Regulation 802/2004.
1111. Article 23 of Regulation 802/2004.
1112. The Commission is not obliged to take into account comments received after the expiry of the time limit: Article 13 (2), fifth subparagraph of Regulation 802/2004.
1113. Article 17 of Regulation 802/2004.
1114. Article 14 (1) of Regulation 802/2004.
1115. Best Practices on the Conduct of Merger Control Proceedings, point 33 (c)–(e). The Commission may also hear the notifying parties at other stages in the proceedings: Article 14 (3) of Regulation 802/2004.

(ii) *Hearing of Third Parties.*
Natural and legal persons showing a sufficient interest, and especially members of the administration or management bodies of the undertakings concerned or the recognized representatives of employees are entitled to be heard.[1116] However, the Commission may also hear other third parties,[1117] such as competitors, customers and consumer organizations,[1118] thereby contributing to a broader factual knowledge of the case. The Commission informs them in writing of the nature and subject matter of the procedure and sets a time limit, within which the third parties may make known their views.[1119] Third parties may also request to develop their arguments in an oral hearing.[1120] There is no special status of complainants in merger cases.[1121] However, they may 'intervene' in the proceedings to the same extent as third persons showing a sufficient interest. They may make submissions in writing on the nature and subject matter of the procedure on which they are informed by the Commission,[1122] including a non-confidential version of the Statement of Objections from which business secrets have been removed.[1123] The Commission may, upon request, grant access to the file in so far as this is necessary for the purposes of preparing their comments.[1124] They may also attend a triangular meeting together with the notifying parties.[1125] Although the regulation does not provide for any formal right of third parties to complain, the Commission will have to take due account of observations made by competitors or consumers, because they are entitled to appeal the final decision under the second paragraph of Article 230 of the EC Treaty.[1126]

Advisory Committee.
The Advisory Committee is to be consulted before any decision at the end of the second phase (Article 19 of Regulation 139/2004) and any decision imposing fines or penalty payments. The procedure is similar to that under Regulation

---

1116. Article 18 (4) of Regulation 139/2004.
1117. Article 16 (3) of Regulation 802/2004.
1118. Best Practices on the Conduct of Merger Control Proceedings, point 34. To this effect, the DGCOMP has appointed a Consumer Liaison Officer.
1119. Article 16 (1) and (2) of Regulation 802/2004.
1120. Article 14 (2) of Regulation 802/2004.
1121. Best Practices on the Conduct of Merger Control Proceedings, fn. 22.
1122. This may include information on 'key documents' and 'key submissions': Best Practices on Merger Control Proceedings, point 45.
1123. Best Practices on the Conduct of Merger Control Proceedings, point 36.
1124. Article 17 (2) of Regulation 802/2004. *See* Article 18 (3) of Regulation 139/2004 (access to the file 'at least' to the parties directly involved).
1125. Best Practices on the Conduct of Merger Control Proceedings, points 38–39.
1126. E.g., *Kaysersberg*, CFI Nov. 27, 1997, 1997 ECR II-2137; *ARD/Kirch Pay-TV-British Sky*, CFI Sept. 30, 2003, T-158/00, paras 11–20.

1/2003,[1127] but the amended version of Article 19 extends the consultation to the parties' commitments which must be included in the set of documents to be communicated to the Advisory Committee. A notable difference is that the Advisory Committee's opinion may be, and usually is, published (Article 19 (7) of Regulation 139/2004).[1128] The Committee may have to be consulted a second time if the notifying parties submit new undertakings in order to render the transaction compatible with the Common Market.[1129]

Decisions Declaring the Transaction Compatible with the Common Market. If the Commission finds during the second phase proceedings that the transaction does not significantly impede effective competition, it must issue a decision declaring the transaction compatible with the Common Market (Article 8 (1) of Regulation 139/2004) and, in the case of full-function joint ventures, also with Article 81 (3) (Articles 2 (4) and 8 (1) of Regulation 139/2004). Since proceedings are opened only if there is serious suspicion that the transaction may impair competition, the Commission will grant clearance only if this suspicion has been dispelled or if the firms concerned have amended or agreed to amend the terms of the notified agreements or plans to its satisfaction. Decisions pursuant Article 8 must be published in all official languages (which explains the sometimes considerable delay of publication),whereas decisions pursuant Article 6 are taken only in the language of the proceedings. The Commission's decision must also cover ancillary restrictions that are 'directly related and necessary to the implementation' of the transaction in order to guarantee the transfer to the acquirer of the full value of the assets acquired (Article 8 (2), third subparagraph, and Article 6 (1) (b), second subparagraph), which is discussed in section D.3. *supra*. In cases of 'full-function cooperative joint ventures', the decision also covers the coordination of competitive behavior (Article 2 (4)), which is discussed in section D.2.g. *supra*.

Decision of Compatibility Subject to Conditions.
A Commission clearance decision taken in the second phase may be subject to conditions and obligations intended to ensure compliance with commitments designed to make the transaction compatible with the Common Market (Article 8 (2)).[1130] In order to ensure compliance with commitments to divest companies or business units the Commission may take, or order the parties to take, the ap-

1127. *See infra* Chapter X.E.5.
1128. The Council and the Commission had made a joint statement that the arrangements for publication of the opinion will be reviewed after four years in the light of experience: Statements, re Article 19, which reconfirmed these arrangements when adopting Regulation 1310/97. The opinions published up to now show a large concordance between Commission and Advisory Committee.
1129. E.g. *Bertelsmann/Kirch/Première*, 1999 OJ C 57/18 and 19.
1130. *See* Article 20 of Regulation 802/2004.

propriate measures which include the obligation not to exercise the voting rights attached to the shares to be transferred, to maintain the value of the company in order to remain an active competing force and to appoint a trustee to conduct business operations independently, to evaluate prospective independent purchasers and to dispose of the assets acquired.[1131]

Decisions Declaring the Transactions Incompatible with the Common Market.

If the Commission finds that a notified or unnotified transaction would significantly impede effective competition in the Common Market or in a significant part of it, the Commission declares the transaction incompatible with the Common Market and – if applicable – with the EEA Agreement (Article 2 (3) and 8 (3)) and with Article 81 where a joint venture does not fulfill the criteria laid down in this provision.[1132] When the transaction has not been consummated in conformity with the waiting requirement under Article 7, the Commission decision is limited to a declaration of incompatibility. When it is implemented the Commission may take the appropriate measures in order to restore conditions of effective competition (divestiture) according to Article 8 (4) of Regulation 139/2004. When a transaction that does not have a Community dimension is referred by a member state to the Commission, its decision may have effects with respect to the entire Community, whereas under Article 22 (5) of the prior Regulation 1310/97 it had to be limited to measures strictly necessary to maintain or restore effective competition with the territory of the member state(s) at the request of which it intervenes.[1133]

Decisions Ordering the Dissolution of a Merger.

Article 8 (4) of Regulation 139/2004 provides that where a merger:

- has already been implemented (legally as in cases referred by the national authorities to the Commission or of public bids)[1134] and has been declared incompatible with the Common Market,[1135] or

1131. Under the EC merger control regulation: Article 8 (4); *Blokker/Toys 'R' Us*, D.Comm. June 26, 1997, 1998 OJ L 316/1, paras 130–132. Under the ECSC merger rules Article 66 §5 (second subparagraph): *Ruhrkohle AG/Saarbergwerke/Preussag Anthrazit*, D.Comm. July 29, 1998, ECSC.1252, points 43–47. Under Article 83 (1) of the Euratom Treaty: *ANF Lingen*, D.Comm. Aug. 1, 1990, 1990 OJ L 209/27.

1132. Article 8 (3) of Regulation 139/2004.

1133. *See Blokker/Toys 'R' Us*, D.Comm. June 26, 1997, 1998 OJ L 316/1. However, a national competition authority that decides on a case referred to it by the Commission must take only the measures strictly necessary to safeguard or restore competition on the market concerned: Article 9 (8) of Regulation 139/2004.

1134. E.g., *Blokker/Toys 'R' Us*, D.Comm. June 26, 1997, 1998 OJ L 316/1.

1135. Examples: *Schneider/Legrand*, D.Comm. Jan. 30, 2002, M.2283 and *Tetra/Sidel*, D.Comm. Jan. 30, 2002, M.2416. Both decisions have been annulled by the Court of First Instance as a consequence of the annulment of the prohibition decisions on which they were based.

– has been implemented in contravention of a condition (non-compliance with a commitment), which is tantamount to the implementation of a non-notified merger without authorization,[1136]

the Commission may require the dissolution of the merger or may, where the prevailing situation cannot be restored, take any other measure appropriate to achieve such restoration as fast as possible or order any other restorative measures (e.g., obligation not to exercise voting rights, to appoint an independent trustee or to report to the Commission), which may be ordered by way of interim measures.[1137] However, the interim measure may, by its very nature, not impose the 'restoration' of effective competition because it must be provisional and not prejudge the final decision (which orders the restoration).[1138] The measures may be imposed in the prohibition decision[1139] or by separate decision.[1140] The Commission's order aims at restoring the situation prior to the (illegal) merger, which consists in the *complete* separation of the assets acquired in order to reestablish effective competition; an ownership interest of only 5% normally does not have negative effects on competition.[1141] Accordingly, the Commission ordered in *Tetra Laval/Sidel* the divestiture of the whole participation of Tetra Laval in Sidel without retaining a minority shareholding,[1142] whereas the maintenance maintenance of a minority shareholding of 20% was accepted in *Blokker/Toys 'R' Us*.[1143]

Mandatory Consultation of the Advisory Committee.
According to Article 19 (3) the Advisory Committee must be consulted before any decision is taken under Article 8 (declaration of incompatibility) and Articles 14 and 15 (fines and penalty payments).

Cooperation with Competition Authorities of Third Countries.
The Commission cooperates closely with competition authorities in third countries within the ICN (International Competition Network). Examples of coordination with the U.S. Federal Trade Commission and the U.S. Department of Justice in-

1136. *See* Recital 31 to Regulation 139/2004. In this case the Commission is not bound by the time limits of Article 10: Article 8 (7) of Regulation 139/2004.
1137. Article 8 (5) of Regulation 139/2004.
1138. *Van der Bergh Foods*, CFI July 7, 1998, 1998 ECR II-2641, para. 62.
1139. *RTL/Veronica/Endemol*, D.Comm. July 17, 1996, 1996 OJ L 134/32, point 116; *aff'd* CFI April 28, 1999, 1999 ECR II-1299; *Blokker/Toys 'R' Us*, D.Comm. June 26, 1997, 1998 OJ L 316/1, points 129–133; *Kesko/Tuco*, D.Comm. Nov. 20, 1996, 1997 OJ L 110/53, point 173.
1140. *Schneider/Legrand,* D.Comm. Jan. 30, 2002, 2004 OJ L 101/134; *Tetra Laval/Sidel,* D.Comm. Jan. 30, 2002, 2004 OJ L 38; both decision were reversed by the Court of First Instance because they were based on an illegal prohibition decision: *Schneider,* CFI Oct. 22, 2002, T-310/01, 2002 ECR II-4091, and *Tetra Laval,* CFI Oct. 25, 2002, T-80/02, 2002 ECR II-4381.
1141. *Schneider/Legrand,* D.Comm. Jan. 30, 2002, 2004 OJ L 101/134, M. 2283, points 28–30.
1142. *Tetra Laval/Sidel,* D.Comm. Jan. 30, 2002, 2004 OJ L 38, M.2416, point 40.
1143. *Blokker/Toys 'R' Us*, D.Comm. June 26, 1997, 1998 OJ L 316/1, points 132–133.

clude cases such as *DSM/Roche*,[1144] *Konica/Minolta*[1145] and, in particular, *MCI WorldCom/Sprint*.[1146]

Publication.
An Article 8 decision must be published, including the Advisory Committee's opinion[1147] and the parties' commitments,[1148] while having regard to the legitimate interest of undertakings in the protection of their business secrets (Article 20), which necessitates longer negotiations and explains the rather late publication of these important decisions. The Commission is not bound to publish decisions imposing fines or penalty payments, but it is not prevented from doing so in order to improve the general level of enforcement and compliance with the merger control regulation.[1149] The Commission has imposed fines in several cases but has not yet issued decisions setting forth its reasoning.[1150]

Effects of the Commission Decision.
The Commission's finding of compatibility or incompatibility of a merger with the Common Market is binding on national authorities and national courts, which follows from the sole jurisdiction conferred to it.[1151] However, the mere finding in the decision that the parties to the merger hold a dominant position has no binding effect and does not affect the powers of national authorities and national courts to apply Article 82; even the Commission would have to proceed to a new analysis when effectively applying Article 82.[1152] In the case of a partial referral the Commission decision relates only to those aspects of the merger which it did *not* refer to a national authority and does not prejudge the substantive decision of the national authority, which is not prevented from assessing the merger in a different way, e.g. by considering the merger as not causal for significantly impeding effective competition, such as by the creation or the strengthening of a dominant position.[1153]

1144. *DSM/Roche*, D.Comm. July 23, 2003, M.2972. *See* International Competition Network, 'Recommended Practices for Merger Notification Procedures', Sept. 2002, updated Jan. 2004, http://internationalcompetitionnetwork.org/practices.pdf.
1145. *Konica/Minolta*, D.Comm. July 11, 2003, M.3091.
1146. *MCI WorldCom/Sprint*, D.Comm. June 28, 2000, 2003 OJ L 300/1, points 13 *et seq.*
1147. Article 19 (7) of Regulation 139/2004.
1148. *See WorldCom/MCI*, D.Comm. July 8, 1998, 1999 OJ L 116/1, points 136–164.
1149. *ACF Chemiefarma-Quinine*, ECJ July 15, 1970, 1970 ECR 661, paras 101–104.
1150. Fines have been imposed in *Samsung*, D.Comm. Feb. 11, 1998; DG IV Newsletter 1998–2, p. 71 (rather symbolic fine of ECU 33.000); *Moller*, D.Comm. Feb. 10, 1999, M.969 (fine of EUR 219.000: EUR 15.000 for each of the three non-notified mergers and EUR 6.000 for each day of delay). Fines were considered in *Telefonica/Sogecable/Cablevision*, CFI July 12, 1996, 1996 ECR II-797 (initiation of proceedings followed by a – belated – notification and the abandonment of the current merger plans).
1151. Article 21 (2) of Regulation 139/2004.
1152. *Coca Cola*, CFI March 22, 2000, 2000 ECR II-1733, paras 84–92.
1153. *Royal Philips Electronics*, CFI April 3, 2003, T-119/02, paras 375–379.

7. Withdrawal of Decisions and Fine Proceedings

Withdrawal.

A decision clearing a transaction in the first phase and declarations of incompatibility in the second phase may be revoked if they are based on incorrect information for which the notifying parties are responsible (Article 6 (3) and Article 8 (6)) including information supplied in a reasoned submission or in a supplement to a notification.[1154] An incomplete notification followed by a clearance limited to the described, and not considering the omitted, activities may be held 'incorrect' and lead to a withdrawal decision followed by a new appraisal of the entire case including the possibilities of imposing fines (Article 14 (1) (a)).[1155] The Commission is not bound by the normal time limits (Article 6 (4) and Article 8 (7)).

Fines.

Under Article 14 (1) the Commission may impose on natural persons referred to in Article 3 (1) (b)[1156] and undertakings or associations of undertakings fines not exceeding 1% of the parties' aggregate turnover where the parties intentionally or negligently

- supply incorrect or misleading information in a reasoned submission, certification, notification or supplement thereto,[1157]
- supply incorrect or incomplete information in reply to a discovery request or fail to supply information in reply to a discovery order within the time-limit,[1158]
- produce business records in incomplete form during an on-the-spot investigation, or refuse to submit to an investigation order,
- give incorrect or misleading answers, fail to rectify an answer or fail or refuse to give an answer during an inspection, or
- breach seals affixed during an inspection.

Under Article 14 (2) fines of up to 10% of the party's aggregate turnover may be imposed against any party which intentionally or negligently:

- fails to notify a merger,

1154. *See Sanofi/Synthélabo*, D.Comm. May 19, 1999, M.1397.

1155. In *Sanofi/Synthélabo* the Commission imposed a fine of EUR 40,000: D.Comm. July 28, 1999, M.1397.

1156. I.e., persons which already control at least one or more undertakings (and may therefore be assimilated to 'undertakings').

1157. *See Deutsche Post/Transoflex*, D.Comm. Dec. 14, 1999, 2001 OJ L 97/1 and *Tetra Laval*, D.Comm. July 7, 2004, IP/04/863 (fines of respectively EUR 100,000 and 90,000 for incorrect information supplied in the notification *and* the reply to a discovery request); *Deutsche BP*, D.Comm. June 19, 2002, IP/02/897 (fine of EUR 35.000).

1158. *Mitsubishi/Heavy Industries*, D.Comm. July 12, 2000, Thirtieth Report on Competition Policy, point 287 (fine of EUR 50,000).

- puts a transaction into effect without notification[1159] or in disregard of an automatic or extended suspension or other order, or in breach of a final decision prohibiting the transaction,
- fails to take the action required by a divestiture order (Article 8 (4) or (5)), or
- fails to comply with a condition or obligation that is imposed as a condition of waiving or lifting a suspension or under the terms of a clearance decision.

Daily Penalties.
Under Article 15 the Commission may, in addition, fine natural persons referred to in Article 3 (1) (b) and undertakings or associations of undertakings up to 5% of the average daily aggregate turnover in order to compel undertakings

- to supply complete and correct information,
- to submit to an inspection ordered by the Commission,[1160]
- to comply with an obligation attached to a decision, or
- to comply with any measure ordered by a decision.[1161]

8. JUDICIAL REVIEW

Decisions Subject to Judicial Review.
The Commission's decisions may be appealed by member states, the parties and third parties, which are directly and individually concerned.[1162] Although the Commission enjoys a certain discretion when assessing a transaction under Regulation 139/2004,[1163] actions may be based on grounds of lack of competence, infringement of an essential procedural requirement (in particular insufficient reasons[1164]), infringement of any rule of law or misuse of powers.

Final Decisions Subject to Appeal.
Any measure which produces binding legal effects so as to affect the interest of an individual by bringing about a distinct change in its legal position is an act or

---

1159. *Samsung*, D.Comm. Feb. 11, 1998 (fine of EUR 33,000, not published); *Moller*, D.Comm. Feb. 10, 1999, 1999 OJ L 183/29 (fine of EUR 219,000). A fine was announced in *Hutchison Atlantic*, D.Comm. Oct. 26, 2000, IP/00/1199 (statement of objections); no fine was considered in *Haniel/Cementbouw*, D.Comm. June 26, 2002, M.2650 (although not notified, the operation was cleared with retroactive effect).

1160. *Mitsubishi/Heavy Industries*, D.Comm. July 12, 2000, Thirtieth Report on Competition Policy, point 287 (daily penalties of EUR 900,000 for failing to comply with a discovery order).

1161. *Cf.* the former maximum EUR 25,000 per day fine in Article 15 (1) of Regulation 1310/97. A fine was considered (but finally was not imposed) in *Skanska/Scancem*, D.Comm. Nov. 11, 1998, M.1157, IP/99/982. On fines generally and procedures, *see infra* Chapter X.F.6.(e).

1162. Article 230 of the EC Treaty.

1163. *Verband freier Rohrwerke*, CFI July 8, 2003, T-374/00, para. 105.

1164. *See Verband freier Rohrwerke*, CFI July 8, 2003, T-374/00, paras 184–193.

decision which may be the subject of an action for annulment under Article 230 of the EC Treaty.[1165] This applies to:

- All final decisions taken after formal proceedings (clearance and prohibition decisions) which are subject to judicial review by the Court of First Instance at the request of a party[1166] or an interested third party, in particular an actual[1167] or potential competitor,[1168] and by the Court of Justice if challenged by a member state (Article 230 of the EC Treaty).[1169]
- An Article 6 (1) (a) decision which may be appealed by the parties because the decision states that the transaction is not subject to the one-stop principle of the merger control regulation and therefore needs clearance under Article 81 or the respective national competition laws.[1170] This applies even if the 'clearance' is granted by way of a press release which may have the same legal effects as an Article 6 (1) (a) decision.[1171]
- A clearance decision which is subject to compliance with commitments,[1172] which may be appealed to the same extent as conditions attached to an exemption decision;[1173] the fact that a commitment is given voluntarily does not preclude a judicial review. As the Court of First Instance stated in the case *Coca Cola*, a commitment is 'not a unilateral act unconnected to the decision applying the competition rules because the obligations created by such an undertaking for the applicant must be deemed equivalent to orders requiring an infringement to be brought to an end'.[1174]
- A decision by which certain restrictions described in the merger notification are deemed to be not ancillary to the concentration, because the assessment of ancillary clauses forms an integral part of the subject-matter of the decision approving the concentration.[1175]

1165. *IBM*, ECJ Nov. 11, 1981, 1981 ECR 2639, para. 9; Canal+/*Lagardère*, CFI Nov. 20, 2002, 2002 ECR II-4825, para. 63.
1166. *See Gencor*, CFI March 25, 1999, 1999 ECR II-753; *Airtours*, CFI June 6, 2002, 2002 ECR II-2585; *Schneider*, CFI Oct. 22, 2002, 2002 ECR II-4091; *Tetra Laval*, Oct. 25, 2002, 2002 ECR II-4381.
1167. *Royal Philips Electronics*, CFI April 3, 2003, T-119/02; *ARD*, CFI Sept. 30, 2003, T-158/00.
1168. *BaByliss/SEB-Moulinex*, CFI April 3, 2003, T-114/02, paras 99–100.
1169. *See French Republic and SCPA/Kali + Salz-MdK*, ECJ March 31, 1998, 1998 ECR I-1375. Member states may also appeal decisions rejecting a request of referral: Article 9 (9) of Regulation 139/2004.
1170. *Generali/Unicredito*, CFI March 4, 1999, 1999 ECR II-203, paras 37–43.
1171. *Air France*, CFI May 19, 1994, 1994 ECR II-323, paras 44–59.
1172. *Coca Cola*, CFI March 22, 2000, 2000 ECR II-1733, para. 104.
1173. *Transocean Marine Paint Association*, ECJ Oct. 23, 1974, 1974 ECR 1063.
1174. *Coca Cola*, CFI March 22, 2000, 2000 ECR II-1733, para. 64.
1175. *See* Article 8 (2), third subparagraph, 'shall also cover restrictions directly related and necessary to the implementation of the concentration': *Canal+/Lagardère*, CFI Nov. 20, 2002, 2002 ECR II-4825, para. 74.

- A decision implementing a clearance decision which is subject to the divestiture of assets, e.g. a decision rejecting the approval of a third company as a suitable acquiror of assets to be divested.[1176]
- A decision rejecting a complaint because of failure to act against a non-notified merger with a Community dimension.[1177]
- A decision imposing a substantive or procedural sanction.[1178]

However, a simple letter by the Commission stating that an operation is not a 'merger' is not open to appeal,[1179] except where such a letter has been issued within the first phase of a notification procedure and may therefore be tantamount to an Article 6 (1) (a) decision.[1180] Similarly, a mere finding in a clearance decision that the parties hold a dominant position is not open to appeal because this statement has no binding effects and does not prejudge any future behaviour which may have to be assessed under Article 82.[1181]

Provisional v. Final Decisions.
Decisions to open formal proceedings (Article 6 (1) (c)) are not appealable because they are merely a step in the procedure leading to a final determination of the case.[1182] However, a decision referring a case to a national authority may be appealed because it excludes the application of the Community merger regulation and subjects the operation to exclusive review by the national authority and affects third parties 'in the same way as it would have been affected by an approval decision had the referral not been made.'[1183] A decision rejecting the transfer of a case may be appealed by the national authority. Decisions ordering an undertaking to submit to an on-the-spot investigation may be appealed by the undertaking concerned, which may also request interim measures.[1184]

1176. *Petrolessence, SG2R*, CFI April 3, 2003, T-342/00, paras 101–121.
1177. E.g., *Express International, DHL*, ECJ June 16, 1994, 1994 ECR I-2681. *See* under Articles 81 and 82: *IECC*, CFI Sept. 16, 1998, 1998 ECR II-3645, para. 176.
1178. The rare decisions imposing fines (mostly procedural fines) have not been appealed.
1179. *See*, with respect of a simple letter stating that there is no state aid: *UPS*, CFI Sept. 30, 1999, 1999 ECR II-2857.
1180. *See Air France*, CFI May 19, 1994, 1994 ECR II-323, paras 44–59.
1181. *Canal+/Lagardère*, CFI Nov. 20, 2002, 2002 ECR II-4825, paras 85–92.
1182. Comparable to a statement of objections which implies the initiation of a procedure: *IBM*, ECJ Nov. 11, 1981, 1981 ECR 2639, para. 9.
1183. *Royal Philips Electronics*, CFI April 3, 2003, T-119/02, paras 280 and 297.
1184. Under Article 14 of the prior Regulation 17 *see Roquette Frères*, ECJ Oct. 22, 2002, ECR I-9011.

Interim Orders.
Where necessary, the Court may suspend a prohibition decision of the Commission[1185] but may not do so where it decides to proceed under an expedited procedure.[1186]

Consequence of the Annulment of a Commission Decision.
When the Court of First Instance annuls a prohibition decision and the Commission does not appeal the judgment the case is deemed to be aborted,[1187] except where the Commission, based on the findings of the Court, decides to adopt a clearance decision subject to new or amended commitments.[1188] When the Court of Justice annuls the whole or part of a Commission decision and the Commission proceeds to a re-assessment, the periods laid down in Article 10 start again from the date of the judgment (Article 10 (5)). With respect of those parts which are annulled, the Commission proceeds to a fresh assessment on the basis of all facts, including those arising between the original notification and the new assessment (assessment *ex nunc*); whereas, with respect to the Commission's decisions which are affirmed, the Court's judgment has the effect of *res iudicata* to the extent that the Commission must base its new assessment on those findings.[1189]

Expedited Procedure before the Court of First Instance.
On 6 December 2000, the Court of First Instance modified, with effect from 1 February 2001, its Rules of Procedure, by including a new Article 76a, in order to allow for the introduction of a new expedited procedure.[1190] This new type of expedited procedure was designed to deal with cases of a particularly urgent nature, such as actions concerning public access to administrative documents held by institutions or decisions regarding the control of mergers or takeovers.[1191] Applications may be lodged at the same time as the application initiating the proceedings or the defence. The Court exercises its discretion on whether to grant the expedited procedure. Once the request is approved the written and oral procedure is slightly modified:

- The case is automatically given priority.

1185. Example under national competition law: *NetCologne*, Higher Court (Oberlandesgericht) Dusseldorf, April 11, 2001, WuW 2001–6, 589. Application for interim relief dismissed in *Petrolessence/SG2R*, CFI Jan. 17, 2001, 2001 ECR II-67, para.53 (no situation liable to jeopardize of the applicants' existence).

1186. *Schneider*, CFI May 30, 2002, 2002 ECR II-4091.

1187. E.g. *First Choice* following the judgment of June 6, 2002, 2002 ECR II-2855; *Schneider* following the judgment of Oct. 22, 2002, ECR II-4091.

1188. E.g. *Tetra Laval/Sidel*, D.Comm. Jan. 13, 2003, M.2416, following the judgment of Oct. 25, 2002, 2002 ECR II-4381; *SEB/Moulinex*, D.Comm. Nov. 11, 2003, M.2226.

1189. E.g., *Kali + Salz-MdK II*, D.Comm. July 9, 1998, M.308, point 10.

1190. 2000 OJ L 322/4.

1191. CFI information notice published on the Court's website.

- The written procedure is simplified.
- The CFI will make greater use of pre-hearing measures.
- Emphasis is placed on the oral procedure.
- The expedited procedure can lead to a judgment within a maximum period of less than 12 months (compared with an average duration of 20 months).

Application of the Expedited Procedure.
In deciding whether to grant a request for expedited procedure, the Court will have regard to the urgency and the circumstances of the case and to the question whether, in view of the complexity and the volume of the pleadings, the case lends itself to essentially oral argument.[1192] The expedited procedure has been granted in two cases at the request of the parties challenging the prohibition of a concentration which has already been implemented,[1193] and in three cases at the request of third parties challenging the conditional clearance of a concentration.[1194] However, cases where the parties to a concentration decided not to proceed with the deal are dealt with under the standard procedure.[1195] The expedited procedure may allow the parties to keep a deal alive pending final judgment. However, they may also withdraw their application following their decision to abandon the transaction.[1196]

F. Assessment of Transactions not Covered by the Merger Regulation

1. Minority Shareholdings

Agreements between Competitors on the Acquisition of a Minority Shareholding.
Agreements between competitors on the acquisition of minority shareholdings may be assessed under various rules:

(a) They may be assessed under the merger control regulation where the minority shareholding confers *control*, which is decisive influence over the target

1192. However, experience shows that urgent cases are granted the benefit of the expedited procedure regardless of their complexity. *See Schneider/Legrand*, CFI Oct. 22, 2002, 2002 ECR II-4091; *Tetra Laval*, CFI Oct. 25, 2002, 2002 ECR II-4381.

1193. *Schneider/Legrand*, D.Comm. Oct. 30, 2001, M.2283; *Tetra Laval/Sidel*, D.Comm. Oct. 30, 2001, M.2416.

1194. *Ineos v. Shell/DEA*, D.Comm. Dec. 20, 2001, M.2389; *BP/E.ON*, D.Comm. Dec. 20, 2001, M.2533; and *BaByliss v. SEB/Moulinex*, D.Comm. Jan. 8, 2002, M.2621.

1195. E.g. *GE/Honeywell*, D.Comm. July 3, 2001, M.2220.

1196. E.g. in the *Schneider/Legrand* case; following the Court's judgment annulling the Commission's prohibition decision (CFI Oct. 22, 2002, 2002 ECR II-4091) the Commission adopted on Dec. 4, 2002 an Article 6(1)(c) decision according to which the notification was withdrawn on Dec. 11, 2002.

company. Decisive influence presupposes the right to co-determine commercial policy, which is conferred by statutary or *de facto* veto rights relating to strategic decisions on its business policy (budget, business plan, major investments and appointment of management) or by representation in the management (interlocking directorates).[1197]

(b) They may be assessed under the merger control regulation and – within the same merger proceedings – under Article 81[1198] where the minority shareholding leads to *joint control* of the target company, which is exercised together by one or more other undertakings, thereby creating a joint venture,[1199] provided the thresholds of Community dimension are met.[1200] In the absence of a Community dimension any anticompetitive coordination must be assessed under Article 81.[1201]

(c) They may be assessed under Articles 81 and 82 where they do not confer decisive influence (control)[1202] but may be used as 'an instrument for *influencing* the commercial conduct of the companies in question so as to restrict or distort competition on the market on which they carry on business.'[1203]

(d) They may not raise any competition concerns where the minority shareholding does not confer rights to control or to influence commercial conduct but is limited to what is necessary to protect the investors' *financial interests*.[1204]

1197. Commission Notice on the Concept of Concentration, 1998 OJ C 66/5, points 18–38.

1198. Article 2 (4) of Regulation 139/2004; Notice on the Concept of Concentrations, points 18–37. This provision presupposes the existence of a joint venture, i.e. 'joint' control. However, in *Newscorp/Telepiù*, D.Comm. Nov. 29, 2002 (Art. 6 (1) (c)), M.2876, the Commission examined the likely anticompetitive coordination between the minority shareholder Telecom Italia holding 20% and Newscorp holding 80% in Stream, which is, according to the Commission, solely (and not jointly) controlled.

1199. E.g. *Electrabel/Totalfina Elf/Photovoltech*, D.Comm. April 18, 2002, M.2712 (42.5% : 34% : 8.5%, but ¾ majority required). Where there are shifting majorities, Article 81 applies: *see Eureko*, D.Comm. April 27, 1992, M.207; *Channel Five*, D.Comm. Dec. 22, 1995, M.673, points 8–14; *Pirelli/Edizione Holding/Olivetti*, D.Comm. Sept. 20, 2001, M.2574.

1200. Article 1 of Regulation 139/2004.

1201. *See Eureko*, D.Comm. April 27, 1992, M.207, point 18.

1202. Unlike certain national merger rules, such as in Germany, Austria, Ireland and Poland, minority shareholdings above 25% that do not confer veto rights are excepted from the Community merger control and the Commission does not intend to extend EU merger control to such minority shareholdings: Green Paper of Dec. 11, 2001, COM(2001)745/6 final, points 106–110.

1203. *Philip Morris/Rothmans*, ECJ Nov. 17, 1987, 1987 ECR 4487, para. 37. Application of the Philip Morris doctrine in *Hudson's Bay II*, IP/88/810, Nineteenth Report on Competition Policy, point 42 (objection to the acquisition of a 35% ownership stake replacing an exclusive purchasing obligation which had been abandoned according to *Hudson's Bay I*, D.Comm. Oct. 28, 1988 (with fines), 1988 OJ L 316/43).

1204. Notice on the Concept of Concentrations, point 22.

Minority Shareholding – Instrument for Acquiring Decisive Influence. Minority shareholdings may lead to joint control[1205] or to sole control[1206] over an enterprise. Joint control may be acquired in the form of veto rights[1207] or the right to co-determine the strategic decisions of an undertaking.[1208] The acquisition of minority shareholdings in a third company by competitors[1209] and cross-shareholdings or ownership of assets in a competitor[1210] may also lead to joint control. A 'qualified minority' may even lead to sole control where the shareholder is highly likely to assemble a majority at the shareholders' meeting, given that the remaining shares are widely dispersed,[1211] or where preferential shares or other rights enable the shareholder to determine the commercial behavior of the target company.[1212] Such minority shareholdings that lead to joint or sole control must be assessed under the merger control regulation, provided they have a Community dimension.

Minority Shareholding – Instrument for Influencing Commercial Conduct. A minority shareholding that does not confer 'control' by one or more undertakings does not constitute a 'concentration' within the meaning of Article 3. Thus, the acquisition of rights below the level of control may not only be subject to Article 81 and Regulation 1/2003 but also to national competition law, provided the shareholding leads to an appreciable restriction or distortion of competition.[1213] The Court of Justice held in *Philip Morris/Rothmans* that minority shareholdings that do not confer joint or sole control may still be used as 'an instrument for influencing the commercial conduct of the companies in question so as to restrict

---

1205. *See Renault/Volvo*, D.Comm. Nov. 7, 1990, M.4 (exchanged shareholdings of 25%).
1206. *Arjomari/Wiggins Teape*, D.Comm. Feb. 10, 1990, M.25; *Société Générale de Belgique/Générale de Banque*, D.Comm. Aug. 3, 1993, M.343.
1207. Notice on the Concept of Concentration, points 21–29.
1208. *Ibid.*, points 18–19 and 30–38.
1209. *See ASKO-Jacobs/ADIA*, D.Comm. May 29, 1991, M.82 (clearance); *Aerospatiale-Alenia/DeHavilland*, D.Comm. Oct. 2, 1991, 1991 OJ L 334/42 (declaration of incompatibility); *Telefonica/Sogecable/Cablevision*, M.709, Twenty-sixth Report on Competition Policy, pp. 65–66 (cancellation of the joint take-over after objection). Under Article 81 *Irish Distillers Group*, Eighteenth Report on Competition Policy, point 80; *Plessey/GEC-Siemens*, Nineteenth Report on Competition Policy, point 66; *BBL*, Twenty-seventh Report on Competition Policy, pp. 154–155.
1210. *Renault/Volvo*, D.Comm. Nov. 7, 1990, M.4. *See IMI/Heilmann I*, Seventh Report on Competition Policy, points 29–32.
1211. *Arjomari/Wiggins Teape*, D.Comm. Feb. 10, 1990, M.25. Further examples of minority shareholdings leading to sole control *see* Section C.3.(b) *supra*.
1212. Notice on the Concept of Concentration, point 14. *See Anglo American Corp./Lonrho*, D.Comm. April 23, 1997, 1998 OJ L 149/21, points 31–39.
1213. Statistics on minority shareholdings are provided in the Twenty-first Report on Competition Policy, p. 422.

or distort competition on the market on which they carry on business' and thereby infringe Article 81.[1214]

Shareholding Links between Competitors and Non-Competitors.
The Court of Justice's analysis in *Philip Morris/Rothmans* was confined to shareholding links between competitors. The Commission has routinely drawn a basic distinction in its evaluation of joint ventures and shareholding links according to whether the parties are competitors or non-competitors and whether or not the shareholding links are reciprocal.[1215] Article 81 is likely to be infringed by shareholding links or joint ventures between *competitors*, but will apply only in rare instances to such holdings between *non-competitors*, unless they involve additional restrictive clauses or agreements, such as non-competition or exclusive dealing obligations which are not strictly necessary in scope or duration.

Minority Shareholdings Strengthening the Restrictive Effect of an Anti-Competitive Agreement.
Irrespective of whether the acquisition of a minority shareholding is, as such, compatible with Community law, the acquisition or existence of such shareholdings may:

- strengthen the anticompetitive effects of an agreement (e.g. through a shareholding in a third company);[1216] therefore, minority shareholdings in third companies (competitors) may have to be included in the overall assessment under Article 81 (3);[1217]
- strengthen the anticompetitive effects of the abuse of a dominant position;[1218]
- preserve or strengthen a dominant position of the parties involved in a concentration (e.g. by assuring preferential treatment);[1219] therefore, a minority

1214. *Philip Morris/Rothmans*, ECJ Nov. 17, 1987, 1987 ECR 4487, para. 37. *See* Section B.3. *supra*.
1215. Joint ventures: *MitchellCotts/Sofiltra*, D.Comm. Dec. 17, 1986, 1987 OJ L 41/3 1; *Olivetti/Canon*, D.Comm. 22 Dec. 1987, 1988 OJ L 52/51; *Elopak/Metal Box*, D.Comm. July 13, 1990, 1990 OJ L 209/15. Unilateral shareholdings: *Philip Morris/Rothmans*, ECJ Nov. 17, 1987, 1987 ECR 4487, para. 37. Cross-shareholdings: *IMI/Heilmann I*, Seventh Report on Competition Policy, points 29–32.
1216. *See British Interactive Broadcasting*, D.Comm. Sept. 15, 1999, 1999 OJ L 312/1, point 176 (exemption granted subject to the establishment of legally separate companies without any structural link through a joint venture).
1217. The acquisition of minority shareholdings is not specifically addressed in the present Commission Guidelines on horizontal cooperation. However, the Commission intends to issue separate guidelines on minority shareholdings, *see* point 10.
1218. *See Deutsche Post I*, D.Comm. March 20, 2001, 2001 OJ L 125/27, IP/01/419, where the German Post created a separate legal entity for business parcel services in order to create a system of transparent and market-based pricing.
1219. Article 2 (3) of Regulation 139/2004. *See BT/Esat*, D.Comm. March 27, 2000, M.1838; *VEBA/VIAG*, D.Comm. June 13, 2000, M.1673.

shareholding of parties to a concentration may have to be included in the overall assessment of a concentration according to Article 2 (3).[1220]

In all of these cases clearance of the agreement or the merger may be made dependent on the divestment or reduction of the minority shareholding in order to prevent any commercial influence and to limit the participation to pure investment protection standards.[1221] Normally the Commission considers a minority shareholding below 10% and without representation in the management[1222] as a mere passive (financial) participation.[1223] Alternatively, the Commission may accept commitments of a minority shareholder not to use its shareholding to influence the market behavior of the operator in which it holds the stake.[1224] However, in some exceptional cases the Commission has not objected to minority shareholdings of 20%.[1225]

Case Examples.

The Commission examined the competitive impact of minority shareholdings under Article 81 in the following cases:

1220. *See Mobil/Exxon*, D.Comm. Sept. 29, 1999, M.1383, points 225–229; *Grupo Villar Mir/EnBW/Hidroeléctrica dal Cantabrico*, D.Comm. Sept. 26, 2001, M.2434, point 69; *Wallenius, Wilhelmsen/Hyundai Merchant Marine*, D.Comm. Nov. 29, 2002, M.2722 (clearance subject to the commitment to withdraw from a shipping conference with their main competitor and not to enter in any similar agreement with any competing carrier).

1221. *Deutsche Post/Trans-o-flex*, D.Comm. May 5, 1999, M.1447 (Article 6 (1) (c) decision concerning Deutsche Post's 24.8% participation in its competitor Trans-o-flex; notification withdrawn accordingly), IP/99/318; *EDF/EnBW*, D.Comm. Feb. 7, 2001, M.1853, p. 27. Similarly the Spanish antitrust authority in *Sogecable/Via Digital*, Nov. 29, 2002, following the Commission's referral decision of Aug. 14, 2002, M.2845; *Hoechst/Rhône Poulenc (Aventis)*, D.Comm. Jan. 30, 2004, M.1378, amending the commitments in its clearance decision of Aug. 9, 1999 by stating: 'It is obvious that there is a potential risk of coordination since Aventis has a share in two firms competing in the same market'.

1222. *See Owens Illinois/BTR Packaging*, D.Comm. April 21, 1998, M.1109; *Akzo Nobel/Courtaulds*, D.Comm. June 30, 1998, M.1182.

1223. *See* Form CO, Section 4. Minority shareholdings below 10% are for investment purposes only: *Anglo American Corp./Lonrho*, D.Comm. April 23, 1997, 1998 OJ L 149/21; *Deutsche Post/DHL*, D.Comm. Feb. 23, 1999, M.1347; *Nordbanken/Postgirot*, D.Comm. Nov. 8, 2001, M.2567.

1224. *Microsoft*, IP/00/569 of April 18, 2000.

1225. *Blokker/Toys 'R' Us*, D.Comm. June 26, 1997, 1998 OJ L 316/1, points 130–133; *British Interactive Broadcasting*, D.Comm. Sept. 15, 1999, 1999 OJ L 312/1, point 167; *Microsoft*, IP/00/569 of April 18, 2000. However, the Court of First Instance held that a participation of 22.498% by Deutsche Post in its competitor in the parcel distribution sector of DHL did not give rise to concerns under Article 82 (and, *a fortiori*, under Article 81 either): *UPS/Deutsche Post*, CFI March 20, 2002, 2002 ECR II-1915, para. 60. The acquisition of full control of DHL by Deutsche Post was unconditionally cleared under the merger control regulation: D.Comm. Oct. 22, 2002, IP/02/1533.

- In the *Mecaniver/PPG* case[1226] the Commission issued a negative clearance for the acquisition of sole control of the Mecaniver flat glass business of the BSN group by the U.S. flat glass producer PPG. The Commission did not consider the BSN-Mecaniver group's retention of minority shareholdings in two competitors in the flat glass industry as conferring the possibility of influencing their behavior because (i) they were effectively controlled by other companies and (ii) the majority shareholders had options to buy out the minority shareholdings from BSN, which was withdrawing completely from the flat glass market.
- In the *AMB/Fondaria* case[1227] the Commission issued a comfort letter for the acquisition by each of two insurance groups of 25% plus one share conferring veto power over Volksfürsorge, a German insurance company with 6.3% of the German life insurance market which nevertheless was guaranteed its continued independence.
- In the *BP/Ruhrgas* case[1228] the Commission authorized a 25% shareholding conferring veto power after the parties gave undertakings to the Commission not to use their representation on the board in such a way as to jeopardize the independence of the companies concerned.
- In the *Enichem/ICI* case[1229] the Commission exempted a restructuring joint venture between competitors on the condition that ICI divested itself of the minority shareholding in a Spanish subsidiary of Solvay, a competitor, and in the meantime did not exercise voting rights.
- In the *Hudson's Bay II* case[1230] the Commission objected under Article 81 to the acquisition of a 35% shareholding by the Danish Fur Breeders' Association in its competitor, Hudson's Bay, because the acquisition was likely to limit competition from Hudson's Bay in collecting furs from members of the Association, thereby strengthening the restrictive effects of the exclusive arrangements between the Association and its members.[1231]
- The *BT/MCI* cases[1232] concerned the creation of a joint venture to develop and market worldwide new international value-added telecommunication services

---

1226. *Mécaniver/PPG*, D.Comm. Dec. 12, 1984, 1985 OJ L 35/54.
1227. *AMB/Fondaria*, 1989 OJ C 210/4 (comfort letter).
1228. *BP/Ruhrgas*, Ninth Report on Competition Policy, points 94–95. In *Renault/Volvo*, D.Comm. Nov. 7, 1990, M.4, also the Commission found that cross-shareholdings of 25% with safeguards for independent conduct did not raise concerns under Article 81.
1229. *Enichem/ICI*, D.Comm. Dec. 22, 1987, 1988 OJ L 50/18.
1230. *Hudson's Bay II*, IP/88/810; 1989 CMLR 353.
1231. *See Hudson's Bay I*, Oct. 28, 1988, 1988 OJ L 316/43; *aff'd* CFI July 2, 1992, 1992 ECR II-1931.
1232. *BT/MCI I*, D.Comm. Sept. 13, 1993, M.353 (Article 6 (1) (a) decision stating that the joint venture was not full-function); an amended operation was declared compatible with the Common Market under the merger control regulation: *BT/MCI II*, D.Comm. July 27, 1994, 1994 OJ L 223/36, point 44 (Article 8 (2) decision). *See also Worldcom/MCI*, D.Comm. July 8, 1998, M.1069, Twenty-eighth Report on Competition Policy, point 164.

in the context of the gradual liberalization and globalization of the telecommunications markets. The parent companies granted the joint venture a license to all of their intellectual property rights, while the joint venture appointed its parents exclusive distributors in their respective territories, i.e., MCI in America and BT in the rest of the world, for the distribution of its services. As a further part of the deal, BT acquired a 20% shareholding in MCI, representation on MCI's board of directors, and BT and MCI each committed not to engage in the core business of the other party in its territory. This reciprocal non-compete clause was tantamount to reciprocal territorial protection in respect to activities outside of the scope of the joint venture's activities. The Commission found that the parent companies were actual competitors in the overall telecommunications market and potential competitors in respect to the international value-added services. By appointing BT as the joint venture's exclusive distributor inside the EEA and by preventing MCI from competing against BT within this territory with respect to activities outside the scope of the joint venture, the arrangement ('strategic alliance') had the effect of isolating the EEA market against a foreign competitor contrary to Article 81. The Commission granted an exemption for the creation of the joint venture after ensuring the possibility of passive sales by MCI inside the EEA with respect to the services provided by the joint venture and after limiting the non-compete obligations of MCI with respect to BT's core business inside the EEA to an initial period of five years. Finally, the parent companies were committed to guarantee access to their networks by third parties on a non-discriminatory basis.[1233] With respect to BT's minority shareholding and representation on the MCI board of directors, the Commission issued a negative clearance stating that it did not lead to anticompetitive coordination because of the limited influence conferred by the 20% shareholding and BT's assurance not to seek access to confidential information.

- The *Olivetti/Digital* case[1234] concerned cooperation in the computer system market involving a five-year technological exclusivity, a minimum purchase requirement and the acquisition by Digital of an 8% shareholding in Olivetti with representation in the board of directors. The Commission granted an exemption with respect to the minimum purchase commitment and issued a negative clearance with respect to the acquisition of the minority shareholding. The Commission found that the board of directors was not involved in decisions on the development of new products or their pricing, which were taken by an independent alliance committee. Therefore, it was unlikely that Digital's representation would lead to coordination of competitive behavior or to an exchange of competitive information.[1235]

1233. *See also BT/France Télécom (Jetphone)*, Twenty-fourth Report on Competition Policy, points 158–159 (access to essential telecommunications networks on a non-discriminatory basis).
1234. *Olivetti/Digital*, D.Comm. Nov. 11, 1994, 1994 OJ L 309/24.
1235. *Ibid.*, points 26–27.

– In the *Deutsche Post/trans-o-flex* case[1236] the Commission objected under the merger control regulation to Deutsche Post increasing its existing minority shareholding of 24.8% in the express service business of trans-o-flex in view of the substantial market shares on markets for national and international parcel services. The parties cancelled the acquisition agreement and withdrew their notification. However, the Commission reserved the possibility of further investigations of the existing minority shareholding, probably, but without saying so, under Article 81.

Paucity of Case Law.

With the paucity of decided cases any general conclusions about the application of Article 81 to shareholding links must be treated with caution. However, some conclusions may be drawn from the treatment of minority shareholdings under Regulation 802/2004 implementing the merger control regulation. Under Section 4 of Form CO the parties to a merger or joint venture must identify personal and financial links with other companies, including minority shareholdings exceeding 10% of the voting rights[1237] or the issued share capital and representations in the board of management and supervisory board of companies active in the affected markets.[1238] Interlocking directorates may give rise to concern because of the access to commercially sensitive information.[1239] The clearance of a transaction may be made subject to the removal of minority shareholdings of 10% or more[1240] and/or of interlocking directorates.[1241] However, minority shareholdings of 10%

1236. *Deutsche Post/trans-o-flex*, D.Comm. May 5, 1999, M.1447, IP/99/378.

1237. Form CO Section 4. Article 3 (5) of Regulation 139/2004 provides that a merger is not deemed to arise when financial institutions and insurance companies acquire companies with a view of reselling them, provided they exercise the voting rights only with the view to preparing the disposal of all or part of that company. It might be concluded that minority shareholdings will not be taken into account if and as long as the voting rights are not exercised. *See Pilkington/BSN*, Tenth Report on Competition Policy, points 152–155.

1238. Form CO, Section 4.

1239. 'Instrument for influencing commercial conduct' within the meaning *of Philip Morris*, ECJ Nov. 17, 1987, 1987 ECR 4487, para. 37.

1240. *Alcatel/Telettra*, D.Comm. April 12, 1991, 1991 OJ L 122/48; *Anglo American Corp./Lonrho*, D.Comm. April 23, 1997, 1998 OJ L 149/21, points 131–137 (reduction of a 27.5% minority shareholding to 9.99%). *See* under German law: *Stadtwerke Garbsen*, Federal Supreme Court (BGH) July 15, 1997, WuWE DE-R 32.

1241. *Owens-Illinois/BTR Packaging*, D.Comm. April 21, 1998, M.1190; *Allianz/AGF*, D.Comm. May 8, 1998, M.1082; *Thyssen/Krupp*, D.Comm. June 2, 1998, M.1080; *Akzo Nobel/Courtaulds*, D.Comm. June 30, 1998, M.1182; *General/INA*, D.Comm. Jan. 12, 2000, M.1712, points 74–76. Under Article 66 of the ECSC Treaty: *Krupp/Südwestfalen*, D.Comm. April 2, 1975, 1975 OJ L 130/13; *Arbed/Neunkirchen/Rodange*, D.Comm. June 6, 1978, 1978 OJ L 164/14.

or less[1242] or that are clearly for investment purposes only are likely not to infringe Article 81.[1243]

Guidance as to the Assessment of Minority Shareholdings.
The following cases may be distinguished:

- A minority shareholding in a *competitor* may be anticompetitive because it may serve as an instrument for restricting or distorting competition in the market in which the competitors carry on business. A distinction can be drawn according to whether the minority shareholding confers the right of, and is effectively linked with, *representation on the board of directors*. In such a case the minority shareholder normally gains access to commercially sensitive information of a competitor (particularly investment and production plans and marketing strategy), which allows the shareholder to take this information into account when adopting its own commercial decisions (risk of anticompetitive coordination).[1244]
- A further distinction must be drawn according to whether the minority shareholding in a *competitor* confers the *right of veto power* over key business decisions. Equity stakes that do *not* confer the right of representation on the board of directors nor give the holder power to veto important corporate decisions will not of themselves infringe Article 81, but may do so if the parties' market shares and the structure of the relevant market together with other agreements between them provides an instrument for influencing the commercial conduct of the companies in question.[1245]
- The acquisition of a shareholding of 10% or less in a *competitor* which is not associated with a representation on the board or veto rights may be considered as a *purely passive* shareholding for investment purposes.[1246]

1242. *Schibstedt/Telenor/Telia*, D.Comm. May 27, 1998, JV. 1; *Anglo American Corp./Lonrho*, D.Comm. April 23, 1997, M.754 (9.99%). *See also* under Article 66 of the ECSC Treaty: *CLIF/Marine*, D.Comm. March 5, 1975, 1975 OJ L 196/27 (in this case the Commission made its exemption of a steel joint venture conditional on the reduction of an existing shareholding held by one parent in the other to 10%).
1243. *Deutsche Post/DHL*, D.Comm. Feb. 23, 1999, M.1347.
1244. This is contrary to the 'requirement of economic independence' recognized by the Court of Justice in *Sugar*, ECJ Dec. 16, 1975, 1975 ECR 1663, para. 174, and by the Court of First Instance in *John Deere – UK Agricultural Tractor Registration Exchange*, CFI Oct. 27, 1994, 1994 ECR II-957, paras 50–52.
1245. *Philip Morris/Rothmans*, ECJ Nov. 17, 1987, 1987 ECR 4487, 4577, paras 38–40. *See* under the merger control regulation: *Arvin/Sogefi*, D.Comm. Sept. 23, 1993, M.360; *Bertelsmann/Kirch/Première*, D.Comm. May 27, 1998, 1999 OJ L 53/1, point 138.
1246. In *BP-Ruhrgas* (Ninth Report on Competition Policy, points 94–95) the Commission authorized a 25% shareholding conferring veto power after the parties gave the undertaking not to use their representation on the board in such a way as to jeopardize the independence of the companies concerned. *See also Blokker Toys 'R' Us*, D.Comm. June 26, 1997, 1998 OJ L 316/1, points 132–133.

- The acquisition of a minority shareholding in a *non-competitor* does not in itself infringe Article 81 but may result in an infringement under exceptional circumstances, in particular when a dominant company has a minority shareholding in companies acting on the upstream or downstream market, and the shareholding may serve as an instrument for exclusive or preferential treatment, thereby impeding competitors and strengthening its dominant position.[1247]

2. Non Full-Function Joint Ventures

(a) General Criteria

Applicability of Article 81.
Full-function joint ventures that do not have a Community dimension and joint ventures that do not perform on a lasting basis all the functions of an autonomous economic entity[1248] are not covered by Regulation 139/2004. Instead, they are subject to an assessment under Article 81 by the Commission, the national competition authorties or the national courts. With respect to full-function joint ventures the general criteria as described in section D.2.(g) above apply. With respect to 'non full-function joint ventures' the general criteria of horizontal[1249] or vertical cooperation[1250] apply dependent on whether the parent companies of the joint venture are actual or potential competitors on the same or related markets or undertakings each of which operates at a different level of the production or distribution chain.[1251] Joint venture agreements are normally not covered by Article 81 (1):

- if they do not have as their object or effect an appreciable restriction of competition, which occurs where the parties' market shares do not exceed 10% in the case of horizontal agreements and 15% in the case of vertical agreements,[1252] or
- if they do not appreciably affect trade between member states, which occurs where the parties' market shares are less than 5% and their turnover does not exceed EUR 40 million.[1253]

The Commission's Notice Concerning the Assessment of Cooperative Joint Ventures[1254] lists the following cases as not being subject to Article 81:

1247. *See* Twenty-eighth Report on Competition Policy, points 155–157.
1248. Article 3 (4) of Regulation 139/2004.
1249. Chapter III and Guidelines on horizontal cooperation, 2001 OJ C 3/2.
1250. Chapter IV and Guidelines on vertical restrictions, 2000 OJ C 291/3.
1251. Article 2 of Regulation 2790/1999.
1252. *De Minimis Notice*, 2001 OJ C 368/13, point 7.
1253. Notice on the effect on trade concept, 2004 C 101/81, point 52.
1254. 1993 OJ C 43/2, points 14–15.

- joint ventures created by companies belonging to the same group;[1255]
- joint ventures that have as their sole object the procurement of non-confidential information,[1256] activities which are not concerned with the supply of goods or services or economic decisions,[1257] or that merely deal with exchange of experience,[1258] technical arrangements,[1259] setting up consortia between companies which do not compete or are unable to execute orders alone[1260] or cooperation in fields removed from the parties' market activities;[1261] and
- joint ventures whose direct and immediate effects on competition are limited to the territory of one member state or EEA country or to territories outside the Community and EEA, provided there are no appreciable repercussions on the trade between member states or with or among EEA countries.[1262]

The Guidelines on the Application of Article 81 (3)[1263] highlight the criteria which must be considered when assessing the four criteria of this provision, in particular with respect to the different categories of efficiencies and the gain for the consumer. The following discussion is limited to several categories of joint ventures in the light of the Commission's administrative practice.

Partial-Function Joint Ventures between Competitors – The 'Group Effect'. The formation and operation of a partial-function joint venture may infringe Article 81 (1) if it gives rise to anticompetitive coordination between the parent companies or between one of them and the joint venture. Even in the framework of a 'joint' enterprise each party may play its own particular role according to its own commercial interests, and any mechanism agreed between them which prevents internal conflicts and rivalries may therefore constitute an infringement of Article 81 (1).[1264] The risk of such anticompetitve coordination is the greatest when the parent companies are actual or potential competitors. Anticompetitive coordination may result from express provisions in the joint venture agreement or related agreements, but it may also be inherent to the establishing of the joint venture by competitors. This is because of the natural tendency of partners in a joint venture to align or to coordinate their conduct in fields related to the joint venture. This indirect coordination of competing parent companies has traditionally been

1255. Commission Notice on the Concept of Concentration, point 8.
1256. *See CEPI Cartonboard II*, Twenty-sixth Report on Competition Policy, pp. 127–130.
1257. *See Belgian Pharmaceutical Association*, D.Comm. Dec. 14, 1989, 1990 OJ L 18/35.
1258. *See EUCAR*, Twenty-seventh Report on Competition Policy, p. 138.
1259. *See Iridium*, D.Comm. Dec. 18, 1996, 1997 OJ L 16/87.
1260. *See Konsortium 900*, D.Comm. July 27, 1990, 1990 OJ L 228/31; *International Private Satellite Partners*, D.Comm. Dec. 15, 1994, 1994 OJ L 354/75.
1261. *See Eurogypsum*, D.Comm. Feb. 26, 1968, 1968 OJ L 57/9.
1262. *See* Chapter I.E.4.(b) and (c).
1263. 2004 OJ C 101/97.
1264. *Nintendo*, D.Comm. Oct. 30, 2002, 2003 OJ L 255/33, point 260.

called the 'group effect' under the ECSC merger control rules, as first recognized in the *Sidmar* case involving a joint production venture between Belgian, French and Luxembourg steel makers:

> '... where the controlling enterprises produce the same or much the same products as the enterprise controlled, competition among all the participant enterprises in respect of the products in question is bound to be affected by the group control, since in the exercise of joint control, i.e. in fixing the prices of the enterprise controlled, the controlling enterprises will inevitably take into account their own prices for the same or similar products, and very possibly agree on all prices ("group effect").'[1265]

Because the Commission considers the 'group effect' an inherent consequence of joint control over a joint venture, it is not assessed as a separate restriction of competition but rather as part of the overall evaluation of the transaction.[1266] The consequence of the 'group effect' or 'spill-over effect'[1267] is that the establishment of the joint venture itself is caught by Article 81 (1) and therefore requires exemption under Article 81 (3) even though no express restrictive clauses are found in the relevant agreements. For example, the establishment of a joint sales organization between competitors does not need an express non-compete clause because any competitive act of the parent companies competing against the joint venture would be counterproductive and frustrate the joint efforts of creating an effective sales organization. However, express non-compete clauses may reinforce the inherent anticompetitive 'group effect' and may be challenged.[1268] On the other hand, the anticompetitive 'group effect' may be reduced by express provisions prohibiting the parent companies from exchanging commercially sensitive information concerning prices, markets and customers; the Commission may therefore subject an exemption of a partial-function joint venture between actual or potential competitors to a commitment or condition to establish a 'Chinese wall' between the parent companies.[1269]

1265. *Sidmar*, High Authority, April 25, 1962, Eleventh ECSC General Report, points 346–349. The 'group effect' may be assimilated to the larger 'spill over effect'. *See* Article 7 of Decision 25/67 (1967 OJ No 154/11).
1266. Wagenführ Report (Report on the Activities and Future Policy of the European Coal and Steel Industry 1952–1962), point 29.
1267. Twenty-eighth Report on Competition Policy, point 180 (insert 7).
1268. Under ECSC law: *Röchling/Possehl*, D.Comm. Feb. 5, 1986, 1986 OJ L 39/57; under EC law: *Danish Furs*, CFI May 8, 1992, 1992 ECR II-1713.
1269. *Optical Fibers*, D.Comm. July 14, 1986, 1986 OJ L 236/30, 37; *Exxon/Shell I*, D.Comm. May 18, 1994, 1994 OJ L 144/20.

Partial-Function Joint Ventures between non-Competitors – No 'Group Effect'.
When the parties to a partial-function joint venture have complementary skills or are in a vertical supplier-purchaser relationship, competition may be restricted to the same extent as in the context of other agreements between non-competing companies.[1270] No 'group effect' can be assumed if the parties to a joint venture are not competitors and the joint venture does not involve the creation of a network of competing joint ventures.[1271] However, competition may be restricted by exclusive supply or purchasing agreements which affect the access of third companies to inputs or to distribution outlets. Similarly, in conglomerate (often termed 'complementary') joint ventures where the parents operate neither on the same nor on vertically related markets as the joint venture, the most common restrictions of competition do not arise from the joint venture itself ('group effect') but from express non-compete clauses preventing the parent companies from engaging in active competition on the market of the joint venture. Such coordination between one parent company and the joint venture is not privileged by the intra-enterprise conspiracy doctrine[1272] as shown in the Commission's practice to examine the anticompetitive effects of supply arrangements between a parent company and a merger-type joint venture if they are exclusive, long-term and not limited to an initial start-up period.[1273]

Application of Block Exemptions or Individual Evaluation.
Certain partial-function joint ventures may be covered by block exemption regulations: Regulation 2659/2000 on R&D Agreements, Regulation 2658/2000 on Specialization Agreements, Regulation 772/2004 on Technology Transfer Agreements, or, in the case of a vertical joint venture agreement, Regulation 2790/1999. If partial-function joint ventures are not covered by one of these block exemption regulations, in particular because the parties' market shares exceed the thresholds of these regulations, they must be assessed on a case-by-case basis. The Commission's administrative practice and the case law of the Court prior to the amendment of the merger regulation is still relevant. This also applies to 'ancillary restrictions' attached to the joint venture. They must be evaluated according to the Commission's practice and the Court's case law and in conformity with the new approach under Regulation 139/2004. The block exemptions and case law generally favor the creation of a new product or service and a new operator likely

1270. *See* Chapter IV.A.2.

1271. In *Shell Chemie/Elf Atochem* (D.Comm. Dec. 22, 1994, M.475) the Commission considered a joint industrial processing company 'full-function' and unlikely to lead to any anticompetitive coordination. *See also Optical Fibers*, D.Comm. July 14, 1986, 1986 OJ L 236/30 (joint ventures between non-competitors but in the context of a network).

1272. *See* Chapter I.D.3.

1273. Notice on Full-Function Joint Ventures, point 14.

to compete against existing operators. The Commission has also granted clearance for a limited start-up period (e.g. for 3–5 years[1274]) for temporary exclusive sales and purchasing relationships between parent firms and the joint venture and other forms of start-up management, marketing and distribution assistance, provided that after the start-up period the joint venture assumes all of the tasks of a full-function joint venture. Furthermore, restrictions contained in such agreements may be considered as 'ancillary' if they are 'strictly necessary for the formation and the proper operation of the joint venture', including non-compete clauses and exclusive supply and purchase obligations. Even restrictions that are not 'strictly necessary' may still be covered by a block exemption regulation or qualify for an individual clearance under Article 81 (3).

(b) R&D Joint Ventures[1275]

Pure R&D Joint Ventures Usually Covered by Regulation 2659/2000.
Joint ventures devoted to R&D up to the stage of industrial application are, if they are restrictive of competition at all, to be evaluated under Regulation 2659/2000, in particular with respect to the free use of the results of the joint R&D by the parent firms and the limited recognition of non-compete clauses. Continued access upon termination or dissolution of the joint venture (in consideration for 'reasonable' royalties) to the jointly developed technology is deemed necessary in order to enable the parents to continue the business independently.[1276] Non-compete clauses on the parent companies (obligations not to research individually in fields which are connected with that of the joint R&D) are covered by the block exemption.[1277]

R&D Joint Ventures Block Exempted up to 25% Market Share.
R&D agreements extending beyond the stage of industrial application and involving joint or coordinated production, including exclusive purchasing arrangements (but not joint marketing), are exempted under Regulation 2659/2000, provided the parties' market shares do not exceed 25%. If the parties' market shares exceed 25% the conditions of Article 81 (3) may be satisfied, provided the products jointly developed and jointly manufactured are marketed by the parent companies separately and in competition with each other, in particular where the parents use different trade marks.[1278]

1274. Three years: *TPS (Television Par Satellite)*, D.Comm. March 3, 1999, 1999 OJ L 90/6; five years: 2004 Draft Notice on Ancillary Restrictions, point 33.

1275. *See* in greater detail Chapter III.B.2. and C.3.

1276. *De Laval Stork I*, D.Comm. July 25, 1977, 1977 OJ L 11, 18–19; *ICI/Montedison*, Seventh Report on Competition Policy, points 156–159: *Rockwell/Iveco*, D.Comm. July 13, 1983, 1983 OJ L 224/19, 28; *Philips/Osram*, D.Comm. Dec. 23, 1994, 1994 OJ L 378/37.

1277. Only non-compete clauses with respect to individual research in unconnected fields are blacklisted: Article 5 (1) (a) of Regulation 2659/2000.

1278. *Continental/Michelin*, D.Comm. Oct. 11, 1988, 1988 OJ L 395/33; *Volkswagen/Ford*, D.Comm. 23 Dec. 1992, 1993 OJ L 20/15, point 34.

R&D Joint Ventures including Joint Marketing to be Assessed under the Merger Control Regulation.
R&D joint ventures which extend to joint production and joint marketing are tantamount to a full-function joint venture and are subject to notification and clearance under Regulation 139/2004, provided they have a Community dimension, even if the market shares do *not* exceed 10%. In the absence of a Community dimension the joint venture agreement needs individual assessment under Article 81.

(c) Production Joint Ventures

Specialization Joint Ventures Exempted under Regulation 2658/2000 up to 20%.
Regulation 2658/2000 exempts joint ventures aiming at specializing production between the parties, including exclusive purchase arrangements but excluding joint marketing, up to 20%. The regulation extends to joint ventures by way of unilateral specialization or subcontracting.[1279]

Specialization Joint Ventures Including Joint Marketing to be Assessed under the Merger Control Regulation.
Specialization joint ventures that assume all the functions of an autonomous economic entity constitute a merger and are, if they have a Community dimension, subject to the merger control regulation, even if their market share is below the *de minimis* threshold (10%) or that of the specialization block exemption Regulation 2658/2000 (20%). In the absence of a Community dimension the joint venture must satisfy the conditions of Regulation 2658/2000 or, in the case of market shares exceeding 20%, the conditions of Article 81 (3). In the case of higher market shares of 40% or more, in particular on oligopolistic markets, high efficiency gains cannot be expected.[1280] However, efficiencies may be expected where a joint venture is set up to contribute to rationalization and reduction of capacity

1279. However, the Commission's Guidelines on Horizontal Cooperation (points 80, 81 and 100) are quite confusing: Subcontracting agreements, which were traditionally assessed under the Notice on Subcontracting Agreements (which provided for no market share limit (1979 OJ C 1/2)), (i) may not infringe Article 81 (1) at all where the parties' market shares do not exceed the limits of the *De Minimis* Notice, which are 10–15% (2001 OJ C 368/13), (ii) may infringe Article 81 (1) but satisfy the technology transfer block exemption regulation if the transfer of technology is involved (market share limit of 20 or 30%), (iii) may be covered by Regulation 2790/1999 if they are of a vertical nature (market share limit of 30%), or (iv) by Regulation 2658/2000 if they constitute a unilateral specialization (market share limit of 20%), (v) Regulation 2659/2000 if they are part of joint R&D (market share limit of 25%), or (vi) may need individual assessment if they contribute to a foreclosure of the market.

1280. Guidelines on Horizontal Cooperation, points 106–107.

(restructuring joint ventures), possibly associated with investment to modernize the remaining facilities.[1281]

Additional Capacity Joint Ventures to be Assessed Individually.
If two competitors decide to establish a joint venture which is to produce additional increments of certain products for supply to each of the parents at cost for sale alongside similar products of their own manufacture, such a joint venture may require individual clearance under Article 81. In the *Solmer II* case, decided under Article 65 of the ECSC Treaty and concerning a joint production venture between the two leading steel groups in France and Germany, the Commission held:

> 'Because Solmer will be controlled in common ... and because the joint investment in Solmer is considerable, each group will be guided in its own investment decisions regarding those sectors of production ... by the investment decisions made jointly with its partners in Solmer. In planning its production each group will naturally bear in mind its share in Solmer's output and regulate its own production accordingly. Joint control of Solmer will thus lead to a restriction of competition between the groups when it comes to making decisions concerning investment and production in the flat products sector.'[1282]

The Commission applied the same principles under Article 81 in the *Exxon/Shell I* case, which concerned a joint production venture between two leading oil companies to produce polyethylene to be supplied to each of the parents at cost for sale alongside similar products of their own manufacture. The Commission granted an exemption under Article 81 (3) on grounds which are similar to specialization agreements in which the parties renounce, for reasons of cost savings and production rationalization, any increase in their own capacity in favor of joint additional production. However, the Commission made the exemption subject to the parties' commitments (i) to provide the possibility for both parent companies to purchase the output of the joint venture according to their individual requirements and the joint venture's availability and to increase their own capacity individually at their own cost, and (ii) to renounce any exchange of information on outlets, markets and prices ('Chinese wall').[1283]

1281. *BASF/Shell*, D.Comm. Dec. 23, 1997, M.1041 (clearance subject to commitments in order to reduce the risk of coordination on the upstream market).
1282. *Solmer II*, D.Comm. Nov. 20, 1974, 1974 OJ L 49/13, 17–18. It is noteworthy that the Commission reasoning anticipates the Court of Justice's 'economic independence' concept as established in *Sugar*, ECJ Dec. 16, 1975, 1975 ECR 1663, paras 173–174.
1283. *Exxon/Shell I*, D.Comm. May 18, 1994, 1994 OJ L 144/20. In *Exxon/Shell II* (D.Comm. July 8, 1998, M.1137) the Commission qualified the joint venture as 'full-function' although the parent companies acted as distributors for the joint venture. Similarly under the merger control

(d) Distribution Joint Ventures

Joint Distribution Among Competitors Ordinarily not Exemptible.
Joint ventures set up solely for distribution are traditionally partial-function joint ventures and must be assessed under Article 81. If the parent firms are competitors the joint venture leads to a clear opportunity for exchanges of sensitive commercial information, particularly on marketing strategy,[1284] and to joint pricing. Even in the absence of a formal obligation, it also leads the parent firms to distribute exclusively through the joint venture,[1285] thereby reducing the number of independent suppliers on the relevant market. In the majority of cases the Commission has considered such arrangements ineligible for exemption because of the substantial harm to competition arising from the coordination of competitors' prices and other terms of sale even if the market shares do not amount to dominance.[1286] This cost savings argument does not justify joint distribution in cases where the individual size of the parent companies enables them to compete effectively individually against other competitors and where the claimed efficiencies consist of savings which result only from elimination of costs that are inherently part of competition.[1287]

Cooperatives with Exclusive Sales Obligations of its Members.
In the *Danish Furs* case[1288] the Court of First Instance ruled that the obligation imposed on the members of the Danish Furs Cooperative not to compete with the cooperative's activities is tantamount to an exclusive supply obligation prohibiting the members from collecting skins for auction sales other than those held by the cooperative (which required no special expertise). The Court of First Instance concluded in the light of the actual economic context that the non-compete obligation significantly curtailed members' freedom of action on the market contrary to Article 81 (l).[1289]

---

regulation: *Anglo American Corp/Lonrho*, D.Comm. April 23, 1997, 1998 OJ L 149/21, point 130; *BT/AT&T*, D.Comm. March 30, 1999, JV. 15.

1284. Commission Guidelines on Horizontal Cooperation, point 146.

1285. Even if the arrangements do not include an express obligation to sell exclusively through the joint venture, the parents will tend not to compete with the joint venture and, if they do, will align their prices with those of the joint venture, as in the *Floral* case, a joint venture set up by the three biggest French fertilizer producers for joint distribution in Germany: *Floral*, D.Comm. Nov. 28, 1979, 1980 OJ L 39/51.

1286. Commission Guidelines on Horizontal Cooperation, point 151. Examples: *ANSAC*, D.Comm. Dec. 19, 1990, 1991 OJ L 152/54, points 23–30 (cease and desist order); *FIFA*, D.Comm. Oct. 27, 1992, 1992 OJ L 326/31, point 96 (cease and desist order); *ASTRA*, D.Comm. Dec. 23, 1992, 1993 OJ L 20/23, points 19–31 (cease and desist order).

1287. Commission Guidelines on Horizontal Cooperation, point 152. *ANSAC*, D.Comm. Dec. 19, 1990, 1991 OJ L 152/54, points 19 and 24. *See* Notice on the assessment of cooperative joint ventures, point 60.

1288. *Danish Furs*, CFI May 8, 1992, 1992 ECR II-1713.

1289. *Ibid.*, paras 98–110.

Joint Distribution in New Geographical Markets.

Joint sales organizations set up by competitors within the Community for exporting their products or providing services to clients in a new geographic market infringes Article 81 (1) only if there are appreciable repercussions on the competitive structure within the Community.[1290] It is rarely the case that a joint sales organization solely regulating sales totally outside the EU and the EEA infringes Article 81 (1).

- In *Telenor/Canal+/Canal Digital*[1291] the Commission cleared an agreement relating to the joint conduct of pay-TV operations in the Nordic region via a jointly owned satellite platform.
- In *Banksys/Interpay*[1292] the Commission cleared an agreement relating to the creation of a joint venture for international credit and credit cards processing services outside the home markets of the parties (Italy, Belgium and the Netherlands).
- In *VVVF*[1293] the Commission issued a negative clearance for the creation of an association between Dutch paint producers with respect to third countries.
- However, in the *CSV* case a distribution joint venture between two Dutch fertilizer producers which coordinated sales in the Netherlands and in non-EC countries but did not formally govern exports to other member states was nevertheless found to infringe Article 81 (1) because of inevitable spill-over effects on competition in other member states.[1294]

Joint Distribution into the EU by Non-EC Competitors.

Joint sales organizations set up by competitors in non-EC countries for marketing their products in the Community may restrict competition in the Common Market and infringe Article 81 (1). For example, the Commission has challenged such organizations exporting wood pulp from North America and Scandinavia[1295] and soda ash from the U.S.[1296]

1290. *See* Guidelines on Horizontal Cooperation, point 147.
1291. *Telenor/Canal+/Canal Digital*, D.Comm. June 26, 2003, 2003 OJ C 149/16.
1292. *Banksys/Interpay*, D.Comm. Dec. 12, 2003, 2003 OJ C 311/33.
1293. *VVVF*, D.Comm. June 25, 1969, 1969 OJ L 168/22. *See also DECA*, D.Comm. Oct. 22, 1964, 1964 OJ L 276/1; *Machine Tools*, D.Comm. July 17, 1968, 1968 OJ L 201/1.
1294. *CSV*, D.Comm. July 20, 1978, 1978 OJ L 242/15, overruling the former '*Cobelaz* doctrine', which accepted national distribution joint ventures whose activities were limited to a single member state, because it was considered as not affecting trade between member states: *Cobelaz/Febelaz*, D.Comm. Nov. 6, 1968, 1968 OJ L 276/13.
1295. *Wood Pulp I*, ECJ Sept. 27, 1988, 1988 ECR 5193, paras 12–13. The authorization of such cartels in the country of origin (e.g., by the Webb-Pomerene Act) does not prevent the application of Article 81: *ibid*, at para. 20; *see ANSAC*, D.Comm. Dec. 19, 1990, 1991 OJ L 152/54, point 2.
1296. *ANSAC*, D.Comm. Dec. 19, 1990, 1991 OJ L 152/54.

Joint Selling Arrangements between Non-Competitors or Minor Competitors.
Joint selling arrangements between non-competitors do not restrict competition.[1297] A joint sales organization set up by small or medium-sized firms that are minor competitors in the home market in order to enter a new geographic market also may not restrict competition sufficiently to bring the arrangement within Article 81 (1).[1298] However, where a joint venture is set up by important competitors to enter a new geographic market, the collaborative arrangement must be the only reasonably feasible way to achieve increased competition on that market. If the parties fail to demonstrate such need the sales joint venture might infringe Article 81 (1).[1299] In that case, whether an exemption can be granted will mainly depend on the structure of the market and the position on it occupied by the participants.[1300]

(e) Purchasing Joint Ventures

Possibly Restrictive but Likely to Fulfill the Conditions of Article 81 (3).
Joint ventures set up solely for joint purchasing are normally partial-function joint ventures and must be assessed under Article 81. Joint ventures between actual or potential competitors for purchasing may restrict competition, because they reduce the number of independent purchasers and lead to common purchase prices for products which may account for a significant proportion of demand, thereby creating buying power. Whilst the creation of buying power can lead to lower purchasing costs and to lower prices for consumers,[1301] it is not always pro-competitive and may even, under certain circumstances, cause severe negative effects on competition.[1302] These effects may be moderated but will still be apparent if the parent firms are not committed to make purchases exclusively through the joint

1297. Commission's Guidelines on Horizontal Cooperation, point 143. *See* Guidelines on the Application of Article 81 (3), point 18.

1298. *See Deutscher Fussballbund*, 1999 OJ C 6/10 and 2003 OJ C 261/13 (comfort letter for central marketing of the television and radio broadcasting rights with an exception, however, for the international games).

1299. *Floral*, D.Comm. Nov. 28, 1979, 1980 OJ L 39/51; *ANSAC*, D.Comm. Dec. 19, 1990, 1991 OJ L 152/54, point 21. In *Kali + Salz/MdK* (D.Comm. Dec. 14, 1993, 1994 OJ L 186/30) the Commission made the authorization of the merger subject to the condition that Kali + Salz terminate its joint venture held together with its major competitor SCPA for jointly selling potash products from Canada, but the Court of Justice annulled the decision, *inter alia*, on procedural grounds (because SCPA was not duly heard) (ECJ March 31, 1998, 1998 ECR I-1375) and the Commission later cleared the merger without that condition (D.Comm. July 9, 1998, M.308).

1300. *See Ruhr Coal Sales Agency III*, ECJ July 15, 1964, 1964 ECR 533, paras 547–550 (grant of authorization to two local coal selling syndicates exposed to competition from coal importers and suppliers of alternative fuels upheld).

1301. *See Covisint*, D.Comm. July 31, 2001, IP/01/1155 (creation by five major vehicle manufacturers of a B2B internet market place).

1302. Commission Guidelines on Horizontal Cooperation, point 127.

venture or are committed only to purchasing certain minimum quantities or a certain minimum percentage through it.[1303] Therefore, the possibility of meeting the conditions for exemption under Article 81 (3) will depend upon the extent of the restrictions and the market position of the parties and their competitors, the limit being that of creating undue buyer power.[1304] The Commission has challenged exclusive[1305] or minimum[1306] purchase obligations in joint purchasing arrangements between competitors holding a large combined market share and exclusive obligations imposed on a seller which prevented the seller from dealing with third parties.[1307]

Cooperatives with Exclusive Purchase Obligations of its Members.
In the *Rennet* case[1308] the Court of Justice held that the rules of a cooperative which requires its members (accounting for more than 90% of Netherlands cheese output) to purchase all their requirements of rennet and coloring agents for cheese from the cooperative, preventing the members from obtaining supplies from other suppliers, infringed Article 81 (1) and did not fulfill the conditions of Article 81 (3) in view of the exclusive nature of the obligation, which was reinforced by an obligation to pay a not inconsiderable penalty payment in the event of a withdrawal or expulsion.[1309]

The *Eurovision (EBU)* Case.
This case[1310] concerned the Eurovision system operated by the European Broadcasting Union (EBU), an association of public sector European broadcasters entrusted by its members with exchanging television programmes, especially sports programmes, and the joint purchasing of the relevant broadcasting rights. The Commission held that the joint purchasing of broadcasting rights for inter-

---

1303. *National Sulphuric Acid Association I*, D.Comm. July 9, 1980, 1980 OJ L 260/24, 29, 31 (25% purchase requirement exempted). Exemption extended: *National Sulphuric Acid Association II*, D.Comm. June 9, 1989, 1989 OJ L 190/22.

1304. *See* case example in the Commission Notice on horizontal cooperation, point 135.

1305. *Rennet*, ECJ March 25, 1981, 1981 ECR 851, paras 17–18; *National Sulphuric Acid Association I*, D.Comm. July 9, 1980, 1980 OJ L 260/24, 25. Similarly under Article 65 of the ECSC Treaty: *Steelmaking Supplies*, D.Comm. Sept. 21, 1984, 1984 OJ L 268/35; *NICIA*, D.Comm. March 21, 1986, 1986 OJ L 115/19.

1306. *Olivetti/Digital*, D.Comm. Nov. 11, 1994, 1994 OJ L 309/24, point 21 and Twenty-fourth Report on Competition Policy, point 162.

1307. *ARD/MGM*, D.Comm. Sept. 15, 1989, 1989 OJ L 284/36 (joint purchasing of film rights by German broadcasters, where the Commission made the exemption subject to the possibility of the seller granting licences for films during certain periods to firms other than the members of the joint purchasing organization).

1308. *Rennet*, ECJ March 25, 1981, 1981 ECR 831.

1309. *Ibid.*, paras 12 and 18.

1310. *Eurovision*, D.Comm. July 11, 1993, 1993 OJ L 179/23; Twenty-third Report on Competition Policy, point 220.

national sporting events restricted competition because of the combined purchasing power enjoyed by EBU members in joint negotiations. However, the system allowed cost savings and a wider range of programmes which especially benefited the members from smaller countries. The Commission granted an exemption subject to the improvement of the rights of non-members, including commercial broadcasters, to obtain access to the sports programmes, in particular to live transmissions of sporting events which the EBU members do not themselves broadcast live. The Court of First Instance annulled the decision, holding that even the amended version did not fulfil the indispensability requirement of Article 81 (3). The Court found that the criteria for admitting commercial channels were too vague and imprecise and could not form the basis for uniform, non-discriminatory application and that the Commission was not in a position to assess during the exemption period whether the membership conditions were applied 'in an appropriate, reasonable and non-discriminatory way'.[1311]

Joint Purchasing between Minor Competitors.

On the other hand, Article 81 (1) is inapplicable in *de minimis* cases where the common purchasing agreement covers only a very small part of the market, as in the *Intergroup* case, in which the 'Spar' food chains operating in several member states established Intergroup as a joint buying organization which accounted for only a minor percentage of the products affected.[1312]

(f) Advertising and Promotion Joint Ventures

Usually Unobjectionable.

Joint ventures that are limited merely to advertising and sales promotion normally do not infringe Article 81 (1).[1313] However, trade fairs are a common form of joint promotion which can fall foul of Article 81 (1) because of exclusivity obligations on the participants: exhibitors often have to agree not to participate in rival trade fairs for a certain period before and after the event in question. Such a restriction on participating in competing trade fairs infringes Article 81(1), but can qualify for exemption provided the restriction is kept to reasonable limits, i.e., a period that does not prevent participation in other major trade fairs.[1314]

1311. *Eurovision*, CFI July 11, 1996, 1996 ECR II-649, paras 93–95. The second *Euovision II* decision of May 10, 2000, 2000 OJ L 151/18, was also annulled: *MG, Antena 3, Gestévision, SIC/UER*, CFI Oct. 8, 2002, 2002 ECR II-3805.

1312. *Intergroup*, D.Comm. July 14, 1975, 1975 OJ L 212/23 (accounting for up to 5.9% for pineapples and 2.4% of other fruits imported into the member state of destination and for only 0.02%–3.82% of total grocery sales in EC member countries). *See also SOCEMAS*, D.Comm. July 17, 1968, 1968 OJ L 201/4.

1313. Commission Notice on Cooperation Agreements, under II.7; *Eurogypsum*, D.Comm. Feb. 28, 1968, 1968 OJ L 57/9.

1314. The Commission's longstanding practice was affirmed by the Court of Justice in *ANCIDES*, ECJ July 9, 1987, 1987 ECR 3131. *See also CEMATEX II*, D.Comm. May 24, 1983, 1983

Exceptionally Full-Function but Likely to be Cleared.
If competitors create a joint venture in order to promote products or services via an internet platform the joint venture may act to the greatest possible extent in an autonomous way, thereby coming within the merger control regulation. Such a joint venture may lead to cost savings, greater efficiencies and, possibly, lower prices. A clearance may be expected where the parents have non-discriminatory access to the platform, are not prevented from establishing competing platforms and the joint use of the platform does not affect the competitive position of third parties.[1315]

(g) Network Joint Ventures

Various Types of Joint Venture Networks.
A single company may engage in establishing in the same sector various joint ventures with a different competitor in each country, the effect of which is a restriction of competition not only between the parties to each joint venture but also between the various joint ventures.[1316] Likewise, multiple competitors may establish multiple joint ventures with different competing firms in each country, the effect of which is a restriction of competition between the parties and, if they are major market players, a foreclosure of the market.[1317] The Commission stated in its Notice Concerning the Assessment of Cooperative Joint Ventures:

> 'Joint venture networks can particularly restrict competition because they increase the influence of the individual joint venture on the business policy of the parents and on the market position of third parties. The assessment under competition law must take into account the different ways of arranging joint venture networks just as much as the cumulative effects of parallel networks.'[1318]

OJ L 140/27; *UNIDI II*, D.Comm. Nov. 23, 1984, 1984 OJ L 322/10; *International Dental Exhibition*, D.Comm. Sept. 18, 1987, 1987 OJ L 293/58; *British Dental Trade Association*, D.Comm. July 11, 1988, 1988 OJ L 233/15. In the case relating to the *Joint Selling of Media Rights to the German Bundesliga* the Commission granted clearance to the (amended) statutes of the League Association which included also the joint performance of socio-political responsibilities, in particular promoting youth and amateur sports activities: D.Comm. Oct. 30, 2003, 2003 OJ C 261/13; *Football Association Premier League*, D.Comm. April 30, 2004, 2004 OJ C 115/3.

1315. E.g. *Newhouse/Jupiter/Scudder/M&G – Cofunds*, D.Comm. Sept. 1, 2000, M.2075, point 20.

1316. *See Optical Fibers*, D.Comm. July 14, 1986, 1986 OJ 1236/30.

1317. *Industrial Gases*, Nineteenth Report on Competition Policy, point 62; joint construction of infrastructure for telecommunications services: *BIB (British Interactive Broadcasting)*, 1998 OJ C 322/6; *BT/ESB/AIG*, D.Comm. May 19, 1998, M.1132.

1318. 1998 OJ C 66/1, point 27.

Likely to be Challenged.

Joint venture networks are critically viewed irrespective of whether the arrangements come within Article 81 or the merger control regulation. In both cases the cumulative effects of the networks must be assessed in their overall context.[1319] They require particular attention and justify exemption only if the anticompetitive risk (exchange of commercially sensitive information) is reduced[1320] and the rights of third parties to access the market are reasonably preserved.[1321] An example is the *Optical Fibers* case.[1322] This case concerned the creation of a joint venture network in the telecommunications cable sector which was initially cleared under Article 81 but would today have to be assessed under Regulation 139/2004. Corning Glass Works, the U.S. parent firm, held numerous patents for the manufacture of optical fibres, one of whose uses is in high-performance telecommunications cables which are likely to replace conventional copper wire or coaxial cables. Corning was the largest manufacturer of optical fibres in the world, but did not manufacture any cable. Accordingly, Corning decided to licence its optical fibre technology to the major suppliers of telecommunications cables in the Community. Corning granted exclusive licences or distribution rights (except with respect to Corning itself) to Pirelli of Italy, CGE of France and to joint venture companies established between itself and BICC of the United Kingdom, COFO of France and Siemens of Germany. Corning also granted a non-exclusive license to Philips of the Netherlands. The UK joint venture was limited to manufacturing and selling optical fibres; the German joint venture, however, could also sell finished optical cables.[1323] The joint ventures supplied optical fibre to BICC and to Siemens for cabling, but could also supply other cable manufacturers. The parent firms were not subject to any non-compete restrictions or special purchasing obligations. However, the Commission insisted on a number of amendments to the original agreements before authorizing the arrangements under Article 81 (3). The principal amendments were as follows:[1324]

- The European partners were given an option to take a licence to continue to utilize Corning's optical fibre technology after termination of the joint ventures in return for a reasonable royalty.
- The patent licences were made non-exclusive, and no joint venture was granted an exclusive sales territory.

1319. *Telia/Sonera/Lietuvos Telecomas* and *Telia/Sonera/UAB Omnitel*, D.Comm. Aug. 14 and 18, 1998, JV. 7 and JV. 9.

1320. *E*.g. by a 'Chinese wall' preventing a flow of commercially sensitive information: *Optical Fibers*, D.Comm. July 14, 1986, 1986 OJ L 236/30, 36–37.

1321. *See BIB (British Interactive Broadcasting)*, 1998 OJ C 322/6, point 5.3.3.

1322. *Optical Fibers*, D.Comm. July 14, 1986, 1986 OJ L 236/30.

1323. The joint ventures may today be considered as 'full-function' and covered by the amended control regulation.

1324. *Optical Fibers*, D.Comm. July 14, 1986, 1986 OJ L 236/30, 34–35.

- Active marketing efforts were permitted among the joint ventures and their European parent firms in all member states, except in countries where Corning had appointed an exclusive licensee, in which case only passive sales would be permitted.[1325]
- The European parties retained the right unilaterally, and at their own expense, to require expansion of the joint venture's output.
- Corning's representation on the joint ventures' governing bodies was reduced so that it would no longer have a decisive influence over their operations.[1326]
- Furthermore, the exemption was made subject to the condition that the companies concerned (parent companies and joint ventures) would not exchange any commercially sensitive information concerning prices, costs, sales, production and marketing plans ('Chinese wall').[1327]

In other cases of joint venture networks the Commission granted clearance for the creation of one joint venture only under the condition that the party also wind up, or to reduce participation in, another joint venture established with a competitor.[1328]

1325. This less liberal treatment of territorial restrictions than in the patent and know-how license regulations was required because of the Commission's strong influence over all the joint ventures, and to a lesser extent over licensees, and because of the tendency of national telecommunications authorities to buy from local firms.

1326. *Optical Fibers*, D.Comm. July 14, 1986, 1986 OJ L 236/30, 39.

1327. *Ibid.*, point 83.

1328. *Veba/Degussa*, D.Comm. Dec. 3, 1997, M.942; *Allianz/AGF*, D.Comm. May 8, 1998, M.1082. Under Articles 81 and 82 *see BSN/St. Gobain*, Fifth Report on Competition Policy, point 34; Bull. EC 4–1977, point 2.1.25; 1977–2 CMLR 687; *Industrial Gases*, Nineteenth Report on Competition Policy, point 62.

Chapter VII

Industrial and Intellectual Property Rights and EC Law

CONTENTS

A. Introduction

1. Industrial and Intellectual Property Law v. Competition Law

Different Objectives of Industrial and Intellectual Property Law and Competition Law.
Applying competition law to transactions involving industrial and intellectual property rights[1] – patents, utility rights ('petty patents'), plant variety rights, rights to ornamental designs, copyrights and trademarks as well as related rights such as trade secrets and know-how – raises special issues because competition and industrial property laws pursue different goals which are sometimes difficult to reconcile. Competition law protects competition from undue restraints and is concerned with maintaining free and open markets. In contrast, the strongest form of industrial property right, namely a patent, confers on the inventor of a new product or process the exclusive right to make, use and sell the invention and the corresponding legal right to prevent others from exploiting the protected invention without its consent.[2] These exclusive rights to make, use and sell the invention may provide a powerful competitive stimulus for innovation. On the other hand, there is a risk that the patentee may abuse the right of exclusivity in an anticompetitive manner, such as to engage unlawful 'tying' or to establish absolute territorial protection among licensees. This risk is greatest if the intellectual property right gives the right holder substantial market power or even a monopoly for a particular type of product. Therefore, the parallel application of competition and industrial property laws requires careful evaluation and balancing of their underlying functions in order to minimize potential conflicts and avoid frustrating the essential objectives of either of these laws.[3]

1. The Commission uses the term 'intellectual property rights' as covering both industrial and intellectual property rights, *see* the Commission's proposed Directive for for the Enforcement of Intellectual Property Rights, IP/03/144.
2. The Commission's proposed Directive for the Enforcement of Intellectual Property Rights, IP/03/144, aims at bolstering the fight against piracy and counterfeiting, thereby helping to combat illegal activities. The proposal complements the proposal for a Regulation to facilitate seizures by customs of counterfeit products from outside the EU, IP/03/75.
3. For a more comprehensive account of the industrial property law and EC Competition rules, *see* Anderman, *EC Competition Law and Intellectual Property Rights*, 1998; Cohen Jehoram, 'International Exhaustion versus Importation Right', GRUR Int. 1996, 280; Cornish, *Intellectual Property: Patents, Copyright, Trade Marks and Allied Rights,* 2nd ed., London 1989; Groves, *Intellectual Property and the Internal Market of the European Community,* 1993; Marenco/Banks, 'Intellectual Property and the Community Rules on Free Movement: Discrimination Unearthed', 15 ELR 224 (1990).

Harmonization of National Industrial Properties Laws v. Application of Existing EC Law.
Article 295 of the EC Treaty provides that it shall not prejudice the rules in member states governing the system of property ownership which include industrial property rights. However, the scope of protection afforded by industrial property law differs in each member state. This leaves gaps in protection in certain member states, thereby allowing unauthorized exploitation in certain parts of the Community. Therefore, there is a need for harmonizing the national laws. The EEA Agreement provides for harmonization of the national industrial property laws of the EEA (non-EC member) countries in such a way as to guarantee the same level of protection as under EC standards and to adhere to the respective international agreements on industrial property rights.[4] Directive 2004/48/CE on the Enforcement oofIntellectual Property Rights[5] aims at improving the means of enforcing in order to ensure that the substantive law on intellectual property rights is applied effectively throughout the Community.[6]

2. Actual State of Harmonization of Industrial and Intellectual Property Law

Results of Harmonization.
Up to now, there has been substantial harmonization of national industrial property laws:

(a) Patents
– The *European Patent Convention,* signed at Munich in 1973 ('Munich Convention'), entered into force in 1978.[7] The Convention has provided for a centralized examination system which allows applicants with a single filing to obtain a bundle of national patents in the Convention member states, which include some non-EC countries. States that have adopted the European Patent Convention are all the EC member states except Ireland and Portugal plus Liechtenstein and Switzerland. A new European Patent Office was established in Munich, Germany pursuant to the Convention. With the accession of Hungary, the number of members of the EPC has increased to 26. The membership on January 1, 2003 was as follows: Austria, Belgium, Bulgaria, Cyprus, Czech Republic, Denmark, Estonia, Finland, France, Germany, Greece, Hungary,

4. Articles 1 and 5 of Protocol 28 of the EEA Agreement, 1994 OJ L 1/1, 194.
5. 2004 OJ L 157/45.
6. In particular with respect to provisional measures, the calculation of dmages and the arrangtements for applying injunctions.
7. *See also* Annex XVII to the EEA Agreement as amended by Decision 21/2000 of the EEA Joint Committee, 2001 OJ L 103/44. The Patent Cooperation Treaty (PCT) of June 19, 1970 concerns international cooperation of national patent offices.

Ireland, Italy, Liechtenstein, Luxembourg, Monaco, Netherlands, Portugal, Slovakia, Slovenia, Spain, Sweden, Switzerland, Turkey, United Kingdom.

- The *Community Patent Convention* ('Luxembourg Convention'), originally signed in 1975[8] and amended in 1989,[9] but not yet in force: The Convention provides the basis for a unitary EC patent, which will confer a uniform standard of protection and make management of rights easier as registration will be renewable for the whole EC at once. The Community patent is not designed to replace national patents but to provide patent protection covering the whole Community.[10] On November 21, 2003 the Commission submitted a new proposal for a Council regulation for a Community patent.[11] The key issues concern language arrangements, financial arrangements, the role of the national patent offices, the compliance with the 'acquis communautaire' and judicial control.[12]
- A *Supplementary Protection Certificate for Medical Products* can be applied for and granted under Council Regulation 1768/92[13] by the holder of a national or a Community patent in each member state. The reason for such supplementary protection is the insufficient duration of protection under the patent to cover the investment put into pharmaceutical research.[14] Accordingly, the duration of the supplementary protection is calculated based on the duration between the date of the application of the basic patent and the date of the first marketing authorization minus 5 years.
- A proposal for a directive on the protection by patents of computer-implemented inventions aims at harmonizing the way in which national patent laws deal with inventions using software.[15]

---

8. 1976 OJ L 17.
9. 1989 OJ L 401/10.
10. According to Article 3 (1) of the Protocol of the EEA Agreement the parties are committed to undertake their best efforts to finalize the Community Patent Convention within three years, i.e. before the end of 1997 (1994 OJ L 1/194), but the Convention is not yet in force.
11. 15086/03. *See* Commission Staff Working Paper on a Community policy for the realization of the Community patent in the context of a revision of the European patent convention of May 7, 2001, SEC(2001)744.
12. The Council failed to reach an agreement on March 11, 2004: MEMO/04/58.
13. 1992 OJ L 182/1. These rights are, for the purposes of technology transfer block exemption regulation, assimilated to patents. *See* the Commission's proposals for a review of the EU pharmaceutical legislation: MEMO/03/262 of Dec. 18, 2003. *See also* the agreement by the member states on pharmaceutical reforms, IP/03/785 of June 2, 2003.
14. Where an active ingredient is covered by a basic patent, the certificate is capable of covering the active ingredient as such and also its various derived forms: *Farmitalia Carlo Erba,* ECJ Sept. 16, 1999, 1999 ECR I-5553, para. 21.
15. Commission proposal of February 20, 2002, COM(2002)92 final, IP/02/277. *See* in greater detail MEMO/02/32.

(b) Utility Models

The national legal protection for *utility models* ('petty patents') differs from member state to member state. Some accord protection similar to a patent (although in a simplified procedure and for a shorter duration, i.e. 6–10 years)[16] whereas others do not provide for any specific protection.[17] The Commission submitted in June 1999 to the Council an amended proposal for a directive on the protection of inventions by utility model.[18] The proposed directive aims at harmonizing the main provisions of national laws, including the introduction of this protection in member states where it does not exist. The main features are the lower level of inventiveness than required for a patent, the absence of a prior examination of the innovation prior to registration, and a limited protection period of no more than ten years. The Commission is evaluating the impact of a Community utility model with a view of updating its Green Paper.[19]

(c) Plant Variety Rights

Council Regulation 2100/94 on Community Plant Variety Rights[20] provides, in the absence of approximation of national laws, for a Community regime which, although co-existing with national regimes, allows for the grant of industrial property rights valid throughout the Community[21] to protect production, multiplication, selling, exporting, importing and stocking of the variety constituents or harvested material of the protected variety (Article 13).[22]

(d) Ornamental and Design Rights

– *European Parliament and Council Directive 98/71 on the Legal Protection of Designs*.[23] This directive undertakes a partial approximation of the design laws of the member states protecting design rights to the extent that they are new and have individual character, excluding, however, 'the existing legal provisions relating to the use of the design of a component part used for the purpose of the

16. Germany, France (*'certificat d'utilité'*), Italy, Austria, Spain and the Netherlands. *See* the Hague Agreement concerning the international deposit of industrial designs, Nov. 6, 1925, as revised in London, June 2, 1934, in The Hague, Nov. 28, 1960 and Geneva, Aug. 29, 1975.
17. United Kingdom, Luxembourg and Sweden.
18. Proposal of June 30, 1999 amending the 1997 proposal (COM/97/691 final) and taking into account the European Parliament's opinion of March 1999.
19. SEC/2001/1307 of March 1, 2002.
20. 1994 OJL 227/1.
21. Excluding any double protection by national plant variety or patent rights (Article 92). *See* the Commission's proposal for a Council Directive on the legal protection of biotechnological inventions (including living matters), 1989 OJ C 10/3, and the International Convention for the Protection of New Varieties of Plants, Dec. 2, 1961, as revised at Geneva, Nov. 10, 1972, Oct. 23, 1978 and March 19, 1991.
22. *See* also the Convention Constituting the Union for the Protection of New Varieties of Plants, 1961.
23. 1998 OJ L 289/28.

repair of a complex product so as to restore its original appearance' which may be maintained by the member states for a transitional period of three years.[24]

- *Council Regulation 6/2002 on the European Community Design.*[25] The Regulation provides for two types of design protection, directly applicable in each member state: the 'Registered Community Design' which must be registered with the Office for Harmonisation in the Internal Market' (OHIM), and the 'Unregistered Design'. In both cases, to be eligible for protection, designs must be new and must have an individual character. In other words, it must be apparent to the public that they are different from products which existed previously. The main difference in the level of protection afforded will be that a Registered Community Design will be protected against deliberate copying and the independent development of a similar design; an unregistered design will be protected only against deliberate copying.[26] The Community design has a duration of between five and twenty-five years, and coexists with national designs, under rules harmonized by Directive 98/71/EC. The Directive excludes, for the time being, the registration and protection of designs of spare components of complex products, such as visible car spare parts (products upon whose appearance the protected design is dependent), thereby allowing member states to maintain their existing rules and to change them only if the purpose is to liberalize the market of such parts.

(e) Copyrights

- *Council Directive 93/98/EC to Approximate the Duration of Copyrights and Related Rights.*[27] This directive provides for a unified duration of seventy years for copyrights and fifty years for related rights.[28]
- *Council Directive 91/250/EC on the Legal Protection of Computer Programs.*[29]

---

24. The Commission stated, however, that it will immediately start consultations involving manufacturers in order to arrive at a voluntary agreement (Commission statement re. Article 18). Recital 20 emphasizes that the transitional provisions may not be construed as constituting an obstacle to the free movement of a product which constitutes a component part.
25. 2002 OJ L 3/1.
26. On Oct. 21, 2002 the Commission adopted Regulation 2245/2002 implementing Regulation 6/2002 (in particular on the application procedure) (2002 OJ L 341/28) and on Dec. 19, 2002 Regulation 2246/2002 setting the registration fees which allows the Office of Marks and Designs already established in Alicante, Spain, to register Community designs from April 1, 2003 (2002 OJ L 341/54).
27. IP/01/1803. *See* the Bern Convention for the Protection of the Literary and Artistic Works, Paris 1971 (Article 5 (1) (b) Protocol 28 of the EEA Agreement) and International Agreement Concerning the Protection of Authors and Manufacturers of Sound Records, Madrid, 1961 (Article 5 (1) (c) Protocol 28 of the EEA Agreement).
28. However, the directive does not preclude a shorter duration of protection of phonograms under national law: *see Butterfly/CEMED,* ECJ June 29, 1999, 1999 ECR I-3939.
29. 1991 OJ L 122/42. *See also* the proposal for a directive on the protection by patents of computer-implemented inventions which aims at harmonizing the way in which national patent laws deal with inventions using software: COM(2002)92 final, IP/02/277.

This directive aims at protecting computer programs, including their preparatory design material, by copyright, as literary works within the Berne Convention for literary and artistic works for 50 years.

- *European Parliament and Council Directive 96/9/EC on the Legal Protection of Databases.*[30] This directive provides for the legal protection of databases in any form, i.e. collections of independent works, data or other materials arranged in a systematic or methodical way and individually accessible by electronic or other means.
- *Council Directive 87/54/EC on the Legal Protection of Topographies of Semiconductor Products.*[31] The directive provides for a protection of semiconductor products, thereby filling a gap between patent and copyright protection.
- *Council Directive 92/100/EC on the Rental and Lending Rights Concerning Copyrights and Rights Related to Copyrights.*[32] This directive recognizes a special right of rental or lending independently of other forms of distribution which may be granted exclusively and is not exhausted by the first marketing.[33]
- *Council Directive 93/83/EC on the Coordination of Certain Rules Concerning Copyrights and Rights Related to Copyright Applicable to Satellite Broadcasting and Cable Retransmission.*[34] This directive provides for an exclusive right for the author to authorize the communication of copyrighted works by satellite or by cable that may be exercised only by a collective agreement between the collecting society and the broadcasting or cable operator.
- *European Parliament and Council Directive 2001/29/EC on the Harmonization of Certain Aspects of Copyright and Related Rights in the Information Society* ('*Multimedia Directive*').[35] The directive aims at adjusting and complementing the existing legal framework, with particular emphasis on new products and services containing intellectual property in order to facilitate cross-border trade in copyright-protected goods and services. This directive is based on the Commission's Greenbook on 'Copyrights and Rights Related to Copyrights in a Multimedia Society'.[36] It provides, *inter alia*, for Community-wide (not international) exhaustion of copyrights, which replaces the national exhaustion of these rights.[37]

---

30. 1996 OJ L 77/20.
31. 1987 OJ L 24/36.
32. 1992 OJ L 346/61.
33. *See Metronome Musik/Music Point Hokamp,* ECJ April 28, 1998, 1998 ECR I-1953.
34. 1993 OJ L 248/15.
35. 2001 OJ L 167/10.
36. COM(95)382 final.
37. Article 4 of the Directive. *See* IP/01/528 of April 9, 2001; Buschle, Joller, 'Multimedia und Urheberrecht', *European Law Reporter* 3/1998, pp. 113–118.

(f) Trademarks

- *First Council Directive 89/104/EC to Approximate the Laws of the Member States Relating to Trademarks,*[38] as amended by the EEA Agreement.[39] This directive deals in particular with the grounds for refusal to register or for declaration of invalidity, e.g., the existence of older identical or confusingly similar trademarks (Articles 3–4); with the rights and exhaustion of rights within the Community (Articles 5–7); and with revocation of the trademark if it has not been put to genuine use within five years of registration (Articles 10–13). The national trademark laws have been amended in order to comply with this directive.[40]
- *Council Regulation 40/94 on the Community Trademark,*[41] amended by Council Regulation 1992/2003[42] and Council Regulation 422/2004.[43] This regulation[44] provides for a new Community-wide protection of trademarks co-existing with the national protection of marks – as harmonized according to the First Council Directive – to be registered at the new Community Trademark Office (Office for Harmonization in the Internal Market – OHIM) established in Alicante, Spain. This system of regulation was completed by Regulation 2868/95 establishing the rules of procedure of the office,[45] Regulation 2869/95 on the fees

38. 1989 OJ L 40/1. *See* the Madrid Agreement Concerning the International Registration of Marks, April 14, 1891, as revised at Nice, June 15, 1957, at Stockholm, July 14, 1967 and at Madrid, June 28, 1989. Not all member states are a party, but they are committed to adhere (Article 5 (1) (d) Protocol 28 of the EEA Agreement).
39. Article 65 (2) and Appendix XVII, point 4 (c) of the the EEA Agreement: 'The trademark shall not entitle the proprietor to prohibit its use in relation to goods which have been put on the market in one of the Contracting States under that trademark by the proprietor or with his consent.'
40. Austria: Amendment of Trademark law in 1993 (BGB11 1993/109); Benelux: existing Benelux Trademark Act of Dec. 2, 1992, in force since Jan. 1, 1996, already in line with the directive; Denmark: Act No. 341 of June 6, 1991; Finland: Trademark Law amended on Dec. 22, 1995; France: Trademark Law 91/7 of Jan. 4, 1991, amended by Law 94–361 of May 14, 1994 and Law 95–4 of Jan. 3, 1995; Germany: new Trademark Law of Oct. 25, 1994, amended by Law of July 19, 1996; Greece: Decret présidentiel 2239/1994 of Nov. 1, 1994; Ireland: Irish Trademarks Act 1996; Italy: Decreto legge No. 480 of Dec. 4, 1992, amended by Decreto No. 480 of March 19, 1996; Portugal: Lei No. 16/1995 of Jan. 24, 1995; Spain: Lei No. 32/1988 of May 11, 1988 (which incorporates already the later directive); Sweden: Amendment of Trademark Law by Law No. 150 of Dec. 16, 1994; United Kingdom: Trademark Act 1994 of Oct. 31, 1994. *See* Bumiller, *Durchsetzung der Gemeinschaftsmarke in der Union,* 1997.
41. 1994 OJ L 11/1.
42. 2003 OJ L 296/1.
43. 2004 OJ L 70/1.
44. Which is based on Article 308 of the EC Treaty. This provision entitles the Council to take the appropriate action which is necessary to attain one of the objectives of the Treaty and this Treaty does not provide the necessary powers.
45. 1995 OJ L 303/1.

payable to the OHIM[46] and Regulation 216/96 on the rules of procedure of the (internal) board of appeal.[47]

– *Regulation 2309/93 on a EU Procedure for the Granting of Marketing Authorization for Medicinal Products.*[48] The regulation provides for two separate procedures: (i) a centralized procedure leading to a single marketing authorization valid throughout the Community, which is mandatory for medicinal products developed by means of biotechnological processes, and optional for certain other categories, and (ii) a mutual recognition procedure for products which are not eligible for the centralized procedure but has to be used where an application for marketing authorization concerns two or more member states. A new Commission proposal tends to open the centralized procedure to a broader range of medicinal products.[49]

(g) Know-How

Know-how[50] is not protected by any national industrial property rights. Its unauthorized use may only constitute an act of unfair competition and lead to the appropriate actions provided for under the national laws which are substantially different, but for which no harmonization directives are envisaged up to now.[51] Because their character is similar to industrial property, know-how licence agreements are treated under competition law in a similar way as patent licence agreements.[52]

3. DIVERGENT OBJECTIVES TO COMPETITION LAW

National Protection of Industrial Property Rights v. Principle of a Unified Community Market.

Despite the progress in approximating national laws, the rights of exclusivity conferred by national industrial property laws have to be reconciled with the achievement of a unified Community marketplace. The problems are particularly complex because national industrial property law provides protection only on the sovereign territory of the member state that grants the right. This is referred to as

46. 1995 OJ L 303/33.
47. 1996 OJ L 28. The decisions of the Board of Appeal may be appealed successively to the Court of First Instance and to the Court of Justice. *See Procter & Gamble,* CFI July 8, 1999, 1999 ECR II-2383 (refusal to register 'Baby-dry') and CFI Feb. 16, 2000, 2000 ECR II-265 (refusal to register a tri-dimension trademark).
48. 2003 OJ L 214/1.
49. 'Reform of EU Pharmaceutical Legislation', MEMO/03/262. *See* Commission's Communication on Parallel Imports of Proprietary Medicines, COM(2003)839 final.
50. Defined as unpatented (whether patentable or not), secret and valuable technology.
51. Besides specific issues such as comparative misleading publicity: Proposal for a Council Directive, 1991 OJ C 180 and 1994 OJ C 136/4.
52. *See* Section E.1.(c) *infra.*

the 'territoriality' principle.[53] Thus, the holder of a patent, trademark or copyright must seek protection for its industrial property under the laws of each individual member state and typically exploits its rights separately through different affiliates or licensees in each member state. This territorial limitation of industrial property rights, together with the exclusivity of the rights, mean that they can be used as a legal means of protecting national markets from imports of similar goods from other member states. Before Community law began to have an influence, national courts had generally – with the exception of certain rulings with respect to trademarks[54] – interpreted the exclusivity conferred by national law in accordance with the territoriality principle, which precluded taking into account conduct or events occurring outside national territory, such as the fact that the protected product had been marketed in another member state in full conformity with that country's industrial property laws.[55] Thus, the holder of an industrial property right could assert it to prevent the importation of products produced by authorized third parties, such as a licensee, or even by the holder itself through its own subsidiary or affiliate operating in a neighbouring member state. This allowed holders of parallel industrial property rights in different member states to isolate national markets along national lines without needing to enter into specific agreements to that end. This explains the different U.S. approach, as laid out in the Antitrust Guidelines for the Licensing of Intellectual Property issued in April 1995 by the Department of Justice and Federal Trade Commission, which generally consider licensing unique U.S.-wide intellectual property rights to be pro-competitive because they

53. *Ideal Standard,* ECJ June 22, 1994, 1994 ECR I-2789 para. 22. *See* the Commission's explanation in *Deutsche Grammophon,* ECJ June 8, 1971, 1971 ECR 487, 495–496. The territoriality of national intellectual property rights – which can bring such rights into conflict with the Community rules on free internal trade – is not changed by the harmonization of national laws or by the introduction of new EC-wide rights alongside the national rights: Advocate General Jacobs in *Hag II,* ECJ Oct. 17, 1990, 1990 ECR 3711, para. 55.

54. These exceptions include, for instance: Germany: *Maja,* German Federal Supreme Court, Jan. 22, 1964, WuWE/BGH 620; *Cinzano,* German Federal Supreme Court Feb. 2, 1973, 1973 GRUR Int. 562 (revised, however, more recently in *Dyed Levi's Jeans,* Dec. 14, 1995, GRUR Int. 1996, 271); Netherlands: *Grundig,* Dutch Supreme Court, Dec. 14, 1956, 1957 GRUR Int. 259; United Kingdom: *Heidsieck,* English High Court, 1931 *Reports on Patent Cases* XLVII 28; but *see Colgate,* English High Court, April 18, 1988, 1989 GRUR Int. 320. Sweden: *Polycolor,* Supreme Court, Oct. 17, 1967, 1968 GRUR Int. 22; Austria: *Agfa,* Supreme Court, Nov. 30, 1970, 1971 GRUR Int. 90. Non-member states – Switzerland: SABA, Supreme Court, *Entscheidungen des schweizerischen Bundesgerichtes* 84 IV 124 (1958). United States: (with respect to companies belonging to the same group) *COPIAT* (*K-Mart v. Cartier*), U.S. Supreme Court, May 31, 1988 – 486 U.S. 281; 6 USPQ 2d 1987; 36 PTCJ 177, 1989 GRUR Int. 68, the first sale doctrine was applicable to imported copies under U.S. copyright law: *Quality King Dist. v. Lanza Research Int.,* U.S. Supreme Court, March 9, 1998, 118 S.Ct. 1125; ELR 1998–4, 142.

55. *See*, e.g., *Voran,* German Supreme Court, Feb. 29, 1968, WuWE BGH 939, with respect to plant breeders' rights and (indirectly) patents.

are less likely to be used as a means of territorial partitioning of a market which has already all the characteristics of a single internal market.[56]

Reconciling the Divergent Objectives.
The isolation of national markets stands in contradiction to the central objective of the EC Treaty, which is to create a unified common market. If industrial property rights can be enforced under national legislation to frustrate this objective, then clearly some limitation on the rights is necessary. After a controversial discussion[57] and first cautious attempts in cases where industrial property rights had been 'abused' for anticompetitive purposes, the Commission and the Court of Justice developed three principles that are designed to reconcile this conflict:

1. *Existence v. Exercise*. Community law may not prejudice the *existence* of national industrial property rights because Article 295 of the EEC Treaty states that the Treaty shall in no way prejudice the rules in member states governing the system of property ownership; however, the *exercise* of such rights – the circumstances under which the rights may be enforced, e.g., in an infringement action – is limited by Community law, especially the rules on competition and the rules on the free movement of goods and services.[58]
2. *'Exhaustion' of Rights*. Under national industrial property laws, industrial property rights are ordinarily 'exhausted' with the first marketing, by the right-holder or with its consent, of products manufactured using the right. The same principle applies under Community law to marketing in another member state. Export of the product to another member state is protected by the principle of free movement of goods between member states under Article 28, and cannot be restricted under Article 30.[59] Accordingly, once a product that is the subject

56. CCH Trade Reg. Rep. § 13, 132; *see* Commission evaluation report, of Dec. 20, 2001, COM/2001/786 final, points 46–58.
57. *See* in particular *Gotzen*, GRUR Int. 1958, 224. This doctrine trying to limit the applicability of the principles of free movement of goods and competition to cases of 'abuse' is being reanimated in the form of the 'proportionality' test trying to introduce a sort of 'rule of reason' rather than applying the stricter prohibitions of both Articles 28/30 and Articles 81/82*; see* A. Reindl, 'Intellectual Property and Intra-Community Trade', Fordham Journal of International Law & Policy, (1996), p. 453.
58. *See Grundig/Consten,* ECJ July 13, 1966, 1966 ECR 299, 344–346*; Deutsche Grammophon,* ECJ June 8, 1971, 1971 ECR 487, paras 11–12.
59. *Deutsche Grammophon,* ECJ June 8, 1971, 1971 ECR 487, para. 13. Articles 28 and 30 apply with respect to the new member states from the date of their accession and not from the end of the transitional period: *Centrafarm/Winthrop,* ECJ Oct. 31, 1974, 1974 ECR 1183, paras 24–30. A temporary exception to the principle of free movement of goods applies to pharmaceutical products under Articles 47 and 209 of the Acts of Accession of Spain and Portugal (and additionally food in the case of Portugal). This exemption applies until the end of the third year after these member states extend patentability to Pharmaceuticals (probably until 1995).

of an industrial property right is put onto the market in a legal manner in one member state or in an EEA country[60] by the owner of such right or with its consent, i.e., under licence, the parallel industrial property right held in another member state or in an EEA country may not be exercised to prevent its importation there.[61]

3. *Application of Articles 81 and 82*. The exercise of industrial property rights in such a way as to prevent imports from other member states of products lawfully distributed there will be caught by Article 81 if it is the subject, the means or the result of an agreement – for example, a licence or assignment of the rights – or a concerted practice.[62] Certain limited restrictions may be warranted to protect the essence of the industrial property right.[63] For example, the grant of an exclusive territory for an introductory period may be justified under Article 81 to induce a licensee to accept the risk of marketing goods manufactured with a new technology.[64] However, the granting of absolute territorial protection to a licensee beyond an introductory period infringes Article 81. Article 82 is not infringed by the mere grant of an exclusive right under national industrial property law. If, however, the industrial property right confers a dominant position or the holder otherwise enjoys a dominant position in the relevant market, that position must not be abusively exploited, such as by imposing exorbitant royalties or other unfair or abusive terms that distort competition.[65]

60. Art. 2 of Protocol 28 of the EEA Agreement, 1994 OJ L 1/1, 194.
61. *See* in particular Art. 7 of the Council Directive to Approximating the National Laws Relating to Trademarks, which recognizes that the owner's rights are exhausted once the product has been put on the market within the Community or – according to Article 2 of Protocol 28 of the EEA Agreement – within the EEA.
62. *See* Directive 2004/48/CE on the Enforcement of Intellectual Property Rights, Recital 12 (2004 OJ L 157/45).
63. *Sirena,* ECJ Feb. 18, 1971, 1971 ECR 69, 82, para. 9; *Deutsche Grammophon,* ECJ June 8, 1971, 1971 ECR 487, para. 6; *Windsurfing,* ECJ Feb. 25, 1986, 1986 ECR 711, para. 36. The latter case shows that under both Articles 28 and 81, the same test is applied to restraints of trade based on protection of industrial property, namely whether they are 'justified for the purpose of safeguarding rights which constitute the specific subject matter of [the] property'. *Centrafarm/Sterling Drug,* ECJ Oct. 31, 1974, 1974 ECR 1147, para. 8. *See also Keurkoop/Nancy Kean Gifts,* ECJ Sept. 14, 1982, 1982 ECR 2853, paras 24–26.
64. *See Maize Seed,* ECJ June 8, 1982, 1982 ECR 2015, paras 55–58.
65. *Renault,* ECJ Oct. 5, 1988, 1988 ECR 6039, paras 14–17; *Parke Davis,* ECJ Feb. 29, 1968, 1968 ECR 55, 72–73.

B. Development and Scope of the 'Exhaustion' Doctrine

1. The Basic Judgments of the Court of Justice

Existence v. Exercise of Rights: Precursor of 'Exhaustion'.
The Court of Justice acknowledged in the *Grundig/Consten* case[66] that the proprietary rights granted under national laws in the form of patents, utility models, trademarks and copyrights may not be prejudiced. However, the 'exercise' of those rights, such as through the imposition of territorial or quantitative restrictions in a licence agreement, may be limited to the extent necessary to give effect to the competition rules. The case concerned a challenge by the Commission to the grant of exclusive trademark and distribution rights that Grundig, a leading German manufacturer of televisions and tape recorders, had conferred on its exclusive distributor in France, Consten. When certain parallel traders began undercutting Consten's prices in France, Consten initiated a trademark infringement action and an unfair competition action under French law to halt the imports. The Court sought a solution to the conflict between industrial property rights and Community law under Article 81. The Court found the underlying exclusive distributorship agreement to be unlawful since it resulted in isolation of the French market and aimed at sheltering Consten's pricing of Grundig products from competition. The Court stated, 'The prohibition [of Article 81 (1)] would be ineffective if Consten could continue to use the trademark to achieve the same object as that pursued by the [exclusive distribution] agreement which has been held to be unlawful …'. The Court went on:

> 'The injunction … to refrain from using rights under national trademark law in order to set an obstacle in the way of parallel imports does not affect the grant of those rights but only limits their exercise to the extent necessary to give effect to the prohibition under Article 85 (1). The power of the Commission to issue such an injunction for which provision is made in Article 3 of Regulation No. 17/62 of the Council is in harmony with the nature of the Community rules on competition which have immediate effect and are directly binding on individuals'.[67]

Thus, the exercise of trademark rights merely as a convenient tool by which to divide national markets among distributors of the genuine goods is not part of the essential functions of the trademark, and therefore is subject to prohibition under the Treaty. The *Parke Davis*[68] and *Sirena*[69] cases followed this line of reasoning

66. *Grundig/Consten,* ECJ July 13, 1966, 1966 ECR 299.
67. *Ibid.,* 345–346.
68. *Parke Davis,* ECJ Feb. 29, 1968, 1968 ECR 55, 72–73.
69. *Sirena,* ECJ Feb. 18, 1971, 1971 ECR 69, paras 9–16.

under the competition rules, Article 81 and Article 82, for patent and trademark law, respectively.

The Article 28 Approach: Adoption of the 'Exhaustion' Principle.
In the *Deutsche Grammophon* case[70] the Court of Justice developed a new doctrine which was not based on Article 81. The case concerned the question of whether Deutsche Grammophon, a German manufacturer of sound recordings, should be granted an injunction under copyright law to prevent importation of genuine Deutsche Grammophon sound recordings that had been marketed in France by its French subsidiary, Polydor, with Deutsche Grammophon's consent. Article 81 could not apply since agreements between a parent and its controlled subsidiary are not caught by Article 81. Instead the Court based its ruling on Articles 28 and 30. Article 28 prohibits governmental restrictions on the free movement of goods among the member states[71] and Article 30 limits this principle to the extent that the restrictions are justified on grounds of 'the protection of industrial and commercial property'. The Court ruled that it was in conflict with the provisions of the Treaty on the free movement of goods for a manufacturer to exercise its copyright, conferred upon it by the legislation of a member state,

> 'in such a way as to prohibit the sale in that State of products placed on the market by him or with his consent in another Member State solely because such distribution did not occur within the territory of the first Member State'.[72]

Thus, the Court of Justice determined that it would frustrate the Community objective of creating a single internal market if a product legally marketed, i.e. by the proprietor or with its consent, in one member state could be blocked from free circulation in other member states of the Community through the exercise of parallel industrial property rights. This has come to be known as the 'exhaustion' principle.[73]

---

70. *Deutsche Grammophon,* ECJ June 8, 1971, 1971 ECR 487.
71. An injunction of a national court prohibiting the import of products legally marketed in another member state constitutes a measure having equivalent effect to a quantitative restriction on imports within the meaning of Article 28: *Graffione/Fransa,* ECJ Nov. 26, 1996, 1996 ECR I-6039, para. 16.
72. *Deutsche Grammophon,* ECJ June 8, 1971, 1971 ECR 487, para. 13. *See also Centrafarm/Sterling Drug,* ECJ Oct. 31, 1974, 1974 ECR 1147, paras 5–15; *Centrafarm/Winthrop,* ECJ Oct. 31, 1974, 1974 ECR 1183, paras 4–12.
73. The wording *of Deutsche Grammophon,* ECJ June 8, 1971, 1971 ECR 487, para. 13, repeated in *Centrafarm/Sterling Drug,* ECJ Oct. 31, 1974, 1974 ECR 1147, para. 15, and *Centrafarm/Winthrop,* ECJ Oct. 31, 1974, 1974 ECR 1183, para. 12, appears to equate the exercise of industrial property rights by individual parties before a national court to a governmental measure subject to the freedom of movement rules. However, clearly it is the governmental action that confers the right to oppose importation and that enforces that right through the courts, and

The *Centrafarm/Sterling Drug* and the *Centrafarm/Winthrop* Cases. In these cases the Court of Justice confirmed and extended to both patents and trademarks the 'exhaustion' principle that it had applied to copyright in the Deutsche Grammophon case. The *Sterling Drug* case[74] concerned the question whether Sterling, a U.S. company that manufactured patented drugs in Germany and the United Kingdom, could assert its Dutch patent rights in order to prevent parallel imports by Centrafarm, a discounter, into the Netherlands from Germany and the United Kingdom where the genuine product had been marketed by subsidiaries of Sterling. In the *Centrafarm/Winthrop* case,[75] Winthrop, a wholly-owned subsidiary of Sterling's UK company, Sterling-Winthrop Group, tried to use its Dutch trademark in order to prevent imports into the Netherlands by Centrafarm of the same drug as in the Sterling Drug case. In both cases the Court concluded in almost identical language as follows:

> 'Inasmuch as it provides an exception to one of the fundamental principles of the Common Market, Article 36 [*now 30*] in fact only admits of derogations from the free movement of goods where such derogations are justified for the purpose of safeguarding rights which constitute the specific subject matter of this property …
>
> An obstacle to the free movement of goods may arise out of the existence, within a national legislation concerning industrial and commercial property, of provisions laying down that a trademark owner's [or a patentee's] right is not exhausted when the product protected by the trademark [or patent] is marketed in another Member State, with the result that the trademark owner [or the patentee] can prevent importation of the product into his own Member State when it has been marketed in another Member State.
>
> Such an obstacle is not justified when the product has been put onto the market in a legal manner in the Member State from which it has been imported, by the trademark owner [or the patentee] himself or with his consent, so that there can be no question of abuse or infringement of the trademark [or patent]'.[76]

---

not the individual exercise of its rights by the right-holder, which falls within Articles 28 and 30. In later judgments, e.g. *Flemish Travel Agents,* ECJ Oct. 1, 1987; 1987 ECR 3801, para. 30, and *Bayer/Süllhöfer,* ECJ Sept. 27, 1988, 1988 ECR 5249, 5285, the Court has made it clear that the freedom of movement rules apply only to governmental measures, not action by firms.

74. *Centrafarm/Sterling Drug,* ECJ Oct. 31, 1974, 1974 ECR 1147.

75. *Centrafarm/Winthrop,* ECJ Oct. 31, 1974, 1974 ECR 1183.

76. *Centrafarm/Winthrop,* ECJ Oct. 31, 1974, 1974 ECR 1183, paras 7–10; bracketed wording from *Centrafarm/Sterling Drug,* ECJ Oct. 31, 1974, 1974 ECR 1147, paras 8–11. *See also Hag II,* ECJ Oct. 17, 1990, 1990 ECR 3711, para. 12; *Ideal Standard,* ECJ June 22, 1994, 1994 ECR 2789, para. 33; *Bristol Myers Squibb/Paranova,* ECJ July 11, 1996, 1996 ECR I-3457, para. 31.

The Article 30 Exception.
In the *Deutscher Apothekerverband/Doc Morris* case[77] the Court of Justice clarified that Article 30 continues to apply in relation to the manufacture and marketing of specialized products as long as the harmonization of national rules has not been fully achieved in those areas. However, national rules having restrictive effects, such as a national prohibition on the sale by mail order of medical products, are compatible with Article 30 only to the extent that they are necessary for the effective protection of health and life of humans. Adequate reasons for prohibiting the mail-order trade are those relating to the need to provide individual advice to the customer and to ensure his protection when he is supplied with medicines and to the need to check that prescriptions are genuine and to guarantee that medicinal products are widely available and sufficient to meet requirements. Prescription medicines need to be strictly controlled. Such control can be justified in view of the risks which medicine present and – this is an *obiter dictum* – 'national legislation fixing prices at which prescription medicines are sold should, in so far as it forms part of the national health system, be maintained.'[78] However, Article 30 cannot be relied upon to justify an absolute prohibition on the sale by mail order of medicinal products that are *not* subject to prescription.[79]

Application of Free Movement Principle to Services.
The Court of Justice extended this case law in principle to services in the *Coditel I* and *Coditel II* cases.[80] These cases concerned the unauthorized cable transmission into Belgium of a German television broadcast of a film that infringed the exclusive copyright licence to the film held by a Belgian distributor. The Court reasoned on the basis of the underlying premise in Article 30 that the distinction

> 'between the *existence* of a right conferred by the legislation of a Member State in regard to the protection of artistic and intellectual property, which cannot be affected by the provisions of the Treaty, and the *exercise* of such right, which might constitute a disguised restriction on trade between Member States, also applies where that right is exercised in the context of the movement of services'. (Emphasis added.)[81]

---

77. *Deutscher Apothekerverband/Doc Morris,* ECJ Dec. 11, 2003, C-322/01.
78. *Ibid.,* paras. 117–122. A national market for prescription medicines could be characterized by non-economic factors with the result that national legislation should, in so far as it forms an integral part of the national health system, be maintained (para. 122).
79. *Ibid.,* para. 124.
80. *Coditel I,* ECJ March 18, 1980, 1980 ECR 881 (Article 49); *Coditel II,* ECJ Oct. 6, 1982, 1982 ECR 3381 (Articles 49 and 81). Similarly *Alpine Investments,* ECJ May 10, 1995, 1995 ECR I-1141, paras 18–22.
81. *Coditel II,* ECJ Oct. 6, 1982, 1982 ECR 3381, 3401, para. 13.

The Court ruled that the mere grant of an exclusive licence to exhibit the film in Belgium which thereby precluded its showing by others did not infringe Articles 49 and 50 on the free movement of services, nor Article 81 on competition.[82] However, the exercise of the copyright by the exclusive licensee may infringe Article 81 where it creates barriers that are artificial or unjustifiable in terms of the needs of the cinematographic industry or results in fees that exceed a fair return on investment or exclusivity for an unduly long period.[83]

Application of the Exhaustion Principle to the Various Property Rights – An Overview.

The 'exhaustion' principle applies to:

– patents[84] and similar rights, such as petty patents and utility models,[85]
– plant breeders' rights,[86]
– registered designs,[87]
– trademarks[88] and trade names,[89]

---

82. *See also M6, Antena 3, Gestévision, SIC/UER, Eurovision II,* CFI Oct. 8, 2002, 2002 ECR II-3805, para. 64.
83. *Coditel II,* ECJ Oct. 6, 1982, 1982 ECR 3381, paras 14–19. *See also Coditel I,* ECJ March 18, 1980, 1980 ECR 881, para. 18; *Debauve,* ECJ March 18, 1980, 1980 ECR 833, para. 16.
84. *Centrafarm/SterlingDrug,* ECJ Oct. 31, 1974, 1974 ECR 1147, paras 8–11; *Merck/Stephar,* ECJ July 14, 1981, 1981 ECR 2063, para. 14. *See* Articles 32 and 81 (1) of the Community Patent Convention: 'The rights conferred by a Community (or by a national patent in a Contracting State) shall not extend to acts concerning a product covered by that patent which are done within the territories of the Contracting States after that product has been put on the market in one of these States by the proprietor or with his express consent, unless there are grounds which, under Community law, would justify the extension of such acts of the rights conferred by the patent'.
85. No cases yet, but *see* the technology transfer block exemption regulation, which assimilates petty patents and utility models to patents. *See* Article 84 of the Community Patent Convention and Article 24 of the Council Regulation 6/2002 on the European Community Design, 2002 OJ L 3/1.
86. *Vriend,* ECJ Feb. 26, 1980, 1980 ECR 327, para. 9 (compulsory membership of a trade association in order to sell plant propagation material); *Maize Seed,* ECJ June 8, 1982, 1982 ECR 2015, paras 41–42; *Sicasov,* D.Comm. Dec. 14, 1998, 1999 OJ L 4/27, points 48–51. *See* Article 16 of Council Regulation 2100/94 on Community Plant Variety Rights.
87. *Keurkoop/Nancy Kean Gifts,* ECJ Sept. 14, 1982, 1982 ECR 2853, para. 29. *See* Article 15 of Directive 98/71/EC.
88. *Hag I,* ECJ July 3, 1974, 1974 ECR 731, paras 7–13; *Centrafarm/Winthrop,* ECJ Oct. 31, 1974, 1974 ECR 1183, paras 9–11; *Bristol-Myers Squibb/Paranova,* ECJ July 11, 1996, 1996 ECR I-3457, para. 34. *See* Article 7 of the Council Regulation on the Community Trademark and Article 7 of the First Trademark Directive.
89. *Ringelhan,* ECJ Nov. 6, 1984, 1984 ECR 3651, para. 20 (use of unfair competition law to prevent imports).

- copyrighted products,[90] and
- copyrighted services.[91]

The precise scope of the rights that are 'exhausted' depends on the *specific subject matter* of the relevant property right, which will be discussed in detail under section C. Certain aspects of the exhaustion principle which are common to all industrial and intellectual property rights are described in the following sub-sections.

2. The Geographic Scope of the Exhaustion Principle

Extension to EEA Countries.
The EEA Agreement[92] provides for an extension of the exhaustion principle to the EEA countries (Norway, Iceland and Liechtenstein[93]). Therefore, the Court's ruling applies to cases where the protected product has been put onto the market in the Community or in any EEA country. The reason is that the EEA Agreement is directly applicable law that contains the same principles of free movement of goods and services as Articles 28 and 49 of the EC Treaty.[94]

No Exhaustion Principle with Respect to Imports from Third Countries – No Worldwide Exhaustion Principle.
The exhaustion principle based on the free movement *between* member states applies only to products marketed by the right-holder or with its consent in one of the EC or EEA countries. The provisions contained in the EFTA Agreement and in the more recent European Agreements concluded with certain East-European countries, although drafted in the same way, do not have the same legal quality of directly applicable law with regard to the exercise of industrial and commercial property rights. Therefore, the exhaustion principle does not apply with respect to these countries even if the product was marketed there by the right-holder or

90. *Deutsche Grammophon,* ECJ June 8, 1971, 1971 ECR 487, para. 13; *Membran and K'tel/GEMA,* ECJ Jan. 20, 1981, 1981 ECR 147, para. 21; *Dansk Supermarked,* ECJ Jan. 22, 1981, 1981 ECR 181, para. 12. *See* Article 5 (5) of Council Directive on the Legal Protection of Topographies of Semiconductor Products, 1987 OJ L 24/36, and Article 4 (2) of Directive 2001/29/EC on the Harmonization of Certain Aspects of Copyright and Related Rights in the Information Society, 2001 OJ L 167/10.
91. *Coditel II,* ECJ Oct. 6, 1982, 1982 ECR 3381, paras 14–19; *M6, Antena 3, Gestévision, SIC/UER, (Eurovision II),* CFI Oct. 8, 2002, 2002 ECR II-3805, para. 64.
92. Article 2 of Protocol 28, 1994 OJ L 1/194.
93. Switzerland, although a contracting party, did not join the EEA, being however party to the EFTA agreement.
94. *See Maglite,* EFTA Court of Justice, Dec. 3, 1997, E-2/97, 1998 CMLR 331.

with its consent.[95] The EC Treaty and the EEA Agreement do not provide for a worldwide exhaustion principle.[96]

However, if the products are imported *from third countries,* the free movement provisions apply only once the products are in free circulation within the EU (Article 23 (2) of the EU Treaty),[97] i.e. after having being put on the market therein by the right-holder or with its consent. This was confirmed by the Court of Justice in the *Phytheron International/Jean Bourdon* case.[98] This case concerned the importation into Germany of a plant health product from Turkey with the consent of the right-holder and later exported to France *without* the consent of the right-holder. The Court of Justice confirmed that Article 7 of the trademark directive which regulates the exhaustion of trademark rights must be interpreted in the light of Articles 28 and 30 as precluding the application of national trademark rights in member state A to oppose importation of a product protected by the mark

> 'where
> – the product has been manufactured in a non-member country,
> – it has been imported into member state B by the owner or by another company in the same group as the owner of the mark,
> – it has been lawfully acquired in the member state B by an independent trader, who has exported it to member state A,
> – it has not been processed and the packaging has not been changed, apart from the addition to the label of certain information to comply with the requirements of the legislation of the member state of import, and
> – the trademark rights are held in member states A and B by the same group'.[99]

95. *Polydor,* ECJ Feb. 9, 1982, 1982 ECR 329, paras 14–22 (concerning imports from Portugal, in those days still an EFTA country). But *see EMI/CBS,* ECJ June 15, 1976, 1976 ECR 811, para 10, where a partitioning of markets between the Community and a third country has been held contrary to Article 81.
96. Article 13 of Regulation 40/96 on the Community Trademark expressly provides for an exhaustion principle limited to EC and EEA countries abandoning the originally proposed principle of worldwide exhaustion. The same applies to the co-existing national trademark laws, which have been harmonized on the lines of Article 7 of the First Directive to approximate national trademark laws, which corresponds to Article 13 of Regulation 40/94. However, other countries (including EFTA countries such as Switzerland) are not prevented from applying a worldwide exhaustion principle under their national law: *see,* under Swiss law, *Philips* and *OMO,* Swiss Federal Court. BGE 86 II, 279 and BGE 105 II, 53, confirmed more recently in *Chanel,* First Civil Court of Geneva, Oct. 23, 1996, *Markenschutz* No. 85 p. 468.
97. *Donckerwolke,* ECJ Dec. 15, 1976, 1976 ECR 1921, paras 14–18; *see also Taboullot,* ECJ Dec. 18, 1997; 1997 ECR I-7471, para. 21 (inapplicability of Article 90 to products directly imported from non-member countries).
98. *Phytheron International/Jean Bourdon,* ECJ March 20, 1997, 1997 ECR I-1729.
99. *Ibid.,* para. 24.

This ruling was confirmed by the Court of Justice in the *Silhouette* case,[100] which concerned the importation of discontinued-style spectacle-frames that had been originally sold by the Austrian right-owner to a distributor in Bulgaria with an express export prohibition but which were reimported by an Austrian dealer. The Court of Justice ruled that Article 7 of the First Trademark Directive, as amended by the EEA Agreement, does not provide for a complete harmonization of the national trademark laws, does not consider national trademark rights exhausted when the trademarked products have been put on the market outside the EC and the EEA and, consequently, does not oppose the use of the trademark rights for halting these imports (no worldwide exhaustion principle).

Exception in the Case the Right-Holder Expressly or Implicitly Consents to Third Country Imports within the EEA.

In the *Zino Davidoff* case[101] which concerned the import into the UK of goods (Levi Strauss jeans) previously placed on the market outside the EEA and opposed by the proprietor of trademarks in the UK, the Court of Justice held:

> '1. … the consent of a trade mark proprietor to the marketing within the European Economic Area of products bearing that mark which have been previously placed on the market outside European Economic Area by that proprietor or with his consent may be implied, where it follows from facts and circumstances prior to, simultaneous with or subsequent to the placing of the goods on the market outside the European Economic Area which … unequivocably demonstrate that the proprietor has renounced his right to oppose placing of the goods on the market within the European Economic Area.
>
> '2. Implied consent cannot be inferred:
> – from the fact that the proprietor of the trade mark has not communicated to all subsequent purchasers of the goods placed on the market outside the European Economic Area his opposition to marketing within the European Economic Area;
> – from the fact that goods carry no warning of a prohibition of their being placed on the market within the European Economic Area;
> – from the fact that the trade mark proprietor has transferred the ownership of the products bearing the trade mark without imposing any contractual reservations and that, according to the law governing the contract, the property right transferred includes, in the absence of such reservations, an unlimited right of resale or, at the very least, a right to market the goods subsequently within the European Economic Area.

100. *Silhouette,* ECJ July 18, 1998, 1998 ECR I-4799, paras 25–29. *See also Sebago/GB Unic,* ECJ July 1, 1999, 1999 ECR I-4103, paras 16–17.
101. *Zino Davidoff,* ECJ Nov. 20, 2001, 2001 ECR I-8691.

'3. With regard to exhaustion of the trade mark proprietor's exclusive right, it is not relevant:
   – that the importer of goods bearing the trade mark is not aware that the proprietor objects to their being placed on the market in the European Economic Area or sold there by traders other than authorised retailers, or
   – that the authorised retailers and wholesalers have not imposed on their own purchasers contractual reservations setting out such opposition, even though they have been informed of it by the trade mark proprietor.'[102]

This judgment may be interpreted as not precluding *automatically* the exhaustion doctrine in the case of goods placed on the market outside the EEA.[103] However, the consent may not be inferred from the mere silence of the right-holder or the absence of express clauses or warnings. Normally, the consent must be expressly stated and may be implied only 'in some cases', which will be rather exceptional.[104] In the case submitted to the Court of Justice the national court decided that there was no such consent.[105]

Burden of Proof.
In the *Van Doren + Q v. Lifestyle sports* case,[106] which concerned the import in Germany of clothing manufactured in the U.S. of which Van Doren was the exclusive distributor in Germany, the Court of Justice refers to its *Zino Davidoff* judgment by stating that the conditions of exhaustion must, as a rule, be proved by the third party who relies on it. However, the Court qualifies this rule of evidence by ruling that if the third party were required to adduce evidence of the place where the products were first put on the market by the trademark proprietor or with his consent, the trademark proprietor could obstruct the marketing of the goods purchased and prevent the third party from obtaining supplies in future from a member of the exclusive distribution network of the proprietor in the EEA. Accordingly, where there is a real risk of market partitioning contrary to Articles 28 and 30, it is first for the proprietor to prove that the goods in question were initially marketed outside the EEA by him or with his consent (and *not* first put on the market within the EEA), and if such evidence is adduced, it is for the third party to prove the consent of the trademark proprietor to subsequent marketing of the goods inside the EEA.[107]

---

102. *Ibid.*, paras. 60 and 66.
103. *See also Maglite Mag Instrument California Trading,* EFTA Court of Justice Dec. 3, 1997, E-2/97; 1998–1 ELR 2.
104. *Zinc Davidoff*, ECJ Nov. 20, 2001, 2001 ECR I-8691.
105. *Levi Strauss v. Tesco Stores,* England and Wales High Court (Chancery Division), July 31, 2002, 2000 EWHC 1556 (Ch). *See also Nintendo,* D.Comm. Oct. 30, 2002, 2003 OJ L 255/33, point 62 and fn. 52.
106. *Van Doren + Q v. Lifestyle sports,* ECJ April 8, 2003, C-244/00.
107. *Ibid.*, paras 25–42. In general, a dealer will be readily able to show from whom he has purchased goods but he will not be able to make his suppliers reveal the previous supplier or

Exception in the Case of International Agreements.
The Court of Justice does not preclude the possibility of the Community authorities extending the exhaustion doctrine to products put on the market in non-member countries by entering into international agreements.[108] This may apply to countries covered by the TRIPs Agreement (Trade-Related Aspects of Intellectual Property Rights).[109] However, the provisions of TRIPs do *not* as such create a private right of action upon which individuals may rely directly before courts by virtue of Community law, [110] e.g. in order to invoke the exhaustion of industrial or intellectual property rights.

3. General Modalities of the Exhaustion Principle

'Consent' of the Right-Holder.
The judgments establishing the exhaustion principle concerned cases where an independent party effected parallel imports of products which had been marketed lawfully in another member state or in an EEA country by the right-holder or with its 'consent'. The right-holder may have consented directly or indirectly but the consent must be 'unequivocally' demonstrated, in particular in cases where goods have been imported from third countries and where the application of the exhaustion doctrine depends on whether the imported goods were subsequently put on the market *inside* the EEA with the consent of the right-holder.[111] In the absence of a consent the right-holder remains entitled to prevent all third parties from importing the protected goods.[112]

---

identify other links in the distribution chain, and even if he were able to trace the distribution chain back to the trademark proprietor, his supply source would be liable to dry up immediately: *ibid.*, para. 21, as demonstrated in *Nintendo,* D.Comm. Oct. 30, 2002, 2003 OJ L 255/33, points 276–277.

108. *Silhouette,* ECJ July 18, 1998, 1998 ECR I-4799, para. 30.
109. Annexed to the agreement establishing the World Trade Organization, signed in Marrakech on April 15, 1994 concerning the conclusion on behalf of the European Community, as regards matters within its competence, of the agreements reached in the Uruguay Round multilateral negotiations (1986–1994), 1994 OJ L 336/1, 213. *See* D.Comm. Dec. 11, 1998, 1998 OJ L 346/60, stating that the amended section 110 (5) of the U.S. Copyright Act authorizing public communications of musical works to the detriment of Community copyright-holders constitutes an obstacle of trade contrary to the TRIPs agreement.
110. *Dior, Tuk Consultancy,* ECJ Dec. 14, 2000, 2000 ECR I-11307, para. 44.
111. *Zino Davidoff,* ECJ Nov. 20, 2001, 2001 ECR I-8691, para. 47. The judgment concerned a preliminary question of a national court, which subsequently decided that the owner of the Levi Strauss trademark was entitled to use its rights to halt imports which had *not* been marketed within the EU with its 'unequivocal' consent.
112. E.g. with respect to trademarks Articles 5 and 7 of First Council Directive 89/104/EC to Approximate the Laws of the Member States Relating to Trademarks and *Silhouette,* ECJ July 16, 1998, 1998 ECR I-4799, paras 25 and 29*; Zino Davidoff,* ECJ Nov. 20, 2001, 2001 ECR I-8691, para. 39.

Exhaustion in Case of Marketing by the Right-holder or by Enterprises Belonging to the Right-holder's Group of Companies.
Industrial property rights are also exhausted once the products have been put on the market by the right-holder itself or by a company belonging to the same group which comprises the parent companies and affiliate companies under the control of a single enterprise or under the joint control of different enterprises, provided the companies form one single economic unit and are incapable of acting independently.[113] Whether this control is in fact exercised or not is not important; only the possibility of control need be shown.[114] The exhaustion principle does not apply in relation to companies which were once under joint control but have become economically independent, unless the right-holder consents to the exploitation, such as by the grant of a licence.[115]

Exhaustion in Case of Direct Imports by the Right-holder or by its Licensee – Relevance of Licence Terms.
A licence granted without any limitation includes the licensor's consent to the marketing of the licensed products by the licensee. The question arises whether the licensor is entitled to limit the licence to a certain territory with the consequence that the licensee is contractually prohibited from marketing the product outside that territory; in doing so the licensee would act without the 'consent' of the right-holder. The Community conventions and regulations establishing a new Community industrial and intellectual property right entitle the proprietor to grant licences limited to a certain territory and to invoke its rights against a licensee who contravenes contractual provisions with regard to the territory where the right may be used. For instance, Article 22 of the Community Trademark Regulation provides:

> '(1) A Community trademark may be licensed … for the whole or part of the Community. A license may be exclusive or non-exclusive.
> (2) The proprietor of a Community trademark may invoke the rights conferred by that trademark against a licensee who contravenes any provision in his licensing contract with regard to … the territory in which the trademark may be affixed …'.[116]

---

113. *Centrafarm/Sterling Drug,* ECJ Oct. 31, 1974, 1974 ECR 1147, paras 10–12; *Phyteron International/Jean Bourdon,* ECJ March 20, 1997, 1997 ECR I-1729, para. 24. With regard to the definition of 'control' *see* Commission Notice on the Concept of Undertakings Concerned, 1998 OJ C 66/14.
114. *Ideal Standard,* ECJ June 22, 1994, 1994 ECR I-2789, para. 34.
115. *Hag II,* ECJ, Oct. 17, 1990, 1990 ECR I-3711, para. 34; *Ideal Standard,* ECJ June 22, 1994, 1994 ECR I-2789, paras 40–60.
116. *See also* Article 19 of the proposal for a Community Patent Regulation, Article 15 of Directive 98/71 on the Legal Protection of Designs, Article 22 of Regulation 40/94 on the Community Trademark, and Article 27 of Regulation 2100/94 on the Community Plant Variety Rights.

However, the regulations and directives cannot override the rules of Article 28 and 49 on the free movement of goods and services[117] nor the competition rules of the EC Treaty.[118] Thus, the limits imposed on the licensee by the right-holder must be compatible with these rules. It follows:

– that a license which is exclusive or limited to a certain territory may be restrictive of competition, unless it is strictly necessary to the dissimination of a new technology,[119] and needs clearance under Article 81 (3), which is granted by the new technology transfer regulation, provided the parties' market share does not exceed the threshold of the regulation (20% if the parties are competitors, 30% if they are non-competitors);
– that the right-holder normally cannot prevent passive exports by the licensee itself, and
– that the right-holder cannot prevent parallel imports of goods which have been marketed in another member state by itself or with its consent (exhaustion principle).

Exhaustion in Case of Lack of Parallel Protection.
A product which has been put on the market by the right-holder or with its consent must circulate freely in countries where the right-holder does not enjoy corresponding ('*parallel*') protection; in the absence of parallel protection such circulation cannot be prevented because it would cause a partitioning of national markets contrary to the aims of the Treaty. If the product has been put on the market in a country without parallel protection and is exported to a protected country the application of the exhaustion principle depends on whether or not the product has been marketed in that market, notwithstanding the lack of parallel protection, by the licensor itself or by its consent, in particular under a know-how agreement.[120]

117. *Bristol Myers Squibb/Paranova,* ECJ July 11, 1996, 1996 ECR I-3457, paras 36–37; *Phyteron International/Jean Bourdon,* ECJ March 20, 1997, 1997 ECR I-1729, para. 19. However, in these cases the Court of Justice referred to Article 13 of the Community trademark regulation which defines the principle of exhaustion in case of 'consent' and certain exceptions, but not to Article 22 which provides for territorial licences which might limit such consent in case of direct exports.
118. *See* Recital 13 of Council Regulation 6/2002 on the European Community Design, which reserves, in general terms, the applicability of Article 81.
119. *Maize Seed,* ECJ June 8, 1982, 1982 ECR 2015, para. 57.
120. *Merck/Stephar,* ECJ July 14, 1981, 1981 ECR 2063; reconfirmed in *Merck/Primecrown,* ECJ Dec 5, 1996, 1996 ECR I-6285, paras 32, 41 and 48–54 (concerning the import of a pharmaceutical product from Spain where the product was put on the market after the accession, but before it could be protected by a patent).

Irrelevance of Differences in Quality or Composition.
The exhaustion principle applies even if the licensed product is manufactured and marketed, under the control and with the consent of the right-holder, in different qualities, whether with the intention to separate markets ('artificial partitioning of markets') or in order to adapt the products to the particularities of the national demand (i.e. taste of coffee or chocolate). Provided that the differences do not basically alter the product and do not result in consumer confusion,[121] it does not matter whether the control is in fact exercised or not; the single market principle of Articles 28 and 30 obliges the right-holder to bear the consequences of its choice.[122] This applies where a medicinal product has been placed on the market in different versions even if the right-holder withdraws the marketing authorization (granted in accordance with Directive 65/65[123] and implying a parallel import licence [124]), unless it is demonstrated that the coexistence of the two versions constitute a risk to public health.[125] This also applies when the products are manufactured in different member states by different companies of the same group according to a uniform formula and show a 'common origin'.[126] If the products are manufactured by different licensees, the licensor may include contractual obligations to guarantee the quality of the goods or services to be provided by the different licensees.[127] If, however, the condition of the products has been impaired after having been put on the market (e.g. by a parallel importer) the right-holder is entitled to use its right to prohibit marketing of the impaired products.[128]

Exhaustion in Case of Government Regulations in State of Export or Import.
The exhaustion principle applies even in the case of price regulation in the member state of export, which is common in the case of pharmaceutical products. Although such price regulations may, in certain conditions, distort competition between member states, they 'cannot justify the maintenance or introduction by another member state of measures which are incompatible with the rules gov-

121. Confusion of consumers with 'a normal degree of attentiveness' can be prevented by the appropriate information: *De Pijper* (*Centrafarm*), ECJ May 20, 1976, 1976 ECR 613, para. 36; *Bristol Myers Squibb/Paranova,* ECJ July 11, 1996, 1996 ECR I-3457, para. 47; *Kessler,* ECJ Jan. 28, 1999, 1999 ECR I-513, para. 36.
122. *Ideal Standard,* ECJ June 22, 1994, 1994 ECR 2789, paras 34–38, 45; *Bristol Myers Squibb/Paranova,* ECJ July 11, 1996, 1996 ECR I-3457, para. 43.
123. Amended by Council Directive 93/39/EC, 1993 OJ L 214/22.
124. *Ferring/Eurim Pharm,* ECJ Sept. 10, 2002, 2002 ECR I-6891, para. 26.
125. *Ibid.,* paras 33–38; *Paranova,* ECJ May 8, 2003, C-15/01, paras. 22–28. In these cases the various versions of the medicinal products did not differ in quality, efficacity nor non-toxicity. *See Sandoz,* ECJ July 14, 1983, 1983 ECR 2445, para. 18.
126. *Smith & Nephew and Primecrown,* ECJ Nov. 12, 1996, 1996 ECR I-5819, paras 23–24.
127. Article 22 (2) of Council Regulation 40/94 on the Community Trademark.
128. *See* Article 7 (2) of the First Directive on Approximating the Laws of the Member States Relating to Trademarks; *Dior/Evora,* ECJ Nov. 4, 1997, 1997 ECR I-6013, paras 48–55.

erning the free movement of goods, in particular in the field of industrial and commercial property'.[129]

Summary.
The scope of the protection afforded to industrial property rights differs according to the nature of the right and is subject to variations in national law, but never goes so far as to confer the exclusive right to market goods up to the final stage of distribution. Under Community law, the existence – i.e., the ability to serve its essential functions – of the industrial property right may not be prejudiced, but its exercise is subject to the rules on the free movement of goods (Articles 28 and 30) and services (Articles 49 and 50) and on competition (Articles 81 and 82). The holder of an industrial property right ordinarily has the right to bring an infringement action against unauthorized sales of the product in the member state that granted the industrial property right. However, this right is lost when the industrial property right is 'exhausted', namely whenever the protected product or service has been marketed in another member state or any EEA country by the holder of the industrial property right itself or with its consent, i.e., by a licensee or assignee or by a person legally or economically dependent on the right-holder, in full conformity with that state's industrial property laws.[130]

Plan of the Following Sections.
The following sections of this chapter deal in further detail with the concepts introduced above. Section C below addresses the scope and limits of the exercise of various industrial and intellectual property rights according to their specific subject-matter under the rules on free movement of goods and services, namely, Articles 28, 30 and 49. Sections D, E and F below address the limits placed on the exercise of industrial property rights by the competition rules, Articles 81 and 82.

C. Limits on the Exercise of Industrial Property Rights under Articles 28 and 49 According to their Specific Subject Matter

Introduction.
The specific subject matter of the relevant industrial property right determines the scope of the right whose existence may not be prejudiced by the Treaty. The

129. *Centrafarm/Sterling Drug,* ECJ Oct. 31, 1974, 1974 ECR 1147, para. 24; *Musik Membran and K'tel/GEMA,* ECJ Jan. 20, 1981, 1981 ECR 147, para. 24; *Bristol-Myers Squibb* (*Paranova*), ECJ July 11, 1996, 1996 ECR I-3457, para. 46; *Merck Stephar/Primecrown,* ECJ Dec. 5, 1996, 1996 ECR I-6285, para. 47.

130. *Keurkoop/Nancy Kean Gifts,* ECJ Sept. 14, 1982, 1982 ECR 2853, para. 25; *Hag II,* ECJ Oct. 17, 1990, 1990 ECR 3711, para. 15; *see also* Advocate General Jacobs in *Hag II,* para. 63.

specific subject matter is therefore the test for the right that is 'exhausted' upon the first marketing of the relevant product or service by the right-holder or with its consent. It is also a measure for the justification of restrictions that are necessary to preserve the essence of the exclusive rights under the rules on free movement of goods and services found in Articles 28, 30 and 49. Since the specific subject matter differs for various industrial property rights, the categories of restrictions that are justified to protect the essence of the rights also varies.

1. Patents

(a) Specific Subject Matter

The Basic Right.
In *Centrafarm/Sterling Drug* the Court of Justice described the specific subject matter of a patent as follows:

> '[T]he guarantee that the patentee, to reward the creative effort of the inventor, has the exclusive right to use an invention with a view to manufacturing industrial products and putting them into circulation for the first time, either directly or by the grant of licences to third parties, as well as the right to oppose infringements'.[131]

Enforcement of rights of exclusivity against goods produced or marketed without the consent of the patentee is the essence of patent law. The key issue is therefore whether the patentee has directly or indirectly (itself or by an authorized person) given its consent leading to the exhaustion of the patent rights within the EEA-area. The same principle should apply for medicinal products which are no longer patented but protected by a certificate according to Council Regulation 1768/92 ('*Supplementary Protection Certificate for Medicinal Products*') and which are placed on the market by the owner of such certificate or with its consent.[132]

131. *Centrafarm/Sterling Drug,* ECJ Oct. 31, 1974, 1974 ECR 1147, para. 9; *see also Merck/Stephar,* ECJ July 14, 1981, 1981 ECR 2063, paras 9–10; *Allen and Hanburys,* ECJ March 3, 1988, 1988 ECR 1245, para. 11.
132. 1992 OJ L 182/1. *See Biogen/Smithkline,* ECJ Jan. 23, 1997, 1997 ECR I-357; *Yamanouchi,* ECJ June 12, 1997, 1997 ECR I-3251.

(b) Use of the Same Patents by the Owner or its Licensees

Exhaustion.
The *Centrafarm/Sterling Drug* case[133] established the principle that patent rights cannot be used to prevent the importation of goods which have been marketed by the patentee or with its consent in another member state (now also extended to EEA countries). However, what is consent? The patent is exhausted by:

- marketing or sale of the patented product by the patentee or through its subsidiary or affiliate,[134] or
- licence of the patented technology to a licensee.[135]

However, patent rights may be asserted to prevent the importation of goods which have been manufactured in another member state on the basis of a *parallel* invention patented by a legally and economically independent owner; no consent can be assumed in such a case.[136]

Compulsory Licence in State of Export – No Consent.
The Court stated in the *Pharmon/Hoechst* case[137] that a patentee may exercise its patent rights to prevent importation of products originating from a country where a compulsory licence has been granted since the patentee did not consent to the compulsory licence, and thus the patent right had not been 'exhausted'. Hoechst held parallel patents on a manufacturing process for the drug 'frusemide' in Germany, the Netherlands and the United Kingdom. A company located in the United Kingdom had obtained a compulsory licence to produce the drug and sold 'frusemide' tablets to Pharmon, which imported them to the Netherlands. Hoechst sued for patent infringement in the Netherlands. Pharmon argued that when Hoechst applied for a parallel patent in the United Kingdom it must accept the entire body of British legislation, including the possibility that a compulsory licence may be granted. The Court of Justice rejected Pharmon's arguments and ruled that the patentee cannot be deemed to have consented to a compulsory licence which allows a third party to carry out manufacturing and marketing operations which the

133. *Centrafarm/Sterling Drug,* ECJ Oct. 31, 1974, 1974 ECR 1147, paras 8–11.
134. *Ibid.,* paras 19–20; *Phyteron International/Jean Bourdon,* ECJ March 20, 1997, 1997 ECR I-1729, para. 24.
135. *Centrafarm/Sterling Drug,* ECJ Oct. 31, 1974, 1974 ECR 1147, paras 10–12. Assigning patent rights in one member state may be tantamount to a licence, in particular when the risk associated with the exploitation remains with the assignor: Advocate General Jacobs in *Hag II,* ECJ Oct. 17, 1990, 1990 ECR 3711, para. 63.
136. *Centrafarm/Sterling Drug,* ECJ Oct. 31, 1974, 1974 ECR 1147, paras 11, 13–14.
137. *Pharmon/Hoechst,* ECJ July 9, 1985, 1985 ECR 2281, paras 25–26; *see also Thetford/Fiamma,* ECJ June 30, 1988, 1988 ECR 3585, para. 24, and *Merck/Primecrown,* ECJ Dec. 5, 1996, 1996 ECR I-6285, para. 41.

patentee would normally have the right to prevent.[138] However, what would happen in the reverse situation, namely if the British compulsory licensee had wished to assert its patent rights to prevent importation into the UK of Hoechst's product from the Netherlands or Germany? The answer is not clear since there are no decided cases. However, it is arguable that the British compulsory licensee would not be able to prevent importation into the United Kingdom of Hoechst's products from the Netherlands or Germany. Otherwise, one would have the perverse result that a compulsory licensee would in many cases be in a better position than a firm to which the patentee had licensed the patent voluntarily, in that it would enjoy automatic territorial exclusivity. Furthermore, the argument that the parties had accepted the implications of the UK compulsory licensing regime in the form of lack of protection from possible imports might well hold as against the beneficiary of the system, the compulsory licensee, although the Court rejected it in relation to the original patentee.[139]

Licence of Right in State of Importation – No Prevention of Imports through Licence Terms – Consent Irrelevant.

In the *Allen and Hanburys*[140] case, the holder of a UK patent for a pharmaceutical product that was subject to 'licences of right' (the grant of a licence on demand) asserted a 'no-imports' condition on such licences under UK legislation against a UK importer desiring to import the same product manufactured in Italy by a firm having no financial or contractual links with Allen and Hanburys. The Court of Justice noted:

> 'that in the United Kingdom, in contrast to the proprietor of an ordinary patent, the proprietor of a patent endorsed "licences of right" cannot oppose the grant of such a licence to a third party who applies for a licence in order to manufacture and market the product in question in that Member State but he retains the right merely to obtain a fair return.
>
> In those circumstances it must be considered that the power of national courts to prohibit the importation of the product in question may be justified

138. This case concerned *direct* exports by the compulsory licensee. Therefore, it is still an open question whether the right-holder should not be entitled to oppose *parallel* imports of products which have been put on the market within the compulsory licensee's territory with its consent.

139. *See* Article 45 of the Community Patent Convention which excludes the applicability of the exhaustion principle (Article 28) with respect to imports of products marketed by a compulsory licensee. A compulsory licence is to be distinguished from a sequestration (expropriation) of rights where the common origin between the former and the new owner is definitively severed and a risk of consumer confusion exists, as the Court of Justice stated in the *Hag II* case, ECJ Oct. 17, 1990, 1990 ECR 3711, paras 15–19.

140. *Allen and Hanburys,* ECJ March 3, 1988, 1988 ECR 1245, paras 13–23. *See* Joliet, 'Geistiges Eigentum und freier Warenverkehr', 1989 GRUR Int. 177, 180.

under the provisions of Article 36 [*now 30*] on the protection of industrial and commercial property only if that prohibition is necessary in order to ensure that the proprietor of such a patent has, vis-à-vis importers, the same rights as he enjoys as against producers who manufacture the product in the national territory, that is to say the right to a fair return from his patent'.[141]

The fact was, however, that patentees had greater rights against importers than against domestic manufacturers because importers could be barred from obtaining licences of right. Because of this 'arbitrary discrimination' the Court concluded that Articles 28 and 30 do not allow the courts of a member state to issue an injunction prohibiting the importation from another member state of a product which infringes a patent endorsed 'licences of right' against an importer who has undertaken to take a licence on the terms prescribed by law, where no such injunction could be issued in the same circumstances against an infringer who manufactures the product in the national territory.[142]

(c) Lack of Parallel Protection in Different Member States

Lack of Protection in State of Export.
The fact that the relevant product may not benefit or no longer benefits from a parallel industrial property right in the member state in which it first entered the channels of trade is irrelevant as long as it was first marketed there by the holder of the industrial property right or with its consent, such as in the form of a know-how licence. On the other hand, imported products of a manufacturer operating without the consent of the right-holder in a country in which no parallel industrial property right may be obtained may properly be the subject of an infringement action.[143]

Consent to Marketing Notwithstanding Lack of Protection in State of Export – The *Merck I* Case.
The *Merck/Stephar* case[144] concerned parallel imports into the Netherlands of a hypertension drug for which Merck held Dutch patents. The imports originated from Italy, where Merck marketed the same drug without patent protection because Italian patent law prohibited the grant of patents for drugs. The Court of Justice decided that these parallel imports into the Netherlands were protected under the 'exhaustion' doctrine. The Court held:

---

141. *Allen and Hanburys,* ECJ March 3, 1988, 1988 ECR 1245, paras 13–14.
142. The grant of a compulsory licence itself may be scrutinized under Articles 28 and 30: *Commission/UK and Northern Ireland,* ECJ Feb. 18, 1992, 1992 ECR I-829; *Generics, Harris/Smith Kline,* ECJ Oct. 27, 1992, 1992 ECR 5335. *See* Article 29 of Council Regulation on Community Plant Variety Rights, 1994 OJ L 227/1.
143. *Centrafarm/Sterling Drug,* ECJ Oct. 31, 1974, 1974 ECR 1147, paras 10–12.
144. *Merck/Stephar,* ECJ July 14, 1981, 1981 ECR 2063.

'... the substance of a patent right lies essentially in according the inventor an exclusive right of first placing the product on the market.

That right of first placing a product on the market enables the inventor, by allowing him a monopoly in exploiting his product, to obtain the reward for his creative effort without, however, guaranteeing that he will obtain such a reward in all circumstances.

It is for the proprietor of the patent to decide, in the light of all the circumstances, under what conditions he will market his product, including the possibility of marketing it in a Member State where the law does not provide patent protection for the product in question. If he decides to do so he must then accept the consequences of his choice as regards the free movement of the product within the Common Market, which is a fundamental principle forming part of the legal and economic circumstances which must be taken into account by the proprietor of the patent in determining the manner in which his exclusive right will be exercised ...

Under those conditions to permit an inventor, or one claiming under him, to invoke a patent held by him in one Member State in order to prevent the importation of the product freely marketed by him in another Member State where that product is not patentable would bring about a partitioning of the national markets which would be contrary to the aims of the Treaty.'[145]

Confirmation in the *Merck II* Case.

In the *Merck II* case the Court of Justice confirmed this conclusion.[146] The case concerned very similar facts, namely the question whether Articles 28 and 30 preclude the exercise, by Merck, of its patent rights in one member state in order to prevent the importation of pharmaceutical products which had been marketed in Spain and Portugal with its consent but at a time when patent protection was not available. Spain and Portugal were obliged under the Act of Accession[147] to provide for patent protection for pharmaceutical and chemical products. After several years of delay both countries complied with these obligations. However, patent protection was not retroactively available for products which were already on the market and therefore failed to meet the novelty requirement. The Advocate General suggested overruling the *Merck I* position, arguing that consent to marketing can be relevant only where it is accompanied by an exclusive patent right and effective patent protection; otherwise the patent holder would be prevented

145. *Merck/Stephar,* ECJ July 14, 1981, 1981 ECR 2063, paras 9–13. The Court issued this ruling despite the fact that the Italian Constitutional Court had declared the prohibition against patentability of drugs under the Italian Patent Law as unconstitutional. Merck had attempted to obtain an Italian patent after this ruling but was precluded from doing so because the product no longer fulfilled the condition of novelty for obtaining a patent. *See also Allen and Hanburys,* ECJ March 3, 1988, 1988 ECR 1245, para. 31.

146. *Merck/Primecrown,* ECJ Dec. 5, 1996, 1996 ECR I-6285.

147. Articles 49 and 209 respectively.

from receiving its monopoly reward by virtue of low-priced imports.[148] The Court of Justice refused to follow the Advocate General's opinion repeating that, unlike compulsory licences preventing the right-holder from freely consenting to the marketing,[149] a proprietor who decides to market the products in a country without patent protection has to bear the consequences of its choice as regards the free movement of goods within the Common Market.[150] With this judgment the Court of Justice maintained its market integration concept in order to avoid any artificial partitioning of the Common Market. Consent is irrelevant only where the patent holder is under a genuine, legal (not only ethical) obligation to market the product.[151]

Unauthorized Manufacture in State without Patent Protection – The *Thetford/Fiamma* Case.

The *Thetford/Fiamma* case[152] concerned a patent in one member state for an invention (a portable toilet) that appeared in a patent specification filed more than 50 years previously but was too old to be eligible for patent protection in a second member state, where an *unauthorized* manufacturer undertook production without consent of the patentee. Referring back to *Parke Davis*,[153] the Court of Justice concluded that in the present state of Community law the patentability of inventions was a matter solely for national law. Consequently, a patentee could enforce its patent rights against importation of infringing products marketed without its consent in another member state where patent protection was not available.[154]

---

148. The Advocate General tends to deny 'the discipline of the Common Market where it does not in fact exist', 1996 ECR I-6285, para. 111, following the study of Remit Consultants, sponsored by the Commission, on the impediments to parallel trade in Pharmaceuticals within the European Community (1991), para. 84.
149. As in the case *Pharmon/Hoechst,* ECJ July 9, 1985, 1985 ECR 2281, para. 25; *Merck/Primecrown,* ECJ Dec. 5, 1996 ECR I-6285, para. 41.
150. *Merck/Primecrown,* ECJ Dec. 5, 1996, 1996 ECR I-6285, para. 36.
151. *Ibid.,* paras 48–54.
152. *Thetford/Fiamma,* ECJ June 30, 1988, 1988 ECR 3585, paras 11–15, 24.
153. *Parke Davis,* ECJ Feb. 29, 1968, 1968 ECR 55, 71, 72. However, this case failed to address the issue of whether Parke Davis had consented to manufacture in Italy on the basis of a know-how licence.
154. In *EMI/Patricia,* a case concerning only copyright law, the Court of Justice found that the owner of a copyright in one member state was entitled to assert its exclusive rights to prevent imports from another member state where the copyright protection had expired and consequently where the products had been put on the market by a third party without the consent of the copyright holder: *EMI/Patricia,* ECJ Jan. 24, 1989, 1989 ECR 79, paras 11–14.

(d) Price Control Regulations

Price Control Regulations in State of Export no Justification for Use of Patent Rights to Prevent Imports.

The principle of the free movement of goods applies even to the export of goods that is stimulated because price regulation in the exporting country keeps prices artificially low. Although the imposition of price controls may distort competition between member states and low-priced imports may affect the return of investments necessary for the research and development of new pharmaceutical products,[155] the presence of such regulations in one member state does not excuse or justify the adoption of countermeasures by the holder of the industrial property right or by other member states that are incompatible with the principle of the free movement of goods.[156] Under such circumstances, the Commission has a duty not only to enforce the competition rules, but also the task of either assuring that the regulatory measures are harmonized or prohibiting such measures as are contrary to Community law insofar as they may affect trade between member states and have as their object or effect the prevention, restriction or distortion of competition within the Community.[157] The same reasoning applies to quality or labelling regulations designed to protect the public against defective products. Member states may depart from the rules on the free movement of goods under Article 30 to protect health and life, but these regulations must be 'proportional' (reasonable). Every importer is obliged to observe national health regulations and to take measures that may be necessary in order to avoid defective products. However, once these health regulations are observed in one member state the products may circulate freely provided the importer is capable of demonstrating

155. A. Reindl, 'Intellectual Property and Intra-Community Trade', *Fordham International Law & Policy* (1996), pp. 453, 463–464.

156. *Merck/Primecrown,* ECJ Dec. 5, 1996, 1996 ECR I-6285, para. 47. Effective protection of health requires distribution of pharmaceuticals at the lowest prices possible: *De Pijper (Centrafarm),* ECJ May 20, 1976, 1976 ECR 613, para. 25. In *Deutscher Apothekerverband/Doc Morris* the Court of Justice ruled that national legislation fixing the prices for the sale of prescription medicinal products may be compatible with Articles 28 and 30 insofar as it forms an integral part of the national health system: 'it is not impossible that the risk of seriously undermining the financial balance of the social security system may constitute an overriding general-interest reason capable of justifying a restriction of that kind' (i.e. the resale price maintenance): CFI Dec. 11, 2003, C-322/01, para. 122. However, the national health system does not seem to be necessarily jeopardized if an identical product which is marketed in another member state with the consent of the rightholder is parallel imported in conformity with the exhaustion principle and resold at a lower price.

157. *Centrafarm/Sterling Drug,* ECJ Oct. 31, 1974, 1974 ECR 1147, paras 23–24; *Membran K'tel/GEMA,* ECJ Jan. 20, 1981, 1981 ECR 147, para. 24; *Bristol-Myers Squibb,* ECJ July 11, 1996, 1996 ECR I-3457, para. 46; *Merck/Primecrown,* ECJ Dec. 5, 1996, 1996 ECR I-6285, para. 47 (in this respect in accordance with the Advocate General's opinion). The regulatory measures may be contrary to Article 28 or to the second paragraph of Article 10 in combination with Article 81 or Article 86 (1) (*see Ahmed Saeed,* ECJ April 11, 1989, 1989 ECR 803, para. 48).

that the necessary approval has been obtained.[158] Furthermore, a licensee may not misuse such rules to retain control over the marketing of products that have once been marketed in the Community by it or with its consent.[159]

2. PLANT VARIETY RIGHTS

Specific Subject Matter.

Plant breeders' rights aim at protection and conservation of plant varieties. Council Regulation 2100/94 provides for the protection of varieties (plant groupings), provided they are distinct, uniform, stable and new.[160] The regulation establishes a system of Community-wide registration of 'Community plant variety rights'. Only the holder of plant breeders' rights may produce or sell seed of the protected variety for commercial purposes. The specific subject matter of the protected right is to subject to the breeder's prior authorization all acts relating to the production, reproduction (multiplication), conditioning, putting up for sale, marketing, export, import and stocking of the seeds of the protected variety.[161] Thus, the legal position of the holder of plant breeders' rights is basically similar to that of an owner of a patent.[162] However, the national legal position is influenced by Community legislation. Under Community directives seed cannot be marketed unless it has been officially examined and certified by a public agency in one of the member states. The directives distinguish between basic seed and certified seed. Basic seed is seed produced under the responsibility of the breeder and is intended for the production of certified seed. Certified seed is seed directly descended from basic seed and intended for purposes other than the production of seed, i.e., for direct or indirect sale to farmers for sowing. The directives ensure free movement within the Community of basic and certified seed which meet their requirements. Ordinarily no new registration procedure for seed approval in one member state may be imposed when the seed is imported into another member state.[163]

158. *Eurim Pharm I*, ECJ April 16, 1991, 1991 ECR 1747; *Eurim Pharm II*, ECJ July 1, 1993, 1993 ECR 3741.

159. *Centrafarm/Sterling Drug*, ECJ Oct. 31, 1974, 1974 ECR 1147, paras 26–29. Parallel imports may not be prevented by claiming copyrights on the summary of products characteristics accompanying patented pharmaceutical products: *Norway/Astra Norge*, EFTA Court of Justice, Nov. 24, 1998, 1998 EFTACR 140, para. 26.

160. Article 5 of Council Regulation 2100/94, 1994 OJ L 227/1.

161. *Sicasov*, D.Comm. Dec. 14, 1998, 1999 OJ L 4/27, point 49.

162. *Maize Seed*, ECJ June 8, 1982, 1982 ECR 2015, paras 40–43; *Hesbignonne*, ECJ April 19, 1988, 1988 ECR 1919, para. 10.

163. The Community directives, however, leave member states free for some species to allow two generations of seed descended from basic seed to be certified. In that case, first-generation certified seed can be used to produce second-generation certified seed in the same way as basic seed is used, and justifies close control of its use by the plant breeder. Consequently, holders of breeders' rights are allowed to impose contractual export prohibitions on licensees in respect of first-generation seed to countries that allow two or more generations. *Hesbignonne*, ECJ

Government Marketing Bodies.
A national law which reserves to persons affiliated to a governmental body or a regulated institution the right to market plant varieties, including to import and export, infringes Article 28. Such a law violates the principle of the free movement of goods because it hinders imports from other member states even if the product was first legally marketed there.[164]

Similar Treatment to Patents.
The rulings of the Court of Justice on the subject of plant breeders' rights in the *Maize Seed*[165] and *Hesbignonne* cases[166] lead to the conclusion that certified seeds marketed by or with the consent of the breeder within the Community are as fully subject to the exhaustion principle as patented goods.[167] The Court accepted, however, that a person who has made considerable efforts to develop varieties of basic seed which may be the subject of plant breeders' rights must be allowed to protect himself against any improper handling of the seed varieties and therefore to prohibit licensees who multiply (propagate) the seed from selling and exporting it.[168]

3. Utility Models

Specific Subject Matter.
A utility model, sometimes also referred to as a registered industrial design, aims at protecting technical inventions that may meet lower standards of inventiveness than for a patent.[169] Utility models are 'petty patents' and therefore justify a narrower scope of protection for a more limited period. In Germany, for instance, protection lasts for three years and may be extended for a further term of three years and for two further terms of two years each, making ten years in all. The specific subject matter is to confer a right of exclusivity employed in a manner very similar to patents.

April 19, 1988, 1988 ECR 1919 para. 10; *Comasso,* 1990 OJ C 6/3; 1990–4 CMLR 269; *Sicasov,* D.Comm. Dec. 14, 1998, 1999 OJ L 4/27, points 23 and 46.

164. *Vriend,* ECJ Feb. 26, 1980, 1980 ECR 327, para. 10.
165. *Maize Seed,* ECJ June 8, 1982, 1982 ECR 2015, paras 40–43.
166. *Hesbignonne,* ECJ April 19, 1988, 1988 ECR 1919, para. 10. Under Article 81, *Comasso,* 1990 OJ C 6/3. The exhaustion principle is included in Council Regulation 2100/94 on Community plant Variety Rights.
167. Including direct export activities of the right-holder or its licensee: Article 16 of Council Regulation ('disposed to others in any part of the Community').
168. *See also Sicasov,* D.Comm. Dec. 14, 1998, 1999 OJ L 4/27, points 50–51.
169. The requirements for the registration of utility models are not identical in those member states providing for such protection, some member states, in particular Germany and France, requiring the same level of inventiveness without, however, previous examination which explains the shorter duration.

Similar Treatment to Patents.
Although there is no Court of Justice ruling on the subject, utility models are probably subject to the same limitations under the free movement of goods principles as patents. Although the economic significance of industrial designs is undisputed,[170] little has been done so far to harmonize national laws most of which are in need of reform. The field of industrial design law has therefore rightly been called the 'orphan of industrial property protection'.[171]

4. Designs and Models

Specific Subject Matter.
New designs[172] and models that are duly registered enjoy protection against unauthorized copying or imitation for a limited period. If aesthetic or artistic features predominate, then the designs are protected in certain member states partly via special design registration laws and partly by copyright laws. If there are also technical features and these predominate, then protection may be conferred under utility model laws. But this protection does not in itself justify restrictions on trade between the member states once the goods have been lawfully marketed in one of them.[173]

Exhaustion: The *Keurkoop/Nancy Kean Gifts* Case.
This case[174] concerned the question of whether enforcement of rights under the newly adopted Uniform Benelux Law on Designs infringed Articles 28 and 30. An enforcement action was brought by the Dutch holder of a registered design for ladies' handbags, which it purchased from Taiwanese sources, against imports of the same design of handbag from other Taiwanese sources. The Benelux Law on Designs had certain peculiar characteristics: the exclusive right to a design was acquired by the first person to file and was in no way based on the presumption that the person filing the design was its author. The Court of Justice decided that the adoption of this new national law was not incompatible with Community law given the then current unharmonized state of Community law; the EC Treaty also allowed the introduction of new national laws on industrial property rights. Yet the limitations of Articles 28 and 30 still applied. The Court of Justice ruled that

170. Apart from a preliminary study by the European Industry-Designer Association on the question of necessity, commissioned by DG XIII in 1988.
171. Beier, 'Industrial Property and the Free Movement of Goods in the Internal European Market', 21–2 IIC 131, 133 (1990).
172. In Article 3 of Regulation 6/2002 on the European Community Design, 2002 OJ L 3/1 defined as 'the appearance of the whole or a part of a product resulting from the specific features of the lines, contours, colours, shape and/or materials of the product itself and/or its ornamentation' requiring novelty and an individual character (Articles 4–6).
173. *Dansk Supermarket*, ECJ Jan. 22, 1981, 1981 ECR 181, para. 12.
174. *Keurkoop/Nancy Kean Gifts,* ECJ Sept. 14, 1982, 1982 ECR 2853, paras 14–29.

the owner of the registered design may legally oppose importation of products of identical appearance to the registered design without infringing Articles 28 and 30, provided that:

- the products in issue were not marketed by, or with the consent of, the owner of the industrial property right or an affiliate,[175]
- there were no anticompetitive agreements or concerted practices among the parties[176] and
- the respective industrial property rights of the owners of the design in the various member states had been established independently one another.

Lack of Consent: The *Renault* Case.
In this case[177] the French automobile and truck manufacturer, Renault, exercised its rights in design of body panels for its vehicles under the Italian law on ornamental designs in order to prevent the manufacture or marketing in Italy, or export to other member states, of replacement panels produced by an Italian firm without Renault's consent. The Court of Justice confirmed that this exercise of industrial property rights under the Italian law on ornamental design did not infringe Article 28, but accepted the applicability of Article 82 in cases of arbitrary refusal of supply and unfair licence fees.

5. Copyrights

(a) Specific Subject Matter

The Basic Right.
A copyright confers rights similar to an industrial property right on the creator of an individual artistic and/or creative work of literature, music, science or applied art.[178] Although the scope of protection varies, a copyright prohibits unauthorized copying or other acts that compromise the integrity of the work and entitles the holder[179] to royalties for placing the work at disposal of the public. It is clear from the case law of the Court of Justice that the grounds of protection of industrial and

175. *See* also *Volvo/Veng*, ECJ Oct. 5, 1988, 1988 ECR 6211, paras 7–8.
176. An anticompetitive agreement was found in the *Industrial Design Foundation* case reported in the Fifth Report on Competition Policy, point 69.
177. *Renault*, ECJ Oct. 5, 1988, 1988 ECR 6039, para. 13. Similarly, *Volvo/Veng*, ECJ Oct. 5, 1988, 1988 ECR 6211, para. 8.
178. All EC member states belong to the Berne Convention for the Protection of Literary and Artistic Works (1886) as amended in 1979, published in *Copyright Laws and Treaties of the World*, compilation by UNESCO. *See* Melville B. Nimmer and Paul Edward Geller (eds.), *International Copyright Law and Practice* (2003) and esp. the section 'The Law of the EEC and Copyright' by H.C. Jehoram and Ch. Gielen.
179. Independently of his EC nationality (Article 17): *Phil Collins/Patricia*, ECJ Oct. 20, 1993, 1993 ECR I-5145.

commercial property referred to in Article 30 include the protection conferred by copyright. The Court of Justice stated in the *Metronome/Music Point* case:

> 'that the protection of literary and artistic property, which is a category of industrial and commercial property within the meaning of Article 36 [*now 30*] of the Treaty, constitutes a ground of general interest which may justify restrictions on the free movement of goods.'[180]

In the *Dior/Evora* case the Court of Justice ruled that:

> 'literary and artistic works may be the subject of commercial exploitation, whether by way of public performance or by way of the reproduction and marketing of the recordings made of them, and the two essential rights of the author, namely the exclusive right of performance and the exclusive right of reproduction, are not called in question by the rules of the Treaty.'[181]

Consequently, exercise of the copyright may only be restricted insofar as the restriction corresponds to objectives of general interest, which include the *social* function of the copyright, and do not constitute in relation to the aim pursued 'a disproportionate and intolerable interference, impairing the very substance of the rights guaranteed.'[182] Similarly, the use of copyrights is not *per se* abusive contrary to Article 82 but only under exceptional circumstances.[183]

Free Movement of Copyrighted Goods and Services.
The application of the free movement principles is necessarily different for copyrighted *goods,* such as books, records and video-cassettes which are placed at the disposal of the public in material form, than for copyrighted *services* or *intangibles,* such as the showing of a film which is made available to the public by performances which may be indefinitely repeated.[184]

(b) Copyrighted Goods

The Exhaustion Principle.
The Court of Justice stated in the *Deutsche Grammophon* case[185] that a copyright holder who exercises its copyright in such a way as to prohibit the sale in one

180. *Metronome Musik/Music Point Hokamp,* ECJ April 28, 1998, 1998 ECR I-1953, para. 23.
181. *Dior/Evora,* ECJ Nov. 4, 1997, 1997 ECR I-6013, para. 57. *See also Warner Brothers/Christiansen,* ECJ May 17, 1988, 1988 ECR 2605, para. 13.
182. *Metronome Musik/Music Point Hokamp,* ECJ April 28, 1998, 1998 ECR I-1953, para. 21.
183. *Micro Leader Business/Microsoft,* CFI Dec. 16, 1999, 1999 ECR II-3989, para. 56; *NDC/IMS Health,* ECJ April 11, 2002, 2002 ECR I-3401, para. 64.
184. *Coditel II,* ECJ Oct. 6, 1982, 1982 ECR 3381, paras 16–19.
185. *Metro/Deutsche Grammophon,* ECJ June 8, 1971, 1971 ECR 487, paras 12–13.

member state of a product placed on the market in another member state by the copyright holder or with its consent infringes Article 28 on the free movement of goods. The manufacturer's copyright is 'exhausted' once the product has been lawfully distributed on the market in any EC or EEA country by the actual proprietor or with its consent.[186] Similarly, the EFTA Court of Justice ruled that the EEA rules on free movement of goods (Articles 11 and 13 of the EEA Agreement, which correspond to Articles 28 and 30 of the EC Treaty)

> 'are to be interpreted as not permitting the protection of a direct importer's[187] national copyright in a Summary of Product Characteristics, approved by the competent medical products authority, which would have the consequence that the medical product may not give out, approve or lay down the same Summary of Product Characteristics for a product imported by way of parallel import without the consent of the direct importer'.[188]

Accordingly, the right-holder cannot invoke its copyrights to prevent parallel trade within the EU of products which have been legally put on the market by itself (or by one of its subsidiaries) or with its consent; any prohibition on the licensee not to resell the products outside the allocated territory is only accepted if it is covered by the Regulation 2790/1999 on Vertical Restraints or, if the block exemption does not apply, satisfies the conditions of Article 81 (3).[189]

Distinction between Distribution and Rental or Lending.
A distinction must be drawn between the distribution right and the specific rental and lending right recognized by Article 9 of Council Directive 92/100/EEC on the Rental and Lending Rights Concerning Copyrights and Rights Related to Copyrights.[190] Whereas the distribution right is exhausted upon the first sale in the

---

186. *Micro Leader Business/Microsoft,* CFI Dec. 16, 1999, 1999 ECR II-3989, paras. 34 and 54; *Membran and K'tel/GEMA,* ECJ Jan. 20, 1981, 1981 ECR 147, paras 10 and 15; *Dior/Evora,* ECJ Nov. 4, 1997, 1997 ECR I-6013, para. 57; *Metronome Musik/Music Point Hokamp,* ECJ April 28, 1998, 1998 ECR I-1953, para. 14. *See* Article 4 (c) of Council Directive 91/250/EEC on the Legal Protection of Computer Programs, 1991 OJ L 122/42, and Article 4 of Council Directive 2001/29/EC on the Harmonization of Certain Aspects of Copyrights and Rights Related to Copyrights in the Information Society ('Multimedia Directive'), 2001 OJ L 167/10.
187. The official importer of the pharmaceutical product who claims copyrights on the summary of product characteristics which describe, from a therapeutic point of view, the same medicinal product.
188. Advisory Opinion of the EFTA Court of Justice, Nov. 24, 1998, E-1/98, ELR 1999–1, 34, paras 25–26. *See Micro Leader Business/Microsoft,* CFI Dec. 16, 1999, 1999 ECR II-3989, para. 56.
189. Regulation 2790/1999 applies to copyright licences that do not constitute the primary object of the agreement: Article 2 (3) of Regulation 2790/1999; Guidelines on Vertical Agreements, 2000 OJ C-291/2, points 39–41.
190. 1992 OJ L 346/61.

Community by the right-holder or with its consent, the rental and lending right is not exhausted by the sale or any other kind of distribution. The Court of Justice affirmed the validity of Article 9 of the Directive in the *Metronome/Music Point* case by arguing that the exclusive rental right appears justified 'by the protection of the extremely high and risky investments which are required for the production of phonograms and are essential if authors are to go on creating new works'.[191] Consequently, a licence of a copyright may be limited to a single field of use, the distribution by way of sale and/or the rental or lending of the copyrighted good.

Consent by Direct or Statutory Licence.

The principle of free movement applies independently of where in the Community the goods have been first lawfully marketed, and independently of whether the licence has been granted by the licensor directly or by statute. In the case of a statutory licence for musical works which is provided for in Section 8 of the United Kingdom Copyright Act 1956, generally the copyright owner's rights are limited to the payment of royalties (as in the case of patents endorsed as subject to 'licences of right') and the right to prevent unauthorized copying but do not include the right to prevent imports of goods first lawfully marketed elsewhere in the EU or EEA.[192]

No Second Royalty Payment.

The Commission has taken the position that a licence granted by a copyright collecting society in the Community for the manufacture and distribution of a copyrighted product, such as records or tapes, is valid throughout the entire Community, wherever it takes place.[193] The importation of copyrighted recordings which have been legally marketed in one member state may not be subject to payment of a second royalty in another member state.[194] The Commission reasons that a separate requirement to pay royalties to the national copyright collecting society in the importing member state under the rates applicable there would practically mean imposition of double royalties which would lead to the reestablishment of national barriers between member states. The Court of Justice stated in the *Membran and K'tel/GEMA* case[195] that a demand for even the difference between the

191. *Metronome Musik/Music Point Hokamp,* ECJ April 28, 1998, 1998 ECR I-1953, para. 16–18; referring to *Warner and Metronome Video/Christiansen,* ECJ May 17, 1988, 1988 ECR 2605, paras 17–18.
192. With respect to licences of right under patent law, *see Allen and Hanburys,* ECJ March 3, 1988, 1988 ECR 1245, para. 23, and discussion in section C.1.(b) *supra.*
193. *BIEM/IFPI,* Thirteenth Report on Competition Policy, points 147–150, and *GEMA IV,* Fifteenth Report on Competition Policy, point 81.
194. *See CICG-ZVEI/ZPU,* D.Comm. Feb. 1, 1971, 1971 OJ L 34/13; *GEMA I,* D.Comm. June 2, 1971, 1971 OJ L 134/15; *GEMA II,* 1984–1 CMLR 308; *GEMA IV,* Fifteenth Report on Competition Policy, point 81.
195. *Membran and K'tel/GEMA,* ECJ Jan. 20, 1981, 1981 ECR 147, para. 27. The surplus royalties

higher royalty paid to a copyright collecting society in the state of importation and the lower royalty paid in the state where the copyrighted work was placed into circulation infringes Articles 28 and 30.

Exceptions for Supplementary Royalties.
An exception applies if the country of origin does not provide any comparable mechanism for charging such a royalty for a particular form of exploitation as is imposed in the country in which the copyrighted work is exploited. In the *SACEM* cases[196] the Court of Justice ruled that the payment of a so-called 'supplementary mechanical reproduction fee' in addition to the customary performance royalty, on the public performance of sound recordings, such as in discotheques, on juke boxes or in radio broadcasts, was permissible if the supplementary royalty was not separately provided for in the country in which the sound recordings were lawfully placed on the market and was therefore included in the mechanical reproduction fee. The same rule was applied in the *Warner Brothers/Christiansen* case[197] which concerned a special royalty on the rental of video cassettes in Denmark that had no parallel under United Kingdom law where the video cassettes were originally purchased. The Court ruled that collecting a royalty on the rental of video cassettes under Danish copyright law did not infringe Article 28 even though the video cassettes in question had already been put into circulation with the consent of the copyright holder in another member state whose legislation did not enable the author to prohibit rentals. This statement was reconfirmed in the *Metronome/Music Point* case;[198] by accepting distribution by way of sale and rental/lending as different fields of using the copyright, the Court of Justice also accepts different licence fees in both cases.

Exclusive Licences and Direct Exports.
If the owner of the copyrights grants to a licensee the exclusive right to produce and market goods in the territory of a single member state, it might be argued that the licensee would infringe the owner's copyright in another member state if the licensee itself exported *directly* to that member state. The *Membran and K'tel/GEMA* case[199] concerned such direct export activities, albeit by a sister company of the licensee. The Court of Justice merely confirmed in general terms the application of the exhaustion doctrine to copyrighted works without deciding whether the doctrine applies to *direct* exports of copyrighted works. On remand the German

have in principle to be refunded: *Membran/GEMA,* German Federal Supreme Court, April 28, 1988, 1988 EWiR 897. *See also SACEM III,* ECJ July 13, 1989, 1989 ECR 2521, para. 11.

196. *SACEM I,* ECJ April 9, 1987, 1987 ECR 1747, paras 14–17; *SACEM III,* ECJ July 13, 1989, 1989 ECR 2811, paras 10–13, and *SACEM IV,* ECJ 12 Dec. 1990, 1990 ECR I-4607 (identical to the *SACEM I* case).

197. *Warner Brothers/Christiansen,* ECJ May 17, 1988, 1988 ECR 2605, paras 10–13.

198. *Metronome/Music Point Hokamp,* ECJ April 28, 1988, 1988 ECR I-1953.

199. *Membran and K'tel/GEMA,* ECJ Jan. 20, 1981, 1981 ECR 147.

Federal Supreme Court decided on its own authority that a copyright is exhausted whenever the copyrighted product is offered by the licensee to any potential buyer in a given member state, including importers from another member state.[200] However, the Court of Justice has not yet expressly ruled on this issue.[201]

Expiration of Copyright in the Exporting Country.
The owner of a copyright in one member state may assert its exclusive rights to prevent imports from another member state where the copyright protection has expired and where the products have been put on the market neither by the copyright holder nor with its consent. This was the general conclusion of the Court of Justice in the *EMI/Patricia* case.[202] In this case EMI UK had transferred its copyright for reproducing and marketing certain sound recordings to its German subsidiary. Two other German firms, one called Patricia, started manufacturing the same recordings in Germany without the consent of EMI at the request of a Danish firm. The recordings were exported to Denmark where the copyright protection had already expired and were then partially reexported and resold back into Germany. The Court of Justice ruled that under these circumstances the exercise of the German copyright to halt importation from Denmark did not infringe Articles 28 and 30 since the copyright holder had not consented to the sale in Denmark. The copyright holder's consent had neither been given nor was required in order for the copyrighted work to be marketed in Denmark where the copyright protection had expired.[203]

Special Features of Functional Designs.
Copyright protection varies considerably from member state to member state in the absence of any Community regulation.[204] Protection used to extend farthest in

200. *Membran/GEMA,* German Federal Supreme Court, Feb. 20, 1986, 1986 GRUR 668. With respect to plants variety rights Article 16 of Council Regulation 2100/94 defines the exhaustion principle as including direct export activities ('disposed to others').
201. One might argue that copyright laws are different from patent and trademark laws (*see supra* section B.3.) in that they do not provide for the right of invoking copyrights against a licensee who contravenes a contractual obligation not to market the copyrighted goods outside its territory; consequently copyrights may be held exhausted, i.e. may not be invoked against direct imports of goods which have been put on the 'export market' by the right-owner or with its consent. However, with respect to trademarks the Commission stated in its Communication on parallel imports of proprietary medicinal products (MEMO/04/7) that the trademark rights are exhausted throughout the entire EU when the trademarked product is put into circulation for the first time, either directly or by the grant of licences to third parties irrespective of whether the products which are marketed in this way are identical or 'sufficiently similar'.
202. *EMI/Patricia,* ECJ Jan. 24, 1989, 1989 ECR 79, para. 14.
203. *See* Commission's Communication on Parallel Imports of Proprietary Medicinal Products of December 30, 2003 (COM(2003)839 final), which states that the withdrawal of the marketing authorization in one member state does not automatically affect the validity of the import licence in another member state.
204. *See,* however, Regulation 6/2002 on the European Community design, 2002 OJ L 3/1.

the United Kingdom, where even technical drawings of functional objects and the products produced with their assistance, e.g., replacement body panels for automobiles, benefited from design copyright protection. The Commission has stated that enforcement of copyright to prevent imports of goods legally manufactured and marketed in other member states could constitute a disguised restriction of trade.[205] The Copyright, Designs and Patents Act 1988 removed copyright protection from most industrially produced functional articles and severely restricted the possibilities of obtaining new design registrations, although designs registered prior to the new legislation continued to enjoy a protection for the remainder of the 15 year period after registration.[206]

(c) Copyrighted Services

Performing Rights.
In the *Coditel I* and *Coditel II* cases[207] the Court of Justice stated that the exercise of copyright in a film to be shown to the public by cinema exhibition or television had to be compatible with Articles 49 and 50 on the free movement of services. However, the cinematographic industry in Europe had special characteristics, especially relating to dubbing and subtitling for the benefit of different language groups, to the possibilities of television broadcast and to the system of financing cinematographic productions.[208] Furthermore, a film producer has a legitimate interest in calculating the royalty for the actual or probable number of cinema performances in the licensed territory, whereas the legitimate interests of a producer of a copyrighted physical object such as a book or a record are satisfied by the payment of the royalty received on first sale irrespective of where it took place in the Community.[209] Based on these considerations, the Court of Justice held that the mere fact that the owner of the copyright in a film has granted to a sole licensee the exclusive right to exhibit that film in the territory of a member state and, consequently, to prevent during a specific period its showing by others is not, in itself, incompatible with Article 49.[210] However, an exclusive licence

205. Answer of the Commission to Written Question No. 855/83 from the European Parliament, 1983 OJ C 335/17; Resolution of the European Parliament on Copyright Protection in the United Kingdom, 1984 OJ C 172/155.
206. Ford undertook to reduce the fifteen year duration to five or three years in order to meet the requirements of the Commission: *Ford Body Panels II,* IP(90)4. The cases decided by the Court of Justice, *Volvo/Veng,* ECJ Oct. 5, 1988, 1988 ECR 6211, and *Renault,* ECJ Oct. 5, 1988, 1988 ECR 6039, deal only with specific questions of the applicability of Article 82.
207. *Coditel I,* ECJ March 18, 1980, 1980 ECR 881, para. 15; *Coditel II,* ECJ Oct. 6, 1982, 1982 ECR 3381, paras 14–15. They followed an earlier judgment in *Sacchi/Tele Biella,* ECJ April 30, 1974, 1974 ECR 409, paras 6–8.
208. *Coditel II,* ECJ Oct. 6, 1982, 1982 ECR 3381, para. 16.
209. *Coditel I,* ECJ March 18, 1980, 1980 ECR 881, para. 13.
210. *Coditel II,* ECJ Oct. 6, 1982, 1982 ECR 3381, paras 16–17.

which is a means of extracting unfairly high royalties or is in force for an unduly long duration may infringe Article 81 (1).[211]

Prohibiting Imported Cable Broadcasts.

In *Coditel I* the copyright holder in a motion picture granted to different companies licences to show the film in Germany by televising it and in Belgium by exhibiting it in cinemas. A German television broadcast of the film could be picked up in Belgium via cable television, thus threatening the economic viability of the Belgian distributor's showing of the film in cinemas. Yet the original owner of the copyrighted work had clearly consented to the distribution of the work in Germany via broadcast television and 40 months after its cinema release on Belgian television. The Court ruled that the television broadcast could be halted, stating that

> 'The provisions of the Treaty relating to the freedom to provide services do not preclude an assignee of the performing right in a cinematographic film in a Member State from relying upon his right to prohibit the exhibition of that film in that State, without his authority, by means of cable diffusion if the film so exhibited is picked up and transmitted after being broadcast in another Member State by a third party with the consent of the original owner of the right'.[212]

Field-of-Use Limitations.

Copyright licences may be restricted to certain fields of use. The Commission accepted in its early *GEMA* case[213] decided under Article 82 that a licence could be limited to certain forms of utilization of copyrights, for example:

- the general performing right;
- the radio broadcasting right;
- the right to repeat radio broadcasts;
- the television rights;
- the right to repeat television broadcasts;
- the right of cinematographic exhibition;
- the right of mechanical reproduction and distribution;
- the right to play mechanically reproduced works;
- the film production right;
- the right to produce, copy and distribute videotaped works;
- the exploitation rights resulting from technical developments or a future change in legislation.

211. *See ARD/MGM,* D.Comm. Sept 15, 1989, 1989 OJ L 284/36.
212. *Coditel I,* ECJ March 18, 1980, 1980 ECR 881, para. 18.
213. *GEMA I,* D.Comm. June 2, 1971, 1971 OJ L 134/15, 22; *GEMA II* (amending *GEMA I*), D.Comm. July 6, 1972, 1972 OJ L 166/22, 22–23.

According to Articles 1 and 9 of the Council Directive 92/100/EEC,[214] a licence limited to a certain field of use may be held necessary on grounds of legitimate protection of the licensed copyright both under the principles of free movement and under competition law with the effect that the distribution and the rental right may be exclusive, i.e. that the distribution right is not exhausted by the first rental within the Community by the right-owner or with its consent nor is the rental right exhausted by the first sale.[215]

Territorial Limitation of the Different Forms of Utilization.
The further consequence of the permissibility of field-of-use restrictions is that a licence can be limited to a single form of exploitation in particular member states. Accordingly, cable transmissions that cross the frontiers of two member states are subject to payment of royalties in the state of reception.[216]

Timing of Different Forms of Exploitation.
The licence of one or the other form of exploitation can also be limited by imposing an interval between one form and another, such as by giving cinemas exclusive performance rights prior to the other forms of performance like television or video cassettes. In the *Cinetheque* case the Court of Justice concluded that Article 28 did not prevent national legislation on motion pictures from

> 'prohibiting their simultaneous exploitation in cinemas and in video-cassette form for a limited period, provided that the prohibition applies to domestically produced and imported cassettes alike and any barriers to intra-Community trade to which its implementation may give rise do not exceed what is necessary for ensuring that the exploitation in cinemas of cinematographic works of all origins retains priority over other means of distribution'.[217]

In this case the intervals varied in different member states between three and twelve months.[218]

214. 1992 OJ 346/61.
215. *Metronome Musik/Music Point Hokamp,* ECJ April 28, 1998, 1998 ECR I-1953, paras 14–23.
216. *See Coditel II,* ECJ Oct. 6, 1982, 1982 ECR 3381, para. 15. The reason is to protect the holder's right to maximize royalties in each recording to the number and value of public performances: *Coditel I,* ECJ March 18, 1980, 1980 ECR 881, para. 18; *SACEM III,* ECJ July 13, 1989, 1989 ECR 2521, para. 19.
217. *Cinéthèque,* ECJ July 11, 1985, 1985 ECR 2605, para. 24.
218. In the case of first release in cinemas and later showings on television the intervals may be longer. In *Coditel I* the interval was 40 months: *Coditel I,* ECJ March 18, 1980, 1980 ECR 881, para. 13.

(d) Copyrighted Computer Programs

Council Directive 96/9/EC.
Computer programs, i.e. sets of instructions to information processing computerized devices causing them to perform certain operations, are protected under the various national copyright laws if the computer program satisfies the same conditions as regards its originality as apply to other literary works. The intellectual effort and the financial investment which may be necessary for the creation of programs and the ease with which they may be copied merit adequate legal protection. Divergences between the copyright laws of the member states as to the availability and scope of the protection caused the Commission and the Council to issue Directive 91/250/EC on the Legal Protection of Computer Programs.[219] This directive does not aim at removing all differences between national protection, but is limited to those which adversely affect the functioning of the Common Market to a substantial degree, i.e. establishing that member states should accord protection to computer programs under copyright law as literary works and to establishing who and what should be protected. According to Articles 4 and 5 the exclusive right includes *inter alia* the authorization of reproduction, translation, adaptation, arrangement and any other alteration of a computer program except where the acts are 'necessary for the use of the computer program by the lawful acquirer in accordance with its intended purpose'. The relationship between Community law and national copyright is governed by the usual distinction between the existence and the exercise of the intellectual property rights in question. The first sale in the Community of a copy of a program by the right-holder or with its consent exhausts the distribution right within the Community of that copy, with exceptions for the right to control further rental of the program or a copy thereof.[220]

6. TRADEMARKS

(a) Specific Subject Matter

The Basic Right.
A trademark may consist, according to Article 4 of the Council Regulation 40/94 on the Community Trademark,[221] of any signs capable of being represented graphically, particularly words, including personal names,[222] designs, letters, numerals,[223] the shape of goods or of their packaging, provided that such signs

219. 1991 OJ L 122/42.
220. Article 4 (c) of the Council Directive 91/250/EC on the Legal Protection of Computer Programs.
221. 1994 OJ L 11/1.
222. Including firm signets: *Ringelhan,* ECJ Nov. 6, 1984, 1984 ECR 3651.
223. *See* the revocation of the trademark protection of the Italian numeral 'quattro' in Germany: *Deutsche Renault/Audi,* ECJ Nov. 30, 1993, 1993 ECR I-6260, para. 6.

are capable of distinguishing the goods or services of one undertaking from those of other undertakings.[224] The Court of Justice has stated that the specific subject matter of a trademark is

> 'the guarantee that the owner of the trademark has the exclusive right to use that trademark, for the purpose of putting products protected by the trademark into circulation for the first time, and is therefore intended to protect him against competitors wishing to take advantage of the status and the reputation of the trademark by selling products illegally bearing that trademark'.[225]

The rights conferred by a trademark have been described in Article 9 (1) of Council Regulation 40/94 on the Community Trademark as follows:

> 'A Community trademark shall confer on the proprietor exclusive rights therein. The proprietor shall be entitled to prevent all third parties not having his consent from using in the course of trade:
> (a) any sign which is identical with the Community trademark in relation to goods or services which are identical with those for which the Community trademark is registered;
> (b) any sign where, because of its identity with or similarity to the Community trademark and the identity or similarity of the goods or services covered by the Community trademark and the sign, there exists a likelihood of confusion on the part of the public; the likelihood of confusion includes the likelihood of association between the sign and the trademark ....'

Article 5 (2) of the First Trademark Directive[226] provides furthermore that the proprietor of a national trademark shall be entitled 'to prevent all third parties not having his consent from using in the course of trade any sign ... where the use of that sign without due cause takes unfair advantage of, or is detrimental to, the distinctive character or the repute of the trademark'.[227] It follows from this provi-

---

224. Including trademarks which consist exclusively of signs or indications which have become customary in the current language or in the *bona fide* and established practices in the trade: *Merz & Krell,* ECJ Oct. 4, 2001, C-517/99, para. 41. *See also Koninklijke Philips Electronics,* ECJ June 18, 2002, C-299/99, para. 65.

225. *Centrafarm/Winthrop,* ECJ Oct. 31, 1974, 1974 ECR 1183, para. 8; *Hag II,* ECJ Oct. 17, 1990, 1990 ECR I-3711, para. 14; *Deutsche Renault/Audi,* ECJ Nov. 30, 1993, 1993 ECR I-6260, para. 30.

226. First Council Directive 89/104/EC to Approximate the Laws of the Member States Relating to Trademarks, 1989 OJ L 40/1.

227. *See Philips/Remington,* ECJ June 18, 2002, 2002 ECR I-5475, paras 30–34 and 65. In *Adidas* the Court of Justice ruled that the proprietor of a trademark with a reputation cannot prevent the use of a similar sign viewed purely as a decorative motif; however, there can be an infringement to the trademark when the degree of similarity between the trademark and the sign

sion, as interpreted by the Court of Justice in the *Dior/Evora* case,[228] that a licence granted by the proprietor of a trademark to resell the products includes the right to make use of the trademark to bring to the public's attention the further commercialization of those goods. To this effect, 'a balance must be struck between the legitimate interest of the trademark owner in being protected against resellers using his trademark for advertising in a manner which could damage the reputation of the trademark and the reseller's legitimate interest in being able to resell the goods in question by using advertising methods which are customary in this sector of trade' and, e.g. in the case of parallel imported perfumes, not 'affecting the value of the trademark by detracting from the allure and prestigious image of the goods in question and from the aura of luxury.'[229]

(b) Exhaustion of Rights Principle

Codification.

The exhaustion principle has been codified in Article 13 of the Council Regulation on the Community Trademark[230] and in Article 7 of the First Council Directive to Approximate the Laws of the Member States Relating to Trademarks[231] as follows:

'1. The [Community] trademark shall not entitle the proprietor to prohibit its use in relation to goods which have been put on the market in the Community under that trademark by the proprietor or with his consent.
2. Paragraph 1 shall not apply where there exist legitimate reasons for the proprietor to oppose further commercialization of the goods, especially where the condition of the goods is changed or impaired after they have been put on the market.'

This provision has to be read together with Article 5 of the Council Regulation 40/94/EEC, referred to above, and does not entitle the proprietor of the trademark, as stated by the Court of Justice in the *Dior/Evora* case,

> 'to oppose the use of the trademark, by a reseller who habitually markets articles of the same kind, but not necessarily of the same quality as the trademarked goods, as was customary in the reseller's sector of trade, for the purpose of bringing to the public's attention the further commercialization of

has the effect that the public establishes a link between the sign and the trademark without necessarily confusing them: *Adidas/Fitness World,* ECJ Oct. 23, 2003, C-408/01.

228. *Bristol-Myers Squibb,* ECJ July 11, 1996, 1996 ECR I-3457, para. 27; *Dior/Evora,* ECJ Nov. 4, 1997, 1997 ECR I-6013, paras 32–38.
229. *Dior/Evora,* ECJ Nov. 4, 1997, 1997 ECR I-6013, paras 44–45.
230. 1994 OI L 11/1.
231. 1989 OJ L 40/1.

> those products, unless it is established that, given the specific circumstances of the case, the use of the trademark for this purpose seriously damages the reputation of the trademark'.[232]

The case in question concerned luxury cosmetic products manufactured by Dior, parallel imported by a Dutch distributor, which was not member of Dior's selective distribution system, and advertised by him for sale during a Christmas promotion period. The Court of Justice argued that a distributor which legally imported those goods must not only be free to resell the goods but also free to use the trademark for advertising purposes in a manner customary to retailers in this market sector.[233] In the *Paranova/AstraZeneca* case, which concerned the parallel import of a medicinal product into Finland after the withdrawal of a marketing authorization of the parallel import, the Court of Justice stated that the withdrawal of the marketing authorization of reference did not entail that of the parallel import licence, except for reasons relating to the protection of public health (which the Court denied in the present case), and that therefore the trademark rights could not be used for preventing parallel imports.[234]

Application of the Exhaustion Principle in the Case of Direct Exports by a Licensee or Exclusive Distributor.
It is not decided yet by the Court of Justice whether the exhaustion principle applies when the licensee or exclusive distributor designated in one member state exports the product directly into another member state which is allocated to another licensee or exclusive distributor. The Community trademark regulation and directive entitle the proprietor to invoke its rights against a licensee which contravenes contractual licence limitations by selling to customers outside its assigned territory. However, these contractual limitations must be compatible with Article 81. Obligations on a trademark licensee not to resell products passively outside its territory infringe Article 81 (1) and constitute hard core restrictions under Article 4 (b) of Regulation 2790/1999 on vertical agreements,[235] whereas active sales bans are block exempted up to a market share of 30%.[236]

232. *Dior/Evora,* ECJ Nov. 4, 1997, 1997 ECR I-6013, para. 48.
233. The further commercialization of legally imported pharmaceutical products cannot be prevented by claiming copyrights on the summary of the product characteristics: *Astra,* EFTA Court of Justice Nov. 24, 1998, 1998 EFTACR 140, para. 26.
234. *Paranova/AstraZeneca,* ECJ May 8, 2003, C-113/01, paras 31–34.
235. Regulation 2790/1999 applies to distribution agreements which relate to the use of trademark rights, provided that those provisions do not constitute the primary object of such agreements: Article 2 (3) of Regulation 2790/1999; Guidelines on Vertical Agreements, 2000 OJ C 291/2, point 38. *See*, under the prior Regulation 67/67, *TEPEA,* ECJ June 20, 1978, 1978 ECR 1391, paras 40–45.
236. Article 4 (b), first indent, of Regulation 2790/1999.

Application of the Exhaustion Principle Inside v. Outside the Common Market and EEA Countries.

The exhaustion principle applies only to goods which have been put onto the market by the trademark owner or with its consent within the Community or the EEA countries (Norway, Iceland and Liechtenstein).[237] The principle of exhaustion does not apply with respect to products first marketed in third countries.[238] By contrast to earlier drafts which provided for the principle of international (third country) exhaustion,[239] both Council Regulation 40/94 on the Community Trademark (Article 13) and the First Council Directive to Approximate the Laws of the Member states Relating to trademarks (Article 7) limit the exhaustion principle to the EU and EEA countries.[240] With regard to products imported from *third* countries (even if they were legally marketed there) the exhaustion principle applies only if they are marketed by the right-holder or with its consent first in an EU or EEA country and then imported into another EU country,[241] or the trademark owner gives unequivocal (not implied) consent to importation into the territory of the EU or EEA[242] or where international agreements provide for a further extension of the exhaustion principle, as the TRIPs Agreements.[243]

---

237. Article 2 and Article 3 (6) of Protocol 28 of the EEA Agreement, 1994 OJ L 194/1, 194; *Donckerwolke,* ECJ Dec. 15, 1976, 1976 ECR 1938. *See* Section B.2. *supra.*
238. *Polydor,* ECJ Feb. 9, 1982, 1982 ECR 329, para. 22 (copyrighted products); *Silhouette International Schmied/Hartlauer,* ECJ July 18, 1998, 1998 ECR I-4799, paras 25–29. *See also Nintendo II,* D.Comm. Oct. 30, 2002, 2003 OJ L 255/33, point 62 (copyrighted video games).
239. The principle of international exhaustion has been applied by different national courts under national trademark law, *see* the cases quoted at note 40 *supra,* and is the basis of Article 3 (d) of Regulation 1983/83 which provides that the block exemption for exclusive distribution agreements is not applicable if one or both of the parties makes it difficult for intermediaries or users to obtain the contract product from outside the Common Market (in particular by using trademark rights) if no alternative source of supply is available inside the Common Market.
240. *Silhouette International Schmied/Hartlauer,* ECJ July 18, 1998, 1998 ECR I-4799, paras 25–26; *Sebago/GB Unic,* ECJ July 1, 1999, 1999 ECR I-4103, paras 16–17. However, the Commission first proposal for trademark harmonization provided for an international exhaustion: 1980 OJ C 351/1, which was subsequently reduced to a Community exhaustion.
241. Article 23 (2) of the EU Treaty and *Phyteron International/Jean Bourdon,* ECJ March 20, 1997, 1997 ECR I-1729.
242. This is the possible result of the reasoning in *Zino Davidoff,* ECJ Nov. 20, 2001, 2001 ECR I-8691.
243. EEA: *Silhouette,*ECJ July 18, 1998, 1998 ECR I-4799, paras. 25–26; EFTA Court of Justice, Nov. 24, 1998, E-1/98, paras 25–26. TRIPs (including the U.S.): *Maglite Mag Instrument/ California,* EFTA Court of Justice Dec. 3, 1997, E-2/97, 1998–1 ELR 2; D.Comm. Dec. 11, 1998, 1998 OJ L 346/60, para. 6.

(c) Use of the Same Trademark by the Same Owner or its Licensees

The Exhaustion Principle.
Articles 28 and 30 will be infringed if the owner can assert its trademark to prohibit importation of genuine goods from one member state to another. In the *Centrafarm/Winthrop* case[244] the Court of Justice concluded that enforcement of a Dutch trademark to prohibit importation of genuine products from the United Kingdom that the trademark owner had marketed there infringed Articles 28 and 30.[245] The specific subject matter of trademark law is to provide a guarantee of origin and therefore does not extend to controlling the channels of distribution.

Lack of Parallel Trademark Protection in the Country of Import: The *Graffione/Fransa* Case.
This case[246] concerned the use of the trademark 'Cottonelle' by the Scott Multinational Group within the Common Market for toilet paper and disposable handkerchiefs. This trademark was declared void under Italian trademark law because it might mislead consumers into thinking that the products in question actually contained cotton, whereas the trademark was upheld in other member states. Fransa, an Italian supermarket, tried to resell products imported from France where the trademark remained valid and where Cottonelle products were put on the market with the trademark owner's consent. Article 12 (2) (b) of the First Council Directive 89/104/EC to Approximate the Laws of the Member States Relating to Trademarks permits revocation of a trademark right insofar as it is liable to mislead consumers. However, the Court of Justice argued, on the basis of the fifth and sixth recitals of the preamble of the directive, that the First Directive does not aim to bring about complete harmonization of member states' trademark laws and that the member states therefore remain free to determine the effects of revocation or invalidity of trademarks; thus, the directive does not preclude a prohibition on the marketing of products coming from other member states even if they have been lawfully marketed there, provided that the prohibition is necessary in order to ensure consumer protection and that these objectives cannot be achieved by measures which are less restrictive of intra-Community trade.[247]

---

244. *Centrafarm/Winthrop*, ECJ Oct. 31, 1974, 1974 ECR 1183, para. 8.
245. This is constant practice, *see Graffione/Fransa,* ECJ Nov. 26, 1996, 1996 ECR I-6039, paras 16–17.
246. *Graffione/Fransa,* ECJ Nov. 26, 1996, 1996 ECR I-6039.
247. *Ibid.*, para. 27. This principle applies to cases where a trademark has been refused from registration because of absolute grounds for refusal (for example a numeral as in the case *Quattro – Deutsche Renault/Audi,* ECJ Nov. 30, 1993, 1993 ECR I-6260, para. 23) or because of identity or similarity with a previously registered trademark (Articles 7 and 8 of Regulation 40/94 on the Community Trademark).

Product Differentiation by the Trademark Owner or its Licensees. The trademark owner may market in different member states a nearly identical product in a slightly different composition likely to affect the internal or external condition of the product, for example by varying the colour or the content of a phial or ampoule or the taste of a product according to the particularities of the national demand (for example the taste of coffee or chocolate). The Court of Justice interprets Article 30 in the light of Article 7 of the First Council Directive 89/104/EC to Approximate the Laws of the Member States Relating to Trademarks, which is identical to Article 13 of Council Regulation 40/94 on the Community Trademark.[248] According to Article 7 (1) the trademark owner is prevented from opposing the further commercialization of a product which was put on the market in another member state by the owner or with its consent. The exception of Article 7 (2) concerns the case where there are legitimate reasons for the proprietor to oppose the further commercialization, 'especially' where the condition of the product has been changed or impaired since it was put on the market. This usually occurs when a third person (i.e. an importer) alters the product after it was put on the market by the trademark owner or with its consent. If the owner or its licensee affixes the same trademark to a slightly different, but basically identical, product, in particular where the owner has put an identical[249] pharmaceutical product on the market in several member states in various forms of packaging, and the repackaging carried out by the importer is necessary in order to market the product in the member state of importation and in such a form that the original condition of the product cannot be affected,[250] the trademark owner still guarantees the identity and quality of the products manufactured under its control and responsibility.[251] The Commission's Communication on parallel imports of proprietary medicinal products[252] defines a medicinal product as being similar to an authorized product[253] if it is manufactured according to the same formulation, using the same active ingredients and has the same therapeutic effects. However, if quality differences result in consumer confusion, the trademark owner has to bear the consequences of its choice of differentiating the products and to take the appropriate measures in

248. *Bristol-Myers Squibb/Paranova,* ECJ July 11, 1996, 1996 ECR I-3457, para. 43; *Dior/Evora,* ECJ Nov. 4, 1997, 1997 ECR I-6013, para. 53; *Loendersloot/Ballantine,* ECJ Nov. 11, 1997, 1997 ECR I-6227, paras 18–23.
249. Or different medical preparations of the same product, i.e. variants of a pharmaceutical product without therapeutic relevance as shown by the information or documents produced by the manufacturer: *De Peijper/Centrafarm,* ECJ May 20, 1976, 1976 ECR 613, para. 36.
250. *See* in greater detail the following subsection.
251. *Ideal Standard,* ECJ June 22, 1994, 1994 ECR I-2789, para. 38. Under Article 8 (2) of the First Council Directive 89/104 to Approximate the Laws of the Member States Relating to Trademarks the trademark owner has the right to sue for trademark infringement if the licensee fails to meet the quality standards provided for in the licence agreement.
252. MEMO/04/7 of January 19, 2004.
253. Marketing authorization under Regulation 2309/93, 1993 OJ L 214/1.

order to avoid such confusion.[254] However, the likelihood of such a confusion presupposes a normal degree of attentiveness of the 'average consumer reasonably well informed and reasonably observant and circumspect'.[255] According to the case law of the Court of Justice, the risk of misleading consumers cannot override the requirements of the free movement of goods and so justify barriers to trade, unless that risk is sufficiently serious and cannot be prevented by less restrictive means ('proportionality principle'), i.e. by issuing the necessary user instructions and information in order to prevent misleading consumers.[256] Maintaining or creating the impression of different products sold under the same trademark might be seen as an artificial partitioning of markets.[257] Hence, it does not qualify for an exception from the exhaustion principle under Article 7 (2) of the First Trademark Directive or Article 30 unless the trademark owner is subject to a genuine, legal (not only ethical) obligation to satisfy national demand.[258] Conforming to these principles the Court of Justice concluded that imported proprietary medical products are covered by the marketing authorization of the competent authority of a member state B where the products are manufactured by an independent company in member state A pursuant to a licence agreement and where the products, although not identical in all aspects, have at least been manufactured according to the same formulation using the same ingredients and have the same therapeutic effects.[259] It may be concluded that the exhaustion principle applies under such circumstances provided the importer is able to prove that the medical products are substantially the same.

254. The right-holder is entitled to oblige its licensees to respect a certain quality of goods or services: Article 7 (2) of the First Directive 89/104/EC to Approximate the Laws of the Member States Relating to Trademarks. *See Ideal Standard,* ECJ June 22, 1994, 1994 ECR I-2789, para. 38; *Dior/Evora,* ECJ Nov. 4, 1997, 1997 ECR I-6013.

255. *Bristol Myers Squibb/Paranova,* ECJ July 11, 1996, 1996 ECR I-3457, paras 36–37; *Estée Lauder/Lancaster,* ECJ Jan. 13, 2000, 2000 ECR I-117, para. 32. Similarly *Lloyd Schuhfabrik Meyer/Klijsen Handel,* ECJ June 22, 1999, 1999 ECR I-3819, paras. 17–18, and *Colin and Biggs,* ECJ June 3, 1999, 1999 ECR I-3175, paras 41–44 (presupposing a 'polyglot' consumer).

256. The licensor cannot claim copyrights on its user instructions and information: *Norway/Astra Norge,* EFTA Court of Justice Nov. 24, 1998, E-1/98, ELR 1999–1, 34; *Kessler,* ECJ Jan. 28, 1999, 1999 ECR I-513, para. 36.

257. Example for artificial partitioning of the markets by way of a restrictive agreement held contrary to Article 81*: Montedison/Stähler,* D.Comm. June 24, 1993, 1993 OJ L 272/28, points 61–92.

258. *Merck/Primecrown,* ECJ Dec. 5, 1996, 1996 ECR I-6285, paras 47–54.

259. *Eurim Pharm II,* ECJ July 1, 1993, 1993 ECR I-3741, para. 26. *See also Hoffmann-La Roche/Centrafarm,* ECJ May 23, 1978, 1978 ECR 1139; *Smith & Nephew and Primecrown,* ECJ Nov. 12, 1996, 1996 ECR I-5819.

Repackaging – Five Conditions for Applying the Exhaustion Principle in Case of Repackaging and Reaffixing the Trademark on Pharmaceutical Products.

The repackaging of a product may be grounds for the enforcement of trademark rights if the repackaging jeopardizes the trademark's function as a guarantee of the origin of the goods in their original condition. Article 7 (1) of the First Council Directive 89/104/EC to Approximate the Laws of the Member States Relating to Trademarks[260] precludes a trademark owner from relying on its rights as owner to prevent an importer from marketing a product which was put on the market in another member state by the owner or with its consent. However, under Article 7 (2) the owner of a trademark may oppose the further commercialization of products where there is a legitimate reason for doing so, especially where the condition of the products has been changed or impaired since they were put on the market, which would be the case, as stated in general terms by the Court of Justice in *Dior/Evora* case,[261] by affecting the value and reputation of the trademark and damaging seriously the proprietor's legitimate interests. The conditions under which legally acquired pharmaceutical products may be repackaged and put onto the market in another member by a parallel importer were clarified in greater detail in the three parallel cases *Bristol Myers Squibb/ Paranova*[262] *Eurim Pharm/Beiersdorf*[263] and *MPA Pharma/Rhône Poulenc Pharma.*[264] In these cases, Paranova, Eurim Pharm and MPA Pharma each bought pharmaceutical products in low-price countries such as Spain, Portugal, France, Greece and the United Kingdom, repackaged them and imported the new packages into Denmark and Germany. The repackaging included putting blister strips into new external packaging, replacing parts of the original package or cutting the original blister strips to achieve a package with a number of tablets that was marketable in the country of import. In almost all cases the parallel importer also added information in the language of the country of import. The Court of Justice held that its case law under Article 30 must be taken as a basis for determining whether, under Article 7 of the First Directive, a trademark owner may oppose the marketing of repackaged products to which the trademark has been reaffixed. Since Article 30 allows derogations from the fundamental principle of free movement of goods only insofar as such derogations are justified in order to safeguard the rights which constitute the specific subject-matter of the industrial and commercial property in question, Article 7 (2) of the First Directive must be interpreted as meaning that a trademark owner may legitimately oppose the further marketing of a pharmaceutical product even

260. 1989 OJ L 40/1.
261. *Dior/Evora,* ECJ Nov. 4, 1997, 1997 ECR I-6013, paras 39–48.
262. *Bristol Myers Squibb/Paranova*, ECJ July 11, 1996, 1996 ECR I-3457, paras. 53–54. Similarly *Merck/Paranova,* ECJ April 23, 2002, 2002 ECR I-3703, para. 26, and *Boehringer Ingelheim,* ECJ April 23, 2002, 2002 ECR I-3759.
263. *Eurim Pharm/Beiersdorf,* ECJ July 11, 1996, 1996 ECR I-3603.
264. *MPA Pharma/Rhône Poulenc Pharma*, ECJ July 11, 1996, 1996 ECR I-3671.

if the importer has repackaged it and reaffixed the trademark without the owner's authorization, unless the following five conditions are met:

> '– it is established that reliance on trademark rights by the owner in order to oppose the marketing of repackaged products under that trademark would contribute to the artificial partitioning of markets between member states; such is the case, in particular, where the owner has put an identical pharmaceutical product[265] on the market in several member states in various forms of packaging, and the repackaging carried out by the importer is necessary in order to market the product in the member state of importation, and is carried out in such conditions that the original condition of the product cannot be affected by it; that condition does not, however, imply that it must be established that the trademark owner deliberately sought to partition the markets between member states;
>
> – it is shown that the repackaging cannot affect the original condition of the product inside the packaging; such is the case, in particular, where the importer has merely carried out operations involving no risk of the product being affected, such as, for example, the removal of the blister packs,[266] flasks, phials, ampoules or inhalers from the original external packaging and their replacement in new external packaging,[267] the fixing of self-stick labels on the inner packaging of the product, the addition to the packaging of new user instructions or information[268] or the insertion of an extra article; it is for the national court to verify that the original condition of the product inside the packaging is not indirectly affected, for example, by the fact that the external or inner packaging of the repackaged product or new user instructions or information omits certain important information or gives inaccurate information, or the fact that an extra article inserted in the packaging by the importer and designed for the ingestion and dosage of the product does not comply with the method of use and the doses envisaged by the manufacturer;[269]
>
> – the new packaging clearly states who repackaged the product and the name of the manufacturer in print such that a person with normal eyesight, exercising the normal degree of attentiveness, would be in a position to understand; similarly, the origin of an extra article from a source other than

265. Or a pharmaceutical product of the same composition according to a uniform formula: *Smith & Nephew and Primecrown,* ECJ Nov. 12, 1996, 1996 ECR I-5819, para. 23.
266. *Pfizer/Eurimpharm I,* ECJ Dec. 3, 1981, 1981 ECR 2913, para. 13.
267. In particular repackaging a pharmaceutical product into larger packages for use in hospitals with newly printed labels without affecting the internal condition of the products: *Hoffmann-La Roche/Centrafarm,* ECJ May 23, 1978, 1978 ECR 1139, paras 9–10.
268. *See Eurim Pharm I,* ECJ July 11, 1993, 1993 ECR I-3741.
269. *See Pfizer/Eurim Pharm II,* ECJ April 16, 1991, 1991 ECR I-1747.

the trademark owner is responsible for it;[270] however, it is not necessary to indicate that the repackaging was carried out without the authorization of the trademark owner;

- the presentation of the repackaged product is not such as to be liable to damage the reputation of the trademark and of its owner, thus, the packaging must not be defective, of poor quality, or untidy;[271] and
- the importer gives notice to the trademark owner before the repackaged product is put on sale, and, on demand, supplies him with a specimen of the repackaged product.'[272]

Removing Labels and Reaffixing Trademarks – Four Conditions for Applying the Exhaustion Principle.

The approach of the Court of Justice in the case of repackaging was applied by analogy in the *Loendersloot/Ballantine* case[273] with regard to removing labels and reaffixing trademarks. The case concerned the marketing, by the Scottish company Ballantine, of a whisky product in bottles bearing the trademark 'Ballantine', the indication 'pure' followed by the name of the contract distributor in the member state where it has been put on the market and an identification number in order to control the distribution network. A Dutch transport and warehouse firm engaged in parallel trade acquired the product in a low-price country, removed the label and reaffixed the trademark without the distributor's name and the identification number and resold it in higher-price countries of the Community. The Court of Justice stated that the criteria of exhaustion developed in the case of repackaged products apply in principle, also in the case of removed and reaffixed labels and trademarks. The national court has to decide whether derogations from the principle of free movement of goods are justified in order to safeguard the reputation of the product and of the trademark or whether the use of that trademark to oppose the marketing of relabelled products would contribute to artificial partitioning of markets. However, since the condition of the product was, in this case, unaffected, neither changed nor impaired the parallel importer is under no obligation to supply the manufacturer with a specimen of the relabelled product; a simple notice suffices.[274] The Court of Justice therefore stated that the trademark owner may legitimately oppose the further marketing of the relabelled product unless the following four conditions are met:

---

270. *See Norway/Astra Norge,* EFTA Court of Justice Nov. 24, 1998, E-1/98, ELR 1999–1, 34.
271. This condition has been added in the light of Article 7 (2) of the First Council Directive 89/104/EC to Approximate the Laws of the Member States Relating to Trademarks.
272. *Bristol-Myers Squibb/Paranova,* ECJ July 11, 1996, 1996 ECR I-3457, para. 79; *Eurim-Pharm/Beiersdorf,* ECJ July 11, 1996, 1996 ECR I-3603, para. 70, and *MPA Pharma/Rhône Poulenc Pharma,* ECJ July 11, 1996, 1996 ECR I-3671, para. 49.
273. *Loendersloot/Ballantine,* ECJ Nov. 11, 1997, 1997 ECR I-6227. *See also Boehringer Ingelheim,* ECJ April 23, 2002, 2002 ECR I-3759, paras. 67–68; *Merck/Paranova,* ECJ April 23, 2002, 2002 ECR I-3703, para. 33.
274. According to the proportionability test: *ibid.,* para. 49.

'– it is established that the use of the trademark rights by the owner to oppose the marketing of the relabelled products under that trademark would contribute to artificial partitioning of the markets between member states;[275]
– it is shown that the relabelling cannot affect the original condition of the product;[276]
– the presentation of the relabelled product is not such as to be liable to damage the reputation of the trademark and its owner; and
– the person who relabels the products informs the trademark owner of the relabelling before the relabelled products are put on sale.'[277]

In the similar case *Upjohn/Paranova*[278] the Court of Justice reaffirmed that intellectual property rights may not be used in order to prevent parallel imports of legally rebranded goods.

(d) Use of Different Trademarks by the Same Owner

Guarantee of Origin v. Market Partitioning.
One and the same product may be marketed by the same manufacturer in different member states under different trademarks. Even if the products are virtually identical and at most reflect varying tastes, the question arises as to whether the parallel importation of these products may be protected by the exhaustion doctrine.[279] The Court of Justice addressed this issue in the *Centrafarm/American Home Products* case.[280] The American Home Products Group sold certain drugs in

275. Affixing the indication 'pure', the name of the contract distributor in the different member states and an identification number may be justified for complying with legal obligations (in particular concerning the conservation of food) or for acting against imitations, but unjustified for controlling the distribution network and preventing a parallel trader from reselling the product in a member state different from that of the contract distributor indicated by the trademark owner (*ibid.*, paras 36–38). For this reason the Court of First Instance held that adding identification numbers are restrictive of competition and unsuitable for exemption in the context of selective distribution systems: *Dunlop/Slazenger II,* CFI July 7, 1994, 1994 ECR II-441, para. 127.
276. This was excluded in the present case (bottled whisky).
277. *Loendersloot/Ballantine,* ECJ Nov. 11, 1997, 1997 ECR I-6227, para. 50. *See also Eurimpharm/Beiersdorf,* ECJ July 11, 1996, 1996 ECR I-3603 (the German Federal Supreme Court, which submitted the repackaging question in this case, ruled that the conditions established by the Court of Justice for considering a repackaging as permissible were fulfilled in the present case: *Sermion II,* BGH April 10, 1997, EuZW 1997–15, 476).
278. *Upjohn/Paranova,* ECJ Oct. 12, 1999, 1999 ECR I-6927, para. 46.
279. On public health grounds it is not contrary to Articles 28 and 30 for pharmacists to be required to dispense the specific branded drug prescribed by the doctor and not the parallel imported therapeutic equivalent product manufactured by the same company in another member state but bearing another trademark: *Royal Pharmaceutical Society,* ECJ May 18, 1989, 1989 ECR 1295, para. 24.
280. *Centrafarm/American Home Products,* ECJ Oct. 10, 1978, 1978 ECR 1823, paras 18–22.

the United Kingdom under the 'Serenid D' trademark and in the Netherlands under the 'Seresta' trademark. Centrafarm, a parallel importer, attempted to export the product from the United Kingdom to the Netherlands and sell it there under the 'Seresta' trademark under a new label which Centrafarm affixed to the goods. The Court of Justice declared enforcement of the American Home Products trademark to be compatible with the Common Market because a third party does not have the right to replace a product's trademark; that is contrary to the essential function of the trademark as a guarantee of the origin of the product. A disguised restriction of trade between member states under Article 30 may nevertheless occur if the owner uses different marks for the same product in different member states in order to 'partition the markets artificially'. The Court of Justice has not further clarified its decision. It is conceivable that an 'artificial' partitioning will exist if a manufacturer that operates throughout the Community decides to introduce a new product under one trademark in certain member states and with knowledge of the consequences selects a different trademark for other member states in order to maintain national price disparities and the selection of the different marks has no other objectively justifiable explanation. It may be argued that the trademark owner may not use its trademark in one member state in order to prevent the parallel importation of genuine products under the trademark used by it or with its consent if the trademarks are almost identical (e.g. 'Aspirin', 'Aspirine', 'Aspirina'). However, the Court of Justice did clarify that the right-holder cannot prevent parallel imports by marketing within the Community different versions of a (substantially identical) product; in order to avoid an artificial market partitioning they must be capable of coexisting, unless it is demonstrated that there is a rsik to public health.[281] Nor is the right-holder entitled to prevent parallel imports by invoking its copyrights with respect to the summary of medicinal product description which the importer annexes to the imported product.[282]

Commission's Communication on Parallel Imports of Proprietary Medicines.

In its Communication on parallel imports of proprietary medicines[283] the Commission clarified how the principle of free movement of goods within the EU applies in practice to parallel import of medicinal products. The communication may be summarized as follows:

281. *Ferring/Eurim-Pharm,* ECJ Sept. 10, 2002, 2002 ECR I-6891, paras. 33–36; *Paranova,* ECJ May 8, 2003, C-15/01, para. 24.
282. *Norway/Astra Norge,* EFTA Court of Justice, Nov. 24, 1998, 1998 EFTACR 140, para. 26.
283. Commission Communication on parallel imports of proprietary medicinal products for which marketing authorizations have already been granted, December 30, 2003, COM(2003)839 final, MEMO/04/07 of Jan. 19, 2004.

- Parallel imports play an important role in preventing the compartmentalization of national markets.[284]
- Medicinal products which have been put on the market in one country of the Community or EEA by the rightowner or with his consent may be imported freely into another country. The rightowner may put the product into circulation for the first time either directly or by the grant of licences to third parties in any member state, thereby including direct exports into the country of destination.
- A medicinal product may be imported in parallel on the basis of a marketing authorization granted either at the national or Community level. National authorities may not obstruct parallel imports by requiring parallel importers to satisfy the same requirements as those which are applicable to undertakings applying *for the first time* for a marketing authoritzation[285] or by holding that the withdrawal of the marketing authorization automatically affects the validity of the import licence.[286]
- The products must not be identical in all respects, provided they are 'similar' to an authorized product, i.e., are manufactured according to the same formulation by using the same active ingredients and have the same therapeutic effects.
- The principle of free circulation applies to all proprietary medicinal products, both prescription medicines and those sold 'over the counter'.[287]
- The parallel importer cannot change the product itself but may repackage it according to the criteria established by the Court of Justice.
- Member states may adopt restrictive measures which aim at protecting human health and life, provided they are necessary and proportionate.

(e) Use of the Same or Confusingly Similar Trademarks by Different Owners

Trademarks Originally Registered to Different Owners.
Although national trademark laws have been largely harmonized,[288] they still permit the same trademark or confusingly similar trademarks to be registered in

284. *Pippig Augenoptik/Hartlauer Handelsgesellschaft,* ECJ April 8, 2003, C-44/01, para. 63.
285. *See De Peijper*, ECJ May 20, 1996, 1976 ECR 613; *Smith & Nephew and Primecrown,* ECJ Dec. 16, 1999, 1999 ECR I-8789.
286. *Ferring,* ECJ Sept. 10, 2003, C-172/00, para. 40.
287. With respect to sales by mail order the Court of Justice ruled that medicinal products subject to prescription can be sold only in pharmacies in the member state where the original prescription is issued. However, an absolute prohibition on the sale by mail order of products that are not subject to prescription in the member state concerned is not justified: *Deutscher Apothekerverband/Doc Morris,* ECJ Dec. 11, 2003, C-322/01, para. 124.
288. Council Regulation 40/94 on the Community Trademark providing for Community-wide protection with a single filing at the new trademark office in Alicante, Spain has lead to numerous applications but in most cases the national trademarks, in particular the well-known trademarks, subsist for an unlimited period and may again be owned by different unrelated undertakings.

two different member states to different owners who have no legal or economic connection with one another. If the exercise of the trademark rights is neither the purpose, the means or the effect of an agreement prohibited by the Treaty nor a means of arbitrary discrimination or a disguised restriction on trade between member states, each trademark may be enforced in its state of registration to prevent the importation of products first marketed under the same or a similar name in another member state that could give rise to confusion. In the *Terrapin/Terranova* case,[289] trademarks had been registered by unrelated firms in the United Kingdom ('Terrapin') and in Germany ('Terra' and 'Terranova') for the same class of products, namely, house-building components and materials. The German Federal Supreme Court[290] considered the trademarks to be confusingly similar and that the lower courts had been correct in prohibiting use of the trademark 'Terrapin' in Germany.[291] The Court of Justice stated that it would not attempt to judge the issue of trademark infringement under national law. The Court ruled that an industrial property right acquired in one member state may legally be used to prevent the importation of 'products marketed under a name giving rise to confusion where the rights in question have been acquired by different and independent proprietors under different national laws'. Otherwise the specific objective of industrial property rights would be undermined. Accordingly, the Court of Justice held that it is

> 'compatible with the provisions of the EEC Treaty relating to the free movement of goods for an undertaking established in a Member State … to prevent the importation of products of an undertaking established in another Member State and bearing by virtue of the legislation of that state a name giving rise to confusion with the trademark and commercial name of the first undertaking, provided that there are no agreements restricting competition and no legal or economic ties between the undertakings and that their respective rights have arisen independently of one another.'[292]

This reasoning was confirmed in the *Deutsche Renault/Audi* judgment.[293] This case concerned the question whether the German car manufacturer Audi was

---

289. *Terrapin/Terranova,* ECJ June 22, 1976, 1976 ECR 1039, para. 7.
290. As quoted in *Terrapin/Terranova,* ECJ June 22, 1976, 1976 ECR 1039, 1042–1043. *See* with regard to confusingly similar trademarks: *Sabel/Puma,* ECJ Nov. 11, 1997, 1997 ECR I-6191, paras 18–26; *Canon/Metro-Goldwyn-Mayer,* ECJ Sept. 29, 1998, 1998 ECR I-5507, paras 24–29.
291. However, the likelihood of such a confusion presupposes a normal degree of attentiveness of the 'average consumer reasonably well informed and reasonably observant and circumspect': *Bristol Myers Squibb/Paranova,* ECJ July 11, 1996, 1996 ECR I-3457, paras 36–37; *Estée Lauder/Lancaster,* ECJ Jan. 13, 2000, 2000 ECR I-117, para. 32. Similarly *Lloyd Schuhfabrik Meyer/Klijsen Handel,* ECJ June 22, 1999, 1999 ECR I-3819, paras 17–18.
292. *Terrapin/Terranova,* ECJ June 22, 1976, 1976 ECR 1039, para. 8.
293. *Deutsche Renault/Audi,* ECJ Nov. 30, 1993, 1993 ECR I-6260.

entitled to rely on its trademark 'quattro' to prevent the use of the trademark 'quadra' by its French competitor Renault for imports into Germany. The Court of Justice denied a conflict with Articles 28 and 30. However, the question arises whether the same principle applies if the trademark was once held by one and the same owner and was only later registered to different, unrelated parties in several member states, for example as a result of expropriation during wartime or assignment. The likelihood of confusion depends, as the Court of Justice ruled in the *Canon/Cannon* case, on 'the risk that the public might believe that the goods or services in question come from the same undertaking or, as the case may be, from economically-linked undertakings', whereas a likelihood of confusion as to the place of production is not sufficient.[294]

Different Owners after Expropriation of Rights: *Hag I* v. *Hag II*.
In its first judgment in this case in 1974,[295] the Court of Justice held that the common origin of a trademark disqualified the owners who had acquired their rights via expropriation from asserting their rights to prevent imports bearing the original owner's mark. The 'Hag' trademark had come into possession of different owners in Belgium and Luxembourg after it had been expropriated from the German firm that had registered it there. When the original German started exporting the product to Luxembourg, the Court of Justice held that the right-holders in Belgium and Luxembourg could not stop them, owing to the mark's common origin.[296] The *Hag II* case,[297] by contrast, concerned the reverse situation, namely the attempt of the Belgian right-holders to export their products to Germany. It might have been argued that the German right-holder's trademark was not exhausted by this export activity because an expropriation of rights has similar effects to those of a compulsory licence, namely effects limited to the territory for which the rights have been granted.[298] However, the Court of Justice found that the common (historical) origin of the trademark was irrelevant to the question whether a restriction of imports was justified in order to safeguard the trademark's essential function of guaranteeing the identical commercial origin of the products. The owners of the

294. *Canon/Cannon,* ECJ Sept. 29, 1998, 1998 ECR I-5507, paras 39–40; *Kessler,* ECJ Jan. 28, 1999, 1999 ECR I-513, para. 36.
295. *Hag I,* ECJ July 3, 1974, 1974 ECR 731, paras 9–15.
296. This judgment has been confirmed by an *obiter dictum* in the case *Terrapin/Terranova,* ECJ June 22, 1976, 1976 ECR 1039, where the Court of Justice stated that the proprietor of an industrial or commercial right cannot rely on that right to prevent the importation of a product which has been lawfully marketed in another member state 'when the right relied on is the result of the subdivision, either by voluntary act or as a result of public constraint, of a trademark which originally belonged to one and the same proprietor; in these cases the basic function of the trademark to guarantee to consumers that the product has the same origin is already undermined by the subdivision of the original right' (para. 6).
297. *Hag II,* ECJ Oct. 17, 1990, 1990 ECR I-3711, paras 13–19.
298. *See* Article 45 of the Community Patent Convention which expressly derogates the exhaustion principle of Article 28.

'Hag' trademark in Belgium/Luxembourg and Germany were in exactly the same position as owners of identical or confusingly similar trademarks that did not have a common origin. Neither had consented to the use of the trademark by the other owner in the other owner's territory. Not to allow them to prevent imports from the other territory would jeopardize the continued existence of their mark as a reliable guarantee of origin.[299]

Different Owners after Assignment of Rights.

In the *Ideal Standard* case[300] the Court of Justice extended the *Hag II* reasoning to the assignment of trademarks. The case concerned the exportation of heating material to Germany bearing the trademark 'Ideal Standard' which had been assigned in France by the French Ideal Standard company to an independent French undertaking. The German Ideal Standard company asserted that the French assignee's exports to Germany infringed the German 'Ideal Standard' trademark registered for both heating and sanitary applications. The Court of Justice held[301] that relying on the German trademark was compatible with Articles 28 and 30 on grounds of the risk of consumer confusion over a device having the same origin, even if the French manufacturer is using that name in its country of origin under a trademark protected there.[302] This unitary control is severed not only by an act of expropriation (as in the *Hag* case) but equally by the voluntary assignment of a trademark whereby the assignor loses the possibility of controlling the product manufactured

299. The distinction between the common *commercial* origin of goods which is the essential function of a trademark to guarantee and the common *historical* origin of a trademark is made by Advocate General Jacobs in his opinion, paras 18–24. It may be noted that under Article 48 of the Community Patent Convention the exhaustion principle is only excluded with regard to the compulsory licensee's territory.

300. *Ideal Standard,* ECJ June 22, 1994, 1994 ECR I-2789.

301. *Ibid.,* para. 60. Contrary to the Advocat General's conclusions, in particular paras 76–102, arguing that, at least, parallel imports by third parties (not by the assignee itself) should not be opposed by the use of the assigned trademark because 'such a result will therefore lead to a complete partitioning of national markets' (para. 136).

302. The Court of Justice ruled, referring to Article 6 *quater of* the Paris Convention, that national trademark rights are independent (Article 9 *ter* allows the registration of the transfer of an international trademark limited to some countries) and may be assigned in some countries without the need of transferring part of the undertaking. Only under the Uniform Benelux Trademark Law and the Council Regulation on the Community Trademark (Article 16) does a single registered trademark apply in multiple member states. However, the Community trademark provisions do not affect the further independence of national trademarks which may still be assigned separately as long as these laws are not harmonized by a directive based on Article 95 (*Ideal Standard,* ECJ June 22, 1994, 1994 ECR I-2789, paras 58–59; *Graffione/Fransa,* ECJ Nov. 26, 1996, 1996 ECR I-6039, para. 29 with respect to Article 12 (2) of the First Trademark Directive providing for the revocation of trademarks the extent of which is left to national law). *See also Deutsche Renault/Audi,* ECJ Nov. 30, 1993, 1993 ECR I-6260, paras 31–33, noting that there is nothing to suggest that the German courts make a broad interpretation of the concept of confusion.

by the assignee. Therefore the trademarks no longer coexist in one and the same territory and may be used by the respective owners in order to prevent imports from the other's territory where they have been placed on the market without its consent.[303] However, the Court of Justice admitted the possibility that assignments may be (i) 'manipulations' in order to grant absolute territorial protection to an affiliate or an exclusive distributor and then would be contrary to Article 30 or (ii) restrictive of competition contrary to Article 81 (although this is not necessarily the case).[304] The Commission objected consistently, under Article 81, to assignments constituting a restrictive agreement having the object or effect of territorial protection, as in *Grundig/Consten,*[305] *Advocat Zwarte Kip,*[306] *Sirdar/Phildar,*[307] *Quantel/Continuum*[308] and *Fyffes/Chiquita.*[309]

(f) Resolving Conflicts Resulting from Different Ownership

Restrictive Agreements on the Use of Similar Trademarks by Different Owners: The *Toltecs/Dorcet* Case.
An example of a restrictive agreement on the use of similar trademarks by different owners was *Toltecs/Dorcet.*[310] This case concerned an agreement between BAT, a leading European tobacco manufacturer, and Segers, a small Dutch manufacturer of fine cut tobacco, to settle a trademark infringement dispute. The Court of Justice upheld the Commission's decision under Article 81 finding that the agreement constituted a disguised market sharing arrangement which, *inter alia,* restricted the use of Seger's trademark 'Toltecs' in Germany to the sale of a certain type of tobacco. Another example is the agreement on the use of identical or similar trademarks in the context of the transfer of a business or part of a business.

---

303. *Ideal Standard,* ECJ June 22, 1994, 1994 ECR I-2789, paras 40–48.
304. *Ibid.,* paras 34–36 and 59. Examples for applying Article 81 to agreements by which parallel trademark rights have been subdivided between several proprietors by contract of assignment: *Sirena,* ECJ Feb. 18, 1971, 1971 ECR 69; *EMI/CBS,* ECJ June 15, 1976, 1976 ECR 811, 871 and 913 (isolating the Common Market from third countries' imports by assigning the respective trademark rights).
305. *Grundig/Consten,* ECJ July 13, 1966, 1966 ECR 299, 345 (agreement authorizing registration of a trademark in the name of an exclusive distributor with the effect of granting absolute territorial protection in using the trademark rights against parallel imports).
306. *Advocaat Zwarte Kip,* D.Comm. July 24, 1974, 1974 OJ L 237/12 (market sharing trademark assignment agreement).
307. *Sirdar/Phildar,* D.Comm. March 5, 1975, 1975 OJ L 125/27 (restrictive trademark delimitation agreement with the effect of market sharing).
308. *Quantel Intemational-Continuum/Quantel,* D.Comm. July 27, 1992, 1992 OJ L 235/9 (market sharing in the framework of the transfer of business).
309. *Fyffes/Chiquita,* Twenty-second Report on Competition Policy, points 168–176 (market sharing in the framework of the transfer of trademarks). *See,* however, *Michelin/Continental,* 1996 OJ C 236/9, where the Commission seems to accept the separation of the European market from the non-European markets with respect to the trademark 'Uniroyal'.
310. *Toltecs/Dorcet,* ECJ Jan. 30, 1985, 1985 ECR 363, paras 33–37.

Such agreements may contain territorial limitations on the use of the trademarks assigned as part of the transferred business which may be tantamount to a market sharing prohibited under Article 81.[311]

Non-Restrictive Coexistence Agreements: The *Penneys* and *Persil* Cases. The problem of market divisions caused by identical or similar trademarks held by different firms may be resolved by agreements allowing the marks to coexist or by introducing distinguishing marks or features. The larger the trademark owners are and the more they are accustomed to selling in all markets, the greater the likelihood they will have a common interest in finding a solution by a non-restrictive agreement, such as by adding distinguishing marks or features. Such agreements are generally favoured by the Commission.[312] Thus, Penney America, a clothing retailer, agreed not to trade under the 'Penneys' name in Ireland, while Penneys Ireland, also a clothing retailer, agreed not to use 'Penneys' as a trademark anywhere in the world and to use it as a business name only in Ireland. The Commission found that the agreement, in settlement of trademark litigation in various jurisdictions, did not infringe Article 81 (1).[313] In the *Persil* case Henkel, the owner of the 'Persil' mark in Germany, adopted red letters with the name 'Henkel' in smaller letters in a red oval alongside it. Unilever, owner of the same 'Persil' trademark in France and the United Kingdom,[314] adopted green letters for the trademark.[315]

---

311. *EMI/CBS,* ECJ June 15, 1976, 1976 ECR 811, paras 38–39; *Gillette/Wilkinson,* D.Comm. Nov. 10, 1992, 1993 OJ L 116/21.
312. This was already contemplated by the Court of Justice in *Hag I,* ECJ July 3, 1974, 1974 ECR 731, paras 9–15, and more explicitly in *Ideal Standard,* ECJ June 22, 1994, 1994 ECR 2789, para. 52.
313. *Penneys,* D.Comm. Dec. 23, 1977, 1978 OJ L 60/19. *See also Osram/Airam,* Eleventh Report on Competition Policy, point 97; *Bayer/Tanabe,* Eighth Report on Competition Policy, points 125–127; *Winninger Domgarten,* Tenth Report on Competition Policy, points 133–134; *Hershey/Herschl,* Twentieth Report on Competition Policy, point 111.
314. Due to expropriation during the Second World War.
315. *Persil,* Seventh Report on Competition Policy, points 138–140. *See also* Advocate General Jabobs in *Hag II,* ECJ Oct. 17, 1990, 1990 ECR I-3711, paras 33–45, expressing scepticism about the practicability of distinguishing additions or simply allowing trademarks to be used concurrently, by both owners, for which there are precedents in national law ('honest concurrent user' in English law – *GE/GEC,* House of Lords, 1973 *Reports on Patent Cases* 297 – and the 1959 German law dealing with trademark conflicts arising from the integration of the Saarland into Germany – BGBl 1959 I–388). *See,* however, Articles 29–35 of the Benelux Trademark Convention ('Eenvormige Beneluxwet op de warenmarken') of March 19, 1962, *Tractatenblad van het Koninkrijk der Nederlanden* 1962 No. 52, which precluded concurrent use of trademarks owned by different right-holders in different countries throughout the Benelux in the transitional period before registration as Benelux marks.

7. Know-How

Know-How not an Industrial Property Right.
Know-how is secret technical or commercial knowledge that provides a competitive advantage to the user.[316] Know-how is not an industrial property right, although it can be equally valuable. Unlike patents and utility models, no exclusive right to produce or market the products manufactured under the know-how exists, no matter what the commercial value of this secret knowledge. Only the confidential character of know-how is protected by national laws and court decisions against industrial espionage, misappropriation and other unfair methods of obtaining access to confidential business information.[317] Hence, no import or export restrictions can be justified by the nature or essence of know-how under Articles 28 and 30.[318] Import or export restrictions can only be based on contractual obligations insofar as they satisfy the conditions of the block exemption regulation on transfer of technology agreements.

8. Rights against Unfair Competition

Unfair Competition Law not an Industrial Property Right.
Unfair competition law is neither an industrial property right nor a matter of 'public policy' under Article 30. However, the Court has recognized the importance of consumer protection and fair trading when interpreting Article 28[319] but has subjected them to two principles: non-discrimination and proportionality. The Court has consistently held, in particular in *Commission* v. *Ireland*,[320] *Allen and Hanburys*[321] and more recently in *Graffione v. Fransa*[322] that obstacles to intra-Community trade resulting from disparities between provisions of national unfair competition law must be accepted in so far as such provisions are applicable to

---

316. *Renter/BASF,* D.Comm. July 26, 1976, 1976 OJ L 254/40, 47.
317. With respect to the international protection of know-how as an act of unfair competition *see* – in very general terms – Article 1 bis of the Paris Convention (The Hague 1925) and – more explicitly – Article 39 of TRIPs: Trade Related Aspects of Intellectual Property Rights (part of the WTO), 1994 OJ L 336/1, 213.
318. Unless the business information can be qualified as a right *sui generis* as in the case of the legal protection of databases under Article 7 of Directive 96/9/EC on the Legal Protection of Databases, 1996 OJ L 77/20.
319. *Ringelhan,* ECJ Nov. 6, 1984, 1984 ECR 3651, para. 19; *GB-INNO-BM,* ECJ March 7, 1990, 1990 ECR I-667, paras 14–16.
320. *Commission v. Ireland,* ECJ June 17, 1981, 1981 ECR 1625, paras 8–10.
321. *Allen and Hanburys,* ECJ March 3, 1988, 1988 ECR 1245, para. 35.
322. *Graffione/Fransa,* ECJ Nov. 26, 1996, 1996 ECR I-6039, para. 17, referring to recital 6 of the First Council Directive to Approximate the Laws of the Member States Relating to Trademarks (*supra* notes 37 and 38), which states that 'this directive does not exclude the application to trademarks of provisions of law of the Member States other than trademark law, such as the provisions relating to unfair competition, civil liability or consumer protection'.

domestic and imported products without distinction and may be justified as being necessary in order to satisfy overriding requirements relating *inter alia* to consumer protection or fair trading. However, in order to be permissible, such provisions must be proportionate to the objective pursued and that objective must not be capable of being achieved by measures which are less restrictive of intra-Community trade.

Non-Discrimination.
The respective national unfair competition rules must apply without discrimination to both domestic and imported products and they must be justified as necessary in order to satisfy essential requirements relating to consumer protection or fair trading.[323] However, the Court of Justice has ruled that certain national rules, although applying equally to domestic and imported products, may unduly restrict the possibility of marketing the imported products and limit the volume of imports, thereby infringing the free movement principle.[324] By contrast, in *Keck*[325] the Court of Justice ruled that national rules concerning only the *modalities* of marketing – as opposed to strictly *product-related* rules – are not likely to discriminate unlawfully against imports.[326] Examples include national rules prohibiting sales below cost,[327] sales of or publicity for para-pharmaceutical products outside pharmacies,[328] and the use of television for advertising[329] or sales after shop closing hours.[330]

Proportionality.
National laws on unfair competition vary substantially through the Community. The limitations that result from the differences in national laws and regulations must be accepted to the extent that they are necessary in order to fulfil essen-

---

323. i.e. non-discriminatory application of national unfair competition rules, in particular with respect to the prohibition of unfairly deceptive imitations from another member state under the same standards as for prohibiting domestically produced imitations: *Beguelin,* ECJ Nov. 25, 1971, 1971 ECR 949 (paras 14–15); *Dansk Supermarket* ECJ Jan. 22, 1981, 1981 ECR 181, paras 15–16.
324. *Dassonville,* ECJ July 11, 1974, 1974 ECR 837; *GB-INNO-BM,* ECJ March 7, 1990, 1990 ECR I-667, para. 7 (prohibition of advertising); *Yves Rocher,* ECJ May 18, 1993, 1993 ECR I-2361 (prohibition of comparing prices of imported with domestic products); *Alpine Investments,* ECJ May 10, 1995, 1995 ECR I-1141, paras 28, 33–39, 45–56 (prohibition of 'cold calling', i.e. to offer financial services by phone to users in other member states without their previous written consent).
325. *Keck,* ECJ Nov. 24, 1993, 1993 ECR I-6097, para. 17.
326. The difference between product- and marketing-related rules has been reaffirmed in *Konsumentenombudsman/Gourmet International,* ECJ March 8, 2001, 2001 ECR I-1795.
327. *Keck,* ECJ Nov. 24, 1993, 1993 ECR I-6097, paras 16–18.
328. *Contact Lenses,* ECJ May 25, 1993, 1993 ECR I-2899; *Hünermund,* ECJ Dec. 15, 1993, 1993 ECR I-6787; *Commission v. Greece,* ECJ June 29, 1995, 1995 ECR I-1623.
329. *Leclerc/Siplec,* ECJ Feb. 9, 1995, 1995 ECR I-179, paras 19–22.
330. *t'Heuske,* ECJ June 2, 1994, 1994 ECR I-2199.

tial public purposes; among these the Court of Justice has considered protecting consumers against being misled[331] or disadvantaged.[332] However, such risk of confusing or misleading customers must be sufficiently serious[333] assuming a 'normal degree of attentiveness'.[334] Any measures to avoid consumer confusion must be 'proportional' (reasonable), that is to say, they must not extend beyond what is necessary to achieve the intended purpose and must not be capable of being achieved with less restrictive means.[335] Any assessment must take account of all the relevant factors, including the circumstances in which the products are sold, the information set out on the packaging and the clarity with which it is displayed, the presentation and content of advertising material, and the risk of error in relation to the group of consumers concerned.[336] For example, distinguishing the origin when trademarks or get-up are similar may be sufficient rather than the more severe forms of marketing restriction.[337] The proportionality test must be based on the objective of Community law to avoid segmentation of national markets.[338]

Piracy and Counterfeiting.

The Commission proposed a directive on the enforcement of intellectual and industrial property rights, such as copyright and related rights, trademarks, designs or patents, against counterfeiting and piracy. The directive would require all member states to apply effective, dissuasive and proportionate remedies and penalties against those engaged in counterfeiting and piracy.[339]

331. *Cassis de Dijon,* ECJ Feb. 20, 1979, 1979 ECR 649, para. 8; *Nissan,* ECJ Jan. 16, 1992, 1992 ECR I-146; *Mars,* ECJ July 6, 1995, 1995 ECR I-1923, para. 15.
332. *Mars,* ECJ July 6, 1995, 1995 ECR I-1923, para. 20.
333. *Graffione/Fransa,* ECJ Nov. 26, 1996, 1996 ECR I-6039, paras 17, 27.
334. *Bristol Myers Squibb/Paranova,* ECJ July 11, 1996, 1996 ECR I-3457, paras 36–37 and 47; *Estée Lauder/Lancaster,* ECJ Jan. 13, 2000, 2000 ECR I-117, para. 32. Similarly *Lloyd Schuhfabrik Meyer/Klijsen Handel,*ECJ June 22, 1999, 1999 ECR I-3819, paras 17–18.
335. *Pall/Dahlhausen,* ECJ Dec. 13, 1990, 1990 ECR I-4844, para. 12; *Yves Rocher,* ECJ May 18, 1993, 1993 ECR I-2361, para. 12; *Alpine Investments,* ECJ May 10, 1995, 1995 ECR I-1141, para. 45; *Mars,* ECJ July 6, 1995, 1995 ECR I-1923, para. 15; *Graffione/Fransa,* ECJ Nov. 26, 1996, 1996 ECR I-6039, para. 27. Similarly *EFTA/Norway,* EFTA Court of Justice, April 5, 2001, E-3/00, para. 26.
336. *Graffione/Fransa,* ECJ Nov. 26, 1996, 1996 ECR I-6039, para. 27.
337. *Ringelhan,* ECJ Nov. 6, 1984, 1984 ECR 3651, paras 15–19; *Industrie Diensten Group,* ECJ March 2, 1982, 1982 ECR 707, para. 10. What is to be termed a 'slavish imitation' is a matter for national courts; it is not a matter that may be determined by contract at the discretion of a licensor and its licensees. Such a form of private regulation may be a prohibited restriction of competition under Article 81 (1): *see* the Advocate General's opinion in the case *Industrie Diensten Group,* 1982 ECR 707, 722–723.
338. *Cassis de Dijon,* ECJ Feb. 20, 1979, 1979 ECR 649, para. 14; *Pall/Dahlhausen,* ECJ Dec. 13, 1990, 1990 ECR I-4844, para. 12; *Mars,* ECJ July 6, 1995, 1995 ECR I-1923, para. 15.
339. IP/03/144 and IP/04/316 of March 9, 2004 (support of the European Parliament).

9. Multiple Protection of the Same Item by Different Property Rights

No Artificial Extension of Property Rights.
A product may be covered in parallel by different property rights, e.g. a pencil by patent, design and trademark rights. The Court of Justice has not ruled expressly on the parallel exercise of such rights.[340] However, the block exemption regulation on transfer of technology agreements extends to mixed intellectual property rights agreements and clarifies that territorial restrictions are exempted as long as the licensed rights are protected.[341] However, the duration of trademark protection (which is unlimited) does not determine the duration of territorial restrictions in mixed agreements where the trademark licence is only ancillary; e.g. copyright protection may not be extended by including ancillary trademark aspects.[342]

D. Limits on the Exercise of Industrial and Intellectual Property Rights under Article 81

1. Complementarity of the Principle of Free Movement of Goods and Services and the EC Competition Rules

Existence v. Exercise.
Agreements to assign or license industrial or intellectual property rights do not in themselves infringe Article 81 any more than does conferring distribution or manufacturing rights. However, the exercise of industrial or intellectual property rights or of contractual rights in accordance with limitations or restrictions in a licence may be caught by Article 81.[343] There are two methods of demonstrating that a restriction of competition in a licence agreement is permissible. First, the restriction may be necessary on grounds of legitimate protection of the licensed right, and this will be determined by the specific subject matter of the individual right.[344] Second, a restriction that extends beyond the specific subject matter of the industrial property right may be justified under Article 81 (3). A balancing of competitive benefits and detriments is not made under Article 81 (1) but under the exemption provision of Article 81 (3) or pursuant to a block exemption regula-

340. *See Dior/Evora,* ECJ Nov. 4, 1997, 1997 ECR I-6013.
341. Article 2 of Regulation 772/2004, which grants territorial protection to know-how agreements for as long as the know-how remains secret and not, as under Article 1 (3) and (4) of Regulation 240/96, only for ten years from the date when the protected product is first put on the market within the EU by one of the licensees.
342. *Dior/Evora,* ECJ Nov. 4, 1997, 1997 ECR I-6013, para. 58.
343. *M6, Antena 3, Gestévision, SIC/UER, Eurovision,* CFI Oct. 8, 2002, T-185/00, para. 64.
344. *Sirena,* ECJ Feb. 18, 1971, 1971 ECR 69, para. 9; *Windsurfing,* ECJ Feb. 25, 1986, 1986 ECR 611, para. 36; *Ottung/Klee & Weilbach,* ECJ May 12, 1989, 1989 ECR 1177, para. 10.

tion.[345] This section discusses these principles in the context of licence agreements likely to be scrutinized under Article 81 and the applicable block exemption regulation, whereas agreements on joint research and development are discussed in Chapter III under Sections B.3. and C.2. and the limits on the exercise of industrial or intellectual property rights under Article 82 in Chapter V. under Section D.6.(d).

Existence Including Limitations of a Licence within the Scope of the Protected Right.
The owner of an industrial property right is entitled to decide whether to exploit the right itself and/or to assign or to grant a licence, and, if so, to whom. The owner is free to grant a licence to a single licensee for all products or services, for the whole territory and for the whole duration protected by its right. It may also divide its rights by allocating territories or fields of use between licensees and itself and limit the duration of the licence. The effect of such limitations is that the licensees receive a right to use the owner's right within those limits (i.e. territory, field of use and duration). Should the licensees use the right beyond those limits, they are subject to actions, by the right-holder, for infringement and breach of their contractual obligations set forth in the licence.[346] In other words: the right-holder is entitled to limit the licensee's exploitation of the licensed right within the scope of the protected right and up to the stage where these rights are 'exhausted', i.e. where the products manufactured using the rights are first marketed by the right-holder or with its consent.

Congruity between the Principle of Free Movement of Goods and Services and the Rules of Competition.
The aims of industrial and intellectual property rights, i.e. protecting and rewarding innovation,[347] and the aims of competition rules, i.e. ensuring undistorted competition,[348] must be interpreted to complement each other because they both aim at promoting consumer welfare and efficient allocation of resources.[349] The scope of industrial and intellectual property rights is determined by the respective national or Community industrial and intellectual property law. Limitations within

345. *Métropole télévision – TPS,* CFI Sept. 18, 2001, 2001 ECR II-2459, paras 72–78.
346. The regulations establishing a Community industrial and intellectual property rigth provide that the proprietor may invoke its right against a licensee who contravenes any provision in the licensing agreement with regard to territory and exclusivity, provided the terms of the agreement conform to the rules of the EC Treaty (including, e.g., Regulation 772/2004), *see* Directive 2004/48/EC on the Enforcement of Intellectual Property Rights, Recital 12 (2004 OJ L 157/45) and Chapter VII.B.3 *supra*.
347. *NDC/IMS Health I,* CFI Oct. 26, 2001, 2001 ECR II-3193, para. 143; *IMS Health II,*ECJ April 29, 2004, C-418/01, para. 52.
348. Article 3 (g) of the EC Treaty.
349. Commission Evaluation Report, COM/2001/786 final, point 29.

this scope are accepted whereas restrictions beyond the scope of the protected right are subject to Article 81. The exercise of these rights within their protected scope cannot be incompatible with EC law on free movement in Articles 28 and 30 nor with competition law in Articles 81 and 82. For example, a contractual provision in a licence agreement reserving the licensor's right to exercise the right outside the licensed territory is normally not deemed restrictive of competition. It follows that a licence agreement may contain severable parts: the licence and its limitations as far as they remain within the scope of the protected rights and the additional contractual restrictions or conduct going beyond this scope. The consequence is that a restrictive clause which is beyond the scope of the protected right and restricts competition in a manner incompatible with Article 81 leads to the nullity of this clause according to the principle of partial nullity as applied under national law. This means that such an unlawful restrictive clause cannot be enforced against a licensee, but the licensee is still subject to the other limits in the licence agreement, i.e. the licensee is not free to use the protected rights outside those limits and remains bound by obligations such as confidentiality and royalties.

How to Examine Restrictive Clauses in Licence Agreements under Article 81.

Any evaluation of licence agreements should include the following steps. The first aspect to consider is whether the licence agreement has been concluded:

- between companies belonging to the same group; in this case the licence is not covered by Article 81;[350]
- between independent companies in the framework of a joint venture or the transfer of a business; in this case they are subject to a specific *ancillarity* test;[351] or
- between independent companies in the framework of a simple or reciprocal licence agreement or a joint research and development agreement; in this case they require full scrutiny under Article 81 (1) and (3).[352]

The second aspect to consider is whether the licence agreement contains restrictions which:

- are within the specific subject matter of the protected right;
- are not appreciable; under the *De Minimis* Notice the restrictions are not appreciable if the parties to the licence agreement do not exceed a market share

350. *Christiani Nielsen,* D.Comm. June 18, 1969, 1969 OJ L 165/12; *Nintendo,* D.Comm. Oct. 30, 2002, 2003 OJ L 255/33, point 245. *See* the definition of 'connected undertakings' in the Notice on Agreements of Minor Importance, 2001 OJ C 368/13, point 12.2.

351. *See* Chapter VI.D.3.(g).

352. *See* Chapter III.B.3.

of 10% of the relevant market if they are competitors and of 15%[353] if they are not competitors, unless the agreement contains hardcore restrictions, such as price or territorial restrictions, that are likely to be caught by Article 81 (1) irrespective of the parties' market shares;[354]

- do not affect trade between member states to an appreciable extent; under the Notice on the Effect on Trade Concept agreements are not capable of appreciably affecting trade between member states when the aggregate market shares of the parties on any relevant market within the Community affected by the agreement does not exceed 5% and the aggregate annual Community turnover does not exceed EUR 40 million;[355]
- infringe Article 81 (1) but are block exempted under Regulation 772/2004 on Transfer of Technology Agreements, which applies if the aggregate market share of the parties on a relevant technology or product market does not exceed 20% in the case of horizontal agreements and 30% in the case of vertical or conglomerate agreements;
- are not covered by this block exemption but satisfy the conditions for exemption under Article 81 (3); or
- do not fulfill the conditions for exemption under Article 81 (3), and therefore are prohibited and exposed to fines[356] and civil sanctions.[357]

However, for *practical* reasons, it is usually more appropriate to start with the applicability of the block exemption regulation because this regulation applies to contractual obligations irrespective of whether they are, or are not, necessary on grounds of legitimate protection of the specific subject matter of the licensed right ('safe harbour' established by the block exemption[358]). Insofar as contractual clauses in technology agreements are covered by Article 81 (1) and block-exempted under Article 81 (3), the block exemption regulation provides for the necessary legal certainty. Only insofar as clauses are not covered by a block exemption regulation do they need individual evaluation under both Article 81 (1) and (3) by the parties themselves or national courts. Even if licence agreements are *not* covered by the block exemption it is still arguable that they are compatible with Article 81 (1)[359] or satisfy the conditions of Article 81 (3), no prior decision to that

---

353. Commission's Notice on Agreements of Minor Importance, para. 7. In case of mixed horizontal/vertical licence agreements the market share limit of 10% applies.
354. Commission's Notice on Agreements of Minor Importance, para. 11.
355. Commission Notice on the Effect on Trade Concept, point 52.
356. However, fines are quite exceptional. *See Windsurfing,* ECJ Feb. 256, 1986, 1986 ECR 611; in this case the rather low fine of ECU 50,000 imposed by the Commission was reduced by the Court of Justice to ECU 25,000.
357. *See* Chapter X.I.2.
358. TT-Guidelines, point 65. *See BaByliss/SEB-Moulinex,* CFI April 3, 2003, T-114/02, para. 424.
359. TT-Guidelines, point 9: 'the great majority of licence agreements are therefore compatible with Article 81'.

effect being required.[360] In cases of novel or unresolved questions the parties may request informal guidance by the Commission.[361]

The following sections of this chapter therefore focus on the origin (Section D.2.) and content of the block exemption regulation on transfer of technology (Section E), followed by a discussion of restrictions in licence agreements for which no block exemption regulation yet exists and which therefore need individual evaluation (Section F).

2. The Origin of the Commission's Practice of Applying Article 81 to License Agreements on Industrial and Intellectual Property Rights

Legal Uncertainty.
The question whether and to which extent licence agreements are subject to Article 81 (1) was disputed from the very beginning of its effective application under Regulation 17/62. The Commission's Notice of December 24, 1962,[362] which was withdrawn in 1984 after the issuance of the patent licence block exemption regulation,[363] considered certain clauses as being 'covered by the patent' or 'justified by the legitimate interest of the licensor' and therefore not caught by Article 81 (1). However, in its subsequent practice the Commission took a more critical approach, in particular with respect to territorial restrictions in licence agreements likely to divide the Common Market.[364] The first case which reached the Court of Justice for clarifying the disputed applicability of Article 81 (1) to a licence agreement was the *Maize Seed* case.

The *Maize Seed* Case.
This case[365] concerned a licence of plant breeders' rights, an industrial property right similar to a patent. The French Institut National de la Recherche Agronomique (INRA), a public corporation entrusted with research and development of plant varieties, the originator of certain maize seed varieties, and Société française des semences de mais, which had been charged by INRA with their commercial exploitation, had granted an exclusive licence of the plant breeders' rights in the seeds to the German partnership Nungesser KG and its owner, Mr. Eisele. The Commission had decided in 1978[366] that certain provisions of the agreements

360. Article 1 (2) of Regulation 1/2003 (abandoning the prior notification system under Regulation 17).
361. Recital 38 to Regulation 1/2003; Commission's Notice on Guidance Letters.
362. 1962 OJ 2922.
363. 1984 OJ C 220/35.
364. *See* e.g. the cease and desist order in *AOIP/Beyrard,* D.Comm. Dec. 2, 1975, 1976 OJ L 6/8 (not appealed before the Court of Justice).
365. *Maize Seed,* ECJ June 8, 1982, 1982 ECR 2015.
366. *Maize Seed,* D.Comm. Sept. 21, 1978, 1978 OJ L 286/23.

infringed Article 81 (1) and could not be exempted under Article 81 (3). The Court considered that, as the maize seed varieties in question had not been known to German consumers when the cooperation between the parties started, a certain protection of new technology seemed to be justified:

> 'In fact, in the case of a licence of breeders' rights over hybrid maize seeds newly developed in one Member State, an undertaking established in another Member State which was not certain that it would not encounter competition from other licensees for the territory granted to it, or from the owner of the right himself, might be deterred from accepting the risk of cultivating and marketing that product; such a result would be damaging to the dissemination of a new technology and would prejudice competition in the Community between the new product and similar existing products.'[367]

The Court drew a distinction between 'open' and 'closed' exclusive licences. An 'open' exclusive licence (sole licence) exists when the licensor is prevented only from granting other licences or from exploiting the technology itself in the territory granted to the licensee, leaving parallel importers and other licensees free to sell into the 'open' exclusive territory. Under a 'closed' exclusive licence the licensor also prohibits other licensees or traders from importing the product into the licensee's territory, and the exclusive licensee is granted the right to bring an infringement action to prevent importation of the product into its territory – in other words, the licensee is given absolute territorial protection. The Court consequently held that, having regard to the specific nature of the products in question and the dissemination of a new technology, in a case such as the one at hand, the grant of an open exclusive licence, that is a licence which did not affect the position of third parties – parallel importers and other licensees for other territories – was not in itself incompatible with Article 81 (1). It annulled in this respect the Commission's decision which had taken a stricter view that even an open exclusive licence infringes Article 81 (1). The Court confirmed, however, that all the aspects of the agreements which gave the licensee absolute territorial protection were incompatible with Article 81 (1).[368] Other parts of the Commission's decision prohibiting price fixing, non-compete clauses and obligations to produce limited quantities had not been appealed.

The Need for a Block Exemption.

The *Maize Seed* judgment settled a long public debate that had ensued about the treatment of exclusive licences in a proposed regulation for patent licence agreements that was first published as a draft in 1979.[369] It left many other licensing

367. *Maize Seed,* ECJ June 8, 1982, 1982 ECR 2015, para. 57.
368. *Maize Seed,* ECJ June 8, 1982, 1982 ECR 2015, paras 52–67.
369. The debate went back to the Commission's 'Christmas Message' of Dec. 24, 1962 (1962 OJ 2922, withdrawn by Notice in 1984 OJ C 220/14) where the Commission considered exclusive

issues unanswered, even with respect to exclusive licences. While concluding that an exclusive licence could be justified in order to protect the introduction of a new technology, the Court did not state expressly that this protection must be limited in duration. However, this conclusion seems obvious. It is in line with the Court of Justice's statements in cases involving exclusive copyright licences that an exclusive licence may infringe Article 81 (1) if it is for an excessively long duration.[370] Therefore, it may concluded that a mere exclusive licence may be caught by Article 81 (1) if the licence is granted for a new technology for an unduly long period of time or if the licence is for a technology that is no longer new. Furthermore, an exclusive licence may infringe Article 81 (1) or Article 82 if it protects a dominant licensee against the grant of further licences and prevents other potential competitors from getting a licence.[371] Another unanswered question was the extent of territorial protection in the relationship between licensor and licensee and between different licensees of the same licensor as well as the extent of manufacturing and marketing limitations. The use of the block exemption has enabled the Commission to avoid a complex discussion of the precise scope of Article 81 (1) and instead set limits on how far limitations in licence agreements, if and insofar as caught by Article 81 (1), can go if they are to qualify for exemption under Article 81 (3).

From a Legalistic to an Economic Assessment:[372] From Regulation 2349/84 to the New Block Exemption Regulation 772/2004.

- *Regulation 2349/84*[373] was the first block exemption regulation on licences of patents and ancillary know-how which entered into force on January 1, 1985. Due to the lack of experience at the time of preparing the first regulation, Regulation 556/89 on pure know-how as well as mixed know-how/patent licence agreements entered into force on April 1, 1989. Regulation 556/89 was designed to be complementary to the first regulation.
- *Regulation 240/96*[374] on technology transfer agreements, which replaces both preceding regulations and continues in force for a transitional period until March 31, 2006, is characterized by a more liberal approach although maintaining the principle of a rather broad application of Article 81 (1). This regulation is more

licences as unlikely to affect trade between member states 'at present', whereas the Commission's subsequent practice was to consider exclusive licences as requiring the grant of an exemption under Article 81 (3): *Davidson Rubber,* D.Comm. June 9, 1972, 1972 OJ L 143/31; *Kabelmetal/Luchaire,* D.Comm. July 18, 1975, 1975 OJ L 222/34; *AOIP/Beyrard,* D.Comm. Dec. 2, 1975, 1976 OJ L 6/8.

370. *Coditel II,* ECJ 6 Oct. 1982 ECR 3381 paras 16–19.
371. *Tetra Pak I,* D.Comm. July 26, 1988, 1988 OJ L 272/27; *aff'd* CFI July 10, 1990, 1990 ECR II-309 (licensee having a market share of more than 90%).
372. Commission Evaluation Report, COM/2001/786final, point 3.
373. 1984 OJ L 219/15.
374. 1996 OJ L 31/2.

flexible in shortening the blacklist and shifting more clauses to scrutiny under the opposition procedure (which was retained after long debate).[375] However, the new regulation follows the same rationale underlying its practice going back to the *Grundig/ Consten* case, which concerned trademarks,[376] and further developed by the Court of Justice in cases of patent,[377] plant variety,[378] copyright[379] and franchise agreements[380] condemning absolute territorial protection, quantity and price restrictions.

- *The new Regulation 772/2004 on the application of Article 81 (3) of the Treaty to categories of technology transfer agreements*,[381] which repeals Regulation 240/96, aims at a more economic oriented approach in line with the recent reforms concerning vertical and horizontal agreements. In particular, the new regulation introduces market share thresholds (20% in the case of horizontal and 30% in the case of vertical agreements) below which the benefit of the block exemption applies, and deletes the 'whitelist' and 'grey list' of practices included in the former regulation.

Plan of the Following Sections.

The following Sections discuss transfer of technology agreements under the new block exemption regulation with particular emphasis on those agreements and clauses which are covered by the block exemption and those which are *not* covered and therefore need individual clearance under Article 81 (1) and (3) (E.) and of other licence agreements for which no block exemption exists yet (F.), whereas R&D agreements are discussed in the framework of horizontal cooperation (Chapter III.C.2.).

375. Regulation 240/96 also eliminates the need to distinguish between mixed patent and know-how licences in which the patent element predominated (formerly governed by Regulation 2349/84) and those in which know-how predominated (formerly governed by Regulation 556/89).
376. *Grundig/Consten*, ECJ July 13, 1966, 1966 ECR 299, 344–350.
377. *Windsurfing*, ECJ Feb. 5, 1986, 1986 ECR 611, para. 99.
378. *Maize Seed*, ECJ June 8, 1982, 1982 ECR 2015, para. 53.
379. *Coditel II*, ECJ Oct. 6, 1982, 1982 ECR 3381, para. 19.
380. *Pronuptia*, ECJ Jan. 29, 1986, 1986 ECR 353, paras 15–26.
381. 2004 OJ L 123/11.

E. The New Technology Transfer Block Exemption Regulation 722/2004

1. The Scope of the Block Exemption

(a) The Main Features of the Regulation and its Guidelines

Block Exemption Subject to Market Share Thresholds.
The new Regulation 772/2004 provides for a broader, umbrella-type block exemption by exempting technology transfer agreements up to a market share threshold of 20% (where the parties are competitors) or 30% (where the parties are non-competing undertakings), except where the agreements contain hardcore restrictions. The main features therefore are:

- distinguishing more clearly between license agreements between actual or potential competitors and agreements between non-competitors by applying market share thresholds of respectively 20 and 30%,[382]
- dropping the 'white list' enumerating those clauses which do not infringe Article 81 (1) or are exemptible under Article 81 (3) and the 'grey list' of clauses which are covered by the block exemption only if they were duly notified to, and not opposed by, the Commission,
- maintaining a limited 'hardcore list' of those clauses which are not covered by the block exemption and normally are not eligible for exemption, such as price fixing and territorial and customer restrictions,[383] and
- taking a more cautious approach toward the exploitation of a new technology by way of patent pools and multiparty licensing.

The most important consequence of the new legal framework is that licence agreements containing restrictive clauses, which were whitelisted under the former block exemption irrespective the parties' market shares, now require individual assessment under Article 81 once the new market share thresholds noted above are exceeded and that, according to Regulation 1/2003, the parties can no longer request clearance by notifying the agreements to the Commission but instead must assess for themselves whether they are compatible with Article 81 (1) or satisfy the conditions of Article 81 (3).

Guidelines Complementing the Block Exemption Regulation.
The principles for the assessment of technology transfer agreements are set out in the Commission's Guidelines on the Application of Article 81 to Technology

382. Commission Evaluation Report, COM/2001/786final, points 183 and 187.
383. *Ibid.*, points 184–186.

Transfer Agreements (hereafter 'TT-Guidelines').[384] The purpose of the Guidelines is to provide guidance on the application of the block exemption regulation and on the application of Article 81 (1) and (3) to agreements which are not covered by the new block exemption regulation, stressing however that each case must be assessed on its own facts and merits.

(b) Transfer of Technology Agreements Covered by the Block Exemption

Licensing or Assignment Agreements.
The new block exemption covers technology transfer agreements, decisions by associations and concerted practices.[385] It applies to licensing agreements on intellectual property rights as well as to agreements on the assignment of such rights that are tantamount to a licensing relationship, namely where the risk associated with the exploitation of the technology remains with the assignor, in particular where the sum payable by the assignee is dependent on products manufactured, sold or provided with the assigned technology.[386] As a rule, however, a simple assignment is not restrictive of competition since the assignor transfers the rights for the purpose of allowing the use by the assignee, and the assignor ceases to use them itself. It is therefore to be compared to a sales agreement which is not restrictive of competition.

Transfer of Technology as Primary Object of the Agreements.
The transfer of technology must be the primary object of the agreements permitting the *production* of the contract product on the basis of the licensed technology.[387] Agreements which contain only ancillary provisions on the use of industrial or intellectual property rights, such as in a mere *distribution* agreement, are not covered by the block exemption on transfer of technology agreements but may instead be covered by Regulation 2790/1999 on Vertical Restraints if they are concluded between non-competitors [388] or by Regulation 2658/2000 on specialization agreements or Regulation 2659/2000 on R & D agreements if they are concluded between competitors.[389]

384. Guidelines on the Application of Article 81 to Technology Transfer Agreements, 2004 OJ C 101/2 (hereafter 'TT-Guidelines').
385. Article 1 (1) (a) of Regulation 772/2004.
386. *Ibid.*, Article 1 (1) (b).
387. Article 2 of Regulation 772/2004.
388. Article 2 (3) of Regulation 2790/1999 and Recital 3. Both regulations are, however, 'closely related': TT-Guidelines, point 62.
389. *See* TT-Guidelines, points 57–60.

Agreements between Two Undertakings for the Manufacture or Provision of Contract Products.

In order to receive the benefit of the new block exemption in technology transfer agreements, the relevant agreement must be concluded between two undertakings permitting the production[390] of contract products or services[391] and may include the following categories of agreement:

- *Licensing and sublicencing agreements:* The block exemption covers both licensing and sublicensing agreements, provided they are granted for the exploitation of the technology.[392] An agreement by which the licensor grants a licence solely for the purpose (i) of granting sublicences to third parties or (ii) of enabling the licensee to carry out further research is not an agreement that permits the production of final or intermediate products and services and therefore falls outside the block exemption.[393]
- *Licensing agreements between competitors and between non-competitors:* The block exemption covers both licensing agreements between competitors and between non-competitors, but with certain differences with respect to the applicable market share thresholds and prohibited hardcore restrictions.[394]
- *Reciprocal and non-reciprocal licensing agreement*: The block exemption covers both reciprocal and non-reciprocal licensing agreements, but with certain differences as to output and territorial restrictions.[395]
- *Subcontracting:* The block exemption covers subcontracting agreements for the purpose of producing products or services,[396] by which the contractor provides to the subcontractor a particular technology (possibly also equipment) necessary for the manufacture of goods which may be supplied only to the contractor, provided the transfer of technology is the primary object of the agreement.[397] In addition, the Commission's Notice on subcontracting agreements[398] remains applicable, in particular with respect to the obligation on the subcontractor to

390. Article 2, first para. of Regulation 772/2004. The licence agreement may extend to the distribution stage, stipulating, for instance, the obligations that the licensee must or may impose on resellers of the products manufactured under the licence.
391. Article 1 (1) (e) of Regulation 772/2004.
392. TT-Guidelines, points 42 and 48.
393. Article 2, first paragraph, and Article 1 (1) (e) of Regulation 772/2004.
394. Articles 3 and 4 of Regulation 772/2004.
395. Article 4 (1) and (2) of Regulation 772/2004.
396. TT-Guidelines, point 44, which must be read in the light of the Notice on Subcontracting Agreements, point 2 (1979 OJ C 1/2), which is still applicable: Horizontal Guidelines, points 80–82. Agreements for the purpose of subcontracting R&D are not covered: Recital 7 to Regulation 772/2004.
397. Where the primary object is specialization whereby the contractor ceases unilaterally production of the products, which are the subject of the subcontracting agreement, Regulation 2658/2000 on specialization agreements applies up to the market share threshold of 20%.
398. 1979 OJ C 1/2.

produce certain products exclusively for the contractor.[399] Agreements between non-competitors which do not involve the transfer of technology may be covered by Regulation 2790/1999 on vertical restraints up to a market share limit of 30%.

- *OEM agreements*: OEM agreements may be covered by Regulation 772/2004 to the same extent as subcontracting agreements, namely insofar as they involve the licence of secret, substantial and identified know-how or industrial property rights to the licensee.
- *Multiple licensing:* The regulation applies to multiple licensing, i.e. the parallel conclusion of licence agreements between a licensor and multiple licensees, because the various licence agreements give rise to the same issues as simple licence agreements.[400] However, the block exemption does not apply to agreements between two or more licensors to grant licences to the same licensee or licensees or to enter into a technology pool whereby two or more licensors agree to pool their technologies and to licence them as a package.[401]
- *Joint ventures:* In the case where undertakings hold interests in a joint venture the parent companies may transfer or licence the technology necessary for the implementation of the joint venture, which may be considered ancillary to the creation of the joint venture.[402]
- *Settlement agreements:* Licence agreements and cross licensing may be an important means of settling or avoiding conflicts on the exploitation of technology (patents and know-how). They are covered by the block exemption (subject to the market share thresholds) where they allow the use of the licensor's technology for the production of goods or services.[403]
- *Technology pools:* Technology pools are agreements between the rightholders of competing or complementary technologies which allow a licensee to operate on the market on the basis on a single licence. Such an agreement is concluded between competitors not for manufacturing or providing goods or services but for establishing a pool (joint venture) with a view of granting licenses to third parties. The horizontal agreement establishing the technology pool is not covered by the block exemption, but the licence agreements concluded between

399. TT-Guidelines, point 44.

400. *See* the very comprehensive Report on Multiparty Licensing by Charles River Associates (Lind, Kleymenova, Miauton and Muysert) of April 22, 2003, DG COMP's website.

401. TT-Guidelines, point 41.

402. Commission Notice on Ancillary Restraints, 2001 OJ C 188/5, points 21–24; *Baxter/Nestle/Salvia,* D.Comm. Feb. 6, 1991, M.58. *See* TT-Guidelines, points 57–60; 2004 Draft Notice on Ancillary Restrictions, points 41–42. Where the parent companies are competitors the block exemption of Regulation 240/96 did not apply according to its Article 5 (1) (2) because of the likely anticompetitive collusion when concluding parallel licence agreements with their jointly controlled undertaking.

403. TT-Guidelines, points 204–206.

the pool and the third parties are block exempted, provided the conditions of Regulation 772/2004 are fulfilled.[404]

- *Franchise agreements:* Such agreements are governed by the new block exemption regulation on technology transfer agreements insofar as the transfer of substantial technology or know-how is the primary object of such agreements;[405] otherwise Regulation 2790/1999 on Vertical Restraints applies.[406] However, the application of both regulations may lead to the same result since both include a list of similarly prohibited hardcore restrictions and market share thresholds (30% in cases of agreements between non-competitors).
- *Supply and distribution agreements:* Supply and distribution agreements in which technology transfer is not the predominant object of the agreement are not covered by the block exemption.[407] They must be assessed under under Regulation 2790/1999 on Vertical Restraints, in particular in cases of bottling agreements.[408]
- *Agreements on joint research and development*: R & D agreements are subject to Regulation 2659/2000 on R&D agreements, although the line between R& D and licensing agreements is difficult to draw because licensing agreements normally include the further development of the licensed technology. However, Regulation 772/2004 applies where the licensee is obliged to carry out development work before obtaining a product that is ready for commercial exploitation, provided that a contract product has been identified.[409]

---

404. *Ibid.*, points 41 and 210–235.
405. Article 1 (1) (b) of Regulation 772/2004; TT-Guidelines, point 49. E.g., *Carlsberg/Watney,* D.Comm. July 12, 1984, 1984 OJ L 207/26 (individual exemption granted prior to Regulation 559/89 on Know-How Licensing Agreements).
406. Article 2 (2) (b) of Regulation 2790/1999 on Vertical Restraints (replacing Regulation 4087/88 on franchising agreements, 1988 OJ L 359/46). Examples: *Campari,* D.Comm. Dec.23, 1977, 1978 OJ L 70/69; *Moosehead/Whitbread,* D.Comm. March 23, 1989, 1989 OJ L 100/32 (both cases were the subject of individual clearances but would be covered by Regulation 2790/1999).
407. Article 1 (1) (b) of Regulation 772/2004 and TT-Guidelines, point 49. *See also* Article 5 (1) (5) of Regulation 240/96. Example: the agreement by which Grundig granted its exclusive distributors a trademark licence (GINT = Grundig International) limited to their exclusive territory in order ensure absolute territorial protection: *Grundig,* ECJ July 13, 1966, 1966 ECR 299.
408. Bottling normally does not adduce appreciable added value in terms of technology, *see Campari,* D.Comm. Dec. 23, 1977, 1978 OJ L 70/69; *Carlsberg/Watney,* D.Comm. July 12, 1984, 1984 OJ L 207/26 (licence for brewing beer under Carlsberg's trademark).
409. TT-Guidelines, point 45.

(c) The Industrial and Intellectual Property Rights Covered by the Block Exemption

The Intellectual Property Rights Covered by the Block Exemption. The block exemption applies only to the licensing or assigning of property rights which are listed in Article 1 (1) (b) and only for as long as the licensed rights are protected (Article 2, para. 2).

The Positive List of Article 1 (1) (b) of the New Block Exemption on Technology Transfer Agreements. The block exemption applies to the licensing or assigning of the following intellectual property rights or a combination thereof:

- patents, including patent applications,
- utility models, including applications for utility models ('petty patents'),
- designs,
- topographies of semiconductor products,
- supplementary protection certificates for medicinal products,
- know-how,
- plant breeder's certificates, and
- software copyrights.

Other intellectual property rights (e.g. copyrights, trademarks and neighbouring rights) are only covered if they do not constitute the primary object of the agreement and are directly related to the manufacture or provision of the licensed products or services.[410] Trademark licences which are ancillary to distribution or franchise agreements must be assessed under Regulation 2790/1999 on Vertical Restraints.[411]

---

410. Article 1 (1) (e) of Regulation 772/2004. *See* TT-Guidelines, points 49–50. Article 10 (15) of the old Regulation 240/96 used the term 'ancillary provisions', i.e. 'provisions relating to the exploitation of intellectual property rights other than patents, which contain no obligations restrictive of competition other than those attached to the licensed know-how or patents and exempted under this regulation.' Article 1 (1) (b) of Regulation 772/2004 states that the block exemption applies to provisions which 'do not constitute the primary object of the agreement and are directly related to the production of the contract products'. The consequence is quite similar: directly related provisions that are *not* 'ancillary' or *do* constitute the 'primary object' of the licence agreement, are normally caught by Article 81 (1), but may be exempt automatically under the block exemption regulation ('safe harbour'); only if these conditions are not fulfilled they need individual assessment under Article 81 (3).

411. Article 2 (3) of Regulation 2790/1999. Example of a bottling agreement: *Campari,* D.Comm. Dec. 23, 1977, 1978 OJ L 70/69; *Carlsberg/Watney,* D.Comm. July 12, 1984, 1984 OJ L 207/26 (licence for brewing beer under Carlsberg's trademark).

Patents.
The block exemption applies to patents and know-how licensing agreements and mixed patent and know-how licensing agreements.[412] The licence agreement may relate to a national patent, a European patent granted for member states or, once Community patents are available, to a Community patent, irrespective of whether the patent has already been issued or has only been applied for or will be applied for within the time limits set by national law. The block exemption also applies to supplementary protection certificates for medicinal products or other products for which a supplementary protection certificate to the basic patent may be obtained.[413]

Know-How.
Know-how means a package of non-patented practical information, resulting from experience and testing, which is secret, substantial and identified.[414]

– The essence of know-how is its secrecy. 'Secret' means that the know-how package as a body or in the precise configuration and assembly of its components is not generally known or easily accessible, so that part of its value consists in the lead which the licensee gains when it is communicated to him; it is not limited to the narrow sense that each individual component of the know-how should be totally unknown or unobtainable outside the licensor's business.
– 'Substantial' means that the know-how includes information which is significant and useful for the production of the products covered by the licence agreement, i.e., can reasonably be expected at the date of conclusion of the agreement to be capable of improving the competitive position of the licensee, for example by helping him to enter a new market or giving him an advantage in competition with other manufacturers or providers of services who do not have access to the licensed secret know-how or other comparable secret know-how.
– 'Identified' means that the know-how is described in a sufficiently comprehensive manner as to make it possible to verify that it fulfils the criteria of secrecy and substantiality, thereby ensuring that the licensee is not unduly restricted in his exploitation of his own technology. The know-how can either be identified

412. Article 1 (1) (b), (f) and (i) of Regulation 772/2004. *See*, more explicitly, Article 1 of Regulation 240/96.
413. Article 1 (1) (h) of Regulation 772/2004. *See* Article 8 (1) and (2) of Regulation 240/96. *See also* Council Regulation 1768/92 on the supplementary protection of medicinal products (1992 OJ L 182/1).
414. Article 1 (1) (i) of Regulation 772/2004 and TT-Guidelines, point 47. It is appropriate to specify high standards for know-how in order to prevent the parties to a know-how agreement – who may be competitors – from using it as a pretext for dividing markets, as in *Racal Decca*, D.Comm. Dec. 21, 1988, 1989 OJ L 43/27, with respect to copyright licences. *See* in greater detail Article 10 (2)–(4) of Regulation 240/96.

in the licence agreement or in a separate document or recorded in any other appropriate form.[415] The same principle should also apply to additional know-how communicated to the other party in the course of the agreement in order to avoid conflicts on the disclosure of licensed (original and additional) know-how to third parties.[416]

In contrast to a patent, know-how does not confer any exclusive rights, but its secret character may be protected under unfair competition law in the event of unauthorized disclosure. Know-how can be of as much or even greater value than a patent, and may contribute just as much to technological advancement as a patent. Although a particular invention may be patentable, the inventor may prefer to retain its invention as a trade secret rather than to disclose it to the world as required when obtaining a patent. From research undertaken prior to the issuance of block exemptions, the Commission had found that pure know-how licences were at least as common as pure patent licences in the Community, and that royalties from know-how licences were roughly equal to those under patent licence agreements. The assignment or licensing of technical or industrial know-how typically includes the right to use a method of manufacturing or an industrial process together with a wide range of related technical, commercial, administrative, financial or other accumulated practical experience.

Utility Models.
The block exemption applies to registered utility models as well as to applications for registration of utility models, which protect technical inventions that may meet lower standards of inventiveness than for a patent ('petty patent'). They are assimilated to patents for the purposes of the block exemption to the same extent as *certificats d'utilité d'addition* and applications for such certificates under French law.[417]

Design Rights.
Designs enjoy protection against unauthorized copying or imitation for a limited period if they are registered, which requires 'newness' in the light of their esthetic or artistic features. Examples include licence agreements on high-quality design furniture used to equip public buildings, hotels and large offices[418] and cases where an original equipment manufacturer (OEM) undertakes to supply certain products for incorporation and resale under the supplier's design, but under the buyer's

415. *See* Article 10 (2)–(4) of Regulation 240/96.
416. *See* Article 5 (2) of Regulation 772/2004, which does not maintain the previous reversal of proof established by Article 2 (1) (18) of Regulation 240/96.
417. Article 1 (1) (h) of Regulation 772/2004.
418. Example: *Knoll/Hille*, Thirteenth Report on Competition Policy, points 142–146.

trademark. The application of the block exemption depends on whether or not the agreements involve the transfer of substantial technology.[419]

Topographies of Semiconductor Products.
The development of topographies of semiconductor products requires the investment of considerable resources, human, technical and financial, while they can be copied at a minor fraction of the cost needed to develop them independently. Topographies of semiconductor products are therefore protected in a way similar to patents.[420] As with patented products, the exclusive right granted for topographies of semiconductor products may not be asserted to prevent their free movement within the Community and the EEA countries once the topography of the semiconductor product has been put on the market in a member state or an EEA country by the owner or with its consent.

Plant Breeder's Rights.
Plant breeder's rights hold the same status as patents.[421] Under EU law a plant breeder's right may be granted only for plant varieties which are distinct, uniform, stable, and new.[422] A key distinction must be made between basic seeds and the reproduced and certified varieties. Granting the right to reproduce seeds, obliging the licensee not resell, nor to reproduce basic seeds for third parties is necessary in order to protect the licensor's selection of licensees, who made major investments, and to avoid improper handling of the basic seed.[423]

Software Copyrights.
Computer software, like any other creative work, is in many countries protected by copyright against misappropriation and, in particular, against unauthorized reproduction, adaptation or distribution. Differences between national protection

419. TT-Guidelines, points 43–45. Examples which were subject to individual assessment under Article 81: *ICL/Fujitsu,* Sixteenth Report on Competition Policy, point 72; *Siemens/Fanuc,* D.Comm. Dec. 16, 1985, 1985 OJ L 376/28.

420. Article 1 (1) (h) of Regulation 772/2004. *See* Council Directive 87/54/EC on the Legal Protection of Topographies of Semiconductor Products, 1987 OJ L 24/36. The directive contains a definition of the protected product (Article 1) and of the scope of the exclusive rights attenuated by the principle of exhaustion (Articles 2 and 5 (5)).

421. Article 1 (1) (h) of Regulation 772/2004. Licence agreements in respect of plant breeder's rights were included in Regulation 240/96 (Article 8 (1) (h)) but were excluded from Regulation 2349/84 (Article 5 (1) (4)). *See Sicasov,* D.Comm. Dec. 14, 1998, 1999 OJ L 4/27, points 72–73.

422. Article 6 of Council Regulation 2100/94 on Community Plant Variety Rights.

423. *Hesbignonne,* ECJ April 19, 1988, 1988 ECR 1919, paras 10–11; *Plant Royalty Bureau,* Ninth Report on Competition Policy, point 120. The particular substantive and procedural provisions of Regulation 26/62 apply only if the agreements in question form an integral part of a national market organization or are necessary for the attainment of the objectives of Article 33 of the EC Treaty. *See Sicasov,* D.Comm. Dec. 14, 1998, 1999 OJ L 4/27, point 65.

are removed by Council Directive 91/250/EC,[424] which defines the scope of the exclusive right and its exhaustion in a similar way as for patent rights.[425] The block exemption applies to software copyright licensing and assignment agreements, including agreements containing provisions which relate to the sale and purchase of the licensed products.[426]

Trademark and Copyrights other than Software Copyrights.
Regulation 772/2004 covers the licensing of trademarks and copyrights only to the extent that they are directly related to the exploitation of the licensed technology and do not constitute the primary object of the agreement. Normally trademark licensing occurs in the context of the distribution and resale of products and is therefore governed by Regulation 2790/1999 on vertical restraints.[427] The licensing of copyright for the purpose of reproduction and distribution of the protected work, i.e. the production of books, records and video-cassettes, is considered to be of the same nature as technology transfer agreements and normally raise similar issues. Although these agreements are not directly covered by the new block exemption on technology transfer agreements, the Commission will apply, as a general rule, the principles set out in the block exemption.[428] The principles applying to the licensing of copyrights for copyrighted services or intangibles, such as the showing of a film which is made available to the public by performances which may be indefinitely repeatable, are necessarily different for copyrighted goods which are placed at the disposal of the public in material form. The licensing of copyrights in performances and other related copyrights raise special issues and are therefore not covered by the block exemption but subject to individual assessment. [429]

Duration of Protection.
The exemption applies to a license agreement only for so long as the rights to the licensed technology have not expired, lapsed or been declared invalid or, in the case of know-how, for so long as the know-how remains secret, except in the event where the know-how becomes publicly known as a result of action by the licensee, in which case the exemption shall continue to apply for the duration of the agreement.[430]

---

424. 1991 OJ L 122/42.
425. *See supra* section C.5 (d).
426. Article 1 (1) (b) of Regulation 772/2004.
427. TT-Guidelines, point 53.
428. TT-Guidelines, point 51. *See Neilson-Hordell/Richmark,* Twelfth Report on Competition Policy, points 88–89.
429. TT-Guidelines, point 52. *See Dior/Evora,* ECJ Nov. 4, 1997, 1997 ECR I-6013, para. 57.
430. Article 2, subparagraph 2, of Regulation 772/2004; TT-Guidelines, point 54. Article 3 (7) of Regulation 240/96 precluded any extension of territorial limitations by concluding separate licence agreements on additional or complementary technology through automatic prolongation of the initial duration of the agreement by the inclusion of any new improvements, whether

(d) Duration of the Block Exemption and Transitional Period

Ten-Year Duration.
The new block exemption will remain in force for ten years, until April 30, 2014.[431] The block exemption applies with respect to each individual licensing agreement, according to Article 2 , second paragraph, for as long as the licensed property right has not expired, lapsed or been declared invalid or, in the case of know-how, for as long as the licensed know-how remains secret,[432] except where the know-how becomes publicly known as a result of action by the licensee, in which case the exemption applies for the duration of the agreement. This constitutes an important difference to Regulation 240/96. According to Article 1 (3) of the prior Regulation 240/96 the exemption formerly applied to active sales restrictions for ten years and to passive sales restrictions for five years from the date when the licensed product was first put on the market within the EU by one of the licensees.[433] The new Regulation 772/2004 permits certain *active* sales bans in licence agreements for the entire duration of the agreement. *Passive* sales bans are permitted in agreements between *non-competitors* for two years into an exclusive territory or customer group allocated to another licensee, and between both competitors and non-competitors in a non-reciprocal agreement for the duration of the agreement or the life of the applicable technology for passive sales into an exclusive territory or customer group reserved to the licensor.[434]

Transitional Period.
Article 10 of the new Regulation 772/2004 provides for a transitional period up to March 31, 2006 in respect of agreements which do not satisfy the conditions of the new block exemption regulation but which satisfy the conditions of Regulation 240/96. This is of particular importance for licence agreements containing passive territorial restrictions against a licensee selling into the territory of another licensee which are entirely precluded as between competitors and are treated less favorably as between non-competitors under the new block exemption but were exempted under Regulation 240/96 up to five years. Therefore, such a

---

patented or not. *See Alcatel/Novasam,* ECJ Oct. 5, 1988, 1988 ECR 5987, para. 10 (automatic extension of a leasing contract for fiftenn years may be abusive).

431. Article 11 of Regulation 772/2004.
432. TT-Guidelines, point 47.
433. *See* Article 1 (2)–(3) of Regulation 240/96. *See also Maize Seed,* ECJ June 8, 1982, 1982 ECR 2015, para. 57. The normal life time of valuable secret know-how is between five and ten years anyway, except in cases of secret formulae (which are, however, rarely fully disclosed). In addition, Article 1 (3), fourth subparagraph, of Regulation 240/96 provides that the block exemption applies only where the parties have identified in any appropriate form the initial know-how (this corresponds to Article 1 (1) (g) of the new Regulation 772/2004) as well as any subsequent improvements to it which become available to one party and are communicated to the other party. The new Regulation 772/2004 should be interpreted in the same way.
434. Article 4 (1) (c) (iv)–(v) and Article 4 (2) (b) (i)–(ii) of Regulation 772/2004.

passive sales ban agreed for five years in a licensing agreement already in force on April 30, 2004 can only be enforced until March 31, 2006. Agreements concluded after April 30, 2004 must conform to the two-year standard under Regulation 772/2004.[435]

2. Distinction between Licence Agreements between Competitors and Non-Competitors Subject to Market Share Thresholds

Different Assessment under Regulation 240/96 and Regulation 772/2004. The prior Regulation 240/96 exempted licensing agreements irrespective of whether the parties are competitors or non-competitors. That regulation excluded reciprocal agreements between competitors,[436] except where they were not subject to any territorial restriction.[437] The new Regulation 772/2004 follows the Court's and the Commission's established practice to distinguish between agreements between *competitors* and *non-competitors*.

- Agreements between *competitors*: Agreements between competitors are covered by the block exemption if the parties' combined market share *does not exceed 20%* of the affected relevant technology and the relevant product market. This market share limit corresponds to the market share threshold of the block exemption regulation on specialization agreements,[438] whereas the block exemption regulation on R&D agreements (although closer to reciprocal licensing agreements) establishes a market share threshold of 25%.[439]
- Agreements between *non-competitors*: Agreements between non-competitors are covered by the block exemption if the market share of each of the parties *does not exceed 30%* of the relevant technology and product market. This market share limit corresponds to the market share limit of Regulation 2790/1999 on vertical restraints.[440]

If the respective market share is initially not more than respectively 20% and 30%, the block exemption continues to apply for a period of two consecutive

---

435. Article 2, para. 2, of Regulation 772/2004; TT-Guidelines, point 54. Article 3 (7) of Regulation 240/96 precluded any extension of territorial limitations by concluding separate license agreements on additional or complementary technology or by including, through automatic prolongation of the duration of the agreement by inclusion of any new improvements, whether patented or not. *See Alsatel/Novosam,* ECJ Oct. 5, 1988, 1988 ECR 5987, para. 10 (automatic extension of a leasing contract for fifteen years may be abusive).
436. Article 5 (1) (3) of Regulation 240/96.
437. Article 5 (2) (2) of Regulation 240/96.
438. Regulation 2658/2000, 2000 OJ L 304/3.
439. Regulation 2659/2000, 2000 OJ L 304/7.
440. 1999 OJ L 336/21. However, Article 3 of Regulation 2790/1999 on Vertical Restraints normally considers the market share held by the supplier and only in the case of exclusive supply obligation that held by the buyer.

calendar years following the year in which the threshold was first exceeded.[441] The block exemption is therefore limited to these market share thresholds,[442] provided the agreements do not contain hardcore restrictions. The definition of 'hardcore' restrictions differs according to whether the agreements are concluded between competitors or between non-competitors and, with respect to agreements between competitors, whether they are reciprocal or non-reciprocal.[443] Reciprocal licensing agreements which are concluded between competitors are subject to stricter conditions, in particular with respect to output limitations, certain territorial restrictions and direct and indirect restrictions of the use of the parties' *own* technologies that are different from the licensed technologies.

Licensing Agreements between Competitors v. Licensing Agreements between Non-Competitors.

According to Article 1 (1) (j) of Regulation 772/2004 the parties may be:

- *Actual* competitors if they both compete on the relevant technology market (including by granting licences to competing technologies[444]) or are both active on the relevant product and geographic market on which the contract products are sold without infringing each others' intellectual property rights.[445] The parties do not need to be active on the same geographic market; they are competitors if without the agreement the licensee would be able to use its own technology for entering another geographic market, unless such entry is precluded by objective factors, such as entry barriers and/or sunk costs.[446]
- *Potential* competitors if, in the absence of the agreement and without infringing the intellectual property rights of the other party, it is likely that they would, on realistic grounds, undertake the necessary additional investments or other necessary switching costs so that they could enter the relevant product and geographic markets in response to a small and permanent increase in relative prices. In order to constitute a realistic competitive restraint entry has to be likely within a short period of one to two years.[447]
- *Non-competitors* where the licensor is neither an actual nor potential supplier of the products on the relevant market and the licensee, already present on the product market, is not licensing out a competing technology even if it owns a competing technology and produces on the basis of that technology.[448] However, the parties become competitors if at a later point in time the licensee starts

441. Article 8 (2) of Regulation 772/2004.
442. Recital 11; Article 3 (1) and (2) of Regulation 772/2004.
443. Article 4 (1) and (2).
444. Article 1 (1) (j) (i) of Regulation 772/2004; TT-Guidelines, point 66.
445. Article 1 (1) (j) (ii) of Regulation 772/2004; TT-Guidelines, points 28 and 67.
446. TT-Guidelines, point 138.
447. TT-Guidelines, point 29; examples under point 73.
448. TT-Guidelines, point 68; examples under point 73.

licensing out its technology or the licensor becomes an actual or potential supplier of products on the relevant market. In that case the hardcore list relevant for agreements between non-competitors will continue to apply, unless the agreement is subsequently amended in any material aspect,[449] e.g. with respect to reciprocal output limitations.

3. The New Market Share Thresholds

Calculation of Market Shares.
The block exemption applies where the parties' combined market shares do not exceed respectively 20% (between competitors) and 30% (between non-competitors) on the affected relevant technology *and* product markets. The relevant *technology* market is that of the licensed technology and substitutable existing technologies, i.e. regarded by the licensees as interchangeable with or substitutable for the licensed technology by reason of the technology's characteristics, royalties and their intended use, which can be used without infringing each others' industrial or intellectual property rights.[450] The relevant technology market may also include innovation markets for products capable of replacing existing products as a source of potential competition.[451] However, the regulation recognizes the difficulty of calculating market shares on the relevant technology market, which would have to be based on the number of technologies[452] or on the total licensing income from royalties, which are mostly unknown.[453] The market share on the relevant technology market is therefore defined in terms of the 'presence of the licensed technology on the relevant product market(s),' which comprise the contract products (intermediate[454] and final products[455]) produced by the licensor

449. Article 4 (3) of Regulation 772/2004; TT-Guidelines, point 31.
450. Article 1 (1) (j) (i) of Regulation 772/2004. Substitutable (= competing) technologies as opposed to complementary (= non-competing) technologies, in particular in the case of technologies that are in a one-way or two-way blocking position (TT-Guidelines, points 204–209). However, the distinction between complementary and substitutable technologies is recognized in the TT-Guidelines (point 204) as not clear-cut.
451. TT-Guidelines, point 25. *See* Article 4 (2) of Regulation 2659/2000 on R&D agreements. The definition of the substitutable products and the accurate calculation of market shares will be extremely difficult in some situations to the extent that the parties to a licensing agreement may have to proceed to an evaluation under both the block exemption and Article 81 (3).
452. TT-Guidelines, points 24 and 131. It is therefore important to assess whether the parties' competitors on the downstream market will be able to source the best technology at hand from a number of credible alternative suppliers, *see Alcan/Pechiney,* D.Comm. Sept. 29, 2003, M.3225, point 22.
453. TT-Guidelines, point 23.
454. Where products are used by the parties as components for manufacturing other products reference shall be made to the markets of such of those products for which the components represent a significant part. *See* Chapter IV.B.6(c).
455. TT-Guidelines, point 21.

and its licensees.[456] The market share is calculated on the basis of the market sales value data or, if such data are not available, on other reliable market information, including market sales volumes, relating to the preceding calender year.[457] In order to increase legal certainty, the Commission's Guidelines state that 'outside the area of hardcore restrictions Article 81 is unlikely to be infringed where there are four or more independently controlled technologies in addition to the technologies controlled by the parties to the agreement that may be substitutable for the licensed technology at a comparable cost to the user.'[458] However, if the shares on the technology market are calculated on the basis of the number of competing technologies the Guidelines only confirm the block exemption: in the absence of hardcore restrictions licensing agreements between competitors enjoy legal certainty if the parties' market shares do not exceed the threshold of 20%.

Difficulties of Evaluating the Impact of Potential Competition.
Potential competition is impossible to calculate in terms of market shares and is therefore not taken into account when assessing the market share thresholds of the block exemption.[459] Potential competition must, however, be included in the individual assessment of the market position of the parties and their actual and potential competitors.[460] For instance, newly developed products may be in an advanced stage of development ('pipeline products' in the pharmaceutical sector[461]) and therefore capable of entering the market of the existing products in the near term. They may represent such 'drastic innovation' that the technology which the licensee is using for manufacturing the relevant products becomes obsolete or uncompetitive, or they may be unlikely to be substitutable in the foreseeable future. Therefore, the assessment may change once the potential competition becomes effective. Where the licensor and licensee are neither actual nor potential competitors at the time of the conclusion of the agreement, but become competitors afterwards, the hardcore restrictions for non-competing firms apply for the full life of the agreement, unless the agreement is subsequently amended in any material respect,[462] e.g., by introducing reciprocal output limitations.[463]

456. Article 3 (3) of Regulation 772/2004.
457. Article 8 (1) of Regulation 772/2004.
458. TT-Guidelines, point 131.
459. TT-Guidelines, points 30 and 66.
460. TT-Guidelines, points 29 and 135–138.
461. *See Ciba-Geigy,* D.Comm. July 16, 1996, 1997 OJ L 201/1, point 42.
462. Article 4 (3) of Regulation 772/2004.
463. Article 4 (1) (b) of Regulation 772/2004.

4. Evaluation of the Most Common Clauses in Licensing Agreements under Regulation 772/2004

(a) Structure of the Block Exemption

Regulation 772/2004 is structured as follows:

- Article 2 contains a general provision which block exempts restrictions of competition which are categorized as neither hardcore nor excluded under the regulation but fall within the scope of Article 81 (1). Such restrictions benefit from the block exemption up to the market share threshold of 20% (between competitors) and 30% (between non-competitors). Article 2 covers in general terms the clauses which were 'white-listed' under Regulation 240/96, namely the clauses which are generally restrictive of competition but merited block exemption (Article 3 of Regulation 240/96) and the clauses which are generally not restrictive of competition but block exempted to the extent that they, under exceptional circumstances, constitute a restriction of competition (Article 2 of Regulation 240/96);
- Article 4 contains a list of *hardcore restrictions* which preclude the applicability of the block exemption to the *entire agreement* irrespective of the parties' market share; and
- Article 5 contains a list of *excluded restrictions* which preclude the applicability of the block exemption to the *particular clause* without affecting the entire agreement, again irrespective of the parties' market share.

With respect to hardcore and excluded restrictions governed by Articles 4 and 5, important distinctions are made according to whether the licensing agreements are concluded between competitors or non-competitors[464] and whether the agreements between competitors are reciprocal or non-reciprocal. However, the block exemption granted in Article 2 applies to all other restrictions, up to the applicable market share thresholds, irrespective of whether or not the parties are competitors. The various clauses therefore need separate discussion.

The plan of this section is:

- to deal with those clauses which are generally not restrictive of competition (section 4 (b)),
- to evaluate the restrictive clauses in agreements between competitors, first in non-reciprocal agreements, followed by a section highlighting the particulars

464. This is new; Regulation 240/96 applied irrespective of whether or not the parties are competitors, except with respect of field-of-use restrictions (Article 3 (4)), licensing agreements relating to the activity of a joint venture (Article 5 (1) (2)) and reciprocal licensing agreements (Article 5 (1) (3)).

of reciprocal agreements between competitors (which are treated more strictly in certain respects) (section 4 (c)), and
- to evaluate restrictions in licensing agreements between non-competitors which are generally treated more permissibly (section 4 (d)).

Section 5 will discuss the conditions for withdrawing the benefit of the block exemption and section 6 the individual assessment of certain agreements and clauses under Article 81 which do not benefit from the block exemption.

Copyright and trademark licensing agreements which are, as such, precluded from the block exemption will be discussed in a separate Section F.

(b) Obligations which are Generally Held Non-Restrictive of Competition

Application of the Block Exemption as Safe Harbour.
Obligations which are generally not restrictive of competition irrespective of whether or not the parties to the licence agreement are competitors do not infringe Article 81 (1) but are covered by the general provision of Article 2 of Regulation 772/2004 for reasons of legal certainty ('safe harbour principle'). The obligations include, among others:

- obligations on the licensee not to divulge the licensed technology;[465]
- obligations on licensees not to sublicence the licensed technology;[466]
- obligations in subcontracting agreements, whereby the subcontractor undertakes to produce certain products exclusively for the contractor,[467]
- obligations not to use the licensed technology after the expiry of the agreement, provided that the licensed technology remains valid and in force;[468]
- obligations to assist the licensor in enforcing the licensed intellectual property rights;[469]
- obligations to pay minimum royalties or to produce a minimum quantity of the licensed product;[470]
- obligations to observe minimum quality specifications and to allow the licensor to carry out related checks;[471] and
- obligations to use the licensor's trademark or indicate the name of the licensor on the contract product;[472] to this extent the agreement may include the grant of

465. TT-Guidelines, point 155. *See* Article 2 (1) (1) of Regulation 240/96.
466. TT-Guidelines, point 155. *See* Article 2 (1) (2) of Regulation 240/96.
467. TT-Guidelines, point 44; Notice on subcontracting agreements (which remains applicable), point 2.
468. TT-Guidelines, point 155. *See* Article 2 (1) (3) of Regulation 240/96.
469. TT-Guidelines, point 155. *See* Article 2 (1) (6) of Regulation 240/96.
470. TT-Guidelines, point 155. *See* Article 2 (1) (9) of Regulation 240/96.
471. *See* Article 2 (1) (5) of Regulation 240/96.
472. TT-Guidelines, point 64. *See* Article 2 (1) (11) of Regulation 240/96.

a trademark licence, provided it is ancillary,[473] i.e. it does not contain additional restrictions which go beyond those agreed under the transfer of technology agreement.[474]

Insofar as such obligations constitute a restriction of competition they are covered by the block exemption under Article 2 of Regulation 772/2004, in which case the market share thresholds of 20% (between competitors) and 30% (between non-competitors) apply.

(c) Evaluation of Restrictions in Agreements between Competitors under Regulation 772/2004

(i) Distinction between Reciprocal v. Non-Reciprocal Licence Agreements

Articles 4 and 5 of Regulation 772/2004 distinguish between non-reciprocal and reciprocal licensing agreements between competitors, by applying stricter conditions to reciprocal agreements because they are more likely to amount to a market sharing between competitors.

- *Non-Reciprocal Licence Agreements.* Non-reciprocal agreements are agreements where one undertaking grants another undertaking a technology licence, or where two undertakings grant each other such a licence but where these licences do not concern competing (substitutable) technologies and cannot be used for the production of competing products.[475] The main motive of non-reciprocal licence agreements between competitors is to increase the rightholder's reward for its invention by granting a licence to an undertaking operating on another geographic market or within another technical field of use or another product market rather than exploiting the invention on its own.
- *Reciprocal agreements* are defined in Article 1 (1) (c) of Regulation 772/2004 as a technology transfer agreement where two undertakings grant each other, in the same or separate contracts, a technology licence and where these licences concern competing technologies[476] or can be used for the production of competing products.[477] Although it is not expressly stated, reciprocal licences may be exchanged directly or via a joint venture and may be concluded following a

473. TT-Guidelines, point 50. *See* Article 5 (1) (4) of Regulation 240/96.
474. *See Norway/Astra Norge,* EFTA Court of Justice, Nov. 24, 1998, E-1/98, ELR 1999–1, 34.
475. Article 1 (1) (d) of Regulation 772/2004.
476. I.e., technologies which may be exploited without infringing each others' industrial or intellectual property rights: Article 1 (1) (j) (i) of Regulation 772/2004.
477. Article 1 (1) (j) (ii) of Regulation 772/2004. *See also* Article 5 (1) (3) of the former Regulation 240/96. Cross licensing technologies which are not competing (e.g., complementary) are not included within the definition of a reciprocal agreement: TT-Guidelines, point 78.

joint research and development phase.[478] Reciprocal licence agreements commonly have different motives. First, they may end disputes between parties in a one-way or two-way blocking position due to their overlapping industrial property rights. Second, they may provide for the joint exploitation of these complementary rights without further cost for research and development. (Regulation 2659/2000 applies in the event the parties undertake joint R&D). In both instances the main threat to competition is that the parties may – depending on their competitive relationship and their collective market share[479] – agree not only on a momentary, but also a long-term exchange of technology which may lead to cross-fertilization and enrichment of the technology but also make it difficult or impossible for the partners to achieve a competitive advantage in the relevant field by their own individual efforts.[480] A further possible threat to competition arises in the case of joint control of the common technology, which may be an impediment to market entry by third parties if a licence may be granted only with the consent of all the participants to the arrangement.[481]

(ii) Evaluation of Restrictions in *Non-Reciprocal* Licensing Agreements between Competitors

Restriction of a Party's Ability to Determine its Prices when Selling Products to Third Parties (Article 4 (1) (a) of Regulation 772/2004).

Any kind of price-fixing is a hard core restriction in agreements between competitors, including the determination of components of prices or discounts for the licensed products or services.[482] Fixing maximum or recommended prices is also, unlike in cases of licence agreements between non-competitors,[483] a hardcore restriction,[484] which is in accord with the Commission's administrative practice with regard to horizontal cooperation.[485] Royalty obligations and payment schemes may be employed in cross-licences between competitors as a means to coordinate prices or reduce output, and therefore will be subjected to closer scrutiny.[486] In

478. E.g. *Philips/Sony,* D.Comm. Aug. 7, 2003, IP/03/1152.
479. Reciprocal licence agreements between firms with market shares of up to 10% (horizontal) or 15% (vertical) are of minor importance and therefore do not infringe Article 81 (1).
480. They must therefore be distinguished from a grant-back relating to improvements to or new applications of the technology licensed by one party (Recital 8 of Regulation 240/96). *See Henkel/Colgate,* D.Comm. Dec. 23, 1971, 1972 OJ L 14/14, 16.
481. E.g., *APS System,* IP/98/353 of April 15, 1998 (settlement after commitment to grant licences to third parties before the end of the development of the new system).
482. *See* Article 3 (1) of Regulation 240/96.
483. Article 4 (2) (a) of Regulation 772/2004.
484. Article 4 (1) (a); *see also* Article 3 (1) of Regulation 240/96.
485. *See Cement,* CFI March 15, 2000, 2000 ECR II-491, para. 4517 (maximum prices); *Fire Insurance,* ECJ Jan. 27, 1987, 1987 ECR I-405, paras 34–43 (recommended prices).
486. Guidelines on Technology Transfer Agreements, points 135 and 199.

cases of multiple licences concluded between competitors price-fixing imposed on multiple licensees by the same licensor amounts to horizontal price-fixing between the different licensees.[487] An obligation on the licensee to pay a minimum royalty is, however, not in itself restrictive of competition.[488]

Limitation of Output (Article 4 (1) (b) of Regulation 772/2004). Limitations of the output of the contract products imposed on the licensee in a non-reciprocal agreement are, unlike in reciprocal agreements, not hardcore restrictions, and are block exempted up to the market share limit of 20%. Output limitations restrict the capacity or quantity to be produced by exploiting the respective licensed technology. They normally have pro-competitive effects and may be necessary to induce the licensor to disseminate its technology as widely as possible.[489] A licensor may also be reluctant to licence a competitor if he could not limit the licence to a particular site with a specific capacity (site licence).[490] However, output imitations with respect to the parties' own technologies (which are not licensed) are always black-listed.[491]

Allocation of Markets or Customers (Article 4 (1) (c) of Regulation 772/2004). This hardcore provision precludes the imposition of territorial or customer restrictions, which are, in the context of agreements between competitors, tantamount to market sharing, except in the following cases:

– *Sole licences.* In non-reciprocal agreements between competitors the licensor may undertake not to licence the technology to another licensee in a particular territory (the territory which is reserved to the licensee).[492] The territory allocated to the licensee may cover the whole world, which implies that the licensor abstains from entering or remaining on the market.[493]
– *Production and sales restrictions between licensor and licensee(s).* In non-reciprocal agreements both the licensor and the licensee may be obliged not to produce in territories reserved for the other party[494] and not to sell actively or passively[495] into the exclusive territory or to the exclusive customer group reserved for the other party.[496]

---

487. *Hesbignonne,* ECJ April 19, 1988, 1988 ECR I-1919, para. 15.
488. TT-Guiudelines, point 79. *See* Article 2 (1) (9) of Regulation 240/96.
489. TT-Guidelines, points 82–83.
490. TT-Guidelines, point 175.
491. Article 4 (1) (d) of Regulation 772/2004; TT-Guidelines, point 82. *See* Article 3 (5) of Regulation 240/96.
492. Article 4 (1) (c) (iii) of Regulation 772/2004.
493. TT-Guidelines, points 86 and 162.
494. Article 4 (1) (c) (ii) of Regulation 772/2004.
495. Active and passive sales as defined in the Commission's Guidelines on Vertical Restraints, 2000 OJ C 291/2, point 50.
496. Article 4 (1) (c) (iv) of Regulation 772/2004.

- *Sales restrictions between various licensees.* In non-reciprocal agreements the licensor may impose on its licensees the obligation not to sell actively into the exclusive territory or to the exclusive sustomer group allocated to another licensee, provided the latter was not a competing undertaking of the licensor at the time of the conclusion of its own licence.[497] However, a ban on passive sales by one licensee to customers located in the territory reserved to another licensee is a hardcore restriction.[498] Passive sales are supplies in response to an unsolicited order.[499] Passive sales restrictions may be the result of the obligation not to sell to certain customers or in certain territories but also of the obligation to refer orders from these customers to other licensees or of indirect measures, such as financial incentives or a monitoring system aimed at verifying the effective destination of the licensed products;[500] even quantity limitations which are normally permitted may be an indirect means to restrict passive sales, although the Commission does not assume that quantity limitations as such serve such purpose.[501] Internet sales, which are deemed to be (permitted) passive sales, are likely to reduce considerably the degree of territorial protection ensured by the (exempted) active sales bans.[502]
- *Field-of-use restrictions.* Non-reciprocal agreements between competitors that limit the licensee to a particular technical field of use or to one or more product markets are block exempted up to the market share limit of 20%.[503] Non-reciprocal agreements may also provide for the obligation on the licensor and/or licensee not to produce with the licensed technology within one or more technical fields or one or more product markets.[504] This means that a field of use restriction may be symmetrial, i.e. limited to the same fields(s) or product market(s), or asymmetrical, i.e. to different fields of use or different

497. Article 4 (1) (c) (v) of Regulation 772/2004.
498. This differs from Article Article 1 (1) (6) and (3) of Regulation 240/96 which block exempted such passive sales bans upt to five years.
499. *See* Article (1) (9) of Regulation 240/96.
500. *See Nintendo,* D.Comm. Oct. 30, 2002, 2003 OJ L 255/3, points 276–277.
501. TT-Guidelines, point 98.
502. Unlike in agreements between non-competitors, Article 4 (1) does not provide for exceptions with respect to sales within a selective distribution network (in particular the obligation to sell only to authorized distributors, which have been selected on the basis of specific criteria, which implies the obligation not to sell – not even passively – to unauthorized distributors in territories allocated to another licensee). The obligation by the licensor on its licensees to establish and to implement such a selective distribution system may therefore appear as a hardcore restriction in agreements between competitors. In agreements between competitors, the licensee must be free to establish, at its own initiative, an exclusive or selective distribution system, provided the agreements concluded between the licensee and its distributors comply with Regulation 2790/1999. *See* TT-Guidelines, points 61–62.
503. Article 4 (1) (c) (i) of Regulation 772/2004. This is an important difference to Article 3 (4) of Regulation 240/96 which black-listed field of use restrictions where the parties were already competitors before the grant of the licence.
504. Article 4 (1) (c) (ii) of Regulation 772/2004.

product markets.[505] According to the Guidelines, the block exemption extends to both symmetrical or asymmetrical field of use restrictions because it gives the licensee an incentive to invest in and develop the licensed technology[506] without necessarily leading to a market sharing.[507] However, in the case of market shares above the 20% market share limitation such agreements may be unlikely to satisfy the conditions of Article 81 (3) because of the risk of market sharing and market foreclosure.

- *Captive use restrictions.* The obligation on the licensee to produce the contract product only for its own use is block exempted, provided the licensee is not restricted in selling the contract product actively and passively as spare parts for its own products.[508] The licensee may be obliged to use the contract products only as an input for incorporating into its own production (including production by way of subcontracting). Captive use restrictions are normally likely to promote the dissemination of technology.[509]
- *Second source of supply limitation.* The obligation on the licensee to produce the contract products only for a particular customer in order to create a second source of supply is block exempted in non-reciprocal agreement between competitors.[510]

Restrictions on the Licensee's Ability to Use its Own Technology (Article 4 (1) (d) of Regulation 772/2004).

Restrictions of the licensee's ability to exploit its own technology or the restriction of the ability of the parties to the agreement to carry out research and development are black-listed in licensing agreements between competitors, unless such latter restriction is indispensable to prevent the disclosure of the licensed know-how to third parties. [511] The provision extends to clauses with a similar effect, such as the obligation to pay royalties irrespective of whether the products are produced under the licensed technology or the licensee's own technology because it limits the licensee's ability to use freely its own technology.[512] The licensee's ability to exploit its own technology and own improvements to the licensed technology includes the possibility to grant licences to third parties without being bound to grant exclusive licences or to assign such developments to the licensor (which is required under Article 5 (1) (a) and (b) of Regulation 772/2004). The ability to carry out further R&D includes the freedom to cooperate with third parties[513]

505. TT-Guidelines, point 183.
506. *See* in greater detail TT-Guidelines, point 91.
507. TT-Guidelines, points 86 and 91.
508. Article 4 (1) (c) (vi) of Regulation 772/2004.
509. TT-Guidelines, points 186–190.
510. Article 4 (1) (c) (vii) of Regulation 772/2004. *See* Article 2 (1) (13) of Regulation 240/96.
511. Article 4 (1) (d) of Regulation 772/2004.
512. Article 4 (1) (d) of Regulation 772/2004 and Guidelines, points 157 and 160.
513. *See* Article 5 (a)–(b) of Regulation 2659/2000 on R&D agreements.

but is subject to the important exception that it must not lead to the disclosure of the licensed know-how.[514] The decisive question therefore is whether the licensee's own developments are 'severable' from the licensed technology[515] or, as formulated in Regulation 2659/2000 on R&D Agreements, relate to an 'unconnected' field.[516] The risk of disclosure of the licensed technology may be reduced by a licensee designating particular employees to be involved in research and development of its own 'severable' technology.[517] Regulation 240/96 provided expressly for the possibility of the licensor to require the licensee to prove that the licensed know-how is *not* being used for the production of products and provision of services other than those licensed.[518] Such clauses, which are ancillary to the obligation not to divulge the licensed know-how, may be covered by the general provision of Article 2 of Regulation 772/2004. In cases where the licensee has the necessary skills and assets, the prohibition not to carry out its own research and not to create a new competitor is unlikely to satisfy the conditions of Article 81 (3) where only a few technologies are available. Foreclosure of competing technologies reduces competitive pressure and reduces competition between the incumbent technologies by limiting the possibilities for licensees to substitute between competing technologies and facilitates collusion between competitors.[519] On the other hand, where several technologies are available and the parties do not possess special assets or skills, such a restraint may promote the dissemination of a new technology by assuring the licensor that the licence does not create a new competitor and by inducing the licensee to exploit and develop the licensed technology.[520]

Obligations with Respect to the Use of the Licensee's Own Severable Improvements of the Licensed Technology (Article 5 (1) (a)–(b) of Regulation 772/2204).

The block exemption does not exempt *exclusive* grant backs or the *assignment* back to the licensor of severable improvements of the licensed technology. An improvement is severable where it can be exploited without infringing upon the licensed technology.[521] The obligation to grant an exclusive licence does not preclude the licensee from using its own improvement, but it precludes the licensee

514. Article 4 (1) (d); *see,* in the case of agreements between non-competitors, Article 5 (2) of Regulation 772/2004. Patented inventions of the licensor cannot be used by the licensee toward third parties anyway. *See also* Article 2 (1) (12) of Regulation 240/96.
515. Article 5 (1) (a) of Regulation 772/2004.
516. *See* Article 5 (a) of Regulation 2659/2000 on R&D Agreements.
517. TT-Guidelines, point 94 (a kind of 'Chinese wall' provision).
518. Article 2 (1) (18) of Regulation 240/96.
519. TT-Guidelines, point 198.
520. TT-Guidelines, point 116. *See* Article 6 (a) of Regulation 2659/2000 on R&D agreements (hardcore restriction in the case of research in unconected fields); *Reuter/BASF,* D.Comm. June 26, 1976, 1976 OJ L 254/20.
521. Article 1 (1) (n) of Regulation 772/2004.

from granting licences to third parties and is therefore likely to reduce its incentive to innovate. However, *non-exclusive* grant-backs are block exempted. Such obligations may be non-reciprocal or reciprocal, thereby including the dissemination of improvements received by the licensor from the various licensees and licensed back to the others in order to allow them to be on an equal footing.[522] However, the stronger the position of the licensor, the more likely it is that exclusive grant back obligations will have restrictive effects on a potential source of competition and innovation from the licensee.[523] In particular in cases of cross licensing between competitors it is unlikely that exclusive grant back obligations will satisfy the conditions of Article 81 (3).[524]

Obligation not to Challenge the Licensed Technology (Article 5 (1) (c) of Regulation 772/2004).
The block exemption does not exempt any direct or indirect obligation on the licensee not to challenge the validity of intellectual property rights which the licensor holds in the EU, without prejudice to the possibility to provide for termination of the licence agreement in the event that the licensee challenges the validity of one or more of the licensed technology rights.[525] Challenging invalid intellectual property rights is in the interest of undistorted competition[526] and in conformity with the principles underlying the protection of intellectual property rights.[527] However, the licensee may be prevented from challenging the secrecy and the substantiality of the licensed know-how because this know-how is, once disclosed, impossible or very difficult to recover.[528] This provision follows the flexible approach of the Court of Justice with respect to no-challenge clauses,[529] thereby taking into account the fact that a licensor cannot be prevented from discontinuing the communication of additional secret know-how anyway.[530]

Tying and Bundling of Technologies.
Tying occurs when the licensor makes the licensing of one technology (the tying product) conditional upon the licensee taking a licence for another technology or purchasing a product from the licensor or someone designated by him (the tied

522. TT-Guidelines, point 109.
523. TT-Guidelines, point 110.
524. TT-Guidelines, point 111.
525. Article 5 (1) (c) of Regulation 772/2004. *See* Article 2 (1) (18) of Regulation 240/96.
526. Competition is distorted by the fact that the licensee is obliged to pay royalties for an invalid and unvaluable technology.
527. TT-Guidelines, point 112.
528. *Ibid.* This differs from Article 4 (2) (b) of Regulation 240/96.
529. *Bayer/Süllhöfer*, ECJ Sept. 27, 1988, 1988 ECR 5249, paras 15–21. A no-challenge clause is particularly unjustified in the case of an obsolete technology with the effect of limiting the licensee's ability to innovate: *Santa Cruz/Microsoft*, Twenty-fourth Report on Competition Policy, point 79.
530. *See* Article 2 (1) (18) of Regulation 240/96.

product). Bundling occurs where two technologies or a technology and a product are only sold together as a bundle. In both cases, however, it is a condition that the products and technologies involved are distinct in the sense that there is a distinct demand for each of the products or technologies forming part of the tie or the bundle.[531] Tying may not be restrictive of competition, in particular where the product and/or technologies must be tied in order to ensure a technically proper exploitation of the licensed technology[532] or it allows the licensee to exploit the licensed technology significantly more efficiently.[533] Tying and bundling in licensing agreements between competitors are neither expressly exempted nor designated as 'hardcore' restrictions under Regulation 772/2004, and are therefore exempted under Article 2 of this regulation, provided the parties' combined market shares do not exceed the market share thresholds of 20%. However, such arrangements need careful evaluation in cases of substantial market power because of the likely effects of foreclosing competing technologies.[534]

(iii) Particulars when Assessing Restrictions in *Reciprocal* Licensing Agreements between Competitors

Article 4 of Regulation 772/2004 provides special more stringent rules for reciprocal agreements between competitors because of their greater likelihood of restricting competition in both innovation and product markets. The cases decided by the Commission demonstrate the anticompetitive risk of reciprocal licensing agreements that are concluded between competitors, in particular where they lead to market sharing between parties with significant market power. In *Siemens/Fanuc* the Commission objected to the reciprocal grant of a licence and the attribution of exclusive territories.[535] In *IMI/Heilmann* the Commission objected to coordination between competitors based on a reciprocal licence and the creation of a joint venture.[536] In *Video Cassette Recorders* it opposed the exchange of licences between competitors which prevented the parties from further developing their own technology and using the technology of third parties.[537] However, in *Concast/Mannesmann* the Commission granted clearance to reciprocal licences which permitted each party to use the technologies freely, including by granting a licence to third parties to its own technology together with a sub-licence to the

531. TT-Guidelines, point 191.
532. *See* Article 2 (1) (5) of Regulation 240/96. Under Article 3 (9) of the first technology transfer Regulation 2349/84 package licences were blacklisted where the licensee was induced at the time of the agreement was entered into to accept further licences which he does not want.
533. TT-Guidelines, points 194–195; *see* Article 2 (1)–(5) of Regulation 240/96.
534. TT-Guidelines, points 191–195.
535. *Siemens/Fanuc,* D.Comm. Dec. 19, 1985, 1985 OJ L 376/29.
536. *IMI/Heilmann I,* Seventh Report on Competition Policy, points 29–32.
537. *Video-Cassette Recorders,* D.Comm. Dec. 20, 1977, 1978 OJ L 47/42.

other party's technology.[538] The Commission also views with suspicion grant-back clauses that may be the basis for, or incorporated into, a more general cooperation between the licensor and several (competing) licensees.[539] Particularly where the licences are exclusive the parties may be prevented from competing effectively with each other and from exploiting freely and independently their own technology with respect to third parties.[540] Accordingly, reciprocal agreements are subject to the very strict conditions provided for by the block exemption.

Price Restrictions (Article 4 (1) (a) of Regulation 772/2004).
Any kind of price fixing is a hardcore restriction in agreements between competitors. Royalty obligations and payment schemes may be employed in cross-licences between competitors as a sham to coordinate prices or reduce output, and are therefore subject to closer scrutiny.[541] However, the Commission will only treat cross licences with reciprocal running royalties as price fixing where the agreement is devoid of any pro-competitive purpose and therefore does not constititute a *bona fide* licensing agreement.[542] In cases of multiple licences price fixing imposed on multiple licensees by the same licensor amounts to horizontal price-fixing between the different licensees.[543] Royalties which extend to products produced solely with the licensee's own technology or with a technology licensed from a third party constitute a hardcore restriction in agreements between competitors because they restrict the licensee's ability to use freely its own technology.[544]

Limitation of Output (Article 4 (1) (b) of Regulation 772/2004).
When competitors agree to impose output limitations in a reciprocal agreement the object and the likely effect is to reduce output in the market to the disadvantage of consumers[545] and may also create, like other forms of horizontal cooperation, foreclosure problems and other negative effects towards third parties.[546] Article 4 (1) (b) covers clauses which, 'directly or indirectly, in isolation or in combination with other factors', have the same object or effect, e.g., the obligation to make

538. *Concast/Mannesmann,* Eleventh Report on Competition Policy, point 93.
539. In general, however, agreements are not 'reciprocal' merely because they contain a grant-back obligation. A 'reciprocal' agreement is a cross-licensing agreement where the licensed technologies are competing technologies or can be used for the production of competing products, *see* Article 1 (1) (c) of Regulation 772/2004; TT-Guidelines, point 78.
540. Even if the party is entitled to grant licences to third parties the value of such licences is less because it is necessarily non-exclusive.
541. TT-Guidelines, point 157.
542. TT-Guidelines, point 80. However, it will be difficult to assess whether a licence agreement is '*bona fide*' or a '*sham*' to a cartel.
543. *Hesbignonne,* ECJ April 19, 1988, 1988 ECR I-1919, para. 15.
544. TT-Guidelines, points 81 and 95.
545. *See* TT-Guidelines, point 82. *See* Article 3 (5) of Regulation 240/96.
546. Guidelines on horizontal cooperation, point 85.

payments if a certain level of output is exceeded, which reduces the parties' incentive to expand output.[547] An output limitation imposed on *only one* of the licensees is, however, block exempted because it creates less risks of anticompetitive coordination between the different (competing) licensees.

Allocation of Markets or Customers (Article 4 (1) (c) of Regulation 772/2004).

Territorial and customer restrictions in reciprocal agreements between competitors are treated more strictly in the following respects:

- *Production and sales restrictions between licensor and licensee(s).* It is a hardcore restriction for a competing licensor and licensee in a reciprocal licence agreement to each agree not to produce in territories reserved to other parties[548] or not to sell actively or passively into the exclusive territory or to the exclusive customer group reserved for the other party.[549] Similarly, the licensees may not agree to refrain from selling actively or passively into the territory or to the customer group reserved to other licensees[550] because such restrictions are likely to eliminate any form of intra-technology competition and result in a hardcore market sharing between competitors.[551] However, sole licences without such territorial or customer restrictions are exempted in reciprocal agreements between competitors to the same extent as in non-reciprocal agreements.[552]
- *Field of use restrictions.* A reciprocal agreement between competitors may include the obligation on the *licensee(s)* to produce only in a specific field of use or product market.[553] However, a field of use restriction imposed on the *licensor and/or licensee* is a hardcore restriction in reciprocal agreements when the fields of use are asymmetrical, i.e. obliging each other to use the licensed technology in different fields or product markets.[554] Such a restriction constitutes a hardcore restriction because of the risk of market sharing between competitors,[555] whereas one-way field of use restrictions are block exempted up to the market share limit of 20%.[556]

---

547. TT-Guidelines, point 82.
548. Article 4 (1) (c) (ii) of Regulation 772/2004.
549. Article 4 (1) (c) (iv) of Regulation 772/2004.
550. Article 4 (1) (c) (v) of Regulation 772/2004.
551. The Commission has intervened against such market sharing agreements: *Siemens/Fanuc,* D.Comm. Dec. 19, 1985, 1985 OJ L 376/29; *IMI/Heilmann,* Seventh Report on Competition Policy, points 29–32.
552. Article 4 (1) (c) (iii) of Regulation 772/2004.
553. Article 4 (1) (c) (i) of Regulation 772/2004.
554. Article 4 (1) (c) (ii) of Regulation 772/2004.
555. Theoretical example: two producers of pharmaceuticals agree to grant each other licences on their competing technologies reserving one party the use of the technology for veterinary products and the other party for human use.
556. However, the Guidelines, points 86–95 and 183 are not entirely clear in this respect.

- *Captive use restrictions.* Such obligations are block exempted irrespective of whether the agreements between competitors are reciprocal or non-reciprocal.[557] Where the parties' combined market share exceeds 20% it is necessary to examine carefully the pro- and anti-competitive effects in the light of the structure of the relevant market of spare parts.[558]
- *Second Source of Supply Obligations.* Such restrictions are hardcore restrictions in reciprocal agreements between competitors[559]

Restrictions on the Use of the Licensee's Own Technology and of its Own Severable Improvements to the Licensed Technology and on Challenging the Technology Rights (Article 4 (1) (d) and Article 5 (1) of Regulation 772/2004).
Under Article 4 (1) (d) of Regulation 772/2004, any restriction of the licensee's ability to exploit its own technology or restriction of the ability of the parties to the agreement to carry out research and development is a hardcore restriction, unless it is indispensable to prevent the disclosure of the licensed know-how to third parties. The consequence of including such a restriction is loss of the benefit of block exemption to the *entire agreement* as is the case for other hardcore restrictions governed by Article 4.

Under Article 5 (1) (a)–(c), exclusive grant back and assignment obligations with respect to the use of the licensee's own severable improvements and obligations not to challenge the licensed technology rights are excluded from the block exemption in reciprocal agreements. The consequences are less severe: the offending obligations are not block exempted, but the benefit of the block exemption continues to apply to the rest of the agreement.

(iv) Evaluation of Restrictions in Licensing Agreements between Non-Competitors

Less Strict Conditions.
Licensing agreements between non-competitors are subject to less strict conditions than licensing agreements between competitors. The list of hardcore restrictions of Article 4 (2) of Regulation 772/2004 is shorter than the list which applies to agreements between competitors. In addition, licence agreements between non-competitors are block exempted up to a market share threshold of 30% (instead of 20% for agreements between competitors).

Price Restrictions (Article 4 (2) (a) of Regulation 772/2004).
Price restrictions are hardcore restrictions to the same extent as in agreements between competitors. However, the licensor may impose a maximum or a recom-

557. Article 4 (1) (c) (vi) of Regulation 772/2004.
558. TT-Guidelines, point 186.
559. Article 4 (1) (c) (vii) of Regulation 772/2004.

mended sale price, provided it does not amount to a fixed or minimum sales price as a result of pressure from, or incentives offered by, any of the parties,[560] e.g., by fixing the margin, the maximum level of discounts or linking the price to the sales prices of competitors, in particular where it is combined with a price monitoring system.[561] Most favored licensee clauses, i.e. the obligation on the licensor to grant the licensee any more favorable terms that the licensor may grant to another licensee, are normally unobjectionable, but may constitute a means of indirect price fixing because of the powerful incentive created for the licensee not to lower its selling price.[562]

Restrictions on Passive Sales Imposed on the Licensee(s) (Article 4 (2) (b) of Regulation 772/2004).

The list of hardcore restrictions does not extend generally to the allocation of markets or customers, except certain types of *passive* sales restrictions imposed on the licensee(s).[563]

- Accordingly, the licensee may also be obliged to produce minimum[564] and fixed quantities[565] in order to ensure an appropriate use of the licensed technology[566] and to exploit the licensed technology in only a specific technical field or one or more product markets,[567] and the licensor may be prevented from granting licences to another licensee and from producing or selling actively or passively into the territory or to the exclusive customer group reserved to the other party, provided the market share limit of 30% is not exceeded.[568]
- *Active* sales bans imposed on the licensor and/or the licensee(s) are exempted by operation of Articles 2 and 4 (2) (b) of Regulation 772/2004, provided that the parties' combined market share does not exceed 30%. This favorable treatment is based on the assumption that such restrictions promote investments, improve the quality of services and solve free rider and hold-up problems.[569]

---

560. *Similarly* Article 4 (a) of Regulation 2790/1999 on Vertical Restraints.
561. TT-Guidelines, point 97.
562. TT-Guidelines, point 97. *See* Article 2 (1) (10) of Regulation 240/96.
563. Passive sales are supplies of the contract products 'in response to an unsolicited order', *see* Article 1 (1) (6) of Regulation 240/96.
564. *See* Article 2 (1) (9) of Regulation 240/96.
565. Not a hardcore restriction under Regulation 772/2004 on technology transfer agreements. *See* however Article 3 (5) of Regulation 240/96 (blacklisted).
566. *See* the best endeavours clause accepted under Article 2 (1) (17) of Regulation 240/96.
567. Field-of-use and product market limitations are not black-listed and therefore included in the general exemption provision of Article 2, which corresponds to Article 2 (8) and (13) of Regulation 240/96.
568. Such restrictions are covered by the general provision of Article 2, paragraph 2, of Regulation 772/2004.
569. TT-Guidelines, points 99–100.

– *Passive* sales bans may be imposed on the licensor with respect to the licensee's territory or customer group[570] and may be imposed on the licensee(s) with respect to the licensor's territory or customer group.[571] However, passive sales bans imposed on the licensees with respect *another licensee's territory or customer group* are block exempted, provided they are limited to the first *two years* that the other licensee is selling the contract product in that territory or to that customer group irrespective of the duration of the agreement or the life of the applicable technology.[572] Such restrictions may be necessary for the licensee to commit substantial investments and promotional activities in order to start up and develop a new market.[573] In cases of market shares exceeding 30% they need careful evaluation but may satisfy the conditions of Article 81 (3) where they are necessary, on a short-term basis (normally not longer than two years[574]), to penetrate a new market. [575] This constitutes an important difference from Regulation 240/96 under which active sales bans in know-how licensing agreements were permitted only up to ten years and passive sales bans up to five years from the date when the licensed product was first put on the market within the EU by one of the licensees.[576] As a rule, a licensee also may not be obliged by the licensor to impose on its distributors territorial or customer restrictions that do not conform to Regulation 2790/1999.

Restrictions of Sales within a Selective Distribution System (Article 4 (2) (c) of Regulation 772/2004).
Unlike agreements between competitors, agreements between non-competitors may contain obligations relating to the establishment and the implementation of particular distribution systems, such as an exclusive or selective distribution system. Following Regulation 2790/1999, Regulation 772/2004 does not distinguish between qualitative and quantitative selective distribution systems. The block exemption extends to:

– the obligation not to sell actively or passively to unauthorized distributors, i.e., who do not satisfy the selective distributions criteria,[577] whereas supplies to authorized distributors may not be restricted;

570. *Ibid.*
571. Article 4 (2) (b) (i) of Regulation 772/2004; TT-Guidelines, point 100.
572. Article 4 (2) (b) (ii) of Regulation 772/2004; TT-Guidelines, points 12 (b) and 101.
573. TT-Guidelines, point 101.
574. TT-Guidelines, point 174.
575. TT-Guidelines, point 101.
576. *See* Article 1 (1) (5) and (3), first paragraph, of Regulation 240/96. Under both regulations the duration of any exempted restriction cannot exceed the actual life of the relevant patent protection in the respective territories: Article 2, second paragraph, of the new technology transfer Regulation; Article 1 (4), third paragraph, of Regulation 240/96.
577. Article 4 (2) (b) (vi) of Regulation 772/2004.

- the obligation not to sell actively[578] or passively[579] to end-users by a licensee which operates on a *wholesale* level; and
- the prohibition against a retail member of the selective distribution system from operating out of an unauthorized place of establishment (location clause).[580]

However, obligations on a licensee operating on the *retail* level not to sell, actively or passively, to end-users,[581] in particular in territories attributed or reserved to other licensees, is blacklisted as a hardcore restriction. The provision conforms to the established case law stating that members of a selective distribution system must be free to sell to other (authorized) members of the distribution system and to end users of their choice irrespective of where they are located, without prejudice to the possibility of prohibiting a member of the system from operating out of an unauthorized place of establishment (location clause).[582] The same applies to licence agreements on plant breeders' rights, which raise similar issues as selective distribution systems: the licensees may not be prevented from reselling actively or passively the basic seed to other licensees of the same licensor, whereas sales to unauthorized third parties may be prohibited.[583] This implies that an agreement between non-competitors may contain the obligation on the licensee to set up a selective distribution system,[584] provided the parties' combined market share does not exceed the market share limit of 30%.

Restrictions on a Licensee's Ability to Exploit its Own Technology (Article 5 (2) of Regulation 772/2004).
Article 5 (2) of Regulation 772/2004 is similar to Article 4 (1) (d) of Regulation 772/2004, but differs with respect to the legal consequences: the inclusion of a non-compete clause in agreements between competitors results in the non-application of the block exemption regulation to the entire agreement, but in agreements between non-competitors results only in the non-applicability of the block exemption to this clause without affecting the entire agreement.[585] The provision states that the exemption shall not apply to any direct or indirect obligation limiting the licensee's ability to exploit its own technology or limiting the ability of any of the parties to carry out research and development, unless the latter provision is indispensable to prevent the disclosure of the licensed know-how to third

578. Article 2 of Regulation 772/2004.
579. Article 4 (2) (b) (v)–(c) of Regulation 772/2004.
580. Article 4 (2) (c) of Regulation 772/2004.
581. Article 4 (2) (b) (v) of Regulation 772/2004.
582. *See* Chapter IV.B.5 (b).
583. *Hesbignonne,* ECJ April 19, 1988, 1988 ECR 1919, paras 9–11.
584. Recital 19 to Regulation 772/2004 and TT-Guidelines, point 63. This is new and fills a gap left by Regulation 240/96, which remained silent on this issue.
585. Article 5 (2) of Regulation 772/2004; TT-Guidelines, point 114. *See* Article 3 (1) of Regulation 240/96.

Summary of the Evaluation of Restrictions in Licensing Agreements under Regulation 772/2004.

Restrictions	*Agreements between competitors*		*Agreements between non-competitors*
	non-reciprocal	reciprocal	
Price restrictions	HC	HC	HC
Maximum and recommended prices	HC	HC	BE
Limitations of output	BE	HC	BE
Only on one licensee	BE	BE	BE
Allocation of markets or customers			
– sole licence = obligation not to grant licences to others	BE	BE	BE
– exclusivity between licensor and licensee = obligation not to produce and not to sell actively and passively	BE	HC	BE
– exclusivity between licensees			
active sales ban	BE	HC	BE
passive sales ban	HC	HC	BE (2 years)
– field of use restrictions			
imposed on the licensee	BE	BE	BE
imposed on licensor and/or licensee	BE	HC	BE
– own use restrictions	BE	BE	BE
– second source restriction	BE	HC	BE
Non-compete clause	HC	HC	ER
Grant back obligations			
– exclusive licence or assignment	ER	ER	ER
– non-exclusive licence	BE	BE	BE
Non-challenge clause	ER	ER	ER

HC Hardcore restrictions which preclude the applicability of the block exemption to the entire agreement even if the parties' combined market share does not exceed the market share thresholds of 20% (between competitors) or 30% between non-competitors).

ER Excluded restrictions which preclude the applicability of the block exemption only to the particular clause without affecting the entire agreement.

BE Block exempted up to the market share limits of respectively 20% and 30%.

parties. For instance, an obligation on the licensee to pay royalties not only on the basis of the products incorporating the licensed technology but also on the basis of the products produced with its own technology may be an indirect means of restricting the use of its own technology and may therefore be excluded from the block exemption.[586] Since the main competitive risk presented by non-compete obligations is the foreclosure of competing technologies such a foreclosure will mainly arise where the licensor has a significant decree of market power or where, by a cumulative effect of agreements concluded by several competitors, more than 50% of the market is tied, which would not be covered by the block exemption or would necessitate withdrawal of its benefit according to Articles 6 and 7 of Regulation 772/2004.[587]

Restrictions on the Use of the Licensee's Own Severable Improvements of the Licensed Technology and on Challenging the Technology Rights (Article 5 (1) (a)–(c) of Regulation 772/2004).
Any restriction of the licensee's ability to use its own severable improvements of the licensed technology, except the grant-back of a non-exclusive license, and of its possibility to challenge the liecned technology rights is precluded from the block exemption to the same extent as in agreements between competitors.

5. Withdrawal of the Block Exemption

Conditions of Withdrawing the Benefit of the Block Exemption.
According to Article 6, the Commission and the national authorities may withdraw the benefit of the block exemption with prospective (*ex nunc)* effect[588] if the conditions of Article 81 (3) are not fulfilled, in particular where:

- access of third parties to the market is restricted, for instance by the cumulative effect of parallel networks of similar restrictive agreements prohibiting imposing licensees from using third party technologies;
- access of potential licensees to the market is restricted, for instance by the cumulative effect of parallel networks of similar agreements preventing licensors from licensing to other licensees,[589] or
- without any objectively valid reason the parties refrain from exploiting the licensed technology.[590]

---

586. TT-Guidelines, 115.
587. TT-Guidelines, points 198–199.With respect to the 50% limit *see* Article 8 of Regulation 2790/199 on vertical restraints.
588. *See* Article 29 (2) of Regulation 1/2003. *See also* Guidelines on Vertical Restraints, point 75.
589. TT-Guidelines, point 118 .
590. However, the licensor may impose on the licensee the obligation to produce minimum quantities or to use its best endeavours (*see* Article 7 (d) of Regulation 240/96) and, if the licensee fails to comply with these obligations, to terminate the license agreement.

National authorities may withdraw the benefit of the block exemption where the agreement has anticompetitive effects in the territory of a member state, which has all the characteristics of a distinct market, and the effect of the withdrawal is limited to that territory.[591] However, member states must ensure that the exercise of this power does not prejudice the uniform application of the Competition rules throughout the Common Market.[592]

Direct Applicability of Article 82 without Prior Withdrawal.
In cases where the conclusion or implementation of a transfer of technology agreement constitutes an abuse of a dominant position Article 82 is directly applicable without the need of prior withdrawal of the benefit of the block exemption.[593]

Scarce Case Law – The *Tetra Pak* Case.
The Commission tested the withdrawal procedure under Regulation 2349/84 with regard to licence agreements in the *Tetra Pak I* case.[594] The case concerned an exclusive patent licence relating to a new technology for sterilizing cartons suitable for UHT-treated milk having a shelf life of several months. Tetra Pak acquired this exclusive licence when it took over Liquipak, a small United States producer of milk packing machines which had been granted an exclusive licence for the technology in question by the British Technology Group, a UK public corporation having the object of licensing the results of public research. The case originated from a complaint by Elopak, a smaller competitor of Tetra Pak which had been cooperating with Liquipak to develop to a commercial stage of exploitation a machine incorporating the new sterilization technology suitable for packaging UHT-treated milk in cartons, a field in which Tetra Pak had over 90% of the market. When Tetra Pak acquired Liquipak and the exclusive licence to the new technology, Tetra Pak gained control over the only commercially proven competing process in the Community for filling cartons with UHT-treated liquids. This not only deprived Elopak of access to this technology, thereby seriously delaying its attempt to enter the market for packaging long-life milk, but also strengthened Tetra Pak's own dominant position in this field. The Commission concluded first that Tetra Pak's acquisition of Liquipak constituted an abuse of a dominant position in this market under Article 82, and secondly that the exclusive licence which otherwise met the conditions of Regulation 2349/84 nevertheless had prevented any new potential competitors from using the technology to enter an already very

591. Under Article 7 of Regulation 240/96 only the Commission was empowered to withdraw the benefit of the block exemption. No such withdrawal decision was adopted under that regulation, but *see* the discussion of the *Tetra Pak* case below.
592. Recital 17 of Regulation 772/2004.
593. *Ibid.*, Recital 20. *See Tetra Pak I*, CFI July 10, 1990, 1990 ECR II-309, paras 21–38; *Hilti*, ECJ March 2, 1994, 1994 ECR I-667.
594. *Tetra Pak I*, D.Comm. July 26, 1988, 1988 OJ L 272/27, 41–43; *aff'd* CFI July 10, 1990, 1990 ECR II-309, paras 21–38.

highly concentrated market, and therefore was incompatible with the conditions for exemption laid down in Article 81 (3). The Commission therefore threatened to withdraw the benefit of the patent licence block exemption and to declare that the exclusive licence infringed Article 81 (1). The licensor and Tetra Pak avoided such a withdrawal by entering into negotiations to grant Elopak a non-exclusive licence to enable it to exploit the new sterilization technology and by granting licences to other competing companies.[595] This was the only case where the Commission considered the withdrawal procedure in regard to a technology transfer agreement.[596]

6. Individual Assessment of Agreements and Restrictions other than those Covered by the Block Exemption

(a) General Criteria for an Individual Assessment

Different Scenarios.
A licence agreement may not be covered by the block exemption because:

- The parties' combined market shares exceed the market share threshold of 20% in the case of competitors and 30% in the case of non-competitors (Article 3); this is the most important difference compared to Regulation 240/96;
- The agreement contains one or more hardcore restrictions which preclude the entire agreement from receiving the benefit of the block exemption (Article 4) or specific restrictions are excluded from the exemption in which case only these restrictions are excluded (Article 5), or
- The agreement is not a 'technology transfer agreement' as defined by Article 1 (1) (b), in particular, in the case of settlement and non-assertion agreements and technology pools.

The TT-Guidelines indicate numerous factors and criteria which may be relevant for an individual assessment under Article 81 (1) and (3).[597]

General Criteria for Assessing Licensing Agreemens between Parties with Market Shares Exceeding the Thresholds of the Block Exemption.
There is no presumption that technology transfer agreements between parties with market shares exceeding the thresholds of Article 3 of Regulation 772/2004 necessarily infringe Article 81 (1), provided they do not contain hardcore restrictions.[598]

---

595. *See also,* under Regulation 1983/83, *Langnese-Iglo,* CFI June 8, 1995, 1995 ECR II-1533, para. 174.
596. Commission evaluation report, point 90.
597. TT-Guidelines, points 130–235.
598. Recital 12 to Regulation 772/2004; TT-Guidelines, point 130.

On the contrary, most licensing agreements do not restrict competition and create pro-competitve efficiencies by leading to dissemination of technology and promoting innovation and therefore are compatible with Article 81.[599] However, even in the absence of hardcore restrictions they may restrict competition, in particular by foreclosing the market. Restrictions which are normally not restrictive of competition when employed in agreements between firms whose combined market shares are below the thresholds in Article 3 of Regulation 772/2004 may, if applied by parties with substantial market power, have an anticompetitive effect on third parties. For instance, an exclusive license granted by a resourceful new competitor to a dominant licensee is likely to foreclose third party licensees and allow the dominant licensee to preserve or strengthen its market power. Such an agreement is unlikely to satisfy the conditions of Article 81 (3)[600] and constitute also an infringement of Article 82.[601] Similarly, an exclusive cross-licence agreement by which the parties undertake not to grant licences to third parties may create a *de facto* closed industry standard reserved for the parties and preclude entry by third parties.[602] However, the Commission takes the view that Article 81 is unlikely to be infringed 'where there are four or more independently controlled technologies in addition to the technologies controlled by the parties to the agreement that may be substitutable for the licensed technology at a comparable cost to the user.'[603] This statement only confirms the limits of the block exemption, namely 20% of the market comprising five competing technologies, but does not give any further guidance for assessing agreements between parties with higher market shares, in particular the 'grey zone' between the market share limits of the block exemption and any single or collective dominant position.

General Criteria for Assessing Licensing Agreements Containing Hardcore Restrictions.

Hardcore restrictions are normally unlikely to fulfill the conditions of Article 81 (3).[604] However, even hardcore restrictions may under exceptional circumstances fulfill the conditions of Article 81 (3) if the restraints are objectively necessary for a licensee to penetrate a new market.[605] However, this statement only underlines the need for assessing the agreement in its overall context, including an evaluation of:

599. TT-Guidelines, point 9.
600. TT-Guidelines, point 166.
601. *Tetra Pak I*, CFI July 10, 190, 190 ECR I-309.
602. TT-Guidelines, point 167.
603. TT-Guidelines, point 131.
604. TT-Guidelines, point 14.
605. TT-Guidelines, point 18. This approach is more consistent with the Commission's practice than point 12 (b) where the Guidelines state that territorial restraints may *fall outside Article 81 (1)* if they are objectively necessary to penetrate a new market.

- *pro-competitive effects*, thereby keeping in mind that the creation of industrial or intellectual property rights often entails substantial *ex ante* investment and that the investor should normaly be free to seek compensation in order to maintain investment incentives and that the licensee may also be requested to make significant sunk investments;[606]
- *anticompetitive effects* on intra-technology competition, in particular by facilitating collusion on the market, and in inter-technology competition, in particular by foreclosing third parties from the market[607] and
- the application of the *indispensability test*, by examining whether the restraints make it possible to perform the activity in question more efficiently than would have been in the absence of the restraint, and whether the restraints are commercially realistic and less restrictive alternatives would lead to a significant loss of efficiencies.[608]

Such agreements require a careful balancing of the pro- and anticompetitive effects. The higher the parties' combined market share the less likely that hardcore restrictions will satisfy the rigorous standards of Article 81 (3). For instance, a passive sales ban agreed not for two, but for five, years is unlikely to satisfy the conditions of Article 81 (3); in most instances the parties' substantial market power does not justify a longer period for penetrating a new market than usually accepted.[609] The assessment requires evaluating the objects (purposes) and the likely effects of the agreement on competition, the market position of other parties and their competitors, the market position of the buyers or customers, entry barriers, maturity of the market and the cumulative effects of parallel agreements in the sector.[610]

The following sections deal with the the individual assessment of the most common clauses in licensing agreements and with settlement and non-assertion agreements and technology pools.

(b) Individual Assessment of the Most Common Restrictions that are not *Covered by the Block Exemption*

(i) Price Restrictions

Restrictions on the free determination of a licensee's prices are hardcore restrictions and unlikely to satisfy the conditions of an individual clearance.[611] Price

606. TT-Guidelines, point 8.
607. TT-Guidelines, points 12, 141–145.
608. TT-Guidelines, points 12 (b) and 149.
609. *See* TT-Guidelines, point 174.
610. *See* TT-Guidelines, points 132–140.
611. TT-Guidelines, point 79.

fixing restricts appreciably intra-technology competition not only between licensor and its licensee(s) but also – and more particularly – between various licensees. However, the block exemption does not preclude a maximum or recommended sales price in agreements between non-competing firms. In agreements between non-competitors that exceed the market share threshold maximum and recommended sales prices do not inherently infringe Article 81 (1) so long as they are not employed as a means to foster collusion among multiple licensees.

(ii) Royalty Obligations

Royalties are normally freely determined by the parties without being caught by Article 81 (1).[612] When royalties are calculated on the basis of the individual sales of the products incorporating the licensed technology the amount of royalty has a direct impact on the marginal cost of the product and thus a direct impact on product price.[613] Therefore, cross-licensing between competitors that jointly have market power can lead to coordinating prices on downstream product markets and is unlikely to satisfy the conditions of Article 81 (3).[614] Royalty obligations which are calculated on the basis of all products irrespective of whether the licensed technology is being used are of doubtful validity because of the appreciable foreclosure effects similar to a non-compete clause.[615] Exceptionally, however, royalties may be calculated on such a basis if it is otherwise impossible or unduly difficult to calculate or monitor the royalty payable by the licensee, for instance because the licensor's technology leaves no visible trace on the final product and practicable alternative monitoring methods are unavailable.[616] An anticompetitive risk can be avoided by a less restrictive payment scheme such as a lump-sum payment or one-way payment of net royalties.[617] The Commission has challenged a contractual obligation to base royalties due to collecting societies on the average retail price of records in the country of sale, taking into account the prices charged by competing record manufacturers, rather than on the manufacturer's published selling prices to retailers of that country. In the *BIEM/IFPI* case[618] the Commission considered this practice as preventing any cost or price advantage that arose in the country of manufacture from being passed on to consumers in the country of sale. The case was settled when the collecting societies agreed to base royalties on the manufacturer's published selling prices to retailers.

612. TT-Guidelines, point 156.
613. TT-Guidelines, point 80.
614. *Ibid.*
615. Article 4 (1) (d) and Article 4 (3) of Regulation 772/2004; TT-Guidelines, points 81 and 157. In the case of software licensing royalties may be calculated on the basis of the number of the users or 'per machine': point 156.
616. TT-Guidelines, point 81.
617. *See also* Commission Guidelines on the Application of Article 81 (3), point 86.
618. *BIEM/IPFI,* Thirteenth Report on Competition Policy, points 147–150.

(iii) Output Restrictions

Output restrictions that are not covered by the block exemption (in reciprocal agreements between competitors) or covered only up to a market share limit of 20% (in non-reciprocal agreements between competitors[619]) and of 30% (in agreements between non competitors[620]) may be necessary to ensure dissemination of the licensor's technology.[621] However, output restrictions are likely to restrict significantly intra- and inter-technology competition and lead to market partitioning, including the incentive to proceed to passive sales into other licensees' territories[622] where the parties have a 'significant' degree of market power, which may be the case where the parties' market shares approach or exceed 40 – 50%.[623] Output restrictions are more generally unlikely to satisfy the conditions of Article 81 (3) where they are applied to multiple licensees and combined with passive sales restrictions because of the risk of an anti-competitive market partitioning.[624] Whereas the Commission has previously considered output restrictions of any kind to be very suspect, it has now adopted a more flexible, economic-oriented approach. For instance, its Guidelines acknowledge that an output restriction may be necessary to induce the licensor to disseminate his technology as widely as possible. A licensor may be reluctant to license his competitors if he cannot limit the licence to a particular production site with a specific capacity.[625] Maximum ouput restrictions are unlikely to satisfy the conditions of Article 81 (3) where the licensee is prevented from satisfying demand for the products incorporating the licensed technology.[626] Likewise, any direct or indirect obligation limiting the licensee's ability to exploit its own technology or limiting any of the parties to carry out R&D would be tantamount to an indirect non-compete restriction unless it is necessary to prevent disclosure of the license know-how to third parties.[627]

---

619. Article 4 (1) (b) of Regulation 772/2004.
620. Covered by the general provision of Article 2, para. 2 of Regulation 772/2004.
621. TT-Guidelines, point 178.
622. Output restrictions may have the same effect as export bans: Recital 24 to Regulation 240/96.
623. *See* Article 7 of Regulation 772/2004.
624. TT-Guidelines, points 175–177.
625. TT-Guidelines, point 175. Site limitations, i.e., limitating the licensee's production to a specific facility, may be justified for a certain period in connection with the creation of a joint venture: *Elopak/Metalbox,* D.Comm. July 13, 1990, 1990 OJ L 209/15, point 36. *See,* however, Article 2 (1) (12) and (13) of Regulation 240/96, which permitted the obligation on the licensee to supply only a limited quantity to a particular customer, so that the customer might have a second source of supply, and may be used as guidance. *See also Arco/Repsol Quimica,* Commission Evaluation Report, fn. 81.
626. TT-Guidelines, point 176.
627. Article 4 (1) (d) and Article 5 (2) of Regulation 772/2004.

(iv) Territorial and Customer Restrictions

Territorial and customer restrictions must be assessed in the context of the various forms in which they appear:

- *Sole licences,* i.e. *obligation on the licensor not to grant a licence to other undertakings in the licensee's territory.* Such restrictions are, if restrictive at all,[628] covered by the block exemption[629] because they normally induce the licensee to make the large investments necessary for the exploitation of the licensed technology.[630] Where the licensee has a dominant position a mere open exclusive licence (without further territorial protection) may foreclose third party licensees and allow the contract licensee to preserve or strengthen its position contrary to both Article 81 (3) and Article 82 if entry into the technology market is difficult and the licensed technology constitutes a real source of competition on the market. [631] In addition, the benefit of the block exemption may be withdrawn if the access of third parties' technology or potential licensees to the market is restricted,[632] for instance by the cumulative effect of parallel networks of similar agreements prohibiting licensees from using third parties' technologies or prohibiting licensors from licensing to other licensees. In particular the regulation may be declared inapplicable where parallel networks of similar technology transfer agreements cover more than 50% of a relevant market.[633] This shows that the critical limit of substantial foreclosure effects may be situated around 50%: Individual clearance is unlikely only where the parties' market shares exceed 50% or where there are no real alternatives to the licensor's technology on the market or such alternatives are already licensed by the licensee, thereby placing the licensee in a dominant position.[634] Finally, cross licence agreements between competitors with market power may create a *de facto* industry standard reserved to the parties, to which third parties must have access in order to compete effectively on the market, and therefore fail to satisfy the conditions of Article 81 (3). In such cases the Commission has required that the technologies which support the standard be licensed to third parties on reasonable terms.[635]

---

628. *Maize Seed,* ECJ June 8, 1982, 1982 ECR 2015, para. 58; TT-Guidelines, points 86 and 165.
629. Covered by the general provision of Article 2, para. 2 and Article 4 (1) (c) (iii)–(v) of Regulation 772/2004; *see also* Article 1 (1) (1) and (2) of Regulation 240/96.
630. TT-Guidelines, points 147 and 162.
631. TT-Guidelines, point 166; *Tetra Pak I,* CFI July 10, 1990, 1990 ECR II-309. *See* Recital 20.
632. Article 6 (1) (a) and (b) of Regulation 772/2004.
633. Article 7 of Regulation 772/2004.
634. *See,* under Article 82, *Tetra Pak I,* CFI July 10, 1990, 1990 ECR II-309, para. 30.
635. TT-Guidelines, point 167. *See Canon/Kodak,* 1997 OJ C 330/10; *IGR Stereo Television,* Eleventh Report on Competition Policy, point 94.

- *Open exclusive licences,* i.e. *the additional protection of the licensor's and licensee's territories against competition from each other.* The obligation on the licensee not to exploit[636] the licensed technology within the territory reserved to the licensor is block exempted, except in cases of reciprocal agreements between competitors.[637] Even in the case where the market shares exceed the limits of the block exemption, such protection for the licensor may be justified as an incentive for licensors to dissiminate technology and to create intra-technology competition rather than limiting use of the technology to themselves.[638] This may apply even where the parties hold 'significant' market shares.[639] However, open exclusive licensing between competitors in reciprocal agreements, which is block exempted up a market share of 20%, may facilitate collusion and restrict substantially both intra- and inter-technology competition where the parties have significant market power.[640] With respect to open exclusive licensing between non-competitors the Commission will intervene only exceptionally, irrespective of the territorial scope of the licence, which may be world wide,[641] except where there are substantial foreclosure effects as in the case of a dominant licensee.
- *Closed exclusive licences,* i.e. *absolute territorial protection in the relationship between multiple licensees*: A prohibition against *active* sales activities in other licensees' territories is covered by the new block exemption, even where licensor and licensees are competitors, provided that the agreement is non-reciprocal.[642] Normally a ban on active sales into the exclusive territory reserved to the licensor meets the conditions of Article 81 (3) even if the parties' market shares exceed the thresholds of the block exemption, except where the licensees have substantial market power and where it is difficult for resellers and users to obtain the licensed products from outside, or to put them on the market, in the licensed territory.[643] However, in reciprocal licensing agreements between competitors it may be tantamount to an illegal market sharing arrangement.[644] *Passive* sales bans are only exempted in licensing agreements between non-competitors and only during the first two years that the protected licensee

636. Exploitation in the sense of any use of the licensed technology, in particular production, active and passive sales, *see* Article 10 (10) of Regulation 240/96.
637. Article 4 (1) (c) (ii) and (iv) of Regulation 772/2004.
638. The Guidelines go as far as stating, 'A technology owner cannot normally be expected to create direct competition with himself inside its own technology' (point 172), which justifies intra-technology restrictions without the need of a block exemption. However, this statement conflicts with the Court of Justice' fundamental approach in the *Maize Seed* case (*see supra* Section D.2.)
639. *Knoll/Hille-Form,* Thirteenth Report on Competition Policy, points 142–146 (design rights).
640. TT-Guidelines, point 163.
641. TT-Guidelines, points 162 and 165.
642. Article 4 (1) (c) (ii) and (iv) of Regulation 772/2004.
643. *See* Article 7 (3) (b) of Regulation 240/96.
644. TT-Guidelines, point 169.

is selling the contract product. According to the Commission's Guidelines, passive sales restrictions exceeding this two-year period are unlikely to satisfy the conditions of Article 81 (3).[645] However, exceptional circumstances may justify an exception, for instance where the dissemination of a new technology requiring very substantial investment by licensees justifies a longer period of, say, 4–5 years.[646] In any event, the licensee may not prevent parallel imports by imposing export bans on its buyers.[647]

- *Territorial limitations with respect to territories outside the EU and EEA*: The block exemption applies to licence agreements relating to territories outside the EU and EEA.[648] Where licensing agreements are concluded for third countries or territories which extend beyond the frontiers of the EU and EEA, Recital 7 to former Regulation 240/96 stated that the block exemption applied insofar as such agreements had appreciable anticompetitive effects within the EU or EEA and were therefore likely to fall within the scope of Article 81 (1).[649] The new regulation on technology transfer agreements does not expressly repeat this statement but may be interpreted in the same sense.
- *Output limitations*: Output limitations in a licence agreement between non-competitors are covered by the block exemption[650] and may, if the parties' market shares exceed the limits of the block exemption, be cleared if the

645. TT-Guidelines, point 174.

646. This would accord with Article 1 (1) (6) and Article 1 (3) (2) of Regulation 240/96 according to which passive sales bans were accepted up to five years from the date when the products were first put on the market within the Community, and with the Commission's practice in *Sicasov,* D.Comm. Dec. 14, 1998, 1999 OJ L 4/27, points 74–76.

647. *Sicasov,* D.Comm. Dec. 14, 1998, 1999 OJ L 4/27, point 77.

648. Territorial restrictions with respect to the EEA countries are prohibited under Article 53 of the EEA Agreement and subject to a similar block exemption regulation adopted according to Protocol 21 to that agreement. Territorial restrictions with respect to third countries do not infringe Article 81, provided they are not part of a broader cooperation including the Common Market or a part of it. *See EMI/CBS,* ECJ June 15, 1976, 1976 ECR 811, paras 25–29.

649. Territorial restrictions may be imposed in order to prevent imports into the EU or EEA without the consent of the rightholder insofar as such imports could be prevented by the exercise of the (not exhausted) intellectual property rights anyway: *see Silhouette,* ECJ June 16, 1998, 1998 ECR I-4799, para. 26 (in this case the agreement with a Bulgarian distributor contained an express export prohibition); *Zino Davidoff/Levis,* ECJ Nov. 20, 2001, 2001 ECR I-8691, paras 60 and 66 (in this case no express export prohibition was imposed). *See also* Chapter VII.B.2. *supra.*

650. This follows from the exemption granted in Article 2 and the absence of any qualification for output restrictions in agreements between non-competitors in Article 4 (2) of Regulation 772/2004. However, the acceptance of captive use restrictions may conflict with Regulation 1400/2002 on vertical agreements in the motor vehicle sector, which aims at ensuring more competition between the (potential) suppliers of spare parts (*see* Article 4 (1) (h)–(l) of Regulation 1400/2002); such restrictions may therefore need a careful evaluation of the pro- and anti-competitive effects. The obligation on a licensee to limit its production to part or all of the needs of a particular customer and otherwise not to supply the market is normally compatible with Article 81.

pro-competitive effects of inducing the licensor to disseminate its technology counterbalance the anti-competitive risk of reducing intra-technology competition and facilitating the partitioning of market between different licensees.[651] Even output restrictions in a licence between competitors are recognized as justifiable provided the obligation is non-reciprocal. For instance, the Guidelines note that 'a licensor may be reluctant to license his competitors if he cannot limit the licence to a particular production site with a specific capacity (a site licence).'[652] In such a case the restriction may fulfill the conditions of Article 81 (3). However, this is unlikely where the parties have substantial market power.

– *Field of use and product market restrictions*: Field of use restrictions between non-competitors are generally recognized as non-restrictive or efficiency enhancing.[653] The individual assessment of field of use and product market restrictions[654] which are contained in agreements between actual or potential competitors will be heavily influenced by whether the fields of use or product markets allocated are identical ('symmetrical') or different ('asymmetrical') from the field of use or product market which is permitted or reserved to the other party and whether the parties may use their own technology outside the licensed field of use or product market restriction.[655] Symmetrical field of use restrictions, whereby the parties are licensed to use each others' technologies within the same field of use, are unlikely to be caught by Article 81 (1) at all.[656] However, asymmetrical field of use restrictions, whereby one party is permitted to use the licensed technology within one product market or technical field and the other party is permitted to use it in another product market or technical field of use, may be caught by Article 81 (1). If the field of use restriction causes the licensee to reduce its output outside the licensed field of use the arrangement may amount to sham market partitioning unlikely to satisfy the conditions of Article 81 (3).[657] For instance, this may be the case where the restrictions are agreed between parties with substantial market power, such as in the pharmaceutical industry, in particular where the products, although manufactured by the same technical process, are designed for different uses, such as pharmaceuticals for human and veterinary uses, pharmaceuticals for hospitals (in larger packaging) and for pharmacies (in smaller packaging) or,

651. TT-Guidelines, points 175–178, especially 178.
652. TT-Guidelines, point 175.
653. TT-Guidelines, point 184.
654. However, captive use restrictions and obligations to serve only one customer as an alternative source of supply are excluded from the list of hardcore restrictions according to Article 4 (1) (c) (vi) and (vii) of Regulation 772/2004, but may pose similar problems when assessing agreements between parties with market shares exceeding the thresholds of the block exemption.
655. TT-Guidelines, point 183.
656. *Ibid.*
657. *Ibid.*

in more general terms, products designed for markets with distinct competitive conditions.[658]

(v) Restrictions Going Beyond the Licensed Technology – Tying and Non-Compete Clauses

Various Forms.
Licence agreements may restrict the exploitation of technologies of the licensor or the licensee(s) that are different (severable) from the licensed technology:

- The licensor may make the licensing of one technology conditional upon the licensee(s) taking a licence for another technology or purchasing a product from the licensor or someone designated by the licensor (tying or bundling).[659]
- A licence agreement may restrict the licensee's ability to exploit its own or a third party's technology or to carry out research and development (non-compete clauses).

Tying and Bundling: Covered by the Block Exemption up to the Market Share Thresholds.
Tying and bundling clauses are block exempted up to the market share threshold of 20% if the parties are competitors and of 30% if the parties are non-competitors. Above these thresholds they are compatible with Article 81 unless the licensor has a significant degree of market power in the tying product so as to restrict competition in the tied product.[660] Tying and bundling are not restrictive of competition when the tied or bundled products are necessary for a technically satisfactory exploitation of the licensed technology or for ensuring that the licensee's production activities conform to the quality standards that are respected by the licensor and other licensees;[661] this is not considered as 'tying', provided the technologies and products do not belong to different markets, i.e. the technology cannot be exploited at all or not in a technically satisfactory way without the product.[662] According to the Commission's longstanding practice, the licensee may be

658. However, any disguised customer restriction within the same technological field of use or the same product market is blacklisted: Guidelines, point 180. *See* Article 3 (4) of Regulation 240/96, which was a more lenient approach to field-of-use limitations than the prior Regulation 2349/84. *See Windsurfing,* ECJ Feb. 25, 1986, 1986 ECR 611, paras 45–53 (restrictions on the use of the patented product for different price classes).

659. TT-Guidelines, point 191.

660. TT-Guidelines, point 192–193.

661. TT-Guidelines, points 194. *See Vaessen/Morris,* D.Comm. Jan. 10, 1979, 1979 OJ L 19/32, 35 and Article 2 (1) (5) of the former Regulation 240/96. With respect to design licences: *Benneton/Time,* 1994 OJ C 242/3 (comfort letter). *Cf.* discussion of the necessity of qualitative specifications in: *Windsurfing,* ECJ Feb. 25, 1986, 1986 ECR 611, paras 45–49

662. The licensees may also be required to submit to checks on quality, *see* Article 2 (1) (5) of Regulation 240/96.

obliged to accept further licences only if he has the right to refuse licences he does not want or considers not necessary or to terminate the agreement at reasonable intervals, (e.g. three years after the initial term).

Indispensability Test.
The principle of proportionality applies to tying arrangements: They are not permissible if less restrictive means would be sufficient, especially if using objective quality control criteria is a practical solution. A patent may not be employed as the basis for extending the licensor's control over, and/or exacting royalties for, items that are not covered by the patent. Similarly, imposing requirements to obtain unpatented products from the licensor that are not necessary for a proper exploitation of the patent amounts to illicit tying. The leading case in this respect is *Windsurfing*.[663] The case concerned patent licence agreements between Windsurfing International, a California-based company founded by Hoyle Schweitzer, the inventor of the windsurfer, and a number of licensees in Germany, the principal European country with patent protection. The relevant market was limited to the rig of the sailboard. Nevertheless, Windsurfing also claimed patent protection for the board itself, and on this basis required of its licensees in Germany the following conditions which the Court concluded were incompatible with Article 81: (i) that new sailboard models be approved by the licensor, and (ii) that component parts, particularly the patented rig, were not to be sold separately. The Court confirmed that both of these restrictions infringed Article 81. Pre-approval of new sailboard models could not be objectively justified on grounds of quality control or safety[664] and the prohibition against selling the patented rig alone was an arbitrary restriction.[665]

Restrictions on the Exploitation of Own and Third Party Technology: Normally Hardcore Restrictions.
Restrictions that hinder licensee(s) from the development and exploitation of their own and third party technology are hardcore restrictions in agreements between

663. *Windsurfing,* ECJ Feb. 25, 1986, 1986 ECR 611. *See Sony,* Twenty-eighth Report on Competition Policy, p. 159. In this case the Commission intervened against a network of licensing agreements, with a view of allowing licensor and licensees to compete amongst themselves in the market for products (video games) compatible with its equipment (video games consoles). Restrictions hindering parallel trade of video games and consoles were fined in *Nintendo,* D.Comm. Oct. 30, 2002, 2003 OJ L 255/3. *See also Hilti,* Fifteenth Report on Competition Policy, point 49; *Hilti,* D.Comm. Dec. 22, 1987, 1988 OJ L 65/19, 36; *aff'd* CFI Dec. 12, 1991, 1991 ECR II-1439 and ECJ March 2, 1994, 1994 ECR I-667; amending the application properties of a product which effectively forecloses access to competitors' operating systems: *Racal Decca,* D.Comm. Dec. 21, 1988, 1989 OJ L 43/27, points 108–110; or the refusal to make available to smaller competitors sufficiently in advance of new product launches the necessary interface information: *IBM,* Fourteenth Report on Competition Policy, points 94–95

664. *Ibid.* paras 46–48.

665. *Ibid.* para. 57.

competitors up to a market share of 20%, unless the restriction is indispensable to prevent the disclosure of the licensed know-how to third parties; if the parties to the agreement are non-competitors, a market share limit of 30% applies.[666] The main competitive risk is that the licensees are prevented from substituting between competing technologies, thereby leading to a foreclosure of the market which poses a significant anticompetitive risk if the licensor has a significant degree of market power. Application of Article 81 (3) becomes very unlikely when 50% or more of the market is subject to such a restriction.[667] However, the practical problem is to determine whether the development and use of own or third party technology is realisticly possible without using and disclosing the licensed know-how for purposes other than those licensed. The decisive question is therefore whether the technologies are sufficiently distinct or severable.[668] It is therefore of utmost importance to identify and document in the appropriate way (by letter or in the licence agreement) as specifically as possible: (i) the know-how which has been licensed to the licensee, (ii) the know-how which the licensee has granted back to the licensor and (iii) the additional know-how which the licensor grants to the licensee during the term of the agreement.[669]

Free Exploitation of Own Improvements v. Confidentiality of the Licensed Know-How.

Since the essence of know-how is its secrecy, it is permissible to oblige the licensee and the sub-licensee not to divulge know-how communicated by the licensor even after the expiration of the agreement.[670] Such a clause is justified irrespective of the parties' market shares. However, one of the special features and practical difficulties with know-how agreements is that know-how is ordinarily related to a particular manufacturing process and is described in terms of the end product, i.e., know-how for manufacturing a particular product. If the licensee were permitted to manufacture competing products without limitation using the licensed or a different technology, then the licensor could be harmed by the licensee's failure to pay fair royalties for use of the licensed technology or failure to exploit the technology adequately.[671]

666. Article 4 (1) (d) and Article 5 (2) of Regulation 772/2004; TT-Guidelines, point 197.
667. TT-Guidelines, points 198–200.
668. *See* Article 4 (1) (d); Article 5 (3).
669. Article 2 (1) (18) of Regulation 240/96 therefore provided for a reversal of proof, i.e. the requirement that the licensee prove that that licensed know-how is *not* being used for the exploitation of the licensee's own developments.
670. TT-Guidelines, points 94–95, 114–116, and 155. *See also* Article 2 (1) (1) of Regulation 240/96.
671. *Delta Chemie/DDD,* D.Comm. Oct. 13, 1988, 1988 OJ L 309/34, 40–41.

(c) Particulars when Assessing Agreements other than 'Technology Transfer Agreements'

(i) Settlement and Non-Assertion Agreements

Possibly Outside Article 81 (1), but also Competitive Risks of Market Foreclosure.
If competitors agree, in settling or avoiding conflicts on the exploitation of substitutable or complementary technologies, not to use or to continue use of an industrial property right in each other's territory or in a particular field of use, this may lead to a disguised division of markets.[672] Agreements that aim *solely* at settling claims by ensuring that one party does not invoke its property rights to prevent the other party from exploiting its own technology (non-assertion agreements) without using the licensor's technology for the production of goods are not covered by the block exemption because they are not technology *transfer* agreements for the manufacture or provision of contract products.[673] Non-assertion agreements may not be restrictive of competition at all, because they allow the parties to compete, provided both parties are free independently to exploit their rights, including the right to grant licences on their own technology and sublicences on the other party's technology to third parties. However, in the event that major competitors grant each other reciprocal licences to future innovation is likely to lead to further technological cooperation and to prevent the parties from gaining a competitive advantage over each other.[674]

An Example: The *Bayer/Süllhöfer* Case. [675]
This case concerned the settlement of a dispute about the validity of patents and utility models for manufacturing polyurethane foam components between Süllhöfer on the one hand and Hennecke and its parent company Bayer on the other. The dispute was resolved by Süllhöfer granting Hennecke and Bayer a non-exclusive licence to its patent and utility model, including the right to grant sub-licences. The licence was royalty-free with respect to the rights in Germany and royalty-bearing with respect to the rights in other member states. In return Bayer granted Sullhöfer a non-exclusive licence to its rights in Germany and agreed together with Hennecke no longer to challenge the rights of Sullhöfer. Sullhöfer agreed to pay a royalty of 3% unless it decided to buy the basic products for the process from

672. *EMI/CBS,* ECJ June 15, 1976, 1976 ECR 811, 871, 913; *Quantel International – Continuum/Quantel,* D.Comm. July 27, 1992, 1992 OJ L 235/9. However, the Court of Justice accepted as compatible with Articles 28 and 30 the existence and use of trademark rights against imports by independent undertakings as a result of the sale of part of assets and trademarks in certain countries: *Ideal Standard,* ECJ June 22, 1994, 1994 ECR I-2789.
673. TT-Guidelines, point 209. *See* Article 2 of Regulation 772/2004.
674. TT-Guidelines, point 208.
675. *Bayer/Süllhöfer,* ECJ Sept. 27, 1988, 1988 ECR 5249.

Bayer; in that case the royalty was included in the sale price. The Court of Justice found that the settlement agreement under these circumstances did not infringe Article 81 (1). Similarly, the Court of Justice held in its *Windsurfing* judgment[676] that whether a no-challenge clause restricted competition depended on its legal and economic context. A no-challenge clause would not restrict competition (i) if the licence were royalty-free and hence did not lead to the possible competitive disadvantages associated with royalty payments or (ii) if a royalty-bearing licence were for a process which was technically outdated and not used by the licensee. A royalty-bearing licence would have to be evaluated to determine whether it affected the freedom of action of the licensee.[677] This case led to a reconsideration of the effects of no-contest clauses and to accept such clauses, provided the holder of the right is free to terminate the licence agreement. [678] The TT-Guidelines state that non-challenge clauses in the context of a settlement and non-assertion agreement are generally considered to fall outside Article 81 (1) since the very purpose of the agreement to settle existing disputes and/or to avoid future disputes.[679]

(ii) Technology Pools

Substitutable v. Complementary Technologies.
Pools between actual or potential competitors which bundle competing technologies raise serious competition concerns. They are not covered by the regulation because they are not concluded 'for the manufacture or provision of contract products' in the sense of Article 2 of the new block exemption on technology transfer agreements but instead for agreeing to grant bundled licences to third parties.[680] The competitive risks resulting from technology pools depend mainly on whether pooled technologies are substitutes or complements (although the distinction is not clear-cut). Two technologies (patents and other industrial and intellectual property rights) are complements as opposed to substitutes when they are both required to produce the product or carry out the process to which the technologies relate.[681]

---

676. *Windsurfing*, ECJ Feb. 25, 1986, 1986 ECR 611, para. 92.
677. Neither the Court of Justice nor the German Federal Supreme Court dealt with the reasonable assumption that charging a royalty when the licensee purchases the basic product (which was neither patented technology nor the subject of know-how) from the licensor might constitute a tying clause covering products that were not necessary for a technically satisfactory exploitation of the technology (*see* Article 2 (1) (1) of Regulation 2349/84) and consequently might be caught by Article 81 (1).
678. Article 5 (1) (c) of Regulation 772/2004.
679. TT-Guidelines, point 209.
680. TT-Guidelines, points 215–235. Technology pools were also excluded from Regulation 240/96 (Article 5 (1) (1)).
681. TT-Guidelines, points 215–216.

Pooling Complementary Technologies Normally outside Article 81 (1). Pooling complementary technologies is normally outside the scope of Article 81 (1) irrespective of the parties' market position, provided the pool includes only essential technologies; where non-essential technologies are included there is a risk of foreclosure of third party technologies (turning into a pool of substitute technologies).[682]

Pooling Substitutable Technologies Normally Restrictive of Competiton. Pooling substitutable technologies normally constitutes an infringement of Article 81 (1) and is unlikely to satisfy the conditions of Article 81 (3) even if the parties, which are competitors, remain free to license independently.[683] Bundling competing technologies prevents licensees from picking the technology of their choice and from licensing on a bilateral basis at individual terms and fees instead of one license granted by the pool at terms and fees agreed collectively by the pool members. Technology pools may lead to horizontal anticompetitive collusion between competitors and therefore infringe Article 81 (1).[684]

An Example: The IGR Stereo Television Case. In the IGR Stereo Television case the Commission took action against the pooling and joint administration of stereo television patents which disadvantaged third parties through collective limitations on the granting of licences and the number of sets to be manufactured as well as by the joint setting of royalties.[685] The anticompetitive risk of technology pools is highlighted in the 3G Patent Platform Partnership case.[686] This case concerned the bundling of five different third generation ('3G') mobile technologies each of which can be used to produce 3G equipment. Manufacturers who want to produce 3G equipment need to have access to the patents that are indispensable for using a particular technology ('essential patents'). In order to safeguard competition between those essential patents for the different 3G technologies, the parties agreed no longer to combine all essential patents in one single platform but to establish five different sets of arrangements, one for each technology, to grant licences under non-discriminatory terms (instead of terms and fees collectively agreed by the pool members) and to abandon the exchange of commercially sensitive information and non-compete clauses which were likely to discourage further R&D and innovation in the mobile telecommunication sector.

682. TT-Guidelines, points 220–221.
683. TT-Guidelines, point 219.
684. *Ibid.*, point 205.
685. *IGR Stereo Television I,* Eleventh Report on Competition Policy, point 94; *IGR Stereo Television II,* Fourteenth Report on Competition Policy, point 92.
686. *3G Patent Platform Partnership,* D.Comm. July 16, 2003, IP/03/1026 (*see also* IP/02/1651).

Indispensability Test.
Technology pools which need assessment under Article 81 (3) must satisfy the indispensability test. In particular, pools that hold a strong market position must satisfy the following conditions:

- they must not extend to non-essential technologies;[687]
- they must not extend to the exchange of sensitive information, such as price or output data, which are likely to facilitate collusion;[688]
- they must be open (voluntary membership)[689] and non-exclusive (the licensors retain the freedom to license outside the pool);[690]
- access must be granted to third parties in a non-discriminatory manner,[691] and
- the parties must not be prevented from creating, or participating in, alternative pools.[692]

Finally, the licence agreements concluded between the pool and third parties must satisfy the conditions of Regulation 772/2004.[693]

Technology Pools for the Purpose of Creating Industry Standards.
A pooling of patents or know-how is often associated with the creation of an industry standard.[694] Such agreements are not covered by the block exemption because they are not concluded 'for the manufacture or provisions of contract products' in the sense of Article 2 of the new block exemption on technology transfer agreements but instead for supporting an industry standard which is open to the industry concerned.[695] However, they are often pro-competitive,[696] except where the members have a strong collective market position and create difficulties for market entry by third parties ('blocking strategy').[697] Such pools satisfy the conditions of Article 81 (3) only if the pooled technologies are selected in an objective way, by preference by an independent expert[698] and if they are non-

687. TT-Guidelines, point 222.
688. TT-Guidelines, point 234. *See John Deere,* ECJ May 28, 1998, 1998 ECR I-3111, para. 76.
689. TT-Guidelines, point 224.
690. TT-Guidelines, point 222.
691. TT-Guidelines, point 224.
692. *Ibid. See Concast/Mannesmann,* Eleventh Report on Competition Policy, point 93.
693. TT-Guidelines, point 223.
694. TT-Guidelines, points 225–235.
695. *Ibid.,* points 212 and 224. Examples: *X/Open Group,* D.Comm. Dec. 15, 1986, 1987 OJ L 35/36; *Philips/Matsushita – DCC,* Twenty-third Report on Competition Policy, p. 460.
696. *See X-Open Group,* D.Comm. Dec. 15, 1986, 1987 OJ L 35/36; *Philips/Matsushita,* Twenty-third Report on Competition Policy, p. 460; TT-Guidelines, point 214.
697. TT-Guidelines, points 203 and 220. *See DVD Standard,* D.Comm. Oct. 9, 2000, IP/00/1135; *MPEG-2* (industry standard for patents essential to transmitting and storing video signals), D.Comm. Dec. 18, 1998, IP/98/1155.
698. TT-Guidelines, points 225 and 232–233.

exclusive, i.e., if licensors and licensees are free to develop competing products and standards and if they are free to grant and obtain licences outside the pool.[699]

(iii) Licensing Agreements between Competitors in the Framework of Joint Ventures

Patent or know-how licences between actual or potential competitors who hold interests in a joint venture or between one of them and the joint venture may be ancillary, i.e. directly related and necessary for the creation and implementation of the joint venture;[700] in this case they must be assessed in the framework of the joint venture itself. Where the licenses go beyond the 'directly related and necessary' standard they may be covered by the block exemption, provided the parties' collective market shares do not exceed 20%.[701] Agreements between competitors with market shares exceeding these limits may justify individual clearance only if the exclusivity of the licences granted by the joint venture is limited to an introductory period of three years, as in the *TPS* case (television by satellite)[702] or if third parties are ensured free access to the technology on non-discriminatory terms.[703] However, the block exemption does not apply to arrangements by which the parent companies license their technologies to the joint venture for the purpose of granting licences on the bundled technologies (e.g. football broadcasting rights) to third parties.[704] Such joint ventures may come within Article 81 (1), in particular because the creation of a joint venture leads *de facto* to a uniform licensing policy (including uniform royalties) and to an exclusivity: even if the parties

699. TT-Guidelines, point 227.
700. *See Elopak/Metalbox,* D.Comm. July 13, 1990, 1990 OJ L 209/15.
701. Although the agreements involve more than two undertakings, the block exemption applies, possibly by analogy. Such licence agreements were subject to the same market share limit of 20% under Article 5 (2) (1) of the former Regulation 240/96.
702. *TPS,* D.Comm. March 3, 1999, 1999 OJ L 90/6, *aff'd* CFI Sept. 18, 2001, 2001 ECR II-2459, in particular para. 116.
703. *Atlas,* D.Comm. July 17, 1996, 1996 OJ L 239/23; *Phoenix/Global One,* July 17, 1996, 1996 OJ L 239/57; *British Interactive Broadcasting,* D.Comm. Sept. 15, 1999, 1999 OJ L 312/1. *See also Olivetti/Canon,* D.Comm. Dec. 22, 1987, 1988 OJ L 52/51; *BT/MCI,* D.Comm. July 27, 1994, 1994 OJ L 223/36, point 43; *Fujitsu AMD Semiconductor,* D.Comm. Dec. 12, 1994, 1994 OJ L 341/66, point 32.
704. *UEFA Broadcasting Regulations,* D.Comm. April 19, 2001, 2001 OJ L 171/12 (negative clearance following amendments) and *UEFA Champions League,* July 24, 2003, IP/03/1105 and MEMO/03/156; *Bundesliga Broadcasting Rights,* D.Comm. July 24, 2003, IP/03/1106 (clearance following commitments that rights to broadcast first and second devision Bundesliga matches will no longer be sold to a single broadcaster in one package); *Football Association Premier League,* D.Comm. April 30, 2004, 2004 OJ C 115/3 (clearance following commitments to allow the football clubs individual exploitation in the event that the right packages are not sold by the association). *See also UIP,* D.Comm. July 12, 1989, 1989 OJ L 226/25 (jointly distributing and licensing motion pictures).

remain legally free to license independently, the parties have little incentive to do so in order not to undermine the pool.[705]

F. Assessment of Licensing Agreements on Intellectual Property Rights other than those Covered by the Block Exemption Regulation

1. Copyright Licensing

Copyright Licensing not Covered by the New Block Exemption on Technology Transfer Agreements.
Copyright licences are not expressly covered by the new regulation on technology transfer agreements, except to the extent they constitute software copyright licences. Agreements which relate to the licensing of other copyrights are only covered when they do not constitute the primary object of the technology transfer agreement.[706] However, licensing for the purpose of reproduction and distribution of copyrighted tangibles, such as books, records and video-cassettes, which are placed to the public in material form, raise similar issues. By contrast, licensing copyrights for copyrighted services or intangibles raise particular issues insofar as value is created not by the reproduction and sales of copies but by each individual performance of the protected work, by making it available to the public by performances which are indefinitely repeatable (theater performances, showing (broadcasting) or renting of protected material such as movies, music or sport events).[707]

(a) Licensing of Copyrighted Tangible Works

Licensing of Copyrights for the Purpose of Reproduction and Distribution of Tangible Works.
Since the licensing of copyrights for purpose of reproduction and distribution of tangible works raises similar issues as technology transfer agreements that are covered by the block exemption, the Commission will apply the principles of the block exemption by analogy.[708] As with other industrial property rights, the Commission and the Court of Justice are mostly concerned with any kind of territorial restriction, price or royalty provision aimed at maintaining unjustified price differences between member states or artificial barriers to market access.[709]

705. *See* Chapter VI.D.2.(g).
706. Article 1 (1) (b) and (g) of Regulation 772/2004.
707. TT-Guidelines, points 49–51.
708. *Ibid.*, point 51.
709. *Deutsche Grammophon*, ECJ July 8, 1970, 1970 ECR 705, paras 12–13; *Dior/Evora*, ECJ Nov. 4, 1997, 1997 ECR I-6013, para. 57.

Furthermore, potentially restrictive clauses may be evaluated more critically when the copyright licences are acquired jointly by competitors[710] or by a firm holding substantial market power.[711] In cases where copyright and trademark licences are granted in parallel the Court of Justice has ruled that the protection conferred by copyright may, in any event, not be broader than that which is conferred on a trademark owner in the same circumstances.[712] On the other hand, it might be argued that any provisions relating to copyright that are 'ancillary'[713] are not caught by Article 81 (1) and therefore do not need individual clearance under Article 81 (3). The evaluation of any restriction depends, more generally, on the legal and factual circumstances and the subject matter of the copyrighted product or service that is being licensed, in particular on the specific right which has been licensed (copyrighted product or service), on whether the licence has been granted by the author himself (primary exploitation rights)[714] or sub-licensed by the licensee for different performances (secondary exploitation rights).[715] If a copyright licence is 'ancillary' to a distribution or franchise agreement, it is included under the block exemption of Regulation 2790/1999, provided it does not contain hardcore restrictions and the parties' market share does not exceed 30%.[716]

(b) Licensing of Copyrights in Performances

Individual Assessment.

The assessment of licensing of copyrights in performances must take account of the specific subject matter of the copyrighted service and the legal and factual cir-

---

710. Exemption rejected in *Screensport/EBV* (*Eurosport*), D.Comm. Feb. 19, 1991, 1991 OJ L 63/32; *Eurovision,* CFI July 11, 1996, 1996 ECR II-649 (annulling the Commission's decision of June 11, 1993, 1993 OJ L 179/23); objected to in *IGR I,* Eleventh Report on Competition Policy, point 94; *IGR II,* Fourteenth Report on Competition Policy, point 92; exemption granted *in ARD/Degebo,* D.Comm. Sept. 15, 1989, 1989 OJ L 284/36 (after attenuation of the exclusivity to the extent that further licences could be granted during certain periods of non-use); *UIP,* D.Comm. July 13, 1989, 1989 OJ L 26/25 (exemption).
711. *Magill,* CFI July 10, 1991, 1991 ECR II-485 para. 73; *aff'd* ECJ April 6, 1995, 1995 ECR I-743; *BSB Football,* Twenty-third Report on Competition Policy, p. 459.
712. *Dior/Evora,* ECJ Nov. 4, 1997, 1997 ECR I-6013, para. 58.
713. Regulation 772/2004 on technology transfer agreements does not use the term 'ancillary', unlike Article 10 (15) of the old Regulation 240/96, which defined 'ancillary provisions' as 'provisions relating to the exploitation of intellectual property rights other than patents, which contain no obligations restrictive of competition other than those attached to the licensed know-how or patents and exempted under this regulation.'
714. In this respect the term of protection is seventy years for copyrights, fifty years for related rights (Articles 1 and 3 of the Council Directive Approximating the Duration of Protection of Copyrights, 1993 OJ L 290/9) and fifteen years for data bases (Article 10 of Directive 96/9/EC on the Legal Protection of Databases, 1996 OJ L 77/20).
715. *See* the listing of uses in *GEMA I,* D.Comm. June 2, 1971, 1971 OJ L 134/15 and *GEMA II,* D.Comm. July 6, 1972, 1972 OJ L 166/22.
716. Article 2 (3) of Regulation 2790/1999.

cumstances, in particular the structure of the market, the parties' position on that market and the level of vertical integration.[717] According to the Court of Justice's ruling in *Coditel II*[718] exclusive copyright licences may be held compatible with Article 81,[719] unless they are agreed for an 'unduly long period' or at unfairly high fees[720] or applied by companies that have a dominant position.[721] The main issues when assessing copyright licences therefore are exclusivity, scope and duration of the licensing agreements.

The Single Buyer Issue.

The single buyer issue concerns the case where one single buyer acquires all the rights at stake, which is likely to prevent competitors from gaining access to the licensed rights. The degree of this restriction depends on the duration of the licences and the existence of alternative ways of exploitation.

– In the case *Film Purchases by German Television Stations*[722] the Commission objected under Article 81 (1) to the exclusive licence granted by MGM and United Artists to one of the German public TV stations, ARD, because the licence was disproportionate in scope, namely covering a very large number of attractive films, such as James Bond films, and in duration, namely for a very long period ranging between 15 and 16 years, was limited to Germany and excluded the grant of sub-licences to others than associated undertakings. The agreement thereby precluded any broadcasting outside Germany and prevented competitors, such as the other public TV station (ZDF) and other private stations, from gaining access to an important segment of the market for broadcasting rights. The Commission exempted the agreement only after reduction of the degree of exclusivity by conceding a large number of 'windows' lifting

---

717. *M6, Antena 3, Gestévision, SIC/UER/Eurovision II,* CFI Oct 8, 2002, 2002 ECR II-3805, paras 64 and 68.

718. *Coditel/Cine Vog Films,* ECJ Oct. 6, 1982, 1982 ECR 3381.

719. *Tierce/Ladbroke,* CFI June 12, 1997, 1997 ECR II-923, para. 132.

720. *Coditel/Cine Vog Films,* ECJ Oct. 6, 1982, 1982 ECR 3381 paras 15–19. *See also Basset/SACEM,* ECJ April 9, 1987, 1987 ECR 1747; *Warner Brothers and Metronome/Christiansen,* ECJ May 17, 1988, 1988 ECR 2605. In *SACEM/SABAM* (Fourth Report on Competition Policy, points 112–113) the Commission considered a duration of fifty years as excessive. In a case of licences to films of horse races the Commission accepted a duration of 5 years as reasonable: *PMI/DSV* (*Ladbroke*), D.Comm. Jan. 31, 1995, 1995 OJ L 221/34, point 7. In *Alsatel/Novasam* the Court accepted that the automatic extension of a leasing contract for 15 years may be abusive: ECJ Oct. 5, 1988, 1988 ECR 5987, para. 10. In *Music Choice Europe,* 1997 OJ C 70/7, the Commission accepted a duration of forty years in the light of the substantial investments.

721. *BSB/Football Association,* Twenty-third Report on Competition Policy, p. 459 (broadcast of transmission of sport events).

722. *Film Purchase by German Television Stations,* D.Comm. Sept. 15, 1989, 1989 OJ L 284/36.

exclusivity for a relatively short period (ranging from two to six years) and permitting the grant of broadcast licences to third parties.[723]

- In the *Eurovision* case the Commission granted individual exemption to the Eurovision system, the framework for the exchange of programs among the members of the European Broadcasting Union (EBU), with respect to joint acquisition and sharing of sports television rights following amendments which made it possible for other broadcasters to obtain sub-licences.[724] The Court of First Instance annulled this decision because the EBU rules led, even after amendment, to a discrimination between public and private broadcasters.[725] Subsequently, the EBU submitted new rules granting sublicences to Eurovision rights for broadcasting on pay-channel television. The Commission granted a new exemption[726] which was again annulled by the Court of First Instance because the new rules did not enable competitors of the EBU members to obtain sub-licences for the live broadcast of unused television rights rather than sub-licences to transmit roundups of competitions under extremely restrictive conditions.[727]

The Single Seller Issue.

The single seller issue concerns the grant of an exclusive licence by individual right-holders to a joint selling body, whereby the individual rightholders are prevented from granting further licences. The severity of this restriction depends on whether individual licensing is excluded with respect to all types of rights (e.g. including satellite and cable) and for an excessively long period.

The *IFPI* case[728] concerned a model reciprocal agreement between collecting societies acting on behalf of record companies. The purpose was to facilitate the grant of international copyright licences to radio and TV broadcasters who wish to engage in simulcasting (transmission by radio and TV stations simultaneously and unaltered both via the traditional means, such as air, cable and satellite, and the internet), thereby making musical works available to the public via the internet. The agreement allowed for international exploitation (the grant of 'one stop shop' multi-repertoire and multi-territorial licences by a single society) instead of limiting their activities to their own territories. The agreement was granted exemption under Article 81 (3) for a limited period (up to December 31, 2004), thereby recognizing the necessity and advantage of avoiding a multiplicity of individual

723. According to the Commission, even this reduced exclusivity still infringed Article 81 (1) and needed exemption under Article 81 (3) (point 45).
724. *EBU/Eurovision I,* D.Comm. June 11, 1993, 1993 OJ L 179/23.
725. *EBU/Eurovision I,* CFI July 11, 1996, 1996 ECR II-649. *See* the critical comments of V. Korah, *Cases & Materials on EC Competition Law* (1997), pp. 167–168.
726. *EBU/Eurovision II,* D.Comm. May 10, 2000, 2000 OJ L 151/18.
727. *M6, Antena 3, Gestevision, SIC, DSF, RTI/Eurovision I,* CFI Oct. 8, 2002, 2002 ECR II-3805, para. 79–86.
728. *IFPI,* D.Comm. Oct. 8, 2002, 2003 OJ L 107/58.

lengthy negotiations by users across the EEA with each individual collecting society.[729] However, the exemption was subject to the following amendments:

- Under the original version broadcasters were required to approach the producer's collecting society in their own member state; the amended version allows broadcasters to approach the collecting society of their choice in order to obtain a multi-territorial and multi-repertoire simulcastsing licence.
- The original agreement obliged the collection societies to respect the tariffs of the country of destination and to combine administration fees (which are different from society to society) and copyright royalties;[730] the amended version provides for a separation of administration fees and the global licence fee, thereby identifying the actual administration costs incurred by the grantor society in respect of the granting of multi-territorial and multi-repertoire licences.[731]

(c) Case Law on Copyright Licensing

Joint Buying *and* Selling of Copyrights – The UEFA Champions League Case.
Both joint buying and joint selling may, if applied by undertakings with substantial market power, lead to the strengthening of a dominant position incompatible with Article 82[732] or, in the case of a merger, with the merger control regulation, unless appropriate remedies can be found.[733] However, joint buying and selling arrangements may foster pro-competitive efficiencies and therefore meet the criteria for exemption under Article 81 (3). *UEFA Champions League*[734] was such a case. This case concerned the joint buying and selling arrangements regarding the media

729. Responding to increasing competitive pressure and a changing market place driven by globalization: Guidelines on horizontal cooperation, 2001 OJ C 3/2, point 3.
730. Royalty fee for a proper remuneration of the right-holders, such as phonogram producers, performers or authors, which was recognized in *Coditel I,* ECJ March 18, 1980, 1980 ECR 881, para. 14.
731. It has to be seen to whether the amended agreement leads effectively to more transparency and competition in terms of price between the EEA-based collecting societies. *See* the previous proceedings against agreements incolving *IFPI,* Thirteenth Report on Competition Policy, points 147–150.
732. *See GEMA I,* D.Comm. June 2, 1971, 1971 OJ L 134/15.
733. E.g. *ARD/Kirch Pay-TV, British Sky,* CFI Sept. 30, 2003, T-158/00; *Vivendi/Seagram/Canal+,* D.Comm. Oct. 13, 2000, M.2050; *Newscorp/Telepiù,* D.Comm. April 2, 2003, M.2876 (in both cases the Commission concluded that the operation would lead to the creation or strengthening of a dominant position for the acquisition of pay-TV rights on premium films and football events following commitments to reduce the exclusivity in scope and duration) ; *Sogecable/Canalsatéllite/Via Digital,* D.Comm. Aug. 14, 2002, M.2845 (referral to the Spanish authority) and decision of the Spanish authority Nov. 29, 2002 (clearance subject to the condition that the duration be reduced to 2–3 years).
734. *UEFA Champions League,* D.Comm. July 23, 2003, 2003 OJ L 291/25.

rights (radio, television, internet and UMTS) of the UEFA Champions League, a pan-European football competition, which is granted the exclusive right to sell certain copyrights on behalf of the participating football clubs. The arrangement restricts competition among the football clubs to the extent that it has the effect of coordinating the pricing policy and other trading conditions. However, the Commission exempted the arrangement because it provides the consumer with the benefit of league focused media products from this pan-European football club competition that is sold via a single point of sale and which would not otherwise be produced and distributed so efficiently. The Commission found that the conditions of Article 81 (3) were satisfied under the exceptional circumstances of the case,[735] subject to the condition that the football clubs must not be prevented from selling their live TV rights to free-TV broadcasters where there is no reasonable offer from any pay-TV broadcaster in order to reduce the impact of the restriction.[736]

From Territorial Licences toward Open Internet-Induced Markets. Exclusive licences may be granted for a certain territory, provided they do not include a prohibition against selling (including publicity or promotion activity) in other licensees' territories[737] or confer the right to invoke the copyright against copyrighted goods which have been put on the market, within the EC and EEA countries by the right-owner or with its consent.[738] Consequently, agreements between national copyright collecting societies providing for reciprocal representation of their copyrighted works in each other's respective home markets were challenged under Article 81 (1) if they required the collecting society to refuse to license foreign users and instead required them to refer foreign enquirers to their own national collecting society.[739] Likewise, if the collecting societies engaged in a concerted practice whereby they systematically refused to license foreign users and this conduct was not objectively justified, for example, by the impracticability of installing a system of monitoring exploitation of the copyrighted work in the other party's home market, this also infringed Article 81 (1).[740]

However, the use of the internet and the digital format for products protected by copyright resulted in the ability to monitor copyright usage from a distance, thereby rendering meaningless the need for physical monitoring, which was the

---

735. *See* the Commission's explanations in the background note, MEMO/03/156.
736. *UEFA Champions League,* D.Comm. July 23, 2003, 2003 OJ L 291/25, points 188–192.
737. *See Dior/Evora,* ECJ Nov. 4, 1997, 1997 ECR I-6013, paras 55–57.
738. This does not apply to imports from third countries: *Polydor,* ECJ Feb. 9, 1982, 1982 ECR 329 (copyrighted records), unless the extension of the exhaustion principle is in conformity with international agreements, such as the EEA and the TRIPs Agreement: *Silhouette,* ECJ July 18, 1998, 1998 ECR I-4799, para. 26; *Sebago/GB-Unic,* ECJ July 1, 1999, 1999 ECR I-4103, paras 16–17 (with respect to trademarks).
739. *SACEM II,* ECJ July 13, 1989, 1989 ECR 2811, paras 11–14; *SACEM III,* ECJ July 13, 1989, 1989 ECR 2521, paras 16–20.
740. *SACEM II,* ECJ July 13, 1989, 1989 ECR 2811, paras 15–17; *SACEM III,* 1989 ECR 2521, paras 21–23; *Tremblay, Lacazeau/SELL,* CFI Jan. 24, 1995, 1995 ECR II-147 para. 30.

traditional justification for reciprocal arrangements between collecting societies containing territorial restrictions. Such territorial restrictions are no longer objectively indispensible since radio and TV broadcasters are able to choose the most efficient society in the EEA for the grant of a multi-territorial copyright licence allowing for an international exploitation of the sound recordings administered by the collecting societies through means of the internet.[741]

Field-of-Use Limitations.

On the basis of longstanding administrative practice and case law, a copyright licence may be limited to a specific field of use.[742] Consequently, the right-owner may grant exclusive distribution rights to licensee A and exclusive rental rights to licensee B[743] subject to the consequence that the exhaustion principle applies. In the *Warner Brothers and Metronome Video/Christiansen* case the Court of Justice pointed out that

> 'literary and artistic works may be the subject of commercial exploitation by means other than the sale of the recordings made of them. That applies, for example, to the rental of video-cassettes, which reaches a different public from the market for their sale and constitutes an important potential source of revenue for makers of films .... By authorising the collection of royalties only on sales to private individuals and to persons hiring out video-cassettes, it is impossible to guarantee to makers of films a remuneration which reflects the number of occasions on which the video-cassettes are actually hired out and which secures for them a satisfactory share on the rental market. Laws which provide specific protection of the right to hire out video-cassettes are therefore clearly justified on grounds of the protection of industrial and commercial property pursuant to Article 36.... A maker of a film who has offered the video-cassette of that film in a Member State whose legislation confers on him no exclusive right of hiring it out must accept the consequences of his choice and the exhaustion of his rights to restrain the hiring-out of that video-cassette in any other Member State. Where national legislation confers on authors a specific right to hire out

741. *See* Mendes Pereira, From discothèques to websites, a new approach to music copyright licensing, DG IV Newsletter 2003–1, p. 44.

742. *See* the list of different uses of a copyright in *GEMA I,* D.Comm. June 2, 1971, 1971 OJ L 134/15; *GEMA II,* D.Comm. July 6, 1972, 1972 OJ L 166/22.

743. *Warner Brothers and Metronome Video/Christiansen,* ECJ May 17, 1988, 1988 ECR 2605, paras 17–18; *Metronome Musik/Music Point Hokamp,* ECJ April 28, 1998, 1998 ECR I-1953, paras 16–18 and 24. The rental rights are of increasing importance to economic and cultural development as a result of the increasing threat of piracy and must guarantee that authors and performers can receive appropriate income and amortize the especially high and risky investments required, particularly for the production of phonograms and films: *Metronome Musik/Music Point Hokamp,* ECJ April 28, 1998, 1998 ECR I-1953, para. 22.

> video-cassettes, that right would be rendered worthless if its owner were not in a position to authorise the operations for doing so.'[744]

According to the Court of Justice's decision in *Metronome Musik/Music Point Hokamp*[745] the distinction drawn by Directive 92/100/EC on the Rental and Lending Rights Concerning Copyrights and Rights Related to Copyrights[746] between the effects of the specific rental and lending right and those of the distribution right is justified under Article 30 of the EC Treaty. 'The former is exhausted by the sale or any other act of distribution of the object, whereas the latter may be exhausted, but only and specifically upon the first sale in the Community by the right-holder or with his consent'.[747] Thus, a licence limited to distribution and excluding hiring and lending does not infringe Article 81 (1). The same reasoning applies to the grant of licences to show a film in different forms, e.g. in cinemas but not on television, and for different durations.[748] The producer of a cinematographic film may grant the exclusive right to exhibit the film to a film distribution company in one member state and to a television broadcasting organization in another member state and consequently grant the right to each licensee to prohibit, during a specific period, its showing by others, including retransmission by cable television. The Court of Justice stated in *Coditel II* that an exclusive licence limited to one member state and one 'field of use' (cinema exhibition or television) was not caught by Article 81 (1). However, the Court added that

> 'it is for national courts, where appropriate, … in particular to establish whether or not the exercise of the exclusive right to exhibit a cinematographic film creates barriers which are artificial and unjustifiable in terms of the needs of the cinematographic industry, or the possibility of charging fees which exceed a fair return on investment, or an exclusivity the duration of which is disproportionate to those requirements, and whether or not, from a general point of view, such exercise within a given geographic area is such as to prevent, restrict or distort competition within the common market.'[749]

---

744. *Warner Brothers and Metronome Video/Christiansen,* ECJ May 17, 1988, 1988 ECR 2605, paras 15–18; *Metronome Musik/Music Point Hokamp,* ECJ April 28, 1998, 1998 ECR I-1953, paras 15–17.
745. *Metronome Musik/Music Point Hokamp,* ECJ April 28, 1998, 1998 ECR I-1953, paras 16–18 and 24.
746. 1992 OJ L 346/61.
747. *See also Foreningen af Danske Videogramdistributorer/Laserdisken,* ECJ Sept. 22, 1998, 1998 ECR I-5171.
748. *Coditel II,* ECJ Oct. 6, 1982, 1982 ECR 3381, para. 19; *Coditel I,* ECJ March 18, 1980, 1980 ECR 881, para. 13 (film licenced initially for cinema exhibition and 40 months later for television showing). *See* under Article 82 *GEMA I,* D.Comm. June 2, 1971, 1971 OJ L 134/15, 22; under Article 28*: Cinéthèque,* ECJ July 11, 1985, 1985 ECR 2605, para. 24.
749. *Coditel II,* ECJ Oct. 6, 1982, 1982 ECR 3381, para. 19.

Even a collecting society which has a dominant position is not prevented from limiting licences to a particular field of use, provided they constitute separate markets.[750]

Further Case Law on Restrictive Clauses in Copyright Licences.[751]
The following clauses are *likely* to be held *in conformity* with Article 81 (1):

- exclusive licences and field-of-use restrictions, as explained above;
- an obligation not to grant sub-licences or to make sub-licences subject to the licensor's prior approval,[752] unless it is a means of strengthening the licensor's market position and of hindering the market access of third parties;[753]
- an obligation not to contest the licensed copyrights;[754]
- an obligation to pay licence fees for each performance;[755]
- a selective distribution system, provided that it is based on objective or qualitative criteria[756] and applied without discrimination.[757]

The following clauses are *unlikely* to gain clearance under Article 81 (3) or they are blacklisted under the various block exemption regulations which may apply directly or by analogy to Regulation 772/2004 on Technology Transfer Agreements and Regulation 2790/1999 on Vertical Restraints:

- resale price maintenance;[758]

---

750. *GEMA II,* D.Comm. July 6, 1972, 1972 OJ L 166/22 (distinction, accepted by the Commission under Article 82, of performing rights, radio, television or cinematographic rights, film or videotape production rights and rights to play or reproduce).
751. A good overview on the administrative practice is found in the Commission's conclusions submitted at the occasion of the adoption of its proposal for a Council Directive on the Legal Protection of Computer Programs, 1989 OJ C 91/16, which has been adopted: 1991 OJ L 122/42.
752. *PMI/DSV* (*Ladbroke*), D.Comm. Jan. 31, 1995, 1995 OJ L 221/34, points 7 and 11 (needed for the licensor's prior control of the technical skills of the potential sub-licensees); *Tierce Ladbroke,* CFI June 12, 1997, 1997 ECR II-923, para. 132. However, the prohibition to grant sub-licences may, under exceptional circumstances, be held restrictive of competition and need (but merit) individual clearance: *Film Purchases by German TV Stations,* D.Comm. Sept. 15, 1989, 1989 OJ L 284/36, point 41.
753. *M6, Antena 3, Gestevision, SIC,UER/Eurovision,* CFI Oct. 8, 2002, T-185/00, paras 71–75.
754. *PMS/DSV* (*Ladbroke*), D.Comm. Jan. 31, 1995, 1995 OJ L 221/34, point 14.
755. *Coditel II,* ECJ Oct. 6, 1982, 1982 ECR 3381, para. 12; *Warner Brothers and Metronome/ Christiansen,* ECJ May 17, 1988, 1988 ECR 2605, paras 14–15; *Metronome Musik/Music Point Hokamp,* ECJ April 28, 1998, 1998 ECR I-1953, para. 16.
756. *PMI/DSV(Ladbroke),* D.Comm. Jan. 31, 1995, 1995 OJ L 221/34 paras 7 and 12. Under Article 82*: IBM Personal Computers,* D.Comm. April 18, 1984, 1984 OJ L 118/24.
757. *PMI/DSV* (*Ladbroke*), D.Comm. Jan. 31, 1995, 1995 OJ L 221/34 para. 7.
758. It is still an open question whether the individual price maintenance obligation – unlike a collective agreement between different competing right-holders – qualifies for an exemption under Article 81 (3).

- application of discriminatory licence fees,[759] in particular fees which differ substantially according to the country of destination, thereby preventing exports;[760]
- collective refusal to grant licences without objective justification;[761]
- customer and market sharing, except for permissible field-of-use restrictions,[762] including the obligation imposed on licensees to communicate confidential sensitive market information in regard to certain customers or markets, thereby reinforcing territorial restrictions;[763]
- export and import prohibitions pertaining to EC and EEA countries;[764]
- restrictions exceeding the duration[765] or the scope of the protected right, in particular the obligation to pay a second[766] or additional licence fee when marketing in another member state,[767] except for fields of use which were not subject to any fee in the country of origin;[768]
- quantitative restrictions (e.g. limiting television rights to fixed quotas[769] or

---

759. Under Article 82*: SACEM II,* ECJ Sept. 13, 1989, 1989 ECR 2811 paras 21–33; *SACEM III,* ECJ July 13, 1989, 1989 ECR 2521 para. 34.
760. *Stemras,* Eleventh report on Competition Policy, point 98; *K'tel/GEMA,* ECJ Jan. 20, 1981, 1981 ECR 147.
761. *Tierce Ladbroke,* CFI June 12, 1997, 1997 ECR II-923, paras 132–133.
762. *Racal Decca,* D.Comm. Dec. 21, 1988, 1989 OJ L 43/27, 42–43.
763. *PMI/DSV (Ladbroke),* D.Comm. Jan. 31, 1995, 1995 OJ L 221/34 para. 7 (need for the licensor to pre-qualify the technical skills of the potential sublicensees).
764. *Miller International,* D.Comm. Dec. 1, 1976, 1976 OJ L 357/40 (*aff'd* ECJ Feb. 1, 1978, 1978 ECR 131); *WEA Filipacchi,* D.Comm. Dec. 22, 1972, 1972 OJ L 303/52 (cease and desist decisions with fines); *BBC and 'The Old Man and the Sea',* Sixth Report on Competition Policy, points 163 and 164; *'Ernest Benn',* Ninth Report on Competition Policy, point 118; *Stemra,* Eleventh Report on Competition Policy, point 98; *BIEM/IFTI,* Thirteenth Report on Competition Policy, point 150. Territorial restrictions imposed on distributors in third countries are not likely to infringe Article 81 (1) and intellectual property rights may be used to halt reimports in the Common Market: *Silhouette,* ECJ June 16, 1998, 1998 ECR I-4799, paras 23–27.
765. *BRT/SABAM II,* ECJ March 27, 1974, 1974 ECR 313, paras 9–15. The maximum duration of protection is: 70 years for copyrights and 50 years for related rights: Articles 1 and 3 of Council Directive 93/98/EC Approximating the Duration of National Copyrights (1993 OJ L 290/9); 50 years for rights on computer programs: Article 8 of Council Directive 91/250/EC (1991 OJ L 122/42); 15 years for rights on databases: Article 10 of Directive 96/9/EC (1996 OJ L 77/20). *Coditel II,* ECJ Oct. 6, 1982, 1982 ECR 3381, para. 19. In cases of a dominant position affecting market access of third parties the maximum duration may be much shorter: *Auditel,* D.Comm. Nov. 24, 1993, 1993 OJ L 306/50 (five years); *Microsoft,* Twenty-fourth Report on Competition Policy, p. 364 (one year).
766. *K'tel/GEMA,* ECJ Jan. 20, 1981, 1981 ECR 147.
767. *BIEM/IFPI,* Thirteenth Report on Competition Policy, points 147–150; *SACEM I,* ECJ April 9, 1987, 1987 ECR 1747 paras 14–17 (under Article 82).
768. For example rental of copyrighted products: *SACEM I,* ECJ April 9, 987, 1987 ECR 1747; *Video-Cassettes,* ECJ May 17, 1988, 1988 ECR 2605; *SACEM IV,* ECJ Dec. 12, 1990, 1990 ECR I-4607.
769. *Auditel,* D.Comm. Nov. 24, 1993, 1993 OJ L 306/50.

minimum commitments[770]) have only be challenged if they were imposed by a dominant firm; it is still an open question (and seems in fact rather doubtful) that such restrictions are generally prohibited under Article 81;
- restrictions on the manufacture (or sub-contracting) of secondary products. In the *Sega* and *Nintendo* cases[771] the Commission objected to licence agreements concluded by two of the leading manufacturers of video game consoles enabling independent firms to develop and distribute games that were compatible with their consoles that also conferred on Sega and Nintendo a right to veto any game developed by the licensees and obliged the licensees to subcontract the production to the licensor or to a limited number of approved manufacturers with the aim of limiting the ability of the licensees to compete with the licensor;
- tying clauses, for example bundling copyrighted software with computer hardware, unless necessary to ensure a technically satisfactory use of the licensed copyright.[772]

Agreements between a National Copyright Collecting Society and Manufacturers.
The main categories of restrictions in agreements between a national copyright collecting society and manufacturers are as follows:

- *Restricting the Place of Manufacture.* In *GEMA IV*,[773] the Commission challenged the practice of the German collecting society of charging royalties on sound recordings manufactured in Germany, even when the licensee had obtained a licence from a collecting society in another member state. The practice tended to restrict manufacture to the country of licensing, whereas the licence granted by a Community copyright protection society to a manufacturer should, in the Commission's view, be valid throughout the Community and authorize manufacture, even by way of custom pressing, in any member state.
- *Export Bans.* Contractual export bans on copyrighted products are normally caught by Article 81 (1) and rarely qualify for exemption under Article 81 (3). In the context of patent and trademark licences, the Court has ruled that an

770. *Microsoft,* Twenty-fourth Report on Competition Policy, p. 364.
771. Twenty-seventh Report on Competition Policy, point 80.
772. Under Article 82: In the *IBM* case (Fourteenth Report on Competition Policy, points 94–95) the practice of not offering the central processing units without main memory capacity included in the price ('memory bundling') was challenged under Article 82 as an abuse of a dominant position. In *Microsoft* (Twenty-fourth Report on Competition Policy, p. 364) the Commission challenged the use of 'per processor' and 'per system' licences, i.e. clauses requiring payment of a royalty on every computer produced by a PC manufacturer either containing a particular processor or belonging to a particular model series designated by that manufacturer, regardless of whether a particular computer is shipped with pre-installed Microsoft software. Similar practices agreed between different right-holders and licensees would be likely to infringe Article 81 (1).
773. *GEMA IV,* Fifteenth Report on Competition Policy, point 81.

exclusive licence combined with, or leading to, absolute territorial protection against parallel imports is incompatible with Article 81.[774] The Court of Justice has not yet addressed this question in relation to copyright licences. However, the Commission has found that the obligation to export only with the approval of the copyright collecting society of the country of importation was tantamount to an export ban and therefore probably impermissible.[775] It has also challenged territorial restrictions in copyright sub-licences when the licensee held a licence for the whole Common Market[776] or when the copyrighted designs were merely affixed to other products.[777] Export prohibitions on retailers are incompatible with Article 81.[778] Consequently, a copyright collecting society may not require a licensed manufacturer to impose export prohibitions on its distributors.[779]

- *Calculation of Royalties*. The Commission has challenged a contractual obligation to base royalties due to collecting societies on the average retail price of records in the country of sale, taking into account the prices charged by competing record manufacturers, rather than on the manufacturer's published selling prices to retailers of that country. In the *BIEM/IFPI* case[780] the Commission considered this practice as preventing any cost or price advantage that arose in the country of manufacture from being passed on to consumers in the country of sale. The case was settled when the collecting societies agreed to base royalties on the manufacturer's published selling prices to retailers.

Agreements between Authors and National Copyright Collecting Societies. In the past the agreements between authors and composers and the national copyright collecting society which manages their rights typically included an exclusive package licence to all rights to all works and uses of those works within the member state or even worldwide for a long period. This had the effect of preventing the author from granting any further licences and completely blocked access to the author's copyrights by other collecting societies or users. The Commission

774. *Maize Seed,* ECJ June 8, 1982, 1982 ECR 2015, paras 52–67 (plant breeders' rights similar to patents); *Grundig/Consten,* ECJ July 13, 1966, 1966 ECR 299, 342–343 (trademarks, by negative inference from the Court's condemnation of absolute territorial protection through trademark licences). In the *Dior/Evora* case the Court extended this jurisprudence to copyrights although the case concerned only the question whether the right-holder may use its rights to prevent publicity activities of the parallel importer: ECJ Nov. 4, 1997, 1997 ECR I-6013.
775. *Stemra,* Eleventh Report on Competition Policy, point 98. *See also BIEM/IFPI,* Thirteenth Report on Competition Policy, points 147–150.
776. *The Old Man and the Sea,* Sixth Report on Competition Policy, point 164.
777. *BBC/Valley Printing,* Sixth Report on Competition Policy, point 163.
778. *Miller International,* ECJ Feb.1, 1978, 1978 ECR 131; *Ernest Benn Ltd.,* Ninth Report on Competition Policy, points 118–119.
779. There is, however, no case law yet on this issue.
780. *BIEM/IFPI,* Thirteenth Report on Competition Policy, points 147–150.

challenged such restrictions under Article 82 in its *GEMA I* decision[781] as constituting an abuse of the dominant position occupied by the only national copyright collecting society within its national territory. On the other hand, the *GEMA I* decision held that the author and the collecting society are each free to grant an exclusive licence to a particular work for a particular country, field of use or limited period without infringing Article 82. A copyright collecting society also abuses its dominant position if it refuses to enter into management contracts with foreign artists.[782]

Agreements between Individual Performers/Artists and Producers/ Broadcasters.
An artist may normally enter into an exclusive obligation with a producer of films for television limited to only one work and one type of exploitation (television films) without infringing Article 81. In the *Deutsche Grammophon* judgment,[783] the Court of Justice gave consideration, *inter alia,* to the performers' popularity on the market, to the duration and extent of the obligations undertaken and to the opportunities available to other manufacturers of sound recordings to obtain the services of comparable performers. Although the case concerned the applicability of Article 82, the criteria stated by the Court may also be used to establish whether an exclusivity clause is caught by Article 81 (1). In the light of *Coditel II*[784] it seems likely that exclusive long-term arrangements between a famous, world-renowned artist and a manufacturer of sound recordings are only under exceptional circumstances caught by Article 81 (1). In the *RAI/Unitel* case the Commission challenged the exclusive contracts which four international opera singers had entered into with Unitel, a German producer of television films, for the entire duration of the production of a film of the opera 'Don Carlos'. They were also subject to a non-competition clause extending over a considerable period. This exclusivity prevented RAI, the Italian radio and television broadcasting company, from broadcasting live via Eurovision the same opera performed at La Scala in Milan during the opera house's 200th anniversary celebrations. After the Commission intervened, Unitel agreed to limit the noncompetition clause to a shorter period and to waive its exclusive rights in the case of live broadcasts of particularly important cultural events.[785]

781. *GEMA I,* D.Comm. June 2, 1971, 1971 OJ L 134/15, 22–23; *BRT/SABAM II,* ECJ March 27, 1974, 1974 ECR 313, paras 7–15.

782. *GVL,* ECJ March 2, 1983, 1983 ECR 483, paras 47–56. *See also GEMA I,* D.Comm. June 2, 1971, 1971 OJ L 134/15, 21.

783. *Deutsche Grammophon,* ECJ June 8, 1971, 1971 ECR 487, para. 18.

784. *Coditel II,* ECJ Oct. 6, 1982, 1982 ECR 3381, para. 19.

785. *RAI/Unitel,* Twelfth Report on Competition Policy, point 90. For similar reasons the Commission challenged the exclusive licence granted by the English Football League to London Weekend Television which created a dominant position excluding BBC from broadcasting soccer matches: Ninth Report on Competition Policy, points 116–117.

Agreements Licensing the Public Performance of Musical Recordings. Whereas the manufacture of sound recordings is subject to a royalty covering mechanical reproduction and distribution, the right of public performance of recordings (for example, in discotheques) is a distinct right for which a separate royalty has to be paid to the author or collected by the national copyright society. In the *SACEM* cases the Court of Justice dealt with several issues raised by licences of performing rights under Article 82. The practice of copyright collecting societies of 'package licensing' their entire repertory was accepted by the Court, except where it could be shown that access to a certain part of the repertory (e.g., English language works) was likely to safeguard the legitimate interests of the artists by the copyright collecting society without increasing the cost of management.[786] The Court also held that the charging of an additional 'mechanical reproduction' fee with the performance royalty in France did not necessarily represent an abuse of the collecting society's dominant position.[787] However, this would not be the case if the total performance royalty the society charged were unfairly high.[788]

Licences to Manufacture Copyrighted Designs of Functional Products such as Automotive Spare Parts. Under United Kingdom law, designs for purely functional articles such as automotive spare parts used to enjoy far-reaching protection by copyright until this protection was much reduced by the Copyright, Designs and Patents Act 1988. In Italy similar protection was provided under patent law for ornamental designs. Agreements licensing such rights in the United Kingdom under the previous legislation were normally not exclusive, but could contain no-challenge clauses, non-compete clauses, the obligation to pay royalties on products not protected by the right held by the licensor, or a clause requiring the licensee to transfer to the licensor the title to the licensee's rights in any improvements. Following its practice in cases of patent licence agreements, the Commission has regarded these clauses as infringing Article 81 (1) and as unlikely to qualify for exemption under Article 81 (3).[789]

---

786. *SACEM III,* ECJ July 13, 1989 ECR 2521, paras 30–31. *See* under U.S. law: *Broadcast Music, Inc. v. Columbia Broadcasting System, Inc.,* 441 US 1, 60 L.Ed. 2nd 1, 99 S.Ct. 1551 (rule of reason).
787. *SACEM I,* ECJ April 9, 1987, 1987 ECR 1747; *SACEM IV,* ECJ Dec. 12, 1990, 1990 ECR I-4607.
788. *SACEM II,* ECJ July 13, 1989, 1989 ECR 2811, paras 21–33; *SACEM HI,* ECJ July 13, 1989, 1989 ECR 2521, paras 34–46. *See also Coditel II,* ECJ Oct. 6, 1982, 1982 ECR 3381, para. 19; *Renault,* ECJ Oct. 5, 1988, 1988 ECR 6039, para. 16; *Volvo/Veng,* ECJ Oct. 5, 1988, 1988 ECR 6211, para. 9.
789. *Neilson-Hordell/Richmark,* Twelfth Report on Competition Policy, points 88–89. *See also* the Commission's Notice on Subcontracting Agreements, 1979 OJ C 1/2.

2. Trademark Licensing

No Trademark Licence Block Exemption.
The Commission has authority to issue a block exemption regulation on trademark licence agreements on the basis of Regulation 19/65, Article 1 (1) (b), but it has not yet done so. Where a trademark licence is directly related to the sale or resale of products and services and does not constitute the primary object of the respective agreements (including selective distribution and franchising agreements), the licence agreement is covered by Regulation 2790/1999 on vertical restraints.[790] Trademark licences which are ancillary to transfer of technology agreements must be assessed under the new regulation on transfer of technology agreements or individually under Article 81 where the market share limits of the block exemption are exceeded. A specific trade mark block exemption may be appropriate only for pure trademark licences in which exploitation of the trademark rather than patents or know-how is the principal subject of the licence.

Pure Trade Mark Licences.
Particularly well-known or distinctive trademarks (such as for luxury goods like perfume or tobacco products) are often licensed to manufacturers of totally unrelated products (such as clothing or watches) in order to boost sales of the latter products.[791] These licence agreements often contain exclusivity clauses, in particular the obligation on the licensor not to grant further licences to competitors of the licensee, not to purchase or use products of competitors[792] and the obligation on the licensee to use the trademark only for making, distributing or using products specified or approved by the licensor.[793] Although the licensor is not a competitor of the licensee in these cases, such an agreement may lead to an unjustified exclusion of, or discrimination (in particular application of objectively unjustified fees) against, the licensee's competitors.[794] The same reasoning applies to the overreaching use of obligations on the licensee to respect minimum quality standards in order to maintain the high reputation of the licensed trademark.[795] Article 81 (1) applies if the licence agreements contain exclusivity provisions

---

790. Guidelines on Technology Transfer Agreements, point 50.
791. E.g. *Eco/Benneton,* ECJ June 1, 1999, 1999 ECR I-3055, para. 9.
792. *Cadbury Schweppes/Coca Cola,* 1996 OJ C 138/6.
793. *Tennis Balls,* 1996 OJ C 138/6, where the Commission objected to the obligation to use only selected balls at certain tennis tournaments instead of imposing mere objective qualitative criteria. *See also Eco Swiss/Benetton,* ECJ June 1, 1999, 1999 ECR I-3055 (Benetton granting a non-exclusive trademark licence to produce watches marketed by Eco under the 'Benetton' trademark).
794. *'Grüner Punkt'/DSD,* 1997 OJ C 100/4.
795. *Cf.* the whitelisted minimum quality clauses in technology transfer agreements under Article 2 (1) (5) Regulation 240/96. *See* the design licence granted by Benetton (clothing manufacturer) in the context of a joint venture created with Time (a watch manufacturer): 1994 OJ C 242/3 (comfort letter).

likely to restrict assess by other competitors to the market. In the *Green Dot* cases which concerned the collection and recovery of sales packaging waste in Germany[796] and France[797] the Commission intervened against the payment of royalties independently of whether the collection services were effectively provided by the licensor (instead the 'no service, no fee' principle should apply)[798] and against the excessively long duration of exclusivity provisions (longer than four years).[799] Reciprocal trademark licences do not in themselves infringe Article 81, but when they are concluded between competitors and lead to market sharing they infringe Article 81 (1) and will not qualify for exemption.[800]

Trademarks Ancillary to Sale of a Business.

Trademarks may also be the principal object when transferring business assets; exclusive licences and accompanying non-compete clauses may be ancillary (necessary for guaranteeing the full value of the transferred business) and not covered by Article 81 (1) if they are limited in scope and duration.[801] The Commission is likely to raise objections under Article 81 when the clauses go beyond the 'necessary' standard which, as the Commission has stated, means the non-competition covenant must be limited to the products produced and the geographic area served by the selling enterprise.[802] The permissible duration should not exceed two years when only goodwill (i.e. trademarks) is transferred with the sale of business; five years may be justified where technical know-how is also transferred.[803]

Trademark Licence Ancillary to Distribution Agreements with Territorial Exclusivity – The *Grundig/Consten* Case.

This case concerned an agreement by which Grundig authorized its French exclusive distributor, Consten, to register the GINT trademark (for Grundig International) in Consten's name in France.[804] The Court of Justice concluded that

---

796. *DSD,* D.Comm. April 20, 2001, 2001 OJ L 166/1, and D.Comm. Sept. 17, 2001, 2001 L 319/1.
797. *Eco-Emballage,* D.Comm. June 15, 2001, 2001 OJ L 233/37 (negative clearance following amendments).
798. Under Article 82: *DSD I,* D.Comm. April 20, 2001, 2001 OJ L 166/1, points 143–154 (prohibition decision).
799. *DSD II,* D.Comm. Sept. 17, 2001, 2001 L 319/1 (negative clearance granted following amendments); *see* Thirty-first Report on Competition Policy, point 79 and Box 3.
800. *EMI/CBS,* ECJ June 15, 1976, 1976 ECR 811, paras 25–29. *See,* however, *Continental/Michelin,* 1996 OJ C 236/9, where the Commission announced its intention to clear, in the context of a larger cooperation, certain market sharing aspects of a trademark deal between competitors.
801. *Remia/Nutricia,* ECJ July 11, 1985, 1985 ECR 2545, paras 17–20.
802. *Quantel International-Continuum/Quantel,* D.Comm. July 27, 1992, 1992 OJ L 235/9; *Gillette/Wilkinson,* D.Comm. Nov. 10, 1992, 1993 L 116/21, paras 33–39; *Chiquita/Fyffes,* Twenty-second Report on Competition Policy, points 168–176.
803. *Remia/Nutricia,* ECJ July 11, 1985, 1985 ECR 2545, para. 42.
804. *Grundig/Consten,* ECJ July 13, 1966, 1966 ECR 299. Previously, Grundig had granted exclusive licences for its trademark 'Grundig' to its various exclusive distributors, *inter alia,* in the

this grant of trademark rights in support of the grant of the exclusive territory to Consten restricted competition. The Court held:

> 'Consten's right under the contract to the exclusive use in France of the GINT trademark, which may be used in a similar manner in other countries, is intended to make it possible to keep under surveillance and to place an obstacle in the way of parallel imports ....
>
> That agreement therefore is one which may be caught by the prohibition in Article 81 (1). The prohibition would be ineffective if Consten could continue to use the trademark to achieve the same object as that pursued by the agreement which has been held to be unlawful....
>
> [The Community rules on competition do] not allow the improper use of rights under any national trademark law in order to frustrate the Community's law on cartels.'[805]

It was impermissible for trademarks to be used as a means of achieving absolute territorial protection, thereby dividing up the Common Market and artificially maintaining price differences between member states to the disadvantage of customers.[806]

Trademark Licences Ancillary to Distribution Agreements without Territorial Exclusivity.

Trademark licences which are ancillary to distribution and franchising agreements ('not the primary object') are covered by Regulation 2790/1999 on vertical restraints.[807] Distribution agreements with respect to trademarked products may include an obligation to sell the product under the trademark of the licensor and a prohibition against alteration or removal of the trademark. Trademark licences are especially common in franchise agreements, where the franchise chain and/or its products are usually identified by a trademark or business name.[808] In the case of such ancillary trademark licences, the principles established in relation to distribution agreements apply as long as any additional operations performed by the

Netherlands. The parties had tried to prevent parallel imports into the Netherlands due to the lower price in Germany by using the trademark rights, but this practice had been condemned by the Dutch Supreme Court, Dec. 14, 1956, 1957 GRUR Int. 259.

805. *Grundig/Consten,* ECJ July 13, 1966, 1966 ECR 299, 345–346.

806. *See also Beguelin,* ECJ Nov. 25, 1971, 1971 ECR 949, paras 14–15; *Tepea,* ECJ June 20, 1978, 1978 ECR 1391, para. 57; *Toltecs/Dorcet,* ECJ Jan. 30, 1985, 1985 ECR 363, para. 33; *Pronuptia,* ECJ Jan. 30, 1986, 1986 ECR 353, paras 23–24; *Chiquita/Fyffes,* Twenty-second Report on Competition Policy, point 173. The same applies to the exercise of patent rights so as to prevent users or resellers from obtaining products which have been lawfully put on the market within the Common Market by the licensor or with its consent.

807. Recital 3 to and Article 2 (3) of Regulation 2790/1999.

808. *See,* by analogy, Article 1 (3) (a) and (b) and Article 3 (2) (f) of the former Regulation 4087/88 on franchise agreements.

distributor or franchisee do not change the economic identity of the product.[809] If, however, more substantial manufacturing operations are undertaken that include the use of licensed patents of know-how, then the block exemption on technology transfer agreements may apply.

Trademark Licence Ancillary to Refilling Agreements – The *Campari* Case. This case[810] concerned exclusive licences to use the 'Bitter Campari' trademark granted by Campari-Milano SpA to licensees in the Netherlands, Germany, France, Belgium, Luxembourg and Denmark. The licensees were required by these agreements to comply scrupulously with the licensor's instructions as to the manufacture of the relevant products, to ensure that the quality of the raw materials used met the licensor's requirements and to buy from the licensor the herbal mixtures whose composition – a trade secret – gives Bitter Campari its characteristic taste. The licence agreements were not considered as know-how licences because the basic know-how, the recipe for the herbal mixture, was *not* licensed, but the mixture was merely sold as an ingredient in the final product. The agreements also went beyond the limits of a simple distribution agreement governed, in those days, by Regulation 67/67. Nevertheless, the Commission applied largely the same rules as under the exclusive distribution regulation. The Commission considered the following principal restrictions as being caught by Article 81 (1):

- the exclusive right granted to the licensee preventing Campari from granting further trademark licences in the licensee's territories to other parties and from manufacturing itself in those countries,
- a clause that prevented the licensees from handling competing products, which would have had appreciable effects since nearly all the licensees were already distributing a whole range of other beverages, and
- a ban on active sales policies by all parties outside their allotted territories, which prevented the licensees from actively competing in other territories.

The Commission granted an exemption for these restrictions because they ensured that the licensees concentrated their production and sales efforts on the Campari products and on a defined market without excluding – in line with the exclusive distribution regulation – passive sales outside each licensee's assigned territory, and because they promoted investment and did not preclude competition between Campari and numerous suppliers of other bitter drinks.[811]

---

809. *See,* by analogy, Commission's former Notice on Regulations 1983/83 and 1984/83, paras 9–10.
810. *Campari I,* D.Comm. Dec. 23, 1977, 1978 OJ L 70/69. After the expiration of the exemption the agreements were replaced partly by intra-group arrangements and partly by mere distribution agreements: *Campari II,* Eighteenth Report on Competition Policy, point 69.
811. *Campari I,* D.Comm. Dec. 23, 1977, 1978 OJ L 70/69, 75–76.

The Commission did not consider the following restrictions as being caught by Article 81 (1):

- an obligation on the licensee to refrain from exporting directly or indirectly outside the Common Market, since there was already considerable parallel trade in Campari from within the Community,[812]
- an obligation on the licensee to observe the licensor's specifications and to allow the licensor to carry out checks, which included in this case the right to control the place of manufacture and any change in that place (location clause), and
- an obligation on the licensee to buy certain secret ingredients from the licensor as being necessary for protecting the secret recipe which is made available only to the selected licensees.[813]

Regulation 2790/1999 applies to refilling agreements, provided the reseller performs operations which do not add substantial value to the goods and do not change the identity of the goods.[814] Refilling agreements, such as the *Campari* agreements, are covered by this block exemption and need individual clearance only if the market share limits are exceeded.[815]

Trademark Licences Ancillary to Agreements for the Collection and Recycling of Packaging Waste.

Trademarks may be licensed for labelling with a 'green dot' on products (in particular used packaging) which are to be collected for recycling on a country-wide basis. Under Directive 94/62/EC[816] manufacturers and distributors are required to take back and recycle, free of charge, used sales packaging from consumers. Manufacturers and distributors responded by adhering to a comprehensive collection system, which takes the responsibility of collecting, sorting and recycling the packaging waste from consumers. In most countries there is only one company that operates such a system. Competition problems arise from the exclusivity of such systems which have the effect of foreclosing the market to other potentially competitive collection systems. The Commission therefore objected to such an exclusivity and made its approval subject to the following conditions:

- the licensees pay a fee only for the collection and recovery service provided by the system operator and not for the use of the 'green dot' trademark ('no service, no fee' principle),

812. *Campari I,* D.Comm. Dec. 23, 1977, 1978 OJ L 70/69, 74.
813. *Ibid. See also Moosehead/Whitbread,* D.Comm. March 23, 1990, 1990 OJ L 100/32, 35–36.
814. *See,* by analogy, the Commission's former Notice on Regulations 1983/83 and 1984/83, 1984 OJ C 101/2, point 10.
815. The Commission decision in *Campari* did not indicate market shares.
816. 1994 OJ L 365/10.

- the system must extend to imports of all products with a 'green dot' label, and
- recycling companies may not be prevented from contracting with competitors on the sharing of containers or other arrangements for the collection, sorting and recycling of household packinging waste.[817]

Trademark Licences Ancillary to Technology Transfer Agreements – The *Carlsberg* Case.

Trademark licences may be granted in the framework of patent or know-how licences. The new Regulation 772/2004 on transfer of technology agreements implicitly exempts an obligation imposed on the licensee to use only the licensor's trademark or get-up determined by the licensor to distinguish the licensed product from similar products, provided that the licensee is not prevented from identifying itself as manufacturer.[818] Likewise, an exemption is provided for the licensee to be obliged to mark the licensed product with the licensor's mark.[819] On the other hand, an obligation on licensees to use different trademarks for the same product in different member states with the purpose or effect of achieving absolute territorial protection among licensees is likely to infringe Article 81.[820] A trademark licence may not be used to extend the effects (in particular the territorial exclusivity) of a patent or know-how licence beyond the life of the licensed technology.[821] Technology transfer agreements may include other provisions relating to trademarks which are ancillary to the achievement of the licensed technology.[822] This is highlighted in the *Carlsberg/Watney* case.[823] This case, which was cleared by an individual decision under Article 81 (3), concerned an agreement by which the Danish brewing company Carlsberg allowed the British brewing group Watney (belonging to the brewery group Grand Metropolitan) to produce certain Carlsberg beers using the know-how disclosed to it by Carlsberg and to sell them under the Carlsberg label. The agreement was less restrictive in some respects than exclusive distribution or know-how licence agreements because it contained no exclusivity, territorial protection nor any apparent non-compete clause. However, the agreement required Watney to purchase certain minimum quantities of beer from Carlsberg and led to cooperation between two very powerful competitors. Since the overall effect

817. Germany: *Duales System,* D.Comm. April 20, 2001, 2001 OJ L 166/1, points 111–115 (Article 82 decision); *DSD,* D.Comm. Sept. 17, 2001, 2001 OJ L 319/1 (negative clearance following amendments). Austria: *ARA,* D.Comm. D.Comm. Oct. 16, 2003, 2004 OJ L 75/39, points 288–294 (exemption subject to conditions). France: *Eco Emballage,* D.Comm. June 15, 2001, 2001 OJ L 233/37 (negative clearance following the commitment to extend the system to all imports).
818. *See,* by analogy, Article 1 (1) (7) of former Regulation 240/96.
819. *Ibid.,* Article 2 (1) (11) of former Regulation 240/96.
820. *Toltecs/Dorcet,* ECJ 30 Jan. 1985, 1985 ECR 373, para. 33.
821. Article 2 of Regulation 772/2004.
822. Recital 7 to Regulation 772/2004.
823. *Carlsberg/Watney,* D.Comm. July 12, 1984, 1984 OJ L 207/26.

was to increase competition with other brands in an oligopolistic market largely in the hands of national firms, the Commission decided that an exemption was justified. Whereas this case concerned an arrangement designed to facilitate the market access of a potential competitor that was likely to promote competition on the United Kingdom market, three subsequent *Carlsberg* cases concerned the cooperation of an actual competitor, which already had its own sales network, with other important competitors that was likely to reduce competition and impair the competitive structure of the market. The *Carlsberg/Courage* case[824] involved intensive cooperation whereby Carlsberg granted to Courage for ten years the right to brew some of its beers (including a trademark licence) and exclusive distribution rights for other beers in the UK. The *Carlsberg/Allied Lyons* case[825] concerned Carlsberg's intention to consolidate its entire brewing and beer sales activities in the UK with the creation of a joint venture likely to become the third largest brewer in the UK. The *Carlsberg/Interbrew* case[826] concerned a licence agreement and an exclusive sales arrangement between Carlsberg and the dominant brewer in Belgium. The Commission objected to all of these arrangements, arguing that the acquisition of exclusive rights by a leading competitor restricted competition and in Belgium even led to strengthening the dominant position of Interbrew. The Commission obtained settlements in the form of amendments to the agreements with respect to exclusivity, duration and minimum volume requirements.[827] The *Moosehead/Whitbread* case[828] concerned an agreement somewhat similar to that in Carlsberg. The Canadian brewer Moosehead licensed Whitbread to use its know-how and trademark for brewing and marketing Moosehead beer in the United Kingdom. The licence was exclusive and also imposed obligations on the licensee not to sell actively outside the licensed territory and not to produce or promote there any other beer identified as a Canadian beer. The Commission considered that a clause prohibiting the licensee from challenging the ownership or validity of the licensed trademark did not constitute a major barrier to any other company entering or competing in the United Kingdom beer market, because the trademark was relatively new and unknown and therefore unlikely to be contested as a generic or descriptive term.[829] The Commission held that the agreement was not covered by the former Regulation 556/89 because the trademark licence was its main object, rather than being merely ancillary as required by Article 1 (1)

824. Twenty-second Report on Competition Policy, point 130.
825. Twenty-second Report on Competition Policy, point 131–136.
826. Twenty-fourth Report on Competition Policy, p. 351.
827. This demonstrates that minimum volume obligations which are, in simple distribution agreements, whitelisted (*see* Article 2 (3) (a) Regulation 1983/83) may be objected to in the context of (even non-reciprocal) arrangements between competitors in oligopoly markets.
828. *Moosehead/Whitbread,* D.Comm. March 23, 1990, 1990 OJ L 100/32.
829. *Ibid.* pp. 35–36. The facts are distinguishable from *Windsurfing,* ECJ Feb. 25, 1986, 1986 ECR 611, paras 77–80, because that case concerned a well-known trademark that was in danger of becoming generic.

of the regulation; however, it was eligible for individual exemption. It may be argued that the licence of secret know-how for manufacturing beer having the same qualities and taste as the Canadian beer manufactured by the licensor is at least as important as the trademark so that the technology transfer regulation applies to such combined know-how/trademark licences, provided the agreement does not contain hardcore restrictions and the parties' market shares do not exceed the thresholds of the block exemption (which is 20% in such a case of agreements between actual or potential competitors). In the case of higher market shares it is unlikely that the conditions of Article 81 (3) are fulfilled, unless substantial amendments are submitted in order to reduce the risk of market foreclosure.[830]

Trademark Licences Ancillary to Subcontracting Agreements.
Subcontracting agreements frequently include a trademark licence by which the subcontractor is authorized to use a specified trademark, trade name or get-up on the products supplied to the contractor. However, the contractor may prohibit the subcontractor from using the contractor's trademark with respect to any products that the subcontractor is authorized to sell to third persons. Subcontracting agreements are particularly difficult to assess depending on the value of the technology transferred: they may be covered by the new regulation on transfer of technology agreements or may be compatible with Article 81 (1) or need individual assessment under Article 81 (3).[831]

Collective Trademark Licence Agreements.
An agreement between competitors to use a common trademark for their products may serve to promote a common quality standard or improve quality and therefore not raise anticompetitive concerns. Such an agreement may infringe Article 81 (1), however, if it precludes individual producers from also using their own trademark or service mark with the relevant goods or services. Associations for the joint use of a quality label may not not restrict competition if other competitors, whose products objectively met the stipulated quality requirements, could use the label on the same conditions as the members. However, competition could be restricted by obligations governing production, marketing or pricing, as for example if the participating firms agreed to manufacture or sell only products meeting the agreed

830. *See Philip Morris/Tabacalera,* D.Comm. Feb. 23, 2001, IP/01/249 (the case concerned a licence agreement between Philip Morris and the Spanish ex-monopolist Tabacalera having a aggregate market share of 75%, which was granted clearance subject to a reduction of the duration (from 6 to 3 years) and to a phasing out the production exclusivity (progressive adaptation of the volumes).
831. Previously Notice on Subcontracting Agreements, under 4;.which is replaced by the Guidelines on the new regulation on technology transfer agreements relating to transfer of technology agreements, points 36–40, and Guidelines on Horizontal Cooperation, 2001 OJ C 3/2, points 80, 100 and 114.

quality standard.[832] In *Anseau,* a standard conformity label which could be applied only to goods sold through an official distribution network was used to impede parallel imports, contrary to the principles of a unified Common Market.[833] In *Transocean Marine Paint Association* the Commission exempted an agreement between different medium-sized marine paint manufacturers situated all over the world in order to allow them to produce paints of the same quality and composition in order to offer identical products under the same trademark worldwide after the parties' removal of excessive territorial protection.[834]

---

832. *See* Chapter III.C.9(a). E.g., *Relais & Chateaux,* Twenty-seventh Report on Competition Policy, p. 141.
833. *Anseau,* ECJ Nov. 8, 1983, 1983 ECR 3369, 3412, para. 27. *See also Plastic Omnium,* Bull. EC 6–1988, point 2.1.107, and Sixth Report on Competition Policy, point 178.
834. *Transocean Marine Paint Association I,* D.Comm. June 27, 1967, 1967 OJ L 163/10 (condition attached to the exemption annulled by ECJ Oct. 23, 1974, 1974 ECR 1063); reaffirmed after amendment of territorial protection: *Transocean Marine Paint Association II,* D.Comm. Dec. 21, 1973, 1974 OJ L 19/18.

Chapter VIII

Application of Articles 81 and 82 in Special Sectors

CONTENTS

A. Introduction

General Applicability of the EC Competition Rules with some Exceptions. Regulation 1/2003 applies, as did its predecessor Regulation 17, in principle to all sectors of the economy[1] including, from July 21, 2002, the coal and steel industries.[2] Special features apply in the following sectors:

- Agricultural products are exempted from Article 81 (1) in certain narrowly defined circumstances under Article 36 of the EC Treaty and Regulation 26/62,[3] whereas Article 82 is fully applicable.[4]
- Article 83 (2) (c) of the EC Treaty empowers the Council to define, if need be, in the various branches of the economy, the scope of the provisions of Articles 81 and 82. The Council did so by adopting regulations which take into account the special features of particular industries, such as rail, road and inland waterway transport (Regulation 1017/68[5]), sea transport (Regulation 4056/86[6]), air transport (Regulation 3975/87[7]) and insurance (Regulation 1534/91[8]). The transport regulations provided for specific procedural rules which differed slightly from sector to sector and were therefore likely to create confusion.[9] Such difficulties are avoided by Regulation 1/2003[10] which applies, from May 1, 2004, to all sectors.
- Article 86 (2) of the EC Treaty[11] exempts firms 'entrusted with the operation of services of general economic interest' and 'revenue-producing monopolies'[12] from the competition rules to the extent that 'the application of such rules does

---

1. *Fire Insurance*, ECJ Jan. 27, 1987, 1987 ECR 405, paras 12–15; *Nouvelles Frontières* (*Asjes*), ECJ April 30, 1986, 1986 ECR 1425, paras 40–45; *Reiff/Bundesanstalt für den Güterfernverkehr*, ECJ Nov. 17, 1993, 1993 ECR I-5801, para. 12.
2. 2002 OJ C 152; Thirty-second Report on Competition Policy, points 10–12.
3. 1962 OJ 993.
4. *See Irish Sugar*, D.Comm. May 14, 1997, 1997 OJ L 258/1, para. 115.
5. 1968 OJ L 175/1. This regulation refers to the specific provision of Article 71 of the EC Treeaty.
6. 1986 OJ L 378/4. This regulation refers to the specific provision of Article 80 (2) of the EC Treaty.
7. 1987 OJ L 374/1. This regulation also refers to the specific provision of Article 80 (2) of the EC Treaty.
8. 1991 OJ L 143/1. The regulation is the legal basis of the block exemption Regulation 358/2003, 2003 OJ L 53/8.
9. *See* the *UIC* case where the Commission applied Regulation 17 instead of Regulation 1017/68: D.Comm. July 25, 1995, Twenty-fifth Report on Competition Policy, p. 133; *rev'd* CFI June 6, 1995, 1995 ECR II-1503, paras 43–50.
10. 2003 OJ L 1/1.
11. *See also* Article 16 of the EC Treaty and Commission Communication on services of general interest, 2001 OJ C 17/4.
12. 'Revenue-producing monopolies' are state monopolies, such as for liquor and tobacco. There have been no decisions applying Article 86 (2) to such monopolies.

not obstruct the performance, in law or in fact, of the particular tasks assigned to them' and that the 'development of trade [is] not affected to such an extent as would be contrary to the interests of the Community.'[13] Article 86 (3) empowers the Commission to address appropriate directives or decisions to member states. The Commission did so by adopting directives in the telecommunications sector.[14]

- Article 95 of the EC Treaty empowers the Council to adopt measures for the approximation of national law or administrative action which have as their object the establishment and functioning of the internal market. The Council did so by adopting directives in the energy sector.[15]

Competition Rules v. Government Regulation.
Highly regulated industries – such as banking, insurance, transport and energy – are subject to supervision by the national regulatory authorities but also to the EC competition rules as applied by the Commission, the national competition authorities and the national courts. The Commission has issued Guidelines with respect to electronic communications networks and services[16] which set out the principles for use by the national regulatory authorities in the analysis of those markets and effective competition under the new regulatory framework[17] and which resulted, with respect to the telecommunications sector, in the creation of a special unit Task Force 'Telecom Consultation Mechanism' within the DGCOMP according to Article 7 of the Framework Directive 2002/21/EC[18] with a view of achieving harmonized and effective regulatory and competition actions.[19] In fact, the lack of harmonization of national regulatory systems and the incomplete access of firms to other national markets which such regulations sometimes cause does not justify suspending or limiting the application of the Community's competition rules. In the *Fire Insurance* case the Court of Justice held that the requirements of

13. In the *Port of Mertert* case the Court of Justice held that the application of Article 86 (2) '... involves an appraisal of the requirements, on the one hand, of the particular task entrusted to the undertaking concerned and, on the other hand, the protection of the interests of the Community. This appraisal depends on the objectives of general economic policy pursued by the States...' (ECJ July 14, 1971, 1971 ECR 723, paras 14–15).
14. Telecommunications Terminal Equipment Directive (1988 OJ L 131/73); Telecommunications Services Directive (1990 OJ L 192/10). *See* more recent directives in Section F, *infra*.
15. Electricity Directive, 1997 OJ L 27/20, as amended by Directive 2003/54/EC, 2003 OJ L 176/37, and Natural Gas Directive, 1998 OJ L 204/1, as amended by Directive 2003/55/EC, 2003 OJ L 176/57.
16. 2002 OJ C 165/6.
17. Framework Directive (2002 OJ L 108/33); Authorization Directive (2002 OJ L 108/21); Access Directive (2002 OJ L 108/7) and Universal Service Directive (2002 OJ L 108/51); Directive on electronic communications networks and services (2002 OJ L 249/21)
18. 2002 OJ L 108/3.
19. *See* Krüger and Mauro, The Article 7 Consultation Mechanism, Competition Policy Newsletter 2003–3, pp. 336.

the proper supervision of insurance companies did not preclude the application of the competition rules:

> '... [N]ational laws concerning the supervision of insurance companies have a different objective from that of Community competition law and... they may continue to be operative regardless of the manner in which the competition law is applied. The applicant has not been able to show that in this case the application of the prohibitions contained in Articles 85 and 86 (*81 and 82*) of the EEC Treaty might be such as to impede the proper functioning of the national system of supervision of insurers ... Community law does not, however, make the implementation of the provisions of Articles 85 and 86 (*81 and 82*) of the EEC Treaty dependent upon the manner in which the supervision of certain areas of economic activity is organized by national legislation.'[20]

The Court concluded that Articles 81 and 82 and Regulation 17 (now Regulation 1/2003) applied without restriction to industries subject to a national system of supervision such as the insurance industry. However, it went on:

> '[T]hat conclusion in no way implies that Community competition law does not permit the special characteristics of certain branches of the economy to be taken into account. It is for the Commission, within the framework of its power under Article 85 (3) (*81 (3)*) to grant exemption from the prohibitions contained in Article 85 (1) (*81 (1)*), to take account of the particular nature of different branches of the economy and the problems peculiar to them.'[21]

Under Regulation 1/2003 Article 81 (3) may be applied directly by the Commission and the national competition authorities and courts. The Commission lost its exclusive competence but is empowered to initiate proceedings with the effect that national authorities are then relieved of their competence to apply this provision.[22] However, under Regulation 26/62 on the application of Articles 81 and 82 in the agricultural sector the Commission still has sole competence to decide whether a restrictive agreement is necessary for attainment of the objectives of the Common Market organizations because of the precedence of the common agricultural policy.[23]

---

20. *Fire Insurance*, ECJ Jan. 27, 1987, 1987 ECR 405, paras 22–23.
21. *Ibid.*, paras 14–15.
22. Article 11 (6) of Regulation 1/2003.
23. Article 2 (2) of Regulation 26/62; *Milk Marque*, ECJ Sept. 9, 2003, C-137/00, para. 81.

Competition Rules v. Liberalization of Regulated Industries.
Monopolies entrusted to enterprises which are not justified by a service of general economic interest are likely to lead, according to the Commission,[24] to high prices, poorer quality service and backwardness in terms of innovation and investment. That is why the Commission advocates that competition should be introduced in monopoly industries:

- by applying the existing competition rules, subject to the exception of Article 86 (2),
- by opening up of networks (telephone communications, rail transport and energy supply), and
- by liberalizing the industries.

Liberalization may consist of the abolition of exclusive rights (thereby ensuring free access by competitors) or privatization of the industries (thereby ensuring free movement of capital according to Article 56) by adoption of appropriate legislation.

Free Access to Networks.
Monopolies are frequent in network industries, such as transport, energy and telecommunications. In these sectors, the Commission makes a distinction between the infrastructure and the services provided over this infrastructure. While it is often difficult to establish a second, competing infrastructure, for reasons linked to high investment costs and ecnomic efficiency, it is possible and desirable to establish and preserve competitive conditions with respect to the services provided. The Commission has therefore developed the concept of separating infrastructure from commercial activities. The infrastructure is thus merely the vehicle of competition. While the right to exclusive ownership may persist as regards the infrastructure (the telephone or electricity network for example), monopolists must grant access to third parties wishing to compete with them as regards the services offered on their networks (telephone communications, electricity supply or railway services). Refusal of access to essential facilities may constitute an abuse prohibited under Article 82.[25]

Privatization v. Golden Share.
The privatization of government owned businesses or infrastructure requires in particular that the acquisition of shares or securities is no longer subject to restrictions based on the nationality of the investors concerned. In particular, there must be no prohibition against the acquisition by investors from other member

24. European competition policy: a brief overview, Feb. 20, 2003, http://europa.eu.int/comm/competition:liberalization/overview.
25. *See* discussion in Chapter V.D.6.(e).

states of more than a given number of shares and/or the prior authorization for third parties to acquire an interest above a certain level, which is normally 10% ('golden share').[26] These restrictions have been held by the Court as infringing Article 56[27] and Article 43 (since restrictions on freedom of establishment are a direct consequence of the obstacles to the free movement of capital).[28] With respect to the prior authorization of third party ownership the Court, referring to the Commission Communication on certain legal aspects concerning intra-EC investment,[29] stated:

> '...it is undeniable that, depending on the circumstances, certain concerns may justify the retention by Member States of a degree of influence within undertakings that were initially public and subsequently privatised, where those undertakings are active in fields involving the provision of services in the public interest or strategic services.... However, those concerns cannot entitle Member States to plead their own systems of property ownership, referred to in Article 222 [*295*] of the Treaty, by way of justification for obstacles, resulting from privileges attaching to their position as shareholder in a privatised undertaking, to the exercise of the freedoms provided for by the Treaty.... Such a scheme must be proportionate to the aim pursued, inasmuch as the same objective could not be attained by less restrictive measures, in particular a system of declarations *ex post facto*.'[30]

Accordingly, the Commission initiated proceedings under Article 226 against various member states for having granted the government's preferential status and the special rights accorded to the holder of the special 'golden share' in sectors which are subject to privatization, in particular telecommunications. [31] However, the exercise of the state's right must be based on sufficiently precise criteria to indicate to the potential investors the way in which the administrative authority will exercise its discretion, in particular, in the case of a prior approval, the specific, objective circumstances in which such approval will be granted or withheld.[32] In any event, neither a mere financial interest[33] nor the mere limitation of the

26. E.g. in *Cimpor*, D.Comm. Nov. 22, 2000, IP/00/1338; *aff'd* ECJ June 22, 2004, C-42/01.
27. *Commission/Portuguese Republic*, ECJ June 4, 2002, C-367/98, paras. 42 and 53. *See also Markku Juhani Läärä*, ECJ Sept. 21, 1999, 1999 ECR I-6067; *Spain and UK/Commission*, ECJ May 13, 2003, C-463/00 and C-98/01.
28. *Commission/Spain and United Kingdom*, ECJ May 13, 2003, C-463/00, para. 86.
29. 1997 OJ C 220/15.
30. *Commission/Portuguese Republic*, ECJ June 4, 2002, 2002 ECR I-4731, paras. 47–50.
31. *KPN and TPC (Netherlands)*, D.Comm. Feb. 5, 2003, IP/03/180; *Commission/Italy*, ECJ May 25, 2000, 2000 ECR I-3811.
32. *Commission/Spain and United Kingdom*, ECJ May 13, 2003, C-463/00, paras. 74–80.
33. *Commission/Portugal*, ECJ June 4, 2002, 2002 ECR I-4731, para. 52.

government's preferential status in time necessarily precludes an infringement of the EC Treaty.[34]

Possible Justifications.

The government's preferential status *may* be justified in fields involving the provision of services in the general interest or strategic goods or services,[35] including petrol, tobacco, electricity, airports and public saving banks.[36] However, this derogation is interpreted strictly by the Court of Justice, so that their scope cannot be determined unilaterally by each member state without any control by the Community institutions. In the case *Commission/Spain and United Kingdom* the Court of Justice ruled:[37]

> 'Thus, public security may be relied on only if there is a genuine and sufficiently serious threat to a fundamental interest of society.... It is therefore appropriate to ascertain whether the rules at issue ... provide assurance within the Member State concerned, in the event of a genuine and serious threat, that there would be a minimum supply of petroleum products and electricity and a minimum level of telecommunications services and do not go beyond what is necessary for that purpose.'[38]

The legitimate national interest justification is mitigated by the principle of proportionality expressly provided for in Articles 30 (2), 58 (3) and 86 (2) of the EC Treaty and Article 21 (4) of the merger control regulation [39] but has a general significance.[40] In the *Cimpor* case[41] the Commission denied, under Article 21 (2) of the merger control regulation, any legitimate interest of the Portuguese government when opposing the proposed takeover of a Portuguese cement company, in which the Portuguese state held approximately 12% of the shares, including 10% golden shares, by referring to the 'need to protect the shareholding structure with a view of reinforcing the efficiency of the national production apparatus'.[42] The

34. *Commission/Spain and United Kingdom*, ECJ May 13, 2003, C-463/00, para. 81.
35. *See* Article 296.
36. *Commission/Spain and United Kingdom*, ECJ May 13, 2003, C-463/00 and C-98/01; *Commission/Portugal*, ECJ June 4, 2002, 2002 ECR I-4731, para. 47; *Commission/France*, ECJ June 4, 2002, 2002 ECR I-4781, para. 43; *Commission/Belgium*, ECJ June 4, 2002, 2002 ECR I-4809, para. 43.
37. *Commission/Spain and United Kingdom*, ECJ May 13, 2003, C-463/00, paras 72–73.
38. Example: limitation of the obligation to purchase 35% from a state-owned refinery was held compatible with Article 30 in the *Campus Oil* case, ECJ July 10, 1984, 1984 ECR 2727, paras. 34–35.
39. *Commission/Portugal*, ECJ June 4, 2002, 2002 ECR I-4731, paras. 49–50.
40. *Gebhard*, ECJ Nov. 30, 1995, 1995 ECR I-4165, para. 37; *Commission/Spain and United Kingdom*, ECJ May 13, 2003, C-463/00, para. 82.
41. *Secil/Holderbank/Cimpor*, D.Comm. Nov. 22, 2000, M.2171, IP/00/1338.
42. *Ibid.*

proposed takeover of *Cimpor* was notified on 16 June 2000 to the Portuguese authority because the acquisition of more than 10% of voting rights in companies which had not yet entirely been privatized was subject to approval of the competent national authority, and on 4 July 2000 to the Commission because the operation had a Community dimension. By two decisions of 6 July and 11 August 2000 the Portuguese regulatory authority prohibited the notified operation under Portuguese law. On 22 November 2000 the Commission decided that the measures taken by the Portuguese authority were not justified by any legitimate interest, and therefore were incompatible with the EU competition law. [43] Thereafter, the Portuguese government decided to fully privatize Cimpor including the divestment of its 10% in the company.[44] The Portuguese legislation on which the opposition was based had already been challenged by the Commission in 1997 as breaching the right of establishment and the free movement of capital, which was affirmed by the Court of Justice.[45] On June 22, 2004, the Court of Justice affirmed the Commission's Article 21 (2) decision by stating that the Commission was entitled to declare the measure of the Portuguese government incompatible with the general principles of Community law.[46]

This chapter will look closely at how the competition rules are applied to specific sectors: agriculture, transport, banking, insurance and at the emerging policy in the energy, telecommunications and postal sectors.

B. Agriculture

Background.

In the European Community, as elsewhere, the importance of agriculture for food supplies and for maintaining the rural population and the countryside has led to extensive regulation of the industry. The EC Treaty provided for this regulation to be placed on a federal basis under a 'Common Agricultural Policy.' Article 33 lists the objectives of the Common Agricultural Policy as: to increase agricultural productivity, to ensure a fair standard of living for the agricultural community, to stabilize markets, to assure the availability of supplies and to ensure that agricultural products reach customers at reasonable prices. Under the Common Agricultural Policy, the previous national marketing arrangements have been replaced by Common Market organizations for most products. These support prices by buying in surpluses at guaranteed prices, taxing imports from outside the EC and subsidizing exports, and in some cases they support farmers' incomes directly or control production. Nevertheless, at the producer level at least, agricultural markets within

43. *Secil/Holderbank/Cimpor*, D.Comm. Nov. 22, 2000, M.2171, IP/00/1338 (Article 21 (4) decision).
44. IP/00/1338. *See* Chapter VI.C.4 (b).
45. *Commission/Portugal*, ECJ June 4, 2002, 2002 ECR I-4731.
46. *Portuguese Republic*, ECJ June 22, 2004, C-42/01, para. 60.

the Community are often more competitive than those of many other industries, because they are almost completely integrated and because by their nature they involve homogeneous products and a large number of buyers and sellers.

Regulation 26/62.
Article 36 of the EC Treaty empowered the Council to limit the applicability of the competition rules in agriculture. This was done by Regulation 26/62.[47] The basic concept is, as the Court of Justice stated in the *Milk Marque* case,[48]

> 'that the maintenance of effective competition on the market for agricultural products is one of the objectives of the common agricultural policy and the common organization of the relevant market. ... [T]he common organizations of the market are based on the concept of an open market to which every producer has free access under effective conditions of competition.'

Regulation 26/62 declares Article 81 and the implementing regulations applicable, including the provisions on fines,[49] but exempts restrictive practices from Article 81 (1) where they are necessary for attainment of the objectives of the Common Market organization for which the Commission retains sole competence.[50] Article 82, however, remains fully applicable. The procedure is governed by Regulation 1/2003.

Products Subject to Regulation 26/62.
The products covered by Regulation 26/62 are those products of the soil, stock-farming and fisheries and products of the first-stage processing of such products[51] that are listed in Annex II to the EC Treaty, e.g. seeds (plant varieties).[52] They do not include further processed products or products ancillary to the production of Annex II products. For instance, they include:

- meat[53] but not live animals for slaughtering;[54]
- milk[55] but not additives used in cheese-making such as rennet;[56]

---

47. 1962 OJ No. 30/993.
48. *Milk Marque*, ECJ Sept. 9, 2003, C-137/00, paras. 57–59.
49. E.g. *Sugar*, D.Comm. Jan. 2, 1973, 1973 OJ L 140/17, *aff'd* ECJ Dec. 16, 1975, 1975 ECR 163 (fines of ECU 1.59 million); *French Federations in the Beef Sector*, D.Comm. April 2, 2003, 2003 OJ L 209/12 (fines of EUR 16.7 million).
50. Article 2 (2) of Regulation 26/62.
51. Article 32 of the EC Treaty. They include tropical products not produced in the EC such as coffee and bananas.
52. *Sicasov*, D.Comm. Dec. 14, 1998, 1999 OJ L 4/27, point 66.
53. *French Federations in the Beef Sector*, D.Comm. (fines) April 2, 2003, 2003 OJ L 209/12.
54. Under the merger control regulation: *Danish Crown/Vestjyske Slagterier*, D.Comm. March 9, 1999, M.1313.
55. *Milk Promotion Fund*, D.Comm. Dec. 7, 1984, 1985 OJ L 35/35, 38–39; *Meldoc*, D.Comm. Nov. 26, 1986, 1986 OJ L 348/50, 59–60.
56. *Rennet*, ECJ March 25, 1981, 1981 ECR 851, paras 19–21.

- sugar[57] but not synthetic sugar substitutes such as aspartame;[58]
- raw alcohol obtained from agricultural products but not synthetic alcohol[59] nor alcoholic drinks such as cognac[60] or armagnac;[61]
- animals[62] but not furs;[63]
- cultivation of potatoes,[64] cauliflower,[65] and flowers[66] but not weed killers;[67]
- coffee[68] and milk[69] but not mineral water.[70]

The Two Exceptions Made by Regulation 26/62.
Article 2 (1) of the Regulation exempts from Article 81 (1) (but not from Article 82)[71] agreements, decisions and concerted practices which either:

- form an integral part of a national market organization,[72] or
- are necessary for attainment of the objectives set out in Article 33.[73]

The second sentence of Article 2(1) gives an example of arrangements that can fall within the exceptions:

> 'In particular, it shall not apply to agreements, decisions and practices of farmers, farmers' associations, or associations of such associations belonging to a single member state which concern the production or sale of agricultural products or the use of joint facilities for the storage, treatment or

57. *Sugar*, ECJ Dec. 16, 1975, 1975 ECR 1663, paras 603–605.
58. *Aspartame*, Eighteenth Report on Competition Policy, point 53.
59. *BP Kemi/DDSF*, D.Comm. Sept. 5, 1979, 1979 OJ L 286/32.
60. *BNIC I*, ECJ Jan. 30, 1985, 1985 ECR 391, paras 14–15.
61. *BNIA*, D.Comm. July 26, 1976, 1976 OJ L 231/24, 28.
62. *British Cattle and Sheep Breeders Association*, Twenty-second Report on Competition Policy, p. 436.
63. *Danish Furs*, CFI July 2, 1992, 1992 ECR 11–1931, para. 38.
64. *New Potatoes*, D.Comm. Dec. 18, 1987, 1988 OJ L 59/25.
65. *Cauliflower*, D.Comm. Dec. 2, 1977, 1978 OJ L 21/23.
66. *Florimex*, CFI July 14, 1997, 1997 ECR II-693, para. 153. *See FRUBO*, ECJ May 15, 1975, 1975 ECR 563, paras 22–27; *Luttikhuis/Coberco*, Dec. 12, 1995, 1995 ECR I-4515, para. 25.
67. *Gottrup Klim*, ECI Dec. 15, 1994, 1994 ECR I-5641.
68. *Brazilian Coffee*, Sixteenth Report on Competition Policy, point 54.
69. *Meldoc*, D.Comm. Nov. 26, 1986, 1986 OJ L 348/50; *Milk Marketing Board*, Twenty-second Report on Competition Policy, points 161–167.
70. *Mineral Water*, Seventeenth Report on Competition Policy, point 75.
71. Examples of cases in which Article 82 has been applied without consideration of Regulation 26/62 are: *Sugar*, ECJ Dec. 16, 1975, 1975 ECR 1663; *United Brands*, ECJ Feb. 14, 1978, 1978 ECR 207; *Artificial Insemination Crespelle*, CFI Oct. 5, 1994, 1994 ECR I-5077; *British Sugar*, D.Comm. July 18, 1988, 1988 OJ L 284/41; *Irish Sugar*, D.Comm. May 14, 1997, 1997 OJ L 258/1, para. 115.
72. Denied: *Sicasov*, D.Comm. Dec. 14, 1998, 1999 OJ L 4/27, point 67.
73. *Florimex*, CFI May 14, 1997, 1997 ECR II-693.

> processing of agricultural products, and under which there is no obligation to charge identical prices, unless the Commission finds that competition is thereby excluded or that the objectives of Article 39 [*33*] of the Treaty are jeopardized.'[74]

Agreements to charge identical prices normally constitute *per se* infringements of Article 81 (1).[75]

National Market Organizations.
The first exception is of limited importance since national marketing arrangements have mostly been replaced by Community market organizations and, where they remain, they must conform to the rules on free intra-Community trade.[76] It has been found applicable in one case concerning French marketing arrangements for new potatoes, which included the setting of production quotas and withdrawal of produce from the market to stabilize, but not fix, prices.[77]

Arrangements Necessary for Attainment of the Objectives of the Common Agricultural Policy.
So far there have been no cases in which this exception has been found applicable. The objectives of the Common Agricultural Policy are usually taken to be adequately provided for by the arrangements made in the Common Market organization;[78] the exception is taken to be applicable only if the goals of the Policy would actually be jeopardized by application of Article 81;[79] and it is assumed that the restrictive arrangements in question must be necessary to attain all those goals.[80] Thus, the exception must be interpreted restrictively.[81] It has been found inapplicable to arrangements involving dealers where the Common Market organization provided only for agreements between producers,[82] or to schemes

---

74. *See* Second Report on Competition Policy, point 75; *Frubo*, ECJ May 15, 1975, 1975 ECR 563, para. 8.
75. Provided they have an appreciable effect on prices and trade between member states: *Sugar*, ECJ 16 Dec. 1975, 1975 ECR 1663, paras 65–72
76. *Charmasson*, ECJ Dec. 10, 1974, 1974 ECR 1383, paras 6–26 (by definition, national market organizations are arrangements that seek to attain at national level similar goals to those of the Common Agricultural Policy).
77. *New Potatoes*, D.Comm. Dec. 18, 1987, 1988 OJ L 59/25.
78. *See French and Taiwanese Mushroom Packers*, D.Comm. Jan. 8, 1975, 1975 OJ L 29/26, 28–29; *Cauliflowers I*, D.Comm. Dec. 2, 1977, 1978 OJ L 21/23, 29/30; *Milk Promotion Fund*, D.Comm. Dec. 7, 1984, 1985 OJ L 35/35, 38–39; *Meldoc*, D.Comm. Nov. 26, 1986, 1986 OJ L 348/50, 59–60.
79. *Milk Marque*, ECJ Sept. 9, 2003, C-137/00, para. 83.
80. *Frubo*, ECJ May 15 1975, 1975 ECR 563, paras 22–26.
81. *Florimex*, CFI May 14, 1997, 1997 ECR II-693, para. 152; *Sicasov*, D.Comm. Dec. 14, 1998, 1999 OJ L 4/27, point 68.
82. *Cauliflowers 1*, D.Comm. Dec. 2, 1977, 1978 OJ L 21/23, 29–30.

which fixed prices,[83] prevented imports,[84] imposed resale restrictions[85] or gave exclusive territorial protection to a licensee.[86]

No Blanket Exemption for Farmers' Associations or Cooperatives. The specific reference to arrangements between farmers and farmers' associations in the second sentence of Article 2 (1) of Regulation 26/62 does not amount to a blanket exemption for such arrangements, since conditions are attached. The arrangements must not involve an obligation to charge identical prices and the Commission must be satisfied that they do not eliminate competition or jeopardize any of the goals of the agricultural policy.[87] Also, it makes no difference if the association operating the arrangements is run as a non-profit-making cooperative. Non-profit-making associations of firms are subject to Article 81 insofar as their activity or the activities of their member firms are calculated to produce anticompetitive results.[88] In the *Meldoc* case the Commission imposed fines on cooperatives that had participated in quota and price arrangements designed to protect the Dutch milk market against imports.[89] The Commission clarified that associations and cooperatives may not impose exclusive distribution[90] or purchase obligations which hinder market access by competitors[91] or discriminate or prevent members from withdrawing from the organization.[92] In the *Milk Marque* case[93] the Court of Justice ruled that national competition law may be applied against a dairy cooperative which enjoys market power and abuses this position contrary to

83. *French and Taiwanese Mushroom Packers*, D.Comm. Jan. 8, 1975, 1975 OJ L 29/26; *Meldoc*, D.Comm. Nov. 26, 1986, 1986 OJ L 348/50; *Scottish Salmon Board*, D.Comm. July 30, 1992, 1992 OJ L 246/37; *Luttikhuis*, ECJ Dec. 12, 1995, 1995 ECR I-4515; *French Federations in the Beef Sector*, D.Comm. April 2, 2003, 2003 OJ L 209/12.
84. *Meldoc*, D.Comm. Nov. 26, 1986, 1986 OJ L 348/50; *Sugar Beet*, D.Comm. Dec. 19, 1989, 1990 OJ L 31/32, 42–43.
85. For instance, a ban on reselling coffee unroasted (*Brazilian Coffee I*, Fifth Report on Competition Policy, point 33; *Brazilian Coffee II*, Sixteenth Report on Competition Policy, point 54) or sugar otherwise than for denaturing (*Sugar*, ECJ Dec. 16, 1975; 1975 ECR 1663, paras 217–224). However, territorial restrictions imposed by the holder of plant variety rights may be exempted under Article 81 (3): *Sicasov*, D.Comm. Dec. 14, 1998, 1999 OJ L 4/27, points 72–77.
86. *Maize Seed*, ECJ June 8, 1982, 1982 ECR 2015, paras 17–21 and 63–67.
87. E.g. *French Federations in the Beef Sector*, D.Comm. April 2, 2003, 2003 OJ L 209/12.
88. *FEDETAB*, ECJ Oct. 29, 1980, 1980 ECR 3125, para. 88.
89. *Meldoc*, D.Comm. Nov. 26, 1986, 1986 OJ L 348/50.
90. *Flower Auction Aalsmeer*, D.Comm. July 26, 1988, 1988 OJ L 262/27 (risk of vertical integration).
91. *Florimex*, CFI May 14, 1997, 1997 ECR II-693.
92. *Campina*, Twenty-first Report on Competition Policy, point 83 (financial disadavantages in case of withdrawal); *Milk Marketing Board*, Twenty-second Report on Competition Policy, points 161–167 (comfort letter after having imposed a greater flexibility towards competitors willing to join and members willing to withdraw).
93. *Milk Marque*, ECJ Sept. 9, 2003, C-137/00.

the public interest by increasing the price for raw milk above competitive levels (although below the target price set by the Common Market organization).[94]

Parallel Application of EC Competition Law and National Law.
As the Common Market organizations are not a competition-free zone, Community and national competition law apply in parallel in accordance with settled case-law since they consider restrictive practices from different points of view: Community law in the light of obstacles to trade between member states, and national competition law on the basis of considerations peculiar to it.[95] The national authorities therefore retain jurisdiction to apply their national competition law to a cooperative in a powerful position on the national market.[96] However, they are under the obligation to refrain from adopting any measure which might undermine or create exceptions to the common market organization.[97]

Procedure.
The procedure is governed by Regulation 1/2003. However, under Article 2 (2) of Regulation 26/62 the Commission has sole power to determine that agreements fulfill the conditions of Article 2 (1).[98] Before taking a decision applying Article 2 (1), it must consult the member states and give a hearing to the firms or associations concerned and any other person that it considers appropriate.[99] However, it need not follow this special procedure, but may instead follow the ordinary rules when deciding that the exception of Article 2 (1) does *not* apply.[100]

C. Transport

1. Regulated Markets v. Competition

Limited Transitional Powers under Articles 84 and 85.
The transport markets are traditionally characterized by governmental regulation with respect to access, capacity and prices. Opening these markets gradually to

94. *Ibid.* paras. 98–102.
95. *Milk Marque*, ECJ Sept. 9, 2003, C-137/00, para. 61.
96. *Ibid.* para. 67.
97. *Ibid.* para. 94.
98. Like the exclusive jurisdiction to apply Article 81 (3) conferred on the Commission by Article 9 (1) of Regulation 17, this exclusivity relates only to positive findings that the provision is applicable. Hence, national courts have jurisdiction to find that Article 2 (1) is not applicable and that the agreement is null and void *ab initio*. *See Dijkstra/Melkunie*, ECJ Dec. 12, 1995, 1995 ECR I-4471, para. 36.
99. As in *New Potatoes*, D.Comm. Dec. 18, 1987, 1988 OJ L 59/25.
100. *Frubo*, ECJ May 15, 1975, 1975 ECR 563, paras 5–11; *Dijkstra/Campina Melkunie*, ECJ Dec. 12, 1995, 1995 ECR I-4471, para. 36; *Sicasov*, D.Comm. Dec. 14, 1998, 1999 OJ L 4/27, paras 65–69.

competition has required both deregulation by means of Community directives and implementing regulations for the competition rules of Articles 81 and 82.[101] The major objective has been to ensure free access to essential facilities by legislative measures (directives), as in the rail sector, or by applying the competition rules, in particular Article 82, as in the air (airports) and the sea (ports) sectors. However, Regulation 141/62 excluded transport from the ordinary procedural rules for enforcing Articles 81 and 82 laid down in Regulation 17.[102] Instead, the Council was to issue special procedural rules for transport under Article 83 of the Treaty.[103] Until it issued such rules years later as described below, Articles 81 and 82 could only be enforced by means of the transitional rules in Articles 84 and 85.[104] The Commission's own powers under Article 85 were limited,[105] the member states' authorities had never exercised their powers under Article 84, and the Court of Justice had held in the *Bosch* judgment,[106] later confirmed with specific reference to transport in the *Nouvelles Frontières*[107] *Ahmed Saeed*[108] and *Reiff*[109] cases, that national courts could not hold anticompetitive agreements in transport, in particular joint fixing of tariffs, to be automatically void under Article 81 (2) in the absence of a formal ruling by the Commission or the national authority

101. Regulation 141/62 excluded the transport sector from Regulation 17 whereas Articles 81 and 82 were fully applicable, however with the limited administrative means of Article 85.
102. 1962 OJ 2751. Article 1 of Regulation 141 provides: 'Regulation No 17 shall not apply to agreements, decisions or concerted practices in the transport sector which have as their object or effect the fixing of transport rates and conditions, the limitation or control of the supply of transport or the sharing of transport markets; nor shall it apply to the abuse of a dominant position, within the meaning of Article 86 of the Treaty, within the transport market.'
103. A date – subsequently extended – was set for the issuance of the rules for rail, road and inland waterway transport, but not for the other sectors.
104. *Commission v. France*, ECJ April 4, 1974, 1974 ECR 359, paras 17–32; *Nouvelles Frontières*, ECJ April 30, 1986, 1986 ECR 1425, paras 27–45; *Olympic Airways*, D.Comm. Jan. 23, 1985, 1985 OJ L 46/51, 52. Before the issuance of Community rules the transport sector was only subject to national competition law: *Ahmed Saeed*, ECJ April 11, 1989, 1989 ECR 803, paras 32–33.
105. *See* Commission decision of Oct. 28, 2002, closing the proceedings it had initiated in 1996 with a view of examining the alliance between KLM and its US partner Northwest and between Lufthansa, SAS and their US partner United Airlines following commitments likely to remove possible regulatory barriers for new entrants on a number of routes from Frankfurt to the US, IP/02/1569, 2002 OJ C 264. However, the UK competition authority OFT has powers to enforce Article 81 and 82 in relation to air transport between member states and the US. For this reason the OFT took the lead in the case British Midland/United Airlines which has also been closed following commitments (Thirty-second Report on Competition Policy, point 73.
106. *Bosch*, ECJ April 6, 1962, 1962 ECR 45, 51–53.
107. *Nouvelles Frontières (Asjes)*, ECJ April 30, 1986, 1986 ECR 1425, paras 46–69.
108. *Ahmed Saeed*, ECJ April 11, 1989, 1989 ECR 803, paras 10–29.
109. *Reiff/Bundesanstalt für den Güterfernverkehr*, ECJ Nov. 17, 1993, 1993 ECR I-5801, para. 12.

under Articles 85 or 84 respectively.[110] Article 82 was, however, fully applicable by national courts.[111]

Special Regulations for Transport.
The Council issued special regulations in 1968 for rail, road and inland waterway transport (Regulation 1017/68), in 1986 for sea transport (Regulation 4056/86) and in 1987 for air transport (Regulation 3975/87 supplemented by Regulation 2410/92).[112] The specific procedural provisions contained in these regulations are replaced by Regulation 1/2003 as from 1 May 2004. Air transport between Community airports and airports in non-member states is subject to Regulation 847/2004.

Main Issues when Applying the Competition Rules in the Transport Sector.
The main issues when applying the competition rules in the transport sector are the 'classical' forms of restrictions of competition such as price fixing, capacity and market sharing and collective refusal of access to essential facilities (under Article 81) and the application, by a carrier having a dominant position on the relevant market (routes, port, airport), of excessive or discriminatory tariffs[113] or refusing access to an essential facility (under Article 82), [114]whereas it may be more difficult to evaluate cooperation agreements aiming at facilitating access to new markets in the absence of any 'hard core' restriction; such evaluation must, according to the ruling of Court of First Instance in the *European Night Services* case,[115] include the consideration of all legal and factual circumstances and may

110. The Court's reasoning was that until procedural regulations had been issued the procedure and scope for exemptions under Article 81 (3) would be unclear, and as exemptions could be made retroactive it would cause legal uncertainty for courts to declare agreements null and void under Article 81 (2) given this possibility of retroactive validation.
111. *Ahmed Saaed*, ECJ April 11, 1989, 1989 ECR 803, para. 32.
112. In case of multi-modal transport means it was difficult to apply the appropriate regulation: Regulation 17, 1017/68 or 4056/86. Applying the wrong one has led to the annulment of the Commission decision: *Eurocorde Agreements*, 1990 OJ C 162/13 (notice of exemption under Regulations 4056/86 and 1017/68 for agreements on North Atlantic shipping routes followed by a comfort letter); *UIC – Union international des chemins de fer* (*Distribution of Railways Tickets*), CFI June 6, 1995, 1995 ECR II-1503, paras 60–61; *aff'd* ECJ March 11, 1997, 1997 ECR I-1287. Example for applying simultaneously several transport regulations: *TAA*, D.Comm. Oct. 19, 1994, 1994 OJ L 376/1 (rejecting exemption); *Vessel Sharing Agreements* (*VSA*), D.Comm. Sept. 3, 1997, Twenty-seventh Report on Competition Policy, point 84.
113. *Alpha Flight Services/Aéroports de Paris*, D.Comm. June 11, 1998, 1998 OJ L 230/10, *aff'd* CFI Dec. 12, 2000, 2000 ECR II-3929.
114. The substantive rules of the special transport regulations are to be interpreted in the same way as Articles 81 and 82 *see Deutsche Bahn*, CFI Oct. 21, 1997; 1997 ECR II-1689, para. 77 (with regard to Article 8 of Regulation 1017/68).
115. *European Night Services*, CFI Sept. 15, 1998, 1998 ECR II-3141, paras 140–160 and 221 (emphasizing that the free access of third parties is already guaranteed by Directive 91/440).

lead to the conclusion that the cooperation does not restrict competition, thereby not infringing Article 81 (1) and not justifying conditions attached to an exemption under Article 81 (3).

2. Rail, Road and Waterway Transport

Regulatory Background.

The pattern in the rail sector was historically one of state railways with a statutary monopoly. Cross-border services, where they existed at all, were possible only on the basis of cooperation between the national monopolies.[116] Liberalization started with Council Directive 91/440/EC on the development of the Community's railways,[117] which is designed to clarify access to railway networks in order to start new, cross-border container freight services. The directive also introduced the concept of 'international grouping', an association between at least two train operators in different member states to operate cross-border passenger or freight services. With respect to freight services, Directive 2001/12/EC[118] renders individual operators free to provide all types of cross-border freight services, which are, however, limited, for a transitional period, to the so-called Trans-European Rail Freight Network (TERFN). Directive 2001/14/EC[119] provides a framework for conditions of access, such as train routes and track charges.[120] A furthergoing liberalization, in particular with respect to passenger services, is the subject of Directive 2004/51/EC of the European Parliament and of the Council amending Council Directive 91/440/EEC.[121]

Regulation 1017/68 v. Regulation 1/2003.

Despite the still underdeveloped liberalization, the EC competition rules apply in the framework of Regulation 1017/68[122] as amended by Article 36 of Regulation 1/2003. Regulation 1017/68 applies to agreements between rail, road and inland waterway transport operators on rates and conditions of carriage, supply of

---

116. *See* Stehmann and Mackay, Liberalization and competition policy in railways, Competition Policy Newsletter 2003–3, p. 21.
117. 1991 OJ L 237/25.
118. 2001 OJ L 44.
119. 2001 OJ L 75.
120. *See also* Directive 95/19/EC on the allocation of railway infrastructure capacity and the charging of infrastructure fees (1995 OJ L 143/75) as amended by Council Directive 2001/14/EC and Directive 95/18/EC on the licensing of railway undertakings (1995 OJ L 143/70).
121. 2004 OJ L 164/164.
122. 1968 OJ L 175/1. The Commission is proposing to introduce competition into the railways by requiring the separation of ownership of the infrastructure from the operation of services and creation of a right of transit for other railway companies' services over track in other member states: Doc. COM(89)564, 8 Nov. 1989.

services (including ancillary services such as forwarding agents[123] but not for shipping services in seaports[124] and at land frontiers[125] nor the supply of equipment[126] which are subject to the general provisions of Article 81 and Regulation 1/2003), sharing of markets, technical cooperation and joint financing or acquisition of transport equipment, and to abuse of dominant positions on transport markets. The regulation provides for a specific exemption for technical agreements[127] and groups of small and medium-sized undertakings[128] without prejudice to the general exemption of Article 81 (3)[129] and to the direct applicability of Article 82.[130] The procedural provisions are replaced and harmonized by Regulation 1/2003,[131] thereby avoiding legal doubts as to which regulation to apply in the case of combined (land and sea) transport services. [132]

Case Law under the Rail, Road and Waterway Regulation.

(i) *Clearing procompetitive agreements under Article 3 of Regulation 1017/68 or Article 81*: The Commission granted clearance in cases of cooperation between railway companies to offer new transport services via the Chanel Tunnel.[133] In some cases the Commission granted exemption subject to conditions relating to non-discriminatory application and free access to the infrastructure.[134] However, certain exemption decisions subject to such conditions have been reversed by the Court of First Instance, in the *Eurotunnel/British Railway – SNCF* case because the Commission had misinterpreted

123. *UCI*, CFI June 6, 1995, 1995 ECR II-1503, paras 43–50 (annulling the Commission decision Nov. 25, 1992, 1992 OJ L 366/47 which denied the applicability of Regulation 1017/68).
124. E.g. *Sea Containers/Stena Sealink*, D.Comm. Dec. 21, 1993, 1994 OJ L 15/8.
125. *FENEX*, D.Comm. June 5, 1996, 1996 OJ L 181/28, points 22–23.
126. *Eurofima*, Third Report on Competition Policy, points 68–69; 1973 CMLR D217, in which a consortium of national railway companies was made to give up the claim to the industrial property rights in new designs of railway rolling stock ordered from a manufacturer.
127. Article 3.
128. Article 4.
129. The specific exemption for agreements intended to reduce structural disturbances (Article 6) has been repealed: Article 36 (4) of Regulation 1/2003.
130. Previously Article 8.
131. Including the provision on fines, Article 22 of Regulation 1017/68 being replaced by Article 23 of Regulation 1/2003.
132. E.g. *Far Eastern Freight Conference*, D.Comm. Dec. 21, 1994, 1994 OJ L 378/17, points 56–85, in this respect *aff'd* CFI Feb. 28, 2002, 2002 ECR II-1101; *Eurocord Agreements* where the Commission applied Regulations 1017/68 and 4056/86 on multi-modal operations (comfort letter, 1990 OJ C 162/13).
133. *Eurotunnel I*, D.Comm. Oct. 24, 1988, 1988 OJ L 311/36 (negative clearance); *ACI*, D.Comm. July 27, 1994, 1994 OJ L 224/28 (exemption).
134. *Combined International Transport of Goods*, D.Comm. Feb. 24, 1993, 1993 OJ L 145/31. Clearance of a cooperation under the merger control regulation: *First Group/Keolis*, D.Comm. Dec. 9, 2003, IP/03/1675.

the notified agreement with respect to the use of spare capacity[135] and in the *European Night Services* case because the railway undertakings were unable to offer the new services alone and that their cooperation therefore did not infringe Article 81 (1) and did not justify the imposition of a condition on access of third parties.[136]

(ii) *Prohibiting anticompetitive agreements under Article 2 of Regulation 1017/68 (now replaced by the general provision of Article 81,*[137] *possibly, in cases of combined land-sea transport services, in parallel to Regulation 4056/86*: The Commission prohibited agreements on joint fixing of prices, provisions and conditions and limiting of capacities.[138] However, the Commission decision in the *UIC (Union international des chemis de fer)* case, which imposed a fine of ECU 1 million,[139] was annulled by the Court of First Instance because the Commission wrongly disregarded Regulation 1017/68 and did not proceed in the absence of a notification *ex officio* to a comprehensive evaluation of the conditions of Article 81 (3).[140]

(iii) *Prohibiting abuses of a dominant position under Article 8 of Regulation 1017/68 (now replaced by the general provision of Article 82)*: The Commission intervened against predatory tariff discrimination with respect to container transport services between German and Belgian ports.[141] In *TACA (Trans Atlantic Conference Agreement)* the Commission found that the parties to the agreement committed an infringement of Article 81 by fixing prices for inland transport services within the territory of the EU to shippers in combination with other services as part of a multimodal transport operation[142] (which was upheld by the Court of First Instance) and by inducing potential competitors to enter the market as parties to the TACA rather than

---

135. *Eurotunnel/SNCF and British Rail*, D.Comm. Dec. 13, 1994, 1994 OJ L 354/66; *rev'd* CFI Oct. 22, 1996, 1996 ECR II-1491.
136. *European Night Services*, D.Comm. Oct. 21, 1994, 1994 OJ L 259/20, *rev'd* CFI Sept. 15, 1998, 1998 ECR II-3141, paras 139–147.
137. Article 36 (1) of Regulation 1/2003.
138. With respect to the fixing of tariffs for land transport services as part of combined land-sea transport services: *Trans Atlantic Agreement (TAA)*, D.Comm. Oct. 19, 1994, 1994 OJ L 376/1, points 304–312; suspension rejected by CFI March 18, 1995, 1995 ECR II-595 and by ECJ July 19, 1995, 1995 ECR I-2165 and ECJ Nov. 22, 1995, 1995 ECR I-2895 (the agreement was finally abandoned); *TACA (Trans Atlantic Conference Agreement)*, D.Comm. Sept. 16, 1998, 1999 OJ L 95/1, point 385, in this respect upheld by CFI Sept. 30, 2003, T-191–98.
139. *UIC (Distribution of Railway Tickets)*, D.Comm. Nov. 25, 1992, 1992 OJ L 366/47.
140. *UIC*, CFI June 6, 1995, 1995 ECR II-1503, paras. 60–61; *aff'd* ECJ March 11, 1997, 1997 ECR I-1287. *See*, with respect to the immunity from fines, *TACA*, CFI Feb. 28, 2002, 2002 ECR II-1125, paras. 48–53.
141. *Deutsche Bahn – HOV-SVZ/MCN*, D.Comm. March 29, 1994, 1994 OJ L 104/34 (fine of ECU 11 million), *aff'd* (including the fine) CFI Oct. 21, 1997, 1997 ECR I-1689, para. 130; ECJ April 27, 1999, 1999 ECR I-2387 (dismissing the appeal as apparently unfounded).
142. *TACA*, D.Comm. Sept. 16, 1998, 1999 OJ L 95/1, *aff'd* (in substance) CFI Sept. 30, 2003, T-191/98.

concluding individual service contracts in competition with the members of TACA (which was annulled by the Court for lack of evidence).[143]

(iv) *Abusing a dominant position by refusing access to the rail network as an essential facility*: The *GVG/FS* case[144] concerned the refusal by the Italian railway operator Ferrovie dello Stato (FS) to allow the railway operator Georg Verkehrsorganisation GmbH (GVG) to enter into an international grouping under Directive 91/440 to discuss terms for access to the track and to provide traction services (locomotives and train crew). GVG was therefore prevented from providing passenger trains between Basel and Milan in competition with FS (in cooperation with the Swiss railway operator Schweizer Bundesbahn SBB), which would be non-stop and therefore considerably quicker and timed to connect at Basel with intercity trains from and to Germany. GVG had already obtained the necessary train paths in Switzerland but needed to enter an international grouping and traction services for the Italian railway network which only FS is capable of providing because there is no realistic alternative supplier. The Commission therefore found that FS had a dominant position on the Italian rail infrastructure for the provision of traction for rail passengers transport on the Italian segment between Domodossola and Milano,[145] and abused this position by refusing access to the railway network constituting an essential facility, [146] and required FS to allow access to the Italian network at adequate remuneration (adequate return of the capital investment).[147] In order to avoid a prohibition decision FS entered into an international grouping with GVG and agreed on the terms of a traction contract and to use best endeavours to provide GVG with train rights-of-way. Furthermore, FS undertook, for a period of five years, to provide traction services to *other* railway companies. Accordingly, the Commission terminated the case without imposing a fine. The Commission considers this as a landmark decision on the further liberalization of railways, the final goal being that the railway network must be completely separated from the transport service provider in order to avoid conflicts of interest.[148]

3. Sea Transport

Regulation 4056/86 v. Regulation 1/2003.
Regulation 4056/86[149] applies to international maritime transport services from or to one or more Community ports, including purely intra-Community traffic

---

143. *TACA – Atlantic Container Line AB*, CFI Sept. 30, 2003, T-191/98, paras. 560–577 and 1304.
144. *GVG/FS*, D.Comm. Aug. 26, 2003, 2004 OJ L 11/14.
145. *Ibid.*, point 110.
146. *Ibid.*, points 119–152.
147. *Ibid.*, points 137 and 160–161.
148. *See* Regulation 881/2004 establishing a European railway agency for improving the interoperability of railway systems (2004 OJ L 220/3).
149. 1986 OJ L 378/4.

and ferry services.[150] The regulation provides for a block exemption for agreements on rates of carriage between carriers concerning the operation of scheduled maritime transport services because of their 'stabilizing' effect, assuring shippers of reliable services, which cannot be obtained without cooperation,[151] and in order to avoid conflicts with the laws and rules of certain third countries[152] according to the conditions of the United Nations Convention on a Code of Conduct for Liner Conferences.[153] It was issued as part of a liberalization package which also contained Regulation 4055/86 designed to phase out restrictions on other member states' shipping lines in trade between EC countries and between EC and non-EC countries.[154] However, the OECD concluded that antitrust immunity or exemption for price fixing or rate discussions is unjustified.[155] Accordingly, the Commission undertook a review of the exemption in particular in order to verify whether collective rate setting by members of a liner conference is still an indispensible requisite for reliable liner shipping services and whether the exclusion from the scope of the regulation of tramp vessel services is still justified.[156] Whereas the substantive rules continue to apply, including the provisions on the monitoring of exempted practices,[157] the procedural rules are replaced by Regulation 1/2003.[158] Article 82 remains directly applicable, however without reference to Article 8 (1) of Regulation 4056/87.

The Scope of the Regulation.
According to Article 1 (2), Regulation 4056/86 applies only to international transport services from or to one of more Community ports, which are likely to affect trade between member states,[159] thereby excluding:

– international tramp vessels as defined in Article 1 (3) (a) of Regulation 4056/86.[160] Tramp vessel services are excluded since the remuneration for such

150. E.g. *Greek Ferries*, D.Comm. Dec. 9, 1998, 1999 OJ L 109/24, *aff'd Strintzig Lines* CFI Dec. 11, 2003, T-56/99.
151. Recital 8 to Regulation 4056/86; *CEWAL*, ECJ March 16, 2000, 2000 ECR I-1365, paras. 46–49.
152. Recital 15 to Regulation 4056/86.
153. Recital 3 to Regulation 4056/86. The EC Council laid down terms on which the member states should ratify or accede to the Convention in Regulation 954/79, 1979 OJ L 121/1.
154. 1986 OJ L 378/1. The package also contained measures to combat unfair pricing practices by non-EC shipping lines and protectionism by non-EC countries in favor of their shipping lines: Regulations 4057/86 and 4058/86, 1986 OJ L 378/14 and 21, respectively.
155. *See* OECD document DSTI/DOT(2002)2 and Thirty-first Report on Competition Policy, point 159.
156. Commission Consultation Paper on the Review of Council Regulation 4056/86, IP/03/445.
157. Article 7 and 8 (2) of Regulation 4056/87.
158. Article 38 (4) of Regulation 1/2003.
159. *See Compagnie Générale Maritime – Far Eastern Freight Conference*, CFI Feb. 28, 2002, 2002 ECR II-1101, paras. 145–148.
160. Article 32 of Regulation 1/2003.

services is freely negotiated between the shipper and the ship operator case by case in accordance with supply and demand.[161] They are subject to Article 81 without Regulation 1/2003 being applicable (therefore enforceable only within the limits of Article 85 of the EC Treaty);
- maritime transport services that take place exclusively between ports of one and the same member state, which are normally unlikely to affect trade between member states,[162] and remain subject to national competition law;
- inland transportation (including on- and off-carriage of cargo), even if it is part of a transatlantic intermodal transport operation, which may be subject to Regulation 1017/68 and Regulation 1/2003.[163] The reason for this restrictive interpretation is that Article 3 of Regulation 4056/86 provides for an exemption of liner conferences which may extend to the fixing of rates and conditions of carriage whereas collectively fixing of the price for inland transport services is prohibited under Article 81 (1) and unlikely to be exempted.[164]

The Structure of the Regulation.

(i) The main *substantive* provisions of Regulation 4056/86 are:
  - an exception from the prohibition provision of Article 81 (1) for technical agreements (Article 2);[165]
  - an exemption, subject to conditions pursuant to Article 4 and to obligations pursuant to Article 5, for liner conferences and for agreements between liner conferences and shippers for the common fixing of rates and conditions of carriage and to regulate the capacity offered by each member, subject to detailed conditions and obligations especially regarding discrimination and loyalty arrangements (Articles 3–6);[166] however, the condition of fixing of rates, or, as defined in Article 1 (3) (b) of Regulation 4056/86, 'uniform or

161. Recital 4 to Regulation 4056/87.
162. Article 32 (b) of Regumlation 1/2003.
163. *See Compagnie Générale Maritime – Far Eastern Freight Conference*, CFI Feb. 28, 2002, 2002 ECR II-1101, paras. 260–262; in this case the Court of First Instance annulled the Commission's decision which wrongly concluded that in the case of a multimodal operation Regulation 4056/87 applied to both the maritime and the inland transport leg: In *TAA* the Court of First Instance confirmed that the Trans Atlantic Agreement was *not* a liner conference enjoying the exemption under Regulation 4056/87 and that inland transport price fixing and the collective limitation of capacity did not qualify for individual exemption under Article 81 (3): CFI Feb. 28, 2002, 2002 ECR II-875, paras. 368–372 and 395.
164. *Compagnie Générale Maritime – Far Eastern Freight Conference*, CFI Feb. 28, 2002, 2002 ECR II-1101, para. 110.
165. Rejected in *Far East Trade Tariff Charges and Surcharges Agreement (FETTCSA)*, D.Comm. May 16, 2000, 2000 OJ L 268/1, in this respect upheld by CFI March 19, 2003, T-213/00, paras. 175–178, but fine annulled because of limitation.
166. The exemption for price fixing or rate discussions between members of a liner conference is being reviewed and may be amended: Thirty-second Report on Competition Policy, point 126.

common freight rates', is not fulfilled where the agreement establishes at least two rate levels,[167] although this leads, at first glance, to more competition and should more likely obtain clearance.[168] Regulation 4056/86 is not applicable either if the activity of a liner conference concerns only 25% carriage of cargo.[169] However, an agreement providing for non-utilization of capacity is not covered by Article 3 of Regulation 4056/86 if it is used as an instrument to create an artificial peak season and if the capacity withdrawal is combined with an increase in the conference tariff;[170]

- a provision on monitoring exempted agreements, including the possibility of adopting a decision which either prohibits the agreement or withdraws the benefit of the exemption where the parties are in breach of an obligation, in particular of loyalty arrangements and transparency of tariffs (Article 7 as amended by Article 38 of Regulation 1/2003). Where the parties do not comply with a condition pursuant to Article 4 the exemption is automatically null and void;
- an exemption for agreements between transport users and conferences concerning the use of scheduled transport services (Article 6);
- specific provisions on complaints about abusive conduct of conferences, in particular tariff discrimination (Article 8 (2));[171] and
- provision for negotiations with non-EC countries to resolve conflicts (Article 9, as amended by Article 38 (3) of Regulation 1/2003).

The block exemption does not provide for market share thresholds. However, where the effects of a liner conference are incompatible with Article 81 (3), in particular where it is not subject to actual or potential external competition, the Commission may withdraw the benefit of the block exemption under Article 7 (2) (c) (i) of the regulation. The market share limit of 50% established by Article 7 of Regulation 823/2000 on Consortia may be interpreted in the sense that liner conferences whose market share exceeds 50% may give rise to a withdrawal of the benefit of the block exemption or a direct application

---

167. *TAA*, CFI Feb. 28, 2002, 2002 ECR II-875, paras. 135–174. *See North Sea Liner Conference*, D.Comm. Jan. 15, 1997, IP/97/12 (inapplicability of Regulation 4056/86, but individual clearance by comfort letter).
168. In fact, the Commission refused to grant individual clearance and prohibited the agreement, which was upheld in *TAA*, CFI Feb. 28, 2002, 2002 ECR II-875.
169. However, such a liner conference may justify individual clearance, as in *Conference Maritime 'Mer du Nord'*, D.Comm. Jan. 15, 1997, IP/97/17 (exemption by comfort letter).
170. Thirty-first Report on Competition Policy, point 156; *TAA*, D.Comm. Oct. 19, 1984, 1994 OJ L 376/1, point 319, not discussed by the CFI Feb. 28, 2002, 2002 ECR II-875. *See* Article 4 of Regulation 823/2000, 2000 OJ L 100/24.
171. Applied in *Sea Containers/Sealink*, Twenty-third Report on Competition Policy, point 234. Possibility of applying Article 82 in case of discriminatory tariffs: *Corsica Ferries*, ECJ May 17, 1994, 1994 ECR I-1783, *aff'd* CFI Dec. 11, 2003, T-56/99.

of Article 82.[172] Where actual or potential competition is precluded as a result of action of a third country (e.g. preventing the participation of outsiders on a route) the Commission must enter into consultations with the competent authorities of the third country concerned in order to remedy the situation.[173]

(ii) The procedural provisions (Articles 10–25) of Regulation 4056/86 are repealed by Article 38 (4) and replaced by those of Regulation 1/2003, including the possibility of making commitments binding and enforceable. The 'exemptions' of Article 3 and 4 are in fact legal exceptions which are directly applicable, no prior decision to that effect being required. If liner conferences do not comply with a condition (Article 3) the Commission may, acting on a complaint or on its own initiative, initiate proceedings with a view of finding an anfringement and requiring the conference to bring the infringement to an end according to Article 7 of Regulation 1/2003 or of imposing fines according to Article 25 of Regulation 1/2003. In the case of a breach of an obligation the Commission must use the specific powers under Article 7 as amended by Article 38 (1) of Regulation 1/2003.[174] In both cases there is no possibility prior to the decision to publish notices in the Official Journal in order invite third parties to submit comments (unlike the repealed provision of Article 12 of Regulation 4056/86).

Block Exemption Regulation on Liner Shipping Companies (Consortia). Regulation 823/2000 as amended by Regulation 463/2004 grants a block exemption to liner shipping consortia.[175] The purpose is to encourage shipowners to improve and rationalize their operations, thereby reducing costs and freight rates while allowing them to offer better-quality service along with greater frequency. It applies only to international liner shipping services to or from one or more Community ports intended exclusively for the carriage of cargo, chiefly by container,[176] and only if the consortium possesses, with respect of the ranges of

---

172. Article 7 of Regulation 823/2000 has been de;eted by Regulation 463/2004 in order to abolish notification and opposition procedure in accordnace with Regulation 1/2003. However, the market share ceiling of 50% remains a valid indicator for the individual assessment of consortia under Article 81 (3) or 82 by the Commission or the national authorities.

173. Article 7 (2) (c) (i) of Regulation 4056/86.

174. Article 9(5) of Regulation 463/2004 on consortia (2004 OJ L 77/23) provides for a system of notifying the agreement to the Commission in order to be able to claim the benefit of the regulation.

175. 2000 OJ L 100/24 and 2004 OJ L 77/23, both based on Council Regulation 479/92, 1992 OJ L 55/3. *See also* Regulation 954/89 (1989 OJ L 121/1) ratifying the United Nations's code of conduct for liner conferences. According to the Statements Relating to Regulation 1310/97, the Commission stated that the merger control regulation does not apply to consortia in the liner trades sector (Re Article 3 (2)).

176. This condition was not fulfilled in the *Baltic Liner Conference* case, Twenty-sixth Report on Competition Policy, point 87, which concerned a largely non-containerized consortium, meriting however an individual exemption

ports it serves, a share of trade of under 30% for operations within a conference or 35% for operations outside a conference.[177] Consortia above this market share ceiling need individual assessment under Article 81 (3) by the Commission or the national authorities.[178] They may satisfy this provision if the conditions and obligations of the block exemption are met, in particular if the market share does not exceed 50%.[179] The block exemption regulation has lead to the clearance of about 30 notifications of consortium agreements.[180] Regulation 463/2004[181] brings Regulation 823/2000 in line with Regulation 1/2003.

Case Law under the Maritime Transport Regulations.

- *Prohibition against fixing maritime transport rates (possibly as part of multimodal transport agreements which provide for both inland and maritime transport services)*: Setting common tariffs to be charged for maritime transport services clearly infringes Article 81 (1), even if it is current practice among all transport companies to exchange information on prices or conditions.[182] The Commission has prohibited multimodal transport agreements which fixed not only the maritime transport rates but also inland transport rates as not being covered by the block exemption of Regulation 4056/86 and as not satisfying the conditions for an individual clearance under Article 81 (3).[183] In *Transatlantic Conference Agreement* (*TACA*) the Commission prohibited joint price fixing that included the inland portions within the Community of intermodal services,[184] which was affirmed by the Court of First Instance.[185] Article 81 (1) also prohibits agree-

177. Article 6 of Regulation 823/2000. Example of a non-opposition under the predecessor regulation 870/95: *VSA2/CSAV* (joint liner service across the Atlantic between Northern Europe and East Coast of South Africa, having a market share of 31.5%), Twenty-nineth Report on Competition Policy, pp. 151–152. *See also Liner Shipping Consortia*, IP/97/357.
178. Article 9 (5) of Regulation 823/2000 as amended by Regulation 463/2004.
179. Although Regulation 463/2004 abolishes notification and opposition procedure of Article 7 of Regulation 823/2000 in accordance with Regulation 1/2003 the 50% limit remains a valid indicator.
180. *VSA2/CSAV*, (joint liner service across the Atlantic), Twenty-nineth Report on Competition Policy, p. 151; *Grand Alliance Consortium* (joint liner shipping service between ports in Northern and Southern Europe), Thirtieth Report on Competition Policy, point 197.
181. 2004 OJ L 77/23.
182. *Marlines – Greek Ferries*, CFI Dec. 11, 2003, T-56/99, paras. 51–58. *See also P&O/Stena Sealink*, D.Comm. Oct. 30, 1996, 1997 OJ L 26/23, paras 56–58.
183. *See Far Eastern Freight Conference*, D.Comm. Dec. 21, 1994, 1994 OJ L 378/17; *aff'd* CFI Feb. 28, 2002, 2002 ECR II-1101, paras. 484–485 (the Court upheld the decision in substance although annulling the (symbolic) fine on grounds of legitimate expectations).
184. *TACA I*, D.Comm. Nov. 26, 1996, Twenty-fifth Report on Competition Policy, point 73 (Article 15 (6) Regulation 17 decision) and *TACA II*, D.Comm. Sept. 16, 1998, 1999 OJ L 95/1 (final prohibition decision).
185. *Atlantic Container Line AB*, CFI Sept. 30, 2003, T-191/98 (affirming the Commission decision with respect to Article 81).

ments that have as their object or effect the sharing of markets or limiting access by other shipowers to a conference.[186]

- *Individual clearance of conference agreements.* The Commission has granted individual clearance to conference agreements, provided they no longer fix inland rates but instead establish a 'not-below-cost rule', i.e. the agreement not to charge a price less than the direct out-of-pocket cost incurred for inland transport services supplied within the EEA in combination with the maritime transport services.[187] Accordingly, all major conferences serving Europe have abandoned inland price-fixing[188] in line with the Court of First Instance affirming the Commission's prohibition of the agreement with respect to that part of the transport services.[189] The Commission is reconsidering the antitrust immunity granted by Regulation 4056/86 to shipping companies when they operate liner conferences on the assumption that the rate-setting of liner conferences leads to stable freight rates, which in turn assures shippers of reliable scheduled maritime transport services.[190]
- *Consortia.* Consortia not covered by Regulation 823/2000 as amended by Regulation 463/2004 are subject to individual evaluation.[191] Until 1 May 2004 they could be notifed to the Commission under Article 12 of Regulation 4056/86 and were exempted if the Commission does not oppose them within six months. However, after 1 May 2004 notifications lapse.[192] In the absence of a transitional provision it may be argued that the parties enjoy legitimate expectations where the Commission initiates, without having opposed to the notification, proceedings with a view to imposing fines.
- *Capacity management agreements.* In the EATA (Europe-Asia Trades Agreement) case[193] the Commission prohibited and fined a capacity management program between shipping companies in order to improve revenues which was tantamount to a price cartel. The Commission held that the agreement was not a liner conference in the strict sense of Regulation 4056/86 and did not

---

186. *French-West-African Shipowners' Committee*, D.Comm. April 1, 1992, 1992 OJ L 134/1 (with fines); *CEWAL*, D.Comm. Dec. 23, 1992, 1993 OJ L 34/20 (with high fines); *aff'd* CFI Oct. 8, 1996, 1996 ECR II-1201 (however reducing the fines by 10%). *See also* Recital 16 to Regulation 823/2000.
187. *TACA III*, D.Comm. Dec. 3, 2001, IP/01/1713, and Thirty-first Report on Competition Policy, points 153–157. One might doubt, however, whether the 'not below cost rule' does not imply mutual price and cost information and may therefore lead to indirect tariff fixing. *See also* *TACA New*, D.Comm. Nov. 17, 2002, 2003 OJ L 26/53, points 74–78 and 90.
188. Twenty-ninth Report on Competition Policy, point 98.
189. *FEFC*, CFI Feb. 28, 2002, 2002 ECR II-875, paras. 266–271.
190. IP/03/445, based on the Commission's Consultation Paper on the Review of Council Regulation 4056/86.
191. E.g. *Fincarrier*, *Poseidon* and *Baltic Liner Conference*, Twenty-sixth Report on Competition Policy, point 87.
192. Article 34 (1) of Regulation 1/2003.
193. D.Comm. April 30, 1999, 1999 OJ L 193/23.

fulfil the conditions for individual clearance under Article 81 (3). In *French-West-African Shipowners Committee*[194] the Commission fined the members of an agreement that aimed at sharing the carrying capacity among the members and refusing membership to competitors or making membership economically uninteresting. Similarly, the Commission intervened against an agreement on the non-utilization of capacity.[195]

- *Pooling lines by way of joint ventures.* The creation of a joint venture is not covered by Regulation 4056/86 but may justify an individual clearance, provided the cooperation does not lead to an oligopolistic dominant position, as in the case of the joint venture between P&O and Stena operating cross-Channel ferry services.[196]
- *Applying predatory practices under Article 82*: The Commission intervened against the *CEWAL Liner Conference* for having applied predatory pricing, fidelity rebates and exclusive arrangements aiming at eliminating competitors, which was affirmed by the Court of First Instance.[197] However, in *TACA II* the Court of First Instance annulled a Commission decision with respect to Article 82 by stating that the Commission failed to demonstrate that the association had taken predatory measures in order to induce competitors to join the association and to become subject to the joint discipline rather than concluding service contracts in competition with the members of the association.[198]

---

194. *French-West-African Shipowners' Committee*, D. Comm. April 1, 1992, 1992 OJ L 134/1 (parallel application of Articles 81 and 82; fines of ECU 15.3 million). *See East-African Conference*, Twenty-third Report on Competition Policy, point 230.
195. *Grand Alliance Consortium*, Thirty-first Report on Competition Policy, point 197; *Grand Alliance/Americana Consortium* and *Europe to Caribbean Consortium*, Thirty-first Report on Competition Policy, point 158. Market instability (possibly as a result of uneconomic investment decisions) do not justify arrangements on rates or non-utilization of capacity: *FEFC*, D.Comm. Dec. 21, 1994, 1994 OJ L 378/17, *aff'd* CFI Feb. 28, 2002, 2002 ECR II-1101; *EATA*, D.Comm. April 30, 1999, 1999 OJ L 193/23, points 148–176 and 197–203. *See also TACA II*, D.Comm. Sept. 16, 1999, 1999 OJ L 95/1, points 415–416, and *TACA New*, D.Comm. Nov. 14, 2002, 2003 OJ L 26/53, point 85. With respect to jointly fixing a surcharge following the devaluation of the pound: *P&O/Stena*, D.Comm. Oct. 30, 1996, 1997 OJ L 26/23, point 58.
196. *P&O/Stena I*, Twenty-seventh report on Competition Policy, point 85 (setting-up of a joint venture for pooling their cross-Channel ferry business); *P&O Stena II*, D.Comm. Jan. 26, 1999, 1999 OJ L 163/21 (exemption of pooling lines, rejection of complaint by competitor Sea France); *P&O/Stena III* (extension), D.Comm. June 7, 2001, IP/01/830. *See also Helsinborg/Helsingor*, Twenty-second Report on Competition Policy, p. 438 (application of the non-opposition procedure of Article 12 of Regulation 4056/86).
197. *CEWAL*, D.Comm. Dec. 23, 1992, 1993 OJ L 34/20, fines of ECU million 10.1, reduced by 10% by CFI Oct. 8, 1996, 1996 ECR II-1201, *aff'd* (with exception of the fine imposed on the association) ECJ March 16, 2000, 2000 ECR I-1365, paras. 130–135 (with respect to Article 82, the infringement of Article 81 not being appealed).:
198. *TACA II – Atlantic Container Line AB*, CFI Sept. 30, 2003, T-191/98, paras 1255–1292.

Fair Access to Port Facilities.
Port authorities may abuse their natural monopolies by refusing or limiting access to port facilities which competitors find essential in order to provide services to their customers ('essential facilities'). Ensuring a competitive Common Market through freer access to port facilities is developing through case law of the Commission and the Court of Justice under Article 82 rather than through new regulations or directives. In the *Sea Containers/Stena Sealink* case[199] the Commission defined an 'essential facility' as 'a facility or infrastructure, without access to which competitors cannot provide services to their customers.'[200] This definition of the Commission is consistent with the approach of the Court of Justice in its *Porto di Genova* cases.[201]

Abusive Refusal of Access to Essential Facilities.
Cases when the Commission found an abuse of a dominant position have concerned the refusal by the owner and operator of a port to grant access to the infrastructure or to grant access on discriminatory conditions. In *Port of Rodby*[202] the Commission intervened on the basis of Article 82 combined with Article 86 against the operator of the terminals in the Danish port of Rodby, which was owned and managed by a public undertaking having the status of a department of the Danish Transport Ministry which also operated ferry services between Denmark and Puttgarden, Germany, for having refused access to two competing operators of ferry services.[203] In both cases the Commission applied a narrow market definition holding that a single port was a geographically relevant market because of competitors' need to have access to this 'essential facility.' The *Sea Containers/ Stena Sealink* case[204] concerned the application of an interim measure against the refusal, by the operator of the port of Holyhead (Wales), which was also operator of a ferry line linking Holyhead with Ireland, to grant access to a company that wished to introduce a new fast ferry service that was not offered yet by the operator itself. The Commission stated that there was a sufficient *prima facie* case of a pattern of behaviour constituting abuse under Article 82 and admitted that 'a decision on interim measures may be just as necessary, to ensure that any final decision of the Commission is effective, in a case of a complainant

199. *Sea Containers/Stena Sealink*, D.Comm. Dec. 21, 1993, 1994 OJ L 15/8.
200. *Ibid.* para. 66. Similarly *Port of Rodby*, D.Comm. Dec. 21, 1993, 1994 OJ L 55/52.
201. *Porto di Genova I*, ECJ Dec. 10, 1991, 1991 ECR I-5889; *Porto di Genova II* (*Diego Cali & Figli*), ECJ March 18, 1997, 1997 ECR I-1547.
202. *Port of Rodby*, D.Comm. Dec. 21, 1993, 1994 OJ L 55/52 (excluding access from commercially viable sailing times); similarly *Harbour of Roscoff*, D.Comm. May 16, 1995, Twenty-fifth Report on Competition Policy, point 43 and p. 120.
203. The access to a port as an essential facility is not subject to Regulation 4056/86, but the general provision of Article 82: *B&I/Sealink*, D.Comm. June 11, 1992, Twenty-second Report on Competition Policy, point 219.
204. *Sea Containers/Stena Sealink*, D.Comm. Dec. 21, 1993, 1994 OJ L 15/8.

who is a new entrant as it is in the case of an already established competitor' but rejected an interim measure because the condition of urgency arising from the danger of serious and irreparable harm was not fulfilled.[205] A port operator may also abuse its dominant position by obstructing access to the port infrastructure in respect of loading and unloading operations at ports.[206] In the *Porto di Genova* case[207] the Court of Justice ruled that the port operator abused its exclusive rights granted by the Italian legislation in requiring the staff to be Italian workers. Another case involving the port of Geneva concerned the discriminatory application of a cabotage licence fee for providing piloting services.[208]

4. Air Transport

Regulatory Background.

International air transport is regulated by a network of international agreements, bilateral agreements between countries and bilateral and multilateral agreements between air carriers. The intergovernmental agreements often limit the number of carriers that are authorized to fly routes and the capacity that may be provided. The private bilateral and multilateral agreements between airlines fix fares and conditions and flight schedules. In Europe, as elsewhere, this regulated and cartelized system has stifled competition and led to higher fares.[209] It has also been a barrier to integration of the Common Market. In June 1986 the EC member states finally agreed to liberalize air transport in the Community by 1992,[210] but to proceed in stages so as to give the industry time to adapt.[211] In December 1987, a package of measures was agreed which, as well as the first phase of liberalization of fares, capacity and market access,[212] contained procedural rules for applying

205. *Ibid.*, points 67 and 79.
206. Port charges as state aid: *Enirisorse*, ECJ Nov. 27, 2003, C-34/01.
207. *Porto di Genova I*, ECJ Dec. 10, 1991, 1991 ECR I-5889. *Similarly Italian Dock Labour Legislation*, D.Comm. Oct. 21, 1997, 1997 OJ L 301/17, where the Commission found that a port administration might abuse its exclusive rights with regard to temporary labour and subcontracting labour-intensive services because of a conflict of interest (subsequently the Italian Government put an end to the infringement: Twenty-eighth Report on Competition Policy, point 110).
208. *Corsica Ferries I*, ECJ May 7, 1994, 1994 ECR I-1783. In the *Corsica Ferries II* case, however, the Court of Justice denied discriminatory tariffs the differences being justified by the need to supply a universal service: ECJ June 18, 1998, 1998 ECR I-3949.
209. House of Lords Select Committee on the European Communities, *European Air Fares*, 49th Report 1979/80 Session; *id.*, *Civil Aviation. A Free Market By 1992?*, 16th Report 1989/90 Session. *See* Van Houtte, *Competition, Liberalization and State Monopolies: Air Transport*, University of Liege, Nov. 5, 1998.
210. Recital 10 to Regulation 3976/87, 1987 OJ L 374/1.
211. Recital 4 to Regulation 3976/87.
212. Council Directive 87/601 (fares) and Council Decision 87/602 (capacity and market access), 1987 OJ L 374/12 and 19 respectively. These were in force until June 30, 1990.

the competition rules to air transport (Regulation 3975/87) and enabling legislation (Regulation 3976/87)[213] for temporary block exemptions of certain restrictive practices pending full liberalization. Before adoption of the package, the Commission had started proceedings against several EC airlines for their anticompetitive agreements under the temporary procedural provisions of Article 85.[214] In June 1990 the EC Council agreed to go a stage further in dismantling restrictions on capacity, market access and fares. This second package of liberalization measures was introduced on 1 November 1990.[215] The third package of liberalization was completed on 1 January 1993 (with respect to restrictions on cabotage on 1 April 1997). This third package consists of the following measures:

- Council Regulation 2407/92 on the licensing of air carriers[216] providing, *inter alia*, that a member state must accept onto its national register, without discriminatory fee or delay, aircraft owned by nationals of another member state;
- Council Regulation 2408/92 on access for Community air carriers to intra-Community air routes;[217]
- Council Regulation 2409/92 on fares and rates for air services;[218]
- Council Regulation 2410/92 laying down the procedure for the application of the rules of competition to undertakings in the air transport sector;[219]
- Council Regulation 2411/92 amending Regulation 3976/87 on the application of Article 81 (3) to certain categories of agreements and concerted practices in the air transport sector;[220]
- Council Regulation 95/93/EC on common rules for the allocation of slots at Community airports.[221]

---

213. 1987 OJ L 374/9.
214. Bull. EC 7/8–1986, point 2.1.60; Bull. EC 7/8–1987, point 2.1.90. Sixteenth Report on Competition Policy, point 36; Seventeenth Report on Competition Policy, point 46.
215. Regulations 2342 and 2343/90, 1990 OJ L 217/1 and 8. In December 1989 the member states agreed in principle to end guaranteed capacity allocations for national flag-carrying airlines and the right of a single national government to veto fare applications by 1993. *See* Nineteenth Report on Competition Policy, point 23.
216. 1992 OJ L 240/1.
217. 1992 OJ L 240/8. The Commission intervened against the refusal by the French authorities to license *Viva Air* to operate on the Paris-Madrid route and stated that the French authorities had misapplied Article 8a of Regulation 2408/92: D.Comm. May 28, 1993, 1993 OJ L 140/51 and the *TAT* cases: Paris-London, Paris-Marseille and Paris-Toulouse, D.Comm. April 27, 1994, 1994 OJ L 127/22, 32. *See also* the Commission intervention in cases of '*open skies deals*', bilateral government-to-government agreements granting US airlines access to the European civil aviation market without, however, requesting reciprocal rights to European Union carriers operating in the US which the Commission intends to guarantee by a comprehensive arrangement to be negotiated on behalf of the EU: IP/98/966 of 5 Nov. 1998.
218. 1992 OJ L 240/15.
219. 1992 OJ L 240/18.
220. 1992 OJ L 240/19.
221. 1993 OJ L 14/1.

A further package of liberalization legislation was agreed between the European Parliament and the Council on 10 December 2003[222] which meets two objectives:

- to establish a decision-making and regulatory framework which will improve air safety (in cooperation with Eurocontrol); and
- to reorganize the provision and supervision of air traffic control services.

The Scope of Regulation 3975/87.

Regulation 3975/87 applies, in its amended version of Regulation 1284/91[223] and Regulation 2410/92,[224] to international air services between airports in different Community countries and domestic services within a member state,[225] whereas international services between a Community and a non-EC airport are subject to the Air Transport Regulation 847/2004 adopted by the Council on 26 February 2004.[226] This regulation ensures a more effective and efficient framework for anti-trust proceedings with regard to air transport between the EU and third countries. The effect is to extend the normal rules of Regulation 1/2003 and to empower the Commission to grant block exemptions for certain categories of agreements restricting competition on those routes. The need for a coordinated international air policy was confirmed by the judgments of the Court of Justice in the *Open Sky Agreement* cases.[227]

Regulation 3975/87 v. Regulation 1/2003.

Article 39 of Regulation 1/2003 repeals most of the substantive provisions of Regulation 3975/87, except Article 2 which provides for an exception for certain technical agreements. The opposition procedure of Article 5 and the other procedural provisions are replaced by the new rules of Regulation 1/2003. However, the block exemptions continue to apply.[228] The current regulations are:

---

222. IP/03/1702.
223. 1991 OJ L 122/2 (providing for interim measures against anticompetitive practices).
224. 1992 OJ L 240/19 (extension to internal flights).
225. Thereby excluding groundhandling services (e.g. *Olympic Airways*, D.Comm. Jan. 23, 1985, 1985 OJ L 46/51) and computer reservation systems (e.g. *Sabena*, D.Comm. Nov. 4, 1988, 1988 OJ L 317/47, 50–51), which were subject to Regulation 17 (now Regulation 1/2003).
226. 2004 OJ L 157/7. Prior to this regulation airline transactions having an impact on routes between the EU and third countries were subject to Article 85 which does not confer effective enforcement powers: *Nouvelles Frontieres*, ECJ April 30, 1986, 1986 ECR 1425; *Ahmed Saeed*, ECJ April 11, 1989, 1989 ECR 803, para. 21. The Commission investigated under Article 85 the air alliances *KLM/Northwest* and *Lufthansa/SAS/United Airlines* and closed the proceedings, in the first case with, in the second case without commitments: D.Comm. Oct. 29, 2002, IP/02/1569. In *Midland/United Airlines* the Commission closed its proceedings in view of the larger powers of the UK competition authority in relation to air transport between member states and third countries: Thirty-second Report on Competition Policy, point 111.
227. ECJ Nov. 5, 2002, 2002 ECR I-9855. *See* Regulation 551/2004 on the organisation and use of the airspace in the single European sky, 2004 OJ L 96/20.
228. Article 34 (2) of Regulation 1/2003.

- Regulation 1105/2002[229] renews Regulation 1617/93[230] as amended by Regulation 1324/2001.[231] By Regulation 1617/93 the Commission granted a block exemption for certain categories of restrictive agreements in four areas, joint planning and coordination of airline schedules, joint operation of a scheduled air service on a new or low-density route, consultations on tariffs for the carriage of passengers,[232] and slot allocation[233] and airport scheduling. Regulation 1617/93 was last amended by Regulation 1324/2001, which extended the block exemption in respect of consultations on passenger tariffs (thereby excluding consultation on cargo tariffs[234]), until 30 June 2002 and the block exemption in respect of slot allocation and airport scheduling, until 30 June 2004. Regulation 1105/2002 renews the block exemption of consultations on passenger tariffs (thereby enlarging the data collection system) because the IATA passenger tariff conferences[235] secure an important benefit in form of interlining and without the tariff conferences the consumers would have a smaller choice of flexible fares and smaller airlines might have fewer interlining opportunities. The regulation also extends the block exemption for slot allocation and airport scheduling by Regulation 95/93[236] as amended by Regulation 894/2002.[237] Regulation 1105/2002 and Regulation 894/2002, read together, set out the conditions under which air carriers can take part in the scheduling conferences at which slots at congested airports are allocated.[238]
- Regulation 3652/93[239] replacing Regulation 83/91[240] exempts agreements relating to computerized reservation systems for air transport services. The exemption is subject to conditions to safeguard competition between compu-

229. 2002 OJ L 167.
230. 1993 OJ L 155/18.
231. 2001 OJ L 177/56.
232. *See Ahmed Saeed*, ECJ April 11, 1989, 1989 ECR 803, paras 14–17. The preceding Regulation 2671/88 also exempted revenue pools, but European airlines have now abandoned these in favor of less restrictive arrangements.
233. Slot allocation used to be exempted under Regulation 84/91 (1991 OJ L 10/14) which aimed at reconciling the 'grandfather rights' (right to continue the use of slots in the next period) with provisions allowing new entrants.
234. The reason was that airlines had had, since Council Regulation 3976/87 was adopted, sufficient time to adapt to the new environment and that there was no longer any justification for an exemption and that the prices fixed by tariff conferences appeared to be much higher that the market rates. Therefore the Commission objected to the *IATA Cargo Tariff Consultations* with the effect that the members agreed to fix cargo rates individually by beginning of 2002: Thirty-first Report on Competition Policy, points 144–148.
235. Most of EEA airlines (including all flag carriers) are members of IATA and take part of the twice-yearly conferences where they agree on fares for interline journeys.
236. 1993 OJ L 14/1.
237. 2002 OJ L 142/3.
238. Thirty-second Report on Competition Policy, point 107.
239. 1993 OJ L 333/37.
240. 1991 OJ L 10/9.

terized reservation systems and between air carriers, which necessitates free access to, and free withdrawal from, systems and absence of display bias.[241] According to Article 3, the system vendor has to grant access on an equal and non-discriminatory basis within the available capacity and shall not make it a condition that the participating carrier may not at the same time be a participant in another system.

– Regulation 82/91 exempts agreements between airlines and suppliers of ground handling services, has expired and not been replaced after the full liberalization of these services.[242] On 15 October 1996 the Council adopted a directive on ground-handling activities on airports in the European Union.[243] It provides for opening up to competition ground handling services at airports subject to certain derogations to be approved by the Commission in the event of lack of space or capacity. The application of the competition rules ensures in particular that agreements between airlines and suppliers of airport ground handling services do not oblige air carriers to obtain services exclusively from a particular supplier, that the supply of services is not tied to the conclusion of contracts for other goods or services and that each airline is free to choose from the range of services offered those that it wants to take from a particular supplier.[244] However, this directive must be complemented by applying Articles 81 and 82 against companies or Article 86 against member states where access to airport facilities is prevented by restrictive agreements or abusive practices or by state measures contrary to the competition rules.[245]

Case Law under the Air Transport Regulations.

– *Hindering new entrants to a specific airline market – Slot allocation and interlining*: Interlining agreements are objectionable where interlining is refused to a new entrant on a route operated by dominant airlines. The Commission intervened under Article 82 against such agreements or granted clearance under Article 81 only if interlining facilities are offered to competitors.[246] In the

---

241. *See also Sabena*, D.Comm. Nov. 4, 1988, 1988 OJ L 317/47; Eighteenth Report on Competition Policy, point 28. The EC has now introduced a mandatory code of conduct based on the principle of non-discrimination for all computer reservation systems, including the two joint ventures Amadeus and Galileo: Council Regulation 2299/89, 1989 OJ L 220/1.
242. Twenty-fifth Report on Competition Policy, points 121–122.
243. Council Directive 96/67/EC, 1996 OJ L 272/36; Twenty-sixth Report on Competition Policy, points 121–122.
244. *Brussels Airport*, D.Comm. June 28, 1995, 1995 OJ L 216/8. *Paris Airports*, Twenty-sixth Report on Competition Policy, p. 142; *Olympic Airways*, Twenty-sixth Report on Competition Policy, point 129.
245. Twenty-sixth Report on Competition Policy, point 129.
246. The Commission grants clearance only if access of competitors is not unduly prevented, *see Lufthansa/SAS*, D.Comm. Jan. 16, 1996, 1996 OJ L 54/28; *Austrian Airlines/Lufthansa*, D.Comm. July 5, 2002, 2002 OJ L 242/25; *Air France/Alitalia*, D.Comm. April 7, 2004, COMP/38.284.

absence of a regulation extending the Commission's powers to routes linking the Community to non-member countries[247] the Commission intervened under Article 85 against certain bilateral alliances likely to foreclose competitors by their interlining.[248] The Commission is unlikely to oppose to the setting-up of an airline joint venture by non-airline companies.[249]

- *Air Alliances*: The Commission normally approves air alliances under Article 81 provided they do not prevent access by competitors, in terms of landing rights and/or slots, to the relevant market (which are the destinations served jointly by the partners to the alliance).[250] However, certain air alliances may be so wide-ranging that the Commission regards the alliance as a merger to be assessed under the merger control regulation and may be cleared only under substantive commitments in order to prevent the creation of a dominant position on certain routes.[251] In the *Air France/Alitalia* case[252] the Commission granted clearance only after having obtained commitments to make available to competitors a number of of take-off and landing slots aimed at supporting new services on seven routes and to allow new entrants to participate in their frequent flyer programs.
- *Computer reservation systems*: Regulation 2652/93 contains a block exemption of agreements on computer reservation systems, provided access to this system is granted to airlines on non-discriminatory and reasonable terms. Agreements leading to unjustified refusal of access is likely to infringe Article 82[253] or will be cleared only if non-discriminatory and reasonable access is guaranteed.[254]
- *Open access to ground handling market*: Council Directive 96/67/EC[255] provides for a gradual opening of ground handling (passenger, baggage, freight,

247. *See* however the Commission's proposal, COM(2003).
248. *British Airways/American Airlines*, *Lufthansa/United*, *Swissair/Sabena*, *Austrian Airlines/Delta*, *KLM/Northwest*, Twenty-seventh Report on Competition Policy, point 92; Twenty-eighth Report on Competition Policy, points 101–104; 1998 OJ C 239/5 and 10.
249. *Premiair*, D.Comm. 18 Dec. 1995, Twenty-fifth Report on Competition Policy, p. 134 (applying the opposition procedure of Regulation 3975/87).
250. Exemption subject to substantive commitments: *Lufthansa/SAS*, D.Comm. Jan. 16, 1996, 1996 OJ L 54/28; *Austrian Airlines/Lufthansa*, D.Comm. July 5, 2002, 2002 OJ L 242/25; *British Airways/Brussels Airlines*, D.Comm. March 10, 2003, IP/03/350 (comfort letter).
251. *See Alitalia/KLM*, D.Comm. Aug. 11, 1999, JV. 19. The commitments go further than undertakings obtained at the time of *Sabena/Swiss Air* merger (1995 OJ C 200) or *Lufthansa/SAS*, D.Comm. Jan. 16, 1996, 1996 OJ L 54/28 (clearance under Article 81). *See also SAS/Spanair*, D.Comm. March 5, 2002, M.2672.
252. *Air France/Alitalia*, D.Comm. April 7, 2004, COMP/38.284.
253. *London European/Sabena*, D.Comm. Nov. 4, 1988, 1988 OJ L 317/47; point 31 (fine of ECU 100.000). *See also*, under Articles 8 and 16 of Council Regulation 2299/89 on a code of conduct for computerized reservation systems (1999 OJ L 220/1): *Lufthansa*, D.Comm. July 20, 1999, IP/99/542 (fine of EUR 10,000).
254. *ACRISS*, 1993 OJ C 149/9; *Amadeus/Sabre*, IP/91/784 of Aug. 2, 1991; *Sabre/Air France and Iberia*, Twenty-third Report on Competition Policy, point 238.
255. 1996 OJ L 272/36.

mail, ramp handling and catering services) to competition.[256] The Commission intervened in cases of unjustified refusal of access by the airport administration.[257] In a second phase the Commission intervened against the application of discriminatory landing charges or discounts.[258]

- *Prohibiting tariff fixing and market sharing*: Article 81 (1) is clearly infringed if airlines agree on common cargo rates,[259] whereas fixing passenger rates remains, for the time being, block exempted. However, the Commission did not oppose to a global freight exchange distribution channel set up by *Lufthansa, British Airways and Air France*.[260] Article 81 (1) is also clearly infringed if two airlines agree on sharing markets (instead of merely interlining).[261]
- Prohibiting fidelity rebates under Article 82: The Commission has held that British Airways infringed Article 82 for having abused its dominant position by granting travel agents in the UK fidelity rebates, which prevented competitors, such as Virgin Airlines, from obtaining fair access to customers. [262] The Court of First Instance affirmed the decision.[263]

---

256. Twenty-sixth Report on Competition Policy, point 128.
257. Under Article 82: *Airport of Frankfurt I*, D.Comm. Jan. 14,1998,1998 OJ L 72/30; Under Articles 86/82: *Olympic Airways*, Twenty-sixth Report on Competition Policy, point 129.
258. Under Article 82: *Airport Frankfurt II*, IP/98/ of Sept. 8, 1998 (intervention against long-term groundhandling service agreements replacing the former monopoly); *Aeroports de Paris* (*Roissy, Charles-de-Gaulle and Orly*), D.Comm. June 11, 1998, 1998 OJ L 230/10, *aff'd* CFI Dec. 12, 2000, 2000 ECR II-3929; *Ilmailulaitos/Luftfartsverket (Finnish Airports)*, D.Comm. Feb. 10, 1999, 1999 OJ L 69/24 (application of discriminatory rebates for ground-handling services); under Article 82 in conjunction with Article 86: *Brussels National Airport*, D.Comm. June 28, 1995, 1995 OJ L 216/8 applying reductions of 50% and 60% for domestic flights); *Portuguese Airports*, D.Comm. Feb. 10, 1999, 1999 OJ L 69/31; *Airport of Athens*, Twenty-seventh Report on Competition Policy, p. 166; *Brussels Airport*, Twenty-fifth Report on Competition Policy, point 120; *Spanish Airports*, D.Comm. July 26, 2000, 2000 OJ L 208/36.
259. *P&O*, *Stena-Sealink*, *Brittany Ferries*, *Sea France* and *North Sea Ferries*, D.Comm. Oct. 30, 1996, 1997 OJ L 26/23 (agreement on the amount and introduction date of a surcharge on freight shipments following the devaluation of the pound sterling; fine of ECU 645,000).
260. Thirty-second Report on Competition Policy, point 116.
261. *SAS/Maersk*, D.Comm. July 18, 2001, 2001 OJ L 265/15 (fines of EUR 52.5 million).
262. *Virgin Airlines/British Airways*, D.Comm. July 14, 1999, 2000 OJ L 30/1 (fines of EUR 6.8 million), *aff'd* CFI Dec. 17, 2003, T-219/99, para. 244.
263. *British Airways*, CFI Dec. 17, 2003, T-219/99, paras. 232–249. The Court also confirmed (para. 100) that the relevant market was that of services of air travel agencies (subject to Regulation 17) which is distinct from the air transport market (subject to Regulation 3975/87). However, this distinction is no longer pertinent because both markets are now subject to Regulation 1/2003.

D. Banking, Insurance and Securities

1. General

Changing Regulatory Framework.
Banking and insurance in the EC are extensively regulated. The regulation is undertaken partly for prudential reasons, i.e., to protect the consumer and maintain confidence in the financial system generally, and partly for purposes of economic management. Thus, there is prudential supervision of such matters as banks' capital and insurance companies' policy conditions and premium rates and there is control of bank lending, interest rates and capital transfers for economic policy reasons. The differences in national regulations have been a major obstacle to the integration of national markets. However, these barriers have been largely removed as result of harmonization directives aiming at a unified financial services market (Monetary Union) under the Maastricht Treaty, which is referred to below.

EC Competition Rules Applicable despite Extensive Regulation.
The Court of Justice has rejected the argument that the extensive regulation of banking and insurance takes them outside the scope of the EC competition rules.[264] Application of the competition rules is perfectly compatible with prudential supervision. The Community competition rules are applicable even if in the context of a particular national supervisory regime the application of national competition law is relaxed.[265] Nor does the regulation of banking as part of national economic management justify private anticompetitive agreements between banks. For instance, the control of international capital transfers by banks for balance-of-payments reasons and the required coordination of national balance-of-payments policies under Articles 101–111 of the EC Treaty do not entitle banks to set common scales of charges for international transfers.[266] Banks and insurance companies may be covered by the exemption from the competition rules provided for by Article 86 (2) insofar as they are entrusted with tasks of general economic interest, e.g. where credit institutions of a comprehensive financial infrastructure provide territorial coverage of essential services in remote or inaccessible areas. The 1998 Report of the Council of Ministers on services of general economic interest in the banking sector[267] concluded that certain credit institutions fulfil tasks

264. *Fire Insurance*, ECJ Jan. 27, 1987, 1987 ECR 405, paras 22–24. *See* Twenty-seventh Report on Competition Policy, point 95.
265. *Ibid.*, para. 23.
266. *Züchner*, ECJ July 14, 1981, 1981 ECR 2021, paras 6–8; *Eurocheques – Helsinki Agreement*, D.Comm. March 25, 1992, 1992 OJ L 95/50 (in substance confirmed by CFI Feb. 23, 1994, 1994 ECR II-49, para. 85).
267. Commission Communication on services of general interest, 2001 OJ C 17/4, point 35.

that constitute services of general interest, but that the compatibility with Article 86 (2) must be assessed on a case-to-case basis.

Government-Induced Distortions.

In a regulated industry it is often difficult to determine whether an anticompetitive practice is the result of action by the regulatory authorities or is the responsibility of the companies concerned. Firms can be called to account under Articles 81 or 82 for conduct that is merely tolerated or approved, but not required, by the state.[268] If the government induces the anticompetitive practice the Commission must take action against the government either under Article 86 (3) (if the firms concerned are government-owned or controlled or have been granted special or exclusive rights by the government) or under Article 226 in conjunction with Article 10, 12 or 31. The Commission first exercised its power under Article 86 (3) to order an individual member state to terminate a requirement placed on public enterprises to infringe the competition rules, contrary to Article 86 (1), in the *Greek Insurance* case.[269] In this case legislation provided that all public property in Greece must be insured by a Greek state-owned insurance company (a market which generated 25% of total premium income) and also obliged state banks (which provided around 80% of total bank credit) to recommend to customers seeking a loan to take out the insurance they required from a state-owned company. The preferential treatment accorded to state-owned companies by these government measures discriminated against both private Greek insurers and Greek subsidiaries or branches of insurance companies from other member states in a manner contrary to Article 86 (1).

2. BANKING

Regulatory Framework.

The main liberalization measure in banking is the First Banking Council Directive 77/780/EC[270] and the Second Banking Council Directive 89/646/EC.[271] Other measures include Council Directive 89/647/EC on the coefficient of solvency.[272]

---

268. *See* Second Report on Competition Policy, point 54 (standard terms of insurance contracts); *Eycke/ASPA*, ECJ Sept. 21, 1988, 1988 ECR 4769 (interest rates on savings accounts); *Consorzio Industrie Fiammiferi*, ECJ Sept. 9, 2003, C-198/01, paras. 45–46.
269. *Greek Insurance*, D.Comm. April 24, 1985, 1985 OJ L 152/25; Fifteenth Report on Competition Policy, point 258; Sixteenth Report on Competition Policy, point 293. Greece's appeal against this decision was dismissed because it was out of time. After Greece still failed to comply, the Commission brought Article 226 proceedings in which the Court found against Greece: *Greek Insurance*, ECJ June 30, 1988, 1988 ECR 3611.
270. 1977 OJ L 322/30.
271. 1989 OJ 386/1.
272. 1989 OJ L 386/14, as amended in 1996 OJ L 85/17.

Target Payment System of the European System of Central Banks ('ESCB').
The target system which is to come into operation at the beginning of the third stage of the economic and monetary union and will be run by the ESCB[273] concerns three categories of payments: payments directly related to monetary policy and involving the ESCB, interbank payments (arbitrage transactions) and payments involving bank customers. The Commission took the view that Article 81 (1) does not apply to payments of the first category (since they are directly related to monetary policy[274]), but does apply to payments of the second and the third categories (since they involve economic operators and customers).[275]

Procompetitive Cross-Border Cooperation between Banks.
Cooperation arrangements between banks which aim at improving cross-border credit transfer services are viewed favourably in the Commission's notice of 27 September 1995.[276] The notice provides guidelines as to how banks can set up cooperation agreements, provided they do not restrain market entry and do not eliminate competition between participating banks. In light of this notice the Commission cleared the *ECU Banking Association's* clearing and settlements system for ECU (now EUR) transactions.[277] Particular interest was paid to price competition, in particular multilateral interchange-fees.[278] Bilateral cooperation agreements may also qualify for exemption under Article 81 (3). In the *Banque Nationale de Paris/Dresdner Bank* case[279] the Commission exempted a worldwide cooperation agreement between the fourth ranking bank in France and the second ranking bank in Germany on their close cooperation leading to an improvement

---

273. *See* Article 4 (a).
274. *See Züchner*, ECJ July 14, 1981, 1981 ECR 2021, paras 6–7, and Sixteenth Report on Competition Policy, point 58, where the Commission reserved its position as to whether banks' policy on interest rates falls under Article 86 (2). Similarly, the Court of Justice ruled that agreements on standard bank conditions, in so far as they enable banks, in contracts for the opening of a current-account credit facility, to change the interest rate at any time for objective reasons, such as changes occurring in the money market, do not have as their object or effect the restriction of competition: *Bagnasco/Associazione Bancaria Italiana*, ECJ Jan. 21, 1999, 1999 ECR I-135, para. 37.
275. Twenty-seventh Report on Competition Policy, point 95.
276. 1995 OJ C 251/3. The Commission's Recommendation 90/109/EC (1990 OJ L 67/39) concerned the transparency of cross-frontier transactions.
277. Twenty-sixth Report on Competition Policy, point 109. This notice is part of a package of measures, including Directive 97/5/EC on cross-border transactions, 1997 OJ L 43/25.
278. *Danish Bankers Association*, *IBOS* and *Eurogiro*, Twenty-sixth Report on Competition Policy, point 109 and pp. 129–130. *See*, however, *Dutch Association of Banks*, D.Comm. Sept. 8, 1999, 1999 OJ L 271/28, points 57–65 (negative clearance concerning an agreement on uniform acceptance giro systems, which was incapable of appreciably affecting trade between member states).
279. D.Comm. June 24, 1996, 1996 OJ L 188/37.

of the distribution of their services after the territorial exclusivity had been removed.

Agreements on Commissions and Restrictions on Market Access Prohibited. Agreements on charges for international money transfers may infringe Article 81 (1) according to the *Züchner* decision of the Court of Justice and the Commission's Notice on Cross-border credit transfer systems.[280] The Commission has challenged agreements on uniform commissions for services to customers and on the value date at which fund transfers are debited or credited.[281] In 1998/1999, at the eve of the introduction of the Euro replacing the national currencies, the Commission started surprise inspections in seven member states which unearthed institutionalized price-fixing schemes. Although the vast majority of banks agreed on a substantial reduction in the charges,[282] the Commission imposed heavy fines on five German banks (EUR 100.8 million)[283] for fixing minimum charges for the exchange of euro-zone currencies and on eight Austrian banks (EUR 124.26 million)[284] for their participation in a price fixing scheme which covered the whole of Austria and all banking products and services.

Further case law includes the *Sarabex* case where the Commission secured amendments to agreements endorsed by the Bank of England between British banks and foreign exchange brokers which restricted the access of non-member firms to the British foreign exchange brokering market.[285] In the *VISA* cases the Commission intervened against exclusive dealing arrangements preventing banks from offering alternative systems and against cross-border exchange fees (interbanking payment made for each transaction carried out under a payment card).[286] Under Article 82 the Commission intervened against the application of discriminatory admission criteria by SWIFT (Society for Worldwide International Financial Telecommunications), which is owned by 2000 banks and aims at an international telecommunications network transferring payment messages specializing in the supply of data transmission and processing services, and granted clearance only after substantial amendments.[287] In the *Clearstream* case the Commission adopted

280. *Züchner*, ECJ July 14, 1981, 1981 ECR 2021, paras 6–8.
281. *Irish Banks*, D.Comm. Sept. 30, 1986, 1986 OJ L 295/28, 29; 1987–2 CMLR 601, 604; *Dutch Banks*, D.Comm. 19 July 1989, 1989 OJ L 253/1, 4–5; *Eurocheque III – Helsinki Agreement*, D.Comm. 25 March 1992, 1992 OJ L 95/50 (in substance upheld by CFI 23 Feb. 1994, 1994 ECR II-49).
282. *See* IP/01/1796 of Dec. 11, 2001.
283. *German Banks*, D.Comm. Dec. 11, 2001, 2003 OJ L 15/1. By contrast, other banks in Germany and other member states reduced their charges to make good vis-à-vis consumers.
284. *Austrian Banks*, D.Comm. June 11, 2002, 2004 OJ L 56/1 ('Lombard Club').
285. *Sarabex*, Eighth Report on Competition Policy, points 35–37; 1979–2 CMLR 262.
286. *Amex, Dean Witter/VISA,* Twenty-sixth Report on Competition Policy, pp. 140–141 (settlement); *VISA International,* D.Comm. July 24 , 2002, 2003 OJ L 84/1 (exemption granted for five-years and subject to substantial amendmends).
287. *SWIFT,* Twenty-seventh Report on Competition Policy, point 68 (settlement).

a decision finding that *Clearstream Banking AG*, the only final custodian of German securities, abused its dominant position as a necessary trading partner for security traders by refusing to supply clearing and settlement services to the German Euroclear Bank during more than two years and by charging an unjustified higher per transaction price to Euroclear Bank than to other securities depositories outside Germany.[288]

Agreements on Interest Rates Beginning to be Challenged.
The Commission has not yet taken action against agreements between banks on the rates of interest charged on overdrawn accounts or paid on positive balances. These rates are influenced by the base lending rates set by national monetary authorities. In many cases the arrangements appear to be more in the nature of guidelines or recommendations than binding agreements.[289] In the *Eycke/ASPA* case,[290] however, the Court held that interbank agreements on maximum interest rates and bonuses paid on savings deposits would infringe Article 81. In the *Eurochèque – Helsinki Agreements* case[291] the Commission imposed a fine under Article 81 and Regulation 17 against the Groupement des Cartes Bancaires which represents all the French banks, members of the Eurocheque system, for concluding an agreement under which they charged French retailers the same commission for cashing foreign Eurocheques as they charged for payments by bank card. However, the Commission seems to accept under Article 81 (3) agreements between banks on an interchange fee limited to the average real costs in case of credit transfers where the sender has asked to bear the costs and the beneficiary's bank cannot charge an additional fee for handling the cross-border transfer.[292] National interbank agreements on operations which are limited to a single member state are unlikely to affect trade between member states and therefore only subject to national competition law.[293] However, price fixing agreements which extend to the entire territory of a member state are normally caught by Article 81. The Commission imposed fines on German banks for having participated in an agreement whose object was to fix the charges for the exchange of in-currency banknotes (i.e. a percentage commission) and a target price level of about 3% to achieve a 90% exchange margin income recovery.[294] The most institutionalized price-fixing

288. *Clearstream Banking,* D.Comm. June 2, 2004, IP/04/705 (declaratory decision without fines in order to clarify a novel legal question).
289. Sixteenth Report on Competition Policy, point 58. *See also Italian Banks*, D.Comm. 12 Dec. 1986, 1987 OJ L 43/51, 53–54; *Dutch Banks*, D.Comm. July 19, 1989, 1989 OJ L 253/1, 3.
290. *Eycke/ASPA*, ECJ Sept. 21, 1988, 1988 ECR 4769; 1990–4 CMLR 330.
291. *Interbank Agreements*, Twenty-second Report on Competition Policy, p. 437.
292. *See Groupement des cartes Bancaires*, 2003 OJ C 80/13 (intention to grant a comfort letter with respect to the amended system); *OUR*, Twenty-fifth Report on Competition Policy, point 48.
293. *Bagnasco/Associazione Bancaria Italiana*, ECJ Jan. 21, 1999, 1999 ECR I-135, para. 53.
294. *German Banks*, D.Comm. Dec. 11, 2001, 2003 OJ L 15/1 (fines of EUR 100.8 million).

cartel was that of eight Austrian banks which covered the entire the entire Austrian territory 'down to the smallest village' with a view of fixing deposit, lending and other rates.[295]

Exemption of Agreements Not Affecting Relations with Customers.
The Commission has exempted interbank agreements on electronic links (the 'Inter-Bank Online System'),[296] on the collection and acceptance of notes, cheques and similar instruments,[297] on simplified clearance procedures for cheques denominated in national and foreign currencies, and on commissions for securities dealings and foreign exchange transfers,[298] on the ground that they promoted standardization, concerned only relations between banks and set only maximum commissions that were not necessarily passed on to consumers. Likewise, the Commission exempted the agreements between the banks that are members of the Eurocheque system, a European-wide payment medium through cheques guaranteed by cheque card. The agreement required members to contract only with authorized firms for the production and finishing of Eurocheques and Eurocheque cards.[299] However, the Commission has imposed fines against agreements fixing identical commissions for cashing foreign Eurocheques.[300]

Negative Clearances for Technical Cooperation.
The Commission has granted negative clearances for agreements on technical cooperation between banks on matters such as:

- the time limits for the execution of international bank transfers, on the ground that the agreements did not restrict competition among banks;[301]
- automatic teller machines, settlement of obligations among banks, standing orders for payment of gas, electricity and telephone bills, foreign exchange dealing, and minimum charges for renting safes and for safe deposit services,

---

295. *Austrian Banks*, D.Comm. June 11, 2002, 2004 OJ L 56/1 (fines of EUR 124.26 million).
296. *IBOS*, Twenty-sixth Report on Competition Policy, p. 129.
297. *Italian Banks*, D.Comm. Dec. 12, 1986, 1987 OJ L 43/51, 57 and 60.
298. *Dutch Banks*, D.Comm. July 19, 1989, 1989 OJ L 253/1, 9–11; *Belgian Banks*, D.Comm. Dec. 11, 1986, 1987 OJ L 7/27, 32–34. In the case *Danish Bankers' Association* (Twenty-sixth Report on Competition Policy, p. 130) the Commission issued a negative clearance because it was *de minimis* (lack of appreciable restriction).
299. *Eurocheques II*, D.Comm. Dec. 19, 1988, 1989 OJ L 36/16.
300. *Eurocheques III – Helsinki Agreement*, D.Comm. March 25, 1992, 1992 OJ L 95/50; *aff'd* CFI Feb. 23, 1994, 1994 ECR II-49. In its previous decision *Eurocheques I*, D.Comm. Dec. 10, 1984, 1985 OJ L 35/43, the Commission accepted, under certain conditions, the clause that no deduction of the fee should be made from the face value at the time of encashment by the foreign banks or retailers. Similarly, the Commission challenged the minimum fee for cross-border payment agreed within the *Eurogiro* grouping European post/girobanks: Twenty-sixth Report on Competition Policy, p. 130.
301. *Italian Banks*, D.Comm. Dec. 12, 1986, 1987 OJ L 43/51, 56–57.

on the ground that they were unlikely to affect trade between the member states even though they could have anticompetitive effects.[302]

Similarly, the Commission has not objected to non-exclusive cooperation agreements between loose groupings of banks in different countries[303] or to agreements on uniform opening hours.[304]

Cooperation Agreements Likely to be Challenged.
The Commission challenged under Article 81 an agreement on the joint control of the Belgian bank Banque Bruxelles Lambert by an insurance and a banking group because each of the parties might make allowance in its decision for the financial interests of the other and gain access to confidential information and adapt its own behavior accordingly.[305] In general, however, arrangements involving operators active in both banking services and insurance are indicative of the growing links between these two sectors, prompting the Commission to look closely at their conglomerate aspects, in particular at the overlap of activities of the parties and competitors.[306] However, joint ventures created between banks may also be 'full function', which must be assessed under the merger control regulation.[307]

3. INSURANCE

Regulatory Framework.
Liberalization legislation in the insurance sector includes: Council Directives 73/239/EC[308] and 88/357/EEC on non-life insurance,[309] Council Directives 79/267/EC,[310] 90/619/EC[311] and 92/96/EC on life insurance[312] and the Commission's Recommendation 92/48/CE on insurance intermediaries.[313]

---

302. *Dutch Banks*, D.Comm. July 20, 1989, 1989 OJ L 253/1, 8–10.
303. *Groupement des cartes Bancaires*, D.Comm. April 3, 2002, 2003 OJ C 80/13 (comfort letter). *See* Eighth Report on Competition Policy, point 33.
304. *Irish Banks*, D.Comm. Sept. 30, 1986, 1986 OJ L 295/28, 30.
305. *Banque Bruxelles Lambert* (*BBL*), Twenty-seventh Report on Competition Policy, pp. 154–155. The case was however wound up after BBL's takeover by another group.
306. *See Fortis/Meers Pierson*, D.Comm. Feb. 6, 1997; *Fortis/ASLK-CGER*, D.Comm. Oct. 2, 1997; *Crédit Suisse/Winterthur*, D.Comm. Oct. 15, 1997; *Merita/Nordbanken*, D.Comm. Dec. 10, 1997; Twenty-seventh Report on Competition Policy, pp. 183–184.
307. E.g. *Lazard/Intersabci/JV*, D.Comm. Feb. 4, 2003, M.2982, points 13–14.
308. 1973 OJ L 28/3.
309. 1988 OJ L 172/1.
310. 1979 OJ L 63/1.
311. 1990 OJ L 330/50.
312. 1992 OJ L 360/1.
313. 1992 OJ L 19/32.

Insurance Block Exemption.
Based on Regulation 1534/91[314] the Commission adopted block exemption Regulation 3932/92[315] which expired on 31 March 2003 and is replaced by Regulation 358/2003 which applies up to 31 March 2010.[316] The regulation was not substantially amended. It covers:

- *Joint carrying-out of studies of risks and exchange of statistical information for the calculation of risks.*[317] Joint calculation of costs and the carrying-out of studies and statistics is, as under Regulation 3932/92, exempted provided they are purely illustrative, do not identify the insurance undertakings concerned and do not include loadings for contingencies, income deriving from reserves, costs comprising commissions payable to intermediaries or the anticipated profit and do not preclude insurance companies from differing from these calculations or tables. This follows from the previous case law of the Commission and the Court of Justice ruling that concerted practices on commercial tariffs, i.e. the premiums actually charged to policyholders and comprising a loading to cover administrative and commercial costs, are not exemptible even if the pure premium tariffs were purely indicative.[318] Even an exchange of detailed tariff information between national associations of insurers in different member states about premiums[319] and a clause prohibiting insurance brokers from passing on part of their commission to customers[320] may be objectionable and preclude applicability of the block exemption.

---

314. 1991 OJ L 143/1.
315. 1992 OJ L 398/7. *See* Report on the block exemption in the field of insurance, COM/1999/192 of 12 May 1999.
316. 2003 OJ L 53/8.
317. Articles 3–4 of Regulation 358/2003. Precedents: *Fire Insurance Germany*, D.Comm. Dec. 5, 1984, 1985 OJ L 35/20 (cease and desist order); *Concordato Incendio*, D.Comm. Dec. 20, 1989, 1990 OJ L 15/25 (exemption).
318. *Fire Insurance*, ECJ Jan. 27, 1987, 1987 ECR 405 (imposing collective across-the-board increase in premiums when these had fallen below costs); *Nuovo CEGAM*, D.Comm. March 30, 1984, 1984 OJ L 99/29 (agreement amended to cover only basic premium rates and to remove other anticompetitive features); *Assuropol*, D.Comm. Jan. 14, 1992, 1992 OJ L 92/1; *Lloyd's Underwriters Association*, D.Comm. Dec. 4, 1992, 1993 OJ L 4/26; similarly, *TEKO*, D.Comm. Dec. 20, 1989, 1990 OJ L 13/34; *Concordato Incendio*, D.Comm. Dec. 20, 1989, 1990 OJ L 15/25. *See also Irish Insurance Intermediaries*, 1987 OJ C 120/5 (agreement between insurers on maximum commissions to intermediaries).
319. Second Report on Competition Policy, point 56. *See also P&I Clubs I*, D.Comm. Dec. 16, 1985, 1985 OJ L 376/2, where the Commission required the elimination of restrictions that made it unattractive to transfer insurance from one club to another and the relaxation of restrictions on premium rates. In *P&I Clubs II* (D.Comm. April 12, 1999, 1999 OJ L 125/12, point 116) concerning marine protection and indemnity ('P&I'), the Commission exempted the recommendation on minimum costs for tankers, as far as they apply to retention costs.
320. *Cf. Flemish Travel Agents*, ECJ Oct. 1, 1987, 1987 ECR 3801, in which the Court found the statutory endorsement of a similar ban on travel agents passing on commission to be contrary to Article 10 of the EC Treaty in conjunction with Article 81.

- *Joint establishment of non-binding standard policy conditions.*[321] The advantage to the consumer of non-binding policy conditions is that it fosters comparability of coverage for the consumer and allowing risks to be classified more uniformly, provided that the conditions are not binding but serve only as models and that they do not exclude systematically particular types of coverage.[322] These reservations are based on the Commission's previous practice, as in the case *P&I Clubs*[323] grouping mutual associations of ship owners and charters which insure their members against third-party liability and certain contractual liabilities connected with ship operation. Previously the Commission required the elimination of restrictions that made it unattractive to transfer insurance from one club to another and the relaxation of restrictions on premium rates. As amended, the system afforded greater scope for competition between the insurance clubs on premiums, although some restrictions on premiums and on the timing of transfers to a new club remained.
- *Joint setting-up and operation of insurance pools.*[324] Such pools allow a greater number of insurance companies to enter the market by increasing the capacity for covering risks that are difficult to cover individually because of their scale, rarity or novelty. [325] However, the exemption is subject to market share limits which have been increased from 10 to 20% for co-insurance and from 15 to 25% for reinsurance pools.[326]
- *Agreements between insurers on technical specifications for safety equipment.*[327] Such specifications are justified provided the insurance undertakings are free to accept other security devices. Agreements may also not be covered by Article 81 (1) at all, in particular when the risks involved (e.g. catastrophic

321. Articles 5–6 of Regulation 358/2003.
322. Precedent: *Concordato Incendio*, D.Comm. Dec. 20, 1989, 1990 OJ L 15/25.
323. *P&I Clubs I*, D.Comm. Dec. 16, 1985, 1985 OJ L 376/2. In *P&I Clubs II*, D.Comm. April 14, 1999, 1999 OJ L 125/12, the Commission granted a negative clearance (with regard to the claim sharing agreement and the restrictions necessary to the proper functioning of this claim-sharing) and exemption under Article 81 (3) (with regard to the quotation procedures, however only after modification of the original restrictions preventing the P&I Clubs from setting rates freely and after adoption of a new minimum common level of cover capable of meeting the shipowners' needs).
324. Article 7–8 of Regulation 358/2003.
325. Twenty-second Report on Competition Policy, point 282. Such agreements (including loss-sharing) have generally been accepted by the Commission (except in case of dominant influence) because they reduce the administrative complexity of the settlement of claims and the length of the reimbursement procedures although it may be argued that the policyholder's negotiating position is considerably affected.
326. Individual exemption granted despite 'substantially' higher market shares in *P&I Clubs II*, D.Comm. April 12, 1999, 1999 OJ L 125/12, points 104 and 113–115. Negative clearance: *Aviation Pools*, Twenty-eighth Report on Competition Policy, points 111—115.
327. Article 9 of Regulation 358/2003.

risks) cannot be covered profitably by one single insurer, therefore requiring the pooling of capacity of different insurers.[328]

Restrictions on Market Access Challenged.
Restrictions on market access are not expressly blacklisted by the regulation. However, they have been challenged in the Commission's practice in several cases besides the *Greek Insurance* case described above.[329] An agreement in Luxembourg which restricted the operation of foreign motor insurance loss-adjusters was abandoned under pressure from the Commission, and the market opened up to firms from other member states.[330] Restrictive arrangements between insurance companies on loss-adjusting for road accident claims in Italy were at issue in the *Ameyde/UCI* case,[331] which also illustrated the difficulty of disentangling the effect of regulatory requirements, which may or may not be open to challenge under Articles 49 and 50 as unjustified restrictions on free cross-frontier provision of services, from that of private restrictions of competition.[332] The currently limited interpenetration of national insurance markets – likely to change with the liberalization moves now under way[333] – make further contractual restrictions particularly serious.[334]

4. SECURITIES MARKETS

Council Market Abuse Directive.
The Council's Market Abuse Directive on trading in securities was adopted on 3 December 2002.[335] The directive aims at reinforcing market integrity, contributing to the harmonization of the rules against market abuse throughout Europe, establishing a strong commitment to transparency and equal treatment of market participants and requiring closer cooperation and a higher degree of exchange of information between national authorities. The directive covers both insider dealing and market manipulation and applies to all transactions admitted to trading on at least one regulated securities market in the EU, including primary markets.

---

328. Individual exemption granted despite 'substantially' higher market shares than 15%: *P&I Clubs II*, D.Comm. April 12, 1999, 1999 OJ L 125/12, points 104 and 113–115. Negative clearance: *Aviation Pools*, Twenty-eigth Report on Competition Policy, points 111–115.
329. *Greek Insurance*, D.Comm. April 24, 1985, 1985 OJ L 152/25.
330. *Motor Vehicle Assessors*, Fifteenth Report on Competition Policy, point 71.
331. *Ameyde/UCI*, ECJ June 9, 1977, 1977 ECR 1091, paras 18–24.
332. In the insurance (free provision of cross-frontier services) case, *Commission v. Germany*, ECJ Dec. 4, 1986, 1986 ECR 3755, para. 41, the Court held that some regulatory requirements that restricted the provision of cover by foreign insurers were justified in the present unharmonized state of Community law.
333. *See supra* section D.I.
334. *Fire Insurance*, ECJ Jan. 27, 1987, 1987 ECR 405, 459, para. 49.
335. IP/02/1789.

Each member state must designate a single administrative regulatory and supervisory authority with a minimum set of responsibilities to tackle insider trading and market manipulation.

E. Energy

1. Applicability of EC Competition Rules

No Statutory Exception.
The EC competition rules apply in principle to the whole energy sector, including the coal industry which was subject to the competition rules of the ECSC Treaty up to 22 July 2002, but is now subject to the general competition rules of the EC Treaty.[336] In the nuclear industry the EC competition rules are applicable except where they are overridden by special provisions of the Euratom Treaty, in particular Articles 67–76 on prices and supply of nuclear materials.[337] There are no statutory exceptions for the oil, electricity and gas industries. However, state monopolies and, in particular, the exclusive export and import rights granted to them are subject to the principle of free movement of goods,[338] which also applies to state monopolies (Article 31) within the limits of public service obligations under Article 86 (2) and Article 16.[339]

2. Special Features of the Energy Market

Different Market Conditions within the Community.
The 'energy market' is in fact a collection of markets for energy suitable for different uses, namely as a raw material, as a fuel or as power. In some of these markets different types of energy compete with one another (e.g., coal, oil, gas and electricity for heating); others are captive to one type of energy (e.g., road transport to oil). Geographically, the degree of integration of EC energy markets

---

336. Article 305 of the EC Treaty establishes the principle of subsidiarity of the ECSC Treaty, which implies the applicability of the EC rules after the expiry of the ECSC Treaty. *See*, with regard to state aids in the steel sector, Sixth Steel Code, D.Comm. 2496/96, 1996 OJ L 338. Administratively, the coal and steel sector is now already integrated into the units dealing with antitrust cases in related sectors.
337. Article 305 (2) of the EC Treaty. For instance, Articles 81 and 82 apply fully to the reprocessing of nuclear fuels: *United Reprocessors* and *KEWA*, D.Comm. Dec. 123, 975, 1976 OJ L 51/7 and 15; Sixteenth Report on Competition Policy, point 69, and to the production and distribution of radioactive materials for research and medical purposes; *Amersham/Buchler*, D.Comm. Oct. 129, 982, 1982 OJ L 314/34.
338. Electricity is considered as 'good': *Almelo*, ECJ April 27, 1994, 1994 ECR I-1477, para. 28.
339. *See* Commission's Communication on services of general interest of 19 January 2001, 2001 OJ C 17/4, points 37–39 and p. 20.

varies from significant in the case of crude oil and refined oil products to low in those of coal (because of insufficient price differences for Community-produced coal to make transport worthwhile)[340] and electricity and gas (because of import restrictions by electricity and gas utilities).

Barriers to Greater Market Integration.
The energy sector is characterized by the existence of natural monopolies: The distribution of electricity and gas requires a fixed infrastructure of transmission lines and pipelines, which is generally owned by suppliers holding a monopoly or a dominant position in their national or local market and cannot be duplicated in an economically feasable way.[341] The national electricity grids and gas pipeline networks are already interconnected in most of the Community; most recently the United Kingdom has been linked to the continental gas network by the pipeline between Norfolk and Zeebrugge (Belgium).[342] The interconnection with other national grids or pipeline networks improves security of supply against the risk of breakdown or disruption and reduces requirements of capacity to meet peak demand levels or as a reserve for emergencies. However, hitherto the national electricity and gas utilities which own the grids and pipelines have been able to control the amount of electricity and gas imported and to determine the price at which it is resold independently of the price level in other member states. As a result, despite substantial price differences between member states national suppliers are still largely insulated from import competition.

Fragmentation of National Markets.
The electricity and gas markets in particular tend to be fragmented along national lines.[343] The barriers to greater integration, which is thought likely to yield considerable economic benefits, have several causes. In some energy sectors, the infrastructure required (e.g., the electricity grid or gas pipelines) makes the industries into natural monopolies and enables their markets to be insulated from foreign competition. Most also have a long history of government regulation for strategic energy supply and other reasons. The structure and organization of energy industries also varies from member state to member state, ranging from national monopolies in France and Italy, through more liberal systems with public or private firms operating more or less independently under regional monopolies in Germany to systems that have recently been opened up to competition in the

340. Coal production in the Community is in general heavily subsidized and the only competition is from imports of cheaper non-EC coal.
341. *See* Monti, Competition Policy Applying EU Competition Law to the Newly Liberalized Energy Markets, Rome, Oct. 6, 2003, SPEECH/03/447.
342. The activities of the Community as formulated by the Maastricht Treaty include the 'encouragement for the establishment and development of trans-European networks,' *see* Article 3 (o) and Articles 154–156 of the EC Treaty.
343. *See EDFI/ESTAG*, D.Comm. March 17, 1998, M.1107 (under the merger control regulation).

Netherlands and the UK, and Sweden and Finland with more liberalized systems.[344] The ongoing opening of national markets is underlined by the increasing number of transnational mergers.[345]

Security of Supply.
In order to justify this fragmentation of national markets, member states and public utilities tend to invoke security of supply as a reason for applying the exception of Article 86 (2) and Article 30.[346] For energy utilities security of public supply may indeed represent a public service obligation. However, in that case they are exempt from the competition rules only insofar as application of the competition rules would *obstruct* the performance of the tasks assigned to them[347] and insofar as the development of trade is not affected to such an extent as would be contrary to the interests of the Community.[348] A possible public interest ground for restricting trade in energy products could be the need to ensure security of supply by exploiting national energy resources and maintaining a certain minimum level of domestic energy production capacity. This principle was recognized by the Court of Justice as justifying an exception from the free trade rules in certain circumstances in the *Campus Oil* case.[349]

The *Campus Oil* Case.
This case concerned an obligation imposed by the Irish Government on all oil importers to purchase 35% of their requirements of petroleum products from a state-owned refinery, the only refinery in the country. The requirement was judged to constitute a measure having equivalent effect to a quantitative restriction on imports contrary to Article 28. The member state claimed that the requirement was justified, however, on grounds of public security which could be seriously affected if domestic production was not maintained at the level necessary to keep national production capacity available in the event of a crisis. The Court of Justice

344. *See* the new legislative package on infrastructure and security of supply as proposed by the Commission on 10 December 2003, IP/2003/1694.
345. *See* Thirty-second Report on Competition Policy, points 88–89.
346. *See* Commission communication on services of general interest, 2001 OJ C 17/4, points 37–39, 50 and pp. 20–22.
347. It is not sufficient to show that the monopoly would suffer certain disadvantages; the performance of its tasks must be put 'in jeopardy' from the economic point of view: *British Telecommunications*, ECJ March 20, 1985, 1985 ECR 873, para. 33.
348. In the *Rendo (IJsselcentrale)* case the Commission argued not only on the basis of the Dutch Electricity Act allowing direct imports by private industrial consumers but also on the fact that the auto-producers were free to produce on their own and to feed their surplus production into the public grid. If auto-production evidently did not interfere with security of public supply, there was no reason why importation should do so: *IJsselcentrale*, D.Comm. Jan. 16, 1991, 1991 OJ L 28/32, 43–44; *aff'd* in this respect CFI Nov. 18, 1992, 1992 ECR II-2917; ECJ Oct. 19, 1995, 1995 ECR I-3319.
349. *Campus Oil*, ECJ July 10, 1984, 1984 ECR 2727.

accepted this argument with certain caveats relating to the proportionality (reasonableness) test. It held:

> '… [P]etroleum products, because of their exceptional importance as an energy source in the modern economy, are of fundamental importance for a country's existence since not only its economy but above all its institutions, its essential public services and even the survival of its inhabitants depend upon them. An interruption of supplies of petroleum products, with the resultant dangers for the country's existence, could therefore seriously affect the public security that Article 36 (*now 31*) allows States to protect.
>
> It is true that … Article 36 refers to matters of a non-economic nature. A Member State cannot be allowed to avoid the effects of measures provided for in the Treaty by pleading the economic difficulties caused by the elimination of barriers to intra-Community trade. However, in the light of the seriousness of the consequences that an interruption in supplies of petroleum products may have for a country's existence, the aim of ensuring a minimum supply of petroleum products at all times is to be regarded as transcending purely economic considerations and thus as capable of constituting an objective covered by the concept of public security.'[350]

The Court went on to evaluate whether the measures were capable of ensuring supplies and whether they were in reasonable proportion to the aim sought, i.e., did not restrict intra-Community trade more than absolutely necessary. It held that the supply requirements had to be limited to the quantity necessary to keep the refinery's production capacity available and that competitive prices would have to be charged by the refinery if competition were not to be unduly distorted. It continued:

> 'If it is not possible by means of industrial and commercial measures to avoid any financial losses resulting from such prices, those losses must be borne by the Member State concerned, subject to the application of Articles 92 and 93 of the Treaty (*now 87 and 88*).'[351]

The judgment thus limited restrictions for the purpose of security of supply to the minimum necessary to achieve the aim in view and required that competition should be allowed to operate in other areas.[352]

---

350. *Campus Oil*, ECJ July 10, 1984, 1984 ECR 2727, paras 34–35 (however, it is possible the Court was swayed by memories of the 1970s energy crisis).
351. *Campus Oil*, ECJ July 10, 1984, 1984 ECR 2727, para. 46.
352. *See also Greek Oil Monopoly*, ECJ Dec. 13, 1990, 1990 ECR I-4747, where the Court of Justice rejected as insufficiently demonstrated the argument that abolishing the monopoly for importing refined oil products would prevent domestic refineries from marketing their own products at competitive prices and so would threaten security of supply.

Further Development of the *Campus Oil* Approach.
The *Campus Oil* approach was further developed in the *Almelo* case.[353] This case concerned the evaluation of an exclusive purchasing obligation imposed on a local electricity distributor in the Netherlands, thereby preventing it from purchasing electricity from other sources, including imports. The Court of Justice examined in particular the extent to which this obligation was necessary to enable the undertaking entrusted with such a task of general economic interest to perform it. The Court ruled that it was necessary to take into consideration the economic conditions in which the undertaking operated, in particular the costs which it had to bear and the legislation, particularly environmental legislation, to which it was subject.[354] Similar criteria have been applied in the evaluation of electricity monopolies. [355] In these cases the Court of Justice rejected the Commission's action under Article 223 against Italy, the Netherlands, France and Spain for having maintained in force exclusive rights to import and export electricity contrary to Article 31, finding that the Commission did not sufficiently substantiate why the application of the competition rules would not have obstructed the performance of the public service tasks assigned to them (Article 86 (2)). [356] This case law constitutes the basis for the Commission's Communication on services of general interest[357] and, more specifically, its legislative framework for the liberalization process in energy market, which requires a balancing of the public service tasks assigned by member states in order to safeguard security of supply against the Community interest in an adequate level of interconnection and exchange between member states (including the new member states as from May 1, 2004).[358]

3. Liberalization Process in the Energy Sector

The Objective of a Single Internal Energy Market.
The European Community aims to integrate its energy markets. The objective was described by the EC Council in 1986 as 'greater integration, free from barriers to trade, of the internal energy market with the aim of improving security of supply, reducing costs and improving economic competitiveness.'[359] The first phase

353. *Almelo*, ECJ April 27, 1994, 1994 ECR I-1477.
354. *Ibid.*, paras. 47–50.
355. *Dutch, Italian, French and Spanish Electricity Monopolies*, ECJ Oct. 23, 1997, 1997 ECR I-5699, 5789, 5815 and 5851, in particular *Italian Electricity Monopoly*, ECJ Oct. 23, 1997, 1997 ECR I-5789, para. 43.
356. *Italian Electricity Monopoly*, ECJ Oct. 23, 1997, 1997 ECR I-5789, paras 46–54. The Commission considers Article 226 proceedings on exclusive rights no longer necessary in view of the recent liberalization directives: Twenty-seventh Report on Competition Policy, point 116.
357. 2001 OJ C 17/4.
358. IP/03/1694.
359. Council Resolution concerning new Community energy policy objectives for 1995 and convergence of the policies of the Member States, Sept. 16, 1986, 1986 OJ C 241/1, 2, section 5 (d).

of this liberalization process started in 1990 with Council Directive 90/547/EEC on the transit of electricity through transmission grids[360] and Council Directive 90/377/EEC concerning a Community procedure to improve the transparency of gas and electricity and electricity prices charged to industrial end-users.[361] The result of the second phase was in 1996 Directive 96/92/EC concerning common rules for the internal market in electricity,[362] and in 1998 Directive 98/30/EC concerning common rules for the internal market in natural gas.[363] Both directives were repealed in 2003 by Directive 2003/54/EC concerning common rules for the internal market in electricity[364] and Directive 2003/55/EC concerning common rules for the internal market in natural gas[365] in order to significantly extend and accelerate the liberalization process. In fact, the liberalization had progressed much more quickly across the Community than expected or required by the Directives. Around 65% of electricity demand and 80% of total European gas demand is already fully open to EU-wide competition.[366] However, the objective of achieving guaranteed security of supply at reasonable prices[367] must be safeguarded under the conditions of the new directives. The new directives are complemented by a new legislative package on infrastructure and security of supply.[368] The objective of this new legislative framework for the liberalization process is the proper functioning of a competitive internal market for energy in order to avoid electricity black-outs, such as occurred in Italy in September 2003.

The Electricity Directives.

- *Directive 96/92/EC* concerning common rules for the internal market in electricity[369] abolished exclusive rights, required unbundling of network activities from generation and supply activities, provided for a gradual opening up of the electricity market for certain customers (‘*eligible customers*’), for a more liberal procedure for authorizing new generation capacities and for better third party access to the network,[370] whereby the member states remained free to choose

360. 1990 OJ L 313/53.
361. 1990 OJ L 185/32.
362. 1997 OJ L 27/20.
363. 1998 OJ L 204/1.
364. 2003 OJ L 176/37.
365. 2003 OJ L 176/57.
366. Commission Communication on services of general interest, 2001 OJ C 17/4, pp. 20–21. With respect to electricity, certain member states have already opened 100% of demand (UK, Finland, Sweden).
367. However, the ‘reasonable price’ is as difficult to determine as the *iustum pretium* at the time of Augustinus.
368. IP/03/1694 of Dec. 10, 2003.
369. 1997 OJ L 27/20.
370. The Community’s average share of the electricity market opening is 34.76% in the period Jan. 1, 2004 to July 1, 2004: 2003 OJ C 321/51.

between the 'negotiated access' (by way of voluntary commercial agreements) or the 'single-buyer system.'[371]

- *Directive 2003/54/EC*[372] opens the electricity market beyond the limits of the previous directive, namely for all non-household customers by July 2004, and for all customers by July 2007. Member states must ensure the implementation of a system of regulated third party access to transmission and distribution systems based on published tariffs, applicable to all eligible customers, except in the case of lack of capacity (Article 20). The directive contains further measures in unbundling, requiring *legal* unbundling of network activities from generation and supply activities,[373] and establishes a regulator in all member states with well defined functions. The directive must be implemented by the member states by July 1, 2004. Although the directive reinforces the universal service obligations in the electricity sector (guarantee of supply at reasonable prices) the member states retain a broad discretion as to the possibility to impose public service (in particular security of supply) obligations which will be monitored by the national regulatory authorities (which already exist or will be designated) and by the national competition authorities and the Commission (with respect to possible abuses of a dominant position). In addition, the *Florence Forum* was created by the Commission in 1998 which convenes twice a year at the European University in Florence and consists of national regulatory authorities, member states, the Commission, transmission system operators, electricity traders, consumers, network users, and power exchanges to discuss issues that are not addressed in the electricity directive, in particular the tariffs for cross border electricity exchanges and the allocation and management of scarce interconnection capacity.

The Natural Gas Directives.

- *Directive 98/30/EC* concerning common rules for the internal market for natural gas[374] was adopted after long discussion due to the overall dependence of the Community on gas supplies from third countries and the strategic and political problems of ensuring long-term supplies as well as the lack of consensus

371. The single buyer system allows larger industrial users and distributors insofar as they supply customers which are themselves eligible to benefit from differences between the prices offered by their traditional supplier and those available from an alternative supplier inside or outside their member state, to negotiate their requirements directly with the alternative supplier and to procure the corresponding quantity via the single buyer by using its transmission system ('hedging contracts').The directive did not consider a more general system of '*common carriage*' whereby transmission capacity would be allocated *pro rata* among all participants.
372. 2003 OJ L 176/37.
373. The Note of DG Energy & Transport on Directives 2003/54/EC and 2003/55/EC on the Internal Market in Electricity and Natural Gas (http://europa.eu.int/comm/energy/electricity/legislation/notes_for_implementation_en.htm) explains the basic elements of the new unbundling regime.
374. 1998 OJ L 204/1.

between the more liberalized member states, such as the United Kingdom and other northern member states, and the member states with nationally-based monopolistic systems, such as France, Italy and Spain. These divergent views made an opening up of the gas market more delicate and complicated. The directive established common rules for the transmission, distribution, supply and storage of natural gas and for access to the market. However, the directive recognized that member states are allowed, under certain conditions, to refrain from applying certain provisions if the fulfilment of the obligations imposed in the general interest would be jeopardized. The overall objective was to liberalize a minimum of 30% of the annual gas consumption upon entry into force of the directive and gradually to extend the liberalized proportion of the market. As under the electricity directive, member states may choose between 'negotiated access' to the network and the 'single buyer' system. The gas directive provided that transmission companies shall not discriminate between different system users, but – unlike the electricity directive – without requiring member states to designate an independent pipeline operator.

– Directive 2003/55/EC[375] opens the natural gas market beyond the limits of the previous directive, namely for all non-household customers by July 2004, and for all customers by July 2007. The directive contains further measures in unbundling (similar to the electricity directive) and establishes a regulator in all member states. In addition, the Madrid Forum has been created which convenes twice a year at the Fundacion de Estudios de Regulacion in Madrid and consists of national regulatory authorities, member states, the Commission, transmission system operators, electricity traders, consumers, network users, and power exchanges which was set up by the Commission in 1998 to discuss issues that are not addressed in the gas directive, in particular the tariffs for cross border gas exchanges and the allocation and management of scarce interconnection capacity and other technical and commercial barriers to the creation of a fully operational internal gas market.

Rules for Access to Networks and Cross-Border Trade of Energy.
The electricity and gas directives are accompanied by regulations and guidelines with regard to cross-border tariffs and the allocation of available interconnection capacities, in order to ensure effective access to transmission systems for the purpose of cross-border transactions and to better integrate the new member states and neighboring regions into a wider European energy market.

– *Regulation 1228/2003* on conditions for access to the network for cross-border exchanges in *electricity*[376] aims at setting fair rules for cross-border exchanges of electricity, taking into account the characteristics of national and regional markets, including a compensation mechanism for cross-border flows of elec-

375. 2003 OJ L 176/57, corr. 2004 OJ L 16/74.
376. 2003 OJ L 176/1.

tricity and the setting of harmonized principles on cross-border transmission charges and the allocation of available capacities of interconnections between national transmission systems.

- The *proposal for a regulation* on conditions for access to the *natural gas* transmission networks[377] aims at setting fair rules for the conditions of access to natural gas transmission systems for both firm and interruptible third party access services, taking into account the characteristics of national and regional markets, including principles for charges for access to the network, the definition of necessary services, harmonized principles for capacity allocation and congestion management, the determination of transparency requirements, balancing and imbalance charges, and the rational and proportional utilization of energy resources.
- *Decision 1229/2003* lays down a series of *guidelines* for trans-European energy networks,[378] which repeals Decision 1254/96/EC.[379] This decision is being updated and amended[380] on the basis of the Second Benchmarking Report on the Implementation of the Internal Electricity and Gas Market in order to take into account the priorities of the enlarged EU as from 1 May 2004.[381] This directive establishes common rules for the cross-border trade of electricity. A regulatory committee will decide on guidelines on compensation of transit flows, on harmonization of tariffs and on allocation of cross-border interconnection capacity. The Florence European Electricity Regulatory Forum ('*Florence Forum*'),[382] whose objective is to eliminate all cross border electricity charges and to harmonize existing rules and to identify complementary measures in order to avoid separate national markets, decided on 9 July 2003 to remove completely the EUR 0.5 MW/h network access charge on exports currently applied by member states. As from 1 January 2004, no additional network charges will apply for cross-border electricity transactions in the internal market, which will be treated in the same way as national transactions.

However, the networks remain a natural monopoly. Access to networks may be refused where the system lacks capacity[383] or where access would prevent the operators from carrying out public service obligations or on the basis of economic and financial difficulties with pay-or-take contracts.[384] However, any refusal must

377. COM(2003)741 of Dec. 10, 2003.
378. 2003 OJ L 176/11.
379. 1996 OJ L 161/47.
380. Commission proposal, *see* MEMO December 2003 on Energy Infrastructures: Increasing Security of Supply in the Union.
381. Commission Staff Working Paper, SEC(2003)448 of April 16, 2003.
382. MEMO/03/153.
383. Directive 2003/54/EC (electricity), Article 20 (2).
384. Directive 2003/55/EC (natural gas), Article 21.

be 'duly substantiated', thereby allowing legal oversight.[385] The most effective means of improving competition in transmission via networks may be the possibility of supplying energy through direct lines,[386] of expanding the network in the case of a lack of capacity or a lack of connection[387] and the right to request the necessary information.[388] Unjustified refusal of access to the network or hindering the expansion of transmission capacity may constititue an infringement of Article 81 or 82 and lead to proceedings before the Commission, the national competition authorties or the national courts.

Energy Infrastructure and Security of Supply.

The Commission proposed a directive to the European Parliament and the Council concerning measures to safeguard security of supply and infrastructure investment.[389] The objective is to ensure that the investors have a stable framework for constructing new transmission capacity and safeguard an ongoing balance between supply and demand by establishing priority projects of European interest meriting support and even state aid.

European Regulators Group.

Both the electricity and the natural gas directives establish independent regulatory authorities in all member states which are coordinated by the *European Regulators Group for Electricity and Gas*.[390] This group will assist the Commission in consolidating the internal market for electricity and gas, in particular by establishing a tighter cooperation between the national regulatory authorities[391] and by ensuring a consistent application in all member states of the electricity and gas directives and of the regulation on cross-border exchanges of electricity. The objective is to promote appropriate incentives to invest in both transmission and distribution networks and to ensure a continuous equilibrium between supply and demand while also allowing for competition between the different suppliers.

---

385. However, it may be difficult to legally judge the reasons of such a refusal, in particular in the case of an indirect refusal by applying a prohibitively high tariff without ending as a tariff regulator or arbiter.
386. Directive 2003/54/EC (electricity), Article 20 (2); Directive 2003/55/EC (natural gas), Article 21 (1).
387. Directive 2003/54/EC (electricity), Article 22; Directive 2003/55/EC (natural gas), Article 24.
388. Article 20 (2) of Directive 2003/54/EC on electricity; Article 22 (4) of Directive 2003/55/EC on natural gas. Examples include the doubling of the interconnector between France and Spain as a condition for clearing a merger on the wholesale market for electricity in Spain: *EnBW/EDP/Cajastur/Hidrocantabrico*, D.Comm. March 19, 2002, M.2684, and the gas pipeline between the Austrian/Slovakian to the Italian border: *Gazprom/ENI*, D.Comm. Oct. 10, 2003, IP/03/1345.
389. COM(2003)743 final of Dec. 10, 2003.
390. Commission Decision of Nov. 11, 2003, 2003 OJ L 296/34.
391. *See* IP/03/1536.

Regulatory Mechanism v. Application of the Competition Rules.
The new liberalization measures (directives, regulations and guidelines) institute a regulatory supervision of the implementation by the national regulatory authorities, which are coordinated by the European Regulators Group.[392] Although nothing prevents the Commission, the national competition authorities and the national courts from applying the competition rules,[393] disputes will be brought in the first instance before the regulatory authorities, which are in a position of conflicting interests: defending the interests of their 'national' operators in which the member states continue to exercise rights of control or influence and the Community interest of safeguarding or encouraging competition between these operators and their competitors. In addition, when fixing or approving tariffs the national regulatory authorities are expressly obliged to base their decision on a proposal *agreed* between the transmission system and distribution operators and the users of the network.[394] Similarly, infrastructure investments are subject to a close monitoring by the national regulatory authorities according to the Commission's proposal for a directive concerning measures to safeguard security of supply and infrastructure investment.[395] This presupposes cooperation between the transmission system operators, which is likely to induce the operators to engage in anticompetitive conduct.[396]

4. Application of the Existing Competition Rules

Interaction of Competition Rules with Single Market Rules.
The enforcement of competition rules ensures in particular that state barriers which are being removed by the electricity and the gas directive are not replaced by anticompetitive behaviour of market operators having the same effect. The adoption of legislation aiming at a progressive liberalization of European energy markets must therefore be accompanied by a strict application of the EC competition rules, including the merger control legislation and the state aid rules.[397] However, the case law is scarce because the application of the competition rules was limited to cases which presented issues not anticipated by legislative developments. The main issues that have arisen are briefly outlined below.[398]

392. Directive 2003/54/EC (electricity), Article 23 and recital 16; Directive 2003/55/EC (natural gas), Article 25 and recital 14.
393. In particular in the case of market dominance and predatory behaviour: Directive 2003/54/EC (electricity), recital 2; Directive 2003/55/EC (natural gas), recital 2.
394. Directive 2003/54/EC (electricity), recital 18; Directive 2003/55/EC (natural gas), recital 16.
395. COM(2003)743 final of Dec. 10, 2003.
396. *See Arduino*, ECJ Feb. 19, 2002, 2002 ECR I-1529, paras. 34–41.
397. Thirty-first Report on Competition Policy, point 101; Thirty-second Report on Competition Policy, points 81–84.
398. *See* Thirty-first Report on Competition Policy, point 96.

Action against Exclusive Export and Import Rights in the Energy Sector. The Commission took action under Article 31 of the EC Treaty against exclusive export and import rights granted to operators of electricity and gas networks by various member states because they constituted infringements of the rules on the free movement of goods. However, the Court of Justice rejected the Commission's intervention as premature (not sufficiently substantiated), but ruled that the Commission may renew its proceedings where exclusive rights are maintained contrary to the liberalization directives.[399]

Favoring Pro-Competitive Cooperations and Mergers. The Commission favors cooperations, joint ventures and mergers which are likely to stimulate competition in markets which were hitherto isolated, provided that the parties do not acquire or strengthen a dominant position on the relevant target market, which is distinct from other national markets on which the parties operate.[400] However, the clearance of such operations may be subject to conditions in order to ensure that there are sufficient possibilities for third parties to acquire, on freely negotiated terms, access to network capacity.[401]

Prohibiting Joint Marketing between Competitors. The Commission intervened against joint sales arrangements between competing suppliers, as in the *GFU* case.[402] This case concerned the joint sale of Norwegian natural gas (accounting for 10% of the EU gas consumption) by Statoil and North Hydro through a single seller, the Gas Negotiation Committee (GFU). The case was closed following a commitment by the parties to discontinue joint marketing and instead to market the gas individually, and by agreeing to reserve certain gas volumes for new customers.[403] Similarly, the Commission intervened against an agreement on the joint sale of Carribean gas within the EEA, [404] against joint

399. ECJ Oct. 23, 1997, 1997 ECR I-5789.

400. *EDFI/ESTAG*, D.Comm. March 17, 1998, M.1107, WuW 1998–6, 628; *see also VIAG/Bayernwerk*, D.Comm. 5 May 1994, M.4170. Examples of transactions cleared by the Commission: *electricity*: *EDF/Edison-ISE*, D.Comm. June 8, 1995, M.568 (joint venture between electricity generator and autoproducer); *natural gas*: *Bayerngas/Gas de France*, D.Comm. July 1, 1996 (joint acquisition of natural gas activities), IP/96/572.

401. Under Article 81: *Gas Interconnector between UK and Belgium*, Twenty-fifth Report on Competition Policy, p. 125. Under the merger regulation: *VIAG/Bayernwerk*, D.Comm. May 6, 1994, M.417.

402. D.Comm. July 17, 2002, IP/02/1084.

403. *See also DONG/DUC*, D.Comm. April 24, 2003, IP/03/91. This case concerned the joint marketing activities of three Danish gas producers (Shell, Maersk and Chevron/Texaco) as well as anticompetitive arrangements in their gas supply contracts with the incumbent wholesaler DONG, which has been settled following a commitment to sell their gas individually in future.

404. *Oil/Statoil/Marathon*, D.Comm. April 20, 2001, IP/01/578.

marketing for Norwegian gas,[405] and against joint marketing of North Sea gas in Denmark[406] because the joint marketing restricted competition between the parties and the access of customers to lower-priced sources of supply. All these cases were settled following commitments to remove anticompetitive provisions, in particular exclusivity, in the supply contracts.

Long-Term Supply Arrangements.
Customers must be free to choose their suppliers and to switch suppliers.[407] However, the Commission takes the view that long-term supply contracts are not *per se* incompatible with the EC competition rules, in particular where they are necessary to amortize significant investments.[408] This applies in particular to long-term agreements for supplying a high-capacity power station inasmuch as the commitment guarantees a stable and sufficiently sizeable outlet and as long as it does not unduly foreclose the market.[409] Agreements between coal and electricity producers under which the latter undertake to buy a certain quantity of coal rather than other primary energy sources, such as oil, on a long-term basis may restrict competition by tying the purchaser to the supplier for longer than is necessary for the purpose of amortizing important investments (in particular pipelines), long-term planning of deliveries and supply, and ultimately ensuring security of supply.[410]

Action against Exclusive and Long-Term Supply and Purchasing Arrangements.
The Commission therefore has acted against exclusive or excessively long-term arrangements:

- *Exclusive supply obligations*: Under Article 81 the Commission intervened against exclusive supply arrangements between the Russian gas producer Gazprom and the Italian wholesaler ENI which prevented Gazprom from supplying other wholesalers and ENI from reselling the gas outside the Italian territory. The case was settled following the parties' commitments to amend

405. *Statoil/North Hydro*, D.Comm. July 17, 2002, IP/02/1084.
406. *Shell, Maersk, Chevron/Texaco*, D.Comm. April 24, 2003, IP/03/91.
407. Directive 2003/54/EC (electricity), recital 20; Directive 2003/55/EC (natural gas), recital 18.
408. Article 18 (3) of the proposed amended gas directive. Thirty-second Report on Competition Policy, point 80.
409. Twenty-sixth Report on Competition Policy, point 103. Example of market foreclosure: *Electrabel/Intermixt*, Twenty-seventh Report on Competition Policy, points 93–94.
410. *See Jahrhundertvertrag*, D.Comm. Dec. 22, 1992, 1993 OJ L 50/14, point 40, *Electrabel*, Twenty-seventh Report on Competition Policy, p. 150; and the comfort letter granted to the long-term agreements between coal and electricity producers in England and Wales (1990 OJ C 191/9) and Scotland (1990 OJ C 245/9). *See* the Commission's proposal for a directive of the European Parliament and of the Council concerning measures to safeguard security of supply and infrastructure investment, COM(2003) 743 final of 10 December 2003, which aims also at ensuring adequate supplies of gas and electricity in both the medium and the long term.

significantly the agreement: Gazprom is now free to sell to other customers in Italy without having to seek ENI's prior approval, and ENI is free to resell outside Italy and indeed agreed to offer significant gas volumes to new customers outside Italy. Furthermore, ENI agreed to increase the capacity of the pipeline via Russian and Slovakia to the Italian border and to grant access to third parties.[411]

- *Long-term purchasing obligations*: Long-term purchasing arrangements prevent the buyer from freely purchasing quantities beyond the contracted terms, and it prevents competing suppliers from supplying such quantities to the buyer. The assessment therefore depends on the foreclosure effect. According to the block exemption on vertical restraints, Regulation 2790/1999, purchasing arrangements may be exclusive (i.e., covering more than 80% of requirements[412]) and agreed for five years, provided the supplier's market share does not exceed 30% of the relevant market.[413] The block exemption does not apply where the buyer has a dominant position or where the parties are actual or potential competitors.[414] This rule also applies to the energy sector. In the case of market shares exceeding 30% the assessment of long-term arrangements depends on balancing of the extent of exclusivity and the duration of the arrangement in the light of the economic circumstances of each case. Based on the Commission's practice, exclusive supply and purchasing arrangements may be concluded for a maximum duration of 10–15 years if they are strictly necessary to amortize important investments, and are subject to a quantitative reduction by 25% of the customer's requirements, in order to allow the buyer to purchase additional quantities from a competing supplier. [415] A decision stating that the supply arrangement is concluded for an excessively long period does

411. *Gazprom/ENI*, D.Comm. Oct. 10, 2003, IP/03/1345 (settlement following commitments). Similarly, the Commission intervened against the agreement between the Algerian gaz producer *Sonatrach*: Monti, SPEECH/03/447.

412. 'Non-compete clauses' in the sense of Article 1 (b) of Regulation 2790/1999.

413. Articles 3 and 5 (a).

414. Article 2 (4) of Regulation 2790/1999, except where competitors enter into non-reciprocal agreements and the buyer has a total annual turnover of not more than EUR 100 million.

415. The Commission opposed 20–30 years exclusivity, but accepted a duration of 15 years in: *Pego*, Twenty-third Report on Competition Policy, points 133a and 222 (electricity Portugal); *Isar Energy*, Twenty-sixth Report on Competition Policy, p. 133 (electricity Italy); *Electrabel*, IP/97/351 (electricity Belgium); *Transgas/Turbogas*, Twenty-sixth Report on Competition Policy, p. 135 (importation of Algerian natural gas by pipeline to Portugal for electricity generation); *Industrial Gases*, Nineteenth Report on Competition Policy, point 62 (supply of industrial gas by special pipeline, co-financed by the gas supplier, to steel producers). Reduction to 12 years: *Endesa/Gas Natural*, D.Comm. March 27, 2000, IP/00/297 (reduced from 18 to 12 years). In the cases *Pego*, *Endesa/Gas Natural* and *Electrabel* (Twenty-seventh Report on Competition Policy, point 94) the exclusive purchasing obligation was reduced to an obligation to buy only 75% from the other party, allowing the remaining 25% to be purchased at buyer's choice from the other party or from a competitor.

not necessarily lead to the nullity of the entire agreement but only of that part which exceeds the permissible duration.[416] One of the Commission's tools for avoiding excessively long-term obligations is to make the clearance subject to the commitment to grant early termination rights.[417]

Action against Resale and Use Restrictions and Non-Compete Clauses.
Obligations not to resell to other customers clearly infringe Article 81.[418] Use restrictions which prevent the customer from using energy supplies for other purposes than, say, power production, are tantamount to resale restrictions.[419] Similary, clauses which allow the supplier to reduce the quantities supplied if the customer were to start selling gas to competitors are indirect resale restrictions which infringe Article 81.[420] The customer may not be prevented from using the gas supplied for other production sites[421] or for other fields (chemicals rather than generation of electricity) than the sites or fields imposed by the supplier,[422] and may not be prevented from establishing new production facilities or from developing and using their own alternative energy sources, in particular from becoming a producer of energy for its own consumption.[423]

Action against Price Discrimination.
Undue discrimination as between customers is prohibited under Article 82, such as when an electricity supplier charges comparable large customers unduly discriminatory prices[424] or purchases surplus electricity generated by 'autoproducers'

---

416. *See Nutricia*, D.Comm. Dec. 12, 1983, 1983 OJ L 376/22, *aff'd* ECJ July 11, 1985, 1985 ECR 2545, 2575, which concludes that the non-compete clause is prohibited (and void) 'from 1 October 1983', i.e., from the end of four years which both the Commission and the Court accepted as reasonable duration.
417. *GVS/EnBW/ENI*, D.Comm. Dec. 17, 2002, M.2822.
418. *See Endesa/Gas Natural*, D.Comm. March 27, 2000, IP/00/297; *Nigeria LNG*, D.Comm. Dec. 12, 2002, IP/02/1869; *Gazprom/ENI*, D.Comm. Oct. 10, 2003, IP/03/1345; *Nigeria LNP*, D.Comm. Dec. 12, 2002, IP/02/1869. In the context of a joint venture: *Synergen*, D.Comm. May 31, 2002, IP/02/792.
419. *Endesa/Gas Natural*, D.Comm. March 27, 2000, IP/00/297.
420. *EdF/Wingas*, D.Comm. Sept. 12, 2002, 2002, IP/02/1293. *See also HFC Bank/British Gas Trading*, Twenty-seventh Report on Competition Policy, p. 132; *Pego*, Twenty-third Report on Competition Policy, point 222 (reduced from 28 to 15 years); *REN/Turbogas*, 1996 OJ C 118/7 (reduced from 20 to 15 years); *ISAB/ENEL*, 1996 OJ C 138/3 (reduced from 20 to 15 years).
421. This is a territorial restriction which is black-listed by Article 4 of Regulation 2790/2000.
422. *Endesa/Gas Natural*, D.Comm. March 27, 2000, IP/00/297. *See* Thirty-first Report on Competition Policy, point 100.
423. Second Report on Competition Policy, point 66; Council Recommendation to promote cooperation between public utilities and auto-producers of electricity, 1988 OJ L 335/29.
424. In case of a state-owned supplier the application of an unjustified low price to one large customer as compared to other customers may constitute a state aid, which was however denied in: *EDF/Usinor-Sacilor* and *Exxon Chemicals*, Twentieth Report on Competition Policy, points 185–186.

at unduly low prices as compared to other generators.[425] However, under the new directives, terms, conditions and tariffs will be monitored by the national regulatory authorities in order to avoid any abusive behaviour.[426]

Action against Unjustified Refusal of Access to the Network.
Article 81 (1) applies to any agreement or concerted practice among energy utilities to divide liberalized markets,[427] institutionalize coordination and supplies between their networks, to avoid competing in each other's territories or to discourage third parties, in particular from other member states, from gaining access to their markets for purposes of import or export.[428] Article 82 applies if access to the existing network is refused in the absence of any realistic alternatives (essential facility).[429] This provision may apply even after the implementation of the Council directives on electricity and natural gas if the owner or operator of the network unduly restricts access. The reasons which are likely to justify the refusal of access to a network are mainly those stated in the directives: lack of capacity or lack of connection (gas and electricity), serious difficulties with pay-or-take contracts (gas) and, more generally and more difficult to prove, the risk of obstructing the performance of the public service obligations (gas and electricity).[430] The Commission may ensure free access to an interconnected grid by making the approval of a merger subject to commitments to reserve a certain part of the transmission capacity to third companies,[431] make the access fees transparent,[432] increase the transmission capacity,[433] or secure access through long-term transit contracts.[434]

---

425. Council Recommendation 88/611/EC to promote cooperation between public utilities and auto-producers of electricity, 1988 OJ L 335/29. *See* the German Court of Appeal Düsseldorf, Feb. 25, 1997, WuW DE-R 156.
426. Directive 2003/54/EC (electricity), Article 23; Directive 2003/55/EC (natural gas), Article 25; Regulation 1228/2003 (conditions for access to the network), Article 9.
427. In the *Ruhrgas/Thyssengas* case the German antitrust authority (Bundeskartellamt) issued a prohibition decision on 18 April 1994 based on both Article 81 (1) and German antitrust law (RdE 1994–4, 154).
428. *IJsselcentrale*, D.Comm. Jan. 16, 1991, 1991 OJ L 28/32, 40–42.
429. In the *SHG/EDF-ENEL* case (Twenty-second Report on Competition Policy, points 142–145) the Commission challenged under Article 81 a horizontal agreement between the French and the Italian monopolists preventing a smaller generator from exporting directly quantities it produced by using their grids; the refusal of granting access could have been challenged also as abuse of a dominant position. In the *IJsselcentrale* case, D.Comm. 16 Jan. 1991, 1991 OJ L 28/32, the Commission challenged an agreement between the different Dutch generators preventing direct imports by Dutch customers situated at the frontier; in this respect the Commission decision has not been appealed.
430. *See DISMA*, Twenty-third Report on Competition Policy, point 223.
431. *See EdF/EnBW*, D.Comm. Feb. 7, 2001, M.1853.
432. E.g. *VEBA/VIAG*, D.Comm. June 13, 2000, M.1673, points 222–224.
433. *Grupo Vilar Mir/Hidroelectrica del Cantabrico*, D.Comm. Sept. 26, 2001, M.2434; *EnBW/EDP/Cajastur/Hidrocantabrico*, D.Comm. March 19, 2002, M.2684.
434. *Gas de France-Ruhrgas*, D.Comm. June 7, 2002, M.2791 (no coordination effect found between the two major competitors).

Various Means of Improving Access to Networks.
Access to the network, in particular a gas pipeline, does not necessarily mean the use of the network for a physical flow of third parties' gas through the pipeline but the possibility of capacity reservations in accordance with the 'contractual path', i.e. of booking the capacity at the points of entry where they intend to inject gas (entry points) and separately at the points where they envisage to off-take gas (exit points). This 'entry/exit system' has been introduced by BEB, a joint venture between ExxonMobil and Shell, in response to the Commission's objections, under Article 82, to BEB's refusal to grant the Norwegian gas producer Marathon access to the Northern German pipeline.[435] The case was settled following commitments to improve transparency, to use storage facilities, to introduce a 'use it or lose it' principle for capacity reservations and to introduce an entry/exit system which allows booking capacity separately at the relevant entry and exit points.[436] The advantage of a transparent entry/exit system is that the owner of the pipeline will be open to discuss with adjacent pipeline system operators possible cooperation to extend the system to larger territories.[437]

F. Telecommunications

1. Intense Liberalization Process

Technological Change Spurring Liberalization.
The situation in EC telecommunications was until recently similar to that in the energy sector. The markets for both telecommunications services and equipment were divided on national lines. Public monopolies, combining responsibility for postal services and telecommunications, owned and operated the telecommunications network and provided all services. Transmission and terminal equipment was largely purchased from national suppliers, and there was little standardization. This situation has now changed, partly as a result of conscious liberalization moves by the EC administration and, in some cases, national governments and partly as a result of technological change, which is making the old nationally-based monopolistic systems increasingly obsolete. The liberalization drive is being led by the Commission with a wide-ranging programme aimed at standardization and EC-wide type approval, the opening up of public telecommunications authorities' equipment purchases to EC-wide competition, and the abolition of monopolies for

---

435. *Marathon/BEB*, D.Comm. July 29, 2003, IP/03/1129. Similarly *Marathon II*, D.Comm. April 30, 2004, IP/04/573, which concerned the refusal by the French and German gas companies Gaz de France and Ruhrgas to grant the Norwegian subsidiary access to their gas networks.
436. *See also Marathon/Thyssengas*, D.Comm. Nov. 23, 2001, IP/01/1641, *Marathon/Gasunie*, D.Comm. April 16, 2003, IP/03/547, and *UK/Belgium Gas Interconnector*, D.Comm. March 13, 2002, IP/02/401.
437. *Marathon/BEB*, D.Comm. July 29, 2003, IP/03/1129.

the supply of terminal equipment and most services and for the liberalization of the telecommunications networks and services.[438] National governments are joining in this process of their own accord, convinced of the increasing importance for economic competitiveness of an efficient, inexpensive and modern telecommunications system. Thus, telecommunications operators are being privatized or placed on a more commercial basis and competition is being allowed in ever more services.[439]

The *British Telecommunications* Case.

In *British Telecommunications*,[440] the UK telecommunications authority, since privatized, was ordered to end its ban on private message-forwarding agencies relaying telex messages between foreign countries over the UK network, on the ground that this was an abuse of its dominant position contrary to Article 82. The decision was upheld in an appeal filed by the Italian Government.[441] The Court of Justice confirmed the Commission's view that the retransmission of telex messages was not covered by the Article 86 (2) exception for public service obligations and that the network operator was not entitled to restrict third parties' use of the network for commercial services in competition with the network operator or with network operators in other member states.[442] This has encouraged the Commission to press for the opening of virtually all telecommunications services to competition.[443]

The Instruments of Liberalization.

In the EC liberalization programme the main instruments being used are the rules on harmonization of laws (Article 95), free interstate trade in goods and services (Articles 28 and 49), non-discrimination (Article 12), state monopolies (Article

438. Commission, Green Paper on the Development of the Common Market for Telecommunications Services and Equipment (COM(87)290), Brussels 1987, Communication on the Implementation of the Green Paper by 1992 (COM(88)48), Brussels 1988, and the second part of the Green Paper on the liberalization of the telecommunications infrastructures by 1995 (COM(95)158); House of Lords Select Committee on the European Communities, European Community Telecommunications Policy, 6th Report 1987–88 Session. Baker & McKenzie's *Telecommunication Laws in Europe* (1998).

439. E.g., British Telecom was privatized in 1985 with a second network operator, Mercury, allowed to enter the market. In 1989 the German Bundespost was converted from a government department into three commercially run organizations responsible for postal services, telecommunications and banking activities.

440. *British Telecommunications*, D.Comm. Dec. 10, 1982, 1982 OJ L 360/36.

441. *British Telecommunications*, ECJ March 20, 1985, 1985 ECR 873.

442. *Ibid.*, paras 21–34. *Cf.* in relation to monopolies in broadcasting, *Sacchi/Tele Biella*, ECJ April 30, 1974, 1974 ECR 409; *Telemarketing*, ECJ Oct. 3, 1985, 1985 ECR 3261.

443. *See infra* this section regarding the Telecommunications Services directive. A decisive influence was also exerted by the Court's ruling in *Telemarketing* that the extension of a monopoly to adjoining service markets was an abuse of dominant position under Article 82: *Télémarketing*, ECJ Oct. 3, 1985, 1985 ECR 3261, paras 19–27.

31) and the competition rules (chiefly Article 82), alone or in conjunction with Article 86. The discussion below is an overview of actions taken under the monopoly and competition provisions. It divides roughly into general directives addressed to all member states and actions against individual governments or telecommunications administrations.

The EC Liberalization Directives.
The liberalization process started during the 1980s with various Green Papers stressing the need for Community policy to promote an advanced and competitive European telecommunications infrastructure with a Community-wide market for equipment and services.[444] These Green Papers were followed by liberalization directives, issued either by the Commission under Article 86 (3) or by the Council under Article 95 in order to establish a clear regulatory framework to ensure full competition in the telecommunications sector within the time-frame agreed by the Council.[445]

The First Phase of Liberalization: Directives Based on Article 86 (3).
The Commission started the liberalization process with two directives based on Article 86 (3) which empowers the Commission to address 'appropriate directives' to member states after consultation, but without formal approval of the European Parliament and the Council:

- Directive 88/301/EEC on competition in the markets for telecommunications terminal equipment.[446] This directive orders the member states to end the monopolies traditionally enjoyed by telecommunications administrations for the supply, connection and maintenance of terminal equipment. The directive follows the settlement of the actions in the *British Telecom* case described above. The member states are also required to publish their technical specifications and details of their type-approval procedures for terminal equipment. In the preamble to the directive the Commission states that the Article 90 (2) exception does not apply to the supply of terminal equipment, whatever may be the position regarding the provision and operation of the public network. On appeal the Court of Justice upheld the directive by stating that the Commission did not abuse its powers under Article 86 (3). However, the Court annulled the

444. Green Paper on the development of the Common Market for telecommunications services and equipment, COM(87)290; Green Paper on a common approach in the field of satellite communications in the European Community, COM(90)490; Green Paper on a common approach to mobile and personal communications in the European Union, COM(94) 145; Green Paper on liberalization of telecommunications infrastructure and cable televisions networks, COM(94)682 and COM(94)682.

445. Council Resolution of 22 Dec. 1994 on the principles and the timetable for the liberalization of telecommunications infrastructures (1994 OJ C 379/4).

446. 1988 OJ L 131/73.

directive insofar as it had ordered the member states to cease certain anticompetitive practices, namely exclusionary long-term contracts with customers, which were not attributable to government compulsion or pressure.[447]

- Directive 90/388/EEC on competition in the markets for telecommunications services.[448] This directive ordered the member states to abolish monopolies for the supply of telecommunications services other than voice telephony, telex, mobile communications, radio-paging and satellite services and to make any licensing procedures objective, non-discriminatory and transparent. The Court of Justice upheld this directive.[449] The directive was adopted simultaneously with a basic directive adopted by the Council on telecommunications network standards or 'Open Network Provision' (ONP).[450]

Second Phase of Liberalization: Directives Amending Directive 90/388. The Commission amended Directive 90/388:

- with regard to satellite communications: Commission Directive 94/46/EC;[451]
- with regard to the abolition of the restrictions on the use of cable television networks for the already liberalized telecommunications services: Commission Directive 95/51/EC;[452]
- with regard to mobile and personal communications: Commmission Directive 96/2/EC;[453]
- with regard to the implementation of full competition in telecommunications markets, including the necessary rebalancing of tariffs for the provision of voice telephony: Commission Directive 96/19/EC,[454]
- in order to ensure that telecommunications networks and cable TV networks owned by a single operator are separate legal entities: Commission Directive 1999/64/EC.[455]

These directives persue the same fundamental principles as Directive 90/388/EC, namely (i) the abolition of existing exclusive and special rights and the prohibition

447. *France/Commission*, ECJ March 19, 1991, 1991 ECR I-1223, paras. 16–18.
448. 1991 OJ L 192/10.
449. CFI Nov. 17, 1992, 1992 ECR I-5833.
450. 1990 OJ L 192/10.
451. 1994 OJ L 268/15.
452. 1995 OJ L 256/49.
453. 1996 OJ L 20/59. With regard to the processing of personal data: Directive 97/66/EC, 1998 OJ L 24/1.
454. 1996 OJ L 74/13. Spain did not comply with the obligations under this directive: *Commission/Spain*, ECJ Jan. 7, 2004, C-500/01.
455. 1999 OJ L 175/39. *See also* Commission communication concerning the review under competition rules of the joint provision of telecommunications and cable networks by a single operator and the abolition of restrictions on the provision of cable TV capacity over telecommunications networks, 1998 OJ C 71/4.

of the granting of new exclusive and special rights in the electronic telecommunications sector, and (ii) the recognition of the right of undertakings to exercise their fundamental freedom of establishment and to provide services within an undistorted competition framework.[456] The Commission's action aims at providing the legal predictibility and regulatory flexibility necessary for this sector, thereby complementing the Europe objective of achieving competitive local access over broadband networks as cheaply as possible on a sustainable basis.[457]

The Commission issued communications on the status of voice on the internet under Directive 90/388[458] and proceeded in 1999 to a review of the existing directives on competition in the telecommunications sector.[459]

Third Phase: New Regulatory Framework.
Based on the Commission's Sixth Report on the implementation of the telecommunications regulatory package,[460] the Council adopted on 14 February 2002 a new regulatory framework for the regulation of electronic telecommunications networks and services in order to simplify and consolidate previous directives.[461] The new legislative package is made up by five directives:

- Directive 2002/21/EC on a common regulatory framework for electronic communications networks and services ('Framework Directive')[462] as complemented by the Commission Recommendation of 11 February 2003 on the definition of relevant product and service markets on which national regulatory authorities are recommended to base their market analysis,[463] the Commission Recommendation on the harmonization of the provision of public access to public electronic communications networks and services,[464] and the Commission Recommendation on a single European emergency call number;[465]
- Access Directive 2002/19;[466] replacing Directive 97/33/EC,[467] and complementing Regulation 2887/2000/EC on unbundled access to the local loop,[468]

456. Thirty-second Report on Competition Policy, point 99.
457. IP/03/1121 of July 25, 2003.
458. 1998 OJ C 6/4 and 2000 OJ C 369/3.
459. IP/00/766.
460. COM(2000)814.
461. 2002 OJ L 108.
462. 2002 OJ L 108/33.
463. COM(2003)497.
464. 2003 OJ L 78/12.
465. 2003 OJ L 189/49, referring to Directive 91/396/EC 1991 OJ L 217/31.
466. 2002 OJ L 108/7.
467. 1997 OJ L 117/15. This directive was held incomplete in the case *Telefonica de España*, ECJ Dec. 13, 2001, 2001 ECR I-10075, paras. 29 *et seq*.
468. 2000 OJ L 336/4; Commission Communication on the unbundled assess to the local loop, 2000 OJ C 272/55.

- Authorization Directive 2002/20/EC;[469] replacing Directive 97/13/EC[470] and transforming the individual licence into a general licence and amending the system of calculation and allocation of the administrative fees,[471]
- Universal Service Directive 2002/22/EC;[472] replacing Directive 98/10/EC,[473] including the methods of financing universal service,[474] complemented by Commission Decision on the minimum set of leased lines with harmonized characteristics and associated standards,[475]
- Privacy and Electronic Communications Directive 2002/58/EC,[476] replacing Directive 97/6/EC;[477] and
- Commission Directive 2002/77/EC with regard to competition in the markets for electronic communications networks and services.[478]

The legislative package is complemented by Guidelines on market analysis and the calculation of significant market power under Article 14 of Directive 2002/21/ EC.[479]

The new package aims at treating all transmission networks in an equivalent manner, thereby ensuring that market players are regulated only where necessary and in a consistent manner across the EU. The main criteria of the regulatory approach is the notion of 'significant market power'[480] which deviates from the previous market share threshold of 25%.[481] The definition follows that of a dominant position as defined by the Court of Justice in *Hoffmann/La-Roche* 'as a position of economic strength affording an undertaking the power to behave to an appreciable extent independently of competitors, customers and ultimately consumers'.[482] Accordingly, the new notion 'significant market power' ('SMP') is not substantially different from 'dominance'[483] and is rather

469. 2002 OJ L 108/21.
470. 1997 OJ L 117/15.
471. Recital 31 and Article 12 of Directive 2002/20/EC.
472. 2002 OJ L 108/51.
473. 1998 OJ L 101/24.
474. Articles 12–13 of Directive 2002/22/EC. However, cross-subsidization may constitute an illegal state aid: recital 18 to Directive 2002/22/EC.
475. 2003 OJ L 186/43.
476. 2002 OJ L 201.
477. 1998 OJ L 24/1.
478. 2002 OJ L 249/21.
479. 2002 OJ C 165/6.
480. Commission Guidelines on market analysis and the assessment of significant market power under the Community regulatory framework for electronic communications and services, 2003 OJ C 165/6, points 72–88.
481. Article 4 (3) of Directive 97/33/EC 1997 OJ L 199/32.
482. *Hoffmann/La Roche*, ECJ Feb. 14, 1978, 1978 ECR 228, para. 207.
483. By contrast, Article 2 of the amended merger Regulation 139/2004 did enlarge the notion by using the term 'significantly impede effective competition, *in particular* as a result of the creation or strengthening of a dominant position'.

a new label.[484] The notion of 'significant market power' is the basis for the intervention of the national regulatory authorities on all the markets concerned by the directives. The national regulatory authorities are supposed to intervene only where the markets are considered not to be effectively competitive as a result of such undertakings being in a position equivalent to dominance within the meaning of Article 82. In that respect the Commission adopted Guidelines for market analysis and the assessment of 'significant market power', setting out the methodology and competition law principles that the national regulatory authorities should follow (in close cooperation with the national competition authorities[485]) when carrying out their market analysis,[486] in particular criteria for defining the relevant market, for assessing single and collective dominance, and investigation and cooperation procedures.[487]

Monitoring the Implementation of the Directives.
The implementation of the telecommunications directives and their predecessors is monitored by the Commission which has led to several infringement proceedings, e.g. against Portugal, Greece, Belgium[488] and France.[489] By July 2003 five member states had transposed new regulatory national law on time.[490]

Independent Regulators Group – IRG and ERG.
The implementation of the directives is monitored by the national regulatory authorities, which are coordinated by the Independent Regulators Group (IRG). This Group was established in 1997 as a group of European National Telecommunications Regulatory Authorities (NRA's) to share experience and points of common interest, such as interconnection, prices, and universal service. To fulfill its mission, the IRG has implemented several working groups and is developing an integrated information system between all the NRA's, which creates the possibility for users to visit just one rather than 29 different sites when looking for information in the telecommunications sector. The IRG is juxtaposed by the European Regulators Group for Telecommunications Networks and Services (ERG)

484. However, the Commission states that 'the new definition will have the effect of raising the regulatory barrier while at the same time ensuring consistency between the *ex ante* regulation and *ex post* enforcement of the competition rules concerning dominant undertakings': Thirty-second Report on Competition Policy, point 95.
485. Article 3 (5) of the Framework Directive.
486. Commission Guidelines on market analysis and assessment of significant market power, 2002 OJ C 165/6, point 1.
487. *Ibid.*, respectively points 38–69, 70–106 (including leverage of market power), and 126–143.
488. Twenty-ninth Report on Competition Policy, point 72–73; Thirty-first Report on Competition Policy, points 120–124.
489. Reasoned opinion for having failed to comply with the 'Cable' Directive 95/51, sent on April 9, 2003, IP/03/520.
490. IP/03/1121 of July 25, 2003.

established by Commission Decision of 29 July 2002.[491] The task of the ERG is to advise and assist the Commission and to ensure the consistent application in all member states of the new regulatory framework. Whereas the IRG acts as sectoral information portal, the ERG is designed as a coordination vehicle. It is composed of the heads of each national regulatory authority and of officials of the Commission, which also provides the secretariat of the group.[492] In fact, both the IRG and ERG act as a single entity.

Regulatory Mechanism v. Application of the Competition Rules.
The regulatory framework for liberalizing the telecommunications sector maintains a sector-specific regulation in place, but introduces a number of criteria derived from EC competition law, thereby handing over the task of safeguarding competition from the competition authorities to the regulatory authorities. When applying competition rules, these regulatory authorities are in a conflict of interest:[493] assessing the behavior of telecommunications operators in which member states continue to have ownership and rights of control or veto powers versus safeguarding or restoring competition in the Community's interest. However, the Commission intends to ensure that EC competition law will be applied 'alongside' the regulatory mechanism and that both are complementary.[494]

2. APPLICATION OF EXISTING COMPETITION RULES

Commission Communication on the Application of the Competition Rules.
No regulations have been adopted under Article 83 (2) (c) in order to define the scope of Articles 81 and 82 in the telecommunications sector. Therefore, the general EC competition rules apply. In 1991 the Commission issued Guidelines on the application of the EC competition rules in the telecommunications sector[495] which intend to advise telecommunications operators, suppliers and users about the general legal and economic principles which have been and are being followed by the Commission (relevant market, provision of facilities and reserved services, non-reserved services and terminal equipment, research and development, the different forms of abuse under Article 82 and particular issues in the field of satellites). A second notice issued in 1998 concerns more specifically the application of the competition rules to access agreements in the telecommunications

491. 2002 OJ L 200/38.
492. Article 4 of Commission Decision of July 29, 2002, 2002 OJ L 200/38.
493. Although the member states must guarantee the independence of the national regulatory authorities by ensuring that they are legally distinct from and funcionally independent of all organizations providing communications networks: Recital 2 to Commission decision of July 29, 2002, 2002 OJ L 200/38.
494. *See* Klotz. Wettbewerb in der Telekommunikation: Brauchen wir eine ex-ante-Regulierung noch? ZWR 2003, 283, 315.
495. 1991 OJ C 233/2.

sector,[496] which deals in particular with the remedies under the competition rules if a network operator refuses access without technical or commercial justification and with the anti-competitive effects of some access agreements that are likely to serve as a means to coordinate prices, share markets, have exclusionary effects on third parties or lead to an exchange of commercially sensitive information.[497]

Powers of the Commission to Act against Infringements of Member States or Telecommunications Operators.
The Commission is entitled to take action under Article 86 (1) and (3) against measures enacted or maintained in force by a member state with respect to a telecommunications administration if they are contrary to the rules of the EC Treaty, in particular Articles 28 and 31, or under Regulation 1/2003 against anticompetitive behaviour by the telecommunications administration itself if it is contrary to Articles 81 or 82. The choice between these two alternatives depends on whether the telecommunications administration has been forced or induced to act in this manner by the government or whether it is acting on its own initiative.[498]

Actions Involving Member States under Article 86 (3).
The Commission has taken decisions based on Article 86 (3) in several cases. It intervened against member states acting through their telecommunications administrations:

- for extending the network operator's monopoly to other telecommunications services,[499]
- for tying of the sale and leasing of equipment to the provision of telecommunication network services,[500]
- for controlling imports,[501]
- for preventing the establishment of an alternative telecommunication network

496. Commission Notice on the application of the competition rules to access agreements in the telecommunications sector, 1998 OJ C 265/2.
497. *Ibid.*, points 130 and 134.
498. *Telecommunications Directive*, ECJ March 19, 1991, 1991 ECR I-1223, paras 55–56.
499. *Telemarketing*, ECJ 3 Oct. 1985, 1985 ECR 3261 (television advertising); *Omnitel Pronto Italia*, D.Comm. Oct. 4, 1995, 1995 OJ L 280/49, point 17 (mobile telephone services).
500. *RTT/GB-INNO-GM*, ECJ Dec. 13, 1991, 1991 ECR I-5941 (by establishing and controlling standards for import of terminal equipment leading to conflict of interests); *Bundespost II (Cordless Telephones)*, Fifteenth Report on Competition Policy, point 260; *Bundespost III (Modems)*, Fifteenth Report on Competition Policy, point 261; Sixteenth Report on Competition Policy, point 294; *Italian Telecommunications*, Sixteenth Report on Competition Policy, point 296 and Seventeenth Report on Competition Policy, point 283 (modems).
501. *Greek Television*, ECJ June 23, 1991, 1991 ECR I-2925 (conflict of interests by importing television films).

for a service based on a new technology which was not used by the monopoly itself,[502]

- for granting to the private Belgian television company VTM the exclusive right to broadcast television advertising which had the effect of excluding any operator from another member state,[503]
- for making it more difficult for new GSM operators to enter the market by imposing unreasonable or discriminatory licence fees, thereby distorting competition between the first (state-owned) and the second mobile telephone operator.[504]

Action Involving Telecommunications Operators under Articles 81 and 82.

(i) *Infringements of Article 81* may be found under the following circumstances:
  - concerted pricing or exchanging price data,[505]
  - market sharing,[506]
  - quota and tying arrangements;[507]
  - joint distribution,[508] except in the case of jointly selling TV rights to football events on behalf of football clubs which is considered by the Commission an efficient way to promote the branding of a league and therefore likely to benefit from an exemption under Article 81 (3);[509] and
  - joint acquisition and licensing of broadcasting rights (e.g. of sports events) by way of agreements[510] or joint ventures.[511]

---

502. *Vebacom*, Twenty-fifth Report on Competition Policy, point 111. *See Broadcasting of span events and competition law*, DG IV Newsletter 1998–2, pp. 18–28.
503. *VTM*, D.Comm. June 26, 1997, 1997 OJ L 244 (*aff'd* CFI July 8, 1999, 1999 ECR II-2329).
504. *GSM Spain*, D.Comm. Dec. 18, 1996, 1997 OJ L 76/19; *see* Twenty-fifth Report on Competition Policy, point 108; Twenty-sixth Report on Competition Policy, point 120; Twenty-seventh Report on Competition Policy, points 107–108.
505. *Global European Network*, D.Comm. March 20, 1997, IP/97/242. *Uniworld*, Feb. 12, 1997, 1997 OJ C 44/4 (comfort letters). *See* Twenty-eighth Report on Competition Policy, points 79–82.
506. *Auditel*, D.Comm. Nov. 24, 1993,1993 OJ L 306/50. *See*, however, *Canal+/Bertelsmann*, D.Comm. comfort letter, 1995 OJ C 168/8.
507. *Auditel*, D.Comm. Nov. 24, 1993, 1993 OJ L 306/50.
508. *UIP I – Pay TV*, D.Comm. March 17, 1991, IP/91/221; *UIP II*, D.Comm. July 26, 1999, 1999 OJ C 205 (announcement of comfort letter following commitment not to tie the grant of licenses on film performance rights).
509. Thirty-second Report on Competition Policy, points 135–137. *See UEFA Champions League*, D.Comm. July 23, 2003, 2003 OJ L 291/25; (conditional clearance); *Football Association Premier League*, D.Comm. April 30, 2004, 2004 OJ C 115/3 (clearance granted to an amended agreement, in particular commitment to offer the TV rights in several packages without exclusivity).
510. *See Téléfonica/Sogécable*, D.Comm. Nov. 23, 2000, Thirtieth Report on Competition Policy, point 220 (notification blocked by announcing an Article 15 (6) decision and subsequently withdrawn). The parties entered into a merger which was referred by Commission decision of Aug. 14, 2002, M.2845, to the national authorities. However, the referral decision was

(ii) *Clearance* in the form of an exemption, negative clearance or comfort letter has been granted with regard to the following forms of cooperation:
- strategic alliances for the provision of telecommunications services on a larger scale;[512]
- creation of a joint venture between competitors for entering a new market (e.g. pay-TV or free-to-air TV[513] or digital platforms);[514]

---

appealed and the national proceedings suspended in view of the outcome of the appeal. The *Sogécable/Via Digital* merger was cleared subject to commitments concerning the access of third companies: D.Comm. May 8, 2003, IP/03/655.

511. Broadcasting organizations discriminating purely commercial channels: *EBU/Eurovision I*, D.Comm. June 11, 1993, 1993 OJ L 179/23 (Commission exemption reversed CFI July 11, 1996, 1996 ECR II-649); *EBU/Eurovision II*, D.Comm. May 10, 2000, 2000 OJ L 151/18 (Commission exemption reversed: *M6, Antena 3, Gestévision, SIC/UER*, CFI Oct. 8, 2002, 2002 ECR II- 3805); *Eurovision III: Métropole Télévision SA*, CFI March 21, 2001, 2001 ECR II-1087 (annulling the Commission decision rejecting the continued discrimination of purely commercial channels despite the Court's decision of July 11, 1996). *See also* the following clearances: *INFONET*, 1992 OJ C 7/3 (comfort letter after releasing the discriminatory and cross-subsidiation clauses); *BT/MCJ*, D.Comm. July 27, 1994, 1994 OJ L 223/36 (exemption); *International Private Satellite Partners*, D.Comm. Dec. 15, 1994, 1994 OJ L 354/75 (negative clearance). *See* however the rejection of exemption under Article 81 (3): *ASTRA I*, D.Comm. Dec. 23, 1992, 1993 OJ L 20/23 (objecting to exclusivity with regard to uplinking services and price alignment); *INTRAX*, Twenty-third Report on Competition Policy, point 218.

512. Clearances under Article 81: *see BT/MCI I*, D.Comm. July 27, 1994, 1994 OJ L 223/36; under the merger regulation: *see BT/MCI II*, D.Comm. May 14, 1997, Twenty-seventh Report on Competition Policy, point 189. Exemption subject to conditions of opening the market to third operators: *Atlas* and *Global One*, D.Comm. July 17, 1996, 1996 OJ L 239/23 (joint ventures aiming at providing telecommunication services to large users after having accepted an open network access and conditional on the granting of the first infrastructure licenses in France and Germany, condition which has been fulfilled: 1997 OJ C 47/8). *See also Iridium*, D.Comm. Dec. 18, 1996, 1997 OJ L 16/87 (negative clearance), *Inmarsat* (comfort letter, Twenty-fifth Report on Competition Policy, point 59, and Twenty-eighth Report on Competition Policy, points 90–91); *Channel Five Broadcasting*, Twenty-sixth Report on Competition Policy, point 125; *BT/News International*, March 6, 1997, 1997 OJ C 65/26; *Uniworld* and *Unisource*, D.Comm. March 19, 1997, 1997 OJ L 318/1 and 24; *Global European Network (GEN)*, Twenty-seventh Report on Competition Policy, point 73.

513. Thirty-second Report on Competition Policy, points 140–144.

514. *International Private Satellite Partners*, D.Comm. Dec. 15, 1994, 1994 OJ L 354/75; *Iridium*, D.Comm. Dec. 18, 1996, 1997 OJ L 16/87 (negative clearances; these decisions seem in line with the Court of First Instance's finding that non-compete clauses in cooperation agreements for entering a new market do not necessarily infringe Article 81 (1): *European Night Services*, CFI Sept. 15, 1998, 1998 ECR I-3141); *TPS*, D.Comm. March 3, 1999, 1999 OJ L 90/6 (three-year exemption as regards the obligation of the four broadcasters to grant TPS exclusive distribution rights to their general interest channels). *See also British Interactive Broadcasting (BIB)*, Twenty-eighth Report on Competition Policy, points 98–99.

– joint construction of an additional infrastructure by a railways and a telecommunications operator;[515]
– agreements on broadcasting sports broadcasting rights, provided the access of third companies is not unduly limited,[516] which means that the broadcasting rights will no longer be sold to a single broadcaster in one package but will be unbundled and offered for sale transparently in a number of separate packages in order to reach more broadcasters as well as internet and telephone operators;[517]
– agreements between mobile telephone operators using the GSM standard in order to coordinate GSM network: sharing the basic network infrastructure, which does not restrict competition, and the use of each other's network to provide services to their respective customers (national roaming), including limitations on the sale of national roaming rights, which was exempted under Article 81 (3) for certain periods in order to promote market entry and a better and quicker coverage of the population;[518] and
– creation of 'Infonet' telecommunications services by telecommunications administration of the Community and of third countries.[519]

(iii) *Infringements of Article 82* have been found under the following circumstances:
– extension, without any objective necessity, of an existing monopoly to neighbouring, but separate markets;[520]
– unjustified refusal to transmit international messages on behalf of third parties;[521]

515. *SNCF/CEGETEL*, D.Comm. (comfort letter under Article 81 (3)), Twenty-eighth Report on Competition Policy, points 88–89.
516. *UEFA I*, D.Comm. April 19, 2001, 2001 OJ L 171/12 (negative clearance); *UEFA II*, D.Comm. Aug. 17, 2002, 2000 OJ C 196/3 (clearance subject to commitments), Thirty-first Report on Competition Policy, points 165–166, and Thirty-second Report on Competition Policy, point 138.
517. *Téléfonica/Sogecable*, D.Comm. May 8, 2003, IP/03/655; *UEFA III*, D.Comm. July 24, 2003, IP/03/11/05; *Bundesliga Broadcasting Rights*, D.Comm. July 24, 2003, IP/03/11/06; *Telenor/ Canal+*, D.Comm. Jan. 5, 2004, IP/04/2 (clearance for five years of the exclusive cooperation between Norway's Telenor, its satellite TV platform Canal Digital and Canal+ Nordic for the satellite distribution of Canal+ premium pay-TV channels in the Nordic region, subject to the condition to shorten substantially the duration).
518. Two parallel cases on 3rd Generation ('3G') mobile network sharing in the UK (*O2 UK Limited/T-Mobile Limited 'UK Network Sharing Agreement'*, D.Comm. April 30, 2003, 2003 OJ L 200/59) and Germany (*T-Mobile/O2 Germany – 'Network Sharing Rahmenvertrag'*, D.Comm. July 16, 2003, 2004 OJ L 75/34).
519. *Infonet*, 1992 OJ C 7/3 (comfort letter). *See* Thirtieth Report on Competition Policy, points 209–215.
520. *Télémarketing*, ECJ Oct. 3, 1985, 1985 ECR 3261, paras 26–27; *VTM*, Twenty-seventh Report on Competition Policy, p. 131.
521. *British Telecommunications*, ECJ March 20, 1985, 1985 ECR 873, para. 26.

- unreasonable or excessive prices which may be established by a cost analysis or an analysis of price levels in comparative markets,[522] e.g., application of excessively high fees concerning access to the public telephone network,[523] the provision of carrier-preselection and number portability,[524] the access to subscriber data for the publication of telephone directories,[525] or the unbundled access to the local loop;[526]
- discriminatory or predatory pricing practices, such as selling goods or services below cost for a sustained period of time, with the intention of deterring entry,[527] or putting a rival out of business);[528] or substantial reduction of telephone tariffs for large customers where the dominant firm faced competition from new market entrants while maintaining at the same level tariffs for other users and for lines leased to new entrants;[529]
- request by a dominant firm to comply with a previous agreement for the supply of telephone directories subscriber data relating to the surrender of various commercial know-how and intellectual property rights which is, however, only abusive if (i) the legal action can only serve to harass a competitor and (ii) it had been conceived in the framework of a plan aimed at eliminating competition;[530]

522. *Deutsche Telekom*, D.Comm. May 21, 2003, 2003 OJ L 263/9 (fine of EUR 12.6 million). *See* Commission's notice on access agreements in the telecommunications sector, 1998 OJ C 3645/2, point 106, and the Commission's price surveys, Twenty-eighth Report on Competition Policy, points 75–82. *See* M. Haag and R. Klotz, *Commission practice concerning excessive pricing in telecommunications*, DG IV Newsletter 1998–2, p. 35.
523. *Deutsche Telekom I*, IP/96/915; DG IV Newsletter 1998-2, p. 37 (settlement after reduction of fees in the range between 38% and 78%); the actions undertaken by the Commission against Belgium, Italy and Spain have been settled following substantive reduction of the fees for leased lines by 30–40%: Thirty-second Report on Competition Policy, points 102–103.
524. *Deutsche Telekom II*, IP/98/430 of May 13, 1998; DG IV Newsletter 1998-2, p. 37 (settlement after reduction of fees by almost 50%).
525. *ITT Promedia/Belgacom I*, Twenty-seventh Report on Competition Policy, p. 152 and DG IV Newsletter 1998-2, p. 36 (settlement after reduction of fees by more than 90% and commitment to apply a cost-orientated method).
526. France Télécom has been committed by the French regulatory authority ART (Autorité de Régulation des Télécommunications), by decision of April 16, 2002 (02–323), to reduce the monthly sharing fee from EUR 6.1 to EUR 2.85. Klotz/Delgado/Fehrenbach (Commission officials) argue that local unbundling, initially heralded as major breaktrough, may turn out to be nothing more than a wasteful regulatory experiment with little benefit for competition and that one of the major challenges for both regulators and competition authorities is to ensure coherent principles of a fair and non-discriminatory pricing are implemented: WuW 2003–4, 346–358.
527. *Wanadoo*, D.Comm. July 16, 2003, IP/03/1025 (fine of EUR 10.35 million).
528. Commission's notice on access agreements in the telecommunications sector, 1998 OJ C 365/2, point 110.
529. *Deutsche Telekom*, Twenty-sixth Report on Competition Policy, point 71.
530. *ITT Promedia/Belgacom II, aff'd CFI* July 17, 1998, 1998 ECR II-2937.

– long-term contracts preventing competitors from entering the market[531] and automatic prolongation of leasing contracts;[532] and
– tying practices.[533]

(iv) The merger control regulation has been applied in several cases involving telecommunications operations, e.g. in view of the creation of a new pay-TV platform which was cleared in *Newscorp/Telepiù*,[534] and in cases of high combined market shares of 55–70%, as in *Telia/Telenor*,[535] subject to commitments ensuring that the merged entity does not foreclose competitors in the dominated markets (Sweden and Finland). However, the Commission cleared, under the merger control regulation, the creation of express courier joint ventures by different national postal administrations in order to establish a new autonomous competitor, provided that access by third parties[536] or the acquisition of minority participations in private express courier services[537] is not restricted, and in cases where the transaction is likely to create or strengthen a dominant position, subject to divestment commitments.[538]

G. Postal Services

Regulatory Background.
In 1991 the Commission issued a Green Paper containing guidelines for a liberalization of the postal sector.[539] The fundamental problem arising from the

531. However, action must be taken against the responsible telecommunication administration under Article 82, not against the member states under Article 86 (3): *Telecommunications Directive Terminal Equipment*, ECJ March 19, 1991, 1991 ECR I-1223, paras 55–57; *Telecommunications Directive – Services*, CFI Nov. 17, 1992, 1992 ECR I-5833, para. 24.
532. *Alsatel/Novasam*, ECJ Oct. 5, 1988, 1988 ECR 5987, para. 10.
533. *Mobile Telefonie*, D.Comm. Dec. 18, 1996, Twenty-sixth Report on Competition Policy, point 120; *Unisource-Telefonica*, D.Comm. Feb. 12, 1997 OJ C 44/15. *See* Commission's notice on access agreements in the telecommunications sector, 1998 OJ C 365/2, point 103.
534. *Newscorp/Telepiù*, D.Comm. April 2, 2003, M.2876.
535. *Telia/Telenor*, D.Comm. Oct. 13, 1999, M.1439. *See also BSkyB/Kirch Pay-TV*, D.Comm. March 21, 2000, JV. 37, *aff'd ARD*, CFI Sept. 30, 2003, T-158/00; *Telia/Sonera*, D.Comm. July 10, 2002, M.2803 (market shares of 55–70% in Sweden and Finland). However, in the latter case the commitments did not preclude the merged entity from abusing its dominant position by applying predatory prices, which prevented the development of alternative infrastructure and the entry of competing service providers: IP/03/1797 of 19 Dec. 2003.
536. *PTT'Post/TNT/GD Express Worldwide*, D.Comm. Nov. 8, 1991, M.843, amended D.Comm. July 24, 1996, and D.Comm. 12 Dec. 1996; *TNT/Canada Post, DBF Postdienst, La Poste, PTT Post and Sweden Post*, D.Comm. Dec. 2, 1991 (*see SFEI*, CFI 15 Jan. 1997, 1997 ECR II-4, para. 74).
537. *DHL/Deutsche Post I*, D.Comm. June 26, 1998, M.1168; *DHL/Deutsche Post II*, D.Comm. Oct. 21, 2002, M.2908.
538. *The Post Office/TPG/SPPL*, D.Comm. March 13, 2001, M.1915, point 165.
539. COM(91)476 final; Twenty-fourth Report on Competition Policy, point 512.

liberalization policy is how 'to bring a reform in the postal service that will benefit the customers through both universal service and competition at the same time'.[540] The liberalization process includes a harmonization directive and a Commission notice on the application of the competition rules in the light of Article 86 (2).[541]

Harmonization Directive.

Following the Council resolution of February 7, 1994,[542] the European Parliament and the Council adopted Directive 97/67/EC on common rules for the development of Community postal services and improved quality of services,[543] which was amended by Directive 2002/39/EC.[544] The directive aims at providing postal services throughout the Community to all citizens at affordable prices with a high degree of quality, including in remote areas. It establishes common rules concerning the provision of a universal service, the criteria defining the reserved activities (delivery of letters, books, newspapers and parcels within certain price and weight limits and registered and insured items), the tariff principles and transparency of accounts for universal service provision,[545] the harmonization of quality and technical standards and the creation of independent national regulatory authorities.[546] The main changes introduced by Directive 2002/39/EC are:

- a further opening of the market with a progressive reduction of the reserved area as of January 1, 2003 (letters weighing more than 100 g) and as of January 1, 2006 (letters weighting more than 50 g) with the view of completing the internal postal market in 2009,
- the liberalization of outgoing cross-border mail except for those member states where it needs to be part of the reserved service in order to ensure the provision of the universal service,[547]
- the prohibition of cross-subsidization of universal services outside the reserved area out of revenues from services in the reserved area, unless this is strictly necessary to fulfil specific universal services obligations imposed in the competitive area,[548] and

540. V.V. Comandini, *Liberalization Policies of the Postal Sector in the European Union*, University of Liege, Nov. 5–6, 1998, referring to a statement of the World Bank (1996).
541. *See* Commission Communication on services of general interest, 2001 OJ C 17/4, point 17.
542. 1994 OJ C 48/3.
543. 1998 OJ L 15/14.
544. 2002 OJ L 176/21.
545. *See Asempre/Entitad Publica Empresarial Correos y Telegrafos*, ECJ March 11, 2004, C-240/02, paras 30–34.
546. *See* Twenty-fifth Report on Competition Policy, point 118.
547. *See* Commission Communication on services of general interest, 2001 OJ C 17/4, point 16.
548. *See German Post*, D.Comm. June 19, 2002, 2002 OJ L 247/27 (decision ordering the recovery of the illegal state aid by cross-subsidization of EUR 572 million).

– the application of the principles of transparency and non-discrimination whenever universal service providers apply special tariffs.[549]

Commission Notice on Postal Services.
The Commission issued a communication on the application of the competition rules in the postal sector in taking into account the special tasks of general interest of that sector, in particular with regard to Article 86 (2).[550] The notice clarifies that the monopoly power left to the national post offices may not be abusively extended to activities that are open for competition nor discriminate between large customers and small users, whereas they may not be prevented from charging postal rates which are necessary to enable the undertaking to operate the universal postal service under economically viable conditions.[551]

The Article 86 (2) Exception in the Light of the *Corbeau* Case.
Article 86 (2) is, as any exception, construed and interpreted narrowly. A typical case where the Court of Justice accepted the applicability of this exception was *Corbeau*.[552] The Court held that the post office is entrusted with the operation of a service of a general economic interest consisting of the duty to collect mail transport and deliver, on behalf of all users at uniform prices, regardless of the distance and the degree of economic profitability of each individual operation thereby compensating losses in some areas by profits in others. Companies concentrating their business in profitable sectors and offering there cheaper prices would obstruct the performance of the post office. However, this would not apply to additional services to the service of general interest, such as home collection of mail, Mr. Corbeau's business.[553]

Application of Existing Competition Rules in Individual Cases.
The competition rules of Articles 81 and 82 apply in the postal sector, subject to the exception of Article 86 (2). The EC competition rules coexist with national competition rules. The competition rules may be applied by the Community and national antitrust authorities, by the regulatory authorities[554] and the national courts.[555] The Commission distinguishes two markets, namely the basic ('universal') postal service market and the express postal service market. Express postal service includes specific services, such as home collection of packages, delivery

549. 2002 OJ L 176/21.
550. 1998 OJ C 39; Twenty-seventh Report on Competition Policy, point 125, Twenty-eighth Report on Competition Policy, points 92–94.
551. *TNT Traco*, ECJ May 17, 2001, 2001 ECR I-4109, para. 63.
552. *Corbeau*, ECJ May 19, 1993, 1993 ECR I-2533, para. 21.
553. Similarly, *FFSA*, CFI Feb. 27, 1997, 1997 ECR II-229, para. 108. *See* in greater detail cases where Article 86 (2) has been applied and rejected in Chapter IX, section C.3.
554. Article 22 (3) of Directive 97/67/EC.
555. *See Remailing*, German Federal Supreme Court (BGH), Oct. 7, 1997, WuWE DE-R 1.

to the addressee in person, the possibility of changing destination or address in transit, acknowledgement of receipt, keeping track of packages, individual attention given to customers, *à la carte* service[556] and guarantee of mail delivery by a specified date.[557] The Commission has applied Article 82:

- by imposing fines on national postal offices for surcharging international mail,[558] not deducting the terminal dues,[559] for predatory pricing[560] or tying practices;[561]
- by adopting decisions under Article 86 (3) against the respective member states for attempting to extend its postal monopoly in the reserved area (letter mail) to services in areas open to competition (e.g. B2B mail or express services),[562] and for abusing the French La Poste's dominant position encouraged by the conflict of interests in the relationship between La Poste and firms specializing in private mail-preparation, which are at the same time its competitors and partners.[563]

However, the Commission exempted, under the merger control regulation, the creation of express courier joint ventures by different national postal administrations in order to establish a new autonomous competitor, provided that access by third parties[564] or the acquisition of minority participations in private express courier services[565] is not restricted, and in cases where the transaction was likely to create or strengthen a dominant position, subject to divestment commitments.[566]

556. *Dutch PTT*, D.Comm. Dec. 20, 1989, 1990 OJ L 10/47, point 3.
557. *Express Courier Service Spain*, D.Comm. Aug. 1, 1990, 1990 OJ L 233/19, point 2.
558. *German Post II*, D.Comm. July 25, 2001, 2001OJ L 331/40 (symbolic fine of EUR 1,000). However, the payment of postal dues equivalent to the postage charge normally applicable to the undertaking responsible for the universal service does not constitute an abuse: *TNT Traco*, ECJ May 17, 2001, 2001 ECR I-4109; *Deutsche Post/GZS*, ECJ Feb. 10, 2000, 2000 ECR I-825, para. 61.
559. *Deutsche Post/GZS*, ECJ Feb. 10, 2000, 2000 ECR I-825, para. 61.
560. *German Post I*, D.Comm. March 20, 2001, 2001 OJ L 125/27 (EUR 39.6 million).
561. *Belgian Post*, D.Comm. Dec. 5, 2001, 2001 OJ L 61/32 (EUR 2.5 million).
562. *Dutch PTT*, D.Comm. Dec. 20, 1989, 1990 OJ L 10/47 (*rev'd* CFI Feb. 12, 1992, 1992 ECR I-565 for non-respect of the interested parties' right of being heard); *Express Courier Service Spain*, D.Comm. August 1, 1990, 1990 OJ L 233/19; *Bundespost I*, Fifteenth Report on Competition Policy, point 259; *An Post – Ireland*, Sixteenth Report on Competition Policy, point 298; *Italian International Courier Services*, Nineteenth Report on Competition Policy, point 228. *Provision of Certain New Postal Services with a Guaranteed Day- or Time-Certain Delivery in Italy*, D.Comm. Dec. 21, 2000, 2001 OJ L 63/59
563. *La Poste*, D.Comm. Oct. 23, 2001, 2002 OJ L 120/19.
564. *PTT Post/TNT/GD Express Worldwide*, D.Comm. Nov. 8, 1991, M.843, amended D.Comm. July 24, 1996, and D.Comm. 12 Dec. 1996; *TNT/Canada Post, DBF Postdienst, La Poste, PTT Post and Sweden Post*, D.Comm. Dec. 2, 1991 (*see SFEI*, CFI 15 Jan. 1997, 1997 ECR II-4, para. 74).
565. *DHL/Deutsche Post I*, D.Comm. June 26, 1998, M.1168; *DHL/Deutsche Post II*, D.Comm. Oct. 21, 2002, M.2908.
566. *The Post Office/TPG/SPPL*, D.Comm. March 13, 2001, M.1915, point 165.

The *International Express Carriers Conference* (*IECC*) v. *Public Postal Operators* (*PPO*) Cases – The *REIMS I* Agreement.
The Commission investigated a complaint lodged by the IECC, a grouping of companies whose members are involved in '*remail*' services: the provider of a remail service collects bulk mail from a sender in country A and remails it in a second country B for delivery by the ordinary post to final destinations in country A (remailing type ABA) or in country C (remailing type ABC). A number of PPO's considered the emergence of such services as a threat to their own activities and in abusive circumvention of the postal monopoly. In the case of an ABA type remailing system the Commission issued a statement of objections stating that Article 81 had been infringed by the so-called *CEPT* agreement between 16 PPO's in regard to two issues:

- the aim of deliberately seeking to eliminate competition from remailing companies by fixing the remuneration due for the delivery of cross-border mail (the so-called 'terminal dues') (the originating PPO in country A is prevented from delivering the mail itself from country A to the final destination in country B because of the still existing postal monopolies[567]) and
- the practice of intercepting, returning or charging extra postage on letters which had been posted in a country other than that of the sender.

However, the Commission did not pursue the infringement procedure in view of he PPO's commitments to introduce a new, more objective system based on the real delivery costs ('Agreement for the Remuneration of Mandatory Deliveries of Cross-Border Mail,' the so-called *REIMS I* Agreement).[568] However, the Court of First Instance annulled this decision with respect to ABA mail on the ground that the Commission erred in finding that interceptions of commercial ABA remail did not constitute an abuse within the meaning of Article 82,[569] which was confirmed by the Court of Justice.[570] In the case of an ABC type of remailing the Court of First Instance upheld the Commission decision; since the German and British postal authorities had given undertakings that they would no longer intercept ABC remail, and in fact there was no evidence of interception by the French postal authorities, the Commission had acted properly in dismissing this aspect of the proceedings.[571]

567. Council Directive 97/67/EC does not touch this monopoly. Interception of cross-border mail is therefore only justified and does not constitute an abuse within the meaning of Article 82 to the extent to which commercial remail companies violate the postal monopoly thereby threatening within the meaning of Article 86 (2) the fulfilment of the task of guaranteeing a universal service: Twenty-fifth Report on Competition Policy, p. 142. *See Remailing*, German Supreme Court (BGH), Oct. 7, 1997, WuWE DE-R 1, and 8 Dec. 1998, WuW DE-R 217.
568. *REIMS I*, 1996 OJ C 42/7; Twenty-fifth Report on Competition Policy, p. 141.
569. *IECC*, CFI Sept. 16, 1998, 1998 ECR II-3645, paras 94–106.
570. *IECC*, ECJ May 17, 2001, 2001 ECR I- 3247.
571. *IECC*, CFI Sept. 16, 1998, 1998 ECR II-3645, paras 125–130.

The *REIMS II Agreement.*

Subsequent to these proceedings, seventeen national postal operators[572] entered into a revised agreement (the *REIMS II Agreement*) with respect to the system of terminal dues, i.e., the remuneration postal operators pay to each other for the delivery of cross-border mail in the country of destination. Although the system is restrictive of competition because it reduces the signatories' freedom to set individually the prices for the delivery of incoming cross-border mail, the Commission granted clearance under Article 81 (3) on 15 September 1999 until 2003[573] and on 23 October 2003 until 2006[574] because the agreement contributed to improving the quality, in particular the speed, of cross-border mail to the benefit for consumers. In its 2003 decision the Commission sets forth the following principles:

- Terminal dues must reflect the actual costs of delivery; the charges for incoming cross-border mail can be increased gradually up to 78.5% of the domestic tariff.
- Stringent quality-of-service targets must be established, accompanied by appropriate penalties.
- The signatories are obliged to deliver incoming cross-border mail on behalf of private operators under the same terms and conditions as they apply among each other, including attractive domestic rates, which the signatories increasingly use in the country of delivery.

---

572. The incumbent postal operators of all member states, other than the Netherlands, and of Norway, Iceland and Switzerland.

573. *REIMS II*, D.Comm. Sept. 15, 1999, 1999 OJ L 275/17, points 69–80, extended by comfort letter of April 23, 2003 IP/03/557. *See also* the Commission clearance of the bilateral agreement between the Dutch and Swedish postal operators which served as a model for the multilateral *REIMS II* Agreement: Commission Notice of Oct. 6, 1998.

574. *REIMS II renewed*, D.Comm. Oct. 23, 2003, 2004 OJ L 56/76.

Chapter IX

Government-Induced Distortions of Competition

CONTENTS

A. Obligation of Member States not to Distort Competition as Complement to Obligation of Enterprises not to Distort Competition and Right to Compete on Equal Terms

The Rules of the EC Treaty Apply to Government Intervention in the Economy.
Member states are in principle free to have their own system of property ownership including state-owned enterprises.[1] They are free to carry on a given commercial activity themselves, to franchise it to publicly or privately owned firms or to leave it entirely to private firms without any state influence.[2] Member states are also not precluded from granting exclusive or special rights[3] or concessions[4] or from entrusting, by way of an act of public authority, selected firms with the operation of services of general economic interest,[5] thereby enjoying a broad discretion.[6] However, Article 3 (g) of the EC Treaty provides for the institution of a system ensuring that competition in the Common Market is not distorted. Competition may be distorted by both governmental measures and the behaviour of enterprises. The Treaty therefore provides for a complete set of legal instruments to prevent distortions of competition regardless of whether they are caused by member states or by public or private undertakings, provided they are engaged in an economic activity,[7] thereby excluding acts of sovereignty:[8]

- member states may not distort competition by imposing quantitative restrictions on imports or exports or measures having equivalent effects (Articles

---

1. Article 295 of the EC Treaty. *See British Telecommunications*, ECJ March 20, 1985, 1985 ECR 873, paras 21–22. *See also Costa/ENEL*, ECJ July 15, 1964, 1964 ECR 585, 598 (Article 31 – state monopolies); *Sacchi/Tele Biella*, ECJ April 30, 1974, 1974 ECR 409, para. 14 (Article 86 – public enterprises).
2. *See Funeral Services*, ECJ May 4, 1988, 1988 ECR 2479, para. 14; *Transparency Directive*, ECJ June 16, 1987, 1987 ECR 2599, paras 7–8.
3. *Silvano Raso* (*Porto di Geneva II*), ECJ Feb. 12, 1998, 1998 ECR I-593, para. 27.
4. Commission Communication on services of general interest, 2001 OJ C 17/4, point 22. *See ERT*, ECJ June 18, 1991, 1991 ECR I-2915, para. 18; *Italian Electricity Monopoly*, ECJ Oct. 23, 1997, 1997 ECR I-5789, para. 29.
5. *Italian Electricity Monopoly*, ECJ Oct. 23, 1997, 1997 ECR I-5789, paras 41–43. *See Franzen/Swedish Alcohol Monopoly*, ECJ Oct. 23, 1997, 1997 ECR I-5909, paras 43–51 (selection of dealers based on objective qualitative criteria).
6. *Coe Clerici Logistics*, CFI June 17, 2003, T-52/00, para. 86.
7. *Höfner/Macrotron*, ECJ April 23, 1991, 1991, ECR I-1979, para. 21; *CSND*, ECJ March 30, 2000, 2000 ECR II-1807, para. 36; *FENIN*, CFI March 4, 2003, T-319/99, para. 36. Purely social activities do not constitute an economic activity: *FENIN*, CFI March 4, 2003, T-319/99, para. 37.
8. *SAT/Eurocontrol*, ECJ Jan. 19, 1994, 1994 ECR I-43, para. 30; *Diego Cali & Figli* (*Porto di Genova II*), ECJ March 18, 1997, 1997 ECR I-1547, paras 16–24 (the mere fact of paying a fee is not decisive). *See* Article 45 (1) of the EC Treaty ('exercise of official authority').

28–30) or on the freedom to provide services within the Community (Articles 49–55);
- member states must progressively adjust existing, and may not introduce new, state trading monopolies (Article 31);[9]
- member states may not distort competition by granting state aid favouring certain undertakings (Articles 87–89);
- member states may not distort competition by imposing discriminatory taxes on imported products (Articles 90–93);[10]
- member states may not take, with regard to public undertakings or undertakings vested with exclusive or special rights, measures contrary to the Treaty and in particular the competition rules (Article 86 (1));
- member states may not distort competition by compelling the conclusion of, or facilitating, anti-competitive agreements between undertakings (Article 10 combined with Articles 81 and 82);[11]
- member states may not distort competition by discriminating on grounds of nationality (Article 12);
- private undertakings may not distort competition by concluding anti-competitive agreements (Article 81), abusing a dominant position (Article 82) or by mergers likely to create or strengthen a dominant position (Regulation 139/2004 on merger control);
- public undertakings or undertakings vested with exclusive or special rights are generally subject to the same obligations as private undertakings (Article 86).

The obligations imposed on member states and private or public undertakings are subject to the general derogation of Article 86 (2), which provides that enterprises 'entrusted with the operation of services of general economic interest' or 'having the character of a revenue-producing monopoly' shall be subject to the rules contained in the EC Treaty, and in particular the rules on competition, insofar as the application of those rules does not obstruct the performance of the particular tasks assigned to them. However, the development of trade in the Community must not be affected to such an extent as would be contrary to the interests of the Community.[12] This exception applies to both government distortions of competition and anti-competitive behavior of state or private enterprises.

---

9. Similarly Article 16 of the EEA Agreement. *See also Norwegian Alcohol Monopoly*, EFTA Court of Justice, Dec. 3, 1997, E-1/97 (discriminatory taxation of beer).
10. These provisions are not discussed. *See*, however, the leading case *Sociaal Fonds voor de Diamantarbeiders*, ECJ July 1, 1969, 1969 ECR 211, and *Outokumpu Oy*, ECJ April 2, 1998, C-213/96.
11. Similarly Articles 53–57 of the EEA Agreement.
12. Article 86 (2) is interpreted in the Commission communication on services of general interest, 2001 OJ C 17/4, which updates the previous communication of 1996, 1996 OJ C 281/3.

The Right to Compete on Equal Terms and Non-Discriminatory Enforcement of the Competition Provisions.

The system as described in Article 3 (g) of the EC Treaty, to ensure that competition within the Community is not distorted, requires that public and private enterprises as well as public authorities exercising economic activities be able to compete on equal terms.[13] This right mandates that distortions of competition, regardless of whether they are caused by member states or enterprises, may be challenged in actions before the national courts, Community courts and before the Commission. When exercising its powers under Article 211,[14] the Commission must act in a non-discriminatory manner against both governmental and entrepreneurial distortions of competition.[15] The Commission may have to act against the member state which causes a distortion of competition in breach of its obligations under the Treaty (Article 10 or Article 86 (1)) and against a public or private enterprise which causes a distortion of competition in breach of its obligations under Article 81, Article 82 or the merger control regulation.

Governmental v. Entrepreneurial Distortions of Competition: *Sugar v. Cognac*.

In many cases it may be difficult to establish who is responsible for the anti-competitive conduct: the state by requiring the conduct or influencing it in a decisive way ('compelling'[16]), the enterprise by engaging in anti-competitive activities based on its own initiative[17] notwithstanding the backing it receives

13. *GM-Inno-BM*, ECJ 13 Dec. 1991, 1991 ECR I-5941, para. 25.
14. Article 211 provides: 'In order to ensure the proper functioning and development of the common market, the Commission shall:
    - ensure that the provisions of this Treaty and measures taken by the institutions pursuant thereto are applied;
    - formulate recommendations or deliver opinions on matters dealt with in this Treaty, if it expressly provides or if the Commission considers it necessary;
    - have its own power of decision and participate in the shaping of measures taken by the Council and by the European Parliament in the manner provided for in this Treaty;
    - exercise the powers conferred on it by the Council for the implementation of the rules laid down in the latter.'

    The Commission is therefore called the *'guardian'* of the Treaty: *CNSD*, ECJ June 18, 1998, 1998 ECR I-3831, para. 26; *IECC II*, ECJ Sept. 16, 1998, 1998 ECR I-3605, paras 53–54.
15. *See Netherlands Postal Services*, ECJ Feb. 12, 1992, 1992 ECR I-565, paras 27–30. Example for acting against discriminatory landing charges under Article 82: *Ilmailulaitos/Luftfartverket*, D.Comm. Feb. 10, 1999, 1999 OJ L 69/24, and under Article 86 in conjunction with Article 82: *Portuguese Airports*, D.Comm Feb. 10, 1999, 1999 OJ L 69/31.
16. *See Bodson – Funeral Services*, ECJ May 4, 1988, 1988 ECR 2479, paras 13–15; *Glöckner*, ECJ Oct. 25, 2001, 2001 ECR I-8089, para. 39 ('led to commit such abuses').
17. *Asia Motor France*, CFI Sept. 18, 1996, 1996 ECR II-961, para. 61; *Ladbroke III*, ECJ Nov. 11, 1997, 1997 ECR I-6265, para. 33; *see British Telecommunications*, ECJ March 20, 1985, 1985 ECR 873, paras 18–20; *Telecommunications Directive Terminal Equipment*, ECJ March 19, 1991, 1991 ECR I-1223, para. 55; *GB-Inno-BM*, ECJ Dec. 13, 1991, 1991 ECR I-5941, para. 20.

from the State, or indeed both.[18] In the *Sugar* case the Commission fined Italian sugar producers under Article 81 for having limited import quantities and fixed import prices, although such imports were affected by a price surcharge imposed by the Italian government (a governmental levy called '*sovvraprezzo*'). The Commission argued that the anti-competitive coordination between the producers infringed Article 81 (1) because it had not been compelled by Italian regulations.[19] However, the Court of Justice held that the government system had 'substantially reduced the opportunities available to the parties concerned to negotiate a price which would have resulted from the operation of free market forces of supply and demand.'[20] Following this Court judgment the Commission took action against the government measure.[21] The *BNIC* case[22] concerned the fixing of a minimum purchase price for potable spirits by the French National Inter-trade Board for Cognac ('BNIC'), intended to ensure a minimum income for the farmers. The Court of Justice ruled that Article 81 (1) applies if minimum prices are discussed and fixed by the members of the association irrespective of whether the board was an institution of public law, whether certain members of the board were appointed by the Minister for Agriculture and whether fixing the minimum price was subsequently approved or declared generally binding by the government. Accordingly, it is only when a firm's conduct is so fundamentally restricted ('compelled') by governmental measures that it cannot engage in meaningful competitive conduct that Articles 81 and 82 do not apply.[23] The more recent case law follows this line of reasoning. The Court of Justice ruled in the *Arduino* case that a firm's conduct is fundamentally restricted when it 'conducts itself like an arm of the State working in the public interest.'[24] If this test is not met the Commission may have to act against both the government and the undertakings where both are responsible for

18. *See*, e.g., the analysis in *Funeral Services*, ECJ May 4, 1988, 1988 ECR 2479, paras 32–33. *See also Ladbroke*, CFI Sept. 18, 1995, 1995 ECR II-2539, paras 46–48.
19. *Sugar*, D.Comm. Jan. 2, 1973, 1973 OJ L 140/17, 32; *Rendo*, CFI Nov. 18, 1992, 1992 ECR II-2417, para. 106 (conduct that conforms to legal provisions does not infringe Article 81 (1)). Similarly *Welded Steel Mesh – Ferriere Nord*, ECJ July 17, 1997, 1997 ECR I-4411, paras 35–39 (even production quotas fixed by the government do not exclude the responsibility of the companies for anticompetitive arrangements on the market in question).
20. *Sugar*, ECJ Dec. 15, 1975, 1975 ECR 1663, para. 68.
21. Fifth Report on Competition Policy, point 20.
22. *BNIC I*, ECJ Jan. 30, 1985, 1985 ECR 391.
23. *GM-Inno-BM*, ECJ Dec. 13, 1991, 1991 ECR I-5941, para. 20; *SSI*, ECJ Oct. 10, 1985, 1985 ECR 3831, paras 24–29; *Polypropylene – Montecatini*, ECJ July 8, 1999, 1999 ECR I-4539, para. 127. *See FEDETAB*, ECJ Oct. 29, 1980, 1980 ECR 3125, paras 123–134; *Rendo/IJsselcentrale*, CFI Nov. 18, 1992, 1992 ECR II-2417, para. 106; *aff'd* ECJ Oct. 19, 1995 ECR I-3319; *Asia Motor France II*, CFI Sept. 18, 1996, 1996 ECR II-961, para. 61; *aff'd* ECJ May 7, 1998, 1998 ECR I-2587. The member state may, however, be held responsible under Article 10 in conjunction with Article 81 when it reinforces the effects of a private price fixing by making it legally binding for all undertakings, including those who did not participate in the price fixing: *see infra* section F.
24. *Arduino*, ECJ Feb. 19, 2002, 2002 ECR I-1529, para. 39.

the anticompetitive conduct, for instance, where the government establishes the legal framework for fixing prices and the undertakings agree on common prices.[25] In the absence of such governmental inducement the undertakings remain responsible for their anti-competitive conduct.[26]

Responsibility of Enterprises in Case of 'Voluntary Restraint Agreements'. Enterprises may infringe Article 81 if a government, instead of taking sovereign measures, encourages them to enter into so-called 'voluntary restraint agreements.'

In the *French-Japanese Ballbearings Agreement* case,[27] the Commission intervened against an agreement between French and Japanese manufacturers of ball bearings which increased the price of Japanese imports into France. The Commission found that the agreement was neither the implementation of a measure of external commercial policy nor imposed by the Japanese or French governments and therefore infringed Article 81 (1). In the *Aluminium* case the Commission followed the same reasoning.[28] In the *Asia Motor France* case[29] the French government limited imports of Japanese cars to a maximum of 3% of the cars registered in France. The Commission investigated, on the complainant's request, the alleged agreement by which the importers partitioned the corresponding quantity amongst themselves. The rejection of this complaint was annulled by the Court

25. E.g. in the *CSND* case referred to *infra*. The governmental measures may be adopted directly by a governmental body, such as fixing prices (*Giuseppe Conte*, ECJ Nov. 29, 2001, 2001 ECR I-9359, concerning fees for architects; *Commission/Italy*, ECJ Nov. 29, 2001, 2001 ECR I-9319, concerning fees for dentists; *Arduino*, ECJ Feb. 19, 2002, 2002 ECR I-1529, para. 44, concerning fees for lawyers; *see*, however, *Belgian Architects*, D.Comm. June 24, 2004, IP/04/800, where the association was held responsible for fixing fees), or preventing free imports (*Sugar*, D.Comm. Jan. 2, 1973, 1973 OJ L 140/17, 32; *Rendo*, CFI Nov. 18, 1992, 1992 ECR II-2417, para. 106, *aff'd* ECJ Sept 18, 1998, 1998 ECR I-2587; *Asia Motors France*, CFI Sept. 18, 1996, 1996 ECR II-961, paras 60–73), or by an undertaking to which the government confers sovereign powers (*Bodson – Funeral Services*, ECJ May 4, 1988, 1988 ECR 2479; *SAT – Eurocontrol*, ECJ Jan. 19, 1994, 1994 ECR I-43, concerning fees for supervising the air space; *Portuguese Airports*, D.Comm. Feb. 10, 1999, 1999 OJ L 69/31, *aff'd* ECJ March 29, 2001, 2001 ECR I-2613).
26. *See Polypropylene – Montedison*, ECJ July 8, 1999, 1999 ECR I-4539, para. 127; *CNSD*, CFI March 30, 2000, 2000 ECR II-1807, paras 54–60 (absence of public interest indicates lack of governmental influence); *AAMS*, CFI Nov. 22, 2001, 2001 ECR II-3413.
27. *French-Japanese Ballbearings Agreement*, D.Comm. Nov. 29, 1974, 1974 OJ L 343/19, 23, point II. 1. (without fines). Similarly: *French and Taiwanese Mushroom Packers*, D.Comm. Jan. 8, 1975, 1975 OJ L 29/26, 28 (with fines). *See also* Commission Notice on Japanese imports, 1972 OJ C 111/13.
28. *Aluminium Imports from Eastern Europe*, D.Comm. Dec. 19, 1984, 1985 OJ L 92, 1, 37–38.
29. *Asia Motor France III*, CFI Sept. 18, 1996, 1996 ECR II-961, 60–69; *aff'd* ECJ 7 May 1998, 1998 ECR I-2587.

of First Instance because of insufficient reasoning.[30] The fact that undertakings are induced by government measures to enter into anticompetitive agreements[31] or that the agreement is concluded in the presence of a government official,[32] encouraged,[33] endorsed or approved[34] or generally accepted[35] by a government measure does not preclude the application of Article 81,[36] although it may justify either lower fines[37] or the non-imposition of fines at all if the firms in question did not have any realistic alternative.[38]

Non-Discriminatory Treatment of Governmental and Entrepreneurial Distortions of Competition: The *CNSD* Case.
In cases where both the government and enterprises are responsible for a distortion of competition the Commission may have to act against both. In the *CSND* case,[39] the Italian Government required customs clearance agents to establish a tariff fixing arrangement without fixing the amount. The agents' association fixed the tariffs. The Commission acted under Article 81 and Regulation 17 against the association because of the anti-competitive tariff fixing arrangement. It also acted under Articles 10, 81 and 226 against the Italian government because of legal provisions declaring this agreement generally binding and thereby reinforcing the

30. This judgment was preceded by two other judgments dealing with the same allegation: *Asia Motor France I*, CFI Sept. 18, 1992, 1992 ECR II-2285 (appeal rejected); *Asia Motor France II*, CFI June 29, 1993, 1993 ECR II-669 (annulling the Commission's rejection of the complaint).
31. It may be argued that the government measure induced or facilitated the conclusion of the anticompetitive agreement in breach of Articles 10 and 81, but the Commission did not take action against the French government. However, the omission of such action does not preclude any action against anticompetitive behaviour insofar as it is based on the initiative of the parties: *FEDETAB*, ECJ Oct. 29, 1980, 1980 ECR 3125, para. 84.
32. *BNIA*, D.Comm. July 26, 1976, 1976 OJ L 231/24.
33. *INNO/ATAB*, ECJ Nov. 16, 1977, 1977 ECR 2115, para. 34.
34. *French-Japanese Ballbearings Agreement*, D.Comm. Nov. 29, 1974, 1974 OJ L 343/19, 23, para. 1.c; *BNIA* (*Armagnac*), D.Comm. July 26, 1976, 1976 OJ L 231/24, 27 (without fines); *BNIC* (*Cognac*), D.Comm. Dec. 15, 1982, 1982 OJ 379/1, 10, paras 49–50 (with fines).
35. *COAPI*, D.Comm. Feb. 2, 1995, 1995 OJ L 122/37. An exemption granted under national competition law does not prevent the application of Article 81 (1), *see Woodpulp*, ECJ Sept. 27, 1988, 1966 ECR 5193, para. 20, and Chapter I.C.2.
36. *Van Hazel*, ECJ May 18, 1977, 1977 ECR 901; *Asia Motors*, CFI June 29, 1993, 1993 ECR II-669, para. 71; *CNSD*, D.Comm. June 30, 1993, 1993 OJ L 203/27, point 44; *COAPI*, D.Comm. Feb. 2, 1995, 1995 OJ L 122/37, 49, point 46.
37. *French and Taiwanese Mushroom Packers*, D.Comm. Jan. 8, 1975, 1975 OJ L 29/26. *See also Dutch Construction Works*, D.Comm. Feb. 5, 1992, 1992 OJ L 92/1, *aff'd* CFI July 16, 1992, 1992 ECR II-2161, paras 39–42; *Greek Ferries*, D.Comm. Dec. 9, 1998, 1999 OJ L 109/24, points 98–108; *aff'd Strintzig Lines Shipping*, CFI Dec. 11, 2003, T-65/99.
38. *Aluminium Imports from Eastern Europe*, D.Comm. Dec. 19, 1984, 1985 OJ L 92, 1, 53, point 17.2.; *French-Japanese Ballbearings Agreement*, D.Comm. Nov. 29, 1974, 1974 OJ L 343/19.
39. *CNSD*, D.Comm. June 30, 1993, 1993 OJ L 203/27.

effects of the anti-competitive arrangement.[40] The Court of Justice upheld this approach.[41]

Different Enforcement Procedures.

The Commission is empowered to act against member states that cause a distortion of competition under the rules established by Article 31, Article 86 (3) and Article 226 of the EC Treaty. The Commission is also empowered to act under Article 226 in cases where a member state infringes the rules on free movement of goods, free provision of services, monopolies and discrimination.[42] If the Commission intends to act against the public or private enterprise that caused the distortion of competition, it must apply Articles 81 and 82 in the procedural framework of Regulation 1/2003 or of Regulation 139/2004 on merger control.[43] It may well be that one and the same state body is acting in part as a commercial enterprise and in part as an organ of government. For example, the Commission intervened under Article 82 against the German post and telecommunications authority's obstruction of private international courier services[44] and for tying the sale and leasing of modems and other terminal equipment to the supply of telecommunications network services.[45] It proceeded under the state monopoly provisions of Article 31 when the German government planned to extend the Bundespost's monopoly, by regulation, to cordless telephones.[46] Similarly, the Commission acted under Article 82 against the Italian tobacco monopoly in its capacity as wholesaler for having abusively limited the access of competitors to the market.[47] It proceeded under Article 31 against the Greek government for having established a system of marketing quotas for imported petroleum products in order to protect the state's oil monopoly.[48] Thus, the Commission can take various types of action against

40. Explained in greater detail in: Twenty-third Report on Competition Policy, point 219.
41. With respect to Article 10 EC Treaty: *CSND II*, ECJ June 18, 1998, 1998 ECR I-3831, paras 37–51; with respect to Article 81: *CNSD I*, CFI March 30, 2000, 2000 ECR II-1807, paras 56–74.
42. *Ente National di Cellulosa*, ECJ ECJ June 18, 1975, 1975 ECR 699, paras 32–36; *SAT/Eurocontrol*, ECJ Jan. 19, 1994, 1994 ECR I-43; *Diego Cali & Figli*, ECJ March 18, 1997, 1997 ECR I-1547, para. 16.
43. Under the former merger control regulation *see AAMS – Italian Tobacco Monopoly*, D.Comm. June 16, 1998, IP/98/536 (fine of ECU 6 million), *aff'd* CFI Nov. 22, 2001, 2001 ECR II-3417.
44. Fifteenth Report on Competition Policy, point 259. *See also Dutch Express Mail Services*,D. Comm. Dec. 20, 1989, 1989 OJ L 10/47; *Italian International Courier Services*, Nineteenth Report on Competition Policy, point 228.
45. Sixteenth Report on Competition Policy, point 294.
46. Fifteenth Report on Competition Policy, point 261.
47. *AAMS*, D.Comm. June 16, 1998, 1998 OJ L 252/47, *aff'd* CFI Nov. 22, 2001, 2001 ECR II-3417.
48. *Greek Oil Monopoly*, ECJ Dec. 13, 1990, 1990 ECR I-4747. *See also Franzen/Swedish Alcohol Monopoly*, ECJ Oct. 23, 1997, 1997 ECR I-5909.

anti-competitive practices according to the governmental or entrepreneurial nature of the anticompetitive practice:

- action under Regulation 1/2003 to enforce Article 81 or 82 or Regulation 139/2004 on merger control against *public or private enterprises or enterprises granted special or exclusive rights* insofar as they exercise a commercial activity,[49]
- action under Article 86 (3) *against a member state* which is in breach of Article 86 (1) by enacting or maintaining in force a measure with respect to such enterprises that is contrary to Article 81 or 82 or the anti-discrimination provision, Article 12;[50]
- action under Article 88 directed *against a member state* which grants a state aid which distorts competition and is incompatible with the Common Market;[51] and
- action under Article 226 before the Court of Justice *against a member state* which has failed to fulfil an obligation under the Treaty (including Article 31[52]) or to comply with a Commission decision, in particular under Article 86 (3).[53]

B. Article 86 (1): Obligation of Member States to Refrain from Government-Induced Distortions of Competition

Introduction: Rationale of Article 86 (1).
Article 86 (1) provides that member states shall neither enact nor maintain in force any measure contrary to the rules of the EC Treaty, in particular to Article 12 and the competition rules, with regard to public undertakings or undertakings to which the member states grant special or exclusive rights.[54] Even within the

---

49. *British Telecommunications*, D.Comm. Dec. 10, 1982, 1982 OJ L 360/36, *aff'd* ECJ March 20, 1985, 1985 ECR 873; *General Motors*, D.Comm. Dec. 19, 1974, 1975 OJ L 29/14, *aff'd* ECJ Nov. 13, 1975, 1975 ECR 1361; *British Leyland*, D.Comm. July 2, 1984, 1984 OJ L 207/11, *aff'd* ECJ Nov. 11, 1986, 1986 ECR 3263; *Telecommunications Directive Terminal Equipment*, ECJ March 19, 1991, 1991 ECR I-1223, paras 55–57; *Telecommunications Directive Services*, ECJ Nov. 17, 1992, 1992 ECR I-5833, para. 24; *Silvano Raso*, ECJ Feb. 12, 1998, 1998 ECR I-593, paras 28–31; *Corsica Ferries II*, ECJ June 18, 1998, 1998 ECR I-3949, para. 39; *AAMS (Italian Tobacco Monopoly)*, D.Comm. June 17, 1998, 1998 OJ L 252/47, *aff'd* CFI Nov. 22, 2001, 2001 ECR II-3417.
50. *Greek Insurance*, D.Comm. April 24, 1985, 1985 OJ L 152/25; *Portuguese Airports*, D.Comm. Feb. 10, 1999, 1999 OJ L 69/31; *VTM*, CFI July 8, 1999, 1999 ECR II-2329, paras 34 and 112. *See* in greater detail section D. *infra*.
51. *See* in greater detail section G, *infra*.
52. *Greek Oil Monopoly*, ECJ Dec. 13, 1990, 1990 ECR I-4747 (failure to reform trading monopoly, in contravention of Article 31). *See* in greater detail section E.3. *infra*.
53. *Greek Insurance*, ECJ June 30, 1988, 1988 ECR 3611.
54. *Cf.* the similar provision in Article 59 of the EEA Agreement and in Art. VIII (1) and (5) of the General Agreement on Trade in Services (GATS), 1994 OJ L 336/195.

framework of Article 86 (1) the competition rules have direct effect and confer on individuals rights which national courts must protect: National courts must refuse to apply any conflicting provisions of national law, even if adopted subsequently.[55] Addressees of this provision are member states, including national governments as well as regional or local authorities.[56] Article 86 (1) was included in the Treaty mainly because of the influence governments may exert over the commercial decisions of public enterprises or undertakings with close links to the state, causing them to distort competitive conditions within the Community. That influence may be exerted by virtue of financial relationships or of rules on how such enterprises operate. Private firms determine their industrial and commercial strategy mainly by reference to requirements of profitability. Decisions of public enterprises, on the other hand, may, under the influence of the government, be affected by considerations related to the pursuit of public interest objectives, and such decisions may distort competition no less than agreements between private enterprises.[57]

1. Growing Importance of Article 86 (1)

The Original Approach of the Court of Justice: *Sacchi/Tele Biella.*
The original approach of the Court of Justice to Article 86 (1) was that, in principle, the mere existence of an exclusive right was not, in itself, incompatible with the provisions of the EC Treaty. In the *Sacchi*[58] case, which concerned an exclusive right granted to an undertaking to transmit television signals, the ECJ stated that Article 86 (1) permitted member states *inter alia* to grant special or exclusive rights to undertakings. The Court of Justice concluded that the exclusive right to broadcast advertisements by television granted by the state was not incompatible with the Treaty:

> 'Nothing in the Treaty prevents Member States, for considerations of public interest, of a non-economic nature, from removing radio and television transmissions, including cable transmissions, from the field of competition by conferring on one or more establishments an exclusive right to conduct them.'[59]

However, the undertaking entrusted with the exclusive right remained subject to the general principle of non-discrimination and the competition rules in the performance of activities of an economic nature. As a result of this judgment

55. *CARRA*, ECJ June 8, 2000, 2000 ECR I-4217, para. 17.
56. *Funeral Services*, ECJ 4 May 1988, 1988 ECR 2479, para. 33. *See* the Commission's Transparency Directive, 1980 OJ L 195/35.
57. *Transparency Directive I*, ECJ July 6, 1982, 1982 ECR 2545, paras 21 and 24–26.
58. *Sacchi/Tele Biella*, ECJ April 30, 1974, 1974, ECR 409.
59. *Ibid.*, para. 14.

it was thought that the grant of exclusive rights by a member state could not of itself constitute a breach of Article 86 (1) but that Article 82 would apply if the undertaking to which exclusive rights are granted commits an abuse[60] or is 'led to commit such abuses'.[61]

The New Approach of the Court of Justice: The *Telecommunications Directive* Case.

The Court of Justice modified its approach, ruling that the grant of an exclusive right can itself constitute a state measure in breach of Article 86 (1), in particular where such measures have the effect of robbing provisions of the EC Treaty (notably Articles 28, 81 or 82) of their effectiveness. This new approach was adopted in the *Telecommunications Directive Terminal Equipment* case.[62] The Court of Justice held that the grant of such rights was the proper subject of scrutiny under Article 86. The case concerned an action brought by France for the annulment of Commission Directive 88/301 on competition in the telecommunications terminal equipment market. Article 2 of this directive provided that member states which had granted exclusive rights to undertakings to import, market, connect and maintain terminal equipment were to ensure that such rights were withdrawn. France contended that the Commission had exceeded its powers in requiring the withdrawal of exclusive rights. The Court of Justice rejected Advocate General Tesauro's submission that Article 86 (1) presupposed the grant of such rights and consequently that they could not constitute a 'measure' within the meaning of Article 86 (1).[63] Referring to Article 86 (3), the Court ruled that:

> '... even though that article presupposes the existence of undertakings which have special or exclusive rights, it does not follow that all such rights were necessarily compatible with the Treaty. That depends on the different rules, to which Article 90 (1) refers.'[64]

Unfortunately the Court of Justice did not use the occasion to shed light on the circumstances in which the mere existence of special or exclusive rights would be

60. *See RTL*, ECJ Oct. 3, 1985, 1985 ECR 3261, para. 16.
61. *Pavlov*, ECJ Sept. 12, 2000, 2000 ECR I-6451, para. 127; *Glöckner*, ECJ Oct. 25, 2001, 2001 ECR I-8089, para. 39.
62. *Telecommunications Directive Terminal Equipment* (*French Republic v. Commission of the European Communities*), ECJ March 19, 1991, 1991 ECR I-1223.
63. 'I would reiterate that the fact that a monopoly – and often, in practice, other similar arrangements – is likely to impair the proper functioning of the common market and freedom of competition was duly considered by the draftsmen of the Treaty, who nonetheless chose to tolerate it, so that the Commission Directive ... by simply abolishing the monopoly or the system of exclusive rights without taking the trouble of providing an appropriate statement of reasons, radically alters the basic framework set out in Article 90 (1),' *ibid.*, at para. 35.
64. *Ibid.*, para. 22.

incompatible with the Treaty. However, the Court clarified this new approach in its subsequent case law.

Subsequent Case Law.

In the *Mediawet II* case[65] the Court of Justice extended the reasoning of its *Telecommunications Directive Terminal Equipments* judgment to services. In *RTT/GB-INNO*,[66] the Court of Justice held that the extension of a monopoly without any objective justification constituted an infringement of Article 86 (1) in conjunction with Article 82. While Article 86 (1) clearly contemplates the creation of exclusive rights, developments in the jurisprudence of the Court of Justice since 1991 interpreting Article 86 reveal that the grant or broadening of exclusive rights is valid only if it is objectively necessary for the performance of a task of general economic interest within the meaning of Article 86 (2). In the *Corbeau* case[67] the Court of Justice elaborated on the new principle without stating expressly that it was reinterpreting Article 86 (1). In this case, which concerned criminal proceedings brought against Mr. Corbeau for infringing the Belgium postal monopoly, the Court of Justice held that Article 86 (1) 'must be read in conjunction with Article 90 (2) [*now 86 (2)*]' which:

> '… provision permits Member States to confer on undertakings to which they entrust the operation of services of general economic interest, exclusive rights which may hinder the application of the rules of the Treaty on competition in so far as restrictions on competition, or even the exclusion of all competition by other economic operators, are necessary to ensure the performance of the particular tasks assigned to the undertakings possessed of the exclusive rights.'

Applying the Court's reasoning in *Corbeau*, it would appear that an exclusive or special right can only be created if it is necessary for the performance of a task of general economic interest, i.e. the 'necessity test' of Article 86 (2).[68] According to the Commission's Communication on services of general interest,[69] Article 86 is neutral as regards the appropriateness of public or private ownership and member states retain fundamental freedom to define services of general interest but the 'proportionality' principle applies in order to avoid unnecessary distortions of trade. This provision, which must be read in the light of the new Article 17,[70]

65. *Stichting Antennevoorziening Gouda* (*Mediawet II*), ECJ July 25, 1991, 1991 ECR I-4007, paras 34–37.
66. *RTT/GB-INNO-GM*, ECJ Dec. 13, 1991, 1991 ECR 5941.
67. *Corbeau*, ECJ May 19, 1993, 1993 ECR 2533, para. 13.
68. *VTM*, CFI July 8, 1999, 1999 ECR II-2329, paras 106–112.
69. 2001 OJ C 17/4, points 21–23.
70. Introduced by the Treaty of Amsterdam. *See infra* section C.I.

requires therefore a balance to be struck between the competition rules and the fulfilment of missions of general economic interest.

Article 86 (1) as a Means of Liberalizing Markets.
According to this new case law of the Court of Justice, the mere existence of exclusive rights where the particular tasks assigned can be carried out without the grant of exclusive rights may infringe Community rules. The rules are infringed if the exclusive rights result, directly or indirectly, in discrimination between domestic products and imported products, to the detriment of the latter, impede the free circulation of goods or the cross border provision of services or results in an infringement of the rules on competition.[71] Therefore, Article 86 (1) is an instrument that may be used, and has been used, for liberalizing markets, such as telecommunications,[72] energy[73] and postal services.[74] This development of the Court of Justice's interpretation of Article 86 (1) is therefore considered as a '*milestone*' in Community competition policy.[75] The directives issued in specific sectors, such as energy and telecommunications, are based on this fundamental approach.[76]

2. ENTERPRISES COVERED BY ARTICLE 86 (1)

Public Undertakings.
The term 'public undertaking' is not defined in Article 86 (1). According to the Commission's directive ordering member states to disclose financial transfers to their public enterprises (the 'Transparency Directive'),[77] the expression 'public undertaking' means any business enterprise over which a public authority may

---

71. *Greek Television Monopoly*, ECJ 18 June 1991, 1991 ECR I-2925, paras 34–36. *See* D. Geradin, *The Opening to Competition of State Monopolies: An Overview of the Main Issues of the Liberalization Process*, Liege, Nov. 5–6, 1998.
72. *Telecommunications Directive Terminal Equipment*, 1988 OJ L 131/73, para. 8, *aff'd* ECJ March 19, 1991, 1991 ECR I-1223, paras 34–36; *Telecommunications Directive Services*, 1990 OJ L 192/10, para. 17, *aff'd* ECJ Nov. 17, 1992, 1992 ECR I-5833, paras 20–22 (both directives based on Article 86 (3)).
73. Electricity: *Directive 2003/54/EC concerning common rules for the internal market in electricity*, 2003 OJ L 176/37, para. 16; natural gas: *Directive 2003/55/EC concerning common rules for the internal market for natural gas*, 2003 OJ L 176/57 (both directives based on Article 95).
74. Directive 97/67/EC on postal services, 1998 OJ L 15/14 (based on Article 95) as amended by Directive 2002/39/EC, 2002 OJ L 176/21.
75. Gardner, *The Velvet Revolution: Article 90 and the Triumph of the Free Market in Europe's Regulated Sectors*, 1995 ECLR 78, 79; Pappalardo, *State Measures and Public Undertakings: Article 90 of the EEC Treaty*, 1991 ECLR 29, 37.
76. *See* in greater detail Chapter VIII.
77. Directive 2000/52/EC on the transparency of financial relations between member states and public undertakings, 2000 OJ L 193/75.

exercise, directly or indirectly, a dominant influence by virtue of its ownership thereof, a financial participation therein, or the articles or other rules that govern the business' operations.[78] Such influence is to be presumed when a public authority directly or indirectly holds a majority of the undertaking's subscribed capital or voting rights, or can appoint more than half of the members of its board of directors.[79] It is irrelevant whether the undertaking has its own legal personality,[80] is an integral part of a member state's administration,[81] or how it is financed.[82] However, the activities delegated to a public or private body must be of an economic nature.[83] Social activities[84] or acts of sovereignty[85] are clearly excluded

78. Article 2 of the Commission's Directive. *See Transparency Directive I*, ECJ July 6, 1982, 1982 ECR 2545, paras 25–26; *Alpha Flight/Aéroports de Paris*, D.Comm. 11 June 1998, 1998 OJ L 230/10, point 50; *Ilmailulaitos/Luftfartverket*, D.Comm. 10 Feb. 1999, 1999 OJ L 69/24, points 21–22.
79. *Cf.* the definition of 'control' in Article 3 (2) of Regulation 139/2004.
80. *Ente Nazionale per la Cellulosa*, ECJ June 18, 1975, 1975 ECR 699, paras 32–36; *British Telecommunications*, ECJ March 20, 1985, 1985 ECR 873, paras 21–22; *Brussels Airport*, D.Comm. June 28, 1995, 1995 OJ L 216/8, para. 7; *Lufthansa/SAS*, D.Comm. Jan. 16, 1996, 1996 OJ L 54/28; *Airport of Frankfurt*, D.Comm. Jan. 14, 1988, 1988 OJ L 72/30; *Airports of Paris* (*Roissy, Charles de Gaulle* and *Orly*), D.Comm. June 18, 1998, 1998 OJ L 230/10. *See also*, under Article 65 ECSC Treaty, *National Carbonizing*, D.Comm. Oct. 29, 1975, 1975 OJ L 35/6.
81. *Transparency Directive II*, June 16, 1987, 1987 ECR 2599, paras 5–10; *Ilmailulaitos/Luftfartverket*, D.Comm. Feb. 10, 1999, 1999 OJ L 69/24, points 21–22. The Commission's communication based on Article 10 of this directive was annulled: *Transparency Directive II*, ECJ June 16, 1993, 1993 ECR I-3283. *See also Decoster*, ECJ Oct. 27, 1993, 1993 ECR I-5335, para. 11. Cases in which the Commission intervened against a public administration engaged in anticompetitive behaviour include *Brazilian Coffee*, Fifth Report on Competition Policy, point 33; *BBC/Valley Printing*, Sixth Report on Competition Policy, point 163; *Sarabex/Bank of England*, Eighth Report on Competition Policy, points 35–37; *Suralmo*, Ninth Report on Competition Policy, points 114–115; *SEITA* (*state monopoly*), Tenth Report on Competition Policy, point 124; *Aluminium Imports from Eastern Europe*, D.Comm. Dec. 19, 1984, 1985 OJ L 92/1.
82. *FENIN*, CFI March 4, 2003, T-319/99, para. 35.
83. In *Höfner/Macrotron* the Court of Justice stated 'that the concept of an undertaking encompasses every activity engaged in an economic activity, regardless of the legal status of the entity and the way in which it is financed': ECJ April 23, 1991, 1991 ECR I-1979, para. 21; *see also Decoster*, ECJ Oct. 27, 1993, 1993 ECR I-5335, para. 11; *CNSD*, ECJ June 18, 1998, 1998 ECR I-3851, para. 36.
84. *AOK Bundesverband v. Ichthyol-Gesellschaft Cordes*, ECJ March 16, 2004, C-264/01: in determining ceilings for payments in respect of certain medicinal products, the sickness fund association did not act as undertakings engaging in economic activity, but performed their task, imposed by legislation, as part of the German social security system. *See also Poucet*, ECJ Feb. 18, 1993, 1993 ECR I-637; *Job Center II*, ECJ Dec. 11, 1997, 1987 ECR I-7119.
85. *LTU*, ECJ Oct. 14, 1976, 1976 ECR 1541; *Leclerc – French Gasoline Prices*, ECJ Jan. 29, 1985, 1985 ECR 305; *Funeral Services*, ECJ May 4, 1988, 1988 ECR 2479; *SAT/Eurocontrol*, ECJ Jan. 19, 1994, 1994 ECR I-43, para. 30; *Diego Cali & Figli* (*Porto di Genova II*), ECJ March 17, 1997, 1997 ECR I-1547, para. 23; *Job Center*, ECJ Dec. 11, 1997, 1997 ECR I-7119. With regard to 'acts of state': *BEUC and National Consumer Council*, CFI May 18, 1994, 1994 ECR II-285, para. 68; *BRD/Delta*, ECJ June 9, 1994, 1994 ECR I-2517.

from Article 86 (1), since the competition rules of Articles 81 and 82 only apply to commercial activities,[86] provided that the sovereign character can be established by the very nature of the activity and does not result from a simple declaration of the state to this effect.[87] However, this does not preclude a body from being an undertaking in its dealings with certain classes of third parties, notwithstanding the fact that, in other matters, it acts as a social institution.[88]

Undertakings to which Member States Grant Exclusive or Special Rights.
The inclusion in Article 86 (1) of firms which have been granted 'special or exclusive rights' by the government is based on the fact that such firms tend to be dependent on the government and to act in accordance with its wishes and that, independently of the wishes of the government, firms may abuse such rights. Article 86 (1) requires an express act by which a member state or regional or local authorities grant exclusive or special rights to certain undertakings.[89]

'Exclusive Rights'.
Exclusive rights are rights which reserve a certain activity in a given geographic area to a single undertaking by excluding competitors. Examples of exclusive rights are monopolies for importing, supplying, connecting, putting into service and maintaining goods or equipment, such as telecommunications terminal equipment,[90] the exclusive right to provide telecommunications services,[91] the exclusive right or franchise for commercial television advertising,[92] the exclusive right to operate an employment agency,[93] the exclusive right to collect and distribute mail,[94] the grant of exclusive licenses for collecting waste oil,[95] the exclusive

86. *See Airport of Brussels* (*Landing Fees*), D.Comm. June 28, 1995, OJ L 216/8, where the Commission dissociated the commercial activities exercised by the entity in charge of the airport from its activities relating to the security of the air traffic; *Ilmailulaitos/Luftfartverket*, D.Comm. Feb. 10, 1999, 1999 OJ L 69/24, point 22.
87. *Höfner/Macrotron*, ECJ April 23, 1991, 1991 ECR I-1979, para. 22. *See also Job Center*, ECJ Dec. 11, 1997, 1997 ECR I-7119.
88. *FENIN*, March 4, 2003, T-319/99, para. 25, referring to *Poucet and Pistre*, ECJ Feb. 17, 1993, 1993 ECR I-637, paras 18–20.
89. *Portuguese Airports*, D.Comm. Feb. 10, 1999, 1999 OJ L 69/31, points 11–13. This excludes those cases where certain rights are granted to an unlimited number of undertakings: *INNO/ATAB* ECJ Nov. 16, 1977, 1977 ECR 2115, para. 42.
90. *Telecommunications Directive Terminal Equipment*, ECJ March 19, 1991, 1991 ECR I-1223, paras 31–44.
91. *Telecommunications Directive Services*, ECJ Nov. 17, 1992, 1992 ECR I-5833.
92. *Sacchi/Tele Biella*, ECJ April 30, 1974, 1974 ECR 409, paras 12–15; *Telemarketing*, ECJ Oct. 3, 1985, 1985 ECR 3261, paras 11–18.
93. *Höfner/Macrotron*, ECJ April 23, 1991, 1991 ECR I-1979, para. 25.
94. *Corbeau*, ECJ May 19, 1993, 1993 ECR I-2533; Commission's Notice on Postal Services, 1998 OJ C 39/2, 4, interpreting Directive 97/67/EC on Postal Services, 1998 OJ L 15/14.
95. *SNFR/Inter-Huile*, ECJ March 10, 1983, 1983 ECR 555.

right to insure certain types of insurance risks,[96] to issue conformity certificates for imported vehicles[97] or telecommunications terminals[98] or to provide funeral services within a certain geographic area.[99]

'Special' Rights.

Special rights are defined in Commission Directive 94/46 on satellite telecommunications[100] with regard to telecommunication services as rights

> 'that are granted by a Member State to a limited number of undertakings through any legislative, regulatory or administrative instrument which, within a given geographic area,
> – limits to two or more undertakings authorized to provide a service or undertake any activity, otherwise than according to objective, proportional and non-discriminatory criteria, or
> – designates, otherwise than according to such criteria, several competing undertakings as being authorized to provide a service or undertake an activity, or
> – confers on any undertaking or undertakings, otherwise than according to such criteria, legal or regulatory advantages which substantially affect the ability of any other undertaking to provide the same telecommunications service or to undertake the same activity in the same geographic area under substantially equivalent conditions.'

Special rights may include the franchise of mobile telephone services,[101] the distribution of alcohol products based on objective, non-discriminatory selective criteria,[102] and the selection of a limited number of specialized undertakings for waste recovery.[103]

---

96. *Ameyde/UCI*, ECJ June 9, 1977, 1977 ECR 1091, paras 18–22.
97. *General Motors*, ECJ Nov. 13, 1975, 1975 ECR 1367, paras 4–10; *British Leyland*, ECJ Nov. 11, 1986, 1986 ECR 3263, paras 3–10. *See also Decoster*, ECJ Oct. 27, 1993, 1993 ECR I-5335, para. 22; a product for which a conformity certificate has been issued in another member state cannot be subject to a second certificate requirement in the country of import: *Lagauche*, ECJ Oct. 27, 1993, 1993 ECR I-5262, para. 51.
98. *Telecommunications Directive Terminal Equipment*, ECJ March 19, 1991, 1991 ECR I-1223, paras 34–36.
99. *Funeral Services*, ECJ May 4, 1988, 1988 ECR 2479, para. 16.
100. 1994 OJ L 268/15, recital 11.
101. *Omnitel Pronto Italia*, D.Comm. Oct. 4, 1995, 1995 OJ L 280/49, para. 6. However, in the *Telecommunications Directive* cases the Court of Justice found that the Commission had not satisfactorily described the nature and effects of 'special rights': ECJ March 19, 1991, 1991 ECR I-1223, paras 45–47, and ECJ Nov. 17, 1992, 1992 ECR I-5833, para. 30.
102. *Franzen/Swedish Alcohol Monopoly*, ECJ Oct. 23, 1997, 1997 ECR I-5909, paras 53–57. However, the Court of Justice did not discuss whether and under which conditions the selection of distributors based on quantitative criteria may be tantamount to a discrimination against imports.
103. *FFAD*, ECJ May 23, 2000, 2000 ECR I-3743, para. 83.

3. Measures Contrary to the EC Treaty, in Particular to the Competition Rules

(a) The Grant of Exclusive Rights in Breach of the EC Treaty

Compatibility of Exclusive Rights and its Limits.
In principle the mere existence of an exclusive right is not incompatible with the Treaty, but only the abuse is subject to Article 82,[104] which is directly applicable even in the context of Article 86.[105] Yet the grant of the such rights may, as mentioned above, infringe the Community rules if it results in discrimination against imports[106] or cross-frontier provision of services.[107] Examples of the grant of such rights include:

- exclusive rights of telecommunications organizations with regard to terminal equipment connected to the public telecommunications network;[108]
- exclusive rights of telecommunications organizations with regard to services other than voice telephony,[109]
- exclusive rights for non-reserved postal services,[110]
- exclusive rights to import and export electricity or natural gas,[111] and
- exclusive rights granted to a private television company.[112]

104. *Sacchi/Tele Biella*, ECJ April 30, 1974, 1974 ECR 409, para. 14; *Höfner/Macrotron*, ECJ April 23, 1991, 1991 ECR I-1979, paras 28–29; *Telecommunications Directive Services*, ECJ Nov. 17, 1992, 1992 ECR I-5833, paras 35–37; *Crespelle*, ECJ Oct. 5, 1994, 1994 ECR I-5077, para. 22; *Silvano Raso* (*Port of Geneva*), ECJ Feb. 12, 1998, 1998 ECR I-593 para. 27.
105. *Commission/Portugal*, ECJ June 8, 2000, 2000 ECR I-4217; *Giovanni Carra*, ECJ June 8, 2000, 2000 ECR I-4217, para. 11.
106. *INNO/ATAB*, ECJ Nov. 16, 1977, 1977 ECR 2115, para. 35; *Telecommunications Directive Terminal Equipment*, ECJ March 19, 1991, 1991 ECR I-1223, paras 31–44; *Greek Television*, ECJ June 18, 1991, 1991 ECR I-2925, paras 15–16; *Franzen/Swedish Alcohol Monopoly*, ECJ Oct. 23, 1997, 1997 ECR I-5909, paras 38–40.
107. *Ameyde/UCI*, ECJ June 9, 1977, 1977 ECR 1091, paras 26–30.
108. Article 2 of the Commission Directive on *Telecommunications Terminal Equipment*, 1988 OJ L 131/73; ECJ March 19, 1991, 1991 ECR I-1223, para. 31.
109. Article 2 of the *Commission Directive on Telecommunications Services*, 1990 OJ L 192/10, ECJ Nov. 17, 1992, 1992 ECR I-5833, para. 31.
110. Article 9 of Commission Directive on postal services, 1998 OJ L 15/14.
111. *Italian Electricity Monopoly*, ECJ Oct. 23, 1997, 1997 ECR I-5789, para. 28, subject, however, to possible justifications under Article 86 (2).
112. The grant of exclusive rights with regard to television advertising considered incompatible with Article 43 (freedom of establishment): *VTM*, D.Comm. June 26, 1997, 1997 OJ L 244/18, points 11–12; *aff'd* CFI July 8, 1999, 1999 ECR II-2329, paras 106–122. *See Telecommunications Directive – Terminal Equipment*, ECJ March 19, 1991, 1991 ECR I-1223, paras 22–36; *Mediawet*, ECJ July 25, 1991, 1991 ECR I-4069, para. 34.

However, the directives issued in specific sectors, such as energy and telecommunications, aim at gradually abolishing exclusive rights with a view to a greater integration of the internal market in these sectors.[113]

(b) Forfeiting Exclusive Rights because of Non-Use ('Fallow Field Doctrine') or of Inherent Abuse (Conflict of Interest)

The 'Fallow Field' Monopolies – The *Höfner/Macrotron* Case.
This case[114] concerned the employment service in Germany established under the Law of Promotion of Employment with the goal of achieving and maintaining a high level of employment. This law entrusted the attainment of this goal exclusively to the Federal Office for Employment, which did not charge a fee for its services. As a result private employment agencies were generally unlawful in Germany, except that cross-frontier activities could be undertaken by other institutions with the consent of the Federal Office for Employment. Despite the German law, certain private employment agencies operated in Germany and charged a fee for their services, especially for the recruitment of executives. In a circular the Federal Office for Employment stated that it would tolerate certain activities of these consultants. The proceedings before the German courts concerned the claim, by a consultant, for payment of a fee due from an executive in violation of the German law (because this activity was reserved to the monopoly). The Court of Justice ruled:

> 'As regards the manner in which a public procurement agency enjoying an exclusive right of employment procurement conducts itself in relation to executive recruitment undertaken by private recruitment consultancy companies, it must be stated that the application of Article 86 of the Treaty cannot obstruct the performance of the particular tasks assigned to that agency in so far as the latter is manifestly not in a position to satisfy demand in that area of the market and in fact allows its exclusive rights to be encroached on by those companies. Whilst it is true that Article 86 *[now 82]* concerns undertakings and may be applied within the limits laid down by Article 90 (2) [*now 86*] to public undertakings or undertakings vested with exclusive rights or special rights, the fact nevertheless remains that the Treaty requires the Member States not to take or to maintain in force measures which could destroy the effectiveness of that provision....'[115]

Manifest Incapacity – 'Fallow Field'.
The decisive aspect of this reasoning is the 'manifest incapacity' of the exclusive right-owner to satisfy the market demand for its services. Under such circum-

113. *See* Chapter VIII.E. and F.
114. *Höfner/Macrotron*, ECJ April 23, 1991, 1991 ECR I-1979.
115. *Ibid.*, paras 25 and 26. Similarly *Job Center*, ECJ Dec. 11, 1997, 1997 ECR I-7119.

stances the right may not be used in order to prevent third parties from carrying out the activity which the right-owner itself does not exercise. This reasoning is similar to the conditions under which a compulsory license may be granted with respect to patents. Articles 21 and 22 of the Community Patent Convention in its amended (although not yet ratified) version[116] provide for the grant of compulsory licenses on grounds of lack or insufficiency of exploitation and incapacity of satisfying the needs in a certain territory. To use an agricultural analogy, the right-owner may be compared with a farmer who does not cultivate a field although he could do so in order to satisfy the needs of consumers. The approach of the Court of Justice may therefore be described as the 'fallow field' doctrine. The Court of Justice re-affirmed this approach in its *Giovanni Carra* judgment[117] with respect of public placement offices by stating:

> 'Public placement offices are subject to the prohibition contained in Article 86 *(now 82)* of the EC Treaty, so long as the application of that provision does not obstruct the particular task conferred on them. A Member State which prohibits any activity as intermediary between supply and demand on the employment market, unless it is carried out by those offices, is in breach of Article 90 *(now 86)* (1) of the EC Treaty where it creates a situation in which those offices cannot avoid infringing Article 86 *(now 82)*. That is the case, in particular, in the following circumstances:
> – the public placement offices are manifestly unable to satisfy demand on the market for all typpes of activities; and
> – the actual placement of employees by private companies is rendered impossible by the maintenance in force of statutory provisions under which such activities are prohibited and non-observance of that prohibition gives rise to penal and administrative sanctions; and
> – the placement activities in question could extend to the nationals or the territory of other Member States.'

Forfeiting Exclusive Rights because of Conflict of Interest – Inducement to Abuse.

An enterprise to which exclusive rights are granted by a member state may be induced, because of a conflict of interest, to engage in abusive practices, such as discrimination or fixing abusively high prices. In the *Greek Television Monopoly* case[118] the Court of Justice stated:

116. Commission proposal of 16 April 2003, 7159/03 PI 24. *See* Chapter VII.A.2(a).
117. *Giovanni Carra*, ECJ June 8, 2000, 2000 ECR I-4217, para. 17. *See also Glöckner*, ECJ Oct. 25, 2001, 2001 ECR I-8089, para. 40.
118. ECJ June 18, 1991, 1991 ECR I-2925, para. 38. *See also Telecommunications Directive – Terminal Equipment*, ECJ March 19, 1991, 1991 ECR I-1223, paras 34–36; *RTT/GB-Inno-BM*, ECJ Dec. 13, 1991, 1991 ECR I-5941; *Decoster*, ECJ Oct. 27, 1993, 1993 ECR I-5335, para. 18.

> 'that Article 90 (1) [*now 86 (1)*] of the Treaty prohibits the granting of an exclusive right to transmit and an exclusive right to retransmit television broadcasts to a single undertaking, where those rights are liable to create a situation in which that undertaking is led to infringe Article 86 *[now 82]* by virtue of discriminatory broadcasting policy which favours its own programmes, unless the application of Article 86 [*now 82*] obstructs the performance of the particular tasks entrusted to it.'

It is settled case law of the Court of Justice[119] and the Commission[120] that it is *not* necessary to wait until undertakings *actually* commit abuses, and that it is sufficient for such undertakings to be legally placed in a position in which they may be *induced* to commit abuses if they have an interest which makes the exclusive right itself incompatible with the EC Treaty. Article 86 (1) therefore extends beyond Article 82, which requires actual conduct constituting an abuse. Some authors refer to it as it the 'automatic abuse theory,' whereby the granting of an exclusive right is only held compatible with EC law where the member state ensures that the exercise of this right will not lead to an abuse within the meaning of Article 82.[121] Where the undertaking will *necessarily* abuse its dominant position, resulting from the exclusive right, the existence of this right infringes Article 86.[122]

(c) Unjustified Extension of Existing Monopolies to Unrelated Markets

The Telecommunication Cases.
The leading case is *Telemarketing*,[123] which concerned the Luxembourg radio and television station RTL. The state had conferred exclusive television rights on RTL, and RTL extended these rights to telesales or telemarketing whereby an advertiser placed on the television an advertisement carrying a telephone number to which viewers could respond. The first telemarketing operation was organized by a company which had the exclusive right to conduct telemarketing operations on RTL, thereby preventing advertising for telephone calls directed to any other telephone number. The Court held:

> 'that an abuse within the meaning of Article 86 is committed where, without any objective necessity, an undertaking holding a dominant position on a

119. *GM-INNO-BM*, ECJ March 7, 1990, 1990 ECR I-667, paras 23–29; *Silvano Raso* (*Port of Genova II*), ECJ Feb. 12, 1998, 1998 ECR I-593, paras 28–31.
120. *Italian Ports*, D.Comm. Oct. 21, 1997, 1997 OJ L 301/17, para. 30.c.
121. M. van der Woude, 'Competing for competence', in *European Law Review*, suppl. 1991, 1992, p. 60; R. Kovar, '"La peau de chagrin": ou comment le droit communautaire opère la reduction des monopoles publics', in *Europe*, July 1992.
122. *See also* for an application of this theory: *Porto di Genova I*, ECJ Dec. 10, 1991, 1991 ECR I-5889.
123. *Télémarketing*, ECJ Oct. 3, 1985, 1985 ECR 3261.

particular market reserves to itself or to an undertaking belonging to the same group an ancillary activity which might be carried out by another undertaking as part of its activities on a neighbouring but separate market, with the possibility of eliminating all competition from such undertaking.'[124]

Other examples of abusive extension of exclusive rights to neighbouring markets include the extension of the television monopoly to not directly related, but closely connected, products or services,[125] of the postal monopoly to express courier service, to cordless telephones[126] and the control of imported telephones,[127] and the extension of the exclusive rights conferred to an airport operator to ground-handling and ramp-handling services,[128] and exclusion of competition from competing private couriers.[129]

(d) Other Forms of Abuse Contrary to Article 82

Discriminatory Means.

The privileged position of a public undertaking as well as exclusive or special rights granted to enterprises may be abused, in particular, by the following means:

- the unjustified refusal of access to a network,[130] port, airport[131] or infrastructure[132] with respect to which exclusive rights are granted,
- the discriminatory treatment of equivalent transactions,[133]

124. *Ibid.*, para, 27. Similarly: *RTT/GM-Inno-BM*, ECJ Dec. 13, 1991, 1991 ECR I-5941, paras 18, 24.
125. E.g., extension to terminal equipment: *Telecommunications Directive Terminal Equipment*, ECJ March 19, 1991, 1991 ECR I-1223, paras 22–36; telecommunication services: *Telecommunications Directive – Services*, ECJ Nov. 17, 1992, 1992 ECR I-5833, paras 35–37; television advertising: *VTM*, CFI July 8, 1999, 1999 ECR II-2329, paras 106–122.
126. Sixteenth Report on Competition Policy, point 294.
127. *RTT/GB-INNO-BM*, ECJ Dec. 13, 1991, 1991 ECR I-5941; *Telecommunications Directive I (Terminal Equipment)*, ECJ Nov. 17, 1992, 1992 ECR I-5833, paras 36–37.
128. *British Airways*, CFI Dec. 17, 2003, T-219/99, para. 127; *Airport of Frankfurt*, D.Comm. Jan. 14, 1998, 1998 OJ L 72/30, para. 71.
129. *Netherlands PTT*, ECJ Feb. 12, 1992, 1992 ECR I-565. In this case the Court accepted a double violation of the competition rules, one committed by the postal monopoly (Article 82) and another by the government (Article 86 (l)/82). However, the Court annulled the Commission's decision based on Article 86 (3) for procedural reasons (non-respect of the rights of defence).
130. *See* in greater detail Chapter V.
131. *Airport of Frankfurt*, D.Comm. Jan. 14, 1998, 1998 OJ L 72/30, paras 70–73.
132. *VEBACOM/Deutsche Telekom*, D.Comm. Nov. 23, 1995, Twenty-fifth Report on Competition Policy, point 111.
133. *Airports of Paris (Roissy, Charles de Gaulle and Orly)*, D.Comm. June 18, 1998, 1998 OJ L 230/10, point 83; *Ilmailulaitos/Luftfartverket*, D.Comm. Feb. 10, 1999, 1999 OJ L 69/24, points 39–56; *Portuguese Airports*, D.Comm. Feb. 10, 1999, 1999 OJ L 69/31, points 33–40 (under Article 86). *See Corsica Ferries I*, ECJ May 17, 1994, 1994 ECR I-1783, para. 45.

- the application of unreasonable or discriminatory prices or fees[134] or rebates,[135]
- discriminatory[136] or predatory[137] fees or rebates,[138] and
- cross-subsidization as a predatory practice,[139] except insofar as it is justified to guarantee a universal service in the general interest.[140]

C. Article 86 (2): Balancing Public Service Obligations of Member States and Interests of the Community

1. The Central Role of Article 86 (2)

Article 86 (2) v. Article 16.
Article 86 (2) provides that undertakings 'entrusted with the operation of services of general economic interest' or 'having the character of a revenue-producing monopoly' are subject to the rules of the Treaty, and in particular to the rules of competition, insofar as the application of such rules do not obstruct the performance, in law or in fact, of the particular tasks assigned to them, and provided the development of trade is not affected to such an extent as would be contrary to the interests of the Community.[141] This requires a balancing of general economic interests and Community interests and involves the application of the proportionality test. The central role of this provision is emphasized in Article 16 (as introduced by the Amsterdam Treaty), which provides:

134. *Funeral Services*, ECJ May 4, 1988, 1988 ECR 2479, para. 32; *Ahmed Saaed*, ECJ April 11, 1989, 1989 ECR 803, para. 43; *GT-Link/Statsbaner*, ECJ July 17, 1997, 1997 ECR I-4449, para. 27; *Omnitel Pronto Italia*, D.Comm. Oct. 4, 1995, 1995 OJ L 280/49; *GSM Spain*, D.Comm. Dec. 18, 1996, 1997 OJ L 76/19.
135. *Corsica Ferries*, ECJ May 17, 1994, 1994 ECR I-1783, paras. 43–45; *Airport of Brussels (Landing fees)*, D.Comm. June 28, 1995, 1995 OJ L 216/8; *Portuguese Airports*, D.Comm. Feb. 10, 1999,
136. *Aéroports de Paris*, D.Comm. June 11, 1998, 1998 OJ L 230/10, points 83–127.
137. *Ground-handling services at airports*, Twenty-third Report on Competition Policy, points 367–369; *Airport of Frankfurt*, D.Comm. Jan. 14, 1998, 1998 OJ L 72/30; *Aéroports de Paris*, D.Comm. June 11, 1998, 1998 OJ L 230/10, points 116–123.
138. *Corsica Ferries*, ECJ May 17, 1994, 1994 ECR I-1783, paras. 43–45; *Portuguese Airports*, D.Comm. Feb. 10, 1999, 1999 OJ L 69/31, *aff'd* ECJ March 29, 2001, 2001 ECR I-2631. However, additional costs or additional services for imported products may justify different prices: *Crespelle*, ECJ Oct. 5, 1994, 1994 ECR I-5077, para. 36.
139. Commission's Guidelines on telecommunications, 1991 OJ C 233/2, paras 102–110.
140. Directive 97/67/EC on postal services, 1998 OJ L 15/14 as amended by Directive 2002/39/EC, 2002 OJ L 176/21.
141. *See FFAD*, ECJ May 23, 2000, 2000 ECR I-5743, para. 51; *TNT*, ECJ May 17, 2001, 2001 ECR I-4109, para. 52.

> 'Without prejudice to Articles 73, 86 and 87, and given the place occupied by services of general economic interest in the shared values of the Union as well as their role in promoting social and territorial cohesion, the Community and the Member States, each within their respective powers and within the scope of this Treaty, shall take care that such services operate on the basis of principles and conditions which enable them to fulfil their missions.'

This provision expresses the intention of the Community and the member states to emphasize the importance of services of general economic interest, without amending the legal scope of Article 86 (2).[142] It may, however, be interpreted as conferring greater freedom on member states to entrust public or private undertakings with specific tasks of a general economic interest.[143]

Commission Communication on Services of General Interest.
In 2001 the Commission issued a communication on services of general interest[144] which updates the 1996 communication.[145] The communication complements Commission guidelines on the application of the competition rules in particular sectors, such as telecommunications,[146] postal services[147] and the banking sector.[148] The 2001 Communication aims at providing further clarification on the proper role of public authorities and of the internal market provisions and at further developing the European framework relating to the sound functioning of services of general interest. It clarifies the scope and criteria of application of internal market and competition rules, which is based on three principles:

- neutrality with regard to the public and private ownership of companies;
- member states' freedom to define services of general interest, subject to control for manifest error;
- proportionality, requiring that restrictions of competition and limitations of the freedom of the single market do not exceed what is necessary to guarantee effective fulfilment of the mission.[149]

142. As stressed in the declaration of the contracting parties at the occasion of the conclusion of the Amsterdam Treaty. If this is so, it may be argued that Article 16 is in fact superfluous, *see* Mestmacker, 'Daseinsvorsorge und Universaldienst im europaischen Kontext', *Festschrift Zächer*, 1998, pp. 635, 651.
143. *See* Twenty-seventh Report on Competition Policy, points 96–100.
144. 2001 OJ C 17/4. *See* Thirty-second Report on Competition Policy, points 580–616, summarizing the Commission's and the Court's case law.
145. 1996 OJ C 281/3.
146. 1991 OJ C 233/2.
147. 1998 OJ C 39.
148. Commission's Communication on services of general economic interest in the banking sector, adopted June 17, 1998.
149. Communication on services of general economic interest (2001 OJ C 17/4), points 21–23.

Narrow Interpretation Prevails in the Case Law.
As in the case of any exception to a general rule – including the exceptions to the free trade rules found in Article 30,[150] Article 86 (2) is narrowly interpreted.[151] The burden of proof lies on the party invoking the exception[152] which is directly applicable,[153] (unless that party gives sufficient explanations which must be rebutted by the other party).[154] The narrow interpretation relates in particular to the term 'entrust,' which presupposes an express act of state, i.e., a delegation by a public authority in the 'general economic interest.'[155] The term 'economic' interest excludes social[156] or cultural[157] interests, ensuring internal or external security,[158] or exercising powers which are typically those of a public authority such as anti-pollution surveillance.[159] Instead, the term 'general' economic interest requires an

150. *Buy Irish*, ECJ June 17, 1981, 1981 ECR 1625, paras 7–8; *Beer Purity Law*, ECJ March 12, 1987, 1987 ECR 1227, paras 40–53; *Pasta I*, ECJ July 14, 1988, 1988 ECR 4233, paras 12–28; *Pasta II*, July 14, 1988, 1988 ECR 4285, paras 12–28.
151. *BRT/SABAM*, ECJ March 21, 1974, 1974 ECR 313, paras 19–23; *FFSA*, CFI Feb. 27, 1997, 1997 ECR II-229, para. 173; *Air Inter*, CFI June 19, 1997, 1997 ECR II-997, para. 144; *Airport of Frankfurt*, D.Comm. Jan. 14, 1998, 1998 OJ L 72/30, point 100.
152. *Magill*, CFI July 10, 1991, 1991 ECR II-485, para. 83. It is therefore consistent to examine Article 86 (2) before examining the conditions of an exemption under Article 81 (3): *Jahrhundertvertrag*, D.Comm. Dec. 22, 1992, 1993 OJ L 50/14, but *see EBU/Eurovision*, D.Comm. June 11, 1993, 1993 OJ L 179/23). Article 86 (2) arguments are in certain cases discussed in the context of Article 81 (3) without expressly referring to Article 86 (2), e.g., *Lufthansa/SAS*, D.Comm. Jan. 16, 1996, 1996 OJ L 54/28.
153. *Rendo*, ECJ Oct. 19, 1995, 1995 ECR I-3319, paras 17–18. *See Port of Metert*, ECJ July 14, 1971, 1971 ECR 723, paras 14–16, excluding, however, the second sentence of Article 86 (2) which national courts are unable to evaluate.
154. *Italian Electricity Monopoly*, ECJ Oct. 23, 1997, 1997 ECR I-5789, paras 46–61.
155. *BRT/SABAM* and *Fonior*, ECJ March 27, 1974, 1974 ECR 313, para. 35. However, 'entrusting' may be done by way of a concession (*Anseau*, D.Comm. Dec. 17, 1981, 1982 OJ L 169/39/48) or by way of an 'agreement or concession' (which is, as such, not covered by Article 81: *Funeral Services*, ECJ May 4, 1988, 1988 ECR 2479, para. 18; *Almelo*, ECJ April 27, 1994, 1994 ECR I-1477, paras 29–30). However, the mere fact of granting a license does not suffice: *BRT/SABAM II*, ECJ March 27, 1974, 1974 ECR 313, 318, paras 17–23; *GVL*, ECJ March 2, 1983, 1983 ECR 483, 504, paras 29–32; *Eurocheques I*, D.Comm. Dec. 10, 1984, 1985 OJ L 35/43, 48.
156. Commission Communication on services of general interest, points 30 and 68. *See Poucet/Assurances Generales*, ECJ Feb. 17, 1993, 1993 ECR I-637, para. 6; *FENIN*, CFI March 4, 2003, T-319/99, paras 25 and 37 (however, a body may be an undertaking in its dealings with certain third parties although acting in other matters as social institution).
157. *GEMA I*, D.Comm. June 2, 1971, 1971 OJ L 134/15, 27; *GVL*, ECJ March 2, 1983, 1983 ECR 483, 504. However, cultural policy and the preservation of pluralism in the media may constitute imperative requirements in the public interest, provided the means are limited to what is necessary: *VTM*, D.Comm. June 26, 1997, 1997 OJ L 244/18, point 13; *aff'd* CFI July 8, 1999, 1999 ECR II-2329, para. 120.
158. E.g. *SAT Eurocontrol*, ECJ Jan. 19, 1994, 1994 ECR I-43 (supervising air space).
159. *Diego Cali & Figli*, ECJ March 18, 1997, 1997 ECR I-1547; *FFAD*, ECJ May 23, 2000, 2000 ECR I-3743, para. 51. *See* Commission Communication on services of general interest, point 28.

essential economic need of consumers throughout a defined territory ('territorial coverage').[160] The term 'obstruct' signifies that the performance of the tasks assigned must be made impossible and not merely made more difficult.[161]

Activities *not* covered by Article 86 (2) include copyright collecting societies,[162] associations for the protection of plant breeders' rights,[163] port facilities[164] and banks.[165] Activities *covered* by Article 86 (2) have been telecommunications, postal services and public transport utilities.[166]

Character of a Revenue-Producing Monopoly.

The exception set forth in Article 86 (2) extends to revenue-producing monopolies which do not have a strictly economic character, but are also entrusted with services of a non-economic character. Possible examples are the tobacco and alcohol monopolies, although the non-economic character was not discussed in the Commission's recommendations. However, it may be argued that such a monopoly may be justified in accordance with Article 30, in particular on grounds of public health.[167]

2. Enterprises Entrusted with the Operation of Services of General Economic Interest

A Leading Case: *Corbeau.*

This case[168] concerned the activities of an individual, Mr. Corbeau, who provided mail delivery services in Liege, Belgium and its surrounding districts. The service consisted in Mr. Corbeau collecting mail from the home of the sender and delivering it by midday the following day, provided that the addressee resided

160. *Corbeau*, ECJ May 19, 1993, 1993 ECR I-2533, paras 14–18; Commission Communication on services of general interest, point 10.
161. *Ahmed Saaed*, ECJ April 11, 1989, 1989 ECR 803, para. 58; *Greek Oil Monopoly*, ECJ Dec. 13, 1990, 1990 ECR I-4747, para. 58; *Höfner/Macrotron*, ECJ April 23, 1991, 1991 ECR I-1979, paras 24–25; *Porto di Genova I*, ECJ Dec. 10, 1991, 1991 ECR I-5889, paras 26–28; *Air Inter*, CFI June 19, 1997, 1997 ECR II-997.
162. *GEMA I*, D.Comm. June 23, 1971, 1971 OJ L 134/15, 27; *Greenwich/SACEM*, ECJ Oct. 25, 1979 ECR 3275, paras 10–13; *GVL*, ECJ March 2, 1983, 1983 ECR 483, paras 29–32.
163. *Maize Seed*, D.Comm. Sept. 21, 1978, 1978 OJ L 286/23, 33.
164. *Harbour of Rodby*, D.Comm. Dec. 21, 1993, 1993 OJ L 55/52, para. 18.
165. *Züchner/Bayrische Vereinsbank*, ECJ July 14, 1981, 1981 ECR 2021, paras 6–9; *Austrian Banks (Lombard Club)*, D.Comm. June 11, 2002, IP/02/844. By contrast, certain insurance activities (loss-making accounts) may constitute a service of general economic interest: *Ameyde/UCI*, ECJ June 9, 1977, 1977 ECR 1091, paras 18–22.
166. See Chapter VIII.C, F and G
167. *Franzen/Swedish AlcoholMonopoly*, ECJ Oct. 23, 1997, 1997 ECR I-5909, paras 74–77; *Glöckner* (emergency transport), ECJ Oct. 25, 2001, 2001 ECR I-8089, para. 58 (subject, however, to the proportionality test).
168. *Corbeau*, ECJ May 19, 1993, 1993 ECR I-2533. *See* Twenty-third Report on Competition Policy, point 372 and Article 3 of Directive 97/67/EC on Postal Services, 1998 OJ L 15/14.

within the city. If addressees resided elsewhere, Mr. Corbeau collected the mail from the sender's home and dispatched it by post. Mr. Corbeau was charged in criminal proceedings for having contravened the postal monopoly. Ruling on the preliminary question of whether the monopoly was compatible with Article 86, the Court of Justice held that member states must not take measures which might thwart the full effectiveness of Articles 86 and 82, read in conjunction with Article 86 (2). The Court held that the post office had been entrusted with the operation of a service of a general economic interest consisting of the duty to collect, transport and deliver mail on behalf of all users at uniform prices, regardless of the degree of economic profitability of each individual operation. Ensuring this meant compensating losses in some areas by profits in others. Companies concentrating their business in profitable sectors and offering cheaper prices in those sectors would obstruct the performance of the post office.[169] However, this would not apply to additional services that are necessarily performed together with the service of general interest, such as home collection of mail.[170]

Application of the *Corbeau* Test.

The *Corbeau* test was applied in the *Almelo* case.[171] This case concerned the evaluation of an exclusive purchasing obligation imposed on a local electricity distributor in the Netherlands preventing it from purchasing electricity from other sources, including imports. The Court of Justice examined in particular the extent to which this obligation was necessary to enable the undertaking entrusted with such a task of general economic interest to perform it. The Court ruled that it was necessary to take into consideration the economic conditions in which the undertaking operated, in particular the costs which it had to bear and the legislation, particularly environmental legislation, to which it was subject.[172] Similar criteria have been applied in the evaluation of electricity monopolies[173] and the postal monopoly.[174]

169. *Ibid.*, para. 21. Similarly *Ahmed Saaed*, ECJ April 11, 1989, 1989 ECR 803, para. 55 (transport enterprises subject to the obligation to provide an *universal service* irrespective the profitability of certain lines); *Glöckner*, ECJ Oct. 25, 2001, 2001 ECR I-8089, para. 57. *See* Commission Communication on services of general interest, points 16 and 39.

170. *Corbeau*, ECJ May 19, 1993 ECR I-2533, para. 19; Directive 97/67/EC on postal services, 1998 OJ L 15/14, recital 21 (justification and limits of a *universal service* to be provided by the postal monopolies); *IECC II*, ECJ Sept. 16, 1998, 1998 ECR I-3645, paras 94–106, *aff'd* ECJ May 17, 2001, 2001 ECR I-3247.

171. *Almelo*, ECJ April 27, 1994, 1994 ECR I-1477.

172. *Ibid.*, para. 49.

173. *Italian Electricity Monopoly*, ECJ Oct. 23, 1997, 1997 ECR I-5789, paras 46–54.

174. Directive 97/67/EC on postal services, 1998 OJ L 15/14 and Commission's notice on this directive, in particular para. 5.5. *See also IECC*, CFI Sept. 15, 1998, 1998 ECR II-3605; *Dutch and Swedish Postal Monopolies*, Oct. 6, 1998, Twenty-eigth Report on Competition Policy, points 92–94 (comfort letters).

General Economic Interest: Universal Interest v. Public Interest. Services of a general economic interest are characterized by the obligation imposed by a member state or its authorities to perform a service for the public within a determined geographic area and to make sure, irrespective of profitability, that all persons enjoy equal access to the service in question at affordable prices ('universal service').[175] This applies typically to the distribution of water,[176] electricity,[177] gas,[178] coal,[179] oil,[180] public services related to transport by rail, road and inland waterway,[181] scheduled air services,[182] broadcasting and television societies,[183] private television companies serving cultural policy and the maintenance of pluralism,[184] postal services,[185] port[186] and airport administration, including – subject to the proportionality test[187] – related services such as ground- or ramp-handling[188] and activities related to the protection of the environment.[189]

175. Commission Communication on services of general interest, 2001 OJ C 17/4, points 14 and 39.
176. *Anseau*, D.Comm. Dec. 17, 1981, 1982 OJ L 169/39.
177. Council Directive 96/92/EC concerning common rules for the internal market in electricity, 1997 OJ L 27/20, recital 17; *Italian Electricity Monopoly*, ECJ Oct. 23, 1997, 1997 ECR I-5789, paras 42–55; *IJsselcentrale*, D.Comm. Jan. 16, 1991, 1991 OJ L 28/34; *Jahrhundertvertrag*, D.Comm. Dec. 22, 1992, 1993 OJ L 50/14; *Almelo* (*IJsselcentrale*), ECJ April 27, 1994, 1994 ECR I-1477.
178. Council Directive 98/30/EC concerning common rules for the internal market for natural gas, 1998 OJ L 204/1.
179. *Jahrhundertvertrag*, D.Comm Dec. 22, 1992, 1993 OJ L 50/14.
180. *Campus Oil*, ECJ July 10, 1984, 1984 ECR 2727, 2751.
181. *See* Council Regulation 1893/91 on action by member states concerning the obligations inherent in the concept of a public service in transport by rail, road and inland waterway, 1991 OJ L 169/1.
182. Regulation 2408/92 (1992 OJ L 240/8) permits member states to impose a public service obligation, which is defined in Article 2 (o), as meaning 'any obligation imposed on an air carrier to take, in respect of any route on which it is licensed to operate by a Member State, all necessary measures to ensure the provision of a service satisfying fixed standards of continuity, regularity, capacity and pricing, which standards the air carrier would not assume if it were solely considering its commercial interest'. *See Ahmed Saaed*, ECJ April 11, 1989, 1989 ECR 803, paras 54–56.
183. *EBU-Eurovision-System*, D.Comm. June 11, 1993, 1993 OJ L 179/23.
184. *VTM*, D.Comm. June 26, 1997, 1997 OJ L 244/18, points 11–12; *aff'd* CFI July 8, 1999, 1999 ECR II-2329, para. 120; Twenty-seventh Report on Competition Policy, points 112–114. *See* Article 21 (4) of Regulation 139/2004 on merger control providing for a protection of legitimate national interests, including plurality of the media.
185. *Corbeau*, ECJ May 19, 1993, 1993 ECR I-2533; *FFSA*, CFI Feb. 27, 1997, 1997 ECR II-229, para. 106; *Chronopost*, ECJ July 3, 2003, C-83/01, para. 34. Directive 97/67/EC on postal services, 1998 OJ L 15/14.
186. *Corsica Ferries II*, ECJ June 18, 1998, 1998 ECR I-3949, para. 44.
187. Commission Communication on services of general interest, point 23.
188. *Airport of Frankfurt*, D.Comm. Jan. 14, 1998, 1998 OJ L 72/30, paras 99–102.
189. *SNFR/Inter-Huile*, ECJ March 10, 1983, 1983 ECR 555; *Diego Cali & Figli*, ECJ March 18, 1997, 1997 ECR I-1547; Commission Communication on Services of general interest, point 28.

The common objective is the protection of the consumer.[190] This narrow interpretation of 'general economic interest' in the sense of 'universal service' contrasts with the term 'public interest' which may include functions and tasks of industrial policy.[191] Although Article 157 of the EC Treaty seems to address industrial policy issues, the same provision also states that 'this title shall not provide a basis for the introduction by the Community of any measure which could lead to a distortion of competition.' This confirms the appropriateness of a narrow interpretation of Article 86 (2).

Universal Service v. Cross-Subsidization.

The performance of a universal service obligation as interpreted by the Court of Justice[192] raises the question of the extent to which cross-subsidization is necessary to 'offset less profitable sectors' or results in abusive predatory behavior.[193] In its *Glöckner* judgment the Court of Justice held that in making the determination whether a restriction of competition is necessary to enable the holder of an exclusive right to perform its task of general interest under economically acceptable conditions the premise must be

> 'that the obligation, on the part of the undertaking entrusted with such a task, to perform its services in conditions of economic equilibrium presupposes that it will be possible to offset less profitable sectors against the profitable sectors and hence justifies a restriction of competition from individual undertakings in economically profitable sectors.'[194]

It may be concluded that cross-subsidization is not in itself a problem under competition rules, but competition problems could arise where funds are used which derive from excessive or discriminatory prices in the reserved market or are used for predatory purtposes in markets open to competition[195] or where such funds derive from illegal or misused state aid.[196]

---

190. This corresponds to the 'economic and social cohesion' as stressed by Articles 16 and 158 of the EC Treaty.
191. The Court of Justice seems to use the term 'public interest' in the sense of a non-economic nature, *see Sacchi/Tele Biella*, ECJ April 30, 1974, 1974 ECR 409, para. 14; *Autotrasporti Librandi/Cuttica spedizioni*, ECJ Oct. 1, 1998, 1998 ECR I-5955, paras 38–41, although the term 'public interest' appears to be broader, including acts of sovereignty.
192. *See Corbeau*, ECJ May 19, 1993, 1993 ECR I-2533; *Almelo*, ECJ April 27, 1994, 1994 ECR I-1477; *Glöckner*, Oct. 25, 2001, 2001 ECR I-8089, paras 56–57.
193. Commission Guidelines on the application of the EC competition rules in the telecommunications sector, 1991 OJ C 233/2, point 86; Commission Notice on the application of the EC competition rules to the postal sector, 1998 OJ C 39/2, point 3.
194. *Glöckner*, ECJ Oct. 25, 2001, 2001 ECR I-8089, para. 57.
195. *UPS/Deutsche Post*, CFI March 20, 2002, 2002 ECR II-1915, paras 55 and 62.
196. *Deutsche Post II*, D.Comm. June 19, 2002, 2002 OJ L 247/27 (by this decision the Commission ordered the government to recover those funds).

3. Balancing the Interests by the Commission

Potential Justifications.
Cases where the *mere existence* of an exclusive right or the extension of a monopoly to related markets is in breach of Community law require the examination of any potential justification under Article 86 (2).[197] Reasons of security of networks may justify certain rights to subject imports to technical approval;[198] reasons of security of supply in the energy sector may be a *prima facie* argument for justifying exclusive export and import rights in general,[199] but such arguments cannot be used, in particular, for justifying exclusive supply obligations imposed on larger customers because such obligations would affect the development of trade between member states to an 'extent contrary to the interests af the Community' (Article 86 (2) (2)).[200]

Disproportionate Means.
The Court of Justice has refused to accept a justification under Article 86 (2) in cases where the means applied are *disproportionate* to the aim sought. The very specific nature of certain products or services has been found to justify marketing via recognized centers[201] or dealers[202] or only after technical approval.[203] Similarly, the Commission stated that cross-subsidization (allocation of costs of certain services to other loss-making services) is justified in the postal sector insofar as it is necessary to safeguard a universal service, including unprofitable mail delivery in rural areas.[204] However, type-approval, administered by the

---

197. To be examined by the national court (which may however be in a difficult position to judge such a complex question): *Greek Television Monopoly*, ECJ June 18, 1991, 1991 ECR I-2925.
198. *Procureur du Roi* (*walkie-talkie*), ECJ Oct. 27, 1993, 1993 ECR I-5267, para. 51.
199. Leading case: *Campus Oil*, ECJ July 10, 1984, 1984 ECR 2727. *See* the *Electricity Monopoly* cases, ECJ Oct. 23, 1997, 1997 ECR I-5699, 5789, 5815 and 5851; *Rendo* (*IJsselcentrale*), CFI Nov. 18, 1992, 1992 ECR II-2417, para. 128, *aff'd* ECJ April 27, 1994, 1994 ECR I-1477; *Jahrhundertvertrag*, D.Comm. Dec. 22, 1992, 1993 OJ L 50/14; *Airport of Frankfurt*, D.Comm. Jan. 14, 1998, 1998 OJ L 72/30, points 99–102.
200. Articles 20–23 of Directive 2003/54/EC concerning common rules for the internal market in electricity, 2003 OJ L 176/37; *Almelo*, ECJ April 27, 1994, 1994 ECR I-1477.
201. *Crespelle* (artificial insemination of cattle), ECJ Oct. 5, 1994, 1994 ECR I-5077, paras 36–40.
202. *Franzen/Swedish Alcohol Monopoly*, ECJ Oct. 23, 1997, 1997 ECR I-5909, paras 43–51; *Corsica Ferries II*, ECJ June 18, 1998, 1998 ECR I-3949, paras 29–32 and 47.
203. *Procureur du Roi/Lagauche* (*walkie-talkie*), ECJ Oct. 27, 1993, 1993 ECR I-5267, para. 51.
204. Directive 97/67/EC on postal services, 1998 OJ L 15/14; Commission notice on this directive, 1998 OJ C 39/2, points 3.1.-3.4. In the telecommunications sector cross-subsidization is generally held to be abusive: Commission's Guidelines on the Application of the EC Competition Rules in the Telecommunications sector, 1991 OJ C 233/2, points 102–110. Similarly with regard to interlining: *AirInter*, CFI June 19, 1997, 1997 ECR II-997, paras

operator of the network vested with exclusive rights and not by an independent body,[205] may lead to a conflict of interests and thereby to a distortion of competition.[206]

No Justification.
Cases in which the Commission has declined to find a justification under Article 86 (2) concern typical forms of abuse under Article 82 or restrictions under Article 81 when the tasks assigned could have been performed with less restrictive or non-abusive means:

- unreasonable or excessive prices[207] or coordinated prices[208] are typical examples of means disproportionate to the aims sought,
- discriminatory transport tariffs or rebates,[209]
- discriminatory application of costs for stocking imported products,[210]
- the grant of rebates on landing fees favoring certain airlines by state-owned airport administrations,[211]
- discriminatory fees for ground handling services,[212]
- discriminatory treatment of workers for loading and unloading on grounds of nationality (Article 12);[213]
- discrimination in the granting of landing/take-off slots,[214]

139–140 and loading/unloading services at ports: *Corsica Ferries II*, ECJ June 18, 1998, 1998 ECR I-3949, paras 42–47.

205. *Decoster*, ECJ Oct. 27, 1993, 1993 ECR I-5335, para. 22.
206. 'As competition may not be eliminated in that manner, it may not be distorted either.' *GB-INNO-BM*, ECJ March 7, 1990, 1990 ECR I-667, para. 24.
207. *Ahmed Saaed*, ECJ April 11, 1989, 1989 ECR 803, paras 43–52. An unreasonable price applied to certain parties may be discriminatory with regard to others: *GT-Link/De Dansk Statsbaner*, ECJ July 17, 1997, 1997 ECR I-4449, para. 27. Even the tendency, inherent in the use of exclusive rights, to apply excessive prices: *Silvano Raso* (*Port of Genova II*), ECJ Feb. 12, 1998, 1998 ECR I-593, paras 30–31.
208. *See BNIA*, D.Comm. July 26, 1976, 1976 OJ L 231/24, 28; *General Motors*, D.Comm. Dec. 19, 1974, 1975 OJ L 29/14, 16; *Anseau I*, D.Comm. Dec. 17, 1981, 1982 OJ L 167/39, 48.
209. Sea transport: *Ahmed Saaed*, ECJ April 11, 1989, 1989 ECR 803, para. 43. Air transport: Airport *of Brussels*, D.Comm. June 28, 1995, 1995 OJ L 216/8.
210. *Crespelle*, ECJ Oct. 5, 1994, 1994 ECR I-5077, para. 36.
211. *Airport of Brussels*, D.Comm. June 28, 1995, 1995 OJ L 216/8. *See also Airports of Paris I*, Twenty-sixth Report on Competition Policy, p. 142; *Alpha Flight Service/Airports of Paris II*, D.Comm. June 18, 1998, 1998 OJ L 230/10, *aff'd* CFI Oct. 24, 2002, C-82/01.
212. *Ground-handling Services at Airports*, Twenty-third Report on Competition Policy, points 365–369; *Airport of Frankfurt*, D.Comm. Jan. 14, 1998, 1998 OJ L 72/30, points 70–98.
213. *Porto di Genova I*, ECJ Dec. 10, 1991, 1991 ECJ I–5889, para. 11; *Silvano Raso* (*Port of Genova II*), ECJ March 12, 1998, 1998 ECR I-533.
214. Under Article 81 (3): *SAS/Lufthansa*, D.Comm. Jan. 16, 1996, 1996 OJ L 54/28 (not expressly referring to Article 86 (2), but discussing the issues under Article 81 (3)).

- the refusal of access to interlining,[215] to airport[216] or harbor disembarkation facilities,[217]
- discrimination against private express courier services,[218]
- restrictions on parallel imports by reserving the issuance of conformity labels for washing machines to the 'official' (i.e. exclusive) importers.[219]

4. Consideration of Non-Economic Reasons

Possible Parallel Application of Articles 30 and 86 (2).
Exceptions based on non-economic reasons are contained in Article 30 and Article 296 and may have to be included in the examination of whether the application of Community law would obstruct the performance of the particular tasks assigned to the enterprises concerned, e.g., measures guaranteeing the financial balance of the social security system.[220] Both Article 30 and Article 86 (2) recognize prevailing national interests subject to the proportionality test,[221] provided that trade between member states is not affected to such an extent as would be 'arbitrary' (Article 30 (2)) or 'contrary to the interests of the Community' (Article 86 (2) (2)).[222]

Article 30.
The leading case dealing with Article 30 is *Campus Oil.* [223] This case concerned the obligation imposed on all Irish oil importers to purchase 35% of their re-

---

215. *Air Inter*, ECJ June 19, 1997, 1997 ECR I-997; *Lufthansa/SAS*, D.Comm. Jan. 16, 1996, 1996 OJ L 54/28.
216. *Airport of Frankfurt*, D.Comm. Jan. 14, 1998, 1998 OJ L 72/30, points 99–102.
217. *Eniricorse*, ECJ Nov. 27, 2003, C-34/01, para. 33; *Coe Clerici Logistics*, CFI June 17, 2003, T-52/00, para. 104; *Corsica Ferries*, ECJ May 17, 1994, 1994 ECR I-1783; *Sea Containers/Stena Sealink*, D.Comm. Dec. 21, 1993, 1994 OJ L 15/8 (refusal of request for interim measures); *Harbour of Rodby*, D.Comm. Dec. 21, 1993, 1994 OJ L 55/52, para. 18; *Harbour of Roscoff*, D.Comm. May 17, 1995, Twenty-fifth Report on Competition Policy, points 43 and 120.
218. *Netherlands PTT*, D.Comm. Dec. 20, 1989, 1990 OJ L 10/47, annulled for procedural reasons (non-respect of the right to be heard) by ECJ Feb. 12, 1992, 1992 ECR I-565.
219. *Anseau II*, D.Comm. Nov. 4, 1982, 1982 OJ L 325/20, *aff'd* ECJ Nov. 8, 1983, 1983 ECR 3369 (without, however, discussing the applicability of Article 86 (2)); *Decoster*, ECJ Oct. 27, 1993, 1993 ECR I-5335, para. 22. In *CECED* (D.Comm. Jan. 24, 1999, 2000 OJ L 187/47) the Commission granted a negative clearance to non-compulsory Eco label system.
220. *Deutscher Apothekerverband/DocMorris*, ECJ Dec. 11, 2003, C-322/01, para. 122. *See also Ferring*, ECJ Nov. 22, 2001, 2001 ECR I-9067, paras 30–33.
221. The proportionality test concerns the question whether the aim can be achieved by less restrictive means: *Denkavit*, ECJ May 17, 1984, 1984 ECR 2171, para. 25; *Air Inter*, CFI June 19, 1997, 1997 ECR II-997, para. 144; *Franzen/Swedish Alcohol Monopoly*, ECJ Oct. 23, 1997, 1997 ECR I-5909, paras 75–76.
222. *See Dohms/Levasseur*, DG IV Newsletter 1998–1, p. 18, 22. In *Italian Electricity Monopoly*, ECJ Oct. 23, 1997, 1997 ECR I-5789, paras 33–42, the Court of Justice examined only the applicability of Article 86 (2) as possible justification of a state monopoly which is incompatible with Article 31.
223. *Campus Oil*, ECJ July 10, 1984, 1984 ECR 2727.

quirements from a state-owned refinery, which was considered of fundamental importance to the country's existence and even for the survival of its inhabitants.[224] Non-economic justifications include public health[225] and environmental concerns, provided the measures taken are proportionate, non-discriminatory, transparent and consistent,[226] which presupposes, in particular, that a legitimate aim can not be achieved with less restrictive means,[227] except in cases where the control of environmental pollution[228] or of air transport safety[229] is part of the sovereign right of the state concerned and are, for that reason, excluded from the scope of Article 86 (1).

Article 296 – National Security.

Article 296 of the EC Treaty provides an exception from the general provisions of the Treaty on grounds of national security.[230] It allows a member state to take 'such measures as it considers necessary for the protection of the essential interests of its security which are concerned with the production of or trade in arms, munitions and war material,'[231] provided that such measures do not affect competitive conditions for 'products which are not intended specifically for military purposes.' To date the Article 296 exception has never been raised as a major issue in a competition decision.[232]

---

224. It is possible that the Court of Justice was swayed by memories of the 1970s energy crisis, *see* in greater detail discussion in Chapter VIII.E.2.
225. *EFTA Surveillance Authority/Kingdom of Norway*, EFTA ECJ April 5, 2001, E-3/00, para. 27; *Deutscher Apothekerverband*, ECJ Dec. 11, 2003, C-322/01, paras 125–131 (safeguard of public health recognized as primary concern with respect to prescription medicinal products). *See also German Alcohol Monopoly*, Recommendation Comm. Dec. 22, 1969, 1970 OJ L 31/20; *Portuguese Alcohol Monopoly*, Rec. Comm. Oct. 8, 1987, 1987 OJ L 306/32; *Swedish Alcohol Monopoly*, ECJ Oct. 23, 1997, 1997 ECR I-5909, paras 53–57; *Norwegian Alcohol Monopoly*, EFTA ECJ Dec. 3, 1997, E-1/97. Marketing via recognized centers in case of artificial insemination of cattle: *Crespelle*, ECJ Oct. 5, 1994, 1994 ECR I-5077, paras 36–40.
226. *EFTA Surveillance Authority/Kingdom of Norway*, EFTA ECJ April 5, 2001, E-3/00, para. 26.
227. *Denkavit*, ECJ May 17, 1984, 1984 ECR 2171, para. 25; *Air Inter*, CFI June 19, 1997, 1997 ECR II-997, para. 144; *Franzen/Swedish Alcohol Monopoly*, ECJ Oct. Oct. 23, 1997, 1997 ECR I-5909, paras 74–77; *FFAD*, ECJ May 23, 2000, 2000 ECR I-3743, para. 51.
228. *Diego Cali & Figli*, ECJ March 18, 1997, 1997 ECR I-1547, para. 23.
229. *SAT/Eurocontrol*, ECJ Jan. 19, 1994, 1994 ECR I-43.
230. *See* Commission Communication on services of general interest, 2001 OJ C 17/4, point 28.
231. An unpublished list of arms, munitions and war material for the purposes of Article 296 exists, which was adopted by EC Council decision on 15 April 1958 under Article 296 (2). *See* Commission recommendations to France of 22 Dec. 1969, 1970 OJ L 31/24. The list is still applicable. *See* Written Answer to Parliamentary Question No. 2711/86, 1988 OJ C 23/11.
232. *See*, however, *GEC Marconi/Alenia*, D.Comm. Aug. 28, 1998, M.1258, where the parties only notified the civil aspects of the operation to the Commission, upon instructions of the governments of the United Kingdom and Italy not to notify information which related to their military activities; *Suralmo*, Ninth Report on Competition Policy, points 114–115, and Commission recommendation to France of Dec. 22, 1969, 1970 OJ L 31/24. Article 296 only applies

D. Article 86 (3): Procedural Provisions for Enforcing the Obligations under Article 86 (1)

The Means of Enforcement.
Article 86 (3) provides that the Commission shall ensure the application of the provisions of Article 86 (1) and shall, if necessary, address appropriate directives or decisions to member states. According to Article 249 a directive is binding, as to the result to be achieved, upon each member state to which it is addressed, but it leaves to the national authorities the choice of form and methods,[233] whereas a decision is binding in its entirety. Directives are designed to specify the obligations of the member states under Article 86 (including the clarification of the financial relationship between a national government and its public undertakings[234]) whereas a decision states a violation of the rules of competition by a governmental measure (e.g. fixing prices or tariffs to be applied by a state-owned enterprise).[235]

Directives v. Decisions.
The supervisory power conferred on the Commission under Article 86 (3) includes the possibility of 'specifying' obligations arising under Article 86 (1).[236] The power to issue directives[237] is different from Article 95, which provides for the adoption of measures for the approximation of the provisions laid down by law, regulation or administrative action[238] and from Article 83 (c), which empowers the Commission to define the scope of Articles 81 and 82 in specific branches of the economy[239] and to adopt any appropriate regulations or directives to give

---

to government measures; thus, agreements, concerted practices and abuses of a dominant position by private arms manufacturers and traders are fully subject to Articles 81 and 82.

233. For this reason a directive can only be of a preventive nature by specifying the obligations under Article 86.
234. *Transparency Directive II*, 1993 OJ L 254/16 (a first directive was annulled by the Court of Justice because of its provision of a minimum turnover: ECJ June 16, 1993, 1993 ECR I-3283).
235. *See Airport of Brussels*, D.Comm. June 28, 1995, 1995 OJ L 216/8; *Portuguese Airports*, D.Comm. Feb. 10, 1999, 1999 OJ L 69/31.
236. *Telecommunications Directive Terminal Equipment*, ECJ March 19, 1991, 1991 ECR I-1223, paras 21–27.
237. *See France, Italy, United Kingdom v. Commission* (*state aid transparency directive*), ECJ July 6, 1982, 1982 ECR 2545: the three member states challenged the competence of the Commission to adopt directives. The Court, however, confirmed this power of the Commission under Article 86 (3).
238. Examples: Directive 2003/54/EC concerning common rules for the internal market in electricity, 2003 OJ L 176/37; Directive 2003/55/EC on common rules for the development of the internal market of Community postal services, 2003 OJ L 176/57.
239. Example: Regulation 1400/2002 on motor vehicles.

effect to the principles set out in Articles 81 and 82.[240] The directives taken under Article 86 (3) involve an appreciation of the obligations of the member states in the light of Community law and specify the consequences with due regard to the requirements for the performance of the particular tasks assigned to an undertaking entrusted with the operation of services of general interest.[241] The power to proceed to decisions under Article 86 (3) addressed to member states is different from the power to adopt directives, which are limited to setting the obligations of the member states under Article 86 (1) and (2), or from the guarantees provided by Article 226 in case a member state has failed to fulfill its obligations under the Treaty. Both ways are open to the Commission, Article 86 (3) having the advantage of making an assessment, by way of decision, of the measures enacted or maintained in force contrary to Article 86 (1)[242] and likely to be appealed to the Court under Article 226. If the decision is not appealed it may form the basis of an application under Article 226 for failure to comply with that decision. In this case the member state is prevented from invoking the nullity of the decision.[243]

Example: The Telecommunications Directives.
Article 86 (3) is also used by the Commission as a means of introducing competition into the markets for telecommunications equipment and services. The lack of competition is due to exclusive or special rights given by the member states to their national telecommunications administrations. A first directive[244] issued in 1988 ordered member states to withdraw the special or exclusive rights which they had granted to their telecommunications authorities for the supply of terminal equipment, in order to give other suppliers the right to import, market, connect, put into service and maintain terminal equipment and to ensure greater transparency and non-discrimination in the implementation of type approval procedures. The Court of Justice upheld the directive on appeal.[245] The Court of Justice did so with respect to the second directive, which required the member states to abolish

240. *Telecommunications Directive Terminal Equipment*, ECJ March 19, 1991, 1991 ECR I-1223, paras 23–25.
241. *Netherlands PTT*, ECJ Feb. 12, 1992, 1992 ECR I-565, para. 27.
242. *Ibid.*, paras 35–36. See Commission decisions based on Article 86 (3) *in the cases Airport of Brussels*, June 28, 1995, 1995 OJ L 216/8; *Omnitel Pronto Italia*, Oct. 4, 1995, 1995 OJ L 280/49; *Second GSM Operator Spain*, Dec. 18, 1996, 1997 OJ L 76/19; *Italian Ports Legislation Relating to Employment*, Oct. 21, 1997, 1997 OJ L 301/17; *Tariffs for Piloting in the Port of Genova*, Oct. 21, 1997, 1997 OJ L 301/27; *Portuguese Airports*, D.Comm. Feb. 10, 1999, 1999 OJ L 69/31; and the termination of infringement proceedings in the cases *Second GSM Operator Italy*, *VTM* (television in Belgium) and *Athens Airport*, Twenty-seventh Report on Competition Policy, pp. 165–167.
243. *Greek Insurance*, ECJ June 30, 1988, 1988 ECR 3611, para. 14.
244. *Telecommunications Directive Terminal Equipment*, 1988 OJ L 131/78.
245. *Telecommunications Directive Terminal Equipment*, ECJ March 19, 1991, 1991 ECR I-1223. The only points on which the Court found against the Commission were in requiring the abolition of 'special rights,' as opposed to 'exclusive rights' (i.e., monopolies) – the 'special rights' were not properly identified in the directive – and in using Article 86 (3) to order telecommu-

monopolies on certain services, in order to afford access to the public network for private service providers.[246]

Commission Directives v. Council Directives.
Although the Court of Justice approved the Commission's approach to issue its own directives based on Article 86 (3), the Commission preferred to proceed to the liberalization of other sectors, such as energy and post, by way of directives based on Article 158 which imply a broader political consensus by engaging the Council and the European Parliament.[247]

Control Mechanism.
A directive or decision addressed to a member state may be appealed by the addressees according to Article 230 (2) of the EC Treaty[248] and, under exceptional circumstances, by individuals provided that they are directly and individually concerned.[249]

However, the Commission enjoys a broad discretion as to when and how to make use of its powers under Article 86 (3) without being limited in this exercise by the existence of complaints made by third parties. This means that individuals have no standing to complain against the Commission's failure to act or to appeal the rejection of a complaint, save in exceptional circumstances.[250] An action against the Commission for failure to act was considered admissible by the Court of First Instance for the first time in its *TF1* judgment holding that the complainant has the right to have the Commission examine its complaint in a diligent and impartial manner.[251] The Court of First Instance confirmed this approach in its *Max.mobil* judgment.[252] This means that the role of the Community courts in evaluating the Commission's actions focuses on three points: (i) whether the Commission's act included a statement of reasons which was *prima facie* consist-

---

nications administrations to terminate long-term contracts with customers, which were private in character and therefore not amenable to action under Article 86 (3) but only under Article 81 or 82 (paras 45–47 and 53–57).

246. *Telecommunications Directive Services*, 1990 OJ L 192/10. For more details on both directives, *see infra* Chapter VIII.F.
247. This is the reason why, for instance, Directive 67/97/EC on common rules for the development of Community postal services (1998 OJ L 15/14) is based on the Commission's proposal, but adopted by the European Parliament and the Council. *See supra* note 238.
248. *See Telecommunications Directive Terminal Equipment*, ECJ March 19, 1991, 1991 ECR I-1223.
249. *See Zégo-Quéré*, CFI May 3, 2002, 2002 ECR II-2365, paras 50–51 (reconsidering the previous stricter interpretation by the Court of Justice); *Coe Clerici Logistics*, CFI June 17, 2003, T-52/00, para. 88.
250. *Bundesverband der Bilanzbuchhalter*, ECJ Feb. 20, 1997, 1997 ECR I-947.
251. *TF1 – Télévision Française 1*, CFI June 3, 1999, 1999 ECR II-1757, paras 49–57. On appeal, the ECJ did not rule on the admissibility of that action: ECJ July 12, 2001, 2001 ECR I-5603.
252. *Max.mobil*, CFI Jan. 30, 2002, 2002 ECR II-313, paras 48–52.

ent and reflected due consideration for the relevant facts of the case, (ii) whether the facts relied on were materially accurate, and (iii) whether the *prima facie* assessment of those facts was not vitiated by any manifest error,[253] including any violation of the proportionality principle.[254]

E. Article 31: Obligation of Member States to 'Adjust' Existing and to Refrain from Creating New State Monopolies

1. Rationale of Article 31

Article 31 as *Lex Specialis*.
Article 31[255] requires member states to 'progressively adjust' state trading monopolies which affect imports or exports by the end of a transitional period for the abolition of customs duties and quantitative restrictions[256] so as to remove discrimination between nationals of member states regarding the conditions under which goods are procured and marketed.[257] Article 31 constitues a *lex specialis*. It supplements the rules for the elimination of quantitative restrictions on intra-EC trade with regard to *existing* state trading monopolies. Article 31 contains specific rules providing for:

- a progressive adaptation rather than a prohibition with immediate effect;
- a smoother procedure starting with recommendations (Article 31 (6)) rather than compulsory decisions (Article 86 (3)) or actions under Article 226;
- a prohibition against introducing new exclusive rights as a substitute for existing monopolies (Article 31 (2)) rather than a general prohibition against introducing any new exclusive rights likely to affect trade between member states, which is subject to Article 86 (1) combined with Article 31 (prohibition against creating new quantitative restrictions on the import of goods) and Article 51 (prohibition against creating new restrictions on the freedom to provide

253. Confirmed in *Coe Clerici Logistics*, CFI June 17, 2003, T-52/00, paras. 86–94.
254. *Portuguese Republic*, ECJ March 29, 2001, 2001 ECR I-2613, para. 20.
255. Similarly Article 16 of the EEA Agreement. *See Norwegian Alcohol Monopoly*, EFTA Court of Justice, Dec. 3, 1997, E-1/97; Twenty-seventh Report on Competition Policy, points 140–143.
256. The transitional period ended with regard to the founding member states on Dec. 31, 1969; with regard to the 'new' member states specific time limits have been fixed in the respective accession treaties, e.g., on Dec.31, 1997 with regard to the Austrian tobacco monopoly: Twenty-fifth Report on Competition Policy, point 129, and with regard to the Austrian, Swedish and Finnish alcohol monopolies: Twenty-sixth Report on Competition Policy, points 133–135, and Twenty-seventh Report on Competition Policy, point 139.
257. Article 31 largely restates Articles 17 and 20 of the GATT Agreement.

services within the Community).[258]

However, with regard to *new* exclusive rights Article 86 (l)–(2) and Article 16 [259] are the central provisions (rather than Article 31 (2)) for considering such rights and for balancing public service and Community interests.[260]

Application Only to Products, not Services.
Article 31 applies to trade in goods, including the importation of products designed to be processed, not to production or processing, although exclusive production or processing rights may be incompatible with the freedom to provide services as guaranteed under Article 49.[261] Article 31 applies only to goods,[262] and not to services, such as cross-frontier provision of television broadcasting or funeral services, which are governed by Articles 49 to 55.[263] However, Article 31 applies to service monopolies that also extend to goods which themselves are separable from those services, e.g., extending a monopoly on telecommunications to telephone hardware.[264]

Examples of State Monopolies.
State monopolies are typically bodies to which the state has granted, by an express act of state, exclusive rights to make, import, export or sell certain goods.[265] The concept is broadly construed. State monopolies may consist of any body through which a member state, in law or in fact, directly or indirectly supervises, determines or appreciably influences imports or exports between member states,[266]

---

258. Cases where the Commission intervened under Article 31 (2) against the creation of new exclusive rights are rare; *see*, however, the Commission's intervention against the German government's plan to extend the Bundespost's monopoly to cordless telephones: Fifteenth Report on Competition Policy, point 260.
259. *See* C.I. *above* and Twenty-seventh Report on Competition Policy, points 96–100.
260. *Italian Electricity Monopoly*, ECJ Oct. 23, 1997, 1997 ECR I-5789, para. 43.
261. In the *Greek Oil Monopoly* case, the Commission challenged under Article 31 only the monopoly for importing refined products, but might have challenged the refinery monopoly under Article 49: ECJ Dec. 13, 1990, 1990 ECR1–4747, paras 31–36. *See Terminal Equipment* 1988 OJ L 131/73, recital 7; *Telecommunications Directive Services*, 1990 OJ L 192/10, recital 6.
262. Electricity is a 'good', not a 'service': *Almelo*, ECJ April 27, 1994, 1994 ECR I-1477, para. 28; *Italian Electricity Monopoly*, ECJ Oct. 23, 1997, 1997 ECR I-5789, paras 16–17.
263. *Sacchi Tele Biella*, ECJ April 30, 1974, 1974 ECR 409, para. 10; *Commission v. France*, June 28, 1983, 1983 ECR 2057; *Funeral Service*, ECJ May 4, 1988, 1988 ECR 2479, para. 10; *Procureur du Roi v. Lagauche*, ECJ Oct. 27, 1993, 1993 ECR I-5267, paras 33–34.
264. *See Bundespost III*, Sixteenth Report on Competition Policy, point 294.
265. *Franzen/Swedish Alcohol Monopoly*, ECJ Oct. 23, 1997, 1997 ECR I-5909, paras 75–76. The exclusive rights may be limited to certain fields of distribution, e.g., to the transport of electricity on the high-voltage interconnected system: *Spanish Electricity Monopoly*, ECJ Oct. 23, 1997, 1997 ECR I-5851, paras 18–21.
266. Article 31 applies even if trade between member states increases: *Italian Electricity Monopoly*, ECJ Oct. 23, 1997, 1997 ECR I-5789, para. 32.

irrespective of whether the monopoly is reserved to the state or delegated by the state to others.[267] The right to grant concessions for marketing products[268] or to fix minimum prices[269] remains subject to Article 28, and fiscal measures are subject to Article 90.[270] Examples of state monopolies are monopolies serving the interests of national security (e.g. oil, arms production), products serving to facilitate collection of tax revenues (e.g., tobacco, matches, liquor), or the protection of local production (e.g., fertilizer). They may be organized as governmental units, public bodies or as independent private legal entities.[271] Article 31 has to be interpreted in an exhaustive way: state trading monopolies which are *not* in breach of Article 31 cannot be held to be contrary to Article 86 (1) in combination with Article 82. For example, the grant of exclusive rights in a certain geographically defined area or the selection of distributors based on objective criteria[272] is not necessarily in breach of Article 86 (1), provided imported products are not excluded from such distribution outlets.[273]

2. Means of Eliminating Discrimination

Elimination of Exclusive Rights.
The objective of Article 31 is to eliminate discrimination between foreign and domestic products[274] that results from a conflict of interest if they are marketed by a single body,[275] and to prohibit the introduction of new discriminatory measures,[276] thereby ensuring the free movement of goods within the Community, including the goods marketed by state monopolies. However, the means to achieve this objective may consist of gradual steps, by progressively opening the market to

267. Second paragraph of Article 31 (1). *Italian Electricity Monopoly*, ECJ Oct. 23, 1997, 1997 ECR I-5789, paras 23–24. *See Commission v. France*, ECJ June 28, 1983, 1983 ECR 2079, paras 9–19.
268. *GB-Inno-BM*, ECJ 13 Dec. 1991, 1991 ECR I-5941; *DIP/Communedi Bassano del Grappa*, ECJ Oct. 17, 1995, 1995 ECR I-3257.
269. *Greek Oil Monopoly*, ECJ Dec. 13, 1990, 1990 ECR I-4747.
270. *Pabst & Richarz*, ECJ April 29, 1982, 1982 ECR 1331.
271. *Cassis de Dijon*, ECJ Feb. 20, 1979, 1979 ECR 649, para. 7. State monopolies in the agriculatural field are subject to specific rules due to the existence of the common market organizations according to Article 31 (4): *Pigs Marketing*, ECJ Nov. 29, 1978, 1978 ECR 2347.
272. Objective criteria may include reasons of public health: *Franzen/Swedish Alcohol Monopoly*, ECJ Oct. 23, 1997, 1997 ECR I-5909, paras 53–57.
273. *Manghera*, ECJ Feb. 3, 1976, 1976 ECR 91, para. 5; *Crespelle*, ECJ Oct. 5, 1994, 1994 ECR I–5077, paras 17–22; *Banchero*, ECJ Dec. 14, 1995, 1995 ECR I-4663, paras 27, 55; *Franzen/ Swedish Alcohol Monopoly*, ECJ Oct. 23, 1997, 1997 ECR I-5909, paras 38–40.
274. *Keck*, ECJ Nov. 24, 1993, 1993 ECR I-6097, para. 16; *Dassonville*, ECJ July 11, 1994, 1994 ECR I-837; *Italian Electricity Monopoly*, ECJ Oct. 23, 1997, 1997 ECR I-5789, para. 25.
275. *Telecommunications Directive Terminal Equipment*, ECJ March 19, 1991, 1991 ECR I-1223, paras 40–43; *Greek Television Monopoly*, ECJ June 23, 1991, 1991 ECR I-2925, paras 15–23.
276. Article 31 (2).

imported products, e.g. by providing periodic increases in import quotas.[277] The best way to comply with the obligation to 'adjust' the existing state monopolies, however – according to the Commission's interpretation in its 1969 recommendations[278] – is the complete 'elimination' of exclusive rights.

Practices Equivalent to Exclusive Import Rights.
The obligation to adjust state monopolies includes the prohibition against introducing 'measures having equivalent effect.'[279] The main means of substituting exclusive rights are the introduction of an import license[280] and the conclusion of exclusive or quasi-exclusive long-term distribution agreements between a foreign supplier and the domestic monopolist. Such agreements deprive the foreign supplier of the opportunity to build its own distribution network and are likely to discriminate against imports because of the conflict of interest[281] when distributing competing national and imported products through a single buyer.[282] Such practices may camouflage new exclusive import rights prohibited under Article 31 (2).[283] The Commission therefore acted against such exclusive distribution arrangements[284] and concession systems making the import of oil products subject to the condition of refinery facilities within the country of destination[285] or to the obligation to supply all retailers established on the national territory (contrary to the established freedom of wholesalers to select their retailers).[286] However, the distribution of imported products through distributors selected according to objective qualitative criteria has been accepted for reasons of public health, provided the selected distributors are free to choose their supplier.[287] In its electricity directives, the Commission requires a single buyer which is part of a vertically integrated electricity undertaking to operate separately from the generation and distribution activities of the integrated undertaking.[288]

277. *See* Seventeenth Report on Competition Policy, points 289–295.
278. E.g. *German Alcohol Monopoly*, Commission recommendation 22 Dec. 1969, 1970 OJ L 31/20. *See* Third Report on Competition Policy, point 41.
279. *See Hansen*, ECJ March 13, 1979, 1979 ECR 935, para. 8; *Manghera*, ECJ Feb. 3, 1976, 1976 ECR 91, paras 5–6; *Commission v. Italy*, ECJ June 7, 1983, 1983 ECR 1955, paras 11–12.
280. *Franzen/Swedish Alcohol Monopoly*, ECJ Oct. 23, 1997, 1997 ECR I-5909, paras 75–76.
281. *Greek Television*, ECJ June 18, 1991, 1991 ECR I-2925, paras 15–23; *RTT/GB-INNO-BM*, ECJ Dec. 13, 1991, 1991 ECR I-5941; *Telecommunications Directive Terminal Equipment*, ECJ March 19, 1991, 1991 ECR I-1223, paras 48–52.
282. *Swedish Match*, Twenty-seventh Report on Competition Policy, point 66; *Hydro Texaco/Preem*, Twenty-seventh Report on Competition Policy, point 54.
283. *SEITA*, Tenth Report on Competition Policy, point 124.
284. *Swedish Matches*, Twenty-seventh Report on Competition Policy, point 66.
285. *French Oil Monopoly*, Sixteenth Report on Competition Policy, point 299.
286. *Austrian Tobacco Monopoly*, Twenty-seventh Report on Competition Policy, point 144.
287. *Franzen/Swedish Alcohol Monopoly*, ECJ Oct. 23, 1997, 1997 ECR I-5909, paras 43–51. Similarly, *Norwegian Alcohol Monopoly*, EFTA Court of Justice, Dec. 3, 1997, E-1/97, Twenty-seventh Report on Competition Policy, points 140–143.
288. Article 15 of Directive 96/92/EC as amended by Directive 2003/54/EC, 2003 OJ L 176/37.

Exceptions under Article 86 (2) – The Electricity and Gas Monopoly Cases. Since Article 31 is construed as a *lex specialis* to the general provisions of Articles 28–30, its application includes considerations of the general principle of Article 28 as well as the public interest considerations contained in Article 30[289] and, more generally, the proportionality test.[290] Thus, a state trading monopoly deemed incompatible with Article 31 does not need to be examined under Articles 28, 29 and 30, but may well be justified under Article 86 (2). This is subject to the proviso that the obligation on member states pursuant to Article 31 does not obstruct the performance of the task of general economic interest assigned to the monopoly or constitute a means of arbitrary discrimination or a disguised restriction on trade between member states.[291] In the case of the electricity and gas state monopolies which existed in Italy, the Netherlands, France and Spain, the Commission took action under Article 226 against exclusive rights to import and export electricity and gas conferred by national law in these countries which were incompatible with Article 31.[292] The Court of Justice[293] found that the exclusive import and export rights were incompatible with Article 31, but that the Commission had not submitted sufficient legal and economic reasons to assess the applicability of the exception contained in Article 86 (2) which was invoked by the state monopolies and the member states. The Court of Justice therefore rejected the Commission's application.[294] The jurisprudence of the Court of Justice must be viewed in the context of the liberalization of the energy market. In the electricity sector Directive 96/92/EC of December 1996[295] obliges member states to take the steps necessary to comply with the directive 'not later than 19 February 1999', and Directive 2003/54/EC[296] sets a new time limit of 1 July 2004 for non-domestic consumers and 1 July 2007 for all other consumers. The directive mandates liberalization of the distribution system and ensures a limited right of access to the network. It might be argued that the abolition of exclusive import and export rights was unlikely to lead to greater freedom of movement of energy as long as access to the network and the free

289. A qualitative *and* quantitative selection of distributors may be justified on grounds of public health without expressly referring to Article 30: *Franzen/Swedish Alcohol Monopoly*, ECJ Oct. 23, 1997, 1997 ECR I-5909, paras 53–57.

290. The test is whether a monopoly could exercise its activity with less restrictive means: *Franzen/Swedish Alcohol Monopoly*, ECJ Oct. 23, 1997, 1997 ECR I-5909, paras 75–76.

291. *Campus Oil*, ECJ July 10, 1984, 1984 ECR 2727; *Greek Oil Monopoly*, ECJ Dec. 13, 1990, 1990 ECR I-4747; *Italian Electricity Monopoly*, ECJ Oct. 23, 1997, 1997 ECR I-5789, paras 41–42.

292. *See* the Commission's regular Benchmarking Reports on the implementation of the internal electricity and gas market: http://europa/eu.int/comm/energy/electricity/benchmarking/index_en.htm.

293. *Italian*, *French*, *Dutch* and *Spanish Electricity Monopolies*, ECJ Oct. 23, 1997, 1997 ECR I-5789, 5699, 5815 and 5851.

294. *Italian Electricity Monopoly*, ECJ Oct. 23, 1997, 1997 ECR I-5789, paras 28 and 46–61.

295. 1997 OJ L 27/20.

296. 2003 OJ L 176/37.

distribution of the imported energy were not guaranteed.

3. Enforcement

Recommendations v. Direct Legal Action against Member States.
The Commission issued recommendations to the member states concerned pursuant to Article 31 (6), during the transitional period for phasing out exclusive export or import rights.[297] Subsequently the Commission brought infringement proceedings under Article 226 against certain member states that failed to fulfill their obligations under Article 31.[298] Article 31 (1) became directly applicable, i.e. enforceable by individual firms through national courts, after the transitional period expired.[299] Like Article 86 (1), Article 31 (2) also prohibits new discriminatory measures and has direct legal effect as of the date of the entry into force of the Treaty or accession, as the case may be.[300]

Actions in Case of Liberalized Monopolies.
Traditional monopolies, such as telecommunications, postal services or energy monopolies, have been liberalized by directives of the Commission based on Article 86 (3) or directives of the Council based on Article 95.[301] In these cases the Commission has to ensure compliance with the obligations under the directives and is empowered to bring action under Article 226 against those member states which do not fulfill these obligations.[302]

Direct Legal Actions against State Monopolies as 'Undertakings.'
A state monopoly is not only a body exercising a government mandate; it also performs, in its capacity as producer, wholesaler and distributor, the functions of an undertaking. The Commission has applied Article 82 when a state monopoly, after elimination of the exclusive import and export rights, concluded exclusive

---

297. *See*, e.g., Commission's recommendations to France of 22 Dec. 1969, 1970 OJ L 31/24 and 26; to Spain, Portugal and France, Seventeenth Report on Competition Policy, points 291 and 293–295. *See also* the Commission recommendation of Sept. 20, 1974 addressed to France with regard to the new member states: 1974 OJ L 278/16 and of Nov. 18, 1974 addressed to the Italian Republic: 1974 OJ L 326/29.

298. *See*, e.g., *Greek Oil Monopoly*, ECJ Dec.13, 1990, 1990 ECR I-4747; *Commission/Portugal*, ECJ Jan. 19, 1993, 1993 ECR I-95 and 117.

299. *Manghera*, ECJ Feb. 3, 1976, 1976 ECR 91, paras 14–15; *REWE/Hauptzollamt Landau/Pfalz*, ECJ Feb. 17, 1976, 1976 ECR 181, paras 22–24; *Miritz*, ECJ Feb. 17, 1976, 1976 ECR 217, paras 7–11.

300. *Costa/ENEL*, ECJ July 15, 1964, 1964 ECR 585, 597–598.

301. Directives may be issued in combination with Article 31: *Telecommunications Directive Terminal Equipment*, 1988 OJ L 131/73, recital 4.

302. E.g. *Commission/Greece*, ECJ July 13, 1995, 1995 ECR I-1951. *See also* the cases quoted in the Twenty-seventh Report on Competition Policy, points 102–104, and, under the EEA agreement, *Erla Maria Sveinbjorndottir*, EFTA Court of Justice, Dec. 10, 1998, E-9/97, ECR 1999–1, 2.

distribution agreements with foreign manufacturers with the effect of maintaining its monopolistic position on the wholesale and distribution level.[303] In the *AAMS – Italian Tobacco Monopoly* case[304] the Commission applied Article 82 against AAMS when it abused its dominant position by imposing wholesale distribution contracts on tobacco producers in other member states which limited access of foreign cigarettes to the Italian market and imposed a fine of ECU 6 million.

F. Article 10 (2): Obligation of Member States to Refrain from Compelling or Facilitating Anticompetitive Behavior of Enterprises Contrary to Article 81 or 82

1. Article 10 (2) in the Context of Other Provisions Ensuring a System of Undistorted Competition

Rationale of Article 10 (2) – The European State Action Doctrine.
Article 10 (2) obliges member states to refrain from any measures which would jeopardize the attainment of the objectives of the Treaty. This provision, read together with Article 3 (g) and Articles 81 and 82, requires member states not to introduce or maintain in force measures, even of a legislative nature,which may render ineffective the competition rules applicable to enterprises.[305] The scope of Article 10 (2) is different from that of Article 86 (1), which prohibits member states from using their influence on enterprises vested with special or exclusive rights to induce anticompetitive conduct. Article 10 (2) in conjunction with Article 3 (g) and Articles 81 and 82 applies where a governmental measure compels enterprises to engage in anticompetitive conduct, which would, without the government intervention, constitute an infringement of Article 81 or 82.[306]

The Scope of Article 10 (2) – The *CNSD* Case.
The application of Article 10 (2) has been strictly circumscribed. It does not prevent member states from adopting legislation to regulate prices or market access, or to

303. *Swedish Match/Skandinavisk Tobakskompagni*, Twenty-seventh Report on Competition Policy, point 66.
304. *AAMS*, D.Comm. June 17, 1998, 1998 OJ L 252/49, *aff'd* CFI Nov. 22, 2001, 2001 ECR II-3413.
305. *See Flemish Travel Agents*, ECJ Oct. 1, 1987, 1987 ECR 3801, paras 30–35,
306. This may be compared to the *'state action' doctrine* in the United States which generally requests (i) the challenged restraint to be clearly articulated and affirmatively expressed as state policy, and (ii) actively supervised by the state itself: *California Retail Liquor Dealers Ass'n. v. Midcal Aluminium, Inc.* 445 U.S. 97 (1980). The purpose of the active supervision requirement 'is to determine whether the State has exercised sufficient independent judgment and control so that the details of the rates or prices have been established as a product of deliberate state intervention, not simply by agreement among private parties': *FTC v. Ticor Title Ins.*, 504 U.S. 621.634 (1992).

fulfill other regulatory functions within the scope of their duties under Article 28, 49 and 86 (1).[307] However, Article 10 (2) does strictly prohibit the member states from facilitating or imposing a structure whereby undertakings reach agreements or engage in conduct that is prohibited by Article 81 or 82.[308] The Court of Justice acknowleged the applicability of Article 10 (2) in the *CNSD* case. This case concerned the National Council of Custom Agents (CNSD), an association governed by public law, which was required by a law adopted and maintained in force by the Italian government to adopt a decision consisting of setting a compulsory tariff for all customs agents subject to disciplinary measures. Accordingly, the association adopted a decision setting a uniform tariff, which was subsequently approved and declared generally binding by the government. The Commission took two actions, (i) against the member state under Article 226 for having infringed Article 10 in conjunction with Article 81,[309] and (ii) against the association under Regulation 17 for having infringed Article 81.[310] The Court of Justice confirmed this double approach.

(i) The Court of Justice held that the Italian government was responsible under Article 10 for imposing a compulsory, uniform tariff and prohibiting agents from derogating from that tariff with the effect of facilitating the application of the tariffs by the agents and of deterring customers who might wish to contest the prices demanded by the customs agents.

> 'Although Article 85 (*now 81)* of the Treaty is, in itself, concerned solely with the conduct of undertakings and not with measures adopted by Member States by law or regulation, the fact nevertheless remains that Article 85 of the Treaty, in conjunction with Article 5 *(now 10)*, requires the Member States not to introduce or maintain in force measures, even of a legislative nature, which may render ineffective the competition rules applicable to undertakings ... Such would be the case if a member state were to require or favour the adoption of agreements, decisions or concerted practices contrary to Article 85 *(now 81)* or to reinforce their effects, or to deprive its own rules of the character of legislation by delegating to private economic operators

307. *Corsica Ferries II*, ECJ June 18, 1998, 1998 ECR I-3949, para. 54; *Van Eycke/ASPA*, ECJ Nov. 21, 1988, 1988 ECR 4769, para. 19.
308. *Altair* and *ENEL*, ECJ Sept. 11, 2003, C-207/01, para. 30, referring to *Ladbroke Racing*, ECJ Nov. 11, 1997, 1997 ECR I-6265, para. 33. *See also Flemish Travel Agents*, ECJ Oct. 1, 1987, 1987 ECR 3801, paras 30–35; *Van Eycke/ASPA*, ECJ Nov. 21, 1988, 1988 ECR 4769, para. 16; *Bundesanstalt für den Güterfernverkehr/Reiff*, ECJ Nov.17, 1993, 1993 ECR I-5801, para. 14: *Ohm*, ECJ Nov. 17, 1993, 1993 ECR I-5851, para. 15; *Delta Schiffahrts- und Speditionsgesellschaft*, ECJ June 9, 1994, 1994 ECR I-2517, para. 14; *Peralta*, ECJ July 14, 1995, 1995 ECR I-3453, para. 21; *Esso Espagnola*, ECJ Nov. 30, 1995, 1995 ECR I-4223, paras 18–19; *CNSD*, ECJ June 18, 1998, 1998 ECR I-3831, para. 53; *Autotrasporti Librandi/Cuttica spedizioni*, ECJ Oct. 1, 1998, 1998 ECR I-5955, para. 37. For Article 82 *see GB-Inno-BM*, ECJ Nov. 16, 1977, 1977 ECR 2115, para. 31.
309. *See CNSD II*, ECJ June 18, 1998, 1998 ECR I-3831.
310. *CNSD I*, D.Comm. June 30, 1993, 1993 OJ L 203/27 (cease and desist order without fines).

responsibility for taking decisions affecting the economic sphere.'[311]

(ii) On the other hand, the Court of Justice stated that the association was responsible for setting a uniform tariff for all customs agents and that its decision restricted competition within the meaning of Article 81 (1), even if the government imposed tariff fixing without fixing the amount and the modalities which was determined by an autonomous decision of the association.[312]

In the *TACA II* case which concerned the Commission prohibition decision under Article 81 against the members of the Transatlantic Liner Conference for having entered into an autonomous agreement on prices for inland transport services as part of a multimodal transport operation[313] the Court of First Instance took the same position by affirming:

> 'Articles 85 and 86 [*now 81 and 82*] may apply, by contrast, if it is found that the national legislation does not preclude undertakings from engaging in autonomous conduct which prevents, restricts or distorts competition ... Consequently, if a national law merely allows, encourages or makes it easier for undertakings to engage in autonomous anti-competitive conduct, those undertakings remain subject to the Treaty competition rules ... In this case, in so far as the applicants point out that certain of the practices mentioned are permitted or even made easier by US law, it is therefore to be observed that that circumstance alone has no bearing on the application of Article 86 (*now 82)* of the Treaty to those practices, since in such a case it remains possible for the TACA parties to adapt their conduct to comply with both Community and US law.'[314]

Accordingly, the Court of First Instance upheld the Commission decision with respect to the infringement of Article 81 but annulled the decision (including the imposition of fines) with respect to the alleged infringement of Article 82 because the Commission had failed to demonstrate to the requisite legal standard that the TACA parties induced potential competitors to join the TACA by the abusive measures referred to in the Commission decision.[315]

Liability of both Member states and Undertakings.

In *Consorzio Industrie Fiammiferi* which concerned fixing of the retail selling prices by a ministry and the allocation of production by a consortium entrusted by the government, the Court of Justice ruled:

---

311. *CNSD II*, ECJ June 18, 1998, 1998 ECR I-3831, paras 41–43 and 53–54; *Arduino*, ECJ Feb. 19, 2002, 2002 ECR I-1529, para. 34.
312. *CNSD I*, CFI March 30, 2000, 2000 ECR II-1807, paras 56–74.
313. *TACA*, D.Comm. Sept. 16, 1998, 1999 OJ L 95/1.
314. *TACA – Atlantic Container Line*, CFI Sept. 30, 2003, T-191/98, paras 1130–1131.
315. *Ibid.*, para. 1368.

'that, where undertakings engage in conduct contrary to Article 81 (1) EC and where that conduct is required or facilitated by national legislation which legitimises or reinforces the effects of the conduct, specifically with regard to price-fixing or market sharing arrangements, a national authority, one of whose responsibilities is to ensure that Article 81 (1) is observed:
– has the duty to disapply the national legislation;
– may not impose penalties in respect of past conduct on the undertakings concerned when the conduct was required by national legislation;
– may not impose penalties on the undertakings concerned in respect of conduct subsequent to the decision to disapply the national legislation, once the decision has become definitive in their regard;
– may impose penalties on the undertakings concerned in respect of past conduct where the conduct was merely facilitated or encouraged by national legislation, whilst taking due account of the specific features of the legislative framework in which the undertakings acted.'[316]

In this case the governmental pre-determination of the sales prices of matches did not rule out all scope of competitive conduct, in particular with respect to the transfer or exchange of production quotas.[317] Thus, the undertakings were liable for distortion of competition going beyond that already brought about the legal obligation.[318]

2. Governmental Measures Compelling or Inducing Firms to Engage in Anticompetitive Conduct Contrary to Article 10

Application of Article 10 (2).
On the basis of the Court of Justice's case law Article 10 (2) in conjunction with Articles 81 and 82 applies to governmental measures such as:

- Legislative measures *compelling* enterprises to partition imports of cars amongst themselves according to fixed quotas,[319] to apply identical minimum prices,[320] to apply a system of fixed prices (without, however, fixing the amount and modalitites),[321] to respect the prices fixed by the tour operators, thereby

316. *Consorzio Industrie Fiammiferi*, ECJ Sept. 9, 2003, C-198/01, para. 58.
317. *Ibid.*, paras 67–69.
318. *Ibid.*, paras 71–72.
319. *Asia Motors France*, CFI Sept. 18, 1996, 1996 ECR II-961.
320. *Van Tiggele*, ECJ Jan. 14, 1978, 1978 ECR 25.
321. *CNSD II*, ECJ June 18, 1998, 1998 ECR I-3831, paras 41–43. However, governmental measures which establish a system of obligatory prices or tariffs without any participation of undertakings or associations of undertakings may be contrary to Articles 28, 43 and 49 of the EC Treaty, *see* Section F.3. below.

prohibiting the travel agencies to share commissions with their clients,[322] or to apply a tariff for services even if this tariff is based on a proposal which the undertakings concerned are compelled to apply.[323] However, Article 10 does not preclude national legislation which provides that the members of a profession (e.g., architects) may set at their discretion the fees for certain services which they perform,[324] which approves a tariff fixing minimum and maximum fees for members of the bar based, in particular, on the monetary value of the disputes[325] or which prohibits or approves any multi-disciplinary partnership between members of the Bar and accountants, provided it is necessary for the proper exercise of the legal function.[326]

- Legislative measures *reinforcing* the anticompetitive effects of a price fixing agreement between enterprises by making it generally binding and therefore compulsory even for those who did not participate in the conclusion of the agreement.[327] However, Article 10 may not apply in cases where an anticompetitive agreement is induced by a governmental measure, i.e. a national collective price maintenance agreement in the book sector, but where the assessment of such agreement under Article 81 (1) and (3) is, in the absence of relevant case law, not sufficiently clarified.[328] The conclusion of an anticompetitive agreement may be facilitated where a governmental measure formally *approves* a price fixing agreement,[329] although the parties to such an agreement may be liable for an infringement of Article 81.[330]
- Governmental measures *facilitating* or *encouraging*[331] the conclusion of an anticompetitive agreement, in particular where governments, instead of taking compulsory measures, proceed to informal actions or measures which aim at

322. *Flemish Travel Agents*, ECJ Oct. 1, 1987, 1987 ECR 3801, para. 24.
323. *Arduino*, ECJ Feb. 19, 2002, 2002 ECR I-1529, paras 34–36.
324. *Conte*, ECJ Nov. 29, 2001, 2001 ECR I-9359, para. 28.
325. *Arduino*, ECJ Feb. 19, 2002, 2002 ECR I-1529, paras 38–44.
326. *Wouters*, ECJ Feb. 19, 2002, 2002 ECR I-1577, para. 123. *See Orde van de Vlaamse Balies*, D.Comm. Sept. 3, 2003, 2003 OJ C 207/22 (comfort letter issued under Article 81 for a decision of the Flemish Bars to prohibit any association between members of the Bars and accountants).
327. *Ohra*, ECJ Nov. 17, 1993, 1993 ECR I-5851, para. 15. The possibility of declaring agreements generally binding ('algemeenverbindingverklaring') was provided for under Dutch and Belgian law and has frequently been used. However, the Dutch competition law, which entered into force on 1 January 1998, no longer provides this possibility in order to adapt national law to the Community standards.
328. *Leclerc-French Book Prices*, ECJ Jan. 10, 1985, 1985 ECR 1, para. 19. However, Article 10 does not prevent a member state from declaring an agreement fixing tariffs for the inland waterway traffic generally binding if the government could have substituted the agreement by a legislative measure on grounds of public interest: *Delta Schiffahrts- und Speditionsgesellschaft*, ECJ June 9, 1994, 1994 ECR I-2517, paras 112–123.
329. *See Ahmed Saeed*, ECJ April 11, 1989, 1989 ECR 803, paras 49–50.
330. E.g., *Franco-Japanese Ballbearings Agreement*, D.Comm. Nov. 29, 1974, 1974 OJ L 343/19, 23.
331. *Arduino*, ECJ Feb. 19, 2002, 2002 ECR I-1529, para. 43.

encouraging enterprises to enter into anticompetitive arrangements. Examples include so-called 'voluntary restraints' agreements whereby third country producers and their competitors within the Common Market enter into anticompetitive agreements in order to align prices of imported products to those of the national products[332] or to reduce the imported quantities.[333] Further examples are proceedings against government measures reinforcing a collective resale price maintenance agreement between Belgian producers and importers of tobacco,[334] against the uniform price-regulating rules of the Dutch building and construction industry,[335] against collective price fixing within the association of Dutch wholesalers of electrotechnical material,[336] and against a recommended minimum fee scale of the Belgian Architects' Association.[337] However, Article 10 may not apply where an anticompetitive agreement is induced by a governmental measure, but where the assessment of such an agreement under Article 81 (1) and (3) is, in the absence of relevant case law, not sufficiently clarified, e.g., with respect to a national collective price maintenance agreement in the book sector.[338]

Exceptions of Applicability of Article 10 (2).
The precondition for the application of Article 10 (2) is an agreement between companies that is compelled, reinforced or facilitated by a governmental measure. Therefore, Article 10 (2) does not apply where the member state acts in its sovereign capacity[339] or where the governmental measure in itself constitutes an infringement of the principle of the free movement of goods and services (Articles 28 and 43), without prejudice to the provisions which guarantee the performance of services of general interest, such as Articles 16, 30, 46 and 86 (2).[340] For

332. *French-Japanese Ballbearings Agreement*, D.Comm. Nov. 29, 1974, 1974 OJ L 343/19, 23 (without fines); *French and Taiwanese Mushroom Packers*, D.Comm. Jan. 8, 1975, 1975 OJ L 29/26, 28 (with fines).
333. *Asia Motor France I*, CFI Sept. 18, 1992, 1992 ECR II-2285; *Asia Motor France II*, CFI June 29, 1993, 1993 ECR II-669; *aff'd* ECJ May 7, 1998, 1998 ECR I-2587.
334. *FEDETAB*, D.Comm. July 20, 1978, 1978 OJ L 224/29; *aff'd* ECJ Oct. 29, 1980, 1980 ECR 3125.
335. *Dutch Construction Works*, D.Comm. Feb. 5, 1992, 1992 OJ L 92/1; *aff'd* CFI Feb. 21, 1995, 1995 ECR II-289.
336. *Nederlandse Federatieve Vereniging voor de Groothandel op Elektrotechnisch Gebied*, CFI Dec. 16, 2003, T-5/00, para. 296.
337. Commission's Statement of Objections of Nov. 5, 2003, IP/03/1500.
338. *Leclerc/French Book Prices*, ECJ Jan. 10, 1985, 1985 ECR 1, para. 19.
339. *SAT/Eurocontrol*, ECJ Jan. 19, 1994, 1994 ECR I-43, para. 27 (maintenance of air navigation safety). *See* the reference to 'measures of external commercial policy' in the Commission decision *in the French-Japanese Ballbearings Agreement*, D.Comm. Nov. 29, 1974, 1974 OJ L 343/19, 23.
340. *See Ahmed Saaed*, ECJ April 11, 1989, 1989 ECR 803, paras 55–58 (fixing air transport tariffs); *Bundesanstalt für den Güterfernverkehr/Reiff*, ECJ Nov. 17, 1993, 1993 ECR I-5801, paras 13–19 (fixing road haulage tariffs).

instance, Article 43 does not preclude national legislation from prohibiting multidisciplinary partnerships between members of the bar and accountants in so far as the regulation is necessary for the proper practice of the profession, provided it is necessary to guarantee professional ethics, integrity and experience, thereby considering grounds of public policy, as recognized in Articles 30 and 46 and that it cannot be guaranteed by a less extreme measure.[341] Such regulation, despite the inherent restrictive effects, is necessary for the proper practice of the profession. The member state is not liable for an infringement of Articles 43 and 49 and neither are the members of the association for an infringement of Article 81 (1).[342]

Responsibility of Undertakings for Anticompetitive Conduct but Lower Fines. Although the undertakings remain responsible for their anticompetitive conduct, the Commission takes into account the governmental measures when imposing fines because these measures could have led the parties to believe that their activities were condoned by the state.[343] The Court approved this argument as a mitigating factor[344] and rejected the argument that the Commission should have commenced actions against the governmental measures stating that

> 'even on the assumption that the Commission has failed to fulfill certain of its obligations under Article 155 of the Treaty by failing to ensure the application of the Community law on competition and the adjustment of state monopolies in the manufactured tobacco sector, that fact cannot justify any infringements of the Community law on competition committed in the same sector in the present cases by the applicants.'[345]

The Court of Justice thereby acknowledged the Commission's responsibility also to act against governmental measures, under Article 10 (2) in conjunction with Articles 81 or 82 and in the framework of an Article 226 proceeding, even if the measures do not compel, but only encourage or facilitate an anticompetitive behavior.[346]

Direct Applicability of Article 10 (2).
The most important consequence of an infringement of Article 10 (2) is its direct applicability. An infringement of Article 10 (2) in conjunction with Article 81 or

341. *Wouters*, ECJ Feb. 19, 2002, 2002 ECR I-1577, paras 90–110.
342. *Ibid.*, para. 110. Both Article 28 and 43 are subject to the public policy exception of Articles 46 and 55. Under Article 81: *Orde van Vlaamse Balies*, D.Comm. Sept. 3, 2003, 2003 OJ C 207/22 (comfort letter issued for an agreement of the Flemish Bars which contained a general prohibition for lawyers to enter into an association with non-lawyers with the intent to cooperate professionally).
343. Twenty-second Report of Competition Policy, point 193.
344. *Dutch Construction Works*, CFI Feb. 5, 1995, 1995 ECR II-289, paras 378–379.
345. *FEDETAB*, ECJ Oct. 29, 1980, 1980 ECR 3125, para. 84.
346. *Inno/ATAB*, ECJ Nov. 16, 1977, 1977 ECR 2115, paras 36–38.

82 has the same direct effect as an infringement of Article 81 or an infringement of Article 86 (1) in conjunction with Article 81 or 82.[347] The direct effect of nullity or non-enforceability can be invoked against the governmental measure in order to avoid any governmental sanction and against the other parties to the agreement, including the association, in order to avoid any penalty payments or other consequences of civil law, in particular termination of the contract. In the case of an agreement which is contrary to Article 81 and declared generally binding by a governmental measure contrary to Article 10 (2), the direct effect of Article 10 (2) protects both the parties who are part of the illegal agreement and the outsiders which are subject to the illegal governmental order.[348] In the case *Consorzio Industrie Fiammiferi,*[349] which concerned the fixing of prices and allocation of production quotas for matches by the Italian State, the Court of Justice clarified that a national authority has the duty to disapply the illegal governmental order. In addition, the Commission and the national authorities may:

- compel undertakings to disapply the illegal legislation with respect to their *future* conduct;
- impose fines on firms whose illegal conduct was facilitated or promoted by the national legislation or for *future* conduct;
- not impose sanctions in respect of *past* conduct required by the national legislation, except where the firms concerned are engaged in autonomous conduct restricting the residual forms of competition and therefore also liable for an infringement of Article 81 (1).

It follows that tariffs fixed for members of a professional organization are not legally binding and enforceable irrespective of whether they have been fixed, compelled or induced by the national government contrary to Article 10 (2) in conjunction with Article 81 (1) or fixed by associations of undertakings contrary to Article 81 (1). The important question is who is responsible for the infringement: the government, the association and/or its members or both. Article 10 (2) applies where, as in the *Arduino* case,[350] which concerned the fixing of minimum and maximum fees for members of the Italian Bar, the professional organization is required to produce a draft tariff for services taking into account not only the interests of the undertakings or associations in the sector which has appointed them but also the public interest, and which is finally adopted by the government. Article 81 (1) applies where, as in the *Belgian Architects* case,[351] a recommended fee

347. *Sacchi/Tele Biella*, ECJ April 30, 1974, 1974 ECR 431, para. 18; *Porto di Genova I*, ECJ Dec. 10, 1991, 1991 ECR I-5923, para. 24; *Almelo (IJsselcentrale)*, ECJ April 24, 1994, 1994 ECR I-1477, paras 35–36.

348. *CNSD*, ECJ June 18, 1998, 1998 ECR I-3857. *See Price Waterhouse*, Amsterdam Court of First Instance, Feb. 7, 1997, Twenty-seventh Report on Competition Policy, point 349.

349. *Consorzio Industrie Fiammiferi,* ECJ Sept. 8, 2003, C-198/01, paras 67-80.

350. *Arduino,* ECJ Feb. 19, 2002, C-35/99, paras 36-37.

351. *Belgian Architects,* D.Comm. June 24, 2004, IP/04/800, points 46-49 (fine of EUR 100,000).

scale applied by the Belgian Architects' Association is more than a mere proposal for the government and likely to be used as a means for coordinating the pricing behaviour of the Belgian architects. Even where national legislation delegates competence to fix retail selling prices of a product and power to allocate production to a consortium to which the relevant producers are obliged to belong, the undertakings concerned still may engage in autonomous conduct restricting the residual forms of competition (such as secret discounts or rebates) which remains prohibited under Article 81 (1). [352] On the other hand, Articles 81 and 82 are not intended to eliminate differences between member states, which are, e.g., caused by different tax regimes, and do not preclude a national law which provides for the levy of surcharges (which is collected by a company on behalf of the state) for the purpose of restoring the competitiveness of economic operators.[353]

3. Governmental Measures Contrary to Article 28 or 49

The Principle of the Rules of the Free Circulation of Goods and Services. Articles 28 and 49 of the EC Treaty are intended to prohibit all rules or other measures having equivalent effect to quantitative measures enacted by member states, which are capable of hindering, directly or indirectly, actually or potentially, intra-Community trade.[354] However, it is also settled case law that a member state is entitled to take measures to prevent certain of its nationals, under the cover of the freedoms created by the Treaty, from wrongfully evading the application of their national legislation, e.g., to restrict exports of goods for the sole purpose of being reimported in order to circumvent a national rule.[355] In its landmark *Keck* decision,[356] the Court clarified and refined its previous case law[357] by ruling that *modalities* of marketing having only effects within one member state do not in-

352. *See*, in particular, *Centro Servizi Spediporto*, ECJ Oct. 5, 1995, 1995 ECR I-2883, para. 42; *Autotrasporti Librandi/Cuttica Spedizioni*, ECJ Oct. 1, 1998, 1998 ECR I-5955, paras 37 and 52 (road-haulage tariffs approved and brought into force by the state on the basis of proposals submitted by a committee, where that committee is composed of a majority of representatives of the public authorities and a minority of representatives of the economic operators concerned and its proposals must observe certain public interest criteria, and where, moreover, the public authorities do not relinquish their rights and powers by taking into consideration, before the proposals are approved, the observations of other public and private bodies, or even by fixing tariffs *ex officio*. Under these conditions even collective agreements are not restrictive of competition (lack of entrepreneurial responsibility)).
353. *Altair Chimica/ENEL*, ECJ Sept. 11, 2003, C-207/01, paras 35–37. Similarly, *Commission/Italy*, 1980 ECR 1533, para. 22 (governmental surcharge on the price of imported sugar paid to an equalization fund for the redistribution to the Italian sugar industry, which 'substantially reduced the opportunities available to the parties to negotiate a price': *Sugar*, ECJ Dec. 16, 1975, 1975 ECR 1663, para. 68).
354. *Dassonville*, ECJ July 11, 1974, 1974 ECR 837, para. 5.
355. *Milk Marque Ltd*, ECJ Sept. 9, 2003, C-137/00, paras 114–115 (with further references).
356. *Keck*, ECJ Nov. 24, 1993, 1993 ECR I-6097.
357. *See Cassis de Dijon*, ECJ Feb. 20, 1979, 1979 ECR 649.

fringe Article 28 or 49,[358] provided they apply without discrimination to national and imported products.[359] On the other hand, *product-related* measures continue to be considered as likely to affect imports and therefore infringe Article 28 or 49.[360]

Application of this Principle.
Article 28 has been held applicable to governmental measures:

- which limit imported quantities;[361]
- which limit the importation by mail order of medicinal products that are not subject to prescription;[362]
- which fix prices solely on the basis of the ex-refinery prices of national refineries;[363]
- which fix low trading charges likely to preclude imports;[364]
- whose maximum prices for national and imported tobacco products are under the specific factual circumstances likely to affect imports;[365]
- which recommend the purchase of national products;[366]
- which require formalities for imported products such as licenses;[367]
- which prohibits advertising the sale (import) of lawfully marketed medicinal products over the internet.[368]

On the other hand, the application of Article 28 has been rejected where the governmental measure is unlikely to discriminate against imports, in particular where it concerns only the modalities of marketing which apply to national as well to imported products.[369]

358. Article 28: *Keck*, ECJ Nov. 24, 1993, 1993 ECR I-6097, paras 14–17; *Honermund*, ECJ Dec. 15, 1993, 1993 ECR I-6787, para. 21; *Lederc/Siplec*, ECJ Feb. 9, 1995, 1995 ECR I-179, para. 21; *Belgapom*, ECJ Aug. 11, 1995, 1995 ECR I-2486, para. 12. Article 49: *Höfner/Macrotron*, ECJ April 23, 1991, 1991 ECR I-1979, para. 37.
359. E.g., *Pal/Dahlhausen*, ECJ Dec. 13, 1990, 1990 ECR I-4844; *Konsumentenombudsman/Gourmet International*, ECJ March 8, 2001, 2001 ECR I-1795.
360. Modalities such as sales below costs and other means of unfair competition: *Dansk Supermarked*, ECJ Jan. 22, 1981, 1981 ECR 181; *Mars/Verein gegen das Unwesen in Handel und Gewerbe*, ECJ July 6, 1995, 1995 ECR I-1923; *Groupement national des commercants en pommes de terre de Belgique*, ECJ Aug. 11, 1995, 1995 ECR I-2486. Product-related provisions such as the markup: *Alpine*, ECJ May 10, 1995, 1995 ECR I-1175; *Pistre*, ECJ May 7, 1997, 1997 ECR I-2343.
361. *Geddo*, ECJ July 12, 1973, 1973 ECR 865, para. 7.
362. *Deutscher Apothekerverband*, ECJ Dec. 11, 2003, C-322/01, paras 125–131.
363. *Leclerc-French Gasoline Prices*, ECJ Jan. 29, 1985, 1985 ECR 305, paras 19–34.
364. *Belgacom*, ECJ Aug. 11, 1995, 1995 ECR I-2486, para. 12.
365. *Inno/ATAB*, ECJ Nov. 16, 1977, 1977 ECR 2115, paras 43–56.
366. *Buy Irish*, ECJ Nov. 24, 1982, 1982 ECR 4005.
367. *Commission/Italy*, ECJ Sept. 20, 1994, 1994 ECR I-4311.
368. *Deutscher Apothekerverband*, ECJ Dec. 11, 2003, C-322/01, para. 149.
369. *See* the *Keck* doctrine discussed *above*.

Possible Justifications on Grounds of Public Exceptions of Applicability of Articles 28 and 49.

The applicability of Articles 28, 49 and 59 is excluded if the governmental measure is justified on grounds of public policy or public security or protection of health, provided it does not constitute a means of arbitrary discrimination or a disguised restriction on trade between member states (Article 30).[370] These exceptions are subject to the proportionality test of whether the objective can be achieved by less restrictive means.[371] For instance, the Article 30 exception can be relied upon to justify a national prohibition on the sale by mail of medicinal products that are subject to prescription.[372]

G. Articles 87–89: Obligation of Member States not to Distort Competition by Granting State Aids

1. Legal Framework

General.

The more the European Community becomes integrated, the more firms are likely to be affected by state aid given to their competitors. More open markets therefore call for tighter control over state aids. This control is to be further intensified in the run-up to full economic and monetary union. Tackling the volume of state aids is also an important way of reducing the gap between the poorer countries on the periphery and the richer countries expending far greater amounts on state aid than their poorer neighbors. The provisions of the EC Treaty were designed to prohibit discriminatory terms likely to jeopardize the free, non-discriminatory movement of goods, services, persons and capital.

Prohibition Mitigated by Exceptions.

Article 87 (1) of the EC Treaty and Article 61 (1) of the EEA Agreement[373] contain a general prohibition against granting state aids that distort or threaten to

---

370. With respect to the free movement of goods (Article 30): *Beer Purity*, ECJ March 12, 1987, 1987 ECR 1227; *DIP/Commune di Bassano del Grappa*, ECJ Oct. 17, 1995, 1995 ECR I-3257, paras 29–31. With respect to free movement of services (Articles 55 and 46): *De Agostini/TV-Shop*, ECJ July 9, 1997, 1997 ECR I-3843, para. 54; *Corsica Ferries II*, ECJ June 18, 1998, 1998 ECR I-3949, para. 61.

371. *See Donckerwolke*, ECJ Dec. 15, 1976, 1976 ECR 1921; *Eurim Pharm*, ECJ April 16, 1991, 1991 ECR I-1747.

372. *Deutscher Apothekerverband/Doc Morris*, ECJ Dec. 11, 2003, C-322/01, paras 117–124. In an *obiter dictum* the Court stated that a national legislation fixing the prices for such products 'should be maintained' in so far as they form an integral part of a national social security system: *ibid.*, para. 122.

373. Articles 61 and 62 and the guidelines of the EFTA Supervisory Authority (1994 OJ L 231/1. *See Folketrydloven*, EFTA Court of Justice, May 20, 1999, E-6/98, paras 12–15 and 52–63.

distort competition by favoring undertakings or the production of certain goods, including, since 23 July 2002, in the coal and steel sectors,[374] provided they affect trade between member states.[375] The EC rules will apply, from May 2004, immediately to the new member states, with only some limited transitional arrangements.[376] The prohibition is mitigated by legal exceptions (Article 87 (2)) and exemptions (Article 87 (3)) granted by individual decision or by regulation (block exemption).

Modernization of the State Aid Control – Proposal of *De Minimis* Rules. The Commission is undertaking a reform of both the procedural and substantive aspects of the state aid rules. In a way similar to the modernization of the application of Articles 81 and 82, this reform package aims at:

- streamlining procedures and freeing the process of examining state aid from unnecessary procedural burdens, thereby facilitating speedy decisions and reserving major resources for the most contentious questions,
- developing transparent and sound economic criteria for the implementation of state aid measures,
- revising existing frameworks and guidelines, in particular on multisectoral framework[377] and employment aid,[378] and
- achieving major improvements in cooperation with member states by raising the awareness of state aid issues among regional, local and national authorities in order to increase its long-term competitiveness.[379]

This reform corresponds to the Council's conclusions on 16 March 2002 at the Barcelona conference, which invited the Commission in particular to continue its efforts to reduce state aid levels[380] and to give priority to reducing, with a view of

374. IP/02/835 of 7 July 2002; Decision 2002/827/ECSC, 2002 OJ L 296/80.
375. The criteria of 'affect trade between Member States' (not only 'likely to affect' as under Articles 81 and 82) is interpreted in a broad sense: D.Comm. 87/16/EC April 23, 1986, 1987 OJ L 12/27, 29 (artificial advantage of the recipient of the aid compared to its competitors in other member states); *Philip Morris*, ECJ Sept. 17, 1980, 1980 ECR 2671, para. 11 (expansion of production capacity leading to an artificial increase of the recipient's capability to export in other member states); *France/Commission*, ECJ Sept. 14, 1994, 1994 ECR I-4103, para. 19 (artificial maintenance of production facilities likely to reduce the ability of competitors in other states to export in the recipient's country).
376. Thirty-third Report on Competition Policy, points 626–651. *See* Monti, New Developments in State Aid Policy, British Chamber of Commerce of Dec. 1, 2003.
377. Commission Communication on multisectoral framework for regional aid for large investment projects, 2002 OJ C 70/8.
378. Commission Regulation on employment aid, 2002 OJ L 337/3.
379. Thirty-second Report on Competition Policy, points 332–355.
380. Total state aid amounted in 2002 to EUR 49 billion = 0.56% of the GDP or 0.39% excluding agriculture and fisheries. *See* Chêne, 'The Commission's Current Agenda in European State Aid Control', *European State Aid Law Quarterly*, 2004, pp. 7–10.

eliminating, aid which has the greatest distortive effects. Accordingly the reform includes:

- Commission Regulation 794/2004 implementing Council Regulation 659/1999 laying down detailed rules for the application of Article 88 of the EC Treaty;[381]
- Commission Regulation 1/2004 on the application of Articles 87 and 88 of the EC Treaty to state aid to small and medium-sized enterprises active in the production, processing and marketing of agricultural products;[382]
- a draft directive amending Directive 80/723/EC on the transparency of financial relations between member states and public undertakings, in particular requiring undertakings enjoying special or exclusive rights or entrusted with the operation of a service of general economic interest to maintain separate accounts;
- a draft Commission decision under Article 86 (3) which contains a block exemption of state aid of lesser amounts and state aid granted to hospitals and social housing undertakings; and
- a draft Community framework for state aid in the form of public service compensation. [383]

The proposed measures pursue the same objectives as those adopted under Articles 81 and 82 with a view of modernizing the application of these provisions: a more economic assessment, the issuance of block exemptions and guidelines for the asssessment of cases which are not covered by block exemptions in order to enable the Commission to give priority to cases with the most harmful effects, thereby leaving the assessment of the legality of the measures or conduct for the national courts, which must apply Article 87 to assess their legality and determine the consequences under national law as regards both the validity of agreements or decisions and restitution.[384]

In view of the complexity of the matter and the steady development of the rules and guidelines issued by the Commission[385] the present section is limited to a short summary.

---

381. 2004 OJ L 140/1–134.
382. 2004 OJ L 1/1.
383. IP/04/235 of 18 February 2004. *See* COM(2002)555 final of 16 October 2002.
384. Under Articles 81 and 82: *BRT/SABAM I*, ECJ Jan. 30, 1974, 1974 ECR 51, para. 16; under Article 88 (3): *Eniricorse*, ECJ Nov. 27, 2003, C-34/01, para. 42.
385. *See* http://europa.eu.int/comm/competition/state_aid/legislation/aid3.html, and Thirty-second Report on Competition Policy, points 329–579.

2. Definition and Schemes of State Aids

Broad Definition of State Aids.
For a measure to involve state aid within the meaning of Article 87 (1), the aid must, according to the Court's judgment in the *Altmark GmbH* case,[386] fulfill the following conditions:

- first, it must be granted by a member state or through state resources;
- secondly, the intervention must be liable to affect trade between member states,
- thirdly, it must confer an advantage on the recipient,
- fourthly, certain undertakings or activities must be favored over others ('selectivity' principle), and
- fifthly, it must distort or threaten to distort competition.

The first three conditions generally determine whether a given measure qualifies at all as state aid, while the fourth and fifth provide qualifications as to the effects of the aid which make it fall within the scope of Article 87 (1) and thus be *prima facie* incompatible with the Common Market.

(i) Grant of State Resources

State aid may result from real financial advantages received directly from the state or from state resources,[387] even if the aid is financed by means of compulsory contributions,[388] or from its regional or local authorities.[389] It may also result from certain parafiscal charges depending on the use to which the revenue from those charges is put as well as from the collection of a contribution constituting a parafiscal charge.[390] The aid can take a variety of forms:

- state grants,[391]
- interest relief,[392]
- tax relief,[393]

---

386. *See Altmark GmbH*, ECJ July 24, 2003, C-280/00, para. 75; *Eniricorse*, ECJ Nov. 27, 2003, C-34/01, paras 26–29; *Chronopost*, ECJ July 3, 2003, C-83/01 P, para. 28. *See also* Versterdorf, 'A Comment on the New State Aid as (Re)shaped by Altmark', *European State Aid Law Quarterly*, 2004, pp. 11–19.
387. *See Preussen Elektra*, ECJ March 13, 2001, 2001 ECR I-2099, para. 58.
388. *Eniricorse*, ECJ Nov. 27, 2003, C-34/01, para. 44.
389. *See* Article 2 of Commission Directive 80/723, 1980 OJ L 195.
390. *Eniricorse*, ECJ Nov. 27, 2003, C-34/01, para. 43.
391. *See Stardust*, ECJ May 16, 2002, 2002 ECR I-4397, para. 36
392. Capital injections must be remunerated at market rates in order not to be considered as state aid: *WestLB*, CFI March 6, 2003, T-228/99
393. *Banco di Credito Industrial*, ECJ March 15, 1994, 1994 ECR I-877; *French Post Office*, CFI Feb. 27, 1997, 1997 ECR II-229; *Ferring*, ECJ Nov. 22, 2001, 2001 ECR I-9067, para. 21;

- state guarantees or shareholdings,[394] or
- provision by the state of goods or services on preferential terms,[395]
- the application of excessively low energy prices;[396]
- the grant of specific rebates giving national producers an unjustified competitive advantage;[397]
- credit facilities and preferential interest rates on loans;[398]
- cross-subsidization;[399]
- state guarantees against exchange risks;[400]
- levies to be charged on imports or remitted on exports;[401]
- indirect advantages such as the sale or lease of land for industrial development by public authorities at non-market prices;[402]
- tax deductions or concessions in favor of public enterprises;[403] and
- participation of the government in companies experiencing financial difficulties.[404]

Altmark GmbH, ECJ July 24, 2003, C-280/00, para. 86. *See* Thirthy-third Report on Competition Policy, points 368–385.

394. *See WestLB*, D.Comm. March 27, 2002, Thirty-third Report on Competition Policy, points 360–366.

395. 'Advantage to a firm or firms': *SIC*, CFI May 10, 2000, 2000 ECR II-2125, para. 83.

396. Fifteenth Report on Competition Policy, point 182; *Dutch Natural Gas Tariffs I*, ECJ Feb. 2, 1988, 1988 ECR 219; *Dutch Natural Gas Tariffs II*, ECJ July 12, 1990, 1990 ECR I-3083; *Adria Wien Pipeline*, ECJ Nov. 8, 2001, 2001 ECR I-8365.

397. *Dutch Natural Gas Prices II*, ECJ July 12, 1990, 1990 ECR I-3083. *See*, however, the approval of the amended scheme by the Commission on 29 Dec.1992, Twenty-second Report on Competition Policy, points 434–437, *aff'd* ECJ Feb. 29, 1996, 1996 ECR I-723.

398. *France/Commission*, ECJ Feb. 14, 1990, 1990 ECR I-307, para. 41.

399. Cross-subsidization must be determined according to the fully distributed cost method, thereby taking account of the incremental costs: *La Poste/SFMI-Chronopost*, ECJ July 3, 2003, C-83/01 P, para. 40; Commission Notice on postal services, 1998 OJ C 39/2, point 3.4.; *Deutsche Post III*, D.Comm. June 19, 2002, 2002 OJ L 247/27, points 89–104. Commission communication concerning the application of Articles 87 and 88 to short-term export credit insurance, 1997 OJ C 281/4; *German Railway Company* (*Deutsche Bundesbahn*), Twenty-third Report on Competition Policy, point 534. *See* Hancher/Buendia Sierra, 35 CMLR, 901, 906 (1998); Faulhaber, American Economy Review 65 (1975), 967–977.

400. *Special Financing Scheme for Investments to Increase Exporting Firms' Production Capacity in France*, D.Comm. May 18, 1979, 1979 OJ L 138/30.

401. Twenty-third Report on Competition Policy, point 391.

402. *Naumburg*, D.Comm. Jan. 20, 1999, 1999 OJ L 107/21; *Potsdamer Platz in Berlin*, Twenty-fourth Report on Competition Policy, point 346; Commission communication on state aid elements in sales of land and buildings by public authorities, 1997 OJ C 209/3. The transfer of assets at non-market prices, thereby containing an element of state aid, may strengthen artificially the financial and economic position of the acquiror and must be considered when assessing the merger: *RJB Mining*, CFI Jan. 31, 2001, 2001 ECR II-337, paras 122–125.

403. *Banco di Credito Industrial*, ECJ March 15, 1994, 1994 ECR I-877; *La Poste*, CFI Jan. 15, 1997, 1997 ECR II-229.

404. *Intermills*, ECJ Nov. 21, 1984, 1084 ECR 3809; the criteria being the principle of market-orientated private investors, *see Spain/Commission*, ECJ Sept. 14, 1994, 1994 ECR I-4103 and Twenty-fourth Report on Competition Policy, point 344.

The close relationship between government and public undertakings and undertakings vested with exclusive or special rights in the sense of Article 86 (1) led to the adoption of the Transparency Directive.[405]

(ii) Effect on Trade between Member States

Unlike under Article 81[406] there is no threshold or percentage below which it may be considered that trade between member states is not affected.[407] The Commission is not required to demonstrate the actual effects of the aid on competition and on trade between member states.[408] For instance, port charges allocated to undertakings in a port and paid by shipping companies in respect of the loading and unloading of goods, whatever their origin, are likely to affect trade between member states.[409] The effect on trade between member states does not depend on the local or regional character of the services supplied but on the likely harm to undertakings established in other member states having less chance of providing their services.[410]

(iii) Advantage on the Recipient – The Prudent Investor Principle

The state measure must be likely directly or indirectly to favour certain undertakings or to constitute an economic advantage which the recipient undertaking would not have obtained in normal market conditions,[411] including the grant of special or exclusive rights. [412] The concept of state aid embraces not only positive contributions, such as subsidies themselves, but also measures which, in various forms, mitigate the charges which are normally included in the budget of an undertaking and which, without therefore being subsidies in the strict meaning of the word, are similar in character and have the same effects.[413] However, the compensation for the services provided by the recipient undertakings in order to

---

405. Commission Directive 2000/52/EC on the transparency of financial relations between member states and public undertakings, 2000 OJ L 193/75.
406. *See* Commission Guidelines on the Effect on Trade Concept, 2004 OJ C 101/81, point 52.
407. *Altmark GmbH*, ECJ July 24, 2003, C-280/00, para. 81; *Eniricorse*, ECJ Nov. 27, 2003, C-34/01, para. 28.
408. *P&O European Ferries*, CFI Aug. 3, 2003, T-116/01, para. 142.
409. *Eniricorse*, ECJ Nov. 27, 2003, C-34/01, para. 28. Similarly, Commission Guidelines on the Effect on Trade Concept, points 97–99.
410. *Altmark*, ECJ July 24, 2003, C-280/00, paras 77–78 and 82. *See* Thirty-second Report on Competition Policy, points 403–404.
411. *Altmark GmbH*, ECJ July 24, 2003, C-280/00, para. 84; *Eniricorse*, ECJ Nov. 27, 2003, C-34/01, para. 30. *See also Banco Exterior de Espana*, ECJ March 15, 1994, 1994 ECR I-877, para. 34; *SFEI*, ECJ July 11, 1996, 1996 ECR I-3547, paras 59–62; *La Poste/SFMI-Chronopost*, ECJ July 3, 2003, C-83/01 P, paras 31–41.
412. Recent administrative practice: Thirty-second Report on Competition Policy, points 360–400.
413. *Altmark*, ECJ July 24, 2003, C-280/00, para. 15.

discharge public-service obligations, so that those undertakings do not enjoy a real financial advantage and that the measure does not therefore have the effect of putting them in a more favourable competitive position than their competitors, cannot be classified as state aid,[414] provided the conditions of operating a service of general economic interest are fulfilled.[415] For assessing whether such advantages constitute a state aid the 'prudent investor principle'[416] applies as stated by the Court of Justice:

> '... it is necessary to assess whether, in similar circumstances, a private investor of a dimension comparable to that of the bodies managing the public sector could have been prevailed upon to make capital contributions of the same size, having regard in particular to the information available and foreseeable developments at the date of those contributions.
>
> In this case, it is undisputed between the parties that, in order to examine whether or not the State has adopted the conduct of a prudent investor operating in a market economy, it is necessary to place oneself in the context of the period during which the financial support measures were taken in order to assess the economic rationality of the State's conduct, and thus to refrain from any assessment based on a later situation.'[417]

However, the concept of normal market conditions does not apply where an undertaking is entrusted with a universal service of general economic interest, such as a postal network which has no equivalent in the market. In the *Chronopost* case,[418] which concerned the question whether the logistical and commercial assistance afforded by the French Post Office constituted state aid, the Court of Justice held that:

> '... in the absence of any possibility of comparing the situation of La Poste with that of a private group of undertakings not operating in a reserved sector, normal market conditions, which are necessarily hypothetical, must be assessed by reference to the objective and verifiable elements which are available. In the present case, the costs borne by La Poste in respect of the provision to its subsidiary of logistical and commercial assistance can constitute such objective and verifiable elements. On that basis, there is no question of state aid if, first, it is established that the price charged properly

---

414. *Altmark*, ECJ July 24, 2003, C-280/00, para. 87; *Eniricorse*, ECJ Nov. 27, 2003, C-34/01, para. 31.
415. *See below* Section G.3.
416. *See Gröditzer Stahlwerke*, ECJ Jan. 28, 2003, C-334/99, para. 133; Matthew Parish, On the private investor principle, (2003) 28 ELRev 70.
417. *French Republic*, ECJ May 16, 2002, 2002 ECR I-4397, paras 70–71. *See also Gröditzer Stahlwerke*, ECJ Jan. 28, 2003, C-334/99.
418. *Chronopost*, ECJ July 3, 2003, C-83/01 P.

> covers all the additional, variable costs incurred in providing the logistcal and commercial assistance … and if, second, there is nothing to suggest that those elements have been underestimated or fixed in an arbitrary fashion.'[419]

(iv) Selectivity

A state measure favoring certain undertakings must satisfy the condition of *selectivity* which defines state aid as laid down by Article 87 (1).[420] It follows that, where a member state imposes public service obligations on *all* operators in a specific economic sector and grants compensations necessary to cover the costs incurred in discharging the public service obligations do not constitute a state aid,[421] except where they are subject to competition from suppliers of substitutable products, as, for instance, the producers of (subsidized) coal which are subject to competition from suppliers of natural gas with respect to the generation of electricity.[422]

(v) Threat to Distort Competition

The state measure must distort or threaten to distort competition[423] by affecting the balance between the beneficiary and its competitors.[424]

3. PROHIBITED STATE AID V. COMPENSATION ALLOWED FOR THE OPERATION OF SERVICES OF GENERAL ECONOMIC INTEREST

Services of General Economic Interest – The *Altmark* Case.
Public subsidies intended to support the operation of services of general economic interest are not caught by Article 87 (1) (and are, therefore, not subject to preventive control) where such subsidies are to be regarded as compensation for the

419. *Ibid.*, paras 38–40. *See also SFEI/La Poste*, ECJ July 11, 1996, 1996 ECR I-3547.
420. *Ministère de l'économie des finances et de l'industrie*, ECJ Nov. 20, 2003, C-126/01, para. 35. *See also Deufil*, ECJ Feb. 24, 1987, 1987 ECR 901, para. 8; *Preussen Elektra*, ECJ March 8, 2001, 2001 ECR I-1975, para. 58; *UK Climate Change Levy*, D.Comm. April 3, 2002, C 18/2001, Thirty-second Report on Competition Policy, points 378 and 394.
421. *See Ferring*, ECJ Nov. 22, 2001, 2001 ECR I-9067, para. 29: a compensation of all pharmaceutical wholesalers for discharging the public service obligation to manage their stocks of medicines so as to ensure availability at all times does not constitute a state aid as long as it does not exceed the additional costs that they bear in discharging the public service obligation.
422. *See* Council Regulation 1407/2002 on state aid to the coal industry, 2002 OJ L 205/1.
423. The distortion does not need to be substantial or significant; the fact that the amount of aid is small does not rule out the distortion of competition: *Belgium/Commission*, CFI Oct. 23, 2002, T-269/99. *See*, however, the block exemptions for *de minimis* cases of state aid (Regulation 69/2001/EC, 2001 OJ L 10/30) and for small and medium sized undertakings (Regulation 70/2001, 2001 OJ L 10/33).
424. Similarly *Eniricorse*, ECJ Nov. 27, 2003, C-34/01, paras 26–30.

services in order to discharge public service obligations.[425] In the *Altmark Trans GmbH* case, which concerned the grant of licences for scheduled bus transport services within a certain region in Germany and public subsidies for operating those services,[426] the Court of Justice requested the national court to ascertain whether the following conditions are satisfied:

- 'first, the recipient undertaking is actually required to discharge public service obligations and those obligations have been clearly defined;[427]
- 'second, the parameters on the basis of which the compensation is calculated have been established beforehand in an objective and transparent manner;
- 'third, the compensation does not exceed what is necessary to cover all or part of the costs incurred in discharging the public service obligations, taking into account the relevant receipts and a reasonable profit for discharging those obligations;
- 'fourth, where the undertaking which is to discharge the public service obligations is not chosen in a public procurement procedure, the level of compensation needed has been determined on the basis of an analysis of the costs which a typical undertaking, well run and adequately provided with means of transport so as to be able to meet the necessary public interest requirements, would have incurred in discharging those obligations, taking into account the relevant receipts and a reasonable profit for discharging those obligations.'[428]

If one or more of these conditions are *not* fulfilled the subsidies are incompatible with the prohibition of Article 88 (3), last sentence,[429] and subject to nullity

425. Communication from the Commission 2001 OJ C 17/4; Commission's 'Non-Paper' on services of general economic interest and state aid, 12 November 2002; *Transparency Directive*, ECJ June 16, 1987, 1987 ECR 2599, para. 7. With respect to further case law, *see* Thirty-second Report on Competition Policy, points 580–611.

426. *Altmark*, ECJ July 24, 2003, C-280/00, para. 95. *See* Rapp-Jung, 'State Financing of Public Services – The Commission's New Approach', *European State Aid Law Quarterly*, 2004, pp. 21–31.

427. The reason is that, in order to satisfy the requirement of legal certainty, individuals should have the benefit of a clear and precise legal situation enabling them to ascertain the full extent of their rights and, where appropriate, to rely on them before national courts: *Altmark*, ECJ July 24, 2003, C-280/00, para. 59.

428. *Altmark Trans GmbH*, ECJ July 24, 2003, C-280/00, operative part of the Article 234 decision. *See FFSA – French Post Office*, CFI Feb. 27, 1997, 1997 ECR II-229; *La Poste/SFMI-Chronopost*, ECJ July 3, 2003, C-83/01 P, para. 41, *annulling* CFI Dec. 14, 2001 Dec. 14, 2000, 2000 ECR II-4055, and *affirming* D.Comm. Oct. 1, 1997, 1998 OJ L 164/37 (*UFEX*), which denied the state aid character of the grant of logistic and commercial aid by the French Post to an express delivery company (access to its infrastructure). These judgments reevaluate the 'effect utile' of Article 86 (2) which risked becoming ineffective (Advocate General Léger, March 19, 2002, C-280/00, para. 79) according to previous judgments, such as *Wouters*, ECJ Feb. 19, 2002, 2002 ECR I-1577, para. 97, and *Ferring*, ECJ Nov. 22, 2001, 2001 ECR I-9067.

429. *See Lorenz*, ECJ Nov. 21, 1991, 1991 ECR I-5505; *Altmark*, ECJ July 24, 2003, C-280/00, para. 94.

resulting from a non-notified state aid.[430]

The *Altmark* judgment clarifies the preceding case law of the Court of First Instance and the Court of Justice which established somewhat divergent criteria for classifying compensation for the operation of services of general economic interest as state aid. Some judgments tended to a legal approach which aimed at considering any financial compensation as state aid, which had to be notified but was likely to be cleared according to the specific circumstances of the case, in particular where the conditions of Article 86 (2) were fulfilled.[431] Other judgments tended to a more economic approach which aimed at considering only the amount of compensation that exceeds what is necessary for discharging the public service obligation.[432] The new approach of the Court of Justice in the *Altmark* case is more balanced, thereby examining more closely the operation of public service obligations and the services supplied in connection with the discharge of the public service obligation,[433] which will not be recognized whenever the undertakings' activities have 'no connection' with the provision of public service obligations.[434] The further administrative practice and the Court's case law will determine whether this new approach is satisfactory or still too theoretical for relying on 'a typical undertaking, well run and adequately provided', except in cases of public procurement, where it is presumed that market conditions prevail.[435] The Commission reviews the regulatory framework applicable when a member state compensates undertakings that provide public services.[436]

4. Incompatible v. Compatible State Aids

Prohibition Mitigated by Exceptions and Exemptions.

Article 87 (1) contains a general prohibition of any state aid which distorts or threatens to distort competition insofar as it is affects trade between member states. This prohibition is tempered by exceptions and exemptions:

---

430. German Federal Supreme Court, April 4, 2003, EuZW 2003–14, 444.
431. *See FFSA*, CFI Feb. 27, 1997, 1997 ECR II-229, *aff'd* ECJ March 25, 1998, 1998 ECR I-1303; *SIC*, CFI May 10, 2000, 2000 ECR II-2125; *Banco Exterior de España*, ECJ March 15, 1994, 1994 ECR I-877; *CELF*, ECJ June 22, 2000, 2000 ECR I-4833. This approach is similar to the Commission's approach under Article 81, considering first the applicability of Article 81 (1) and (3) followed by the assessment of Article 86 (2) (thereby presupposing the notification of the restrictive agreement), *see Jahrhundertvertrag*, D.Comm. Dec. 12, 1992, 1993 OJ L 50/14.
432. *See Ferring*, ECJ Nov. 22, 2001, 2001 ECR I-9067, para. 33.
433. *Altmark*, ECJ July 24, 2003, C-280/00, para. 91.
434. *Ferring*, ECJ Nov. 22, 2001, 2001 ECR I- 9067, para. 34.
435. *See* Massimo Merola, De l'arrêt Ferring à l'arrêt Altmark : Continuité ou revirement dans l'approche du financement des services publics, Les Cahiers du droit européen, no 5/6 2003.
436. IP/04/235. *See* the Commission's proposals dealing with the same matter: (i) New Framework for the Assessment of State Aid which has Limited effects on Intra-Community Trade, (ii) Community Framework for State Aid in the Form of Public Service Compensation, (iii) Commission Decision on the Application of Article 86 to State Aid in the Form of Public Service Compensation.

- According to Article 87 (2) the following forms of state aid are allowed (compatible with the Common Market):
  - aid having a social character, granted to individual consumers,[437] and
  - aid to make good the damage caused by natural disasters or exceptional occurences.[438]
- According to Article 87 (3) the following forms of state aid may be declared compatible with the Common Market:
  - aid designed to promote economic development of underdeveloped areas,
  - aid designed to promote the execution of an important project of common European interest, or to remedy a serious disturbance in the economy of a member state,
  - aid designed to facilitate the development of certain activities or areas,
  - aid designed to promote culture and heritage conservation, and
  - aid designed to implement issues specified by a Council decision.

However, both excepted and exemptible forms of state aid must be notified to the Commission.[439]

Block Exemptions and Schemes of State Aid.

The Commission adopted regulations to exempt certain categories of aid with so-called 'horizontal' objectives (as opposed to sectoral and regional objectives), based on the Council's enabling Regulation 994/98,[440] and launched various state aid schemes in order to give guidance as to how to apply Article 87 (2) and (3) to various forms of state aid:[441]

- *Research and development aid* is subject to the Community framework for state aid for research and development.[442] The Commission takes a generally favourable attitude toward aid for research and development,[443] which is underscored by Article 163 of the EC Treaty. However, the distinction is difficult to draw between aid aimed at promoting research and development versus operating aid, which is normally not designed to finance productive investments

437. E.g. *Benedetti/Munari*, ECJ Feb. 3, 1977, 1977 ECR 163; *P&O European Ferries*, CFI Aug. 5, 2003, T-116/01, paras 162–170.
438. Examples: Thirty-second Report on Competition Policy, points 522–523.
439. *Commission/Italy*, ECJ March 27, 1984, 1984 ECR 1603.
440. 1998 OJ L 142/1.
441. Regulation 364/2004 on aid for R&D, 2004 OJ L 63/22.
442. 1996 OJ 45/3.
443. *See* Twenty-seventh Report on Competition Policy, points 287–289; Thirty-second Report on Competition Policy, points 421–426; Thirty-third Report on Competition Policy, points 421–426. The generally favourable attitude corresponds to the favourable attitude to cooperation between undertakings under Article 81, *see* Regulation 2659/2000 on research and development agreements.

and therefore is unlikely to be exempted under Article 87 (3).[444] Aid granted to promote basic research and development without benefiting any particular enterprise is normally not an aid.[445]

- *Environmental aid* is subject to Community guidelines on state aid for environmental protection.[446] The guidelines provide a comprehensive and user-friendly framework,[447] at the same time moving towards the full application of the 'polluter pays' principle (Article 174), so as to encourage voluntary action to reduce pollution in excess of legal requirements.[448]
- *Rescue and restructuring aid* is subject to the Community guidelines on state aid for rescuing and restructuring firms in difficulty.[449] The guidelines elaborate the conditions under which such aid may be regarded as compatible with the Common Market, in particular the requirement to present a viable restructuring plan designed to solve structural (as opposed to cyclical or conjunctural) problems.[450] According to the ruling of the Court of Justice in *Intermills*,[451] the Commission must show

  > 'why the applicants' activities on the market, following the conversion of its production with the assistance of the aid granted, were likely to have such an adverse effect on trading conditions that the undertaking's disappearance would have been preferable to its rescue.'[452]

  Accordingly, the Commission gave conditional approval to the state aid granted by France to *Bull*[453] following assurances that the loan was given at market based interest rates and that the rescue loan was limited to the short-term rescue costs.
- Criteria for assessing *employment aids* are provided for in Regulation

444. *See Italian Tax Reductions*, D.Comm. July 25, 1990, 1992 OJ L 207/47; *Bull*, D.Comm. C37/91, 1992 OJ C 244/2.
445. *See Friuli-Venezia*, D.Comm. May 28, 1991, 1991 OJ L 262/29.
446. Guidelines for state aid for environmental protection, 2001 OJ C 37/3 and Revised Guidelines of the EFTA Surveillance Authority, 2001 OJ L 237/16. E.g., *Fleuren Compost*, ECJ Jan. 14, 2004, C-109/01, paras 109–115.
447. Example: The Commission granted exemption decisions concerning excise duty rates on biofuels: Thirty-second Report on Competion Policy, points 414–415.
448. Twenty-third Report on Competition Policy, points 419, 166 and 384; Thirty-first Report on Competition Policy, points 382–388.
449. 1999 OJ C 288/2, as complemented by the 2002 Community Guidelines applying Articles 87 and 88 to the granting of urgency and/or restructuring aid to firms in difficulty. *See British Airways/Commission, Air France*, CFI June 25, 1998, 1998 ECR II-2405, para. 82; *BFM/EFIM*, CFI Sept. 15, 1998, 1998 ECR II-3442, para. 99.
450. *See General Textile Espana*, D.Comm. 25 March 1992, 1992 OJ L 176/57; *GAN*, D.Comm. July 30, 1997, 1998 OJ L 78/1, 10–12; *Eniricorse*, D.Comm. April 16, 1997, 1998 OJ L 80/32. *See* Thirty-second Report on Competition Policy, points 412–413 and the similar approach under Article 81 (3), Chapter III.C.4.
451. *Intermills*, ECJ Nov. 21, 1984, 1984 ECR 3809, 3832.
452. In the absence of sufficient reasoning the Commission decision may be annulled: *Netherlands* and *Leeuwarder Papierwarenfabriek*, ECJ March 13, 1985, 1985 ECR 817, 825.
453. *Bull*, D.Comm. Nov. 13, 2002, Thirty-third Report on Competition Policy, points 406–408.

2204/2002.[454] The regulation creates a block exemption for certain types of state aid up to certain ceilings, meaning that member states do not need to notify them to the Commission for clearance. Via this framework, the Commission encourages member states to opt for a reduction in labor costs in the form of general measures rather than in the form of aid.[455] Conversely, the French textile plan,[456] which reduced labor costs in a specific sector at the expense of other sectors, was regarded as operating aid held incompatible with the Common Market that had to be repaid. State aids for maintaining jobs are accepted only if they are limited in time and justified by exceptional circumstances.[457]

- *Export aids* for the export of products or services to EU or EEA countries distort competition and directly affect trade between member states. Such aid can rarely be justified under Article 87 (3).[458] Export aid for products exported to third countries may be tolerated,[459] for example, in the shipbuilding sector.[460]
- *Regional state aids* are subject to detailed evaluation methods issued in the Commission guidelines of December 16, 1997.[461] The guidelines contain in particular quantitative criteria for determining the regions to be considered and methods for measuring the socio-economic disparities in question.[462] Large regional aid projects are the subject of the Commission Communication on 'Multisectoral Framework on Regional Aid'.[463] The links between regional and competition policy are explained in the Commission's 1998 Communication to the member states.[464]
- *Sectoral state aids.* Special rules have been issued with respect to state aids aimed at specific sectoral problems, such as:
  - agriculture (Article 36),[465]

454. 2002 OJ L 337/3.
455. Example: *Maribel*, D.Comm. Dec. 4, 1996, 1997 OJ L 95/25.
456. *French Textile Plan*, D.Comm. April 9, 1997, 1997 OJ L 334/25; Twenty-seventh Report on Competition Policy, points 292–293.
457. Twenty-third Report on Competition Policy, points 439–443.
458. *See France/Commission*, ECJ Dec. 10, 1969, 1969 ECR 523; *Greece Special Tax*, D.Comm. May 3, 1989, 1989 OJ L 394/1 (tax exemption granted in respect of profits from exports to other member states); *Italian Levies on Paper, Board and Cellulose*, D.Comm. April 24, 1991, 1991 OJ L 47/19 (refund of the levies imposed on the exports to other member states).
459. *See* Article 132 of the EC Treaty. Examples: Thirty-second Report on Competition Policy, points 443–447. *See also* Commission notice on the application of Articles 87 and 88 to short-term export credit insurance, 2001 OJ C 217/2.
460. Framework on state aid to shipbuilding, 2003 OJ C 317/11, point 3.3.4.
461. 1998 OJ C 74/9 and 1998 OJ C 107/7, amended 2000 OJ C 258/5. *See* Twenty-seventh Report on Competition Policy, points 206–209.
462. Examples: *Germany/Commission*, ECJ Oct. 14, 1987, 1987 ECR 4013, para. 19; *PYRSA*, ECJ Jan. 14, 1997, 1997 ECR I-135; *FIAT*, D.Comm. Sept. 29, 1999; *Azores*, Thirty-second Report on Competition Policy, points 430–435. *See*, however, *Folketrydloven*, EFTA Court of Justice, May 20, 1999, E-6/98.
463. 2003 OJ C 263/3.
464. 1998 OJ C 16/5.
465. New Guidelines for state aid in the agricultural sector, 2000 OJ C 232/17; *see also* Regulation

- fisheries,[466] in particular rules for assessing aid to producers' organizations,[467]
- coal; [468]
- broadcasting: state funding of public service broadcasting,[469]
- electricity: criteria for assessing the compatibility of state aid aiming at compensating stranded costs in the electricity sector (investment costs incurred prior to the liberalization),[470]
- motor vehicle industry,[471]
- shipbuilding,[472]
- synthetic fibers,[473] and
- transport.[474]

– Multisectoral state aids concern government support to large investment projects. The Commission's Communication 'Multisectoral Framework on Regional aid for Large Investment Projects'[475] sets out the rules for the evaluation of state aid for such projects and eliminates the need for prior notification. At the same time the framework brings together and consolidates in a single text the different sectoral rules which applied previously in particular in the steel, synthetic fibers and automobile sectors.[476]

1/2004 on state aid for small and medium-sized undertakings in the agricultural sector, 2004 OJ L 1/1.

466. Guidelines, 2001 OJ C 19/7.
467. Regulation 1924/2000, 2000 OJ L 230/5; Regulation 2369/2002, 2002 OJ L 358/49.
468. Now covered by the general provisions of the EC Treaty: Regulation 1407/2002, 2002 OJ L 205/1.
469. Commission Communication 2001 OJ C 320/5. *See* IP/01/1429.
470. Commission Communication of 26 July 2001, *see* IP/01/1077 and Thirty-second Report on Competition Policy, points 389–393.
471. Commission Communication 2001 OJ C 368/10. New rules on aids to the automobile sector are contained in the multisectoral framework for regional investment aid, 2002 OJ C 107/7, Thirty-second Report on Competition Policy, Box 2. *See Volkswagen-Dresden*, D.Comm. July 18, 2001, Thirty-first Report on Competition Policy, point 426 (decision to reduce planed regional investment aid to be granted to Volkswagen for a new car plant in Dresden); *Opel Portugal*, D.Comm. Oct. 2, 2002, Thirty-second Report on Competition Policy, point 469 (approval following an in-depth investigation).
472. Council Regulation 1177/2002, 2002 OJ L 172/1; Framework on state aid to shipbuilding, 2003 OJ C 317/11.
473. New rules on the synthetic fibers sectors are contained in the multisectoral framework for regional investment aid, 2002 OJ C 107/7. *See Zellstoff Stendal*, D.Comm. June 19, 2002 and *Capro Schwedt*, D.Comm. Nov. 13, 2002, Thirty-second Report on Competition Policy, points 439, 442 and Box 2.
474. Regulation 543/97, amending Regulation 1893/91, 1991 OJ L 169/1; Guidelines 2004 OJ C 13/3. *See Altmark GmbH*, ECJ July 24, 2003, C-280/00, paras 58–66. Examples: Thirty-first Report on Competition Policy, points 428–455, and Thirty-second Report on Competition Policy, points 481–511.
475. 2002 OJ C 70.
476. Thirty-second Report on Competition Policy, point 341.

A complete list of the relevant regulations, communications, guidelines, frameworks and letters can be found in the Commission's website.[477]

5. The Control Mechanism

(a) Role of the Commission in Monitoring State Aid

Powers of the Commission.
The Commission is entitled to monitor existing state aid (Article 88 (1)), to scrutinize existing and new state aid (Article 88 (2))[478] and to require that illegally granted state aid be repaid by recipients to public authorities which granted it.

Procedural Provisions.
Plans of member states to grant or alter state aid must be notified to the Commission (Article 88 (3)). The necessary procedural provisions are contained in Council Regulation 659/1999 as implemented by Commission Regulation 794/2004.[479] Regulation 659/1999 aims at increasing transparency and legal certainty by the codification and clarification of the procedural rules developed through the Commission's practice and the jurisprudence of the Court of Justice. The regulation deals in particular with the following matters: notification, standstill (suspension of the effects of a notified aid), preliminary evaluation, requests for information, hearing, decisions, interim measures, recovery of unlawful aids, reporting obligations, monitoring powers, co-operation with national independent supervisory bodies and third party rights.[480] The rights of defence are similar to those guaranteed by Regulation 1/2003.[481] Regulation 794/2004 establishes a compulsory standard notification form and sets out detailed provisions on member states' annual reporting obligation to enable the Commission to monitor aid.

Preventive Control – Obligation of Member States to Notify New State Aids to the Commission.
According to Article 88 (1), the Commission must keep all existing state aids under constant review,[482] including those authorized by the Commission, due to increasing integration and the changing environment of the Community. Any plans to grant or alter aid prohibited under Article 87 (1) and not authorized under Article 87 (2) or

477. http://europa.eu.int/comm/competition/state_aid/legislation/aid3.html
478. With respect to aid existing in the new member states and exceptions agreed in some cases for a limited transitional period: Thirty-second Report on Competition Policy, points 626–651.
479. 1999 OJ L 83/1 and 2004 OJ L 140/1.
480. Including complainants' right to claim for a declaration of failure to act; 2003 OJ C 116/3, *see Sytraval*, CFI Sept. 28, 1995, 1995 ECR II-2654 , para. 62; *Télévision Française 1*, CFI June 3, 1999, 1999 EC R II-1757, paras 72–81.
481. *See UFEX*, CFI Dec. 14, 2000, 2000 ECR II-4055, paras 85–90.
482. *See* Monitoring of existing aid under Article 88 (3), in 'EU/Competition – State Aid', under points 73–84.

any general aid scheme or guideline of the Commission have to be notified to the Commission according to Article 88 (3). Notification shall take place in due time, i.e. at least two months or, as the case may be, 30 days before the projected entry into force, and no payments shall be made in violation of Article 88 (3). The standard notification form specifies the information which the Commission deems necessary for examining aids. Regulation 794/2004 also provides for a simplified notification procedure in certain specified circumstances. The Commission considers a notification compulsory even where the exceptions under Article 87 (2) are fulfilled.[483]

Discretionary Power of the Commission to Exempt State Aid under Article 87 (3).
The Commission enjoys a broad discretionary power when assessing a state aid under Article 87 (3).[484] The Commission must evaluate, in the light of complex economic circumstances, whether the aid is necessary for the achievement of Community objectives, i.e. whether the objective could not have been obtained under normal market conditions[485] and whether the duration, intensity and scope of the aid is proportional to the importance of the intended result,[486] or whether such aid is 'misused', which means that it is actually used for purposes other than authorized by the Commission, e.g., aid for restructuring being used as for covering merely operational costs.[487] If it considers that any such plan is not compatible with the Common Market, it must without delay initate the procedure provided for in Article 88 (2). If it does so, under the last sentence of Article 88 (3), the member state concerned is prohibited from putting its proposed measures into effect until the procedure has resulted in a final decision.[488] If the state aid is declared incompatible the member state concerned may be ordered to recover the state aid, except in cases of absolute impossibility,[489] and this obligation to recover the state aid may not be jeopardized by the member state concerned or by national proceedings.[490] A state aid may be declared compatible up to a certain amount and incompatible with respect to the exceeding amount.[491] In cases where state aid has been granted

483. *Commission/Italy*, ECJ March 27, 1984, 1984 ECR 1603.
484. *Boussac*, ECJ Feb. 14, 1990, 1990 ECR I-307, para. 15; *British Aerospace and Rover*, ECJ Feb. 4, 1992, 1992 ECR I-493, para. 10; *Textilwerke Deggendorf*, ECJ May 15, 1997, 1997 ECR I-2564, para. 26; *British Airways*, CFI June 25, 1998, 1998 ECR II-2405, para. 79.
485. 'Compensatory compensation' principle which presupposes a contribution, by the beneficiary, over and above the effects of the normal play of the market forces in the achievement of the Community objectives contained in the derogations of Article 87 (3): Tenth Report on Competition Policy, point 213.
486. *Philip Morris*, ECJ Sept. 17, 1980, 1980 ECR 2671, paras 17–25. *See* Twelfth Report on Competition Policy, point 160.
487. *See* Gonzalés y Diaz, D.Comm. April 10, 2003, 2003 OJ C 87/17.
488. *See Republic of Austria*, ECJ Feb. 15, 2001, 2001 ECR I-1101, para. 31; *Belgium/Commission*, ECJ June 26, 2003, C-182/03 R, para. 118.
489. *Portugal*, ECJ June 27, 2000, 2000 ECR I-4897, para. 40.
490. *Banks/Naloo*, ECJ Sept. 20, 2001, 2001 ECR I-6117, para. 122.
491. E.g., *BMW Leipzig*, Dcomm. Dec. 11, 2002, 2003 OJ L 128/12.

for setting-up a joint venture or for restructuring a company by means of a merger, the Commission proceeds in parallel under two different procedures, a procedure for assessing the transaction under the competition provisions of Article 81,[492] and a procedure for assessing the state aid.[493] In merger cases, the Court tends to request the Commission to consider state aid when assessing the compatibility of the merger with the Common Market. [494] If the Commission must proceed to an overall coherent[495] assessment under both Article 88 and the competition rules, it does so within two separate proceedings.[496]

Aid Put into Effect without Prior Notification.

Article 1 (f) of Regulation 659/1999 laying down detailed rules for the application of Article 88 provides that a new aid[497] is 'unlawful' if it is put into effect in contravention of Article 88 (3), i.e., without prior notification.[498] This prohibition on implementation contained in the last sentence of Article 88 (3) has a direct effect and gives rise to rights of individuals, which national courts are bound to safeguard.[499] Failure to notify can lead to an action by the Commission under Article 226[500] or by individuals (complainants, in particular competitors) before the Commission.[501] In addition, the Commission may, after giving the member state concerned the opportunity to submit its comments, adopt a decision or an interim measure[502] requiring the member state to suspend any unlawful aid until the Commission has taken a decision on the compatibility of the aid with the Common Market.[503] If the member state fails to suspend payment of the aid the

492. *Ford-Volkswagen*, D.Comm. Dec. 23, 1992, 1993 OJ L 20/1, *aff'd Matra/Ford-Volkswagen*, CFI July 15, 1994, 1994 ECR II-595, paras 44–48.
493. *Matra/Ford-Volkswagen*, ECJ June 15, 1993, 1993 ECR I-3250, para. 44; *RAG/Saarbergwerke/Preussag*, D.Comm. July 29, 1998, IV/ECSC/1252, point 54 (under Article 66 ECSC Treaty), *rev'd* CFI Jan. 31, 2001, 2001 ECR II-337, paras 62 and 122–125.
494. *RAG/Saarbergwerke/Preussag*, D.Comm. 29 July 1998, IV/ECSC/1252, point 54 (under Article 66 ECSC Treaty), *rev'd* CFI Jan. 31, 2001, 2001 ECR II-337, paras 62 and 122–125.
495. *See* Communication of the Commission of Mar. 17, 1998 on the links between regional and competition policy (98/C90/03).
496. *See* in *RAG/Saarbergwerke/Preussag*, 2000 OJ C 101/3 (clearance of the merger), and D.Comm. May 7, 2002, 2002 OJ L 203/52 (stating that there is no element of state aid).
497. With regard to existing aid in sectors that are being liberalized, *see* Thirty-first Report in Competition Policy, point 480.
498. 1999 OJ L 83/1.
499. *Eniricorse*, ECJ Nov. 27, 2003, C-34/01, para. 42.
500. *Portugal/Commission*, ECJ May 3, 2001, 2001 ECR I-3175.
501. *SFEI*, ECJ July 11, 1996, 1996 ECR I-3547. *See* Form for the submission of complaints concerning alleged unlawful state aid, 2003 OJ C 116/3, and legal status of complainants as explained in 'EU/Competition – State aid' under points 85–86.
502. *France*, ECJ Feb. 14, 1990, 1990 ECR I-307, paras 18–20; *Belgium*, ECJ June 26, 2003, C-182/03R and C-217/03R, para. 118.
503. Article 88 (3) and Article 11 of Regulation 659/1999, formalizing the Commission's practice as confirmed by the Court of Justice: *Boussac*, ECJ Feb. 14, 1990, 1990 ECR I-307, para. 19. *See* Twenty-eighth Report on Competition Policy, points 287–289.

Commission may bring the matter directly before the Court.[504] The allocation by the state of a significant proportion of certain charges constitutes state aid does not preclude that allocation from also giving rise to abuse of a dominant position by that undertaking, contrary to Article 82 and 86.[505]

First Phase of Assessment.

The Commission must complete its initial assessment[506] within a period of two months as required by the Court of Justice.[507] The Commission may prolong this preliminary procedure by requesting further information which is necessary for the preliminary examination without, however, repeatedly asking new irrelevant questions.[508] This first assessment may result in the compatibility of the aids or, in case of serious doubts about its compatibility,[509] in the initiation of the procedure to enjoin the aids from entering into effect.[510] In the event that the Commission fails to take one of these decisions within the two-month period, the state aid is automatically approved,[511] the Commission is prevented from acting against such aid,[512] and the member state concerned may put the aid into effect.[513]

Second Phase of Assessment.

After the initiation of proceedings, the Commission informs the member states and other interested parties by issuing a notice in the Official Journal.[514] The Commission may proceed (on the basis of its powers under Articles 211 and 284) with the necessary investigation by addressing requests for information to member states,

---

504. *Boussac*, ECJ Feb. 14, 1990, 1990 ECR I-307, para. 23.
505. *Eniricorse*, ECJ Nov. 27, 2003, C-34/01, para. 50.
506. This does not necessarily include the hearing of complainants: *Sytraval*, ECJ April 2, 1998, 1998 ECR I-1719.
507. Rules of Procedure, Article 4 (5). *See Germany/Commission*, ECJ March 20, 1984, 1984 ECR 1451, para. 11; *Matra/Ford-Volkswagen*, ECJ June 15, 1993, 1993 ECR I-3250, paras 33–39. An accelerated procedure applies for the clearance of state aids for small and medium-sized enterprises and for employment aid (1995 OJ C 334/4, point 26: twenty days).
508. *Republic of Austria*, ECJ Feb. 25, 2001, 2001 ECR I-1101, para. 50.
509. *See Matra/Commission*, ECJ June 15, 1993, 1993 ECR 3258, 3260, paras 33–39. The Commission is, in case of serious doubts, obliged to initiate proceedings: *Sytraval II*, ECJ April 2, 1998, 1998 ECR I-1719.
510. *Commission/French Republic*, ECJ March 20, 1983, 1983 ECR 2621.
511. *Lorenz*, ECJ Dec. 11, 1973, 1973 ECR 1471; *Commission/French Republic*, ECJ March 20, 1983, 1983 ECR 2621; *German Republic/Commission*, ECJ March 20, 1984, 1984 ECR 1451.
512. *Spain/Commission*, ECJ June 30, 1992, 1992 ECR I-4117.
513. *Lorenz*, ECJ Dec. 11, 1973, 1973 ECR 1471; *Spain/Commission*, ECJ June 30, 1992, 1992 ECR I-4145.
514. About 80% of the cases notified to the Commission are approved without opening the formal investigation procedure, some 5% are subject to a formal investigation and around 15% are withdrawn by the member states following the Commission's objections: Thirty-second Report on Competition Policy, point 339. This percentage corresponds roughly to the proportion of merger cases in which the Commission initiates, because of 'serious doubts', the second phase of procedure.

enterprises or associations, including competitors. It may also hear from interested member states, third parties and complainants, without, however, any *legal* obligation to do so. However, this does not release the Commission from the duty to examine complaints carefully and to proceed to a thorough market analysis in the absence of which the complainant may appeal the Commission decision.[515]

Enforceability of the Commission Decision.

A decision stating that the notified aid is compatible with the Common Market in the sense of Article 88 (3)[516] or justified under Article 86 (2)[517] is enforceable to the extent that the state aid may be put into effect. If the Commission finds that the aid is incompatible on substantive grounds,[518] it orders the state concerned to abolish or alter such aid within a period of time to be determined by the Commission[519] and to take the necessary steps to recover the illegal state aid from the beneficiary in accordance with the procedures under the national law of the member state concerned.[520] An illegally granted state aid has to be refunded,[521] even if this would lead to the bankruptcy of the company in question.[522] Recovery may also be ordered by the national court because of the direct effect of the prohibition provision.[523] The aid to be recovered must include interest from the date

---

515. Hearing of complainants: *Matra/Ford-Volkswagen*, ECJ June 15, 1993, 1993 ECR I-3250. Hearing of member states: *British Airways/Commission, Air France*, CFI June 25, 1998, 1998 ECR II-2405, paras 75–77. The fact that a complainant participated actively during the Commission proceedings may be a decisive factor for the admissibility of the complainant's appeal: *AUFFASS/Hualon*, CFI Dec. 12, 1996, 1996 ECR II-2169. Hearing of unions: *Comite d'entreprise de la societe frangaise de production/Commission*, CFI Feb. 18, 1998, 1998 ECR II-335.
516. *British Airways/Commission, Air France*, CFI June 25, 1998, 1998 ECR II-2405. The state aid may be authorized by the Commission even if that aid has already been paid before the decision was adopted: *RJB Mining*, CFI Sept. 9, 1999, 1999 ECR II-2585, paras 65–83.
517. *Commission/Italy*, ECJ April 4, 1995, 1995 ECR I-673, para. 21; *FFSA*, CFI Feb. 27, 1997, 1997 ECR II-229.
518. The Commission cannot take a recovery decision on the sole ground of unlawfulness of measures for procedural grounds: *Boussac*, ECJ Feb. 14, 1990, 1990 ECR I-351.
519. Article 88 (3).
520. Article 14 of Regulation 659/1999 and Commission Communication on the recovery of aid granted unlawfully, 1995 OJ C 156/5. *See Nouvelle Filiature Lainière de Roubaix*, D.Comm. Nov. 4, 1998, 1999 OJ L 145, *aff'd* ECJ March 22, 2001, 2001 ECR I-2537; *Commission/Belgium*, ECJ Jan. 15, 1986, 1986 ECR 89, para. 14. The obligation to recover aid is subject to a limitation period of ten years (Art. 15 of Regulation 659/1999).
521. *See Commission/Italy*, ECJ April 4, 1985, 1985 ECR I-673, para. 18. *See* Niejahr, 'The Art of Recovering Unlawful State Aid – A Review of the Court's Case Law', *European State Aid Law Quarterly*, 2004, pp. 43–49.
522. Commission Communication to the Member States on the recovery of unlawful aid of June 22, 1995. *See Meura & Boch*, ECJ July 10, 1986, 1986 ECR 2263; Twenty-seventh Report on Competition Policy, point 314.
523. *Fédération nationale du commerce extérieur des produits alimentaires*, ECJ Nov. 28, 1991, 1991 ECR I-5505.

on which it was at the disposal of the beneficiary until the date of its recovery, and interest must be calculated on the basis of the reference rate used for calculating the grant equivalent of regional aid.[524] Failure of a member state to recover an illegal aid constitutes a breach of its Treaty obligations under Article 226. While the only defence available to a member state in opposing such an application by the Commission is to plead that it was absolutely impossible for it to implement the decision properly, the Court of Justice has ruled that the fact:

> 'that implementation was absolutely impossible does not prevent a State which, in giving effect to a Commission decision on state aid, encounters unforeseen and unforeseeable difficulties or becomes aware of consequences overlooked by the Commission, from submitting those problems to the Commission for consideration, together with proposals for suitable amendments to the decision in question.'[525]

The non-recovery of the illegally granted aid by the member states constitutes a further violation of the Treaty[526] and the Commission may oppose the exemption of a new aid.[527] A negative decision of the Commission can be overruled by the Council at the request of a member state in exceptional circumstances (Article 88 (2), (3) and (4)).[528]

Failure to Comply with a Commission Decision.
If the state concerned does not comply with the Commission decision, the Commission or any other interested state may, in derogation of Articles 226 and 227, refer the matter to the Court of Justice directly (Article 88 (2)).[529] Where a decision is not appealed or affirmed by the Court of Justice, the Commission requests the competent national authorities to recover the illegal aid.

---

524. Article 9 of Regulation 794/2004; Commission Communication on the interest rates to be applied when aid granted unlawfully is being recovered, 2003 OJ C 110/21. E.g. *Deutsche Post III*, D.Comm. June 19, 2002, 2002 OJ L 247/27, Article 2.
525. *Commission/Belgium*, ECJ July 3, 2001, 2001 ECR I-5107, paras 30–31. *See also Commission/Portugal*, ECJ June 27, 2000, 2000 ECR I-4897; *Commission/France*, ECJ March 22, 2001, 2001 ECR I-2537, para. 23.
526. *Lautex GmbH*, D.Comm. July 20, 1999, 2000 OJ L 42. *See Commission/Belgium*, ECJ Jan. 15, 1986, 1986 ECR 89, para. 14; *Commission/Italy*, ECJ April 4, 1995, 1995 ECR I-673, paras 24–30; France, ECJ March 20, 2001, 2001 ECR I-2481.
527. *Textilwerk Deggendorf*, ECJ May 15, 1997, 1997 ECR I-2549, paras 24–28.
528. This possibility has been used only in the agricultural sector. *See* Twenty-second Report on Competition Policy, point 502.
529. If the Court of Justice finds that the member state concerned has not complied with its judgment, it may impose a lump sum or penalty payment according to the new provision of Article 228 (2) (2) as amended by the Maastricht Treaty. The Commission issued guidelines on the calculation of such lump sum: Commission notice on the method of setting penalty payments, 1997 OJ C 63/2.

(b) Actions before National Courts

Direct Applicability.

Third parties, in particular competitors, injured or threatened with injury through illegal aid, can take action before national courts.[530] The prohibition against granting aid without prior authorization by the Commission is absolute and, as such, is directly enforceable in national courts.[531] Therefore, third parties may be able to obtain an injunction from a national court or a judgment that the decision of the public authorities granting the aid was illegal and unenforceable.[532] Third parties may also request the recovery of the illegal aid.[533] A national court may nullify an agreement containing an element of state aid which was declared illegal by the Commission[534] or which was not notified to the Commission. [535] The parties cannot rely on their ignorance of the applicable rules nor invoke the principle of justified expectations, save exceptional circumstances.[536]

Cooperation between the Commission and the National Courts.

By virtue of the rule imposing on the member states and the Community institutions a duty of genuine cooperation which underlies, in particular, Article 10 of the Treaty, the Commission and the member state must work together in good faith with a view to overcoming the difficulties whilst fully observing the Treaty provisions and, in particular, any potential inconsistencies in their respective assessments of the state aid concerned.[537] National courts which have to decide on

530. *See* Massimo Merola, Legal position of third parties in the procedure governing matters of state aid, in Droit européen de la concurrence: un nouveau rôle pour les Etats membres, Bruyland, Bruxelles 2001.
531. *Federation nationale du commerce exterieur des produits alimentaires*, ECJ Nov. 21, 1991, 1991 ECR I-5505, paras 11–14; *Eniricorse*, ECJ Nov. 27, 2003, C-34/01, para.42.
532. Commission Notice on unnotified aid, 1983 OJ C 318/3, point 3. Example: *Rynair*, Tribunal correctionnel de Strassbourg, July 24, 2003.
533. However, the national court may consult the Commission, which must supply the necessary information on the compatibility or incompatibility of the aid; the mere absence of notification does not suffice: *Boussac*, ECJ Feb. 14, 1990, 1990 ECR I-307, paras 19–21; *SFEI*, ECJ July 11, 1996, 1996 ECR I-3547, para. 43. *See SKET/SMM* (*Treuhandanstalt*), D.Comm. June 26, 1997, 1997 OJ L 314/20.
534. By decision of 20 January 1999 the Commission stated that the price at which real estate was purchased contained an illegal state aid and ordered the covery of this aid (*Naumburg*, D.Comm. 1999 OJ L 107/21). On April 4, 2003 the German Federal Supreme Court (Bundesgerichtshof) decided that the acquiror had to pay the higher price, i.e. the transaction price negotiated between buyer and seller increased by the amount of state aid (V ZR 314/02, EuZW 2003–14, 444).
535. The illegality of state aid found by the national court is not remedied by a subsequent notification to the Commission (even a declaration of compatibility would not have a retroactive effect): *Federation nationale du commerce exterieur des produits alimentaires*, ECJ Nov. 21, 1991, 1991 ECR I-5505; *SFEI*, ECJ July 11, 1996, 1996 ECR I-3547.
536. *Fleuren Compost*, CFI Jan. 14, 2004, T-109/01, paras 140–142.
537. *Commission/Belgium*, ECJ July 3, 2001, 2001 ECR I-5107, para. 31.

the legal consequences, including interim measures, against a non-notified aid or an aid declared incompatible by the Commission may request assistance and information from the Commission in accordance with the Notice on the cooperation between national courts and the Commission in the state aid field.[538] The national court is entitled to submit preliminary questions to the Court of Justice according to Article 234.[539]

(c) Judicial Review

A Commission decision declaring a state aid incompatible with the Common Market may be appealed by the member state concerned (Article 230 (1)) and by the beneficiary (Article 230 (4)). A decision exempting a state aid[540] and a decision not to initiate proceedings under Article 88 (3)[541] may be appealed by any member state and third parties (normally competitors), provided those parties are directly and individually concerned.[542] The appeal must be lodged within two months following the day the decision came to its knowledge or, in the absence thereof, by the fifteenth day after publication in the Official Journal.[543] Exemption decisions are enforceable unless the Court of Justice issues interim measures according to Article 243.[544] The Commission has a broad power of assessment;[545] it is not for the Court to substitute its own economic assessment.[546] The appeal must therefore be based on lack of reasoning[547] or a manifest error in assessment likely to have a decisive effect on the outcome.[548] The recipient of the aid can invoke the principle

538. 1995 OJ C 312/8. *See SFEI*, ECJ July 11, 1996, 1996 ECR I-3547, para. 50.
539. E.g. *Eniricorse*, ECJ Nov. 27, 2003, C-34/01.
540. *Kahn*, CFI June 5, 1996, 1996 ECR II-477.
541. *Portugal/Commission*, ECJ May 3, 2001, 2001 ECR I-3175.
542. Article 230 (2). E.g., *Landbouwschap/Commission*, ECJ Sept. 30, 1992, 1992 ECR I-5003; *British Airways/Air France*, CFI June 25, 1998, 1998 ECR I-2405, para. 58 (lack of sufficient reasoning). Under Article 33 of the ECSC Treaty third persons did not have the same rights of appeal: *Walton Region/Commission*, CFI Sept. 29, 1997, 1997 ECR II-1513, para. 24.
543. Articles 102 and 101 (b) of Rules of Procedure of the Court of First Instance. *See Cofindustria*, CFI Jan. 19, 2001, 2001 ECR II-85.
544. Appeals of individuals are brought before the Tribunal of First Instance whereas appeals of member states have to be addressed to the Court of Justice. *See Cofaz*, ECJ Jan. 28, 1986, 1986 ECR 391; *French Republic/Commission* (*Air Inter/TAT*), ECJ Oct. 26, 1994, 1994 ECR I-5229. *Dutch Natural Gas Prices I*, ECJ Feb. 2, 1988, 1988 ECR 219, para. 59; *Sytraval and Brinks France*, ECJ Sept. 28, 1995, 1995 ECR II-2654, para. 52, *aff'd* ECJ April 2, 1998, 1998 ECR I-1719.
545. *Philip Morris*, ECJ Sept. 17, 1980, 1980 ECR 2671, paras 17 and 24; *Graphischer Maschinenbau*, CFI May 14, 2002, 2002 ECR II-2427, para. 32.
546. *Max.mobil*, CFI Jan. 30, 2002, 2002 ECR II-313, para. 54.
547. E.g. *Westdeutsche Landesbank*, CFI March 6, 2003, T-228/99 and T-233/99 (with respect to the interest rate).
548. *Graphischer Maschinenbau*, CFI May 14, 2002, 2002 ECR II-2427, para. 49.

of good faith only where he could have had a legitimate expectation that the aid was granted in accordance with the procedure laid down in Article 88.[549]

549. *Fleuren Compost*, ECJ Jan. 14, 2004, C-109/01, paras 134–142. *See also Alcan*, March 20, 1997, 1997 ECR I-1591, paras 25 and 43; Twenty-seventh Report on Competition Policy, points 311–314.

Chapter X

Enforcement and Procedure

CONTENTS

A. Introduction

1. Means of Enforcement

Impact of the Direct Effect of Articles 81 and 82.
The provisions of Articles 81 and 82 of the EC Treaty and Articles 53 and 54 of the EEA Agreement are directly applicable, including, from May 1, 2004, Article 81 (3),[1] and can therefore be enforced by the Commission and by the EFTA Surveillance Authority according to their procedural rules, acting upon applications (notifications or complaints) or *ex officio* (on their own initiative). They may also be invoked by national authorities insofar as they are empowered to apply these provisions according to their national procedural rules and by national courts acting on applications of natural or legal persons (private actions).[2]

The New Procedural Rules Applicable from May 1, 2004: Regulation 1/2003.
Regulation 1/2003 replaces Regulation 17 and the special procedural rules established in the transport sectors.[3] The new rules apply from May 1, 2004.[4] It applies to all economic sectors except agriculture, which remains subject to Regulation 26/62.[5] The Commission has the same powers to apply the competition rules of the EEA Agreement under similar rules adopted pursuant to this Agreement.[6]

Main Features of the New Regulation and Implementing Provisions.
The new regulation shifts the Article 81 (3) exemption system toward a system of decentralized evaluation of potentially anticompetitive conduct. Notifications to the Commission are abandoned,[7] and the Commission no longer has exclusive competence to grant exemptions. Beginning May 1, 2004 national competition authorities and national courts have authority to apply Articles 81 and 82 in full, including the assessment under Article 81 (3).[8] In order to assure uniform applica-

1. Article 1 (2) of Regulation 2003.
2. With regard Articles 81 and 82: *Van Gend & Loos*, ECJ Feb.5, 1963, 1963 ECR 1, para. 21; *BRT/SABAM I*, ECJ Jan. 30, 1974, 1974 ECR 51, para. 16; *Benim*, CFI Jan. 24, 1995, 1995 ECR II-147, para. 62; with regard to Articles 53 and 54 of the EEA Agreement: *Erla Maria Sveinbjörnsdottir*, EFTA Court of Justice, Dec. 10, 1998, E-9/97, para. 59; however, limited direct effect under Articles 65 and 66 of the ECSC Treaty: *Banks/British Coal*, ECJ April 27, 1994, 1994 ECR I-1477, paras 17–18.
3. 2003 OJ L 1/1.
4. Article 45 of Regulation 1/2003.
5. 1962 OJ 993.
6. Article 1 of Protocol 21 of the EEA Agreement, 1994 OJ L 1/181.
7. The parties to an anticompetitive agreement which gives rise to genuine uncertainty may seek informal guidance from the Commission on the applicability of the EC competition rules pursuant to Recital 38 to Regulation 1/2003, provided the case presents novel and unresolved questions.
8. Articles 5 and 6 of Regulation 1/2003.

tion, the regulation provides for close cooperation between national courts and the national competition authorities and the EC Commission.[9] Whenever national authorities and national courts apply national law, they are also required to apply European competition law, provided trade between member states is likely to be affected. In order to assure the uniform appliocation of Article 81, national law may not lead to the prohibition of restrictions that do not infringe Article 81 (1) or meet the conditions for exemption under Article 81 (3), but member states may adopt and apply stricter national law that prohibits unilateral conduct or predominantly pursues an objective different from that pursued by Articles 81 and 82.[10] This 'decentralization' requires close cooperation between the Commission and the national competition authorities (in particular with respect to the allocation of cases and the exchange of information) and the national courts (in particular with respect to mutual information and the *amicus curiae* function of the Commission).

Regulation 1/2003 is complemented by a package of regulations and notices:

- Regulation 773/2004 Relating to Proceedings by the Commission Pursuant to Articles 81 and 82, 2004 OJ L 123/18;
- Notice on the Handling of Complaints, 2004 OJ C 101/65;
- Notice on Informal Guidance Relating to Novel Questions Concerning Articles 81 and 82 that Arise in Individual Cases (Guidance Letters), 2004 OJ C 101/78;
- Notice on the Cooperation within the Network of Competition Authorities (European Competition Network – ECN), 2004 OJ C 101/43;
- Notice on the Cooperation between the Commission and the Courts of the EU Member States, 2004 OJ C 101/54.

Further measures may be adopted by the Commission pursuant to Article 33 of Regulation 1/2003 with respect to the practical arrangements for the exchange of information and consultations provided for in Article 11 of Regulation 1/2003 and the practical arrangements for the hearings.

Specific procedural rules have been adopted for implementing Regulation 139/2004 on merger control (Regulation 773/2004, 2004 OJ L 123/18) and for implementing Council Regulation 659/1999 on state aid (Regulation 794/2004, 2004 OJ L 140/1), which are discussed in respectively Chapters VI and IX.

The new procedural rules take largely account of the previous case law and administrative practice, which may therefore constitute a valuable basis for the subject of this Chapter.

9. Articles 11 and 15 of Regulation 1/2003.
10. Article 3 of Regulation 1/2003.

Plan of this Chapter.
This Chapter discusses the new procedural rules (with reference to the current rules where appropriate): cooperation within the European Competition Network (section B), initiation of proceedings by the Commission (section C), fact-finding (section D), due process (section E), decisions and settlements (section F), the judicial review of decisions by the Court of Justice (section G), special features of proceedings against member states (section H) and enforcement by national courts (section I).

2. Enforcement Authorities and Powers

(a) EC Commission

Structure and Decision-Making.
The EC Commission, based in Brussels, is the central enforcement agency with general responsibility for policing and securing compliance with the EC (and ECSC) competition rules (Article 211). Formal decisions in individual cases and on general matters, such as legislation, are taken by a majority of the full 25–member Commission at the proposal of the member of the Commission ('Commissioner') with special responsibility for competition policy (Articles 213 and 219). Ten commissioners will be, as of 1 May 2004, associated with ten collegues of the new member states, becoming their 'junior' partners for a running-in period before competences will be reallocated (after this reallocation the actual 30 members will be reduced to 25). Details of the decision-making process are contained in the Commission's rules of procedure.[11] According to these rules of procedure Commission decisions may be taken either orally within the Commission meetings (oral procedure) or by non-opposition to proposals circulated for approval by the responsible member to all other members of the Commission (written procedure).[12] Proposed decisions in competition matters are prepared by the Directorate-General for Competition – DG COMP (formerly DG IV).[13]

DG COMP.
The Directorate-General for Competition (DG COMP) is the staff department of the Commission which carries out the day-to-day work of fact-finding, preparing decisions and formulating policy in competition matters under the supervision of

---

11. Articles III–255–257 of the Treaty Establishing a Constitution for Europe; Rules of procedure, 1999 OJ L 252/41. The previous rules were discussed in detail in *Steel Beams – Eurofer*, CFI March 11, 1999, 1999 ECR II-263, paras 57–82.
12. If some members disagree or request a discussion, the proposal is discussed at the weekly meeting of the Commission, where a simple majority is required for adoption. *See* in greater detail section E.I. *infra*.
13. There are currently 23 specialized directorates-general serving the Commission, plus a small number of general departments such as the Legal Service.

the Commissioner. DG COMP has a total staff of approximately 600, approximately half of whom are professionals (mainly lawyers and economists).[14] At present DG COMP consists of nine directorates with the following responsibilities:

- Directorate R: Strategic Planning and Resources,
- Directorate A: Policy and Strategic Support,
- Directorates B, C, D, E and F – each of which is an examining directorate responsible for preparing antitrust cases under Articles 81, 82 and 86 of the EC Treaty, Articles 53 and 54 of the EEA Agreement and the merger control regulation, which are allocated to them according to the sector concerned,
- Directorates G and H: State Aids, which are in charge of monitoring national government subsidies to industry.

The directorates are subdivided into more specialized units or 'divisions'. The Commission's legal department, the Legal Service, assists DG COMP when preparing major decisions, and represents the Commission before the Court of Justice. Other departments of the Commission are informed or consulted as and when the subject matter concerns them.

Powers.

The Commission has direct powers to investigate and order the termination of infringements of the competition rules of the EC Treaty[15] and of the EEA Agreement,[16] subject to judicial review by the Court of Justice. It does not have to act through the member states' authorities, although it cooperates with their competition authorities in and informs and consults them about its work and can ask them for information and for assistance with investigations on firms' premises. The Commission also has direct powers to impose fines for substantive or procedural infringements, including daily fines for refusal to obey cease-and-desist orders or orders to disclose information or submit to investigations.[17] Fines are enforceable in the member states under Article 256 of the EC Treaty[18] in the same way as judgments or orders of national courts.

---

14. The Chief Economist is attached to the Dirctor General; the Hearing Officers are directly responsible to the Commissioner for competition.
15. Incorporating the powers under the ECSC Treaty after the expiry of that Treaty on July 23, 2002, *see* draft Thirty-second Report on Competition Policy, points 10–14.
16. The Commission has the same powers to apply Articles 53 and 54 of the EEA Agreement as under Regulation 17 (new Regulation 1/2003): Article 4 of the Protocol 21 of the EEA Agreement, 1994 OJ L 1/181.
17. Articles 23 and 24 of Regulation 1/2003. Daily fines are officially called 'periodic penalty payments'.
18. Article 92 of the ECSC Treaty.

Procedural Safeguards and Due Process.
The Commission is required to observe procedural safeguards to protect the interests of firms directly or indirectly affected by its decisions. Some safeguards are provided for in Regulation 1/2003, while others have been introduced in response to rulings of the Court of Justice on procedural issues or to outside criticism of the fairness and impartiality of its procedures.[19] Among the specific safeguards provided in the regulations are protection from disclosure of trade secrets and confidential business information. Additional safeguards preserve the basic rights of defendants in proceedings leading up to an adverse decision to reply to the Commission's charges before the decision is taken and the right of complainants and other interested parties to object to proposed decisions favorable to other firms. These 'due process' rights have been clarified in recent years with respect to access to documents in the Commission's files and legal professional privilege, and a neutral Hearing Officer has been appointed to conduct oral hearings. In addition to these specific procedural safeguards, the Commission is obliged in its competition enforcement procedures to observe the general principles of law and fundamental rights which the Court of Justice has recognized from a common constitutional tradition of the member states and which are part of Community law.[20] These general legal principles and fundamental rights include the principle of proportionality (reasonableness),[21] the right to a fair hearing,[22] respect of privacy[23] (including, within certain limits, protection

19. *See* House of Lords Select Committee on the European Communities, *Competition Practice*, 8th Report Session 1981–82, London 1982. Much of the criticism stems from a basic constitutional objection to competition enforcement by the executive branch of government rather than through the courts, on the ground that the executive is less open, more arbitrary and less likely to arrive at fair, well-balanced decisions. However, the Court of Justice has rejected the basic constitutional objection to the Commission's combination of the functions of prosecution and adjudication, subject to proper observance of procedural safeguards: *FEDETAB*, ECJ Oct. 29, 1980, 1980 ECR 3125, paras 79–81; *Pioneer*, ECJ June 7, 1983, 1983 ECR 1825, paras 6–11.
20. Article 6 (2) of the Treaty on European Union, and Recital 37 to Regulation 1/2003. *See Stauder v. Ulm*, ECJ Nov. 12, 1969, 1969 ECR 419, para. 7; *Internationale Handelsgesellschaft*, ECJ Dec. 17, 1970, 1970 ECR 1125, paras 3–4; *Testa*, ECJ June 19, 1980, 1980 ECR 1979, paras 17–19; *Hoechst – PVC/LdPE*, ECJ Sept. 21, 1989, 1989 ECR 2859, paras 12–14; *Solvay*, ECJ 18 Oct. 1989, 1989 ECR 3255, para. 29; *Zwartfeld*, ECJ July 13, 1990, 1990 ECR I-3365, para. 16; *Van der Wal*, CFI March 19, 1998, 1998 ECR II-545, para. 46; *Ke Kelit*, CFI March 20, 2002, 2002 ECR II-1647, paras 109–128; *LVM*, ECJ Oct. 15, 2002, 2002 ECR I-8375, para. 167.
21. E.g., in relation to the size of fines, *United Brands*, ECJ Feb. 14, 1978, 1978 ECR 207, para. 302; or to the investigative methods used, *National Panasonic*, ECJ June 26, 1980, 1980 ECR 2033, paras 28–30.
22. *Van der Wal*, CFI March 19, 1998, 1998 ECR II-545, para. 47; *HFB Holding*, CFI March 20, 2002, 2002 ECR II-1847, paras 294–295.
23. *National Panasonic*, ECJ June 26, 1980, 1980 ECR 2033, paras 19 *et seq.*; *Hoechst-PVC/LdPE*, ECJ Sept. 21, 1989, 1989 ECR 2859, paras 17–19: *see infra* section D.7.

against self-incrimination[24]), legitimate expectations,[25] legal certainty[26] and the related principles of prescription[27] and estoppel,[28] and protection against double jeopardy.[29] Finally, addressees of and interested parties to any formal decision by the Commission have the ultimate safeguard of the right of appeal to the European Court of Justice. Appeals from competition decisions are first heard by the lower chamber of the European Court, the European Court of First Instance, with a further appeal on points of law to the Court of Justice itself.

(b) EFTA Surveillance Authority

Similar Competition Rules.
Articles 53, 54 and 57 of the EEA Agreement contain competition rules similar to Articles 81 and 82 and Regulation 139/2004 on merger control. These rules are applied by the EFTA surveillance authority[30] where more than one third of the turnover of the undertakings concerned or the thresholds of the merger regulation are attained in a territory covered by the EEA Agreement.[31] Cooperation between the EFTA surveillance authority and the Commission involves the mutual exchange of information on notifications and complaints, case allocation,[32] and exchange of information about investigations, subject to the respect of business secrets and other confidential information, and mutual assistance upon request.[33]

---

24. *Solvay*, ECJ Oct. 18, 1989, 1989 ECR 3255, paras 15–28; *Orkem*, ECJ Oct. 18, 1989, 1989 ECR 2183, paras 18–31; *Postbank*, ECJ Nov. 10, 1993, 1993 ECR I-5683, para. 12; *LVM*, ECJ Oct. 15, 2002, 2002 ECR I-8375, para. 279.
25. *Far East Freight Conference*, CFI Feb. 28, 2002, 2002 ECR II-1101, para. 485; *CMA SGM FETTCSA*, CFI March 19, 2003, T-213/00, para. 336.
26. *See infra* section G.3.
27. Article 25 of Regulation 1/2003, replacing Council Regulation 2988/74 which introduced in 1974 a statute of limitations for fines, making up for an omission from Regulation 17.
28. Similar to the concept in civil law countries of 'protection of legitimate expectations'. For instance, the Commission might be stopped from imposing fines for conduct which it had appeared to clear in a general notice or a comfort letter (or 'guidance letter'): *Sugar*, ECJ Dec. 16, 1975, 1975 ECR 1663, paras 555–557; *Pre-Insulated Pipes – LR af 1998 A/S*, CFI March 20, 2002, 2002 ECR II-1705, paras 241–248; *Van der Bergh Foods*, CFI Oct. 23, 2003, T-65/98, para. 192.
29. *Boehringer II* (*Interpretation*), ECJ Dec. 14, 1972, 1972 ECR 1281, para. 3. *See also infra* section F.6.
30. Agreement on the EFTA Surveillance Authority and Court of Justice, 1994 OJ L 344/1.
31. Articles 56 (1) and 57 (2) of the EEA Agreement. *See P & I Clubs*, D.Comm. April 12, 1999, 1999 OJ L 125/12, point 139.
32. Including a referral of cases by the EFTA Surveillance Authority to the Commission: *see ARA*, D.Comm. Oct. 16, 2003, 2004 OJ L 75/39, point 2 (when referring the case to the Commission Austria was still member of EFTA).
33. Protocols 23 and 24 of the EEA Agreement, 1994 OJ L 344, 186–191. The cooperation on mergers is provided for in cases where 25% the aggregate turnover of the undertakings concerned is achieved in EEA countries and the turnover at least two undertakings in the EEA countries is more than EUR 250 million (Article 2 of Protocol 24).

(c) National Competition Authorities

Role of the National Authorities in EC Law Enforcement. National competition authorities also have jurisdiction to enforce Articles 81 and 82 independently of the Commission, once their respective national laws provide the necessary powers for investigating, deciding and fining infringements of Article 81 or 82.[34] From May 1, 2004 this also applies to the evaluation of Article 81 (3). However, mergers having a Community dimension are subject to the exclusive competence of the Commission, subject to the possibility of referring a case from and to national competition authorities.[35] National authorities lose their competence when the Commission initiates proceedings.[36] National authorities are regularly involved in the Commission's enforcement in close cooperation between each other.[37] National officials are present when the Commission carries out on-the-spot investigations of firms, and if a firm refuses to submit to a duly ordered investigation they must call on national enforcement powers to secure submission. National authorities may be required to supply information to the Commission and are themselves kept informed of enforcement actions by the Commission and consulted on proposed decisions and legislation through the Advisory Committee on Restrictive Practices and Monopolies. In addition, national competition authorities give advice to firms about the EC law implications of their arrangements, the formalities of notification to the Commission, and other matters.

Concurrent Application of Community and National Competition Law. National antitrust authorities may also apply their national antitrust law concurrently with the application of Community competition law by the Commission, provided the application does 'not prejudice the uniform application throughout the common market of the Community rules on cartels and the full effect of the measures adopted in implementation of those rules'.[38] However, the application of national

---

34. Normally, the national laws confer to the national authorities the necessary powers, including to proceed to investigations and to sanction infringements. Article 5 of Regulation 1/2003 provides for powers of the national competition authorities requiring that an infringement be brought to an end, ordering interim measures, accepting commitments and imposing fines insofar as the national law does not provide for such powers yet. However, there are doubts whether the Council is empowered under Article 83 of the EC Treaty to complement the national procedural rules.
35. Article 22 (1) and Article 9 (1) of Regulation 139/2004.
36. Article 11 (6) of Regulation 1/2003, *see* Article 9 (1) of Regulation 17.
37. Article 11 of Regulation 1/2003 and Notice on Cooperation within the ECN, points 16–30, which replace Article 10 of Regulation 17 and Notice on Cooperation between National Competition Authorities and the Commission, 1977 OJ C 313/3.
38. *Van Gend & Loos*, ECJ Feb. 5, 1963, 1963 ECR 1, para. 21; *Walt Wilhelm*, ECJ Feb. 13, 1969, 1969 ECR 1, para. 6; *Welded Steel Mesh – Sotralentz*, CFI April 6, 1995, 1995 ECR II-1 127, paras 26–29. However, the coal and steel industry is pre-empted by the ECSC Treaty competition rules (Articles 65 and 66), which apply to any restriction and merger.

competition law may not lead to the prohibition of an agreement which does not restrict competition or fulfills the criteria of Article 81 (3), except where the national law pursues an objective different from that pursued by Articles 81 and 82.

(d) National Courts

Duty to Enforce EC Rules and Grant Remedies.
The decentralized, private enforcement of antitrust law in the national courts is important as it tends to raise the general level of enforcement and voluntary compliance with the law. The Court of Justice confirmed the direct applicability of Articles 81 and 82 'in full' and the right of individuals to invoke infringements before the national courts. In the EC, the private enforcement of competition law is relatively new and still developing. The competition rules themselves contain only a general statement in Article 81 (2) that agreements contrary to Article 81 (1) are automatically void. It has been left to the Court of Justice to clarify the rights the competition rules confer on private firms and individuals and the duty of courts to enforce these rights. It is now clear that national courts must refuse to enforce agreements contrary to Articles 81 or 82 against parties or third parties and must grant the civil remedies available under national law to third parties injured or threatened with injury by conduct in breach of these Articles. The grant of injunctions in relation to breaches of EC competition law has become fairly common, and a right of action for damages has been recognized in principle in many member states, although few awards of damages have been made so far. The present state of Community and national law regarding the enforcement of Articles 81 and 82 by national courts is set out in greater detail in section I.

(e) European Court of Justice

Preliminary Rulings and Judicial Review.
The role of the European Court of Justice in enforcing the competition rules is twofold. Under Article 234, the Court gives preliminary rulings on questions of Community law concerning the EC competition rules referred to it by national courts. Its second function is that of judicial review of Commission decisions, or of the Commission's failure to act, under Articles 230 and 232 of the EC Treaty. Since 1989 appeals against competition decisions by the Commission are heard by the Court of First Instance, from whose decision a further appeal may be made on a point of law to the Court of Justice. Appeals against decisions by the EFTA Surveillance Authority under Articles 53, 54 and 57 of the EEA Agreement are heard by the EFTA Court of Justice.[39] The main features of the judicial review are set out in section G of this Chapter.

39. Articles 36 and 37 of the Agreement establishing the EFTA Surveillance Authority and the EFTA Court of Justice, 1994 OJ L 344/1 (identical to Articles 230 and 231 of the EC Treaty).

B. European Competition Network

1. Need for Close Cooperation at Community and National Level

Concurrent Application of Community Competition Law.
Following the removal of the Commission's exclusive competence to grant exemptions, Community competition law may be applied in parallel by the Commission, the national competition authorities and the national courts. However, national authorities are obliged under Article 10 (2) of the EC Treaty to constant and loyal cooperation with the Commission ('cooperation in good faith').[40] This raises the question of reciprocal information, case allocation and further cooperation during the respective proceedings. National courts must apply Community competition law in such a way as to avoid conflicts with decisions adopted or contemplated by the Commission.[41]

Concurrent Application of Community and National Competition Law.
National competition law continues to be applied by the national competition authorities and the national courts. However, in cases which are likely to affect trade between member states[42] national authorities and courts must also apply Community competition law.[43] Thereby they are subject to the same obligation to cooperate closely and to avoid conflicting decisions. There are three exceptions:

- National authorities and courts may apply stricter national law where it prohibits unilateral conduct of a dominant or non-dominant firm that is not prohibited by EC competition law.[44]
- National authorities and courts may apply national law that predominantly pursues an objective different from that pursued by Articles 81 and 82.[45]

40. Article 11 of Regulation 1/2003, replacing the previous Cooperation Notice (1997 OJ C 313/3). *See Van Munster/Rijksdienst voor Pensioenen*, ECJ Oct. 5, 1994, 1994 ECR I-4661, para. 32.
41. Article 16 (1) of Regulation 1/2003.
42. The Commission applies *de minimis* rules for measuring the likely effect on trade between member states by fixing a minimum market share of 5% and a minimum overall turnover of EUR 40 million. However, the *de minimis* rule contains a negative definition of appreciability which does not imply that agreements which exceed the thresholds are likely to appreciably affect trade between member states in this sense. *See* Commission Guidelines on the Effect on Trade Doctrine, 2004 OJ C 101/81.
43. Article 3 of Regulation 1/2003. This provision is based on Article 83 (2) (e) of the EC Treaty which empowers the Council to determine the relationship between national law and Articles 81 and 82.
44. This exception relates mainly to §20 (2) of the German Act Against Restraints of Competition which prohibits discriminatory conduct towards obligatory trading partners without necessarily involving a dominant position.
45. Article 3 (3) of Regulation 1/2003. This exception relates mainly to national provisions that prohibit unfair trade practices (Recital 9 to Regulation 1/2003).

- National authorities are not precluded from applying national law to joint ventures which do not have a Community dimension or to operations which are referred to them by the Commission.[46]

2. Cooperation between National Authorities and the Commission

Exchange of Information within the ECN.
The objective of close cooperation between the Commission and the national competition authorities is to encourage (in accordance with the subsidiarity principle of Article 5 of the Treaty) the national competition authorities to apply Community competition rules in cases where they are in a better position to do so and have more detailed and precise knowledge of the relevant markets so as to avoid duplication of proceedings. The new system aims at assuring the uniform application of Community competition law not only between the Commission and the national authority of each member state but also between various national authorities, thereby creating a European Competition Network (ECN) as a framework for the cooperation.[47] The cooperation starts in an early stage of proceedings in order to allocate cases. To this effect, the national authorities, before dealing with a case under the EC competition rules,[48] must inform the Commission and the other authorities in writing (e-mail) and without delay.

Confidential Information.
Information which the Commission and the national authorities collect on their own behalf or on behalf of the Commission[49] or other national authorities[50] may be exchanged between them, and the exchange may include confidential information.[51] However, information acquired under the respective investigation procedures may be used only for the purposes for which it was acquired.[52] The Commission is not prevented from communicating information received from one national authority to other national authorities which may be concerned, especially where access of firms from those countries to such information is significantly impeded.[53]

---

46. Article 21 (1) and Article 22 (1) of Regulation 139/2004.
47. Thirty-second Report on Competition Policy, point 17.
48. National law must normally be applied in conjunction with the EC competition rules, Article 3 (2) of Regulation 1/2003.
49. Article 22 (2) of Regulation 1/2003.
50. Article 22 (1) of Regulation 1/2003.
51. Article 12 (1). *See*, however, under Regulation 17: *Spanish Banks*, ECJ July 16, 1992, 1992 ECR I-4785, paras 39–43.
52. Article 28 (1) of Regulation 1/2003. Use of information acquired in a particular case (concerning sector A) cannot directly be used as evidence in a similar case (sector B) unless the authority proceeds to a new request: *LVM – PVC II*, ECJ Oct. 15, 2002, 2002 ECR I-8375, paras 305–306 (protection against 'fishing expeditions').
53. Notice on the Cooperation within the ECN, points 27 and 48–49.

Case Allocation.
On the basis of the information exchanged, the Commission and national competition authorities decide by mutual agreement which authority is best placed to initiate proceedings. They are not prevented from starting parallel proceedings, in particular where an infringement has been committed in several member states and requires action by the competent authorities (which have territorially limited jurisdiction). However, the fact that one national authority is dealing with a case shall be sufficient grounds for other authorities to suspend their proceedings.[54] In the case where the national authorities disagree on the case allocation or where more than three member states are affected the Commission may, in order to ensure effective enforcement, decide to initiate proceedings which relieves the national authorities of their competence to apply Articles 81 and 82; in cases where a national authority is already acting in the case, the Commission will do so only after consulting that national authority.[55] The Commission may do so in particular in cases where the national authority might adopt a decision in conflict with the Community case law, where the national authority does not act or where the Commission intends to develop the Community competition policy.

The Guardian-Function of the Commission.
The regular contact and consultation among the Commission and the national authorities is designed to provide a valuable safeguard against divergent application of the Community competition provisions. The Commission is the guardian ensuring that the decisions taken by national authorities are consistent and that the antitrust rules are applied in a uniform manner, thereby avoiding conflicting decisions.[56] For that purpose, the national authorities must, no later than 30 days before the adoption a prohibition decision, provide the Commission with a summary of the case and the draft decision; they may extend this consultation to other authorities.[57] The Commission consults the Advisory Committee before taking a decision.[58]

3. Cooperation between National Courts and the Commission

Duty to Enforce EC Rules and Grant Remedies.
The decentralized, private enforcement of antitrust law in the national courts is important as it tends to raise the general level of enforcement and of voluntary compliance with the law. The Court of Justice has confirmed the direct applicability of Articles 81 and 82 and the right of individuals to invoke infringements

54. Article 13 (1) of Regulation 1/2003.
55. Article 11 (6) of Regulation 1/2003.
56. Article 11 (4) and (5).
57. Article 11 (4) of Regulation 1/2003.
58. Article 14 (3) of Regulation 1/2003.

before the national courts.[59] In the EC, the private enforcement of competition law is relatively new and still developing. The competition rules themselves contain only a general statement in Article 81 that agreements contrary to Article 81 are automatically void. It has been left to the Court of Justice to clarify the rights the competition rules confer on private firms and individuals and the duty of courts to enforce these rights. It is now clear that national courts must refuse to enforce agreements contrary to Articles 81 or 82 against parties or third parties and must grant the civil remedies available under national law to third parties injured or threatened with injury by conduct in breach of these Articles. The grant of injunctions in relation to breaches of EC competition law has become fairly common, and a right of action for damages has been recognized in principle in the member states, although few awards of damages have been made so far.

Close Cooperation.
National courts are to act in close cooperation with the Commission whenever they apply Community competition law, either alone or in conjunction with national competition law[60] in order to assure uniform application of Community competition law.[61] The national authorities must forward to the Commission any judgment of national courts on the application of Articles 81 and 82.[62] Where a national court has already adopted a decision which conflicts with a decision of the Commission but has been appealed, the court of appeal may suspend its proceedings or submit questions to the Court of Justice; where such a decision is not (or is no longer) subject to a judicial remedy the decision may be made subject to appeal under national law[63] in order to remove the conflict or to avoid any sanction resulting from the decision of the national court.[64]

---

59. Commission Notice on the cooperation between the Commission and the national courts (hereafter 'Notice on national courts'), 2004 OJ C 101/54, (which replaces the previous Notice 1993 OJ C 39/5), points 6 and 9. *See BRT/SABAM I,* ECJ Jan. 30, 1974, 1974 ECR 51, paras 16–17.
60. The provisions of national law relating to the application of the EC competition rules must be compatible with the general principles of Community law: Notice on national courts, point 10 with references to the relevant case law.
61. However, it is still an open question whether information, in particular confidential information, that has been collected by the Commission for the purposes of investigating and sanctioning a suspected infringement of Articles 81 and 82 can be used, as such, by national courts for awarding damages under national civil law. *See* with respect to fines against individuals which are provided for under national, but not under Community law: Notice on national courts, point 28 (b).
62. Article 15 (2).
63. By analogy to Article 98 of the Court's Rules of Procedure.
64. *Masterfoods*, ECJ Dec. 14, 2000, 2000 ECR I-11369, para. 48.

Amicus Curiae.
The cooperation between the national courts and Commission includes the right to ask the Commission to transmit information or opinions concerning the application of Articles 81 and 82. Its role is limited to that of an *amicus curiae* without the intention to intervene on the side of either party. National authorities and the Commission may submit to the court written or oral observations and may request the transmission of any document necessary for the assessment of the case,[65] which is without prejudice to wider powers of national authorities under their national law.[66]

Territorially Limited Jurisdiction of National Authorities and Courts.
By applying Community competition law, national authorities and courts may only take the measures necessary to safeguard or restore effective competition on their national market.[67] Although national authorities *may* reject a complaint where a similar complaint is already dealt with by another national authority[68] there are no express provisions on parallel proceedings of different national authorities concerning the same case. The jurisdiction of national authorities is limited to their territory, and their decisions can only cover practices insofar as they have foreseeable (immediate and substantial) effects within that territory.[69] Therefore, a decision adopted by a national authority cannot preclude another national authority from taking action in the same case although the close cooperation established between them in the framework of the ECN[70] is designed to prevent double proceedings and conflicting decisions.

4. COOPERATION BETWEEN THE COMMISSION AND THE COMPETITION AUTHORITIES OF THIRD COUNTRIES

Increasing Number of Cases implying the Parallel Application of Different Competition Laws.
International cartels are subject to parallel investigations and parallel proceedings (including sanctions) by various antitrust authorites within and outside the Community. Examples include cases such as *Graphite Electrodes*,[71] *Vitamins*[72] *and Citric Acid*.[73] The competent authorities are therefore inclined to exchange

65. Notice on National Courts, point 39.
66. E.g. §90 of the German Law against Restraints of Competition (GWB).
67. *Cf.* in the case of a Commission referral: Article 9 (8) of the Merger Control Regulation.
68. Article 13 (2).
69. *See Gencor/Lonrho*, CFI March 25, 1999, 1999 ECR II-753, para. 90.
70. Article 11 and Notice within the ECN, point 5.
71. D.Comm. July 18, 2001, 2002 OJ L 100/1.
72. D.Comm. Nov. 21, 2001, 2003 OJ L 6/1.
73. D.Comm. Dec. 5, 2001, 2002 OJ L 239/32.

information and cooperation to the extent permissible under applicable regulation and international cooperation agreements.

Cooperation between the Commission and Third Country Authorities.
The cooperation between the Commission and the competition authorities of third countries is subject to bilateral arrangements, such as with the United States,[74] Canada,[75] Japan,[76] other OECD countries,[77] the EFTA Surveillance Authority,[78] and within the framework of the International Competition Nework (ICN).[79]

Positive Comity.
The cooperation may extend to positive comity principles. The Agreement between the European Communities and the U.S. provides for the right of one party to request the other party to investigate and, if warranted, to remedy anticompetitive activities which occur in the territory of one party and are adversely affecting the interests of the other party. The cooperative procedures aim at achieving the effective and efficient enforcement of competition law, namely to encourage the competition authorities to take effective enforcement action against anticompetitive activities within that authority's jurisdiction that may be directed toward the other party's territory.

C. Initiation of Investigations[80]

1. General

Sources and Selection of Cases.
There are three main routes that prompt the Commission to begin an investigation: informal sources of information that prompt an inquiry on the Commission's

74. 1995 OJ L 95/45, Thirty-second Report on Competition Policy, points 655–659 *See also* Agreement between the European Communities and the Government of the United States of America on the Application of Positive Comity Principles in the Enforcement of their Competition Laws, 1998 OJ L 173.
75. 1997 OJ L 175, *see* Thirty-second Report on Competition Policy, points 660–661.
76. *See* Thirty-second Report on Competition Policy, points 662–663; IP/00/739.
77. *See* the 1995 OECD Revised Council Recommendation concerning cooperation between member countries, OECD Doc. COM(95)130 final, which provides a framework for concluding bi-lateral cooperation agreements.
78. Protocol 23 concerning the cooperation between EFTA Surveillance Authority and Commission.
79. Thirty-second Report on Competition Policy, point 666. Report from the Commission to the Council and the European Parliament on the application of the agreements, COM(2002)505 final.
80. *See* the Commission's booklet *Dealing with the Commission*, which explains the most important aspects, in particular notifications, investigation, infringement proceedings and rights to be heard (1997), http://europa.eu.int.

own initiative, complaints and clearance requests. In a typical year[81] the Commission may receive 70–100 tips[82] or other information leading to an investigation on its own initiative,[83] about 110–170 complaints, and – up to now – it used to receive about 100 requests for clearance (notifications). With such a large number of cases and finite staff resources, the Commission is forced to be selective in the cases it takes up for a large-scale investigation, possibly leading to a formal decision.[84] It therefore concentrates on important cases such as major cartels, abuses of dominant position causing damage to complainant firms, complaints displaying a Community interest and cases which clarify or develop the law, for example preparing the way for a block exemption regulation.[85]

Investigation of Cases.

Investigations are initially informal, and in the vast majority of cases are closed without reaching the stage of a formal decision.[86] In the course of them the Commission may or may not use its fact-finding powers to obtain the discovery of information or documents and to carry out investigations on firms' premises.[87] If the Commission decides to take a case through to a formal decision, it must commence formal proceedings. During the formal proceedings defendants and interested parties are given the opportunity to object to the proposed decision, the national authorities are consulted and the draft decision is circulated to other interested departments of the Commission and to the Commission itself.[88] However, formal proceedings do not always lead to a final formal decision. In many cases the proceedings are closed beforehand on the basis of an informal settlement with the parties or a comfort letter.

Decisions.

The Commission can take a decision at the end of formal proceedings in the form of an *adverse* decision finding an infringement, ordering parties to cease

---

81. *See* Thirty-second Report on Competition Policy, points 5–8.
82. Including the increasing number of self-reporting cases in order to obtain immunity from fines under the Commission Notice 2002 OJ C45/3.
83. Comparative annual statistics in: Thirty-first Report on Competition Policy, after point 243.
84. Formal decisions make considerable calls on resources both within and outside DG COMP. Besides drafting work and extensive intradepartmental and interdepartmental consultations, the resultant decisions must be translated in order to be published into all the (now nineteen) EC languages.
85. E.g., *BMW*, D.Comm. Dec. 13, 1974, 1975 OJ L 29/1 (vehicle distribution); *Maize Seed*, D.Comm. Sept. 21, 1978, 1978 OJ L 286/23 (patent licensing); *Pronuptia*, D.Comm. Dec. 17, 1986, 1987 OJ L 13/39; *Yves Rocher*, D.Comm. Dec. 17, 1986, 1987 OJ L 8/49 (franchising); *Boussois/Interpane*, D.Comm. Dec. 15, 1986, 1987 OJ L 50/30 (know-how licensing).
86. In the years 1996–2001 the number of formal decisions annually was limited to 21–68, whereas 300–500 cases were closed without formal decision: Thirty-first Report on Competition Policy, after point 243.
87. *See infra* section D.
88. *See infra* sections E and F.

and desist from an infringement,[89] and possibly threatening or imposing fines or periodic penalty payments,[90] or *a favourable* decision stating that Article 81 (1) is not applicable or that the conditions of Article 81 (3) are fulfilled.[91] In the course of formal proceedings decisions threatening or imposing fines for procedural infringements are also possible. However, the Commission may also close a case by issuing a comfort letter, rejecting a complaint, discontinuing proceedings or accepting a settlement (subject to commitments).[92]

2. Initiation of Proceedings on the Commission's Own Initiative

Importance of Proceedings Commenced on the Commission's own Initiative.

The Commission may investigate and prosecute infringements of Article 81 or 82 on its own initiative (*ex officio* proceedings).[93] While evidence unearthed in the course of investigations of other infringements sometimes leads the Commission to initiate proceedings on its own initiative, more frequently the trigger is information received from informal complainants or informants, including parties to a secret cartel, which inform the Commission about the existence of the cartel in order to enjoy immunity from fines. The validity of an own investigation commenced on the Commission's own initiative is not affected by whether or not the source of the Commission's information had a legitimate interest to file a formal complaint.[94]

Termination of *ex officio* Proceedings.

Ex officio proceedings may be terminated by a formal decision:

- imposing a fine,[95]
- requiring the companies to bring the infringement to an end,[96]
- concluding that the commitments offered by the parties meet the Commission's competition concerns and that there are no longer grounds for action,[97] or
- if there is a legitimate reason in doing so, finding that an infringement has been committed *in the past*.[98]

89. Articles 7 and 8 of Regulation 1/2003.
90. Articles 23 and 24 of Regulation 1/2003.
91. Article 10 of Regulation 1/2003.
92. *See* Article 5 *et seq*. of Regulation 1/2003.
93. Article 7 (1) of Regulation 1/2003.
94. *BMW Belgium*, ECJ July 12, 1979, 1979 ECR 2435, para. 18.
95. Article 23 of Regulation 1/2003.
96. Article 7 (1) of Regulation 1/2003.
97. Article 9 (1) of Regulation 1/2003.
98. Article 7 (1) of Regulation 1/2003.

Ex officio proceedings may also be terminated by closing or discontinuing the case.

3. COMPLAINTS

Important Enforcement Tool.

Article 7 of Regulation 1/2003 provides for the filing of formal 'complaints' to the Commission.[99] A complaint is both an important source of information about antitrust violations which helps the Commission in its enforcement tasks and an important avenue of redress for persons injured by antitrust violations.[100] A complainant enjoys certain procedural rights, including the right to be heard and the right to appeal a decision addressed to, or directly and individually concerning, the complainant. A complaint may be a more certain (and cheaper) alternative to private enforcement through the courts, which is still relatively undeveloped in the EU, although civil remedies are being encouraged by the Commission as a means of satisfying complainants' interests and reserving Commission intervention for cases of Community interest. Although a complaint may also be submitted by a member state, its main use is by injured firms and individuals, not only weak market partners complaining against behaviour of powerful firms, but also by large firms complaining against the behaviour of their competitors.[101]

Complaint to Initiate or Reopen Proceedings.

A complaintant may request the Commission to *initiate* proceedings with the view of investigating and finding an infringement of Article 81 or 82,[102] including the adoption of interim measures,[103] or to *reopen* proceedings:

– where there has been a material change in any of the facts on which a Commission decision was based,

---

99. *Cf.* Article 3 of Regulation 17. The handling of complaints under Regulation 1/2003 is comprehensively described in the Commission Notice on Complaints, 2004 OJ C 101/65. However, the merger control regulation and the rules on state aids do not provide for formal complaints; 'complaints' may be submitted, but complainants do not have the same procedural rights as the parties to the transaction or the recipients of a state aid: *see* Chapter VI.E. at p. 682 and Chapter IX.G. at p. 1019. *See Sytraval*, ECJ April 4, 1998, 1998 ECR I-1719.

100. The purpose of antitrust enforcement is not only to maintain effective competition in markets but also to protect individual firms and consumers from anticompetitive conduct insofar as they contribute to effective competition: *Sugar (intervention)*, ECJ Dec. 11, 1973, 1973 ECR 1465, 1469. *See also Hoechst – PVC/LdPE*, ECJ Sept. 21, 1989, 1989 ECR 2859, para. 25.

101. *See* the complaints of Mars against *Langnese* (CFI June 8, 1995, 1995 ECR II-1533, para. 3; *aff'd* ECJ Oct. 1, 1998, 1998 ECR I-5609) and the complaint of *Reynolds Tobacco* against *Philip Morris* (ECJ Nov. 17, 1987, 1987 ECR 4566, para. 3).

102. Article 7 (1) of Regulation 1/2003.

103. Article 8 (1) of Regulation 1/2003. The national authorities and the national courts may be equally well placed to adopt interim measures: Commission Notice on the Handling of Complaints, point 80.

- where the undertakings concerned act contrary to their commitments, or
- where the decision was based on imcomplete, incorrect or misleading information provided by the parties.[104]

Need for 'Legitimate Interest'.

Any person having a 'legitimate interest' may complain to the Commission about an agreement or practice which may infringe Article 81 or 82 and ask the Commission to issue a cease-and-desist order.[105] Those having a legitimate interest include the parties to the agreement or practice,[106] associations of enterprises,[107] consumer associations[108] and third parties suffering or threatened with loss as a direct result of it, such as traders,[109] competitors[110] and would-be purchasers to whom a firm refuses to sell.[111] To be able to demonstrate a sufficiently direct interest, third parties must normally be businesses, although occasionally the Commission has accepted complaints from consumers[112] and even trade unions.[113] A third party clearly has a legitimate interest to complain if the Commission is proposing to clear an agreement which allegedly injures him, since an exemption, being binding on national courts would prevent any further legal challenge.[114] However, member states do not need to justify any legitimate interest.[115]

---

104. Article 9 (2) of Regulation 1/2003.
105. Commission Notice on the Handling of Complaints, points 33–40.
106. The Commission has accepted for consideration complaints from parties to license agreements (*Roses*, D.Comm. Dec. 13, 1985, 1985 OJ L 369/9), contracts for sale of a business (*Reuter/BASF*, D.Comm. July 26, 1976, 1976 OJ L 254/40; *Continuum/Quantel*, D.Comm. July 27, 1992, 1992 OJ L 235/9), and contractual arrangements between suppliers and purchasers of goods or services (*Distillers I*, D.Comm. Dec. 20, 1977, 1978 OJ L 50/16) and between trade associations and their members (*FRUBO*, D.Comm. July 25, 1974, 1974 OJ L 237/16).
107. *BEMIM*, CFI Jan. 24, 1995, 1995 ECR II-147.
108. Commission Notice on the Handling of Complaints, points 35–37. *See IECC/Reims II*, ECJ May 17, 2001, 2001 ECR I-3247.
109. *Novalliance/Systemform*, D.Comm. Dec. 4, 1996, 1997 OJ L 47/11.
110. *Matra/Volkswagen-Ford*, CFI July 15, 1994, 1994 ECR II-595; *Eurovision*, CFI July 11, 1996, 1996 ECR II-649 (Article 81); *French-West-African Shipowners' Committees*, D.Comm. April 1, 1992, 1992 OJ L 134/1 (Articles 81 and 82); *ECS/Akzo II*, D.Comm. Dec. 14, 1985, 1985 OJ L 374/1 (Article 82); *aff'd* ECJ July 3, 1991, 1991 ECR I-3359; *SCPA/Kali + Salz*, CFI March 31, 1998, 1998 ECR I-1375.
111. *Zoja/Commercial Solvents*, D.Comm. Dec. 14, 1972, 1972 OJ L 299/51; *aff'd* ECJ March 6, 1974, 1974 ECR 223; *United Brands*, ECJ Feb. 14, 1978, 1978 ECR 207, paras 189–202; *British Sugar/Napier Brown*, D.Comm. July 18, 1988, 1988 OJ L 284/41, points 65–68.
112. *Kawasaki*, D.Comm. Dec. 12, 1978, 1979 OJ L 16/9; associations of consumers: *BEUC and National Consumer Council*, CFI May 18, 1994, 1994 ECR II-285.
113. *Nestlé Perrier (Trade Unions)*, CFI April 27, 1995, 1995 ECR II-1213.
114. Such persons also have standing to appeal the exemption decision: *SABA I*, ECJ Oct. 25, 1977, 1977 ECR 1875, para. 13.
115. With respect to Article 81: *CEWAL*, D.Comm. Dec. 23, 1992, 1993 OJ L 34/20, *aff'd* (in substance) CFI Oct. 8, 1996, 1996 ECR II-1201; with respect to Article 86 (3): *Port of Rodby*, D.Comm. Dec. 21, 1993, 1994 OJ L 55/52.

Main Concern of a Complaint.
The main concern of a complainant is to have the alleged infringing conduct brought to an end or altered. If such conduct is terminated or if it can be assumed that the conduct will be altered in a manner conducive to the public interest, a complainant no longer has a legitimate interest in requesting a formal Commission decision stating that such conduct *was* contrary to the EC competition rules.[116]

Individual Interests v. Community Interests.
Articles 81 and 82 aim at both protecting an effective competitive structure within the Community (protection of competition as an institution) and protecting individuals affected by anticompetitive behaviour.[117] Accordingly, individuals may justify a complaint by proving that they have been individually injured and that the intervention of the Commission is necessary in order to obtain a remedy which they would probably not obtain in an action before the national courts.[118] The Commission's obligations are, on the other hand, to be considered in the light of Article 85 of the EC Treaty, which constitutes the specific expression of the general supervisory role conferred on it by Article 211 of the Treaty.[119] Accordingly, the Commission is not prevented from giving priority to cases where the Community interest in improving or restoring the competitive structure of the market is strong. In *Automec II* [120] the Court of First Instance conceded to the Commission a certain discretion in fixing its priorities according to the degree of Community interest.[121] This implies the right of the Commission to reject a complaint when it considers that the case does not display a sufficient Community interest to justify initiation of proceedings and further investigation of the case.[122] Where the Commission rejects a complaint for lack of Community interest, the judicial review which the Court must undertake focuses on whether or not the contested decision is based on materially incorrect facts, or is vitiated by an error of law, a manifest error of appraisal or misuse of powers.[123] A complaint cannot therefore oblige the Commission to initiate proceedings and to take action, but can only urge the Commission to examine 'with all due care' the factual and legal aspects of the

116. *IECC*, CFI Sept. 16, 1998, 1998 ECR II-3605, paras 56–59.
117. *Generale Sucrière* (*Sugar*), ECJ Dec. 11, 1973, 1973 ECR 1465, 1469. *See also Hoechst-PVC/LdPE*, ECJ Sept. 21, 1989, 1989 ECR 2859, para. 25.
118. Commission Notice on Complaints, point 44.
119. *Parker Pen*, CFI July 14, 1994, 1994 ECR II-531, para. 63; *IECC*, CFI Sept. 16, 1998, 1998 ECR II-3605, para. 54.
120. *Automec II*, CFI Sept. 18, 1992, 1992 ECR II-2223, paras 72–73.
121. *See IECC/Reims II*, ECJ May 17, 2001, 2001 ECR I-3247, para. 42.
122. *Automec II*, CFI Sept. 18, 1992, 1992 ECR II-2223, paras 74–76; *SFEI*, CFI Jan. 15, 1997, 1997 ECR II-l, para. 29; *IECC*, CFI Sept. 16, 1998, 1998 ECR II-3605, para. 46.
123. *Automec II*, CFI Sept 18, 1992, 1992 ECR II-2223, para. 80; *BEUC*, CFI May 18, 1994, 1994 ECR II-285, para. 45; *Koelmann*, CFI Jan. 9, 1996, 1996 ECR II-1, para. 56; *IECC*, CFI Sept. 16, 1998, 1998 ECR II-3605, para. 47. Similarly under ECSC law: *NALOO*, CFI Sept. 24, 1996, 1996 ECR II-1019.

complaint.[124] In cases when an alleged infringement has ceased the Commission may have to investigate as to whether the harmful effects on competition may be continuing but the complainant cannot oblige the Commission to do so.[125] On the other hand, when a complainant is unable to demonstrate a legitimate interest, the Commission is not prevented from initiating, where appropriate, proceedings *ex officio*.[126]

Formalities.

Formal complaints must be made by using Form C, which rather recalls the information to be supplied,[127] and submitted to the Commission by respecting the general rules as described in the Commission Recommendations.[128] The complainant must properly identify itself and the respondent, state the facts alleged, indicate the basis for the claim that the agreement or practice infringes Article 81 or 82 and that there is an affect on trade between member states and furnish any evidence (e.g., correspondence, names of witnesses). The complainant must also demonstrate how its interests are directly affected by the agreement or practice. Technical details of relevant products or processes should be given, and an explaination of why intervention by the Commission is necessary rather than action before a national court (principle of subsidiarity). Where the complaint is lodged by a representative, proof of authority to act for the complainant must be provided. Confidential information which the complainant does not wish the Commission to disclose to the respondent should be marked or preferably put in a separate annex. The complainant may ask the Commission to issue an interim order to maintain the *status quo* pending its determination of the complaint.[129] Individuals may address *informal* complaints to the Commission suggesting the initiation of *ex officio* proceedings[130] without having procedural rights. The Commission must respect

124. *Automec II*, CFI Sept. 18, 1992, 1992 ECR II-2223, para. 74; *Guérin Automobiles*, CFI June 27, 1995, 1995 ECR II-1753, para. 23; *Dalmasso*, CFI Jan. 21, 1999, 1999 ECR II-93, para. 48.
125. *Ufex*,CFI May 25, 2000, 2000 ECR II-2167, annulling a Commission decision rejecting a complaint because of lack of a Community interest (however, this was the third Court decision in that case).
126. *IECC*, CFI Sept. 16, 1998, 1998 ECR II-3645, para. 79, *aff'd* ECJ May 17, 2001, 2001 ECR I-3247, para. 36; *Kruidvat*, ECJ Nov. 17, 1998, 1998 ECR I-7183.
127. Article 5 (2) of Regulation 773/2004 and Commission's Notice on the Handling of Complaints, point 30; Annex (Form C) and Recommendation for the submission of complaints and antitrust correspondence, updated May 1, 2004 (Commission's website). *See Automec II*, CFI Sept. 18, 1992, 1992 ECR II-2223 para. 72.
128. Commission's Recommendations for the Submission of Complaints and Antitrust Correspondence, in particular with respect to the use of electronic file carrier.
129. *See infra* section F.3.
130. *IECC*, CFI Sept. 16, 1998, 1998 ECR II-3645, para. 79. Informal complaints are an important source of information for the Commission, e.g. *COAPI*, D.Comm. Jan. 30, 1995, 1995 OJ L 122/37; *FENEX*, D.Comm. June 5, 1996, 1996 OJ L 181/28.

the confidentiality of informants and also of supporting documents which might identify the complainant thereby exposing him to measures of retaliation.[131]

No Duty of Commission to Take a Decision but to Examine Carefully. Complaints do not oblige the Commission to initiate proceedings[132] or to adopt a decision finding an infringement of Article 81 or 82[133] but to react within a reasonable period of time.[134] The Commission is not obliged to mount a full-scale investigation of every complaint.[135] This would overstretch its resources. It is only required to investigate a complaint sufficiently to establish whether a violation of Articles 81 or 82 has been or is being committed and, if so, whether it is advisable or necessary for it to intervene, given the alternative means of redress available to complainants, notably through national courts.[136] The Commission usually informs the complainant within four months whether the Commission will further investigate the case. If the conduct complained of has ceased, is not a particularly serious infringement or arises out of a civil dispute between the parties that is already before, or suitable for adjudication by, a national court or a national authority,[137] only a brief investigation will usually be made.

Duty to Investigate Past Anticompetitive Conduct v. Legitimate Expectations. A complaint must be lodged within a reasonable time after having discovered a past suspected anticompetitive conduct. The principle of legal certainty or legitimate expectations does not prevent the Commission from examining such past conduct but the Commission cannot indefinitely extend the period granted to a complainant for the purpose of providing evidence to substantiate its complaint.[138]

---

131. Non-respect of confidentiality may lead to damage claims: *Adams*, ECJ Nov. 7, 1985, 1985 ECR 3539.
132. *Automec II*, CFI Sept. 18, 1992, 1992 ECR II-223, para. 74. *See also Asia Motor I*, ECJ June 12, 1992, 1992 ECR I-3935.
133. *BEMIM II*, CFI Jan. 24, 1995, 1995 ECR II-147, para. 62; *IECC*, CFI Sept. 16, 1998, 1998 ECR II-3605, para. 46. *See GEMA*, ECJ Oct. 18, 1979, 1979 ECR 3173 para. 17; *Automec II*, CFI Sept. 18, 1992, 1992 ECR II-2223 paras 75–76; *Rendo*, CFI Nov. 18, 1992, 1992 ECR II-2417; *Ladbroke II*, CFI Oct. 27, 1994, 1994 ECR I-1015 paras 37–39; *Ladbroke III*, CFI Sept. 18, 1995, 1995 ECR II-2568 para. 45; *Guérin*, CFI June 27, 1995, 1995 ECR II-1753 para. 22; *Koelmann*, CFI Jan. 9, 1996, 1996 ECR II-l, para. 39.
134. The period depends on the complexity of the case: Commission Notice on the Handling of Complaints, point 60; *see Nederlandse Kraanhuurbedrijf (SCK)*, CFI Oct. 22, 1997, 1997 ECR II-1739, para. 57.
135. *Automec II*, CFI Sept. 18, 1992, 1992 ECR II-2223 para. 76; *Asia Motors III*, CFI June 29, 1993, 1993 ECR II-669, para. 36.
136. *Max. mobil*, CFI Jan. 30, 2002, 2002 ECR II-313, paras 48–56.
137. Commission Notice on the Handling of Complaints, points 44 and 58. *See La Cinq*, CFI Jan. 24, 1992, 1992 ECR II-1 para. 61; *Ladbroke III*, CFI Sept. 18, 1995, 1995 ECR II-2568 para. 50.
138. *International Power/NALOO*, ECJ Oct. 2, 2003, C-172/01 P, paras 109–110 and 179.

Parallel Complaints at Community and National Level.
A complainant may report the same conduct to the Commission and to one or several national competition authorities.[139] In order to avoid such a complaint being dealt with simultaneously by several antitrust authorities (acting on the complaint or on their own initative) the priority rule applies: the authority which is already acting continues its proceedings, and the other authorities may suspend their investigation or decline to take action on the complaint.[140]

Judicial Review in Cases of Rejection or Failure to Act.
If the Commission does not find a reason for intervention it must reject the complaint by reasoned 'letter'[141] or, but not necessarily,[142] by decision,[143] after having given the complainant the opportunity to comment.[144] If the Commission, after receiving the complainant's comments, is still unconvinced that the complaint is justified, it generally sends the complainant, if it wishes, 'within a reasonable period'[145] a notice of *formal rejection* which is appealable to the Court under Article 230 of the EC Treaty. The reasoning must be such as to enable the party concerned to ascertain the grounds justifying it so that it can defend its rights and ascertain the legal grounds on which the decision is based[146] and whether it is well founded or not.[147] In cases entailing a complex economic assessment, the Court's judicial review of a rejection letter will be confined to verifying compliance with procedural rules and those relating to the statement of reasoning,[148] verifying

139. Expressly provided for in Article 5 of Regulation 1/2003.
140. Article 13 of Regulation 1/2003.
141. Stating that there is no reason for further action: *Storck Amsterdam*, CFI Feb. 17, 2000, 2000 ECR II-309, paras 63–68.
142. *Max.mobil*, CFI Jan. 30, 2002, 2002 ECR II-313, para. 55.
143. The Commission may, by exempting the agreement which is the subject of the complaint, reject the complaint implicitly; the complainant is in this case entitled to appeal the exemption decision: *Florimex*, CFI May 14, 1997, 1997 ECR II-693. Similarly in case of settlement: *Philip Morris*, ECJ Nov. 17, 1987, 1987 ECR 4487, para. 19; *NALOO*, CFI Sept. 24, 1996, 1996 ECR II-1019, paras 275–276.
144. Article 7 of Regulation 773/2004, *see* CFI, CFI June 3, 1999, 1999 ECR II-1757, para. 88. Such a letter is only an intermediary act preparing the final 'decision' (decision in two phases) and is therefore not subject to appeal: *Automec I*, CFI July 10, 1990, 1990 ECR II-367; *GEMA II*, ECJ Oct. 18, 1979, 1979 ECR 3173, paras 17–18; *Asia Motors II*, CFI Sept. 18, 1992, 1992 ECR II-2285. The letter is characterized by the fixing of a period for introducing eventual remarks: *Peugeot*, CFI May 2, 1997, 1997 ECR II-663, para. 34; whereas the letter rejecting the complaint does not set such a period.
145. *IECC*, CFI Sept. 16, 1998, 1998 ECR II-3597, para. 15.
146. E.g. Articles 81, 82 or 86: *Tierce/Ladbroke II*, CFI Jan. 24, 1995, 1995 ECR 11–115, para. 60; *Tierce/Ladbroke III*, CFI Sept. 18, 1995, 1995 ECR II-2568 paras 46–50.
147. *La Cinq*, CFI Jan. 24, 1992, 1992 ECR II-1, paras 41–43; *Asia Motors II*, CFI June 29, 1993, 1993 ECR II-669, para. 30.
148. The Commission may, however, refer, in its final assessment, to the reason exposed in its letter pursuant to Article 7 of Regulation 773/2004: *Tierce/Ladbroke IV*, CFI June 12, 1997, 1997 ECR II-923.

the material accuracy of facts and the absence of manifest errors of assessment or misuse of power.[149] A complainant whose complaint is rejected implicitly by the Commission in a formal decision of exemption or negative clearance for the agreement or practice complained of also has a right of appeal to the Court against the decision under Article 230.[150] The notice merely rejects the complaint on the known facts; it is not a definitive ruling that the agreement or practice complained of does not infringe Article 81 or 82.[151] The standards applied by the Court of Justice are strict and have led to the annulment in numerous cases of the Commission's decision to reject a complaint[152] to such an extent that the Commission, although not obliged to act, has a limited margin of manoeuvre.[153] If the Commission *fails to act*[154] within two months of being called upon to act, the complainant is entitled to bring an action, within a further period of two months, before the Court of Justice against the Commission under Article 232 of the EC Treaty for failure to act.[155]

149. *La Cinq*, CFI Jan. 24, 1992, 1992 ECR II-l, paras 41–43; *Asia Motors III*, CFI June 29, 1993, 1993 ECR II-669, paras 30–33; *BEUC*, May 18, 1994, 1994 ECR II-285 para. 45; *Koelmann*, CFI Jan. 9, 1996, 1996 ECR II-1 para. 56.

150. *Rendo*, CFI Dec. 12, 1996, 1996 ECR II-1827. *See also Timex v. Council and Commission*, ECJ March 20, 1985, 1985 ECR 849 (dumping); *COFAZ v. Commission*, ECJ Jan. 28, 1986, 1986 ECR 391 (state aids).

151. Which would require a full, formal investigation: *GEMA II*, ECJ Oct. 18, 1979, 1979 ECR 3173, para. 18. The notice may introduce additional arguments against the complainant's submissions further to those stated in the Article 6 letter: *Philip Morris/Rothmans*, ECJ Nov. 17, 1987, 1987 ECR 4487, paras 26–27.

152. *Asia Motor France*, CFI June 29, 1993, 1993 ECR II-669; *Ladbroke II*, CFI Sept. 18, 1995, 1995 ECR II-2568; *Rendo*, CFI Dec. 12, 1996, 1996 ECR II-1827; *Florimex*, CFI May 14, 1997, 1997 ECR II-693; *Ladbroke III*, CFI June 12, 1997, 1997 ECR II-6265. Similarly, in cases of state aids: *Sytraval and Brinks France*, CFI Sept. 28, 1995, 1995 ECR II-2654; *aff'd* CFI April 2, 1998, 1998 ECR I-1719; *IECC*, CFI Sept. 16, 1998, 1998 ECR II-3645.

153. *See* e.g. *Asia Motor II*, CFI June 29, 1993, 1993 EC II–669, and *Asia Motor III*, CFI Sept. 18, 1996, 1996 ECR II-961, *aff'd Somaco*, ECJ May 7, 1998, 1998 ECR I-2587. The Commission must act within a 'reasonable' period of time: CFI June 3, 1999, 1999 ECR II-1757; *UPS*, CFI Sept. 9, 1999, 1999 ECR II-2633, paras 42–47.

154. This does not necessarily imply the final evaluation of the complaint, but at least a reaction (e.g. investigation or an Article 6 letter): *Guérin automobiles*, CFI June 27, 1995, 1995 ECR II-1753, para. 25. If the Commission acts *after* the action under Article 232 was brought before the Court the action before the Court becomes devoid of purpose: *Asia Motors III*, CFI Sept. 18, 1992 ECR II-2285, para. 37; *IECC*, CFI Sept. 16, 1998, 1998 ECR II-3597, para. 15.

155. *Demo/Revox*, ECJ Oct. 11, 1983, 1983 ECR 3045, paras 19 and 22; *CICCE*, ECJ March 28, 1985, 1985 ECR 1105, para. 18; *Ladbroke II*, CFI Jan. 24, 1995, 1995 ECR II-115, paras 39–40. In *Asia Motors III*, CFI Sept. 18, 1992, 1992 ECR II-2285, the Court of First Instance rejected the action under Article 232 because it had become devoid of purpose in the light of the measures taken by the Commission after initiation of that action, but the Commission had to bear the costs.

Action on Complaint.

If the Commission considers a complaint, *prima facie*, well-founded, it may begin its investigation by demanding information from the respondent or third parties or carrying out investigations on their premises. It may also, especially in cases involving the commercial relations between the complainant and respondent, first send a copy of the complaint (with any confidential information deleted) to the respondent, asking for its reactions. According to its fact-finding the Commission may seek a settlement[156] before bringing formal proceedings against the respondent. Before taking a cease-and-desist order the Commission must inform the complainants of the Statement of Objections, thereby respecting business secrets, and give them the opportunity to comment.[157] Complainants are not entitled to assist at an oral hearing; however, the complainant may be, and is in practice often, invited.[158] Complainants are informed on the termination of preceedings initiated on their behalf[159] and may appeal a cease-and-desist order if its terms are not to their satisfaction; otherwise they may intervene.[160] If the Commission exempts the agreement concerned by the complaint, the complainant may appeal this decision because it implies the rejection of its complaint.[161] If the Commission decides to settle the case, the complainant may also appeal the settlement because it also implies the rejection of its complaint.[162]

Informal Complaints.

Some persons wish to inform the Commission about suspected infringements of Article 81 or 82 without having their identity revealed to the undertakings concerned by the allegations. These persons may contact the Commission but do not have any procedural rights. The Commission is bound to respect an informant's request for anonymity,[163] unless the request is manifestly unjustified.[164]

---

156. *See infra* section F.5.
157. Article 6 (1) of Regulation 773/2004. *See FEDETAB*, ECJ Oct. 29, 1980, 1980 ECR 3125, para. 34.
158. However, the Commission is not obliged to invite complainants to the oral hearing if it has given them an opportunity to make written submissions: *Deutscher Komponistenverband*, ECJ July 13, 1971, 1971 ECR 705. *See infra* section E.3.
159. Article 8 of Regulation 773/2004.
160. *See VBBB/VBVB*, ECJ Jan. 17, 1984, 1984 ECR 19.
161. *SABA I*, ECJ Oct. 25, 1977, 1977 ECR 1875; *Eurovision*, CFI July 11, 1996 ECR II-9. In a more recent case the Commission rejected the complaint by separate decision: *Whitbread*, D.Comm. Feb. 24, 1999, 1999 OJ L 88/26 (exemption) and March 11, 1999 (rejection of complaint).
162. *Philip Morris/Rothmans*, ECJ Nov. 17, 1987 ECR 4487, paras 23–24. *See Ufex*, ECJ April 3, 1999, C-199/97 (annulling a Commission decision rejecting a complaint without having investigated the possibly continuing harmful effect of the alleged infringement although it had formally been ceased). On the disclosure of defendants' evidence to complainants.
163. *Adams*, ECJ Nov. 7, 1985, 1985 ECR 3539.
164. Commission Notice on the Handling of Complaints, point 81. However, the *Adams* case referred to above shows the risk of damage claims in the case the Commission reveals the informant's identity.

4. Requests for Clearance

(a) Clearance under Regulation 17

Types of Clearance.
Regulation 17 provided for two possibilities of clearance by the Commission:

- negative clearance by which the Commission stated that on the known facts it found no ground for action on its part,[165] because Article 81 (1) is not infringed ('strong' negative clearance) or because the Commission uses its discretionary power in favor of non-intervention ('weak' negative clearance), and
- exemption by which the Commission declared the provisions of Article 81 (1) inapplicable according to Article 81 (3) because the procompetitive effects of the agreement outweighed the anticompetitive effects of the restrictions contained in it.

In both cases, the agreements for which clearance was sought were to be notified to the Commission by using the form A/B under Regulation 3385/94.[166] Clearance by decision was legally binding on national authorities and national courts (supremacy of Community law).[167] However, a comfort letter was not legally binding, but was of 'persuasive authority'.[168]

Advantages of Notification.
Notification not only rendered an agreement formally eligible for exemption, but also confered immunity from fines from the date of notification, should the Commission decide to condemn the agreement.[169] Another advantage of notification was that it afforded some defence against litigation in national courts. As an exemption could be backdated to the date of notification,[170] a national court could be more easily dissuaded from holding a notified agreement void under Article 81 (2). By contrast, if an agreement has not been notified and thus is not eligible

165. Article 2 of Regulation 17.
166. 1994 OJ L 377/28. Under Regulation 2843/98 a new single Form TR similar to Form A/B applies for the notification of restrictive agreements in road, rail and inland waterway transport sectors and in sea and air transport sectors under Regulations 1017/68, 4056/86 and 3975/87 (1998 OJ L 354/22).
167. *See* Chapter I.F.3.
168. *Guerlain*, ECJ July 10, 1980, 1980 ECR 2327, para. 13.
169. Article 15 (5) of Regulation 17. But not for any period before notification: *Pittsburgh Corning*, D.Comm. Nov. 23, 1972, 1972 OJ L 272/35, 39; *Hasselblad*, ECJ Feb. 21, 1984, 1984 ECR 883, paras 54–55. Conduct prohibited by Article 82 may also escape fines if it is related to a notified agreement: *United Brands*, D.Comm. Dec. 17, 1975, 1976 OJ L 95/1, 18. Regulation 1017/68 does not provide for immunity: *TACA*, CFI Feb. 28, 2002, 2002 ECR II-1125, para. 48.
170. *See* former Article 6 (1) of Regulation 17.

for exemption, judgment could be given against it in a national court without the possibility of a subsequent reversal of the judgment as a result of the grant of an exemption.[171]

(b) Clearance under Regulation 1/2003

Decisions Finding the Inapplicability of Article 81.
According to Article 10 of Regulation 1/2003 the Commission, acting on its own initiative, may find that Article 81 is not applicable to an agreement either because the conditions of Article 81 (1) are not fulfilled, or because the conditions of Article 81 (3) are satisfied, as the case may be, after amendments or commitments to order to meet the Commission's competition concerns.[172] The Commission may adopt a decision of a declaratory nature finding that Article 81 (1) or 82 are not infringed 'where the Community interest ... so requires', with the view of clarifying the law and ensuring its consistent application throughout the Community.[173] Possible examples include strategic alliances,[174] creation of infrastructure networks,[175] pools of intellectual property rights[176] or other forms of joint marketing,[177] the clearance of which is subject to likely free access commitments. Any decision must be preceded by a publication of a concise summary of the proposed course of action in order to hear interested third parties[178] and after having consulted the Advisory Committee.[179] However, there is no *right* of the parties to an agreement likely to fall within Article 81 (1), and for which they may wish clearance under Article 81 (3), to obtain a Commission finding on inapplicability of Article 81.

Effect of the Finding of Inapplicability.
According to Recital 14 to Regulation 1/2003 the Commission decision is of a declaratory nature. However, a decision by which a certain anticompetitive conduct is 'declared not liable' (a decision declaring that Article 81 or 82 does not apply to a certain conduct), precludes national competition authorities from taking another decision on the same conduct (*non bis in idem* principle).[180] Furthermore,

---

171. *See infra* section I.
172. Article 9 (1) of Regulation 1/2003.
173. Recital 14 to Regulation 1/2003.
174. *See Austrian Airlines/Lufthansa*, D.Comm. July 5, 2002, 2002 OJ L 242/15.
175. *See T-Mobile*, IP/02/1277; *Telenor/Canal+/Digital*, Article 19 (3) publication 2003 OJ C 149/16; *TACA II*, D.Comm. Nov. 14, 2002, 2003 OJ L 26/53.
176. *See IFTI Simulcasting*, D.Comm. Oct. 8, 2002, 2003 OJ L 107/58.
177. E.g. of natural gas (IP/03/566) or football rights (IP/03/655).
178. Article 27 (4) of Regulation 1/2003. Depending on the reaction of the parties, comments or complaints of interested third parties, the Commission may proceed to a comfort letter (in particular in case of amendment) or to initiating a formal proceeding, including a statement of objections, in order to adopt a cease-and-desist order.
179. Article 14 (1) of Regulation 1/2003.
180. *PVC II – LVM*, ECJ Oct. 15, 2002, 2002 ECR I-8375, para. 59.

a Commission decision stating that the conditions of Article 81 (3) are fulfilled constituted, under the Commission's sole competence for applying this provision, a 'positive, though indirect, action' within the meaning of the *Walt Wilhelm* judgment (deference to an exemption).[181] Under Regulation 1/2003 this results from the effects of the Commission's initiation of proceedings which precedes a decision of inapplicability. The Commission decision relieves the national authorities of their competence to apply Article 81 or 82[182] and prevents national courts from taking decisions 'running counter' to such a Commission decision.[183]

Informal Guidance.
According to Recital 38, the Commission may, at the request of individual undertakings, issue 'informal guidance' where a case gives rise to genuine uncertainty because it presents novel or unsolved questions.[184]

Cases where the Commission may Provide Informal Guidance.
The Commission may provide informal guidance only insofar as this is compatible with the Commission's enforcement priorities. According to the Commission Notice on Guidance Letters the issuing of guidance letters will only be considered if the following cumulative conditions are fulfilled:

- absence of sufficient case law,
- economic importance, in particular widespread economic usage in the market place[185] or important investments related to structural operations, such as non-full-function joint ventures;
- no need for further fact-finding.[186]

Request for Informal Guidance.
There is no form. However, the applicants must submit a memorandum to the Commission which clearly states:

- the identity of the undertakings concerned,
- the specific questions on which guidance is sought,
- a detailed reasoning why the request presents novel and unsolved questions,[187]
- full and exhaustive information on the parties, the relevant market, their market

181. *Walt Wilhelm*, ECJ Feb. 13, 1969, 1969 ECR 1, 13.
182. Article 11 (6) of Regulation 1/2003.
183. Article 16 (1) of Regulation 1/2003.
184. *See* Commission Notice on Informal Guidance (Guidance Letters), 2004 OJ C 101/78.
185. E.g. Community-wide selective distribution systems.
186. Point 8 (c) of the Commission Notice on Guidance Letters.
187. The Commission may not consider a request on issues raised in a case pending before the Court of Justice or the Court of First Instance or subject to proceedings pending before a national competition authority or a national court.

position and their most important competitors, which allows the Commission to adopt an informal assessment without the need of further investigation.[188]

Information given in submissions to the Commission in order to obtain informal guidance must be truthful and exhaustive. Incomplete, incorrect or misleading information is not subject to sanctions but may lead to reopening the proceedings according to Article 9 (2) of Regulation 1/2003, which may apply not only in the case of a formal decision but also in the case of informal guidance.

Processing of the Request.
The Notice on Guidance Letters gives the Commission a broad discretion:

- it may, possibly after consultation with the national competition authorities, issue the guidance letter which sets out a summary description of the facts (the information supplied by the applicant and, possibly, additional information at the Commission's disposal) and the principal reasoning.[189] The letter may be limited to part of the questions raised and may also include additional aspects; it is published on the DG COMP's web-site;[190]
- it may not pursue the request where it does not concern a novel or unresolved question or where the information supplied is incomplete or would require further fact-finding; in this case the applicant will be informed accordingly;
- it can use the information supplied in the request in subsequent procedures under Regulation 1/2003 on its own initiative with the view of adopting a decision finding an infringement and requiring that the infringement be brought to an end or terminating proceedings following commitments.[191]

Effects of Guidance Letters.
Guidance letters are primarily intended to help undertakings carry out an informed assessment themselves.[192] They are not legally binding but the Commission normally takes a guidance letter into account and will reconsider the case only in the light of any development in the case law of the European Courts or on the basis of new facts or elements (in particular received from complainants).[193] Unlike a notification under Article 15 (5) of Regulation 17, a request for informal guidance

188. Point 14 of the Commission Notice on Guidance Letters.
189. Example (still under Regulation 17 – but with continuing effect under Article 34 (2) of Regulation 1/2003): *Football Association Premier League*, D.Comm. April 30, 2004 2004 OJ C 115/3.
190. Point 22 of the Commission Notice on Guidance Letters.
191. *Ibid.*, point 25.
192. *Ibid.*, point 23.
193. *Ibid.*, point 25. The guidance letter is therefore similar to a negative clearance under Article 2 of Regulation 17 which is explicitly based 'on the basis of facts in its possession'.

does not provide for immunity from fines.[194] However, with respect to Regulation 1017/68, which does not provide for immunity from fines (unlike Regulation 17 and other transport regulations), the Commission interpreted the Court's ruling in the *TACA* case[195] by stating that, 'even if Regulation 1017/68 does not expressly provide for immunity from fines, it must be regarded as a general principle of EU competition law that formal notification has that consequence'.[196] It may therefore be argued that a request for informal guidance, which brings potentially anticompetitive conduct to the Commission's knowledge, is likely to create legitimate expectations to the extent that no fines will be imposed within the limits of the conduct described in the request where the Commission fails to inform the applicant within a reasonable time[197] of its intention to initiate proceedings on its own initiative.[198]

Transitional Provision of Regulation 1/2003.

Notifications made under Regulation 17 lapse as from May 1, 2004, whereas procedural steps and, in particular, exemptions granted under Regulation 17 continue to have effect.[199] This means that parties which submitted a notification under Regulation 17 cannot request an exemption decision but may, based on the information supplied in the notification, seek informal guidance from the Commission. The Commission is not prevented from continuing proceedings initiated under Regulation 17 with a view to finding and terminating an infringement of Article 81,[200] possibly subject to commitments,[201] or to issue a guidance (comfort) letter.

---

194. Moreover, notifications made under the current Regulation 17 lapse as from the date of application of the new regulation (May 1, 2004), which includes their effect of immunity: Article 34 (1) of Regulation 1/2003.
195. *TACA I (*Article 15 (6) decision), CFI Feb. 28, 2002, 2002 ECR II-1125, paras 48–53.
196. Thirty-second Report on Competition Policy, point 124. In TACA II (decision imposing fines) the Court of First Instance set aside the fines imposed by the Commission because the parties voluntarily submitted a notification, thereby revealing, on their own initiative, practices regarded by the Commission as constituting an abuse. Therefore, even if a notification does not give immunity from fines there was no justification for imposing a fine: CFI Sept. 30, 2003, T-191/98, paras 1597–1633.
197. *See*, with respect to complaints, *Guérin*, ECJ March 18, 1997, 1997 ECR I-1503, para. 37; Commission Notice on the Handling of Complaints, point 60.
198. *See CMA CGM/FETTCSA*, CFI March 19, 2003, T-213/00, para. 336. The Court of First Instance ruled, under Regulation 17, that the Commission 'cannot postpone indefinitely its position in relation to an application for clearance under Article 81 (3)': CFI June 3, 1999, 1999 ECR II-1757, para. 74, *aff'd* ECJ July 12, 2001, 2001 ECR I-5603.
199. Article 34 of Regulation 1/2003.
200. Article 7 of Regulation 1/2003.
201. Article 9 of Regulation 1/2003.

5. Initiation of Proceedings

Parallel Competences of Competition Authorities.
Regulation 1/2003 is based on a system of parallel competences in which all competition authorities have the power to apply Articles 81 and 82 and are responsible for an efficient allocation of cases which may be dealt with by:

- a single national competition authority, possibly with the assistance of the competition authority of another member state, or
- several national competition authorities in parallel, or
- the Commission.[202]

The basic principle is to find out which authority is the best placed for conducting an investigation, thereby taking account of the territory affected by the alleged infringement, the means of gathering evidence, the possibilities to effectively bring to an end the entire infringement or to sanction adequately the infringement, and, possibly, the need to develop Community competition policy or to ensure effective and coherent enforcement.[203]

Mechanism of Cooperation for the Purpose of Case Allocation.
Regulation 1/2003 provides for mutual exchange of information between competition authorities with the view of reaching an agreed case allocation and assistance, normally within a period of two months.[204] Where a case is already being dealt with by a competition authority the mutual consultation includes the stay or closure of proceedings or parts of a proceeding, in particular in cases of complaints.[205] The Commission is empowered to intiate proceedings on its own initiative with the effect of precluding national competition authorities from applying Articles 81 and 82 but is bound to consult the national authority in question beforehand.[206] The national authorities may ask for a meeting of the Advisory Committee; the Commission will normally not adopt a decision which is in conflict with the outcome of the consultation within the Advisory Committee.[207] The

202. Commission Notice on Cooperation within the Network of Competition Authorities, points 5 and 15: The Commission is better placed in particular where agreements cover more than three member states or when a new competition issue arises. *See* 2004 Draft Notice on Case Allocation in merger cases.
203. Commission Notice on Cooperation within the Network of Competition Authorities, point 8 and examples under points 10–15.
204. Article 11 of Regulation 1/2003; Commission Notice on Cooperation within the Network of Competition Authorities, points 16–19.
205. Commission Notice on Cooperation within the Network of Competition Authorities, points 20–25.
206. Article 11 (6) and Article 14 (7) of Regulation 1/2003.
207. Article 14 (7) of Regulation 1/2003; Commission Notice on Cooperation within the Network of Competition Authorities, points 56–57.

mechanism of cooperation applies to the entire proceeding, including investigation and the decision-making process.[208]

Significance of Formal Proceedings.
The Commission may decide to initiate proceedings with a view to adopting a decision persuant to Articles 7 to 10 of Regulation 1/2003 (finding and termination of infringement, interim measures, commitments and finding of inapplicability).[209] It is not necessary for the Commission to initiate proceedings before exercising its powers of investigation and before rejecting a complaint.[210] As under Regulation 17, the initiation of proceedings will normally be combined with the statement of objections,[211] which must be communicated to the parties[212] and the complainant.[213] The initiation of proceedings may be published.[214]

Implication on National Proceedings.
The initiation of proceedings is 'an authoritative act of the Commission, evidencing its intention of taking a decision'.[215] Pursuant to Article 11 (6) of Regulation 1/2003 the initiation of proceedings by the Commission relieves the national authorities of their competence to apply Articles 81 and 82.[216] Where a case is already being dealt with by a national competition authority (which informs the Commission without delay after commencing the first formal investigative measure[217]) the Commission can initiate proceedings on its initiative but must inform that member state on its *intention* to do so because of the precluding effect of Article 11 (6).[218] The member state in question may then request the Advisory Committee to include the case on the agenda for consultation on the case allocation.[219] However, the national courts remain competent to apply Articles 81 and 82 but must

---

208. Commission Notice on Cooperation within the Network of Competition Authorities, points 43–57.
209. Article 2 of Regulation 773/2004 (which replaces Regulations 3385/94 and 2842/98).
210. Article 2 (4) of Regulation 773/2004.
211. Article 10 of Regulation 773/2004. *See*, under Regulation 17: *Dyestuffs – ACNA*, ECJ July 12, 1972, 1972 ECR 933, paras 9–13.
212. Article 10 of Regulation 773/2004
213. Article 7 of Regulation 773/2004.
214. Article 2 (2) of Regulation 773/2004. The corresponding provision of Article 3 (2) of the previous Regulation 2842/98 has never been used.
215. *Haecht II*, ECJ Feb. 6, 1973, 1973 ECR 77; Commission Notice on Cooperation within the ECN, point 52. However, the initiation of proceedings is not subject to a separate appeal: *IBM*, ECJ Nov. 11, 1981, 1981 ECR 2639, paras 7–21.
216. 'Authorities' include judicial authorities in those countries where the national competition authority brings an action before a court that is separate and different from the prosecuting authority: Article 35 (3)–(4) of Regulation 1/2003.
217. Article 11 (3) of Regulation 1/2003.
218. Commission Notice on Cooperation within the Network of Competition Authorities, point 56.
219. Article 14 (7) of Regulation 1/2003.

avoid taking decisions which would conflict with a decision contemplated by the Commission and assess whether it is necessary to stay its proceedings.[220]

D. Fact-Finding

1. Introduction

Role of Compulsory Investigative Powers.
Much of the information used by the Commission in its competition enforcement is disclosed to it voluntarily by the parties,[221] reported by third parties,[222] or gleaned from the specialist press and publicly available reports and statistics. But the Commission could hardly perform its enforcement role effectively if it were restricted to information coming to it from these sources and if it were unable to verify or supplement that information. It has, therefore, been given active information-gathering powers.[223] The Commission's investigatory powers include:

- power to obtain information from the national competition authorities,[224]
- requests for information,[225]
- power to take statements (hearing of witnesses during or outside an on-the-spot-investigation),[226]
- on-the-spot investigations: inspections of the undertakings' premises,[227] and other premises,[228]
- sector enquiries.[229]

Investigations may also be carried out by a national competition authority in its own territory on its own behalf or at the Commission's request.[230] These powers can, if necessary, be backed by coercive measures in the form of formal orders

220. Article 16 (1) and Article 35 (3) of Regulation 1/2003. *See* Notice on the Cooperation between the Commission and the Courts of the EC Member States, points 11–14.
221. E.g., requests for informal guidance.
222. E.g., informal or anonymous complaints (*see supra* section C.3), allegations by informants, questions by members of the European Parliament.
223. With respect to sectors which are still excluded from the existing regulations (e.g. air transport between the Community and third countries), the general powers under Article 85 apply ('investigate cases of suspected infringement' of Articles 81 and 82), without, however, any compulsory investigatory measures.
224. Article 12 (1) of Regulation 1/2003.
225. Article 18 of Regulation 1/2003.
226. New powers conferred by Article 19 of Regulation 1/2003.
227. Article 20 of Regulation 1/2003.
228. New powers conferred by Article 21 of Regulation 1/2003.
229. Article 17 of Regulation 1/2003.
230. Article 22 of Regulation 1/2003.

and possible fines. The Commission's procedures in on-the-spot investigations have met with considerable legal challenge but have been largely vindicated and clarified by the Court of Justice.[231]

Use and Addressees of Powers.

These powers can be exercised at any stage in the procedure and any number of times in a particular case,[232] and it is a matter of the Commission's discretion whether it is necessary to employ them.[233] They are not confined to parties, i.e., the firms actually under investigation for an antitrust violation (or for clearance or exemption of their arrangements), but can be directed equally at third parties believed by the Commission to have information that may shed light on the case, such as competitors, traders or customers (consumers), provided they are 'firms' or 'associations'. Non-EC firms operating in the EC may also be required to produce information or documents relating to suspected infringements committed within the EC and may be subjected to on-the-spot investigations at premises situated within the EC.[234]

Suspected Infringement of Article 81 or 82 as Requirement for Exercising the Commission's Investigative Powers.

Any formal investigation must, according to Article 18 (2) and Article 20 (3)–(4) of Regulation 1/2003, specify the subject-matter, the legal basis and the 'purpose' of the request. This has been interpreted in the sense of Article 85, i.e. that the request has to explain briefly the 'suspected' infringement by providing *prima facie* reasoning. In order to show that it acts within the limits of its powers, the Commission must demonstrate, as the Court of Justice held in *Société Générale*:

> 'that the information requested of the undertakings concerned is justified and also to enable those undertakings to assess the scope of their duty to cooper-

231. Notably in *Brescia*, ECJ April 14, 1960, 1960 ECR 71; *National Panasonic*, ECJ June 26, 1980, 1980 ECR 2033; *AM&S*, ECJ May 18, 1982, 1982 ECR 1575; *Akzo II*, ECJ Sept. 23, 1986, 1986 ECR 2585; *Hoechst – PVC/LdPE*, ECJ Sept. 21, 1989, 1989 ECR 2859; *Dow Benelux*, ECJ 17 Oct. 1989, 1989 ECR 3137; *Dow Iberica*, ECJ Oct. 17, 1989, 1989 ECR 3165; *SEP*, Dec. 12, 1991, 1991 ECR II-1497; *Société Générale*, CFI March 8, 1995, 1995 ECR II-545; *Peugeot*, CFI May 2, 1997, 1997 ECR II-663.

232. The limits are those of Article 25 of Regulation 1/2003 (replacing Regulation 2988/74): a period of five years running upon the day on which the suspected infringement was committed or ceased, which can be interrupted by a Commission action up to a maximum period equal to twice the limitation period (Article 1 and 2 (3)). An investigation period of five years was held 'reasonable' in complex cases, such as *PVC II*, CFI April 20, 1999, 199 ECR II-931, paras 120–130; *aff'd* ECJ Oct. 15, 2002, 2002 ECR I-8375.

233. *Solvay*, ECJ Oct. 18, 1989, 1989 ECR 3255, para. 12–13; *Orkem*, ECJ Oct. 18, 1989, 1989 ECR 3283, paras 15–16; *Hoechst – PVC/LdPE*, ECJ Sept. 21, 1989, 1989 ECR 2859, para. 25.

234. For details, *see infra* Section D.5.

> ate while at the same time safeguarding their rights of defence. It follows that the Commission is entitled to require the disclosure only of information which may enable it to investigate putative infringements which justify the conduct of the enquiry and are set out in the request for information.'[235]

The Commission must clearly[236] indicate the alleged facts which it intends to investigate but is not obliged to disclose all the facts known. It must give a concise indication of the suspected infringement of the competition rules and of how the firm concerned is believed to be involved.[237] Accordingly, a decision requiring the addressee to supply all the information at its disposal 'in order to assess the extent to which the terms on which a French bank handles foreign Eurocheques might infringe Community rules on competition and that the request was made in the context of the application for an exemption for the New Package Deal Agreement concluded on …' was held as containing the 'essential constituents' required by Article 11 of Regulation 17.[238]

Confidentiality.

The information obtained may be used only for the purpose of the particular antitrust investigation concerned, and the usual confidentiality obligation applies to any such information that is technically or commercially sensitive. Consequently, firms cannot refuse to hand over evidence on the ground that it could be used against them for another offense[239] or that it is secret or confidential and should

235. *Société Générale*, CFI March 8, 1995, 1995 ECR II-545, para. 40 (with respect to requests for information). *See also Hoechst*, ECJ Sept. 21, 1989, 1989 ECR 2859, para. 29 (with respect to investigations); *SEP*, CFI Dec. 12, 1991, 1991 ECR II-1497, para. 25. It is not necessary to indicate which other firms are thought to be involved or what evidence the Commission has: *National Panasonic*, ECJ June 26, 1980, 1980 ECR 2033, paras 24–27, concerning the statement of reasons in a decision ordering an on-the-spot investigation.

236. The Commission must not give rise to any ambiguity, which can, however, be removed by subsequently providing further details: *ibid.*, paras 44 and 63; *Hoechst*, ECJ Sept. 21, 1989, 1989 ECR 2859, para. 41; *Dow Benelux*, ECJ Oct. 17, 1989, 1989 ECR 3137, para. 9.

237. The Commission decision must enable the undertakings to assess the scope of their duty to cooperate: *Strintzis – Greek Ferries,* CFI Dec. 11, 2003, T-65/9, point 44. *See National Panasonic*, ECJ June 26, 1980, 1980 ECR 2033, paras 24–27; *Hoechst – PVC/LdPE*, ECJ Sept. 21, 1989, 1989 ECR 2859, paras 39–43; *Dow Benelux*, ECJ Oct. 17, 1989, 1989 ECR 3137, paras 6–11; *Dow Iberica*, ECJ Oct. 17, 1989, 1989 ECR 3165, paras 43–48. *See also Hoechst – PVC/LdPE* (*Injunction*), ECJ March 26, 1987, 1987 ECR 1549; *Brescia*, ECJ April 14, 1960, 1960 ECR 71, para. 4. In answer to criticism that its failure to explain properly the subject matter of investigations was leading to 'fishing expeditions', the Commission promised in the Eleventh Report on Competition Policy, point 18, to be more specific.

238. *Société Générale*, CFI March 8, 1994, 1994 ECR II-545, para. 63. Such clarification prevents any 'fishing expedition'.

239. Obviously not on the ground that it is incriminating and could be used against them in a prosecution by the Commission for the antitrust offence it is investigating. *See infra* Section D at page 1064.

not be revealed to other parties or authorities.[240] However, an exception is made for correspondence with firms' lawyers.[241] Information obtained during an investigation that is *not* covered by the subject matter may not be used as such for other purposes, but the Commission is not prevented from using the knowledge as circumstantial evidence for initiating new proceedings and to undertake further verifications.[242]

2. Power to Obtain Information from the National Competition Authorities

The Commission is empowered to obtain information from the national competition authorities.[243] The information may include confidential information and can be used as evidence for the purpose of applying Article 81 or 82[244] and in respect of the subject-matter for which it was collected by the transmitting authority.[245]

3. Power to Obtain Information from Undertakings and Associations of Undertakings

Under Article 18 of Regulation 1/2003 the Commission is empowered to obtain information by simple request or by decision, whereas Article 11 of Regulation 17 provided for a two-stage procedure: first sending a simple request and to issue a formal compulsory order only if the addressee of the request refuses or fails to comply with an initial request. Under the new regulation the Commission may use both forms alternatively according the circumstances of the case. However, the Commission may proceed to a decision only where a refusal to comply with a simple request is to be expected.[246] Fines can be imposed for supplying incorrect

---

240. *SEP*, ECJ May 19, 1994, 1994 ECR I-1911, para. 41.
241. Attorney-client or 'legal professional' privilege; *see infra* section D.5. at page 1077.
242. *Dow Benelux*, ECJ Oct. 24, 1989, 1989 ECR 3150, para. 19. *See* with respect to information communicated by the Commission to national antitrust authorities: *Spanish Banks*, ECJ July 18, 1992, 1992 ECR I-4785, paras 35–39.
243. Article 18 (6) of Regulation 1/2003.
244. Information transmitted by the Commission can be used by the national competition authority for the purpose of applying national competition law only if the national law is applied in the same case and in parallel to Community competition law and if it does not lead to a different outcome: Article 12 (2). The use of information for imposing fines on natural persons (Article 12 (3) of Regulation 1/2003) is rather theoretical because it presupposes that the law of both the transmitting and the receiving authority foresee sanctions of a similar kind (which is not the case for EC competition rules).
245. Article 12 (1) and (2) of Regulation 1/2003. This is new; under Regulation 17 confidential information supplied by the Commission to national competition authorities could not be used as direct evidence: *Spanish Banks*, ECJ July 16, 1992, 1992 ECR I-4785, paras 39–43.
246. Example: *CSV*, D.Comm. June 25, 1976, 1976 OJ L 192/27 (refusal to produce documents because this might result in certain of CSV's employees facing criminal charges in Switzerland).

or misleading information in reply to both a discovery request or formal discovery order.[247]

Addressees.

As noted above, discovery can be ordered not only from the firms or associations whose arrangements the Commission is investigating, but also from third parties, such as competitors and customers, even if they themselves have triggered the investigation by a complaint. This also applies to accounting or consulting firms suspected of aiding and abetting their client firms in operating a cartel,[248] though perhaps not to accountants (or banks) providing routine services. Law firms can invoke attorney-client privilege against revealing information about a client's involvement in antitrust violations, just as their clients can invoke the privilege in relation to correspondence with the law firm.[249] Discovery requests must be answered by the owners of the undertakings, by persons authorized to represent the undertaking or association or a lawyer, provided he is duly authorized by the client and the client remains fully responsible for any incomplete, incorrect or misleading information.[250]

Non-EC Firms.

The Commission frequently uses its discovery powers to obtain information from non-EC firms about conduct within the EC. To avoid jurisdictional complications,[251] the discovery request or order is normally served on a business establishment situated within the EC, such as a sales office, branch or subsidiary.[252] If the firm has no EC office or subsidiary, the Commission writes directly

---

247. Article 23 (1) (a) of Regulation 1/2003. *See Telos*, D.Comm. Nov. 25, 1981, 1981 OJ L 58/19, 28; *Baccarat*, D.Comm. March 15, 1991, 1991 OJ L 97/16.

248. In *Fides*, D.Comm. Jan. 31, 1979, 1979 OJ L 57/33, the Commission refused to recognize the fiduciary relation of accountants to their clients as a ground for refusing to submit to an on-the-spot investigation in such circumstances. Indeed, Fides was later held jointly responsible for the infringement: *Italian Cast Glass*, D.Comm. Dec. 17, 1980, 1980 OJ L 383/19, 26.

249. *See infra* section D.6. This would not apply if the law firm were involved in running a cartel.

250. Article 18 (4) of Regulation 1/2003. Less clear under Article 11 (4) of Regulation 17.

251. On the vexed question of the extraterritorial application and enforcement of antitrust law, *see* D. M. Jacobs, 'Extraterritorial Application of Competition Laws: An English View', 1979 *International Lawyer*, 645; 'Problems arising from Extraterritorial Application of Competition Laws', 1980 ECLR 199; Torremans, 'Extraterritorial Application of EC and U.S. Competition Law', 1996–21 ELRev 280. *See* the confirmation of the 'extraterritorial' application of the EC merger control regulation, provided there are foreseeable, immediate and substantial effects within the Community in: *Gencor/Lonrho*, CFI March 25, 1999, 1999 ECR II-753, para. 92.

252. Either on the business establishment alone or on it and the registered office of the foreign company. Service of procedural documents, such as statements of objections and decisions, has been judged by the Court of Justice to have been properly effected both when it was made through branches or subsidiaries in the EC (*ICI-Dyestuffs*, ECJ July 14, 1972, 1972 ECR 619, paras 34–44) and when it was made directly on the registered office of the foreign company

to the head office of the foreign company.[253] In this case, too, a formal information request may be made if the information is required for clearance of an agreement to which the non-EC company is a party; otherwise, an informal request without reference to the Commission's powers will be sent.

Extent of Inquiry.

The information required must be 'necessary' for, or 'conducive' to, the enforcement of the competition rules. What is necessary is a matter for the Commission's discretion, and the Commission does not have to justify in detail the need for the information, provided that the demand respects the limits of proportionality and reasonableness and is therefore not manifestly excessive or unreasonable.[254] The request has to stick to specific questions of fact, and avoid questions about the firm's involvement in a restrictive practice which are so broad as to be tantamount to asking for a confession.[255] On the other hand, the information demanded need not be confined to the firm's own business, but may extend to questions about the background of the industry and the market as far as the requested information is available to, or can be estimated by, the addressee. Firms cannot refuse to produce information on the basis of arguments on the merits of the case.[256] The request for information is normally not published but may be published in cases of general interest.[257]

(*Geigy-Dyestuffs*, ECJ July 14, 1972, 1972 ECR 787, paras 10–12; *Continental Can*, ECJ Feb. 21, 1973, 1973 ECR 215, paras 9–10). Documents are properly served when they are put into the possession of the addressee, wherever service takes place: *ALMA*, ECJ Dec. 10, 1957, 1957 ECR 95, 99.

253. In accordance with OECD Council Recommendation Concerning Cooperation between Member Countries on Restrictive Business Practices Affecting International Trade, July 27–28, 1995, C(95)130 final, the government of the foreign company's country and those of other non-EC countries affected would be informed. Any formal request for information will normally *not* indicate penalties.
254. *SEP*, CFI Dec. 12, 1991, 1991 ECR II-1497, paras 25–26. *Cf.* the similar investigative powers under Article 47 of the ECSC Treaty (which are also expressed as being exercisable where 'necessary' or 'required') in *Brescia*, ECJ April 14, 1960, 1960 ECR 71, paras 1–4; *San Michele*, ECJ Dec. 14, 1962, 1962 ECR 449, 461–462. *See also Solvay*, ECJ Oct. 18, 1989, 1989 ECR 3255, paras 12–13; *Orkem*, Oct. 18, 1989, 1989 ECR 3283, paras 15–16.
255. This would infringe the rights of the defence: *Solvay*, ECJ Oct. 18, 1989, 1989 ECR 3255, paras 29–37; *Orkem*, ECJ Oct. 18, 1989, 1989 ECR 3283, paras 32–41; *Otto/Postbank*, ECJ Nov. 10, 1993, 1993 ECR I-5683, para. 12.
256. As in *CICG-ZVEI/ZPU*, D.Comm. Feb. 1, 1971, 1971 OJ L 34/13, 15; *RAI/Unitel*, D.Comm. May 26, 1978, 1978 OJ L 157/39; *Fire Insurance* (*Discovery*), D.Comm. Dec. 9, 1981, 1982 OJ L 80/36; *Olympic Airways*, D.Comm. Jan. 23, 1985, 1985 OJ L 46/51.
257. E.g. *CSV*, D.Comm. June 25, 1976, 1976 OJ L 192/27.

Discovery of Documents.
The information required may be included in documents. The Commission therefore can, and does, require the production of copies of documents.[258]

Self-incrimination.
There is no right of the addressee of the enquiry to refuse discovery of information or documents because they are incriminating, i.e., may be used to establish, against itself or another undertaking, the existence of anticompetitive conduct,[259] and would expose the firm to fines by the Commission or administrative penalties or civil damages in member states. In order to preserve 'l'effet utile' of the Commission's investigatory powers[260] and its ability to prosecute antitrust infringements the Commission can oblige companies to provide all information concerning *facts* and related documents.[261] However, the Commission may not ask questions that may undermine the rights of defence of the undertaking concerned by compelling to provide it with answers which might involve an *admission* on its part of the existence of an infringement which it is incumbent upon the Commission to prove,[262] nor can the refusal of discovery be used as evidence.[263] In *Orkem*

258. *Solvay*, ECJ Oct. 18, 1989, 1989 ECR 3255, paras 10–11 and 31; *Orkem*, ECJ Oct. 18, 1989, 1989 ECR 3283, paras 13–14 and 34.
259. *Orkem*, ECJ Oct. 18, 1989, 1989 ECR 3255, para. 34; *Seamless Steel Tubes – Mannesmann*, Feb. 20, 2001, 2001 ECR II-729, paras 84–88. Recital 23 to Regulation 1/2003.
260. *Seamless Steel Tubes – Mannesmann*, Feb. 20, 2001, 2001 ECR II-729, para. 65.
261. *Ibid.* This principle was finally established in *Orkem*, ECJ Oct. 18, 1989, 1989 ECR 3283, paras 27–31; *Solvay*, ECJ Oct. 18, 1989, 1989 ECR 3255, paras 24–28; *Société Générale*, CFI March 8, 1995, 1995 ECR II-545, para. 74, in which the Court of Justice pointed out that neither the national laws of member states of the EC nor Article 6 of the European Convention for the Protection of Human Rights and Fundamental Freedoms (4 Nov. 1950, 213 U.N.T.S. 221) nor Article 14 of the International Covenant on Civil and Political Rights (19 Dec. 1966, 999 U.N.T.S. 171; *see Funke*, European Court of Human Rights, 25 Feb. 1993, para. 44; *Murray*, Court of Human Rights, 17 Dec. 1996, para. 47) provide for a privilege against self-incrimination by corporations being investigated for non-criminal antitrust violations. The right not to give evidence against oneself or to confess guilt relates only to *persons* accused of a criminal offence in court proceedings and thus has no bearing on proceedings against *firms*. Under EC law, unlike the U.S. and German antitrust laws (*see* §59 (5) of the German Act Against Restrictions of Competition), only firms (not their individual executives or officers) are liable to penalties for antitrust infringements: *see* Stessens, 'The Obligation to Produce Documents Versus the Privilege Against Self-incrimination: Human Rights Protection Extended Too Far?' (1997) 22 ELRev 45. The privilege against self-incrimination for the purpose of an EC antitrust investigation, which has been successfully pleaded as a defence to discovery *inter partes* in UK civil proceedings, does not apply to discovery ordered by a statutory authority such as the Commission. However, it might present an obstacle to civil actions in UK courts under EC competition law: *see infra* section I.2.
262. *Orkem*, ECJ Oct. 18, 1989, 1989 ECR 3255, para. 35; *Seamless Steel Tubes – Mannesmann*, Feb. 20, 2001, 2001 ECR II-729, para. 74; *PVC – LVM*, ECJ Oct. 15, 2002, 2002 ECR I-8375, para. 279.
263. *PVC II*, CFI April 20, 1999, 1999 ECR II-931, para. 489 ('The refusal to reply … cannot in

the Court of Justice ruled that the Commission may not ask for clarification on 'every step or concerted measure which may have been envisaged or adopted to support such price initiatives' (which is tantamount to requiring a confession), whereas it may ask for information of a purely factual nature, e.g., on the circumstances in which meetings are held, on participants and documents relating thereto.[264] Recital 23 to Regulation 1/2003 affirms the power of the Commission to require such information by decision under Article 18 (3):

> 'When complying with a decision of the Commission, undertakings cannot be forced to admit that they have committed an infringement, but they are in any event obliged to answer factual questions and to provide documents, even if this information may be used to establish against them or against another undertaking the existence of an infringement.'[265]

The admittedly increased danger of prosecution or civil damages before national courts or authorities which an EC antitrust conviction might bring also is not a valid defence as it, too, would defeat the effective enforcement of EC antitrust law.[266] More controversial is the right to refuse discovery on the basis that discovery itself is against the law of a non-EC country and would render the company or its officers liable to criminal sanctions there.[267] In the *CSV* case where a Dutch company refused to produce documents because this would have resulted in certain of its employees facing criminal charges in Switzerland, the Commission was unsympathetic to such claims.[268]

---

itself constitute proof of an undertaking's participation in an agreement.'), *aff'd LVM – PVC*, ECJ Oct. 15, 2002, 2002 ECR I-8375, paras 258–292.

264. *Orkem*, ECJ Oct. 18, 1989, 1989 ECR 3255, paras 37–38. *See also Société Générale*, CFI March 8, 1995, 1995 ECR II-545, para. 74.
265. It is therefore correct to draw a distinction between a simple request for information and a decision requiring information, which additionally subjects an undertaking to a penalty: *LVM – PVC*, ECJ Oct. 15, 2002, 2002 ECR I-8375, para. 279.
266. *SEP*, CFI Nov. 21, 1990, 1990 ECR II-649. Although the Commission and national authorities are prohibited by Article 28 (1) and (2) of Regulation 1/2003 from using themselves, or handing over to other authorities or courts for use, in other proceedings, evidence which came into their possession in the course of the particular EC antitrust proceedings concerned, the summary of the evidence in the published Commission decision recording the conviction and the fact of the conviction itself may well greatly assist a national prosecution or damages claim.
267. When Regulation 17 was being drafted, the EEC Assembly proposed including in Article 11 a right for persons to refuse to provide information that might expose them to 'penal sanctions', but the Council did not take up the suggestion, because only businesses, and not individual employees or directors, are liable to penalties under EC antitrust law.
268. *CSV (Discovery)*, ECJ June 25, 1976, 1976 OJ L 192/27.

Claims of Fiduciary Duty or Confidentiality.
Breach of fiduciary duty[269] or of a trade association's rules if information is disclosed[270] is likewise not accepted as a valid defence to discovery. Nor is confidentiality, as the Commission and national authorities are not prevented from using confidential information as evidence for proving an infringement of Article 81 or 82, provided the rights of the undertakings concerned of being heard are respected.[271]

Discovery Requests.
Discovery 'requests' are made in the form of a letter containing a list of questions to be answered and of documents to be supplied.[272] The signing of information requests is delegated to a Director of one of the Directorates of DG COMP. The letter must refer to the legal basis, specify the purpose for which the information or documents are required and state the penalties for supplying incorrect information.[273] A time limit is set for supplying the information which, depending on the estimated amount of work involved in assembling the information, can be between two and four weeks. An extension is granted if there are good reasons. Discovery requests may be made orally, provided it is confirmed in writing.[274]

Formalities of Discovery Orders.
A discovery 'order' must specify the information required, including the purpose,[275] set a time limit for supplying it, warn the company of the risk of fines for refusal,[276] and inform it of its right to judicial review of the order by the European Court of Justice.[277] The making of discovery orders is delegated to the member of the Commission responsible for competition.[278] The addressee may apply to the

269. *Fides*, D.Comm. Jan. 31, 1979, 1979 OJ L 57/33. But *cf.* legal professional privilege, *infra* section D.5.
270. *Fédération Nationale de l'Industrie de la Chaussure de France*, D.Comm. Oct. 27, 1982, 1982 OJ L 319/12.
271. *See Hoffmann-La Roche*, ECJ Feb. 13, 1979, 1979 ECR 461, para. 11.
272. *Seamless Steel Tubes – Mannesmann*, CFI Feb. 20, 2001, 2001 ECR II-729, paras 71–72.
273. Article 18 (2) of Regulation 1/2003.
274. *Kish Glass*, CFI March 30, 2000, 2000 ECR II-1885, para. 38, *aff'd* ECJ Oct 18, 2001, 2001 ECR I-7759.
275. *Solvay*, ECJ Oct. 18, 1989, 1989 ECR 3255, paras 5–9; *Orkem*, ECJ Oct. 18, 1989, 1989 ECR 3283, paras 8–11. This does not make the investigation order into a statement of objections against which the firm must be allowed to defend itself: *ibid.*
276. The amount of the fine per day of refusal and the date from which fines will be imposed may already be stated in the order, as in CSV, D.Comm. June 25, 1976, 1976 OJ L 192/27; *Baccarat*, D.Comm. March 15, 1991, 1991 OJ L 97/16; *Eurocheques*, D.Comm. April 1, 1993 (not published).
277. Article 18 (3) of Regulation 1/2003.
278. Approved for decisions ordering investigations in *Akzo II*, ECJ Sept. 23, 1986, 1986 ECR 2585, paras 280.

Court of Justice for judicial review of the order, but unless the Court granted a stay of execution, the addressee would meanwhile have to comply.[279]

Comply with the Discovery Request or Order.

Information which the firm does not wish to have disclosed to third parties should be marked and, preferably, placed in a separate annex. As the firm can be fined for applying incorrect information, the reply should be prepared carefully and authorized at the highest level.[280]

Liaison with Member States.

The national competition authority of the member state in which the addressee of the request is based must be sent a copy of the request for information or the order, but there is no requirement to consult the national authorities.[281] There is no provision for the Commission also to send the member state a copy of the reply but, if the Commission later contemplates a formal decision of some kind, the replies to discovery requests or orders may well be among the main documents of the case that have to be shown to all member states under the consultation requirements.[282]

Sanctions.

Supplying incorrect or misleading in formation or refusal to supply information or documents within the time limit was subject to fines ranging from EUR 100 to 5,000 under Article 15 of Regulation 17,[283] but is substantially higher, up to 1% of the total turnover under Article 23 (1) of Regulation 1/2003.[284] 'Incorrect' is

279. *SEP*, CFI Nov. 21, 1990, 1990 ECR II-649.

280. Article 23 (1) of Regulation 1/2003. However, it is free to retract or correct statements provided this is done promptly: *United Brands*, ECJ Feb. 14, 1978, 1978 ECR 207, paras 259–268.

281. Article 18 (5) of Regulation 1/2003.

282. Article 12 (1) of Regulation 1/2003. Confidential documents are not automatically excluded because the national authorities have to take the necessary measures to ensure such documents not to be disclosed (Article 28 (2) of Regulation 1/2003). However, this protection may be insufficient in cases where the member state is a major shareowner of a competitor and might be tempted to use the confidential information (conflict of interests): *SEP*, CFI May 19, 1994, 1994 ECR I-1911, paras 27–31, correcting CFI Dec. 12, 1991, 1991 ECR II-1497, paras 57–60. The Commission may therefore withhold such confidential information: *SEP*, CFI May 3, 1991, 1991 ECR I-2043.

283. E.g., *Baccarat*, D.Comm. March 15, 1991, 1991 OJ L 97/16 (ECU 10,000); *Anheuser-Busch*, D.Comm. Dec. 14, 1999, 2000 OJ L 49/17 (EUR 3,000). *See also Theal/Watts*, D.Comm. Dec. 21, 1976, 1977 OJ L 39/19; *National Panasonic* (*Belgium*), D.Comm. Dec. 11, 1981, 1982 OJ L 113/18; *Telos*, D.Comm. Nov. 25, 1981, 1982 OJ L 58/19; *National Panasonic* (*France*), D.Comm. Dec. 11, 1981, 1982 OJ L 211/32 (ECU 5,000 each); *Peugeot*, D.Comm. Sept. 25, 1986, 1986 OJ L 295/19 (ECU 4,000); *Sécretama*, D.Comm. Dec. 19, 1990, 1991 OJ L 35/23 (ECU 5,000).

284. Similarly Article 14 (1) of Regulation 139/2004 on Merger Control.

taken to mean evasive or misleading answers[285] as well as untruthful statements.[286] Periodic penalty payments up to 5% of the average daily turnover per day may be imposed in order to compel submission of complete and correct information requested by decision.[287] Decisions imposing procedural fines must be preceded by the usual procedures to safeguard the rights of the defence and third parties and consultation of the member states.[288]

Judicial Review of Information Orders.
The addressee may apply to the Court of Justice for judicial review of the order, but unless the Court granted a stay of execution, the addressee would meanwhile have to comply.[289] An order may be appealed even if the information has already been supplied and a final decision adopted.[290] In the case of a successful appeal the information supplied under the illegal request cannot be used as evidence of an infringement of Article 81 or 82. However, the decision may be upheld if the remaining evidence is sufficient.

4. Power to Take Statements

Powers to Interview Persons.
Unlike Regulation 17, the new Regulation 1/2003 empowers the Commission to interview any natural or legal person who consents to be interviewed for the purpose of collecting information relating to the subject-matter of an investigation.[291] The interview may be conducted by any means including telephone or electronic means. However, the Commission has no power to summon witnesses nor to hear them under oath and may not impose fines in the case of incorrect or misleading information.[292] If the Commission makes a record of the statement it shall make it available to the person interviewed, who may communicate any correction.[293]

---

285. *See AKZO*, D.Comm. Oct. 14, 1994, 1994 OJ L 294/31.
286. *Telos*, D.Comm: Nov. 25, 1981, 1982 OJ L 58/19.
287. Article 24 (1) (d) of Regulation 1/2003 (under Article 16 of Regulation 17 the periodic penalty payments were limited to EUR 1,000 per day). E.g. *Baccarat*, D.Comm. March 15, 1991, 1991 OJ L 97/16; in this case a lower fine than the maximum to which the firm was liable was imposed because of extenuating circumstances, namely ECU 10,000 instead of ECU 43,000 – Article 16 (2) of Regulation 17.
288. *See infra* sections F.6.(e).
289. *See SEP*, CFI Nov. 21, 1990, 1989 ECR II-649.
290. *See Seamlesss Steel Tubes – Mannesmann*, CFI Feb. 20, 2001, 2001 ECR II-729.
291. Article 19 (1) of Regulation 1/2003; Article 3 of Regulation 773/2004. Regulation 17 did not provide for such powers.
292. *See* Article 23 (1) (a) of Regulation 1/2003 (no possibility of imposing fines on natural persons).
293. Article 3 (3) of Regulation 773/2004.

Oral Questions during Inspections.
The Commission is empowered to ask, during inspections, representatives or staff of the undertaking in question for oral explanations.[294] Where a member of the staff is not authorized to make statements on behalf of the undertaking the Commission sets a time-limit within which the undertaking can communicate any rectification to be added to the statement made by such member of staff.[295]

No Sanctions in the Case of Incorrect or Misleading Information.
The Commission may impose fines up to 1% of the annual turnover on the *undertaking*:

- where the undertaking gives an incorrect or misleading answer,
- where the undertaking fails to rectify within the time-limit an incorrect, incomplete or misleading answer given by a member of its staff, or
- the undertaking fails or refuses to provide a complete answer on facts relating to the subject matter and purpose of the inspection ordered by decision.[296]

However, unlike the merger control regulation,[297] the Commission may not impose sanctions on natural persons who give incorrect or misleading information or refuse to give a complete answer during the inspection. If a member of the staff of the undertaking that is being investigated gives incorrect or misleading information or refuses to provide a complete answer that undertaking may be held responsible and subject to a fine (but not to penalty payments). The undertaking may, in any event, be interested to cooperate with the Commission in order to benefit of the leniency program.[298]

5. On-the-Spot Investigations

Different Uses of Discovery and Investigation Powers.
The Commission is empowered to conduct all necessary inspections of undertakings or associations of undertakings.[299] Whereas written discovery of information is typically employed to elicit particulars of contractual arrangements and firms' market position, often in cases where no adverse decision is contemplated, on-the-spot investigations are usually carried out to obtain direct evidence of hard-core

294. Article 20 (4) of Regulation 1/2003; Article 4 of Regulation 773/2004. Under Article 14 (1) (e) of Regulation 17 the Commission was empowered to ask for oral explanations, however, without any sanction.
295. Article 4 (3) of Regulation 773/2004.
296. Article 23 (1) (d) of Regulation 1/2003.
297. Articles 14 and 15 of Regulation 139/2004.
298. Commission Notice on immunity from fines and reduction of fines in cartel cases, 2002 OJ C 45/3.
299. Article 18 of Regulation 1/2003.

infringements such as cartels. There are cases where both discovery and on-the-spot investigations are used in tandem. But the powers remain basically distinct and independent. For example, the Commission need not attempt to obtain the evidence it seeks by discovery before it sends in the inspectors.[300]

Differences of Procedure.
The different circumstances of discovery and on-the-spot investigations account for some important differences of procedure. One is the possibility of surprise; the Commission need not give the firm prior notice of an on-the-spot investigation.[301] Another difference is that although there is provision for two types of warrant: (1) a non-compulsory 'authorization to investigate', and (2) a compulsory order, an order can be made without first attempting the investigation under a simple warrant.[302]

Subjects of Investigation.
As with discovery, there is no restriction on the nature of the firms or associations that can be investigated. These can include third parties whose own conduct is not under investigation and the EC establishments of non-EC firms. Likewise, there is no restriction on the number of times in a particular case or the stage in the procedure at which the powers can be exercised.[303] There is analogous provision for fines for incomplete production of files or for refusal to submit to an investigation for which a formal order has been made.[304]

Choice between Announced or Surprise Investigations, under Warrant or Order.
As already noted, investigations may or may not be announced to the firm beforehand,[305] and the inspectors may come armed with either a non-compulsory warrant ('authorization to investigate')[306] or a formal investigation order ('deci-

300. *See Brescia*, ECJ April 14, 1960, 1960 ECR 71, para. 3.
301. Unannounced investigations (or 'dawn raids', as they are rather sensationally called – the inspectors in fact come during office hours) have been held by the Court of Justice not to infringe fundamental rights: *National Panasonic*, ECJ June 26, 1980, 1980 ECR 2033, paras 17–20.
302. Unlike the two-stage procedure for discovery under Regulation 17. *See National Panasonic*, ECJ June 26, 1980, 1980 ECR 2033, paras 8–16; *Hoechst – PVC/LdPE*, ECJ Sept. 21, 1989, 1989 ECR 2859, para. 22.
303. The powers can even be used after the sending of the statement of objections: *Dyestuffs – Francolor*, ECJ July 14, 1972, 1972 ECR 851, paras 15–18. In many cases, especially where surprise is called for, investigations are carried out simultaneously on firms in different locations and often different countries.
304. Article 23 (1) of Regulation 1/2003.
305. Usually by telephone.
306. Article 20 (3) of Regulation 1/2003 ('Authorization to investigate').

sion').[307] Announced investigations are conducted under warrant. Investigation orders are issued for surprise investigation or investigations of which the firm has been warned if it has indicated that it may not submit to a warrant.[308]

Issuance of Warrants and Orders.

Warrants are signed by the Director-General of DGCOMP on the authority of the member of the Commission responsible for competition, while investigation orders ('decisions') are issued and normally signed by the latter personally.[309] The authorities of the member state in which the investigation is to take place must be informed of the investigation (and of the inspectors' identity) beforehand if only a warrant is being issued and must be 'consulted' beforehand if a formal order for the investigation is being made.[310] The firm investigated has no right to put its case against the issue of an investigation order before the order is made.[311]

Specification of Subject Matter and Purpose in Warrants and Decisions.

Both warrants and orders must state the 'subject matter and purpose' of the investigation.[312] The statement of subject matter and purpose in a warrant is apt to be briefer[313] than in an order, which must, in its quality of a 'decision', satisfy the requirement of reasoning under Article 253 of the EC Treaty.[314] However, the Commission need not adduce detailed evidence for its suspicions,[315] give a precise definition of the relevant market,[316] or provide a list of the documents it wishes

307. Article 20 (4) of Regulation 1/2003.
308. *See* Guerrin, 'Changement important dans la structure de la DG IV', DG IV News Letter, 1999–1, 22.
309. The delegation of power to take decisions ordering on-the-spot investigations to the Commissioner responsible for competition policy was upheld by the Court in *Akzo II*, ECJ Sept. 23, 1986, 1986 ECR 2585, paras 28–30. *See also Hoechst – PVC/LdPE*, ECJ Sept. 21, 1989, 1989 ECR 2859, paras 44–47; *Dow Iberica*, ECJ Oct. 17, 1989, 1989 ECR 3165, paras 57–59.
310. Article 20 (5) and (6) of Regulation 1/2003. The consultation may be informal, and even by telephone: *Akzo II*, ECJ Sept. 23, 1986, 1986 ECR 2585, paras 21–24. The requirement for consultation does not mean that the Commission would have to follow the member state's advice if it were to oppose the investigation.
311. Surprise is legitimate: *National Panasonic*, ECJ June 26, 1980, 1980 ECR 2033, para. 21. Consequently, there are no statements of objections or other defence rights at this stage. But *cf. infra* this section re judicial review.
312. Article 20 (3) of Regulation 1/2003.
313. However, in investigations conducted under warrant the inspectors are prepared to elaborate on the information given in it.
314. *See Akzo II*, ECJ Sept. 23, 1986, 1986 ECR 2585, paras 18–20.
315. *Dow Benelux*, ECJ Oct. 17, 1989, 1989 ECR 3137, paras 13 and 16. *See also Hoechst – PVC/LdPE*, ECJ Sept. 21, 1989, 1989 ECR 2859, para. 41; *Dow Iberica*, ECJ Oct. 17, 1989, 1989 ECR 3165, para. 45.
316. *Dow Benelux*, ECJ Oct. 17, 1989, 1989 ECR 3137, paras 6 and 10; *Dow Iberica*, ECJ Oct. 17, 1989, 1989 ECR 3165, paras 43, 46 and 50–51.

to see.[317] Nor must it state in a formal order why this procedure (as opposed to an investigation under warrant only) is thought necessary; this is a matter for the Commission's discretion.[318]

Other Formalities.

Warrants state the names of the Commission's inspectors authorized to conduct the investigation and warn of fines for incomplete production of documents.[319] Formal orders must in addition specify the date on which the investigation is to commence, warn of fines for refusal to submit to the investigation, and inform the company of its right to judicial review.[320] An identical order can be served on several companies believed to be involved in the same infringement which are to be investigated simultaneously. Investigation orders issued following a refusal to submit to investigation voluntarily under a warrant are occasionally published.[321]

Cooperation in Good Faith with National Authorities.

Community authorities and national authorities are called upon to cooperate in the attainment of the objectives of the Treaty by the coordinated exercise of their respective duties,[322] which applies in particular in the case of inspections.[323] The officials or other accompanying persons authorized by the Commission shall be actively assisted by officials or persons authorized or appointed by the competition authority of the member state in whose territory the inspection is to be conducted. They must afford them the necessary assistance, requiring where appropriate the assistance of the police or of an equivalent enforcement authority, so as to enable them to conduct the inspection.

Authorization by a National Judicial Authority.

If the assistance of the national competition authority requires authorization from a judicial authority according to national rules, such authorization must be applied for. Such authorization may also be applied for as a precautionary measure even if the national rules do not so require.[324] To this effect the Commission must *give notice* of the inspection (without decision) to the competent authority of the mem-

317. *Hoechst – PVC/LdPE*, ECJ Sept. 21, 1989, 1989 ECR 2859, para. 27; *Dow Benelux*, ECJ Oct. 17, 1989, 1989 ECR 3137, para. 38.
318. *National Panasonic*, ECJ June 26, 1980, 1980 ECR 2033, paras 28–30.
319. Article 20 (3) of Regulation 1/2003.
320. Article 20 (4) of Regulation 1/2003.
321. As in *Fides*, D.Comm. Jan. 31, 1979, 1979 OJ L 57/33; *AM&S*, D.Comm. July 6, 1979, 1979 OJ L 199/31.
322. Duty to cooperate in good faith as enshrined in Article 10 of the Treaty and Article 11 (1) of Regulation 1/2003.
323. *Roquettes Frères*, ECJ Oct. 22, 2002, 2002 ECR I-9011, paras 30–32.
324. Article 20 (7) of Regulation 1/2003. Commission Notice on the cooperation between the Commission and the national courts, 2004 OJ C 101/54, points 38–41.

ber state in whose territory it is to be conducted[325] but must *consult* that authority before it takes a decision to proceed to inspections.[326] Where authorization of a national court is required the national court must control that the Commission decision is authentic and that the coercive measures envisaged are neither arbitrary nor excessive (proportionality test).[327] As clarified by the Court in the *Roquettes Frères* case[328] the Commission must ensure that the national court has at its disposal all the information necessary to carry out the review, including:

- a description of the essential features of the suspected infringement, at the very least an indication of the market thought to be affected and of the nature of the suspected restrictions of competition,
- explanations concerning the manner in which the undertaking at which the coercive measures are aimed is thought to be involved in the infringement in question,
- detailed explanations showing that the Commission possesses solid factual information and evidence providing grounds for suspecting such infringement on the part of the undertaking concerned,
- as precise as possible an indication of the evidence sought, of the matters to which the investigation must relate and of the powers conferred on the Community investigators,
- a specification of the premises to be inspected, and in the case of non-business premises by stating reasons that have led the Commission to conclude that books or other records related to the business and to the subject matter of the investigation are being kept at other premises,[329] and
- in the event of a precautionary measure, in order to overcome any opposition on the part of the undertaking concerned, explanations enabling the national court to satisfy itself that, if authorization for the coercive measures were not granted on precautionary grounds, it would be impossible, or very difficult, to establish the facts amounting to the infringement.[330]

However, the national judicial authority may not call into question the necessity for the inspection nor demand that it be provided with the information (evidence) in the Commission's file; the lawfulness of the Commission decision is subject to review only by the Court of Justice.[331]

325. Article 20 (3) of Regulation 1/2003.
326. Article 20 (4) of Regulation 1/2003.
327. Article 20 (8) of Regulation 1/2003, which follows the administrative practice under Article 14 (6) of Regulation 17.
328. *Roquettes Frères*, ECJ Oct. 22, 2002, 2002 ECR I-9011, para. 99; *Schneider*, CFI Oct. 22, 2002, 2002 ECR II-4091, paras 30–36.
329. Article 21 (2) of Regulation 1/2003.
330. *See also* Recital 27 to Regulation 1/2003.
331. Article 20 (8) of Regulation 1/2003.

Submission to On-the-Spot Investigation.

On arriving at the offices of the firm to be investigated, the Commission inspectors, accompanied by an official from the national competition authority,[332] identify themselves at the reception desk and ask to see a senior manager. They present the manager with the warrant ('authorization to investigate') and investigation order, if any,[333] plus an explanatory note setting out the rights and duties of the company in relation to the investigation and explaining the procedure. If the inspectors only have a warrant, the manager is asked whether the company submits to the investigation. This submission cannot be withdrawn in the course of the investigation. If, after agreeing to submit, the firm later refuses to show certain files or open certain desks, it is liable to a fine for incomplete production of records,[334] for incomplete access to the company's premises[335] or for refusal of copying documents.[336] A similar refusal in the course of an investigation under a formal order would count as a constructive refusal to submit to the investigation and also render the firm liable to a fine. If the company refuses to submit to an investigation for which the inspectors only have a warrant, the refusal is minuted and the investigation abandoned until the inspectors can return with a formal investigation order. If a company refuses to submit to an investigation order, the inspectors call on the national official to get the order enforced via local enforcement procedures and the Commission may impose penalty payments in order to compel the undertaking to submit to the inspection.[337]

Presence of Legal Advisers.

The inspectors will wait a short time for a company's external legal adviser to arrive if it does not have an in-house lawyer.[338] Requesting a unreasonably long delay may be tantamount to refusal to the investigation and justify the imposition of a fine.[339]

332. Article 20 (5) of Regulation 1/2003.
333. Service of an investigation order immediately before the investigation begins was judged lawful by the Court in *National Panasonic*, ECJ June 26, 1980, 1980 ECR 2033, para. 20; prior service would of course defeat the purpose of surprise.
334. Article 23 (1) (c) of Regulation 1/2003. Fines have been imposed for this reason in the following cases: *Raffinerie Tirlemontoise*, Bull. EC 11–1971, 55; *Fédération Nationale de l'Industrie de la Chaussure de France*, D.Comm. Oct. 27, 1982, 1982 OJ L 319/12; *PVC II*, CFI April 20, 1999, 1999 ECR II-931, para. 421.
335. *Akzo*, D.Comm. Oct. 14, 1994, 1994 OJ L 294/31.
336. *CSM*, D.Comm. Oct. 7, 1992, 1992 OJ L 305/16.
337. Article 24 (1) (e) of Regulation 1/2003.
338. *See National Panasonic*, ECJ June 26, 1980, 1980 ECR 2033, 2045–2046, 2064 and 2069 (the claim that failure to await the arrival of its lawyer infringed its fundamental rights was implicitly rejected by the Court).
339. *MEVAC*, D.Comm. Dec. 17, 1992, 1993 OJ L 20/6.

Premises to be Inspected.

The Commission officials and other authorized persons may enter any premises, lands or means of transport.[340] In addition, Article 21 of Regulation 1/2003 provides for the possibility to inspect by decision other premises, including the homes of directors, managers and other members of the staff, provided the decision indicates a reasonable suspicion that books or other records related to the business and to the subject-matter of the inspection, which may be relevant to prove a serious infringement, are being kept in such other premises.[341]

Access to Offices.

If the firm has submitted to the investigation, the inspectors may not be confined to a meeting room while the files are brought to them, but for obvious reasons insist on being present in the offices where the files are kept when they are taken out. They may enter any office and order any filing cabinet, desk, brief case, etc., to be opened and its contents produced for inspection.[342] If any documents are temporarily off the premises, the inspectors can order that they be fetched and produced,[343] or the Commission may proceed, pursuant to Article 21 of Regulation 1/2003, to the inspection of the premises where the documents are being kept. The inspectors may ask to use the firm's photocopying facilities. The inspectors' right to access may be enforced by the national officials who assist the Commission using national powers; the refusal of access or incomplete access is subject to a fine.[344]

Inspectors' Powers.

Once the investigation begins, the Commission inspectors are entitled:

---

340. Article 20 (2) (a) of Regulation 1/2003.

341. The European Human Rights Convention does not preclude homes from being inspected: *Schneider*, CFI Oct. 22, 2002, 2002 ECR II-4091, paras 23–28; *LVM –PVC*, ECJ Oct. 15, 2002, 2002 ECR I-8375, paras 236–256.

342. Investigations do not breach the fundamental right of privacy as this does not apply to business premises: *Hoechst – PVC/LdPE*, ECJ Sept. 21, 1989, 1989 ECR 2859, paras 17–18; *Dow Benelux*, ECJ Oct. 17, 1989, 1989 ECR 3137, paras 22–29; *Dow Iberica*, ECJ Oct. 17, 1989, 1989 ECR 3165, paras 7–35. Access to all parts of the firm's premises is necessary for a full investigation: *Hoechst – PVC/LdPE*, ECJ Sept. 21, 1989, 1989 ECR 2859, paras 26–27; *Dow Benelux*, ECJ Oct. 17, 1989, 1989 ECR 3137, paras 37–38.

343. *See Stahlwerke Röchling Burbach*, D.Comm. July 27, 1977, 1977 OJ L 243/20. This, too, was made clear in the ECSC inspections Decision, Article 1 (a), by the addition of the words 'wherever such books or business records are kept'. The ECSC Decision, Article 1 (d), also stated that the Commission can carry out investigations on third parties (e.g., computer bureaus) with which books or business records have been deposited.

344. *See* Article 20 (6) and (7) of Regulation 1/2003; Commission's Notice on Cooperation between the Commission and the National Courts, points 38–41.

– to examine 'books and other business records', to ask for 'oral explanations on the spot', and to enter any premises, land or vehicles of the company.[345] 'Books and business records' are understood in a broad sense as any records a business keeps for business purposes,[346] including correspondence, minutes of meetings, internal notes and memoranda, and the expense accounts and appointments diaries of managers, and regardless of the storage medium on which the records are kept, be it paper, film, audio or video tape, diskettes or computer.[347] In the latter cases inspectors are entitled to ask the 'password' in order to get access. The Commission does not have to provide a list of the documents it wishes to see before the investigation, under its obligation to specify the 'purpose and subject matter' of the investigation.[348] The inspectors ask where files are kept and order the files or specific documents to be produced.[349] They determine which documents are relevant;[350]
– to take or obtain in any form copies or or extracts from such books or records;[351]
– to seal premises and books or records for the period and to the extent necessary for the inspection, normally for not more than 72 hours;[352]
– to interview any representative or member of the staff for the purpose of collecting information (explanations on facts or documents) relating to the subject-matter of the inspection.[353]

345. Article 20 (1) of Regulation 1/2003.
346. Private correspondence is excluded. In cases of doubt, however, the inspector may have to take a rough glance.
347. Expressly provided in Article 20 (2) (b) of Regulation 1/2003.
348. *Hoechst – PVC/LdPE*, ECJ Sept. 21, 1989, 1989 ECR 2859, para. 27; *Dow Benelux*, ECJ Oct. 17, 1989, 1989 ECR 3137, para. 38.
349. Even when the firm refuses to cooperate and the Commission has to call on the national authorities to help it carry out the investigation, the Commission does not itself have powers of search, but must rely on the assistance of the national officials to locate and obtain the documents it wishes to inspect: *Hoechst – PVC/LdPE*, ECJ Sept. 21, 1989, 1989 ECR 2859, paras 31–32 and 37; *Dow Benelux*, ECJ 17 Oct. 1989, 1989 ECR 3137, paras 42–43 and 48; *Dow Iberica*, ECJ Oct. 17, 1989, 1989 ECR 3165, paras 28–29 and 34.
350. *AM&S*, ECJ May 18, 1982, 1982 ECR 1575, para. 17. The ECSC inspections Decision, Article 1 (d), specified that the inspectors may have sight of the books and business records to satisfy themselves that they are relevant.
351. Article 20 (1) (c) of Regulation 1/2003.
352. Article 20 (2) (d) and Recital 25 to Regulation 1/2003. Under Regulation 139/2004 on merger control seals should be used for the period of time strictly necessary for the inspection, normally not for more than 48 hours: Recital 39 to Regulation 139/2004.
353. Article 20 (2) (e) and Article 19 (2) of Regulation 1/2003.

Cooperation and Oral Explanations.
The firm investigated is under a duty not merely to submit passively, but to cooperate actively with the investigation.[354] This applies not only to the physical opening of filing cabinets and desks for the inspectors but also to the furnishing of 'oral explanations'. Thus, the firm's representatives must tell the inspectors where certain offices or archives are located,[355] explain the filing system, identify the writers of letters and memos from their initials, and elucidate incidental matters arising from documents found, such as the purpose of a meeting, who was present at it, the meaning of abbreviations and jargon used in memoranda, etc. If the firm produces the required books or records in incomplete form,[356] provides incorrect oral information[357] or fails to provide clear explanations leading to relevant documents being examined, the firm will be liable to a fine for incomplete production.[358] An absolute refusal to submit to an investigation[359] or to provide explanations to facilitate an investigation under order will also attract a fine[360] or penalty payments.[361]

Legal Professional or 'Attorney-Client' Privilege.[362]
The only documents which a company can refuse to produce for the inspectors to read are papers and correspondence exchanged (or written for the purpose of being exchanged) between the company and its outside lawyers for the purpose of seeking or giving advice about the practices or arrangements under investigation or preparing the company's defence to a possible or actual prosecution.[363] Thus, papers and correspondence with lawyers in any way concerning the case, and not just those dating from after the opening of formal proceedings, are privileged. The inspectors may not read them but may have sufficient sight of them or other relevant material to satisfy themselves that they are indeed privileged.[364] Inter-

354. *Hoechst -PVC/LdPE*, ECJ Sept. 21, 1989, 1989 ECR 2859, paras 31 and 63–64; *Dow Benelux*, ECJ Oct. 17, 1989, 1989 ECR 3137, para. 42; *Dow Iberica*, ECJ Oct. 17, 1989, 1989 ECR 3165, para. 28; *PVC II*, CFI April 20, 1999, 1999 ECR II-931, para. 444.
355. E.g., *Akzo Chemicals*, D.Comm. Oct. 14, 1994, 1994 OJ L 294/31.
356. *CSM*, D.Comm. Oct. 7, 1992, 1992 OJ L 305/16.
357. *Akzo Chemicals*, D.Comm. Oct. 14, 1994, 1994 OJ L 294/31.
358. *Fabbrica Pisana* and *Fabbrica Sciarra*, D.Comm. Dec. 20, 1979, 1980 OJ L 75/30 and 35.
359. *UKWAL*, D.Comm. April 6, 1992, 1992 OJ L 121/45.
360. Article 23 (1) (c) of Regulation 1/2003. *See MEWAC*, D.Comm. Dec. 17, 1992, 1993 OJ L 20/6.
361. This is new: Article 24 (1) (e) of Regulation 1/2003.
362. *See AM&S*, ECJ May 18, 1982, 1982 ECR 1575; *Hilti* (*Discovery*), CFI April 4, 1990, 1990 ECR II-163; Twelfth Report on Competition Policy, points 33 and 50–54.
363. *AM&S*, ECJ May 18, 1982 ECR 1575, para. 29; *Volkswagen I*, D.Comm. Jan. 28, 1998, 1998 OJ L 124/60, paras 198–199, *aff'd* ECJ Sept. 18, 2003, C-338/00 P.
364. In case of dispute the Commission could order discovery of the documents as in the *AM&S* case, and if the parties appealed the matter could be adjudicated by the Court of Justice: *AM&S*, ECJ May 18, 1982 ECR 1575, para. 31.

nal memoranda from and with in-house lawyers[365] and with non-EC lawyers[366] were originally not covered by attorney-client privilege. However, in *Akzo Nobel Chemicals* the Court of First Instance extended the priviledge to lawyers employed by an undertaking on a permanent basis, provided that they are subject to certain rules of professional conduct,[367] and the Commission recognizes the priviledge of *bona fide* legal advice sought or rendered by non-EC lawyers.

Modalities of Protecting the Legal Professional Priviledge.
The undertaking under investigation is not bound to reveal the content of the documents in question in order to prove whether the documents merit protection. The Commission's official must refrain from reading the document immediately[368] or casting even a cursory glance over the documents, unless the undertaking gives its unreserved consent.[369] The procedure which the Commission must follow consists of the following three stages:[370]

– If the undertaking relies on professional priviledge and on that ground refuses to produce documents, it must demonstrate that the substantive conditions

365. Drafted for the sole purpose of obtaining legal advice: *AM&S*, ECJ May 18, 1982, 1982 ECR 1575, paras 24 and 27; *Akzo Nobel Chemicals*, CFI Oct. 30, 2003, T-125/03 R, para. 108. In *Hilti* (*Discovery*), CFI April 4, 1990, 1990 ECR II-163, para. 18, on an application by the plaintiff to withhold certain documents from intervenors, the Court of First Instance ruled that legal professional privilege also extended to internal memoranda that merely reported outside legal advice.
366. *AM&S*, ECJ May 18, 1982, 1982 ECR 1575, paras 25–26. However, in practice it would generally do so, as was its practice before the *AM&S* judgment, *see* Thirteenth Report on Competition Policy, point 78.
367. *Akzo Nobel Chemicals*, CFI Oct. 30, 2003, T-125/03 R, paras 124–130; arguing that there is no presumption that the link between a lawyer and an undertaking will always, and as a matter of principle, affect the independence necessary for the effective exercise of the role of collaborating in the administration of justice by the courts if the lawyer is bound by strict rules of professional conduct (para. 126).
368. *Akzo Nobel Chemicals*, CFI Oct. 30, 2003, T-125/03 R, para. 146.
369. *AM&S*, ECJ May 18, 1982, 1982 ECR 1575; *Akzo Nobel Chemicals*, CFI Oct. 30, 2003, T-125/03 R, paras 138–140 and 148. However, in practice it may be difficult to form an opinion on the professional privilege nature of a document without 'casting even a cursory glance' on a document, such as the memorandum from the General Manager to one of his superiors, unless it is clear from external indications, such as a lawyer's letterhead: *Akzo Nobel Chemicals*, CFI Oct. 30, 2003, T-125/03 R, para. 138. If the Commission's inspector realizes, after having casted a glance, that the document satisfies the criteria of legal professional priviledge, he is prevented from taking a copy and the document cannot be used as evidence; however, the mere knowledge is innocuous. In *PVC* the Commission was not prevented from using the knowledge of a document discovered by accident during an investigation of another case and launching a new investigation: *LVM – PVC*, ECJ Oct. 15, 2002, 2002 ECR I-8375, paras 305–306. *See also Spanish Banks*, ECJ July 16, 1992, 1992 ECR I-4785, paras 39–42.
370. *AM&S*, ECJ May 18, 1982, 1982 ECR 1575, para. 29; *Akzo Nobel Chemicals*, CFI Oct. 30, 2003, T-125/03 R, para. 74.

required by the case-law are satisfied, although it is not obliged to reveal the contents of the documents. To this effect it may be appropriate to place a copy of the documents in question in a sealed envelope[371] and to order their production by decision which would allow the Court of First Instance to resolve the dispute.[372]

- If the Commission is not satisfied it must order, by decision, production of the documents in question.
- If the undertaking continues to maintain that the documents are covered by professional priviledge, it is for the Court of First Instance to resolve the dispute.

Other grounds for refusing to produce documents in investigations, such as self-incrimination or confidentiality, are not recognized any more than they are in the case of discovery.[373]

Fines.
The level of fines that can be imposed for refusing to submit to an investigation ordered by decision, for failing to produce all the material relevant to the investigation or for giving an incorrect or misleading answer given by a member of staff are the same as for discovery offenses.[374]

Investigations by National Authorities Acting on Commission's Behalf.
Investigations may be carried out by national authorities on the Commission's behalf (which is being more frequently used). In this case the powers of the national authorities are those of Article 14 in accordance with national law.[375] However, the same anticompetitive conduct may be investigated in parallel by the Commission under Community law and the national authorities under national law and the result may be used for their respective proceedings within the limits of Articles 11 and 12 of Regulation 1/2003.[376]

---

371. This is what the Court of Justice ordered the Commission to do in the *AM&S* case: ECJ Feb. 4, 1982, 155/79 (interim measure, not published).
372. *Akzo Nobel Chemicals*, CFI Oct. 30, 2003, T-125/03 R, para. 141. In *AM&S*, the Court of Justice rejected the suggestion of an independent expert: ECJ May 18, 1982, 1982 ECR 1575, paras 7 and 30.
373. *Fédération Nationale de l'Industrie de la Chaussure de France*, D.Comm. Oct. 27, 1982, 1982 OJ L 319/12.
374. Article 23 (1) of Regulation 1/2003. Daily fines were imposed in the *Hoechst* case: *Hoechst – PVC/LdPE*, ECJ Sept. 21, 1989, 1989 ECR 2859, and announced in *Akzo*, D.Comm. Oct. 19, 1993, IP/93/893.
375. Article 22 (2) of Regulation 1/2003.
376. *See supra* Section B.2.

Judicial Review of Investigation Orders.
Companies are entitled to judicial review of an investigation order by the Court of Justice under Article 230 of the EC Treaty.[377] Along with the application for judicial review, they may ask for a stay of execution of the order under Article 242 if the investigation has not already taken place or has not been completed. The system of judicial review in the Treaty is however essentially retrospective: the act appealed against is valid and enforceable until set aside by the Court.[378] In the case of an on-the-spot investigation a successful appeal would mean that the Commission was barred from using any evidence collected during the investigation.[379] Stays of execution under Article 242 are an exception from the usual procedure of retrospective review and are only granted where the act would cause irreparable injury to the applicant, an argument so far dismissed by the Court in the cases it has decided of applications for stays of execution of on-the-spot investigations.[380] Until a stay is granted the Commission is entitled to proceed with the investigation. If a stay were ever granted in time to prevent an investigation going ahead (which with modern telecommunications methods is physically possible), the conditions of the stay would have to include safeguards against the destruction or removal of evidence.[381] If the appeal is successful the Commission may be requested to return (and not to use) documents that are illegally collected.[382] However, the validity of the decision ordering the investigation cannot itself be affected by acts subsequent to its adoption, i.e., the validity of the acts implementing the decision.[383] Decisions subsequent to a decision ordering the investigation which are subject to judicial review include:

– a decision ordering the production of documents for which the legal legal professional privilege is claimed;[384]

377. Article 21 (3) of Regulation 1/2003.
378. The first sentence of Article 242 of the EEC Treaty ('Actions brought before the Court of Justice shall not have suspensory effect.') and *Granaria BV v. Hoofdproduktschap voor Akkerbouwprodukten*, ECJ Feb. 13, 1979, 1979 ECR 623, para. 5.
379. *Roquette Frères*, CFI Oct. 22, 2002, 2002 ECR II-9011.
380. *Brescia* (*Injunction*), ECJ June 26, 1959, 1960 ECR 98, 99–100; *Hoechst – PVC/LdPE* (*Injunction*), ECJ March 26, 1987, 1987 ECR 1549, para. 34. Dow's application for an injunction restraining the Commission from using the evidence gathered during an investigation was dismissed as unnecessary: *Dow Chemical Nederland* (*Injunction*), ECJ Oct. 28, 1987, 1987 ECR 4367.
381. Such as the sealing of filing cabinets, desks and offices thought to contain evidence. But unlike the case where only a few documents for which the firm claims attorney-client privilege are involved, as in *AM&S*, ECJ May 18, 1982, 1982 ECR 1575, the practical difficulties of sealing would be enormous.
382. Discussed but not decided in *Schneider*, CFI Oct. 22, 2002, 2002 ECR II-4091.
383. *Akzo Nobel Chemicals*, CFI Oct. 30, 2003, T-125/03 R, para. 69. *See*, however, *Elf/Atochem*, CFI July 9, 1997, 1997 ECR II-909, para. 20; *Dysan Magnetics*, CFI March 14, 1996, 1996 ECR II-181, para. 20.
384. E.g., *AM&S*, ECJ May 18, 1982, 1982 ECR 1575.

– a decision or letter of the Commission rejecting the request for the return of documents and for confirmation that all the copies will be destroyed.[385]

6. Sector Enquiries

Broad Powers Seldom Employed.
The Commission may use its discovery and investigative powers to investigate suspicious pricing behaviour or other conduct suggesting an antitrust violation across a whole industry.[386] Under this procedure strong evidence of violations is not required, but the Advisory Committee must be consulted and a formal decision taken by the Commission to launch the enquiry. Under Regulation 17 the procedure has been used only twice: to investigate the margarine industry[387] and the tying of 'public houses' (bars) to breweries.[388] In both cases there was doubt as to whether the conduct constituted a violation.[389] Under Article 17 of Regulation 1/2003 the procedure may be used for investigations of the suspected sector (e.g. the pharmaceutical sector) or a particular type of agreements across various sectors (e.g. license agreements). The Commission may request the undertakings concerned to supply information necessary for giving effect to Articles 81 and 82, including the communication of all agreements, and may carry out any inspection necessary for that purpose.[390]

7. Use and Disclosure of Information

Restrictions on the Use of Information v. Obligation of Professional Secrecy.
The Commission and the national competition authorities as well as their officials and experts may not disclose information acquired or exchanged which is 'of the kind of professional secrecy'. Article 28 (2) of Regulation 1/2003 only repeats the obligation of Article 287 of the EC Treaty, whereas Article 28 (1) of Regulation 1/2003 restricts the official use of incriminating material 'only for the purpose for

385. Successfully appealed in *Akzo Nobel Chemicals*, CFI Oct. 30, 2003, T-125/03 R, paras 61–65.
386. Article 17 of Regulation 1/2003.
387. Bull. EEC 8–1965, 35 and Bull. EC 8–1970, 66.
388. 1969 OJ C 148/3. *See Alsacienne de Brasserie*, *Union de Brasseries* and *Maes*, D.Comm. June 18, 1971, 1971 OJ L 161/2, 6 and 10.
389. In the margarine industry the Commission wanted to establish whether the virtual absence of interstate trade and large price differences between member states were due to private restrictive practices or to government regulation; in the event both were found to be factors and the enquiry led to the abandonment of certain restrictive practices by a dominant supplier. In the beer industry there was doubt whether the breweries' networks of 'public houses' (bars) tied to purchasing their brands of beer prevented market entry and thereby interstate trade. *See also* First Report on Competition Policy, point 124.
390. The specific provision relating to the possibly abusive behavior of dominant undertakings (Article 12 (3) of Regulation 17) is repealed.

which it was acquired'.[391] Article 28 (2) essentially protects information acquired in the performance of an investigation duties which is 'of the kind covered by the obligation of professional secrecy'.[392] The obligation of 'professional' secrecy here refers to the duty of official bodies – government agencies – not to disclose private information that a business or individual has supplied about themselves and is not widely known or publicly available,[393] in particular information on business relations or their cost components.[394] Within the generality of protected private information, the special category of business (or trade) secrets enjoys special protection, as recognized in Articles 27 (4) and 30 (2) of Regulation 1/2003. 'Business secret' is not defined but can be taken to mean especially confidential information arising from or used in a trade or business which is commercially sensitive, such that its disclosure would harm the firm from which it came.[395] The term encompasses both valuable technical know-how and commercial and financial information on prices, costs, actual and forecast sales, market shares, contracts with customers or suppliers, investment plans, and details of product development and advertising campaigns, etc. The use and disclosure of confidential information acquired pursuant to the Regulation is restricted in order to protect the providers of the information and to overcome reluctance to providing information among firms under investigation and third parties.

Safeguard against Arbitrary, Unspecific Use of Fact-Finding Powers, in Particular Fishing Expeditions.

Both the Commission and the national competition authorities may use information obtained by use of their respective fact-finding powers only for the particular antitrust investigations in which the powers were exercised and in respect to the

391. Information supplied voluntarily by a complainant or informant is normally not of an incriminating nature.
392. The term 'professional secrecy' is a translation of the French *'secret professionnel'* and the German *'Berufsgeheimnis'*, but there is no exact or concise equivalent of these concepts in English. Article 28 (2) is a specification of the confidentiality obligation imposed on the members of the EC governing institutions and committees and on EC officials by Article 287 of the EC Treaty, which specifically refers to information about firms, their business relations and their costs.
393. Information divulged only to certain individuals, such as the members of a trade association, is not public: *FEDETAB*, ECJ Oct. 29, 1980, 1980 ECR 3125, para. 46.
394. Article 287.
395. However, information may be used in general publications or surveys provided that references to individual firms are removed (Article 20 (3) of Regulation 17, not expressly repeated in Article 28 of Regulation 1/2003). *Cf. Celanese Corporation v. Commission*, ECJ March 30, 1982, 1982 ECR 1183, the proposed definition of 'trade secret' under Canadian law (Coleman, 'Reform of Canadian Trade Secrets Law', 1987 EIPR 228), and the criterion for confidential, non-disclosable information in EC anti-dumping proceedings (Regulation 2423/88, 1988 OJ L 209/1, Article 8 (3)): '... if its disclosure is likely to have a significantly adverse effect upon the supplier or the source of the information'. *See also* Eighteenth Report on Competition Policy, point 43.

subject-matter for which it was collected.[396] Therefore, the Commission (DG COMP) may not pass information on to other departments of the Commission (e.g., agriculture, transport or fraud prevention) for use by them. This restriction on the use of information obtained by means of the Commission's fact-finding powers helps protect firms from arbitrary use of the powers. This also prevents 'fishing expeditions', investigations undertaken without genuine suspicion of a specific antitrust violation (e.g. by 'accident'). It thereby reinforces the requirement for the Commission to specify the subject matter and purpose of discovery demands and on-the-spot investigations.[397] The use restriction means in practice that the Commission may not directly use material found while investigating one infringement (e.g., a cartel on the polypropylene market) in order to bring a prosecution for a different antitrust infringement (such as a cartel for PVC). However, if the Commission uncovers evidence of another infringement during an investigation, it is entitled to launch a new investigation to obtain more complete evidence of this infringement.[398] The restriction does not prevent the Commission from using evidence found during an investigation of one firm implicating another firm in the same offence (which was the subject of the investigation) against the second firm.[399]

Use of Information by National Competition Authorities.
Information collected by the Commission or the national competition authorities for the purpose of applying Article 81 and 82 may be exchanged among them, including confidential information.[400] Nor are the national authorities prevented from using information obtained during an EC on-the-spot investigation at which their officials were present to support a case they themselves were bringing under EC competition law.[401] Also, if national competition authority officials carried out a joint on-the-spot investigation with the Commission under their own law, they would be able to use the evidence in a national antitrust prosecution, but probably not (though this would depend on national law) for other offenses. However, the national competition authorities must ensure the respect of confidentiality, in particular:

---

396. Article 28 (1) of Regulation 1/2003; Article 16 of Regulation 773/2004.
397. *See supra* sections D.3.–5.
398. *PVC – LVM*, ECJ Oct. 15, 2002, 2002 ECR I-8375, paras 305–306. *See Dow Benelux*, ECJ Oct. 17, 1989, 1989 ECR 3137, paras 14 and 17–20. The Commission may also order discovery of this evidence: *Solvay*, ECJ Oct. 18, 1989, 1989 ECR 3255, para. 11; *Orkem*, ECJ Oct. 18, 1989, 1989 ECR 3283, para. 14.
399. *Dow Benelux*, ECJ Oct. 17, 1989, 1989 ECR 3137.
400. Article 12 (1) and 27 (2) of Regulation 1/2003; Article 15 (3) of Regulation 773/2004; Notice on the ECN, points 27–28; Joint Statement of the Council and Commission on the Fonctioning of the Network of Competition Authorities of Dec. 10, 2002, 15435/02 ADD 1, point 10. *See LVM – PVC,* ECJ Oct. 15, 2002, 2002 ECR I-8375, paras 305–306.
401. *See Total*, Eighteenth Report on Competition Policy, point 22.

- by refusing access of third parties, including complainants, to confidential information supplied by undertakings which are the subjects of investigation,[402]
- by refusing access of certain addressees to confidential information supplied by other addressees because this would result in the exchange of commercially sensitive information between competitors.

To this effect, the Commission requests undertakings that provide information to identify those documents which contain confidential information to substantiate their claim for confidentiality with respect to each individual document and to provide the Commission with a non-confidential version and a concise description of each piece of deleted information.[403] Where the Commission intends to disclose information for which confidentiality is claimed it must set out the reasons and, in case of disagreement, adopt a decision that is subject to appeal.[404] However, the competition authorities are not prevented from using confidential information for the purposes of proving an infringement, provided the rights of defence are observed.[405]

Use of Information by National Courts.
Information obtained during the Commission's investigation may be used by national courts. The parties to the Commission's proceedings may rely on the facts collected by the Commission and which are communicated to them in a Statement of Objections (although it is provisional) or referred to in the hearing report or in the final decision of the Commission. The Commission is not prohibited from transmitting, and the national courts are not prohibited from using confidential information, provided they ensure the respect of the confidentiality according to Article 287 of the EC Treaty.[406]

---

402. Article 9 (1) of Regulation 773/2004. *See*, under Regulation 1049/2001 on Public Assess to Commission Documents, 2001 OJ L 145/43. *See*, with respect to the previous Regulation 94/90, 1994 OJ L 46/58: *see Van der Wal*, ECJ Jan. 11, 2000, 2000 ECR I-1, paras 20–22; *Mattila*, CFI Jan. 22, 2004, C-353/01 P.
403. Article 16 (3) of Regulation 773/2004.
404. Articles 16 and 17 of Regulation 773/2004. In case of disagreement, the decision is adopted by the Commission and no longer by the Hearing Officer as provided for by Commission decision 2001/462/EC, 2001 OJ L 162/21, *see Commerzbank II*, CFI July 9, 2003, T-219/01 (appeal against the Hearing Officer's decision not to grant access to the file).
405. Article 27 (2) of Regulation 1/2003 and Article 15 (3) of Regulation 773/2004. *See* Commission Notice on Cooperation within the ECN, point 28.
406. Commission Notice on National Courts, 2004 OJ C 101/54, points 24–25; *Zwartveld*, ECJ July 13, 1990, 1990 ECR I-4405, paras 10–11; *Postbank*, CFI Sept. 18, 1996, 1996 ECR II-921, paras 65–67 and 93. *See Information Resources v. Dun & Bradstreet*, U.S. District Court, Dec. 7, 1998, 96 Civ. 5716 (LLS); *Ree Japanese Elec. Prods. Antitrust Litig.*, 723 F.2nd 238, 268, 273 (3rd Cir. 1983).

Legal Consequences of Non-Respect of Confidentiality.
The legal consequence of a non-respect of this obligation is liability according to Article 288 of the EC Treaty, which provides for the restitution of damage caused by the Community institutions or its servants. Damages were successfully claimed in the *Hoffmann-La Roche*[407] case because of the disclosure of an informant's identity.[408] Subsequently, the Commission has issued instructions to DG COMP not to reveal the identity of informants who could face criminal prosecution in a non-EC country without first obtaining their consent and warning them of the possible consequences, and not to disclose even information supplied anonymously if this could lead to the informant being traced and prosecuted.[409]

Exceptions from the General Confidentiality Obligation.
There are four exceptions to the general confidentiality obligation:

- the Commission is not prevented from disclosing and using information necessary to prove an infringement of Article 81 or 82,[410] subject, however, to the obligation to inform the undertakings beforehand in writing, thereby inviting them to submit their views.[411]
- publication of general information or survey;[412]
- disclosure in published decisions which must have regard to firms' legitimate interest in the protection of their business secrets;[413] and
- disclosure to prospective addressees of decisions and third parties where necessary for observance of due process, i.e. to guarantee the rights of prospective addressees of decisions to reply to the Commission's case against them and of third parties to support or object to a proposed decision. The procedure for the disclosure of evidence to parties and third parties as part of their rights to a fair hearing and the safeguards to prevent wrongful disclosure are set out in section E. below.

---

407. *Hoffmann-La Roche*, ECJ 13 Feb. 1979, 1979 ECR 461.
408. *Adams I*, ECJ Nov. 7, 1985, 1985 ECR 3539.
409. Fifteenth Report on Competition Policy, point 51; *British Plaster Board*, ECJ April 6, 1995, 1995 ECR I-865, paras 21–27; *Endemol*, CFI April 28, 1999, 1999 ECR II-1299, para. 60. *Cf. CSV (Discovery)*, D.Comm. June 25, 1976, 1976 OJ L 192/27, in which the Commission refused to recognize the possibility of prosecution in Switzerland for disclosure of commercial secrets as a defence to discovery.
410. Article 15 (3) of Regulation 773/2004. *See Tokai Carbon – Graphite Electrodes*, CFI April 29, 2004, T-236/01, para. 403.
411. Article 17 of Regulation 773/2004. In the case of disagreement the Commission must adopt a decision. The mandate of the Hearing Officer (Commission Decision 2001/462/EC 2001 OJ L 162/21) provided for a settlement of disagreements by the Hearing Officer, *see Commerzbank II*, CFI July 9, 2003, C-219/01, para. 13.
412. Article 20 (3) of Regulation 17, not expressly repeated in Article 28 of Regulation 1/2003.
413. Article 30 (2) of Regulation 1/2003.

E. Due Process

1. Introduction

Due Process Obligations.
While not a court, the Commission exercises quasi-judicial functions. This quasi-judicial character is most marked in decisions imposing fines[414] or ruling on complaints.[415] The Commission is obliged to observe the principles of natural justice or due process of law in relation to the persons to whom its decision is addressed or whom will be affected by it. The basic principle is that of *'audi alteram partem'*, i.e. the obligation to give the prospective addressees and interested third parties a 'fair hearing'; in relation to adverse decisions this becomes an obligation to observe the 'rights of defence'.[416] The Commission can, in its decisions, deal only with objections in respect of which the addressees have been able to comment.[417]

Toward Prospective Addressees of Decisions.
The general duty of the Commission to give a fair hearing to the prospective addressees of decisions and to respect their rights of defence is stated in Article 27 (1) of Regulation 1/2003. It applies to all formal or substantive decisions adverse to the addressee, e.g., cease-and-desist orders,[418] including interim orders,[419] decisions imposing fines,[420] or periodic penalty payments,[421] deci-

414. However, these are expressly stated to be non-criminal in nature (Article 23 (5) of Regulation 1/2003).
415. In such cases the proceedings assume an adversarial character and the Commission's role may resemble that of a civil court or an arbitration panel adjudicating a civil dispute.
416. Article 6 (1) of the EU Charter of Fundamental Rights: 'Right of every person to have his or her affairs handled impartially and within a reasonable time limit' . *See Baustahlgewerbe*, ECJ Dec. 17, 1998, 1998 ECR I-8417, paras 20–21; *LVM – PVC*, ECJ Oct. 15, 2002, 2002 ECR I-8375, para. 915. The importance of due process in decisions by the EC executive which directly affect the interests of individual businesses has also been established in other areas of EC law enforcement, such as anti-dumping (*see*, e.g., *Timex v. Council and Commission*, ECJ March 20, 1985, 1985 ECR 849, paras 18–31), government subsidies (*Belgium v. Commission (Meura)*, ECJ July 10, 1986, 1986 ECR 2263, paras 25–30; *Belgium v. Commission (Boch)*, ECJ July 10, 1986, 1986 ECR 2321, paras 25–31; *Walloon Regional Executive v. Commission (Glaverbel)*, ECJ March 8, 1988, 1988 ECR 1573, paras 36–39), and production and price controls in the steel industry (*Krupp v. Commission*, ECJ Nov. 12, 1985, 1985 ECR 3609, paras 5–10; *Manchester Steel v. Commission*, ECJ July 10, 1986, 1986 ECR 2351, paras 11–17).
417. Article 11 (2) of Regulation 773/2004.
418. Article 7 of Regulation 1/2003. *See infra* section F.2 (a).
419. Articles 8 and 27 (1) of Regulation 1/2003. *See* under Regulation 17: *Camera Care*, ECJ Jan. 17, 1980, 1980 ECR 119, para. 19.
420. Articles 23 (2) and 27 (1) of Regulation 1/2003.
421. Article 24 of Regulation 1/2003.

sions revoking the benefit of a block exemption,[422] and decisions rejecting a complaint.[423] It also applies to decisions which are basically favourable to the addressee, e.g., declarations of inapplicability or settlement which are subject to conditions (commitments).[424] It does not, however, apply to procedural decisions such as discovery and investigation orders,[425] or a decision to initiate[426] or reopen proceedings.[427] The rights of defence include:

(i) *Legal Guarantee of a 'Statement of Objections'*: The Commission is obliged to deal in its decisions only with objections on which the prospective addressees have been afforded the opportunity to be heard.[428]
(ii) *Right of Access to the File*: The Commission is obliged to disclose the documentary evidence on which it relies in support of its allegations,[429] except where such evidence contains business secrets or other confidential information protected from disclosure by virtue of Article 28 (2) of Regulation 1/2003.
(iii) *Right to a Written Response*: Prospective addressees of a Commission decision must be afforded the opportunity to make their views known in writing on the objections raised against them.[430]
(iv) *Right to a Hearing*: The prospective addressees of a Commission decision must also have the right to develop their arguments at an oral hearing.[431]

---

422. Article 29 of Regulation 1/2003.
423. Articles 7 and 13 of Regulation 773/2004.
424. Articles 7, 9 and 27 (1) of Regulation 1/2003. *See* under Regulation 17: *Transocean Marine Paint Association*, ECJ Oct. 23, 1974, 1974 ECR 1063, where the Court of Justice established that the Commission must give the prospective addressees of exemption decisions an opportunity to object to any conditions it proposes to attach to the exemption.
425. *See* under Regulation 17: *National Panasonic*, ECJ June 26, 1980, 1980 ECR 2033, para. 21. Regarding decisions rejecting complaints, *see infra* this section and section E.3.
426. Article 11 (6) of Regulation 1/2003.
427. Article 9 (2) of Regulation 1/2003.
428. Article 27 (1) of Regulation 1/2003; Article 11 (2) of Regulation 773/2004.
429. Article 27 (2) of Regulation 1/2003 and Article 15 of Regulation 773/2004. *See* in particular *Hoffmann-La Roche*, ECJ Feb. 13, 1979, 1979 ECR 461, para. 11: defendants 'must have been afforded the opportunity during the administrative procedure to make known their views on the truth and relevance of the facts and circumstances alleged and on the documents used by the Commission to support its claim that there has been an infringement of Articles 85 and 86 of the Treaty.' *See also Pioneer*, ECJ June 7, 1983, 1983 ECR 1825, paras 24–30; *AEG-Telefunken*, ECJ Oct. 25, 1983, 1983 ECR 3151, paras 21–30; *Boussac*, ECJ Feb. 14, 1990, 1990 ECR I-351, paras 29–31.
430. Article 10 of Regulation 773/2004.
431. The right of being 'heard' includes both the right of being heard in writing and the right to an oral hearing.

The non-respect of the prospective addressees' rights of defence constitutes a procedural irregularity and may lead to the annulment of the entire decision or part of it.[432]

Toward Complainants.
Complainants who show 'a sufficient interest' in order to be entitled to lodge a complaint pursuant to Article 7 of Regulation 1/2003[433] must be given a fair hearing as set forth in Article 27 of Regulation 1/2003. Complainants must be 'associated closely' with the proceedings.[434] The right to be heard includes:

(i) *Reasons for Denying a Complaint*: Complainants have the right to be informed of the reasons in cases where the Commission considers that on the basis of the information in its possession there are insufficient grounds for acting on the complaint,[435]
(ii) *Access to Statement of Objections*: Complainants have the right to obtain a non-confidential version of the statement of objections in case the Commission raises objections relating to an issue of the complaint,[436]
(iii) *Limited Access to the File*: Evidence of defendants may be disclosed to complainants where it is necessary to do so for a proper conduct of the case, but defendant's business secrets may under no circumstances be disclosed; otherwise, complainants might file complaints solely to gain access to competitors' secrets,[437] However, where the Commission intends to reject the complaint the complainant may request access to documents on which the Commission bases its provisional assessment.[438]

432. *See esp. Distillers v. Commission*, ECJ July 10, 1980, 1980 ECR 2229, para. 26; *Europay*, CFI Feb. 23, 1994, 1994 ECR II-49, para. 47. *See also* Article 51 of the Protocol on the Statute of the Court of Justice of the European Economic Community, which states that one of the grounds of appeal to the Court of Justice from a decision of the Court of First Instance shall be 'a breach of procedure before it *which adversely affects the interests of the appellant'* (emphasis added).
433. Article 5 of Regulation 773/2004; Commission Notice on the handling of complaints, points 33–40. As a rule, in the absence of a Community interest there is no legitimate interest of a complainant in a Commission's intervention, *see* Commission's Notice on the handling of complaints, points 12–25.
434. Article 27 (1), third sentence, of Regulation 1/2003; Articles 5–9 of Regulation 773/2004; Commission's Notice on the handling of complaints.
435. Article 7 of Regulation 773/2004.
436. Article 6 (1) of Regulation 773/2004.
437. *Akzo I*, ECJ June 24, 1986, 1986 ECR 1965, paras 28–29; *Matra/Ford-Volkswagen,* CFI July 15, 1994, 1994 ECR II-595, para. 34.
438. Article 9 of Regulation 773/2004. The documents to which the complainant is granted access can only be used by the complainant for the application of Articles 81 and 82; Article 8 (2) of Regulation 773/2004.

(iv) *Right to Written Comment*: Complainants must be afforded the opportunity to make their views known in writing,[439]
(v) *Opportunity to Assist to the Oral Hearing*: Complainants may be afforded, where appropriate, the opportunity of orally expressing their views.[440]

Toward Other Interested Third Parties.
The Commission's due process obligation towards interested parties are set forth in Article 27 (3) of Regulation 1/2003 and Article 13 of Regulation 773/2004.[441] It is obliged to hear the views of third parties who show a sufficiently direct interest in the outcome of the case. A 'sufficient interest' of a third party may be compared to the 'interest in the result of the case' which an individual must demonstrate in order to be entitled to intervene in proceedings before the Court of Justice,[442] which may include representative associations.[443] Hearing third parties and considering their views is both in their interest and also in the interest of a broader and more comprehensive investigation and evaluation of all factual and legal aspects of the case in question. The Commission may therefore hear representations from third parties not having themselves a direct interest. Third parties may make critical comments on proposed negative clearances, exemptions or settlements which the Commission must take into account. The right of third parties to be heard is, however, not as extensive as that of defendants.[444] These rights include the opportunity to make their views known in writing or to ask questions during the oral hearing (with the Hearing Officer's approval).[445] However, third parties are not granted access to the file.[446] The Commission is bound by the general principle that business secrets may not in any circumstances be disclosed to a complainant or other third party.[447]

Guarantee of a Fair Hearing by the Hearing Officer.
The position of the Hearing Officer was created in 1982. His initial responsibility was limited primarily to the organization, chairing and conduct of the oral hearing. The Hearing Officer's duties were expanded in 1994 to ensure adequate protection of the rights of the parties, in particular the confidentiality of documents and business secrets and adequate access to the files of the Commission.[448] On May

439. Article 6 (2) of Regulation 773/2004.
440. Article 13 (3) of Regulation 773/2004.
441. Replacing Regulation 2842/98 (Article 19).
442. Article 40 (2) of the Statute of the Court of Justice.
443. E.g., in cases before the Court of First Instance: *Akzo Nobel Chemicals*, CFI Oct. 30, 2003, T-125/03 R, paras 43–54; in cases before the Commission Consumer associations, Twenty-nineth Report on Competition Policy, point 64.
444. Article 13 of Regulation 773/2004.
445. Article 14 (7) of Regulation 773/2004.
446. *Nestlé-Perrier*, April 27, 1995, 1995 ECR II-1213, para. 64.
447. Article 16 of Regulation 773/2004.
448. Commission Decision on the Terms of Reference of the Hearing Officer, 1994 OJ L 330/67.

23, 2001 the Commission adopted a new mandate,[449] which maintains the core aspects of the hearing officer's functions and strengthens its functions in the decision-making process. The Hearing Officer[450] is now attached for administrative purposes to the competition Commissioner and reports directly to him rather than to the Director-General for Competition, as was previously the case. The Hearing Officer is kept informed about how a proceeding is developing up to the stage of the draft decision to be submitted to the Competition Commissioner. He may present observations at this early stage of proceedings. The Hearing Officer ensures in particular that, in the preparation of a draft decision, due account is taken of all the relevant facts, whether favourable or unfavourable to the parties concerned, including the factual elements related to the gravity of any infringement.[451] He decides on applications to be heard from third parties, whereas disagreement on confidential information is no longer settled by the Hearing Officer[452] but by Commission decision.[453]

The following subsections describe in greater detail the due process requirements in relation to prospective addressees of decisions and interested third parties.

2. Hearing of Prospective Addressees of a Decision

(a) Statement of Objections

Allegation of Facts and Legal Assessment.

The Statement of Objections informs the defendant of the objections raised against him. It must set out clearly, albeit concisely, all the essential facts alleged against the defendant and the Commission's submissions on how the alleged acts of the defendant infringe Article 81 or 82,[455] and must indicate the action which the Commission proposes to take by way of orders or fines. Thus, a Statement of Objections contains two elements: a statement of facts and a legal assessment

449. 2001 OJ L 162/21. Similarly the EFTA Surveillance Authority Decision of 30 October 2002 concerning proceedings under Articles 53, 54 and 57 of the EEA Agreement, 2003 OJ L 80/27.
450. There are two hearing officers for conducting hearings under Article 81 and 82 and two hearing officers for conducting hearings under the merger control regulation.
451. Article 5 of the Commission Decision 2001/462.
452. *See Commerzbank II*, CFI July 7, 2003, T-219/01; *Bank Austria Creditanstalt*, CFI Nov 7, 2003, T-198/03 R, paras 33–43; *Aalborg Portland – Cement*, ECJ Jan. 7, 2004, C-204/00P, para. 66.
453. Article 17 of Regulation 773/2004.
454. *ACF Chemiefarma-Quinine*, ECJ July 15, 1970, 1970 ECR 661, para. 26; *Continental Can*, ECJ Feb. 21, 1973, 1973 ECR 215, para. 5; *United Brands*, ECJ Feb. 14, 1978, 1978 ECR 207, paras 274–276; *Hoffmann-La Roche*, ECJ Feb. 13, 1979, 1979 ECR 461, para. 10; *Pioneer*, ECJ June 7, 1983, 1983 ECR 1825, para. 14; *VBVB/VBBB*, ECJ Jan. 17, 1984, 1984 ECR 19, para. 20.

demonstrating how the alleged conduct is considered to have infringed the competition rules. It must refer to documentary evidence and indicate the conclusions to be drawn.[455] As noted earlier the final decision can only deal with objections in respect of which the defendant has been afforded the opportunity to make his views known. However, the final decision need not be an exact replica of the Statement of Objections.[456] The Commission may restructure facts and arguments, taking into account the defendant's comments and arguments, omitting some elements and incorporating others. If, however, in the light of new evidence or the defendant's reply to the Statement of Objections the Commission later decides to change its allegations, for example with regard to the duration or gravity of the infringement or on new legal grounds, it must send the defendant a supplementary Statement of Objections.[457] But a further formal statement is not necessary in the case of additional corroborating evidence of the infringement, provided such evidence is communicated to the defendant in some form.[458]

Particulars in the Case of Sanctions.

In proceedings in which sanctions may be imposed, the observance of the rights of defence requires that the Statement of Objections specify unequivocally the essential factors taken into consideration, the classification of those facts, the evidence on which the Commission relies and the legal person on whom sanctions may be imposed (and to whom the Statement of Objections must be addressed)[459] and the degree of the individual involvement of the defendants. The Commission

455. *Polypropylene – Shell*, CFI March 10, 1992, 1992 ECR II-757, para. 55; *Polypropylene – BASF*, CFI Dec. 17, 1992, 1992 ECR II-1523, para. 36.
456. *Quinine – ACF Chemiefarma*, ECJ July 15, 1970, 1970 ECR 661, paras 90–96; *Dyestuffs – ICI*, ECJ July 14, 1972, 1972 ECR 619, paras 21–25; *FEDETAB*, ECJ Oct. 29, 1980, 1980 ECR 3125, para. 68; *Pioneer*, ECJ June 7, 1983, 1983 ECR 1825, paras 12–17; *Anseau*, ECJ Nov. 8, 1983, 1983 ECR 3369, paras 9–11.
457. *Pioneer*, ECJ June 7, 1983, 1983 ECR 1825, paras 12–17. Supplementary statements were sent, for example, in *Frubo*, ECJ May 15, 1975, 1975 ECR 563, para. 12; *FEDETAB*, ECJ Oct. 29, 1980, 1980 ECR 3125, paras 67–68; *Polypropylene – Petrofina*, CFI Oct. 24, 1991, 1991 ECR II-1087, para. 39; *Cimenteries*, CFI Dec. 18, 1992, 1992 ECR II-2667, paras; 35–36. A Statement of Objections may be followed by further investigations (and a new hearing of the results is to be used as evidence): *Francolor – Dyestuffs*, ECJ July 14, 1972, 1972 ECR 851, paras 15–18. A new hearing is *not* necessary where the Commission's decision has been annulled on procedural grounds (e.g., for lack of authentication): *PVC II*, CFI April 20, 1999, 1999 ECR II-931, para. 261, *aff'd* ECJ Oct. 15, 2002, 2002 ECR I-8375, para. 75.
458. *ACNA-Dyestuffs*, ECJ July 14, 1972, 1972 ECR 933, paras 14–16; *Francolor-Dyestuffs*, ECJ July 14, 1972, 1972 ECR 851, paras 15–18 (fresh investigations); *FRUBO*, ECJ May 15, 1975, 1975 ECR 563, paras 12–14 (amendment of challenged agreement); *FEDETAB*, ECJ Oct. 29, 1980, 1980 ECR 3125, paras 29–35 (further complaints); *AEG-Telefunken*, ECJ Oct. 25, 1983, 1983 ECR 3151, para. 29 (evidence from another retailer).
459. *ARBED*, ECJ Oct. 2, 2003, C-176/99 P, paras 20–21; *Compagnie Maritime Belge Transports*, ECJ March 16, 2000, 2000 ECR I-1365, paras 143 and 146.

must, without giving absolute figures,[460] indicate, in the light of the Commission's Guidelines on the Method of Setting Fines, the *general* criteria for fixing the fine and calculating the amount, including gravity and duration of the suspected infringement and aggravating and attenuating circumstances, which the final decision translates into figures insofar as they are capable of being quantified.[461]

Several Defendants.

The same Statement of Objections may be served on all the defendants who were in varying ways involved in the infringement, provided that it states how each is alleged to have been implicated and whether and the extent to which they are collectively responsible for the infringement.[462] Where there are many defendants, the Statement of Objections is served on each individually but may be served on their joint agent if they have appointed one.[463] Non-EC firms may be served directly at their headquarters or through an EC branch office or subsidiary, or both.[464] As the Statement of Objections is merely a preliminary procedural document and not the Commission's final verdict on the case, there is no right of appeal to the Court of Justice.[465]

---

460. *Pioneer*, ECJ June 7, 1983, 1983 ECR 1825, paras 20–22; *Michelin*, ECJ Nov. 9, 1983, 1983 ECR 3461, paras 17–21.
461. *KNP BT – Carton*, CFI Nov. 16, 2000, 2000 ECR II-9641, paras 28–29; *HFB Holding, Isoplus – Pre-Insulated Pipes*, CFI March 20, 2002, 2002 ECR II-1487, paras 628–636.
462. *Sugar*, ECJ Dec. 16, 1975, 1975 ECR 1663, paras 423–428; *Krupp-Thyssen*, CFI Dec. 13, 2001, 2001 ECR II-3757, paras 62–68.
463. Article 10 (1) of Regulation 773/2004.
464. The non-EC defendants in the *Dyestuffs* case (the British firm ICI and the Swiss firms Sandoz and Geigy) were served with the statement of objections at their headquarters, while Continental Can was served through its EC subsidiary, after Continental had itself requested that correspondence be addressed to the subsidiary: *Geigy-Dyestuffs*, ECJ July 14, 1972, 1972 ECR 787, paras 10–12; *Continental Can*, ECJ Feb. 21, 1973, 1973 ECR 215, paras 2–3. Pleas of denial of due process because of improper service of statements of objections were dismissed by the Court in *Bayer* (*Bayo-n-ox*), CFI May 29, 1991, 1991 ECR II-219; *aff'd* ECJ Dec. 15, 1994, 1994 ECR I-5619. *See also ALMA*, ECJ Dec. 10, 1957, 1957 ECR 95, 99 (documents are properly served when they are put into the possession of the addressee wherever service takes place); *Continental Can*, *ibid.*, and *FRUBO*, ECJ May 15, 1975, 1975 ECR 563, paras 12–14 (in the latter case, service only on members of an association, not on the association itself), as were the similar pleas of ICI, Sandoz and Geigy, concerning service of the final decision on EC subsidiaries: *ICI-Dyestuffs*, July 14, 1972, 1972 ECR 619, paras 34–44; *Geigy-Dyestuffs*, July 14, 1972, 1972 ECR 787, paras 16–19.
465. *IBM*, ECJ Nov. 11, 1981, 1981 ECR 2639, para. 21. *See also Omni-Partijen Akkoord*, CFI Dec. 13, 1990, 1990 ECR II-797; *SFEI/DHL*, CFI Nov. 30, 1992, 1992 ECR II-2479; *Cimenteries*, CFI Dec. 18, 1992, 1992 ECR II-2667.

Authority to Sign the Statement of Objections and Date for Reply.
The Statement of Objections is signed by the Commissioner and sent under cover of a letter signed by the Director-General of DG COMP.[466] The letter announces that the Commission has opened proceedings against the defendant[467] with a view to a finding of a violation of Article 81 or 82. The letter explains the defendant's rights of defence, in particular: the right of access to the file in form of a CD-Rom containing the accessible documents,[468] the right to reply to the charges in writing, to produce evidence and supporting testimony from third parties[469] and to be granted an oral hearing for which a tentative date may be scheduled should the defendant request a hearing.[470] The time allowed for filing the written defence must take into account the time required for preparation of comments and the urgency.[471] The minimum time limit is two weeks, which applies to interim measures. In complex cases the time limit is normally six weeks, but may be extended if the addresses cannot with good reason comply.[472] The Commission is not obliged to take into account written submissions received after that date.[473]

Language.
The languages to be used are determined by Regulation 1/58.[474] The Commission has to respect the language selected by the addressee or the language of the member state of the jurisdiction to which the addressee is subject.[475] This applies also to the relevant extracts of any annexed documentary evidence.[476] The entire document need not be translated.[477] In multilateral cartel cases in which the co-defendants communicate with one another in one common language, usually English, the Statement of Objections may be sent to them in that language. There

---

466. The decision to commence proceedings and send the Statement of Objections is taken by the responsible member of the Commission: *ICI-Dyestuffs*, ECJ July 14, 1972, 1972 ECR 619, paras 11–14; *VCH*, ECJ Oct. 17, 1972, 1972 ECR 977, paras 10–14; *VBVB/VBBB*, ECJ Jan. 17, 1984, 1984 ECR 19, paras 12–14; *PVC II*, CFI April 20, 1999, 1999 ECR II-931, para. 330.
467. The defendant need not be informed of the opening of proceedings separately: *ACNA-Dyestuffs*, ECJ July 14, 1972, 1972 ECR 933, paras 9–13.
468. E.g., *Concrete Reinforcing Bar Cartel*, D.Comm. Dec. 17, 2002, IP/02/1908.
469. Article 13 (3) of Regulation 802/2004.
470. Article 14 of Regulation 802/2004.
471. Article 10 (2) of Regulation 773/2004.
472. Two months are sufficient even in complex cases: *PVC II*, CFI April 20, 1999, 1999 ECR II-931, para. 349, *aff'd* ECJ Oct. 15, 2002, 2002 ECR I-8375. Possibility of extension: Article 17 (4) of Regulation 773/2004.
473. Article 10 (2), second subparagraph of Regulation 773/2004.
474. 1958 OJ 385. The languages to be used under the EEA Agreement are determined by Article 12 of Protocol 23 to the EEA Agreement.
475. Article 3 of Regulation 1/58.
476. *PVC II*, CFI April 20, 1999, 1999 ECR II-931, para. 338; *Steel Mesh – Tréfilunion*, CFI April 6, 1995, 1995 ECR II-1063, para. 21; *Carton – Finnboard*, CFI May 14, 1998, 1998 ECR II-1617, para. 53; *Cement*, CFI March 15, 2000, 2000 ECR II-491, paras 631–643.
477. *Suiker Unie*, ECJ Dec. 16, 1975, 1975 ECR 1663, para. 430.

is no obligation to send a non-EC defendant the Statement of Objections in his language.[478]

Speedy Trial Principle.
The Commission is not obliged to respect certain time limits between sending of the Statement of Objection and the final decision, subject, however, to the limitation period.[479] The Commission can fix priorities at its discretion without giving the undertakings concerned the right to invoke the principle of reasonable expectation (estoppel).[480] The duration must be viewed in the light of the complexity of the case in question and the need of further examination.[481] However, a duration which goes beyond the standard of 'reasonable time'[482] and is 'exceptionally long' may justify lower fines.[483]

(b) Access to Documents

Principles.
Due process requires that the defendant be given access to the documentary evidence on which the Commission relies to support the allegations against him. Article 27 (2) of Regulation 1/2003 and Article 15 of Regulation 773/2004 codify the right of access to the file,[484] which has developed step by step under Regulation 17, starting with the Commission's practice annexing to the Statement of Objections copies of the documentary evidence on which the Commission relied,[485] and

478. Japanese defendants, for example, usually send the statement of objections in English. Including eventual amendments. *See Carton – Finnboard*, CFI May 14, 1998, 1998 ECR II-1617, paras 49–52.
479. Article 25 of Regulation 1/2003.
480. *Dutch Cranes*, CFI Oct. 22, 1997, 1997 ECR II-1739, para. 67.
481. *See Nederlandse Federatieve Vereniging voor de Groothandel op Elektrotechnisch Gebied*, CFI Dec. 16, 2003, T-5/00, para. 89.
482. *LVM – PVC*, ECJ Oct. 15, 2002, 2002 ECR I-8375, para. 199.
483. *CMA CGM – FETTSCA*, CFI March 19, 2003, T-213/00, paras 324–325 (reduction by EUR 100,000 by reason of fairness). *See also Irish Sugar*, CFI Oct. 7, 1999, 1999 ECR II-2969, para. 283 (ten months between written submission to Statement of Objections and the adoption of the decision); *Commercial Solvents*, ECJ March 6, 1974, 1974 ECR 223, para. 51.
484. *See* in particular, *Aalborg Portland – Cement*, ECJ Jan. 7, 2004, C-204/00P, paras 68–77. In addition, Council Regulation 1049/2001 (2001 OJ L 145/43) establishes the right of public access to documents of the European Parliament, the Council and the Commission, the refusal of which may be successfully pleaded. *See Mattila*, CFI Jan. 22, 2004, C-353/01 P.
485. This was accepted by the Court of Justice which held that the Commission is not obliged to give the defendant access to its entire file. *See Hoffmann-La Roche*, ECJ Feb. 13, 1979, 1979 ECR 461, para. 11; *FEDETAB*, ECJ Oct. 29, 1980, 1980 ECR 3125, para. 39; *Michelin*, ECJ Nov. 9, 1983, 1983 ECR 3461, para. 7; *AEG-Telefunken*, ECJ Oct. 25, 1983, 1983 ECR 3151, para. 30; *VBVB/VBBB*, ECJ Jan. 17, 1984, 1984 ECR 19, paras 24–25; *Philip Morris/Rothmans (Discovery)*, ECJ June 18, 1986, 1986 ECR 1899, para. 7; *Cimenteries*, CFI Dec. 18, 1992, 1992 ECR II-2667, paras 38–39.

followed by annexing a list of the entirely or partly accessible documents which could be consulted in the Commission's office. This practice had been criticized as permitting a Commission official to select certain documents and, contrary to the principle of 'equality of arms', does not allow the systematic inclusion of documents likely to exonerate the defendants. In the *Soda Ash* case the Court annulled the Commission's decision because the Commission refused to give all the defendants (members of an alleged cartel) access to all the documents disclosed by the other defendants during inspections.[486] In addition to documents used as evidence, the Commission's file usually contains material which, though not confidential, is not relevant to the case. It must be guaranteed that the accessible part includes both incriminating evidence and exculpatory evidence, whereas the non-accessible parts consist of internal documents of the Commsission and other confidential information.[487]

Business Secrets and Other Confidential Information Excluded. Documents containing business secrets and other confidential information are not accessible.[488] Business secrets are those described under Article 287 of the EC Treaty as 'information covered by the obligation of professional secrecy', in particular information relating to business relations and cost components. Business secrets include strategic information concerning the essential interests of a firm, operations and development of the business, e.g., manufacturing and distribution costs, production and trade secrets including investments, quantities produced and sold, source of supply, market shares, customer and distributor lists, cost price structure, sales policy and information concerning internal organization. Documents relating to facts or figures older than five years may lose their confidential character.[489] Confidential information must be identified and substantiated.[490] A general classification of 'confidential' will not suffice.[491] Confidential information includes the identity of a complainant, where the complainant wishes to remain anonymous because of the risk of retaliatory measures.[492] In cases of abuse of a dominant position, the Commission may not disclose to the dominant firm letters and documents received from competitors, trading partners, customers or suppliers

486. *Solvay – Soda Ash*, CFI June 29, 1995, 1995 ECR II-1775, paras 82–97; *Cement*, CFI March 15, 2000, 2000 ECR II-491, para. 317. *See also* House of Lords Select Committee on the European Communities, *Competition Practice*, 8th Report Session 1981–82, vii–viii.
487. *Aalborg Portland – Cement*, ECJ Jan. 7, 2004, C-204/00 P, para. 68. The practical problem is, however, that a complete 'file' does not exist and that access is granted by annexing to the Statement of Objections in electronic form all the documents which are considered to constitute the entire accessible file.
488. Article 16 of Regulation 773/2004.
489. *Steel Beams*, CFI June 19, 1996, 1996 ECR II-537, para. 27.
490. Article 16 (3) of Regulation 773/2004.
491. *Soda Ash – Solvay*, CFI June 29, 1995, 1995 ECR II-1775, para. 91.
492. *Adams I*, ECJ Nov. 7, 1985, 1985 ECR 3539; *British Plaster Board*, ECJ April 6, 1995, 1995 ECR I-865, para. 26.

on account of the risk of considerable economic and commercial pressure which third parties may face.[493] In the case of a multilateral cartel the co-defendants may waive the confidentiality of their documents with regard to other co-defendants.[494] If documents contain partly confidential information, this may be deleted, blackened or summarized.[495] The conflict between respecting confidentiality and disclosure as evidence may be solved by establishing non-confidential versions.[496] However, confidentiality cannot be claimed by one defendant vis-à-vis co-defendants for documents necessary to prove an infringement.[497] In the case of major and necessary evidence, confidentiality may have to yield to the public interest in effective enforcement.[498]

Internal Documents Excluded.

Access to internal documents is not permitted.[499] Internal documents include drafts, briefings, internal notes to the hierarchy and other Commission services,[500] internal reports on-the-spot investigations,[501] contacts with national authorities and the Advisory Committee[502] and the internal hearing report of the Hearing Officer.[503] During the inspection, documents containing confidential information from other undertakings[504] and internal Commission documents are inacces-

---

493. *British Plaster Board*, ECJ April 6, 1995, 1995 ECR I-865, para. 26.
494. *Polypropylene – Atochem*, CFI Oct. 24, 1991, 1991 ECR II-1177, paras 54, 166, 172, 182, 228.
495. *Soda Ash – Solvay*, CFI June 29, 1995, 1995 ECR II-1775, para. 92; *British Plaster Board*, ECJ April 6, 1996, 1996 ECR I-865, paras 29–32; *Steel Beams* (*Confidentiality*), CFI June 19, 1996, 1996 ECR II-537, para. 24. However, the defence of one defendant cannot depend on the goodwill of the other to waive confidentiality: *PVC II*, CFI April 20, 1999, 1999 ECR II-931, para. 1015. The confidentiality of certain documents does not justify refusal to grant access if partial access can be considered: *Mattila*, ECJ Jan. 22, 2004, C-353/01 P, paras 25–34 (under Council Regulation 1049/2001 on public access to documents of the European Parliament, Council and Commission, 2001 OJ L 145/43).
496. Article 16 (3) of Regulation 773/2004. *See Soda Ash – ICI*, CFI June 29, 1995, 1995 ECR II-1847, paras 98 and 103; *Endemol*, CFI April 28, 1999, 1999 ECR II-1299, para. 67
497. Article 15 (3) of Regulation 773/2004. *See Cement*, CFI March 15, 2000, 2000 ECR I-491, para. 317.
498. Article 27 (2), last subparagraph of Regulation 1/2003.
499. Article 15 (2) of Regulation 773/2004. *See Cement*, CFI March 15, 2000, 2000 ECR II-491, para. 428; *Krupp-Thyssen*, CFI Dec. 13, 2001, 2001 ECR II-3757, para. 89. The Court of Justice itself does not claim access to the Commission's internal file, unless it suspects that the Commission's decision was motivated by factors extraneous to antitrust enforcement and hence involved a misuse of power: *Philip Morris/Rothmans* (*Discovery*), ECJ June 18, 1986, 1986 ECR 1899, para. 11.
500. *NHM Steel*, CFI Dec. 10, 1997, 1997 ECR II-2293.
501. *British Plaster Board*, ECJ April 6, 1996, 1996 ECR I-865, para. 28.
502. Article 27 (2) of Regulation 1/2003; Article 15 (2) of Regulation 773/2004. *See Pioneer*, ECJ June 7, 1983, 1983 ECR 1825, paras 34–36.
503. *Polypropylene – ICI*, ECJ Dec. 11, 1986 (not published in ECR); 1987–2 CMLR 500.
504. Firms are asked when replying to discovery requests and statements of objections to indicate information which they regard as confidential and if possible to place it in a separate annex:

sible.[505] Studies commissioned by the Commission are accessible if they are used directly or indirectly in the proceedings, irrespective of their intrinsic value.[506] However, documents and studies which are already in the public domain do not need to be included.[507]

Disputes on Confidentiality to be Settled by the Hearing Officer or Decided by the Commission.

Where the Commission intends to disclose information which the informants consider confidential, it shall inform them in writing of its intention and of its reasons. In the case of disagreement the Commission adopts a decision on the disclosure.[508] This decision may be appealed.[509]

Consequences of a Violation of the Right of Access to the File.

The right of access to the file is ancillary to the Statement of Objections in cases involving decisions on infringements, decisions rejecting complaints and decisions imposing interim measures.[510] The right cannot therefore be exercised during the investigative proceedings nor after the adoption of the decision.[511] Documents which have not been made accessible cannot be used as evidence.[512] A violation of the right of access to the file constitutes an infringement of an essential procedural requirement, where the defendant adequately demonstrates, 'not that the Commission's decision would have been different in content, but rather that it would

Article 16 (2) of Regulation 773/2004. But in many cases their classification is too sweeping and confidentiality is claimed for whole documents or for parts which are merely embarrassing rather than commercially sensitive.

505. By, for example, being clipped together in the file or removed from it. In the case of material from other firms, confidential passages may be deleted or a non-confidential summary prepared.

506. Statistics, market studies and economic analyses are accessible except where such analyses are established by the Commission for national authorities: *Van der Wal*, ECJ Jan. 11, 2000, 2000 ECR I-1, paras 20–23.

507. *British Plaster Board*, ECJ April 6, 1995, 1995 ECR I-865, para. 22.

508. Article 17 of Regulation 773/2004.

509. Prior to Regulation 1/2003 such disputes were settled by decision of the Hearing Officer which was appealable: *see Commerzbank I*, CFI Dec. 5, 2001, 2001 ECR II-3501, para. 41 (refusing one party access to certain documents relating to the abandonment of procedure against other parties may not be appealed before any decision finding an infringement and possibly imposing a penalty on it is adopted); *Commerzbank II*, CFI July 9, 2003, T-219/01, paras 65–73.

510. *Cimenteries*, CFI Dec. 18, 1992, 1992 ECR II-2667, para. 38.

511. *Baustahlgewerbe*, ECJ Dec. 17, 1998, 1998 ECR I-8417, para. 330; *Cement* CFI March 15, 2000, 2000 ECR II-491, para. 431.

512. Article 11 (2) of Regulation 773/2004. *See esp. Hoffmann-La Roche*, ECJ Feb. 13, 1979, 1979 ECR 461, para. 14; *Pioneer*, ECJ June 7, 1983, 1983 ECR 1825, paras 24–29; *AEG-Telefunken*, ECJ Oct. 25, 1983, 1983 ECR 3151, paras 21–30; *Michelin*, ECJ Nov. 11, 1983, 1983 ECR 3461, paras 5–8; *Soda Ash – Solvay*, CFI June 29, 1995, 1995 ECR II-1775, paras 81–97; *Cement*, CFI March 15, 2000, 2000 ECR II-491, para. 382.

have been better able to ensure its defence had there been no error'.[513] Failure to communicate a document is therefore a breach of the rights of defence only if the undertaking concerned shows, first, that the Commission relied on that document to support its objection concerning the existence of an infringement, and, second, that the objection could be proved only by reference to that document.[514] With respect to an exculpatory document the undertaking concerned must establish that it was indispensible for its defence[515] or, according the new standards set by the Court of Justice, that its non-disclosure was able to influence, to its disadvantage, the course of proceedings and the content of the decision of the Commission.[516] A violation of the right of access to the file can be remedied during a later stage of the administrative procedure before the Commission only if the right of defence is fully respected prior to the adoption of a decision, but not during the subsequent judicial proceedings.[517]

(c) Written Observations

Written Comments.
Parties may make known their views in writing by the date set by the Commission. The Commission is not obliged to take into account written comments received after the time limit has expired.[518] Parties are, however, not obliged to comment and may nevertheless contest the facts before the Court of Justice.[519] The Commission may proceed to further fact-finding, provided it affords the parties the opportunity of making their views known if it intends to deal with such new facts (objections) in the final decision.

(d) Oral Hearing

Nature.
The defendants may request in their written comments the opportunity to develop their arguments in an oral hearing without needing to show a sufficient interest.

513. *Thyssen Stahl*, ECJ Oct. 2, 2003, C-194/99 P, para. 31.
514. *Aalborg Portland – Cement*, ECJ Jan. 7, 2004, C-204/00 P, para. 71.
515. *LVM – PVC*, ECJ Oct. 15, 2002, 2002 ECR I-8375, para. 341.
516. *Aalborg Portland – Cement*, ECJ Jan. 7, 2004, C-204/00 P, para. 74.
517. *LVM – PVC*, ECJ Oct. 15, 2002, 2002 ECR I-8375, para. 325; *Aalborg Portland – Cement*, ECJ Jan. 7, 2004, C-204/00 P, para. 104. *See also Soda Ash – Solvay*, CFI June 29, 1995, 1995 ECR II-1795, para. 103, which overruled the earlier ruling in *Hoffmann-La Roche*, ECJ Feb. 13, 1979, 1979 ECR 461, paras 15–17.
518. Article 10 (3) of Regulation 773/2004. *See*, with respect to the procedure before the Court of Justice, Article 44 (1) of the Rules of Procedure, and *Branco*, CFI Dec. 13, 1995, 1995 ECR II-2993, para. 9.
519. *Hilti*, CFI Dec. 12, 1991, 1991 ECR II-1439, para. 38. *See*, however, the previous comments of Advocate General Warner in *Distillers*, 1980 ECR 2267, 2291.

Only third parties are required to show a 'sufficient interest' in being heard.[520] The hearing is ancillary to the written procedure. Its purpose is to give the parties an opportunity to elaborate on points raised in their written answer. There is no obligation on the defendants' representatives to reply. The hearing is thus not a trial.[521] As the procedure before the Commission is purely an administrative procedure, the Commission is not required to afford the opportunity to cross-examine a particular witness and to analyse his statements at the investigation stage.[522] Nor can the Commission constrain the parties to admit infringements because this would constitute a breach of the right not to give self-incriminating evidence.[523] However, questions and replies may clarify statements and avoid misunderstandings. The oral hearing is relatively brief, rarely lasting more than one or two days, except in cases involving many defendants or complex Article 82 cases, where it may last a week or more. The date for the hearing is set by the Hearing Officer, a tentative date being scheduled in the covering letter accompanying the Statement of Objections.

Preparation and Conduct of the Hearing.
The Hearing Officer ensures that the hearing is properly prepared and that the rights of the defence are respected.[524] The Hearing Officer determines the date, the duration and the place of the hearing.[525] He may hold a preparatory meeting with the parties and the Commission staff in order to clarify questions of fact. He may supply in advance to the parties invited to the hearing a list of questions on which he wishes them to make known their views.[526] The Hearing Officer is fully responsible for the conduct of the hearing and decides in particular whether fresh documents should be admitted and persons heard separately or in the presence of the others. The Hearing Officer also settles disputes on the confidentiality of certain documents (the decision being left to the Commission[527]) and whether persons should be heard *in camera* after the representatives of other firms have

---

520. Article 13 of Regulation 773/2004; Article 27 (3) of Regulation 1/2003. However, the Commission normally grants third parties the right to submit written observations as this is a way for it to get more information on the case under investigation.
521. *See* Johannes, 'The Role of the Hearing Officer', 1989 Fordham Corp.L.Inst. 429.
522. *Aalborg Portland – Cement*, ECJ Jan. 7, 2004, C-204/00 P, para. 200.
523. *Ibid.*, paras 206–209.
524. Article 14 of Regulation 773/2004; Commission Decision of 23 May 2001 on the terms of reference of Hearing Officers, 2001 OJ L 162/21; Decision of the EFTA Surveillance Authority of Oct. 30, 2002, 2003 OJ L 80/27.
525. Article 12 of the Commission Decision on the Hearing Officer, 2001 OJ L 162/21.
526. Article 11 of the Commission Decision on the Hearing Officer.
527. Article 17 of Regulation 773/2004. This decision is appealable: *Peugeot*, CFI May 2, 1997, 1997 ECR II-663.

left the room.[528] The Hearing Officer may afford the persons heard the opportunity to submit within a fixed time limit written comments after the oral hearing.[529]

Participation.

Firms cannot be represented solely by outside counsel, but must send officers or employees of the firm as well.[530] They can ask the Commission to hear testimony from any third party, expert or other witnesses.[531] If the Commission acts on a complaint it informs the complainant of its reasons by sending a non-confidential copy of the Statement of Objections and affords the complainant the opportunity to orally expressing its views, if it so requests in its written comments.[532] Testimony is not given under oath. Representatives of member states' authorities are usually present.[533] Hearings are not open to the public.[534] Thus, parties may not participate in the hearing merely as observers.

Minutes of the Oral Hearing.

Pursuant to the old Regulation 99/63, after the hearing, minutes (practically a verbatim transcript of the tape in the original languages[535]) were drawn up by the Hearing Officer and sent to the parties for comment and any necessary corrections.[536] This practice was extremely time-consuming, so under Regulation 4064/89 on merger control, the statements of each person heard were recorded and the tape was made available to each person heard on request. This procedure has been adopted in Article 14 (8) of Regulation 773/2004. The tape is made available to the participants, but the Commission must take the necessary precautions to ensure that the entitlement of the undertakings concerned to to protection of confidential information is not undermined. An outright prohibition by the

---

528. Article 12 (3) of the Commission Decision on the Hearing Officer.
529. Article 12 (4) of the Commission Decision on the Hearing Officer. However, this may imply that other defendants must be given the opportunity to comment on such additional written submissions.
530. Article 14 (4) and (5) of Regulation 773/2004: The parties may be 'assisted' by their lawyers. Non-EC lawyers are generally admitted.
531. However, the Commission can refuse witnesses: *FEDETAB*, ECJ Oct. 29, 1980, 1980 ECR 3125, paras 20–25; *VBVB/VBBB*, ECJ Jan. 17, 1984, 1984 ECR 19, paras 17–18, though this rarely happens. The decision is taken by the Hearing Officer after consultation with the Director responsible.
532. Article 6 (1) Regulation 773/2004. Defendants and complainants are, however, heard separately if their evidence is confidential.
533. Article 14 (3) of Regulation 773/2004.
534. Article 14 (6) of Regulation 773/2004.
535. *Parker Pen*, July 14, 1994, 1994 ECR II-549, para. 74.
536. Article 9 (4) of Regulation 99/63. Complaints of inaccuracies in minutes and infringements of the defendant's rights by inordinate delay in sending them were dismissed in *Boehringer-Quinine*, ECJ July 15, 1970 ECR 769, paras 16–18, and in two of the *Dyestuffs* cases (*Bayer-Dyestuffs*, ECJ July 14, 1972, 1972 ECR 745, paras 16–18, and *ICI-Dyestuffs*, ECJ July 14, 1972, 1972 ECR 619, paras 27–33).

Commission of such access would be incompatible with the principle of sincere cooperation between Commission and national courts and would also undermine the rights of litigants deriving from the direct effect of Articles 81 and 82 in relations between individuals which the national courts may safeguard.[537]

Hearing Officer's Report.

The Hearing Officer reports to the competent member of the Commission[538] on the hearing, and the conclusions he draws from it, with respect of the right to be heard. His report concerns procedural issues (in particular the objectivity of any enquiry) but may also include observations on the further progress of the proceedings (need for further information, withdrawal or reformulation of objections).[539] On the basis of the draft decision the Hearing Officer prepares his final report which is submitted as an appendix to the draft decision (i) to the Advisory Committee, (ii) to the competent member of the Commission and (iii) to the Commission, in order to ensure that the Commission is fully apprised of all relevant issues of the proceedings. The final report is communicated to the addressees of the decision[540] and published together with the decision.[541] Finally, the Hearing Officer decides on the disclosure of confidential information in the published version of the decision.

Closure of Defence Procedure.

After the oral hearing the defendant may only make further submissions if this was agreed at the hearing. However, should the Commission continue its investigations after the hearing and wish to make new allegations or use new evidence against the defendant, the defence procedure will be restarted with the sending of a new or a supplementary Statement of Objections and the holding of another hearing. After the defence procedure is closed, the Commission must consult the Advisory Committee on Restrictive Practices and Monopolies, which is composed of representatives of national antitrust authorities.[542] This acts as a final procedural safeguard, prior to the adoption of the decision, to ensure that the defendant has been treated fairly.

---

537. *Postbank*, CFI Sept. 18, 1996, 1996 ECR II-921, paras 63–69 (annulling the Commission decision which allowed third parties participating to the hearing to use the minutes before a national court).
538. A copy is given to the Director-General for Competition.
539. Article 13 of the Commission Decision on the Hearing Officer.
540. Previously, the report was treated as an internal document: *Pre-Insulated Pipes – HFB*, CFI March 20, 2002, 2002 ECR II-1847, para. 40.
541. Articles 15 and 16 of the Commission Decision on the Hearing Officer.
542. Article 14 of Regulation 1/2003. *See infra* section E.5.

3. Hearing of Complainants

Not the Same Procedural Rights as Defendants.
A complainant does not have the same rights as the defendants. However, a complainant is entitled to participate in proceedings where the Commission issues a Statement of Objections relating to a matter in respect of which it has received a complaint[543] and a complainant must be heard when the Commission considers that on the basis of the information received there are insufficient grounds for action.[544]

Prior to Adverse Decisions.[545]
In the proceedings leading up to a contemplated cease and desist order and/or sanction, a complainant may, after having submitted its written comments on the non-confidential version of the Statement of Objections,[546] participate in the oral hearing and orally express its views.[547] Complainants may show a legitimate interest[548] in the outcome of the proceedings, including the conditions and modalities of a contemplated decision,[549] which they are entitled to appeal.[550] The Commission must guarantee both defendants and complainant confidentiality of information received from the other side. However, the proceedings at the oral hearing are not contradictory (no cross-examination).[551] If the Commission wishes to release information which the defendant claims is confidential, it must first give the defendant the opportunity of challenging the disclosure before the Court.[552]

Prior to Rejection of Complaint.[553]
A complainant must be heard before the Commission rejects its complaint:

- because there are insufficient grounds on which to take action, including insufficient Community interest,[554]

---

543. Article 6 of Regulation 773/2004.
544. Article 7 of Regulation 773/2004.
545. *See* Commission Notice on the handling of complaints, points 64–73.
546. Articles 6 (1) and 16 (2) of Regulation 773/2004.
547. Article 13 (3) of Regulation 773/2004.
548. Article 5 (1) of Regulation 773/2004.
549. *See also Philip Morris/Rothmans*, ECJ Nov. 17, 1987, 1987 ECR 3801; *NALOO*, CFI Sept. 24, 1996, 1996 ECR II-1019.
550. They are normally directly and individually concerned in the sense of Article 230 (4) of the EC Treaty.
551. *Philip Morris/Rothmans*, ECJ Nov. 17, 1987, 1987 ECR 3801, para. 20; *NALOO*, CFI Sept. 24, 1996, 1996 ECR II-1019, para. 320.
552. *Akzo I*, ECJ June 24, 1986, 1986 ECR 1965, para. 29 (although this procedure is likely to considerably delay proceedings).
553. *See* Commission Notice on the handling of complaints, points 74–79.
554. Article 7 (1) of Regulation 773/2004.

- because the Commission intends to find that Articles 81 and 82 are not, or are no longer, applicable or that the conditions of Article 81 (3) are satisfied,[555] or
- because a national competition authority is dealing with the case.[556]

It informs the complainant of its reasons and gives the complainant the opportunity to make known its views in writing within the time-limit set by the Commission.[557] The complainant may request access to the documents on which the Commission bases its provisional assessment (which is less than access to 'the file').[558] However, the Commission normally does not grant a formal oral hearing.[559] If the written submission does not lead to a different assessment the Commission rejects the complaint by decision (which may be appealed). If the complainant fails to make known its views within this time-limit the complaint is deemed to have been withdrawn.[560]

4. HEARING OF OTHER INTERESTED PARTIES

Right of Being Heard.
Interested parties potentially affected by a decision addressed to other firms do not have as far-reaching rights to a hearing as do the direct addresses of the decision.[561] If the third parties show a sufficient interest, the Commission informs them in writing of the nature and subject matter of the procedure, but normally does not provide a non-confidential version of the Statement of Objections.[562] The intereested parties may make appropriate observations in writing and orally develop their views.[563] The Commission may invite any other person (even those which did not show a sufficient interest) to express their views.[564]

555. *See Rendo/IJsselcentrale*, CFI Dec. 12, 1996, 1996 ECR II-1827; *Matra/Ford-Volkswagen*, CFI July 15, 1994, 1994 ECR II-595, para. 34.
556. Article 13 (1) of Regulation 1/2003. In this case the Commission informs the complainant of the national competition authority which is dealing or has already dealt with the case: Article 9 of Regulation 773/2004. Likewise, a national competition authority may reject a complaint where the case has already been dealt with by another national competition authority: Article 13 (2) of Regulation 1/2003.
557. Article 7 (1) and (2) of Regulation 773/2004.
558. Article 8 of Regulation 773/2004. *See Matra/Ford-Volkswagen*, CFI July 15, 1994, 1994 ECR II-595, para. 34. However, a complainant has no right to receive or consult confidential information: *FEDETAB*, ECJ Oct. 29, 1980, 1980 ECR 3125, para. 46.
559. *See Philip Morris/Rothmans*, ECJ Nov. 17, 1987, 1987 ECR 3801, para. 19; *NALOO*, CFI Sept. 24, 1996, 1996 ECR II-1019, paras 275–276.
560. Article 7 (3) of Regulation 773/2004.
561. Article 13 of Regulation 773/2004.
562. Article 13 (1) of Regulation 773/2004.
563. Article 14 (7) of Regulation 773/2004. The Commission may refuse to give third parties an oral hearing where the written observations received do not need further oral explanation: *Deutscher Komponistenverband*, ECJ July 13, 1971, 1971 ECR 705; *VBVB/VBBB*, ECJ Jan. 17, 1984, 1984 ECR 19, paras 16–19.
564. Article 27 (3) of Regulation 1/003; Article 13 (4) of Regulation 773/2004.

No Access to File.
Third parties are normally not granted access to the file.[565] The Commission may communicate non-confidential documents to third parties only where necessary for a proper submission of observations.

5. HEARING (CONSULTATION) OF THE ADVISORY COMMITTEE

Liaison with National Authorities.
Before taking formal decisions, whether favourable or adverse to the addressee, including interim measures, the Commission is required to consult the Advisory Committee on Restrictive Practices and Monopolies, which is composed of representatives of the member states' competition authorities.[566] The meeting takes place not earlier than 14 days after the dispatch of the notice convening it, together with a summary of the case, an indication of the most important documents (in particular the Statement of Objections, the defendant's written defence and replies to discovery requests) and the draft decision, and 7 days in the case of a draft interim measure. A shorter period may be agreed by mutual consent of all members of the Advisory Committee.[567] Consultation may also take place by written procedure (non-opposition within a fixed time limit). The Committee's meeting is not open to the defendants or members of the general public. The Committee's opinion is attached to the draft decision which is sent to the Commissioners for approval, and may, at the recommendation of the Committee, be published.[568] It is not binding on the Commission but the Commission shall take 'the utmost account' of the opinion.[569]

F. Decisions, Orders, Fines and Informal Settlements

1. COMMON PROCEDURAL REQUIREMENTS OF DECISIONS

Introduction: The Importance of 'Decisions'.
The Commission makes a formal determination, or 'decision', in only a minority of the cases it investigates. The vast majority of cases are closed without a formal decision. Decisions, however, are more important than settlements, both in terms

565. *See Nestlé/Perrier*, CFI April 27, 1995, 1995 ECR II-1213, para. 64.
566. Article 14 of Regulation 1/2003.
567. *See* already *Kaysersberg/Procter & Gamble*, CFI Nov. 27, 1997, 1997 ECR II-2137, para. 88 (stating that a shorter notice is not necessarily 'unduly' likely to make the decision unlawful).
568. Similarly Article 19 (7) of the merger control regulation. Article 10 (6) of Regulation 17 did not provide for any publication, *see Pioneer*, ECJ June 7, 1983, 1983 ECR 1825, paras 34–36.
569. Article 14 (5) of Regulation 1/2003.

of their immediate legal effects and in terms of their status as precedents and guides to Commission policy. They are therefore subject to detailed requirements in the procedure leading up to and surrounding their adoption and to the right of judicial review by the Court of Justice.[570] After a description of procedures and requirements common to all decisions, this section will deal with the main types of decision in turn. It will conclude with a brief description of settlements.

Types of Decision.

The most common types of decisions are cease-and-desist orders, sanctions (for substantive or procedural infringements), decisions rejecting complaints, decisions stating the inapplicability of Article 81 or 82, and, more rarely, temporary injunctions (interim orders). Finally, there are the purely procedural discovery and investigation orders, the procedure for which has already been described. Several kinds of decisions addressed to the same parties may be handed down in a single decision. For example, cease-and-desist orders may often also impose fines on the parties,[571] and a decision rejecting a complaint may also state the inapplicability of Article 81 or 82[572] or conclude that the conditions of Article 81 (3) are satisfied.[573] In addition, other administrative acts of the Commission, such as letters rejecting a complaint[574] or closing proceedings (which may indirectly reject a complaint), may affect the legal position of the addressee or third parties and therefore be appealable.

Drafting and Adoption.

Decisions are drafted by DG COMP in consultation with the Commission's Legal Service and other interested departments and under the supervision of the Commissioner responsible for competition. Substantive decisions are approved by majority vote of the full Commission in an '*oral procedure*'.[575] This is the rule for important decisions, such as decisions imposing fines. Other substantive decisions may be approved by way of non-opposition to a draft submitted to all Commissioners in a '*written procedure*';[576] in case of opposition the decision will be orally discussed and approved by the full Commission. The decisions must be approved by the Commission in the procedural languages; only linguistic and orthographic corrections may be made thereafter by the competent Commissioner whereas the reasoning of the decision may not be amended irrespective of its

570. *See infra* section G.
571. *See German Banks*, D.Comm. Dec. 11, 2001, 2003 OJ L 15/1.
572. Article 10 of Regulation 1/2003. *See SFEI*, CFI Jan. 15, 1997, 1997 ECR II-1.
573. Under Regulation 17 *see Storck Amsterdam*, CFI Feb 17, 2000, 2000 ECR II-309; *M6, Antena 3, Gestevision, SIC/UER/Eurovision*, CFI Oct. 8, 2002, 2002 ECR II-3805.
574. *See UPS/Deutsche Post*, CFI March 20, 2002, 2002 ECR II-1915.
575. *See Steel Beams – British Steel*, CFI March 11, 1999, 1999 ECR II-263, paras 117–141.
576. In *Quinine*, the Court dismissed the plea that the whole file on a case had to be circulated to each Commissioner: *Buchler-Quinine*, ECJ July 15, 1970, 1970 ECR 733, paras 21–23.

importance or relevance.[577] The adoption of the decision in the other languages can, however, be delegated to the responsible Commissioner.[578] Decisions of the Commission have to be signed by the President and the Secretary General.[579] Certain procedural decisions may be taken by an individual member of the Commission to whom decision powers have been delegated (in competition matters) by the Commissioner responsible for DG COMP), subject to the control of the whole Commission.[580] This '*delegation procedure*' applies to orders for production of information or documents;[581] carrying out investigations of firms on their premises;[582] commencing formal proceedings in a case;[583] sending 'statements of objections';[584] publishing notices of proposed clearances;[585] withdrawing the benefit of a block exemption regulation,[586] communicating confidential information[587] and decisions on the application of third parties to be heard.[588] The signature of many procedural documents, such as simple requests for information and warrants, and other responsibilities, such as preparing and chairing oral hearings and meetings of the Advisory Committee on Restrictive Practices and Monopolies,

577. *LdPE*, CFI April 6, 1995, 1995 ECR II-729, paras 84 and 120.
578. *PVC*, ECJ June 15, 1994, 1994 ECR I-2629, para. 71; *Soda Ash – Solvay*, CFI June 29, 1995, 1995 ECR II-1825, paras 73–76.
579. The lack of this formality was the reason for annulling *PVC*, ECJ June 15, 1994, 1994 ECR I-2555, paras 75–77 and *Soda Ash – ICI*, June 29, 1995 ECR II-1901, paras 28–31 (not to a non-existing decision as ruled by the Court of First Instance: Feb. 27, 1992, 1992 ECR II-315 para. 68); *IECC*, CFI Sept. 16, 1998, 1998 ECR II-3597, para. 117. *See also Steel Beams – British Steel*, CFI March 11, 1999, 1999 ECR II-263, paras 143–154 (with respect to the 'authentication' of the decision in the languages of the proceedings).
580. *PVC*, CFI Feb. 27, 1992, 1992 ECR II-318, para. 57; *aff'd* ECJ June 15, 1994, 1994 ECR II-2629, para. 71. In *Akzo II*, ECJ Sept. 23, 1986, 1986 ECR 2585, paras 35–39, the Court upheld the principle of delegating 'simple administrative decisions' to individual Commissioners, subject to the control of the whole Commission, but recommended that the decisions to delegate be published. However, the delegation procedure must be limited to clearly defined management or administrative measures in the sense of Article 13 of the Commission's Rules of Procedure of Sept. 25, 1999, 1999 OJ L 252/41; *see ASPEC*, CFI April 27, 1995, 1995 ECR II-1281 para. 107.
581. Simple requests for information can be signed by the competent director: *Dyestuffs – ICI*, ECJ July 14, 1972, 1972 ECR 619, 653; *VBVB*, ECJ March 31, 1982, 1982 ECR 1241.
582. *Akzo II*, ECJ Sept. 23, 1986, 1986 ECR 2558, para. 39; *Dow Iberica*, ECJ Oct. 17, 1989, 1989 ECR 3165, para. 58; *Hoechst*, CFI Sept. 21, 1989, 1989 ECR II-2859, paras 44–46.
583. *Akzo II*, ECJ Sept. 23, 1986, 1986 ECR 2558, para. 33.
584. *Dyestuffs – Geigy*, ECJ July 14, 1972, 1972 ECR 961, para. 4; *VCH*, ECJ Oct. 17, 1972, 1972 ECR 787, para. 10.
585. No longer compulsory as under Article 19 (3) of Regulation 17, *see Akzo II*, ECJ Sept. 23, 1986, 1986 ECR 2558, para. 36.
586. Article 29 of Regulation 1/2003.
587. *Akzo II*, ECJ June 24, 1986, 1986 ECR 1965 para. 27. For the purposes of the oral hearing the hearing officer is delegated to take the necessary decisions: Article 5 (1) and (2) of the Commission's decision of Dec. 12, 1994, 1994 OJ L 330/67.
588. Delegated to the hearing officer.

are sub-delegated to officials.[589]

Reasoning.

Under Article 253 of the EC Treaty, decisions must be properly reasoned, that is, must present the evidence and legal and economic argument justifying them. This requirement also applies to responses to complaints[590] and to interim measures.[591] According to the Court of First Instance in *IECC,* the statement of reasons for an individual decision must be such:

> 'as, first, to enable the person to whom it is addressed to ascertain the matters justifying the measure adopted so that he can, if necessary, defend his rights and verify whether or not the decision is well founded and, second, to enable the Community judicature to exercise its powers of review.'[592]

Decisions which fail to meet the required standard may be struck down for breach of an essential procedural requirement.[593] The amount of detail required in the reasoning of a decision varies according to the type of decision and its novelty. Procedural decisions need not be explained in as much detail as decisions making substantive findings, or routine decisions as much as those departing from earlier precedents.[594] The Commission need not refute in detail all the parties' submissions in the text of the decision.[595] The reasoning may be limited to the essential factual and legal aspects[596] but must result from the decision itself and not from additional declarations of the Commission or Commission officials, e.g. during a press conference.[597]

---

589. Article 11 (2) of the Commission's Rules of Procedure.
590. This is because under Article 232 the Commission can be taken to the Court for failing to 'define its position' on requests for it to take action of some kind, which implies a satisfactory degree of reasoning in its response: *see GEMA II*, ECJ Oct. 18, 1979, 1979 ECR 3173, paras 5, 11 and 19–20 (a complaint); *Deutscher Komponistenverband*, ECJ July 13, 1971, 1971 ECR 705 (a request for an oral hearing).
591. *Noordwijks Cement Accoord*, ECJ March 15, 1967, 1967 ECR 75 (Article 15 (6) decision).
592. *IECC*, CFI Sept. 16, 1998, 1998 ECR II-3597, para. 125. *See also Fleuren Compost*, CFI Jan. 14, 2004, T-109/01, para. 119.
593. *M6, Antena 3, Gestévision, SIC/UER – Eurovision II*, CFI Oct. 8, 2002, 2002 ECR II-3805. *See also Belgian Wallpaper*, ECJ Nov. 26, 1975, 1975 ECR 1491, paras 22–35, where the Court cancelled the fine because the Commission had failed to show an effect on trade; *Continental Can*, ECJ Feb. 21, 1973, 1973 ECR 215, paras 28–37, and *Kali-Chemie*, ECJ May 14, 1975, 1975 ECR 499, where the decisions were quashed because of doubts about the Commission's market definition.
594. *Belgian Wallpaper*, ECJ Nov. 26, 1975, 1975 ECR 1491, paras 30–31.
595. E.g., *Carton – Mayr-Melnhof*, CFI May 14, 1998, 1998 ECR II-1751, para. 42; *PVC II*, CFI April 20, 1999, 1999 ECR II-931, paras 386–388; *Asia Motor II*, CFI June 29, 1993, 1993 ECR II-669, para. 31 (rejection of complaint).
596. *NALOO*, CFI Sept. 24, 1996, 1996 ECR II-1019, para. 299.
597. *Hilti*, Dec. 12, 1991, 1991 ECR II-1439, para. 136; *Danish Furs*, CFI July 2, 1992, 1992 ECR II-1931, para. 131; *Carton – SCA*, CFI May 14, 1998, 1998 ECR II-1373, para. 204.

Form.

The background and reasons for the decision are placed in a lengthy preamble, divided into a 'Facts' and a 'Legal Assessment' section. The terms of the decision are stated concisely in a series of numbered articles at the end ('operative part'), which also lists the names and addresses of the addressees. In the case of cease-and-desist orders and fining decisions, this 'operative part' begins with a finding that the agreement in question was, or is, a breach of Articles 81 or 82 (or the procedural rules) and informs the addressees that the decision is enforceable.[598] The operative part must be interpreted in the light of the statement of reasons.[599] Mistakes in the operative part of the decision, such as the omission of the name of one of the addressees, can have serious consequences,[600] but the Court has shown itself tolerant of obvious clerical errors or misprints.[601] Occasionally, the Commission has issued new decisions to correct mistakes or to vary the terms of an original decision.[602] There is no need for the Commission to inform the addressees of their right to judicial review.[603]

Language.

The language in which the decision is served must be one of the official languages of the EC and EEA countries selected by the applicant or, in case of *ex officio* proceedings, that of the addressee's country of residence,[604] but for non-EC firms any EC language may be used, usually English.[605]

598. The operative part of the decision determines its scope and appealability: *Dutch Banks Association*, CFI Sept. 17, 1992, 1992 ECR II-2182, para. 32.
599. *Sugar – Suiker Unie*, ECJ Dec. 16, 1975, 1975 ECR 1663, para. 122; *Carton – Sarrio*, CFI May 14, 1998, 1998 ECR II-1439, para. 274.
600. Making the decision inapplicable to that firm: *Sugar*, ECJ Dec. 16, 1975, 1975 ECR 1663, paras 311–317.
601. Such as differences between the title of the decision given in the version served on the addressee and that in the published version: *Continental Can*, ECJ Feb. 21, 1973, 1973 ECR 215, paras 7–8. Only obvious infringements of essential procedural requirements are likely to lead to annulment of the decision: *NALOO*, CFI Sept. 24, 1996, 1996 ECR II-1019, para. 111.
602. As in *GEMA I*, D.Comm. June 2, 1971, 1971 OJ L 134/15, and *GEMA II*, D.Comm. July 6, 1972, 1972 OJ L 166/22 (substitution of different positive obligations); *Anseau I*, D.Comm. Dec. 17, 1981, 1982 OJ L 167/39, and *Anseau II*, D.Comm. Nov. 4, 1982, 1982 OJ L 325/20, *Anseau III*, D.Comm. Dec. 5, 1983, 1983 OJ L 376/7 (repeal of fine imposed on wrong person and imposition on correct one).
603. *ACF Chemiefarma-Quinine*, ECJ July 15, 1970, 1970 ECR 661, paras 97–98. Guérin automobiles, ECJ March 5, 1999, 1999 ECR I-1441.
604. Articles 2 and 3 of Regulation 1/58 (1958 OJ 385) and Article 12 of Protocol 23 to the EEA Agreement. Article 8 of the EC Treaty as amended by the Amsterdam Treaty refers, with regard to the languages to be used by Community citizens, to Article 248 which would include Gaelic (although not mentioned in Regulation 1/58 as amended in 1994 OJ C 241/285.
605. *See supra* section E.2 (a).

Service.

To be enforceable, decisions must be served on their addressees.[606] There is no prescribed method of service,[607] and the usual method is by recorded delivery mail. Non-EC firms may be served directly by mail to their headquarters,[608] through diplomatic channels, or through an EC subsidiary or branch.[609] From the date of service the two-month period for appeal starts to run.[610] A copy of the decision or order is simultaneously sent to the authorities of the addressee's member state.[611] Non-EC countries' authorities are also generally informed of decisions addressed to their nationals.[612] Irregularities of service do not affect the validity of the decision;[613] they may only lead to a later start of the appeal period.[614] The addressee has to bear the consequences of internal irregularities after service.[615]

Publication.

Cease-and-desist orders (Article 7), interim measures (Article 8), decisions on commitments (Article 9), decisions stating the inapplicability of Article 81 or 82 (Article 10) and decisions imposing sanctions (Articles 23 and 24) must be published according to Article 30 of Regulation 1/2003.[616] Procedural decisions may be published if of sufficient general interest.[617] Publication is in the EC *Official Journal,* 'L' (legislation) series. Confidential business data, such as unpublished sales figures or market shares, are deleted from the published version. Publication

606. Article 254 (3) of the EC Treaty.
607. All that is required is that the decision be brought to the cognisance of the addressee: *ALMA*, ECJ Dec. 10, 1957, 1957 ECR 95, 99; *Continental Can*, ECJ Feb. 21, 1973, 1973 ECR 215, paras 9–10.
608. *Continental Can*, ECJ Feb. 21, 1973, 1973 ECR 215, paras 9–10.
609. *ICI-Dyestuffs*, ECJ July 14, 1972, 1972 ECR 619, paras 34–44.
610. Third paragraph of Article 230 of the EEC Treaty. The period begins to run on the day following receipt: Article 81 (1) of the Rules of Procedure of the Court of Justice. The period is extended for all firms except those based in Luxembourg by a certain number of days or weeks, depending on distance. The period within which interested third parties may appeal begins to run on the 15th day after publication of the decision in the EC *Official Journal.*
611. Under the general liaison requirement in Article 11 of Regulation 1/2003.
612. Under agreements with EFTA and other OECD countries. *See supra* section D.2 (a).
613. *Dunlop Slazenger*, CFI July 7, 1994, 1994 ECR II-447, para. 25. Irregularities of service to one party do not affect the validity of the decision *vis-à-vis* the other parties anyway: *Dalmine*, CFI June 24, 1998, 1998 ECR II-2383, para. 40.
614. *Geigy*, ECJ July 14, 1972, 1972 ECR 787, para. 18; *Fiatagri*, CFI Oct. 27, 1994, 1994 ECR II-905, para. 27. However, irregularities of service are irrelevant if the addressee is duly informed: *Dalmine*, CFI June 24, 1998, 1998 ECR II-2383, para. 39.
615. *Bayer* (*Adạlat*), CFI Dec. 15, 1994, 1994 ECR II-5619, para. 21.
616. Article 30 of Regulation 1/2003. Article 20 of Regulation 17 did not expressly provide for publication of fining decisions, which was however commended by the Court in *ACF Chemiefarma-Quinine*, ECJ July 15, 1970, 1970 ECR 661, para. 104, because it assists enforcement.
617. Especially discovery orders of general importance, but also occasionally investigation orders.

is at present required in all EC languages,[618] the versions in the language(s) of the addressee(s) being regarded as authoritative. The publication may, however, be limited to the 'main content' of the decision.[619] Press releases may be issued about decisions.[620] The decisions must be published in all official languages. The Court has found it a 'regrettable' practice, however, for the Commission to release information to the press before the decision has been served on the addressees.[621] Decisions are also reported in the monthly EC Bulletin and the Commission's annual Reports on Competition Policy. The two-month period for appeal by interested parties, to which the decision has not been served, runs from the 15th day after publication in the *Official Journal*.[622]

2. Cease-and-Desist Orders

Desist Orders.

According to Article 7 (1) of Regulation 1/2003, the Commission may, if it finds that there is infringement of Article 81 or 82, require the undertakings concerned to bring the offended conduct to an end, provided the order is necessary and proportionate.[623] The Commission may also order infringers to refrain from similar

618. This explains the sometimes very long delay of publication (up to 2–3 years). The full decision is not even available on the Commission's website as long as there is not agreement between the Commission and the addressees on the confidentiality of certain data which must be deleted in the public version.
619. Article 30 (2). Mostly the Commission publishes the entire decision except the confidential data. In the *Microsoft* case the Commission considers, however, to publish a summary: MEMO/04/70.
620. *See* the Commission Press Releases about cases such as *Quinine*, D.Comm. July 16, 1969, 1969 OJ L 192/5, and *Pre-insulated Pipes*, D.Comm. Oct. 21, 1998, 1999 OJ L 24/1.
621. *ACF Chemiefarma-Quinine*, ECJ July 15, 1970, 1970 ECR 661, paras 99–105; *United Brands*, ECJ Feb. 14, 1978, 1978 ECR 207, paras 284–288; *Volkswagen*, CFI July 6, 2000, 2000 ECR II-2707, para. 283; *aff'd* ECJ Sept. 18, 2003, C-388/00P, para. 163. The same applies to publication before service: *Anseau*, ECJ Nov. 8, 1983, 1983 ECR 3369, paras 12 and 16; *Polypropylene – ICI*, ECJ Dec. 11, 1986, 212/86; 1987–2 CMLR 500, para. 14.
622. Or on the date it comes to their knowledge, if earlier: third paragraph of Article 230 of the EC Treaty. *See infra* section G.2.
623. *Irish Sugar*, CFI Oct. 7, 1999, 1999 ECR II-2969, para. 298; *Tetra Pak II*, CFI Oct. 6, 1994, 1994 ECR II-755, para. 220; *Carton – Stora*, CFI May 14, 1998, 1998 ECR II-2111, paras 97–98, *aff'd* ECJ Feb. 28, 2002, 2002 ECR I-843; *PVC II*, CFI April 20, 1999, 1999 ECR II-931, paras 1254–1258. To be on the safe side, the Commission frequently orders the addressees to desist from the violation insofar as they have not already done so: *see*, e.g., *Polypropylene*, D.Comm. April 23, 1986, 1986 OJ L 230/1, 36; *Pre-insulated Pipes*, D.Comm. Oct. 21, 1998, 1999 OJ L 24/1 (Article 2 of the decision). This practice seems legally doubtful and in practice unenforceable because the non-respect of such an order requires a new proceeding anyway in order to investigate and state that the new conduct was 'similar' to, and as incompatible as, the old conduct. According to the judgment of the Court of First Instance in the *Carton* case, the Commission was right in finding that the exchange of commercially sensitive information was

conduct in the future, although such a measure is of a mere declaratory nature.[624] The Commission may order the parties to *desist* from actions (negative orders) or to *perform* affirmative acts (positive orders).[625] For instance, the Commission may order that export bans no longer apply or require repeal of such bans,[626] that price information exchange cease[627] or, under Article 82, that the parties refrain from predatory practices[628] or from exclusivity clauses,[629] or not apply discriminatory fees or rebates[630] or tying practices.[631] The Commission may order the infringers not only to bring the infringement to an end but also to refrain from continuing or repeating the conduct or from taking measures having the same or a similar effect.[632] However, the order may not exceed what is appropriate and necessary to attain the objective sought, namely to restore compliance with the rules infringed.[633] In the *Carton* case the Court of First Instance annulled the Commission's order insofar as it extended to the exchange of information which had *not* been held unlawful by the Commission in its statement of reasons.[634] In the *Langnese-Iglo* case the Court of First Instance annulled the Commission's order insofar as it prohibited *any* kind of future exclusive purchasing agreement including agreements likely to be covered by a block exemption regulation.[635]

---

infringed Article 81 but erred in ordering the parties to refrain from *any* exchange of information, including global statistics: *Stora*, CFI May 14, 1998, 1998 ECR II-2111, paras 111–112.

624. *Steel Beams – Eurofer*, CFI March 11, 1999, 1999 ECR II-263, para. 138; the order must be 'sufficiently precise' in order to be enforceable: *ibid.* paras 226–227.
625. *Irish Sugar*, CFI Oct. 7, 1999, 1999 ECR II-2969, para. 298. *See Commercial Solvents*, ECJ March 6, 1074, 1974 ECR 223, para. 45.
626. *VW/Audi*, D.Comm. Jan. 28, 1998, 1998 OJ L 124/60, Article 2.
627. *UK Agricultural Tractor Registration Exchange*, D.Comm. Feb. 17, 1992, 1992 OJ L 68/19; *aff'd John Deere*, ECJ May 28, 1998, 1998 ECR I-3111.
628. *ECS/AKZO*, D.Comm. July 29, 1983, 1983 L 252/13; *aff'd* ECJ April 30, 1986, 1986 ECR 1503.
629. E.g., from freezer exclusivity: *Van den Berg Foods*, D.Comm. March 11, 1998, 1998 OJ L 246/1, points 272–280; *aff'd* CFI Oct. 23, 2003, T-65/98.
630. *Irish Sugar*, D.Comm. May 14, 1997, 1997 OJ L 258/1; *Alpha Flight Services – Aéroports de Paris*, D.Comm. June 11, 1998, 1998 OJ L 230/10 (Article 2 of the decision), *aff'd* ECJ Oct. 24, 2002, 2002 ECR I-9297.
631. *Tetra Pak II*, D.Comm. July 24, 1991, 1991 OJ L 72/1; *aff'd* ECJ Nov. 14, 996, 1996 ECR I-5951.
632. *Tetra Pak II*, CFI Oct. 6, 1994, 1994 ECR II-755, para. 220; *Carton – Stora*, CFI May 14, 1998, 1998 ECR II-2111, para. 97. *See DSD ('Green Dot')*, D.Comm. April 20, 2001, 2001 OJ L 166/1, Article 2 of the decision and points 161–167.
633. *Magill-RTE and ITP*, ECJ April 6, 1995, 1995 ECR I-743, para. 93; *Carton-Sarrio*, CFI May 14, 1998, 1998 ECR II-1439, para. 267; *PVC II*, CFI April 20, 1999, 1999 ECR II-931, para. 1250.
634. *Carton – Stora*, CFI May 14, 1998, 1998 ECR II-2111, paras 111–112.
635. *Langnese-Iglo*, CFI 8 June 1995, 1995 ECR 11–1533, paras 205–209.

Behavioral v. Structural Remedies.
The Commission may impose any behavioral or structural remedies which are proportionate to the infringement committed and necessary to bring the infringement effectively to an end. Structural remedies can only be imposed if there is no equally effective behavioral remedy, in particular where there is a substantial risk of a lasting or repeated infringement that derives from the very structure of the undertaking, or where any equally effective behavioral remedy would be more burdensome for the undertaking concerned than a structural remedy.[636] In the *Deutsche Post* case[637] the Commission found that the German Postal operator abused its dominant position by granting fidelity rebates and engaging in predatory pricing by way of cross-subsidization in the market for business parcel services and ordered this infringement be brought to an end. As a result of this decision the German Post created a separate legal entity and introduced market-based pricing, thereby separating competitive parcel services from the letter monopoly in order to prevent any cross-subsidization.[638] Normally, however, structural remedies are limited to cases of joint ventures[639] or mergers[640] where the firms may be requested to divest or to retransfer certain assets or activities.

Special Features of Positive Orders (Injunctions).
Orders with respect to Article 81 normally do not justify positive acts (injunctions).[641] However, certain infringements of Article 82 may require (within the limits of the proportionality principle[642]) the performance of positive acts, e.g. an order to resume deliveries,[643] to grant a licence[644] or to grant access to an essential facility[645] or the submission of proposals if several courses of action are possible.[646] Such positive acts may be required in the case of interim measures (temporary injunctions) necessary to avert serious and irreparable harm caused by

636. Article 7 of Regulation 1/2003 and Recital 12.
637. *Deutsche Post*, D.Comm. March 20, 2001, 2001 OJ L 125/27.
638. IP/01/419.
639. *Gillette/Wilkinson*, D.Comm. Nov. 10, 1992, 1993 OJ L 16/21.
640. *See Blokker/Toys 'R' Us*, D.Comm. June 26, 1997, 1998 OJ L 316/1, points 129–133.
641. *Automec II*, CFI Sept. 18, 1992, 1992 ECR II-2223, paras 50–53.
642. *RTE and ITP* (*Magill*), ECJ April 6, 1995, 1995 ECR I-743 para. 90.
643. *Commercial Solvents*, D.Comm. Dec. 14, 1972, 1972 OJ L 299/51, 56; *aff'd* ECJ March 6, 1974, 1974 ECR 223, paras 42–46; *Hugin/Liptons*, D.Comm. Dec. 8, 1977, 1978 OJ L 22/23, 35; *Boosey & Hawkes*, D.Comm. July 29, 1987, 1987 OJ L 286/36.
644. *Magill TV Guide*, D.Comm. Dec. 21, 1988, 1989 OJ L 78/43, 51; *aff'd* ECJ April 6, 1995, 1995 ECR I-743, para. 90. *See also IGR I and II*, Eleventh Report on Competition Policy, point 94 and Fourteenth Report on Competition Policy, point 92.
645. *Airport of Frankfurt*, D.Comm. Jan. 14, 1998, 1998 OJ L 72/30, Article 1.
646. *Magill TV Guide*, D.Comm. Dec. 21, 1988, 1989 OJ L 78/43, 51; *aff'd* ECJ April 6, 1995, 1995 ECR I-743. *See Continental Can*, D.Comm. Dec. 9, 1971, 1972 OJ L 7/25, 39; *VBBB/VBVB*, D.Comm. Nov. 25, 1981, 1982 OJ L 54/36, paras 64–65.

a probable violation of Article 81 or 82 until a full hearing can be held.[647] In any event, the Commission may not replace entrepreneurial decisions by its own judgment and normally does not impose the conclusion of a predetermined contract[648] but instead obliges the undertakings to submit proposals.[649]

Information Orders.
Firms may be ordered to inform customers[650] or members of a trade association[651] about changes in contracts which the Commission has ordered or to inform the Commission of the action they have taken to remedy the violation and to submit regular compliance reports.[652]

Procedural Requirements.
Orders are often coupled with the imposition of fines in respect of the infringement[653] and occasionally with the threat of daily fines should the addressees fail to comply. The usual procedural requirements of due process, consultation with the Advisory Committee and publication apply. This implies that the Commission has to hear any third party which might be affected by an order, e.g., by the obligation to terminate cooperation agreements with a competitor.[654]

Commitments in Order to Avoid a Cease-and-Desist Order.
Where the Commission intends to adopt a cease-and-desist order the undertakings concerned may offer commitments to meet the Commission's competitive con-

647. *See Peugeot*, D.Comm. March 26, 1990 (not published in OJ), *aff'd* CFI July 12, 1991, 1991 ECR II-653.
648. *Automec II*, CFI Sept. 18, 1992, 1992 ECR II-2223, paras 44–53.
649. *Continental Can*, D.Comm. Dec. 9, 1971, 1972 OJ L 7/25; *Hugin Uptons*, D.Comm. Dec. 8, 1977, 1978 OJ L 22/23, 35; *IJsselcentrale*, D.Comm. Nov. 28, 1990, 1990 OJ L 351/46. *See*, however, *Magill – RTE*, April 6, 1995, 1995 ECR I-743, para. 91 (in case of compulsory licence).
650. *Schöller*, CFI June 8, 1995, 1995 ECR II-1611, para. 158; *VW/Audi*, D.Comm. Jan. 28, 1998, 1998 OJ L 124/60, Article 2; *Van den Bergh Foods*, D.Comm. March 11, 1998, 1998 OJ L 246/1. *See also Hasselblad*, D.Comm. Dec. 2, 1981, 1982 OJ L 161/18, 33; *VBBB/VBVB*, D.Comm. Nov. 25, 1981, 1982 OJ L 54/36, 50; *Astra*, D.Comm. Dec. 23, 1992, 1993 OJ L 20/23.
651. *CNSD*, D.Comm. June 30, 1993, 1993 OJ L 203/27; *COAPI*, D.Comm. Jan. 30, 1995, 1995 OJ L 122/37, 50.
652. *Italian Tobacco Monopoly AAMS*, D.Comm. June 17, 1998, 1998 OJ L 252/47. *See also ECS/Akzo II*, D.Comm. July 29, 1983, 1983 OJ L 252/13; *aff'd* ECJ April 30, 1986, 1986 ECR 1503; *United Brands*, D.Comm. Dec. 17, 1975, 1976 OJ L 95/1, 20.
653. *See infra* section F.6.(e). If the infringement has ceased, the fining decision merely establishes the past infringement and is then not strictly speaking a cease and desist order, but is certainly a warning as to future conduct: *see Michelin*, D.Comm. Oct. 7, 1981, 1981 OJ L 353/33, 46, *aff'd* ECJ Nov. 9, 1983, 1983 ECR 3461; *Fatty Acids*, D.Comm. Dec. 2, 1986, 1987 OJ L 3/17, 25.
654. Under the merger control regulation: *SCPA/Kali + Salz/MdK*, ECJ March 31, 1998, 1998 ECR I-1375, para. 67.

cerns expressed in its preliminary statement (Statement of Objections).[655] Where the Commission is satisfied with these commitments it takes a decision making them binding (for a specific period) and concluding that there are no longer grounds for action. The implementation of the commitments can be enforced by fines and periodic penalty payments in the same way as a cease-and-desist order.[656]

3. Interim Measures (Temporary Injunctions)

Significance and Procedure of Interim Measures.
Interim measures are a form of injunctive relief designed to prevent anticompetitive practices from being continued or enforced. The legal basis for interim cease-and-desist orders used to be Article 3 of Regulation 17. Although the provision does not expressly refer to such power,[657] it was recognized in 1980 by the Court of Justice[658] as a legal basis for taking the necessary interim measures which can be enforced by daily fines should the addressee fail to comply with the order. Such interim measures are 'decisions' likely to be appealed by the defendant.[659] The defendant must therefore be given a fair hearing, subject to the shorter time limits clearly necessary in injunction proceedings.[660] The Commission is not obliged to consult the Advisory Committee, but may well do so. Such decisions must be reasoned and may be, but are not necessarily, published.[661] Regulation 1/2003 provides expressly for interim measures. According to Article 8 the Commission may, in cases of urgency due to the risk of serious and irreparable damage to competition, order interim measures which are based on a *prima facie* finding of infringement.

655. Article 9 of Regulation 1/2003.
656. Article 23 (2) (c) and Article 24 (1) (c) of Regulation 1/2003.
657. *See*, however, third paragraph of Article 66 (5). First exercised after the Court of Justice's order in *Miles Druce (Injunction) I*, ECJ Oct. 11, 1973, 1973 ECR 1049, and extended to abuse of dominant positions (Article 66 (7)) by the Court's order in *National Carbonizing*, ECJ Oct. 22, 1975, 1975 ECR 1193. Cases: Fourth Report on Competition Policy, points 141–143; *National Carbonizing*, D.Comm. Oct. 29, 1975, 1976 OJ L 35/6.
658. By the Court of Justice in *Camera Care*, ECJ, Jan. 17, 1980, 1980 ECR 119. Confirmed in *Cosimex*, CFI Dec. 6, 1989, 1990 ECR 1990 II-1, para. 11.
659. *Camera Care*, ECJ Jan. 17, 1980, 1980 ECR 119, paras 19–20; *Langnese-Iglo*, CFI June 16, 1992, 1992 ECR II-1839.
660. The defendant is sent a Statement of Objections and given an oral hearing. Thus, interim orders are not *ex parte*, and are therefore likely to take longer to obtain (weeks, if not months) than an *ex parte* preliminary injunction from a national court: *see infra* section I. It is arguable that if a refusal to supply were life-threatening for a smaller firm, the Commission could grant an interim order *ex parte*; the addressee would be protected by the right to ask the Court of Justice to set aside the order under Article 242 of the EC Treaty. *See also* Recital 11 to Regulation 1/2003.
661. *See National Carbonizing*, D.Comm. Oct. 29, 1975, 1976 OJ L 35/6; *Akzo*, D.Comm. July 29, 1983, 1983 OJ L 252/13.

Conditions of Interim Cease-and-Desist Orders.

Interim measures may be granted only where the practices in question *prima facie*[662] constitute a breach of the EC competition rules for which a penalty could be imposed by the Commission's final decision and involve a risk of serious and irreparable damage which implies the urgent need for protective measures.[663]

- *Prima facie* means *fumus boni iuris,* as developed by the Court with respect to interim measures under Article 243 of the EC Treaty.[664] *Fumus boni iuris* is not necessarily excluded where the law is novel.[665]
- An interim measure can be issued only in cases of proven urgency, which must be assessed in the light of the need for an interlocutory order to avoid serious and irreparable damage to the party seeking relief and foreseeability with a sufficient degree of probability.[666] Losses of a purely financial nature cannot, save exceptional circumstances, be regarded as irreparable or reparable with difficulty if it can ultimately be the subject of financial reparation; the losses alleged must be such as to threaten the party's survival.[667] The assessment of a serious and irreparable damage therefore requires a balance of the interests involved.[668]
- The order must be provisional and not prejudge the Commission's decision on the substance. It must merely preserve the *status quo* pending the final determination of the issue and so be fair to the addressee.[669]

Examples of interim measures include orders to refrain from exclusive purchase obligations,[670] to resume deliveries[671] or to refrain from discriminatory[672] or preda-

662. In the sense of 'probability': *La Cinq*, CFI Jan. 24, 1992, 1992 ECR II-1, para. 32.
663. *NDC/IMS Health*, CFI Oct. 26, 2001, 2001 ECR I-3193, paras 52–75, *aff'd* ECJ April 11, 2002, 2002 ECR I—3401.
664. *See Cement*, CFI March 23, 1992, 1992 ECR II-1571, para. 56; *SNCF and British Railways/Eurotunnel*, CFI May 12, 1995, 1995 ECR II-1433.
665. *NDC/IMS Health*, CFI Oct. 26, 2001, 2001 ECR I-3193, para. 93. However, a compulsory licence may be ordered by way of interim measure only under exceptional circumstances: *ibid.*, paras 103–106. The Commission withdrew its interim measure according to the Court's judgments: *NDC/IMS Health II*, D.Comm. Aug. 13, 2003, 2003 OJ L 268/69.
666. *La Cinq*, CFI Jan. 24, 1992, 1992 ECR II-l, paras 27–29; *NDC/IMS Health*, CFI Oct. 26, 2001, 2001 ECR I-3193, para. 116.
667. *NDC/IMS Health*, CFI Oct. 26, 2001, 2001 ECR I-3193, paras 119–121.
668. *NDC/IMS Health*, CFI Oct. 26, 2001, 2001 ECR I-3193, para. 133.
669. *Camera Care*, ECJ Oct. 17, 1980, 1980 ECR 119, para. 18; *Goldstein*, CFI Feb. 27, 1996, (not published in ECR); 1996–5 CMLR 106, para. 22.
670. *Mars/Langnese-Iglo*, CFI June 16, 1992, 1992 ECR II-1839, para. 32.
671. *AKZO*, ECJ April 30, 1986, 1986 ECR 1503, para. 14. *Eco Peugeot*, CFI July 12, 1991, 1991 ECR II-653; *Boosey & Hawkes*, D.Comm. July 29, 1987, 1987 OJ L 286/36.
672. *La Cinq*, CFI Jan. 24, 1992, 1992 ECR II-1 (Commission's rejection of interim measure reversed).

tory practices.[673] Interim measures were rejected or reversed where the interim orders would anticipate the final assessment about access of third parties to an exclusive distribution system,[674] to exclusive property rights (compulsory licence),[675] or to a shore facility despite doubts regarding the likelihood of the complainant being unable to operate a commercially viable service.[676]

Commission's Own Initiative.
Article 8 of Regulation 1/2003 provides that interim measures may be taken on the Commission's own initiative. This seems to reflect the Court of Justice' general statement that the primary purpose of applying the competition rules is to prevent distortions of competition and especially to safeguard interests of consumers, rather than to protect the position of particular competitors.[677] In fact, however, only complainants can provide the Commission with the necessary data justifying interim measures.[678] In fact, in all the cases of the interim measures taken or rejected by the Commission, the Commission acted on behalf of a complainant who may therefore appeal the rejection of interim measures. However, the role of the Community judiciary is to carry out a legal review of the Commission's action, including suspending an interim measure imposed by the Commission,[679] but not to act in the place of the Commission in the exercise of its powers.[680]

Reasons for Poor Administrative Practice.
The main reasons for the relatively poor administrative practice is the complicated procedure, which includes extensive hearing of the parties and the consultation

673. *ECS/AKZO*, D.Comm. July 29, 1983, 1983 OJ L 252/13.
674. *Ford*, ECJ Feb. 28, 1984, 1984 ECR 1129, para. 21.
675. *NDC/IMS Health*, CFI Oct. 26, 2001, 2001 ECR I-3193, para. 147.
676. *Sea Containers/Stena Sealink*, D.Comm. Dec. 21, 1993, 1994 OJ L 15/8, point 79.
677. *NDC/IMS Health*, CFI Oct. 26, 2001, 2001 ECR I-3193, para. 145, following the Advocate General in *Bronner*, 1998 ECR I-7991, para. 58. Following the Court's judgment the Commission withdrew its interim measure: *NDC/IMS Health II*, D.Comm. Aug. 13, 2003, 2003 OJ L 268/69.
678. Complainants are therefore entitled to appeal the Commission decision directly or indirectly rejecting their complaint: *see Cosimex*, CFI Dec. 6, 1989, 1989 ECR II-1; *La Cinq*, CFI Jan. 24, 1992, 1992 ECR II-1; *EBU/Eurovision*, CFI Dec. 14, 1993, 1993 ECR II-1409. Under state aids provisions: *Tsimenta Halkidos*, CFI Aug. 11, 1995, 1995 ECR II-2237.
679. *Mars/Langnese-Iglo*, CFI June 16, 1992, 1992 ECR II-1839; *Postbank*, CFI Dec. 1, 1994, 1994 ECR II-1141, para. 27; *Goldstein*, CFI Feb. 27, 1996, 1996–7 CMLR 106, paras 36–37 (not published in ECR). *See Hasselblad*, ECJ May 7, 1982, 1982 ECR 1555.
680. *Cosimex*, CFI Dec. 6, 1989, 1990 ECR 1990 II-1, paras 11–14; *Camera Care*, ECJ Jan. 17, 1980, 1980 ECR 119, para. 20; *Gestévision*, CFI Dec. 14, 1993, 1993 ECR II-1409, para. 24; *Union Carbide*, CFI Dec. 2, 1994, 1994 ECR II-1159, para. 27; *Goldstein*, CFI Feb. 27, 1996, 1996–7 CMLR 106, para. 40.

of the Advisory Committee.[681] However, the mere contemplation of interim measures may cause the defendant to cease the offending conduct.[682]

4. Declarations Stating an Infringement in the Past

Clarifying Legal Positions or Preventing Recurrences.
If the Commission has a legitimate interest in doing so, it may issue formal decisions declaring that conduct which is known to have ceased was an infringement of Article 81 or 82, even when no fine is imposed.[683] The purpose may be to clarify the legal position with respect to new types of agreements and practices that have not been settled in the existing case-law[684] (and for this reason refraining from imposing a fine[685]) or to prevent recurrences.[686] An alternative is a declaration decision combined with a small fine ('symbolic' fine).[687]

Recommendations.
Article 3 (3) of Regulation 17 provided the possibility for the Commission to issue a recommendation to firms to terminate an infringement before going on, if necessary, to serve a binding cease-and-desist order on them. However, this provision has been hardly used,[688] due probably to the fact that it was found that the Statement of Objections (sent to defendants before a cease-and-desist order is issued) serves the same purpose and is often more effective in getting them to desist from an infringement (even without a final decision) than a recommendation would be.[689] Regulation 1/2003 no longer provides for recommendations.

---

681. However, Article 14 (3) of Regulation 1/2003 provides for dispatching only the operative part of the draft decision and for a shorter consultation period of seven days.
682. *See IGR Stereo Television I*, Eleventh Report on Competition Policy, point 94; *Amicon/Fortia, ibid.*, point 112, or gave an undertaking to do so: *Hilti (Settlement)*, Fifteenth Report on Competition Policy, point 49; *Ford UK*, Fifteenth Report on Competition Policy, point 49; *British Sugar (Settlement)*, Sixteenth Report on Competition Policy, point 74.
683. Under Regulation 17 e.g., *IFTRA Aluminium*, D.Comm. July 15, 1975, 1975OJ L 228/3; *Wirtschaftsvereinigung Stahl*, D.Comm. Nov. 26, 1998, 1998 OJ L 72/30; *Montedison/Stähler*, D.Comm. June 23, 1993, 1993 OJ L 272/28; *Auditel*, D.Comm. Nov. 24, 1993, 1993 OJ L 306/50; *Seacontainer/Sealink*, D.Comm. Dec. 21, 1993, 1994 OJ L 15/8, point 47, where the Commission apparently affirmed the need of clarifying the legal position although the parties had reached a mutual understanding. Under Regulation 1/2003 *see* Recital 11.
684. *Eurofer*, CFI March 11, 1999, 1999 ECR II-263, para. 138; *EATA*, D.Comm. April 30, 1999, 1999 OJ L 193/23, points 182–186; Recital 14 to Regulation 1/2003.
685. E.g. *Deutsche Post*, D.Comm. March 20, 2001, 2001 OJ L 125/27.
686. Practice upheld by the Court of Justice in *GVL*, ECJ March 2, 1983, 1983 ECR 483, paras 16–28, and in *ANTIB*, ECJ May 20, 1987, 1987 ECR 2201, para. 15.
687. *See FENEX*, D.Comm. June 5, 1996, 1996 OJ L 181/28 (ECU 1,000). However, in *Far Eastern Freight Conference* even a symbolic fine was annulled by CFI Feb. 28, 2002, 2002 ECR II-1101.
688. In fact, only on one occasion: *Convention Faïence*, First Report on Competition Policy, point 20.
689. *Camera Care*, ECJ Jan. 17, 1980, 1980 ECR 119, para. 16.

5. Decisions of Inapplicability, no Further Action Decisions and Informal Guidance

Finding of Inapplicability by Individual Decision.
According to Article 10 of Regulation 1/2003 the Commission, acting on its own initiative, may, by way of a declaratory decision,[690] find that Article 81 is not applicable to an agreement either because the conditions of Article 81 (1) are not fulfilled, or because the conditions of Article 81 (3) are satisfied. Such a decision will be taken by the Commission 'where the Community interest ... so requires'. Any decision must be preceded by a publication of a concise summary of the proposed course of action in order to hear interested third parties[691] and after having consulted the Advisory Committee.[692] The decision is of a declaratory nature.[693] However, after the initiation of proceedings by the Commission national competition authorities are and remain relieved of their competence to apply Article 81,[694] and national courts must avoid giving decisions which would conflict with the Commission's decision,[695] as the case may be, after amendments or commitments to order to meet the Commission's competition concerns.[696] The effect of the Commission decision on the inapplicability of Article 81 depends on the nature of the decision:

- If the decision states that the conditions of Article 81 (3) are satisfied it is legally binding in the same way as an exemption used to be under the *Walt Wilhelm* doctrine.[697]
- If the decision states that the conditions of Article 81 (1) are not fulfilled the firms cannot be held liable for the same conduct according the principle *non bis in idem*.[698]

690. Recital 14 to Regulation 1/2003.
691. Article 27 (4) of Regulation 1/2003. Depending on the reaction of the parties, comments or complaints of interested third parties, the Commission may proceed to a comfort letter (in particular in case of amendment) or to initiating a formal proceeding, including a statement of objections, in order to adopt a cease-and-desist order.
692. Article 14 (1) of Regulation 1/2003.
693. Recital 14 to Regulation 1/2003.
694. Article 11 (6) of Regulation 1/2003. However, if the Commission, after having initiated proceedings, closes the file because of lack of Community interest the national authorities are not precluded from applying national and Community competiton law according to Article 3 (1) of Regulation 1/2003.
695. Article 16 (1) of Regulation 1/2003.
696. Article 9 (1) of Regulation 1/2003.
697. *Walt Wilhelm*, ECJ Feb. 13, 1969, 1969 ECR 1, 14.
698. *PVC II – LVM*, ECJ Oct. 15, 2002, 2002 ECR I-8375, para. 59.

Finding of Inapplicability by Individual Informal Guidance.
According to recital 38, the Commission may, at the request of individual undertakings, issue 'informal guidance' where cases give rise to genuine uncertainty because they present novel or unresolved questions. There is no right to request such informal guidance nor any kind of notification. However, parties may have a legitimate interest in such an informal guidance where the assessment raises unresolved legal issues, where the agreement is of particular economic importance or involves important investments (licence or R&D agreements) or the creation of structures which are difficult to divest (partial-function joint ventures). The formalities of such a request may be similar to those actually used for pre-notification discussions, which include a detailed description of the agreement and additional information on the parties, the relevant market, their market position and their most important competitors. The information must be complete and correct in order to allow the Commission to grant informal guidance without the need of any further investigation. Normally, such informal guidance only represents the Commission's opinion and does not legally bind national authorities and courts.[699] Such a letter may be compared with a *comfort letter* and a closing letter (settlement)[700] in the Commission's administrative practice under Regulation 17. Because such letters are not legally binding,[701] they do not preclude the Commission from re-opening the file[702] and may be appealed where the issuance of the comfort letter implies the rejection of a complaint.[703]

Finding of Inapplicability by Block Exemption.
The block exemptions adopted by the Commission and the power to issue further block exemptions under Regulation 19/65 (vertical and licence agreements),[704] Regulation 2821/71 (certain horizontal agreements),[705] Regulation 3976/87 (air transport),[706] Regulation 1534/91(insurance),[707] or Regulation 479/92 (maritime

699. However, the persuasive authority of such letters depends on the depth of the factual and legal assessment, such as in *Football Association Premier League*, D.Comm. April 30, 2004, 2004 OJ C 115/3.
700. E.g. *L'Oreal*, ECJ Dec. 11, 1980, 1980 ECR 3775, para. 11.
701. They are, however, self-binding to the same extent as Commission notices (*Pre-insulated Pipes – LR af 1998*, March 20, 2002, 2002 ECR II-1705, para. 360) and they have 'persuasive authority' (*Sateba II*, ECJ July 17, 1998, 1998 ECR II-1523, para. 36) and constitute a factor to be considered by national courts (*Guerlain*, ECJ July 10, 1980, 1980 ECR 2327, para. 13).
702. Article 9 (2) of Regulation 1/2003. *See Telecom Development*, 1998 OJ 293/4 (comfort letter limited in time).
703. *See Automec II*, CFI Sept. 18, 1992, 1992 ECR II-2223, para. 80; *Koelman*, CFI Jan. 9, 1996, 1996 ECR II-1, para. 41–44.
704. 1965 OJ 533.
705. 1971 OJ L 285/46.
706. 1987 OJ L 374/9, as amended by 1990 OJ L 217/15.
707. 1991 OJ L 143/1.

transport)[708] remain in force.[709] The benefit of a block exemption may be withdrawn by the Commission[710] or a national competition authority (in this case only with respect to the territory of that member state)[711] when in any particular case an agreement, a decision or a concerted practice has certain effects which are incompatible with Article 81 (3). Such a decision has only *ex nunc* effect.

Decisions Stating that there is no Ground for Further Action.
The Commission may, after having initiated proceedings, come to the conclusion that there are not sufficient reasons for taking a formal decision because its competitive concerns are met by commitments offered by the parties and made binding by the Commission. The non-implementation of commitments is subject to sanctions.[712] Commitments do not prevent national courts from subsequently finding an infringment and adopting the appropriate remedies. However, national authorites are bound by the *non bis in idem* principle.[713]

Commitments under Regulation 17.
Under Regulation 17 some cases were settled after negotiations with the parties to get them to change their arrangements or conduct. In the case of a notification the Commission could issue an exemption subject to conditions or obligations.[714] Conditions may concern the implementation of commitments offered by the parties, such as to prevent collusive behavior or to grant access to essential facilities (ports and airports)[715] In the case of a complaint or *ex officio* proceedings the Commission may settle the case subject to the right to monitor the situation and to reopen proceedings, if necessary.[716] As part of a settlement the parties may also agree to introduce a compliance programme.[717] In cases where proceedings originate from a complaint, the letter accepting the commitments and closing the file implies the rejection of the complaint and may be appealed by the complainant.[718] Exemption decisions adopted under Regulation 17 continue to have effect unless they are withdrawn by the Commission.[719]

---

708. 1992 OJ L 55/3.
709. Article 29 of Regulation 1/2003.
710. Article 29 (1) of Regulation 1/2003.
711. Article 29 (2) of Regulation 1/2003.
712. Article 23 (2) (c) and Article 24 (1) (c) of Regulation 1/2003.
713. *PVC II – LVM*, ECJ Oct. 15, 2002, 2002 ECR I-8375, para. 59.
714. Article 8 (1) of Regulation 17.
715. Example of far-reaching conditions and obligations: *Lufthansa/SAS*, D.Comm. Jan. 16, 1996, 1996 OJ L 54/28; *Austrian Airlines/Lufthansa*, D.Comm. July 5, 2002, 2002 OJ L 242/25.
716. *See IBM*, Fourteenth Report on Competition Policy, points 94–95; Sixteenth Report on Competition Policy, point 75; Seventeenth Report on Competition Policy, point 85.
717. This may also be a mitigating factor in the assessment of the fine: *National Panasonic*, D.Comm. Dec. 7, 1982, 1982 OJ L 354/28, 34.
718. *Philip Morris/Rothmans*, ECJ Nov. 17, 1987, 1987 ECR 4487, para. 12.
719. Articles 34 and 43 of Regulation 1/2003.

Commitments under Regulation 1/2003.

Article 9 of Regulation 1/2003 adopts the practice on commitments under the merger control regulation. The undertakings concerned by a Commission proceeding may, normally after having received the Statement of Objections but also in an earlier stage of proceedings, offer commitments to meet the concerns of the Commission expressed in its preliminary assessment. If the Commission agrees to the proposal or, if necessary, its amendments, it may take a decision which makes those commitments binding on the undertakings. Such a decision may be adopted for a specific period and concludes that there are no longer grounds for action by the decision. The decision must be published[720] and is appealable by third parties if their legal position is directly and individually affected.[721] Failure to comply with the commitments can, unlike under Regulation 17, be enforced by fines[722] and periodic penalty payments.[723]

Clearance Subject to Commitments.

According to Article 10, the Commission may, where the Community public interest so requires, take a decision finding that the conditions of Article 81 (3) are fulfilled. The Commission may do so after having sent a Statement of Objections and after having received commitments which are likely to meet the Commission's competition concerns.[724] This corresponds to what the Commission used to do under Regulation 17.

Reopening of Proceedings.

The Commission may reopen proceedings (under Article 9 (2) of Regulation 1/2003) where there has been a material change in any of the facts on which the decision was based, where the parties commit a breach of any obligation or commitment, or where the decision is based on incomplete, incorrect or misleading information provided by the parties.[725] However, the practical application of this possibility (for which the usual procedure for final decisions applies) may be under Regulation 1/2003 as rare as under Regulation 17.[726]

---

720. Article 30 (1) of Regulation 1/2003.
721. This possibility of appeal may induce the Commission to contact third parties before taking its decision to the same extent as it is used to do under the merger control regulation.
722. Article 23 (2) (c) of Regulation 1/2003.
723. Article 24 (1) (c) of Regulation 1/2003.
724. Article 9 of Regulation 1/2003.
725. Article 9 (2) of Regulation 1/2003. If the application of a block exempted agreement constitutes an abuse (as mentioned in Article 8), the Commission may apply Article 82 directly without the need to withdraw the block exemption: *Tetra Pak I*, D.Comm. July 26, 1988, 1988 OJ L 272/27, 41–42; *aff'd* CFI July 10, 1990, 1990 ECR II-309, para. 30, and ECJ Oct. 1, 1998, 1998 ECR I-5609.
726. Amending an exemption decision: *Bayer/BP Chemicals*, D.Comm. July 11, 1994, 1994 OJ L 137/34; *Unisource II*, D.Comm. Dec. 29, 2000, 2001 OJ L 52/30. Withdrawal of a block exemption: *Langnese-Iglo*, D.Comm. Dec. 23, 1992, 1993 OJ L 183/1 and 19, *aff'd* CFI June 8, 1995, 1995 ECR II-1533 and 1611; *aff'd* ECJ Oct. 1, 1998, 1998 ECR I-5609.

6. Sanctions

(a) Introduction

Substantive Fines.
The Commission may impose fines for substantive infringements of Articles 81 or 82 up to 10% of the total worldwide turnover of the preceding business year where undertakings or associations of undertakings, either intentionally or negligently,

- infringe Article 81 or Article 82, or
- contravene a decision ordering interim measures, or
- fail to comply with a commitment made binding by a Commission decision.[727]

Because fines themselves can be quite heavy and inevitably generate adverse publicity for the company, the threat of fines can be a strong deterrent to anti-competitive conduct,[728] whereas cease-and-desist orders alone in many cases would not. In relation to some types of long-term contractual arrangements, such as licensing or joint ventures, the danger of unenforceability if the contract were to be litigated may be a greater disincentive than the possibility of fines. However, civil damage actions are not yet a major deterrent in the EC,[729] unlike in the United States where they have become the main motor of enforcement.[730] Since the entry into force of the Maastricht Treaty member states may be liable to penalty payments to be fixed at the discretion of the Court of Justice if they infringe an obligation under the EC Treaty and fail to take the necessary measures to comply with the Court's judgment.[731]

Procedural Sanctions.
Procedural fines up to 1% of the total turnover in the preceding business year are provided for where undertakings or associations of undertakings, either intentionally or negligently,

727. Article 23 (2) of Regulation 1/2003, which corresponds to Article 15 (2) of Regulation 17, making however the implementation of commitment also subject to fines. Under Article 15 (2) of Regulation 17, the fine may range between EUR 1,000 to EUR 1,000,000, or a sum in excess thereof but not exceeding 10% of the turnover in the preceding business year.
728. *Eurocheques – Helsinki*, CFI Feb. 23, 1994, 1994 ECR II-49, para. 137; *PVC II*, CFI April 20, 1999, 1999 ECR II-931, para. 1173 ('dissuasive effect').
729. *See infra* Section I.
730. *See* the long list of quotations testifying to the effectiveness of private damages suits as an enforcement medium in the U.S., in Temple Lang, 'Community Antitrust Law – Compliance and Enforcement', 1981 CMLRev 335–362, 341, note 13.
731. Article 228 (2) (2). Methods of calculating the amount of penalty payments have been issued by the Commission in 1996 OJ C 242/6 and 1997 OJ C 63/2.

- supply incorrect or misleading information in response to a request for information,
- supply incorrect, incomplete or misleading information or do not supply information within the required time-limit in response to a request made by decision,
- produce books or other business records in incomplete form during an inspection or refuse to submit to inspections ordered by decision,
- give incorrect or misleading answers, do not rectify an incorrect, incomplete or misleading answer given by a member of their staff, or fail or refuse to provide a complete answer in response to question asked during an inspection, or
- break seals affixed by the Commission.[732]

Daily fines[733] up to 5% of average daily turnover may be imposed to compel companies to obey cease-and-desist orders or procedural (discovery or investigation) orders. Procedural and daily fines will be discussed separately at the end of this section.

'Non-Criminal' Nature.
The fines imposed are stated to be 'non-criminal',[734] but they are little different from fines imposed by a criminal court save for the fact that they cannot be imposed on natural persons.[735] Their purpose is not only to force the offender to give up a current violation but also to fine violations that have already ceased,[736] thereby deterring both the offender and others from further violations in future[737] ('dissuasive effect'[738]).

732. Article 23 (1) of Regulation 1/2003, which extends the list of Article 15 (1) of Regulation 17, including in particular fines with respect to the correctness of answers given during an inspection and with respect to seals affixed by the Commission.
733. Article 24 of Regulation 1/2003. Similar to fines for contempt of court in the UK.
734. Article 23 (5) of Regulation 1/2003. The word 'punish' is used in *Pioneer*, ECJ June 7, 1983, 1983 ECR 1825, para. 105. Article 15 (4) of Regulation 17 was inserted to avoid constitutional problems arising from a transfer of criminal jurisdiction to the EC Commission. *See also* the discussions of the issue by Advocate General Gand in *ACF Chemiefarma-Quinine*, ECJ July 15, 1970, 1970 ECR 661, 722–723, and by Advocate General Mayras in *Sugar*, ECJ Dec. 16, 1975, 1975 ECR 1663, 2119–2120.
735. Fines can be imposed on natural persons by national competition law, by Community competition law only if natural persons constitute an enterprise, *see* Recital 8 to Regulation 1/2003.
736. *See ACF Chemiefarma-Quinine*, ECJ July 15, 1970, 1970 ECR 661, para. 175.
737. Thirteenth Report on Competition Policy, points 62–65; *CEWAL*, CFI Oct. 8, 1996, 1996 ECR II-1201, para. 235; *Carton – Finnboard*, CFI May 14, 1998, 1998 ECR II-1617, para. 301; *CMA CGM – FETTCSA*, CFI March 19, 2003, T-213/00, paras 340–341.
738. *PVC – LVM*, ECJ Oct. 15, 2002, 2002 ECR I-8375, para. 465.

Statute of Limitations (Substantive Infringements).
The fining of firms for substantive infringements of Article 81 or 82 is time-barred[739] five years after the infringement was committed or, in the case of continuing or repeated infringements, after the infringement ceased,[740] unless during that period the Commission or the national competition authority (not only on the Commission's behalf but also independently[741]) has taken formal steps to investigate or prosecute the infringement. In such a case, the limitation period is extended for a further five years from each such step, up to a maximum total period of ten years after the violation was committed or ceased.[742] However, the period may not be extended by a request for information the sole purpose of which is to prolong the limitation period artificially.[743] If a decision is taken within the relevant limitation period and is appealed, however, the limitation period is interrupted by the appeal and continues to run after judgment on the appeal is delivered, even if the total period then exceeds ten years.[744] The formal steps commencing the investigation which start the limitation period running afresh include the service of discovery requests or orders,[745] investigation warrants or orders, or statements of objections, and the commencement of formal proceedings.[746] The limitation period is extended for all the firms involved in an infringement by any of these acts directed at any one of the firms.[747] The time bar on fines does not apply to 'declaratory' prohibition orders without fines.[748]

---

739. Article 25 of Regulation 1/2003 (which replaces Article 1 of Regulation 2988/74, 1974 OJ L 319/1).
740. A continuing infringement only ceases when the agreement or the restrictive clauses are removed: *Toltecs/Dorcet*, D.Comm. Dec. 15, 1982, 1982 OJ L 379/19, 28; *Polypropylene – Hercules*, CFI Dec. 17, 1991, 1991 ECR II-1715, para. 310; *aff'd Polypropylene-Montecatini*, ECJ July 8, 1999, 1999 ECR I-4539, para. 195. *See*, however, under German penal law Supreme Court May 3, 1990, WuWE BGH 2429 (a repeated infringement presupposes a general intent and not only a repetition of a similar conduct following the same scheme).
741. Recital 31 to Regulation 1/2003.
742. Article 25 (2) and (5) of Regulation 1/2003. In *CMA CGM – FETTCSA* the fine imposed by the Commission was annulled because the total period exceeded ten years: CFI March 19, 2003, T-213/00, para. 517.
743. *CMA CGM – FETTCSA*, CFI March 19, 2003, T-213/00, para. 488.
744. Article 25 (6) of Regulation 1/2003. This provision was inserted under Regulation 2988/74 to enable the Commission to take a second decision imposing fines if the first decision was struck down for procedural reasons. *See PVC II*, CFI April 20, 1999, 1999 ECR II-931, paras 1101–1105; *aff'd* ECJ Oct. 15, 2002, 2002 ECR I-8375, para. 162–199. *See also CMA CGM – FETTCSA*, CFI March 19, 2003, T-213/00, paras 468–491.
745. However, a request for information on turnover, the sole purpose of which is to prolong the limitation period artificially, does not suffice: *Austria*, ECJ Feb. 15, 2001, 2001 ECR II-1101, paras 45–67; *CMA CGM – FETTCSA*, CFI March 19, 2003, T-213/00, para. 488.
746. Article 25 (3) of Regulation 1/2003; *PVC II*, CFI 20 April 1999, 1999 ECR II-931 *a.o.*, para. 1099.
747. Article 25 (4) of Regulation 1/2003.
748. *See supra* section F.2.

Limitation v. Speedy Trial Principle.
Commission proceedings are subject only to the above-mentioned time limitations. The Commission can fix priorities at its discretion without giving the undertakings concerned the right to invoke the principle of reasonable expectation (estoppel).[749] The duration must be viewed in the light of the complexity of the case in question and may be of four[750] or five years.[751] However, an exceptionally long duration of proceedings may contrast with the immediate enforceability of a cease-and-desist order[752] or justify lower fines.[753] An excessively long duration of the proceedings before the Court of First Instance may lead to a reduction of fines.[754]

Limits of Imposing Fines where Infringement is Brought to the Commission's Attention.

(i) *Infringements of Article 81.* Agreements notified to the Commission used to be exempt from fines for infringements of Article 81 committed under the agreement between the date of notification and that of the Commission's decision, unless the Commission withdraws the immunity of fines by way of an Article 15 (6) decision. Fines could, however, be imposed for the period before notification,[755] for infringements not disclosed in the notification[756] and for conduct caught by Article 82.[757] Agreements are not safe from fines if they were not notified because of being dispensed from notification for the

749. *Dutch Cranes*, CFI Oct. 22, 1997, 1997 ECR II-1739, para. 67.
750. *Ibid.*, para. 57.
751. *Tetra Pak II*, CFI Oct. 6, 1994, 1994 ECR II-755, para. 30; *Thyssen Stahl*, CFI Oct. 2, 2003, T-194/99, para. 165.
752. *Net Book Agreement*, ECJ June 13, 1989, 1989 ECR 1693, para. 35. *See Nederlandse Federatieve Vereniging voor de Groothandel op Elektrotechnisch Gebied*, CFI Dec. 16, 2003, T-5/00, paras 435–438.
753. *Irish Sugar*, CFI Oct. 7, 1999, 1999 ECR II-2969, para. 283 (ten months between written submission to Statement of Objections and the adoption of the decision); *Commercial Solvents*, ECJ March 6, 1974, 1974 ECR 223, para. 51.
754. *Welded Steel Mesh*, ECJ Dec. 17, 1998, 1998 ECR I-8417: reduction of the fine imposed by the Commission and confirmed by the Court of First Instance by ECU 50,000 (ECU 2,950,000 instead of ECU 3,000,000) because of the excessive duration of the proceedings before the Court of First Instance (4½ years), which does not infringe the Human Rights Convention ('principle of promptitude') but is contrary to a general principle of Community law as developed in the ECJ's opinion 28 March 1996, 1996 ECR I-1759, para. 33.
755. As in *Pittsburgh Corning*, D.Comm. Nov. 23, 1972, 1972 OJ L 272/35, 39; *Floral*, D.Comm. Nov. 28, 1979, 1980 OJ L 39/51, 59; *Hudson's Bay I*, D.Comm. Oct. 28, 1988, 1988 OJ L 316/43. In *SSI*, D.Comm. July 15, 1982, 1982 OJ L 232/1, 36, fines were considered for periods before notification. *See also Pioneer*, ECJ June 7, 1983, 1983 ECR 1825, para. 93.
756. *See Sperry New Holland*, D.Comm. Dec. 16, 1985, 1985 OJ L 376/21. The suppression of important facts in notifications also attracts procedural fines: *see infra* this section.
757. *TACA II*, D.Comm. Sept. 16, 1998, 1999 OJ L 95/1, point 585; *aff'd* in this respect CFI Sept. 3, 2003, T-191/98, para. 1628.

purposes of exemption.[758] This is the general rule under Regulation 1/2003, which no longer provides for notification; requests for informal guidance[759] do not give any immunity from fines. However, fines may not be appropriate where the parties bring agreements which contain restrictions of competition voluntarily to the Commission's attention, in particular by requesting informal guidance on questions which they consider novel or unresolved.[760] In such a case the principle of legitimate expectation[761] may prevent the parties from being fined to the same extent as a company that is the first to disclose the existence of an anticompetitive agreement or conduct, thereby meriting immunity from fines.[762]

(ii) *Infringements of Article 82.* Where abusive practices have been brought to the Commission's attention (under Regulation 17 by way of notification) the Commission did not impose a fine.[763] The same may apply where they are brought to the Commission's attention by way of informal guidance requests or disclosure in order to benefit from leniency.[764]

(b) Addressees

Undertakings.
Addressees of a fine decision are the undertakings which committed the infringement.

– *Responsibility of the Acting Undertaking.* Only firms or associations, not their senior employees or directors, can be fined under EC competition law.[765] The

758. *SSI*, ECJ Dec. 10, 1985, 1985 ECR 3831, paras 73–78; *SPO*, CFI Feb. 21, 1995, 1995 ECR II-289, para. 342; *aff'd* ECJ March 25, 1996, 1996 ECR I-1611. Fines were imposed for agreements recognized as being covered by Article 4 (2) in *Belasco*, D.Comm. July 10, 1986, 1986 OJ L 232/15, 29, and were considered, but waived, in *Vaessen/Moris*, D.Comm. Jan. 10, 1979, 1979 OJ L 19/32, 35–36. *See also Pioneer*, ECJ June 7, 1983, 1983 ECR 1825, para. 93.

759. Recital 38 to Regulation 1/2003.

760. *Ibid.*, Notice on Informal Guidance Letters.

761. *See Van der Bergh Foods*, CFI Oct. 23, 2003, T- 65/98, para. 192.

762. *Christie's and Sotheby's*, D.Comm. Oct. 30, 2002, IP/02/1585. This 'grey-hound principle' may appear unfair, particularly in a case such as *Vitamins* (in the US) where the first request was submitted only a few hours before the second. *See* Klusmann, WuW 2001–9, 820, 826.

763. E.g., *Racal Decca*, D.Comm. Dec. 21, 1988, 1989 OJ L 43/27; *United Brands*, Dec. 17, 1975, 1976 OJ L 95/1 (with respect to the prohibition not to resell bananas while still green because it appeared as part of the – notified – general conditions of sale); *Atlantic Container Line – TACA*, CFI Sept. 30, 2003, T-191/98, paras 1628–1633.

764. However, the abusive practices must be brought to the Commission's attention prior to any investigatory measures being commenced by the Commission: *Michelin*, CFI Sept. 30, 2003, T-203/01, para. 302.

765. With respect to the similar issue under the prior Article 65 (5) of the ECSC Treaty, *see Steel Beams – Eurofer*, CFI March 11, 1999, 1999 ECR II-263, para. 98.

criteria of intention or negligence relate to natural persons who committed the offending conduct. Since natural persons are not themselves subject to fines, their unlawful conduct must be imputed to the undertaking on the behalf of which they acted when committing the infringement,[766] irrespective of their position within the undertaking,.[767] Liability to fines is not extinguished by changes in the legal identity or ownership of the firm that committed the violation, provided the new entity continues the relevant business.[768]

– *Responsibility of the Controlling Undertaking*. The anticompetitive conduct of an undertaking can be attributed to its parent company where it has not decided independently upon its own conduct on the market,[769] but has carried out, in all material aspects, the instructions given to it by that parent company, having regard in particular to the economic and legal links between them.[770] Thus, parent companies controlling a subsidiary which committed an infringement are liable for the anticompetitive conduct of a subsidiary if they have the possibility of exerting decisive influence on the subsidiary's commercial policy, unless it can be proved that the subsidiary acted in an autonomous way.[771] Where it is difficult to apportion responsibility, both the individual subsidiary or parent company may be held collectively responsible.[772] In this case, a single fine is imposed jointly on parent and subsidiary,[773] or, where parent and subsidiary

766. *Carton – Stora*, ECJ Nov. 16, 2000, 2000 ECR I-9925, para. 28.
767. *Pioneer*, D.Comm. Dec. 17, 1982, 1982 OJ L 167/39, 49.
768. *Polypropylene – Enichem*, CFI Dec. 17, 1991, 1991 ECR II-1628, para. 238; *Deutsche Bahn*, CFI Oct. 21, 1997, 1997 ECR II-1689, para. 105. *See*, in particular, *Industrial Copper Tubes*, D.Comm. Dec. 16, 2003, IP/03/1746, paras 234–262 (general principles for establishing liability).
769. Examples: BMW Belgium, and not its German parent, in *BMW Belgium*, D.Comm. Dec. 23, 1977, 1978 OJ L 46/33, 42; Nederlandse Banden-Industrie Michelin, and not the French parent company, in *Michelin*, D.Comm. Oct. 7, 1981, 1981 OJ L 353/33; Vernante Pennitalia and Fabbrica Pisana, and not their American and French parents, PPG Industries and Saint Gobain, respectively, in *Italian Flat Glass II*, D.Comm. Dec. 7, 1988, 1989 OJ L 33/44 (not annulled by CFI 10 March 1992, 1992 ECRII–1403 in this respect); Shell International Chemical Company, and not the two group holding companies of the Royal Dutch/Shell Group, in *PVC*, D.Comm. July 29, 1994, 1994 OJ L 239/14, para. 46; *aff'd* CFI April 20, 1999, 1999 ECR II-931, para. 960.
770. *Dyestuffs – ICI*, ECJ July 14, 1972, 1972 ECR 619, paras 132–133; *Carton – Metsa Serla*, ECJ Nov. 16, 2000, 2000 ECR I-10065, para. 27; *Krupp Thyssen*, CFI Dec. 13, 2001, 2001 ECR II-3757, para. 189.
771. *Carton – Stora*, ECJ Nov. 16, 2000, 2000 ECR I-9925, para. 28. However, a holding may be held responsible even if the subsidiary is construed as a separate profit center: *Carton – SCA Holding*, CFI May 14, 1998, 1998 ECR II-1373, para. 63; *Enichem/ Anic*, CFI Sept. 17, 1991, 1991 ECR II-1623, para. 55.
772. *Commercial Solvents*, ECJ March 6, 1974, 1974 ECR 223, para. 51; *Pre-insulated Pipes*, CFI March 20, 2002, 2002 ECR II-1847, para.527.
773. E.g., *Commercial Solvents*, D.Comm. Dec. 14, 1972, 1972 OJ L 299/51, 52; *Carton*, D.Comm. July 13, 1994, 1994 OJ L 243/1, points 173–174; *aff'd Finnboard*, CFI May 14, 1998, 1998 ECR II-1617.

were involved in different ways or degrees, they may be fined separately for the same infringement.[774] Firms based in non-EC countries are liable to fines for infringements of the EC competition rules committed in the Community, whether they committed the violation themselves (e.g., in selling directly to EC customers)[775] or through subsidiaries, branches or agents in the Community.[776]

- *Responsibility of an Undertaking which Changed its Legal Form or Name.* A change in the legal form and name of an undertaking does not necessarily have the effect of creating a new undertaking free of liability for the anti-competitive conduct when, from an economic point of view, the two are identical.[777]
- *Responsibility of the Acquiring Company.* In principle, it falls to the legal or natural person managing the undertaking in question when the infringement was committed to answer for that infringement, even if, when the infringement was adopted, another person has assumed responsibility for running the undertaking.[778] Thus, a company responsible for a violation may still be fined after it has sold the business concerned to another company, provided that there is no structural link between them.[779] The acquiring company is liable for conduct of the acquired company if both constitute the same economic entity.[780] However, if the company responsible has been completely absorbed by another company, including a newly created company,[781] and so has ceased to exist as an independent entity, the successor company will be liable,[782] provided it continues

774. E.g., *Benelux Flat Glass*, D.Comm. July 23, 1984, 1984 OJ L 212/13, 21 (BSN and Glaverbel, Saint Gobain and Saint-Roch).
775. *Wood Pulp*, ECJ Sept. 27, 1988, 1988 ECR 5193, 5243, paras 16–17; *Vegetable Parchment*, D.Comm. Dec. 23, 1977, 1978 OJ L 70/54 (a Finnish firm).
776. *Polypropylene – Chemie Linz*, CFI March 10, 1992, 1992 ECR II-1275, para. 350.
777. *CRAM and Rheinzink*, ECJ March 28, 1984, 1984 ECR 1679, para. 9; *Aalborg Portland – Cement*, ECJ Jan. 7, 2004, C-204/00 P, para. 59.
778. *Carton – Cascades*, ECJ Nov. 16, 2000, 2000 ECR I-9693, para. 78; *Krupp-Thyssen*, CFI Dec. 13, 2001, 2001 ECR II-3757, para. 57.
779. *Aalborg Portland – Cement*, ECJ Jan. 7, 2004, C-204/00P, para. 359. Examples: ANIC, and not Montepolimeri, in *Polypropylene*, CFI Dec. 17, 1991, 1991 ECR II-1623, paras 235–238; Trefilunion and not ACOR in *Welded Steel Mesh*, D.Comm. Aug. 2, 1989, 1989 OJ L 260/1, 40; *aff'd Trefilunion*, CFI April 6, 1995, 1995 ECR II-791; *Cascades – Carton*, ECJ Nov. 16, 2000, 2000 ECR I-9693, paras 77–82.
780. *Aalborg Portland – Cement*, ECJ Jan. 7, 2004, C-204/00P, paras 59 and 357. No economic entity found in *Krupp-Thyssen*, CFI Dec. 13, 2001, 2001 ECR II-3757, para. 78.
781. *Alloy Surcharge*, D.Comm. Jan. 21, 1998, 1998 OJ L 100/55, point 102; *Aalborg Portland – Cement*, ECJ Jan. 7, 2004, C-204/00 P, para. 357.
782. *Asturienne-Rheinzink*, ECJ March 28, 1984, 1984 ECR 1679, para. 8; *Polypropylene – Enichem*, CFI Dec. 17, 1991, 1991 ECR II-1628, para. 237. This applies where the company responsible becomes affiliated to a new parent company: *Carton*, D.Comm. July 13, 1994, 1994 OJ L 243/1, point 147; *aff'd Cascades*, CFI May 14, 1998, 1998 ECR II-925, para. 158; *Mayr-Melnhof*, CFI May 14, 1998, 1998 ECR II-1751, paras 388–390; *Stora*, CFI May 14, 1998, 1998 ECR II-2111, para. 85.

the relevant business.[783]

Associations.
Associations may be fined if the responsibility for an infringement of Article 81 or 82 may be imputed to the association and not, or not only, on its members.[784] Associations may be fined if they are a legal entity[785] and assume responsibility for autonomous market behavior.[786] Where the infringement relates to the activities of its members, the fine shall not exceed 10% of the total turnover of each member active on the market affected by the infringement[787] while taking account of the situation of small or medium-sized enterprises.[788] Where the fine is imposed on the association and the association is not solvent, it must call for contributions from its members,[789] or the Commission may require the payment of the fine, or payment of the balance, directly by any of the undertakings whose representatives were members of the decision-making bodies of the association[790] and who are therefore responsible for the association's conduct,[791] provided the financial liability does not exceed 10% of the total turnover of the member concerned in the preceding business year.[792] Associations may be fined where they are active in manufacturing, purchasing or selling the goods in respect of which competition has been restricted or where they played an active role, as an 'undertaking'[793]

783. *All Weather Sports Benelux*, CFI April 28, 1994, 1994 ECR II-211, para. 30; *PVC II*, CFI April 20, 1999, 1999 ECR II-931, para. 969 (continuing business through joint venture) and para. 981; *Krupp Thyssen*, CFI Dec. 13, 2001, 2001 ECR II-3757, para. 62; *Pre-insulated Pipes – HFB Holding*, CFI March 20, 2002, 2002 ECR II-1487, paras 103–118.
784. *Nederlandse Federatieve Vereniging voor de Groothandel op Elektrotechnisch Gebied*, CFI Dec. 16, 2003, T-5/00, paras 351–362.
785. In case of an association without the status of a legal entity the members are responsible and liable according to their degree of participation: *CEWAL*, CFI Oct. 8, 1996, 1996 ECR II-1201, para. 232.
786. *SPO*, ECJ Feb. 21, 1995, 1995 ECR II-289 para. 385; *Dutch Cranes (Injunction)*, CFI June 4, 1996, 1996 ECR II-407 para. 33. Own responsibility of the association (e.g. joint sales organization) affirmed: *Eurocheques*, CFI Feb. 23, 1994, 1994 ECR II-49, paras 137–139; denied: *Woodpulp II*, ECJ Sept. 27, 1988, 1988 ECR 5193 paras 24–27; *PVC II*, CFI April 20, 1999, 1999 ECR II-931, paras 983–989 (holding company).
787. Article 23 (2), second and third subparagraph, of Regulation 1/2003; *Eurocheque Helsinki*, CFI Feb. 23, 1994, 1994 ECR II-49, para. 137.
788. Recital 30 to Regulation 1/2003.
789. *Eurocheque Helsinki*, CFI Feb. 23, 1994, 1994 ECR II-49, para. 139.
790. Members which did not participate cannot be held liable: *Eurofer*, CFI March 11, 1999, 1999 ECR II-263, paras 98–99 and 131.
791. *NAVEVA*, D.Comm. July 15, 1982, 1982 OJ L 232/1, 37.
792. Article 23 (4) of Regulation 1/2003.
793. *Carton*, D.Comm. July 13, 1994, 1994 OJ L 243/1, point 173; *aff'd Carton – Finnboard*, CFI May 14, 1998, 1998 ECR II-1617, paras 282–283 (joint sales organization; the relevant turnover is, however, based on the sales of its members and not on its commissions).

rather than an 'association of undertakings,[794] in executing the restrictive agreement or organizing the restriction of competition.[795] In such cases a fine may only be imposed (according to their responsibility) on the association,[796] on the members of the association[797] or on both the association and its members.[798] If the association did not play an independent role but was merely a forum or a vehicle for coordinating the behaviour of its members, imposing a fine on the association will not be appropriate.[799]

Intention v. Negligence.
Fines may be imposed where an infringement of Article 81 or Article 82 has been committed intentionally or negligently.

- The term '*intention*' implies that the author of the infringement has acted intentionally with the will to commit an act which he knew was unlawful and prohibited by the Treaty and conscious of the unlawful consequences of his behaviour.[800] An undertaking acts intentionally where it is fully aware or could not have been unaware[801] that its conduct was of such a nature as to

---

794. *Dutch Construction Works*, CFI Feb. 23, 1995, 1995 ECR II-289, para. 385; *Dutch Cranes*, CFI Oct. 22, 1997, 1997 ECR II-1739, para. 253. *See BNIC*, D.Comm. Dec. 15, 1982, 1982 OJ L 379/1, 13; *Anseau I*, D.Comm. Dec. 17, 1981, 1982 OJ L 167/39, 49–50. This point was not contested before the Court when it affirmed the Commission's decision: *Anseau*, ECJ Nov. 8, 1983, 1983 ECR 3369); *Belasco*, D.Comm. July 10, 1986, 1985 OJ L 232/15, 30. *See also Welded Steel Mesh*, D.Comm. Aug. 2, 1989, 1989 OJ L 260/1, 42; *aff'd* CFI April 6, 1995, 1995 ECR II-987; *CEWAL*, CFI Oct. 8, 1996, 1996 ECR II-1201, para. 232.
795. *Eurofer – Steel Beams*, CFI March 11, 1999, 1999 ECR II-263, paras 98–99 and 131.
796. In this case the amount of the fine is calculated on the turnover of its members which reflect the association's importance: *British Dental Trade Association*, D.Comm. July 13, 1988, 1988 OJ L 233/15; *Hudson's Bay I*, D.Comm. Dec. 8, 1977, 1978 OJ L 22/23; *Eurocheques*, D.Comm. March 25, 1992, 1992 OJ L 95/50, *aff'd Europay*, CFI Feb. 23, 1994, 1994 ECR II-49, paras 136–137; *Dutch Construction Works* (*SPO*), D.Comm. Feb. 5, 1992, 1992 OJ L 92/1; *aff'd* CFI Feb. 21, 1995, 1995 ECR II-289, para. 385, and ECJ March 25, 1996, 1996 ECR 1–611; *FENEX*, D.Comm. June 5, 1992, 1992 OJ L 181/28. It is a matter for the association and its members in which proportion the fine is attributed internally: *Dutch Cranes*, CFI Oct. 22, 1997, 1997 ECR II-1739, para. 253 (in this case the fine was based only on the association's turnover); *Eurocheques*, CFI Feb. 23. 1994, 1994 ECR II-49 para. 139.
797. *SSI*, D.Comm. July 15, 1982, 1982 OJ L 232/1, paras 166–169; *CEWAL*, CFI Oct. 8, 1996, 1996 ECR II-1201, para. 232 (because the association lacked legal personality).
798. *Belasco*, D.Comm. July 11, 1986, 1986 OJ L 232/15, point 115; *aff'd* ECJ July 11, 1989, 1989 ECR 2117, paras 41–44; *Cement*, D.Comm. Nov. 30, 1994, 1994 OJ L 343/1, point 65.3–6; *Carton – Finnboard*, CFI May 14, 1998, 1998 ECR II-1617, paras 282–283; *Nederlandse Federatieve Vereniging voor de Groothandel op Elektrotechnisch Gebied*, CFI Dec. 16, 2003, T-5/00, paras 390–393.
799. *Wood Pulp I*, ECJ Sept. 27, 1988, 1988 ECR 5193, 5245, paras 148–163. *See Floral*, D.Comm. Nov. 28, 1979, 1980 OJ L 39/51.
800. *See Cement*, CFI March 15, 2000, 2000 ECR II-1213, para. 4784.
801. *Volkswagen*, ECJ Sept. 18, 2003, C-338/00 P, para. 94; *Opel*, CFI Oct. 21, 2003, T-368/00, para. 198.

enter into or encourage restrictions on competition,[802] even if the actions are undertaken by employees, least of all, actions by senior employees.[803] As a rule, an undertaking is responsible for the conduct of all persons within its sphere of influence or responsibility.[804] However, the intentional nature of the infringement is established without demanding the identification of persons who had acted improperly within the undertaking or who ought to have been the responsible for any defective organization of the undertaking.[805] In case of an infringement involving a multitude of undertakings it must be established that the undertaking concerned intended to contribute by its own conduct to the common objectives pursued by all the participants and that it was aware of the actual conduct planned or put into effect by other undertakings in pursuit of the same objectives or that it could reasonably have foreseen it and that it was prepared to take that risk.[806]

- The concept of '*negligence*' must be applied where the author of the infringement, although acting without any in tention to perform an unlawful act, has not foreseen the consequences of his action in circumstances where a person who is normally informed and sufficiently attentive could not have failed to foresee them.[807]
- *Non-implementation of an anticompetitive agreement* does not preclude fines because it constitutes infringement by its very object. The parties are not liable only if they did not implement the cartel *and* were not aware or have actively distanced themselves from it before the Commission's initiation of proceedings.[808]
- *A mistake of facts or law* excludes 'intention' but does not preclude fines where the mistake is due to negligence.[809] This may be interpreted in the same sense as the Commission's 2001 *de minimis* Notice,[810] stating that the Commission will not impose fines where undertakings assume 'in good faith' that an agreement is covered by this notice.

802. *Pioneer*, ECJ June 7, 1983, 1983 ECR 1825, para. 112.
803. Advocate-General Slynn in *Pioneer*, 1983 ECR 1825, para. 168.
804. *Pioneer*, ECJ June 7, 1983, 1983 ECR 1825, para. 97.
805. *Volkswagen*, ECJ Sept. 18, 2003, C-338/00 P, para. 98.
806. *Aalborg Portland – Cement*, ECJ Jan. 7, 2004, C-204/00 P, para. 291.
807. Advocate-General Mayras in *General Motors*, ECJ Nov. 13, 1975, 1975 ECR 1367, 1388–1389.
808. *See* Article 23 (4), fourth subparagraph, of Regulation 1/2003.
809. *Strintzis Lines – Greek Ferries*, CFI Dec. 11, 2003, T-65/99, para. 171. *See also* opinion of Advocate-General Mayras in *General Motors* (1975 ECR 1367, 1382 *et seq*.;) and Reischl in *Hoffman-La Roche (*1979 ECR 461, 596).
810. Commission 2001 *de minimis* Notice (2001 OJ C 368/13), point 4.

– *Legitimate self-protection (state of necessity)* may preclude fines only if it is demonstrated that the offender's existence would be threatened,[811] which must be assessed in the light of the proportionality principle.[812]

(c) Method of Calculating Fines

Discretion of the Commission.
Fines imposed for substantive infringements of the EC competition rules must be in proportion to the gravity and duration of the infringement.[813] The Commission does not apply a scale of fines for particular infringements, but decides each case on its merits. Fine assessment is thus a typical exercise of discretion, involving the weighing of many factors.[814] The Court of Justice recognizes the Commission's discretion and its right to issue guidelines, which do, however, not prejudge the assessment of the fine by the Court in the light of its unlimited jurisdiction.[815] The Court does not repeat the whole assessment process, but only reviews it in relation to particular objections raised by each defendant according to its degree of responsibility and participation in the infringements[816] and the principle of proportionality.[817] The Court will reduce the fines from the level set by the Commission if the objections are sustained. The Commission's discretion includes the power not to fine without being exposed to a discriminatory treatment.[818] Nor is the Commission prevented from raising the general level of fines in order to

811. Rejected in *Pioneer*, ECJ June 7, 1983, 1983 ECR 1825, paras 88–91, and Opinion of Advocate-General Slynn, para. 161. (no justification of self-protection against the damaging effects of 'parasitical trade').
812. *Valsabbia*, ECJ March 18, 1980, 1980 ECR 907, para. 143.
813. Article 23 (2) of Regulation 1/2003; Commission Guidelines on the method of setting fines, 2003 OJ C 10/16, which are binding on the Commission: *LR af 1998 – Pre-insulated Pipes*, CFI March 20, 2002, 2002 ECR II-1705, para. 360.
814. *CMA CGM – FETTCSA*, CFI March 19, 2003, T-213/00, para. 252.
815. *Opel*, CFI Oct. 21, 2003, T-368/00, para. 188.
816. *Polypropylene-Atochem*, CFI Oct. 24, 1991, 1991 ECR II-1177, paras 213–218; *SSI*, ECJ Dec. 10, 1985, 1985 ECR 3831, paras 100–101 (responsibility of one defendant less than that of others, yet same percentage turnover base used to calculate fine); *PVC II*, D.Comm. July 27, 1994, 1994 OJ L 239/14, point 53; *Pre-insulated Pipes*, D.Comm. Oct. 21, 1998, 1999 OJ L 24/1, point 167. Even smaller firms may be held co-responsible: *Welded Steel Mesh -Trefilunion*, CFI April 6, 1995, 1995 ECR II-797, para. 102.
817. *British Plaster Board*, CFI April 1, 1993, 1993 ECR II-389, para. 168; *Pre-insulated Pipes*, D.Comm. Oct. 21, 1998, 1999 OJ L 24/1, point 166.
818. There is no principle requiring pursuit all offenders in the same way or even simultaneously: *Polypropylene – Rhône Poulenc*, CFI Oct. 24, 1991, 1991 ECR II-867 para. 147; *Parker Pen*, CFI July 14, 1994, 1994 ECR II-549, para. 86. *See* with regard to the 'principle of equal punishment': Commission Guidelines on the method of setting fines, 2003 OJ C 10/16. *See Aalborg Portland – Cement*, ECJ Jan. 7, 2004, C-204/00 P, para. 285.

increase their deterrent effect, as it did in 1979, starting with the *Pioneer* case.[819] A complete list of the cases in which fines have been imposed for substantive or procedural infringements of the EC competition rules is given at the end of this chapter.

Single v. Continuous Nature of the Infringement.
An infringement of Article 81 (1) may result from an isolated act or from a series of acts or from continuous conduct. When different actions form part of an overall plan, because their identical object distorts competition, the Commission is entitled to impute responsibility for those actions on the basis of participation in the infringement considered as a whole.[820] The same anticompetitive economic aim may, however, be embodied in various unlawful measures.[821]

Plurality of Infringements.
In the absence of an overall plan[822] conduct that follows periodically the same pattern and has the same anticompetitive purpose constitutes separate infringements, for instance when price collusion alternates with periods of price competition. The same conduct may constitute an infringement of both Article 81 and Article 82, justifying a decision which states an infringement of both provisions. The Commission imposes a single fine[823] based on the infringement which is considered the more serious, in order to avoid double liability contrary to the principle of *non bis in idem*.[824] However, where the parties supply incorrect or misleading information in the same case both in a notification and in response to a request for information the Commission may find two separate infringements and impose a fine which exceeds the maximum fixed for a single infringement.[825]

---

819. Upheld by the Court of Justice in *Pioneer*, ECJ June 7, 1983, 1983 ECR 1825, paras 101–109. *See also Pre-insulated Pipes – Ke Kelit*, CFI March 20, 2002, 2002 ECR II-1647, paras 119–128.
820. *Aalborg Portland – Cement*, ECJ Jan. 7, 2004, C-204/00 P, para. 258. *See* under German penal law the Federal Supreme Court decision of 3 May 1990, WuWE BGH 2429 (a repeated infringement presupposes a general intent and not only a repetition of a similar conduct following the same scheme).
821. *Aalborg Portland – Cement*, ECJ Jan. 7, 2004, C-204/00 P, para. 325.
822. *Ibid.*, para. 309.
823. *Michelin*, CFI Sept. 30, 2003, T-203/01, para. 265.
824. *Aalborg Portland – Cement*, ECJ Jan. 7, 2004, C-204/00 P, para. 316.
825. *Tetra Laval*, D.Comm. July 7, 2004, IP/04/863 (fine of EUR 90,000 for the two separate infringements compared to the maximum of EUR 50,000 for a single infringement under Regulation 1310/97, which is increased up to 1% of the turnover under Article 14 of Regulation 139/2004). The existence of these infringements was discovered during the monitoring work after the prohibition decision of Oct. 30, 2001, 2004 OJ L 43/13, which was annulled by the Court of First Instance on Oct. 25, 2002, 2002 ECR II-4381, and which was followed – with respect to an amended operation – by the conditional clearance decision of Jan. 13, 2003, M.2416.

Individual Determination of Fines.

The amount of fines must be determined individually for each undertaking participating in the infringement.[826] However, the Commission is not prevented from determining the overall amount of the fines to be imposed and then from spreading that total amount among the undertakings according to their 'specific impact'.[827] The method of setting fines is explained in the Commission's Guidelines of 16 January 2003.[828] This method does not imply a mechanical recourse to arithmetic formulae.[829] The Commission proceeds to calculation of fines as follows:

- First, the Commission determines the *basic amount* of the fine according to the gravity and duration of the infringement.
- Secondly, the Commission *adjusts this basic amount* to take account of the participants' size and their overall resources in order to ensure that the fine has a sufficient deterrent effect[830] and to respect the principle of equal punishment.[831]
- Thirdly, the Commission considers the *aggravating and attenuating circumstances.*
- Fourthly, the Commission considers the *degree of cooperation* of the various offenders which may lead to immunity from, or reduction of, fines.

Finally, the Commission verifies whether the amount of fines calculated according this method *does not exceed 10% of the total worldwide turnover* of each undertaking in the preceding business year.[832]

Basic Amount of Fines.

The basic amount is determined by the gravity and duration of the infringement as follows:[833]

---

826. *LVM – PVC*, ECJ Oct. 15, 2002, 2002 ECR I-8375, para. 573. *Opel*, CFI Oct. 21, 2003, T-368/00, para. 92.
827. *CMA CGM – FETTCSA*, CFI March 19, 2003, T-213/00, paras 385 and 396.
828. 2003 OJ C 10/6. Recent example of how these Guidelines are being applied: *Industrial Copper Tubes*, D.Comm. Dec. 16, 2003, IP/03/1746, points 291–432.
829. *PVC – LVM*, ECJ Oct 15, 2002 ECR I-8375, para. 464. Guidelines on the method of setting fines, under 2.A.
830. *Cement*, CFI March 15, 2000, 2000 ECR II-1213, para. 4846; *Opel*, CFI Oct. 21, 2003, T-368/00, para. 189; *Aalborg Portland – Cement*, ECJ Jan. 7, 2004, C-204/00P, para. 90. *See German Banks*, D.Comm. Dec. 11, 2001, 2003 OJ L 15/1, points 192–194 (leading in this case to doubling the basic amount with respect to the most important undertakings).
831. *Nintendo*, D.Comm. Oct. 30, 2002, 2003 OJ L 255/33, points 385–391. *See Cement*, CFI March 15, 2000, 2000 ECR II-1213, para. 123.
832. The basic amount may exceed the limit of 10% if the final amount remains within this limit: *Pre-insulated Pipes – ABB Brown Boveri*, CFI March 20, 2002, 2002 ECR II-1881, para. 184.
833. Article 23 (3) of Regulation 1/2003.

– *Gravity*: The assessment of the gravity depends on the nature of the infringement, its impact on the market,[834] and the size of the relevant market.[835] *Minor* infringements, such as vertical restrictions with a limited market impact, may be fined EUR 1,000 to EUR 1 million. For *serious* infringements,[836] such as horizontal or vertical restrictions, more rigorously applied and with a wider market impact, fines range from EUR 1 million to EUR 20 million. For *very serious* infringements, such as price fixing, market sharing or other practices likely to jeopardize the proper functioning of the single market,[837] fines may exceed EUR 20 million.[838]
– *Duration*: A short duration (less than one year) will result in no increase, a medium duration (one to five years) in an increase of up to 50%, and long duration in an increase of 10% per year.[839]

Adjustment of the Basic Amount.
The scale of fines permits a differential treatment of the undertakings concerned according to the nature of the infringement concerned and the effective economic capacity of the offenders.[840] The Commission therefore adjusts this basic amount of fines to take account of the participants' size and their overall resources in order to ensure that the fine has a sufficient deterrent effect[841] and to respect the principle of equal punishment.[842] This may lead to doubling the basic amount of fines.[843]

834. Guidelines on the method of setting fines.
835. However, there is no need for proving damage caused to consumers: Under Article 81: *Nederlandse Federatieve Vereniging voor de Groothandel op Elektrotechnisch Gebied*, CFI Dec. 16, 2003, T-5/00, para. 317; under Article 82: *British Airways*, CFI Dec. 17, 2003, T-219/99, para. 311.
836. More serious infringements imply intent, even in case of new legal interpretations: *Deutsche Bahn*, CFI Oct. 21, 1997, 1997 ECR II-1689, paras 127–130. *See also Tetra Pak II*, CFI Oct. 6, 1994, 1994 ECR II-755, paras 238–243.
837. 'Hardcore' restrictions: *Cement*, D.Comm. Nov. 30, 1994, 1994 OJ L 343/1, point 45; *Pre-insulated Pipes*, D.Comm. Oct. 21, 1998, 1999 OJ L 24/1, points 164 and 168–169. In the vertical context: *Pioneer*, ECJ June 7, 1983, 1983 ECR 1825, paras 106–107. Significant damage to other operators, in particular customers: *see Sugar-Suiker Unie*, ECJ Dec. 16, 1975, 1975 ECR 1663, para. 621; *Irish Sugar*, D.Comm. May 14, 1998, 1998 OJ L 258/1, point 167; *aff'd* ECJ July 10, 2001, 2001 ECR I-5333; *British Sugar/Napier Brown*, D.Comm. Oct. 14, 1998, 1999 OJ L 76/1, point 204, *aff'd* CFI July 12, 2001, 2001 ECR II-2035.
838. *See* the list of fines imposed by the Commission at the end of this Chapter.
839. *Amino Acids*, CFI July 9, 2003, T-220/00, paras 128–144. *See Pre-insulated Pipes*, D.Comm. Oct. 21, 1998, 1999 OJ L 24/1, points 166 and 170; *Industrial Copper Tubes*, D.Comm. Dec. 16, 2003, IP/03/1746, points 263–284.
840. *See Austrian Banks*, D.Comm. June 11, 2002, 2004 OJ L 56/1, points 504–542.
841. *Cement*, CFI March 15, 2000, 2000 ECR II-1213, para. 4846.
842. *See Cement*, CFI March 15, 2000, 2000 ECR II-1213, para. 123 and 285; *Amino Acids*, CFI July 9, 2003, T-220/00, paras 104–115.
843. E.g. *German Banks*, D.Comm. Dec. 11, 2001, 2003 OJ L 15/1, points 192–194.

Aggravating and Attenuating Circumstances.
The basic amount of the fine is adjusted by aggravating and attenuating circumstances,[844] which are reviewed in detail by the Court of First Instance.[845]

- *Aggravating circumstances*: Long duration,[846] repeated infringements,[847] a refusal to cooperate,[848] assuming the role of leader or instigator,[849] retaliatory measures or a need to increase the fine in order to exceed the amount of gains improperly made as a result of the infringement[850] are considered aggravating circumstances.
- *Attenuating circumstances*: Assuming a minor, passive or 'follow-my-leader' role,[851] non-implementation[852] or termination, as soon as the Commission interevenes,[853] the financial situation,[854] depressed or difficult market conditions,[855]

---

844. Example: *Industrial Copper Tubes*, D.Comm. Dec. 16, 2003, IP/03/1746, points 348–425.
845. *Amino Acids*, CFI July 9, 2003, T-220/00, paras 223–231.
846. *Ibid.*, paras 128–144.
847. *See Nintendo*, D.Comm. Oct. 30, 2002, 2003 OJ L 255/33, point 412. *See also* Thirty-second Report on Competition Policy, point 35; *Soda Ash*, D.Comm. Dec. 13, 2000, 2000 OJ L 10/1, 10 and 33; *TACA*, D.Comm. Sept. 16, 1998 (this cartel succeeded a previous anticompetitive arrangement between the same parties, which was prohibited by the Commission: *Transatlantic Agreement* (*TAA*), D.Comm. Oct. 19, 1994, 1994 OJ L 376/1); *Plasterboard*, D.Comm. Nov. 27, 2002, IP/02/1744 . *See*, however, *Steel Beams – Thyssen Stahl*, CFI March 11, 1999, 1999 ECR II-347, paras 614–625.
848. *Welded Steel Mesh – Baustahlgewerbe*, CFI April 6, 1995, 1995 ECR II-987, paras 123–124; *Steel Beams Carton*, D.Comm. July 13, 1994, 1994 OJ L 243/1, point 165.
849. *Carton – Koninklijke KNP*, CFI May 14, 1998, 1998 ECR II-1007, para. 94; *Pre-insulated Pipes*, D.Comm. Oct. 21, 1998, 1999 OJ L 24/1, point 171 (increase by 50%).
850. But *cf. Kawasaki*, D.Comm. Dec. 12, 1978, 1979 OJ L 16/9, 15–16; *Eurocheques*, D.Comm. March 25, 1992, 1992 OJ L 95/50, point 81; *aff'd* CFI Feb. 23, 1994, 1994 ECR II-49, para. 144; *Pre-insulated Pipes*, D.Comm. Oct. 21, 1998, 1999 OJ L 24/1, point 164. Monopoly profits are sometimes referred to as having been taken into account, e.g., in *United Brands*, D.Comm. Dec. 17, 1975, 1976 OJ L 95/1, 18, or as being a proper factor to take into account, e.g., by the Court of Justice in *Pioneer*, ECJ June 7, 1983, 1983 ECR 1825, para. 108, but are notoriously difficult to calculate. *Cf.* the German Act Against Restraints of Competition (GWB), Section 34, where the upper limit on fines is triple the extra profits earned by infringing the law.
851. *Aalborg Portland – Cement*, ECJ Jan. 7, 2004, C-204/00 P, para. 328; *Carton*, D.Comm. July 13, 1994, 1994 OJ L 243/1, point 171.
852. *Nintendo*, D.Comm. Oct. 30, 2002, 2003 OJ L 255/33, points 434–437.
853. *Ibid.*, points 438–439; *Aalborg Portland – Cement*, ECJ Jan. 7, 2004, C-204/00 P, para. 382.
854. *CMA GCM – FETTCSA*, CFI March 19, 2003, T-213/00, paras 351–352; in *Tokai Carbon – Graphite Electrodes,* CFI April 29, 2004, T-236/01, the Court of First Instance stated: 'The difficult situation in the graphite electrodes industry does not constitute a "specific" economic context within the meaning of point 5 (b) of the Guidelines. As stated above, cartels come into being, in particular, at a time when a sector is experiencing difficulties.' (para. 369). *See also Industrial Copper Tubes,* D.Comm. Dec. 16, 2003, IP/03/1746, points 370–377.
855. *See Cement*, D.Comm. Nov. 30, 1994, 1994 OJ L 343/1, point 65.6. Government regulations which reduce the scope of competition may be (*see Sugar*, ECJ Dec. 16, 1975, 1975 ECR

existence of reasonable doubt,[856] negligence[857] or effective cooperation with the Commission[858] constitute attenuating circumstances.

Assessment of the Cooperation of the Offenders with the Commission – Leniency Program.

On 14 February 2002 the Commission issued a new Notice on its the leniency program[859] which replaces its previous 1996 notice.[860] The Notice aims at increasing in the transparency and certainty of the conditions on which immunity from and any reduction of fines will be granted. The Court of First Instance carefully reviews the application of the Guidelines for calculating fines and the lenience program,[861] leading frequently to corrections of the amount of fines, even by the Court of Justice.[862] A company, which considers collaboration in the detection of a secret cartel, should be able to calculate chances and risks of such collaboration.

– *Immunity from fines*. The notice provides for a full immunity from fines under the following conditions:
  (i) The Commission must be unaware of the alleged cartel and the company be the first to disclose its existence.[863]
  (ii) The company must provide evidence and information enabling the Commission to proceed to surprise inspections.
  (iii) The collaboration must be full, on a continuous basis and expeditious.

1663, paras 613–620), but are not usually, regarded as a mitigating factor (*Johnson & Johnson*, D.Comm. Nov. 26, 1980, 1980 OJ L 377/16, 26–27).

856. New legal interpretations and applications may preclude the imposition of fines: *see Racal Decca*, D.Comm. Dec. 21, 1988, 1988 OJ L 43/27, points 133; *Atlantic Container Line – TACA*, CFI Sept. 30, 2003, T-191/98, paras 1597–1633, in particular para 1630, or justify lower fines: *see Far Eastern Freight Conference*, D.Comm. Dec. 21, 1994, 1994 OJ L 378/17, point 159 (rather symbolic fine of ECU 10,000), which was, however, annulled by CFI Feb. 28, 2002, 2002 ECR II-1101, para. 485 because of legitimate expectations); *FENEX*, D.Comm. June 5, 1996, 1996 OJ L 181/28 (symbolic fine of EUR 1.000).

857. Intent warrants a higher fine than negligence: *Woodpulp*, ECJ March 31, 1993, 1993 ECR I-1307, para. 195. A lawyer's opinion does not exclude negligence: *Windsurfing*, ECJ Feb. 25, 1986, 1986 ECR 611, para. 106; *BASF Coatings*, CFI May 19, 1999, 1999 ECR II-1581, para. 152.

858. *Carton*, D.Comm. July 13, 1994, 1994 OJ L 243/1, point 172, *aff'd Stora*, CFI May 14, 1998, 1998 ECR II-2111, paras 156–159. A compliance programme is not necessarily a mitigating factor: *Strintzis Lines – Greek Ferries*, CFI Dec. 11, 2003, T-65/99, para. 201.

859. 2002 OJ C 45/3.

860. 1996 OJ C 207/4.

861. E.g., *See Amino Acids*, CFI July 9, 2003, T-220/00, paras. 215–231.

862. E.g., *Aalborg Portland – Cement*, ECJ Jan. 7, 2004, C-204/00 P.

863. *Christie's and Sotheby's*, D.Comm. Oct. 30, 2002, IP/02/1585. This 'grey-hound principle' may appear unfair, particularly in a case such as *Vitamins* (in the US) where the first request was submitted only a few hours before the second. *See* Klusmann, WuW 2001–9, 820, 826.

(iv) The company must immediately cease its involvement in the cartel.[864]
(v) The company must not have coerced other companies to participate in the illegal cartel.[865]

In order to enjoy immunity, the company must submit a request for immunity, which may be preceded by a contact 'in hypothetical terms' in order to check whether the conditions for immunity would be met. If the conditions are likely to be met the Commission grants conditional immunity in writing during the procedure and confirms immunity in the final decision. It is important to note that only the first undertaking revealing the existence of an illegal cartel gets immunity from fines (even if the undertaking is not aware of an earlier submission); the Commission will not consider other applications before it has taken its position on the first application. An undertaking which fails to submit evidence recognized by the Commission as disclosing a cartel may withdraw the evidence disclosed but the Commission may use its normal investigation powers to get that evidence.[866]

– Full immunity has been granted in several recent cases,[867] which show that more and more companies are willing to reveal a cartel to the Commission in order to be granted full immunity. In cases where decisive evidence ('smoking gun evidence') has been submitted but 'not entirely spontaneously' or only after having received a request for information, full immunity will not be granted but only a reduction of fines of 70–90% (not only 50% as mentioned under point 23 of the notice).[868] Although not expressly mentioned in the Commission

864. In the case of horizontal price fixing between numerous competitors it is difficult for the Commission to accept a price decrease by company A as ending its involvement in the cartel without giving the impression of replacing the higher cartel price by a lower but still identical regulated price. *See* the banks case regarding change cash conversion charges for euro-currency notes: *SNS Banks Netherlands*, IP/01/554; *Ulster Bank Ireland*, IP/01/635; *Bayerische Landesbank Girozentrale Germany*, IP/01/634; *Dutch and Belgian Banks*, IP/01/650.

865. In the *Belgium Brewers – private label* case Interbrew did not benefit from full immunity 'because it was one of the instigators of the cartel' (having 'coerced' the others): D.Comm. Dec. 5, 2001, IP/01/1739, whereas Interbrew was not the instigator and did benefit from full immunity in the *Luxembourg Brewer* case: D.Comm. Dec. 5, 2001, 2002 OJ L 253/21, points 102–108. *See* also *British Sugar*, CFI July 12, 2001, 2001 ECR II-2035, para. 120 ('initiator and organisator').

866. Leniency Notice, point 17. *See* already *French-West-African Shipowners' Committee*, D.Comm. April 1, 1992, 1992 OJ L 134/1.

867. *Carbonless Paper*, D.Comm. Dec. 20, 2001, IP/01/1892 (Sappi); *Methionin*, D.Comm. July 2, 2002, 2003 OJ L 255/1 (Merck); *Speciality graphites cartel*, D.Comm. Dec. 17, 2002, IP/02/1906 (Graph Tec); *Food flavour enhancers cartel*, D.Comm. Dec. 17, 2002, IP/02/1907 (Takeda); *Vitamins*, D.Comm. Nov. 21, 2001, 2002 OJ L 239/18 (however, in this case the company Aventis got full immunity with respect to vitamin A but was fined with respect to Vitamin D3).

868. 70%: *Graphite electrodes*, D.Comm. July 18, 2001, 2002 OJ L 100/1; 80%: *Sodium gluconate*, D.Comm. Oct. 2, 2001, IP/01/1355; 90%: *Citric Acid*, D.Comm. Dec. 5, 2001, IP/01/1743.

Notice, no fines may be imposed where there is legal uncertainty,[869] or where a company is a victim, rather than a member of a cartel.[870]

– *Reduction of fines*. Undertakings may obtain a reduction of the fine that would otherwise be imposed if they provide the Commission with evidence that represents significant added value with respect to the evidence which is already in the Commission's possession. However to benefit, the undertakings must terminate their involvement in the suspected infringement not later than the time at which they submit the evidence.[871] The concept of 'added value' refers to the extent to which the evidence provided strengthens the Commission's ability to prove the case. The reductions are as follows:
  - 50% to 30% for the first company providing evidence;[872]
  - 30% to 20% for the second, and
  - up to 20% for subsequent companies.[873]

  The level of reduction depends on the extent and continuity of collaboration and whether the evidence provided is directly or only indirectly relevant to the facts.[874]
– *Proceeding*. The Commission will acknowledge receipt and will not consider any further submission of other evidence before it has taken a position on any existing application. It will come to the preliminary conclusion that the evidence provided constitutes added value[875] and will inform the party in writing, no later than in the Statement of Objections, of its intention to reduce a fine and explain the reasons in the final decision.[876]

869. *See Duales System*, D.Comm. April 20, 2001, 2001 OJ L 166/1; *Deutsche Post II*, D.Comm. July 25, 2001, 2001 OJ L 331/40; *Cement*, CFI March 15, 2000, 2000 ECR II-491, para. 4913. However, cases imposing a symbolic fine (according to the Guidelines on the Method of Setting Fines, point 5 (d)), are carefully reviewed. *See Far Eastern Freight Conference*, CFI Feb. 28, 2002, 2002 ECR II-1101, paras 484–485. The non-imposition of fines does not protect against damage claims under national civil law.
870. *Pre-Insulated Pipes*, D.Comm. Oct. 21, 1998, 1999 OJ L 24/1, point 18
871. 2002 Leniency Notice (2002 OJ C 45/3), points 20–23.
872. This, again, may appear unfair, *see supra*.
873. Not contesting the facts exposed in the statement of objections merits only a 10% reduction: *Austrian Banks*, D.Comm. June 11, 2002, IP/02/844.
874. *See Nintendo*, D.Comm. Oct. 30, 2002, 2003 OJ L 255/33, points 450–457.
875. The Commission distinguishes 'crucial evidence' (*Vitamins*, D.Comm. Nov. 21, 2001, IP/01/2001), evidence that 'corroborates' existing evidence (*Sodium gluconate*, D.Comm. Oct. 2, 2001, IP/01/1355)), 'some' more or less material evidence (*Belgian Brewers*, D.Comm. Dec. 5, 2001, IP/01/1739) and information 'that helped to shed further light on the unlawful practice', which is far from any significant added value (*Carbonless Paper*, D.Comm. Dec. 20, 2001, IP/01/1892). No reduction of fines will be granted when the evidence is mainly gathered during the Commission investigation: *SAS/Maersk*, D.Comm. July 18, 2001, 2001 OJ L 265/15.
876. Leniency Notice (2002 OJ C 45/3), points 24–27.

Calculating and Reasoning any Percentage Increases or Reductions Reflecting Aggravating or Mitigating Circumstances.
Any percentage increases or reductions that reflect aggravating or mitigating circumstances must be applied to the basic amount of the fine set by reference to the gravity and duration of the infringement, not to the amount of any increase already applied for the duration of the infringement or to the figure resulting from any initial increase or reduction to reflect aggravating or mitigating circumstances, thereby ensuring equal treatment between the various companies involved in a cartel.[877] The application of the Leniency Notice must be reasoned in such a way as to enable the addressee to know which factors were taken into account by the Commission and to provide the competent court with sufficient material for it to exercise its power of review.[878]

Absolute Limits on Size of Fines.
Fines for substantive infringements of the EC competition rules, i.e., for violations of Article 81 or 82 of the EC Treaty, can range up to 10% of the firm's total sales in the preceding business year.[879] Under the EC competition rules the sales-related upper limit for fines refers to the total (worldwide) sales of all products, not just those concerned in the infringement.[880] In its administrative practice[881] the Commission, when assessing the duration and gravity of each party's infringement and degree of responsibility (without differentiating in relation to the different infringements[882]), considers the companies' world-wide turnover as a basis on which to measure the firm's size and market position of each offender. In its *Preinsulated Pipes* decision the Commission stated that the particular gravity of the infringement in question (bid-rigging) justified fines by reference to the

---

877. *Cheil Jedang – Amino Acids,* CFI July 9, 2003, T-220/00, para. 229.
878. *Aalborg Portland – Cement,* ECJ Jan. 7, 2004, C-204/00, paras 370-375.
879. Article 23 (2) of Regulation 1/2003. For credit and other financial institutions 'sales' may be replaced by analogy to Article 5 (3) of the merger control regulation, by one-tenth of total assets. However, this issue was not decided in *Eurocheques*, CFI Feb. 23, 1994, 1994 ECR II-49.
880. *Pioneer*, ECJ June 7, 1983, 1983 ECR 1825, paras 113–121; *Tipp-Ex*, ECJ Feb. 8, 1990, 1990 ECR I-261, paras 37–39.
881. The Commission started its practice in the *Quinine* case with fines totalling ECU 500,000 (D.Comm. July 16, 1969, 1969 OJ L 192/5), increased the amount of fines considerably in *Pioneer* (ECU 6.95 million; D.Comm. Dec. 14, 1979, 1980 OJ L 60/21; *aff'd* ECJ June 7, 1983, 1983 ECR 1825), imposed a fine of ECU 102 million in *Volkswagen/Audi*, D.Comm. Jan. 28, 1998, 1998 OJ L 124/60 (reduced by CFI July 6, 2000, 2000 ECR II-2707 to EUR 90 million, which was affirmed by ECJ Sept. 18, 2003, C-338/00 P) and an even higher fine of EUR 149 million in *Nintendo*, D.Comm. Oct. 30, 2002, 2003 OJ L 255/33.
882. *Tetra Pak*, CFI Oct. 6, 1994, 1994 ECR II-755, paras 241–244; *PVC II*, CFI April 20, 1999, 1999 ECR II-931, paras 986 and 1175; *Polypropylene -Montecatini*, ECJ July 8, 1999, 1999 ECR II-4539, para. 207.

parties' total turnover.[883] In the *Carton* case the Court of First Instance held that a fine corresponding to 9% of the total annual turnover was reasonable and proportionate.[884]

***Non Bis in Idem* (Double Jeopardy).**

The principle of concurrent application of both Community and national (including third country) competition rules may lead to parallel proceedings and to double sanctions. However, as the Court of Justice ruled in the *Walt Wilhelm* case,[885] equity requires that the earlier sanction should be taken into account in determining the level of the later sanctions to be imposed; any fine imposed in other national jurisdictions within the EC for the same offence is set off against the fine considered appropriate by the Commission,[886] except where the object of the offence is different[887] or the territorial scope of application does not overlap, as in cases of fines imposed outside the EC for different conduct.[888] Such a territorial overlap may, however, be argued in cases where the relevant market is the world market and the cartel implements the restrictions worldwide.[889]

883. *See Pre-insulated Pipes*, D.Comm. Oct. 21, 1998, 1999 OJ L 24/1 and Press Release of the same day (fines totalling ECU 92.2 million), *aff'd Pre-insulated Pipes – Sigma*, CFI March 20, 2002, 2002 ECR II-1845, para. 91.

884. *Carton – SCA Holding*, CFI May 14, 1998, 1998 ECR II-1373, paras 179 and 201. In *Sotheby* the fine represented 6% of the total worldwide turnover: Thirty-second Report on Competition Policy, point 47.

885. *Walt Wilhelm*, ECJ, Feb. 13, 1969, 1969 ECR 1, 14; *Tokai Carbon – Graphite Electrodes*, CFI April 29, 2004, T-236/01, paras 132–134.

886. *Ibid.*, p. 15; *Cast Iron and Steel Rolls*, D.Comm. Oct. 17, 1983, 1983 OJ L 317/1, 15; *Welded Steel Mesh*, D.Comm. Aug. 2, 1989, 1989 OJ L 260/1, 41–42; *aff'd Sotralentz*, CFI April 6, 1995, 1995 ECR II-1191, para. 29; and *Baustahlgewerbe*, CFI April 6, 1995, 1995 ECR II-987, para. 132. *See also* second paragraph of Article 90 of the ECSC Treaty which expressly provides for set-off.

887. *Aalborg – Cement*, ECJ Jan. 7, 2004, C-2004/00 P, paras 316–339.

888. *Walt Wilhelm*, ECJ Feb. 13, 1969, 1969 ECR 1, 14. However, in *Vitamins*, D.Comm. Nov. 21, 2001, 2002 OJ L 239/1, point 333, the Commission argued that the territorial scope does not overlap because the sanctions are limited to the anticompetitive effects within the respective territories.

889. The majority of recent cases concern worldwide cartels and have lead to parallel prosecution and sanctions by different authorities inside and outside the Community, such as in *Lysine*, D.Comm. June 7, 2000, 2001 OJ L 152/24; *Graphite electrodes*, D.Comm. July 18, 2001, 2002 OJ L 100/1, points 177–183; *Vitamins*, D.Comm. Nov. 21, 2001, 2002 OJ L 239/1, points 327–335; *Citric Acid*, D.Comm. Dec. 5, 2001, IP/01/1743; *Zinc Phosphate*, D.Comm. Dec. 11, 2001, IP/01/1797; *Carbonless Paper*, D.Comm. Dec. 20, 2001, IP/01/1892; *Christie's and Sotheby's*, D.Comm. Oct. 30, 2002, IP/02/1585. *See* Kuck, Wirtschaft und Wettbewerb 2002–7/8, 689.

(d) Due Process and Enforcement

Due Process.
The defendant must be told in the Statement of Objections of the Commission's intention to impose fines and how seriously it views the infringement, so as to give an idea of the factors to be considered when assessing the size of the fine (gravity, duration, aggravating and attenuating circumstances), but not the proposed amount of the fine.[890] The Advisory Committee must be consulted on the approximate size of fine proposed.[891]

Payment and Enforcement.
Fines are now denominated in EUR (€).[892] The decision gives the number of one or more bank accounts held by the Commission into which the fine must be paid[893] and states the period (between one and three months) from the date of service of the decision on the addressee, within which it must be paid. The Commission usually states in the decision that after this period interest will be charged.[894] If the decision is appealed, the liability to pay the fine is not automatically suspended.[895] However, since 1981 the Commission has agreed to suspend collection on condition that the companies provide security and agree to pay interest on the eventual fine.[896] Firms may also be given further time to pay after the appeal is decided or allowed to pay by installment.[897] If necessary, the Commission can ask the authorities of the defendant's country to enforce payment of the fine. The enforcement order is issued by the national authorities[898] without any formality other

890. This is due to the fact that the Statement of Objections is approved by the Commissioner whereas the fine is imposed by the full Commission in the light of the written and oral hearing of the parties. There is, under EC competition law, no plea bargaining: Commission Answer to Parliamentary Question 2006/82, 1983 OJ C 118/21.
891. Article 14 (3) of Regulation 1/2003.
892. Council Regulation 2866/98, 1998 OJ L 359/1.
893. Usually in an EC defendant's own country and in an EC country in the case of a non-EC defendant.
894. 7.5% considered necessary to discourage dilatory behavior accepted in *Pre-insulated Pipes – LR af 1998*, CFI March 20, 2002, 2002 ECR II-1705, para. 398. An interest rate of 10.5% was approved in *Steel Mesh*, CFI April 6, 1995, 1995 ECR II-867, paras 138–139; *Tokai Carbon – Graphite Electrodes*, CFI April 29, 2004, T-236/01, paras 476–477.
895. Under Article 242 of the EC Treaty and Article 39 of the ECSC Treaty, an appeal to the Court does not automatically suspend enforcement of the challenged act but the Court itself may so order.
896. Bank guarantee to be provided and normally not suspended: *Dutch Cranes*, CFI June 4, 1996, 1996 ECR II-407 para. 38. A bank guarantee is not an additional fine: *CB Cartes Bancaires*, CFI July 14, 1995, 1995 ECR II-2169 paras 52–53; *Atlantic Container Line – TACA*, CFI Sept. 30, 2003, T-191/98, paras 1637–1643, but necessary to discourage dilatory behaviour: *LR af 1998 – Pre-insulated Pipes*, CFI March 20, 2002, 2002 ECR II-1705, para. 398.
897. Mentioned in *Pioneer*, ECJ June 7, 1983, 1983 ECR 1825, para. 135.
898. Usually the justice ministry or equivalent body.

than verification of the authenticity of the decision and can only be set aside by the European Court of Justice.[899] The limitation period for the collection of fines is five years from the date the decision[900] imposing the fine was served on the addressee or the last action to collect the fine was undertaken, plus any time the addressee was allowed to pay and any time the decision was under appeal before the Court of Justice.

(e) Sanctions for Procedural Infringements

Fines.

For violations of the procedural rules fines up to 1% of the average daily turnover can be imposed by the Commission.[901] Fines for procedural breaches can be levied together with fines for substantive infringements.[902] The imposition of procedural fines is time-barred three years after termination of the infringement,[903] but the period is extended up to a maximum of six years by each act to investigate or prosecute.[904] The procedural infringements for which firms can be fined under Regulation 1/2003 are (a) incorrect or misleading answers in response to a discovery request,[905] (b) incorrect, incomplete or misleading answers in response to, or disregard of, a discovery decision,[906] (c) incomplete production of records during an on-the-spot investigation or refusal to submit to an investigation order,[907] (d) failure to reply truthfully or to correct an incorrect, incomplete or misleading answer given during an on-the-spot investigation, or (e) breaking seals affixed by officials or others authorized by the Commission.[908]

Daily Fines.

To compel the addressee to comply with an interim or final cease-and-desist order,[909]

---

899. Fourth paragraph of Article 256 of the EC Treaty and of Article 92 of the ECSC Treaty.
900. Or a Commission decision varying the original one or refusing to vary it.
901. Article 23 (1) of Regulation 1/2003. Article 15 (1) of Regulation 17 provided for much lower fines (from EUR 100 to 5,000).
902. As in *Theal/Watts*, D.Comm. Dec. 21, 1976, 1977 OJ L 39/19.
903. In relation to infringements involving misleading statements in notifications, the infringement is only regarded as having ended when the Commission is freed from the misconception: *Theal/Watts*, D.Comm. Dec. 21, 1976, 1977 OJ L 39/19, 20; *aff'd Tepea*, ECJ June 20, 1978, 1978 ECR 1391, paras 69–72.
904. Article 25 (1) and (5) of Regulation 1/2003.
905. What is incorrect or misleading was clarified in *Records*, ECJ March 20, 1980, 1980 ECR 1137, para. 11.
906. *See AKZO Chemicals*, D.Comm. Oct. 14, 1994, 1994 OJ L 294/31.
907. *See UKWAL*, D.Comm. April 6, 1992, 1992 OJ L 121/45; *CSM*, D.Comm. Oct. 7, 1992, 1992 OJ L 305/16.
908. Article 23 (1) (a)–(e) of Regulation 1/2003.
909. Or ancillary obligations imposed under it. *See*, e.g., *Commercial Solvents*, D.Comm. Dec. 14, 1972, 1972 OJ L 299/51, 57–58 (two fines threatened in respect of two obligations); *United*

commitments made binding by Commission decision, or a discovery[910] or investigation order,[911] the Commission may impose periodic penalty payments up to 5% of the average daily turnover per day.[912] Daily fines are imposed in two stages:

- by an order threatening a daily fine in case the addressee does not comply with the initial order within a certain time limit. This order may be, but is not necessarily, combined with the cease-and-desist, discovery or investigation order. This order is not enforceable and cannot be appealed.
- by an order imposing the daily fines because the addressee did not comply with the first order. This order is open to appeal.[913]

Before the final decision imposing the penalty payments is taken, the defendant must be sent a Statement of Objections and the Advisory Committee must be consulted,[914] whereas decisions threatening a daily fine (mostly combined with the order to supply information or to submit to an investigation) do not require the previous hearing of the addressees or the Advisory Committee.[915] Where the firms have satisfied the obligation which the periodic penalty payment was intended to enforce, the Commission has discretion whether or not to fine the defendant the full amount due.[916] The general limitation period for collection of fines applies. In practice, it is usually not necessary to impose the fine, as the defendant complies.[917] If, however, the defendant does not comply the Commission may

Brands, D.Comm. Dec. 17, 1975, 1976 OJ L 95/1, 20; *Hugin/Liptons*, D.Comm. Dec. 8, 1977, 1978 OJ L 22/23, 35; *IMA Rules*, D.Comm. Sept. 18, 1980, 1980 OJ L 318/1, 15; *Hasselblad*, D.Comm. Dec. 2, 1981, 1982 OJ L 161/18, 34 (two fines threatened for two obligations); *ECS/Akzo I*, D. Comm July 29, 1983, 1983 OJ L 252/13, 21; *ECS/Akzo II*, D.Comm. Dec. 14, 1985, 1985 OJ L 374/1, 27 (both interim and final order, two fines for two obligations in the latter); *Boosey & Hawkes I*, D.Comm. July 29, 1987, 1987 OJ L 286/36, 43.

910. *CSV*, D.Comm. June 25, 1976, 1976 OJ L 192/27, 29; *Eurocheques*, D.Comm. April 1, 1993 (not published).
911. *Fides*, D.Comm. Jan. 31, 1979, 1979 OJ L 57/33, 34.
912. Article 24 of Regulation 1/2003. The amount of penalty payments under Article 16 of Regulation 17 were much lower (from EUR 50 to EUR 1,000).
913. *Dalmine*, CFI June 24, 1998, 1998 ECR II-2383, paras 29–31. There may, therefore, be three decisions of an investigation: the decision to submit to the investigation, a second announcing a fine and a third imposing the fine, as in *Hoechst*, D.Comm. Jan. 15, 1987, 3 Feb. 1987 and May 26, 1988, *aff'd* ECJ Sept. 21, 1989, 1989 ECR 2859. *See also Peugeot*, CFI May 2, 1997, 1997 ECR II-663, para. 32.
914. Article 27 (1) of Regulation 1/2003. *See Hoechst-PVC/LdPE*, D.Comm. May 26, 1988, Seventeenth Report on Competition Policy, point 57, *aff'd* ECJ Sept. 21, 1989, 1989 ECR 2859, paras 49–58.
915. Articles 18 (2) and 20 (4) of Regulation 1/2003.
916. Article 24 (2) of Regulation 1/2003. In this case the decision imposes a 'fine' for the past conduct rather than compelling future conduct by 'periodic penalty payments', *see Baccarat*, D.Comm. March 15, 1991, 1991 OJ L 97/16.
917. The only two exceptions under the EC rules have so far been Hoechst, which was fined ECU 55,000 for its refusal to submit to an on-the-spot investigation for 55 days: *Hoechst-*

legally apply both fines according to Article 23 (1) and periodic penalty payments according to Article 24, although in practice it will not do so.[918]

Judicial Review – Unlimited Jurisdiction.
Decisions that impose sanctions may be appealed by the addressee. The Court of Justice has unlimited jurisdiction; it may cancel, reduce or increase the fine or periodic payment imposed by the Commission. The Court of First Instance has a broad power of assessment which includes a review of the essential factors which the Commission takes into consideration when setting the amount of fine. The Court of First Instance examines in particular whether the Commission applied correctly Guidelines which create legitimate expectations,[919] which may lead to cancelling[920] or reducing the fine imposed by the Commission.[921] The Court of Justice's task is limited to examining whether, in exercising its power of review, the Court of First Instance made an error of law, in particular whether there has been any manifest error of appraisal or misuse of powers, without substituting its own assessment for that of the Court of First Instance,[922] which may lead to a further reduction of the fine already reduced by the Court of First Instance.[923]

7. Revisions or Amendments of Decisions

Corrections of Assessment v. *Res Iudicata.*
Matters settled by an unappealable Commission decision or by a judicial decision cannot lead to a fresh re-assessment, except where it is expressly provided for[924] or where the assessment is based on new facts;[925] they become *res iudicata*. This

---

PVC/LdPE, ECJ Sept. 21, 1989, 1989 ECR 2859; and *Baccarat*, D.Comm. March 15, 1991, 1991 OJ L 97/16, which was fined ECU 10,000 for failure to comply with a discovery order.

918. No *non bis in idem* because of the different character of the penalties.
919. *See Tokai Carbon – Graphite Electrodes,* CFI April 29, 2004, T-236/01, paras 155.
920. E.g., *Far Eastern Freight Conference,* CFI Feb. 28, 2002, 2002 ECR II-1101.
921. E.g., reducing a fine because of an unreasonably long duration of the administrative proceedings: *Irish Sugar,* CFI Oct. 7, 1999, 1999 ECR II-2969, para. 283 (arithmetic reduction from EUR 8,800,000 to EUR 7,883,326), or because of a too small reduction reflecting attenuating circumstances: *Krupp-Thyssen,* CFI Dec. 13, 2001, 2001 ECR II-3501, para. 281 (not only 10% but further 20% reduction), or because the Commission granted companies a reduction of 10% for not having contested the facts whereas the Court considered a reduction of only 8% appropriate: *Tokai Carbon – Graphite Electrodes,* CFI April 29, 2004, T-236/01, para. 418.
922. *Aalborg Portland – Cement,* ECJ Jan. 7, 2004, C-204/00, paras 47 and 279.
923. E.g., *KNP – Carton,* ECJ Nov. 16, 2000, 2000 ECR I-9641 (reduction of a fine that was already reduced by the Court of First Instance from EUR 2.7 million to EUR 2.6 million); *Aalborg Portland – Cement,* ECJ Jan. 7, 2004, C-204/00, paras 381–384 (miscalculation of the fine by including the turnover of the Spanish and Greek subsidiaries on which the defendant Ciments Français had not assumed control when committing the infringement).
924. E.g. in the case of withdrawal, *see* Article 29 of Regulation 1/2003.
925. *LVM – PVC,* ECJ Oct. 15, 2002, 2002 ECR I-8375, paras 41–45.

principle precludes an undertaking from being found guilty or proceedings from being brought against it a second time on the grounds of conduct in respect of which it has been penalized or declared not liable by previous unappealable decisions.[926] However, this does not preclude the resumption of proceedings where the first decision was annulled for procedural reasons and therefore cannot be regarded as an 'acquittal', as was the case in *PVC II* where the first Commission decision was annulled by the Court for procedural reasons.[927] Undertakings which did not appeal a decision addressed to them cannot rely on the nullity of that decision pronounced by the Court with respect to other addressees which did appeal the decision; decisions in competition matters have an *inter partes* effect.[928] In the *Woodpulp-AssiDomän* case[929] the Court of Justice ruled that the principle of legal security precludes any necessity to re-examine a decision with regard to parties which did not challenge the decision. This case concerned a decision by which the Commission found that 43 firms had infringed Article 81 by concerting prices and imposed fines on them.[930] On appeal of 26 addressees the Court of Justice partly annulled the decision and partly reduced the fines imposed.[931] Some of the addressees who did not challenge the decision, in particular AssiDomän, requested the Commission to review the decision in their respect in the light of the Court's judgment. The Commission rejected this request but the Court of First Instance annulled this decision arguing that Article 233 required the Court to re-examine the previous decision with respect to other defendants.[932] On the Commission's appeal the Court of Justice set aside this judgment. The Court of Justice held that an addressee who could have challenged a Commission decision but failed to do so cannot claim the invalidity of the decision even if it were annulled with respect to other parties who challenged the decision. A ruling to the opposite would give such parties the power to overcome the definitive nature of the decision. The Court of Justice concluded:

> 'Where a number of similar individual decisions imposing fines have been adopted pursuant to a common procedure and only some addressees have taken legal action against the decisions concerning them and obtained their annulment, the principle of legal certainty therefore precludes any necessity for the institution which adopted the decisions to re-examine, at the request

926. *Ibid.*, para. 59. Non-interventions, settlements or closures of proceedings do not have the same effect, *see* Chapter I.F.1. at p. 79.
927. *LVM – PVC*, ECJ Oct. 15, 2002, 2002 ECR I-8375, paras 44–75.
928. *PVC II*, CFI April 20, 1999, 1999 ECR II-931, para. 173; *Norsk Hydro*, CFI June 19, 1990, T-106/89 (not published in ECR); *Woodpulp III (AssiDomän)*, ECJ Sept. 14, 1999, 1999 ECR I-5363, paras 49–57; *LVM – PVC*, ECJ Oct. 15, 2002, 2002 ECR I-8375, para. 101.
929. *Commission v. AssiDomän* (*Woodpulp IV*), ECJ Sept. 14, 1999, C-310/97 P.
930. *Woodpulp*, D.Comm. Dec. 19, 1984, 1985 OJ L 85/1.
931. *Woodpulp II*, ECJ March 31, 1993, 1993 ECR I-1307.
932. *Woodpulp III – AssiDomän*, CFI July 10, 1997, 1997 ECR II-1185, paras 82–86.

of the other addressees, in the light of the grounds of the annulling judgment, the legality of the unchallenged decisions and to determine, on the basis of that examination, whether the fines paid must be refunded.'[933]

G. Judicial Review

1. Introduction

Role of Judicial Review.
Like other acts of the European Community's governing bodies, legislation and decisions of the EC Council and Commission in competition matters are subject to judicial review by the EC Court of Justice according to the provisions of the EC Treaty, the Statutes and the Rules of Procedure.[934] Appeals against Commission decisions addressed to individual firms or associations account for the major part of the Court's work in this area.[935] Such decisions may be challenged by their addressees, by third parties in some instances, and by member states.[936] Negative acts, i.e., the refusal or failure to make a decision, may also be appealed.[937] While the appeal is pending, the appellant may be granted an injunction against enforcement of the Commission decision or other interim relief.[938]

Machinery.
The main function of judicial review in competition cases was transferred in 1989 from the Court of Justice to the European lower court attached to the Court of Justice, the Court of First Instance.[939] The Court of First Instance reviews the

---

933. *Woodpulp IV – AssiDomän*, ECJ Sept. 14, 1999, C-310/97, para. 63, arguing on the basis of *Snupat*, ECJ March 22, 1961, 1961 ECR 53, 86–88; *Textilwerke Deggendorf*, ECJ 1994 ECR I-2181, para. 13. Legal basis: Article 233.
934. Last amended on 14 June 2003, 2003 OJ L 147/17 and 22. Decisions and acts of the EFTA Supervisory Authority are subject to review by the EFTA Court of Justice, *see* Articles 27–41 of the Agreement Establishing the EFTA Supervisory Authority and the EFTA Court of Justice, 1994 OJ L 344/1, 5. *See* Sven Norberg, 'The EFTA Court', in R. Plender, European Courts, Practice and Precedents, 1997, 3.01–3.78; Christiansen, 'The EFTA Court', (1997) 22 ELRev. 539.
935. Commission directives addressed to member states under Article 86 (3) (public enterprises) have also been appealed: *Transparency Directive I*, ECJ July 6, 1982; 1982 ECR 2545.
936. Article 230 of the EC Treaty and Article 33 of the ECSC Treaty. In addition, under Articles 229 of the EC Treaty and 36 of the ECSC Treaty the Court has jurisdiction to review fines. The Commission is under no obligation to inform the addressees of its decisions on their right to appeal: *Guérin automobiles*, ECJ March 5, 1999, 1999 ECR I-1441.
937. Article 232 of the EC Treaty.
938. Articles 242 and 243 of the EC Treaty.
939. Council Decision 88/591 of Oct. 24, 1988 (1988 OJ L 319/1). Enabling provisions for establishing the new court were inserted into the EC Treaties by the 1986 amending Treaty, the Single European Act (1987 OJ L 169/1). As well as appeals in EC and ECSC competition

Commission's findings both as regards the facts and the law. On a point of law the decision of the Court of First Instance is open to further appeal to the Court of Justice.[940] The basic features of the judicial review process, including the types of acts open to appeal, limitation periods, standing, grounds of appeal, and the related principles established in the Court of Justice's case law, are unaffected by the new review machinery. However, changes are likely in the lower court's procedure, especially since the Court of First Instance has been charged with the task of scrutinizing the Commission's fact-finding more closely.[941]

This section will discuss the main points of procedure in judicial review and will then deal in turn with the various types of action, namely appeals against actual Commission decisions, proceedings for failure to act and applications for interlocutory relief. The section does not discuss the procedure in preliminary rulings on questions of Community law referred by national courts under Article 234 of the EC Treaty, which have been highly influential on the development of EC competition law. This quintessentially 'supreme court' function continues to be performed by the Court of Justice.[942]

2. Procedure

Rules of Procedure.
The procedure before the Court on First Instance and the Court of Justice are governed by:

– the Statute of the Court of Justice,

---

cases and actions for damages brought against the Commission together with the appeal, the new lower court also hears appeals against Commission decisions on levies and output and price controls under the ECSC Treaty and cases brought by personnel of the EC governing institutions concerning employee benefits, etc.: Article 3 (1) of Decision 88/591. Since March 25, 1994 the CFI has jurisdiction to hear appeals against anti-dumping duties. However, appeals by member states go directly to the ECJ; in cases of parallel appeals by member states and individuals against the same decision the ECJ may suspend its procedure in order to enable the CFI to hear the case and allow individuals a further right of appeal.

940. E.g., Articles 49–54 of the Statute of the Court of Justice.

941. Fourth and sixth recitals of the preamble to Decision 88/591. A Commission decision may be appealed by individuals before the Court of First Instance and by member states before the Court of Justice. Parallel proceedings can be avoided, according to Article 47 (3) of the Statute of the Court of Justice, by suspending the proceedings before of Court of Justice (*see Neue Maxhütte*, CFI Jan. 21, 1999, T-129/95, paras 46, 52, 57) or the proceedings before the Court of First Instance (*see French Republic and SCPA/Commission and Kali + Salz, MDK, Treuhand*, March 31, 1998, 1998 ECR I-1375) or by referring the case to the Court of Justice (*see CNSD*, CFI May 6, 1996, leading to the Court of Justice's judgment of June 18, 1998, 1998 ECR I-3551).

942. For more detailed accounts of judicial review and other actions before the Court of Justice *see* Rodrigues Iglesias, Proceedings of the Court of Justice in 2002, http://curia/eu.int/en/instit.

– the Rules of Procedure of the Court of First Instance,[943] and
– the Rules of Procedure of the Court of Justice.[944]

Limitation Periods.
Appeals against fines and other decisions under Articles 229 and 230 of the EC Treaty by their addressees must be lodged (i.e., received at the Court's registry)[945] within two months of the day following service of the decision on them.[946] Appeals under Article 230 of the EC Treaty by third parties must be lodged within two months of the notification (service) to the addressee,[947] or, in the absence thereof, of the day on which it came to the knowledge of the addressee, or, where the measure is published, from the 15th day after publication in the *Official Journal*.[948] Actions for failure to act under Article 232 of the EC Treaty[949] must be filed within two months of the expiry of the two-month period after the Commission was called upon to act.[950] All the limitation periods are extended for member states other than Luxembourg (the seat of the Court of Justice and the Court of First Instance) by a certain number of days, set out in Annex II to the Court's Rules of Procedure, in order to take account of differences in the distance potential appellants are from the Court. The periods are not interrupted by vacations or public holidays but if ending on a Sunday or public holiday are extended to the following working day.[951] The Court may accept late submission of appeals where there are special circumstances or *force majeure*.[952] The grounds on which appeals

943. Consolidated in 2003 OJ C 193/41.
944. Consolidated in 2003 OJ C 193/1.
945. Article 37 (3) of the Rules of Procedure of the Court of Justice.
946. Third paragraph of Article 230 of the EC Treaty in conjunction with Article 81 (1) of the Rules of Procedure of the Court of Justice and Article 101 (1) of the Rules of Procedure of the Court of First Instance. The limitation period for appeals against decisions under the ECSC Treaty is one month from service: third paragraph of Article 33 of ECSC Treaty. The partial communication of the decision (e.g., the operative terms) before service of the full decision (including the preceding Facts and Assessment sections) does not count as service.
947. *See Dalmine*, CFI June 24, 1998, 1998 ECR II-2383, para. 40.
948. Article 230 (3) of the EC Treaty and Article 102 of the Rules of Procedure of the Court of First Instance.
949. *See infra* section G.4.
950. Article 232 of the EC Treaty.
951. Article 80 (1) and (2) of the Rules of Procedure of the Court of Justice; Article 101 of the Rules of Procedure of the Court of First Instance.
952. Article 42 of the Statute of the Court of Justice. But the Court interprets this exception strictly. For example, in *Norsk Hydro*, CFI June 19, 1990, T-106/89 (not published in ECR), the Court of First Instance dismissed the Norwegian company's appeal against the ECU 750,000 fine imposed by the Commission for its involvement in the PVC cartel although the appeal had been filed only one day late, on 25 April 1989, instead of April 24 (reception of Commission's decision by the plaintiff in Norway on 10 February + 2 months + 2 weeks for distance = 24 April). *See also Filtrona*, CFI July 10, 1990, 1990 ECR II-367, para. 30; *Bayer*, CFI May 29, 1991, 1991 ECR II-219; *aff'd* ECJ Dec. 15, 1994, 1994 ECR I-5619.

are based must be complete and no fresh issues may be raised in the course of the proceedings.[953]

Language.
Appeals and applications may be lodged in any EC language,[954] or, as the case may be, in any EEA language.[955]

Legal Representation.
Parties may be represented by any 'lawyer entitled to practise before a court of a member state' or a court of an EEA state.[956]

Intervention.
Member states, EC governing institutions and 'any other person establishing an interest in the result of the case' may apply, within three months of the notice on the case published in the *Official Journal,* to intervene in the proceedings on the side of the applicant or the defendant Commission.[957] Examples of private third parties who have been allowed to intervene include competitors of the addressees,[958] including complainants[959] (or the firm complained of where the complaint was rejected),[960] consumer associations,[961] marketing companies,[962] and the European

953. Article 42 (2) of the Rules of Procedure; *Peugeot*, CFI May 2, 1997, 1997 ECR II-663, para. 38.
954. Namely, the nineteen national languages plus Irish: Article 29 of the Rules of Procedure of the Court of Justice.
955. Article 20 of the Agreement between the EFTA countries, 1994 OJ L 344/1.
956. Article 17 of the Statute of the Court of Justice; Protocol EEA Agreement 1994 OJ L 1/1, 567.
957. Article 37 of the Statute of the Court of Justice and Article 93 (1) of its Rules of Procedure. *See* Dashwood, 'Intervention in Cases before the Court of Justice of the European Communities', 1983 Law Soc. Gaz. 147. Intervenors – often competitors of the plaintiff – are not given access to documents (or parts of documents) originating from the parties for which the Court accepts the parties' claim of confidentiality: Article 94 (3) of the Rules of Procedure of the Court of Justice. *See Gencor*, CFI 3 June 1997, 1997 ECR II-879. This practice accords with that of the Commission with regard to granting third parties access to parties' business secrets: *see supra* sections D.7. and E.4.
958. E.g. *Frubo*, ECJ May 15, 1975, 1975 ECR 563; *Auditel*, CFI Feb. 6, 1995, 1995 ECR II-239, paras 23–26, 31 (third parties who have contributed actively during the Commission proceeding are supposed to have a legitimate interest); *Polypropylene – Hüls*, ECJ July 8, 1999, 1999 ECR I-4287, paras 49–56 (intervention of a co-defendant claiming the inexistence of the decision). Member states are automatically admitted: Article 37 of the Statute of the Court of Justice.
959. Zoja in *Commercial Solvents*, ECJ March 6, 1974, 1974 ECR 223.
960. Hasselblad in *Camera Care*, ECJ Jan. 17, 1980, 1980 ECR 119.
961. An Italian consumers' association in *Sugar*, ECJ Dec. 11, 1973, 1973 ECR 1465, paras 7–8; BEUC, the European consumers' union, in *Ford I*, ECJ Feb. 28, 1984; 1984 ECR 1129; *Atlantic Container Line*, CFI March 10, 1995, 1995 ECR II-595.
962. *Auditel*, CFI Feb. 6, 1995, 1995 ECR II-239.

Federation of Bar Associations in the *AM&S* case, which involved the issue of attorney-client privilege.[963]

Procedure before the Court of First Instance.

The procedure in the hearing of appeals before the Court of First Instance at present follows the Rules of Procedure of the European Court of Justice.[964] Compared to the Court of Justice, the Court of First Instance follows a much more automatic system of assigning cases. An assignment to the full Court and the appointment of an Advocate General are extreme exceptions. The proceedings are normally heard before a three or five judge chamber.[965] All cases involving important 'national' interests (i.e. dumping and state aid cases) are assigned to a five judge chamber according to a 'tour de role'. The President of the chamber which has received the assignment proposes a reporting judge from that chamber to the President of the Court, who then appoints the judge concerned. Each chamber, following a proposal by the reporting judge, may decide, because of the major or minor importance of the case, either to 'lift' a case from a three judge chamber to a five judge chamber or to 'degrade' a case from a five judge chamber to a three judge chamber. The procedure is initially conducted in writing, with the parties exchanging pleadings. After the written procedure has been closed, the reporting judge makes a preliminary report, which is not disclosed to the parties. On the basis of this report the Court may then order further enquiries, such as the production of documents and information, or the hearing of witnesses and expert testimony. There then follows an oral hearing of the parties' counsel,[966] and some time later[967] the judgment, which is a single majority judgment without the expression of concurring or dissenting opinions. In the Court of First Instance, it is likely that further enquiries, hearing of witnesses and expert testimony, and perhaps the oral hearing of counsel, will assume a more important role than in the

963. *AM&S*, ECJ May 18, 1982, 1982 ECR 1575.

964. Article 2 (3) of Decision 88/591. *See* Statute of the Court of Justice and Rules of Procedure of the Court of Justice.

965. Cases may be heard by a single judge provided they raise only questions already clarified by established case-law or if they form part of a series of cases in which the same relief is sought and of which one has already been finally decided: Article 1 (2) amending Article 14 of the Rules of Procedure, 1999 OJ L 135/92.

966. *See* Practice Directions relating to direct actions and appeals, 2003 OJ L 98/9 (ECJ) and 2003 OJ L 87/48 (CFI).

967. There is no express time limit; however, in the *Welded Steel Mesh* case the Court of Justice ruled that 32 months elapsed between the end of the written procedure and the decision to open the oral procedure and 22 months between the close of the oral procedure and the delivery of the judgment before the Court of the First Instance were too long so that the fine imposed by the Commission was reduced by ECU 50,000: ECJ Dec. 17, 1998, 1998 ECR I-8417. Reopening of the oral procedure only in the case of new facts and evidence: *Polypropylene – ICI*, ECJ July 8, 1999, 1999 ECR I-4399, paras 55–67.

Court of Justice. French is traditionally the working language of both the Court of Justice and the Court of First Instance.[968]

Expedited Procedure before the Court of First Instance.
On 6 December 2000, the Court of First Instance modified, with effect from 1 February 2001, its Rules of Procedure, by including a new Article 76a, in order to allow for the introduction of a new expedited procedure.[969] This new type of expedited procedure was designed to deal with cases of a particularly urgent nature, such as actions concerning public access to administrative documents held by institutions or decisions regarding the control of mergers or takeovers.[970] Applications may be lodged at the same time as the application initiating the proceedings or the defence. The Court exercises its discretion on whether to grant the expedited procedure. Once the request is approved the written and oral procedure is slightly modified:

- The case is automatically given priority.
- The written procedure is simplified.
- The CFI will make greater use of pre-hearing measures.
- Emphasis is placed on the oral procedure.
- The expedited procedure can lead to a judgment within a maximum period of less than 12 months (compared with an average duration of 20 months).

In deciding whether to grant a request for expedited procedure, the Court will have regard to the urgency and the circumstances of the case and to the question whether, in view of the complexity and the volume of the pleadings, the case lends itself to essentially oral argument.[971] The expedited procedure has been granted in two cases at the request of the parties challenging the prohibition of a concentration which has already been implemented,[972] and in three cases at the request of third parties challenging the conditional clearance of a concentration.[973] However, cases where the parties to a concentration decided not to proceed with the deal are dealt with under the standard procedure.[974]

968. This means that briefs are translated only into French for internal purposes and debates.
969. 2000 OJ L 322/4.
970. CFI information notice published on the Court's website.
971. However, experience shows that urgent cases are granted the benefit of the expedited procedure regardless of their complexity, *see Schneider/Legrand*, CFI Oct. 22, 2002, 2002 ECR II-4091; *Tetra Laval*, CFI Oct. 25, 2002, 2002 ECR II-4381.
972. *Schneider/Legrand*, D.Comm. Oct. 30, 2001, M.2283; *Tetra Laval/Sidel*, D.Comm. Oct. 30, 2001, M.2416.
973. *Ineos v. Shell/DEA*, D.Comm. Dec. 20, 2001, M.2389, and *BP/E.ON*, D.Comm. Dec. 20, 2001, M.2533, and *BaByliss v. SEB/Moulinex*, D.Comm. Jan. 8, 2002, M.2621.
974. E.g. *GE/Honeywell*, D.Comm. July 3, 2001, M.2220.

The expedited procedure may allow the parties to keep a deal alive pending final judgment. However, they may also reconsider their deal and decide not to implement or to divest the merger or takeover.[975]

Further Appeal to the Court of Justice.
Parties who were partially or wholly unsuccessful in their submissions to the Court of First Instance have a right of appeal to the Court of Justice within two months on points of law, such as the lower Court's lack of jurisdiction, a procedural breach or an infringement of Community law by the Court. Private intervenors may appeal if they are directly affected by the decision of the Court of First Instance. Member states and the Community's governing institutions, whether they intervened or not, have a right of appeal.[976]

Costs.
Court proceedings as such are free. As regards the parties' costs, the rule is that the unsuccessful party bears the other party's costs.[977] If both parties are partly successful and partly unsuccessful, the Court may order that each bears its own costs.[978] Appeals against Commission decisions are relatively inexpensive even if the appellant loses, because the Commission is usually defended by members of its in-house Legal Service, whose costs other than travel and subsistence expenses are not recoverable.

3. Appeal against Commission Decisions

Broad Concept.
Under the second paragraph of Article 230 in conjunction with Article 231 of the EC Treaty, natural or legal persons have the right to bring actions before the Court of Justice for the annulment of decisions by the Commission which have been addressed to them or, although addressed to another, are of direct and individual concern to them. Only measures producing binding legal effects, so as to affect the applicant's interests by modifying its legal situation in a specific way, constitute acts or decisions within the meaning of Article 230.[979] Under Article 229 of the EC Treaty and Article 31 of Regulation 1/2003, the Court has 'unlimited

975. E.g. in the *Schneider/Legrand* case.
976. Article 225; Articles 49–54 of the Statute of the Court of Justice, as amended by Article 7 of Decision 88/591. *See Polypropylene-Montecatini*, ECJ July 8, 1999, 1999 ECR I-4539, para. 119.
977. Costs include the 'necessary expenses' of a lawyer to be fixed by the Court: *Continental Can*, ECJ April 18, 1975, 1975 ECR 495; *British Aerospace/Rover*, ECJ Feb. 6, 1995; *Opel Austria*, ECJ Jan. 22, 1997, 1997 ECR II-39) and translation expenses: *Air France*, CFI April 17, 1996, 1996 ECR II-235.
978. Articles 69–75 of the Rules of Procedure of the Court of Justice.
979. *Cimenterie del Tirreno*, CFI June 10, 1998, 1998 ECR II-2261.

jurisdiction' to review fines imposed by the Commission for substantive or procedural infringements of the competition rules and may cancel, reduce or increase such fines.

Types of Decision Open to Appeal.
The 'decisions'[980] of the Commission that are open to appeal include, firstly, decisions imposing fines and all other decisions expressly termed such in Regulation 1/2003,[981] e.g. cease-and-desist orders (including interim orders),[982] exemptions[983] and negative clearances,[984] decisions withdrawing or renewing exemptions, and discovery[985] and investigation orders,[986] and decisions making commitments binding on the parties.[987] In addition, a number of other acts by the Commission, not expressly labelled 'decisions' in Regulation 17 or Regulation 1/2003 but which affect the legal position of the addressees[988] have been established as being appealable decisions, even where they have the appearance of simple communications lacking the usual formality of a decision. These include decisions finally rejecting complaints,[989] or refusing to issue an interim order,[990] and decisions to disclose documents for which the originators claim

980. *IBM*, ECJ Nov. 11, 1981, 1981 ECR 2639, paras 8–9; *Dalmine*, CFI June 24, 1998, 1998 ECR II-2383, para. 29.
981. *See* generally *supra* section F.6.
982. E.g., *Ford Europe*, ECJ Feb. 28, 1984, 1984 ECR 1129; *Peugeot*, CFI May 21, 1990, 1990 ECR II-295.
983. Exemptions made subject to conditions or obligations can even be appealed by the addressee: *Transocean Marine Paint Association*, ECJ Oct. 27, 1974, 1974 ECR 1063; *SNCF and British Railways* (*Eurotunnel*), CFI Oct. 22, 1996, 1996 ECR II-1491. The appeal may lead to the annulment of the entire exemption: *European Night Services*, CFI Sept. 15, 1998, 1998 ECR II-3141.
984. However, the reasoning of a negative clearance is not subject to appeal: *Nederlands Bankiersvereniging*, CFI Sept. 17, 1992, 1992 ECR II-2182 para. 32.
985. *Scottish Football Association*, CFI Nov. 9, 1994, 1994 ECR II-1039; *Société Générale*, CFI March 8, 1995, 1995 ECR II-545.
986. Discovery and investigation orders: e.g., *Brescia*, ECJ April 14, 1960, 1960 ECR 98; *National Panasonic* (*UK*) *v. Commission*, ECJ June 26, 1980, 1980 ECR 2033; *AM&S*, ECJ May 18, 1982, 1982 ECR 1575; *Hoechst-PVC/LdPE*, ECJ Sept. 21, 1989, 1989 ECR 2859; *SEP*, CFI Nov. 21, 1990, 1990 ECR II-649.
987. Which may affect the position of third parties and may therefore be appealed.
988. *See IBM*, ECJ Nov. 11, 1981, 1981 ECR 2639, paras 8–13.
989. *CICCE*, ECJ March 28, 1985, 1985 ECR 1105. *See supra* section C.3. Notices of final rejection of complaint may also be drafted as formal decisions, as in *Philip Morris/Rembrandt/Rothmans*, Fourteenth Report on Competition Policy, points 98–100; *Storck Amsterdam*, CFI Feb. 17, 2000, 2000 ECR II-309, para. 68.
990. *Camera Care*, ECJ Jan. 17, 1980, 1980 ECR 119; *Cosimex*, CFI Dec. 6, 1989, 1989 ECR II-l.

confidentiality[991] or to grant third parties access to file.[992] As regards the rejection of complaints, it is settled law that where the Commission has decided to reject a complaint without holding an investigation, the purpose of judicial review by the Court of First Instance is to ensure that the decision at issue is not based on materially incorrect facts, and not vitiated by an error of law, manifest error of assessment or abuse of power.[993]

Final v. Preliminary 'Decisions'.
It is irrelevant whether the act is called a 'decision', provided it has direct legal effects[994] (including final rejection of a complaint[995] and the binding assessment of a merger by the competent Commissioner[996]). It is uncertain whether an appeal lies against 'decisions' to enter or withdraw opposition to the exemption of a notified agreement under the opposition procedure of block exemption regulations or against the refusal to take evidence from third parties. Decisions to commence formal proceedings in a case and to serve a Statement of Objections cannot be appealed.[977] The same almost certainly applies to letters setting out the Commission's preliminary views on the rejection of a complaint or, more generally, in relation to acts taken in the first phase of a two-phase procedure which constitute merely preliminary statements.[998] This includes the rejection of a defendant's request for access to file which can only be objected to when appealing the final Commission decision.[999] Comfort letters have not been subject

---

991. *Akzo I*, ECJ June 24, 1986, 1986 ECR 1965; *Gencor*, CFI June 3, 1997, 1997 ECR II-881. Today, confidentiality claims are decided in two stages: by the competent service of DG COMP and by the Hearing Officer. Only the latter's decision may be appealed. *Peugeot*, CFI May 2, 1997, 1997 ECR II-663, para. 32.
992. *Interporc*, CFI Feb. 6, 1998, 1998 ECR II-231. However, refusal to grant the defendants access to the file can be appealed only in conjunction with the final decision: *Cimenteries*, CFI Dec. 18, 1992, 1992 ECR II-2667, paras 28–31.
993. *ITT Promedia NV*, CFI July 17, 1998, 1998 ECR II-2937.
994. In the *PVC* case the Court of First Instance had qualified the attacked decisions as 'non-existent' because the final text was not certified (authenticated) by the President of the Commission and the General Secretary: CFI Feb. 27, 1992, 1992 ECR II-315, para. 68, whereas the Court of Justice considered the decision as existent but affected by an essential procedural defect leading to its annulment: ECJ June 15, 1994, 1994 ECR I-2555 paras 47–52.
995. *Florimex*, CFI May 14, 1997, 1997 ECR II-693.
996. *Air France*, CFI March 24, 1994, 1994 ECR II-121, paras 50–51.
997. *IBM*, ECJ Nov. 11, 1981, 1981 ECR 2639. Nor are preliminary letters informing parties of the aspects of their agreement which need to be amended in order to receive exemption. *Omni-Partijen Akkoord*, CFI Dec. 13, 1990, 1990 ECR II-797.
998. *Guérin II*, ECJ March 18, 1997, 1997 ECR I-1503, para. 34; *Peugeot*, CFI May 2, 1997, 1997 ECR II-663, para. 32. *See Automec I*, CFI July 10, 1990, 1990 ECR II-367, para. 42.
999. *Cimenteries*, CFI Dec. 18, 1992, 1992 ECR II-2667 para. 28. The rejection to treat information of a third party as confidential and to communicate it to the defendant is, however, final with respect to that third party and subject to appeal: *SEP*, ECJ May 19, 1994, 1994 ECR I-1911 para. 28.

to appeal.[1000] However, the Commissioner's public statement that a merger is compatible with the Common Market constitutes a decision.[1001] An appeal may be conceivable at least in those cases where a comfort letter has been reasoned in a way similar to a decision.[1002] A regulation may be appealed by a member state, the Council, the Commission or by individuals if the regulation is in fact directed at certain individuals and is therefore a disguised decision.[1003] Directives are binding on member states as to the result to be achieved and may be appealed by those states.[1004]

Standing to Appeal.

As well as the direct addressees of the above 'decisions',[1005] which may include associations,[1006] third parties directly affected by them have standing to appeal. Thus, a complainant can appeal against a decision to grant exemption for the practice complained of.[1007] Decisions may be appealed by persons who, although not the addressee of the decision, are directly and individually concerned by it and they are therefore treated as being in a position analogous to that of the

1000. Although the Court seems to give a comfort letter preceded by publication a higher degree of authority: *Guerlain*, ECJ July 10, 1980, 1980 ECR 2327, paras 9–13; *Langnese-Iglo*, CFI June 8, 1995, 1995 ECR II-1533, para. 36.

1001. *Air France*, CFI March 24, 1994, 1994 ECR II-121, paras 50–51.

1002. *See ATR/Alenia/British Aerospace*, comfort letter of Sept. 11, 1995, Twenty-fifth Report on Competition Policy, p. 128. The effects of such a reasoned comfort letter are similar to a letter rejecting a complaint because the conditions of Article 81 (3) are fulfilled, which was held appealable by the Court of First Instance: *Koelmann*, CFI Jan. 9, 1996, 1996 ECR II-1, paras 40–41.

1003. *Codorniù*, ECJ May 18, 1994, 1994 ECR I-1853, para. 19; *Vereniging van Exporteurs van Levende Varkens*, CFI Dec. 13, 1995, 1995 ECR II-2941, para. 50. An antidumping duty imposed by regulation but concerning in the first place specific operators may be appealed by those persons: *Gestetner Holdings*, ECJ March 14, 1990, 1990 ECR I-781. With regard to state aid: *HapagLloyd*, CFI Feb. 11, 1999, 1999 ECR II-179, paras 42–54; *VTM*, CFI July 8, 1999, 1999 ECR II-2329, para. 34.

1004. *See* the *Telecommunications Directive* case: ECJ March 19, 1991, 1991 ECR I-1233, and Nov. 17, 1992, 1992 ECR I-5833.

1005. In *BP*, ECJ June 29, 1978, 1978 ECR 1513, para. 13, the Court noted that firms do not have to have been fined to have an interest in appealing. However, only the decision as determined by its operative part is subject to appeal, not the reasoning: *Dutch Banks Association*, CFI Sep. 17, 1992, 1992 ECR II-2182, para. 32.

1006. *FRUBO*, ECJ May 15, 1975, 1975, ECR 563. Including consumer associations: *Sugar (intervention)*, ECJ Dec. 11, 1973, 1973 ECR 1465; *BEUC*, CFI May 18, 1994, 1994 ECR II 285; *Tremblay*, CFI Jan. 24, 1995, 1995 ECR II-147, para. 28.

1007. E.g., Metro in *SABA I*, ECJ Oct. 25, 1977, 1978 ECR 1875; a horticultural growers' association in *Dutch Natural Gas Prices I*, ECJ Feb. 2, 1988, 1988 ECR 219, paras 17–25. Similarly, a competitor who objected to a proposed exemption in response to the announcement in the Article 19 (3) notice: *ANCIDES*, ECJ July 9, 1987, 1987 ECR 3131. Appeals by complainants are also accepted against anti-dumping decisions: *FEDIOL*, ECJ Oct. 4, 1983, 1983 ECR 3125; *Timex*, ECJ March 20, 1985, 1985 ECR 849.

addressee.[1008] Persons having a legitimate interest in filing a complaint under Article 3 (2) of Regulation 17 are also entitled to appeal.[1009] Persons having actively participated during the Commission proceedings are deemed to be directly and individually concerned.[1010] However, they may be entitled to appeal if they did not participate actively because they were unaware or badly informed of the Commission's proceedings.[1011] Member states have a right of appeal in all cases.[1012]

Grounds of Appeal.

Four grounds on which the appellant can ask the Court to quash a decision are given in Article 230. They are (i) lack of competence (jurisdiction), (ii) infringement of an essential procedural requirement, (iii) infringement of the Treaty or of any rule of law relating to its application, and (iv) misuse of powers. The grounds are couched in broad terms and often overlap. For example, inadequate reasoning would be both an infringement of an essential procedural requirement (ground (ii)) and an infringement of Article 256 of the EC Treaty (ground (iii)). Consequently, appellants usually cite several grounds and the Court does not always specify the grounds on which an appeal is upheld. Whether the Court quashes the Commission's decision in whole or in part or not at all depends on the seriousness of the infringement by the Commission. The appeal must specify all the issues on which it is based, and fresh issues may not be raised in the course of the proceedings unless it is based on matters of law or fact which came to light during the written procedure.[1013]

(i) *Lack of Competence.* This ground has been pleaded successfully against the Commission's alleged assertion of competence in concluding an Agreement between the Community and the United States on the application of their competition laws[1014] and a Commission decision based on an inappropriate

1008. Article 230 (4). *See Plaumann*, ECJ July 15, 1963, 1963 ECR 197; *Codorniù*, ECJ May 18, 1994, 1994 ECR I-1853; *Air France*, CFI March 24, 1994, 1994 ECR II-121, para. 79; *Express International/DHL*, ECJ June 16, 1994, 1994 ECR I-2681; *SPEI (DHL)*, CFI Jan. 15, 1997, 1997 ECR II-1; *Guérin*, ECJ March 18, 1997, 1997 ECR II-1503.

1009. *Benim*, CFI Jan. 24, 1995, 1995 ECR II-185, para. 26.

1010. An exemption decision implies the rejection of the complaint and therefore entitles the complainant to appeal: *SABA*, ECJ Oct. 25, 1977, 1977 ECR 1875, para. 13. Similarly a decision to close the file: *Philip Morris/Rothmans*, ECJ Nov. 17, 1987, 1987 ECR 4566.

1011. *Trade Unions/Commission (Nestlé-Perrier)*, CFI April 27, 1995, 1995 ECR II-1213, paras 26–36; *ASPEC*, CFI April 27, 1995, 1995 ECR II-1281, paras 61–64.

1012. E.g., *British Telecommunications (Italy v. Commission)*, ECJ March 20, 1985, 1985 ECR 873.

1013. Article 42 (2) of the Rules of Procedure of the Court of Justice; Article 48 (2) of the Rules of Procedure of the Court of First Instance. *See Peugeot*, CFI May 2, 1997, 1997 ECR II-663, para. 38; *Polypropylene-Montecatini*, ECJ July 8, 1999, 1999 ECR I-4539, para. 208.

1014. ECJ Aug. 9, 1994, 1994 ECR I-3641 (competence of the Council and not of the Commission).

legal grounds.[1015] An inappropriate legal ground cannot be cured by adducing a new legal ground.[1016] Lack of competence includes the absence of delegation of decision-making authority[1017] or the required signature[1018] by individual Commissioners or officials.[1019] Lack of authority was successfully argued in the *Ford* case against an interim order which the Court held went further than a final cease-and-desist order could have done.[1020] Lack of competence has been pleaded unsuccessfully with respect to extraterritorial jurisdiction over non-EC firms[1021] and information and investigation decisions (including the announcement of penalty payments) taken by the competent commissioner by way of delegation.[1022]

(ii) *Infringement of Procedural Requirements.* Breaches of procedure are pleaded in a great many appeals. If upheld, they may or may not lead the Court to annul or vary the decision. A major breach, such as failure to consult the Advisory Committee[1023] or total disregard of due process[1024] or lack of reasoning,[1025] would entail the annulment of the whole decision. Lesser infringements or minor procedural irregularities might lead to only partial

---

1015. Erroneous assertion of competence based on Regulation 17 rather than Regulation 1017/68: *UIC*, CFI June 6, 1995, 1995 ECR II-1503; *aff'd UIC II*, ECJ March 11, 1997, 1997 ECR I-1287; erroneous assertion of lacking competence for interim measures: *Camera Care*, ECJ Jan. 17, 1980, 1980 ECR 119.

1016. *Leghühner*, ECJ Feb. 23, 1988, 1988 ECR 905; *Dutch Construction Works*, CFI Feb. 21, 1994, 1994 ECR II-289, paras 57–59.

1017. E.g., *Akzo II*, ECJ Sept. 23, 1986, 1986 ECR 2585.

1018. *ICI-Dyestuffs*, ECJ July 14, 1972, 1972 ECR 619, paras 10–14; *VCH*, ECJ Oct. 17, 1972, 1972 ECR 977, paras 10–14; *VBVB/VBBB*, ECJ Jan. 17, 1984, 1984 ECR 19, paras 12–14; *Dow Iberica*, ECJ Oct. 17, 1989, 1989 ECR 3137, paras 55–59.

1019. *PVC*, CFI Feb. 27, 1992, 1992 ECR II-315, para. 65 (Commissioner signing an act after the expiry of his mandate); *PVC*, ECJ June 15, 1994, 1994 ECR I-2555, paras 47–52; *Solvay – Art. 86*, CFI June 29, 1995, 1995 ECR II-729, paras 50–51 (decision not approved by full Commission); *FRUBO*, ECJ May 15, 1975, 1975 ECR 563, para. 20; *Langnese-Iglo*, CFI June 8, 1995, 1995 ECR II-1533, para. 37 (no authority of the signing official).

1020. *Ford I*, ECJ Feb. 28, 1984, 1984 ECR 1129.

1021. E.g., *Continental Can*, ECJ Feb. 21, 1973, 1973 ECR 215, paras 14–17; *ICI-Dyestuffs*, ECJ July 14, 1972, 1972 ECR 619, paras 125–146; *Wood Pulp*, ECJ Sept. 21, 1988, 1988 ECR 5193; *Polypropylene – Linz*, CFI March 10, 1992, 1992 ECR II-1275, paras 383–384; *Gencor/Lonrho*, CFI March 25, 1999, 1999 ECR II-753, paras 89–105.

1022. *AKZO*, ECJ Sept. 23, 1986, 1986 ECR 2585 para. 34; *Hoechst*, ECJ Sept. 21, 1989, 1989 ECR 2859, paras 44–46. *See* however *ASPEC*, CFI April 27, 1995, 1995 ECR II-1281, para. 107 (state aids).

1023. *See Distillers*, ECJ July 10, 1980, 1980 ECR 2229, 2290 (Advocate General Warner); *Ford I*, ECJ Feb. 28, 1984, 1984 ECR 1129, 1173 (Advocate General Slynn).

1024. *Transocean Marine Paint Association*, ECJ Oct. 27, 1974, 1974 ECR 1063. *See also Akzo I*, ECJ June 24, 1986, 1986 ECR 1965, where the Commission's decision to disclose confidential documents to the complainant without asking the originator of the documents was annulled.

1025. *Cimenteries*, ECJ March 15, 1967, 1967 ECR 75. However, the Commission does not need not refute *all* arguments: *Benim*, CFI Jan. 24, 1995, 1995 ECR II-147, para. 41.

annulment or be disregarded by the Court. The test is whether, but for the breach of procedure, the decision might well have been different.[1026] For example, where the Commission has failed to hear the defendant on major allegations, such as regarding the duration of the infringement, the Court has reduced the fine.[1027] On the other hand, where the Commission has refused to show the defendant documents on which it partly based its case on the ground that they contained sensitive information about other firms, but the charges were sufficiently proven by other evidence,[1028] then the Court has not seen fit to vary the decision for this reason. An infringement of the rights of access to the file cannot be remedied by the mere fact that access has been made possible at a later stage, in particular during judicial proceedings.[1029] Other pleas of procedural irregularities which, even if upheld by the Court, have not been regarded as sufficiently serious to meet the above test, include delays in sending defendants the minutes of an oral hearing,[1030] alleged irregularities in the service of the decision[1031] or Statement of Objections[1032] or in the language used therein,[1033] premature publicity,[1034] failure to explore all

---

1026. *See Distillers*, ECJ July 10, 1980, 1980 ECR 2229, paras 25–26; *FEDETAB*, ECJ Oct. 29, 1980, 1980 ECR 3125, para. 47; *PVC II*, CFI April 20, 1999, 1999 ECR II-931, para. 1021.

1027. *Pioneer*, ECJ June 7, 1983, 1983 ECR 1825, paras 12–17 and 130.

1028. *See FEDETAB*, ECJ Oct. 29, 1980, 1980 ECR 3125, paras 36–40; *Pioneer*, ECJ June 7, 1983, 1983 ECR 1825, paras 24–36; *AEG-Telefunken*, ECJ Oct. 25, 1983, 1983 ECR 3151, paras 21–30. However, it seems doubtful whether evidence that was undisclosed during the Commission proceedings may, as a general rule, be made available to the appellant during the proceedings as has been accepted in *Hoffmann-La Roche*, ECJ Feb. 13, 1979, 1979 ECR 461, paras 15–17. *See* Advocate General Warner in *Distillers*, 1980 ECR 2267, 2297; *Soda Ash – Solvay*, CFI June 29, 1995, 1995 ECR II-1775, para. 98.

1029. *LVM – PVC*, ECJ Oct. 15, 2002, 2002 ECR I-8375, para. 325; *Aalborg Portland – Cement*, ECJ Jan. 7, 2004, C-204/00 P, para. 104. *See also Soda Ash – Solvay*, CFI June 29, 1995, 1995 ECR II-1795, para. 103, which overruled the earlier ruling in *Hoffmann-La Roche*, ECJ Feb. 13, 1979, 1979 ECR 461, paras 15–17.

1030. *ICI-Dyestuffs*, ECJ July 14, 1972, 1972 ECR 619, paras 27–32.

1031. However, such irregularity does not affect the validity of the decision but results in a later start of the appeal period: *Magill – RTE*, CFI July 10, 1991, 1991 ECR II-485, para. 27; *Dunlop-Slazenger*, CFI July 7, 1994, 1994 ECR II-447, para. 25; *Kaysersberg*, CFI Nov. 27, 1997, 1997 ECR II-2137, para. 88.

1032. *ICI-Dyestuffs*, ECJ July 14, 1972, 1972 ECR 619, paras 34–43; *Frubo*, ECJ May 15, 1975, 1975 ECR 563, paras 12–14.

1033. *Continental Can*, ECJ Feb. 21, 1973, 1973 ECR 215, paras 11–12; *Sugar*, ECJ Dec. 16, 1975, 1975 ECR 1663, paras 429–430; *ACF Chemiefarma-Quinine*, ECJ July 15, 1970, 1970 ECR 661, para. 52.

1034. The Court considered premature publicity as 'regrettable' but not as affecting the validity of the decision, *see Sugar*, ECJ Dec. 16, 1975, 1975 ECR 1663, paras 89–92); *United Brands*, ECJ Feb. 14, 1978, 1978 ECR 207, paras 284–286; *Anseau*, ECJ Nov. 8, 1983, 1983 ECR 3369, para. 16; *Hilti*, CFI Dec. 12, 1991, 1991 ECR II-1439, para. 136. However, after the decision is taken, information given to the press cannot complement the reasoning of the decision.

avenues of settlement,[1035] unauthorized disclosure of confidential information to third parties,[1036] failure to disclose the entire file to defendants[1037] or to circulate the entire file to the entire Commission,[1038] or failure of Commission officials dealing with the case to be present throughout the oral hearing.[1039] The plea of inadequate proof or reasoning of a decision can fall under this heading or that of a breach of the Treaty. It has been upheld in a few cases and has led to decisions being wholly or partially quashed, including cases where the Commission issued an interim measure,[1040] imposed fines,[1041] refused an exemption[1042] or rejected a complaint.[1043]

(iii) *Infringement of the Treaty or Any Rule of Law Relating to its Application.* This ground has been invoked to assert that decisions are wrong in law, e.g. as regards the scope of application of Article 81 or 82[1044] or of one of the regulations,[1045] have misapplied the law to the facts,[1046] or have breached fundamental principles of law such as 'proportionality' (reasonableness),[1047] non-discrimination,[1048] legitimate expectations (estoppel),[1049] double jeopardy,[1050] and others.[1051] Subject of an application for annulment is only the operative part

1035. *Anseau*, ECJ Nov. 8, 1983, 1983 ECR 3369, paras 12–15; *VBVB/VBBB*, ECJ Jan. 17, 1984, 1984 ECR 19, paras 51–52.
1036. *FEDETAB*, ECJ Oct. 29, 1980, 1980 ECR 3125, paras 41–47.
1037. *Grundig/Consten*, ECJ July 13, 1966, 1966 ECR 299, 338; *VBVB/VBBB*, ECJ Jan. 17, 1984, 1984 ECR 19, paras 23–25.
1038. *Buchler-Quinine*, ECJ July 15, 1970, 1970 ECR 733, paras 19–22.
1039. *VBVB/VBBB*, ECJ Jan. 17, 1984, 1984 ECR 19, paras 15–16.
1040. *Cimenteries*, ECJ March 15, 1967, 1967 ECR 75.
1041. *Belgian Wallpaper*, ECJ Nov. 26, 1975, 1975 ECR 1491.
1042. *Kali Chemie*, ECJ May 14, 1975, 1975 ECR 499.
1043. *Florimex*, CFI May 14, 1997, 1997 ECR II-693. *Cf.*, under the state aids rules: *Sytraval*, CFI Sept. 28, 1995, 1995 ECR II-2654, para. 62, *aff'd* ECJ April 2, 1998, 1998 ECR I-1719.
1044. E.g., *Sugar*, ECJ Dec. 16, 1975, 1975 ECR 1663, paras 473–498; *Maize Seed*, ECJ June 8, 1982, 1982 ECR 2015, paras 44–67.
1045. *VIP I*, CFI June 6, 1995, 1995 ECR II-1503 (erroneous application of Regulation 17 instead of Regulation 1017/68, likely to be qualified as lack of competence; *aff'd VIP II*, ECJ March 11, 1997, 1997 ECR I-1287.
1046. *General Motors*, ECJ Nov. 13, 1975, 1975 ECR 1367. However, when the Commission's findings are based on an appraisal of complex economic facts, the Court confines its review to ensuring that the Commission did not commit any manifest error in its appraisal. *Remia/Nutricia*, ECJ July 11, 1985, 1985 ECR 2545, paras 34–36; *Philip Morris/Rothmans*, ECJ Nov. 17, 1987, 1987 ECR 4487, paras 61–63.
1047. E.g., in relation to the size of fines (*United Brands*, ECJ Feb. 14, 1978, 1978 ECR 207, para. 302) or to the investigative methods used (*National Panasonic*, ECJ June 26, 1980, 1980 ECR 2033, paras 28–30).
1048. *British Leyland*, ECJ Nov. 11, 1986, 1986 ECR 3263, paras 41–43.
1049. *Sugar*, ECJ Dec. 16, 1975, 1975 ECR 1663, paras 555–557.
1050. *Boehringer II*, ECJ Dec. 14, 1972, 1972 ECR 1281.
1051. In particular infringements of human rights. According to Article 6 (2) of the Maastricht Treaty) the European Union shall respect fundamental rights, as guaranteed by the European

of the decision; the grounds (recitals), although constituting an essential basis, are not in themselves capable of forming the subject of appeal.[1052]

(iv) *Misuse of Powers*. This plea has been entered (unsuccessfully) to support claims that the Commission used its powers for purposes for which they were not given or vindictively.[1053]

Outcome of Appeal.

If an appeal is upheld on some or all counts, the Court may, depending on how serious the infringement is, quash the decision in whole or in part[1054] (including cancelling or reducing fines).[1055] The Court does not substitute its discretion for the Commission's.[1056] According to Article 233 the Commission is required to take the necessary measures[1057] to comply with the Court's judgment.[1058] The

---

Convention for the Protection of Human Rights and Fundamental Freedoms signed in Rome on 4 November 1950, since these constitute the expression of the general principles of law which underlie the constitutional traditions common to the member states. *See Nold*, ECJ May 14, 1974, 1974 ECR 491; *Otto/Postbank*, ECJ Nov. 10, 1993, 1993 ECR I-5683; *Polypropylene-Montecatini*, ECJ 8 July 1999, 1999 ECR I-4539, paras 175–176. *See* Charter of Fundamental Rights of the Union as adopted June 2004, in particular Article II-53 referring to the Convention for the Protection of Human Rights.

1052. *CMA CGM/FETTCSA*, CFI March 19, 2003, T-2131/00, para. 186; *Carton – KNP*, ECJ Nov. 16, 2000, 2000 ECR I-9641, para. 106.

1053. *British Leyland*, ECJ Nov. 11, 1986, 1986 ECR 3263, paras 38–39; *Akzo I*, ECJ June 24, 1986, 1986 ECR 1965, para. 24. Lack of powers was successfully argued in the *Ford* case against an interim order which the Court held went further than a final cease and desist order would have done: *Ford*, ECJ Feb. 28, 1984, 1984 ECR 1129.

1054. E.g., *International Power/NALOO*, ECJ Oct. 2, 2003, C-172/01 P, paras 167–172. The question of partial annulment depends on the severability of the part annulled from the whole; the annulment of a condition attached to an exemption normally does not affect the exemption as such: *Transocean Marine Paint Association*, ECJ Oct. 23, 1974, 1974 ECR 1063; *SNCF and British Railways* (*Eurotunnel*), CFI Oct. 22, 1996, 1996 ECR II-1491. Cases in which the Court has wholly quashed the Commission's decision on this ground include: *Cimenteries*, ECJ March 15, 1967, 1967 ECR 75; *Kali-Chemie*, ECJ May 14, 1975, 1975 ECR 499; *Belgian Wallpaper*, ECJ Nov. 26, 1975, 1975 ECR 1491, paras 29–34. The Court may also declare the appeal 'clearly inadmissible': Article 119 of the Rules of Procedure, *see Deutsche Bahn*, ECJ April 27, 1999, 1999 ECR I-2387.

1055. *See* list of decisions imposing fines and the outcomes of appeals against them at the end of this chapter. The Court has never yet increased a fine, however considered in *Hilti*, ECJ March 2, 1994, 1994 ECR II-667 para. 49.

1056. *IECC*, CFI Sept. 16, 1998, 1998 ECR II-3605, para. 33; *Dalmasso*, CFI Jan. 21, 1999, 1999 ECR II-93.

1057. This obligation does not affect any obligation which may result from the liability of the Commission under Article 288 (2). However, even if a decision is annulled the Commission would be liable to the defendants only in case of a serious breach of law and manifest and grave disregard of individuals' interests: *Stahlwerke Salzgitter Peine*, CFI 1991 ECR II-4611.

1058. For instance, in *NDC/IMS Health* the Commission withdrew its cease and desist order of July 3, 2001 (2001 OJ L 59/12) following the annulment by the Court of Justice (ECJ April 11, 2002, 2002 ECR I-3401): *NDC/IMS Health II*, D.Comm. Aug. 13, 2003, 2003 OJ L 268/69.

Court interprets Article 233 as obliging the Commission to reconsider the case with regard not only to the parties to the case but to other parties as well, provided that the reasons for annulling the decision are substantial and affect the whole decision.[1059] Occasionally, the Court encourages the Commission to take a new decision, effectively referring the case back to it.[1060] The Commission is, however, under no obligation to proceed to new investigations.[1061]

Appeals against Judgments of the Court of First Instance.
Judgments of the Court of First Instance may be appealed on points of law only.[1062] In the *Cement* case the Court of Justice clarified that an appeal against the Court of First Instance's decision can only be based on an error of law, recognizing that the Court of First Instance has exclusive jurisdiction to establish the substantive facts and assess these facts.[1063] An appeal can therefore be based only on any manifest error of appraisal or misuse of powers.[1064] It is not sufficient simply to repeat or reproduce verbatim the pleas already put before the Court of First Instance.[1065] The most frequent grounds of appeal against decisions imposing a fine relate to the rights of defence, in particular the right of access to the file,[1066] the establishment

1059. Under Article 249 individual decisions are binding in their entirety on the firm to which they are addressed; therefore, where an addressee did not bring an action for annulment of the decision insofar as it relates to it, the decision continues to be valid and binding on it: *Textilwerke Deggendorf*, ECJ March 9, 1994, 1994 ECR I-833, para. 13; *AssiDomän*, CFI July 10, 1997, 1997 ECR II-1185, paras 56–58; *PVC II*, CFI April 20, 1999, 1999 ECR II-931, para. 168. However, the Commission is not prevented from reconsidering its decision in favour of the addressee (*see Anseau*, D.Comm. Dec. 5, 1983, 1983 OJ L 376/7) and it may be obliged to do so under Article 233 in cases where the Court annuls the Commission decision relating to one addressee but on grounds which affect the entire decision (*AssiDoman*, para. 72). By contrast, a judgment annulling the Commission decision on grounds which relate only to one addressee does not take effect *erga omnes* (*PVC II*, CFI April 20, 1999, 1999 ECR II-931, paras 169–174).

1060. Remand by the Court to the Commission: *Transocean Marine Paint Association*, ECJ Oct. 23, 1974, 1974 ECR 1063, paras 21–22; *SNCF and British Railways* (*Eurotunnel*), CFI Oct. 22, 1996, 1996 ECR II-1491. Remand by the Court of Justice to the Court of First Instance: *Net Book Agreements*, ECJ Jan. 17, 1995, 1995 ECR I-23. Under Articles 87–88: *Dutch Natural Gas Prices II*, ECJ July 12, 1990, 1990 ECR I-3083.

1061. *Tremblay/SELL*, CFI Nov. 27, 1997, 1997 ECR II-2215.

1062. Article 225 (1) of the EC Treaty; Article 51 (1) of the Statute of the Court of Justice; Articles 110–123 of the Rules of Procedure of the Court of Justice. The Court may reject an appeal as 'clearly inadmissible' according to Article 114 of the Rules of Procedure: *Deutsche Bahn*, ECJ April 27, 1999, 1999 ECR I-2387.

1063. *Aalborg Portland – Cement*, ECJ Jan. 7, 2004, C-204/00, paras 47–51.

1064. *Ibid.*, para. 279. Misuse of powers includes unequal treatment: para. 285.

1065. *Ibid.*, para. 51.

1066. The question whether the exclusion of a specific document adversely affects an undertaking's rights of defence is a question of law: *Aalborg Portland – Cement*, ECJ Jan. 7, 2004, C-204/00 P, para. 125.

of the liability of the undertakings and the criteria material to the setting of the fine.[1067] If the appeal is successful the Court of Justice may, according to Article 54 (1) of the Statutes of the Court of Justice, take the final decision if it is capable of doing so[1068] or refer the case back to the Court of First Instance.[1069]

4. Actions for Failure to Act

Standing to Appeal.

Under Article 232 of the EC Treaty,[1070] natural or legal persons (as well as member states or other EC bodies) can bring proceedings against the Commission before the Court for failure to take action which it is required to take under the Treaty or legislation enacted under the Treaty[1071] and which is of direct and individual concern to the applicant.[1072] The action is admissible only if the Commission has first been called upon to act and did not define its position within two months of being so called upon and may be brought within a further period of two months (Article 232 (2)). In competition cases, it is unlikely that this type of action can be used to force the Commission to issue a prohibition decision, which is a matter for the Commission's discretion,[1073] but only to obtain from the Commission a 'definition of its position' on a request to take such action, which, provided adequate reasons are given, may be a refusal of the request.[1074] Any claim in respect of failure to act must be substantiated.[1075] The information given must be sufficiently clear and precise to establish a causal link between the Commission's failure to act and the disadvantage suffered by the applicant.[1076] Actions for failure to act and actions

---

1067. *See* the review of the role of the Court of Justice in an appeal in *Aalborg Portland – Cement*, ECJ Jan. 7, 2004, C-204/00, paras 46–92.

1068. For instance, the Court of Instance reduces itself the amount of fine in cases where the Court of First Instance erred in the assessment of the fines imposed by the Commission: *Aalborg Portland – Cement*, ECJ Jan. 7, 2004, C-204/00 P, paras 384–387 (wrong determination of the duration of the infringement).

1069. *See Express International/DHL*, ECJ June 16, 1994, 1994 ECR I-2681; e.g. *Rendo*, ECJ Oct. 19, 1995, 1995 ECR I-3319; new decision of the CFI on Dec. 12, 1996, 1996 ECR II-1827.

1070. Similarly Article 37 of the EEA Agreement.

1071. The Commission must be under a specific duty to take action: *Lütticke*, ECJ March 1, 1966, 1966 ECR 18, 24–25. *See Deutscher Komponistenverband*, ECJ July 13, 1971, 1971 ECR 487; and *GEMA II*, ECJ Oct. 18, 1979, 1979 ECR 3173.

1072. Found not to be the case in *Bethell*, ECJ June 10, 1982, 1982 ECR 2277.

1073. *GEMA II*, ECJ 18 Oct. 1979, 1979 ECR 3173, paras 10–23; *Dunlop/Slazenger*, CFI July 7, 1994, 1994 ECR II-441 para. 181; *Benim*, CFI Jan. 24, 1995, 1995 ECR II-147 paras 32–34; *Ladbroke*, CFI Jan. 24, 1995, 1995 ECR II-115 para. 75.

1074. *Demo/Revox*, ECJ Oct. 11, 1983, 1983 ECR 3045, paras 17–22; *CICCE*, ECJ March 28, 1985, 1985 ECR 1105, paras 21–29; *Philip Morris/Rothmans*, ECJ Nov. 17, 1987, 1987 ECR 4487, para. 20.

1075. The possibility of national remedies is irrelevant: *TF 1*, CFI June 3, 1999, 1999 ECR II-1757, *aff'd* ECJ July 12, 2001, 2001 ECR I-5603.

1076. *Guérin Automobiles II*, CFI July 10, 1997, 1997 ECR II-1223.

for annulment under Article 230 are mutually exclusive. If the Commission remains silent after being called upon to act it is subject to action under Article 232, whereas any reasoned position taken by the Commission constitutes a 'decision' subject to action under Article 230.[1077]

Outcome of Appeal.
If an action for failure to act is upheld, the Commission will be obliged to take the necessary action.[1078] The Court cannot substitute its judgment for that of the Commission.[1079] However, successful actions for failure to act are rare[1080] because Article 232 requires that notice be given to the Commission, thereby granting the Commission the opportunity to reconsider a request or complaint. The Commission normally does so but sometimes adopts positions which give rise to actions under Article 230.[1081]

5. INTERIM RELIEF PENDING APPEALS

Two Types of Interim Relief.
Where an appeal against a Commission decision, including interim measures,[1082] has been lodged before the Court, the party filing the appeal may additionally ask the Court to grant an injunction suspending enforcement of the Commission decision (Article 242) or providing other interim relief (Article 243).[1083] The first type of interim relief aims at suspending the immediate enforceability of Commission orders, whereas the second aims at protecting parties against certain immediate effects of Commission decisions finding an infringement or granting or rejecting exemptions.[1084] However, both types overlap to the extent that the Court considers both in combination.[1085]

1077. *Guérin Automobiles I*, CFI June 27, 1995, 1995 ECR II-1753, paras 26–30; *Ladbroke*, CFI Jan. 24, 1995, 1995 ECR II-115 para. 66. In the *Camera Care* case the Court of Justice held that irrespective of whether Article 230 or 232 applied, the Commission would be obliged to reconsider the application for interim measures on a new legal ground as interpreted by the Court: ECJ Jan. 17, 1980, 1980 ECR 119.
1078. Article 233 of the EC Treaty. *See Camera Care*, ECJ Jan. 17, 1980, 1980 ECR 119.
1079. *IECC*, CFI Sept. 16, 1998, 1998 ECR II-3605, para. 33. *See Koelmann*, ECJ Nov. 29, 1993, 1993 ECR II-1267; *J/Commission*, CFI April 27, 1994, 1994 ECR II-391, para. 17.
1080. E.g. under Article 66 ECSC Treaty: *National Carbonizing*, ECJ Oct. 22, 1975, 1975, ECR 1975 1193; under Article 3 of Regulation 17: *Camera Care*, ECJ Jan. 17, 1980, 1980 ECR 119; *Ladbroke*, CFI Jan. 24, 1995, 1995 ECR II-115.
1081. Actions under Article 232 were dismissed in *Guérin Automobiles*, CFI June 27, 1995, 1995 ECR II-1753; *Asia Motors*, CFI Sept. 18, 1996, 1996 ECR II-961; *Intertronic*, CFI Feb. 19, 1997, 1997 ECR II-143.
1082. *Ford I*, CFI Feb. 28, 1994, 1994 ECR II-1129 (granted); *Vichy* (Article 15 (6) decision), CFI July 7, 1991, 1991 ECR II-265 (rejected).
1083. *See also* Article 39 of the ECSC Treaty.
1084. *See SCPA, EMC/Kali + Salz-Mdk*, CFI June 15, 1994, 1994 ECR II-403.
1085. *Ibid.*, para. 10.

Procedure.
Applications for interim relief can only be submitted after or at the same time as the main action and set out, by a separate document, the urgent need for interim measures.[1086] The decision which is the subject of an interim application must therefore be open to appeal, thereby excluding decisions adopted by a procedure involving several stages, in particular where they concern a provisional measure intended to pave the way for the final decision, for instance measures refusing access to the file.[1087] Applications are usually decided by the President of the Court in chambers, but not usually *ex parte*.[1088] Interim measures may be granted with respect to the whole or part of the contested decision while leaving the other aspects directly enforceable.[1089]

Conditions of Granting Interim Relief.
According to Article 104 (2) of the Rules of Procedure and the case law of the Court of Justice, an application for interim measures must state:

> 'the circumstances giving rise to urgency and the pleas of fact and law establishing a prima facie case for the interim measure applied for. The measure sought must further be provisional inasmuch as it must not prejudge the points of law or fact in issue or neutralise in advance the effects of the decision subsequently to be given in the main action'.[1090]

Thus, (i) there must be an apparent existence of an infringement ('*fumus boni iuris*'),[1091] (ii) there must be a risk of serious and irreparable harm (a harm which is 'foreseeable with a sufficient degree of probability')[1092] to individuals

1086. Article 83 of the Rules of Procedure of the Court and Article 104 of the Rules of Procedures of the Court of First Instance.
1087. *Commerzbank I*, ECJ Feb. 27, 2002, 2002 ECR I-2129, paras 7–8; *Commerzbank II*, CFI July 9, 2003, T-219/01, para. 53 (these cases concerned the refusal of access to certain documents relating to the abandonment of parallel proceedings against banks other than those which were fined by the Commission in its decision *German Banks*, D.Comm. Dec. 11, 2001, 2003 OJ L 15/1).
1088. *See* Article 36 of the Statute of the Court of Justice and Articles 83–90 of the Court's Rules of Procedure, bearing in mind, however, the changes following the transfer of jurisdiction to the Court of First Instance.
1089. *Langnese-Iglo*, CFI June 16, 1992, 1992 ECR II-1839.
1090. *Van den Bergh Foods*, CFI July 7, 1998, 1998 ECR II-2641, para. 104. *See Atlantic Sea Container II*, ECJ July 19, 1995, 1995 ECR I-2165, para. 22.
1091. *La Cinq*, CFI Jan. 24, 1992, 1992 ECR II-1, para. 35; *Postbank*, CFI Dec. 1, 1994, 1994 ECR II-1141 para. 27; *Bayer-Adalat*, CFI June 3, 1996, 1996 ECR II-381, paras 45–52; *Sogecable*, CFI July 12, 1996, 1996 ECR II-797, paras 41–42; *Van den Bergh Foods*, CFI 7 July 1998, T-68/98R, paras 54–61 (degree of foreclosure effect depends on the final assessment of the exclusivity requirement).
1092. *Van den Bergh Foods*, CFI July 7, 1998, 1998 ECR II-2641, para. 62.

or to the public,[1093] which implies the urgent need for interim relief,[1094] and (iii) the injunctive relief must not prejudice the final decision.[1095] Where the case involves a civil dispute between opposing parties, the balance of convenience will also be taken into account.[1096] Applications for a suspension of the enforcement of fines are no longer necessary as the Commission now does not collect fines under appeal provided the appellant lodges a bank guarantee and agrees to pay interest if the appeal is unsuccessful.[1097] Injunctions against enforcement of cease-and-desist orders have been granted in a number of cases,[1098] but refused in appeals against decisions the immediate enforcement of which is unlikely to lead to serious and irreparable harm.[1099] Information or investigation decisions are normally not suspended,[1100] except decisions

---

1093. *Continental Can* (*Injunction*), ECJ March 21, 1972, 1972 ECR 157, paras 2–4 (no justification for interim measure if the defendant is only obliged to submit proposals to bring an infringement to an end); *AKZO* (*Injunction*), ECJ April 30, 1986, 1986 ECR 1503 (no visible harm if obligation imposed by the Commission were to be respected); *SNCF and British Railways* (*Eurotunnel*), CFI May 12, 1995, 1995 ECR II-1433 (refusal of suspending a condition attached to an exemption because unlikely to have immediate effects).

1094. The urgency is in reality only one aspect of the condition concerning the risk of serious and irreparable damage: *La Cinq*, CFI Jan. 24, 1992, 1992 ECR II-1, para. 29.

1095. *Ford*, ECJ Feb. 28, 1994 ECR 1129; *Transacciones Maritimas*, CFI Oct. 26, 1994, 1994 ECR II-885.

1096. *See*, e.g., *Miles Druce* (*Injunction*), ECJ Oct. 11, 1973, 1973 ECR 1049 (an Article 66 ECSC case); *Commercial Solvents*, ECJ March 14, 1973, 1973 ECR 357; *SABA I*, ECJ July 23, 1976, 1976 ECR 1353; *Peugeot*, CFI May 21, 1990, 1990 ECR II-195; *Vichy*, CFI June 7, 1991, 1991 ECR II-265; *EISA*, CFI July 15, 1994, 1994 ECR II-703; *Van den Bergh Foods*, CFI July 7, 1998, 1998 ECR II-2641, para. 69.

1097. *Carton – Laakmann*, CFI Dec. 21, 1994, 1994 ECR II-1279, paras 10 and 21–27. *See also Welded Steel Mesh-Aristrain*, CFI Aug. 25, 1994, 1994 ECR II-717 (interim measure granted).

1098. E.g., *Langnese-Iglo*, CFI June 16, 1992, 1992 ECR II-1839; *Kali-Chemie*, ECJ April 3, 1974, 1974 ECR 337; *Frubo*, ECJ Oct. 15, 1974, 1974 ECR 1031; *United Brands*, ECJ April 5, 1976, 1976 ECR 425; *FEDETAB*, ECJ Oct. 30, 1978, 1978 ECR 2111; *VBVB/VBBB*, ECJ March 31, 1982, 1982 ECR 1241; *Magill TV Guide*, ECJ May 11, 1989, 1989 ECR 1141; *Net Book Agreement*, ECJ June 13, 1989, 1989 ECR 1693; *Transatlantic Agreement I*, CFI March 10, 1995, 1995 ECR II-467; *aff'd* ECJ July 19, 1995, 1995 ECR I-2165; *Van den Bergh Foods*, CFI July 7, 1998, T-65/98 R. Suspension of a condition attached to a merger clearance: *SCPA*, *EMC*, CFI June 15, 1994, 1994 ECR II-403 (Commission decision annulled by ECJ March 31, 1998, 1998 ECR I-1375; clearance without conditions granted: D.Comm. July 9, 1998, M.308).

1099. E.g., *Continental Can*, ECJ Feb. 21, 1973, 1973 ECR 215; *Akzo III*, ECJ April 30, 1986, 1986 ECR 1503; *Dutch Cranes*, CFI June 4, 1996, 1996 ECR II-407, *aff'd* ECJ Oct. 10, 1996, 1996 ECR I-4971; *Carton – Laakmann*, CFI Dec. 21, 1994, 1994 ECR II-1279; *TAA – Atlantic Container Line*, CFI Nov. 22, 1995, 1995 ECR II-2895. Suspension of a merger clearance decision rejected: *Union Carbide*, Dec. 2, 1994, 1994, ECR II-1159. Suspension of a state aid decision rejected: *EISA*, CFI July 15, 1994, 1994 ECR II-703.

1100. *Otto/Postbank*, CFI Dec. 1, 1994, 1994 ECR II-1141; *Brescia*, ECJ June 25, 1959, 1960 ECR 98; *Hoechst-PVC/LdPE*, ECJ March 26, 1987, 1987 ECR 1549 (both against investigation orders); *Dow Chemical Nederland*, ECJ Oct. 28, 1987, 1987 ECR 4367 (against use of evidence obtained during an on-the-spot investigation); *SEP*, CFI Nov. 21, 1990, 1990 ECR II-649.

on confidentiality.[1101] In actions under Articles 232 and 243, the Court has sometimes declined to grant injunctive relief itself[1102] but has suggested that the Commission do so.[1103] This applies in cases where the Commission finds, pursuant to Article 10 of Regulation 1/2003, that an agreement satisfies the conditions of Article 81 (3) and third parties appeal this decision.[1104]

H. Special Features of Proceedings against Member States

Introduction.
This section summarizes the special features of proceedings under Article 226 of the Treaty against member states for infringements of Article 31 (state commercial monopolies), Article 86 (1) and Article 10 in conjunction with Articles 81 and 82 (government-induced distortions of competition), and Articles 87 and 88 (state aids).[1105]

Broad Discretion of the Commission.
According to Article 211 of the EC Treaty, the Commission may take the necessary measures in order to ensure the implementation of the provisions of the Treaty and measures taken by the institutions pursuant thereto, including the initiation of proceedings under Article 31 (6), 86 (3) and 88 (3). The Commission may initiate proceedings upon its own initiative or upon application (complaint).[1106] However, the Commission has a broad discretionary power, but an individual may not be deprived of the protection of its legitimate interests.[1107] The Commission is therefore not released from the obligation to examine complaints carefully and to carry out a thorough market analysis;[1108] its decisions are, within these limits, subject to

---

Applications for injunction partly granted: *Mars/Langnese-Scholler*, CFI June 16, 1992, 1992 ECR II-1839; *SCPA and EMC/MdK-K+S*, CFI June 15, 1994, 1994 ECR II-403 (suspension of a condition attached to a merger clearance decision).

1101. *AKZO*, ECJ June 24, 1986, 1986 ECR 1965.

1102. *Miles Druce*, ECJ Oct. 11, 1973, 1973 ECR 1049.

1103. *National Carbonizing (Injunction)*, ECJ Oct. 22, 1975, 1975 ECR 1193; *Camera Care*, ECJ Jan. 17, 1980, 1980 ECR 119.

1104. Requests for inerim measures rejected: *Gestévision*, CFI Dec. 14, 1993, 1993 ECR II-1409 (exemption under Article 81 (3)); *Union Carbide*, CFI Dec. 2, 1994, 1994 ECR II-1159 (merger declared compatible).

1105. The substantial rules are discussed in Chapter IX.

1106. *See* Form for the Submission of Complaints Concerning Alleged Unlawful State Aid, 2003 OJ C 116/3.

1107. *Télévision Française 1 SA*, CFI June 3, 1999, 1999 ECR II-1757, paras 50–51, *aff'd* ECJ July 12, 2001, 2001 ECR I-5603.

1108. *See Asia Motors I*, CFI Sept. 18, 1992, 1992 ECR II–2285; *Asia Motors II*, CFI Sept. 18, 1996, 1996 ECR II-961; *aff'd Somaco*, ECJ May 7, 1998, 1998 ECR 1–2587.

a judicial review under Article 230 (2)[1109] and Article 232.[1110]

Investigative Powers of the Commission.
The Commission may request information and proceed to investigations under Article 284 of the EC Treaty without having compulsory powers.[1111] The Commission may hear interested parties or complainants which do not, however, have the same rights as under Article 3 of Regulation 17 and Article 27 (3) of Regulation 1/2004.[1112] The Commission must hear the member state to which the directive or decision is to be addressed.[1113] By analogy to Article 27 (1) of Regulation 1/2003, the Commission may base its decision only on facts as to which the addressee had been afforded the opportunity of making known its views.[1114] The Commission therefore addresses a letter which summarizes the facts, gives a provisional evaluation and invites the member state concerned to submit its observations (which may be compared to the Statement of Objections).[1115] Failure to hear the member state concerned may lead to annulment of the decision.[1116] The Commission is not obliged to hear or inform other member states.[1117] It is the Commission's practice to inform, although not to consult, the Advisory Committee.

Decision of the Commission.
A decision finding an infringement of Article 86 (1) in combination with Article 81 or 82 may impose obligations to bring this infringement to an end[1118] and may

1109. *Star Fruit*, ECJ Feb. 14, 1989, 1989 ECR 291, 301; *Ladbroke*, CFI Sept. 18, 1995, 1995 ECR II-2568, para. 45; *aff'd* in this respect ECJ Nov. 11, 1997, 1997 ECR I-6265; *Sateba*, ECJ July 17, 1998, 1998 ECR I-4913, para. 42.
1110. *Intertronic*, CFI Feb. 19, 1997, 1997 ECR II-143, para. 24. Under state aid provisions: *AITEC*, CFI May 22, 1996, 1996 ECR II-351.
1111. *See*, however, the Commission's proposal for a procedural regulation under Article 89 (state aids): 1998 OJ C 116/13.
1112. *Sytraval*, ECJ April 2, 1998, 1998 ECR I-1719, para. 58; *Sateba*, ECJ July 17, 1998, 1998 ECR I-4913, para. 42. *See Ladbroke*, CFI Sept. 18, 1995, 1995 ECR II-2568, para. 45; *Tremblay*, ECJ Oct. 24, 1996, 1996 ECR I-5547, para. 69; *SFEI*, CFI Jan. 15, 1997, 1997 ECR II-1, para. 116; *Intertronic*, CFI Feb. 19, 1997, 1997 ECR II-141, para. 24.
1113. *Netherlands PTT*, ECJ Feb. 12, 1992, 1992 ECR I-565, para. 37.
1114. *Meura & Boch*, ECJ July 10, 1986, 1986 ECR 2263, 2289.
1115. Expressly provided for under Article 88 (2) when the Commission intends to declare a state aid incompatible with Article 87 and under Article 226 when a member state did not fulfil an obligation under Article 10 in conjunction with Article 81 or 82. Examples include *Rodby*, Twenty-second Report on Competition Policy, point 522; *VEBACOM*, Twenty-fifth Report on Competition Policy, point 111. Need for an additional statement of objections: *Irish Fishery*, ECJ May 21, 1977, 1977 ECR 921.
1116. *Netherlands Courier Express Services*, ECJ Feb. 12, 1992, 1992 ECR I-5654.
1117. *Air France*, CFI June 25, 1998, 1998 ECR II-2405, paras 75–77.
1118. In cases of abusive market foreclosure practices the Commission may impose compulsory licenses: *Omnitel/Pronto*, D.Comm. Oct. 4, 1995, 1995 OJ L 280/49; *VEBACOM*, Twenty-fifth Report on Competition Policy, point 111.

be, and normally is, published.[1119] Commitments undertaken by the member state after initiation of an Article 86 (3) proceeding may lead to a suspension or a letter closing the file.[1120] Under Article 226 the Commission delivers a reasoned opinion after giving the member state concerned the opportunity to submit observations and brings the matter before the Court of Justice if the member state does not comply with the opinion.[1121]

Judicial Review of Commission Directives and Decisions Addressed to Member States.
The Commission directive or decision addressed to member states[1122] can be appealed by the addressee (Article 230 (2)), by any other member state (Article 227))[1123] and by any natural or legal person, provided such person is directly and individually concerned (Article 230 (2)).[1124] Appeals of a member state must be brought before the Court of Justice while appeals of natural or legal persons must be brought before the Court of First Instance. Commission decisions finding incompatibility of a state aid may be appealed by the addressee (the member state) or by the beneficiary.[1125] Decisions declaring a state aid compatible with the EC provisions may be appealed by competitors who are affected by the aid that distorts competition between them and the beneficiary.[1126] Interim measures are

---

1119. Examples of unpublished Article 86 (3) decisions include *GSM Spain*, Twenty-sixth Report on Competition Policy, point 120; *VTM (Flemish Television Monopoly)*, Twenty-seventh Report on Competition Policy, points 112–114; *aff'd* CFI July 8, 1999, 1999 ECR II-2329.

1120. *Deutsche Bundespost*, Fifteenth Report on Competition Policy, point 261; *VEBACOM*, Twenty-fifth Report on Competition Policy, point 111; GSM *Italy*, Twenty-seventh Report on Competition Policy, point 108.

1121. E.g. *Greek Oil Monopoly*, ECJ Dec. 13, 1990, 1990 ECR I-4747 (partially granted); *Electricity Monopolies*, ECJ Oct. 23, 1997, 1997 ECR I-5699, 5789, 5815 and 5851 (rejected). Under Article 88 (2), subparagraph 2, the Commission may, in derogation from Article 226, refer the matter to the Court of Justice directly.

1122. Recommendations, in particular according to Article 31 (6), are not subject to judicial review. *See* Article 230 (1) of the EC Treaty.

1123. *See France/Air Inter-TAT*, ECJ Oct. 26, 1994, 1994 ECR I-5229.

1124. Directives: *see Telecommunications Directive*, ECJ March 19, 1991, 1991 ECR I-1223. Decisions: *see Netherlands PTT*, ECJ Feb. 12, 1992, 1992 ECR I-565; *Bundesverband der Bilanzbuchhalter*, ECJ Feb. 20, 1997, 1997 ECR I-947.

1125. *See Air France*, CFI Dec. 12, 1996, 1996 ECR II-2105. Appeals of the beneficiary may be brought before the Court within two months after being informed by the member state, addressee of the decision or a competitor, *see Alitalia*, Dec. 12, 2000, 2000 ECR II-3871, para. 61.

1126. *See Cofaz*, ECJ Jan. 28, 1986, 1986 ECR 391; *Greek Cement (Herakles)*, CFI July 6, 1995, 1995 ECR II-1971, para. 34 (both appeals leading to the annulment of the Commission decisions). Non-competitors are, however, excluded from appeal: *Asociacion Telefonica de Mutualistas*, CFI Dec. 18, 1997, 1997 ECR II-2529.

rarely granted under Article 243.[1127] Decisions which are not appealed cannot be held void before national courts.[1128]

Non-Respect of a Court Decision.
A member state's non-respect of a directive or decision can be brought before the Court by either the Commission under Article 226 or by another member state under Article 227, and in cases of state aid under Article 88 (2) (2). If the Court states that the member state concerned has not complied with its judgment, it may impose a lump sum penalty payment according to Article 228 (2). The Commission has issued guidelines on the calculation of such lump sums.[1129]

I. Enforcement by National Courts[1130]

1. Introduction

Legal Basis of Private Enforcement.
The Court of Justice has established that Articles 81 and 82 are of 'direct effect' in the member states i.e., the prohibitions of restrictive practices and abuse of dominant positions can be enforced by private firms and individuals through the national courts without, in principle, further action or enactment by the EC authorities.[1131] Firms and individuals can invoke Articles 81 (1) and (3) and 82 both as a 'shield' and as a 'sword', i.e., as a defence in a civil action for enforcement of a prohibited agreement or practice and as a cause of action claiming an injunction, damages or other remedies. Even if parties or third parties do not invoke

1127. *See Tsimentia Halkidos*, CFI Aug. 11, 1995, 1995 ECR II-2237; *France/Air Inter-TAT*, ECJ Oct. 26, 1994, 1994 ECR I-5229 (in both cases rejected).

1128. *National Farmers*, ECJ Oct. 22, 2002, 2002 ECR I-9079.

1129. Commission Notice on the Method of Setting Penalty Payments, 1997 OJ C 63/2. The Commission imposed on 20 Dec. 2002 a daily fine of EUR 21,600 in the case against *Ireland*, IP/02/1950.

1130. *See* Picanol, 'Remedies in National Law for Breach of Articles 85 and 86 of the EEC Treaty: A Review', 1983 *Legal Issues of European Integration* 1; Temple Lang, 'EEC Competition Actions in Member States' Courts – Claims for Damages, Declarations and Injunctions for Breach of Community Antitrust Law', 1984 *Fordham International Law Journal* 389; F. Jacobs, 'Civil Enforcement and EEC Antitrust Law', 1984 *Michigan Law Review* 1364; Louis, *The Community Legal Order*, EC Commission, 2nd. ed., 1990, Chapter III; Whish, 'The Enforcement of EC Competition Law in the Domestic Courts of Member States', 1994 ECLR 60.

1131. *BRT/SABAM I*, ECJ Jan. 30, 1974, 1974 ECR 51, para. 16: 'As the prohibitions of Articles 85 (1) and 86 tend by their very nature to produce direct effects in relations between individuals, these Articles create direct rights in respect of the individuals concerned which the national courts must safeguard'. *See also Sacchi/Tele Biella*, ECJ April 30, 1974, 1974 ECR 409, para. 18; *Delimitis/Henninger Bräu*, ECJ Feb. 28, 1991, 1991 ECR I-935, para. 45.

Articles 81 and 82, national courts have to apply these provisions *ex officio*.[1132] The Community law provides only one consequence of civil law in Article 81 (2): Agreements which are contrary to Article 81 (1) and do not satisfy the conditions of Article 81 (3) are automatically void, no prior decision to that effect being required.[1133] The question whether the agreement is entirely or partly void and whether the infringement justifies damage claims is a matter of national law.[1134]

A Still Underdeveloped Tool.

The enforcement of EC competition law in civil litigation before national courts is still relatively underdeveloped compared with private antitrust enforcement in the United States. However, it is on the increase, as is shown by national courts' rulings in a growing number of cases on the civil consequences of Articles 81 and 82[1135] and by both the Commission[1136] and the Court of Justice[1137] favouring greater private enforcement.[1138] A decentralized application of Community law not only corresponds to the subsidiarity principle as established by Article 5 (2) of the Maastricht Treaty but also raises the general level of voluntary compliance with and enforcement of the law, as is the case in the United States. In addition, it eases the enforcement burden on the Commission which should concentrate on cases presenting a Community interest.[1139] This section will deal first with the remedies available in national courts for breaches of Articles 81 and 82. It then sets out the limitations on the jurisdiction of national courts and finally discusses the main procedural issues arising in private enforcement.

1132. *Van Schijndel*, ECJ Dec. 14, 1995, 1995 ECR I-4705, para. 13; *Van Schijndel*, Dutch Supreme Court Nov. 1, 1997, Twenty-seventh Report on Competition Policy, p. 349.
1133. Article 1 of Regulation 1/2003. *See Delimitis/Henninger Bräu*, ECJ Feb. 28, 1991, 1991 ECR I-935, para. 45; with respect to Article 81 combined with Article 10: *Flemish Travel Agents*, ECJ Oct. 1, 1987, 1987 ECR 3801, paras 22–24; with respect to the EEA Agreement: *Erla Maria Sveinbjörnsdottir*, EFTA Court of Justice Dec. 10, 1998, E-9/97, 1998 EFTACR 95, para. 66.
1134. *See* The Application of Articles 85 and 86 by National Courts in the Member States, 1997, updated http://europa.en.int. The recent Commission Reports on Competition Policy include a section on the application of the Community competition rules by courts of the member states. *See also Tetra Pak I*, CFI July 10, 1990, 1990 ECR II-309, para. 42
1135. E.g., with respect to illegal forms of selective distribution of perfumes, *Depotkosmetik*, German Federal Court, 12 May 1998, WuW DE-R 206.
1136. Commission's Notice on Cooperation between the Commission and the Courts of the EU Member States, para. 16.
1137. *Dalmasso/VAG*, CFI Jan. 21, 1999, 1999 ECR II-93, para. 46.
1138. Not only of competition law, but of EC law generally, such as Articles 28 *et seq*. (free intra-EC trade) and 90 (non-discriminatory taxation).
1139. Commission's Notice on Cooperation between the Commission and the Courts of Member States, points 13–14.

2. Remedies

Remedies a Matter of National Law.
The direct effect of Articles 81 and 82 on private legal relations and the duty of national courts to enforce the resultant rights and obligations are a matter of Community law.[1140] The remedies granted by national courts in order to do so, however, are a matter of national law.[1141] The remedies and the procedural rules for granting them must be no less favorable than those for similar claims under national law *and* may not render practically ineffective the Common Market rules.[1142] For example, a national court may have to grant interim relief even if the national law does not provide for such a remedy, provided it is necessary for guaranteeing the protection of subjective rights under Community law.[1143]

Recognition of Articles 81 and 82 as a Defence; Severance.
The violation of Articles 81 or 82 is a defence to actions for the enforcement of contracts against parties[1144] or of other rights (for example, intellectual property rights or unfair competition law) against third parties.[1145] National courts are nowadays generally disposed to accept such 'Euro-defences' if the violation is clear.[1146] In a number of cases national courts have granted requests for a declaration that

1140. *See*, in particular, the detailed opinion of Advocate General Van Gerwen in the case *Banks/ British Coal*, ECJ April 13, 1994, 1994 ECR I-1209, 1243–1260.

1141. *See* in great detail 'Application of Community law by national courts', the Court's website.

1142. *San Giorgio*, ECJ Nov. 9, 1983, 1983 ECR 3595, para. 14.

1143. *Factorame*, ECJ April 19, 1990, 1990 ECR I-2433, paras 20–21. *See also Eridania*, ECJ Jan. 22, 1986, 1986 ECR 117, paras 37–38; *Peterbroeck*, ECJ Dec. 14, 1995, 1995 ECR I-4615, para. 12; *van Schijndel*, ECJ Dec. 14, 1995, 1995 ECR I-4705, para. 17. *See* Hoskins, 'Tilting the Balance: Supremacy and National Procedural Rules', 1996 ELRev. 365; Rodriguez Iglesias, 'Gedanken zum Entstehen einer Europäischen Rechtsordnung', NJW 1999–1, 1, 6.

1144. Examples of cases decided in UK courts: *Sirdar v. Les Fils de Louis Mulliez*, English High Court, March 19, 1975, 1975–1 CMLR 378; *Dymondv. G.B. Britton & Sons*, English High Court, July 24, 1976, 1976–1 CMLR 133; *Felixstowe Dock & Railway Co. v. British Transport Docks Board*, English Court of Appeal, July 29, 1976, 1976–2 CMLR 655; *Chemidus Wavin v. TERI*, English Court of Appeal, 20 Dec. 1976, 1978–3 CMLR 514. Example of cases decided by German courts: *Polyurethane Foam*, Düsseldorf State Appeals Court, June 19, 1984, WuW/E OLG 3354. *See also* the Belgian case that gave rise to *Flemish Travel Agents*, ECJ Oct. 1, 1987, 1987 ECR 3801.

1145. *Béguelin*, ECJ Nov. 25, 1971, 1971 ECR 949, para. 29. Examples of UK cases: *Application des Gaz v. Folks Veritas*, English Court of Appeal, May 22, 1974, 1974–2 CMLR 75; *British Leyland v. T.I. Silencers*, English Court of Appeal, Nov. 24, 1980; 1981–2CMLR 75; *ICI v. Berk Pharmaceutical Ltd.*, English High Court, July 16, 1980; 1981–2 CMLR 91; *Lansing Bagnall v. Buccaneer Lift Parts*, English Court of Appeal, July 27, 1982; 1984–1 CMLR 224; *British Leyland v. Armstrong Patents*, English Court of Appeal, June 21, 1984, 1984–3 CMLR 102. Example of a German case: *Grundig*, German Federal Court (BGH) Feb. 28, 1985, WuW/E BGH 2187.

1146. Notice on the Cooperation between the Commission and the national courts, points 3–8.

a contract is void or conduct illegal under Articles 81 or 82.[1147] The finding that clauses of a contract are invalid under Article 81 does not, however, mean that the Court will have to dismiss the action if the plaintiffs are seeking the enforcement of clauses (e.g., payment of royalties) or contracts (e.g. sales contracts concluded by a joint venture)[1148] from which the invalid portion of the contract can be severed. The Court of Justice has held that the practical consequences of the nullity of certain clauses of a contract for the enforceability of the remaining clauses are wholly a matter for national law; thus, courts must apply their national rules concerning severance.[1149]

Injunctions.

The most common remedy so far is the injunction. Both prohibitory and mandatory orders have been granted. The types of enjoined behaviour have included refusal to supply, collective boycott and hostile takeover. In many cases damages may be an alternative to an injunction or both remedies may be sought together.[1150]

1147. The leading UK case is *Chemidus Wavin*, English Court of Appeal, Dec. 20, 1976, 1978–3CMLR 514. In Germany the cases include: *Klippan*, Federal Supreme Court (BGH), July 10, 1969, WuW/E BGH 1030; *Ciment/Kerpen*, Saarbrücken State Appeals Court (OLG) May 9, 1984, WuW/E OLG 3243; Stuttgart Higher Regional Court, March 17, 1995, Twenty-fifth Report on Competition Policy, p. 302; in the Netherlands: Supreme Court (Hoge Raad), Dec. 22, 1995, Twenty-fifth Report on Competition Policy, p. 303; in Denmark: Supreme Court April 15, 1997, Twenty-seventh Report on Competition Policy, p. 346; in France: *Espace Diffusion*, Court de Cassation, Oct. 15, 1996, Twenty-seventh Report on Competition Policy, p. 347 (*see also BMW/ Deenik*, ECJ Feb. 23, 1999, C-63/97, in a similar case which was submitted by the Dutch Supreme Court). An arbitral decision stating on the applicability of Article 81 may be null and void only if it is contrary to the public interest: *Eco/Benneton*, ECJ June 1, 1999, 1999 ECR I-3055.

1148. *ASTRA*, D.Comm. Dec. 23, 1992, 1993 OJ L 20/23, para. 33.

1149. *Maschinenbau Ulm*, ECJ June 30, 1966, 1966 ECR 235; *Ciment/Kerpen*, ECJ Dec. 14, 1983, 1983 ECJ 4173, paras 10–12; *VAG France v. Magne*, ECJ Dec. 12, 1986, 1986 ECR 4071, para. 15; *Delimitis/Henninger Bräu*, ECJ Feb. 28, 1991, 1991 ECR I-935, para. 40; *Automec II*, CFI Sept. 18, 1992, 1992 ECR II-2223, paras 92–95. *See* Guidelines on the Application of Article 81 (3), point 41.

1150. Belgium: *Union de Remorquage et de Sauvetage v. Schelde Sleepvaartbedrijf*, Antwerp Commercial Court, July 6, 1964, 1965 CMLR 251; *Belgacom*, Brussels Commercial Court, Twenty-seventh Report on Competition Policy, p. 345; France: *Labinal*, Cour de Cassation Feb. 14, 1995, Twenty-fifth Report on Competition Policy, p. 302; *Lilly France*, French Court de Cassation May 6, 1997, Twenty-seventh Report on Competition Policy, p. 347; Germany: *Metro/Cartier*, German Federal Supreme Court (BGH), Dec. 19, 1989, WuW/E BGH 2608; *Global One*, Düsseldorf Higher Regional Court, Oct. 30, 1996, Twenty-sixth Report on Competition Policy, p. 336; Frankfurt Regional Court, June 4, 1997, Twenty-seventh Report on Competition Policy, p. 344; Düsseldorf Higher Regional Court, August 28, 1998, WuW DE-R 233; Netherlands: *Dutch Cranes*, Gerechtshof Amsterdam Oct. 22, 1997; UK: *Budgett v. British Sugar*, English High Court, Feb. 16, 1979; *Garden Cottage Foods*, English Court of Appeal, May 18, 1982, 1982–2 CMLR 542; *Cutsforth v. Mansfield Inns*, English High Court, Oct. 28, 1985, 1986–1 CMLR 1; *Argyll Group v. Distillers*, Court of Session (Scotland), April 4, 1986, 1986–1 CMLR 764; *Plessey v. GEC/Siemens*, FT Dec. 21, 1988; *Gibbs Mew*, Supreme Court, July 22, 1998, FC3 98/5827/1.

Restitution.

Restitution of moneys paid, e.g., royalties, may be ordered.[1151] This also applies to illegal state aids (not notified or rejected).[1152]

Damages.

A right of action for damages for harm caused by the breach of Article 81 or 82 as a matter of public policy[1153] has now been recognized, in principle, by courts in many member states.[1154] However, damages have been awarded in very few cases[1155] probably on account of the many uncertainties surrounding claims for damages for breach of the EC antitrust rules. Apart from doubts as to the right to damages itself, the uncertainties include, in particular, the causal link between

1151. *See Courage*, ECJ Sept. 20, 2001, 2001 ECR I-6297, para. 30. *See also K'tel/GEMA*, German Supreme Court (BGH) April 28, 1988, 1988 EWiR 897; *Cement/Import*, Saarbrücken State Appeals Court, May 9, 1984, WuW/E OLG 3243, but *see* the German Supreme Court, April 28, 1988, EWiR 1988, 892. *See also* Picanol, 'Remedies in National Law for Breach of Articles 85 and 86 of the EC Treaty', Legal Issues of European Integration, 1983, 10–11, 15. With respect to repayment of an unduly paid fee or duty *see General Motors*, ECJ Nov. 13, 1975, 1975 ECR 1367, paras 19–22; *GT- Link/De Dansk Statsbaner*, ECJ July 17, 1997, 1997 ECR I-4449, para. 61.

1152. *Rheinland Pfalz/Alcan*, ECJ March 20, 1997, 1997 ECR I-1591. Restitution of the illegal state aid has to be claimed by the state having granted the aid; abstention from such claim constitutes an infringement likely to lead to an action by the Commission under Article 226: *Commission/Italy*, Feb. 23, 1995, 1995 ECR I-343.

1153. *Générale Sucrière*, ECJ Dec. 11, 1973, 1973 ECR 1468, para. 7; *Sacchi*, ECJ April 30, 1974, 1974 ECR 409, para. 18; *RTB/SABAM*, ECJ Jan. 30, 1974, 1974 ECR 51, paras 15–17; *Tetra Pak I*, CFI July 10, 1990, 1990 ECR II-347, para. 42; *Foster*, ECJ July 12, 1990, 1990 ECR I-3313, para. 22; *Fiatagri*, CFI Oct. 27, 1994, 1994 ECR II-905, para. 39; *Van Schijndel*, ECJ Dec. 14, 1995, 1995 ECR I-4728, para. 13; *International Power/NALOO*, ECJ Oct. 2, 2003, C-172/01 P, para.88.

1154. Belgium: *Union de Remorquage and Club*, Antwerp Commercial Court, July 6, 1964, 1965 CMLR 251; France: *SACEM*, Cour de Cassation, Dec. 13, 1983, 1984–3 CMLR 233; Germany: *BMW*, Federal Supreme Court (BGH), Oct. 23, 1979, WuW/E BGH 1643; Düsseldorf Regional Court April 16, 1997, Twenty-seventh Report on Competition Policy, p. 344; *Depotkosmetik*, Federal Supreme Court May 12, 1998, WuW DE-R 206; Düsseldorf Higher Regional Court, Aug. 28, 1998, WuW DE-R 233; Ireland: *Cadbury Ireland v. Kerry Cooperative Creameries*, High Court of Ireland, 1982 Irish Law Reports Monthly 77; Italy: Milan Court of Appeal Dec. 24, 1996, Twenty-sixth Report on Competition Policy, p. 337; Netherlands: *Eco Swiss China Time/Benneton*, Supreme Court (Hoge Raad), March 21, 1997, R96/57 HR (reference to the ECJ, C-126/97 (*see* opinion of Advocate General Saggio of Feb. 25, 1999) but not decided yet); UK: *Garden Cottage Foods*, English Court of Appeal, May 18, 1982, 1982–2 CMLR 542; *Bourgoin v. Ministry of Agriculture*, English Court of Appeal, July 29, 1985, 1986–1 CMLR 267; *Gibbs Mew*, Court of Appeal, July 22, 1998, FC3 98/5827/1.

1155. E.g., *Société Palais de l'Auto v. Poch*, Versailles (France) Appeals Court, May 5, 1988, Gazette du Palais, 1988 I Jur. 876 (termination of a car dealership); *Global One*, Düsseldorf High Court, June 16, 1998, WuW 1998–7/8, 713. Possibility of treble damages under US law: *Empagran/Hoffman – LaRoche*, US Court of Appeal, Jan. 17, 2003, 315 F.3d 338 (D.C.Cir. 2003), WuW 2004–1, 101 (vitamins cartel).

the infringement and the calculation of the losses suffered.[1156] In cases when a member state infringes directly applicable Community law (e.g. non-application of a Community directive), the member state in question is liable according to the general principle expressed by Article 288 (2) and is subject to claims for damages from individuals directly affected.[1157]

3. Cooperation between National Courts and the Commission

Concurrent Application of EC Competition Rules by National Courts and Commission.

Under Regulation 1/2003 the Commission and the national courts are both responsible for the implementation of the EC competition rules. The Commission has to act in the public interest while national courts have the task of safeguarding the rights of individuals in their relations with one another. The Commission[1158] and the Court of Justice[1159] favour simultaneous application, provided that this does not impair the effectiveness and uniformity of Community competition rules and the measures taken to enforce them. Furthermore any conflicts which may arise must be solved in accordance with the principle of the precedence of Community law.[1160] In *Consorzio Industrie Fiammiferi* which concerned fixing of the retail selling prices by a ministry and the allocation of production by a consortium entrusted by the government, the Court of Justice ruled:

> 'that, where undertakings engage in conduct contrary to Article 81 (1) EC and where that conduct is required or facilitated by national legislation which legitimises or reinforces the effects of the conduct, specifically with regard to price-fixing or market sharing arrangements, a national authority, one of whose responsibilities is to ensure that Article 81 (1) is observed:
> – has the duty to disapply the national legislation;
> – may not impose penalties in respect of past conduct on the undertakings concerned when the conduct was required by national legislation;
> – may not impose penalties on the undertakings concerned in respect of conduct subsequent to the decision to disapply the national legislation, once the decision has become definitive in their regard;

1156. *Brasserie du Pecheur*, ECJ March 5, 1996, 1996 ECR I-1029, para. 90. *See* under Article 288: *Asia Motors*, CFI Sept. 18, 1996, 1996 ECR II-961, para. 110.
1157. *Francovich*, ECJ Nov. 19, 1991, 1991 ECR I-5357, para. 37; *Brasserie du Pecheur/BRD*, ECJ March 5, 1996, 1996 ECR I-1029, paras 20–38. Similarly under the EEA Agreement: *Erla Maria Sveinbjorndottir*, EFTA Court of Justice. Dec. 10, 1998, E-9/97, ECR 1999–1, 2, para. 69.
1158. Article 15 of Regulation 1/2003.
1159. *Dalmasso*, CFI Jan. 21, 1999, 1999 ECR I-3055.
1160. *See Walt Wilhelm*, ECJ Feb. 13, 1969, 1969 ECR 1, 13–14; *Spanish Banks*, ECJ July 16, 1992, 1992 ECR I-4785, para. 12.

– may impose penalties on the undertakings concerned in respect of past conduct where the conduct was merely facilitated or encouraged by national legislation, whilst taking due account of the specific features of the legislative framework in which the undertakings acted.'[1161]

In order to avoid conflicts, Article 15 of Regulation 1/2003, which replaces the previous Commission Notice,[1162] provides, according to Article 10 of the EC Treaty, for a close, constant and sincere coopeeration between national courts and the Commission, which aims at guaranteeing the strict, effective and consistent application of EC competition law and avoiding conflicts. This cooperation has been described in greater detail in Section B. *supra*.

Impact of the Cooperation.

The Commission reports on the cooperation between the Commission and national courts show an increasing number of requests by national courts and responses given by the Commission. This cooperation is complementary to the Court of Justice's role under Article 234 of the EC Treaty of harmonizing the interpretation of the provisions and is likely to reduce the risk of parallel proceedings and conflicts in cases of concurrent application. It is not inconsistent with the principles of the parallel application of Articles 81 and 82 by the Commission and national courts if a national court applies Article 81 or 82 in a stricter way than the Commission, in particular when the Commission denies a 'Community interest', or if the Commission takes a stricter position than a national court in the same matter. In *Van den Bergh Foods* the Commission stated:

> 'It is not inconsistent with the principles governing the concurrent powers of national courts and the Commission in the application of Article 85 (1) and Article 86 of the Treaty, for the Commission to take a decision which differs from a judgment delivered by a national court, provided that there exists a sufficient Community interest in doing so'.[1163]

1161. *Consorzio Industrie Fiammiferi*, ECJ Sept. 9, 2003, C-198/01, para. 58.
1162. 1993 OJ C 39/5.
1163. *Van den Bergh Foods*, D.Comm. March 11, 1998, 1998 OJ L 246/1, point 279, *aff'd* CFI Oct. 23, 2003, T-65/98.

Table of Fines for infringements of the EC and ECSC Competition Rules

Case	Commission decision	Infringement	Fine	ECJ/CFI judgment	Decision on fine
Quinine	July 16, 1969 1969 OJ L 192/5	Article 85 (*now 81*): Horizontal market sharing, quota arrangements and price fixing	Between ECU 10,000 and 210,000 (Total: ECU 500,000)	July 15, 1970, 1970 ECR 661	Three biggest fines reduced by 10,000 each
Dyestuffs	July 24,1969 1969 OJ L 195/11	Article 85: Horizontal price fixing	Between ECU 40,000 and 50,000 (Total: ECU 490,000)	July 14, 1972, 1972 ECR 619	One company's fine reduced to ECU 30,000
Raffinerie Tirlemontoise	Nov. 1971 1971 Bull. EC 11/55	Article 15(1)(c) of Regulation 17: Incomplete production of records during investigation	ECU 4,000		
Pittsburgh Corning	Nov. 23, 1972 1972 OJ L 272/35	Article 85: Discriminatory pricing to restrain parallel imports	ECU 100,000		
Commercial Solvents	Dec. 14, 1972 1972 OJ L 299/51	Article 86 (*now 82*): Refusal to supply	ECU 200,000	March 6, 1974 1974 ECR 223	Fine reduced to ECU 100,000
WEA- Filipacchi	Dec. 22, 1972 1972 OJ L 303/52	Article 85: Vertical export ban	ECU 60,000		

Case	Commission decision	Infringement	Fine	ECJ/CFI judgment	Decision on fine
Sugar	Jan. 2, 1973 1973 OJ L 140/17	Article 85: Horizontal market sharing, price fixing and collusive tendering; Article 86: Exerting pressure to restrict intra-Community trade	Between ECU 100,.000 and 1.5 mIllion Total: ECU 9 million	Dec. 16, 1975 1975 ECR 1663	Fines on seven companies quashed and those on the others reduced to between 600,000 and 40,000 Total: ECU 1.59 million
Deutsche Philips	Oct. 5, 1973 1973 OJ L 293/40	Article 85: Vertical export ban	ECU 60,000		
Belgian Wallpaper	July 23, 1974 1974 OJ L 237/3	Article 85: Horizontal aggregated rebate cartel and collective boycott	Between ECU 36,000 and 135,000 Total: ECU 358,500	Nov. 26, 1975 1975 ECR 1491	Decision quashed
General Motors	Dec. 19, 1974 1975 OJ L 29/14	Article 86: Obstructing parallel imports by overcharging for conformity certificates	ECU 100,000	Nov. 13, 1975 1975 ECR 1367	Decision quashed
French-Taiwanese Mushroom Packers	Jan. 8, 1975 1975 OJ L 29/26	Article 85: Horizontal export quotas and price fixing	Between ECU 2,000 and 32,000 Total: ECU 100,000		

Case	Commission decision	Infringement	Fine	ECJ/CFI judgment	Decision on fine
United Brands	Dec. 17, 1975 1976 OJ L 95/1	Article 86: Vertical customer restrictions, discriminatory pricing and refusal to supply	ECU 1 million	Feb. 14, 1978 1978 ECR 207	Fine reduced to ECU 850,000
Hoffmann- La Roche	June 9, 1976 1976 OJ L 223/27	Article 86: Fidelity rebates and exclusive dealing arrangements	ECU 300,000	Feb. 13, 1979 1979 ECR 461	Fine reduced to ECU 200,000
Miller International	Dec. 1, 1976 1976 OJ L 357/40	Article 85: Vertical export ban	ECU 70,000	Feb. 1, 1978 1 978 ECR 131	Decision upheld
Theal-Watts	Dec. 21, 1976 1977 0J L 39/19	Article 85: Vertical prevention of parallel imports Article 15(1)(a) of Regulation 17: Supplying false information in notification	2 x ECU 10,000 ECU 5,000	June 20, 1978 1978 ECR 1391	Decision upheld
Hugin/Liptons	Dec. 8, 1977 1978 OJ L 22/23	Article 86: Refusal to supply spare parts	ECU 50,000	May 31, 1979 1979 ECR 1869	Decision quashed

Case	Commission decision	Infringement	Fine	ECJ/CFI judgment	Decision on fine
Vegetable Parchment	Dec. 23, 1977 1978 OJ L 70/54	Article 85: Horizontal market sharing and coordination of price increases	Between ECU 10,000 and 25,000 (Total: ECU 115,000)		
BMW Belgium	Dec. 23, 1977 1978 OJ L 46/33	Article 85: Vertical export ban	Between ECU 1,000 and 150,000 Total: ECU 203,500	July 12, 1979 1979 ECR 2435	Decision upheld
Kawasaki	Dec. 12, 1978 1979 OJ L 16/9	Article 85: Vertical export ban	ECU 100,000		
Floral	Nov. 28, 1979 1980 OJ L 39/51	Article 85: Horizontal joint selling arrangements	3 x ECU 85,000 Total: ECU 255,000		
Pioneer	Dec. 14, 1979 1980 OJ L 60/21	Article 85: Vertical export ban	Between ECU 300,000 and 4,350,800 Total: ECU 6,950,000	June 7, 1983 1983 ECR 1825	Fine reduced to between ECU 200,000 and 2 million. Total: ECU 3.2 million
Fabbrica Pisana	Dec. 20, 1979 1980 OJ L 75/30	Article 15(1)(c) of Regulation 17: Incomplete production of records during investigation	ECU 5,000		

Case	Commission decision	Infringement	Fine	ECJ/CFI judgment	Decision on fine
French and German special steel producers	March 27, 1980 Tenth Report on Competition Policy fixing points 109-110	Article 65 of ECSC Treaty: Quota arrangements and price	ECU 900,000		
Johnson & Johnson	Nov. 25, 1980 1980 OJ L 377/16	Article 85: Vertical export ban	ECU 200,000		
Michelin	Oct. 7, 1981 1981 OJ L 353/33	Article 86: Tying by means of discount and rebate scheme to prevent imports of competing products	ECU 680,000	Nov. 9, 1983 1983 ECR 3461	Fine reduced to ECU 300,000
Comptoir Commercial d'Importation	Nov. 17, 1981 1982 OJ L 27/31	Article 15(1)(b) of Regulation 17: Supplying false information in reply to discovery request	ECU 5,000		
Telos	Nov.25, 1981 1982 OJ L 58/19	Article 15(1)(b) of Regulation 17: Supplying false information in reply to discovery request	ECU 5,000		
Moet & Chandon	Nov. 27, 1981 1982 OJ L 94/7	Article 85: Vertical export ban	ECU 1.1 million		

Case	Commission decision	Infringement	Fine	ECJ/CFI judgment	Decision on fine
National Panasonic (Belgium)	Dec. 11, 1981 1982 OJ L 113/18	Article 15(1)(b) of Regulation 17: Supplying false information in reply to discovery request	ECU 5,000		
National Panasonic (France)	Dec. 11, 1981 1982 OJ L 211/32	Article 15(1)(b) of Regulation 17: Supplying false information in reply to discovery request	ECU 5,000		
Hasselblad	Dec. 2, 1981 1982 OJ L 161/18	Article 85: Vertical. prevention of parallel Imports, Influence on dealers' prices	Manufacturer: ECU 560,000 Distributors: ECU 165,000 and 3 x ECU 10,000 Total: ECU 755,000	Feb. 21,1984 1984 ECR 883	Fine on UK distributor reduced to ECU 80,000
Anseau	Dec. 17,1981 1982 OJ L 167/39	Article 85: Horizontal prevention of parallel imports by means of conformity labelling	Between ECU 9,500 and 76,500 Total: ECU 935,000 (after correction)	Nov. 8, 1983 1983 ECR 3369	Decision upheld
AEG Telefunken	Jan. 6, 1982 1982 OJ L 117/15	Article 85: Vertical restraints on dealers' pricing: discriminatory exclusion of dealers	ECU 1 million	Oct. 25, 1983 1983 ECR 3151	Decision upheld

Case	Commission decision	Infringement	Fine	ECJ/CFI judgment	Decision on fine
SSI (Dutch Cigarettes)	July 15, 1982 1982 OJ L 232/1	Article 85: Horizontal price fixing	Between ECU 100,000 and 425,000 Total: ECU 1,475,000	Dec. 10, 1985 1985 ECR 3801 and 3831	Decision upheld. One fine reduced from ECU 150,000 to 100,000
FN/CF	Oct. 27, 1982 1982 OJ L 319/12	Article 15(1)(c) of Regulation 17: Incomplete production of records during investigation	ECU 5,000		
National Panasonic	Dec. 7, 1982 1982 OJ L 354/28	Article 85: Vertical export ban	ECU 450,000		
Rolled Zinc	Dec. 14, 1982 1982 OJ L 362/40	Article 85: Horizontal market sharing arrangement	ECU 400,000 and 500,000	March 28, 1984 1984 ECR 1679	Fines quashed
BNIC (Cognac)	Dec. 15, 1982 1982 OJ L 379/1	Article 85: Horizontal price fixing	ECU 160,000		
Toltecs/Dorcet	Dec. 15, 1982 1982 OJ L 379/19	Article 85: No-challenge clause in trade mark agreement	ECU 50,000	Jan. 30, 1985 1985 ECR 363	Fine quashed

Case	Commission decision	Infringement	Fine	ECJ/CFI judgment	Decision on fine
Windsurfing	July 11, 1983 1983 OJ L 229/1	Article 85: Restrictions in patent license agreements	Licensor: ECU 50,000 Licensees: between 5,000 and 15,000 Total: ECU 95,000	Feb. 25, 1986 1986 ECR 611	Licensor's fine reduced to ECU 25,000
Cast Iron and Steel Rolls	Oct. 17, 1983 1983 OJ L 317/1	Article 85: Horizontal price fixing and market sharing	Between ECU 8,000 and 111,000 Total: 1,250,000		
IPTC (Anseau Ill)	Dec. 5, 1983 1983 OJ L 376/7	Article 85: Horizontal prevention of parallel imports	ECU 5,000		
Polistil/Arbois	May 16, 1984 1984 OJ L 136/9	Article 85: Vertical prevention of parallel imports	2 x ECU 30,000		
British Leyland	July 2, 1984 1984 OJ L 207/11	Article 86: Obstructing parallel imports by offences in connection with conformity certificates	ECU 350,000	Nov. 11, 1986 1986 ECR 3263	Decision upheld
Benelux Flat Glass	July 23, 1984 1984 OJ L 212/13	Article 85: Horizontal market sharing and price fixing	Between ECU 765,000 and 1,450,000 Total: ECU 4 million		

Case	Commission decision	Infringement	Fine	ECJ/CFI judgment	Decision on fine
Zinc Producer Group	Aug. 6, 1984 1984 OJ L 220/27	Article 85: Horizontal price fixing and market sharing	Between ECU 350,000 and 950,000. Total: ECU 3.3 million		
Peroxygen	Nov. 23, 1984 1985 OJ L 35/I	Article 85: Horizontal price fixing and market sharing	Between ECU 500,000 and 3 million. Total: ECU 9 million		
John Deere	Dec. 14, 1984 1985 OJ L 35/58	Article 85: Vertical export ban	ECU 2 million		
Wood Pulp	Dec. 19, 1984 1985 OJ L 85/I	Article 85: Horizontal price fixing	Between ECU 50,000 and 500,000 Total: ECU 4.125 million	March 31, 1993 1993 ECR I-1307	Partly annulled, partly reduced to total ECU 1.380 million
				July 10, 1997 1997 ECR II-1185	Appeal rejected (res iudicata)
				Sept. 14, 1999 1999 ECR I-5363 'AssiDomän'	Confirming CFI

Case	Commission decision	Infringement	Fine	ECJ/CFI judgment	Decision on fine
ECS/Akzo	Dec. 14, 1985 1985 OJ L 374/1	Article 86. Predatory pricing	ECU 10 million	July 3, 1991 1991 ECR I-3359	Reduced to ECU 7.5 million
Sperry New Holland	Dec. 16, 1985 1985 OJ L 376/21	Article 85: Vertical export ban	ECU 700,000		
Siemens/Fanuc	Dec. 18, 1985 1985 OJ L 376/29	Article 85: Horizontal market sharing	2 x ECU 1 million		
Polypropylene 1991 ECR II -867	Apri1 23, 1986 1986 OJ L 230/1	Article 85. Horizontal price fixing and quota arrangements	Between ECU 500,000 and 11 million Total: ECU 57.85 million	Oct. 24, 1991 1991 ECR II-867, 1087, 1177 Dec. 17, 1991 1991 ECR II 1623, 1715, 1833	Fines partly upheld, partly slightly reduced
				ECJ July 8, 1999 1999 ECR I-4287, 4399, 4537	Appeal rejected
Belasco	July 10, 1986 1986 OJ L 232/15	Article 85: Horizontal price and quota arrangements	Between ECU 15,000 and 420,000 Total: ECU 1 million	July 11, 1989 1989 ECR 2117	Decision upheld

Case	Commission decision	Infringement	Fine	ECJ/CFI judgment	Decision on fine
Peugeot	Sept. 25, 1986 1986 OJ L 295/19	Article 15(1)(b) of Regulation 17: Supplying false information in reply to discovery			
Meldoc	Nov. 26, 1986 1986 OJ L 348/50	Article 85: Horizontal price fixing and quota arrangements	Between ECU 425,000 and 3,150,000. Total: ECU 6,555,000	Appeal withdrawn	
Fatty Acids	Dec. 2, 1986 1987 OJ L 3/17	Article 85: Horizontal exchange of information on sales	3 x ECU 50,000 Total: 150,000		
Tipp-Ex	July 10, 1987 1987 OJ L 222/1	Article 85: Vertical obstruction of parallel imports	ECU 10,000 and 400,000	Feb. 8, 1990 1990 ECR I-261	Decision upheld
Sandoz	July 13, 1987 1987 OJ L 222/28	Article 85: Vertical export ban	ECU 800,000	Jan. 11, 1990 1990 ECR I-45	Decision upheld Fine reduced to ECU 500,000
Fisher-Price	Dec. 18, 1987 1988 OJ L 49/19	Article 85: Vertical export ban	ECU 300,000		
Konica	Dec. 18, 1987 1988 OJ L 78/34	Article 85: Vertical prevention of parallel imports	2 x ECU 75,000		

Case	Commission decision	Infringement	Fine	ECJ/CFI judgment	Decision on fine
Hilti	Dec. 22, 1987 1988 OJ L 65/19	Article 86: Tying and discriminatory practices	ECU 6 million	Dec. 12, 1991 1991 ECR II-1439	Decision upheld
				March 2, 1994 1994 ECR I-667	Appeal rejected
Hoechst	May 26, 1988 17th Report pt. 57	Article 16(1)(d) of Regulation 17: Contempt fines for refusal to submit to investigation	ECU 55,000	Sept. 21, 1989 1989 ECR 2859	Decision upheld
British Dental Trade	July 11, 1988 1988 OJ L 233/15	Article 85: Discrimination against foreign exhibitors at Association trade fairs	ECU 100,000		
British Sugar	July 18, 1988 1988 OJ L 284/41	Article 86: Predatory conduct towards competitor	ECU 3 million		
Hudson's Bay/ DPF	Oct. 28, 1988 1988 OJ L 316/43	Article 85: Horizontal exclusive dealing arrangements	ECU 500,000	July 2, 1992 1992 ECR II-1931	Decision partly annulled, fine reduced to ECU 300,000

Case	Commission decision	Infringement	Fine	ECJ/CFI judgment	Decision on fine
Sabena	Nov. 4, 1988 1988 OJ L 317/47	Article 86: Refusal to allow smaller competitor access to computerized booking system	ECU 100,000		
British Plaster Board	Dec. 5, 1988 1989 OJ L 10/50	Article 86: Exclusive dealing to prevent imports	ECU 3 million and 150,000	April 1, 1993 1993 ECR II-389 April 6, 1995 1995 ECR I-865	Decision upheld Appeal rejected
Italian Flat Glass II	Dec. 7, 1988 1989 OJ L 33/44	Article 85: Horizontal price fixing and quota arrangements Article 86: Collective unfair pricing	ECU 7, 4.7 and 1.7 million. Total: ECU 13.4 million	March 10, 1992 1992 ECR II-1403	Decision partly annulled, fines reduced to 1/7
PVC I	Dec. 21, 1988 1989 OJ L 74/1	Article 85: Horizontal price fixing and quota arrangement	Between ECU 400,000 and 3.5 million. Total: ECU 23.5 million	Feb. 27, 1992 1992 ECR II-315 June 15, 1994 1994 ECR I-2555	Non-existence of decision Decision annulled on procedural grounds

Case	Commission decision	Infringement	Fine	ECJ/CFI judgment	Decision on fine
LdPE	Dec. 21, 1988 1989 OJ L 74/21	Article 85: Horizontal price fixing and quota arrangements	Between ECU 100,000 and 5.5 million. Total: ECU 37 million	Apri1 6, 1995 1995 ECR II-729	Decision annulled on procedural grounds
Welded steel mesh	Aug. 2, 1989 1989 OJ L 260/1	Article 85: Horizontal price fixing and market sharing	Between ECU 13,000 and 4.5 million. Total: ECU 9.5 million	April 6, 1995 1995 ECR II-717	Fines partly reduced to total ECU 7.5 million
				Dec. 17, 1998 1995 ECR II-987	Appeal rejected but fines reduced by ECU 50,000 each
Bayo-N-Ox	Dec. 13, 1989 1990 OJ L 21/71	Article 85: Vertical export ban	ECU 500,000	Oct. 26, 1000 2000 ECR II-3383	Decision squashed
Stainless Steel Cartel	July 18, 1990 Twentieth Report, point 123	Article 65 of ECSC Treaty: Quota arrangements	ECU 425,000		
Secretama	Dec. 19, 1990 1991 OJ L 35/23	Article 16(4) of Regulation 4056/86: Supplying false information in reply to discovery request	ECU 5,000		

Case	Commission decision	Infringement	Fine	ECJ/CFI judgment	Decision on fine
Soda Ash I:	IP(90)1057				
A. Solvay/ICI	Dec. 19, 1990 1991 OJ L 152/1	Article 85: Market sharing	ECU 7 million each	June 29, 1995 1995 ECR II-1775	Decision squashed on procedural grounds
B. Solvay/CFK	Dec. 19, 1990 1991 OJ L 152/16	Article 85: Quota arrangement	ECU 1 and 3 million	June 29, 1995 1995 ECR II-1821	Decision squashed
C. Solvay	Dec. 19, 1990 1991 OJ L 152/21	Article 86: Exclusionary discounts	ECU 20 million	June 29, 1995 1995 ECR II-1825	Decision squashed
D. ICI	Dec. 19, 1990	Article 86: Exclusionary discounts	ECU 10 million	June 29, 1995 1995 ECR II-1901	Decision squashed
Baccarat	March 15, 1991 1991 OJ L 97/16	Article 16(1)(c) of Regulation 17: Fines for refusal to supply information	ECU 10,000		
Gosme/Martell	Dec. 19, 1990 1991 OJ L 35/23	Article 65: Preventing parallel trade	ECU 350,000		

Case	Commission decision	Infringement	Fine	ECJ/CFI judgment	Decision on fine
Viho/Toshiba	June 5, 1991 1991 OJ L 287/39	Article 81: Preventing parallel trade	ECU 2 million		
Tetra Pak II	July 24, 1991 1992 OJ L 72/1	Article 82: Exclusionary practices	ECU 75 million	Oct. 6, 1994 1994 ECR II-755	Fine upheld
Dutch BuildIng Cartel	Feb.5, 1992 1992 OJ L92/I	Article 81: Bid-rigging cartel	ECU 22,250,000	Nov. 14, 1996 1996 ECR I - 5951	Decision upheld
British Midland	Feb.26, 1992 1992 OJ L 96/34	Article 82: Exclusionary practices	ECU 750,000	Feb. 21, 1995 1995 ECR II-289	Decision upheld
Newitt/Dunlop	March 18, 1992 1992 OJ L131/32	Article 81: Preventing parallel trade	ECU 5,550,000	Dunlop: July 7, 1994 1994 ECR II-441 All Weather Sports. April 28, 1994 1994 ECR II-211	Fine reduced to ECU 3 million Fine squashed

Case	Commission decision	Infringement	Fine	ECJ/CFI judgment	Decision on fine
Eurocheques; Helsinki	March 25, 1992 1992 OJ L95/50	Article 81: Commission fixing	ECU 5 million and 1 million	Feb. 23, 1994 1994 ECR II-49	Fine reduced to ECU 2 million Eurocheques' fine squashed
VIHO/Parker – Pen	July 15, 1992 1992 OJ L 233/27	Article 81: Export ban	ECU 740,000	July 14, 1994 1994 ECR II-755	Parker Pen's fine reduced to ECU 500,000 from 700,000
				July 14, 1994 1994 ECR II-531	Herlitz's fine upheld
CSM	Oct. 7, 1992 1992 OJ L 305/16	Art. 15 Reg. 17	ECU 5,000		
MEWAG	Dec. 17, 1992 1993 OJ L 20/6	Art. 18 of Reg. 4056/86: refusal to submit to investigation	ECU 4,000		
CEWAL	Dec. 23, 1992 1993 OJ L 34/20	Articles 81 and 82: Price fixing and market sharing	ECU 10.1 million	Oct. 8, 1996 1996 ECR II-1201	Fine reduced to ECU 9,090,000
				March 16, 2000 2000 ECR I-1365	Decision upheld, but fine on members of CEWAL squashed on procedural grounds

Case	Commission decision	Infringement	Fine	ECJ/CFI judgment	Decision on fine
HOV SVZ/MCN 1994	March 29 1994 OJ L 104/34	Article 82: Discriminatory prices	ECU 11 million	Oct. 22, 1997 1997 ECR II-1689	Decision upheld,
Steel Beams	Feb. 16, 1994 1994 OJ L 116/1	Article 65: Price fixing	Between ECU 13,000 and ECU 12.3 million. Total ECU 20 million	March 11, 1999 1999 ECR II-263, 303, 333, 347, 585, 603, 613, 629, 645, 707	Fines slightly reduced
				Oct. 2, 2003 C-176/99 P a.o.	Appeal dismissed, in one case referred back to the CFI
PVC II (decision of Dec. 21, 1988 renewed)	July 29, 1994 1994 OJ L 239/14	Article 81: Horizontal price fixing and quota	Between ECU 400,000 and ECU 3.2 million. Total ECU 19.25 million	April 20, 1999 1999 ECR II-931	Decision upheld, fines partly upheld, partly slightly reduced to ECU 17.2 million
				Oct. 15, 2002 2002 ECR I-8375	Appeal dissmissed

Case	Commission decision	Infringement	Fine	ECJ/CFI judgment	Decision on fine
Carton Board,	July 13, 1994 1994 OJ L 243/I	Article 81: Price fixing, information exchange	Between ECU 0.2 million and ECU 22.75 million. Total ECU 138 million	May 14, 1998 1998 ECR II-813 925, 869, 1007, 1043, 1129, 1235, 1331, 1373, 1439, 1571, 1617, 1727, 1989, 2111	Decision partly annulled and fines reduced to ECU 128 million
				Nov. 16, 2000 2000 ECR I-9641, 9925, 10265	Appeal rejected, fines in 3 cases slightly reduced, in 2 cases referred to CFI on procedural grounds
				Feb. 28, 2002 2002 ECR II-813, 843	Fines reduced respectively from ECU 11.2 to 4.67 and from 16.2 to 13.5 million
AKZO Chemicals	Oct. 14, 1994 1994 OJ L 294/31	Article 15 of Reg. 17: Supplying false information during investigation	ECU 5,000		

Case	Commission decision	Infringement	Fine	ECJ/CFI judgment	Decision on fine
Cement	Nov. 30, 1994 1994 OJ L 343/I	Article 81: Horizontal price fixing, quota, market sharing	Between ECU 0.4 million and ECU 32.5 million. Total ECU 248 million	March 15, 2000 2000 ECR II-491	Decision partly annulled, fines reduced to ECU 113.3 million
				Jan. 7, 2004 C-204/00 P	Appeal rejected, fines reduced in one out of the five cases from EUR 13.5 to 9.6 million
Far Eastern Freight	Dec. 21, 1994 1994 OJ L378/17	Article 81: Horizontal price fixing	ECU 10,000. Total ECU 140,000	Feb. 28, 2002 2002 ECR II-1101	Decision upheld, fine squashed
Tretorn	Dec. 21, 1994 1994 OJ L378/45	Article 81: Vertical export ban	ECU 600,000 and 10,000	Dec. 11, 1996 1996 ECR II-1799	Decision upheld
BASF/ Accinauto	July 12, 1995 1995 OJ L 272/16	Article 81: Preventing parallel trade	ECU 2.8 million	Apri1 20, 1999 1999 ECR II-1581	Decision upheld
Dutch Cranes	Nov. 29, 1995 1995 OJ L 312/79	Article 82: Exclusionary practices	ECU 11.5 million and 300,000	Oct. 22, 1997 1997 ECR II-1739	Decision upheld; fine of ECU 300,000 reduced to ECU 100,000

Case	Commission decision	Infringement	Fine	ECJ/CFI judgment	Decision on fine
Bayer-Adalat	Jan. 10, 1996 1996 OJ L 201/1	Article 81: Export ban	ECU 3 million	Oct. 26, 2000 2000 ECR II-3383	Decision squashed
				Jan. 6, 2004 C-2/01 P	Appeal Commission rejected
Fenex	June 5, 1996 1996 OJ L 181/28	Article 81: Collectively recommended tariffs	ECU 1,000		
Ferry Operators	Oct. 30, 1996 1997 OJ L26/23	Article 81: Tariff fixing	Between ECU 25,000 and ECU 400,000. Total: ECU 645,000		
Novaillance Systemform	Dec. 4, 1996 1997 OJ L 47/11	Article 81: Preventing parallel trade	ECU 100,000		
Irish Sugar	May 14, 1997 1997 OJ L 258/1	Article 82: Predatory pricing, discriminatory rebates	ECU 8.8 million	Oct. 7, 1999 1999 ECR II-2969	Fine reduced to EUR 7,883,326
				July 10, 2001 2001 ECR I-5333	Appeal rejected

Case	Commission decision	Infringement	Fine	ECJ/CFI judgment	Decision on fine
Alloy Surcharge	Jan. 21, 1998 1998 OJ L 100/55	Article 65: Horizontal fixing alloy surcharge	Between ECU 2.8 and 8.1 million. Total ECU 27.38 million	Dec. 13, 2001 2001 ECR II-3757	Fines partly reduced, partly upheld
VW-Audi	Jan. 28, 1998 1998 OJ L 124/60	Article 81: Preventing parallel imports	ECU 102 million	July 6, 2000 2000 ECR II-2707	Fine reduced to EUR 90 million
Samsung	Feb. 11, 1998 Not published	Article 14 Reg. 4064/89: Non-notified merger	ECU 33,000		
AAMS	June 17, 1998 1998 OJ L 252/47	Article 82: Abusive exclusive purchasing	ECU 6 million	Nov. 22, 2001 2001 ECR II-3413	Decision upheld
TACA	Sept. 19, 1998 1998 OJ L 95/1	Article 82: Abuse of collective dominance in transatlantic container transport	Between ECU 6.88 million and ECU 41.26 million. Total: ECU 273 million	Sept. 30, 2003 T-191/98 a.o.	Decision upheld, fines squashed
British Sugar, Tate & Lyle	Oct. 14, 1998 1999 OJ L 76/1	Article 81: Price fixing	Between ECU 1.8 million and ECU 39.6 million. Total 50.2 million	July 12, 2001 2001 ECR II-2035	Fine on Tate & Lyle reduced from ECU 7 to 5.6 million
				April 29, 2004 C-359/01P	Appeal dismissed

Case	Commission decision	Infringement	Fine	ECJ/CFI judgment	Decision on fine
Pre-insulated Pipes	Oct. 21, 1998 1999 OJ L 24/1	Article 81: Price fixing, quota	Between ECU 0.7 million and ECU ECU 70 million. Total ECU 92.2 million	March 20, 2002 2002 ECR II-1613, 1633, 1647, 1681, 1705, 1845, 1847, 1881	Decision partly annulled, fines slightly reduced
Greek Ferries	Dec. 9, 1998 1999 OJ L 109/28	Article 81: Horizontal price fixing	Between ECU 0.26 million and 3.26 million. Total ECU 7.12 million	Dec. 11, 2003 T-56/99	Affirmed
Möller	Feb. 10, 1999 1999 OJ L 183/29	Article 14 Reg. 4064/89: Implementing non-notified merger	EUR 219,000		
Virgin Airlines, Brittish Airways	July 14, 1999 2000 OJ L 30/1	Article 82: Exclusionary rebates	EUR 6.8 million	Dec. 17, 2003 T-219/99	Affirmed
Lufthansa	July 20, 1999 Not published	Article 16 of Regulation 2299/89 on code of conduct for computer reservation systems	EUR 10,000		

Case	Commission decision	Infringement	Fine	ECJ/CFI judgment	Decision on fine
1998 Football World Cup Finals	July 20, 1999 2000 OJ L 5/55	Article 82 : Discriminatory sales of tickets	EUR 1,000		
Sanofi-Synthélabo	July 28, 1999 Not published	Article 14 of Reg. 4064/89: Incorrect information in notification	EUR 40,000		
Nederlandse Federatieve Vereniging voor de Groothandel op Elektrotechnisch Gebied (FEG)	Oct. 26, 1999 2000 OJ L 39/1	Article 81: Exclusive collective dealing	EUR 4.4 and 2.15 million	Dec. 16, 2003 T-5/00	Affirmed
Seamless Steel Tubes	Dec. 8, 1999 2003 OJ L 140/1	Article 81: Market sharing	EUR 99 million	Dec. 14, 2000 2000 ECR II-4121	Suspension rejected
				March 23, 2001 2001 ECR I-2559	Rejection affirmed
				July 8, 2004 T-44/00	Fines reduced to EUR 86.2 million

Case	Commission decision	Infringement	Fine	ECJ/CFI judgment	Decision on fine
Anheuser-Busch	Dec. 14, 1999 2000 OJ L 49/17	Article 15 (1) (a) Reg. 17 : Supplying incorrect information	EUR 3,000		
Deutsche Post/ Transoflex	Dec. 14, 1999 2001 OJ L 97/1	Article 14 (1) (b) and (c) Reg. 4064/89: misleading and incorrect information in notification	EUR 50,000		
FETTCSA	May 16, 2000 2000 OJ L 268/1	Arts. 81 and 2 Reg. 4056/87: tariff and discount fixing	EUR 7 million	March 19, 2003 T-213/00	Infringement affirmed, fines annulled
Amino Acids (Lysine Cartel)	June 7, 2000 2001 OJ L 152/14	Article 81 fixing prices and quota	EUR 109.9 million	July 9, 2003 T-220/00	Fines reduced by 10%
Editions Nathan	July 5, 2000 2001 OJ L 54/1	Article 81: vertical export ban and resale price fixing	EUR 60,000		
Mitsubishi	July 12, 2000 IP/00/764	Article 14 (1) (c) Reg. 4064/89 and Article 15 (1) (a) for failing to supply information	EUR 50,000 and 900,000		
Opel	Sept. 20, 2000 2001 OJ L 59/1	Article 81: vertical export ban	EUR 43 million	Oct. 21, 2003 T-238/00	Fine reduced to EUR 35.475 million

Case	Commission decision	Infringement	Fine	ECJ/CFI judgment	Decision on fine
Soda Ash II (re-adoption)	Dec. 13, 2000 2003 OJ L 10/1, 10 and 33	Article 81: market sharing and quota.	EUR 6 million		
		Article 82: exclusionary rebates.	EUR 20 and 10 million		
JC Bamford (JCB)	Dec. 21, 2000 2002 OJ L 69/1	Article 81: vertical export restrictions	EUR 39.6 million	CFI Jan. 13, 2004 T-67/01	Fine reduced to EUR 30 million
Deutsche Post I	March 20, 2001 2001 OJ L 125/27	Article 82: fidelity rebates and predatory pricing	EUR 24 million		
Michelin II	June 20, 2001 2002 OJ L 143/1	Article 82: predatory bonus system	EUR 19.76 million	Sept. 30, 2003 T-203/01	Affirmed
Volkswagen II	June 29, 2001 2001 OJ L 262/14	Article 81: vertical export restrictions	EUR 30.96 million	Dec. 3, 2003 T-208/01	Annulling Commission decision
Graphite Electrodes	July 18, 2001 2002 OJ L 100/1	Article 81: horizontal price and market sharing cartel	EUR 218.8 million	April 29, 2004 T-236/01	Affirmed
SAS/Maersk	July 18, 2001 2001 OJ L 265/15	Article 81: market sharing	EUR 39.375 and 13.125 million		

Case	Commission decision	Infringement	Fine	ECJ/CFI judgment	Decision on fine
Deutsche Post II	July 25, 2001 2001 OJ L 331/40	Article 82: surcharging international mail	Symbolic fine of EUR 1,000		
Sodium gluconate	Oct. 2, 2001 IP/01/1355	Article 81: price fixing	EUR 57.53 million		
Daimler Chrysler	Oct. 10, 2001 2002 OJ L 257/1	Article 81: hindering parallel exports	EUR 72 million		
Vitamins	Nov. 21, 2001 2003 OJ L 6/1	Article 81: price fixing	EUR 855.22 million		
La Poste (B)	Dec. 5, 2001 2002 OJ L 61/32	Article 82: tying	EUR 2.5 million		
Citric Acid	Dec. 5, 2001 2002 OJ L 239/18	Article 81: price fixing and market sharing	EUR 135.22 million		
Belgium brewers	Dec. 5, 2001 2003 OJ L 200/1	Article 81: market fixing and price fixing	EUR 91 million		
Luxembourg brewers	Dec. 5, 2001 2002 OJ L 253/21	Article 81: market protection	EUR 448,000		
Zinc phosphate	Dec. 11, 2001 2003 OJ L 153/1	Article 81: price fixing	EUR 11.95 million		

Case	Commission decision	Infringement	Fine	ECJ/CFI judgment	Decision on fine
German banks	Dec. 11, 2001 2003 OJ L 15/1	Article 81: fixing commissions	EUR 100.8 million		
Carbonless paper	Dec. 20, 2001 2004 OJ L 115/1	Article 81: price fixing and market sharing	EUR 317.7 million		
Austrian Banks	June 11, 2002 2004 OJ L 56/1	Article 81: price fixing	EUR 124.26 million		
Deutsche BP	June 19, 2002 2004 OJ L 91/40	Misleading and incorrect information Reg. 4064/89	EUR 35,000		
Methionin	July 2, 2002 2003 OJ L 255/1	Article 81: Exchange of sales information, target price fixing	EUR 127 million		
Dutch Industrial and Medical Gases	July 24, 2002 2003 OJ 84/1 corr. 2003 OJ L 123/49	Article 81: price fixing and customer sharing	EUR 25.7 million		
Christie's	Oct. 30, 2002 IP/02/1585	Article 81: fixing commission fees	EUR 20.4 million		
Nintendo	Oct. 30, 2002 2003 OJ L 255/33	Article 81: vertical agreements preventing parallel trade	EUR 137.8 million		

Case	Commission decision	Infringement	Fine	ECJ/CFI judgment	Decision on fine
Aventis/Merck Methylglucamine	Nov. 27, 2002 2004 OJ L 38/18	Article 81: fixing prices and sharing customers	EUR 2.85 million		
Plasterboard	Nov. 27, 2002 IP/02/1744	Article 81: fixing prices and exchanging information	EUR 478 million		
Food flavour enhancer cartel	Dec. 17, 2002 2004 OJ L 75/1	Article 81: fixing target prices, allocating customers and exchanging price information	EUR 20.56 million		
Concrete reinforcing Bar cartel	Dec. 17, 2002 IP/02/1908	Article 65 ECSC: fixing size of extras to the base price	EUR 85 million		
Speciality graphites cartel	Dec. 17, 2002 IP/02/1906	Article 81: fixing prices	EUR 60.6 million		
French Federations in the Beef Sector	April 2, 2003 2003 OJ L 209/12	Article 81: fixing minimum Prices	EUR 16.68 million		
Deutsche Telecom	May 21, 2003 2003 OJ L 263/9	Article 82: charging discriminatory tariffs for access to local network	EUR 12.6 million		

Case	Commission decision	Infringement	Fine	ECJ/CFI judgment	Decision on fine
Yamaha	July 16, 2003 IP/03/1028	Article 81: partitioning of markets and resale price maintenance	EUR 2.56 million		
Wanadoo	July 16, 2003 IP/03/1025	Article 82: predatory pricing in internet access services	EUR 10.35 million		
Sorbates cartel	Oct. 1, 2003 IP/03/1330	Article 81: collusion on prices and volumes	Between EUR 99 and 10.5 million. Total amount of EUR 138.4 million		
Carbon and graphite products cartel	Dec. 3, 2003 IP/03/1651	Article 81: collusion on prices and customer sharing	Between EUR 43.05 and 1.06 million. Total amount: EUR 101.44 million		
Organic Peroxides	Dec. 10, 2003 IP/03/1700	Article 81: price fixing	Between EUR 1,000 and 43.5 million. Total amount: EUR 70 million		
Industrial Copper Tubes Cartel	Dec. 16, 2003 IP/03/1746	Article 81: price fixing and market sharing	Between EUR 18.1 and 39.8 million. Total amount: EUR 78.6 million		

Case	Commission decision	Infringement	Fine	ECJ/CFI judgment	Decision on fine
Microsoft	March 24, 2004 IP/04/382	Article 82: leveraging a near monopoly onto related markets (operating systems and media players)	EUR 479,196,304		
Topps	May 26, 2004 IP/04/682	Article 81: preventing parallel imports	EUR 1.59 million		
Belgian Architects	June 24, 2004 IP/04/800	Art 81: fixing recommended minimum fees	EUR 100,000		
Tetra Laval	July 7, 2004 IP/04/863	Art. 14 Reg. 1310/97: providing incorrect or misleading information	EUR 90,000		

Index

Landmark decisions are referred to in italics.[1]

1. These references replace an exhaustive table of the Court cases which appeared redundant in the light of access via the internet. The Court's website (http://www.curia.eu.int/jurisp) may be consulted not only by reference to the case number or the parties but also to the Commission decision which is the subject of appeal and under which they are usually known (under 'words in the text'). For instance, the Court's judgment Cheil Jedang (CFI July 9, 2003, T-220/00) can also be found under Lysine (D.Comm. June 7, 2000) and Tokai Carbon (CFI April 29, 2004, T-236/01) under Graphite electrodes (D.Comm. Dec. 17, 2002). Where appropriate reference is therefore made to both the name of the applicant and the – usually better known – name of the Commission's decision which is the subject of the Court's judgment. A complete list of Commission decisions imposing a sanction for infringement of EC competition rules is annexed to Chapter X and includes references to the judgments of the Court of First Instance and the Court of Justice in these cases.